CASES AND MATERIALS

PRODUCTS LIABILITY AND SAFETY

FIFTH EDITION

by

DAVID G. OWEN
Carolina Distinguished Professor of Law
University of South Carolina

JOHN E. MONTGOMERY
Dean Emeritus and Professor of Law
University of South Carolina

MARY J. DAVIS
Stites & Harbison Professor of Law
University of Kentucky

FOUNDATION PRESS

2007

THOMSON
✳ ™
WEST

© 1980, 1989, 1996, 2004 FOUNDATION PRESS
© 2007 By FOUNDATION PRESS
   395 Hudson Street
   New York, NY 10014
   Phone Toll Free 1–877–888–1330
   Fax (212) 367–6799
   foundation–press.com

Printed in the United States of America
ISBN: 978-1-59941-180-4

 TEXT IS PRINTED ON 10% POST CONSUMER RECYCLED PAPER

∞

D.G.O.
To the memory of
Nathan and Janet Owen

*

J.E.M.
To Bonnie, John B., Kelli, Carter, and Riley Montgomery

*

M.J.D.
To Stuart and Virginia Davis Scales

*

and

*

To the memory of
Page Keeton

PREFACE TO THE FIFTH EDITION

The fifth edition captures recent developments in products liability and continues our ongoing quest to enhance the portrait of products liability law, theory, and practice revealed by the cases and materials assembled in prior editions. Although the rate of doctrinal change has slowed substantially from the period of tumultuous growth during the 1960s, 1970s, and early 1980s, courts, legislatures, and commentators continue to search for improved approaches to a large variety of products liability problems. Moreover, products liability "reform" in legislatures and the courts, sometimes as captured by the American Law Institute's *Restatement (Third) of Torts: Products Liability*, continues to affect certain aspects (usually peripheral) of this field of law.

This edition includes a number of new cases and legislative developments, but we have kept the additions modest and have continued to streamline the book, which now is the shortest it has ever been. The new edition continues to stress developments in the evolving meaning of "defectiveness" and problems of proof arising in particular from the Supreme Court's *Daubert v. Merrell Dow* decision. As in previous editions, we have updated and otherwise enriched the chapter exploring class actions and other mass tort developments in toxic substance products liability litigation.

Most footnotes are omitted from the principal materials; original numbering is retained for footnotes that remain. Asterisks designate footnotes of the editors. Ellipses, brackets, and asterisks indicate omissions. Within cases, formatting and citation form generally are standardized; page references to trial transcripts, exhibits, and pleadings ordinarily are omitted without notation; parties generally are identified by their trial designations; some citations are omitted without notation from quotations in the Notes; and certain other minor technical revisions are designed to enhance clarity of presentation.

In the process of revisions, we may have dropped or altered certain materials which various users wish we had retained. To them, we extend our permission to reproduce selected materials from earlier editions for classroom use. Many improvements in the book reflect comments from users of previous editions. We appreciate all such suggestions and hope that users of the fifth edition will continue to pass along their ideas on how the book may be improved.

DAVID G. OWEN
JOHN E. MONTGOMERY
MARY J. DAVIS

owen@sc.edu
jcmontgomery@gwm.sc.edu
mjdavis@email.uky.edu

FEBRUARY 2007

ACKNOWLEDGMENTS

We are grateful for the many valuable suggestions from various law professors and attorneys who have served over the years as special advisers on various editions of this book: Richard Ausness, Carl Bogus, Charles Cantu, William Childs, Robert Felix, Steven Johnson, Susanah Mead, Joseph Page, Barbara Plumeri, Susan Raeker-Jordon, Deborah Robinson, Joseph Sanders, Kathryn Sowle, Rod Surratt, Edmund Ursin, Sean Wajert, and Ellen Wertheimer. We are particularly indebted to Professors Cantu and Surratt who furnished generous research and analytical advice on earlier editions that has helped the book in various ways. We regret that we have lost the services of our valued collaborator and adviser, Paul LeBel, who mysteriously some time ago was captured by the siren call of deaning, that unrepentant thief of time, scholarly productivity, and other things of value. And we remain indebted to Mike Green for his contributions to the second edition.

Prior to the fourth edition, we lost our co-author, the late Dean W. Page Keeton Emeritus of the University of Texas. Dean Keeton played an instrumental role in launching the first edition in 1980, and he continued to contribute to the book in the years that followed. In the 1960s and 1970s, Page Keeton's perceptive and prolific scholarship on products liability law, together with his service as Adviser for the Restatement (Second) of Torts, played a significant role in shaping the direction of products liability law. We continue to miss him as a founding member of the products liability league of scholars, as a collaborator, and as a friend. We are aware of no better tribute to the life of Werdner Page Keeton than the marvelous memorial biography by his colleagues at the University of Texas, David Robertson, David Anderson, and the late Charles Alan Wright. See http://www.utexas.edu/faculty/council/1999-2000/memorials/Keeton/keeton.html, or google "W. Page Keeton."

We are grateful to various law students who furnished research, editorial, and administrative assistance on this edition, to whom we express our appreciation: Karen Miller, Donald Cummings, William Jordan, Adam Lee, MacKenzie Mayes, Steven McFarland, and Sarah Dixon Wendell. Working tirelessly in many ways to bring the new edition to successful completion, Karen Miller deserves the lion share of our thanks. Thanks also are owing to James Coates for skillfully shepherding the manuscript through production, now for the fifth time, to final book.

Our largest debt is to our families, Joan, Wendy, and Ethan Owen, and Megan Dantzler; Bonnie and John B. Montgomery; and Stuart and Virginia Scales, for their good cheer and encouragement throughout the project.

Finally, we acknowledge the cooperation of the following publishers and authors who granted us permission to use various materials included herein.

American Law Institute, 1961 ALI Proceedings. Copyright © 1962 by the American Law Institute. Reprinted with permission.

American Law Institute, Restatement of the Law Second, Torts. Copyright © 1965 by the American Law Institute. Reprinted with permission.

American Law Institute, Restatement of the Law Third, Torts: Products Liability. Copyright © 1998 by the American Law Institute. Reprinted with permission.

American Law Institute, Uniform Commercial Code, Official Text and Comments. Copyright © 1987 by the American Law Institute and the National Conference of Commissioners on Uniform State Laws. Reprinted with permission of the Permanent Editorial Board for the Uniform Commercial Code. All rights are reserved.

Black and Lilienfield, Epidemiologic Proof in Toxic Tort Litigation, 52 Fordham L.Rev. 732 (1984). Reprinted by permission of the authors.

Bogus, War on the Common Law: The Struggle at the Center of Products Liability, 60 Mo.L.Rev. 1 (1995). Reprinted with the permission of the Missouri Law Review.

Bureau of National Affairs, State Tort Reform, reprinted by permission from Product Safety and Liability Reporter, Vol. 16, No. 4, p. 108 (January 22, 1988). Copyright © 1988 by the Bureau of National Affairs, Inc.

Charlotte Observer, "Ford: Faulty Capri Wipers Safer Than Recall Hazards," p. 2A, col. 4 (June 3, 1978). Reprinted with permission of the newspaper.

"Coke on Littleton" (drawing), 43 Cal.L.Rev. 374 (1955). Copyright © 1970, California Law Review, Inc. Reprinted with permission of the California Law Review and Fred B. Rothman & Co.

A. Corbin, Contracts (1963). Copyright © 1952 by West Publishing Co. Reprinted with the permission of West Publishing Company.

Cowan, Some Policy Bases of Products Liability, 17 Stan.L.Rev. 1077 (1965). Copyright © 1965 by the Board of Trustees of the Leland Stanford Junior University. Reprinted with permission of the Stanford Law Review.

Dickerson, Products Liability: How Good Does a Product Have to Be?, 42 Ind.L.J. 301 (1967). Reprinted with the permission of the Indiana Law Journal and Fred B. Rothman & Co.

Eaton, Revisiting the Intersection of Workers' Compensation and Product Liability: An Assessment of a Proposed Federal Solution to an Old Problem, 64 Tenn. L. Rev. 881 (1997). The full text of this article was published originally at 64 Tenn.L.Rev 881 (1997) and this exerpt is reprinted with permission of the author and the Tennessee Law Review Association, Inc.

Epstein, Products Liability: The Search for the Middle Ground, 56 N.C. L.Rev. 643 (1978). Reprinted with the permission of the author.

Feezer, Manufacturers' Liability for Injuries Caused by His Products: Defective Automobiles, 37 Mich.L.Rev. 1 (1938). Reprinted with the permission of the Michigan Law Review.

Gillam, Products Liability in a Nutshell, 37 Or.L.Rev. 119 (1958). Reprinted with the permission of the Oregon Law Review.

Goldberg, Manufacturers Take Cover. Reprinted with permission from the July 1986 issue of ABA Journal, The Lawyer 's Magazine, published by the American Bar Association.

Hamilton, The Ancient Maxim Caveat Emptor. Reprinted by permission of The Yale Law Journal Company and Fred B. Rothman & Co. from The Yale Law Journal, Vol. 40, pp. 1133–65 (1931).

Henderson, Coping With The Time Dimension In Products Liability. Copyright © 1981 California Law Review, Inc. Reprinted from the California Law Review, Vol. 69, No. 4, July 1981, pp. 919–949, by permission.

Henderson, Manufacturers' Liability for Defective Product Design: A Proposed Statutory Reform, 56 N.C.L.Rev. 625 (1978). Reprinted with the permission of the author.

James A. Henderson, Jr. & Aaron D. Twerski, Closing the American Products Liability Frontier: The Rejection of Liability Without Defect, 66 N.Y.U.L.Rev. 1263, 1316–18, 1322–23, 1325–26, 1329–31 (1991). Reprinted with the permission of the New York University Law Review.

Hensler & Peterson, Understanding Mass Personal Injury Litigation: A Socio-legal Analysis, 59 Brook.L.Rev. 961 (1993). Reprinted with the permission of the Brooklyn Law Review.

James, Products Liability (pt. 2), 34 Tex.L.Rev. 227 (1955). Reprinted with the permission of the Texas Law Review.

W.P. Keeton, Torts, Annual Survey of Texas Law, 32 Sw.L.J. 1 (1978). Reprinted with permission of the copyright holder. Copyright © 1978 by Southern Methodist University.

Klemme, The Enterprise Liability Theory of Torts, 47 Colo.L.Rev. 153 (1976). Reprinted with the permission of the Colorado Law Review.

Larson, Workmen's Compensation: Third Party's Action Over Against Employer, 65 Nw.U.L.Rev. 351 (1970). Reprinted with the permission of the Northwestern Law Review.

Leidy, Another New Tort?, 38 Mich.L.Rev. 964 (1940). Reprinted with the permission of the Michigan Law Review.

Merrill, Risk-Benefit Decisionmaking by the Food and Drug Administration, 45 Geo.Wash.L.Rev. 994 (1977). Reprinted with the permission of The George Washington Law Review.

Montgomery & Owen, Reflections on the Theory and Administration of Strict Tort Liability for Defective Products, 27 S.C.L.Rev. 803 (1976). Copyright © 1976 by the South Carolina Law Review. Reprinted by permission.

The New York Times, Art by Niculae Asciu. Copyright © 1985 by The New York Times Company. Reprinted by permission.

R. Nordstrom, Law of Sales (1970). Copyright © 1970 by West Publishing Co. Reprinted with permission of West Publishing Company.

Owen, The Graying of Products Liability Law: Paths Taken and Untaken in the New Restatement, 61 Tenn.L.Rev. 1241 (1994). Originally published by the Tennessee Law Review Association, Inc. Reprinted with permission.

D. Peck, Decision At Law (1961). Reprinted by permission of Dodd, Mead and Company, Inc. from DECISION AT LAW by David W. Peck. Copyright © 1961 by David W. Peck.

Phillips, Contribution and Indemnity in Products Liability. Reprinted with permission of the author and the Tennessee Law Review Association, Inc. from 42 Tennessee Law Review 85 (1974).

Posner, A Theory of Negligence, 1 J.Leg.Stud. 29 (1972). Reprinted with the permission of the Journal of Legal Studies.

Posner, Strict Liability: A Comment, 2 J.Leg.Stud. 205 (1973). Reprinted with the permission of the Journal of Legal Studies.

R. Pound, Social Control Through Law (1942). Copyright © 1942 by Yale University Press from Social Control Through Law by Roscoe Pound. Reprinted in 1968 by Archon Books, Hamden, Connecticut. Reprinted with the permission of the publisher.

Prosser, The Assault Upon the Citadel (Strict Liability to the Consumer). Reprinted by permission of The Yale Law Journal Company and Fred B. Rothman & Co. from The Yale Law Journal, Vol. 69, pp. 1099, 1120–21 (1960).

Prosser, The Fall of the Citadel (Strict Liability to the Consumer). 50 Minn. L.Rev. 791 (1966). Reprinted with the permission of the Minnesota Law Review.

Prosser, The Implied Warranty of Merchantable Quality, 27 Minn.L.Rev. 117 (1943). Reprinted with the permission of the Minnesota Law Review.

Rahdert, Covering Accident Costs (1995). Originally published by Temple University Press. Reprinted with the permission of the publisher.

Rheingold, The Expanding Liability of the Product Supplier: A Primer, 2 Hofstra L.Rev. 521 (1974). Reprinted with the permission of the Hofstra Law Review.

Roberts, Circular Saw Design: A Hazard Analysis, 1 J. of Prod.Liab. 127 (1977). Reprinted with the permission of the author and the Institute of Product Safety.

Rothschild, The Magnuson-Moss Warranty Act: Does It Balance Warrantor and Consumer Interests?, 44 Geo.Wash.L.Rev. 335 (1976). Reprinted with the permission of The George Washington Law Review.

Russell, Manufacturers Liability to the Ultimate Consumer, 21 Ky.L.J. 338 (1933). Reprinted with the permission of the Kentucky Law Journal.

William W. Schwarzer, Alan Hirsch & Edward Sussman, Judicial Federalism: A Proposal to Amend the Multidistrict Litigation Statute to Permit Discovery Coordination of Large-Scale Litigation Pending in State and Federal Courts. Published originally in 73 Texas Law Review 1529 (1995). Copyright © 1995 by The Texas Law Review Association. Reprinted by permission.

Shapo, A Representational Theory of Consumer Protection: Doctrine, Function and Legal Liability for Product Disappointment, 60 Va.L.Rev. 1109 (1974). Reprinted with the permission of the Virginia Law Review Association and Fred B. Rothman & Co.

Speidel, The Virginia "Anti-Privity" Statute: Strict Products Liability Under the Uniform Commercial Code, 51 Va.L.Rev. 804 (1965). Reprinted with the permission of the Virginia Law Review Association and Fred B. Rothman & Co.

"The Toxic Avenger," reprinted by permission. Copyright © 1984, Troma, Inc./The HCH Co. from the motion picture "The Toxic Avenger," a Lloyd Kaufman/Michael Hesz Production. The producer conditioned use of the picture on the inclusion of the following additional credit: "The Toxic Avenger," a horror/comedy motion picture dealing with the consequences of toxic waste, was a tremendous box-office hit for TROMA, INC. in 1985 that enjoyed a successful six-month run in New York City.

J. Thomas, Textbook of Roman Law (1976). Reprinted with the permission of the author and Elsevier-North Holland Publishing Co.

Titus, Restatement (Second) of Torts Section 402A and the Uniform Commercial Code, 22 Stan.L.Rev. 713 (1970). Copyright © 1970 by the

Board of Trustees of the Leland Stanford Junior University. Reprinted with the permission of the Stanford Law Review.

Trial Lawyer's Guide, photographs of defective screws, p. 327 (1971). Reprinted with permission from Trial Lawyer's Guide, 1971 Annual, published by Callaghan & Company, 3201 Old Glenview Road, Wilmette, Illinois 60091.

Twerski, The Many Faces of Misuse, 29 Mercer L.Rev. 403 (1978). Reprinted with the permission of the author and the Mercer Law Review.

Twerski, Weinstein, Donaher & Piehler, The Use and Abuse of Warnings in Products Liability—Design Defect Litigation Comes of Age, 61 Cornell L.Rev. 495 (1976). Copyright © 1976 by Cornell University. Reprinted with the permission of the authors, the Cornell Law Review and Fred B. Rothman & Co.

Wade, On the Nature of Strict Tort Liability for Products, 44 Miss.L.J. 825 (1973). Reprinted with the permission of the Mississippi Law Journal.

The Wall Street Journal, Litigation Load. Reproduced by permission of the Wall Street Journal. Copyright © Dow Jones & Company, Inc. 1976. All rights reserved worldwide.

Weinstein, Ethical Dilemmas in Mass Tort Litigation, 88 Nw.U.L.Rev. 469 (1994). Originally published by The Northwestern University School of Law. Reprinted with permission of the author.

Weintraub, Disclaimers and Limitation of Damages for Breach of Warranty Under the UCC, 53 Tex.L.Rev. 60 (1974). Reprinted with the permission of the Texas Law Review.

Wertheimer, The Smoke Gets in Their Eyes: Products Category Liability and Alternative Feasible Designs in the Third Restatement, 61 Tenn.L. Rev. 1429 (1994). Reprinted by permission of the Tennessee Law Review Association, Inc. from 61 Tenn.L.Rev. 1429 (1994).

J. White & R. Summers, Uniform Commercial Code, Fifth Edition. Copyright © 2000 by West Group. Reprinted with the permission of West Publishing Company.

SUMMARY OF CONTENTS

*

TABLE OF CONTENTS

TABLE OF CASES

Principal cases are in bold type. Non-principal cases are in roman type. References are to Pages.

*

PRODUCTS LIABILITY AND SAFETY

*

CHAPTER 1

An Introduction to Products Liability and Safety Law

Products liability law occupies a central role in America, and increasingly in the world, at the beginning of the 21st century. Products liability litigation and prevention figure prominently in corporate and legal decisionmaking in modern America, as legions of plaintiffs' lawyers across the nation file thousands of products liability suits each year. In an effort to avoid and manage effectively such high stakes litigation, many major corporations and law firms have established separate teams or departments for products liability matters.

The reform of products liability law, a field viewed by many as having developed certain excesses, has taken center stage over the last few decades in many state legislatures, the United States Congress, and the American Law Institute. Nearly every year, various state legislatures continue to reform this area of the law in varying ways. Less frequently, but from time to time, Congress examines and occasionally legislates on various products liability and safety issues. Federal regulatory agencies continue to churn out a profusion of regulations governing product safety, and these agencies, notably the FDA, increasingly assert the preemptive effect of their regulations on products liability law. In 1998, the American Law Institute provided products liability with its own Restatement—the Restatement (Third) of Torts: Products Liability.

This introductory chapter presents an overview of the nature of products liability and safety law, where it came from, and where it stands today. The remaining materials in the book provide a foundation for lawyers to understand this area of the law in a fundamental and comprehensive way that should enable them effectively to manage their clients' products liability problems and to help frame the future direction of products liability and safety law.

1.   THE SOCIAL PROBLEM OF DANGEROUS PRODUCTS

> [T]oday we face an unparalleled profusion of new products spawned by space-age technology. A somber by-product of this proliferation of new products in the home has been the growth of new categories and dimensions of home injuries.

So declared Senator Magnuson in urging the Senate in 1967 to establish a national commission to survey product safety. See Final Report, National Commission on Product Safety 123 (June 1970) [Final Report].

Congress responded. Asserting that "the American Consumer has a right to be protected against unreasonable risk of bodily harm from products purchased on the open market for the use of himself and his family," the United States Congress by Joint Resolution in November 1967 established the National Commission on Product Safety. Public Law 90–146, 90th Cong., S.J.Res. 33, Nov. 20, 1967. The Commission was directed to perform various tasks: (1) to study the nature and magnitude of the problem of accidental injuries associated with the use of consumer products; (2) to determine the extent to which such injuries were attributable to product hazards reasonably avoidable by manufacturers and hence "unnecessary"; (3) to examine the effectiveness of the then-existing structure of regulatory and common-law rules governing products liability and safety; and (4) to propose any appropriate remedial legislation.

In particular, Congress instructed the Commission to "conduct a comprehensive study and investigation of the scope and adequacy of measures now employed to protect consumers against unreasonable risk of injuries which may be caused by hazardous household products" and to identify "categories of household products * * * which may present an unreasonable hazard to the health and safety of the consuming public."

The Commission presented its findings in 1970:

> Americans—20 million of them—are injured each year in the home as a result of incidents connected with consumer products. Of the total, 110,000 are permanently disabled and 30,000 are killed. A significant number could have been spared if more attention had been paid to hazard reduction. The annual cost to the Nation of product-related injuries may exceed $5.5 billion.

> The exposure of consumers to unreasonable consumer product hazards is excessive by any standard of measurement. Final Report at 1.

Because these findings excluded data on product accidents outside the Commission's jurisdiction—accidents (1) in the workplace, and those involving (2) motor vehicles, (3) food, drugs, and cosmetics, (4) insecticides, (5) firearms, (6) cigarettes, (7) radiological hazards, and (8) certain flammable fabrics—the total product accident toll in the U.S. is considerably higher. In the early 21st century, the number of product accidents in America (including injuries from toxic substances) may be roughly estimated at 50 million per year, at an annual cost to the nation of $100 billion.*

————

Final Report, National Commission on Product Safety

Chapter 2, pp. 9–34 (1970).

PRODUCT RISKS TO CONSUMERS: HOUSEHOLD HAZARDS IDENTIFIED

The primary charge to the National Commission on Product Safety was to "consider the identity of categories of household products . . . which may present an unreasonable hazard to the health and safety of the consuming public."

* * *

The role of specific products is, however, difficult to define. The estimate of 6,200 killed by home fires and 1,300,000 injured by burns received at home leaves open the question of cause: matches, stoves, wiring, fabrics, or cigarettes?

Home falls kill about 12,000 a year and injure 6,900,000, but again the precise causes are uncertain: high heels, loose treads, rough floors, flimsy ladders, worn stairs, slippery floors, torn carpets, alcohol?

Every hour of the day, on the average, household hazards in America kill three victims. For every one they kill, more than 1,000 suffer injuries. The injuries restrict activities of about half of the victims and force a third of these to take to bed to recover. A tenth of the bedridden require hospital care. * * *

* See the CPSC's Annual Reports and the National Safety Council's annual editions of Accident Facts.—Eds.

**STATISTICAL SUMMARY OF INJURIES FROM CONSUMER PRODUCTS BASED ON DEPARTMENT
OF HEALTH, EDUCATION AND WELFARE ESTIMATES**

APPLIANCES

burns from gas and electric ranges	100,000
burns from coffeepots	40,000
burns from vaporizers	15,000
burns from irons	20,000
burns from sun and heat lamps	20,000
burns from other sources	30,000
injuries from wringer washing machines	100,000
other injuries from appliances	175,000
TOTAL	**500,000**

HOME FURNISHINGS

injuries involving beds	150,000
injuries involving chairs	100,000
injuries involving tables	60,000
injuries involving stools	50,000
injuries involving sofas	45,000
injuries involving venetian blinds	40,000
other injuries from home furnishings	55,000
TOTAL	**500,000**

HOME FIXTURES

injuries from windows	100,000
injuries from stairs	1,800,000
injuries from tubs and showers	125,000
injuries from glass doors (patio, bath, etc.)	100,000
burns from hot water in bathroom	25,000
injuries from doors other than glass	150,000
other injuries from home fixtures	200,000
TOTAL	**2,500,000**

HEATING DEVICES

burns from furnaces		30,000
gas explosions	20,000	
burns from hot water heaters		10,000
burns from room heaters		35,000
burns from floor furnaces		25,000
burns from other heating devices		35,000
other injuries from heating devices		40,000
TOTAL		**175,000**

HOME WORKSHOP

injuries from power saws	75,000
injuries from power drills	15,000
other injuries from home workshop	35,000
TOTAL	**125,000**

COOKING DEVICES

burns from skillets	80,000
burns from pressure cookers	10,000
other injuries from cooking devices	60,000
TOTAL	**150,000**

KITCHEN GADGETS AND SERVING UTENSILS

injuries from knives	190,000
other injuries from gadgets and utensils	310,000
TOTAL	**500,000**

RECREATIONAL EQUIPMENT

injuries involving tricycles	100,000
other injuries from mobile equipment	200,000
injuries involving skates	200,000
injuries involving winter sports	400,000
injuries involving baseballs	500,000
injuries involving footballs	1,000,000
injuries involving basketballs	800,000
other injuries involving balls	700,000
injuries involving camping	200,000
injuries involving fishing	300,000
other and unknown injuries from sports eqpmt	500,000
poisoning from airplane glue	25,000
other injuries from hobby equipment	375,000
injuries involving toys	700,000
TOTAL	**8,000,000**

INCINERATORS **TOTAL**	**50,000**

FLAMMABLE LIQUIDS

burns from gasoline	40,000
burns from lighter fluid	10,000
other burns from flammable liquids	10,000
poisonings from lighter fluid	15,000
poisonings from kerosene	15,000
poisonings from turpentine	25,000
other poisonings from flammable liquids	10,000
TOTAL	**125,000**

FLAME PRODUCING DEVICES

burns from flame producing devices	75,000
TOTAL	**75,000**

CLOTHING INJURIES OTHER THAN BURNS

TOTAL	**200,000**

HOME TOOLS

injuries involving ladders	180,000
injuries involving saws	100,000
injuries involving hammers	150,000
other injuries from home tools	320,000
TOTAL	750,000

LAUNDERING, CLEANING, POLISHING PRODUCTS

poisonings from soaps, detergents, cleaners	40,000
poisonings from bleach	35,000
poisonings from disinfectants, deodorizers	20,000
poisonings from furniture polish	20,000
poisonings from lye, corrosives	15,000
other poisonings from laundering, cleaning and polishing products	20,000
other injuries from laundering, cleaning and polishing products	100,000
TOTAL	250,000

YARD AND GARDEN EQUIPMENT

injuries from power mowers	140,000
other injuries from yard and garden equipment	360,000
TOTAL	500,000

RECREATIONAL EQUIPMENT

injuries involving swings	500,000
injuries involving slides	200,000
injuries involving seesaws	50,000
other injuries from stationary equipment	250,000
injuries involving bicycles	1,000,000

FIREARMS AND EXPLOSIVES

injuries from firearms	120,000
injuries from fireworks	10,000
other injuries from firearms and explosives	20,000
TOTAL	150,000

COSMETICS

injuries from perfume, toilet water	20,000
injuries from lotions and creams	10,000
other injuries from cosmetics	30,000
TOTAL	60,000

PERSONAL USE ITEMS

injuries from shaving equipment	30,000
other injuries from personal use items	20,000
TOTAL	50,000

PESTICIDES

poisonings from insecticides	35,000
poisonings from rodenticides	20,000
other poisonings from pesticides	20,000
TOTAL	75,000

CONTAINERS

injuries involving cans and jars	160,000
injuries involving bottles	40,000
other injuries involving containers	50,000
TOTAL	250,000

ESTIMATED TOTAL INJURIES FROM LISTED CONSUMER PRODUCTS   14,960,000

EVALUATING HAZARDS

In assessing individual hazards, we studied data relating frequency, severity, duration, and sequelae of injury to the frequency and degree of exposure to the product. Other variables we looked at were the degree of inherent risk, the essentiality of the product, and the feasibility and approximate cost of safety improvements.

We also considered whether there were acceptable alternatives for a hazardous product; effects on the product of aging and wear; the contribution to hazards of defective maintenance and repair; exposure to instructions or warnings; influence of product advertising on behavior; the extent and forms of abnormal uses of the product; effects of storage, distribution, and disposal; and characteristics of the persons injured, including age, sex, skills, training, and experience.

UNREASONABLE HAZARDS

Beyond the foregoing guidelines for defining "unreasonable hazards," we believe that no completely satisfactory definition is possible. Prof. Corwin D. Edwards of the University of Oregon has presented an excellent statement which supplements our guidelines:

"Risks of bodily harm to users are not unreasonable when consumers understand that risks exist, can appraise their probability and severity, know how to cope with them, and voluntarily accept them to get benefits that could not be obtained in less risky ways. When there is a risk of this character, consumers have reasonable opportunity to protect themselves; and public authorities should hesitate to substitute their value judgments about the desirability of the risk for those of the consumers who choose to incur it.

"But preventable risk is not reasonable (*a*) when consumers do not know that it exists; or (*b*) when, though aware of it, consumers are unable to estimate its frequency and severity; or (*c*) when consumers do not know how to cope with it, and hence are likely to incur harm unnecessarily; or (*d*) when risk is unnecessary in ... that it could be reduced or eliminated at a cost in money or in the performance of the product that consumers would willingly incur if they knew the facts and were given the choice.

"Risks that are unreasonable by this definition of unreasonableness seem ... to be common."

* * *

While we prefer to emphasize positive recommendations for the future protection of consumers, we find that within each of the categories discussed in the pages immediately following, there are makes, models, and types of products which constitute "an unreasonable hazard to the health and safety of the consuming public" within the meaning of our mandate.

[The Commission gathered the following data on particular products from physicians, the insurance industry, and hospitals.]

ARCHITECTURAL GLASS

Every year, about 150,000 victims of broken windows, doors, or glass walls discover that what they can't see can hurt them. About 100,000 walked through glass doors last year, probably believing the space to be open. If the doors had been safety glazed, most of the serious injuries would not have occurred. But the fragile, brittle panels of ordinary glass shatter even under a light blow from a child. The crystal knives and daggers slice through the hand or wrist, cut vital organs, and cause permanent disfigurement, paralysis, or death. Victims may bleed to death before medical aid can arrive. * * *

COLOR TELEVISION SETS

[Of] the 85 million TV sets in the United States in 1969, including about 20 million color sets, about 10,000 sets caught fire. * * * [C]olor sets ... require up to and sometimes more than 25,000 volts. If conductors in the set are not well insulated, the high voltage forces a short circuit. Resistance to this flow of current builds up temperatures to the flaming point.

Operating temperatures of color sets are in the 110°–115° F. range. Heat generated in normal circuits in some sets changed the properties of a wax insulating coating around the high-voltage transformer, so that it broke down. This form of insulation has since, for the most part, been replaced by a more durable, less combustible silicone rubber. * * *

The spread of fire is enhanced by the present use of flammable paper or cardboard to enclose capacitors; flammable lubricants; accumulation of dust around components; frayed leads; and closely packed circuitry. Other components considered to be potential fire sources are the deflection yoke around the cathode-ray tube, automatic tuning devices, printed circuit parts in the chassis, the AC switch, and ceramic resistors.

HOT-WATER VAPORIZERS

The McCormack family bought a Hankscraft vaporizer advertised as tipproof, foolproof, and safe. It bore the seals of *Good Housekeeping* and *Parents'* magazines, and the mark of Underwriters' Laboratories. They placed it on a stool in their home, plugged in the house circuit, and waited for the steam to rise. While it was steaming, their 3-year-old daughter caught herself in its electric cord. The vaporizer tipped and spilled scalding water onto the child. Andrea McCormack spent 5 months in the hospital enduring a series of painful operations. She will bear the scars all her life. In 1960 a court awarded damages of $150,000.

As of 1968, there were more than 100 claims open and pending against the Hankscraft Co. in the Travelers Insurance Co. office in Milwaukee. The insurer recommended that Hankscraft recall the model and replace it with a safer design. When the manufacturer did not respond, the insurer reduced the coverage and eventually canceled.

In the 10 reports we studied in depth of burns and scalds related to hot water vaporizers, nine were children under 5. Evidence indicated the product to be at least partially at fault in every instance. [The Underwriters' Laboratories voluntary safety standard for vaporizers is very weak, and cool mist vaporizers are as effective for most conditions as steam vaporizers.]

* * *

HOUSEHOLD CHEMICALS

[Household chemicals pose a major hazard to curious young children]: every liquid or chewable substance is something for them to sample. [For example, many household chemicals look like food, are attractively packaged, and pleasantly scented: some types of of liquid furniture polish resemble milk, strawberry soda, or lemon soda. Yet furniture polish can produce chemical pneumonia if even a small quantity gets into the lungs. The FDA Commissioner estimated that ingestions of potentially harmful household substances range from 500,000 to 1 million a year.]

Parents often are aware that a household chemical may be hazardous but unfamiliar with the degree of hazard [and manufacturers fail to] inform consumer users of the degree of potential injury. Warning labels which conform to the legal requirements of the Hazardous Substances Act fail to list relative alkalinity or toxicity levels. Names of hazardous ingredients and antidotes, as well as instructions for treatment, frequently are missing. * * *

Since almost anything within reach of tiny hands frequently will go into an infant's mouth, repackaging with child-resistant spouts might reduce the hazard. Single-use packets or a substitution of solids for liquid or powdered forms might also help.

Most important, many products can use less hazardous ingredients without loss of function. According to testimony from Cornell Aeronautical Laboratory, all brands of dishwasher detergent, regardless of causticity, are of approximately equal effectiveness. Yet alkalinity (pH value of solutions) ranges from that of lye to that of milk of magnesia. . . .

The unreasonable hazards presented by household chemicals, particularly strong alkaline dishwasher detergents and petroleum-based furniture polishes, can be substantially reduced by standards requiring reformulation and protective packaging as well as by more effective warnings. * * *

ROTARY LAWN MOWERS

On the first warm Saturday in spring, hospital emergency room crews expect a parade of patients holding a bloody towel around a lacerated or amputated hand or foot. On opening day of the grass-grooming season, the rotary power mower begins its work of trimming lawns, fingers, and toes. About 70 percent of the injuries from power mowers are lacerations, amputations, and fractures that result from the cutting and crushing action of the fast whirling blade.

In addition, there are high-velocity ejections of wire, glass, stones, and debris that can puncture vital body parts. * * * Missiles thrown by the rotary blades strike bystanders as well as operators. The blades hurl such debris as pebbles, nails, glass, and wires like shrapnel 50 feet or more, no matter how carefully a lawn is policed before mowing.

NOTES

1. After reviewing these and other product categories, the Commission observed: "It has been our purpose to identify these hazards, but we cannot forbear mention of ways of moderating undue risks," noting that improvements could often be made "in the original concept, in the design, in systems of assuring quality throughout production, storage, and distribution, in information for the consumer and repairman, and in methods of disposal or recycling of the product." Id. at 36.

2. The Commission noted a "dearth of factors motivating producers toward safety" and observed that "[o]nly a few of the largest manufacturers have coherent, articulated safety engineering programs." Id. at 2.* The Commission concluded that government intervention was necessary to reduce the incidence of unreasonably

---

* This has changed. Although products liability and safety still is not a "central focus of most corporate decision makers in the conduct of their business," most major manufacturers have integrated these considerations into the corporate structure in some manner or another. N. Weber, Product Liability: The Corporate Response 15 (Conference Board Report No. 893, 1987).—Eds.

hazardous products facing the consumer. The excerpts from the Final Report that follow illuminate a variety of products liability and safety issues examined throughout this book.

————

Final Report, National Commission on Product Safety

Chapters 1 & 6, pp. 3–4, 69–72 (1970).

PATHS TO SAFETY

* * *

Injury Factors

There are those who believe that safety, like charity, begins at home in the behavior of the family—steadying ladders, storing knives, supervising children. Others believe that safety begins with the home itself, the environment where hazardous products find their uses—good lighting, well-insulated wiring, slipproof bathtubs and rugs, latched cabinets for medicine and household chemicals. A third view is that safety begins in the factory and involves design, construction, hazard analysis, and quality control.

None of these views is wholly right or wrong. The classical concept of epidemiology counts all three factors: host, environment, and agent. Close examination of the three uncovers many subsidiary factors: hosts of different capacities and habits; differing social, political, and psychological as well as physical environments; and agents acting in combination, additively, or serially. * * * [After considering all of these factors,] we have concluded that the greatest promise for reducing risks resides in energizing the manufacturer's ingenuity.

We do not mean that manufacturers by themselves can do all that is needed to achieve an optimal safety record. We mean that with Government stimulation they can accomplish more for safety with less effort and expense than any other body—more than educators, the courts, regulatory agencies, or individual consumers.

Manufacturers have it in their power to design, build, and market products in ways that will reduce if not eliminate most unreasonable and unnecessary hazards. Manufacturers are best able to take the longest strides to safety in the least time. The capacity of individual manufacturers to devise safety programs, without undue extra cost, has been demonstrated repeatedly in the course of our short history: in safety glass, double-insulated power tools, baffles on rotary mowers, noncombustible TV transformers, and releases on wringer washers. * * *

Behavioral Factors

Danger is a regrettable but unavoidable facet of life. Many persons who like to fly, surf, dive, or speed are proud of their ability to cope with it.

Usually, they are keenly conscious of the hazards and take pains to control them.

But everyone, at one time or another, suffers from complacency, a certainty that everything is under control, that injuries happen only to the other fellow. Then in that moment of carefree confidence, disaster strikes. The mower goes over a grade, slips out of control, and the blades chop at the feet. Many, with utmost care, commit themselves to handling dangerous instruments which, for lack of experience, knowledge, or skill, they cannot manage. An ineradicable minority is careless; they will wear a flammable garment near an open fire; use a power saw without a guard; work a lathe without safety glasses. * * *

Manufacturers' Responsibility

Prospects for measurable reform of human behavior are distant. Similarly, there is little hope for an early improvement of the home environment. The limited power of conventional educational methods has been described by our witnesses. [Thus,] while continuing to educate and seeking even better ways, there seems little choice but to concentrate on reducing unreasonable hazards by encouraging additional care in the design and manufacture of products.

The law has tended in recent years to place full responsibility for injuries attributable to defective products upon the manufacturer. [The manufacturer] is in the best position to know what are the safest designs, materials, construction methods, and modes of use. Before anyone else, he must explore the boundaries of potential danger from the use of his product. He must be in a position to advise the buyer competently how to use and how to maintain and repair the product. * * *

TRADE–OFFS

Every transaction implies a decision about safety costs and benefits. But to the consumer, the benefits of a product seem less related to safety than to performance, appearance, ease of operation, durability, freedom from maintenance or repair, price, availability of credit, and low down payment.

To the manufacturer, the chief benefits of a product may be marketability, ease of manufacture, economies of materials or labor, assurance of a continuing or expanding demand, and profit.

For such benefits, both manufacturer and consumer trade off certain costs. But each figures his personal costs and benefits, if he figures at all. Thus, the existing mechanism of the competitive market requires decisions on social costs and benefits by people who customarily calculate personal costs and benefits.

MARKET FORCES

The theoretical function of the market is to arrive at mutually satisfactory cost/benefit ratios for buyers and sellers. As applied to product safety, the market in theory asks, given limited resources, what goods and performance should be traded off at what cost for the removal of specific hazards?

Because absolute safety is unattainable and because every product presents some risks, the seller and buyer are compelled to decide what level of hazard is acceptable.

Increasingly, however, complex technology has diminished the consumer's ability to exercise a rational choice among risks in the market. The forces of supply and demand are distorted by unequal bargaining powers, lack of information, and other intervening factors.

The theory that a free market can reduce undue risks in consumer products is based on the assumption that the consumer has a freedom of choice in the market and, by trial and error if not by rational inquiry, is able to select or reject hazardous products.

Role of Consumer

[One expert testified that a buyer can decide how much safety is worth if he understands the product's risks and the product does not endanger others. But buyers seldom are sufficiently informed, and most product hazards do endanger persons other than the buyer. Nor do consumers generally have any way of knowing how much more they would have to pay to obtain a comparable, but less hazardous product.] Even when aware of a risk in a product, consumers cannot predict the frequency, severity, or probability of injury [and must rely upon the seller or manufacturer for information on product use, their inherent risks, and methods of safe use. As Professor Edwards] observed, "Only people trained to meet risks that they understand can cope with them reliably."

Role of Manufacturer

What can the manufacturer in a free market do to reduce unreasonable hazards? With or without effective methods of informing the consumer, a change in the product's design would seem to be the most effective solution [if it can be done at reasonable cost]. * * *

How High the Risk

One perplexing question [is], What level of risk is acceptable? * * * Presumably, the acceptable risk will vary with the product, its utility, necessity, and inherent dangers. * * *

CONCLUSIONS

As the Council on Trends and Perspectives of the Chamber of Commerce of the United States has recently observed:

> "The time has long since passed when the seller can successfully fall back on the argument that 'rational consumer choice' will protect the buyer...."

The competitive market currently fails to reduce unreasonable hazards because, as a consequence of modern technology, consumers cannot evaluate the risks to themselves or others, and the judgments of buyers and sellers reflect a personal rather than a social interest. Product redesign, whether voluntary or enforced, appears to be the most economical method of protecting consumers from unacceptable product hazards.

Although there remains ample room for private enterprise to reduce undue risks, even in a competitive market, only a Government presence can require prompt compliance with responsible manufacturing practices in the interest of safety.

NOTES

1. The Commission concluded: "Because of the inadequacy of existing controls on product hazards, we find a need for a major Federal role in the development and execution of methods to protect the American consumer." Final Report, supra, at 3. It thus proposed the creation of a federal product safety regulatory agency. In 1972, Congress responded by enacting the Consumer Product Safety Act, which established the Consumer Product Safety Commission (CPSC). 15 U.S.C.A. §§ 2051–2081. Among other duties, the CPSC is directed by the Act (1) to study possible causes and cures for product accidents (§ 5), (2) to establish minimum product safety standards for products containing unreasonable hazards (§ 7), and (3) to ban products containing hazards incapable of being reduced to a reasonable level (§ 8).

2. From its inception, the CPSC was a controversial agency. It has been criticized over the years for being poorly organized, poorly managed, and ineffective in accomplishing its charge of reducing product accidents. President Carter considered abolishing it in 1978, and there was substantial sentiment in the House of Representatives in the late 1980s to restructure the Commission significantly. See Prod. Saf. & Liab. Rep. (BNA) 673 (Sept. 25, 1987). Upon his resignation from the CPSC in 1986, Commissioner Stuart Statler warned of a "cloud on the horizon" for the agency due to the reduction of funding and staff. In the previous six years, funding had declined by 34% and the staff by 41%. Such cuts "mean that, for the future, the agency will be unable to assess emerging risks from new products, or even identify them in the first place.... As a result, more Americans will be maimed and charred and killed before we can even begin to seek solutions." Id. at 673 (March 28, 1986).

3. The Money Tells the Tale. The budgets of the product safety regulatory agencies give some idea of their clout. For fiscal 2007, their budgets were as follows: CPSC—$62 million; OSHA—$484 million; NHTSA—$815 million; and FDA—$1.5 billion.

2.   THE NATURE OF PRODUCTS LIABILITY AND SAFETY LAW

"Products liability" and "product safety" are phrases used to describe the law concerning product-related accidents and illnesses. A central issue in both products liability law and product safety law is the determination of when products are fairly classifiable as "excessively" or "unreasonably" hazardous. Both areas of law are concerned with reducing the toll of accidents from such hazards. But there the parallels stop.

A.   PRODUCT SAFETY LAW

The law of product safety is *regulatory* law—the systems of rules established by legislatures and administrative agencies of federal, state, and occasionally even municipal governments to regulate the safety of products sold to the public. Product safety law operates *ex ante*, by seeking to prevent product-caused accidents and diseases before they occur.

Municipal authorities regulate the safety of certain building products through building codes and sometimes prohibit the sale of miscellaneous other products. At the state level, departments of health, employment safety, fire boards, consumer protection and other agencies administer safety laws on a variety of diverse products, such as glue, architectural glass, industrial tools and machinery, fireworks, mattresses, refrigerators, household chemicals, life preservers, power tools, toys, elevators, BB guns, sling shots, unvented gas heaters, food and drugs, blood, plastic bags and, until recently in Connecticut, used hats. These state and local laws have aptly been described as "a hodgepodge of tragedy-inspired responses" to the product safety problem and are generally characterized by "narrow scope, diffuse jurisdiction, minuscule budgets, absence of enforcement, mild sanctions, and casual administration." The primary administration of such laws is often through education rather than enforcement. See Final Report, National Commission on Product Safety 2, 81–88 (1970). Because of the diversity and relatively minimal impact of such laws on either product safety or liability, there is little further reference to them in this book.

Product safety law at the federal level is much more significant, although regulation even at this level has so far proved to be of questionable effectiveness in many areas. Nevertheless, various federal agencies do exert considerable control over product safety on a national scale. The CPSC, already briefly discussed above, has broad jurisdiction to regulate consumer product safety under (1) the Consumer Product Safety Act (15 U.S.C.A. § 2051 et seq.), (2) the Federal Hazardous Substances Act (15 U.S.C.A. § 1261 et seq.), (3) the Poison Prevention Packaging Act (15 U.S.C.A. § 1471 et seq.), (4) the Flammable Fabrics Act (15 U.S.C.A. § 1191 et seq.), and (5) the Refrigerator Safety Act (15 U.S.C.A. § 1211 et seq.).

Other product safety regulatory jurisdiction of major importance is vested in (1) the National Highway Traffic Safety Administration (NHTSA) of the Department of Transportation (administering the National Traffic and Motor Vehicle Safety Act of 1966, 15 U.S.C.A. § 1381 et seq.), (2) the Food and Drug Administration (FDA) of the Department of Health and Human Services (administering the Federal Food, Drug, and Cosmetic Act, 21 U.S.C.A. § 301 et seq.), (3) the Occupational Safety and Health Administration (OSHA) of the Department of Labor (administering the Occupational Safety and Health Act of 1970, 29 U.S.C.A. § 651 et seq.), (4) the Federal Aviation Administration (FAA) of the Department of Transportation (administering the safety provisions of the Federal Aviation Act of 1958, 49 U.S.C.A. § 1301 et seq.), and (5) the Environmental Protection Agency (EPA) (administering the Toxic Substances Control Act, 15 U.S.C.A. § 2601 et seq., the Federal Insecticide, Fungicide, and Rodenticide Act, 7 U.S.C.A. § 135 et seq., and the Clean Air Act, particularly the regulation of asbestos removal in 42 U.S.C.A. § 7412).

These and other federal agencies also regulate the safety of pesticides, fungicides, meat, poultry, eggs, perishable agricultural commodities, railroad safety appliances, firearms, firearm carriage, cigarette labeling, and boat safety. Federal regulation of product safety is considered at various points in the book.

For general information on federal regulation of product safety, see BNA Product Safety & Liability Reporter; BNA Occupational Safety & Health Reporter, CCH Consumer Product Safety Guide, and CCH Food Drug Cosmetic Law Reports. For Europe, see C. Hodges, European Regulation of Consumer Product Safety (Oxford 2005).

B.   PRODUCTS LIABILITY LAW

The law of products liability governs the private *litigation* of product accidents. Operating *ex post*, after a product accident has already occurred, its rules define the legal responsibility of sellers and other product transferors for the resulting damages.

Products liability law is full of mixtures. It is a mixture of tort law—negligence, strict tort, and deceit—and of the contract law of sales—mostly warranty. It is a mixture of common law, especially on its tort side, and statutory law, generally on its contract side—notably the Uniform Commercial Code. In addition, state legislatures (and Congress) are increasingly enacting products liability "reform" acts which may cover actions in both tort and contract. Because of these hybrid characteristics of products liability law, plaintiffs in such actions often have a variety of available claims. Negligence, strict liability in tort, and breach of implied warranty are all based on the notion that something was wrong with the product, that it was "defective" or excessively dangerous. Remedies for breach of express warranty and tortious misrepresentation are available when a product turns out to have been more dangerous than it was stated to be, even though it may not have been defective or unfit when tested by standards of negligence or implied warranty.

As will be seen throughout the book, many of the most difficult products liability issues facing courts today spring from the doctrinal mixture of contract and tort. This blending of doctrines has generated perplexing questions involving, for example, the standard of liability, defenses, statutes of limitation, and the types of damages recoverable.

A typical products liability case involves a claim for damages against the manufacturer or retailer of a product by a person injured while using the product. The plaintiff seeks to prove that his injury was caused by some deficiency in the way the product was made or marketed—that the product was in some manner "defective." He also seeks to demonstrate that he was using the product properly or at least in a predictable manner. Typically, he claims damages for medical expenses, disability and disfigurement, pain and suffering, lost earnings and earning capacity, perhaps some kind of property damage, and possibly damage to the product itself. The defendant usually attempts to show that the product was *not* defective—that it was in fact reasonably made and reasonably marketed. Further, the defendant often seeks to establish that the accident was largely the result of the plaintiff's (or some other person's) improper use of the product. These are the central issues in a typical case.

In some cases, however, the transaction may not involve a sale. The product may have been leased or merely loaned by the owner. Or the injury-producing "product" may not be a typical, mass-produced chattel but instead a house, a toxic substance, a recipe, electricity, or a poisonous spider in a pair of pants. Or the defendant may be a wholesaler, component part manufacturer, employer, publisher, hospital, trademark owner, or the federal government.

All of these examples raise questions about the outer boundaries of products liability law. What really is a "product"? To what kinds of transactions should products liability principles apply? Where should the line be drawn between products liability and professional malpractice? Environmental law? Workers' compensation?

These are some of the issues of products liability law—the primary topic of this book.

3. Early Products Liability Law

Although products liability cases prior to the last quarter of the 19th century are few in number, the roots of products liability law reach deep into history. Most of its early beginnings are found in the tort-contract hybrid warranties of quality, express and implied.

A. Roman Law

In ancient Rome, the law of tort (*delict*) was quite undeveloped and apparently afforded little if any protection to a person injured by a defective product. Nor did the law of sales (*emptio venditio*) aid the disappointed purchaser much under the early classical law as set forth in the Twelve Tables of 450 B.C. "The original principle [although not the maxim] of the civil law was *caveat emptor* ['let the buyer beware']. The seller was not liable for any defects in the thing unless he had by *stipulation* expressly undertaken such liability." B. Nicholas, An Introduction to Roman Law 181 (1962).

J. Thomas, Textbook of Roman Law
288–90 (1976).

The vendor's liability to warrant against defects in the thing was ... an obligation of gradual evolution and development. The concern is with latent or hidden defects; patent defects, as in modern legal systems, were taken to be accepted by the buyer and even express warranties were deemed not to cover them—if, for instance, a one-eyed dog was sold as sound, it was as a sound one-eyed dog. [I]f the vendor was aware of the defect and did not disclose it, he was guilty of *dolus* [fraud] and would be liable in the *actio empti*; but it could be difficult for the purchaser [who had the burden of proof] to establish the vendor's knowledge. He was also liable if the thing in fact did not match the description which he innocently gave of it [as in modern express warranty]. But, these cases apart, the law imposed no liability upon the vendor, under the contract of sale itself, in respect of latent defects.

Accordingly, a purchaser who sought to safeguard himself against defects in the thing had again to resort to a stipulation [of] the non-existence of concealed defects [which the vendor typically would be reluctant to provide].

N O T E

By the last century b.c., limited implied warranty protection began to extend to the purchase of cattle and slaves under the rule of the curule aediles, magistrates charged (from 367 b.c.) with policing activities in the public market. Early in the first century a.d., the Aedilician Edict may have extended a general implied warranty of quality to the sales of all property. By the time of Justinian (553 a.d.), Roman law appears to have implied a basic warranty of quality against latent defects into the sale of goods in general. The extent of damages recoverable for breach, however, still depended upon whether the seller knew of the defect and failed to disclose it.

Justinian's Digest
Book 19, Tit. 1, Lex 13 (533 A.D.)

In the matter of damages in the action *ex empto* [*actio empti*] Julian, book 15, distinguishes between one who has sold with knowledge and one who has sold in ignorance. For, he says, the unwitting seller of a diseased herd or of unsound timber will have to make good in the action *ex empto* only the amount by which the price would have been reduced had the buyer known the truth, whereas, if the seller knew, but was silent and so deceived the buyer, he will have to make good to the buyer all losses that have fallen on him in consequence of the purchase: thus, if a house has collapsed owing to the unsound timber, he must make good the value of the house, or if the buyer's beasts have perished through being infected by the diseased herd, the damage sustained.

B.   EARLY ENGLISH LAW

As we move from the laws of Justinian to the early English law of the Middle Ages, we observe a shift from a moderately sophisticated system of sales law to one that was crude at best. Indeed, private law, under which an aggrieved purchaser might sue his seller for damages caused by defective goods, was largely unknown in early England. Instead, there developed a rustic and localized criminal law that was designed to protect the public more from being cheated than injured. The late Roman law's insistence on the fair quality of goods sold wended its way to some extent into medieval English law through the dominant role in society of the church, whose scholars were trained in the civil law.

————

Hamilton, The Ancient Maxim Caveat Emptor

40 Yale L.J. 1133, 1136–64 (1931).

Caveat emptor is not to be found among the reputable ideas of the Middle Ages. As custom of trade or rule of law it is not to be met with upon the highways of medieval culture. To priest and lord, to yeoman and villain, and even to burgl[a]r and lawyer, it would have fallen strangely upon the ear. They did not talk that language.

* * *

The church manuals, even as late as the seventeenth century, laid down standards of mercantile conduct for Christians. Aquinas [1225?–1274 A.D.], theologian or lawyer as you will, discusses with his usual common sense and his usual display of neat distinctions, the delicate problems which traffic in wares brings. In his didactic fashion he asks, "Is a sale rendered unlawful by a defect in the thing sold?" He answers that a defect in kind, in quantity, or in quality, if known to the vendor and unrevealed, is sin and fraud, and the sale is void. If the defect be unknown it is no sin. Yet the seller must make good to the buyer his loss, and likewise the buyer must recompense the seller if he discovers that he has received more than he paid for. He next inquires, "Is the seller bound to mention any flaw in the thing sold?" By an argument that moves straight to its appointed result, he concludes that the seller is bound to reveal secret flaws that may occasion loss through a decrease in the value of the article or danger through the ware becoming harmful in use. But if the flaw is manifest, he is not bound to reveal it "by any duty of justice," though to do so would exhibit "the more exuberant virtue."* His judgment accords with an ancient adage that "a buyer's eye is his merchant where the defect is obvious."[21] * * *

It was in the courts of custom, of manor and baron, of leet and tolsey, that secular justice made its most immediate contact with the activities of the people. At the beginning life was lived very close to the soil, a standard

---

* Aquinas references are to THOMAS AQUINAS, SUMMA THEOLOGICA, ETHICUS, II, II, question 77, arts. 2–4.—Eds.

21. ... The eye is to judge where the eye can judge, that is where the defect is obvious. In time the eye became symbolic of all man's faculties, its jurisdiction was enlarged, and the restraint of the last five words was conveniently removed....

hardly up to subsistence prevailed, the list of necessities which demanded protection was short, the wares which came to an intermittent market and fell under control were few. As the crafts increased in number and claimed more followers, the scrutiny of the community was progressively extended. The intent of the folkways, which were just passing into law, was to insure an open market, a fair price, an honest measure, and a quality good after the fashion of the day . . . .

[A system of regulation of quality slowly developed that was more criminal than civil in nature.]

As trade lost its adventitious character, the fair was succeeded by the market town. The b[o]rough . . . claimed over manufacture and sale the control which the manor had exercised over agriculture; upon the ancient foundations, in the spirit of the authoritarian ideal, it erected a detailed and elaborate system of regulation. The gilds, decked out in the trappings of religious orders and dedicated to the worship of God, Our Lady the Virgin, and all the Saints, held themselves out to serve as roundly as any Rotary Club. The conduct of the several handicrafts were regulated by their own statutes, which became rather generally ordinances of the town. Their enforcement rested with the officers of the gild, under the oversight of officials of the city. The Mayor and Alderman constituted an authority which was alike an administrative body and a court. Away from the marts of organized trade were to be found the wayfaring palmer with his relics and trinkets, the peripatetic peddlar with gew-gaws and ornaments, strangers here today and there tomorrow, wayfaring men of no place and without the law. In such wares one had to trade at his peril; there was no authentic test for holy water and bones of the saints, for Venetian glass and spices of Araby. Nor could a standard have been used; before the latent became the obvious fault, the itinerant was far on his unknown way . . . . There, too, was the horse-trader, the erratic properties of whose merchandise could not be reduced to a standard model; he was not expected to cry the uncertain defects of his steed or nag from the house-tops. Among such persons without rank or of mean estate a redress of wrongs was practically not to be had. It took time and the bitterness of experience to subdue the idea into compact language; but here it came to be understood that one's unconsidered bargain was his own tough luck.

How the trick of phrase was turned, and *caveat emptor* came into being we do not know. The wisdom seems to be the afterthought of the good man who has bargained, perhaps in a horse trade, once too often; the manner suggests the lawyer regretfully stating that the grievance seems to be without redress. * * *

The expression *caveat emptor,* in its upward climb, appears in print for the first time well along in the sixteenth century . . . . An ordinance of Lancaster, relating to the purchase of malt, ignored the distinction between obvious and latent defects and restated an old proverb, "let their eye be their chapman."[208] At the beginning of the seventeenth century the expres-

---

208. [Citation.] The date is 1562. "It was proverbial in France, *'qui n'ouvre pas yeux doit ouvrir la bourse.'* "[Citation.]

sion appears to be quite well known.... [A much-quoted passage from Coke on Littleton (1633), provided:] "Note that by the civil law every man is bound to warrant the thing he selleth or conveyeth, albeit there be no express warranty, either in deed or in law; but the common law bindeth him not, for *caveat emptor.*"

Coke on Littleton

N O T E

The maxim of *caveat emptor* first appears in the law reports in 1601. Moore v. Hussey, 80 Eng.Rep. 243. Two years later, the judges and barons of the Exchequer–Chamber decided the famous case of the bezoar stone, Chandler v. Lopus, 79 Eng.Rep. 3 (1603). Plaintiff alleged that the defendant goldsmith sold him a stone "which he affirmed to Lopus to be a bezar-stone ... for one hundred pounds; *ubi revera* it was not a bezar-stone: the defendant pleaded not guilty, and verdict was given and judgment entered for the plaintiff in the King's Bench." Holding the declaration deficient, the Exchequer–Chamber reversed. "[T]he bare affirmation that it was a bezar-stone, without warranting it to be so, is no cause of action: and although he knew it to be no bezar-stone, it is not material; for every one in selling his wares will affirm that his wares are good, or the horse which he sells is sound; yet if he does not warrant them to be so, it is no cause of action...."

As Chandler v. Lopus came to be interpreted, it announced a simple rule governing the rights of the buyer of inferior goods: "He had a cause of action if he had exacted an express warranty at the time of the sale from a seller who knew his representations to be false. An affirmation, no matter how many holy saints were invoked, fell short of a warranty; latent defects, however impervious to ordinary vision, were the purchaser's own lookout. When in time writs were accommodated more sharply to specific complaints, ... the buyer had the alternative of a suit in assumpsit on express warranty or in deceit by proving a *scienter*. The exactions of a ceremonial were set down as an injunction to the buyer to look to himself for protection." Hamilton, *supra,* at 1168–69. For the next two centuries, except for cases of fraud, or breach of express warranty, *caveat emptor* ruled supreme.

C.   Early American Law

In 1804, Chancellor Kent of New York proclaimed that *caveat emptor* applied to latent defects, Seixas v. Woods, 2 Cai. R. 48, 2 Am. Dec. 215 (N.Y. Sup. Ct.1804), and other early nineteenth-century American courts latched onto the rule with a gusto reflecting the new nation's devotion to individualism and free enterprise.* Toward the end of the century, some

---

* That the doctrine of *caveat emptor* was the prevailing legal ethic during the seven- teenth and eighteenth centuries is the con- ventional historical wisdom. See, e.g., Pros-

courts finally began imposing an implied warranty of quality on manufac-turers (and growers), but the *caveat emptor* principle persisted in most states in retailer cases even into the twentieth century. See, e.g., National Oil Co. v. Rankin, 75 P. 1013 (Kan. 1904). Consider Barnard v. Kellogg, 77 U.S. (10 Wall.) 383, 388–89, 19 L. Ed. 987 (1870):

> No principle of the common law has been better established, or more often affirmed, both in this country and in England, than that in sales of personal property, in the absence of express warranty, where the buyer has an opportunity to inspect the commodity, and the seller is guilty of no fraud, and is neither the manufacturer nor grower of the article he sells, the maxim of *caveat emptor* applies. Such a rule, requiring the purchaser to take care of his own interests, has been found best adapted to the wants of trade in the business transactions of life. And there is no hardship in it, because if the purchaser distrusts his judgment he can require of the seller a warranty that the quality or condition of the goods he desires to buy corresponds with the sample exhibited.... Of such universal acceptance is the doctrine of *caveat emptor* in this country, that the courts of all the States in the Union where the common law prevails, with one exception (South Carolina), sanction it.

As the functions of manufacturing and retailing separated during the course of industrialization in the nineteenth century, the law developed yet another obstacle to consumer recovery. Winterbottom v. Wright, 10 M. & W. 109, 152 Eng.Rep. 402 (Ex.1842), and its progeny prohibited actions against "remote" manufacturers with whom plaintiffs had no "privity of contract." E.g., Loop v. Litchfield, 42 N.Y. 351 (1870); Lebourdais v. Vitrified Wheel Co., 80 N.E. 482 (Mass. 1907).

The privity requirement was an effective instrument of social policy for a nation bent on promoting the development of its infant industry. One court explained: "If a contractor who erects a house, who builds a bridge, or performs any other work; a manufacturer who constructs a boiler, a piece of machinery, or a steamship, owes a duty to the whole world, that his work or his machine or his steamship, shall contain no hidden defect, it is difficult to measure the extent of his responsibility, and no prudent man would engage in such occupations upon such conditions. It is safer and wiser to confine such liabilities to the parties immediately concerned." Curtain v. Somerset, 21 A. 244, 245 (Pa. 1891). At least one early scholar disagreed: "To encourage commerce and industry by removing all duty and incentive to protect the public is to invite wholesale sacrifice of individual

ser, The Implied Warranty of Merchantable Quality, 27 Minn. L. Rev. 117 (1943). At least in the eighteenth and early nineteenth centuries, however, there is evidence of some pockets of resistance to the doctrine in the form of support for an implied warranty of quality in a few American jurisdictions and possibly in England, perhaps reflecting aberrational mercantile customs in certain areas. Yet once the nineteenth century was well under way,

apparently all American jurisdictions except South Carolina adhered to the principle of *caveat emptor*. See generally M. Horwitz, The Transformation of American Law, 1780–1860, at 167, 180, 330 n. 13 (1977). Horwitz argues, however, that a "sound price" rule *generally* prevailed during the seventeenth and eighteenth century and that the *caveat emptor* notion did not take hold until about 1800.

rights on the altar of commercial greed. . . . [I]t cannot be to the interest of any community to encourage carelessness and disregard of human life and property therein." Bohlen, The Basis of Affirmative Obligations in the Law of Tort (pt. 3), 53 U. Pa. L. Rev. 337, 355 (1905).

"Modern" products liability law, and Chapter 2, begin with the fall of the privity defense in negligence cases occasioned by MacPherson v. Buick Motor Company in 1916.

N O T E

On the Roman law origins of products liability, see W. Buckland, A Text–Book of Roman Law from Augustus to Justinian 491–94 (3d ed. Stein rev. 1966); R. Lee, The Elements of Roman Law 13, 15, 314–16 (4th ed. 1956); J. Thomas, Textbook of Roman Law 15, 16, 286–88 (1976); F. de Zulueta, The Roman Law of Sale 46–51, 124 (corr. ed. 1945). On its subsequent early history, see Bohlen, The Basis of Affirmative Obligations in the Law of Tort (pts. 2 & 3), 53 U. Pa. L. Rev. 273, 337 (1905); Hamilton, The Ancient Maxim Caveat Emptor, 40 Yale L.J. 1133 (1931); Llewellyn, On Warranty of Quality, and Society (pts. 1 & 2), 36 Colum. L. Rev. 699 (1936), 37 Colum. L. Rev. 341 (1937); Murphy, Medieval Theory and Products Liability, 3 B.C. Indus. & Com. L. Rev. 29 (1961); Prosser, The Implied Warranty of Merchantable Quality, 27 Minn. L. Rev. 117, 118–22 (1943). On its history generally, see D. Owen, Products Liability Law § 1.2 (2d ed. 2008).

4. MODERN PRODUCTS LIABILITY LAW

Products liability law, as we know it today, is of recent origin. As late as 1955, for example, one writer remarked, "Products liability does not yet rank as a term of art in the courts of law." Wilson, Products Liability (pt. 1), 43 Calif. L. Rev. 614 (1955). With the exception of a few cases involving fraud and the sale of defective medicines and food, the appearance of products liability cases in the law reports coincides with the rise of the industrial revolution in the late 1800s. By 1900, such cases begin to appear with some frequency. The birth of modern products liability law may safely be dated at 1916 with the case of MacPherson v. Buick Motor Co., 111 N.E. 1050, decided by Judge Cardozo of the New York Court of Appeals. More spectacular than the birth of modern products liability, however, was its initial forays as a toddler in the late 1950s and its explosive blossoming into adolescence in the 1960s with generalized theories of strict manufacturer liability in warranty and tort.

A. AN ANATOMY OF MODERN PRODUCTS LIABILITY LITIGATION

Prior to studying the modern problems and rules of products liability law presently applied by the courts, it is helpful to examine the broad nature of such litigation. Several studies provide useful empirical information.

Interagency Task Force Study

A comprehensive study of products liability litigation was conducted under the auspices of the Interagency Task Force on Product Liability, formed in 1976 to study the increase in products liability litigation and resulting insurance premiums. Under the direction of Professor Victor Schwartz, working out of The Department of Commerce, the Task Force analyzed hundreds of decisions from 1965–76. The Task Force report, released in 1977, revealed the following information:

The Forum—78% of the cases were tried in state court, 22% in federal court. Suit usually was brought in the state where the injury occurred, usually *not* where the product was manufactured, and almost always in the plaintiff's home state. Juries heard 86% of the cases tried.

Increase in Cases—The number of products liability cases reported in the eight states doubled from 1965–70 to 1971–76.

Type of Product—About ⅓ of the cases involved automobiles, followed in frequency by industrial machinery.

Parties—Manufacturers were defendants in 79% of the cases, retailers in 33%, wholesalers 5%, manufacturers' suppliers 5%, employers 4%, lessors 3%, and installers 5%. Manufacturers were third-party plaintiffs in 15% of the cases in which they were original defendants. Manufacturers were third-party defendants in about 10% of the cases; employers in 8%.

Age of Product—About 10% of the products were over 20 years old. Excluding automobiles, 21% of the products were over 20 years old.

Work–Related Injuries—In 1971–76, 50% of the cases involved work-related injuries from machinery and tools.

Type of Defect—The bases of liability asserted were manufacturing (and inadequate inspection) defects in 42% of the cases, design defects in 39%, and warning defects in 21%. (By comparison, a 1973 survey indicated the following breakdown of 222 cases brought in strict tort: manufacturing defects—28%; design defects—46%; warning defects—25%; and misrepresentation—1%.)

Most automotive and container cases alleged defective manufacture, most machinery and recreational product cases alleged defective design, and most chemical cases alleged inadequate warnings.

Prevailing Party—Plaintiffs prevailed in 50% of all the cases, defendants in 50%. Of cases decided on the merits, plaintiffs prevailed 41% of the time in Arizona, 44% in Illinois, 58% in California, and 63% in Texas. Plaintiffs won 60% of the jury trials but only 44% of the non-jury trials. (Note, however, that businesses are more frequently plaintiffs in non-jury trials.)

From the 1965–70 period to 1971–76, the rate of successful plaintiff cases rose 4%.

Damages—The average damage award in cases in which the plaintiff ultimately prevailed rose from $104,000 in 1965–70 to $222,000 in 1971–76, for an average over the entire period of $181,000. By state, average damage awards for the entire period were as follows: California ($272,000), Texas ($221,000), New York ($170,000), Pennsylvania ($137,000), and Illinois ($119,000). Much of the increase in awards between the two periods was attributable to inflation, especially the cost of medical care which is often the largest component of products liability claims.

NOTE

See Product Liability: Final Report of the Legal Study, vol. 3 (Interagency Task Force on Product Liability: U.S. Dept. of Comm., 1977), summarized in id., vol. 1, at 17–18.

A comprehensive insurance industry survey in 1977 found that less than 4% of all products liability claims went all the way to verdict and, in contrast to the findings of the Task Force, fewer than 25% of the defendants in these cases were found liable. Highlights, Insurance Services Office Product Liability Closed Claim Survey: A Technical Analysis of Survey Results 6 (1977).

Insurance Industry Study

The following statistics are from another insurance industry study of large (in excess of $100,000) products liability claims closed in 1985. Such claims represent only 1–2% of all products liability claims, but they account for 50–60% of insurer payments.

Payments at Various Stages of Litigation—In the 4% of large claims where no suit was filed, the average payment was $232,000. In the 71% of claims where suit was filed, but where settlement was reached before trial, payments averaged $441,000. Where settlement was reached during trial (14% of the cases), payments averaged $649,000. In cases that went to verdict (11%), payments averaged $532,000.

Theory of Liability—Strict liability was the only theory alleged in 22% of the claims; negligence the only theory in 15%; and breach of warranty the only theory in 3%. All three theories of liability were alleged in 30% of the claims.

Strict liability was the main theory relied upon in settlement in 60% of the cases, negligence in 31%, and warranty in 8%.

Type of Defect—Where strict liability was the main theory of liability, defective design was the applicable theory in 75% of the claims, and warning defects in 18%.

Punitive Damages—Punitive damages were demanded in 18% of the incidents; separate payments for such damages were awarded by a jury or paid for in settlement in 1% of the cases. Yet the threat of such damages probably increased the size of other settlements.

Number of Defendants—There was only one defendant in 56% of the cases. There were two defendants in 22%, three defendants in 9%, four defendants in 6%, and more than four in 7%.

Miscellaneous Issues—In the opinion of the claim reviewers, the question of product defect was too technical for the jury to understand and decide in 17% of the incidents; damage, alteration, modification, or misuse was a cause of the accident in 34% of the incidents; and 12% of the products failed to comply with governmental safety standards.

NOTES

1. See A Study of Large Product Liability Claims Closed in 1985, a joint study of the Alliance of American Insurers (L. Soular, Research Dept.) and the American Insurance Ass'n (1986).

2. Another study, based on cases from the late 1970s, found that 19% of products liability claims filed were dropped, and 95% of the remainder were settled. Of the 5% that went to verdict, plaintiffs won 37% and lost 63%. Viscusi, The Determinants of the Disposition of Product Liability Claims and Compensation for Bodily Injury, 15 J.Leg.Stud. 321 (1986). By contrast, a Rand Corporation study indicated that plaintiffs won about 50% of the products liability trials in San Francisco and Cook County, Illinois in the early 1980s. D. Hensler, Summary of Research Results on Products Liability (Institute for Civil Justice, Oct. 1986).

3. The plaintiff success rate and median awards of products liability verdicts vary considerably among regions, as one ABF study revealed: Maricopa County, Arizona: 44%—$135,000; Los Angeles: 44%—$428,000; San Diego: 30%—$255,000; Cook County, Illinois: 35%—$279,000; New York, N.Y.: 61%—$1,132,000. Six cases were tried in Westchester, N.Y. The plaintiff won only one (17%), and recovered $16,710. Daniels & Martin, Jury Verdicts and the "Crisis" in Civil Justice: Some Findings from an Empirical Study (Amer. Bar Found., unpubl'd paper, 1987) (tables 2 & 4).

4. Median and mean products liability awards were reportedly $500,000 and $1.5 million in 1984, and $380,000 and $2 million in 1994, respectively. Current Award Trends in Personal Injury (1996 ed.), Personal Injury Valuation Handbook, Jury Verdict Research Series.

Department of Justice Study

In 2004, the Bureau of Justice Statistics of the U.S. Department of Justice released a new study of state court jury verdicts in all types of civil damages cases during 2001 in the 75 largest counties in the nation. The study examined two types of cases: 126 *ordinary product* cases and 31 involving *asbestos*. Civil Justice Survey of State Courts, 2001—Civil Jury Cases and Verdicts in Large Counties, NCJ–202803 (April 2004):

Proportion of Total—*Ordinary* products liability cases represented 1.1% of the total civil cases, down from 3% of the total ten years earlier, *asbestos* product cases 0.3%, down from the toxic substance total of 2.4% a decade earlier. (By comparison, auto cases were 35.6% of the total, premises liability 10.6%, and medical malpractice 9.7%.)

Time to Verdict—The periods from filing of the civil complaint to verdict were as follows: *Ordinary*—average time, 35.1 months. *Asbestos*—average time, 16.8 months.

Plaintiff Success Rates—Plaintiffs won 40.3% of the *ordinary* product cases, 60% of the *asbestos* cases.

Size of Awards, Generally—The sizes of the awards were as follows: *Ordinary* products—median, $311,000; mean, $2.2 million. *Asbestos*—median, $1.65 million; mean, $4.5 million. Of the awards won by plaintiffs, 31.4% involving *ordinary* products exceeded $1 million as did 59.7% of those involving *asbestos*.

Punitive Damages—Punitive damages were awarded in only one (2%) and two (11%) of the *ordinary* product and *asbestos* cases in which the plaintiff won, respectively. The punitive award was $177,000 in the *ordinary* case and averaged $450,000 in the *asbestos* cases.

Plaintiff Success Rates & Size of Awards, by Location (Jury Trials)—Plaintiff success rates and verdict sizes varied considerably by location. The following data represent, respectively, plaintiff success rates; median awards; mean awards; and median punitive damages awards, considering *all* types of damages cases, not just products:

Los Angeles:	53%;	$120,000;	$390,724;	$35,000.
San Francisco:	52%;	$152,000;	$2,887,857;	$120,000.
Hartford, CT:	57%;	$18,000;	$143,000;	$80,000.
Dade, FL:	57%;	$74,000;	$3,002,713;	$2,300,000.
Fulton, GA:	68%;	$10,000;	$122,626;	$53,000.
Cook, IL:	56%;	$80,000;	$802,487;	$5,000.
Honolulu:	55%;	$550,000;	$1,155,600;	$1,150,000.
Jefferson, KY	44%;	$25,000;	$154,267;	$20,000.
St. Louis	56%;	$16,000;	$84,340;	$14,000.
Essex, NJ	41%;	$38,000;	$268,642;	$2,000.*
New York	46%;	$280,000;	$1,379,376;	$700,000.
Cuyahoga, OH	57%;	$20,000;	$318,783;	$100,000.
Philadelphia	51%;	$74,000;	$1,715,584;	$49,000.
Harris, TX	40%;	$37,000;	$603,090;	$90,000.
King, WA	59%;	$32,000;	$678,029;	$10,000.
Milwaukee	69%;	$15,000;	$109,949;	$2,000.*

* Not a median but the actual amount awarded.

Jury Verdict Research Study

In 2005, Jury Verdict Research published a study entitled Product Liability Claims: An Overview of Jury Awards and Settlements, edited by Brooke Doran. The study arrived at the following data for products liability cases:

Products Liability Cases of All Types

Plaintiff Recovery Probability: 46%

Award Median: $1 million

Awards of $1 million or greater: 52%

Industrial, Construction, Commercial and Farm Products

Plaintiff Recovery Probability: 54%

Award Median: $1 million

Awards of $1 million or greater: 52%

Transportation Products

Plaintiff Recovery Probability: 43%

Award Median: $2.68 million

Awards of $1 million or greater: 70%

General Consumer Products

Plaintiff Recovery Probability: 39%

Award Median: $216,269

Awards of $1 million or greater: 31%

Medical Products

Plaintiff Recovery Probability: 46%

Award Median: $987,500

Awards of $1 million or greater: 51%

NOTE

Interpreting statistics on products liability awards is tricky business—because of the mysteries of statistics and the partisan nature of this field of law. Products liability studies covering the late 1980s and most of the 1990s showed moderation and, in some instances, declines in case filings (at least in non-toxic substance cases), verdicts, and plaintiff success rates. See, e.g., Message from the Chair, ABA TIPS Newsletter 1 (Spring/Summer 1995) (noting that products liability filings in federal court, apart from asbestos cases, declined 36% between 1985 and 1991); Hunter, Product Liability Insurance–Report of the Insurance Group of Consumer Federation of America (June 1998) (showing products liability insurance costs "minute" and declining, from 25¢ per $100 dollars of retail product sales in 1985 to 16¢ in 1996).

But products liability costs and insurance tend to move in waves, sometimes up and sometimes down; and the wave in the early 2000s appears to be on the rise.

Winter, Jury Awards Soar as Lawsuits Decline on Defective Goods

nytimes.com (Jan. 30, 2001).

After years of little change, jury awards to consumers suing over defective products are rising sharply in many industries, from cars and tools to toys and appliances. But at the same time, far fewer such cases are being brought, and many lawyers are turning away clients because their injuries are not debilitating enough to bring in big awards. * * *

The median award—not including punitive damages—has more than tripled since 1993, from $500,300 to over $1.8 million in 1999, according to a study of 2,751 product-liability verdicts to be released today by LRP Publications, one of the only nonpartisan groups to track cases in several states each year. Much of that rise has come the last three years, and awards are now growing at the fastest rate in two decades. * * *

Manufacturers and defense lawyers have long attributed large verdicts in defective product cases to what they call Robin Hood jurors who relish sitting in judgment of powerful corporations, if only for a day. But a growing number of legal scholars say that rising awards are, to a large degree, the unexpected outcome of rules [such as recent limits on expert testimony] that make it harder to sue manufacturers and win. * * *

To better their prospects under the new rules, many plaintiff's lawyers are buttressing their arguments with platoons of experts, and improving their chances of winning by choosing only truly egregious cases involving the most seriously injured parties.

"I've had plenty of defective products, clearly defective, where I won't even talk to the people because their injuries aren't severe enough," said Craig E. Hilborn, president of Hilborn & Hilborn, a small law firm in Birmingham, Mich. "If they're not a quadriplegic, a paraplegic or losing some part of their body, there's no way I'm going to take that case." * * *

"I can't take case on any more unless I am absolutely positive that I have one worth at least $2 million," said James L. Gilbert, president of the Attorney Information Exchange Group, an organization of about 500 plaintiffs' lawyers nationwide. "I can no longer afford to spend $300,000 trying a case that is only worth $500,000, and that's ridiculous." * * *

The insurance industry is blaming the escalating awards for the double-digit increases for basic coverage that many businesses are now facing. They are the highest rate increases since the liability crisis of the mid–1980's, the industry says, when playgrounds were chained shut and diving boards were stripped from pools for fear of the injuries—and lawsuits—they might induce.

"It is cause for alarm," said Dr. Robert P. Hartwig, chief economist of the Insurance Information Institute.... "We've seen a much more aggressive trial bar since the tobacco settlement. The are flush with cash and looking to generate a high rate of return."

But as plaintiff's lawyers seek out more valuable cases, some worry that finding representation has become significantly more difficult, even for those who suffer injuries from truly dangerous products.

"Smaller cases are getting priced out of the market," said Marc Galanter, a professor at the University of Wisconsin law school. "There are people with legitimate injuries who will not be able to take advantage of the redress the law provides." * * *

[The federal courts' tightening up on rules governing the admissibility of expert testimony has led plaintiffs' lawyers to build] fortresses of expert testimony that they hope will withstand any challenges. To prove a car is unsafe, for example, lawyers now routinely hire separate experts to analyze the crash site, the road conditions, the body's response to an impact and the vehicle's design—then pay other experts in the field to verify the findings. * * *

The wave of experts has helped plaintiffs' lawyers improve their batting average in court. While most injured consumers lose defective product suits, their success rate rose from 39 percent in 1993 to 46 percent in 1999, according to [LRP's study].

"It debunks the notion of the frivolous lawsuit," [said] Stephen Daniels, senior research fellow at the American Bar Foundation, a nonpartisan research group. "The plaintiffs' attorneys believe that the tort reform movement has poisoned the jury box, so they're extra prepared." * * *

But many academics believe jurors are surprisingly impartial. Valerie P. Hans, a sociology professor at the University of Delaware who has studied juries the last decade, said juries hold corporations to a higher standard than they do individuals but are equally skeptical of plaintiffs, hesitant to side with them simply to bond with the underdog. * * *

N O T E

Compare Moller & Indig, Products Liability Law Revisited: A Realistic Perspective, 31 Tort & Ins. L.J. 879 (1996), arguing that "products liability cases are among the hardest and costliest suits to initiate and win." Proving that a product was defective and that the defective condition caused the plaintiff's injury "with credible evidence can cost hundreds of thousands of dollars in litigation expenses and costs, including ... fees for high-priced experts." Most such cases "are extremely hard fought" by defendant corporations that "have invested heavily in safety research and are concerned about protecting their corporate image and goodwill. Such corporations ... take an especially hard line approach to products liability claims and are unwilling to settle cases for fear of inviting other claims."

―――

B.   A CASE EXAMPLE

1.   THE PROBLEM

Roberts, Circular Saw Design: A Hazard Analysis
1 J. Prod. Liab. 127 (1977).

The portable electric circular power saw has grown in popularity [such] that there are over 30 million currently in use in the United States alone.

With their ... availability at a low price has come an associated trend toward home use and ... use by the untrained or novice user. The CPSC's Bureau of Epidemiology studied in depth 74 of the 5,000 accidents involving portable circular saws in 1975. [The CPSC's National Electronic Injury Surveillance System (NEISS) estimated that a total of 100,000 saw injuries were treated in American hospitals in 2004.–Eds.]

* * *

The greatest value provided by the in-depth reports is to be found in the narrative discussion of the accident circumstances. Three types of circumstances predominate ...:

(1) *Human Error:* For 33 of the 74 cases, operator error is the only appropriate description of the accident process.... [Many] individuals saw directly into their hands or legs which frequently are beneath the piece they are sawing. It is difficult to conceive of a mechanical solution to this type of accident. * * *

(2) *Guards Which Failed to Operate:* Circular saws are commonly equipped with a retractable lower guard which slides up into the housing over the top of the blade while cutting. The guard is pulled by a spring or falls due to gravity over the lower part of the blade after the cut is completed. [The guards failed to operate properly and prevent the accident in 17 cases.]

These accidents consistently involve the leg of the victim. The usual set of circumstances involves an operator, who when finished with a cut, will lower his hand to his side. The guard fails to return to its position over the bottom of the blade and the still-turning blade cuts deeply into the upper or lower leg.

This injury is interesting because it is so correctable. In a subsequent section the actual circumstances involving a specific saw will be developed and the simple design measure which could have yielded a solution is described.

There were also accidents which implied guard failure wherein the guard apparently operated by gravity. There is an indication from the reports that the saw kickback which caused the injury could have been prevented had a spring with significant retarding force been present to restore the guard before the blade came in contact with the operator. In either event the accidents could not be attributed to the user but rather to the design specifications and manufacturing procedures of the manufacturer....

(3) *Saw Kickback:* [The third predominant cause of circular saw injuries is from "saw kickback." This phenomenon sometimes occurs when the blade binds, or hits a knot or defect in the wood. It usually is preventable by the addition of a safety device, a "riving knife," which "acts as a wedge behind the blade to prevent the wood from closing around the blade and binding."]

Injury Data—Detailed Investigation

. . . This section concerns an analysis of a saw involved in an accident during its first day of use.

Figure 4: Circular Saw with Lower Guard in Down Position

The saw involved was a Skilsaw Model 537 manufactured by the Skil Corporation, Chicago, Illinois. It is powered by a 1⅞ horsepower motor and operates at 5200 r.p.m. At this angular velocity with a 7¼ inch blade, the blade edge velocity is 164.5 feet per second or 112 mph.

At the time of the accident the victim who is regularly employed as a carpentry contractor was using his new saw while working on a ladder to cut rafters over his head. He completed a cut, released the trigger and lowered his arm to his side. The blade guard failed to return to the closed position and as a result the still rotating blade [lacerated] the victim's right thigh.

. . . Figure 4 illustrates the saw as it was received for analysis. Note that the blade guard can be pushed to the full open position and that it will remain open and not snap back to protect the blade.

Physical examination revealed that the action of the blade guard is controlled either manually by the plastic lever at the top of the saw or by stock being cut physically pushing the lower guard up into the housing. As the guard is pushed up a small coil spring attached at one end to the fixed upper guard and at the other to the movable lower guard is stretched around the motor shaft-mandrel.

The stretching of the spring produces a restoring force and associated torque which tends to cause the lower housing to automatically return to the closed position. When the lower guard is fully pushed into the upper position exposing the blade as shown in Figure 5, the string is stretched a total of two and one-half inches. The spring was removed from the saw and found to have a spring constant of one pound of developed force per inch of extension. Thus the maximum force which the spring could develop to return the guard to the down position is two and one half pounds.

Figure 5: Circular Saw with Lower Guard in Up Position
Held in Place by Friction

While the spring was removed, the saw blade was removed as well and the force required to return the guard to the down position measured as shown in Figure 6. The restoring force was measured with a Pelouze tension scale model 10–T modified to record the maximum force exerted. Ten trials produced force values which ranged from three to four and one half pounds. The average force required was three and three quarter pounds.

**Figure 6: Procedure Used to Measure Force Necessary
to Restore Lower Guard to Down Position**

As was indicated earlier, the maximum force which the spring—designed and installed by the manufacturer—could produce was two and one half pounds. Given the physical evidence above, it is easy to see why the guard did not return to the closed position, thus exposing the victim's leg to the still-turning blade.

This particular saw involves both problems of design and manufacturing liability. The blade guard tends to stay in the upper position because of friction and binding between the upper and lower guards. This is usually the result of poor quality control over the dimensional tolerances of the finished parts. Dimensional interference which produce friction and binding can be overcome by the spring. However, the spring must be stiff enough to develop sufficient force when it is extended. If the saw in question had had a spring of proper design or parts of proper dimension, the accident described above could [not] have occurred. * * *

Safe design is not an accident. The circular power saw proves the point.

N O T E

The Roberts article illustrates the type of failure analysis engineers are capable of providing to lawyers handling products liability cases. This type of assistance is invaluable to the lawyer throughout the case, from the initial investigatory stages, in discovery, and through the trial. On experts in products liability litigation, see D. Owen, Products Liability Law § 6.3 (2d ed. 2008).

---

2. THE REGULATORY RESPONSE

Two federal agencies have jurisdiction over the safety of portable circular saws: the Consumer Product Safety Commission and the Occupational Safety and Health Administration. In 1976, the CPSC issued a "Product Profile" on consumer power saws, including portable circular saws, describing the nature and frequency of accidents from such saws. In 1977 the CPSC accorded power saws a "medium" priority for the issuance of safety standards. See 42 Fed. Reg. 47,859 (1977). As of 1995, the agency still had not issued such standards and its staff reported that none will be considered unless injury rates materially increase.

The Occupational Safety and Health Administration has jurisdiction over the safety of portable circular saws used in the workplace. It has issued the following general industry job safety and health standard:

Guarding of Portable Powered Tools

29 C.F.R § 1910.243 (2007).

(a) **Portable powered tool**—(1)*Portable circular saws.* (i) All portable, power-driven circular saws having a blade diameter greater than 2 in. shall be equipped with guards above and below the base plate or shoe. The upper guard shall cover the saw to the depth of the teeth, except for the minimum arc required to permit the base to be tilted for bevel cuts. The lower guard shall cover the saw to the depth of the teeth, except for the minimum arc required to allow proper retraction and contact with the work. When the tool is withdrawn from the work, the lower guard shall automatically and instantly return to covering position.

N O T E

Do you think the OSHA regulation adequately addresses the hazards in portable circular saws? Why do you suppose the CPSC accorded such saws only a "medium" priority for regulation? Why do you suppose this agency never issued safety standards?

Recall Report

34 Prod. Safety & Liab. Rep. 17 (January 9, 2006).

Approximately 196,000 7¼-inch [Porter–Cable] MAG–SAW circular saws recalled because the lower guard on the saws could stick in the open position, posing a risk of severe lacerations to consumers.... Corrective Action: Porter–Cable is providing a free inspection and repair, if necessary.

———

3. THE JUDICIAL RESPONSE

Cavanaugh v. Skil Corporation

Superior Court of New Jersey, Appellate Division, 1999.
331 N.J. Super. 134, 751 A.2d 564, modified on other grounds and aff'd on Appellate
Division's opinion below, Supreme Court of New Jersey, 2000. 751 A.2d 518.

■ KING, P.J.A.D.

Defendant Skil Corporation appeals a $200,155.20 judgment entered upon a jury verdict in this product liability case. Plaintiff, a carpenter, lost one toe and severely damaged another after he had placed down a Skilsaw portable circular saw [manufactured by the defendant] which "travelled" eighteen inches across the subfloor of a house that plaintiff was framing and ran over his right foot. [The judgment below was based on plaintiff's claims that the saw was defectively designed and that the defendant was negligent.] Affirmed.

[After using the Skilsaw to cut a number of 2x4 pieces of lumber, plaintiff released the saw's trigger and heard the saw's motor stop, but the blade continued to "spin pretty fast." Four or five seconds later, he set the saw down on the floor about eighteen inches to his right, whereupon it traveled across the flooring and onto his work boot, cutting off a toe.]

[Plaintiff showed the jury the saw's lower blade guard and how it was "supposed to snap back like that." On the day of the accident, however, for reasons unknown to the plaintiff,] the guard "didn't come down. It stayed in the open position." [Plaintiff further testified that, although he had seen some carpenters use a wedge of wood to keep a circular saw's guard open, he personally had never done so nor had he ever used a saw with the guard wedged open, which] would have slowed his productivity significantly. He would have to wait for about twenty seconds after each cut for the blade to stop spinning. Thus, wedging the guard open would have made his job more difficult and more dangerous. Plaintiff could think of no common sense reason for wedging open the guard. [One of plaintiff's co-workers had never seen the plaintiff wedge the guard open but knew that some carpenters use the wedgie technique to saw rafters.]

[The plaintiff's expert mechanical engineer, Louis E. Howarth, testified that the American National Standards Institute (ANSI) viewed the Underwriters Laboratory (UL) 45 code the proper standard for portable woodworking tools. This code, which was in force when the subject Skilsaw was produced in 1988, provided] that a saw should have a retractable lower guard, which shall automatically retract to the closed position when the saw is not in use.... [Howarth further testified that in 1988, the UL–45 did not require a blade brake on a portable circular saw but contended that, as of 1995, it did. He explained that the] retractable blade guard could work with two different types of springs. The first type operated like a screen door: "when you let go it pulls the door shut." The second type was the torsion spring. The spring was wound up and when released, "it shuts [the lower blade guard and] makes it close," [protecting] the operator from contact with the front of the blade.

Howarth testified that sometimes the lower blade guard would not release after a cut—when for example, it was clogged by wood chips or saw dust. [And when the user released the trigger, the blade continued to rotate for 15–20 seconds. If the user put the saw down while the blade was still spinning and the guard was stuck open, the saw] would "run backwards on the floor on you every time." [A] blade brake [would have prevented this risk.]

In 1988, when the Skilsaw was made, an electronic dynamic brake (also known as a blade brake) existed which would have prevented the blade from continuing to spin after the trigger had been released. [A blade brake would have addressed the risk noted in a Consumer Products Safety Commission "fact sheet" that] a portable saw blade guard could malfunction by "staying in a retracted position after completion of the cut" [even though the blade continued] rotating after the power was stopped. Electronic, or dynamic, braking would cause the blade to stop rotating more quickly. This was the device that should have been on the saw that plaintiff had used. Electronic blade brakes were very reliable.

Howarth showed the jury an Ambitech electronic blade brake that had been available since 1974 and cost only $20 in 1995. According to Ambitech, the brake would stop a blade from spinning in "a fraction of a second." Howarth claimed a blade brake could have been designed into the Skilsaw used by plaintiff.

In 1988, defendant's competitors manufactured portable circular saws with blade brakes. Indeed, Sears manufactured such a saw in 1976 and 1977. Black and Decker also made a portable circular saw with a blade brake as did Makita. The manufacturers of these saws claimed that the blade would stop rotating either instantaneously or within a few seconds [leading Howarth to conclude that the accident saw was defective because it was sold without a blade brake when there was a foreseeable risk that the guard might stick open.]

Howarth did not know why the guard did not work on the day of plaintiff's accident [but surmised that it probably failed to close] "because it jammed up with a—sawdust or chips—wood chips of some sort," [a risk known to manufacturers and hence foreseeable. Howarth concluded that a blade brake would have prevented plaintiff's accident because the brake would have stopped the blade from spinning quickly. Howarth also testified that the benefits of a blade brake "far outweigh[ed] any risk of injury that may occur." A blade brake makes a portable circular saw "much safer"] because "whenever the retractable lower guard is not closed on it and you release the trigger, you're stopping that blade so fast that any motion you have you would probably prevent an injury from occurring because the blade is stopped.''

* * *

[Peter Domeny, who worked as an engineer for the defendant, testified as an expert on its behalf. Since 1969, Domeny has worked on the design and development of power tools and their safety, including accident investigations. In fact,] Domeny helped develop and design the Skilsaw that had injured plaintiff. He was the director of defendant's product safety department and, as such, was responsible for overseeing the development, design, testing and writing of manuals from a "safety point of view." During the course of his employment, Domeny worked with "a broad line of power tools from drills, grinders, circular saws."

Domeny examined the subject saw after the accident. He turned it "on" and then "off" and found that it worked fine. He took measurements and used strobe photography to "show how fast and what is the timing of the guard closure from the open to the fully closed position." Domeny checked the guard system on the saw, "and everything was working fine." When Domeny tested the speed at which the lower guard closed, it was .13 to .14 of a second, using strobe photography. The strobe photography created a permanent record of the progression of the guard from opening to closing.

[Domeny testified that the standard that governed the design of circular saws, UL–45, required the guard to close in .30 of a second. According to Domeny, and contrary to Howarth's testimony, UL–45 still did not mandate electric brakes for portable circular saws.]

Upon examination of the subject saw, Domeny found "quite extensive and strong evidence" of wedging. He also found a concentration of scrape marks that were consistent with pushing an object, be it a nail or wood, between the handle and the outside surface of the upper guard. Domeny removed the saw's blade and found "the strongest evidence of the wedging." The evidence included "gouges." To confirm that the gouges were the result of wedging, Domeny removed the blade. He then explained and demonstrated how the guard could be wedged by sticking a penny nail "between the lower guard and the inner surface of the upper guard." The prying of the nail caused the marks. Domeny showed the jury pictures he had taken of the inside of the saw, which he testified showed the wedge marks and gouges.

Domeny was able to tell when the wedging had been done by examining the saw. First, the aluminum underneath the marks had fresh color. Second, there was no sawdust accumulation in the gouges, which would have occurred over time. Third, no resin had accumulated over the gouges.

* * *

[Domeny testified that] defendant made a conscious decision not to use the [blade brake] technology "because of the benefits and detriments of the feature." [While the brake could prevent some guard-sticking accidents, they in fact represented only two percent of all circular saw accidents. It] would be a good thing to help prevent even two percent of all accidents but only "if the detriment of this device would not cause even more accidents than the two percent benefit that you gain out of it." [A brake would be a detriment in that it would increase the risks to users] of (1) electrocution, (2) switch failure, which would prevent the saw from stopping after the trigger was released and cause a kickback, and (3) unsafe behavior by operators who might view the brake as a back-up system when, in fact, the brake "will not work every time." [Together, these "combined negative aspects" of introducing other hazards into the saw outweighed the potential benefit of saving two percent of all portable circular saw accidents.]

[The jury voted, 5–1, that the Skilsaw was defectively designed and that the defect was the proximate cause of plaintiff's injuries.]

Defendant next contends that it should have been permitted to raise a comparative negligence defense. * * *

In 1972, the Supreme Court of New Jersey considered whether the comparative negligence defense was applicable in a products liability case. Bexiga v. Havir Manufacturing Corp., 60 N.J. 402, 290 A.2d 281 (1972). [The question in *Bexiga* was whether the plaintiff's contributory negligence in injuring his hand while operating a press barred his strict liability in tort design defect claim against the press manufacturer for failing to equip the press with guards. The court there] held the defense inapplicable to the facts of that case because

> The asserted negligence of plaintiff—placing his hand under the ram while at the same time depressing the foot pedal—was the very eventuality the safety devices were designed to guard against. It would be anomalous to hold that defendant has a duty to install safety devices but a breach of that duty results in no liability for the very injury the duty was meant to protect against.

* * *

In Crumb v. Black & Decker (U.S., Inc.), 499 A.2d 530 (N. J. App. Div. 1985), for example, the plaintiff cut into his leg with a circular saw ... while sawing branches at the direction of his employer [when the blade guard stuck open]. The plaintiff's expert testified that the guard failed to close because the guard's spring had wedged itself. The defendant's expert testified that the spring had been wedged intentionally [and] that the plaintiff was using the wrong type of saw for the task and that he handled the saw in a dangerous manner. The plaintiff was sitting on the ground cross-legged while he was cutting. [We there concluded] that the plaintiff was not contributorily negligent because the guard "was designed to protect against the precise inadvertent motion that resulted in plaintiff's accident, i.e., one that would bring an unguarded blade in contact with the user."

* * *

However, defendant offered evidence that the Skilsaw had been purposely wedged open. This evidence goes beyond mere negligence. Indeed, the wedging theory presented by defendant goes to an intentional act on the part of plaintiff that would have created the very situation that gave rise to the accident.... [H]ad plaintiff wedged open the lower guard, he would have voluntarily proceeded to encounter a known risk—a risk he had purposely created. This type of conduct is not exempted by [*Bexiga* and its progeny. But the defendant has argued only comparative fault, not the plaintiff's knowing and voluntary assumption of risk nor the plaintiff's misuse of the product.]

The trial judge thus properly refused to charge the jury on comparative negligence, [and the issues of whether the plaintiff assumed the risk or misused the product are not before this court.]

Affirmed.

N O T E S

1. Having learned of 18 injuries, two fatal, to users of Skil circular saws, the CPSC sought to inspect Skil documents at its premises. The Commission obtained a warrant from a federal magistrate which was upheld by the district court and the court of appeals. In re Establishment Inspection of Skil Corporation, 846 F.2d 1127 (7th Cir. 1988).

2. In Skil Corp. v. Lugsdin, 309 S.E.2d 921, 923 (Ga. Ct. App. 1983), plaintiff cut his hand when the lower blade guard of defendant's circular saw failed to close. Evidence that the manufacturer had received at least 48 complaints and lawsuits involving the failure of the guard was admitted on the issue of defendant's knowledge of a dangerous condition, and hence as relevant to negligence, the strict liability duty to warn, and punitive damages.

[Because the saw was sent in for routine servicing after the accident, it could not be determined whether the saw was defective at the time of the injury. However,] immediately after plaintiff was injured, the lower blade guard, which should have closed automatically and instantaneously after plaintiff completed his cut in the wood, was still in the open position, leaving the blade exposed. Plaintiff's expert witness testified that the cause of the open guard was failure of the spring that should have closed the guard, and that such failure was a defect in the saw. Defendant's expert testified that any failure of the guard to close would have been caused by damage to the saw by banging or dropping and that spring failure was very unlikely.

Held, circumstantial evidence of defect and cause sufficient; plaintiff verdict affirmed. See also Roth v. Black & Decker, U.S., Inc., 737 F.2d 779 (8th Cir. 1984) (failure of guard to retract may have been caused by sawdust clogging spring; verdict for compensatory damages affirmed, punitive damages reversed).

3. Contrast McKinnon v. Skil Corp., 638 F.2d 270 (1st Cir. 1981), where plaintiff cut his foot when he either dropped his circular saw or placed it on the ground. Although he had known for some time that the guard was not retracting properly, he continued to use it. *Held,* defendant's verdict affirmed.

4. Compare Barrash v. Dewalt Ind. Tool Co., 1999 WL 1486278 (N.D. Ga.1999), where plaintiff was sawing a box in his back yard with his DW 936 power circular saw when the lower blade guard failed to retract. In an attempt to free the guard, plaintiff placed his left thumb on the guard and pressed the trigger with his right hand. The unguarded blade began to spin and cut off the plaintiff's thumb. *Held*, plaintiff's claims barred by assumption of risk.

5. Expert Testimony. Increasingly, the quality of expert testimony controls the outcome of products liability litigation. Compare Cuffari v. S–B Power Tool Co., 80 F.App'x 749 (3d Cir. 2003) (allowing exclusion of plaintiffs' expert's testimony that saw was defectively designed because it was not equipped with an electric brake), with Schroeder v. Makita Corp., 2006 WL 335680 (D. Vt. 2006) (allowing plaintiff's expert's testimony that alternative design of switch would have prevented accident).

6. "Plaintiffs' lawyers often avoid product cases involving portable circular saws [because they] have been in use for many years, are very similar in design from manufacturer to manufacturer, and there is a public perception that people injured by a power tool simply were careless." Kalin, Portable Circular Saws, Useful—but Dangerous—Tools, Trial 60 (Nov. 1986).

7. Who is doing a better job, the safety regulators or the courts? Should society spend more money on regulating the safety of portable circular saws so that it may spend less on litigating injuries caused by such saws?

8. Products Liability Resources.

Restatement: Restatement (Third) of Torts: Products Liability (1998).

Hornbook: D. Owen, Products Liability Law (2d ed. 2008).

Treatises: Frumer and Friedman, Products Liability (regularly updated); American Law of Product Liability 3d (regularly updated); M. Shapo, The Law of Products Liability (3d ed. 1994); D. Owen, M.S. Madden, & M. Davis, Madden & Owen on Products Liability (3d ed. 2000, regularly updated).

Nutshell: D. Owen, Products Liability in a Nutshell (8th ed. 2008).

British law: C. J. Miller and R. Goldberg, Product Liability (Oxford University Press, 2004).

European law: Application of the EC Products Liability Directive—Quinquennial Reports to the Council; BIICL Product Liability and Product Safety Database: www.biicl.org (European Cases).

Japanese law: L. Nottage, Product Safety and Liability Law in Japan (Routledge Curzon 2004).

Reporters: CCH Products Liability Reporter (full reports of cases and statutes); BNA Product Safety and Liability Reporter (summaries of important judicial and regulatory decisions and full text of CPSC and NHTSA regulations).

*

PART I

Theories of Manufacturer Liability

This part of the book examines the various theories of recovery that may support a products liability action against a manufacturer. The theories of liability may be divided into three basic groups: (1) negligence; (2) misrepresentation, both tortious and by breach of warranty; and (3) strict liability in tort for defective products. While the principles of these liability theories are often applicable to suppliers generally, they are developed in this part of the book primarily with respect to the manufacturer, the usual defendant. Issues of liability theory more germane to actions against retailers and other defendants are treated later, in Chapter 16. A recurring issue in the materials examined here, pertinent to the development of each of the bases of liability, is the threshold question of whether the manufacturer owes a duty to persons who may be affected by its products but with whom it did not directly deal—the issue of "privity" of contract.

In considering the various claims examined in Chapters 2, 3, 4, and 5, bear in mind that a product supplier may be subject to liability in a single case on two, three, or even more separate bases of recovery. As each new theory is studied, consider its similarities with and variations from the other theories of liability already studied.

Shapo, A Representational Theory of Consumer Protection: Doctrine, Function and Legal Liability for Product Disappointment

60 Va.L.Rev. 1109, 1153–55 (1974).

1. *Theoretical Architectonics*

There are many conceptual shelves, primarily though not exclusively in the "torts" library, from which judges may select answers to product frustration cases. Some theorists emphasize distributional effects and speak the language of "fairness"; others deal primarily with allocational consequences and risk assumption and stress "reasonableness" and utility. Some find answers in philosophical frameworks overlaid on tort history; some may superimpose an economic model on traditional doctrines of personal injury law; others focus on the nature of the transaction as a commercial event, placing varying emphases on the historical and policy bases of common law remedies and of the UCC.

It would be folly to suggest that any of these models, or indeed the one advanced in this study, will cabin neatly the products area under discussion. One can visualize the problem as one of overlapping geometric figures, in which the central concern is the rectangle labeled "product disappointment cases." . . .

2.   *Specific Theories*

Judges have painted product frustration cases in a rainbow of classifications. "Tort" categories have supplied the primary ground of analysis, although there have been frequent excursions into "contract" territory. Conventional tort theory describes a continuum that runs from situations in which the defendant acts deliberately in a way that he knows will cause consequences that society condemns, reaching through "negligent" conduct, and extending to actions that cannot be called "unreasonable" but for which the law imposes compensatory obligations on policy grounds when injury results. In the consumer product area the continuum may be viewed as starting with fraud, in which the defendant makes untrue representations knowingly or reckless of their falsity and with the intent that the plaintiff will rely on them. It continues through negligence to classifications that are technically denominated non-fault. "Strict liability in tort" has received the most attention in the terrain beyond negligence but there are important sibling theories of liability. One of these concepts is "innocent misrepresentation," a specific recent version of which is embodied in the non-fault misrepresentation theory of section 402B of the *Restatement (Second) of Torts*. Closely related contract doctrines are the "implied warranty" theories, both of merchantability and of fitness for a particular purpose. Another contract based doctrine which does not require a showing of fault is the theory of "express warranty." Superimposed upon these theories is a classification of the cases which distinguishes between those that primarily involve hazards to physical safety and those concerned principally with economic injury.

CHAPTER 2

NEGLIGENCE

Most lawyers consider negligence to be the "classic" theory of products liability. And while its importance in products liability litigation waned during the 1960s and 1970s as "strict" theories of manufacturer liability developed and expanded, negligence remains a most important theory of recovery. Several states never did adopt the theory of strict liability in tort. In other states that have this doctrine, there may be good tactical or evidentiary reasons for a plaintiff to base recovery at least in part on negligence. Or the facts of a case, at least in some jurisdictions, may support recovery in negligence but not strict liability in tort. See Phillips v. Cricket Lighters, 841 A.2d 1000 (Pa. 2003) (claim that disposable butane cigarette lighter should have had childproof design lay in negligence, but not strict liability in tort); Blue v. Environmental Engineering, Inc., 828 N.E.2d 1128 (Ill. 2005) (statute of limitations had run on strict liability claim, but not negligence).

Moreover, many judges have stated that the basis of strict liability in design and warning cases is similar—if not identical—to negligence liability. Indeed, many recent "reform" proposals have called for such a return, on a formal basis, to the principles of negligence. Some state legislatures, a few courts, and the new Products Liability Restatement have responded, and negligence principles have begun a pronounced resurgence in the law of products liability. In addition, an important study reveals that jurors respond more favorably to plaintiffs—in terms of both the likelihood of success and verdict size—whose claims are based on negligence rather than strict liability. Cupp & Polage, The Rhetoric of Strict Products Liability Versus Negligence: An Empirical Analysis, 77 N.Y.U. L. Rev. 874 (2002). In short, the doctrine of negligence is both a vital and powerful theory of recovery in products liability litigation.

Following an introductory section on privity, the negligence cases are presented here in the three principal contexts in which a manufacturer may fail in its duties toward consumers: (1) manufacture; (2) the provision of warnings and instructions; and (3) design. Since these are also the three categories of "defectiveness," discussion of the many recurring issues concerning defectiveness in general (such as problems concerning obvious dangers) is delayed until subsequent chapters. Note also that while the various negligence principles are generally applicable to all three contexts, for brevity they usually are developed in one context only.

1. THE PRIVITY OBSTACLE

When the consumer deals with the retailer rather than directly with the manufacturer, he establishes a contractual relation with the retailer to which the manufacturer is not, legally speaking, a party. The manufacturer sells (directly or indirectly) to the retailer; the retailer sells to the consumer. The marketing process is a series of sales—a series of contracts. The parties to these contracts overlap in the middle of the marketing process but not at the ends: there is an ultimate supplier and an ultimate consumer. The retailer has contractual relations with both his supplier and his customer, and so is the connecting link between them. The customer, however, makes no contract with . . . the manufacturer. These two do not deal with one another; typically they are strangers. In legal phraseology, there is no "privity of contract" between them. Gillam, Products Liability in a Nutshell, 37 Or. L. Rev. 119, 131 (1958).

Winterbottom v. Wright, 10 M. & W. 109, 152 Eng. Rep. 402 (Ex.1842), thrust privity to center stage in Anglo–American law. The defendant, Wright, a manufacturer and repairer of stagecoaches, supplied a stagecoach to the Postmaster General under a contract to keep it in good repair. The coach subsequently broke down and overturned, injuring the driver, Winterbottom, who sued Wright for damages. In a decision that was to exert enormous influence over products liability litigation for an entire century, Lord Abinger, C.B., delivered an opinion that substantially reflected the views of all the judges:

I am clearly of the opinion that the defendant is entitled to our judgment. We ought not to permit a doubt to rest upon this subject, for our doing so might be the means of letting in upon us an infinity of actions. . . . There is no privity of contract between these parties; and if the plaintiff can sue, every passenger, or even any person passing along the road, who was injured by the upsetting of the coach, might bring a similar action. Unless we confine the operation of such contracts as this to the parties who entered into them, the most absurd and outrageous consequences, to which I can see no limit, would ensue. . . . By permitting this action, we should be working this injustice, that after the defendant had done everything to the satisfaction of his employer, and after all matters between them had been adjusted, and all accounts settled on the footing of their contract, we should subject them to be ripped open by this action of tort brought against him.

Judgment was given for the defendant. The rule of *Winterbottom,* that no action could be maintained against a remote seller, continued as the law of the land well into the twentieth century. This was so even in *negligence* actions, despite the fact that Mr. Winterbottom had grounded his declaration solely upon the contract between his employer, the Postmaster General, and the defendant.*

---

* That the true holding of the case thus may have been improperly extended to the nascent action in negligence has been argued by some scholars. See Bohlen, The Basis of

By 1900, dissatisfaction with the privity bar rule had generated certain exceptions summarized in Huset v. J.I. Case Threshing Mach. Co., 120 Fed. 865 (8th Cir. 1903) (Sanborn, J.): (1) "an act of negligence of a manufacturer or vendor which is imminently dangerous to the life or health of mankind [in preparing] an article intended to preserve, destroy, or affect human life"; (2) a property owner's negligence that injures a person invited "to use his defective appliance upon the owner's premises"; and (3) providing an article known to be "imminently dangerous to life or limb to another without notice of its qualities."

Although the formulation of these exceptions varied among the cases, the three *Huset* exceptions were widely accepted at the time. To recover against a negligent manufacturer or other remote vendor, a plaintiff had to squeeze his case into one of the three exceptions—which was usually quite hard to do, since most courts at the time interpreted the exceptions narrowly. Clearly the most important exception (Judge Sanborn's exception no. 1) involved the sale of "imminently" or "inherently" dangerous products. When *Huset* was decided in 1903, however, the exception was narrowly confined to products like poisons, drugs, guns, explosives and foodstuffs. Seven years later, a certain Scotsman purchased a quite different kind of product—a marvelous new machine called a "car."

D. Peck, Decision at Law

40–64 (1961).

It was [in 1910] that Donald MacPherson, a stone cutter and dealer in monuments and gravestones, of Galway Village near Saratoga Springs in the state of New York, purchased a new Buick automobile from Close Brothers, local automobile dealers. The car had a front seat for two, a rumble seat for one, and was called a runabout. It had four cylinders of twenty-two horsepower.

Late in July of [1911] Mr. MacPherson drove his car on an errand of mercy—to take a neighbor to the hospital. Mr. MacPherson was accompanied on the ride by the sick man and his brother. The car did not reach the hospital. But Mr. MacPherson did, as a patient, by means of another conveyance. His new Buick automobile ended up in a ditch, with the owner pinioned under the axle.

As he and his two companions described the accident . . . eighteen months later at the trial of MacPherson v. Buick Motor Company, they were driving along at about fifteen miles an hour when the rear of the machine started to skid. The road was dry and there was no apparent

---

Affirmative Obligations in the Law of Tort (pt. 2), 53 U. Pa. L. Rev. 273, 281–84 (1905); Feezer, Tort Liability of Manufacturers and Vendors, 10 Minn. L. Rev. 1, 3 (1925) (calling *Winterbottom*'s progeny in negligence cases "bastard offspring"). But see C.J. Miller & R. Goldberg, Product Liability 5 (2004), a leading English authority on products liability law.

reason for the skid. As they looked back, they heard a crash, like the breaking of wood, and saw the left rear of the car swerve and go down. Mr. MacPherson tried to straighten the car out and bring it to a halt, but it would not respond to his steering; it headed into a telephone pole and overturned.

An inspection at the scene of the accident immediately afterward revealed the left rear wheel detached from the car and lying on the ground, the spokes broken and scattered around.

* * *

When MacPherson, a wiry little Scotsman, sufficiently recovered from his injuries to get around again, called upon Senator Brackett and asked him to take the case, he was somewhat more cordially received as a constituent than as a client. Edgar T. Brackett was the leading lawyer in Saratoga County. He was also the political leader of the county and the state senator from the district.... He resembled a minister both in appearance and adeptness in quoting scripture and Shakespeare. He was thorough in the preparation and persuasive in the presentation of both facts and law, and enjoyed a reputation throughout the state as a master both in the trial of cases and argument of appeals.

Mr. MacPherson thought that he had a simple case of an automobile with a rotten wheel, which had collapsed and fallen apart under normal driving conditions. He felt that he had a claim in simple justice against the manufacturer of the car. Brackett knew better. The claim was novel, not simple. He knew that a long, hard and uncertain legal road lay ahead and that every inch of the way would be closely contested. During the next five years, while the case was in litigation in three courts, MacPherson learned this too [and] that he was a guinea pig for testing out a proposition of law of much larger significance than the amount of any verdict he would receive at the hands of a country jury.

The problem and difficulty, as Brackett explained, was to persuade the court that the Buick Company should be held responsible to MacPherson for any defect in the machine, when he had not bought the car from or had any dealings with the Buick Company. He had bought the car from an independent dealer. The dealer might be liable for selling a bad car, although his liability was more academic than real as it was doubtful that he would be good for any judgment that might be taken against him. But if the Buick Company was to be held responsible directly to MacPherson, with whom it had no contact, a new theory of law would have to be propounded and established—for no court had as yet recognized any responsibility on the part of a manufacturer in favor of a purchaser who did not buy from the manufacturer.

* * *

What would be the consequences if MacPherson won his lawsuit? Investors the country over asked the question and pondered the answer. An automobile might break down for a number of reasons—a cracked axle, blown tire, steering gear out of alignment, faulty brakes, careless operation. It was difficult to tell after a little wear and tear whether the cause was some mechanical failure or human failure or neglect in care of the car. If every breakdown could be made the basis of a claim against the manufacturer, the industry would be subject to risks and hazards beyond calculation. The possible liabilities would be a threat to solvency. The hopes and fears of Detroit, Indianapolis and every other city that boasted of an automobile plant were thus gathered in Saratoga.

No country lawyer was to be trusted with the defense of this case. Disadvantageous as it might be to have a stranger appear against the local idol in the local forum, that was a handicap which had to be accepted. This case could not be won for the defendant on the basis of personality or sympathy. It could be won only on the strength of compelling reason—an overwhelming demonstration that practically nothing more could have been done to assure the production of a safe and sound machine than Buick had done—and a convincing revelation of the dire consequences [from] the imposition of responsibility upon the manufacturers of automobiles.

Not unnaturally the lawyer selected by the defendant came from the automobile capital. William Van Dyke of Detroit was chosen for his knowledge of the automobile industry and his forensic skill.... Both in presence and manner he was a commanding figure, and courts always listened respectfully to his legal learning and cogent argument.

[At trial, plaintiff was nonsuited at the close of his case because of the absence of privity. The nonsuit was reversed on appeal, 138 N.Y.S. 224 (App. Div. 1912), on the ground that one of the exceptions to the privity requirement may have applied, and the case was remanded for a new trial. The following summary of the case presumably is from the second trial.]

Brackett was fairly well satisfied from the start of the case that the jury would accept MacPherson's account of how the accident happened. He was not so sure that he could show the jury what was wrong with the wheel or convince them that the Buick Company was to blame. But that was his immediate task. The trial, therefore, became an inquiry into wheels, the wood from which they were made, and the available means for testing their soundness and strength.

Wheel making was a trade in which many were engaged in those days. The makers of carriage and wagon wheels—a numerous body of artisans— had turned to making automobile wheels. Wheels were made not only in factories, but also in small shops by individual wheelwrights. In fact, wheel making was such a specialty that it had not been integrated into the manufacturing process of any of the automobile companies except Peerless.... All other companies bought their wheels from specialists in wheel making. Buick bought its wheels from the Imperial Wheel Company, a well-known and reliable old company.

As every community had at least one wheelwright among its established and essential occupations, Brackett did not have to go far from home for his expert witnesses.

George A. Palmer from Saratoga Springs had been a carriage maker for thirty years and for the past several years his occupation had been making and repairing automobile wheels. The wheel from MacPherson's Buick, that is, its collected parts, had been brought . . . to Mr. Palmer's shop for examination.

Mr. Palmer pointed out to the judge and jury that the spokes had broken off square, which indicated that the wood was poor. "Apparently the wood was brittle," he said, "coarse grained such as you find in old trees. I never saw a spoke broke off as square as they were. Good quality of sound hickory, when it breaks, brooms up, slivers up. The fact that they are broken square across indicates that they were brittle, of poor quality, trash."

* * *

Adelbert Payne came from the nearby town of Amsterdam, where he had built carriages and made wheels for twenty years. "A good class of carriage requires the best hickory," he said.

"Are you able to tell the quality of a wood from an examination of the surface of the sides of a hickory spoke?" Brackett asked.

"Yes, sir. The integrity of hickory can be determined from an examination of the surface by an experienced eye. A sound, good quality of hickory has a very firm grain that shows distinctly through the outer surface."

The witness conceded that if a wheel came painted one could not tell anything about the grain. "That is why," he explained, "I never let a wheel come painted—so I can see the quality of hickory used." If the wood came painted, the test would be to scrape off sufficient paint to see the grain and fiber of the wood—it was "a perfectly feasible and easy test to determine the character of a spoke that way, and make sure."

* * *

[Anticipating Buick's argument that it could not inspect the grain of the spokes since it received the wheels from the supplier already painted with a prime coat, Brackett went to the Thomas Motor Car Company of Buffalo for his last expert—a wheel tester.] This man testified that the Thomas Company bought its wheels in the natural wood. They were first inspected in the Receiving Department. They then went to the Wheel Department where each wheel was tried out separately under pressure—by hydraulic pressure applied on the hub. Buick made no such test.

Van Dyke, for the defense, approached the problem of proof from a different angle and on a different level. He sought to give the jury a more scientific understanding of wood and the means of determining its suitability for spokes, and to show the virtual impossibility, as a practical matter, of examining or testing the wood after a wheel was made. The automobile companies had to rely on the wheel makers, he said, and he argued that if the companies selected wheel makers who had demonstrated their dependability over the years, that should be regarded as a discharge of their responsibility.

Van Dyke began the defense with the director of the laboratory for testing materials at Purdue University. This man had a long background in the testing of woods for the Forestry Service of the United States. He gave the jury a briefing on the tests to determine the weight, grain and strength of wood. He rejected as unfounded prejudice the notion that wood from young trees was better than that from old trees or that coarseness or fineness of grain affected the strength. The studies of the Forestry Service established, he said, that the fast growing hickories have the greater shock resisting capacity; growth was measured by the count of rings on the stem; good hickory was produced at a rate of growth of from five to twenty-five rings per inch. Shown the spokes from the wheel of MacPherson's Buick, he said that they were first-class, running about fifteen rings per inch.

It would be impossible, he explained, to determine the strength and suitability of a spoke by an examination of the side surface because the rings did not show in that way. It would be necessary to look at the ends to observe the rings, which was impossible in a finished wheel.

The attorney for Buick also called representatives of the leading automobile makers and wheel makers of the day. All uniformly testified that no test was made or could be made by the motor companies to determine the quality or strength of the spokes in wheels supplied by the wheel makers. Any pressure test was ridiculed as worthless—it would tell only that a wheel could carry so much weight, without revealing how it would bear up under the stress and strain of the actual operation of a car. No automobile company employed wood experts to pass on the wood in wheels. None was known to remove any portion of the priming coat for the purpose of examining the grain of the wood.

* * *

After the experts were called and all the other evidence was in, the defense called witnesses from the Buick Company and the Imperial Wheel Company to testify to their experience with wheels over the years. Up to that time Buick had turned out 125,000 cars, with 500,000 wheels, all obtained from the Imperial Company. Never before had a complaint been made of a wheel breaking down, the witnesses testified. Imperial had never received a complaint of a single wheel failing because of the quality of the wheel.

The Buick representative acknowledged that Buick attempted no test of the wheels it received other than the road test given all finished cars. This test consisted of driving the car over a ten-mile course of an ordinary country road as fast as the car could go and taking the turns at ten to twenty-five miles an hour.

So the issues were drawn as to the cause of the accident, the worth of the wheel, and the responsibility of the Buick Company.

[The judge instructed the jury that it should find for the plaintiff if it found (1) that the accident was caused by the crumbling of the spokes of the wheel, and (2) that Buick had failed to employ such tests "that a person skilled in the manufacture of cars ... ought to have used to discover a defect." The jury returned a verdict for MacPherson for $5,000. The intermediate appellate court affirmed the judgment for MacPherson, 145 N.Y.S. 462 (App. Div. 1914), and Buick took the case to the New York Court of Appeals.]

The issue was whether the manufacturer of an article should be held liable to a person injured by reason of a defect in the article—when that person was not one to whom the manufacturer sold the article or with whom the manufacturer had any contact. Or, to put it another way, the question was whether the New York Court of Appeals, in the year 1916, should follow the decision and law established by the Court of [Exchequer of Pleas] in Winterbottom v. Wright in the year 1842, or turn the law about and place a higher responsibility on the manufacturer for the better protection of the ultimate user.

[For Buick, Van Dyke argued that an automobile is not an] "inherently dangerous article." And from that premise he reached the corollary conclusion in law—"An automobile not being an article inherently dangerous, defendant was not liable in simple negligence to a third party not in contractual relation with it." . . . "The maker of an innocuous article, such as a chair, table or buggy, cannot follow it through every hand for all time. He cannot know as to whether it goes into prudent or imprudent hands, or whether it has had minor accidents, or undue exposure, which have weakened it. He cannot trace the history of his article through every subsequent and remote user for all time and in all places." . . .

Senator Brackett, fully sensitive to the legal force of the argument against him, . . . played upon [sympathy], but he . . . put the case in its broad perspective. "The decision of this question," he noted, "is of the utmost interest, not simply to this little tombstone dealer in the remote hamlet of Galway in Saratoga County, but to every person, everywhere, who shall hereafter use this modern means of locomotion." . . . "What substantial difference, what difference in morals, should be made" he pleaded, "in testing this defendant's liability for this maiming of the plaintiff, whether, having first manufactured, it sells this machine directly to MacPherson or sells it to Close Brothers, with the expectation and intention that Close Brothers will sell it to some MacPherson? The defendant was equally culpable in either case. The plaintiff has suffered equal damage; and it is close to, if not quite, immoral and wicked to allow the recovery in one case and deny it in the other."

* * *

With this closing analysis . . . Brackett delivered his client and his case into the hands of the court.

MacPherson v. Buick Motor Co.

Court of Appeals of New York, 1916.
217 N.Y. 382, 111 N.E. 1050.

■ CARDOZO, J.

The defendant is a manufacturer of automobiles. It sold an automobile to a retail dealer. The retail dealer resold to the plaintiff. While the plaintiff was in the car, it suddenly collapsed. He was thrown out and injured. One of the wheels was made of defective wood, and its spokes crumbled into fragments. The wheel was not made by the defendant; it was bought from another manufacturer. There is evidence, however, that its defects could have been discovered by reasonable inspection, and that inspection was omitted. . . . The question to be determined is whether the defendant owed a duty of care and vigilance to any one but the immediate purchaser.

The foundations of this branch of the law, at least in this state, were laid in Thomas v. Winchester (6 N.Y. 397) [1852]. A poison was falsely labeled. The sale was made to a druggist [who] sold to a customer. The customer recovered damages from the seller who affixed the label. "The defendant's negligence," it was said, "put human life in imminent danger." A poison falsely labeled is likely to injure any one who gets it. Because the danger is to be foreseen, there is a duty to avoid the injury. . . .

* * *

. . . The defendant argues that things imminently dangerous to life are poisons, explosives, deadly weapons—things whose normal function it is to injure or destroy. But whatever the rule . . . may once have been, it has no longer that restricted meaning. . . .

* * *

We hold, then, that the principle of Thomas v. Winchester is not limited to poisons, explosives, and things of like nature, to things which in their normal operation are implements of destruction. If the nature of a thing is such that it is reasonably certain to place life and limb in peril when negligently made, it is then a thing of danger. Its nature gives warning of the consequences to be expected. If to the element of danger there is added knowledge that the thing will be used by persons other than the purchaser, and used without new tests, then, irrespective of contract, the manufacturer of this thing of danger is under a duty to make it carefully. . . . We have put aside the notion that the duty to safeguard life and limb, when the consequences of negligence may be foreseen, grows out of contract and nothing else. We have put the source of the obligation where it ought to be. We have put its source in the law.

[T]here thus emerges a definition of the duty of a manufacturer which enables us to measure this defendant's liability. Beyond all question, the nature of an automobile gives warning of probable danger if its construction is defective. This automobile was designed to go fifty miles an hour. Unless its wheels were sound and strong, injury was almost certain. It was as much a thing of danger as a defective engine for a railroad. The defendant knew the danger. It knew also that the car would be used by persons other than the buyer. . . . The dealer was indeed the one person of whom it might be said with some approach to certainty that by him the car would not be used. Yet the defendant would have us say that he was the one person whom it was under a legal duty to protect. The law does not lead us to so inconsequent a conclusion. Precedents drawn from the days of travel by stage coach do not fit the conditions of travel today. The principle that the danger must be imminent does not change, but the things subject to the principle do change. They are whatever the needs of life in a developing civilization require them to be.

* * *

In Winterbottom v. Wright, 10 M. & W. 109 [1842], ... [t]he defendant undertook to provide a mail coach to carry the mail bags. The coach broke down from latent defects in its construction. . . . The court held that he was not liable for injuries to a passenger. . . .

There is nothing anomalous in a rule which imposes upon A, who has contracted with B, a duty to C and D and others according as he knows or does not know that the subject-matter of the contract is intended for their use. . . .

. . . Subtle distinctions are drawn by the defendant between things inherently dangerous and things imminently dangerous, but the case does not turn upon these verbal niceties. If danger was to be expected as reasonably certain, there was a duty of vigilance, and this whether you call the danger inherent or imminent. . . .

We think the defendant was not absolved from a duty of inspection because it bought the wheels from a reputable manufacturer. It was not merely a dealer in automobiles. It was a manufacturer of automobiles. It was responsible for the finished product. It was not at liberty to put the finished product on the market without subjecting the component parts to ordinary and simple tests. . . . The obligation to inspect must vary with the nature of the thing to be inspected. The more probable the danger, the greater the need of caution.

[Affirmed; dissenting opinion of BARTLETT, C.J., omitted.]

NOTES

1. While many courts followed *MacPherson* quite quickly, others did not, and by 1933 the case law on the scope of the "imminently dangerous" exception was in a state of utter confusion. One by one, however, courts swung over to *MacPherson*. By 1955, Professor James could write that "[t]he citadel of privity has crumbled, and today the ordinary tests of duty, negligence and liability are applied widely to the man who supplies a chattel for the use of another." James, Products Liability (pt. 1), 34 Tex. L. Rev. 44 (1955). Lingering on in some states longer than others, the privity requirement in negligence actions was finally abolished in Maine in 1982. The *MacPherson* rule "has become, in short, a general rule imposing negligence liability upon any supplier, for remuneration, of any chattel." Prosser, The Assault Upon the Citadel (Strict Liability to the Consumer), 69 Yale L.J. 1099, 1102 (1960). "Probably no other case has been as frequently cited in following decisions or has made as great an impact on industry." D. Peck, Decision at Law 69 (1961).

2. How can the rise and dogmatic adherence to the privity rule in the 1800s be explained? What accounts for its fall from 1916 to 1982? "This trend was responsive to ever-growing pressure for protection of the consumer coupled with a realization that liability would not unduly inhibit the enterprise of manufacturers and that they were well placed both to profit from its lessons and to distribute its burdens.'' James, Products Liability (pt. 1), 34 Tex. L. Rev. 44 (1955).

3. *MacPherson* was noted in 29 Harv. L. Rev. 866 (1916) and 25 Yale L.J. 679 (1916). See Henderson, MacPherson v. Buick Motor Company: Simplifying the Facts While Reshaping the Law, Torts Stories 41 (R. Rabin & S. Sugarman, eds., Foundation Press, 2003); Probert, Applied Jurisprudence: A Case Study in *Mac-Pherson v. Buick* and Its Precedents, 21 U.C. Davis L. Rev. 789 (1988). England's *MacPherson* came in 1932 in Donoghue v. Stevenson, [1932] A.C. 562, (H.L.). See C.J. Miller & R. Goldberg, Product Liability § 1.18 et seq. (Oxford, 2004); J. Stapleton, Product Liability 20 (Butterworths, 1994).

2. THE MANUFACTURING PROCESS: FABRICATION AND QUALITY CONTROL

The manufacture of products requires the performance of many individual tasks, from the selection or fabrication of materials and component parts to the assembly of those parts into the final product. While the manufacture of even simple products involves many such tasks, the manufacture of complex products, such as cars and sophisticated industrial machinery, involves many thousands. It should therefore be expected that the performance of an occasional manufacturing task, such as the tightening of a nut on a bolt as in the *Jenkins* case that follows, will be done improperly. Nor will the manufacturer's quality control procedures usually be capable of catching all such products that contain production defects. When the manufacturing process goes awry in this manner, and a "flawed" product that deviates from the manufacturer's specifications is thereby produced and sold, persons are sometimes injured as a result. Whether the manufacturer will be liable in negligence to such persons will depend upon a determination of whether the manufacturer's production and quality control procedures were conducted with "reasonable" care.

Jenkins v. General Motors Corp.

United States Court of Appeals, Fifth Circuit, 1971.
446 F.2d 377.

■ INGRAHAM, CIRCUIT JUDGE.

Ione Jenkins was severely injured when the Corvair automobile in which she was a passenger suddenly veered off the road and landed in a ditch on April 15, 1962. She [sued] General Motors Corporation on the grounds of negligent failure to properly tighten and inspect a nut on a bolt in the left rear suspension system. A jury returned a verdict for plaintiff [for] $425,000 and judgment was entered thereon. On this appeal appellant [challenges] the insufficiency of evidence to submit to the jury....

[Jenkins] and her date, Billy Mixon, each sixteen years of age, left a drivein theater near Swainsboro, Georgia on the night of April 15, 1962, and headed toward Swainsboro on a straight and level gravel-top asphalt road. Mixon was driving the two months' old 1962 Corvair which registered about 2200 miles on its odometer. Having traveled approximately 1800 feet, the car suddenly veered and pulled to the left, became "uncontrollable", slammed into a concrete culvert off the left shoulder of the road and turned over into a ditch. As a result appellee Jenkins was permanently paralyzed in a major portion of her body.

Jenkins' witnesses, including the trooper who investigated the accident scene, established that there was no evidence of excessive speed, of use of alcoholic beverages, or of improper driving. Appellee Jenkins and Billy Mixon, the only eyewitnesses to the occurrence, testified that they were driving along when the automobile suddenly veered to the left and became uncontrollable. Mixon tried to counteract this by turning the wheel fully to the right. In response to Miss Jenkins' inquiry, Mixon cried out "I have lost my steering." Mixon testified that he tried to apply his brakes, but that when he hit them, the pedal went to the floor board and he got no braking action.

Jenkins' theory of the cause of the accident was that a nut on a bolt in the left rear suspension system was inadequately torqued during assembly at the appellant's factory and that under normal operation conditions this nut worked loose and dropped off, allowing the bolt to drop out. The absence of this bolt and the concomitant additional stresses and strains on the remaining adjacent bolt caused this second bolt to "wallow out" the hole in which it was placed during normal operation of the car. Consequently, at the time of the accident, this second bolt pulled through leaving the components unsecured and causing the left rear suspension assembly to sweep back, canting the wheel outward and to the rear. Jenkins contends that this not only created the sudden pull to the left, but also resulted in a loss of a portion of the brake assembly and the subsequent brake failure.

[General Motors contends] that the district court erred in denying its motions for a directed verdict and for judgment notwithstanding the verdict[, arguing] that the damage to the rear suspension system was the result, not the cause, of the accident, and that [Jenkins' theory] is so speculative that the jury should not have been permitted to draw the series of inferences required to establish the ultimate fact of appellant's negligence.

* * *

Appellant asserts that the facts are "equiponderant" as to what caused the automobile to strike the culvert. In support of its position at trial, appellant introduced numerous films, exhibits and expert opinion testimony concerning the degree of tightening of the bolt, the shape of the pull-through hole, and of tests conducted on Corvair automobiles. A witness testified that he found the "missing" bolt forty-one feet away from the scene of the accident, and according to appellant's experts the bolt was sheared at impact. This was contrasted with the expert testimony utilized by Jenkins supporting her theory of the case, including evidence of the condition of the brakes, of rotational marks on the left rear axle indicating it was out of position before impact, and of the condition of the left rear wheel, found "canted out" after the accident but with evidence of only minimal damage from impact.

It all boils down to a battle of experts and, as such, the trial court did not err in submitting the case to the jury. The jury was allowed to inspect and even handle the various components of the rear suspension assembly involved, including the "wallowed out" hole and the "missing" bolt. In addition, they viewed the hundreds of photographs, exhibits and the movies that were shown. The jury was not ... forced to accept the testimony of its experts, even if uncontradicted [and] was authorized to make reasonable inferences even if some speculation and conjecture was required....

* * *

[Affirmed.]

NOTES

1. **Accident Reconstruction.** Products liability cases often are like detective stories. In many cases after a product accident has occurred, neither the injured party nor the manufacturer will have any idea what went wrong. And if the person using the product is killed in the accident, no one may know whether the product was being misused at the time of the accident. It is a principal responsibility of the lawyers for the parties, and their experts, to piece together the facts surrounding the accident—to "reconstruct" it—to develop theories of how and why the accident happened.

In *Jenkins,* what was plaintiff's theory of why the car crashed? What was defendant's theory? Which theory appears more plausible from the facts as stated in the reported opinion? By what process was this conflict in theories of causation resolved at trial? Might the jury reasonably have believed the defendant's version of how the accident happened?

2. **Litigation Complexity and the Need for Experts.** Note the complexity—and commensurate expense—of litigating the relatively simple issues in this typical products liability case, where hundreds of photographs, exhibits, and films were shown to the jury. Most products liability cases cannot be tried, as illustrated by the *Jenkins* case, without the assistance of at least one expert. Since the "battle of experts" thus may largely determine the outcome of the case, the selection and effective use of skilled—and credible—expert witnesses is one of the most important tasks facing the products liability lawyer. In an omitted portion of the *Jenkins* opinion, the court held that the trial judge had properly excluded evidence that one of plaintiff's expert witnesses was under indictment for perjury.

Beware of the expert who is a "professional" witness! "Professional expert witnesses are troublesome. [T]he problems posed by the use of expert witnesses now appear to be widely recognized...." Richmond, The "Professional Expert" Witness: Doctor Lichtor, I Presume?, 17 J. Prod. & Toxics Liab. 197, 223 (1995).

3. The Negligence Standard of Liability.

A. In general. Most courts use ordinary negligence parlance in defining the standard of care applicable to products liability cases. When courts attempt any definition of the standard, which often they do not, they generally go no further than to state that the duty is one of "reasonable," "ordinary," or "due" care. See, e.g., Stahlecker v. Ford Motor Co., 667 N.W.2d 244, 253 (Neb. 2003) (whether "conduct was reasonable"; tires); Andrade v. General Motors Corp., 785 N.E.2d 214, 218 (Ill. App. 2003) ("ordinary care"; seats); Roach v. Ivari Int'l Ctrs., Inc., 822 A.2d 316 (Conn. App. 2003) (a "reasonably prudent person under the same circumstances"; hairpiece). Courts sometimes tailor these general notions to the products liability context by setting the standard at a mythical "manufacturer of ordinary prudence in the exercise of ordinary care," or, even more specifically, "a press manufacturer of ordinary prudence."

B. Expertise. In evaluating a manufacturer's conduct, note that manufacturers are "held to the skill of an expert in that business and to an expert's knowledge of the arts, materials, and processes. Thus manufacturers must keep reasonably abreast of scientific knowledge and discoveries touching their products and of techniques and devices used by practical people in their trade." 5 F. Harper, F. James & O. Gray, The Law of Torts 350–51 (2d ed. 1986).

4. Negligent Manufacture as Involving "Unreasonable" Risk.

Liability for negligent manufacture is set forth in § 395 of the Restatement (Second) of Torts (1965) which provides that a manufacturer is subject to liability for failing to exercise reasonable care in manufacturing chattels to avoid an "unreasonable risk" of causing physical harm. Comment *g* to § 395 provides that "the *amount of care* which the manufacturer must exercise is *proportionate to the extent of the risk* involved in using the article if manufactured without the exercise of these precautions." So, "[w]here, in the case of an automobile or high speed machinery or high voltage electrical devices, there is danger of serious bodily harm or death unless the article is substantially perfect, it is reasonable to require the manufacturer to exercise almost meticulous precautions … in order to secure substantial perfection." However, "it would be ridiculous to demand equal care of the manufacturer of an article which, no matter how imperfect, is unlikely to do more than … trivial harm…." Comment *d* to § 395 refers the "unreasonableness" of risk determination to § 291 which provides that "the risk is unreasonable and the act is negligent if the risk is of such magnitude as to outweigh what the law regards as the utility of the act or of the particular manner in which it is done."

Ford Motor Co. v. Zahn

United States Court of Appeals, Eighth Circuit, 1959.
265 F.2d 729.

■ MATTHES, CIRCUIT JUDGE.

This is a Minnesota negligence action, in which appellee-plaintiff received a judgment for $26,350 following jury verdict, as damages for loss of his eye occasioned by a defective ash tray in a Ford automobile manufactured by appellant-defendant. Jurisdiction rests on diversity and amount in controversy. [The trial court denied Ford's post-trial motions, and Ford appealed.]

[P]laintiff was riding as a passenger in the front seat of a 1956 model Ford automobile ... driven by Clarence Dailey.... at 45 to 50 miles per hour. As the automobile approached a crossroad, plaintiff dropped a lighted cigarette. While plaintiff was attempting to retrieve the same from the floor of the vehicle, with his head down, [Dailey jammed on the brakes to avoid hitting a car that suddenly appeared from the crossroad], throwing plaintiff forward and causing his face to [hit] the dashboard.... Immediately following plaintiff's contact with the dashboard, he realized that his right eye had been injured, as it was paining him and blood and liquid was emerging therefrom....

The [car had] an ash tray ... in the center of the dashboard. This tray was found on the floor of the vehicle after plaintiff was injured.... [T]he upper right-hand corner of the front portion of this accessory is not only sharp, but a small protrusion, described by witnesses as a ["jagged"] burr, extends therefrom. Testimony indicated that such a defect would be occasioned by a dull cutting die. This sharp edge and burr is the defect upon which plaintiff predicates his case.

* * *

... Was the defendant negligent? ... We do not understand that defendant seeks to escape [liability] on the theory that the sharp edge of the ash tray with the projecting burr did not constitute a defect—rather, its position is that the inspection made by it, particularly in view of the nature, position, and size of the defect, and the foreseeability of injury resulting therefrom, constituted the exercise of reasonable care on its part.

[T]here is imposed upon the manufacturer of an article for sale or use the duty to exercise reasonable care to prevent defective conditions caused by a miscarriage in the manufacturing process. This duty requires reasonable skill and care in the process of manufacture and for *reasonable inspection or tests* to discover defects. [Citations.]

Applying this general rule to our facts, it appears that the evidence leaves doubt as to whether the subject ash tray was actually inspected. From the testimony of Mr. Van Scoy, the quality control manager for defendant, who was stationed at the Twin City Assembly Plant in St. Paul, where Dailey's automobile was assembled, we find that defendant followed certain practices designed to insure inspection of automobiles. Ash trays were inspected at various stages—in his words they passed "through roughly seven inspectors," but the same witness also testified that insofar as the face of the ash tray was concerned (the portion containing the instant defect) the inspection was a sampling operation. "We don't look over each one individually." This witness stated that the exposed faces of the ash trays are supposed to have rounded corners, and that they were so constructed to prevent injuries. [He further] testified: "I can feel it very easily with my finger. I have done so, both out in the corridor yesterday and here on the witness stand today.... Apparently every one of our inspectors missed that.... If each ash tray had been inspected, this defect that we are concerned with here could possibly have been discovered."

[T]he defendant insists that a reasonably prudent person was not required to anticipate or foresee the unusual occurrence and resulting injury to plaintiff; that the harm to be anticipated from the defect was perhaps a "cut finger" or "snagged clothing," and that since the extent of the foreseeable risk was minimal, the argument follows that the inspection as made, fully complied with the standard of reasonable care so as to completely insulate defendant from liability.

We do not subscribe to the view that the foreseeable risk attending the defective ash tray was minimal and necessarily limited to a lacerated finger or comparable injury. While the risk of danger was perhaps not as great as that which might inhere in a defective wheel or a defective steering mechanism, nevertheless, the fact remains that plaintiff *did* suffer a serious injury, and the jury could properly consider as a circumstance that in this era of fast moving automobiles, emergencies arise frequently which require the sudden application of brakes which in turn throw the occupants of the automobile forward and against the dashboard. The record reveals that defendant was fully conscious of the necessity of guarding against injuries resulting from such occurrences. Mr. Van Scoy testified: "... I would imagine there would be occasions when the brakes are applied suddenly and children and other persons are thrown forward in cars...."

[The negligence question was properly for the jury. Judgment for plaintiff affirmed.]

NOTES

1. Production Errors. As in the first principal case, *Jenkins*, plaintiffs sometimes seek to prove the defendant's negligence in performing a particular assembly line skill, or in improperly adjusting, operating or maintaining an assembly line machine.

In *Zahn*, what failure in Ford's production process was responsible for the flawed ash tray? How might the plaintiff have argued that this failure was negligent? What proofs would have been helpful? How might defendant have responded?

2. Quality Control Failures. As in *Zahn*, many negligent manufacture cases are fought, not on negligence in the production process, but on the adequacy of the defendant's quality control program—the sufficiency of its testing and inspection procedures for *screening out* mistakes made on the assembly line. Why do you suppose that the battles are often fought at this secondary stage of the manufacturing process?

3. In *Zahn*, what was Ford's argument that it had acted with reasonable care even though it produced a defective ashtray? Was the court correct to reject this argument?

4. Assume that Ford was negligent in its production of the ash tray, but not negligent in its inspection of the trays. Should it be liable? Compare Nicklaus v. Hughes Tool Co., 417 F.2d 983, 986 (8th Cir. 1969), citing *Zahn* ("To permit recovery for negligent manufacture, ordinarily plaintiff must show, in addition to lack of reasonable skill and care in the process of manufacture, that the manufacturer failed to make a reasonable inspection or test to discover defects."), with Rest.

(2d) Torts § 437 ("If the actor's negligent conduct is a substantial factor in bringing about harm to another, the fact that after the risk has been created by his negligence the actor has exercised reasonable care to prevent it from taking effect in harm does not prevent him from being liable for the harm.").

5. Recall Judge Cardozo's words in *MacPherson:* "The obligation to inspect must vary with the nature of the thing to be inspected. The more probable the danger the greater the need of caution." 111 N.E. at 1055. This is still good law. See Rest. (2d) Torts § 395, cmt. *e*:

> A garment maker is not required to subject the finished garment to anything like so minute an inspection for the purpose of discovering whether a basting needle has not been left in a seam as is required of the maker of an automobile or of high speed machinery or of electrical devices, in which the slightest inaccuracy may involve danger of death.

6. Manufacturer Responsibility for Defective Materials and Components. Even prior to the production process, a manufacturer may be negligent in the selection, inspection, or testing of materials and component parts.

> The exercise of reasonable care in selecting raw material and parts to be incorporated in the finished article usually requires something more than a mere inspection of the material and parts.... So, too, a manufacturer who incorporates a part made by another manufacturer into his finished product should exercise reasonable care to ascertain not only the material out of which the part is made but also the plan under which it is made.

Rest. (2d) Torts § 395, cmt. *g*. The fact that the assembler purchased the part from a reputable supplier does not relieve it of its responsibility to make its own tests and inspections. E.g., MacPherson v. Buick Motor Co., 111 N.E. 1050, 1055 (N.Y. 1916) (defective wheel for car).

7. Sampling. In *Zahn*, Ford tested or inspected for defects by "sampling" only a fraction of the total number of ash trays. "[I]f proper samples of a certain size are taken for testing, the average of the results for these tests will differ by no more than a measurable amount at an acceptable probability level from the average of the results that would be obtained if all the items were to be tested.... In most cases sufficient information concerning the items can be obtained without going through the time and expense of testing all items." 7 L. Frumer, M. Friedman, and C. Sklaren, Products Liability § 95.06[4] (2006) (section authored by Gaffney, Bein, and Barzelay).

8. Keller v. Coca Cola Bottling Co., 330 P.2d 346, 350 (Or.1958), was a cigar-stub-in-a-Coke case. "Following the filling process the bottles were exposed to strong artificial light while moving along a conveyor chain. Two employees, sometimes only one, had the responsibility to examine the bottles and their contents and at the same time remove the bottles from the conveyor and place them in cases. The employees were so engaged six to eight hours per day. Occasionally, foreign substance was detected. The ability of a person to carefully inspect under these conditions was clearly for the jury to determine." Compare Haynes v. Coca Cola Bottling Co., 350 N.E.2d 20, 23 (Ill. App. 1976) (1200 cans per minute passed by one employee primarily responsible for preventing cans from jamming). In both cases, plaintiff's judgments were affirmed.

3. THE DESIGN PROCESS: THE PRODUCT CONCEPT

Only in recent decades have courts in any number begun to examine the reasonableness of the design of products involved in accidents. Yet the formulation of the product concept is the first and in many ways the most important safety function of manufacturers. For it is at this step that decisions are made that will affect the safety of the entire product line: decisions concerning the types and strengths of raw materials and component parts, the manner in which they will be combined into the finished product, whether safety devices are to be built in, and the overall product concept. The determination of whether the design of any particular product was "adequately" safe—or was, instead, "unreasonably" hazardous—is often a difficult task, particularly since the process generally involves second-guessing (with the benefit of hindsight) the defendant's professional design engineers. Yet "mistakes" of this type sometimes are made, and resulting injuries are sometimes traceable to the manufacturer's failure to exercise reasonable care in designing the product.

Metzgar v. Playskool Inc.

United States Court of Appeals, Third Circuit, 1994.
30 F.3d 459.

■ MANSMANN, CIRCUIT JUDGE.

[Ronald Metzgar placed his 15–month-old son, Matthew, awake and healthy, in his playpen. Ronald left the room for 5 minutes and upon his return found that Matthew was lifeless, having asphyxiated to death on a small play block. Ronald called "911," removed the block lodged in Matthew's throat, and tried unsuccessfully to revive him. The block was a purple half-column Playskool building block manufactured by Playskool and purchased at K–Mart. In a diversity action against Playskool and K–Mart, the parents' claims included negligent design and sale of a toy block of a "size and shape which made the block susceptible of being swallowed and causing a child to choke." The district court rendered summary judgment for the defendants and against the plaintiffs on all counts, and plaintiffs appealed.]

The block which caused Matthew's untimely death is a cylindrical column, ⅞" wide by 1–¾" long, the smallest block among the 49 brightly colored and variously shaped wood blocks marketed by Playskool, Inc. Playskool did not place any warning of a choking hazard on the box containing the blocks, but clearly and boldly imprinted on the front, back and top of the box are the words, "Ages 1½–5." The size and shape of the block satisfied existing federal standards and regulations for risk mitigation and cautionary labeling promulgated and enforced by the Consumer Products Safety Commission, 16 C.F.R. § 1501.4, under the Federal Hazardous Substances Act, 15 U.S.C. §§ 1261–77. The Playskool block also met the small toy and toy part standard established by the American Society for Testing Materials.

* * *

In ruling [for the defendant on its] motion for summary judgment, the district court [ruled] that although the danger of choking was foreseeable, "[t]he historical risk of choking from the Playskool blocks is so small that, even ignoring the issue of parental supervision, the risk from the design as a matter of law is not unreasonable." * * *

We are troubled by the district court's summary judgment disposition of the plaintiffs' negligent design [claim]. [T]he district court properly engaged in a risk-utility analysis. Griggs v. BIC Corp., 981 F.2d 1429, 1435–36 (3d Cir. 1992) (negligence law requires balancing of risk in light of social value of interest at stake, and potential harm, against value of conflicting interest) (citing W. Page Keeton, Dan B. Dobbs, Robert E. Keeton & David G. Owen, Prosser and Keeton on Torts § 31, at 173 (5th ed. 1984)); [citations]; see also Kleinknecht v. Gettysburg College, 989 F.2d 1360, 1369–70 (3d Cir.1993) (the classic risk-utility analysis is used to determine whether a risk is unreasonable in a negligence cause of action). In performing this analysis, the district court relied heavily on the statistical fact that the general population of small children suffer a mortality rate from choking on small toys or toy parts of approximately only one per 720,000 children. We note also that according to Playskool's representative, Charles Fischer, over the past twenty years, the Playskool block in question, of which easily hundreds of thousands have been sold, has not generated any complaints of choking deaths or injuries. Nevertheless, the plaintiffs' expert, E. Patrick McGuire, reported for the record that in one year studied, 1988, there were eleven deaths due to aspiration of small toys or toy parts by children. The record does not indicate the current infant mortality rate due to small toy related asphyxiation, but the plaintiffs submitted a CPSC estimate reported in the House Congressional Record that in each year from 1980–88, an average of 3,200 small children were treated in hospital emergency rooms for toy related ingestion and aspiration injuries. The CPSC also reported that between 1980 and 1991, 186 children choked on small toys, toy parts, and other children's products.

We share the district court's concern that without "at least a realistic threshold of risk," courts should avoid intrusion into product design by too readily weighing risk-utility factors against the defendant, even in those cases where a grievous injury has been suffered. Nonetheless, we believe that an annual mortality rate of eleven is a "realistic threshold of risk" in this case. The fact that the Playskool purple half-column block has not been a contributor to the infant mortality rate until now may be simply happenstance from which we cannot conclude that the block will be safe for future reasonably foreseeable users. We note that although the purple half-column was in technical compliance with CPSC and ASTM standards, the block only minimally met the required standards by protruding in length slightly beyond the ASTM test cylinder. The block's width, however, was slightly narrower than the test cylinder. It appears that a slight modification to the block design could virtually eliminate the choking potential without detracting from the block's utility. We do not believe that the evidence demonstrates, therefore, that the risk of a reasonably foreseeable user choking on the block is so relatively small—measured against the block's decreased utility by modifying its present design—as to permit summary judgment for the defendants on the basis of a risk-utility analysis. Therefore, we will vacate the summary judgment order as it pertains to the claim of negligent design.

[Reversed and remanded] for trial on the merits of the complaint. [Judge Scirica's partial dissent that follows is relocated from footnote 6 to its conventional location below.—Eds.]

■ SCIRICA, CIRCUIT JUDGE, partially dissenting.

[I] would affirm the grant of summary judgment to Playskool on the negligent design claim on the basis of the district court's risk-utility analysis, which noted that the purple block exceeded the CPSC minimum size for toys for children under three. Where there is utility to the toy's size, the toy is safe for children of certain ages or under supervision, it is accompanied by adequate warnings, and the statistical probability of the risk is extremely low, the risk-utility analysis may preclude a negligent design claim. Otherwise, it would appear that every marble would be subject to a negligent design claim. . . .

NOTES

1. **Statutes and Regulations—*Violation*.** Note the judges' concern in *Metzgar* with whether the size of the Playskool block met the minimum standards prescribed by the CPSC. Recall that many courts hold that violation of statute, and perhaps of an administrative regulation, may be negligence *per se*. See, e.g., Steele v. Evenflo Co., 178 S.W.3d 715, 718 (Mo. Ct. App. 2005) (reciting elements: (1) violation; (2) plaintiff in protected class; (3) injury type to be prevented; and (4) violation proximately caused injury). See generally D. Owen, Products Liability Law § 2.3 (2d ed. 2008).

2. **Statutes and Regulations—*Compliance*.**

A. Common law. Most courts agree with the *Metzgar* majority that "compliance with a statutory standard is evidence of due care, [but] it is not conclusive on the issue. Such a standard is no more than a minimum, and it does not necessarily preclude a finding that the actor was negligent in failing to take additional precautions." Prosser & Keeton, supra, at 233. See, e.g., Abadie v. Metropolitan Life Ins. Co., 784 So.2d 46, 81–82 (La. Ct. App. 2001) (negligence; jury charge that "[c]ompliance with government standards is but one element or item of proof of whether of not the product is defective" was correct). See generally D. Owen, Products Liability Law § 14.3 (2d ed. 2008).

B. Preemption. A federal statute or regulation may *preempt* state products liability law, however, in which case compliance *is* a complete defense. The preemption doctrine, which injects an important new dimension into products liability law, is considered below in ch. 9.

3. **Custom.** Recall the famous *T.J. Hooper* rule: While industry practice or custom is important evidence of the reasonableness of the defendant's conduct, it generally is not conclusive, since the industry as a whole may have been derelict in failing to adopt precautionary procedures dictated by ordinary prudence. See The T.J. Hooper, 60 F.2d 737 (2d Cir. 1932) (Hand, C.J.), cert. denied, 287 U.S. 662 (1932); Hillrichs v. Avco Corp., 514 N.W.2d 94, 98 (Iowa 1994) (custom of cornpick-

er manufacturers not to equip them with $50 emergency stop device no defense to claim of negligent design).

4.   Product Testing. Just as there is a duty to test and inspect products for manufacturing flaws, so too does the manufacturer have a duty to test the product prototype for hidden dangers in design. In Banks v. Koehring Co., 538 F.2d 176, 179 (8th Cir. 1976), plaintiff was injured while dislodging sorghum stalks from his new harvester machine that continually clogged: "When a manufacturer offers a machine or equipment to the public ..., the user is entitled to presume that the manufacturer has fully tested the mechanism...."

5.   Risk–Utility Analysis. Explain the risk-utility analysis applied by the court. What risks were weighed against what benefits? Was the court's analysis correct?

6. Compare the "danger-utility" test applied by the court in Exum v. General Electric Co., 819 F.2d 1158 (D.C. Cir. 1987): Negligence in design determined by whether manufacturer exercised due care in the circumstances, which involves " 'a balancing of the likelihood of harm, and the gravity of harm if it happens, against the burden of precaution which would be effective to avoid the harm,' "citing 2 Harper & James, The Law of Torts § 28.4, at 1542 (1956), and Prosser & Keeton on Torts 699 (5th ed. 1984).

7. In Griggs v. BIC Corp., 981 F.2d 1429, 1437 (3d Cir. 1992), cited in *Metzgar*, a 3–year–old boy early one morning took a disposable butane cigarette lighter out of his stepfather's pants pocket and used it to set fire to the bed of his 11–month–old stepbrother, Zachary Griggs, injuring him seriously. Zachary and his mother sued BIC alleging that BIC was negligent in failing to design the lighter in a childproof manner, which BIC conceded was feasible. *Held*, reversing summary judgment for BIC on negligent design claim:

> On balance, the high social value placed on the safety of people and property threatened by childplay fires, the high gravity of risk, the considerable probability of risk, and the likelihood of a reasonably available alternative may outweigh BIC's interest in producing its lighters without childproofing features. In such circumstances, the risk of omission would be unreasonable.

Accord, Phillips v. Cricket Lighters, 841 A.2d 1000 (Pa. 2003).

8.   The Hand Formula. Whether a manufacturer should be considered negligent for designing a product in a particular manner is to be determined by whether the risks involved—the foreseeable accident costs—were greater or less than the "utility" of the conduct. This method of "risk-benefit," "risk-utility," or "cost-benefit" analysis for ascertaining whether a defendant's conduct was negligent was explained by Judge Learned Hand in two cases decided in the 1940s:

> The degree of care demanded of a person by an occasion is the resultant of three factors: [1] the likelihood that his conduct will injure others, taken with [2] the seriousness of the injury if it happens, and balanced against [3] the interest which he must sacrifice to avoid the risk. All these are practically not susceptible of any quantitative estimate, and the second two are generally not so, even theoretically. For this reason a solution always involves some preference, or choice between incommensurables, and it is consigned to a jury because their decision is thought most likely to accord with commonly accepted standards, real or fancied.

Conway v. O'Brien, 111 F.2d 611, 612 (2d Cir. 1940), rev'd on other grounds, 312 U.S. 492 (1941).

> Possibly it serves to bring this notion into relief to state it in algebraic terms: if the probability be called P; the injury, L [for "Loss"]; and the burden [cost of precaution to avoid the loss], B; liability depends upon whether B is less than L multiplied by P: i.e., whether B<PL.

United States v. Carroll Towing Co., 159 F.2d 169, 173 (2d Cir.1947).

Learned Hand's negligence "formula" thus may be described in full as:

$$B < P \times L \Rightarrow N$$

Possibly it serves to understand the Hand formula to reconvert it, cryptically, into English: If the burden of precaution to avoid a loss is less than the value of that loss, discounted by the probability that the loss will occur, the actor's failure to take the precaution implies its negligence.

More simply, if the cost of a precaution to avoid an accident is less than the expected safety benefits, the actor's failure to take the precaution is probably negligent.

Posner, A Theory of Negligence

1 J. Legal Stud. 29, 32–34 (1972).

It is time to take a fresh look at the social function of liability for negligent acts. The essential clue, I believe, is provided by Judge Learned Hand's famous formulation of the negligence standard—one of the few attempts to give content to the deceptively simple concept of ordinary care. . . . In a negligence case, Hand said, the judge (or jury) should attempt to measure three things: the magnitude of the loss if an accident occurs; the probability of the accident's occurring; and the burden of taking precautions that would avert it. If the product of the first two terms exceeds the burden of precautions, the failure to take those precautions is negligence. Hand was adumbrating, perhaps unwittingly, an economic meaning of negligence. Discounting (multiplying) the cost of an accident if it occurs by the probability of occurrence yields a measure of the economic benefit to be anticipated from incurring the costs necessary to prevent the accident. The cost of prevention is what Hand meant by the burden of taking precautions against the accident. It may be the cost of installing safety equipment or otherwise making the activity safer, or the benefit for[e]gone by curtailing or eliminating the activity. If the cost of safety measures or of curtailment—whichever cost is lower—exceeds the benefit in accident avoidance to be gained by incurring that cost, society would be better off, in economic terms, to for[e]go accident prevention. A rule making the enterprise liable for the accidents that occur in such cases cannot be justified on the ground that it will induce the enterprise to increase the safety of its operations. When the cost of accidents is less than the cost of prevention, a rational profit-maximizing enterprise will pay tort judgments to the accident victims rather than incur the larger cost of avoiding liability. Furthermore, overall economic value or welfare would be diminished rather than increased by incurring a higher accident-prevention cost in order to avoid a lower accident cost. If, on the other hand, the benefits in accident avoidance exceed the costs of prevention, society is better off if those costs are incurred and the accident averted, and so in this case the enterprise is made liable, in the expectation that self-interest will lead it to adopt the precautions in order to avoid a greater cost in tort judgments.

* * *

Perhaps, then, the dominant function of the fault system is to generate rules of liability that if followed will bring about, at least approximately, the efficient—the cost-justified—level of accidents and safety. Under this view, damages are assessed against the defendant as a way of measuring the costs of accidents, and the damages so assessed are paid over to the plaintiff (to be divided with his lawyer) as the price of enlisting their participation in the operation of the system. Because we do not like to see resources squandered, a judgment of negligence has inescapable overtones of moral disapproval, for it implies that there was a cheaper alternative to the accident. Conversely, there is no moral indignation in the case in which the cost of prevention would have exceeded the cost of the accident. Where the measures necessary to avert the accident would have consumed excessive resources, there is no occasion to condemn the defendant for not having taken them.

If indignation has its roots in inefficiency, we do not have to decide whether regulation, or compensation, or retribution, or some mixture of these best describes the dominant purpose of negligence law. In any case, the judgment of liability depends ultimately on a weighing of costs and benefits.

NOTES

1. Assume that a punch press manufacturer knows that over a one year period the cost of adding guards to each press (B) will be $1 million and that the cost of injuries thereby averted over a one year period (PxL) will be $2 million. Assuming with Posner that the manufacturer is a "rational profit-maximizing enterprise," will it necessarily add the guards? Why or why not? Is it of interest that only 9% of workers injured by a product on the job (compared to 3% of seriously injured victims of non-work-related product accidents) hire a lawyer? See D. Hensler et al., Compensation for Accidental Injuries in the United States 127 (1991). What other factors might be relevant?

2. Not all scholars agree with Richard Posner's economic analysis of negligence law. Compare, for example, Calabresi & Hirschoff, Toward a Test for Strict Liability in Torts, 81 Yale L.J. 1055 (1972). See also Vandall, Judge Posner's Negligence–Efficiency Theory: A Critique, 35 Emory L.J. 383, 401 (1986): "One of the most disturbing aspects of Posner's efficiency theory is that it enables users of the theory to give pop answers to serious issues that have troubled society and the legal profession for hundreds of years by plugging numbers into formulas."

3. Whatever its weaknesses, the cost-benefit model of negligence responsibility is a powerful analytical tool. It explains the principal formulation of the concept of negligence and its converse, due care. And it probably explains, even if only in rough terms, the core of the negligence litigation process, from the type of proof and argument generally offered by counsel to what may be the predominant decision-making mechanism (even if often unconscious) of juries and courts. See D. Owen, Products Liability Law § 2.2 (2d ed. 2008); 1 D. Owen, M.S. Madden, & M. Davis, Madden & Owen on Products Liability § 2:5 (3d ed. 2000).

Mesman v. Crane Pro Services, a Division of Konecranes, Inc.

United States Court of Appeals, Seventh Circuit, 2005.
409 F.3d 846.

■ POSNER, CIRCUIT JUDGE.

[Mesman, an employee of Infra–Metals, a manufacturer of steel products, was injured] when a load of steel sheets he was unloading from a boxcar fell on him from the crane that was lifting the sheets out of the boxcar. He and his wife brought suit in an Indiana state court under Indiana's products liability law against the firm that had rebuilt the crane, Konecranes, which removed the case to federal district court. A jury awarded the plaintiffs a large verdict, but the judge set it aside and entered judgment for the defendant. . . .

* * *

Built into the plant was a very old crane, which Infra–Metals wanted renovated, for unloading steel sheets from the rail siding that ran into the plant. [As originally designed, the crane was operated from a cab attached to the roof of the plant. Sitting in the cab, the operator controlled a hoist, at the top of which was a "spreader beam" with chains hanging down from its ends. At the bottom of the chains were "scoops" for gripping a load. In redesigning the crane, Konecranes left the operator's cab in place, attached to the ceiling, but rerouted the controls from the cab to] a hand-held remote-control device with which the operator would operate the crane from ground level. To raise the load he would press the up button on the device and to lower it he would press the down button. [The problem with leaving the cab in place] was that when a boxcar was being unloaded underneath the [cab], there was only a foot or two of clearance between the rim of the boxcar and the cab overhead. And if while being lifted by the hoist the spreader beam struck the cab, the load might be jarred loose and fall, hitting anyone standing beneath it.

. . . With the cab no longer being used for anything, it could have been removed to eliminate the danger of its being struck by the spreader beam. Konecranes did not remove the cab; instead it installed alongside the up and down buttons on the remote-control device an emergency-stop button, so that if the operator sensed an impending collision between the load and the cab he could bring the spreader beam to an immediate dead stop by pressing that button. Alternatively, by pressing the down button he could reverse the direction of the hoist; but because the up and down control had a deceleration feature to reduce wear and tear on the crane, the spreader beam would continue to rise for three seconds after the down button was pressed, traversing in that period about a foot, until it stopped and began its reverse motion. Thus, pressing the down button would not arrest the upward motion of the spreader beam and load as fast as pressing the emergency-stop button would.

* * *

On the day of the accident, the crane operator, Van Til, was standing about 20 feet away from a boxcar that was underneath the abandoned cab. Mesman, standing in the boxcar, fastened a load of steel sheets to the scoops beneath the spreader beam and Van Til pressed the up button and the beam and load rose. As they rose [Van Til] saw that the spreader beam was going to hit the cab, but instead of pressing the emergency-stop button, as he should have done to bring the rising load to a dead stop, he pressed the down button. Because of the deceleration feature—of which he was aware—and the narrow clearance between the cab and the rim of the boxcar, the beam continued to rise for three seconds and hit the cab, and the collision caused the load to fall on Mesman.

[The jury assigned] two-thirds of the responsibility for the accident to Infra–Metals, the employer of Van Til (as of Mesman) and only one-third to Konecranes. The design of the renovated crane also contributed to the accident, however; for had Konecranes removed the cab, eliminated the deceleration feature, or [taken other precautions], the accident would have been avoided....

Under Indiana's products liability law, a design defect can be made the basis of a tort suit only if the defect was a result of negligence in the design, Ind. Code § 34–20–2–2; [citations], that is, only if the product could have been redesigned at a reasonable cost to avoid the risk of injury. [Citations.] *Expressly* requiring proof of negligence in a design-defect case, as Indiana law does, though unusual really isn't much of a legal innovation, since "defect" always implied something that should not have been allowed into the product–something, in other words, that could have been removed at a reasonable cost in light of the risk that it created. [Citations]; Powers, "A Modest Proposal to Abandon Strict Products Liability," 1991 *U. Ill. L. Rev.* 639, 652, 654–59.

The risk of a heavy load falling on a worker if the spreader beam struck the disused cab was substantial because of the narrow clearance [beneath the cab]; and if the load did fall on someone it would be likely to kill or seriously injure him....

In a negligence or "defect" case, the risk of injury has to be weighed against the cost of averting it. In Learned Hand's influential negligence formula, *United States v. Carroll Towing Co.*, 159 F.2d 169, 173 (2d Cir. 1947), failure to take a precaution is negligent only if the cost of the precaution (what he called the "burden" of avoiding the accident) is less than the probability of the accident that the precaution would have prevented multiplied by the loss that the accident if it occurred would cause; hence the formula: $B < PL$. E.g., [citations]; W. Page Keeton, Dan B. Dobbs, Robert E. Keeton, and David G. Owen, *Prosser and Keeton on the Law of Torts* § 32, p. 173 n. 46 (5th ed. 1984). The cheaper the precaution, the greater the risk of accident, and the greater the harm caused by the accident, the likelier it is that the failure to take the precaution was negligent.

In this case the risk, which we said was substantial, of an injury that would be likely to be serious could have been eliminated at little cost simply by removing the cab. The cab no longer had any function. It was just a dangerous eyesore. . . . Another alternative would have been to eliminate the deceleration feature, so that pressing the down button while the spreader beam was rising would have brought the beam to an immediate stop. This would not have been an ideal solution, however, because without the feature the crane would wear out sooner. The same drawback would attend another alternative safety precaution—reducing the period of deceleration from three seconds to one, which would have stopped the spreader beam within four inches after the down button was pressed rather than twelve. . . .

* * *

The specific question in the present case is whether there was a sufficient likelihood that the operator of the rebuilt crane would fail to press the emergency-stop button when he saw the spreader beam about to hit the cab that Konecranes should have [adopted one or more available precautions]. This is the question that the jury should have been instructed to focus on. The answer would depend on the likelihood of the kind of mistake that Van Til made and the cost and efficacy of additional precautions, such as removing the cab. It is easy enough to push the wrong button in an emergency or to forget that pushing the down button isn't as effective as pushing the emergency-stop button because of the deceleration feature. This argues for an automatic protective device, of which the cheapest would have been simply to remove the cab, made empty and useless by the removal from it of the crane controls. A jury that concluded that, all things considered, the failure to design the renovated crane in such a way as to protect Mesman against the kind of error that Van Til made was negligent could not be thought unreasonable. [Citations.]

Affirmed in part, reversed in part, and remanded with directions.

NOTES

1. Feasible, Safer Design Alternatives. Note Judge Posner's focus in *Mesman* on the safer design approaches that the defendant failed to adopt. Ordinarily, the very nature of negligent design is the failure to adopt a "feasible" alternative design that would have prevented the accident and been safer overall. *Compare* Richards v. Michelin Tire Corp., 21 F.3d 1048 (11th Cir.1994) (alternative design might have *de*creased overall safety: defendant not negligent), and Garst v. General Motors Corp., 484 P.2d 47 (Kan. 1971) (no way to design 40–ton earth-mover to make it turn or brake quickly: not negligent), *with* South Austin Drive–In Theatre v. Thomison, 421 S.W.2d 933 (Tex. Civ. App.1967) (failure to provide $3 shield to cover rear of power mower: negligent), and Calkins v. Sandven, 129 N.W.2d 1 (Iowa 1964) (failure to install simple, inexpensive shield over exposed conveyor mechanism on power farm wagon, where shield would not interfere with operation: negligent).

2. *Defect* as an Element of Negligence. In *Mesman,* Judge Posner observes that product defectiveness implies negligence. Increasingly, courts recognize the *converse* proposition: that negligence claims in products liability cases necessarily imply the product's defectiveness. See, e.g., Global Ground Support LLC v. Glazer Enterprises, 2006 WL 208639, at *11 (E.D.Pa. 2006) (negligence claim requires proof of defect, that defect resulted from negligence, and proximate cause). This suggests that a negligence claim effectively includes two elements apart from proximate cause: (1) a product defect, and (2) negligence in making or selling the product with that defect. The theory is that a manufacturer cannot ordinarily be negligent for making and selling a non-defective product, a product that is good.

---

4. THE MARKETING PROCESS: WARNINGS AND INSTRUCTIONS

A product may be designed and produced exactly as intended by the manufacturer yet still be unduly hazardous to consumers who do not appreciate its dangerous characteristics. This is increasingly true as consumers are faced with a burgeoning variety of products of ever-increasing complexity, spawned by modern technology. Consumers are often dependent upon the expert manufacturer to supply them with information on product dangers and how to avoid them. Reasonable care may thus obligate the manufacturer "to speak out if the product is capable of harm and does not itself carry a message of danger." Dillard & Hart, Product Liability: Directions for Use and the Duty to Warn, 41 Va. L. Rev. 145, 147 (1955). In most instances, of course, "[t]he purpose of a warning is to apprise a party of a danger of which he is not aware, and thus enable him to protect himself against it." Jonescue v. Jewel Home Shopping Service, 306 N.E.2d 312, 316 (Ill. App. Ct. 1973). In passing along the finished product to the ultimate consumer, the prudent manufacturer must therefore attach whatever information reasonably appears to be necessary to permit the consumer to use the product with reasonable safety. Thus, a manufacturer may be negligent if it fails adequately to warn of dangers in its product or to instruct on methods for its safe use. "It is not necessary that the product be negligently designed or manufactured; the failure to warn of hazards associated with foreseeable uses of a product is itself negligence, and if that negligence proximately results in a plaintiff's injuries, the plaintiff may recover." Laaperi v. Sears, Roebuck & Co., 787 F.2d 726, 729 (1st Cir. 1986).

As was seen in Chapter 1, the maker's obligation to warn of hidden dangers in its products is an ancient one. Its roots reach back into early Roman sales law and the ecclesiastical law of medieval England. It will be recalled that one of the three privity exceptions articulated in *Huset v. J.I. Case Threshing Machine Co.*, supra, was for "one who sells or delivers an article which he knows to be imminently dangerous to life or limb of another without notice of its qualities." Negligence in the failure to supply adequate warnings or instructions continues today to be a central issue in many products liability cases. Since the various issues of warning "defectiveness" receive full consideration in Chapter 8, the focus here is on the nature of the negligence principles at work in the warning context.

Boyl v. California Chemical Co.

United States District Court, District of Oregon, 1963.
221 F. Supp. 669.

■ EAST, DISTRICT JUDGE.

[The case was tried to the court, which found as follows: Defendant, a chemical manufacturer, makes and sells a liquid weed killer called "Triox." A major market for Triox is the "do-it-yourself garden-type consumer."

About] 50% of the Triox solution is a chemical compound referred to as sodium arsenite, which compound is compared as being four to six times as toxic to humans as arsenide trioxide (rat poison); the minimum human lethal dosage of sodium arsenite is 20 to 30 milligrams and it is a very stable compound with long-lasting toxic contamination propensities, and a disabling dosage of the compound, varying in degrees to fatal, can be taken into the human bloodstream by way of absorption through the skin or by inhalation as readily as by ingestion.

* * *

Plaintiff's Use of Triox

During the latter part of May, 1960, plaintiff purchased from a third party retail outlet a quart-sized can of the Triox product for the intended ultimate use on weed growth in and about the driveway of her residence, and the container so purchased exhibited the following pertinent labels and warnings:

[Front of Can]
ORTHO
TRIOX
KILLS VEGETATION
An Arsenical Weed Killer!

Prevents Plant Growth for 1 to 2 years

Use on driveways, brick walks, paths, tile patios, tennis courts, parking areas; along fence lines, curbs and gutters; around garages, house foundations and other structures, where soil can be poisoned and no plant growth is wanted.

POISON
[Skull and crossbones]

Active Ingredient	by Wt.
Sodium Arsenite ($NaAsO_2$)	55%
Inert Ingredients	45%

Equivalent to 41.9% of arsenic trioxide.

Arsenic expressed as metallic, all in water-soluble form 31.7%

Pounds Arsenic Trioxide per gallon at 68° F 6

DO NOT USE ON LAWNS

[Right Side of Can]

TRIOX
KILLS WEEDS IN
[picture]
Tile Patios
[picture]
Curbs and Gutters
[picture]
Brick Walks
Driveways
Paths
Tennis Courts
Parking Areas
Along Fence Lines

USE WHERE SOIL CAN BE POISONED AND NO PLANT GROWTH IS WANTED

[Left Side of Can]

Manufactured by [manufacturer's name and address omitted.]

[Back of Can]

DILUTION TABLE
[omitted]

READ ENTIRE LABEL. USE STRICTLY IN ACCORDANCE WITH LABEL CAUTIONS, WARNINGS AND DIRECTIONS.

TO POISON SOIL AND PREVENT PLANT GROWTH: [Dilution and instruction of preparation of ground—omitted]

TO KILL ANNUAL WEEDS AND TOP GROWTH OF PERENNIAL WEEDS: [Dilution and instruction of application—omitted]

NOTE: INSTRUCTIONS AS TO FREEZING TEMPERATURES [omitted]

WARNING: TRIOX is a strong poison. It should be kept away from children and animals. Avoid breathing spray mist. Avoid contact with skin, eyes, or clothing. Wash thoroughly after using. Avoid getting TRIOX into cuts, sores, etc. Should this occur, wash off at once. Livestock and poultry will be poisoned if allowed to feed on treated areas.[2] Avoid getting TRIOX on

---

2. Indicative of defendant's knowledge of long-lasting earth-contaminating potentials of sodium arsenite.

[Poison skull & cross-bones]

painted surfaces as peeling of paint will occur. Rinse spray hoses thoroughly after use as TRIOX will deteriorate hose materials. *When container is empty, immediately wash thoroughly and destroy.* Never re-use.[3]

ANTIDOTE FOR ARSENIC: Give a tablespoonful of salt in a glass of warm water and repeat until vomit fluid is clear. Then give two tablespoonfuls of Epsom Salts or Milk of Magnesia in water and plenty of milk and water. Have victim lie down and keep quiet. **CALL A PHYSICIAN IMMEDIATELY.**

* * *

On May 27, 1960 (a Friday), plaintiff proceeded to apply the Triox, and after perusing the labels and warnings on the container she put on protective clothing such as gloves and a scarf, and then proceeded, while standing windward, to apply the Triox to the driveway area with the use of a backpack air-pressure spray pump;

That after applying the bulk of the Triox solution in the spray tank, she thereupon rinsed the spray tank with garden hose water and poured out the rinse water containing the tank residue of Triox upon a "waste area" (rough grass area) of the back yard immediately adjoining a clear patio space;

That afternoon plaintiff and her family motored to the Oregon beach area for the Memorial Day weekend, and plaintiff recalls no physical malfunctioning effects or discomforts from her spraying activities except for a bad headache during the same evening.

Injury

On the following Wednesday early afternoon the weather was sunny and warm and plaintiff, while dressed in a "bra and shorts" type sunsuit, had just finished hanging a clothes washing on the dryer rack in the patio area when she unwittingly lay stomach down for a sunning in the rough grass area where she had poured out the Triox rinse;

Very shortly thereafter she noticed a "heat rash" and severe itching about her thighs, and within half an hour she broke out with red spots followed by hives; thereafter, her condition worsened in that her body became generally swollen, and by 6:00 P.M. she was dizzy and confused and had developed muscle tremors and twitching, and by 7:00 to 8:00 P.M. she had been and was hospitalized for the following three days, during the first 24–hour period of which hospitalization her worsened physical condition was listed as critical. No useful purpose will be here served by further describing plaintiff's symptoms, physical malfunctioning and disabilities nor the medical treatment therefor extended over some 18 months, as I am

3. Italicized to indicate defendant's knowledge of the stability of sodium arsenite.

satisfied from the medical expert testimony that plaintiff's acute physical malfunctioning immediately following the exposure, with resulting disability during the slow recovery, was due to the introduction into her blood supply through skin absorption and inhalation of an intolerable quantity of toxic sodium arsenite during the time she lay upon the ground which had been contaminated with the Triox rinse.

Duty to Warn

I conclude that with its experience and expertise the defendant knew or should have known of the stable quality (see n. 3) and long-lasting contamination propensities of the sodium arsenite contained in the Triox solution upon the earth (see n. 2) and of the hazard or danger to humans coming in contact with such contaminated earth;

Further, that a prudent producer of such a potential danger to humans would reasonably foresee an injury such as that sustained by plaintiff in the absence of, or but for some reasonable notice or warning concerning a safe disposal of the rinse residue after the use of the product for the intended purpose for which it was produced and sold....

* * *

[A] manufacturer who undertakes to produce and sell to the general public a product with high risk of human harm must provide specification, instruction, and warning, so that it is reasonably safe for ordinary persons to use it, *not only* for the purposes for which it is produced and intended to be used *but also* all other necessarily incidental and attendant uses (such as storage or disposal) and to give reasonable notice and warning of after or delayed effect or latent or lingering dangers not known or reasonably to be expected by the ordinary user, but which are "foreseeably probable" to the manufacturer with his expertise.[5]

* * *

Defendant's Failure to Warn and Liability

A perusal of the warnings and instructions on the can of Triox here tells us in no uncertain words that Triox is "an arsenical ..." compound and that it contains a large quantity of "sodium arsenite" and that such solution is "poison," as I am sure everyone knows. The warning gives an antidote for *internal* ingestion. Also, directions for prevention of personal injury *while using and applying the liquid;* however, no warning or protective advice whatsoever as to disposal of the fluid or of any risk to unadvised persons from the stability or long-lasting qualities or propensities and lingering risks of the liquid after returning to a dry or solid form is given, or even reasonably inferable. In fact, the directions as to use and advice as to avoiding skin or other personal contact with the liquid or

---

5. The likelihood of an accident taking place and the seriousness of the consequences are always pertinent matters to be considered with respect to the duty to provide a suffi-cient label. See Rest., Torts, §§ 291, 388, Comment *l*, pp. 1051–1052; § 397, Comments *b–d*....

breathing the spray mist of Triox and the washing of the person after using, and total lack of advice as to disposal of the rinse, could mislead a user to concluding that there was no lingering risk after immediate use and airwashing.

From the foregoing, I conclude that the defendant was negligent towards plaintiff in failing to give any reasonable notice or warning of a risk or danger to her personal safety from contact with earth lately contaminated with the Triox solution, and that such negligence on the part of the defendant was the proximate cause of plaintiff's resulting physical malfunctioning and disabilities.

* * *

[Judgment for plaintiff in the amount of $7,910.60.]

NOTES

1. Did defendant warn users that contact of the weed killer with the skin could be dangerous? What language on the label do you suppose defendant relied upon? If defendant did warn users of the danger, why was it held negligent?

2. Do you agree with the court that no warning was given of the long-lasting nature of the danger?

3. Was it really foreseeable that a person informed of the danger of contact with Triox would dump out the chemical residue and then lie down, partially unclothed, on top of it? Compare Jones v. Amazing Products, Inc., 231 F.Supp.2d 1228, 1241 (N.D. Ga. 2002) (foreseeable that consumer might attempt to transfer sulfuric acid drain cleaner to container that would melt; foreseeability "means that which would be foreseeably probable or objectively reasonable to expect, not merely what might occur").

4. Was the decision correct? Did the court use a calculus of risk approach in finding the defendant negligent? Can you?

5. Risk–Benefit Analysis in Warning Cases. Sometimes, but infrequently, courts explicitly apply risk-benefit analysis to warning cases. See, e.g., Holladay v. Chicago, Burlington & Quincy R. Co., 255 F. Supp. 879, 884 (S.D. Iowa 1966) (failure to warn of skin irritation from herbicide) ("In determining the duty of care required of defendant in the case at hand, the likelihood of harm, and the gravity of the harm if it happens, must be weighed against the burden of precaution which would be effective to avoid the harm.")

Perhaps the clearest application of risk-utility principles to a warning claim is Moran v. Faberge, Inc., 332 A.2d 11, 15 (Md. 1975), where the defendant failed to warn that its perfume was flammable:

> To begin with we note that a manufacturer's duty to produce a safe product, with appropriate warnings and instructions when necessary, is no different from the responsibility each of us bears to exercise due care to avoid unreasonable risks of harm to others. 2 Harper & James, The Law of Torts, § 28.3 (1956); Prosser, The Law of Torts, § 31 (4th ed. 1971). Whether any such unreasonable risk exists in a given situation depends on balancing the probability and seriousness of harm, if care is not exercised, against the costs of taking appropriate precautions. 2 Harper & James,

supra, §§ 16.9, 28.4; Restatement, Second, Torts §§ 291–93, 298 (1965). However, we observe that in cases such as this the cost of giving an adequate warning is usually so minimal, amounting only to the expense of adding some more printing to a label, that this balancing process will almost always weigh in favor of an obligation to warn of latent dangers, if the manufacturer is otherwise required to do so.

6. Foreseeability of Danger.

A. In general—Expert in field. A failure to warn may be negligent, of course, only if the danger is reasonably foreseeable to the manufacturer. See generally Note, Foreseeability in Product Design and Duty to Warn Cases—Distinctions and Misconceptions, 1968 Wis. L. Rev. 228. But foreseeability is often viewed from the perspective of an expert in the business who is held to know the characteristics of its products and the uses to which they possibly may be applied. Put another way, a manufacturer is deemed to possess the knowledge of an expert in the field: "In testing the defendant's liability for negligence in failing to warn, the defendant should be held to the standard of care of an expert in its field." Olson v. Prosoco, Inc., 522 N.W.2d 284 (Iowa 1994). See also Stahlheber v. American Cyanamid Co., 451 S.W.2d 48, 61 (Mo. 1970) (manufacturer of polio vaccine "knew or, by using the skill of an expert in defendant's business, could have known of the dangerous potentiality of said product" when administered to adults).

B. Constructive knowledge. Foreseeability is sometimes defined in terms of "constructive knowledge": "Negligence based on the failure to warn requires actual or constructive knowledge of the danger on the part of the manufacturer, and the lack of a warning notice." Smith v. United States, 155 F.Supp. 605, 609 (E.D. Va. 1957). " 'Constructive knowledge' refers to knowledge that one has the opportunity to possess by the exercise of ordinary care." First Nat. Bank v. Nor–Am Agricultural Products, 537 P.2d 682, 690 (N.M. App.1975).

7. Is it foreseeable that cleaning fluid may be splashed in the eye? See Sawyer v. Pine Oil Sales Co., 155 F.2d 855 (5th Cir. 1946) (no). Paint? Haberly v. Reardon Co., 319 S.W.2d 859 (Mo. 1958) (yes).

8. On negligence claims in products liability cases, see D. Owen, Products Liability Law ch.2 (2d ed. 2008); 1 D. Owen, M.S. Madden, & M. Davis, Madden & Owen on Products Liability ch.2 (3d ed. 2000).

CHAPTER 3

Tortious Misrepresentation

There are three primary theories of tortious misrepresentation recognized today by the common law that differ principally according to the defendant's state of mind in making the representation. Fraud and deceit requires a showing of *scienter*, that the defendant knew the matter to be false and intended to mislead the plaintiff, or some similar state of mind. Negligent misrepresentation requires proof only that the defendant was negligent in not knowing the falsity of its representations, or that the defendant communicated them in a negligent manner. In some states, a defendant may be strictly liable in tort for certain public misrepresentations about its products, regardless of its good faith or its exercise of reasonable care. Other differences between these three separate theories of recovery are considered below.

Because fraud and other misrepresentation claims hinge on particular words written or spoken by the defendant, claims of this type require the precise identification and close scrutiny of particular, offending language. Thus, the lawyer must first and foremost isolate the exact words challenged, framing the particular context in which they were communicated, to assess whether they properly give rise to a misrepresentation claim. See, e.g., In re Kings Cty. Tobacco Litig., 727 N.Y.S.2d 241 n.8 (Sup. Ct. 2000) (misrepresentation claim dismissed because of plaintiff's failure to identify particular representations, merely relying on television ads that "made smoking seem cool").

1. Fraud

St. Joseph Hospital v. Corbetta Construction Co.
Illinois Appellate Court, 1974.
21 Ill. App.3d 925, 316 N.E.2d 51.

■ HALLETT, JUSTICE.

* * *

The St. Joseph Hospital (the Hospital) in 1958 entered into a contract with architect Belli & Belli of Missouri (Belli) for the erection of a hospital on a new site in Chicago to replace one erected before the Great Chicago Fire of 1871, and the general construction of the hospital was undertaken by the Corbetta Construction Company (Corbetta). In April of 1965, when the building had been substantially completed, the Hospital was advised by the city collector that its application for a license to operate the Hospital had been disapproved because the wall paneling (General Electric's "Textolite") which covered its rooms and corridors, and had been manufactured and furnished by the General Electric Company (General Electric), did not comply with a Chicago code requirement that such paneling have a "flame spread" rating of not to exceed 15. Actually it had a rating of 255, 17 times the maximum. The city also threatened criminal action against the Hospital for operating without said license.

[The Hospital thereupon filed a complaint for a declaratory judgment against Corbetta, Belli, and General Electric (G.E.) to determine liability for the loss. The jury rendered a verdict for the Hospital on liability, and a subsequent jury awarded damages to the Hospital for the cost of replacing the Textolite paneling with other paneling that complied with the Chicago Building Code. The following portion of the court's opinion pertains only to the liability of G.E., which argued throughout the case that it had informed the parties that Textolite was "not rated."]

On August 28, 1962, a series of flame spread tests were made at the Underwriters Laboratories in Northbrook. Herbert Day, an employee of General Electric, was there. The tests were performed by Walter Haas of Underwriters and seven different products were tested. General Electric's product Textolite (the same as was here installed) was placed in one of the tunnels and the fire turned on. The test lasted only 2 minutes and 16 seconds because by then the flames had traversed the entire (25 feet) length of the tunnel and the sample of Textolite was removed with its surface completely charred. That concluded the test and the flame spread was calculated at 254.6 or 255. The Textolite had the highest flame-spread rating of any of the products tested that day.

On August 31, 1962, Day reported to General Electric by a letter addressed to Mr. Thomas, with copies to Mr. Derbyshire of General Electric, and others. Haas, of Underwriters, explained the nature of the test and the result of the test on Textolite and said that the product was not given a flame-spread rating because they felt that no product testing out over 200 should be given a rating because it would be highly inflammable and dangerous.

On October 26, 1962, 2 months after said test, General Electric entered into its subcontract with Corbetta for the installation of this highly inflammable material on the walls of the plaintiff's hospital in Chicago. No one other than General Electric knew at that time of the disastrous results of this test.

In December of 1962, representatives of General Electric, including Derbyshire, and of Corbetta met and discussed further the installation of Textolite in the plaintiff's hospital. Again, Derbyshire said nothing of the results of said test to Corbetta's representatives, or even to Warner, his own salesman.

On January 3, 1963, Derbyshire wrote Mr. Egidi, of Corbetta, as follows:

"Further at this time I wish to point out that our Batten Panel System does not carry a flame spread rating of any kind. I have brought up the need of a fire rating of this System in several of our initial discussions and again on December 12, 1962. I have been told [by the architect Belli] that it was none of our concern and that everything was taken care of in this respect. Nowhere is a rating mentioned in the specification. If we now find that our System must have a flame spread rating, then our contracted price no longer can apply. We must at this point reevaluate the requirements and reengineer the paneling and pricing accordingly.

"We can supply a U–L flame spread rated panel but not under the terms and drawings submitted in conjunction with the contract."

It should be noted that, again, the fact that the Textolite paneling had actually been flame tested and had tested out a disastrous 17 times the maximum permitted under the Code is masked and concealed. Rather, it was a "coverup." Furthermore, General Electric did not then have (nor has it had since) a wall paneling meeting the flame-spread test fixed in the Chicago Code.

* * *

In view of these facts, we agree, as it said in plaintiff's (and Corbetta's) brief, that:

"Regardless of how many times General Electric might say, either orally or in writing, that 'Our material is not flame rated,' the statement is still a 'gross deception' covering up the real truth namely that General Electric was proposing for installation in this hospital a material which it actually knew was utterly unfit for use in such an institution."

Under these facts, we are of the considered opinion that General Electric is liable to the Hospital on the basis of fraud and deceit in not disclosing that its said paneling had actually been tested by Underwriters Laboratory and had been found to have a flame spread 17 times the maximum under the Chicago Building Code; which theory does not require privity in the traditional sense.

It is well established that a statement which is technically true as far as it goes may nevertheless be fraudulent, where it is misleading because it does not state matters which materially qualify the statement as made. In other words, a half-truth is sometimes more misleading than an outright lie.

* * *

It is also well established that where one has made a statement which at that time is true but subsequently acquires new information which makes it untrue or misleading, he must disclose such information to anyone whom he knows to be acting on the basis of the original statement—or be guilty of fraud or deceit.

It is also well established that in fraud cases based on misrepresentation it is not a prerequisite to recovery that there be privity, at least in the traditional sense. It is enough that the statements by the defendant be made with the intention that it reach the plaintiff and influence his action and that it does reach him and that he does rely upon it, to his damage.

[Verdict for Hospital against G.E. affirmed.]

NOTES

1. One of the earliest reported products liability opinions was based on fraud and deceit. See Langridge v. Levy, 2 M. & W. 519, 150 Eng. Rep. 863 (1836), aff'd, 4 M. & W. 337, 150 Eng. Rep. 1458 (1838).

2. Consider Dobbin v. Pacific Coast Coal Co., 170 P.2d 642, 648 (Wash. 1946) (distributor of defective furnace not liable in fraud): "Of all civil liabilities, fraud is the most difficult to establish." *Dobbin* set out the essential elements as follows:

(1) A representation of an existing fact; (2) its materiality; (3) its falsity; (4) the speaker's knowledge of its falsity or ignorance of its truth; (5) his intent that it should be acted on by the person to whom it is made; (6) ignorance of its falsity on the part of the person to whom it is made; (7) the latter's reliance on the truth of the representation; (8) his right to rely upon it; (9) his consequent damage.

In the principal case, did the complaint make out a case of fraud on each of the *Dobbin* elements? Some courts compress the nine *Dobbin* elements into as few as four for purposes of defining the tort, see, e.g., Lewis v. Lead Indus. Ass'n, Inc., 793 N.E.2d 869 (Ill. App. Ct. 2003), but a fraud case will fail even in those jurisdictions if plaintiff does not establish each of the requirements set forth in *Dobbin*.

3. A misrepresentation may be accomplished by conduct as well as by words, and manufacturers and other sellers have been held liable for fraudulent concealment of a dangerous defect. See Kuelling v. Roderick Lean Mfg. Co., 75 N.E. 1098 (N.Y.1905) (beam on farm machine made of unfit, cross-grained wood with knothole): "[D]efendant concealed this knothole with a plug of soft wood nailed in, and then the knot, the plug, the hole, the cross-grain of the wood, and the kind of wood used were covered up and concealed by the defendant with putty and paint...." This amounted to "an affirmative representation that the [beam] was sound...." See also Woodward v. Miller & Karwisch, 46 S.E. 847 (Ga. 1904) (large crack in axle of buggy covered over with grease). See generally W. P. Keeton, Fraud—Concealment and Nondisclosure, 15 Texas L. Rev. 1 (1936).

4. Most courts hold that the misrepresentation must be of an *existing* fact rather than being a prediction of future facts. However, a promise of future performance made with no present intention of keeping it may satisfy the rule. See Willard v. Chrysler Corp., 148 S.E.2d 867 (S.C. 1966).

5. Puffing. Opinions, including "sales talk" that extol the quality of a product in general terms, will not ordinarily support an action of deceit. See, e.g., Lambert v. Sistrunk, 58 So.2d 434 (Fla. 1952) (step-ladder would "last a lifetime" and customer would "never break it"); Holley v. Central Auto Parts, 347 S.W.2d 341 (Tex. Civ. App.1961) (tire rim was "a good one").

However, "[w]here the party making the representations has superior knowledge regarding the subject matter of his representations, and the other party is so situated that he may reasonably rely on such supposed superior knowledge or special information, the representations may be construed as fact and not opinion." Toole v. Richardson–Merrell Inc., 60 Cal. Rptr. 398, 411 (Ct. App. 1967) (drug that produced serious eye damage to defendant's test animals, and later to humans, advertised as "virtually non-toxic," "safe," and free of "significant side effects"). See generally W.P. Keeton, Fraud: Misrepresentations of Opinion, 21 Minn. L. Rev. 643 (1937).

6. Scienter. Plaintiffs in fraud cases often have difficulty establishing the defendant's "scienter"—the defendant's knowledge of the falsity and/or intent to deceive. See, e.g., Limited Flying Club, Inc. v. Wood, 632 F.2d 51 (8th Cir. 1980). However, some courts liberalize the scienter requirement by holding that "deliberate deception or scienter is not a necessary element of the cause of action for fraud.... It is sufficient if the speaker makes the statement as of his own knowledge without knowing whether it is true or false." Clements Auto Co. v. Service Bureau Corp., 298 F. Supp. 115, 126 (D.Minn.1969). Thus," 'fraud' includes pretense of knowledge, where there is no knowledge." Sgarlata v. Carioto, 201 N.Y.S.2d 384, 385 (Albany City Ct. 1960).

7. Reliance. The misrepresentation must of course be the cause of the plaintiff's harm, and so the element of reliance. See Boeken v. Philip Morris Inc., 26 Cal.Rptr.3d 638, 651–59 (Cal. Ct. App. 2005) (smoker established his reliance on fraudulent ads). Thus, a person who buys a safe solely for burglary protection who loses the safe's contents in a fire cannot ground a fraud claim on the manufacturer's misrepresentation that the safe could withstand fire. See Fitzgerald v. Liberty Safe and Security Products, 80 F. App'x 897 (5th Cir. 2003). And of course a plaintiff who did not hear or see the misrepresentation at all will usually have considerable difficulty with this element. Yet reliance need not be by the plaintiff personally, however, so long as it is by someone–a doctor, family member, or friend– acting on his or her behalf.

8. Many cases of fraud and deceit are against retailers, often used-car dealers, for loss of bargain rather than for personal injury. For example, the dealer may be charged with falsely having said that the car had only been used as a demonstrator, or that it had never been involved in a crash. The recurring problem of used car dealers misrepresenting the mileage by turning back the odometer was addressed by Congress in 1972 in the Motor Vehicle Information and Cost Savings Act, 15 U.S.C.A. § 1981 et seq. Section 1984 provides: "No person shall disconnect, reset, or alter or cause to be disconnected, reset, or altered, the odometer of any motor vehicle with intent to change the number of miles indicated thereon." Purchasers of such vehicles are entitled to (1) the greater of treble damages or $1,500, and (2) costs of suit and reasonable attorneys fees. 15 U.S.C.A. § 1989.

9. Cigarette Litigation and Preemption. Fraud and other misrepresentation claims figure prominently in the ongoing cigarette litigation, as developed further in ch. 19. The basic fraud claim escaped preemption in Cipollone v. Liggett Group, Inc., 505 U.S. 504 (1992), and it remains a major claim in the continuing litigations.

10. Disclaimers. Disclaimers against liability in fraud are void as against public policy. First Nat'l Bank v. Brooks Farms, 1990 WL 6386 (Tenn. Ct. App. 1990) (good discussion), aff'd on this point, 821 S.W.2d 925 (Tenn. 1991).

11. Unfair Trade Practices Acts. Some states have statutes that broadly prohibit false, misleading, unfair or deceptive trade practices. Similar to the federal odometer statute, such laws often provide for treble damages and attorneys fees. Utica Mutual Ins. Co. v. Denwat Corp., 778 F.Supp. 592 (D. Conn. 1991) (separate products liability claim maintainable under such a statute notwithstanding state products liability statute that purports to govern all product actions). Such statutes were generally not enacted, however, to provide remedies to persons suffering physical injuries from defective products, and so their remedies may not be available in such cases. See generally Boswell, Stagg & Myers, Deceptive Trade Practice—Consumer Protection Acts and Their Effect on Product Liability Litigation, 15 Forum 716 (Spring 1980). But see Maldonado v. Nutri/System, Inc., 776 F.Supp. 278 (E.D. Va. 1991) ("loss" under statute included loss of gall bladder caused by defendant's weight loss; food falsely advertised as safe).

12. Pleading and proof. Under the federal rules, and the law of many states, a plaintiff must plead with specificity the facts constituting a fraud. Fed. R. Civ. P. 9(b) provides in part:

> In all averments of fraud or mistake, the circumstances constituting fraud or mistake shall be stated with particularity.

See, e.g., Baryo v. Philip Morris USA, Inc., 435 F.Supp.2d 961, 968–69 (W.D. Mo. 2006) (fraud claims failed to comply with Rule 9(b); plaintiffs allowed to amend complaint). Moreover, because of the accompanying stigma associated with the commission of a fraud, many jurisdictions apply a "clear and convincing evidence" standard of proof to claims of fraudulent misrepresentation. See, e.g., DeVries v. DeLaval, Inc., 2006 WL 1582179, at *7 (D. Idaho 2006).

13. Today, products liability actions involving personal injuries are only infrequently brought in fraud and deceit. Why do you suppose this is so? Depending on the jurisdiction, however, proof of fraud may advantage a plaintiff's case with respect to privity, preemption, the statute of limitations, the effect of a disclaimer, contributory negligence, and possibly punitive damages. Note, however, that in some jurisdictions fraud claims do not survive the death of a party. See, e.g., Faircloth v. Finesod, 938 F.2d 513 (4th Cir. 1991) (South Carolina; *held*, denial of such claims is constitutional).

14. On fraud and deceit in products liability litigation, see generally D. Owen, Products Liability Law § 3.2 (2d ed. 2008); 1 D. Owen, M.S. Madden, & M. Davis, Madden & Owen on Products Liability § 3:2 (3d ed. 2000).

2. NEGLIGENT MISREPRESENTATION

Although a person injured as the result of a misrepresentation is unable to make out a fraud case, as from lack of evidence on the defendant's scienter, he or she nevertheless may be able to prove a claim of negligent misrepresentation. In Pabon v. Hackensack Auto Sales, Inc., 164 A.2d 773, 784 (N.J. Super. Ct.1960), the plaintiff was injured when the steering on his new automobile locked, causing the car to crash. He had noticed a "clicking" and "chopping" sensation in the steering and had brought it to the attention of the defendant's service manager on three occasions prior to the accident. Each time, the service manager without checking the problem said something like, "It's a new car. Don't worry about it. It'll wear out." Holding that a jury could find the defendant liable for negligent misrepresentation on these facts, the court stated:

> Negligence may be inferred not only from Hackensack's failure or refusal to repair or even to examine the reported defect, but also from its representation to Alphonse that the steering deficiency was normal and should cause him no concern. A false statement negligently made, and on which justifiable reliance is placed, may be the basis for the recovery of

damages for injury sustained as a consequence of such reliance. . . . There must be knowledge, or reason to know, on the part of the speaker that the information is desired for a serious purpose, that the seeker of the information intends to rely upon it, and that if the information or opinion is false or erroneous, the relying party will be injured in person or property.

NOTES

1. Most negligent misrepresentation cases involve retailers. The defendant's negligence usually consists in its failure to exercise reasonable care to ascertain the accuracy of its representation. Typical are the used car cases. E.g., Boos v. Claude, 9 N.W.2d 262 (S.D. 1943) (car with defective steering said to be in "perfect mechanical condition," yet "defendants had not used reasonable care in making tests for the purpose of ascertaining defects"); Flies v. Fox Bros. Buick Co., 218 N.W. 855 (Wis.1928) (Owen, J.) (dealer representing car, restored after wreck, to be "in perfect operating condition" negligent in not discovering defective brakes).

2. Manufacturers on occasion are held responsible for negligent misrepresentation, usually in connection with representations on a product's label or in advertising. Typically the product is labeled or advertised to be "harmless" or "safe" when in fact it contains a hidden danger. The manufacturer's failure to warn of the danger in these cases often appears to be as important as its affirmative misrepresentation of safety. See, e.g., Colacicco v. Apotex, Inc., 432 F.Supp.2d 514, 554–55 (E.D.Pa. 2006) (inadequate labeling of drug that caused suicide; but for overriding duty issue, negligent misrepresentation claim would have survived motion to dismiss); Henry v. Crook, 195 N.Y.S. 642 (App. Div. 1922) (sparklers advertised as "A harmless and delightful amusement for children" ignited seven-year-old plaintiff's dress); Crist v. Art Metal Works, 243 N.Y.S. 496 (App. Div.1930), aff'd, 175 N.E. 341 (N.Y. 1931) (toy revolver, advertised as "absolutely harmless," ignited plaintiff's Santa Claus beard and costume during demonstration of product in department store window). Compare Wawrzynek v. Statprobe, Inc., 422 F.Supp.2d 474, 484 (E.D.Pa. 2005) (allowing negligent misrepresentation claim against biostatistical services provider that provided false information about clinical study to medical device manufacturer which led to FDA approval of device that injured plaintiff).

3. Statutory Violations. False labeling or advertising concerning a product's safety may contravene a misbranding, false advertising, or unfair and deceptive trade practices statute and thus support a claim for negligence per se. Although defendant received over 373 complaints of skin irritation over a four year period, it continued to advertise its deodorant, "Arrid," as "safe" and "harmless," and that it "does not irritate the skin." Plaintiff, who suffered a skin disorder from using Arrid, alleged that defendant had misrepresented and falsely advertised its product:

> It is well established that a statutory violation may be the basis for civil liability if the injured person is a member of the class for whose express benefit the statute was enacted and the harm resulting from the violation is of the type that the statute was designed to prevent.

Wright v. Carter Prods., Inc., 244 F.2d 53, 61 (2d Cir. 1957). See also Tetuan v. A.H. Robins Co., 738 P.2d 1210 (Kan. 1987) (false advertising of dangerous Dalkon Shield IUD); Washington State Physicians Ins. Exchange & Ass'n v. Fisons, 858 P.2d 1054 (Wash. 1993) (doctors could sue under Consumer Protection Act for injury to reputation from misprescribing drug with inadequate warnings).

4. The negligent misrepresentation theory of liability has been used infrequently in products liability litigation, especially in actions for personal injuries against manufacturers. Why? A modern, limited role for the theory addresses certifiers of product safety, see ch. 16, § 6, below.

---

3.   STRICT LIABILITY FOR MISREPRESENTATION

Baxter v. Ford Motor Co.

Supreme Court of Washington, 1932.
168 Wash. 456, 12 P.2d 409.

■ HERMAN, J.

[While plaintiff was driving his Model A Ford, a pebble from a passing car struck his windshield, causing small pieces of glass to fly into his eye which he lost as a result. In a suit against Ford Motor Company for misrepresenting the windshield's characteristics in its advertising catalogues, the trial court rendered judgment for the defendant, and plaintiff appealed. The catalogues stated:]

TRIPLEX SHATTER-PROOF GLASS WINDSHIELD. All of the new Ford cars have a Triplex shatter-proof glass windshield—so made that it will not fly or shatter under the hardest impact. This is an important safety factor because it eliminates the dangers of flying glass—the cause of most of the injuries in automobile accidents. In these days of crowded, heavy traffic, the use of this Triplex glass is an absolute necessity. Its extra margin of safety is something that every motorist should look for in the purchase of a car—especially where there are women and children.

Respondent [Ford] contends that there can be no implied or express warranty without privity of contract, and warranties as to personal property do not attach themselves to, and run with, the article sold.

* * *

[Ford represented the car] as having a windshield of non-shatterable glass "so made that it will not fly or shatter under the hardest impact." An ordinary person would be unable to discover by the usual and customary examination of the automobile whether glass which would not fly or shatter was used in the windshield. In that respect, the purchaser was in a position similar to that of the consumer of a wrongly labeled drug, who has bought the same from a retailer, and who has relied upon the manufacturer's representation that the label correctly set forth the contents of the container. For many years, [manufacturers have been held liable to consumers even if they] purchased from a third person the commodity causing the damage. Thomas v. Winchester, 6 N.Y. 397.

The rule in such cases does not rest upon contractual obligations, but rather on the principle that the original act of delivering an article is wrong, when, because of the lack of those qualities which the manufacturer represented it as having, the absence of which could not be readily detected by the consumer, the article is not safe for the purposes for which the consumer would ordinarily use it.

* * *

Since the rule of *caveat emptor* was first formulated, vast changes have taken place in the economic structures of the English speaking peoples. Methods of doing business have undergone a great transition. Radio, bill boards and the products of the printing press have become the means of creating a large part of the demand that causes goods to depart from factories to the ultimate consumer. It would be unjust to recognize a rule that would permit manufacturers of goods to create a demand for their products by representing that they possess qualities which they, in fact, do not possess; and then, because there is no privity of contract existing between the consumer and the manufacturer, deny the consumer the right to recover if damages result from the absence of those qualities, when such absence is not readily noticeable.

[Reversed and remanded.]

N O T E

The case was retried, and plaintiff prevailed. The Supreme Court affirmed, ruling that Ford's belief in the truth of its representations was irrelevant, as was its evidence that the windshield was as good as any made. 35 P.2d 1090 (Wash. 1934). "As to this general field—negligence, deceit, warranty, or whatever the *Baxter* case may really involve—I take it we are feeling our way.... Perhaps we are actually witnessing the birth of a new type of tort liability." Leidy, Another New Tort?, 38 Mich. L. Rev. 964, 986 (1940). See also Feezer, Manufacturer's Liability for Injuries Caused by His Products: Defective Automobiles, 37 Mich. L. Rev. 1, 26 (1938).

Compare Worley v. Procter & Gamble Mfg. Co., 253 S.W.2d 532 (Mo. Ct. App. 1952), defendant manufacturer represented that "Tide is kind to your hands." *Held,* representation could support non-contractual warranty action imposing strict liability for its breach on manufacturer despite absence of privity. Cf. Rogers v. Toni Home Permanent Co., 147 N.E.2d 612 (Ohio 1958).

———

Restatement (Second) of Torts (1965)

§ 402B. Misrepresentation by Seller of Chattels to Consumer

One engaged in the business of selling chattels who, by advertising, labels, or otherwise, makes to the public a misrepresentation of a material fact concerning the character or quality of a chattel sold by him is subject to liability for physical harm to a consumer of the chattel caused by justifiable reliance upon the misrepresentation, even though

(a) it is not made fraudulently or negligently, and

(b) the consumer has not bought the chattel from or entered into any contractual relation with the seller.

————

Hauter v. Zogarts

Supreme Court of California, 1975.
14 Cal.3d 104, 120 Cal. Rptr. 681, 534 P.2d 377.

■ TOBRINER, JUSTICE.

* * *

Defendants[1] manufacture and sell the "Golfing Gizmo" (hereinafter Gizmo), a training device designed to aid unskilled golfers improve their games. Defendants' catalogue states that the Gizmo is a "completely equipped backyard driving range." In 1966, Louise Hauter purchased a Gizmo from the catalogue and gave it to Fred Hauter, her 13½–year–old son, as a Christmas present.

The Gizmo is a simple device consisting of two metal pegs, two cords— one elastic, one cotton—and a regulation golf ball. After the pegs are driven into the ground approximately 25 inches apart, the elastic cord is looped over them. The cotton cord, measuring 21 feet in length, ties to the middle of the elastic cord. The ball is attached to the end of the cotton cord. When the cords are extended, the Gizmo resembles the shape of a large letter "T," with the ball resting at the base.

The user stands by the ball in order to hit his practice shots. The instructions state that when hit correctly, the ball will fly out and spring back near the point of impact; if the ball returns to the left, it indicates a right-hander's "slice"; a shot returning to the right indicates a right-hander's "hook." If the ball is "topped," it does not return and must be retrieved by the player. The label on the shipping carton and the cover of the instruction booklet urge players to "drive the ball with full power" and further state: "COMPLETELY SAFE BALL WILL NOT HIT PLAYER."

. . . Fred Hauter was seriously injured while using defendants' product [and plaintiffs filed this action for tortious misrepresentation, breach of express and implied warranties, and strict liability in tort for defective design.]

Fred Hauter testified at trial that prior to his injury, he had practiced golf 10 to 20 times at driving ranges and had played several rounds of golf. His father instructed him in the correct use of the Gizmo. Fred had read the printed instructions that accompany the product and had used the Gizmo about a dozen times. Before the accident, Fred set up the Gizmo in his front yard according to the printed instructions. The area was free of objects that might have caused the ball to ricochet, and no other persons

----

1. Defendants are Rudy C. Zogarts, who does business as House of Zog [manufactur-   er] and Miles Kimball Company [seller].

were nearby. Fred then took his normal swing with a seven-iron. The last thing he remembers was extreme pain and dizziness. After a period of unconsciousness, he staggered into the house and told his mother that he had been hit on the head by the ball. He suffered brain damage and, in one doctor's opinion, is currently an epileptic.

George Peters, a safety engineer and an expert on the analysis and reconstruction of accidents, testified for plaintiffs. In Peters' opinion, Fred Hauter had hit underneath the ball and had caught the cord with his golf club, thus drawing the cord upwards and toward him on his follow-through. The ball looped over the club producing a "bolo" effect and struck Fred on the left temple. Peters, an expert on the cause of accidents, concluded that the Gizmo is a "major hazard."

Ray Catan, a professional golfer, also testified for plaintiffs. He added that even if the club had hit the lower part of the ball, the same result probably would have occurred. He personally tested the Gizmo, intentionally hitting low shots, and found that his club became entangled in the cord, bringing the ball back toward him as he completed his swing. Describing Fred Hauter as a beginner, Catan stated that since such a golfer's swing usually is very erratic, he rarely hits the ball solidly.

Defendants did not dispute plaintiffs' version of the accident. The manufacturer merely stated that he bought the rights to manufacture and distribute the Gizmo from a former professional golfer in 1962 and that the product had been on the market since that time.

[The jury rendered a unanimous verdict for defendants on each claim, the trial judge granted plaintiffs' j.n.o.v. and new trial motions, and defendants appealed.]

* * *

Plaintiffs' claim of false representation relies on common law tort principles reflected in section 402B of the Restatement Second of Torts. For plaintiffs to recover under this section, defendants' statement "COMPLETELY SAFE BALL WILL NOT HIT PLAYER" must be a misrepresentation of material fact upon which plaintiffs justifiably relied. (Rest. 2d Torts, § 402B, coms. f, g, and j.)

If defendants' assertion of safety is merely a statement of opinion— mere "puffing"—they cannot be held liable for its falsity. [Citations to cases where courts have ruled that a seller's representations were puffing, such as that the product was a "good machine"; "just as good or perhaps better than any"; "first class"; or that the product would "last a lifetime" or was "wonderful."] Defendants' statement is so broad, however, that it properly falls within the ambit of section 402B. The assertion that the Gizmo is completely safe, that the ball will not hit the player, does not indicate the seller's subjective opinion about the merits of his product but rather factually describes an important characteristic of the product. Courts have consistently held similar promises of safety to be representations of fact. [Citations to cases involving representations that a vaporizer was "safe" and "practically foolproof"; that a cosmetic was "safe"; that cigarettes "can cause no ills"; that tires were "safe" within stated limits; that a detergent was safe for all household tasks; and that a permanent wave solution was safe and harmless].

These decisions evidence the trend toward narrowing the scope of "puffing" and expanding the liability that flows from broad statements of manufacturers as to the quality of their products. Courts have come to construe unqualified statements such as the instant one liberally in favor of injured consumers. Furthermore, the illustrations in the Restatement indicate that the assertion "COMPLETELY SAFE BALL WILL NOT HIT PLAYER" constitutes a factual representation. . . .

[T]he materiality of defendants' representation can hardly be questioned; anyone learning to play golf naturally searches for a product that enables him to learn safely. Fred Hauter's testimony that he was impressed with the safety of the item demonstrates the importance of defendants' statement. That Fred's injury occurred while he used the Gizmo as instructed proves the inaccuracy of the assertion on the carton.

Defendants, however, maintain that plaintiffs' reliance upon the assurance of safety is not justifiable. (See Rest. 2d Torts, § 402B, com. j.) Alluding to the danger inherent to the sport, defendants argue that the Gizmo is a "completely safe" training device only when the ball is hit squarely. Defendants repeatedly state that an improperly hit golf shot exposes the player, as well as others nearby, to a serious risk of harm; they point to testimony recounting how an experienced player once hit a shot so poorly that the ball flew between his legs. As a result, contend defendants, plaintiffs cannot reasonably expect the Gizmo to be "completely safe" under all circumstances, particularly those in which the player hits beneath the ball.

[But] Fred Hauter was not "playing golf." He was home on his front lawn *learning* to play the game with the aid of defendants' supposedly danger-free training device. By practicing in an open, isolated area apart from other golfers and free of objects off which a poorly hit shot could ricochet, Fred Hauter *eliminated* most of the dangers present during a normal round of play. Moreover, even though certain dangers are inherent in playing golf, the risk that the golfer's own ball will wrap itself around his club and strike the golfer on the follow-through is not among those dangers. Fred Hauter's injury stemmed from a risk inherent in defendants' product, not a risk inherent in the game of golf.

Additionally, defendants' analysis would render their representation of safety illusory. Were we to adopt their analysis, the words "COMPLETELY SAFE BALL WILL NOT HIT PLAYER" would afford protection to consumers only in *relatively infrequent instances* in which the "duffers" using the Gizmo managed to hit the ball solidly. Yet defendants' instructions supplied with the Gizmo clearly indicate that defendants anticipated the users of their product would "hook," "slice" and "top" the ball. They expected their customers to commit the errors that normally plague beginning golfers. Thus, when they declared their product "completely safe," the only reasonable inference is that the Gizmo was a safe training device for all golfers regardless of ability and regardless of how squarely they hit the ball.

Although defendants claim they did not intend their statement to cover situations such as the one at bar, subjective intent is irrelevant. The question is not what a seller intended, but what the consumer reasonably believed. The rule "is one of strict liability for physical harm to the consumer, resulting from a misrepresentation of the character or quality of the chattel sold, even though the misrepresentation is an innocent one, and not made fraudulently or negligently." (Rest. 2d Torts, § 402B, com. a.)

We conclude that Fred Hauter reasonably believed he could use the Gizmo with safety and agree [that the plaintiffs established all elements of a misrepresentation claim.]

[Affirmed and remanded for trial to determine damages. Concurring opinion of CLARK, J., set forth below, in ch. 4.]

N O T E S

1. Consider the following variations:

A.   Fred set up the Gizmo 10 feet in front of a brick wall and squarely hit the ball which bounced off the wall and struck him in the head.

B.   Fred set up the Gizmo in his yard, hit the ball squarely, but was injured when the ball bounced off a tree—twenty feet away at a 45° angle from where he was standing—and hit him in the head.

C.   Fred's father injured his back when he hit underneath the ball, tangling his club in the cord in a way that caused his back to twist.

D.   Fred was injured exactly as in the case, but the only relevant representation was that the Gizmo was "safe."

E.   Fred was hit in the temple and injured when he missed catching a plastic frisbee that had been advertised as "the best form of safe and wholesome fun."

2. Interpretation: Truth or Falsity. Whether a representation should be interpreted as true or false on the facts of a particular case is sometimes a matter of contention. Plaintiff truck driver sustained injuries to head and chest when another truck hit the side of his vehicle thrusting him against the steering wheel. Plaintiff claimed that the steering column, advertised as "telescopic," failed to telescope adequately, contrary to the representation. Noting that the column would have telescoped more had the collision been head-on, and that it had telescoped somewhat even though plaintiff had been hit at an angle, the court concluded that the representation was not false: "The statement of appellant . . . never asserted that the steering column would telescope under any and all circumstances and conditions." General Motors Corp. v. Howard, 244 So.2d 726, 728 (Miss. 1971).

3. Consider Klages v. General Ordnance Equip. Corp., 367 A.2d 304 (Pa. Super. Ct. 1976). After once being held up by armed robbers, plaintiff, the night clerk at a motel, purchased the defendant's mace weapon for protection. The promotional literature for the weapon stated in part:

"Rapidly vaporizes on face of assailant effecting *instantaneous incapacitation* . . . an attacker is *subdued—instantly* . . . . Time Magazine stated the

Chemical Mace is '. . . a weapon that *disables as effectively* as a gun and yet does no permanent injury' . . . ."

When plaintiff was again held up soon thereafter, he removed the mace from the cash register where it was stored. "Using the cash register as a shield, Klages squirted the mace, hitting the intruder 'right beside the nose.' Klages immediately ducked below the register, but the intruder followed him down and shot him in the head." Rejecting the manufacturer's argument that plaintiff had assumed the risk, a defense subsumed in misrepresentation cases under the umbrella of justifiable reliance, the court affirmed a judgment for the plaintiff on the principles of § 402B.

Is this decision tantamount to holding that the defendant's promotional statements effectively (and inadvertently) extended to users of the mace an insurance policy against criminally inflicted harm when the mace was used, no matter how dangerous the situation?

4. Justifiable Reliance. The plaintiff, an off-duty, general duty policeman riding his personal motorcycle, received head injuries when he collided with a truck and his helmet popped off before he hit the ground. The helmet he was wearing was a general duty model 1601, designed with a special snap harness for quick release to permit an officer to remove the helmet easily in a riot if someone grabbed his head. The police department issued a different helmet (model 1602) to the motorcycle police, as plaintiff knew. Both models were packaged in the same type box, with illustrations on both sides of the box depicting a motorcyclist wearing a helmet. In an action against the manufacturer under § 402B, the plaintiff claimed that he relied upon the illustrations on the box in deciding to use his model 1601 helmet for personal motorcycle riding. In American Safety Equip. Corp. v. Winkler, 640 P.2d 216, 223 (Colo. 1982) (4–3 decision), a bare majority of the court rejected his claim, concluding that he had not justifiably relied upon the representations because he knew that the motorcycle officers were issued model 1602, not 1601: "Justifiable reliance contemplates the reasonable exercise of knowledge and intelligence in assessing the represented facts. Unsupportable subjective reliance is inadequate."

The dissenting judges thought that a jury question on the issue had been made out, since the plaintiff's knowledge that the motorcycle officers used the model 1602 was "not the equivalent of actual knowledge of the unsuitability of helmet model 1601 for motorcycling purposes." Id. at 225. Moreover, two of the dissenters thought that the majority's definition of justifiable reliance incorrectly imposed on the plaintiff an independent duty to investigate the truth of the representation.

5. Puffing. In Berkebile v. Brantly Helicopter Corp., 337 A.2d 893 (Pa. 1975), plaintiff was killed in a helicopter crash when his engine failed. Advertising brochures touted that the craft was "a safe, dependable helicopter" and was "easy to fly" for beginning as well as professional pilots. One of plaintiff's contentions was that the average pilot could not react quickly enough in case of engine failure to activate the helicopter's "auto-rotation" system—an emergency safety system, operated by a "collective pitch stick," that changed the angle of the rotor blades so that the disabled craft could be glided to a safe landing. *Held*, the representations were "mere puffs."

In addition to undermining the materiality and factual character of a representation, how else does the "puffy" nature of a statement weaken a plaintiff's case? See § 402B, comment *j*.

6. What if Fred Hauter had not seen the affirmations of safety on the shipping carton or on the cover of the instruction booklet for the Gizmo, but his mother had? Would it matter whether she saw the representations before or after buying the product? What if neither had noticed the affirmations until after the accident? See § 402B, comment *j.*

7. In *Hauter,* was the testimony of either of plaintiffs' expert witnesses necessary to the § 402B claim?

8. Note that the *Hauter* jury found *unanimously* for the defendants. Assuming that the case was handled competently at trial by plaintiffs' attorney, and considering that the appellate court found for the plaintiffs on *each* of their four theories of recovery *as a matter of law,* what can account for a legal result so at variance with the community's sense of justice?

9. Mini-problem. Vehicle manufacturer tells dealer that new model truck's cooling system can support addition of air conditioner without overheating. Dealer installs air conditioner on truck and passes along the representation to buyer who purchases truck on strength of this information. Engine subsequently overheats and sprays buyer with scalding water when radiator hose bursts. Buyer sues dealer, and dealer seeks indemnification from manufacturer. Can dealer recover over against the manufacturer under § 402B? See Ford Motor Co. v. Russell & Smith Ford Co., 474 S.W.2d 549 (Tex. Civ. App. 1971); § 402B, comments *a, h* and *i.* See also First Nat'l Bank v. Brooks Farms, 821 S.W.2d 925 (Tenn. 1991).

10. There have been very few reported decisions involving § 402B, and most of those have favored the defendant. See, e.g., Evans v. Toyota Motor Corp., 2005 WL 2001141 (S.D. Tex. 2005) (no reliance); Eiser v. Brown & Williamson Tobacco Corp., 2005 WL 1323030 (Pa. Com. Pl. 2005) (no express statement of fact); Prohaska v. Sofamor, S.N.C., 138 F.Supp.2d 422, 447–48 (W.D.N.Y. 2001) (New York never adopted § 402B). Even in states where courts have mentioned the doctrine at one time or another, case authority for the doctrine is generally sparse and often dated. Why do you suppose this is so? Yet the doctrine seems quite firmly accepted—even if infrequently used—in such major jurisdictions as California, Pennsylvania, and Texas.

11. The Case of the Falsely Represented Ankle Alarm. One of the few recent cases to base liability on § 402B is Kirby v. B.I. Inc., 2003 WL 22227694 (N.D. Tex. 2003). Plaintiffs' decedent was murdered by her estranged boyfriend, who had been equipped with an electronic ankle alarm transmitter after being charged with aggravated robbery with a deadly weapon. After cutting the strap of and removing his ankle bracelet, he proceeded to the decedent's house and killed her. The electronic warning system was manufactured and sold by the defendant which stated on its internet site that the electronic ankle bracelet would transmit an alarm to the Monitoring Center and monitoring units located in homes of persons at risk if the stalker/offender came within proximity of the home unit or if the stalker/offender tampered with the ankle transmitter. In fact, the system would send a tampering warning signal only if the tampering occurred within range (about 100 feet) of the home monitoring unit. Because the boyfriend cut off his ankle bracelet at a greater distance from the decedent's home, it never transmitted an alarm. *Held,* the defendant's representations were false and misleading and plaintiff justifiably relied on them, such that defendant was liable under § 402B.

12. Products Liability Restatement. Rather than "restating" § 402B in a black letter section of its own, § 9 of the Third Restatement seemingly readopts § 402B in comment *b:* "The rules governing liability for innocent product misrepresentation are stated in the Restatement, Second, of Torts § 402B."

13. See generally D. Owen, Products Liability Law § 3.4 (2d ed. 2008); 1 D. Owen, M.S. Madden, & M. Davis, Madden & Owen on Products Liability § 3:5 (3d ed. 2000).

CHAPTER 4

WARRANTY

This chapter first examines the three relevant Code warranties: (1) express warranty, (2) the implied warranty of merchantability, and (3) the implied warranty of fitness for particular purpose. The privity of contract problem is then explored. Unlike its current role in tort law, privity is seen in some circumstances to remain a formidable, ongoing obstacle to injured persons seeking to reach a remote seller through the law of warranty. Last to be considered is the system of rules defining the method and extent to which a seller may limit potential liability by disclaimers of responsibility and limitations of remedies.

1. EXPRESS WARRANTY

As with tortious misrepresentation, the lawyer in express warranty cases must focus closely on the precise words claimed to constitute the warranty and frame the complaint specifically in such terms. See Richman v. W.L. Gore & Assoc., 881 F. Supp. 895, 905 (S.D.N.Y. 1995) (conclusory "bare-bones" complaint dismissed for failure to state specifically what was warranted). The importance of linguistic analysis in express warranty cases is demonstrated by the following case.

———

Kolarik v. Cory International Corporation

Supreme Court of Iowa, 2006.
721 N.W.2d 159.

■ CARTER, JUSTICE.

[While eating a salad containing olives he had taken from a jar of defendant's Italica Spanish Olives, plaintiff bit down on an olive pit or pit fragment and fractured a tooth. Among other claims, he sued the importers and wholesalers for breach of express warranty on which claim the trial court granted defendants' motions for summary judgment. Plaintiff appeals to the Supreme Court. *Held*, summary judgement for defendant affirmed on this claim.]

Plaintiff urges the words "minced pimento stuffed," contained on the label of the jar of olives, constituted an express warranty that the olives had been pitted. Iowa Code section 554.2313(1) provides that an express warranty is created by the following:

a. Any affirmation of fact or promise made by the seller to the buyer which relates to the goods and becomes part of the basis of the bargain. . . .

b. Any description of the goods which is made part of the basis of the bargain. . . .

Although both the express-warranty and implied-warranty provisions of the UCC are drafted so as to determine the rights and obligations of the immediate parties to a sales transaction, the Code also provides [that such warranties extend to other persons, such as the plaintiff here].

The vice president of quality control for defendants testified in his deposition that olives must be pitted in order to be stuffed because the pitting process provides the cavity in which the pimento stuffing may be placed. This witness also testified that

[t]here's a reasonable expectation that most of the pits would be removed, and there's some expectation that it's not a perfect world, and some of the pits or fragments may not be removed [in these] natural products. . . . When the olives go into those machines, the machines do very well, but, you know, the olives have different shapes. And the reason they don't get pitted right all the time is because of the different shapes of the olives.

The witness asserted that, because large quantities of pitted and stuffed olives are received in bulk form, no practical method of inspection exists. This witness's statements concerning the inevitability of some pits or pit fragments being in the product was corroborated by plaintiff's own assertion that United States Department of Agriculture standards for pitted olives allow 1.3 pits or pit parts per one hundred olives.

Comment 7 of the official comments that accompany U.C.C. section 2–313, from which Iowa Code section 554.2313 is taken, states:

Of course, all descriptions by merchants must be read against the applicable trade usages with the general rules as to merchantability resolving any doubts.

U.C.C. § 2–313 cmt. 7. In discussing this official comment [by] the UCC drafters, a federal court has declared: "[E]xpress warranties . . . must be read in terms of their significance in the . . . trade and relative to what would normally pass in the trade without objection under the contract description." *Fargo Mach. & Tool Co. v. Kearney & Trecker Corp.*, 428 F.Supp. 364, 373 (E.D.Mich.1977). Given the evidence of how the defendants receive and resell these olives, it is unrealistic to impart to the description "minced pimento stuffed" the meaning that defendants are guaranteeing that the olives in the jar are entirely free of pits or pit fragments. It is much more realistic to interpret the description as only warranting that the particular jar of olives contains pimento-stuffed, green olives that would pass as merchantable without objection in the trade. Plaintiff has provided no evidence that the contents of the jar, taken as a whole, did not live up to this warranty.

[Trial court did not err in granting summary judgment for defendants on plaintiff's express warranty claim.]

Uniform Commercial Code

§ 2–313. Express Warranties by Affirmation, Promise, Description, Sample

(1) Express warranties by the seller are created as follows:

(a) Any affirmation of fact or promise made by the seller to the buyer which relates to the goods and becomes part of the basis of the bargain creates an express warranty that the goods shall conform to the affirmation or promise.

(b) Any description of the goods which is made part of the basis of the bargain creates an express warranty that the goods shall conform to the description.

(c) Any sample or model which is made part of the basis of the bargain creates an express warranty that the whole of the goods shall conform to the sample or model.

(2) It is not necessary to the creation of an express warranty that the seller use formal words such as "warrant" or "guarantee" or that he have a specific intention to make a warranty, but an affirmation merely of the value of the goods or a statement purporting to be merely the seller's opinion or commendation of the goods does not create a warranty.

NOTES

1. "Boned Chicken; No Bones." With Kolarik, compare Lane v. C.A. Swanson & Sons, 278 P.2d 723, 724–26 (Cal. Dist. Ct. App. 1955). Plaintiff was injured while eating canned chicken when a bone lodged in his throat. He sued the producer, Swanson, for breach of an express warranty based on the label's "Boned Chicken" claim and a newspaper advertisement that said: "Swanson Boned Chicken All luscious white and dark meat. *No bones.* No waste. Swanson chicken—finest in the land. Chosen by poultry experts. Specially bred and fed. Swanson-cooked to juicy perfection. Wonderful for salads and casseroles. Quick! Thrifty, too!" (Emphasis added by court.) Plaintiff testified that he had read the advertising prior to purchase.

The trial court found no evidence of an express warranty and entered judgment for the defendants, accepting the defendant's theory "that the term 'Boned Chicken' was merely descriptive of the manner in which the product was prepared and packaged and that it did not constitute a warranty that the contents of the can were wholly free from bones."

On appeal, *held*, reversed. The court noted that many descriptive terms constitute a warranty only of a product's general characteristics—"fireproof," "stainless," "rustproof," "nonskid," "waterproof," "shelled," and "boneless"—*not* a warranty of perfection. Yet the court observed the then-modern tendency "to construe liberally in favor of the buyer language used by the seller in making affirmations respecting the quality of his goods. . . ."

... The question is whether the statement that "boned chicken" contained "no bones" would reasonably be understood by the buying public to mean that the principal bones had been removed but there might be fragments of bone remaining or that all bones, large and small, and all pieces of bone had been removed. From a strictly anatomical standpoint it may be said that if a leg bone of a chicken has been removed with the exception of small fragments the leg bone has been removed; but the fragments of bone that remained would be "bone" to anyone who might attempt to swallow them. "No bones," no doubt, means to the manufacturer that great care has been used to remove all bones and all pieces of bone, but we think it would mean to a buyer that no bones whatever would be found in the product. Unless it can be said that a small piece of bone is no bone at all when it sticks in one's throat it cannot be said that a product which contains one or more bone fragments contains no bones.... Defendants argue that it is impossible to extract the bones of a defunct chicken without leaving in the remains small slivers or pieces of bone and that if they are held to liability ... it will be impossible for them to continue the processing and sale of boned or boneless poultry and that they and many processors of similar products would be forced out of that business. We do not believe this dark outlook is justified....

The court concluded:

[T]he label on the can, coupled with ... the newspaper ads that the contents contained no bones, constituted an express warranty [which] was breached. If there could be a doubt as to the meaning of "boned chicken," it was removed by the statement that it contained no bones.

2. Do you suppose the *Lane* decision forced C.A. Swanson & Sons out of the business of processing and selling boned and boneless poultry, as predicted by counsel? As Swanson's attorney, what advice would you have given after the rendering of this opinion?

3. It is axiomatic that breach of express warranty requires no showing of fault and thus is truly "strict" liability. Moreover, "no 'defect' other than a failure to conform to the warrantor's representations need be shown in order to establish a breach of an express warranty." McCarty v. E.J. Korvette, Inc., 347 A.2d 253, 264 (Md. Ct. Spec. App. 1975) (tire guaranteed against blowouts); Caboni v. General Motors Corp., 398 F.3d 357 (5th Cir. 2005) (airbag failed to deploy; conformity to express warranty depends on whether performance "matched that described by the language of the warranty, rather than whether the [product] performed as it was designed to perform").

4. Interpretation—Truth or Falsity. Perhaps the most prevalent issue in express warranty litigation involves the interpretation of the representation. So, an express warranty claim based on statements in a vehicle owner's manual about when an airbag would deploy depends upon whether those specific statements were true or false, not whether the airbag functioned properly or was defective according to an expert engineer. Caboni v. General Motors Corp., 278 F.3d 448, 454 (5th Cir. 2002).

Information may be communicated through pictures as well as words. In Sylvestri v. Warner & Swasey Co., 398 F.2d 598 (2d Cir. 1968), plaintiff was thrown from the operator's seat of a backhoe manufactured by defendant. The vehicle tipped when its stabilizing outriggers shifted while it was being used to lift boulders and swing them around to different locations. An advertising brochure showed the backhoe lifting a length of pipe and stated that "Hydraulic system provides powerful lift force for material handling." Upholding plaintiff's verdict, the court remarked: "While Sylvestri apparently did not attach the rock to the backhoe in exactly the same manner that the pipe was attached in the brochure picture, and while lifting rock may in some way be different from lifting pipe, [the jury could] determine . . . whether the brochure picture and statements as a whole represented an affirmation of fact or promise that the machine could be used as Sylvestri used it. It is the 'essential idea' conveyed by the advertising representations which is relevant. . . ."

5. Plaintiff fell while skiing and suffered a broken leg when his ski bindings failed to release. In Salk v. Alpine Ski Shop, Inc., 342 A.2d 622, 626 (R.I. 1975), he sued the manufacturer of the bindings in express warranty on the basis of the following advertisements: "Cubco is the precise binding that releases when it's supposed to. . . . Both heel and toe release at the exact tension you set. And release whichever way you fall." *Held,* no recovery for breach of warranty:

> For . . . a breach of express warranty, plaintiff must first establish that Cubco warranted its bindings would release in every situation presenting a danger to the user's limbs. [C]ubco's advertising falls short of this blanket guarantee. [It was shown at trial that] no binding could be set at a tension sufficiently low to release during a slow fall and still keep the skier on his skis during normal skiing, [and that] Cubco bindings had a multi-direction-al release which could be adjusted to operate at a variety of tensions. . . . The advertisements . . . do no more than affirm these uncontroverted facts.

6. "Safe." General representations of safety may create an express warranty. See Drayton v. Jiffee Chem. Corp., 395 F. Supp. 1081 (N.D. Ohio 1975) (advertising claims that particularly caustic drain cleaner was safe for household use).

7. Consider also Whitmer v. Schneble, 331 N.E.2d 115 (Ill. App. Ct. 1975) (female Doberman Pinscher, represented by sellers to be "docile," bit child viewing dog's new puppies two and a half years after sale; *held,* no recovery: "Even a docile dog is known and expected to bite under some circumstances"; moreover, statement pertained to dog's personality at the time of sale and did not mean that its personality could not change); Whittington v. Eli Lilly & Co., 333 F. Supp. 98 (S.D. W. Va. 1971) (birth control pills said to "offer virtually 100% protection" in fact offered 98.1% protection; *held,* no promise of *absolute* protection); Beyette v. Ortho Pharmaceutical Corp., 823 F.2d 990 (6th Cir. 1987) (IUD manufacturer's represen-tations as to (1) estimate of pelvic inflammatory disease rate, and (2) statement that more than a million women had used IUDs successfully; *held,* no recovery for such disease: first representation was merely a future prediction, and second was true, not a warranty of risk-free use).

8. Compare Huebert v. Federal Pac. Elec. Co., 494 P.2d 1210 (Kan. 1972) (current passed through electrical panel injuring plaintiff electrician although handle was in "off" position; *held,* panel manufacturer made and breached express warranty).

9. Mini-problem. Plaintiff's General Electric Smoke Detector alarm fails to go off in a fire, and her house is burned to the ground. Breach of express warranty?

10. Article 2 Amendments. In 2003, the National Conference of Commis-sioners on Uniform State Laws (NCCUSL) and the American Law Institute (ALI), completing their joint revision project on Article 2 (on sales, and its sister provision governing leases, Article 2A), promulgated various Amendments to Articles 2 and 2A. As of 2006, no state has adopted these amendments:

The 2003 amendments to Article 2 and 2A continue to go nowhere. They have only been introduced in three states—Kansas, Nevada, and Oklahoma—and have died unceremonious deaths in all three. Unless NCCUSL and the ALI return to the drawing board and initiate a legislative full court press (neither of which seems likely in the near future), the only amendments to Articles 2 and 2A likely to be of any relevance in the foreseeable future are conforming amendments required by a state's adoption of Revised Article 1 or 7 or amended Articles 3 and 4.

Keith Rowley, Revised Article 1 Legislative Roundup, AALS Contracts Prof Blog, Aug. 23, 2006. Accordingly, the amendments to Article 2 will be set forth in the Statutory Supplement when legislatures begin to adopt them.

Stang v. Hertz Corp.

Court of Appeals of New Mexico, 1971.
83 N.M. 217, 490 P.2d 475.*

■ Wood, Chief Judge.

The automobile accident involved in this case occurred when a tire blew out. The tire, manufactured by Firestone Tire & Rubber Company, was mounted on a car belonging to Hertz Corporation. The car had been rented by a nun, and Catherine Lavan, also a nun, was a passenger in the car when the blowout occurred. Catherine Lavan suffered injuries in the accident resulting in her death.... The verdict was in favor of Firestone. There is no appeal from this verdict. The trial court directed a verdict in favor of Hertz. The dispositive issues in this appeal concern the liability of Hertz. Plaintiffs contend there were issues for the jury concerning: (1) an express warranty and (2) strict liability in tort.

Express warranty.

Plaintiffs assert the rental agreement contains an express warranty. They rely on a statement that the "vehicle" was in good mechanical condition. Defendant contends that "vehicle" does not include tires because twice in the rental agreement "tires" were referred to in a sense separate from "vehicle."

Apart from the rental agreement, a Hertz representative, in a conversation with one of the nuns, stated: "you have got good tires." Plaintiffs contend this statement was also an express warranty as to the tires. Defendant asserts this statement was no more than "puffing." See § 50A–2–313(2), N.M.S.A.1953 (Repl. Vol. 8, pt. 1).

It is not necessary to answer these contentions....

... Under § 50A–2–313(1), supra, the affirmation of fact (the rental agreement) creates an express warranty if it "becomes part of the basis of the bargain." Similarly, the description of the goods (the reference to good

---

* Reversed on other grounds, 83 N.M. 730, 497 P.2d 732 (1972).

tires) creates an express warranty if the description "is made part of the basis of the bargain." . . .

There is no evidence that any of the nuns relied on, or in any way considered, the terms of the rental agreement before agreeing to the rental. See Speed Fastners, Inc. v. Newsom, 382 F.2d 395 (10th Cir. 1967). The comment concerning "good tires" was made after the car had been rented. See Terry v. Moore, 448 P.2d 601 (Wyo. 1968). There is no evidence that either the terms of the rental agreement or the reference to "good tires" were part of the basis of the bargain. There was insufficient evidence for the question of express warranty to be submitted to the jury. * * *

[Affirmed.]

Hauter v. Zogarts

Supreme Court of California, 1975.
14 Cal. 3d 104, 120 Cal. Rptr. 681, 534 P.2d 377.

■ Tobriner, Justice.

[This is the "Golfing Gizmo" case. For the statement of facts and a discussion of defendant's "puffing" defense, see supra, p. 87.]

. . . [T]he claim for breach of express warranty . . . is governed by California Commercial Code section 2313. The key under this section is that the seller's statements—whether fact or opinion—must become "part of the basis of the bargain."[10] (See Cal. U. Com. Code, § 2313, com. 8; Ezer, supra, at p. 287, fn. 39). The basis of the bargain requirement represents a significant change in the law of warranties. Whereas plaintiffs in the past have had to prove their reliance upon specific promises made by the seller (Grinnell v. Charles Pfizer & Co. [79 Cal. Rptr. 369 (Cal. Ct. App. 1969)]), the Uniform Commercial Code requires no such proof. According to official cmt. 3 to the Uniform Commercial Code following section 2313, "no particular reliance . . . need be shown in order to weave [the seller's affirmations of fact] into the fabric of the agreement. Rather, any fact which is to take such affirmations, once made, out of the agreement requires clear affirmative proof."

The commentators have disagreed as to the impact of this new development. (See generally, Note, "Basis of the Bargain"—What Role Reliance? (1972) 34 U. Pitt. L. Rev. 145, 149–150). Some have said that the basis of the bargain requirement merely shifts the burden of proving non-reliance to the seller. (See 1 Carroll, Cal. Commercial Law, supra, § 6.7, p. 210;

---

10. As we explained above, defendants' statement is one of fact and is subject to construction as an express warranty. It is important to note, however, that even statements of opinion can become warranties under the code if they become part of the basis of the bargain. (Cal. U. Com. Code, § 2313, com. 8; Ezer, supra, at p. 287, fn. 39.) Thus the California Uniform Commercial Code expands sellers' liability beyond the former Uniform Sales Act (former Civ. Code, §§ 1732–1736) and provides greater coverage than Restatement Second of Torts, section 402B, discussed earlier.

Boyd, Representing Consumers—The Uniform Commercial Code and Beyond (1968) 9 Ariz. L. Rev. 372, 385.) Indeed, the comments to section 2313 seem to bear out this analysis; they declare that "all of the statements of the seller [become part of the basis of the bargain] *unless good reason is shown to the contrary.*" (Cal. U. Com. Code, § 2313, com. 8 (italics added).)[11]

Other writers, however, find that the code eliminates the concept of reliance altogether. (See Note, supra, 34 U. Pitt. L. Rev. at p. 150; Nordstrom, Sales (1970) §§ 66–68.) Support can be found in the comments to the code for this view also; they declare that "[i]n view of the principle that the whole purpose of the law of warranty is to determine what it is that the seller *has in essence agreed to sell,* the policy is adopted of those cases which refuse except in unusual circumstances to recognize a material deletion of the seller's obligation. Thus, a contract is normally a contract for a sale of something describable and described." (Cal. U. Com. Code, § 2313, com. 4 (italics added).) To these observers, the focus of the warranty shifts from the buyer, who formerly had to rely upon specific statements in order to recover, to the seller, who now must stand behind his words if he has failed adequately to disclaim them. "[T]he seller must show by clear affirmative proof either that the statement was retracted by him before the deal was closed or that the parties understood that the goods would not conform to the affirmation or description. Under such an interpretation, the affirmation, once made, is a part of the agreement, and lack of reliance by the buyer is not a fact which would take the affirmation out of the agreement." (Note, supra, 34 U. Pitt. L. Rev. at p. 151.)[12]

We are not called upon in this case to resolve the reliance issue.[13] The parties do not discuss the changes wrought by the Uniform Commercial Code, and plaintiffs are fully able to meet their burden regardless of which test we employ. Fred Hauter's testimony shows that he read and relied upon defendants' representation; he was impressed by "something on the cover dealing with the safety of the item." More importantly, defendants presented no evidence which could remove their assurance of safety from the basis of the bargain. The trial court properly concluded, therefore, that

---

11. The code relegates "the metaphysical 'buyer's reliance' requirement to secondary status, where it properly belongs." (Ezer, The Impact of the Uniform Commercial Code on the California Law of Sales Warranties (1961) 8 UCLA L. Rev. 281, 285.) Ezer also notes: "The Code's implicit premise is that buyer's reliance is prima facie established from the fact that he made the purchase. If the seller can establish that the buyer in fact did not rely on the seller, that the affirmation or promise was not the 'basis of the bargain,' to use the Code language, then there is no express warranty." (Id. at p. 285, fn. 30.)

12. Thus if a seller agrees to sell a certain quality of product, he cannot avoid liability for selling lower grade goods. No longer can he find solace in the fact that the injured consumer never saw his warranty. [Citations.]

13. Although the code has been the law in California since 1965, we know of no California case which analyzes the basis of the bargain requirement. The scattered cases from other jurisdictions generally have ignored the significance of the new standard and have held that consumer reliance still is a vital ingredient for recovery based on express warranty. (See, e.g., Stang v. Hertz Corp. [490 P.2d 475 (N.M.)], revd. on other grounds, [497 P.2d 732 (N.M. 1972), 52 A.L.R.3d 112]; [citations]).

defendants expressly warranted the safety of their product and are liable for Fred Hauter's injuries which resulted from a breach of that warranty.

[Trial court's judgment for the plaintiff notwithstanding the verdict affirmed; case remanded to determine damages.]

■ CLARK, JUSTICE (concurring).

I concur with the majority that the record here establishes breach of express warranty as a matter of law—requiring affirmance of the judgment and disposing of this appeal. However, beyond this first issue, the majority's discussion [on the Restatement, Second, Torts § 402B] is both unnecessary and unpersuasive.

NOTES

1. Compare, with Justice Clark's concurring opinion in *Hauter,* the following observations of the court in Klages v. General Ordnance Equip. Corp., supra p. 91 n. 3, in support of its adoption of § 402B of the Restatement (Second) of Torts:

> In so doing, we note the extensive similarity between § 2–313 of the Uniform Commercial Code, supra, and § 402B. . . . Because the elimination of the privity requirement allows the buyer to sue the manufacturer directly in assumpsit for noncompliance with his express statements, we see no sound reason for not recognizing a similar cause of action in trespass.

2. Reliance. The requirement of reliance has proved a major stumbling block for plaintiffs in express warranty cases over the years. It was an explicit requirement under § 12 of the Uniform Sales Act. See, e.g., McCully v. Fuller Brush Co., 415 P.2d 7 (Wash. 1966) (insufficient proof that plaintiff, who suffered dermatitis on the hands, had relied on label statement, "It's Kind To Your Hands"). *Stang* illustrates the decisions that still require reliance in express warranty cases, although UCC § 2–313(1) provides only that the representation be "part of the basis of the bargain."

Comment 3 to § 2–313 addresses the issue:

> In actual practice affirmations of fact made by the seller about the goods during a bargain are regarded as part of the description of those goods; hence no particular reliance on such statements need be shown in order to weave them into the fabric of the agreement. Rather, any fact, which is to take such affirmations, once made, out of the agreement requires clear affirmative proof. The issue normally is one of fact.

See Lutz Farms v. Asgrow Seed Co., 948 F.2d 638, 645 (10th Cir. 1991) (most jurisdictions no longer require proof of reliance, citing cases).

3. "What the Code does to the pre-Code reliance requirement is quite unclear. One may argue that [reliance is still effectively required.] We favor [this] interpretation. [O]ne who has not relied on the seller's statement . . . is asking for greater protection than . . . he bargained for. We would send him to the implied warranties." J. White & R. Summers, Handbook of the Law under the Uniform Commercial Code § 9–5, at 356 (5th ed. 2000).

Is the approach recommended by White & Summers harsh and unfair? Consider UCC § 2–314(2)(f), below.

4. Post-sale Statements. With the *Stang* court's treatment of the salesman's "good tires" statement, compare cmt. 7 to § 2–313:

> The precise time when words of description or affirmation are made or samples are shown is not material. The sole question is whether the language or samples or models are fairly to be regarded as part of the contract. If language is used after the closing of the deal (as when the buyer when taking delivery asks and receives an additional assurance), the warranty becomes a modification, and need not be supported by consideration if it is otherwise reasonable and in order (Section 2–209).

For how long after the sale should the seller's affirmations be construed as modifications of the contract? Until buyer has passed over seller's threshold? So long as sale is still "hot"? As long as seller would permit the product to be returned? See Nordstrom, supra, at 205–07; White & Summers, supra, at § 9.5.

Should the seller's public advertisements made shortly after plaintiff purchases a product be held to modify the plaintiff's contract of sale under the principle of cmt. 7? Consider White & Summers, supra, at 355, noting that "section 2–209 contemplates an 'agreement modifying a contract. . . .' It is far from self-evident that a seller's post-sale words uttered during delivery are an 'agreement of modification,' and one can hardly attribute that bilateral connotation to an advertisement that is not published until after the sale. Indeed, Comment 7 seems to contemplate only the cases of face-to-face dealings that occur while the deal is still warm."

Should representations in brochures sealed in a package and thus not read until the package is opened several hours after sale be deemed express warranties under the principles of cmt. 7? See Nordstrom, supra, at 207.

5. What if the affirmations are made before the purchase, but not learned about by plaintiff until after the *accident*? Plaintiff is injured when her new automobile tire is punctured by a nail and blows out. If the manufacturer had advertised the tire on national television as "blowout-proof" prior to purchase, how might plaintiff who did not see or learn about the commercial until after her accident argue that it was nevertheless part of the basis of *her* bargain? Does cmt. 3 help or hurt her case? See R. Nordstrom, Handbook of the Law of Sales 209 (1970):

> The court's task is to determine whether the injury was caused by a defect in the product, and any statements made by the seller designed to induce the public to buy his product are relevant in making this determination. The "basis of the bargain" includes the dickered terms, but is not limited to them. The "basis of the bargain" is also the item purchased, and a part of that bargain includes the statements which the seller made about what he sold.

Compare *Hauter* footnote 12, supra. Might some sort of estoppel argument be in order? Waiver? See § 2–209(4). But see Lowe v. Sporicidin Int'l., 47 F.3d 124 (4th Cir. 1995) (claim failed because no allegation of reliance or causation of any type).

6. Obvious Defects and Inspections. What effect, if any, should the obviousness of a condition contrary to seller's representation have on the existence of an express warranty? Used car dealer sells plaintiff a car with bald tires, representing that "the car is practically new and in excellent shape."

What if prior to purchase buyer submits the product to an inspection that should or does reveal that a latent defect makes the representation false? See Werner v. Montana, 378 A.2d 1130 (N.H. 1977); Nordstrom, supra, at 209–12.

7. Perennial, Perplexing and Persnickety Problems of "Puffs." Note that § 2–313(2) provides in pertinent part that "a statement purporting to be merely the seller's opinion or commendation of the goods does not create a warranty." Was the salesman's "good tires" statement in *Stang* an affirmation of fact or did it purport to be merely the lessor's (possibly prejudiced) personal opinion? Should the fact that the statement was made to a nun affect the result?

As noted by a couple of early cases previously examined, the area of allowable puffing was increasingly being narrowed at the time of those decisions. But predicting whether a particular statement will be construed as fact or opinion is always risky business, particularly now that courts are growing more conservative. "Only a foolish lawyer will be quick to label a seller's statement as puffs or not puffs, and only a reckless one will label a seller's statement at all without carefully examining such factors as the nature of the defect (was it obvious or not) and the buyer's and seller's relative knowledge." White & Summers, supra, at 348. Or, as put by another: "In one sense, every statement made by a seller is nothing more than his opinion as to the goods or how the goods will operate; yet at some point he makes his statement in a manner and under such conditions that the buyer does not understand that *only* this seller's opinion is involved." Nordstrom, supra, at 219.

Compare Carney v. Sears, Roebuck & Co., 309 F.2d 300 (4th Cir. 1962) ("good quality ladder"; *held,* opinion), with Turner v. Central Hardware Co., 186 S.W.2d 603 (Mo. 1945) (ladder "mighty strong and durable"; *held,* fact: "the seller's protection lies in the fact that his is the choice of language and action"). Compare also Jenkins v. Landmark Chevrolet, Inc., 575 So. 2d 1157 (Ala. Civ. App. 1991) (used car "in good shape": puff), with Jones v. Kellner, 451 N.E.2d 548, 550 (Ohio App. 1982) (used car "mechanically A–1": fact) ("although it was unclear how long this warranty would have lasted, it should have lasted at least long enough for the appellee to get the car home").

Carpenter v. Alberto Culver Co., 184 N.W.2d 547 (Mich. App. 1970), was an express warranty action against a drug store for an adverse skin reaction from a hair dye plaintiff bought at the store. "[T]he clerk indicated that several of her friends had used the hair-dyeing product in question, and that her own hair came out 'very nice' and 'very natural' [and that] she 'would get very fine results.' "Both the box and bottle carried warnings of the risk of skin irritation and of the need to make a preliminary patch test. The court remarked in part as follows:

> In determining whether a statement of the seller is to be deemed a warranty, it is important to consider whether in the statement the seller assumes to assert a fact of which the buyer is ignorant, or merely states an opinion or judgment upon a matter of which the seller has no special knowledge and on which the buyer may be expected also to have an opinion and to exercise his judgment. Representations which merely express the seller's opinion, belief, judgment, or estimate do not constitute a warranty. 67 A.L.R.2d 619, § 2, p. 625.

> In the instant case, from all the factual evidence, we cannot agree that such statements made by the retail seller can be considered that of express warranty for use by this plaintiff. From the context in which such statements were made, coupled with the cautionary instructions printed on both the bottle and the box, warning against possible adverse reaction, nothing more existed than an implied warranty that the product was reasonably fit for use as a hair dye.

Should it make any difference how *specific* is the information represented? Whether it is *capable of objective determination*? How specific is "safe"? Do you agree that "safe" should be considered to be a statement of fact rather than opinion? What if a statement is in writing?

Will the Code's statute of frauds present the purchaser relying on oral warranties with additional problems? See UCC § 2–201; Nordstrom, supra, at 213.

8.   Federal Warranty Act. The Magnuson–Moss Warranty Act, 15 U.S.C.A. §§ 2301–12, enacted by Congress in 1975, has had little substantive impact on express warranty litigation in products liability cases. Basically a consumer protection statute, the Act requires that written warranties given in connection with consumer products be complete, comprehensible, and available for review prior to purchase. Certain minimum standards are prescribed if a warranty is designated as a "Full Warranty"; other warranties are to be designated as "Limited." A seller offering a full warranty may not require the return of a warranty registration card as a condition precedent to warranty coverage. See 15 U.S.C.A. § 104(b)(i); 16 C.F.R. § 700.7 (2007).

Two procedural aspects of the Act would seem to have interesting implications for express warranty products liability actions: (1) Consumers are given a federal cause of action, for breach of a written (or implied) warranty; and (2) Consumers who "finally prevail" in such actions may be allowed litigation costs and expenses, including attorney's fees. See § 110(d) of the Act, 15 U.S.C.A. § 2310(d). However, "[c]ourts have uniformly held that the act does not create a federal cause of action for personal injury claims which are otherwise state law claims for breach of warranty." Washington v. Otasco, Inc., 603 F.Supp. 1295, 1296 (N.D. Miss. 1985).

The major substantive changes wrought by the Act affecting personal injury litigation concern certain restrictions on disclaimers, examined below.

9.   On express warranties generally, see R. Nordstrom, Handbook of the Law of Sales §§ 63–73 (1970); J. White & R. Summers, Handbook of the Law under the Uniform Commercial Code §§ 9.3–9.6 (5th ed. 2000); L. Lawrence, 3 Anderson on the Uniform Commercial Code § 2–313:1 et seq. (2002 rev.); D. Owen, Products Liability Law § 4.2 (2d ed. 2008); 1 D. Owen, M.S. Madden, & M. Davis, Madden & Owen on Products Liability § 4:2–:4 (3d ed. 2000).

---

2.   IMPLIED WARRANTY OF MERCHANTABILITY

"It has been said that the concept of implied warranty rests upon the foundation of business ethics and constitutes an exception to the maxim 'let the buyer beware,' itself encompassing the idea that there is no warranty implied with respect to the quality of the goods being sold." Lambert v. Sistrunk, 58 So. 2d 434–35 (Fla. 1952). "Under the rule of *caveat venditor,* a sale 'raises an implied warranty (against latent defects) from the fairness and fullness of the price paid, upon this clear and reasonable ground, that in the contract of sale, the purchaser is not supposed to part with his money, but in expectation of an adequate advantage, or recompense.' Champneys v. Johnson, [2 Brevard 268, 272 (1809)]. 'Selling for a sound price raises an implied warranty that the thing

sold is free from defects, known and unknown (to the seller).' [citation]."
Lane v. Trenholm Bldg. Co., 229 S.E.2d 728, 730 (S.C. 1976).

———

Prosser, The Implied Warranty of Merchantable Quality

27 Minn. L. Rev. 117–22 (1943).

Is there such a thing as a standard warranty of quality presumptively to be implied in every sale of goods made by a dealer? Otherwise stated, are there certain minimum requirements of quality in the thing sold which every purchaser from such a dealer is entitled to demand unless there is express agreement to the contrary, or circumstances are shown which indicate a contrary understanding?

Section 15(2) of the Uniform Sales Act reads as follows:

Where the goods are bought by description from a seller who deals in goods of that description (whether he be the grower or manufacturer or not), there is an implied warranty that the goods shall be of merchantable quality.

This section, which has been enacted thus far in thirty-four states, as well as the District of Columbia, Alaska and Hawaii, was copied almost verbatim from the first part of Section 14(2) of the English Sale of Goods Act of 1894, which was itself a restatement and codification of the common law of England as it existed at that date. As it is stated in the American act, ... it has been recognized as merely declaratory of established common law rules....

HISTORY

In its inception, breach of warranty was a tort. The action was upon the case, for breach of an assumed duty, and the wrong was conceived to be a form of misrepresentation, in the nature of deceit and not at all clearly distinguished from deceit. Warranty has never entirely lost this tort character which it had in the beginning; and this may have important consequences at the present day.... [The tort perspective] has continued to color the substantive law of warranty itself, by introducing some idea of misrepresentation of fact, however innocent, and of reliance on the part of the buyer upon the seller's knowledge, skill or judgment, or some implied assertion concerning the character of the goods sold. * * *

The leading case is Gardiner v. Gray,[19] at nisi prius in 1815.... Lord Ellenborough stated the fundamental principle of the implied warranty of merchantable quality:

[T]he purchaser has a right to expect a saleable article answering the description in the contract. Without any particular warranty, this is an implied term in every such contract. Where there is no opportunity to inspect the commodity, the maxim of

19. (1815) 4 Camp. 144, 171 Eng. Rep. 46....

caveat emptor does not apply. He cannot without a warranty insist that it shall be of any particular quality or fineness, but the intention of both parties must be taken to be, that it shall be saleable in the market under the denomination mentioned in the contract between them. The purchaser cannot be supposed to buy goods to lay them on a dunghill....

A long line of later cases rounded out the picture. The seller's warranty, as a matter of contract, was held to mean not only that the goods delivered must be genuine according to the name, kind or description specified, but that they must be of a quality to pass in the market under that description, and this in turn to mean that they must be reasonably fit for the ordinary uses to which such goods are put....

At about the same time, if not earlier, the idea began to make its appearance that warranties arose by implication "of law" from what had been said and done, and were independent of any intent on the part of the seller to contract with regard to them, or to be bound by them. This idea [was] based upon the increasing practice of reputable sellers to assume responsibility for defective goods sold, together with the feeling that such responsibility is best placed upon the seller as a cost of his business, which he may distribute to the public at large as a part of the price. As a result, it is often said that implied warranties of quality arise by operation of law and are independent of any intention to agree upon their terms as a matter of fact; and there are many cases, at least, in which to hold that the warranty is a term of the contract is "to speak the language of pure fiction."[32]

Uniform Commercial Code

§ 2–314. Implied Warranty: Merchantability; Usage of Trade

(1) Unless excluded or modified (Section 2–316), a warranty that the goods shall be merchantable is implied in a contract for their sale if the seller is a merchant with respect to goods of that kind. Under this section the serving for value of food or drink to be consumed either on the premises or elsewhere is a sale.

(2) Goods to be merchantable must be at least such as

(a) pass without objection in the trade under the contract description; and

(b) in the case of fungible goods, are of fair average quality within the description; and

(c) are fit for the ordinary purposes for which such goods are used; and

(d) run, within the variations permitted by the agreement, of even kind, quality and quantity within each unit and among all units involved; and

----

32. Williston, Liability for Honest Misrepresentation, (1911) 24 Harv. L. Rev. 415, 420; Smith, Surviving Fictions, (1917) 27 Yale L.J. 147, 317, 326.

(e) are adequately contained, packaged, and labeled as the agreement may require; and

(f) conform to the promises or affirmations of fact made on the container or label if any.

(3) Unless excluded or modified (Section 2–316) other implied warranties may arise from course of dealing or usage of trade.

N O T E

Is subsection (2)(f) misplaced? See cmts. 8 and 10.

———

J. White & R. Summers, Uniform Commercial Code*
360–368 (5th ed. 2000).

The implied warranty of merchantability in 2–314 is an important warranty. It is a first cousin to strict tort liability, and "products liability" cases are often tried under the merchantability banner. Section 2–314 is not revolutionary; it is simply a modernized version of the comparable Uniform Sales Act provision.

In a merchantability lawsuit a plaintiff must prove that the defendant deviated from the standard of merchantability and that this deviation caused the plaintiff's injury both proximately and in fact. These make a merchantability claim a first cousin to a negligence claim. Under 2–314, a plaintiff must prove that (1) a merchant sold goods, (2) which were not "merchantable" at the time of sale, (3) injury and damages to the plaintiff or its property (4) which were caused proximately and in fact by the defective nature of the goods, and (5) notice to seller of injury. The plaintiff can fail on any of the points listed; it can also succumb to any of the affirmative defenses that the defendant may raise, for instance, warranty disclaimed, notice of breach not timely, assumption of risk, or statute of limitations expired. Recall too that a merchantability case is likely to be somewhat more difficult for the plaintiff than an express warranty case, for implied warranties are more easily disclaimed than are express warranties, and proof of breach of an explicit express warranty is likely to be easier than is proof of breach of the more diffuse standard of merchantability.

* * *

The most widely quoted of the synonyms in subsection (2) is paragraph (c), which provides that goods must be "fit for the ordinary purposes for which such goods are used." However, in most cases, to say that goods are fit for the ordinary purposes does little to advance the analysis; it simply substitutes one synonym for another. For example, it does not tell a lawyer whether the protective guards around the sides of a rotary lawn mower are sufficient to make it fit for the ordinary purposes or whether the design is fatally defective....

[W]e cannot hope to summarize the thousands of cases that deal with the question of merchantability. We can only suggest where a frustrated lawyer might look for help in determining whether the goods in his particular case ought to be classified as merchantable or nonmerchantable.

Certainly the first place one should look is to the usage in the trade....

Comment 7 to 2–314 suggests another source of information about the parties' intention: [price]. If, for example, there is a dispute on the question whether an airplane that is the subject of a sale must be flyable to be merchantable, it would be revealing to find that the agreed price fell precisely within the price range charged for flyable airplanes and twenty to thirty per cent above the price normally charged for nonflyable airplanes. In that case, the price is an objective manifestation of the intention of the parties to deal over a flyable aircraft.

Obviously, one should also look at the characteristics exhibited by goods of the same class that are manufactured by persons other than the seller in question.

One might get some idea about merchantability in cases from government standards and regulations which are now published by an increasing number of federal and state agencies. If, for example, a used car lacks shoulder harnesses, which are required under federal law for a car made in that year, that fact is powerful evidence that the car is not merchantable.

Finally, how does the merchantability standard differ from the comparable strict tort standard "defective condition, unreasonably dangerous...." [Except in certain limited respects], we believe that the two standards are interchangeable.

NOTE

Compare the observations of R. Nordstrom, Handbook of the Law of Sales 235–36 (1970):*

[Whether a product is "fit for the ordinary purposes for which such goods are used" under U.C.C. § 2–314(2)(c)] is the key thought—the heart—of the merchantability warranty. When a merchant sells goods of the kind in which he deals, there is a warranty that the goods purchased will be fit for their ordinary purpose. Shoes must have their heels attached so that they will not break off under normal use, but if those shoes are used for mountain climbing, there is no implied warranty that the heels will be fit for this extraordinary purpose—unless, of course, the elements of a warranty of fitness for purpose are present. Likewise, shoes are warranted against producing dermatitis, shotgun shells against premature explosion, marine engines against excessive smoking, machinery against defective operation, rivet studs against splitting, and hair lotion against scalp burns.

* * *

The warranty of merchantability is broader than that the goods will do the ordinary job for which they were made. They must also, unless the

---

* Copyright © 1970 by West Publishing Co.

further warranty is disclaimed, do the job safely. The hair lotion might do an excellent job of putting a wave in a woman's hair but, if it also causes dermatitis in a substantial number of users, the lotion is not *fit* for its ordinary purpose.... Thus, fitness for ordinary purpose is a broader concept than just that of doing a single job; it contains ideas of doing that job safely. However, the law does not require that the goods sold be accident-proof. A hammer is fit for its ordinary purpose even though it is capable of mashing thumbs, and shoes may be merchantable even though they slip on wet asphalt. There is no escape from the proposition that the issue is one of fact for the jury: were the goods fit for their ordinary purposes?

Maybank v. S.S. Kresge

Court of Appeals of North Carolina, 1980.
46 N.C. App. 687, 266 S.E.2d 409.*

[Plaintiff sued K–Mart, the retailer of a G.T.E. Sylvania Blue Dot flashcube that exploded in her face, injuring her eye. The carton had warned of the risk that damaged cubes might shatter. There was no evidence that the cube had been damaged prior to use. The trial court severed K–Mart's third party action against Sylvania for trial at a later date, and, after the plaintiff's evidence, directed a verdict for defendant. Plaintiff appealed.]

■ Vaughn, Judge.

* * *

Plaintiff purchased the package of flashcubes for $.88 from defendant's K–Mart store. Defendant was a merchant within the definition of that term in the Uniform Commercial Code as provided in the first clause of G.S. 25–2–104(1). Defendant sold the flashcube to plaintiff and "is a merchant with respect to goods of that kind." G.S. 25–2–314(1).

Whether the flashcube was merchantable can be resolved in part by examining G.S. 25–2–314(2) [(a)–(f)]. These are the minimum standards which a good must have in order to be merchantable. A flashcube which does not work properly and which causes the unexpected harm this flashcube caused is not merchantable. A flashcube can "pass without objection," be "of fair average quality" and "fit for ordinary purposes" and be far short of perfect. But these minimum requirements embodied in G.S. 25–2–314(2)(a), (b), (c) are not met by a flashcube which explodes. Contrast Coffer v. Standard Brands, 226 S.E.2d 534 (N.C. Ct. App. 1976). Such a flashcube is not "within the variations permitted by the agreement." The package contained a warning of possible shattering of a flashcube. The warning of possible shattering or static electricity does not mean that an exploding flashcube has been "adequately contained, packaged and labeled" or that it "conform[ed] to the promises or affirmations of fact made on the container." This was not an adequate warning of the consequences of this case. A flashcube which shatters might be merchantable. An exploding

---

* Modified on other grounds, and affirmed, 273 S.E.2d 681 (N.C. 1981).

flashcube is not, however, merchantable. The attributes listed in G.S. 25–2–314(2) are not exclusive nor exhaustive. The evidence of this case is to the effect that the attributes of merchantability found in subsection (2) of G.S. 25–2–314 were not present in the flashcube. This is sufficient proof that the flashcube was not merchantable to reach the jury. * * *

Reversed and remanded.

N O T E S

1. Which subsection(s) of § 2–314(2) might fairly be applicable to the facts in *Maybank*? What do the words "as the agreement may require" mean in subsection (e)? See cmt. 10 to § 2–314; Nordstrom, Law of Sales 236–37 (1970).

Does it matter whether the container itself is sold? What if a Coke bottle that explodes was "returnable" at which time a deposit was to be returned? Cf. Pettella v. Corp Bros., Inc., 268 A.2d 699 (R.I. 1970).

2. Certain preliminary issues may arise concerning the coverage of a case under § 2–314. For example, the defendant must be a "merchant." See, e.g., Samson v. Riesing, 215 N.W.2d 662 (Wis. 1974) (no recovery under § 2–314 for salmonella food poisoning from turkey salad prepared by Wauwatosa High School Band Mothers, since mothers were not "merchants"); Ballou v. Trahan, 334 A.2d 409 (Vt. 1975) (private person who sold used Porsche to plaintiff not "merchant"). Further, the defendant must be a merchant *with respect to the type of goods sold to the plaintiff*. A bank, for example, which sells a repossessed boat to the plaintiff in an isolated transaction, may not be a "merchant" for purposes of § 2–314. See Donald v. City Nat. Bank, 329 So. 2d 92 (Ala. 1976). Compare McHugh v. Carlton, 369 F. Supp. 1271 (D.S.C. 1974) (service station operator who kept stock of new and used tires held to be merchant with respect to recapped tires, although he did not keep stock of recapped tires and ordered them only on specific request). See cmt. 3 to § 2–314: "A person making an isolated sale of goods is not a 'merchant' within the meaning of the full scope of this section...." See also UCC § 2–104 ("merchant" defined).

There must be a contract for the "sale" of "goods." The lease of realty, therefore, is not covered by § 2–314. Leases of goods are covered in Article 2A. See ch. 17, below.

Comment 1 to § 2–314 provides in part: "The seller's obligation applies to present sales as well as to contracts to sell...." A recurring issue in exploding pop bottle cases is whether the requisite contract exists prior to payment by the purchaser at the check-out counter. In Fender v. Colonial Stores, Inc., 225 S.E.2d 691 (Ga. Ct. App. 1976), plaintiff was injured when a bottle of Coca–Cola exploded as she was placing it on the defendant grocer's check-out counter. Defendant argued that UCC § 2–314 did not apply since a "contract for sale" had not yet been formed at the time of injury. *Held,* that defendant had offered the beverage for sale by placing it on the shelf; that plaintiff had accepted the offer by taking physical possession of the item; and that § 2–314 was thereafter applicable. See also Keaton v. A.B.C. Drug Co., 467 S.E.2d 558 (Ga. 1996) (plaintiff's action in grasping bleach container to remove it from high store shelf with intent to purchase was sufficient "possession" to allow claim of breach of implied warranty of merchantability). See UCC § 2–106(1).

3. Standard of Liability. The meaning of "merchantability," its essential nature, and how it may or may not differ from the standards underlying the other theories of liability are issues of central importance in UCC § 2–314 litigation. As seen in the following chapter on strict liability in tort, some courts attempt to distinguish the notion of "merchantability" from "nondefective" under Restatement (2d) of Torts § 402A. See Denny v. Ford Motor Co., 662 N.E.2d 730 (N.Y. 1995), ch. 5, below. But most courts consider the standard of unfitness under the two theories of liability to be largely if not entirely the same. See, e.g., Lariviere v. Dayton Safety Ladder Co., 525 A.2d 892 (R.I. 1987) (ladder that collapsed); Larsen v. Pacesetter Systems, Inc., 837 P.2d 1273, 1284–85 (Haw. 1992) ("to bring an action in implied warranty for personal injury a plaintiff is required to show product unmerchantability sufficient to avoid summary judgment on the issue of defectiveness in a tort strict products liability suit").

4. Tort Law's Final Victory: "Unmerchantable" = "Defective." If ever there were any doubt, the inherent superiority of tort to contract law was certified authoritatively in 2003 with the approval by NCCUSL and the ALI of the amendments to UCC Article 2. Preliminary Official Comment 7 to UCC § 2–314 as amended explains the interrelationship between the implied warranty of merchantability and tort law, between the notions of an "unmerchantable" product, under UCC § 2–314, and a "defective" product, for purposes of strict products liability in tort:

> 7. Suppose that an unmerchantable lawn mower causes personal injury to the buyer, who is operating the mower. Without more, the buyer can sue the seller for breach of the implied warranty of merchantability and recover for injury to person "proximately resulting" from the breach. Section 2–715(2)(b).
>
> This opportunity does not resolve the tension between warranty law and tort law where goods cause personal injury or property damage. The primary source of that tension arises from disagreement over whether the concept of defect in tort and the concept of merchantability in Article 2 are coextensive where personal injuries are involved, *i.e.*, if goods are merchantable under warranty law can they still be defective under tort law, and if goods are not defective under tort law can they be unmerchantable under warranty law? The answer to both questions should be no, and the tension between merchantability in warranty and defect in tort where personal injury or property damage is involved should be resolved as follows:
>
> > When recovery is sought for injury to person or property, whether goods are merchantable is to be determined by applicable state products liability law. When, however, a claim for injury to person or property is based on an implied warranty of fitness under Section 2–315 or an express warranty under Section 2–313 or an obligation arising under Section 2–313A or 2–313B, this Article determines whether an implied warranty of fitness or an express warranty was made and breached, as well as what damages are recoverable under Section 2–715.
>
> To illustrate, suppose that the seller makes a representation about the safety of a lawnmower that becomes part of the basis of the buyer's bargain. The buyer is injured when the gas tank cracks and a fire breaks out. If the lawnmower without the representation is not defective under applicable tort law, it is not unmerchantable under this section. On the other hand, if the lawnmower did not conform to the representation about safety, the seller made and breached an express warranty and the buyer may sue under Article 2.

* * *

The only problem with this excellent approach is that, as stated earlier, no state has yet adopted these amendments to Article 2 such that tort law's final victory might arguably be seen as not yet totally complete. Nevertheless, under comment 7, *query*:

a. If a jury finds the lawnmower non-defective for purposes of strict liability in tort, does comment 7 permit a jury to find that the product was unmerchantable for purposes of breach of warranty under UCC § 2–314? See note 3, above.

b. If a jury finds the lawnmower merchantable for breach of warranty purposes under UCC § 2–314, does comment 7 preclude a jury from finding that the manufacturer was *negligent* in making and selling it in that condition?

5.   Product Malfunction as "Unmerchantability." If plaintiff can show a malfunction of the product, for example that the brakes or steering on a new car suddenly failed, but is unable to show the specific cause of the failure, has plaintiff established a breach of the implied warranty of merchantability? "When machinery 'malfunctions', it obviously lacks fitness regardless of the cause of the malfunction. Under the theory of warranty, the 'sin' is the lack of fitness as evidenced by the malfunction itself rather than some specific dereliction by the manufacturer in constructing or designing the machinery." Greco v. Bucciconi Eng'g Co., 283 F. Supp. 978, 982 (W.D. Pa. 1967), aff'd, 407 F.2d 87 (3d Cir. 1969). See also DeWitt v. Eveready Battery Co., Inc., 565 S.E.2d 140, 151 (N.C. 2002) (malfunction plus elimination of other possible causes may suffice to prove that product was unmerchantable; plaintiff need not establish specific defect). See generally L. Lawrence, 3 Anderson on the Uniform Commercial Code § 2–314:175 (2002 rev.) (breach of implied warranty of merchantability "may be shown by circumstantial evidence of a failure of the goods to function properly, even thought the buyer fails to establish the specific defect that made it malfunction").

6.   Type of Defect. The type of defect does not matter, and a product may be "unmerchantable" on account of a defect in manufacture, an unsafe design, or an inadequate warning. For example, an inadequate warning of danger may render a product unmerchantable under UCC § 2–314(2)(c), (e) and (f). Reid v. Eckerds Drugs, Inc., 253 S.E.2d 344 (N.C. Ct. App. 1979) (plaintiff liberally applied deodorant, lit a cigarette, and burst into blue flame).

7.   Reliance. "It has never been contended, to our knowledge, that a buyer must prove reliance on the skill or judgment of the manufacturer in order that he may recover for the breach of an implied warranty of merchantability. The warranty is implied because the manufacturer holds himself out as being skilled in the construction of his products and as being able to manufacture them without latent defects in materials or workmanship." Vitro Corp. of America v. Texas Vitrified Supply Co., 376 P.2d 41, 49 (N.M. 1962). Indeed, this is perhaps the central notion that supported the shift from *caveat emptor* to the basic implied warranty of quality (merchantability) in the nineteenth century.

The warranty of merchantability will thus accompany the sale of a product even though the buyer asks for it by trade name. E.g., Dougall v. Brown Bay Boat Works & Sales, Inc., 178 N.W.2d 217 (Minn. 1970). Similarly, the fact that the buyer specifically identifies the product in some other manner, as by selecting it himself from among the seller's stock, will not exclude the implied warranty of merchantability. See cmt. 3.

However, warranty protection generally only arises with respect to hidden, non-obvious defects. See § 2–316(3)(b), discussed below.

**8.   **Prior to or in lieu of adopting the doctrine of strict liability in tort, some states—still including Delaware, Massachusetts, Michigan, North Carolina, and Virginia—have used an implied warranty of quality to fill the void. Some such courts speak of a common law "implied warranty" in tort, while others simply apply

UCC § 2–314. The standard of unfitness of such implied warranties is nearly identical to strict liability in tort.

9. Notice. By UCC § 2–607(3)(a), the buyer must notify the seller of a breach within a reasonable time "or be barred from any remedy." Most courts have refused to bar recovery for unreasonable delay of notice in consumer injury cases, but some courts apply the rule even in this context. See, e.g., Smith v. Robertshaw Controls Co., 410 F.3d 29 (1st Cir. 2005) (Mass. law) (affirming summary judgment for defendant prejudiced by 3–year delay in notice by which time crucial evidence under plaintiff's control was lost); Hearn v. R.J. Reynolds Tobacco Co., 279 F. Supp. 2d 1096, 1116 (D. Ariz. 2003) ("two years constitutes unreasonably delayed notice").

10. On the implied warranty of merchantability, see generally L. Lawrence, 3 Anderson on the Uniform Commercial Code § 2–314:1 et seq. (2002 rev.); D. Owen, Products Liability Law § 4.3 (2d ed. 2008); 1 D. Owen, M.S. Madden, & M. Davis, Madden & Owen on Products Liability § 4:5–:7 (3d ed. 2000).

3. IMPLIED WARRANTY OF FITNESS FOR PARTICULAR PURPOSE

Uniform Commercial Code

§ 2–315. Implied Warranty: Fitness for Particular Purpose

Where the seller at the time of contracting has reason to know any particular purpose for which the goods are required and that the buyer is relying on the seller's skill or judgment to select or furnish suitable goods, there is unless excluded or modified under the next section an implied warranty that the goods shall be fit for such purpose.

Official Comment

2. A "particular purpose" differs from the ordinary purpose for which the goods are used in that it envisages a specific use by the buyer which is peculiar to the nature of his business whereas the ordinary purposes for which goods are used are those envisaged in the concept of merchantability and go to uses which are customarily made of the goods in question. For example, shoes are generally used for the purpose of walking upon ordinary ground, but a seller may know that a particular pair was selected to be used for climbing mountains.

A contract may of course include both a warranty of merchantability and one of fitness for a particular purpose.

Barb v. Wallace

Court of Special Appeals of Maryland, 1980.
45 Md. App. 271, 412 A.2d 1314.

■ COUCH, JUDGE.

[George Barb, age 16, purchased a small, used gasoline engine for $5 from Robert Wallace to use in a go-cart. When George attempted to start the engine, it exploded, injuring his head. George sued Wallace, on various grounds, including breach of implied warranty of fitness for a particular purpose under U.C.C. § 2–315. The trial court granted defendant's motion for summary judgment, and plaintiffs appealed].

George's deposition discloses that George informed appellee that he intended to use the engine in a "go-cart". The appellee responded, according to George, that the engine could be used in a "go-cart" because the "shaft was out the side of the engine" and that the engine "ran good." Appellee admits in his brief that he was apprised of the purpose for which George was purchasing the engine. The issue, then, in our review of the trial court's granting of the motion for summary judgment, is whether there is a genuine dispute as to George's reliance on the appellee's skill or judgment. See Shay v. Joseph, 149 A.2d 3 (Md. 1959).

Appellee, in his brief, relies upon George's statement that at the time he purchased the engine he was taking a course in auto mechanics where he had worked on small engines for the proposition that George's judgment and skill was at least as good as appellee's. We believe this evidence presents a factual dispute as to whether George relied upon himself or actually relied upon appellee's skill and judgment to select or furnish suitable goods. . . . Moreover, Comment 1 to § 2–315 states that the question of whether an implied warranty of fitness for a particular purpose exists in any particular case is basically a question of fact to be determined by the circumstances of the contracting. [Citations.] The fact that George may have had some experience with engines does not necessarily preclude the possibility that he was relying upon appellee's knowledge of the capabilities of this particular engine. [T]his raises a factual dispute which should not have been resolved on a motion for summary judgment.

We note that § 2–315 does not limit the application of an implied warranty of fitness for a particular purpose to merchants only. The official comment to that section states that, "Although normally the warranty will arise only where the seller is a merchant with the appropriate 'skill or judgment', it can arise as to nonmerchants where this is justified by the particular circumstances." Md. Com. Law Code Ann. § 2–315, Comment 4 (1975). The burden of proof carried by the buyer where a nonmerchant seller is involved poses greater difficulties, particularly on the issue of appellee's possession of appropriate skill and judgment, but it does not warrant the granting of a motion for summary judgment. * * *

[Reversed and remanded.]

NOTES

1. The distinction between the implied warranties of merchantability and fitness for a particular purpose is well described in cmt. 2 to § 2–315 set forth above. Courts are split on whether a § 2–315 action will lie if a buyer's *particular* purpose for the product was *also* an *ordinary* one. Compare Crane v. Bagge & Son, Inc., 2005 WL 1576544, at *6 (Cal. Ct. App. 2005) (auto repair shop's equipping BMW with one wrong-size tire may have contributed to accident, but "[a] 'particular purpose' means something other than the ordinary purpose," and "operating the BMW on public roads in all kinds of weather, is the ordinary purpose for which a tire is used"), with Nelson v. Wilkins Dodge, Inc., 256 N.W.2d 472, 476 n. 2 (Minn. 1977) (particular as well as ordinary use of pickup truck was to be driven at sustained high rates of speed). Many courts remain confused. "Such confusion under the Code is inexcusable. Sections 2–314 and 2–315 make plain that the warranty of fitness for a particular purpose is narrower, more specific, and more precise." J. White & R. Summers, Uniform Commercial Code 369 (5th ed. 2000).

One problem arising out of the overlap between the two implied warranties is one of terminology. Especially in earlier years some courts referred to the implied warranty of merchantability as an "implied warranty of fitness." This confusion of labels is contrary to the usage of the Uniform Commercial Code and is only occasionally seen in modern decisions.

The implied warranty of fitness for particular purpose may also overlap with a seller's express warranties. See Filler v. Rayex Corp., 435 F.2d 336, 338 (7th Cir. 1970) (sunglasses advertised as "Baseball Sunglasses," that splintered when hit by baseball, "not fit for baseball playing, the particular purpose for which they were sold").

On the overlap between the warranties, see UCC § 2–317; Ezer, The Impact of the Uniform Commercial Code on the California Law of Sales Warranties, 8 UCLA L.Rev. 281, 299 (1961); Annot., 83 A.L.R.3d 656 (1978).

2. Plaintiffs bought a particular model riding mower upon the recommendation of the defendant's salesman for use on their hilly property, subject to the salesman's inspection of the property to confirm that the mower was appropriate. When the salesman delivered the mower, he inspected the property and pronounced the mower suitable, provided it was driven vertically up the steepest hills. Plaintiff husband was injured when the mower tipped over backwards while he was mowing vertically up a 19° slope. The owner's manual warned against using on slopes in excess of 15°. *Held,* plaintiff's verdict for breach of implied warranty of fitness, affirmed. Klein v. Sears Roebuck and Co., 773 F.2d 1421 (4th Cir. 1985).

3. Non-merchant Sellers. Note that the seller need not be a "merchant" under § 2–315, as in § 2–313, but unlike § 2–314. Why the distinction?

4. Reliance. A fundamental difference between §§ 2–314 and 2–315 is the requirement in § 2–315 that plaintiff establish reliance (and, additionally, the seller's reason to know of it). See, e.g., Stephens v. Paris Cleaners, Inc., 885 A.2d 59, 72 (Pa. Super. Ct. 2005). At common law, there were certain specific exclusions based upon the plaintiff's reliance. For example, plaintiff's inspection of the product, or in some jurisdictions even his opportunity to inspect, negated both the fitness and merchantability implied warranties. Section 15(3) of the Uniform Sales Act restricted this exclusion to actual examinations and defects which ought to have been revealed thereby. The reliance requirement also supported the rule precluding implied warranties of fitness for a particular purpose for articles that were "known, described and definite." Nor could such warranties arise "[i]n the case of a contract to sell or a sale of a specified article under its patent or other trade name...." Uniform Sales Act § 15(4). See generally 1 Williston on Sales §§ 234–36a (rev. ed. 1948). Compare cmt. 5 to § 2–315:

The elimination of the "patent or other trade name" exception constitutes the major extension of the warranty of fitness which has been made by the cases and continued in this Article. Under the present section the existence of a patent or other trade name and the designation of the article by that name, or indeed in any other definite manner, is only one of the facts to be considered on the question of whether the buyer actually relied on the seller, but it is not of itself decisive of the issue. If the buyer himself is insisting on a particular brand he is not relying on the seller's skill and judgment and so no warranty results. But the mere fact that the article purchased has a particular patent or trade name is not sufficient to indicate nonreliance if the article has been recommended by the seller as adequate for the buyer's purposes.

5. Plaintiff's reliance on the seller's skill and judgment is sometimes very clear. See, e.g., Newmark v. Gimbel's Inc., 246 A.2d 11 (N.J. Super. Ct. 1968), aff'd, 258 A.2d 697 (N.J.1969) (beauty shop customer, who suffered injuries to scalp and loss of hair from permanent wave solution, relied on beauty shop operator to select appropriate lotion); Caldwell v. Brown Serv. Funeral Home, 345 So. 2d 1341 (Ala. 1977) (purchasers of casket and vault relied on defendant funeral home to select casket that would fit in vault).

However, a buyer who inspects the product, or otherwise participates in its selection, may have difficulty in establishing his reliance on the seller's judgment in selecting the product. See Carney v. Sears, Roebuck & Co., 309 F.2d 300 (4th Cir. 1962) (plaintiff looked over step-ladders and chose the one recommended by salesman; *held*, no warranty because selection not "exclusively within the control of" salesman; buyer's "discretion and judgment played a major part in the selection"). But compare Peters v. Lyons, 168 N.W.2d 759, 764 (Iowa 1969). Buyer asked for a dog chain strong enough to restrain his 100–120 pound German shepherd. Saleswoman selected the strongest chain, which she and buyer both inspected, and agreed it would be sufficient. It was not, and plaintiff was attacked and injured by the dog. *Held,* since the defect was not discoverable by inspection, reliance on seller's skill and judgment had been established: " 'The buyer's reliance on the seller need not be total reliance. The buyer may rely on his own judgment as to some matters and on the seller's skill and judgment as to others.' "

6. Miscellaneous Applications. Section 2–315 may apply in an action for indemnity or contribution brought by the assembler of a product against its supplier of a component part. See, e.g., Gellenbeck v. Sears, Roebuck & Co., 229 N.W.2d 443 (Mich. Ct. App.1975) (supplier of chains for use in swing sets had reason to know of assembler's reliance on its skill and judgment in selecting chains that could withstand stresses of twisting as well as load-carrying).

An employee may be able to recover under § 2–315 against the supplier of a product sold to his employer that was not fit for the employer's particular purpose. See, e.g., Ploof v. B.I.M. Truck Serv., Inc., 384 N.Y.S.2d 521 (App. Div. 1976) (worker killed when cable, too large for pulley system, snapped).

7. On the implied warranty of fitness for a particular purpose, see J. White & R. Summers, Handbook of the Law under the Uniform Commercial Code §§ 9.10 (5th ed. 2000); D. Owen, Products Liability Law § 4.4 (2d ed. 2008); 1 D. Owen, M.S. Madden, & M. Davis, Madden & Owen on Products Liability § 4:8 (3d ed. 2000).

4. PARTIES AND PRIVITY: PROPER DEFENDANTS AND THIRD PARTY BENEFICIARIES

Privity of contract is once again the topic of discussion. The problem is examined here in terms of the separate notions of "vertical" and "horizontal" privity. The unifying question in both contexts involves the determination of the proper parties in a warranty lawsuit: What defendants are bound by a warranty, and what plaintiffs obtain its benefits?

"Vertical privity" refers to the contractual relationship between the parties up and down the chain of distribution, from suppliers of raw materials and component parts, at the top, through the manufacturer, wholesaler, retailer and, at the bottom of the chain, the purchaser. From the vantage point of the ultimate purchaser, the vertical privity issue may be framed in terms of the question, *Who can be sued?*

The separate issue of "horizontal privity" involves the rights of non-purchasing parties who may be affected by the product and who seek to stand in the purchaser's shoes to obtain the benefits of whatever warranties flowed to him by virtue of his contract of purchase. Such parties, extending horizontally away from the purchaser in decreasing order of affinity, include family, members of the household, guests in the home, employees, and bystanders. Viewed from the perspective of the injured party, the horizontal privity issue may be framed as, *Who can sue?*

———

A. VERTICAL PRIVITY

"In earlier times the one who made the article generally sold it directly to the ultimate user, and thus the consumer, being in privity of contract with the manufacturer, was allowed to recover on the usual warranties for losses caused by defective workmanship." Jeanblanc, Manufacturers' Liability to Persons Other Than Their Immediate Vendees, 24 Va. L. Rev. 134 (1937). Yet, just as the courts began imposing implied warranties of quality on manufacturers in the latter part of the nineteenth century, manufacturers increasingly were spinning off the retail function to third party dealers. This meant, of course, that the typical consumer began to deal contractually only with the retailer. Thus, manufacturers sued in warranty by consumers of defective products in the late 1800s had available the ready-made defense of no privity of contract, a defense that was proving its effectiveness in actions brought in negligence. But the harshness of the rule in cases of consumer injury was readily apparent, and the courts began to riddle it with exceptions at an early date. See Gillam, Products Liability in a Nutshell, 37 Or. L. Rev. 119, 152–55 (1958) (listing 29 such exceptions).

The first decisions to abolish outright the manufacturer's privity defense in *implied* warranty cases were decided at the turn of the century and involved defective foodstuffs. See Mazetti v. Armour & Co., 135 P. 633 (Wash. 1913). Consider Jacob E. Decker & Sons, Inc. v. Capps, 164 S.W.2d 828, 829 (Tex. 1942):

> Liability in such case is [based] on the broad principle of the public policy to protect human health and life. It is a well-known fact that articles of food are manufactured and placed in the channels of commerce, with the intention that they shall pass from hand to hand until they are finally used by some remote customer. It is usually impracticable, if not impossible, for the ultimate customer to analyze the food and ascertain whether or not it is suitable for human consumption. . . . [W]here food products sold for human consumption are unfit for that purpose, there is such an utter failure of the purpose for which the food is sold, and the consequences of eating unsound food are so disastrous to human health and life, that the law imposes a warranty of purity in favor of the ultimate consumer as a matter of public policy.

The breakdown of the remote seller's privity defense in implied warranty cases spread in the 1950s to animal food and products for intimate bodily use, such as soap, hair dye, and permanent wave solution. Then, in the late 1950s and early 1960s, several courts in rapid succession extended the idea to durable goods. It was in 1960, in Henningsen v. Bloomfield Motors, Inc., 161 A.2d 69, 83 (N.J. 1960), that the privity bar was forcefully repudiated in a landmark implied warranty case involving injuries from a defective automobile:

> We see no rational doctrinal basis for differentiating between a fly in a bottle of beverage and a defective automobile. The unwholesome beverage may bring illness to one person, the defective car, with its great potentiality for harm to the driver, occupants, and others, demands even less adherence to the narrow barrier of privity.

In the words of Dean Prosser, *Henningsen* marked the "fall of the citadel of privity." Prosser, The Fall of the Citadel (Strict Liability to the Consumer), 50 Minn. L. Rev. 791 (1966). Courts quickly fell into line after *Henningsen*, and most jurisdictions abolished the manufacturer's vertical privity defense in implied warranty actions involving durable goods.

The absence of privity of contract was also a stumbling block for plaintiffs in early cases who had relied on a manufacturer's *express* warranties in its public advertisements. Because manufacturers make such warranties precisely for the purpose of inducing persons to purchase their goods, the policy arguments against allowing a privity defense in this context are stronger than in the implied warranty situation. Rogers v. Toni Home Permanent Co., 147 N.E.2d 612 (Ohio 1958), is the landmark case abolishing the privity bar in express warranty cases. Noting that the express warranty action derived originally from tort (deceit) rather than contract, the court relied upon *Baxter v. Ford Motor Co.* in extending the privity exception recognized in food cases to products generally, observing as follows:

> [W]hen the goods purchased by the ultimate consumer on the strength of the advertisements aimed squarely at him do not possess their described

qualities and goodness and cause him harm, he should not be permitted to move against the manufacturer to recoup his loss. . . . The warranties made by the manufacturer in his advertisements and by the labels on his products are inducements to the ultimate consumers, and the manufacturer ought to be held to strict accountability to any consumer who buys the product in reliance on such representations and later suffers injury [as a result].

Many courts now hold that express warranties in advertisements run directly to purchasers, despite the absence of privity of contract. Note, however, that § 2–313B of the UCC, as amended in 2003, addresses express warranty rights of remote purchasers arising out of public advertisements. This new section (not yet adopted in any state) provides such purchasers with express warranty rights only with respect to advertisements of which they are aware and on which they reasonably rely.

NOTES

1. The vertical privity defense was expressly abolished by statute in several states. See, e.g., Virginia's "anti-privity" statute, a non-uniform version of UCC § 2–318. Va. Code Ann. § 8.2–318. A number of states have interpreted their "uniform" versions of § 2–318 as abolishing the remote seller's vertical privity defense, as explored below.

2. But some states have retained a vertical privity requirement for warranty claims. In Compex Int'l Co. v. Taylor, 209 S.W.3d 462 (Ky. 2006), plaintiff was injured by the collapse of a chair his parents had bought at K–Mart. In his suit against the chair retailer and manufacturer, K–Mart was dismissed due to its pending bankruptcy. Plaintiff's claim against the manufacturer then was barred for lack of vertical privity on the ground that the legislature's only waiver-of-privity provision in its enactment of UCC Article 2 was § 2–318 (Alt. A), discussed below, which extends warranty benefits to family, household, and guests only of the party who buys a product directly from the defendant seller:

A *seller's* warranty . . . extends to any natural person who is in the family or household of *his* buyer. . . .

Here, K–Mart (not the plaintiff's parents) was the buyer of the chair from (and had privity with) the selling manufacturer. Hence, plaintiff was a third-party beneficiary of K–Mart's warranties to his parents, but not of the manufacturer's warranties to K–Mart.

———

B. HORIZONTAL PRIVITY

Early cases denied warranty recovery to users injured by products which they had not bought themselves. E.g., Chysky v. Drake Bros. Co., 139 N.E. 576 (N.Y. 1923) (waitress bit into nail baked into cake purchased by her employer from defendant). Especially in the context of food purchases for other family members, some courts employed agency principles to avoid the problem and allow recovery. See, e.g., Greenberg v. Lorenz, 213 N.Y.S.2d 39 (N.Y. 1961) (presumption that food purchase by father was made for all members of household).

This issue, at least, is now addressed in § 2–318 of the Uniform Commercial Code.

Uniform Commercial Code

§ 2–318. Third Party Beneficiaries of Warranties Express or Implied

Note: *If this Act is introduced in the Congress of the United States this section should be omitted. (States to select one alternative.)*

Alternative A

A seller's warranty whether express or implied extends to any natural person who is in the family or household of his* buyer or who is a guest in his* home if it is reasonable to expect that such person may use, consume or be affected by the goods and who is injured in person by breach of the warranty. A seller may not exclude or limit the operation of this section.

Alternative B

A seller's warranty whether express or implied extends to any natural person who may reasonably be expected to use, consume or be affected by the goods and who is injured in person by breach of the warranty. A seller may not exclude or limit the operation of this section.

Alternative C

A seller's warranty whether express or implied extends to any person who may reasonably be expected to use, consume or be affected by the goods and who is injured by breach of the warranty. A seller may not exclude or limit the operation of this section with respect to injury to the person of an individual to whom the warranty extends. As amended 1966.

Amendments

The 1966 Amendment added alternatives B and C.

Editorial Board Note on 1966 Amendment

Source:

Colorado, Delaware, South Carolina, South Dakota, Vermont, Wyoming. Compare Proposed Final Draft, Spring 1950, and non-uniform versions enacted in Alabama, Arkansas, Texas, Virginia. The section was omitted in California and Utah.

Reason for Change:

This section as drawn in 1950 was substantially in the form of the new Alternative B. The form shown as Alternative A was substituted in 1951,

----

* In 1992, Wisconsin changed the first "his" to "the seller's" and converted the second to "that buyer's."

limiting beneficiaries to the family, household and guests of the buyer. Beyond this, according to Comment 3, the section was neutral and was not intended to enlarge or restrict "the developing case law." The section was criticized in California as "a step backward," and was omitted from the Code as enacted in California and in Utah. Nonuniform versions were enacted in ten states, and proposals for amendment have been made elsewhere. There appears to be no national consensus as to the scope of warranty protection which is proper, but the promulgation of alternatives may prevent further proliferation of separate variations in state after state. Alternative B is therefore promulgated in substantially the 1950 form, and Alternative C is drawn to reflect the trend of more recent decisions as indicated by Restatement of Torts 2d § 402A (Tentative Draft No. 10, 1965) extending the rule beyond personal injuries.

[Conforming changes were made in pars. 2 and 3 of the Official Comment, infra, in 1966].

Official Comment

2. The purpose of this section is to give certain beneficiaries the benefit of the same warranty which the buyer received in the contract of sale, thereby freeing any such beneficiaries from any technical rules as to "privity." It seeks to accomplish this purpose without any derogation of any right or remedy resting on negligence. It rests primarily upon the merchant-seller's warranty under this Article that the goods sold are merchantable and fit for the ordinary purposes for which such goods are used rather than the warranty of fitness for a particular purpose. Implicit in the section is that any beneficiary of a warranty may bring a direct action for breach of warranty against the seller whose warranty extends to him [As amended in 1966].

3. The first alternative expressly includes as beneficiaries within its provisions the family, household and guests of the purchaser. Beyond this, the section in this form is neutral and is not intended to enlarge or restrict the developing case law on whether the seller's warranties, given to his buyer who resells, extend to other persons in the distributive chain. The second alternative is designed for states where the case law has already developed further and for those that desire to expand the class of beneficiaries. The third alternative goes further, following the trend of modern decisions as indicated by Restatement of Torts § 402A (Tentative Draft No. 10, 1965) in extending the rule beyond injuries to the person [as amended in 1966].

Lukwinski v. Stone Container Corporation

Appellate Court of Illinois, 2000.
312 Ill. App. 3d 385, 244 Ill. Dec. 690, 726 N.E.2d 665.

■ JUSTICE WHITE delivered the opinion of the court:

In this case, plaintiff, John Lukwinski, appeals the order of the circuit court dismissing with prejudice counts III and IV of his sixth amended complaint which alleged claims against defendant, Stone Container Corporation (Stone), for breach of the implied warranties of fitness and merchantability under sections 2–314 and 2–315 of the Uniform Commercial Code—Sales (UCC) (810 ILCS 5/2–314, 2–315 (West 1998)). In dismissing these counts, the court concluded plaintiff could not maintain his warranty claims under section 2–318 of the UCC (810 ILCS 5/2–318 (West 1998)). . . . [F]or the following reasons, we affirm.

[Plaintiff is a truck driver employed by FAB Express ("FAB"), a delivery carrier company. FAB contracted with Stone, a manufacturer of cardboard boxes, to deliver its boxes to its customers, including Coca–Cola. Stone bundles its boxes with pressurized straps and loads the bundles on pallets into FAB's delivery trucks.] Notably, plaintiff was not a party to the sales contract between Stone and Coca–Cola. Plaintiff was simply engaged to deliver Stone's goods to Coca–Cola. [Stone's dispatcher told plaintiff that once he reached the Coca–Cola facility he should help unload the boxes if he was asked to do so, which he was. As plaintiff was adjusting a bundle, the pressurized strapping around the boxes suddenly broke, causing plaintiff to fall and sustain injuries.]

Plaintiff sued Stone for negligence, strict liability, breach of implied warranty of fitness for a particular purpose (count III), and breach of implied warranty of merchantability (count IV). * * *

[Plaintiff asserts] that certain implied warranties ran from Stone to Coca–Cola and its employees pursuant to the sale of Stone's boxes. Plaintiff is not a party to Stone's contract with Coca–Cola and, thus, lacks the necessary privity to assert a direct warranty action against Stone. Plaintiff sought to assert a derivative warranty claim under section 2–318 of the UCC, which extends warranty protections to certain nonprivity persons. In pertinent part, section 2–318 states:

> A seller's warranty whether express or implied extends to any natural person who is in the family or household of his buyer or who is a guest in his home if it is reasonable to expect that such person may use, consume or be affected by the goods and who is injured in person by breach of the warranty. [Citation.]

[Plaintiff asserts 2–318] permits him to seek recovery against Stone for its alleged breach of implied warranties running to Coca–Cola.

[W]e conclude plaintiff falls outside the class of third-party beneficiaries extended warranty protection by section 2–318 and, thus, cannot maintain his warranty claims.

Plaintiff initially urges this court to adopt an expansive reading of section 2–318. Plaintiff claims section 2–318 essentially allows any party in the horizontal chain of the goods distribution to sue the seller under a warranty theory. In this regard, plaintiff asserts the relevant inquiry is not whether the injured party is in the family or household of the buyer, or a guest in the buyer's home, but rather whether it was reasonable to expect that the party would use, consume or be affected by the seller's goods. Thus, plaintiff asserts section 2–318 authorizes any non-privity person who was reasonably expected to use, consume or be affected by the seller's goods to bring a warranty cause of action as a third-party beneficiary. In this case, plaintiff contends it was reasonable to expect he would use or be affected by Stone's boxes during the course of their delivery.

Contrary to plaintiff's suggestion, section 2–318 is not unlimited in scope and does not remove the requirement of privity in all cases. On its face, section 2–318 extends warranties, both expressed and implied, to a certain class of non-privity persons in the horizontal chain of distribution who sustain personal injuries.[2] This class is not limitless, but is confined to members of the buyer's family or household, and guests in the buyer's home. The effect of section 2–318 is to permit parties having a certain relationship with the buyer to maintain warranty claims under the UCC despite a lack of privity with the seller of the good. In this regard, section 2–318 reflects only a limited abolition of privity and is not intended to allow recovery by all persons foreseeably affected by defects in the seller's product. 3A R. Anderson, Anderson on the Uniform Commercial Code, § 2–318:27 at 321 (3d ed. rev. 1995). Parties not covered by section 2–318 must still demonstrate privity. [Citations.]

Section 2–318 was adopted by our General Assembly in 1961 and is identical to the original version drafted by the uniform committee, now commonly known as alternative A. Because many states declined to adopt this version, the uniform committee drafted two alternate versions, B and C, in 1966. Alternatives B and C afford broader coverage than alternative A and extend warranty coverage to a larger class of nonprivity users. Illinois has not adopted either alternative B or C, but instead has elected to retain the original version of the section.

In arguing that he qualifies for third-party beneficiary protection, plaintiff [relies on Alternative B which] extends warranty protections to "any natural person who may reasonably be expected to use, consume or be affected by the goods and who is injured in person by breach of the warranty." [Citation.] [T]his provision is not the law in Illinois and thus cannot be invoked by plaintiff to defeat Stone's motion for dismissal. Acceptance of plaintiff's contention here would render the version of the UCC passed by our legislature ineffective and meaningless.

In the alternative, plaintiff claims he was a "guest" of Coca–Cola at the time he sustained his injuries. Notably, section 2–318 extends warranty protections to persons who are guests in the buyer's *"home."* The UCC

---

2. Horizontal privity concerns the non-privity of consumers and sellers, and refers to those who are not in the distributive chain of a product but who nonetheless use the product and retain a certain relationship with the buyer [whereas] vertical privity refers to the relationship between those who are in the distributive chain of the good. [Citation.]

does not provide a definition of the term "home," and no court of this state has considered the matter of whether the premises or property of a business constitutes a "home" for purposes of section 2–318. Notwithstanding, assuming the word "home" encompasses business property such as Coca–Cola's facility, we conclude plaintiff was not a "guest" as contemplated by the UCC.

In interpreting a statute, our primary aim is to ascertain and effectuate the intent of the legislature, and in doing so our first step is to consider the specific wording of the legislation. [Citation.] Where the intent can be determined from the plain language of the statute, that intent must prevail [citation] and, unless otherwise defined, statutory terms are to be ascribed their ordinary and popularly understood meanings. [Citations.]

The term "guest" is not defined in the UCC. Giving the word its ordinary and popular meaning, it is clear plaintiff does not qualify for warranty protection in this regard. "Guest" is defined, in relevant part, as "a person entertained in one's house ... a person to whom hospitality is extended," particularly "one invited to participate in some activity (as an excursion) at the expense of another" (Webster's Third New International Dictionary, at 989), and "a person who is received and entertained at one's home, club, etc., and who is not a regular member." Black's Law Dictionary, at 707. Here, plaintiff was not invited to be entertained or participate in any activity at Coca–Cola. Rather, plaintiff was at Coca–Cola's facility because he was required to be there as part of his job duties with FAB.

Plaintiff further argues that if he does not qualify as a guest under the statute, he falls within the framework of those decisions that have declined against a literal reading of section 2–318 to find that an employee of a purchaser may sue the seller for an alleged breach of warranty where the contracting parties contemplated that the employee was within the class of persons to be extended warranty protection. In Whitaker v. Lain Feng Machine Company, 509 N.E.2d 591 (Ill. App. Ct. 1987), the plaintiff sued the defendant-vendor under a warranty theory for injuries allegedly suffered as a result of a defective bandsaw that was purchased from the defendant by the plaintiff's employer. The employee was not in privity with the seller and sought to bring himself within the class of nonprivity persons covered under section 2–318.

On review of the circuit court's ruling dismissing the plaintiff's claim, this court determined our legislature intended for the judiciary "to decide, in accord with common law principles and with the guidance of the UCC, whether warranty coverage should further extend to any ... non-purchasing user of a product" beyond those persons specified in section 2–318. *Whitaker,* 509 N.E.2d at 594. According to the court, the designated class is not fixed, but can be expanded to encompass other nonprivity parties in the horizontal chain when warranted by the circumstances of a particular case. *Whitaker,* [citation] (recognizing section 2–318 and its commentary leave "a door at least slightly ajar for future extension of some warranties in appropriate circumstances to nonprivity plaintiffs").

Under *Whitaker,* an employee can sue a seller under section 2–318 "as long as the safety of that employee in the use of the goods was either explicitly or implicitly part of the basis of the bargain when the employer purchased the goods." *Whitaker,* 393 N.E.2d at 595. The court, in finding the plaintiff covered under section 2–318, explained the employer bargained for a bandsaw that was safe as any other merchantable bandsaw, and since "a corporation cannot use the bandsaw at all unless its employees operate it," it concluded the plaintiff's safety was an implicit part of the parties' bargain. *Whitaker,* 509 N.E.2d at 595.

Significantly, *Whitaker* and its progeny concern solely the situation where the injured party is an employee of the buyer. These cases do not address whether any other party can maintain a warranty claim pursuant to section 2–318, and are thus limited in application to the circumstances under which they were decided. Plaintiff in this case was not an employee of Coca–Cola at the time of his injuries, but rather was a third party engaged by the vendor to deliver its products. Consequently, plaintiff cannot rely on *Whitaker* to bring himself within the class of parties to whom that case and similar decisions have extended warranty protection.

Plaintiff, recognizing this dilemma, argues he was akin to an employee of Coca–Cola by virtue of the directive he received from Stone's dispatcher and the request for assistance expressed by Coca Cola's forklift operator. We disagree. The record clearly shows that at the time of his injuries plaintiff was acting within the course of his employment with FAB. The instructions of Stone's dispatcher to assist its customer in unloading its goods and the request of Coca–Cola's operator to remove the boxes from the delivery truck, by themselves, are insufficient to transform plaintiff's employee status for purposes of applying *Whitaker* in this case.

As discussed, the courts may enlarge the scope of section 2–318 where the circumstances of the case warrant. Notwithstanding this discretion, we are extremely reluctant, in light of the express wording of the statute, to expand this section's operation absent a compelling and well-founded reason. The policy underlying the *Whitaker* ruling is quite clear. If coverage was not provided to employees of a corporate buyer, any warranties of the seller would be ineffective and extend to no person since it is impossible for a corporation to be the beneficiary. Plaintiff here, other than asserting the need of protecting the general safety of delivery persons, provides no compelling basis under warranty law for the extension of third-party beneficiary coverage under the facts of the case. We similarly fail to discern any such basis. Plaintiff's relationship with Coca–Cola under the facts is too far removed from those relationships warranting protection under section 2–318. Notably, plaintiff is not without a remedy for his injuries and has other legal theories available under which he can pursue relief.
* * *

Affirmed.

NOTES

1. As *Lukwinski* notes, the court in *Whitaker* had previously concluded that Alternative A covers employees of a purchaser, on grounds of policy. *Whitaker* reasoned that comment 3 to § 2–318 authorized it to continue to expand horizontal privity under "the developing case law." Do you agree that this is a fair reading of comment 3?

More fundamentally, in construing a state statute enacted in 1961, of what relevance is "Official Comment" rewritten by national law revision entities (the ALI and the NCCUSL) in 1966? To the extent that the actual intent of the state legislators is relevant, what do you suppose it was?

2. Some courts have agreed with *Whitaker* that employees are proper plaintiffs under Alternative A. See, e.g., Salvador v. Atlantic Steel Boiler Co., 319 A.2d 903 (Pa. 1974). Others disagree. See, e.g., Hester v. Purex Corp., 534 P.2d 1306 (Okla. 1975) (legislature's adoption of Alternative A language in 1961, and its subsequent failure to substitute either Alternative B or C, precluded suit by employee against manufacturer in warranty; but injured employees not without a remedy since they could sue in negligence and strict tort).

3. McNally v. Nicholson Mfg. Co., 313 A.2d 913, 920 (Me. 1973), held that employees are in the "business family" of their employers for purposes of Alternative A. With a clarity of expression rarely to be seen, the *McNally* court explained why employees are proper beneficiaries of the Code warranties although they do not fall within any of the categories specifically described in Alternative A: "The literal specifications of Section 2–318 are the guideposts of a fundamental course of policy flow adaptable to encompass other relationships which, policy-wise, may be fairly regarded as functionally equivalent to those textually designated." Webber, J., sat at argument but retired before the decision was rendered.

4. Florida has expanded its version of Alternative A to include any person "who is an employee, servant or agent of his buyer." 19A Fla. Stat. Ann. § 672.2–318 (1993).

5. Beyond Employees. By analogy to the "business family" principle of *McNally,* should a soldier injured by defective equipment sold to the military be considered for purposes of Alternative A to be part of the military's "warrior family"? Cf. Miles v. Bell Helicopter Co., 385 F. Supp. 1029, 1031 (N.D. Ga. 1974) (no); or a church member, whose toes froze in the church's freezer, in the church's "family of Christian warriors"? Cf. Crews v. W.A. Brown & Son, Inc., 416 S.E.2d 924 (N.C. App. 1992) (no).

6. Family members who do not live in the purchaser's household have presented a problem for some courts. See, e.g., Wolfe v. Ford Motor Co., 376 N.E.2d 143, 149 (Mass. App. 1978) (niece, not in household, within Alternative A). Is a mother in the "family" of her married daughter? See Lane v. Barringer, 407 N.E.2d 1173 (Ind. App. 1980).

7. Compare Thompson v. Reedman, 199 F. Supp. 120, 121 (E.D. Pa. 1961) ("It is too much of a leap, it seems, to classify a guest passenger in an automobile as a guest in the *home*"; warranty nevertheless ran to plaintiff under "the developing case law" of Pennsylvania). Guests *outside* the home are guests "*in* the home." Handrigan v. Apex Warwick, Inc., 275 A.2d 262 (R.I. 1971) (plaintiff, friend of purchaser of ladder, fell while helping paint friend's house). Cf. Tomczuk v. Town of Cheshire, 217 A.2d 71 (Conn. Super. Ct. 1965) (friend fell from purchaser's bike— no mention of problem of inclusion under § 2–318; moreover, third party beneficiary "guest" is not "buyer" for purposes of § 2–607(3)(a) and so need not "notify the seller of breach or be barred from any remedy"); Miller v. Sears, Roebuck and Co., 500 N.E.2d 557 (Ill. App. 1986) (patron in shop not "guest in home") (partially overruled in *Whitaker*).

8. Verddier v. Neal Blun Co., 196 S.E.2d 469, 470 (Ga. App. 1973), held that a maid whose finger was amputated on her employer's garage door could not maintain a warranty action against a seller of the door because she "simply does not fall into the category of persons benefiting from" Alternative A. Right result?

9. Other classes of plaintiffs have had poor fortune with Alternative A. See, e.g., Stovall & Co. v. Tate, 184 S.E.2d 834 (Ga. App. 1971) (no warranty action for school girl struck in eye by rock thrown by rotary lawnmower through open classroom window); Barry v. Ivarson Inc., 249 So. 2d 44 (Fla. Dist. Ct. App. 1971) (no warranty action for tenant injured by defective table purchased by landlord); Driver v. Burlington Aviation, Inc., 430 S.E.2d 476 (N.C. App. 1993) (airplane manual failed to warn of carburetor icing; passengers not in privity); Snawder v. Cohen, 749 F. Supp. 1473 (W.D. Ky. 1990) (only doctor, not patient who contracted polio from vaccine, in privity with manufacturer).

10. Should a spouse be able to recover for loss of consortium under § 2–318? See Phipps v. General Motors Corp., 363 A.2d 955 (Md. 1976) (Alternative A: yes). What specifically is the issue?

11. Should a divorced wife, who acquires a defective trailer from her ex-husband under the terms of the divorce decree, be entitled to maintain a warranty action against the seller under Alternative A? Cf. Chandler v. Hunter, 340 So. 2d 818 (Ala. Civ. App. 1976) (case decided under Alternative B). What is the issue?

12. While in detention cell, police removed clothing of prisoner known to be suicidal, providing him with paper isolation gown. Prisoner hanged himself with gown. Assuming the gown was unmerchantable because it failed to tear away, would the Appellate Court of Illinois allow a warranty claim by the prisoner's estate against the manufacturer of the gown? See Reed v. City of Chicago, 263 F. Supp. 2d 1123 (N.D. Ill. 2003).

13. Vertical Privity. Recall that Alternative A appears to retain vertical privity. See Compex Int'l Co. v. Taylor, 209 S.W.3d 462 (Ky. 2006) (noting that Alt. A provides: "A *seller's* warranty ... extends to any natural person who is in the family or household of *his* buyer"). By contrast, at least a couple of states have held that the language of Alternatives B and C eliminates vertical as well as horizontal privity. See Bishop v. Sales, 336 So. 2d 1340 (Ala. 1976). See also Gasque v. Eagle Mach. Co., 243 S.E.2d 831 (S.C. 1978). Do you agree?

14. Will any of the § 2–318 alternatives help a retailer, held liable to an injured consumer, reach over a wholesaler for indemnity against a remote manufacturer?

15. Alternative A is presently law in about half the states. The other states have adopted either Alternative B or C, some variation thereon, or some other type of "anti-privity" statute such as that of Virginia. Va. Code Ann. § 8.2–318 (1991). Texas leaves the matter entirely to the courts, Garcia v. Texas Instruments, Inc., 610 S.W.2d 456 (Tex. 1980), and California omitted § 2–318 and requires privity, with limited exceptions, as a matter of common law.

16. On privity, see generally J. White & R. Summers, Handbook of the Law under the Uniform Commercial Code §§ 11.2—11.7 (5th ed. 2000); D. Owen, Products Liability Law § 4.5 (2d ed. 2008); 1 D. Owen, M.S. Madden, & M. Davis, Madden & Owen on Products Liability § 4:9–:10 (3d ed. 2000).

5.   CONTRACTUAL LIMITATIONS ON RESPONSIBILITY

A.   THE PROBLEM AND JUDICIAL SOLUTION

Henningsen v. Bloomfield Motors, Inc.

Supreme Court of New Jersey, 1960.
32 N.J. 358, 161 A.2d 69.

■ FRANCIS, J.

Plaintiff Claus H. Henningsen purchased a Plymouth automobile, manufactured by defendant Chrysler Corporation, from defendant Bloomfield Motors, Inc. [Claus and his wife, Helen, took delivery of the car on May 9 and drove it 468 miles without incident until May 19. On that day, Mrs. Henningsen was driving alone when the car suddenly veered sharply off the highway and into a brick wall, injuring her and destroying the car. The insurance company's appraiser concluded that a mechanical defect in the steering mechanism had caused the failure.] Mrs. Henningsen instituted suit against both defendants to recover damages on account of her injuries. [The trial court dismissed the negligence count and submitted the case] to the jury for determination solely on the issues of implied warranty of merchantability. Verdicts were returned against both defendants and in favor of the plaintiffs. [Defendants appealed.]

The purchase order was a printed form of one page. On the front it contained blanks to be filled in with a description of the automobile to be sold, the various accessories to be included, and the details of the financing. The particular car selected was described as a 1955 Plymouth, Plaza "6," Club Sedan. The type used in the printed parts of the form became smaller in size, different in style, and less readable toward the bottom where the line for the purchaser's signature was placed. The smallest type on the page appears in the two paragraphs, one of two and one-quarter lines and the second of one and one-half lines, on which great stress is laid by the defense in the case....

The two paragraphs are:

"The front and back of this Order comprise the entire agreement affecting this purchase and no other agreement or understanding of any nature concerning same has been made or entered into, or will be recognized. I hereby certify that no credit has been extended to me for the purchase of this motor vehicle except as appears in writing on the face of this agreement.

"I have read the matter printed on the back hereof and agree to it as a part of this order the same as if it were printed above my signature. I certify that I am 21 years of age, or older, and hereby acknowledge receipt of a copy of this order."

[Mr. Henningsen testified that he did not read these two fine print paragraphs, nor the matter referred to on the back, nor did anyone direct his attention to them.]

The reverse side of the contract contains 8½ inches of fine print. It is not as small, however, as the two critical paragraphs described above. The page is headed "Conditions" and contains ten separate paragraphs consisting of 65 lines in all. The paragraphs do not have headnotes or margin notes denoting their particular subject.... In the seventh paragraph, about two-thirds of the way down the page, the warranty, which is the focal point of the case, is set forth. It is as follows:

> "7. It is expressly agreed that there are no warranties, express or implied, *made* by either the dealer or the manufacturer on the motor vehicle, chassis, or parts furnished hereunder except as follows:

> " 'The manufacturer warrants each new motor vehicle (including original equipment placed thereon by the manufacturer except tires), chassis or parts manufactured by it to be free from defects in material or workmanship under normal use and service. Its obligation under this warranty being limited to making good at its factory any part or parts thereof which shall, within ninety (90) days after delivery of such vehicle *to the original purchaser* or before such vehicle has been driven 4,000 miles, whichever event shall first occur, be returned to it with transportation charges prepaid and which its examination shall disclose to its satisfaction to have been thus defective; *this warranty being expressly in lieu of all other warranties expressed or implied, and all other obligations or liabilities on its part*, and it neither assumes nor authorizes any other person to assume for it any other liability in connection with the sale of its vehicles ....' " (Emphasis ours).

* * *

[Addressing the defendants' argument that the disclaimer of liability and limitation of remedy clauses in the warranty shielded them from liability for breach of warranty, the court noted that such attempts at avoiding "the obligations that normally attend a sale ... are not favored, and ... are strictly construed against the seller."]

The terms of the warranty are a sad commentary upon the automobile manufacturers' marketing practices. Warranties developed in the law in the interest of and to protect the ordinary consumer who cannot be expected to have the knowledge or capacity or even the opportunity to make adequate inspection of mechanical instrumentalities, like automobiles, and to decide for himself whether they are reasonably fit for the designed purpose. [Citations.] But the ingenuity of the Automobile Manufacturers Association, by means of its standardized form, has metamorphosed the warranty into a device to limit the maker's liability. * * *

... The language gave little and withdrew much. In return for the delusive remedy of replacement of defective parts at the factory, the buyer is said to have accepted the exclusion of the maker's liability for personal injuries arising from the breach of the warranty, and to have agreed to the elimination of any other express or implied warranty. An instinctively felt sense of justice cries out against such a sharp bargain. But does the doctrine that a person is bound by his signed agreement, in the absence of fraud, stand in the way of any relief?

In the modern consideration of problems such as this, Corbin suggests that practically all judges are "chancellors" and cannot fail to be influenced by any equitable doctrines that are available. And he opines that "there is sufficient flexibility in the concepts of fraud, duress, misrepresentation and undue influence, not to mention differences in economic bargaining power" to enable the courts to avoid enforcement of unconscionable provisions in long printed standardized contracts. 1 Corbin on Contracts (1950) § 128, p. 188. Freedom of contract is not such an immutable doctrine as to admit of no qualification in the area in which we are concerned. . . .

The traditional contract is the result of free bargaining of parties who are brought together by the play of the market, and who meet each other on a footing of approximate economic equality. In such a society there is no danger that freedom of contract will be a threat to the social order as a whole. But in present-day commercial life the standardized mass contract has appeared. * * *

The warranty before us is a standardized form designed for mass use. It is imposed upon the automobile consumer. He takes it or leaves it, and he must take it to buy an automobile. No bargaining is engaged in with respect to it. In fact, the dealer through whom it comes to the buyer is without authority to alter it; his function is ministerial—simply to deliver it. The form warranty is not only standard with Chrysler but . . . is the uniform warranty of the Automobile Manufacturers Association. . . .

The gross inequality of bargaining position occupied by the consumer in the automobile industry is thus apparent. There is no competition among the car makers in the area of the express warranty. Where can the buyer go to negotiate for better protection? Such control and limitation of his remedies are inimical to the public welfare and, at the very least, call for great care by the courts to avoid injustice through application of strict common-law principles of freedom of contract. * * *

It is undisputed that the president of the dealer with whom Henningsen dealt did not specifically call attention to the warranty on the back of the purchase order. The form and the arrangement of its face, as described above, certainly would cause the minds of reasonable men to differ as to whether notice of a yielding of basic rights stemming from the relationship with the manufacturer was adequately given. . . .

But there is more than this. Assuming that a jury might find that the fine print referred to reasonably served the objective of directing a buyer's attention to the warranty on the reverse side, and, therefore, that he should be charged with awareness of its language, can it be said that an ordinary layman would realize what he was relinquishing in return for what he was being granted? Under the law, breach of warranty against defective parts or workmanship which caused personal injuries would entitle a buyer to damages even if due care were used in the manufacturing process. Because of the great potential for harm if the vehicle was defective, that right is the most important and fundamental one arising from the relationship. Difficulties so frequently encountered in establishing negligence in manufacture in the ordinary case make this manifest. [Citations.] Any ordinary layman of reasonable intelligence, looking at the phraseology, might well conclude that Chrysler was agreeing to replace defective parts and perhaps replace anything that went wrong because of defective workmanship during the first 90 days or 4,000 miles of operation, but that he would not be entitled to a new car. It is not unreasonable to believe that the entire scheme being conveyed was a proposed remedy for physical deficiencies in the car. *In the context* of this warranty, only the abandonment of all sense of justice would permit us to hold that, as a matter of law, the phrase "its obligation under this warranty being limited to making good at its factory any part or parts thereof" signifies to an ordinary reasonable person that he is relinquishing any personal injury claim that might flow from the use of a defective automobile. Such claims are nowhere mentioned. The draftsmanship is reflective of the care and skill of the Automobile Manufacturers Association in undertaking to avoid warranty obligations without drawing too much attention to its effort in that regard. No one can doubt that if the will to do so were present, the ability to inform the buying public of the intention to disclaim liability for injury claims arising from breach of warranty would present no problem. * * *

Public policy at a given time finds expression in the Constitution, the statutory law and in judicial decisions. In the area of sale of goods, the legislative will has imposed an implied warranty of merchantability as a general incident of sale of an automobile by description. The warranty does not depend upon the affirmative intention of the parties. It is a child of the law; it annexes itself to the contract because of the very nature of the transaction. [Citation.] The judicial process has recognized a right to recover damages for personal injuries arising from a breach of that warranty. The disclaimer of the implied warranty and exclusion of all obligations except those specifically assumed by the express warranty signify a studied effort to frustrate that protection. * * *

[W]e conclude that the disclaimer of an implied warranty of merchantability by the dealer, as well as the attempted elimination of all obligations other than replacement of defective parts, are violative of public policy and void. * * *

[Affirmed.]

NOTE

Compare Marshall v. Murray Oldsmobile Co., 154 S.E.2d 140 (Va. 1967), where the court explicitly rejected the *Henningsen* approach. Pointing to the legislative approval of disclaimers in § 2–316 of the Uniform Commercial Code, adopted in Virginia in 1966 after the case sub judice had arisen, the court reaffirmed its commitment to the principles of freedom of contract.

B.   DISCLAIMERS UNDER THE UCC

Uniform Commercial Code

§ 2–316. Exclusion or Modification of Warranties

(1) Words or conduct relevant to the creation of an express warranty and words or conduct tending to negate or limit warranty shall be construed wherever reasonable as consistent with each other; but subject to the provisions of this Article on parol or extrinsic evidence (Section 2–202) negation or limitation is inoperative to the extent that such construction is unreasonable.

(2) Subject to subsection (3), to exclude or modify the implied warranty of merchantability or any part of it the language must mention merchantability and in case of a writing must be conspicuous, and to exclude or modify any implied warranty of fitness the exclusion must be by a writing and conspicuous. Language to exclude all implied warranties of fitness is sufficient if it states, for example, that "There are no warranties which extend beyond the description on the face hereof."

(3) Notwithstanding subsection (2)

(a) unless the circumstances indicate otherwise, all implied warranties are excluded by expressions like "as is", "with all faults" or other language which in common understanding calls the buyer's attention to the exclusion of warranties and makes plain that there is no implied warranty; and

(b) when the buyer before entering into the contract has examined the goods or the sample or model as fully as he desired or has refused to examine the goods there is no implied warranty with regard to defects which an examination ought in the circumstances to have revealed to him; and

(c) an implied warranty can also be excluded or modified by course of dealing or course of performance or usage of trade.

(4) Remedies for breach of warranty can be limited in accordance with the provisions of this Article on liquidation or limitation of damages and on contractual modification of remedy (Sections 2–718 and 2–719).

NOTES

1.   Comment 1 to § 2–316 provides:

This section is designed principally to deal with those frequent clauses in sales contracts which seek to exclude "all warranties, express or implied." It seeks to protect a buyer from unexpected and unbargained language of disclaimer by denying effect to such language when inconsistent with language of express warranty and permitting the exclusion of implied warranties only by conspicuous language or other circumstances which protect the buyer from surprise.

2. Plaintiff was injured when the accelerator-carburetor linkage malfunctioned on the used car that he had purchased six days earlier from defendant dealer. The salesman had written "30 day warranty" on the face of the purchase agreement. A printed clause on the back provided in part: "It is expressly agreed that there are no warranties, express or implied, made by either the selling dealer or the manufacturer. . . ." Citing § 2–316(1), the court ruled: "This attempted disclaimer of any express warranties is inoperative since to give effect to the disclaimer would be unreasonable in view of the writing on the face." Realmuto v. Straub Motors, Inc., 322 A.2d 440, 442 n. 2 (N.J. 1974). See also Woodruff v. Clark Cty. Farm Bureau Co–op. Ass'n, 286 N.E.2d 188, 200 (Ind. App. 1972) (noting the "judicial aversion to negation of express warranties").

How can an express warranty and words disclaiming it *ever* be "consistent"? See Neville Constr. Co. v. Cook Paint & Varnish Co., 671 F.2d 1107 (8th Cir. 1982).

Dorman v. International Harvester Co.

Court of Appeals of California, 1975.
46 Cal. App. 3d 11, 120 Cal. Rptr. 516.

■ Stephens, Associate Justice.

* * * Dorman entered into a "Retail Installment Conditional Sales Contract" with I.H. purportedly on October 31, 1968 (he testified that he executed a second contract on November 3) to purchase a new tractor and backhoe for $12,912.26, including finance charges, and had paid a total of $7,233.68 on the contract. Dorman purchased this equipment for use in his earthgrading business and took delivery on November 4, 1968. The evidence adduced at trial shows that Dorman experienced problems with the tractor from the day he took delivery. The tractor broke down on numerous other occasions during the period of November 7, 1968 to August 21, 1969 and it had to be returned to I.H. [International Harvester] for repairs.

[Dorman filed suit against International Harvester in December, 1969, alleging breach of warranty, and I.H. cross-claimed for the return of the equipment. The jury returned verdicts for the plaintiff on both claims but the trial judge granted defendant's motion for judgment notwithstanding the verdicts and reduced plaintiff's verdict to the amount paid on the contract. Both parties appealed. *Held*, reversed, for erroneous rulings on validity of disclaimer and on damages.]

Disclaimer

At the outset of the trial, the court considered the issue of whether the Retail Installment Conditional Sales Contract contained a valid disclaimer of implied warranties. The disclaimer in question is shown in its context in the facsimile below (appearing after paragraph "9. Terms of Payment"):

The court concluded that the disclaimer provision was sufficiently conspicuous to constitute a valid disclaimer of the implied warranties of merchantability and fitness for particular purpose pursuant to California Commercial Code section 2316 [UCC § 2–316]. The court thus limited the issues to be determined at trial to whether I.H. had fulfilled its standard printed warranty.

Contentions

Dorman contends that the trial court erred in its ruling on the validity of the disclaimer provision for the following reasons: (1) the disclaimer provision is not "conspicuous"; (2) the disclaimer provision as interpreted by the court is unconscionable; and (3) the court did not allow the introduction of parol evidence of warranties consistent with the contract provision as well as the parties' interpretation of the provision by their subsequent actions.

(1) Conspicuousness

It was well settled in California under pre-Commercial Code law that a provision disclaiming implied warranties was to be strictly construed (Burr v. Sherwin Williams Co., 268 P.2d 1041 (Cal.)) and was ineffectual unless the buyer assented to the provision or was charged with notice of the disclaimer before the bargain was completed. [Citations.] At trial, Dorman testified that he did not sign the contract dated October 31, 1968 but that he did read it on that date; that on November 3, 1968, he signed but did not read a contract represented to him to be the same as the one he had read on October 31; and that he did not receive a copy of the standard manufacturer's warranty at the time he signed the contract even though the contract contained a clause stating that he acknowledged receipt of the warranty. Although Dorman did not assent to the disclaimer provision and did not read the contract at the time he signed it, the court concluded that the provision was conspicuous and that he should be charged with notice of the disclaimer.

Commercial Code section 2316, subdivision (2) provides that an exclusion of the implied warranty of merchantability "in case of a writing must be conspicuous," and that an exclusion of the implied warranty of fitness for particular purpose "must be by a writing and conspicuous." The code defines "conspicuous" as "so written that a reasonable person against whom it is to operate ought to have noticed it. A printed heading in capital letters (as: NONNEGOTIABLE BILL OF LADING) is conspicuous. Language in the body of a form is 'conspicuous' if it is in larger or other contrasting type or color.... Whether a term or clause is 'conspicuous' or not is for decision by the court." (§ 1201, subd. (10).) [UCC § 1–201]

There is no statutory counterpart of section 1201, subdivision (10) in pre-code law; nor have we found any California cases under the code which have dealt with this section. Therefore, we must rely predominantly on the official comments to sections 2316 and 1201, subdivision (10), and to foreign law. The official comment to subdivision (10) of section 1201 states that the "test [of conspicuousness] is whether attention can reasonably be expected to be called to [the disclaimer provision]." (Cf. Gray v. Zurich Insurance Co., 419 P.2d 168 (Cal.)). We must examine this comment in the light of the official comment to section 2316, which states: "This section is designed principally to deal with those frequent clauses in sales contracts which seek to exclude 'all warranties, express or implied.' It seeks to protect a buyer from *unexpected* and unbargained language of disclaimer by denying effect to such language when inconsistent with language of express warranty and permitting the exclusion of implied warranties only by conspicuous language or other circumstances which protect the buyer from surprise." (Emphasis added.) In other words, section 2316 seeks to protect the buyer from the situation where the salesman's "pitch," advertising brochures, or large print in the contract, giveth, and the disclaimer clause—in fine print—taketh away.

Here, the disclaimer provision appears in close proximity to where Dorman signed the contract, but emphasized (italicized) the implied-warranties wording *"merchantability and fitness for particular purpose shall apply."* Although the disclaimer provision was printed in a slightly larger type face than was the preceding paragraph of the contract, it was not in bold face type, and we are of the opinion that it was not sufficiently conspicuous to have negated the implied warranties, particularly where no "standard printed warranty" was in fact given to Dorman at the time of execution of the contract.[9] The slightly larger type face and location of the disclaimer paragraph are not conclusive. As stated by [another court], "[w]hile there is some slight contrasting set-off, this is not sufficient. *A provision is not conspicuous when there is only a slight contrast* with the balance of the instrument." The instant disclaimer does not reach that level of conspicuousness so as to exclude the right of the buyer to implied warranties which are an integral part of the transaction. (Henningsen v. Bloomfield Motors, Inc. 161 A.2d 69, 76 (N.J. 1960)). It thus violated the underlying rationale of section 2316 as set forth in the official comment of protecting the buyer from an unbargained for limitation in the purchase of a product. In order to have a valid disclaimer provision, it must be in clear and distinct language and prominently set forth in large, bold print in such position as to compel notice. (§ 1201, subd. (10).) In the instant contract, the only large size type (in relation to other type on the page) that may satisfy these criteria is that used for the words "ADDITIONAL PROVISIONS" on the signature page (in a reference to matters on the reverse side of the contract which are extraneous to the warranties disclaimer). Though the size of the type in those words may be large enough, the remainder of the provision is insufficiently "conspicuous." The contract here also failed to have an adequate heading at the beginning of the disclaimer provision, such as "DISCLAIMER OF WARRANTIES," to call the buyer's attention to the disclaimer clause.

The attempted disclaimer of implied warranties in the instant case is ineffective for another reason. Construing the language of the provision strictly [citation], the construction of the wording is ambiguous and could easily be misleading. A purchaser glancing at the provision would reasonably observe the *italicized* language, which reads: *"merchantability and fitness for the particular purpose shall apply,"* and would be lulled into a sense of security. This is directly contrary to the actual intent of the provision.... "An implied warranty ... must be disclaimed by the most precise terms; in other words, so clear, definite and specific as to leave no doubt as to the intent of the contracting parties." [Citation.]

Moreover, the manufacturer's standard printed warranty (which also endeavored to limit the warranties and the introduction of consequential damages) was not included in the contract which Dorman signed on

---

9. There is no indication that a copy of a "Retail Order Form" containing the standard manufacturer's warranty was ever given to Dorman.

November 3, 1968. It was on the reverse side of the purchase order, a separate document not shown to have been signed by Dorman or delivered to him at any time. A disclaimer of warranties must be specifically bargained for so that a disclaimer in a warranty given to the buyer *after* he signs the contract is *not* binding. . . .

We conclude that the disclaimer was insufficiently conspicuous to inform a reasonable buyer that he was waiving his right to have a quality product. As the Supreme Court of the State of Washington succinctly stated in Berg v. Stromme 484 P.2d 380, 385 (Wash. 1971): "The purported disclaimers of warranty in the conditional sale contract form and the waiver of warranty in the purchase order form highlight the absurdity of a rule of law which elevates these bland and substantially meaningless terms and conditions above the individually and expressly negotiated terms and conditions, and gives them controlling effect over specifically agreed upon items and conditions of the contract. To adhere to such a rule means that the law presumes that the buyer of a brand new automobile intends to nullify in general all of the things for which he has specifically bargained and will pay. We would presume the buyer does just the opposite."

(2) Unconscionability

Accordingly, we need not reach the issue of whether the disclaimer provision of implied warranties is unconscionable under California common law.[11] . . .

* * *

[Reversed.]

NOTES

1. What broadly does § 2–316 allow, and what broadly does it prohibit?

2. Compare and contrast the methods of disclaiming responsibility for defective products in subsections (2) and (3)(a). Seller asks you to draft a clause for its purchase contract to shield it from potential implied warranty liability for injuries caused by defects in its power lawnmowers. Would you select the approach of subsection (2) or of subsection (3)? Why? Does your answer make you question whether the policies expressed in cmt. 1, above, are in fact achieved by operation of the section? See Weintraub, Disclaimer of Warranties and Limitation of Damages for Breach of Warranty Under the UCC, 53 Tex. L. Rev. 60, 65–66 (1974).

3. What would have been the effect in *Dorman* of a clause in boldface type providing: "NO IMPLIED WARRANTIES ACCOMPANY THE SALE OF THIS PRODUCT"? Consider § 2–316(2), § 2–316(3)(a), and cmt. 1.

4. Conspicuousness. In Koellmer v. Chrysler Motors Corp., 276 A.2d 807 (Conn. Super. Ct. 1970), the buyer of a new Dodge truck sued the dealer and manufacturer for breach of the implied warranty of merchantability. The defense was the plaintiff's execution of a purchase order form on the back of which was a disclaimer in the 7th of 10 separate paragraphs, printed in the same size and style type, in the same color, totaling over 800 words, and with nothing characteristic

---

11. California did not adopt Uniform Commercial Code section 2302. . . .

about the disclaimer clause to distinguish it from the other paragraphs. *Held,* the disclaimer clause did not satisfy the conspicuousness requirement of § 2–316(2). See also Christopher v. Larson Ford Sales, Inc., 557 P.2d 1009 (Utah 1976) (ditto, "unless it is shown that the provision [on the back of the form] was actually called to his attention"). "The reason for this provision is that it is the policy of the law to look with disfavor upon semi-concealed or obscured self-protective provisions of a contract prepared by one party, which the other is not likely to notice." Id. at 1012.

Compare Houck v. DeBonis, 379 A.2d 765 (Md. Ct. Spec. App. 1977), where a reverse-side disclaimer was held "conspicuous." The court reasoned as follows: "The face of the contract mentions in two separate places that additional terms and conditions are contained on its reverse side. Furthermore, the disclaimer language is separately underscored in Item No. 7, and a heading in capital letters ['DISCLAIMER OF IMPLIED WARRANTY'] demarcates the section." 379 A.2d at 773. Would it have made any difference if half of the reverse side had been underscored and all 12 paragraphs had been preceded by headings in capital letters? Cf. Jones v. Abriani, 350 N.E.2d 635 (Ind. App. 1976).

Suppose the buyer in fact does read an inconspicuous but otherwise effective disclaimer of implied warranty of merchantability. Should the disclaimer be enforced against him? Compare §§ 2–316(2) and 1–201(10) with cmt. 1 to § 2–316. See White and Summers, supra, § 12–5, at 437.

5. **"As Is."** May an "as is" clause alone be effective to disclaim the implied warranty of merchantability? Buettner v. R.W. Martin & Sons, 47 F.3d 116 (4th Cir. 1995) (used good; yes). Need it be *conspicuous*? Consider Fairchild Ind. v. Maritime Air Service, Ltd., 333 A.2d 313 (Md. 1975), where the court split 4 to 3 on the conspicuousness issue. Holding that the conspicuousness requirement of subsection (2) *should* be read into subsection (3), the majority quoted from Gindy Mfg. Corp. v. Cardinale Trucking Corp., 268 A.2d 345, 352–54 (N.J. Super. Ct. 1970): " 'It serves no intelligible design to protect buyers by conspicuous language when the term 'merchantability' is used, but to allow an effective disclaimer when the term 'as is' is buried in fine print.... The expectations of the buyer need as much protection in one case as in another.' " 333 A.2d at 317. Relying upon Lord Mildew's dictum in Bluff v. Father Gray to the effect that "If Parliament does not mean what it says, it must say so" [A.P. Herbert, Uncommon Law 192 (1936)], the position of the dissent was simple: "[I]f this is what the draftsmen meant, they could easily have said so." Id. at 319. Compare Pearson v. Franklin Labs., Inc., 254 N.W.2d 133, 142 (S.D. 1977) ("The phrase '... we accept no responsibility for the results following its use,' buried in the middle of the purported disclaimer is ambiguous at best" and thus ineffective to disclaim liability under subsection (3)(a)).

6. **Timeliness.** In accord with *Dorman*, is Taterka v. Ford Motor Co., 271 N.W.2d 653 (Wis. 1978), where the court similarly ruled that a purchaser is not bound by a disclaimer in the owner's manual delivered with the car subsequent to the signing of the contract of sale.

7. **Obvious and Known Defects.** Should the seller be deemed to have impliedly warranted the absence of defects that are obvious, known, or suspected by the buyer prior to purchase? Plaintiff is injured when the blade of a power saw, which was very wobbly at the time of purchase, flies off during initial use. Warranty of merchantability made and breached? Consider § 2–316(3)(b): "[W]hen the buyer before entering into the contract has examined the goods or the sample or model as fully as he desired or has refused to examine the goods there is no implied warranty with regard to defects which an examination ought in the circumstances to have revealed to him...." See also § 2–314, cmt. 13. See also § 2–316, cmt. 8: "Of course if the buyer discovers the defect and uses the goods anyway, or if he unreasonably fails to examine the goods before he uses them, resulting injuries may be found to result from his own action rather than proximately from a breach of warranty." Compare § 2–715, cmt. 5; Harison–Gulley Chevrolet, Inc. v. Carr, 214 S.E.2d 712 (Ga. App. 1975) (no recovery in implied warranty for death of purchaser of car, where accident may have been caused by oversized steering wheel and tires, since purchaser had inspected and test-driven car prior to purchase).

8. Suppose a fork lift operator is injured when the load he is carrying slips off the raised forks and falls on his head. Further assume that the manufacturer has a nondelegable duty to attach overhead roof guards to all of its lifts, but omitted the guard in this case since the operator's employer needed a lift with low overall height and so specified in its order that the guards be left off. Can the employee maintain a defective design action under § 2–314? "[W]here the buyer gives detailed specifications as to the goods, neither of the implied warranties as to quality will normally apply to the transaction unless consistent with the specifications." Cmt. 9 to § 2–316. See also § 2–317(c) which provides that "Express warranties displace inconsistent implied warranties [of merchantability]."

9. Should a third party beneficiary of a warranty be bound by an otherwise effective disclaimer of which he was not aware? See Comment, 27 Okla. L. Rev. 284 (1974); cf. Matthews v. Ford Motor Co., 479 F.2d 399, 403 (4th Cir. 1973) ("Generally, express warranties and disclaimers do not run with personal property.").

What is the meaning of the last sentence of each alternative to § 2–318? See cmt. 1 thereto. See generally Buettner v. R.W. Martin & Sons, 47 F.3d 116, 119 (4th Cir. 1995) (third parties obtain "both the benefits and limitations of warranties provided to the purchaser").

10. Burden of Pleading and Proof. As an affirmative defense, a disclaimer must be pleaded affirmatively in the defendant's answer. Skeen v. C & G Corp., 185 S.E.2d 493 (W. Va. 1971). And "the burden is upon the party asserting the disclaimer to establish that [it] was delivered at the time of sale and constituted an integral part of the transaction." Noel Transfer & Package Delivery Service, Inc. v. General Motors Corp., 341 F. Supp. 968, 970 (D. Minn. 1972).

11. Attempting to Defeat Diversity by Joinder of Dealer. For various reasons, a person injured in a car accident may to want to litigate a case against the car's manufacturer in state court. In order to defeat diversity jurisdiction, in order to stay in state court, a plaintiff may join the local dealer, asserting a breach of warranty claim against it, in addition to suing the foreign manufacturer on various grounds. If the dealer properly disclaimed all warranties, the warranty claim will fail and the dealer will be considered a fraudulently joined party, in which case diversity jurisdiction will exist and the case will stay in federal court. See Davenport v. Ford Motor Co., 2006 WL 2048308 (N.D.Ga. 2006) (Duffey, J.).

12. Indirect Disclaimers—Conflict of Warranties. Note that inconsistent implied (and possibly express) warranties in a sense are disclaimed by agreements to manufacture a product according to the buyer's specifications. UCC § 2–317(a).

May a manufacturer use § 2–317 to contract away liability for foreseeable misuse? A punch press manufacturer provides in the purchase contract that all warranties are subject to proper safe use pursuant to the operator's manual; the manual prohibits operators from ever putting their hands on the press under the ram. An operator one day disregards this instruction in order to clean away debris accumulated on the press, and an electrical malfunction causes the ram to descend upon and squash the operator's hand. Will the purchase contract serve to "disclaim" the warranty of merchantability? See § 2–317(c) and comments.

13. On disclaimers generally, see J. White & R. Summers, Handbook of the Law under the Uniform Commercial Code ch. 12 (5th ed. 2000); D. Owen, Products Liability Law § 4.7 (2d ed. 2008); 1 D. Owen, M.S. Madden, & M. Davis, Madden & Owen on Products Liability § 4:12–:19 (3d ed. 2000).

———

C. LIMITATIONS UNDER THE UCC

Uniform Commercial Code

§ 2–719. Contractual Modification or Limitation of Remedy

(1) Subject to the provisions of subsections (2) and (3) of this section and of the preceding section on liquidation and limitation of damages,

(a) the agreement may provide for remedies in addition to or in substitution for those provided in this Article and may limit or alter the measure of damages recoverable under this Article, as by limiting the buyer's remedies to return of the goods and repayment of the price or to repair and replacement of non-conforming goods or parts; and

(b) resort to a remedy as provided is optional unless the remedy is expressly agreed to be exclusive, in which case it is the sole remedy.

(2) Where circumstances cause an exclusive or limited remedy to fail of its essential purpose, remedy may be had as provided in this Act.

(3) Consequential damages may be limited or excluded unless the limitation or exclusion is unconscionable. Limitation of consequential damages for injury to the person in the case of consumer goods is prima facie unconscionable but limitation of damages where the loss is commercial is not.

N O T E

1. Freedom to Contract Remedies. Comment 1 provides in part that the "parties are left free to shape their remedies to their particular requirements and reasonable agreements limiting or modifying remedies are to be given effect."

2. Failure of Essential Purpose. But a remedy agreement that does not cure a breach of warranty is not "reasonable." Hence, comment 1 also provides, pursuant to § 2–719(2), that "where an apparently fair and reasonable clause because of circumstances fails in its purpose or operates to deprive either party of the substantial value of the bargain, it must give way to the general remedy provisions of this Article." This is § 2–719's "lemon clause" that typically applies when a seller's repeated repair efforts to cure a defect simply fail to cure the problem. See Pack v. Damon Corp., 434 F.3d 810, 816–17 (6th Cir. 2006).

McCarty v. E.J. Korvette, Inc.

Court of Special Appeals of Maryland, 1975.
28 Md. App. 421, 347 A.2d 253.

■ DAVIDSON, JUDGE.

[Action for breach of express tire warranty. Plaintiffs were injured in an accident caused by the blowout of a tire under warranty. Defendants' motions for directed verdicts were granted at the conclusion of plaintiffs' case. Reversed and remanded. Excerpts from the opinion pertaining to attempted warranty limitations on plaintiffs' remedies follow.

[The "Korvette Tire Centers All–Road–Hazards Tire Guarantee" stated:]

> "*The tires identified hereon are guaranteed for* the number of months (or miles) designated [*36,000 miles*] *against all road hazards* including stone bruises, impact bruises, *blow out*, tread separation, glass cuts and fabric breaks, only when used in normal, non-commercial passenger car service. *If a tire fails to give satisfactory service under the terms of this guarantee*, return it to the nearest Korvette Tire Center. *We will replace the tire* charging only the proportionate part of the sale price for each month elapsed (or mileage used) from date of purchase, plus the full federal tax.

> "The above guarantee does not cover tires run flat, or simply worn out; tires injured by a fire, collision, vandalism, misalignment or mechanical defects of the vehicle. Radial or surface fissures, discoloration or ordinary repairable punctures, do not render tires unfit for service. Punctures will be repaired free.

> "*Neither the manufacturer nor Korvette Tire Centers shall be liable for any consequential damage and our liability is limited solely to replacement of the product.*" (emphasis by court)

[After holding that the first sentence in the "tire guarantee" warranted against blowouts, the court turned to the limitation of remedy issue.]

Questions remain as to what impact the additional language appearing on the invoice has upon the scope and extent of the express warranty. Comm. L. Art., § 2–316[4] specifically recognizes a right on the part of the warrantor to negate, modify or limit an express or implied warranty under certain circumstances. It also implicitly recognizes that warranties may be limited in two different ways—one by "disclaiming" the warranty or a part of the warranty itself in the manner prescribed by subsections (1)–(3), and the other by "limiting the remedy" available upon breach (subsection (4)) in the manner prescribed by Comm. L. Art., §§ 2–718 and 2–719.[5]

4. "§ 2–316. Exclusion or modification of warranties. * * *

"(4) Remedies for breach of warranty can be limited in accordance with the provisions of this subtitle on liquidation or limitation of damages and on contractual modification of remedy (§§ 2–718 and 2–719)." [Emphasis omitted.]

5. The difference between the two modes of negating or modifying a warranty has been clearly expressed in J. White & R. Summers, Uniform Commercial Code § 12–11, at 383–84 (1972):

Here the language which says that the guarantee applies only when the tires are used in normal non-commercial passenger car service, and does not apply to tires that are run flat, or simply worn out, injured by a fire, collision, vandalism, misalignment or mechanical defects of the vehicle, constitutes a disclaimer under Comm.L.Art., § 2–316(1). The language which not only promises to replace the tire if a blowout occurs, but also attempts to avoid consequential damages and restrict the remedies of the buyer solely to replacement, constitutes a limitation of remedies under Comm.L.Art., § 2–316(4), governed by the provisions of Comm.L.Art., § 2–719.[6] Comm.L.Art., § 2–316.1 is inapplicable.[7]

Comm. L. Art., § 2–719 gives the parties considerable latitude in which to fashion their remedies to their particular requirements.[8] It expressly recognizes that parties may limit their remedies to repair and replacement. The parties, however, must accept the legal consequence that there be some fair remedy for breach of the obligations or duties outlined in the contract. Reasonable agreements which limit or modify remedies will be given effect, but the parties are not free to shape their remedies in an unreasonable or unconscionable way. Comm. L. Art., § 2–719(3) recognizes the validity of clauses limiting or excluding consequential damages, otherwise available

"A disclaimer clause is a device used to exclude or limit the seller's warranties; it attempts to control the seller's liability, by reducing the number of situations in which the seller can be in breach. An exclusionary clause [limitation of remedies], on the other hand, restricts the remedies available to one or both parties once a breach is established. Assume, for example, that a new-car buyer sues for breach of warranty, and the seller raises defenses based on disclaimer and exclusionary clauses. The disclaimer defense denies the existence of any cause of action. The exclusionary-clause defense, on the other hand, denies that the buyer is entitled to the remedy he demands—for example, consequential damages...."

6. Comm. L. Art., § 2–316, Official Comment 2, provides, in pertinent part:

"This Title treats the limitation or avoidance of consequential damages as a matter of limiting remedies for breach, separate from the matter of creation of liability under a warranty. If no warranty exists, there is of course no problem of limiting remedies for breach of warranty. Under subsection (4) the question of limitation of remedy is governed by the sections referred to rather than by this section."

7. Comm. L. Art., § 2–316.1, Limitation of exclusion or modification of warranties to consumers, provides, in pertinent part:

"(1) The provisions of § 2–316 [including subsection (4)] do not apply to sales of consumer goods, as defined by § 9–109, services, or both."

The fact that the instant warranty was made on 25 February 1971 precludes the applicability of § 2–316.1 which did not become effective until 1 July 1971. [Citation.]

8. Comm. L. Art., § 2–719, Contractual modification or limitation of remedy [is set out by the court].

Comm. L. Art., § 2–714(3) provides that "[i]n a proper case any incidental and consequential damages under the next section may also be recovered." [Citation.]

Comm. L. Art., § 2–715(2)(b) defines consequential damages as "injury to person or property proximately resulting from any breach of warranty."

Comm. L. Art., § 9–109(1) defines consumer goods as goods "used or bought for use primarily for personal, family or household purposes."

under Comm. L. Art., § 2–714(3), but expressly states that they may not operate in an unconscionable manner. That subsection also establishes that limitation of consequential damages for injury to the person in the case of consumer goods is *prima facie* unconscionable.

Comm. L. Art., § 2–302(1) sets forth the alternatives available to a court when it finds a limitation of remedy to be unconscionable. That section permits the court in its discretion, after a finding of unconscionability, to refuse to enforce the contract as a whole, if it is permeated by the unconscionability, or *to strike any single clause or group of clauses which are so tainted* or which are contrary to the essential purpose of the agreement, or to simply limit unconscionable clauses so as to avoid unconscionable results. Thus, any clause purporting to modify or limit remedies in an unconscionable manner is subject to deletion and will not be given effect.[13]

Here the executory promise to replace the tire in the event of a blowout, found in the first paragraph of the warranty, is, in and of itself, nothing more than an express statement that the remedy of replacement is available in addition to all of the other remedies provided by law.[14] But that executory promise, coupled with the clause purporting to exclude liability for consequential damages and to limit liability solely to replacement, clearly expresses an intent that replacement be the sole remedy under the contract.

The record shows, however, that the warranted tires which Mrs. McCarty purchased were bought for "her" stationwagon, which was ordinarily driven about 150 miles per week; that she did not seek damages for loss of employment; and that her husband was employed as a "locomotive engineer" and did not, therefore, use an automobile for business purposes. This evidence supports a rational inference that the warranted tires here constitute consumer goods as defined by Comm. L. Art., § 9–109,[15] so that the provisions of Comm. L. Art., § 2–719(3) are applicable.

The clause purporting to limit the consumers' remedy solely to replacement of the tire purports to exclude liability for both personal injury and property damage. At trial, the defendants presented no evidence to show that the purported exclusion of consequential damages for personal injury was not unconscionable. Accordingly, to the extent that the clause purports to limit consequential damages for personal injury, it is unconscionable as a matter of law.

In Collins v. Uniroyal Inc., 315 A.2d 16 (N.J.1974), [a case on similar facts, the] Court cogently expressed the reasons for regarding a provision limiting the remedy to replacement of the tire to be "patently" unconscionable, and, therefore, invalid by stating:

13. Comm. L. Art., § 2–719, Official Comment 1.

14. Comm. L. Art., § 2–719(1)(b) creates a presumption that clauses prescribing remedies are cumulative rather than exclusive. If the parties intend such a clause to describe the sole remedy under the contract, such intent must be clearly expressed. [Citation.]

15. See note 8 above.

> "A tire manufacturer warrants against blowouts in order to increase tire sales. Public advertising by defendant relative to these tires stated: 'If it only saves your life once, it's a bargain.' The seller should be held to realize that the purchaser of a tire buying it because so warranted is far more likely to have made the purchase decision in order to protect himself and the passengers in his car from death or personal injury in a blowout accident than to assure himself of a refund of the price of the tire in such an event. That being the natural reliance and the reasonable expectation of the purchaser flowing from the warranty, it appears to us patently unconscionable for the manufacturer to be permitted to limit his damages for a breach of warranty proximately resulting in the purchaser's death to a price refund or a replacement of the tire. [Thus] the statutory presumption of unconscionability was not here overcome...."

While there is no statutory presumption of unconscionability with respect to a limitation of consequential damages for injury to property in the case of consumer goods, the rationale in *Collins* persuades us that the clause here, which attempts to exclude liability for both personal injury and property damage is so tainted by unconscionability as to warrant deletion in its entirety. If the defendants do not want to be liable for consequential damages, they should not expressly warrant the tires against blowouts.[17]

Under the present circumstances, the clause purporting to restrict remedies solely to replacement is ineffective. It cannot serve to convert the express warranty against blowouts into a guarantee that if a tire blew out, "the tire would be replaced."

[Reversed and remanded.]

NOTES

1. "[I]t is virtually impossible to imagine what the disclaiming party can do or show to overcome the 'prima facie' language. In effect we probably have an absolute bar in section 2–719." Franklin, When Worlds Collide: Liability Theories and Disclaimers in Defective–Product Cases, 18 Stan. L. Rev. 974, 1013 (1966). Compare the dissenting opinion of Judge Clifford in Collins v. Uniroyal, Inc., 315 A.2d 16, 18 (N.J. 1974), where the purchaser of a tire manufactured by the defendant and guaranteed against blowouts was killed when the tire blew out. Since the warranty guaranteed against blowouts from external causes as well as from defects in the tires, and since no defect was shown in this case, the dissent argued that the manufacturer's limitation of remedy to repair or replacement should be enforced:

> The drafters presumably had something in mind when they chose the expression "prima facie unconscionable" instead of "per se unconscionable" or simply "unconscionable"....
>
> ... I think it not unreasonable ... to conclude that where the express warranty goes beyond what is required by the Code and the common law of this state, and where the product is found to be free from defect, the prima facie unconscionability contemplated by the Code has been overcome. I

---

17. Comm. L. Art., § 2–719, Official Comment 3, provides:

"The seller in all cases is free to disclaim warranties in the manner provided in Section 2–316."

would so hold. I emphasize that I would limit this holding to the "extra" guarantee case. . . .

See Note, 50 N.Y.U. L. Rev. 148, 174–75 (1975) (limitation of remedies for *nondefective* failures might be viewed as *not* prima facie unconscionable because "such limitations simply do not seem to be unfair if the consumer is given an understanding of their operation and effect").

2. In accord with *McCarty,* on similar facts, is Tuttle v. Kelly–Springfield Tire Co., 585 P.2d 1116, 1120 n. 11 (Okla. 1978), holding that express, no less than implied, warranty is subject to § 2–719(3) presumption: "[White & Summers suggest] somewhat skeptically it could be possible for a seller to rebut the presumption by showing the [remedy limitation] clause was conspicuously printed, that it was explained to the buyer, that the parties bargained over it, and that the buyer knew the products had a tendency to be dangerous."

3. "Consumer Goods." Recall from ch. 1 that approximately one-half of all products liability cases involve commercial, rather than consumer, goods. The prima facie unconscionability clause of § 2–719 does not apply to such transactions. Buettner v. R.W. Martin & Sons, 47 F.3d 116, 120 n. 2 (4th Cir. 1995) (flatwork ironer not a consumer good); McCrimmon v. Tandy Corp., 414 S.E.2d 15 (Ga. App. 1991) (lawyer's computer system; semble). Assume that Ms. McCarty had been a lawyer who used her car, purchased (as were the tires) with law firm assets, 90% for law firm business. Same result? What if she had been a cab driver, and had sought out the very most durable tires she could find?

Should the issue be determined by the nature of (1) *her* principal use, whether she buys the product "primarily for a personal, family, or household purpose," cf. UCC § 2A–103(1)(e) ("consumer lease")? Or should the inquiry concern the nature of (2) the *product's* principal use, whether it is "normally used for personal, family, or household purposes"? Cf. Magnuson–Moss Federal Warranty Act, 15 U.S.C.A. § 2301(1) ("consumer product").

4. Must a remedy limitation be conspicuous? McCrimmon v. Tandy Corp., 414 S.E.2d 15 (Ga. App. 1991) (no, because no explicit requirement of conspicuousness as in § 2–316(2)). Is an inconspicuous limitation unconscionable under § 2–719(3)?

Ford Motor Co. v. Moulton

Supreme Court of Tennessee, 1974.
511 S.W.2d 690, cert. denied, 419 U.S. 870.

■ CHATTIN, JUSTICE.

This is a personal injury suit brought by Moulton and his wife, Pauline, against Ford Motor Company and a retail Ford dealer, Hull–Dobbs.

Moulton seeks $1,000,000.00 in damages and charges the defendants with: negligence; breach of express and implied warranties; tortious misrepresentation based on public advertisement; and strict liability in tort.

[Moulton and his wife filed a complaint on May 13, 1971, alleging that Mr. Moulton purchased a Ford LTD from Hull–Dobbs and took delivery on April 30, 1969; that he was seriously injured while driving on July 5, 1970 when the car "suddenly veered to the right, jumped the guard rail, and fell twenty-six feet to a street below"; and that the loss of control was due to a defect in the steering mechanism of the car. The trial judge dismissed plaintiffs' *tort* claims as barred by the applicable 1–year statute of limitations and their warranty claims for failure to state a cause of action. The Court of Appeals reinstated the tort claims but upheld the dismissal of the warranty counts, and both parties petitioned for review. The Supreme Court reinstated the trial court's dismissal of the entire action. Excerpts from the Supreme Court opinion concerning the validity of the time and mileage limitations on the defendants' warranties follow.]

The Court of Appeals concluded that Hull–Dobbs had not given Moulton an express warranty. This conclusion is supported by the evidence. That Court found that Ford had given Moulton a one-year or twelve thousand mile express warranty. However, the Court of Appeals held that this warranty had expired, thereby precluding an action for its breach.

Both Hull–Dobbs and Ford had disclaimer clauses in their contracts with Moulton, which purportedly disclaimed all implied warranties. The Court of Appeals found these disclaimer clauses to be valid; and, therefore, sufficient to prevent plaintiffs from having a cause of action for breach of implied warranty.

Plaintiffs make three arguments: First, they insist the disclaimer clauses were not properly drawn in that they failed to comply with the provisions of the Uniform Commercial Code; and are, therefore, invalid. Second, if the disclaimer clauses are properly drawn, they are prima facie unconscionable.... Finally, plaintiffs insist that the one-year or twelve thousand mile limitation on the express warranty is prima facie unconscionable under T.C.A. 47–2–719.

T.C.A. 47–2–316(2) provides that implied warranties of merchantability and fitness may be disclaimed if the disclaimer is conspicuous and mentions merchantability, and if it is in writing with reference to the fitness warranty. The Court of Appeals concluded that the requirement of T.C.A. 47–2–316(2) had been complied with; and, consequently, the disclaimers were validly drawn. We agree with this conclusion.

Plaintiffs insist that even if the disclaimers were drawn in accordance with the provisions of T.C.A. 47–2–316 they are, nevertheless, invalid because they violate T.C.A. 47–2–719.

T.C.A. 47–2–719(3) provides:

> Consequential damages may be limited or excluded unless the limitation or exclusion is unconscionable. Limitation of consequential damages for injury to the person in the case of consumer goods is prima facie unconscionable but limitation of damages where the loss is commercial is not.

Plaintiffs' argument is that as a result of the accident Moulton sustained personal injuries; that because of the valid disclaimer of warranties, he is unable to bring an action for consequential damages resulting from the accident; and that such an exclusion is violative of T.C.A. 47–2–719(3) since that section "expressly prohibits exclusion of personal injuries by warranty."

In answer to this argument, the Court of Appeals said:

> ... Plaintiffs misconstrues the scope of this Section. (2–719(3)). Subsection (3) thereof provides the limitation of consequential damages for injury to the person in case of consumer goods is prima facie unconscionable, but that Section does not control disclaimer of implied warranties. Official comment 3 to T.C.A. 47–2–719 states that the seller "in all cases is free to disclaim warranties in the manner provided in Section 2–316."

> The latter Section, which is T.C.A. 47–2–316, provides in subsection (2) that implied warranties of merchantability and fitness may be disclaimed if the disclaimer is conspic[u]ous and mentions merchantability, and if it is in writing with reference to the fitness warranty. The disclaimer here is in writing, and merchantability is explicitly mentioned in the disclaimer of the motor vehicle sales contract.

Most Uniform Commercial Code commentaries agree with the conclusion of the Court of Appeals that disclaimers drawn in accordance with 47–2–316 cannot be considered to violate the provisions of 47–2–719. The following analysis is offered in the one volume treatise of the UCC by White and Summers:

> ... The proposition enunciated by ... (a few courts) ... that a disclaimer that has the effect of modifying or excluding consequential damages may be unconscionable under 2–719(3) ... is out of line with the scheme of the Code. Comment 3 to 2–719(3) provides: ... "Subsection (3) recognizes the validity to clauses limiting or excluding consequential damages but makes it clear that they may not operate in an unconscionable manner. Actually such terms are merely an allocation of unknown or undeterminable risks. The seller in all cases is free to disclaim warranties in a manner provided in Section 2–316."

> The last sentence seems to be telling the seller, "if you really want to limit your liability why don't you disclaim all warranties? Then you won't have to worry about limiting damages." ...

> This implication is buttressed by comment [2] to 2–316 ... "If no warranty exists, there is of course no problem of limiting remedies for breach of warranty."

> The comment's reasoning is elementary: there can be no consequential damages if there is no breach; there can be no breach of warranty if there is no warranty; there can be no warranty if the seller has disclaimed them pursuant to 2–316. Although a particular disclaimer may be unconscionable under 2–302, it seems clear that the scheme of the Code does not permit a court to disregard that disclaimer on the basis that it operates to exclude the consequential damages that could not be excluded under 2–719(3).

We think the Court of Appeals correctly determined that the disclaimer clauses did not violate the provisions of 2–719(3).

Plaintiffs did not argue that the Court of Appeals did not consider the question as to whether a warranty disclaimer which meets the provisions of 2–316 can be considered unconscionable within the meaning of the term as used in 2–302. Most commentaries answer this question in the negative.

See Leff, Unconscionability and the Code, the Emperor's New Clause, 115 U. Pa. L. Rev. 485 (1967).

* * *

The Court of Appeals also rejected Mrs. Moulton's contention that she had a breach of warranty action stating: "... her action being derivative, she is entitled to no greater warranty rights under this Section than the buyer himself. Since Mr. Moulton has no warranty rights ... neither does Mrs. Moulton."

We agree with the foregoing conclusions of the Court of Appeals.

[Court of Appeals' decision upholding dismissal of warranty counts affirmed; action dismissed. Dissenting opinion of FONES, J., omitted.]

NOTES

1. UCC § 2–725(1) provides: "An action for breach of any contract for sale must be commenced within four years after the cause of action has accrued. By the original agreement the parties may reduce the period of limitation to not less than one year but may not extend it." Subsection (2) provides that a cause of action for breach of warranty accrues upon tender of delivery, unless the warranty "explicitly extends to future performance of the goods...."

2. A few courts have held that disclaimers valid under § 2–316 may be invalidated for being unconscionable under § 2–719(3). See, e.g., Walsh v. Ford Motor Co., 298 N.Y.S.2d 538 (1969). There is in fact some academic support for this approach. E.g., Note, 63 Va. L. Rev. 791 (1977).

3. Disclaimers and § 2–302. Given that § 2–719(3) should not be applied to invalidate disclaimers that conform to the requirements of § 2–316, may a court invalidate such a conforming disclaimer under § 2–302, the general section on unconscionability? Relying on Professor Leff's classic article, *Moulton* indicated that there has been little support for such an approach. Professor Weintraub argues, however, that this "seems consistent with Code policy that section 2–302 be used to police against unconscionable warranty disclaimers, even those that have meticulously adhered to the formal requirements of section 2–316." Weintraub, Disclaimers and Limitation of Damages for Breach of Warranty Under the UCC, 53 Tex. L. Rev. 60, 83 (1974) (suggesting the relevance to the unconscionability determination of such factors as (1) the *type of remedy* excluded—lost profits vs. personal injury, (2) *advertence*—whether the buyer understands the disclaimer's meaning and practical consequences, and (3) *adhesion*—whether the buyer could bargain for better terms).

Consider White & Summers, Uniform Commercial Code § 12–11, at 454 (5th ed. 2000):

> Dismal as the prospect is to at least one of [us], we suspect that the courts have the bit in their teeth and that most are determined to apply 2–302 to warranty disclaimers whether or not those disclaimers comply with 2–316. One of us believes that these courts misread the intention of the drafters and that the drafters never intended 2–302 to be an overlay on the disclaimer provisions of 2–316. Nevertheless, lawyers must recognize the judicial hostility to warranty disclaimers, particularly in contracts made with consumers.

4. Is a disclaimer or limitation by a fire or burglary alarm manufacturer (or installer and servicer) against liability for fire or burglary losses unconscionable? See Leon's Bakery, Inc. v. Grinnell Corp., 990 F.2d 44 (2d Cir. 1993) (fire in bakery, disclaimer not unconscionable: no reasonable person would expect cost of system to include fee for fire or burglary insurance which the owner-victim may be expected to carry himself).

5. "The issue of unconscionability presents a question of law for the court; not an issue of fact for the jury." Schroeder v. Fageol Motors, Inc., 544 P.2d 20, 24 (Wash. 1975).

6. What would be the scope and effect of a "secret warranty" extended only to complaining owners after the expiration of the formal express warranty? Cf. Bennett v. Matt Gay Chevrolet Oldsmobile, Inc., 408 S.E.2d 111 (Ga. App. 1991). See generally Sovern, Good Will Adjustment Games: An Economic and Legal Analysis of Secret Warranty Regulation, 60 Mo. L. Rev. 323 (1995).

7. On limitations of remedy, see generally J. White & R. Summers, Handbook of the Law under the Uniform Commercial Code ch. 12 (5th ed. 2000); D. Owen, Products Liability Law § 4.8 (2d ed. 2008); 1 D. Owen, M.S. Madden, & M. Davis, Madden & Owen on Products Liability § 4:20 (3d ed. 2000).

———

D. Statutory Reform

Commentators for years have objected to applying the UCC's disclaimer and limitations provisions to consumer cases. See, e.g., Peters, Remedies for Breach of Contracts Relating to the Sale of Goods Under the Uniform Commercial Code: A Roadmap for Article Two, 73 Yale L.J. 199, 282–83 (1963). As interest in consumer rights increased during the late 1960s and early 1970s, so too did criticisms of the Code's treatment of this problem:

> The disclaimer section of the UCC is the most controversial and ambiguous warranty section. Although its principal purpose is to protect the buyer from unexpected and unbargained-for language of disclaimer, its requirement that any disclaimer must mention "merchantability" almost ensures failure of this purpose because the term conveys so little information to the average consumer. This provision has enabled merchants to continue shifting the risk of loss back to consumers while camouflaging their action with legal jargon. . . .
>
> The Code purports to set the permissible boundaries for contractual terms limiting remedies or liquidating damages with its concepts of reasonableness and unconscionability. These terms, however, are vague, and to the extent that they are vague, they do not sufficiently protect the consumer.

Rothschild, The Magnuson–Moss Warranty Act: Does It Balance Warrantor and Consumer Interests?, 44 Geo. Wash. L. Rev. 335, 343–44 (1976).

In an attempt to tip the scales more in favor of the consumer, several states enacted legislation restricting in consumer transactions the ability of sellers to disclaim warranty liability or to limit the remedies therefor. These statutes vary considerably, from simple amendments to the UCC, the typical approach illustrated by the statutes set forth below, to rather complex consumer protection statutes, as in Kansas, Rhode Island and California.

VT. STAT. ANN. tit. 9A, § 2–316(5) (1994):

The provisions of subdivisions (2), (3) and (4) of this subsection shall not apply to sales of new or unused consumer goods or services. Any language, oral or written, used by a seller or manufacturer of consumer goods and services, which attempts to exclude or modify any implied warranties of merchantability and fitness for a particular purpose or to exclude or modify the consumer's remed ies for breach of those warranties, shall be unenforceable. . . .

ALA. CODE § 7–2–316(5) (1975):

Nothing in subsection (2) or subsection (3)(a) or in Section 7–2–317 shall be construed so as to limit or exclude the seller's liability for damages for injury to the person in the case of consumer goods.

ALA. CODE § 7–2–719(4) (1975):

Nothing in this Section or in Section 7–2–718 shall be construed so as to limit the seller's liability for damages for injury to the person in the case of consumer goods. (Acts 1965, No. 549, p. 811.)

See Cal. Civ. Code § 1790 et seq. (1985 & Supp.1995). See generally Clark & Davis, Beefing Up Product Warranties: A New Dimension in Consumer Protection, 23 U. Kan. L. Rev. 567 (1975).

———

Rothschild, The Magnuson–Moss Warranty Act: Does It Balance Warrantor and Consumer Interests?
44 Geo. Wash. L. Rev. 335, 353–56 (1976).

On January 4, 1975, President Ford signed the Magnuson–Moss Act into law to take effect July 4, 1975. The Act is the culmination of a long line of warranty legislation introduced in both Houses of Congress.

Structure of the Act

The Act[152] provides that any written warranty given for consumer products actually costing the consumer more than $5 must contain the terms and conditions of the written warranty in readily understood language according to standards set by the Federal Trade Commission.[153] Nothing in the Act commands that a consumer product be warranted or that a product be warranted for any specific length of time. If, however, a

---

152. The Act's 12 sections are: section 101, definitions; section 102, warranty provisions; section 103, description of warranties; section 104, federal minimum standards for warranties; section 105, full and limited warranty of a consumer product; section 106, service contracts; section 107, designation of representatives; section 108, limitation on disclaimer of implied warranties; section 109, Commission rules; section 110, remedies; section 111, effect on other laws; and section 112, effective date.

153. Magnuson–Moss Warranty Act § 102(a), (e), 15 U.S.C.A. § 2302(a), (e). The FTC has set $15 as the minimum price for consumer products that will trigger warrantors' and sellers' duties under the Act. . . .

written warranty is offered, full disclosure is required, and the warranty information must be made available to consumers before the product is sold. . . .

If the product actually costs the consumer more than $10, any written warranty must be labeled either "full warranty", indicating that it meets federal standards, or "limited warranty", indicating that it does not meet federal standards. . . .

A "full warranty" designation obligates the warrantor to correct defects, malfunctions, or nonconforming quality defects without charge and within a reasonable time, to disclose clearly on the face of the warranty the exclusions or limitations of consequential damages, and to permit refund or replacement after reasonable but unsuccessful attempts to repair. Further, the warrantor may not limit the duration of implied warranties or impose any duties on the consumer, other than notice, as a condition of remedying defective quality. These duties extend from the "full warranty" warrantor to each person who is a consumer of the warranted product.

. . . Where a written warranty is given or a service contract is entered into, the warrantor may not disclaim or modify any implied warranties, except to limit them to the duration of the written warranty, if that limitation is reasonable, conscionable, and prominently displayed on the face of the warranty in clear, unmistakable language.

Violation of the Warranty Act or a Commission rule is a violation of the Federal Trade Commission Act. The Attorney General or FTC attorneys may sue to restrain deceptive warranties or noncompliance with the Act in the United States district courts. In addition, a consumer who is damaged by a breach of warranty or noncompliance with the Act or with Commission rules promulgated thereunder may sue for injunctive relief, damages, or other legal relief in any state or appropriate United States district court. The court may award costs and expenses, including attorneys' fees, to the consumer if he/she prevails. Nothing in the Act invalidates any right or remedy of a consumer under state law or under any other federal law. At the same time, state laws covering warranty provisions are governed by the Act unless the Commission specifically exempts them.

Magnuson–Moss Act: Restrictions on Disclaimers

The key substantive provision of the Federal Warranty Act relevant to products liability litigation, § 108, limits disclaimers. As codified at 15 U.S.C.A., it provides as follows:

§ 2308. Implied warranties

(a) Restrictions on disclaimers or modifications

No supplier may disclaim or modify (except as provided in subsection (b) of this section) any implied warranty to a consumer with respect to such consumer product if (1) such supplier makes any written warranty to the consumer with respect to such consumer product, or (2) at the time of sale, or within 90 days thereafter, such supplier enters into a service contract with the consumer which applies to such consumer product.

(b) Limitation on duration

For purposes of this chapter (other than section 2304(a)(2) of this title), implied warranties may be limited in duration to the duration of a written warranty of reasonable duration, if such limitation is conscionable and is set forth in clear and unmistakable language and prominently displayed on the face of the warranty.

(c) Effectiveness of disclaimers, modifications, or limitations

A disclaimer, modification, or limitation made in violation of this section shall be ineffective for purposes of this chapter and State law.

NOTES

1. Section 2304(a)(2) provides that the duration of implied warranties may not be limited in the case of "full" warranties.

2. Note that limitations on consequential damages are not prohibited by § 108. Indeed, they are specifically permitted by § 104(a)(3), 15 U.S.C.A. § 2304(a)(3), so long as the "exclusion or limitation conspicuously appears on the face of the warranty." In the case of personal injuries, however, the draftsmen quite clearly intended to leave UCC § 2–719(3) intact. See § 111(b) of the Act, 15 U.S.C.A. § 2311(b).

3. Jurisdiction and Attorney's Fees. Section 2310(d) provides that a consumer damaged by a supplier's failure "to comply with any obligation under this chapter, or under a written warranty, implied warranty, or service contract," (1) may sue for damages in state court or, if the amount in controversy is at least $50,000, in federal court, and (2) may recover attorney's fees, if he finally prevails. Early commentators read this section to open up important new opportunities for injured persons: "[C]onsumers suddenly have a federal forum, as well as the prospect of recovering their attorney's fees, for a violation of UCC section 2–314! In many respects, this 'muscling up' of the UCC could be one of the most important aspects of the Federal Act." Clark & Davis, Beefing Up Product Warranties: A New Dimension in Consumer Protection, 23 Kan. L. Rev. 567, 616 (1975). At least with respect to personal injury actions, however, the courts have disagreed:

We agree with the conclusion of the district court in *Saf–T–Mate:*

> ... Congress was content to let the question of personal injury products liability remain a matter of state-law causes of action, except to the extent that certain substantive provisions in the Magnuson–Moss Act overrule contrary state laws relating to the warrantor's ability to disclaim personal injury liability.

Gorman v. Saf–T–Mate, Inc., N.D. Ind.1981, 513 F. Supp. 1028, 1035. We hold that § 2311(b)(2) of the MMWA prohibits claims arising from personal injury based solely on a breach of warranty, express or implied. One may, however, recover personal injury damages under the MMWA where there has been a violation of the substantive provisions of § 2308 (prohibiting disclaimer of implied warranties), § 2304(a)(2) (prohibiting full warrantors from limiting the duration of implied warranty coverage) or § 2304(a)(3)[17] (prohibiting full warrantors from excluding or limiting consequential damages unless such exclusion or limitation conspicuously appears on the face of the warranty).

Boelens v. Redman Homes, Inc., 748 F.2d 1058, 1068 (5th Cir.1984). "[A]n action for personal injury may be maintained only for substantive violations of §§ 2308 and 2304(a)(2) and (3)." Voelkel v. General Motors Corp., 846 F. Supp. 1468, 1474 (D. Kan. 1994).

Moreover, even such substantive violations of the Act may not give rise to federal claims for personal injuries, for the Act may be interpreted as leaving such claims entirely to state law. Id. at n.2 (adopting the interpretation of Clark & Smith, The Law of Product Warranties). "In short, § 2311(b)(2) does not directly impose personal injury liability but may have the effect of creating the same under state law in the event that a warranty disclaimer or modification or limitation is struck down." Id.

4. Products Covered. The Warranty Act applies only to *consumer* products, defined as products "normally used for personal, family, or household purposes" in § 2301(1), and see 16 C.F.R. § 700.1 (1995), and the disclaimer and limitation provisions apply only to products that cost more than $10. See id. at § 700.6.

5. Would a case like Ford Motor Co. v. Moulton, supra p. 143, be any stronger if it were brought under the Federal Warranty Act rather than under state warranty law alone?

6. On the federal warranty act, see generally J. White & R. Summers, Handbook of the Law under the Uniform Commercial Code § 9–12 (5th ed. 2000); D. Owen, Products Liability Law § 4.9 (2d ed. 2008); 1 D. Owen, M.S. Madden, & M. Davis, Madden & Owen on Products Liability § 4:21–:23 (3d ed. 2000).

---

17. [The statutory reference to § 2304(a)(4) in § 2311(b)(2) was "evidently" an error in draftspersonship.]

CHAPTER 5

STRICT LIABILITY IN TORT

1. DEVELOPMENT

James, Products Liability (Pt. 2)

34 Tex. L. Rev. 192, 227–28 (1955).

As the accident toll of modern life has increased, the urge towards strict liability has grown. Many older forms of liability were vehicles for such a principle but none of them is well adapted to solving our present accident problem. Warranty is a case in point. This was fashioned to serve commercial needs in a commercial context, and however well or ill adapted it is to that end today, its technicalities and limitations reflect those needs. If it occasionally happens to fit the needs of accident law, that is pure coincidence. As a general proposition it does not. If strict liability should be imposed in these cases as a matter of policy, there is no more reason than there is in connection with the negligence doctrine to confine the scope of liability to those in privity of agreement. The need for protection is as wide as the likelihood of this kind of harm, and all such harm may fairly be regarded as a casualty of the supplier's enterprise. Not only the rule of privity, but also many other limitations on warranty liability which we have treated here, are out of place in the context of accident law. They would all be abandoned in a rational scheme of strict liability for injurious products. In some cases this may require legislation. Yet the concept of the warranty implied in law on grounds of policy was devised by courts in the past to meet commercial needs. Why should not the courts of today—entirely within the tradition of a dynamic common law—develop a warranty theory in products liability cases which is tailored to meet modern needs in that field—at least where existing legislation does not positively and clearly forbid such a development? To some extent this has taken place. The process should and no doubt will continue.

NOTE

Other early writings suggesting the need for strict manufacturer responsibility and pointing out the inability of traditional warranty law to meet the need include James, General Products—Should Manufacturers Be Liable Without Negligence?, 24 Tenn. L. Rev. 923 (1957); Noel, Manufacturers of Products—The Drift Toward Strict Liability, 24 Tenn. L. Rev. 963 (1957). On the doctrine's early theoretical development, see generally V. Nolan & E. Ursin, Understanding Enterprise Liability (1995); Priest, The Invention of Enterprise Liability: A Critical History of the

Intellectual Foundations of Modern Tort Law, 14 J. Legal Stud. 461 (1985); D. Owen, Products Liability Law § 5.2 (2d ed. 2008); 1 D. Owen, M.S. Madden, & M. Davis, Madden & Owen on Products Liability § 5:2 (3d ed. 2000).

Escola v. Coca Cola Bottling Co.

Supreme Court of California, 1944.
24 Cal. 2d 453, 150 P.2d 436.

■ GIBSON, CHIEF JUSTICE.

Plaintiff, a waitress in a restaurant, was injured when a bottle of Coca Cola broke in her hand. She alleged that defendant company, which had bottled and delivered the alleged defective bottle to her employer, was negligent in selling "bottles containing said beverage which on account of excessive pressure of gas or by reason of some defect in the bottle was dangerous . . . and likely to explode." This appeal is from a judgment upon a jury verdict in favor of plaintiff.

[Plaintiff testified that the bottle exploded in her hand as she was transferring it from its case to the refrigerator. A fellow employee who saw the accident testified that plaintiff did not knock the bottle against any other object. Unable to prove any specific act of negligence, plaintiff relied entirely upon the doctrine of res ipsa loquitur. Defendant contended that the doctrine did not apply and that the evidence was insufficient to support the judgment.]

Upon an examination of the record, the evidence appears sufficient to support a reasonable inference that the bottle here involved was not damaged by any extraneous force after delivery to the restaurant by defendant. It follows, therefore, that the bottle was in some manner defective at the time defendant relinquished control, because sound and properly prepared bottles of carbonated liquids do not ordinarily explode when carefully handled.

* * *

Although it is not clear in this case whether the explosion was caused by an excessive charge or a defect in the glass there is a sufficient showing that neither cause would ordinarily have been present if due care had been used. Further, defendant had exclusive control over both the charging and inspection of the bottles. Accordingly, all the requirements necessary to entitle plaintiff to rely on the doctrine of res ipsa loquitur to supply an inference of negligence are present.

* * *

The judgment is affirmed.

■ TRAYNOR, JUSTICE.

I concur in the judgment, but I believe the manufacturer's negligence should no longer be singled out as the basis of a plaintiff's right to recover in cases like the present one. In my opinion it should now be recognized that a manufacturer incurs an absolute liability when an article that he has placed on the market, knowing that it is to be used without inspection, proves to have a defect that causes injury to human beings. MacPherson v. Buick Motor Co., 111 N.E. 1050 (N.Y.) established the principle, recognized by this court, that irrespective of privity of contract, the manufacturer is responsible for an injury caused by such an article to any person who comes in lawful contact with it. Sheward v. Virtue, 126 P.2d 345 (Cal.); Kalash v. Los Angeles Ladder Co., 34 P.2d 481 (Cal.). In these cases the source of the manufacturer's liability was his negligence in the manufacturing process or in the inspection of component parts supplied by others. Even if there is no negligence, however, public policy demands that responsibility be fixed wherever it will most effectively reduce the hazards to life and health inherent in defective products that reach the market. It is evident that the manufacturer can anticipate some hazards and guard against the recurrence of others, as the public cannot. Those who suffer injury from defective products are unprepared to meet its consequences. The cost of an injury and the loss of time or health may be an overwhelming misfortune to the person injured, and a needless one, for the risk of injury can be insured by the manufacturer and distributed among the public as a cost of doing business. It is to the public interest to discourage the marketing of products having defects that are a menace to the public. If such products nevertheless find their way into the market it is to the public interest to place the responsibility for whatever injury they may cause upon the manufacturer, who, even if he is not negligent in the manufacture of the product, is responsible for its reaching the market. However intermittently such injuries may occur and however haphazardly they may strike, the risk of their occurrence is a constant risk and a general one. Against such a risk there should be general and constant protection and the manufacturer is best situated to afford such protection.

* * *

The retailer, even though not equipped to test a product, is under an absolute liability to his customer, for the implied warranties of fitness for proposed use and merchantable quality include a warranty of safety of the product. [Citations.] This warranty is not necessarily a contractual one (Chamberlain Co. v. Allis–Chalmers, etc., Co., 125 P.2d 113 (Cal.); see 1 Williston on Sales, 2d ed., §§ 197–201), for public policy requires that the buyer be insured at the seller's expense against injury. [Citations.] The courts recognize, however, that the retailer cannot bear the burden of this warranty, and allow him to recoup any losses by means of the warranty of safety attending the wholesaler's or manufacturer's sale to him. Ward v. Great Atlantic & Pacific Tea Co., supra; see Waite, Retail Responsibility and Judicial Law Making, 34 Mich. L. Rev. 494, 509. Such a procedure, however, is needlessly circuitous and engenders wasteful litigation. Much would be gained if the injured person could base his action directly on the manufacturer's warranty.

The liability of the manufacturer to an immediate buyer injured by a defective product follows without proof of negligence from the implied warranty of safety attending the sale. * * *

This court and many others have extended protection according to such a standard to consumers of food products, taking the view that the right of a consumer injured by unwholesome food does not depend "upon the intricacies of the law of sales" and that the warranty of the manufacturer to the consumer in absence of privity of contract rests on public policy. [Citations.] Dangers to life and health inhere in other consumers' goods that are defective and there is no reason to differentiate them from the dangers of defective food products. [Citations.]

In the food products cases the courts have resorted to various fictions to rationalize the extension of the manufacturer's warranty to the consumer: that a warranty runs with the chattel; that the cause of action of the dealer is assigned to the consumer; that the consumer is a third party beneficiary of the manufacturer's contract with the dealer. * * * Such fictions are not necessary to fix the manufacturer's liability under a warranty if the warranty is severed from the contract of sale between the dealer and the consumer and based on the law of torts (Decker & Sons v. Capps, supra; Prosser, Torts, p. 689) as a strict liability. * * *

As handicrafts have been replaced by mass production with its great markets and transportation facilities, the close relationship between the producer and consumer of a product has been altered. Manufacturing processes, frequently valuable secrets, are ordinarily either inaccessible to or beyond the ken of the general public. The consumer no longer has means or skill enough to investigate for himself the soundness of a product, even when it is not contained in a sealed package, and his erstwhile vigilance has been lulled by the steady efforts of manufacturers to build up confidence by advertising and marketing devices such as trademarks. [Citations.] Consumers no longer approach products warily but accept them on faith, relying on the reputation of the manufacturer or the trademark. * * * The manufacturer's obligation to the consumer must keep pace with the changing relationship between them; it cannot be escaped because the marketing of a product has become so complicated as to require one or more intermediaries. Certainly there is greater reason to impose liability on the manufacturer than on the retailer who is but a conduit of a product that he is not himself able to test. * * *

N O T E

Dean Pound once denounced [Traynor's opinion in *Escola*] as a piece of "authoritarian law," and a major step in the direction of socialism [in New Paths of the Law 39–47 (1950), and Law in the Service State: Freedom versus Equality, 36 A.B.A. J. 977, 981 (1950)]. Assuming that we are not nowadays disposed to flee shrieking in terror from the prospect of a spot of socialism in our law when the public interest demands it, the question remains whether our courts, our legislators, and public sentiment in general, are yet ready to adopt so sweeping a legal philosophy, and to impose so heavy a burden abruptly and all at once upon all producers. Thus far there has been relatively little indication that the time is yet ripe for what may very possibly be the law of fifty years ahead. As in the case of the related agitation for strict liability on the part of all automobile drivers, there are too many vested interests in the way, and the sudden change is likely to be regarded as too radical and disruptive; and progress in the direction of any such broad general rule cannot be expected to be rapid.

Prosser, The Assault Upon the Citadel (Strict Liability to the Consumer), 69 Yale L.J. 1099, 1120–21 (1960). On *Escola*, see Geistfeld, *Escola v. Coca Cola Bottling Co.*: Strict Products Liability Unbounded, Torts Stories 229 (R. Rabin & S. Sugarman, eds., Foundation Press, 2003).

Henningsen v. Bloomfield Motors, Inc.

Supreme Court of New Jersey, 1960.
32 N.J. 358, 161 A.2d 69.

■ FRANCIS, J.

[Mr. and Mrs. Henningsen sued Chrysler Corporation (the manufacturer) and Bloomfield Motors (the dealer) for losses suffered in an accident caused by a steering defect in their Plymouth Plaza 6 Club Sedan ten days after they took delivery from the dealer. *Held,* plaintiffs could recover for breach of an implied warranty of merchantability, despite the absence of privity of contract with Chrysler, and despite provisions in the purchase contract that disclaimed implied warranties and limited remedies to repair or replacement. The opinion is set forth at p. 126 et seq., above.]

Greenman v. Yuba Power Products, Inc.

Supreme Court of California, 1963.
59 Cal. 2d 57, 27 Cal. Rptr. 697, 377 P.2d 897.

■ TRAYNOR, JUSTICE.

Plaintiff brought this action for damages against the retailer and the manufacturer of a Shopsmith, a combination power tool that could be used as a saw, drill, and wood lathe. He saw a Shopsmith demonstrated by the retailer and studied a brochure prepared by the manufacturer. He decided he wanted a Shopsmith for his home workshop, and his wife bought and gave him one for Christmas in 1955. In 1957 he bought the necessary attachments to use the Shopsmith as a lathe for turning a large piece of wood he wished to make into a chalice. After he had worked on the piece of wood several times without difficulty, it suddenly flew out of the machine and struck him on the forehead, inflicting serious injuries. About ten and a half months later, he gave the retailer and the manufacturer written notice of claimed breaches of warranties and filed a complaint against them alleging such breaches and negligence.

After a trial before a jury, the court ruled that there was no evidence that the retailer was negligent or had breached any express warranty and that the manufacturer was not liable for the breach of any implied warranty. Accordingly, it submitted to the jury only the cause of action alleging breach of implied warranties against the retailer and the causes of action alleging negligence and breach of express warranties against the manufacturer. The jury returned a verdict for the retailer against plaintiff and for plaintiff against the manufacturer in the amount of $65,000. The trial court denied the manufacturer's motion for a new trial and entered judgment on the verdict. The manufacturer and plaintiff appeal. * * *

Plaintiff introduced substantial evidence that his injuries were caused by defective design and construction of the Shopsmith. His expert witnesses testified that inadequate set screws were used to hold parts of the machine together so that normal vibration caused the tailstock of the lathe to move away from the piece of wood being turned permitting it to fly out of the lathe. They also testified that there were other more positive ways of fastening the parts of the machine together, the use of which would have prevented the accident. The jury could therefore reasonably have concluded that the manufacturer negligently constructed the Shopsmith. The jury could also reasonably have concluded that statements in the manufacturer's brochure were untrue, that they constituted express warranties,[1] and that plaintiff's injuries were caused by their breach.

The manufacturer contends, however, that plaintiff did not give it notice of breach of warranty within a reasonable time and that therefore his cause of action for breach of warranty is barred by section 1769 of the Civil Code. * * *

Like other provisions of the uniform sales act (Civ. Code, §§ 1721–1800), section 1769 deals with the rights of the parties to a contract of sale or a sale. It does not provide that notice must be given of the breach of a warranty that arises independently of a contract of sale between the parties. Such warranties are not imposed by the sales act, but are the product of common-law decisions that have recognized them in a variety of situations. * * *

The notice requirement of section 1769 * * * is not an appropriate one for the court to adopt in actions by injured consumers against manufacturers with whom they have not dealt. [Citations.] "As between the immediate parties to the sale [the notice requirement] is a sound commercial rule, designed to protect the seller against unduly delayed claims for damages. As applied to personal injuries, and notice to a remote seller, it becomes a booby-trap for the unwary. The injured consumer is seldom 'steeped in the business practice which justifies the rule,' [James, Product Liability, 34

---

1. In this respect the trial court limited the jury to a consideration of two statements in the manufacturer's brochure. (1) "WHEN SHOPSMITH IS IN HORIZONTAL POSI-TION—Rugged construction of frame provides rigid support from end to end. Heavy centerless ground steel tubing insures perfect alignment of components." (2) "SHOPS-MITH maintains its accuracy because every component has positive locks that hold adjustments through rough or precision work."

Texas L. Rev. 44, 192, 197] and at least until he has had legal advice it will not occur to him to give notice to one with whom he has had no dealings." (Prosser, Strict Liability to the Consumer, 69 Yale L.J. 1099, 1130, footnotes omitted.) * * * We conclude, therefore, that even if plaintiff did not give timely notice of breach of warranty to the manufacturer, his cause of action based on the representations contained in the brochure was not barred.

Moreover, to impose strict liability on the manufacturer under the circumstances of this case, it was not necessary for plaintiff to establish an express warranty as defined in section 1732 of the Civil Code. A manufacturer is strictly liable in tort when an article he places on the market, knowing that it is to be used without inspection for defects, proves to have a defect that causes injury to a human being. Recognized first in the case of unwholesome food products, such liability has now been extended to a variety of other products that create as great or greater hazards if defective. [Citations of cases involving a grinding wheel, bottles, a vaccine, an insect spray, a surgical pin, a skirt, a tire, a home permanent, a hair dye, and automobiles, including *Henningsen v. Bloomfield Motors, Inc.*]

Although in these cases strict liability has usually been based on the theory of an express or implied warranty running from the manufacturer to the plaintiff, the abandonment of the requirement of a contract between them, the recognition that the liability is not assumed by agreement but imposed by law [citations], and the refusal to permit the manufacturer to define the scope of its own responsibility for defective products [citations] make clear that the liability is not one governed by the law of contract warranties but by the law of strict liability in tort. Accordingly, rules defining and governing warranties that were developed to meet the needs of commercial transactions cannot properly be invoked to govern the manufacturer's liability to those injured by their defective products unless those rules also serve the purposes for which such liability is imposed.

We need not recanvass the reasons for imposing strict liability on the manufacturer. They have been fully articulated in the cases cited above. (See also 2 Harper and James, Torts, §§ 28.15–28.16, pp. 1569–1574; Prosser, Strict Liability to the Consumer, 69 Yale L.J. 1099; Escola v. Coca Cola Bottling Co., 150 P.2d 436 (Cal.), concurring opinion.) The purpose of such liability is to insure that the costs of injuries resulting from defective products are borne by the manufacturers that put such products on the market rather than by the injured persons who are powerless to protect themselves. Sales warranties serve this purpose fitfully at best. (See Prosser, Strict Liability to the Consumer, 69 Yale L.J. 1099, 1124–1134.) In the present case, for example, plaintiff was able to plead and prove an express warranty only because he read and relied on the representations of the Shopsmith's ruggedness contained in the manufacturer's brochure. Implicit in the machine's presence on the market, however, was a representation that it would safely do the jobs for which it was built. Under these circumstances, it should not be controlling whether plaintiff selected the machine because of the statements in the brochure, or because of the machine's own appearance of excellence that belied the defect lurking beneath the surface, or because he merely assumed that it would safely do the jobs it was built to do. It should not be controlling whether the details of the sales from manufacturer to retailer and from retailer to plaintiff's wife were such that one or more of the implied warranties of the sales act arose. (Civ. Code, § 1735.) "The remedies of injured consumers ought not to be made to depend upon the intricacies of the law of sales." (Ketterer v. Armour & Co., D.C., 200 F. 322, 323) [citation]. To establish the manufacturer's liability it was sufficient that plaintiff proved that he was injured while using the Shopsmith in a way it was intended to be used as a result of a defect in design and manufacture of which plaintiff was not aware that made the Shopsmith unsafe for its intended use.

* * *

The judgment is affirmed.

———

Priest, The Invention of Enterprise Liability: A Critical History of the Intellectual Foundations of Modern Tort Law

14 J. Legal Stud. 459, 507–08 (1985).

The modern synthesis of enterprise liability became law in *Henningsen v. Bloomfield Motors, Inc.*, decided in 1960, and in *Greenman v. Yuba Power Prods., Inc.*, decided in 1963. The powerful arguments of the respective opinions provided the grounds for the subsequent adoption of the strict liability standard in the remaining U.S. jurisdictions. Of substantially more importance, however, these opinions ratified the scholarly consensus on internalization, risk distribution, and the need to protect consumers. This consensus—the theory of enterprise liability—was elaborated and worked out over the next decades to define the contours of our modern tort law regime.

Henningsen marked the effective end of the relevance of contract law in defective product actions involving personal injury. Its holding allows recovery based on an implied warranty of merchantability, but it repudiates every other principle of contract law potentially applicable to product defect actions. As would be rapidly observed, there is no truly contractual—that is, consensual—basis for the implied warranty. *Greenman* completely and unalterably shifted the grounds for decision in product defect cases involving personal injury from contract to tort law. The sequence of *Henningsen* and *Greenman* was not accidental. The delegitimation of contract in *Henningsen* made possible if not compelling the adoption of the purely tort grounds for decision in *Greenman*. In retrospect, *Greenman* is only a logical implication of *Henningsen*.

NOTE

Shortly prior to *Greenman* an important development had begun with the American Law Institute's reconsideration of the rules governing the liability of suppliers of products. This development was summarized by Judge Wisdom in Putman v. Erie City Mfg. Co., 338 F.2d 911, 918–19 (5th Cir. 1964):

> The original Restatement of Torts had no provision for strict liability based on a seller's implied warranty. In April 1961, Tentative Draft No. 6 of the Restatement, Second, recommended adoption of a new section, Section 402A. This section recognized the seller's strict liability but limited liability to claims for "food for human consumption." By April 1962 it had become apparent that "food for human consumption" was too narrow a category. Tentative Draft No. 7 expanded the coverage of the section to include "products intended for intimate bodily use", "whether or not [they] ha[ve] any nutritional value." A comment explained that "intimate bodily use" also included "products intended for external application or contact" where it was "of an intimate character" [such as chewing gum, chewing tobacco, snuff, cigarettes, drugs, clothing, soap, cosmetics, liniments, hair dye, and permanent wave solutions, 338 F.2d at 918–19, n. 16]. In two years even this greatly broadened version was obsolete. In May 1964, the Institute approved the final draft of Section 402A making the rule applicable to all products.

Section 402A was published the next year, 1965, in the Restatement (2d) of Torts.

Restatement (Second) of Torts (1965)

§ 402A. Special Liability of Seller of Product for Physical Harm to User or Consumer

(1) One who sells any product in a defective condition unreasonably dangerous to the user or consumer or to his property is subject to liability for physical harm thereby caused to the ultimate user or consumer, or to his property, if

(a) the seller is engaged in the business of selling such a product, and

(b) it is expected to and does reach the user or consumer without substantial change in the condition in which it is sold.

(2) The rule stated in Subsection (1) applies although

(a) the seller has exercised all possible care in the preparation and sale of his product, and

(b) the user or consumer has not bought the product from or entered into any contractual relation with the seller.

Caveat:

The Institute expresses no opinion as to whether the rules stated in this Section may not apply

(1) to harm to persons other than users or consumers;

(2) to the seller of a product expected to be processed or otherwise substantially changed before it reaches the user or consumer; or

(3) to the seller of a component part of a product to be assembled.

Comment:

a. This Section states a special rule applicable to sellers of products. The rule is one of strict liability, making the seller subject to liability to the user or consumer even though he has exercised all possible care in the preparation and sale of the product. * * * The rule stated here is not exclusive, and does not preclude liability based upon the alternative ground of negligence of the seller, where such negligence can be proved.

* * *

m. *"Warranty."* The liability stated in this Section does not rest upon negligence. It is strict liability, similar in its nature to that covered by Chapters 20 and 21. The basis of liability is purely one of tort.

A number of courts, seeking a theoretical basis for the liability, have resorted to a "warranty," either running with the goods sold, by analogy to covenants running with the land, or made directly to the consumer without contract. In some instances this theory has proved to be an unfortunate one. Although warranty was in its origin a matter of tort liability, and it is generally agreed that a tort action will still lie for its breach, it has become so identified in practice with a contract of sale between the plaintiff and the defendant that the warranty theory has become something of an obstacle to the recognition of the strict liability where there is no such contract. There is nothing in this Section which would prevent any court from treating the rule stated as a matter of "warranty" to the user or consumer. But if this is done, it should be recognized and understood that the "warranty" is a very different kind of warranty from those usually found in the sale of goods, and that it is not subject to the various contract rules which have grown up to surround such sales.

The rule stated in this Section does not require any reliance on the part of the consumer upon the reputation, skill, or judgment of the seller who is to be held liable, nor any representation or undertaking on the part of that seller. The seller is strictly liable although, as is frequently the case, the consumer does not even know who he is at the time of consumption. The rule stated in this Section is not governed by the provisions of the Uniform Sales Act, or those of the Uniform Commercial Code, as to warranties; and it is not affected by limitations on the scope and content of warranties, or by limitation to "buyer" and "seller" in those statutes. Nor is the consumer required to give notice to the seller of his injury within a reasonable time after it occurs, as is provided by the Uniform Act. The consumer's cause of action does not depend upon the validity of his contract with the person from whom he acquires the product, and it is not affected by any disclaimer or other agreement, whether it be between the seller and his immediate buyer, or attached to and accompanying the product into the consumer's hands. In short, "warranty" must be given a new and different meaning if it is used in connection with this Section. It is much simpler to regard the liability here stated as merely one of strict liability in tort.

NOTES

1. "Although the writer was perhaps the first to voice it, the suggestion was sufficiently obvious that all of the trouble lay with the one word 'warranty,' which had been from the outset only a rather transparent device to accomplish the desired result of strict liability. No one disputed that the 'warranty' was a matter of strict liability. No one denied that where there was no privity, liability to the consumer could not sound in contract and must be a matter of tort. Why not, then, talk of the strict liability in tort, a thing familiar enough in the law of animals, abnormally dangerous activities, nuisance, workmen's compensation, libel, misrepresentation, and respondeat superior, and discard the word 'warranty' with all its contract implications?" Prosser, The Fall of the Citadel (Strict Liability to the Consumer), 50 Minn. L. Rev. 791, 802 (1966).

2. "The modern synthesis of the theory of enterprise liability was achieved during the period 1960–64. The synthesis represents the convergence of once independent streams of contracts and torts scholarship. Contracts scholarship established that warranty law was insufficient to protect relatively powerless consumers from the efforts of powerful manufacturers to avoid liability for product-related injuries. Torts scholarship established that society would benefit from internalizing injury costs to manufacturing enterprises to encourage such enterprises either to prevent injuries or to insure for them. The convergence of these streams of thought constitutes the mature theory of enterprise liability that dominates modern tort law today." Priest, The Invention of Enterprise Liability: A Critical History of the Intellectual Foundations of Modern Tort Law, 14 J. Legal Stud. 461, 505 (1985), elegantly critiqued in Owen, The Intellectual Development of Modern Products Liability Law: A Comment on Priest's View of the Cathedral's Foundations, 14 J. Legal Stud. 529 (1985), blithely ignored in Priest, Strict Products Liability: The Original Intent, 10 Cardozo L. Rev. 2301 (1989), indulgently addressed in G. Schwartz, The Beginning and Possible End of the Rise of Modern American Tort Law, 26 Ga. L. Rev. 601 (1992), splendidly illuminated in Owen, The Fault Pit, 26 Ga. L. Rev. 703 (1992), compellingly buttressed in G. Schwartz, Mixed Theories of Tort Law; Affirming Both Deterrence and Corrective Justice, 75 Tex. L. Rev. 1801 (1997), pompously derided in Wright, Justice and Reasonable Care in Negligence Law, 47 Am. J. Juris. 143 (2002).

Phipps v. General Motors Corp.

Court of Appeals of Maryland, 1976.
278 Md. 337, 363 A.2d 955.

■ ELDRIDGE, JUDGE.

[Plaintiff was injured while driving a car manufactured by the defendant when without warning the accelerator suddenly stuck. The car accelerated out of control and crashed into a tree. Plaintiff brought suit against General Motors (GM) in federal district court on grounds of negligence, warranty, and strict liability in tort. GM moved to dismiss the strict tort count, arguing that the doctrine had not been adopted by the Maryland courts. The federal court certified this question to the Maryland Court of Appeals. The Court answered the question, "Yes," pursuant to the theory of strict products liability in tort in the Restatement (Second) of Torts § 402A (1965).]

Various justifications for imposing strict liability in tort on manufacturers have been advanced by the courts. It has been said that the cost of injuries caused by defective products should in equity be "borne by the manufacturers that put such products on the market rather than by the injured persons who are powerless to protect themselves" and that "warranties serve this purpose fitfully at best." Greenman v. Yuba Power Products, Inc., supra, 377 P.2d at 901. It has also been suggested that imposing strict liability on manufacturers for defective products is equitable because it shifts the risk of loss to those better able financially to bear the loss. Seely v. White Motor Company, 403 P.2d 145, 151 (Cal. 1965). Another reason advanced is that a consumer relies upon the seller in expecting that a product is safe for the uses for which it has been marketed, and that this expectation is better fulfilled by the theory of strict liability than traditional negligence or warranty theories. [Citation.]. And still another reason advanced is that the requirement of proof of a defect rendering a product unreasonably dangerous is a sufficient showing of fault on the part of the seller to impose liability without placing an often impossible burden on the plaintiff of proving specific acts of negligence. McCormack v. Hankscraft Company, 154 N.W.2d 488, 500 (Minn. 1967); Dippel v. Sciano, 155 N.W.2d 55, 63 (Wis. 1967).[3]

The essential elements of an action in strict liability are set forth in § 402A. For recovery, it must be established that (1) the product was in a defective condition at the time that it left the possession or control of the seller, (2) that it was unreasonably dangerous to the user or consumer, (3) that the defect was a cause of the injuries, and (4) that the product was expected to and did reach the consumer without substantial change in its condition. However, in an action founded on strict liability in tort, as opposed to a traditional negligence action, the plaintiff need not prove any specific act of negligence on the part of the seller. The relevant inquiry in a strict liability action focuses not on the conduct of the manufacturer but rather on the product itself. See Weinstein, Twerski, Piehler, Donaher, Product Liability: An Interaction of Law and Technology, 12 Duquesne L. Rev. 425, 429 (1974). Thus the standard to be applied in determining whether a product is defective becomes critical.

* * *

---

3. [See generally] Calabresi, Some Thoughts on Risk Distribution and the Law of Torts, 70 Yale L.J. 499 (1961); Keeton, Products Liability—Liability Without Fault and the Requirement of a Defect, 41 Tex. L. Rev. 855 (1963); Shapo, A Representational Theory of Consumer Protection: Doctrine, Function, and Legal Liability for Product Disappointment, 60 Va. L. Rev. 1109 (1974).

In those cases where the defect is a result of an error in the manufacturing process, that is where the product is in a condition not intended by the seller, there is less difficulty in applying the defectiveness test of § 402A. [Citing Frumer and Friedman, Products Liability]. Where, however, the alleged defect is the result of the design process so that the product causing injury was in a condition intended by the manufacturer, the test has proved more difficult to apply. This difficulty has caused some courts and commentators to suggest that the theory of strict liability in tort is not really applicable in cases involving design defects as opposed to construction or manufacturing defects but rather that, analytically, traditional negligence standards still apply. See [citations]; Wade, On the Nature of Strict Tort Liability for Products, 44 Miss. L.J. 825, 836–838 (1973). The reasoning of these authorities is that in a design defect case the standard of defectiveness under § 402A, involving as it does the element of unreasonable danger, still requires a weighing of the utility of risk inherent in the design against the magnitude of the risk. [Citation.] However, there are those kinds of conditions which, whether caused by design or manufacture, can never be said to involve a reasonable risk. For example, the steering mechanism of a new automobile should not cause the car to swerve off the road, Henningsen v. Bloomfield Motors, Inc., [citation]; the drive shaft of a new automobile should not separate from the vehicle when it is driven in a normal manner, Elmore v. American Motors Corporation, 451 P.2d 84 (Cal. 1969); the brakes of a new automobile should not suddenly fail, Sharp v. Chrysler Corporation, 432 S.W.2d 131 (Tex. Civ. App. 1968); and the accelerator of a new automobile should not stick without warning, causing the vehicle suddenly to accelerate. Conditions like these, even if resulting from the design of the products, are defective and unreasonably dangerous without the necessity of weighing and balancing the various factors involved.

Under § 402A, various defenses are still available to the seller in an action based on strict liability in tort [described in the] official comments following § 402A. For example, the seller is not liable where injury results from abnormal handling or use of the product (Comment h), where mishandling or alteration after delivery of the product renders it unsafe (Comment g), or if warnings or instructions supplied with the product are disregarded by the consumer where, if used in accordance with these warnings, the product would be safe (Comment j). Additionally, where the plaintiff unreasonably proceeds to use a product despite a known risk or danger, the defense of assumption of the risk is still available (Comment n). [See generally] Noel, Defective Products: Abnormal Use, Contributory Negligence, and Assumption of Risk, 25 Vand. L. Rev. 93 (1972).

This Court has in prior cases, where the question was raised, declined to adopt the strict liability principles of § 402A, finding that under the facts of those cases § 402A was not applicable and would have afforded no additional basis of liability. * * *

GM argues that we should not adopt the doctrine of strict liability for several reasons. It contends that the warranty provisions of the Maryland

Uniform Commercial Code [UCC] and the doctrine of strict liability in tort are substantially the same ...; ... that even if we were to conclude that the differences between the two theories of liability were significant enough to adopt § 402A of the Restatement, the Legislature in enacting the warranty provisions of the UCC has "preempted the field of products liability law" [; and] that the adoption of strict liability would substantially alter the rights of consumers and sellers as presently defined by the law of negligence and contract, and that the policy reasons advanced by the courts for altering those traditional rights are more properly a matter of legislative rather than judicial determination.

We do not agree with any of GM's contentions. With respect to the differences between strict liability in tort and warranty actions, it is true that the requirement of privity, once an obstacle to recovery under a contract action, and a major reason for the adoption of [§ 402A], has been eliminated by the General Assembly [if] personal injuries result from a breach of warranty. Sections 2–318 and 2–314 of the Maryland Uniform Commercial Code. See [citation]. But there still remain various other requirements and limitations imposed by contract law [in] breach of warranty [actions that are avoided] under the theory of strict liability in tort.

One of the more significant differences between the two theories is the right of the seller to disclaim or limit remedies for breach of warranty. Although the Maryland Legislature has eliminated the right of sellers to disclaim or limit warranties arising from the sale of *consumer* goods, §§ 2–316.1, 2–719(3) of the Maryland Uniform Commercial Code, there is no similar limitation on the right to exclude warranties where the goods involved are not consumer goods.... Under § 402A [disclaimers have no effect] (Comment m). The notice requirement of § 2–607 of the UCC may also prove to be an obstacle to recovery. [The] buyer is still required by § 2–607(3) to give notice or be barred from any recovery for breach of warranty [unlike § 402A which does not require notice]. Also, [warranty claims are] governed by the [4–year-from-delivery] limitations period contained in [UCC § 2–725 whereas a § 402A action is governed by the 3–year statute that] may begin to run at a later time. These are examples of significant differences between actions based upon contract and strict liability in tort.

[Nor do we] agree with GM that the Legislature has preempted the field of product liability law, precluding our adoption of Restatement § 402A. The only authority cited by GM in support of this contention is [a concurring opinion in a case in which the majority] noted in rejecting a similar contention and adopting strict liability, there is no indication that the Legislature, in enacting the UCC, intended to prevent the further development of product liability law by the courts. In the absence of any expression of intent by the Legislature to limit the remedies available to those injured by defective goods exclusively to those provided by the Maryland UCC, we believe that GM's preemption contention is without merit.

Finally, we disagree with GM's argument that adoption of strict liability would result in such a radical change of the rights of sellers and consumers that the matter should be left to the Legislature.... As [Professor Wade] has observed, the doctrine of strict liability is really but another form of negligence per se, in that it is a judicial determination that placing a defective product on the market which is unreasonably dangerous to a user or consumer is itself a negligent act ... (Wade, Strict Tort Liability of Manufacturers, 19 Sw. L.J. 5, 14 (1965)) * * *. Thus, the theory of strict liability is not a radical departure from traditional tort concepts. Despite the use of the term "strict liability" the seller is not an insurer, as absolute liability is not imposed on the seller for any injury resulting from the use of his product. [Citations.] Proof of a defect in the product at the time it leaves the control of the seller implies fault on the part of the seller sufficient to justify imposing liability for injuries caused by the product. Where the seller supplies a defective and unreasonably dangerous product, the seller or someone employed by him has been at fault in designing or constructing the product.

Almost all of the courts of our sister states have adopted the strict liability principles set forth in § 402A of the Restatement (Second) of Torts. Several reasons for adopting strict liability are summarized in Comment c to § 402A as follows:

"[T]he justification for the strict liability has been said to be that the seller, by marketing his product for use and consumption, has undertaken and assumed a special responsibility toward any member of the consuming public who may be injured by it; that the public has the right to and does expect, in the case of products which it needs and for which it is forced to rely upon the seller, that reputable sellers will stand behind their goods; that public policy demands that the burden of accidental injuries caused by products intended for consumption be placed upon those who market them, and be treated as a cost of production against which liability insurance can be obtained; and that the consumer of such products is entitled to the maximum of protection at the hands of someone, and the proper persons to afford it are those who market the products."

We find the above reasons persuasive. [T]here is no reason why a party injured by a defective and unreasonably dangerous product, which when placed on the market is impliedly represented as safe, should bear the loss of that injury when the seller of that product is in a better position to take precautions and protect against the defect. Yet this may be the result where injured parties are forced to comply with the proof requirements of negligence actions or are confronted with the procedural requirements and limitations of warranty actions. Therefore, we adopt the theory of strict liability as expressed in § 402A of the Restatement (Second) of Torts.

For these reasons, we conclude that the third and sixth counts of the complaint state a cause of action under Maryland law. The certified question is answered "Yes."

* * *

NOTES

1. By the time *Phipps* was decided in 1976, the doctrine of strict manufacturer liability in tort had already been adopted by a substantial majority of American jurisdictions. Indeed, the general adoption of the doctrine in this country from 1963 to the mid–1970s is one of the most rapid and dramatic doctrinal developments ever to occur in the law of torts. Within a decade after *Phipps*, all states except Delaware, Massachusetts, Michigan, North Carolina and Virginia had adopted strict products liability in tort. The last adoption was Wyoming, in Ogle v. Caterpillar Tractor Co., 716 P.2d 334 (Wyo. 1986). For citations to adopting cases and statutes, see D. Owen, Products Liability Law § 5.3 (2d ed. 2008).

2. From the start, however, critics complained that (1) the American Law Institute had improperly "restated" a *new* rule of tort law, and (2) the new tort doctrine blatantly intruded into an area that was at the time being expressly addressed by the state legislatures through the warranty provisions of the UCC. See, e.g., Titus, Restatement (Second) of Torts Section 402A and The Uniform Commercial Code, 22 Stan. L. Rev. 713 (1970).

3. Comparison with Other Theories of Liability–In General. Is strict liability in tort in fact any different from warranty, or even from negligence? Consider the answer given by the court in Chestnut v. Ford Motor Co., 445 F.2d 967, 968 (4th Cir.1971): "The standard of safety of goods imposed on the seller or manufacturer of a product is essentially the same whether the theory of liability is labeled warranty or negligence or strict tort liability: the product must not be unreasonably dangerous at the time that it leaves the defendant's possession . . ." Many other courts have agreed. Do you? Has all of the effort to distinguish between the different doctrines been nothing but a tempest in a teapot?

4. Warranty *vs.* Strict Liability in Tort. How, if at all, is strict liability in tort different from warranty?

Denny v. Ford Motor Co.

New York Court of Appeals, 1995.
87 N.Y.2d 248, 639 N.Y.S.2d 250, 662 N.E.2d 730.

■ TITONE, JUDGE.

Are the elements of New York's causes of action for strict products liability and breach of implied warranty always coextensive? If not, can the latter be broader than the former? These are the core issues presented by the questions that the United States Court of Appeals for the Second Circuit has certified to us in this diversity action involving an allegedly defective vehicle. [W]e hold that the causes of action are not identical and that, under the circumstances presented here, it is possible to be liable for breach of implied warranty even though a claim of strict products liability has not been satisfactorily established.

[Plaintiff was injured when she slammed on the brakes of her Ford Bronco II small sport utility vehicle to avoid hitting a deer, and the vehicle rolled over. In an action against Ford, the jury concluded that: (1) the Bronco was not "defective," so that Ford was not liable under strict products liability in tort, but (2) Ford had breached the implied warranty of merchantability and so was liable for plaintiff's injuries. On a certified question, *held*, the claims are not identical and, on the facts, the jury's findings were reconcilable.]

It is [the] negligence-like risk/benefit component of the defect element that differentiates strict-products-liability claims from UCC-based breach-of-implied-warranty claims in cases involving design defects. While the strict products concept of a product that is "not reasonably safe" requires a weighing of the product's dangers against its overall advantages, the UCC's concept of a "defective" product requires an inquiry only into whether the product in question was "fit for the ordinary purposes for which such goods are used" (UCC § 2–314[2][c]). The latter inquiry focuses on the expectations for the performance of the product when used in the customary, usual and reasonably foreseeable manners. The cause of action is one involving true "strict" liability, since recovery may be had upon a showing that the product was not minimally safe for its expected purpose—without regard to the feasibility of alternative designs or the manufacturer's "reasonableness" in marketing it in that unsafe condition.

* * *

[Ford argued at trial] that the design features of which plaintiffs complain, i.e., the Bronco II's high center of gravity, narrow track width, short wheel base and specially tailored suspension system, were important to preserving the vehicles's ability to drive over the highly irregular terrain that typifies off-road travel. Ford's proof in this regard was relevant to the strict-products-liability risk/utility equation, which required the factfinder to determine whether the Bronco II's value as an off-road vehicle outweighed the risk of the rollover accidents that could occur when the vehicle was used for other driving tasks.

On the other hand, plaintiffs' proof focused, in part, on the sale of the Bronco II for suburban driving and everyday road travel [and that it was] unusually susceptible to rollover accidents when used on paved roads. All of this evidence was useful in showing that routine highway and street driving was the "ordinary purpose" for which the Bronco II was sold and that it was not "fit"—or safe—for that purpose.

Thus, under the evidence in this case, a rational factfinder could have simultaneously concluded that the Bronco II's utility as an off-road vehicle outweighed the risk of injury resulting from rollover accidents *and* that the vehicle was not safe for the "ordinary purpose" of daily driving for which it was marketed and sold. Under the law of this State such a set of factual judgments would lead to the concomitant legal conclusion that plaintiffs' strict-products-liability cause of action was not viable but that defendant should nevertheless be held liable for breach of its implied promise that the Bronco II was "merchantable" or "fit" for its "ordinary purpose." Importantly, what makes this case distinctive is that the "ordinary purpose" for which the product was marketed and sold to the plaintiff was not the same as the utility against which the risk was to be weighed. It is these unusual circumstances that give practical significance to the ordinarily theoretical difference between the defect concepts in tort and statutory breach-of-implied warranty....

[Certified questions answered; dissenting opinion of Simons, J., omitted.]

NOTES

1. *Denny* may be alone in this view. Other courts reason that strict liability in tort "is essentially the liability of implied warranty divested of the contract doctrines of privity, disclaimer, and notice." Nave v. Rainbo Tire Service, Inc., 462 N.E.2d 620, 625 (Ill. App. Ct. 1984). "To recover on either theory—implied warranty or strict liability—the plaintiff in a products liability case must satisfy three basics from an evidentiary standpoint: (1) the existence of a defect, (2) the attribution of the defect to the seller, and (3) a causal relation between the defect and the injury." Virgil v. "Kash N' Karry" Service Corp., 484 A.2d 652, 656 (Md. Ct. Spec. App. 1984). See also Larsen v. Pacesetter Systems, Inc., 837 P.2d 1273, 1284–85 (Haw. 1992) ("to bring an action in implied warranty for personal injury a plaintiff is required to show product unmerchantability sufficient to avoid summary judgment on the issue of defectiveness in a tort strict products liability suit").

2. Which is the better view? An early debate included Speidel, The Virginia "Anti–Privity" Statute: Strict Products Liability Under The Uniform Commercial Code, 51 Va. L. Rev. 804, 851 (1965) (warranty is preferable), and Franklin, When Worlds Collide: Liability Theories and Disclaimers in Defective–Product Cases, 18 Stan. L. Rev. 974, 1019–20 (1966) (tort is preferable). Most courts have been little concerned with the argument that strict tort might impermissibly invade a field preempted by the UCC. But see Cline v. Prowler Indus. of Maryland, Inc., 418 A.2d 968, 980 (Del. 1980) ("the General Assembly did not intend to permit the adoption of a competing theory of liability in cases involving the sales of goods and, thus, preempted the field").

3. Negligence *vs.* Strict Liability in Tort. Are you at all uncomfortable with the assertion that the basis of liability in strict tort is essentially the same as that in negligence? Why or why not? While most courts have valiantly attempted over the years to distinguish between negligence and strict liability in tort, many have recognized their similarity, if not identity, in design and warning cases. See, e.g., Jones v. Hutchinson Mfg., Inc., 502 S.W.2d 66, 69–70 (Ky. 1973) (In a design case "the distinction between the so-called strict liability principle and negligence is of no practical significance so far as the standard of conduct required of the defendant is concerned. In either event the standard required is reasonable care."); DiPalma v. Westinghouse Elec. Corp., 938 F.2d 1463 (1st Cir.1991) (warning).

See generally Powers, The Persistence of Fault in Products Liability, 61 Tex. L. Rev. 777, 815 (1983) ("fault is analytically implicit in current products liability law and cannot be purged"); Birnbaum, Unmasking the Test for Design Defect: From Negligence [to Warranty] to Strict Liability to Negligence, 33 Vand. L. Rev. 593, 649 (1980) ("Calling a theory of liability based on a duty of due care and a standard of reasonable conduct anything other than negligence is pure sophistry."); Miller, Design Defect Litigation in Iowa: The Myths of Strict Liability, 40 Drake L. Rev. 465 (1991); Owen, Defectiveness Restated: Exploding the "Strict" Products Liability Myth, 1996 U. Ill. L. Rev. 743 ("It has been an open secret for many years that courts have been purporting to apply 'strict' liability doctrine to design and warnings cases while in fact applying principles that look remarkably like negligence. Quite simply, most courts have been saying one thing while doing quite another—calling a pig a mule.'').

The similarity of strict tort and negligence in certain contexts has given rise to a thorny problem involving inconsistent jury verdicts. Suppose a case is submitted to the jury on both negligence and strict liability in tort and the jury decides for the plaintiff on negligence but for the defendant on strict liability. What is the problem? What should be done? See, e.g., Connelly v. Hyundai Motor Co., 351 F.3d 535 (1st Cir. 2003) (N.H. law) (jury could consistently find that airbag that killed child when it deployed was not defectively designed while finding manufacturer negligent in testing and design); Phillips v. Cricket Lighters, 841 A.2d 1000, 1008–10 (Pa. 2003) (because the elements of the two torts are distinct, it would be ''illogical'' to reject negligence claim solely because of the failure of the claim for strict liability in tort).

Fortunately, this kind of nonsense is rejected by most courts. See, e.g., Higginbotham v. KCS Internat'l, Inc., 85 F. App'x 911, 917 (4th Cir. 2004) (Md. law) (''the elements of proof are the same whether the claim be for strict liability or negligence,'' such that the plaintiffs' failure to establish defect and causation caused all their negligence, breach of warranty, and strict liability claims to fail); Golonka v. General Motors Corp., 65 P.3d 956, 965 (Ariz. App. 2003) (''when a plaintiff's claims for strict liability design and negligent design are factually identical, and the jury employs a risk/benefit analysis to determine that the manufacturer is not at fault for strict liability design, the jury cannot consistently find the product manufacturer at fault for negligent design''). See generally D. Owen, Products Liability Law § 5.9 (2d ed. 2008).

Why *might* a jury find a manufacturer negligent for selling a product *not* in a ''defective condition unreasonably dangerous'' to users? Because of a feeling that even an inadequately designed product, or one carrying inadequate warnings, cannot fairly be considered ''defective'' in the ordinary sense of the word? Cf. Rinker v. Ford Motor Co., 567 S.W.2d 655, 659–60 (Mo. Ct. App. 1978). Because the phrase ''unreasonably dangerous'' may sound to the jury ''as if the requisite proof for a product defect is some form of 'extraordinary' danger.''? Twerski, From Defect to Cause to Comparative Fault—Rethinking Some Product Liability Concepts, 60 Marq. L. Rev. 297, 334 (1977). See generally Blydenburgh, Analyzing Inconsistent Verdicts in Products Liability Cases: How the Law Promotes Them, Why Juries Render Them, and Why Some Courts Permit Them, 73 Def. Couns. J. 46 (2006).

One solution to all this would be to require the plaintiff to elect a single theory upon which to submit the case to the jury, as examined further below. Is this a good idea? Many courts instruct juries on both negligence and strict liability in tort, but some withdraw the negligence count from the jury on grounds that it would be ''superfluous and would tend to confuse the jurors'' if included with a count for strict liability in tort. Mather v. Caterpillar Tractor Corp., 533 P.2d 717, 719 (Ariz. Ct. App. 1975).

4. Abnormally Dangerous Activities. Distinguish the doctrine of strict tort liability for selling defective products (Restatement (Second) of Torts § 402A) from the doctrine of strict tort liability for conducting abnormally dangerous activities (§§ 519–24A). With almost no exceptions, the courts have steadfastly kept these two theories of strict tort liability separate and distinct. See, e.g., Ehlis v. Shire Richwood, Inc., 233 F. Supp. 2d 1189, 1191–93 (D.N.D. 2002) (strict liability for abnormally dangerous or utltrahazardous activity doctrine does not apply to sale of prescription drugs); Merrill v. Navegar, Inc., 89 Cal. Rptr. 2d 146, 190–92 (Ct. App. 1999), superseded on other grounds, 991 P.2d 755 (Cal. 2000) (same: sale of guns);

Copier By and Through Lindsey v. Smith & Wesson Corp., 138 F.3d 833 (10th Cir. 1998) (Utah law) (same); Gaines–Tabb v. ICI Explosives USA, Inc., 995 F. Supp. 1304 (W.D. Okla. 1996) (same: ammonium nitrate, labeled as fertilizer, used as explosive). See generally Cantu, Distinguishing the Concept of Strict Liability for Ultrahazardous Activities from Strict Products Liability under Section 402A of the Restatement (Second) of Torts: Two Parallel Lines of Reasoning that Should Never Meet, 35 Akron L. Rev. 31, 56 (2001) ("the concept of strict liability for ultra-hazardous activities is entirely different from strict liability under Section 402A").

5. Strategy. Many plaintiffs' lawyers generally apply a "shotgun" approach, pleading and trying cases on *all* theories of liability that may be available—typically negligence, breach of implied warranty of merchantability, and strict liability in tort—in order to avoid the risk of omitting the one theory that the court or jury may find appropriate. Other lawyers prefer the "rifle-shot" approach, pleading and trying a case on a single theory—such as negligence or strict liability in tort—in order to keep the issues simpler for a jury which may be confused by the multiple theory approach. Indeed, there is a risk under the shotgun approach that the jury will mistakenly believe that the plaintiff can recover only if he makes his case on *each* separate claim. Another risk of the shotgun approach is that the jury will find that the defendant was negligent, but that the product was not defective, that may lead some courts to strike the former finding as an inconsistent verdict.

Assuming a plaintiff's lawyer takes a case to the jury on a single claim, which should it be, negligence or strict liability? Consider the thoughts of a leading plaintiffs' advocate, Rheingold, The Expanding Liability of the Product Supplier: A Primer, 2 Hofstra L. Rev. 521, 531–32 (1974):

What Difference Does Strict Liability Really Make to the Practitioner?

The advent of strict liability a decade ago was then hailed and still tends to be hailed today as a major change in product liability law. Without question, the "enterprise system" philosophy behind it is a major step forward in the social consciousness of the courts. What strict liability has done in fact for the consumer-plaintiff and his lawyer is another question. In my view, it has accomplished little for the consumer and it has had little impact upon practice.

More plaintiffs would prefer to present their respective cases to a jury on a negligence, rather than on a strict liability, basis. In McLuenesque terms negligence is "hot" and strict liability is "cold." It is easier to prevail by showing that the defendant did something wrong than that there is something technically defective about the product. It is easier to win (and collect substantial damages) by showing that a drug company concealed information about side effects than to show that in fact there was no warning on the labeling about the risks.

If strict liability makes a difference it is in the "impure" defect case. Here it makes counsel's life much easier if he can have the judge instruct the jury that the mere presence of glass in a can of spinach creates liability, than if he has to prove how the defendant carelessly put it in or failed to detect it. But those cases had traditionally been won by plaintiffs—in the rare instance when they weren't settled.

It is sometimes argued that the plaintiff in every type of strict liability case gains a direct benefit by having the defendant barred from proving due care. The trouble with this argument is that the defendant, directly or indirectly, does get this sort of defense before the jury. Not only are many such defenses allowed . . . but also § 402A does not really divorce itself from "negligence talk."

An important empirical study, conducted by a law professor and a psychology professor, confirms these insights. Professors Richard Cupp and Danielle Polage discovered that jurors in fact respond more favorably to plaintiffs—in terms of both the likelihood of success and verdict size—whose claims are based on negligence rather than strict liability. See Cupp & Polage, The Rhetoric of Strict Products Liability Versus Negligence: An Empirical Analysis, 77 N.Y.U. L. Rev. 874 (2002).

6. Privity; Bystanders. One key reason for the development of strict liability in tort was the failure of warranty law to deal adequately with the product accident problem for persons not in privity of contract with the seller of a defective product.

While the existence of any contractual relationship between the parties is irrelevant to liability under subsection (2)(b) of § 402A, and while "users" and "consumers" are defined broadly in comment *l*, the question of whether liability under § 402A extends to "bystanders" (persons who are *not* "users" or "consumers") is expressly left open in caveat (1). See comment *o*. Nevertheless, courts almost unanimously allow recovery for bystanders where injury to them is reasonably foreseeable, reasoning that the policies arguing for user or consumer recovery in strict tort generally apply with equal force to the innocent bystander. See Lunsford v. Saberhagen Holdings, Inc., 106 P.3d 808 (Wash. Ct. App. 2005). Indeed, since the bystander has no choice in the selection of the product (and hence has no control over whether safety or price should be preferred in choosing between products), nor has an opportunity to inspect the product (to "kick the tires") nor to control the manner of its use, it has been argued that he or she deserves if anything even greater protection than the user himself. See Elmore v. American Motors Corp., 451 P.2d 84 (Cal. 1969).

Nor does the extension of strict tort liability to bystanders place any additional burden upon the manufacturer "for the reason that the same precautions required to protect the buyer or user would generally do the same for the bystander." Giberson v. Ford Motor Co., 504 S.W.2d 8 (Mo. 1974) (court permitted strict tort suit by occupants of car involved in pile-up that occurred when engine in police car manufactured by defendant exploded in traffic, creating dense smoke that obscured vision). But the *Palsgraf* doctrine lives on, and the risk to the plaintiff must be reasonably foreseeable. See Kirk v. Michael Reese Hosp. & Med. Center, 513 N.E.2d 387, 394 (Ill. 1987) (passenger injured when driver, who consumed alcohol after taking prescription drugs, lost control of car; *held,* on inadequate warning claim, that manufacturers "[could not] have reasonably foreseen that their drugs would be dispensed without warnings by the physicians, that the patient would be discharged from the hospital, drink alcohol, drive a car, lose control of his car, hit a tree, and injure the passenger [all] on the same day").

Pennsylvania law appears curiously contra, in that § 402A operates only if a product is unsafe for its intended user, *not* for foreseeable victims. Hence, the doctrine does not protect victims of fires started by young children with disposable butane cigarette lighters, not equipped with a childproof design, that are intended only for adults. See Phillips v. Cricket Lighters, 841 A.2d 1000 (Pa. 2003), reaffirmed in Pennsylvania Dep't of Gen. Servs. v. United States Mineral Prods. Co., 898 A.2d 590, 600 (Pa. 2006).

On the extension of strict tort protection to bystanders, see generally Cochran, Dangerous Products and Injured Bystanders, 81 Ky. L.J. 687, 725 (1993) ("The price of dangerous products should include the losses that they cause to bystanders.''); D. Owen, Products Liability Law § 5.3 (2d ed. 2008).

7. Disclaimers. Another key aspect of warranty law that led through warranty and negligence to the development of strict liability in tort was the seller's ability to avoid responsibility by a disclaimer.

A. Negligence. Although there are not many cases, disclaimers in principal are generally effective, but only if they clearly and unequivocally relieve the seller of responsibility for harm caused by his negligence. To most courts this has meant that the word "negligence" or "fault" must appear in the disclaimer provision.

B. Strict tort. Even simpler than the negligence rule is the one applied to strict liability in tort: Manufacturers and other sellers of new products may *not* disclaim strict tort liability for personal injuries caused by defects in their products. See Restatement (Second) of Torts § 402A, comment *m* (a consumer's claim "is not affected by any disclaimer"). See McNichols, Who Says that Strict Tort Disclaimers Can Never Be Effective? The Courts Cannot Agree, 28 Okla. L. Rev. 494 (1975).

Compare Restatement (Third) of Torts: Products Liability § 18: "Disclaimers and limitations of remedies . . . , waivers . . . , and other similar contractual exculpations . . . do not bar or reduce otherwise valid products liability claims against sellers . . . of new products for harm to persons." Most of the difficult problems with disclaimers in strict tort involve their effectiveness in commercial contexts involving economic losses.

8. Variations on a Common Theme. Most courts, like the Maryland court in *Phipps,* have embraced the theory of strict liability in tort by "adopting" § 402A. A few states have been more independent and, while adhering generally to the principles of § 402A and the surrounding jurisprudence, have developed their own strict tort doctrines under other names. One such state is Oklahoma where, in Kirkland v. General Motors Corp., 521 P.2d 1353 (Okla. 1974), the state supreme court adopted an extensively described theory of strict liability in tort, called "Manufacturers' Products Liability." See generally McNichols, The Kirkland v. General Motors Manufacturers' Products Liability Doctrine—What's In a Name?, 27 Okla. L. Rev. 347 (1974). See also Casrell v. Altec Indus., Inc., 335 So. 2d 128 (Ala. 1976), and Atkins v. American Motors Corp., 335 So. 2d 134 (Ala. 1976) ("extended manufacturer's liability," likened to negligence per se). Compare Halphen v. Johns–Manville Sales Corp., 484 So. 2d 110 (La. 1986) (establishing separate classifications of unreasonably dangerous products), superseded in 1988 by the Louisiana Products Liability Act, LSA–R.S. 9:2800.56.

The California Supreme Court, which gave birth to strict liability in tort in *Greenman* in 1963, seemed to adopt § 402A in Pike v. Frank G. Hough Co., 467 P.2d 229 (Cal. 1970), but then repudiated the Restatement formulation of the rule and returned to the *Greenman* approach in Cronin v. J.B.E. Olson Corp., 501 P.2d 1153 (Cal. 1972). Later California developments are explored in subsequent chapters.

Several states have adopted the doctrine by statute. 14 Me. Rev. Stat. Ann. § 221, Or. Rev. Stat. § 30.920, and S.C. Code Ann. §§ 15–73–10 to–30 are nearly verbatim restatements of § 402A. Ark. Code Ann. § 4–86–102, Ga. Code Ann. § 15–1–11 to 11.1 (prescribing action in tort for injuries from unmerchantable products), and Ind. Code §§ 34–20–4–1 all provide variations on the same theme.

Except perhaps for North Carolina, the few other states that have refused to adopt § 402A or a close equivalent, notably Delaware, Massachusetts, Michigan, and Virginia, work nearly similar results through the law of warranty, either statutory or common law. See D. Owen, Products Liability Law § 5.3 (2d ed. 2008).

9.   The literature is replete with discussions of the development and nature of strict liability in tort. Among the classic articles are two by Prosser, The Assault Upon the Citadel (Strict Liability to the Consumer), 69 Yale L.J. 1099 (1960), and The Fall of the Citadel (Strict Liability to the Consumer), 50 Minn. L. Rev. 791 (1966). For Judge Traynor's reflections on the topic, see The Ways and Meanings of Defective Products and Strict Liability, 32 Tenn. L. Rev. 363 (1965). Perhaps the "modern" classic is Dean Wade's article, On the Nature of Strict Tort Liability for Products, 44 Miss. L.J. 825 (1973). See also Cantu, Twenty–Five Years of Strict Product Liability Law: The Transformation and Present Meaning of Section 402A, 25 St. Mary's L.J. 327 (1993). See generally D. Owen, Products Liability Law ch. 5 (2d ed. 2008); 1 D. Owen, M.S. Madden, & M. Davis, Madden & Owen on Products Liability ch. 5 (3d ed. 2000).

2.   Rationales

A.   In General

An understanding of the strengths and weaknesses of the common arguments for strict manufacturer liability is necessary to a reasoned consideration of whether the strict liability principles should be applied in particular contexts. Indeed, a proper resolution of many complex issues of modern products liability law depends upon a clear articulation and evaluation of the competing values and social policies involved. Space constraints preclude extended consideration here of the increasingly rich models of products liability theory developed in recent years based on "justice," "fairness," or economic efficiency. See, e.g., Kysar, The Expectations of Consumers, 103 Colum. L. Rev. 1700, 1790 (2003); Keating, Pressing Precaution Beyond the Point of Cost–Justification, 56 Vand. L. Rev. 653 (2003); Keating, The Theory of Enterprise Liability and Common Law Strict Liability, 54 Vand. L. Rev. 1285 (2001); Hanson and Kysar, Taking Behavioralism Seriously: A Potential Response to Market Manipulation, 6 Roger Williams L. Rev. 259 (2000); Hanson and Kysar, Taking Behavioralism Seriously: Some Evidence of Market Manipulation, 112 Harv. L. Rev. 1420 (1999); Bernstein, How Can a Product be Liable?, 45 Duke L.J. 1 (1995); Croley & Hanson, Rescuing the Revolution: The Revived Case for Enterprise Liability, 91 Mich. L. Rev. 683 (1993); Landes & Posner, A Positive Economic Analysis of Products Liability, 14 J. Legal Stud. 535 (1985); Owen, The Moral Foundations of Products Liability Law: Toward First Principles, 68 Notre Dame L.Rev. 427 (1993); A. Schwartz, Proposals for Products Liability Reform: A Theoretical Synthesis, 97 Yale L.J. 353 (1988).

The materials in this section focus principally upon the traditional policies that widely were thought to support the move toward strict products liability in tort—most particularly, risk spreading and deterrence.

Yet, to truly understand the modern rules and stated policies of products liability law, lawyers need to appreciate that the precepts actually operating behind the rules of law are rooted in more fundamental principles of ethics and political theory. This section thus begins with a brief look at the moral footings of products liability law.

The Moral Foundations of Products Liability Law*

Products liability law lies at the center of the modern world. Whether or not humans have evolved much over the ages as moral creatures, civilization is marching into the twenty-first century in a blaze of advancing technology. To a large extent, persons accomplish their individual and collective objectives, and relate to one another, through the products of science and technology—automobiles, punch presses, tractors, prescription drugs, frozen dinners, tennis rackets, perfumes, greeting cards, and airplanes (civilian and military). Matters concerning the creation and exchange of such products of technology are addressed by the law of property, contracts, and commerce. Products liability law instead concerns the consequences of modern technology gone awry—when products, or the interactions between persons and their products, fail.

But products liability law deals with matters of much greater import than merely the relationship between people and their machines. This rather sterile conception of the subject matter unhappily has dominated the thinking about products liability law since it was "invented" in modern form several decades ago. When a person is injured by a product, the principal question of interest in products liability law is whether the product was too dangerous, according to some standard of product safety. This focus of modern products liability law expressly upon the products—both the one which caused the injury, and some hypothetical one of proper safety—thus tends to direct the liability issue into a barren, technologically-based determination.

Yet the most essential question in any products liability case is not whether certain engineering, production, or informational psychology standards were met or breached. Rather, the relationship between the maker of a product and the victim of a product accident implicates fundamental issues of moral philosophy. By choosing to expose product users and others to certain types and degrees of risk, product makers appropriate to themselves certain interests in safety—in bodily integrity—that may belong to those other persons. Similarly, by choosing to purchase products with certain inherent risks or by choosing to use such products in certain risky ways, and then by choosing to make claim against the maker for harm resulting from such risks or uses, victims of product accidents seek to appropriate to themselves economic interests that may belong to product makers and to other consumers. Both situations involve important ques-

* *From* Owen, The Moral Foundations of Products Liability Law: Toward First Principles, 68 Notre Dame L. Rev. 427, 429–30 (1993).

tions of how persons should treat one another. Ethical theory therefore has much to say as to whether moral responsibility for product accidents lies (in part or in whole) with the maker, the user, or the victim. At bottom, product accidents are moral—not technological—events.

N O T E

In examining the arguments that courts and commentators advanced in the 1960s and 1970s for strict manufacturer liability, formulated in the conventional public policy terms summarized below, consider how these policies draw from more fundamental ethical and political ideals.

––––––

Montgomery & Owen, Reflections on the Theory and Administration of Strict Tort Liability for Defective Products
27 S.C. L. Rev. 803, 809–10 (1976).

(1) Manufacturers convey to the public a general sense of product quality through the use of mass advertising and merchandising practices, causing consumers to rely for their protection upon the skill and expertise of the manufacturing community.

(2) Consumers no longer have the ability to protect themselves adequately from defective products due to the vast number and complexity of products which must be "consumed" in order to function in modern society.

(3) Sellers are often in a better position than consumers to identify the potential product risks, to determine the acceptable levels of such risks, and to confine the risks within those levels.

(4) A majority of product accidents not caused by product abuse are probably attributable to the negligent acts or omissions of manufacturers at some stage of the manufacturing or marketing process, yet the difficulties of discovering and proving this negligence are often practicably insurmountable.

(5) Negligence liability is generally insufficient to induce manufacturers to market adequately safe products.

(6) Sellers almost invariably are in a better position than consumers to absorb or spread the costs of product accidents.

(7) The costs of injuries flowing from typical risks inherent in products can fairly be put upon the enterprises marketing the products as a cost of their doing business, thus assuring that these enterprises will fully "pay their way" in the society from which they derive their profits.

N O T E

Do you agree with each of these rationales for strict liability? Do they in combination make a good case for imposing strict liability on all manufacturers of defective products of all kinds? On some types of manufacturers? On retailers? On sellers of used products? Do the rationales apply with equal force to cases involving inadequate warnings and designs as well as to cases of manufacturing flaws? To cases where the consumer has abused the product?

———

B. THE INSURANCE RATIONALE—"RISK SPREADING"

One of the principal justifications said to support the rule of strict manufacturer liability is to "spread the risk of loss." The next excerpt, by Klemme, summarizes the conventional economic perspective; while the final insurance excerpt, by Rahdert, provides a broad retrospective of the evolving role of the insurance rationale in products liability law.

Risk distribution, through manufacturers of products involved in accidents, may be viewed at bottom as little more than a form of judicially mandated products liability *insurance*. It is "third party" insurance, because a third party (the manufacturer) insures consumers (the first parties) against the risk of (certain types of) product accidents, for which insurance coverage the insureds pay "premiums" to the manufacturer-insurer through incremental increases in product prices. The manufacturer uses the price-premiums to recoup its costs of (1) claims paid (verdicts and settlements), and (2) administration (its own attorneys fees and costs of litigation).

Especially in the 1960s and early 1970s, products liability law was viewed by some as a felicitous instrument of social engineering for bridging the welfare gap, during the forward march of society in an expanding economy, until the time when the state would have adequate social welfare programs take care of the accident compensation problem:

> Until Americans have a comprehensive scheme of social insurance, courts must resolve by a balancing process the head-on collision between the need for adequate recovery and viable enterprises. This balancing task should be approached with a realization that the basic consideration involves a determination of the most just allocation of the risk of loss between the members of the marketing chain.

Helene Curtis Ind., Inc. v. Pruitt, 385 F.2d 841, 862 (5th Cir. 1967), citing Wilson, Products Liability, 43 Calif. L. Rev. 809 (1955).

Even at the start, there were some skeptics. See Plant, Strict Liability of Manufacturers for Injuries Caused by Defects in Products—An Opposing View, 24 Tenn. L. Rev. 938, 946 (1957), arguing that "what is sometimes euphemistically called 'social engineering' . . . frequently turns out to be crass expediency seeking its ends without any particular regard for basic principles." Compare also Markle v. Mulholland's Inc., 509 P.2d 529, 546 (Or. 1973) (Bryson, J., dissenting) (". . . I am not willing to place the court in a position of adopting a law based on a socialistic theory.").

Apart from the soundness of the risk-spreading rationale in terms of *political* theory, are its underlying *empirical* assumptions correct?

Klemme, The Enterprise Liability Theory of Torts

47 Colo. L. Rev. 153, 191–92 n. 107 (1976).

[A]t least today and probably for some time, the courts and legislatures have implicitly recognized that whether a loss was shifted to the defendant or left on the plaintiff, the loss (or a major portion of it) could and would be shifted by the plaintiff or the defendant to other members of the community. Hence the basic "fairness" question is: which group in society ought ultimately to bear the loss—the persons to whom the plaintiff would shift it through his casualty insurance (Blue Cross, employer's sick leave, social security benefits, veteran's benefits, unemployment compensation, welfare programs and the like) or the persons to whom the defendant would shift it through his liability insurance, the market place, or, in some cases, a government subsidy program.

* * *

[T]ext writers have suggested that it is "better" or "fairer" for a loss (tort-like, or otherwise) to be distributed among many people rather than leaving it entirely on the person who sustains it.

* * *

[M]y position as to what is the basic question of fairness in distributing losses ... diverges from those of many text writers and some courts ... on the further assumption that, generally, defendants (actors) are more likely to be carrying liability insurance through which tort losses can be distributed than are accident victims likely to be carrying casualty insurance through which the loss could also be distributed. When Justice Traynor, for example, wrote in *Greenman* ... that it is better to have a loss caused by a defective product distributed via the manufacturer's liability insurance to the members of the public than to leave it on the victim who is "powerless" to protect himself, he could have been thinking either that Mr. Greenman was "powerless" to prevent such losses or that he was "powerless" to provide adequate insurance protection against such losses. My impression of what many text writers and courts have been thinking is the latter, namely, that in most cases involving tort losses, the accident victim is less likely to be covered by casualty or welfare benefits, and therefore it is generally "fairer" to impose liability on actors (who are more likely to be insured) than leave it on victims (who are more likely to be uninsured).

If this is what is considered to be the basic "fairness" justification for distribution of losses under the enterprise liability theory, then a major determinant in establishing liability rules should be: which participants in an enterprise are most likely to be carrying adequate insurance to cover the kind of loss involved, the actors (e.g., manufacturers, wholesalers, and retailers) or victims (e.g., consumers, users, or bystanders)? In short, who is most likely to be able to distribute the loss most widely as well as most efficiently? Probably today in many, if not most, cases the answer to this question, with the exception of losses for pain and suffering, will be that the victim is, through his casualty insurance, employment benefits, and various welfare programs.

NOTES

1. For further, not dissimilar analyses, see Epstein, Products Liability: The Gathering Storm, 1 Regulation 15, 19–20 (Sept./Oct. 1977); Epstein, Products Liability: The Search for the Middle Ground, 56 N.C. L. Rev. 643 (1978); Owen, Rethinking the Policies of Strict Products Liability, 33 Vand. L. Rev. 681, 703–07 (1980). For more recent and further developed spins, see the articles by Epstein, Huber & Priest (and commentary) in 10 Cardozo L. Rev. 2193 et seq. (1989); G. Schwartz, The Ethics and the Economics of Tort Liability Insurance, 75 Cornell L. Rev. 313 (1990).

2. Compare Kalven, Torts: The Quest for Appropriate Standards, 53 Calif. L. Rev. 189, 205–06 (1965) ("The economist would tell us that if we put liability strictly on the manufacturer we are in effect compelling the consumer through increased prices to buy accident insurance for himself."), with Lange, Compensation of Victims—A Pious and Misleading Platitude, 54 Calif. L. Rev. 1559, 1562–63 (1966) ("Whenever it is open to men to decide for themselves upon whom losses should fall, there will be a tendency for them to impose the loss upon the person or persons who can most conveniently insure.").

3. Periodic Insurance Crises. Beginning about 1975, rapidly increasing premiums priced products liability insurance beyond the reach of many small manufacturers and retailers, a condition that recurs from time to time in varying degrees. Is this fact relevant to whether the strict tort principle should be applied to these kinds of defendants? Can manufacturers in fact pass on to consumers the entire cost of products liability insurance? Of products liability judgments?

Who really is paying for what? And who is making the decision?

M. Rahdert, Covering Accident Costs
72, 75–77 (1995).

The Insurance Rationale Coming of Age:
The Era of Product Liability

Until the advent of the post-World War II consumer economy, and the concomitant rise of product liability, reference to insurance considerations in tort cases remained sporadic. Although some commentators during the period prophesied a new trend toward insurance-based tort doctrine, the case law, taken *ensemble*, fails to make a case for broad judicial acceptance of the insurance rationale. Near the end of the war, however, Justice Roger Traynor of the Supreme Court of California ushered in a new generation of judicial tort thinking with his landmark concurrence in *Escola v. Coca Cola Bottling Co.* Traynor took the occasion of an exploding soda bottle case to advance his argument that manufacturers of mass consumer goods should be held strictly liable for injuries caused by defective products. His opinion represents a remarkable departure from the past for many reasons, not the least of which is his explicit advocacy of an insurance rationale.

* * *

[T]he explicit reference to insurance in *Escola* ultimately had an enormous impact on the acceptance of insurance considerations in tort law. The effect was not immediate, since strict tort liability for product defects did not take hold until nearly two decades later. Yet as strict product liability took root and spread during the 1960s and early 1970s, court after court in jurisdiction after jurisdiction turned to Justice Traynor's *Escola* opinion—including its insurance rationale—for support. Thus, by the mid–1970s, most jurisdictions had, in one way or another, incorporated insurance considerations into the set of policy factors to be considered in setting one important group of common-law liability rules. They used the belief that a class of defendants (manufacturers) was better able to spread the costs of accidents than a class of plaintiffs (consumers) as at least a secondary reason for imposing liability. To play upon Judge Benjamin Cardozo's famous metaphor, which William Prosser applied to the advance of strict product liability, the same forces that conquered the "citadel of privity" also tore down the wall of separation between insurance and tort doctrine. The insurance rationale finally had come of age.

* * *

Insurance considerations have figured in numerous product liability developments, including the initial adoption of strict product liability; determination of who qualifies as a "seller" subject to such liability; determination of whether strict product liability applies in cases involving only "economic loss" to the purchaser; extension of product liability to include injuries to individuals other than the ordinary consumer (in particular, the establishment of so-called bystander liability); the determination of what constitutes a product "defect," especially in the area of design defects; determination of what damages are recoverable in product liability; the application of Section 402A's exception from strict liability for sellers of "unavoidably unsafe" products; availability in products cases of defenses, particularly the defense of comparative negligence and the so-called government contractor defense; and the availability, in cases involving failures to warn, of the so-called state-of-the-art defense.

* * *

It would be a mistake, however, to surmise from this catalogue of developments influenced by the insurance rationale that it has always exerted an expansionary, pro-plaintiff effect. Nor would it be accurate to assume that the insurance rationale has overwhelmed other policy considerations in the areas where it has played a role. To the contrary, both within product liability and beyond it, courts have often recognized ways in which insurance considerations support limits on liability. And they have been prepared to let other factors serve as effective counterweights to their desire to achieve effective spreading of accident costs. Moreover, at key points along the way, concurring or dissenting judges have voiced strong reservations about head-long pursuit of risk spreading as a primary function of tort law. They still often counsel against tort rules that would make defendants "insurers" of the safety of their products and services.

Signs of Recent Judicial and Legislative Skepticism

Just as in scholarship, tort practice during the 1980s has been marked by a decline in judicial and legislative enthusiasm for the insurance rationale. To be sure, in cases where courts have adopted expansive liability rules, they have continued the habit developed in the 1960s and 1970s of referring to insurance considerations as one of several factors supporting their decisions. But in many of these cases, dissenting judges have begun to voice the concern that the costs of liability insurance may be getting out of hand. There have also been noteworthy instances where the courts themselves have cut back on liability. And in these instances courts have not infrequently mentioned the escalating cost of liability insurance and the so-called liability insurance crisis as reasons for either containing or limiting liability rules. These developments suggest that courts, like contemporary scholars, have become wary about the dangers of runaway liability.

Skepticism has been even more evident in the legislatures. As a result of a sustained campaign during the 1980s by a coalition of insurers and large corporations, nearly every state legislature has been persuaded to enact at least a few of an array of contemporary measures that insurers, corporations, and others have advocated under the rubric "tort reform." These measures have as their explicit purpose scaling back the monetary burden of tort liability on defendants. It is fair to say, however, that most tort reforms enacted during the 1980s have fiddled at the edges of the tort compensation system, amounting to little more than what one commentator has called a band-aid response. So far at least, most legislatures have resisted pressure to overturn the more expansive liability rules set by courts in the 1960s and 1970s. Instead, they have been content primarily to focus attention on methods for limiting or reducing damages awardable on a finding of tort liability, or on other similar measures designed to reduce the cost of liability, without altering the basic legal structure. Most of the judicial developments mentioned above that depended in part on the insurance rationale have remained intact.

NOTE

For economic analyses of the insurance rationale and products liability reform, see Hanson & Logue, The First–Party Insurance Externality: An Economic Justification for Enterprise Liability, 76 Cornell L. Rev. 129 (1990); Geistfeld, The Political Economy and Neocontractual Proposals for Products Liability Reform, 72 Tex. L. Rev. 803 (1994).

C. THE DETERRENCE RATIONALE—ACCIDENT PREVENTION

First National Bank v. Nor–Am Agricultural Products, Inc.

Court of Appeals of New Mexico, 1975.
88 N.M. 74, 537 P.2d 682.

■ SUTIN, JUDGE.

[Mr. Huckleby fed his hogs grain that unknown to him had been treated with Panogen–15, a seed disinfectant manufactured by the defendant. The disinfectant contained mercury. The Huckleby family ate one of the hogs that had eaten the treated grain, and the children suffered blindness and paralysis from mercury poisoning. In an action against the manufacturer for failure adequately to warn of the danger, the trial court granted the defendant's motion for summary judgment on the claim based on strict liability in tort.]

(1) Public interest in human life, health and safety requires that the law give consumers maximum protection against dangerous product defects.

* * *

(3) The marketing of dangerously defective products can have tragic consequences. Allowing injured plaintiffs to proceed on a theory of a manufacturer's liability, without the necessity of proving negligence, will cause manufacturers to take cautionary steps to prevent the marketing of dangerously defective products. Such preventive measures may avert tragedies such as befell the Huckleby family, and thereby save our system the cost of lawsuits such as this one.

> Where a defendant's product is adjudged by a jury to be dangerously defective, imposition of liability on the manufacturer will cause him to take some steps (or at least make calculations) to improve his product.... We suspect that, in the final analysis, the imposition of liability has a beneficial effect on manufacturers of defective products both in the care they take and in the warning they give.

Phillips v. Kimwood Machine [Co., 525 P.2d 1033, 1041–42 (Or. 1974)].

[Held, summary judgment for defendant on § 402A reversed.]

NOTES

1. Compare Larsen v. Pacesetter Sys., Inc., 837 P.2d 1273, 1287 (Haw. 1992) ("imposing liability on Pacesetter will promote product safety by encouraging manufacturers to anticipate and test for foreseeable defects likely to cause severe injury"). See generally: Arlen, Compensation Systems and Efficient Deterrence, 52 Md. L. Rev. 1093 (1993); Tietz, Strict Products Liability, Design Defects and Corporate Decision–Making: Greater Deterrence Through Stricter Process, 38 Vill. L. Rev. 1361 (1993); Hanson & Logue, The First Party Insurance Externality: An Economic Justification for Enterprise Liability, 76 Cornell L. Rev. 129, 190 (1990) ("an absolute enterprise liability regime is the most efficient"); G. Schwartz, Reality in the Economic Analysis of Tort Law: Does Tort Law Really Deter?, 42 UCLA L. Rev. 377 (1994).

2. Will raising the level of a manufacturer's legal responsibility from "reasonable" care to "strict" accountability in fact increase the manufacturer's care in making and selling its products? Is there any practical distinction between "reasonable" care and "super" care? Some economists argue that the level of safety will not be increased by a strict liability rule: "It is tempting to conclude that strict liability encourages higher, and in the long run more efficient, levels of safety, but this is incorrect. Rather than creating an incentive to engage in research on safety, a rule of strict liability merely shifts that incentive [to consumers]." Posner, Strict Liability: A Comment, 2 J. Legal Stud. 205, 209 (1973). He concludes: "The question whether a general substitution of strict for negligence liability would improve efficiency seems at this stage hopelessly conjectural; the question is at bottom empirical and the empirical work has not been done." Id. at 211–12. See also Sachs, Negligence or Strict Product Liability: Is There Really a Difference in Law or Economics?, 8 Ga. J. Int'l & Comp. L. 259 (1978); Gilles, Negligence, Strict Liability, and the Cheapest Cost–Avoider, 78 Va. L. Rev. 1291 (1992) (arguing the economic formulations of negligence and strict liability are closely "nested").

3. Is Deterrence Relevant? Defense lawyers argue that the standard of legal "defectiveness" (at least in design cases) is too *vague* to be a meaningful deterrent and so instead is often simply ignored. See Raleigh, The "State of the Art" in Product Liability: A New Look at an Old "Defense," 4 Ohio N.U. L. Rev. 249, 250–52 (1977), for a valuable perspective on the dissatisfaction of General Motors' chief products liability lawyer with the prevailing rules of products liability. Others have argued that manufacturers are generally as careful as reasonably possible anyway, regardless of the theory of liability, in order to safeguard their valuable reputations. See Plant, Strict Liability of Manufacturers for Injuries Caused by Defects in Products—An Opposing View, 24 Tenn. L. Rev. 938 (1957). Cf. Sugarman, Doing Away with Tort Law, 73 Calif. L. Rev. 555, 566 (1985) (citing Rand study by Eads & Reuter which found that some manufacturers treat specific case outcomes as "random noise"). For an economic critique of the deterrence rationale, see Williams, Second Best: The Soft Underbelly of Deterrence Theory in Tort, 106 Harv. L. Rev. 932 (1993).

4. It appears quite clear that the increasing impact of products liability has caused many manufacturers to devote more attention, personnel, and money to product safety, and that products today are in general safer as a result. See Final Report, Interagency Task Force on Product Liability VI–47 (1977); N. Weber, Product Liability: The Corporate Response (Conf. Bd.1987); The Benefits of the Modernization of the Tort Law in the Context of the Social Movement for Improved Safety and Quality in the National Economy (Cons. Fed. of Amer. Sept.1987).

5. "Overdeterrence." What of the problem of *too much* deterrence—of discouraging manufacturers from developing and selling inherently dangerous but socially beneficial products, such as football helmets, IUDs, and many prescription drugs. See generally Huber, Safety and the Second Best: The Hazards of Public Risk Management in the Courts, 85 Colum. L. Rev. 277 (1985). But see Comment, 55 U. Chi. L. Rev. 943 (1988) (AIDS vaccine producers *not* overdeterred by strict liability).

6. Damages. Forgotten now by most courts and commentators was the conjunctive link, in early products liability theorizing by tort law scholars, between the expansion of a manufacturer's liability and a commensurate reduction of tort law *damages*. In 1955, Fleming James urged the adoption of "a rational scheme of strict liability for injurious products." James, Products Liability (pt. 2), 34 Tex. L. Rev. 192, 228 (1959). Yet such an enterprise liability scheme would have to be funded, which in James' view meant that victims might have to surrender their common-law right to damages for pain and suffering which he considered predicated on a defendant having been a true "wrongdoer." James, Damages in Accident Cases, 41 Cornell L.Q. 582, 583 (1956). Further, a rational enterprise liability scheme might require victims to surrender compensation even for some of their *pecuniary* losses, because "accidents bring a net pecuniary loss to society ... so that if the victim is made entirely whole, he will fare better than society and will not himself share the economic burden he is asking society to distribute." Id. at 584. The idea of limiting pain and suffering damages was shared by other scholars of the day, including such notables as Albert Ehrenzweig, Louis Jaffe, Leon Green, Marcus Plant, Clarence Morris, and Roger Traynor. See also Prosser, Assault on the Citadel (Strict Liability to the Consumer), 69 Yale L.J. 1099, 1121 (1960). See generally V. Nolan and E. Ursin, Understanding Enterprise Liability ch. 15 (1995).

7. Aggregating Liability Theories—Toward a Unified Products Liability Cause of Action. This section of the book has examined the array of different theories of liability that may be separately applicable to the problem of a consumer suffering a single injury caused by a single product defect. "The resulting complexity of litigation strongly suggests that development of a single theory of recovery for a particular kind of loss would promote a more efficient and just administration of products liability claims." W. P. Keeton, Annual Survey of Texas Law: Torts, 32 Sw. L.J. 1, 2 (1977). The Model Uniform Product Liability Act adopted this position in §§ 102(D) and 103(A), and some products liability reform statutes, as in Louisiana and New Jersey, provide for a single products liability claim that supplants independent theories such as negligence, the implied warranty of merchantability, and strict liability in tort. The Restatement (Third) of Torts: Products Liability § 2 comment *n* favors this kind of unified approach and provides that "two or more factually identical defective-design [or] failure-to-warn claims ... should not be submitted to the trier of fact in the same case under different doctrinal labels."

Do you favor unifying products liability claims in this manner? Do you suppose that courts in the years ahead will turn increasingly toward a single, unified theory of recovery in design and warnings cases? Should manufacturing defect cases be treated the same or differently?

8. Disaggregating Defectiveness—Toward Separate Liability Tests by Type of Defect. A somewhat converse problem, to be kept in mind in the next chapter, is whether "defectiveness," which developed generally as a single issue under whatever theory of liability, should be pulled apart into its three separate components—defects in manufacture, designs and warnings. Should different standards (or theories) of liability be applied to different types of defects? Specifically, should truly "strict" liability be applied only to manufacturing defects, and only negligence liability to defective designs and warnings? This basic approach received early support from some commentators, see, e.g., Henderson, Manufacturers' Liability for Defective Product Design: A Proposed Statutory Reform, 56 N.C. L. Rev. 625 (1978), and it finds support in moral theory, as seen below. The Interagency Task Force on Product Liability adopted this approach, in § 102(D) of The Model Uniform Product Liability Law, which provided for a single "product liability claim" in lieu of separate claims in negligence, warranty and strict tort. The basis for § 102(D) was the Task Force's earlier report, in which it concluded:

> When the product is not made in accord with the manufacturer's own specifications (a defect in construction) and this causes an injury, manufacturers should be strictly liable. On the other hand, when the defect is one of design or failure to warn, it may not be sound to subject a manufacturer to liability unless considerations such as the foreseeability of harm and the

seriousness of harm are balanced against the utility of the product and the burden on the manufacturers to avoid the risk. In sum, open-ended "strict liability" under the *tort system* in these areas does not appear to be sound long-range policy.

Final Report at VII–19 to 20 (1977). See also "The Basic Standard of Responsibility in Product Liability Cases: A Crisis of Confusion," Interagency Task Force on Product Liability, 4 Legal Study Final Report 86–94 (1977) (calling for a "return to negligence" in design and warnings cases).

As will be seen in the chapters that follow, most courts, many state legislatures, and the Products Liability Restatement have all been moving closer and closer toward the position recommended by the Task Force many years ago.

9. Were Judge Traynor, Professor James, and Dean Prosser simply wrong?

*

PART II

The Concept of Defectiveness

[T]he word "defect" has no clear legal meaning.

Denny v. Ford Motor Co., 662 N.E.2d 730, 740 (N.Y. 1995) (Simons, J., dissenting).

———

Part I considered various causes of action that may be available to a plaintiff injured by a defective product. Part II examines the principles and proofs courts use to determine whether particular injury-producing products should be classified as "defective." A central notion pervading many cases is that, ordinarily, perfect safety is not only technologically impossible but also costs too much in both dollars and product usefulness. See G. Calabresi, The Costs of Accidents 17–18 (1970). Reflecting this position, courts routinely assert that manufacturers are not insurers of their products' safety, and that manufacturers do not have a duty to make and sell only the safest possible products. Since absolute safety thus is not to be the rule, at least not in design and (to a lesser extent) warning cases, the safety issue resolves to a question of appropriate *balance*—of judging the soundness of a manufacturer's trade-offs between safety, usefulness, feasibility, and cost. In short, the question of "defectiveness" becomes, "How safe is safe enough?"

Early courts and commentators, generally conceptualizing product defectiveness as a unitary notion, failed to focus on differences in the forms of defect. In *Greenman*, Judge Traynor in 1963 spoke obliquely of evidence of the "defective design and construction" of the Shopsmith lathe, and that the set screws were "inadequate" to hold the machine together. Even by 1972, the California Supreme Court in *Cronin* saw little need to differentiate among defects: "Although it is easier to see the 'defect' in a single imperfectly fashioned product than in an entire line badly conceived, a distinction between manufacture and design defects is not tenable." But as courts continued to address the multiplicity of issues in the distinct contexts of failures in (1) manufacture, (2) design, and (3) warnings, analysis of the separate issues began to segregate and cluster according to the separate defect types. As one judge noted:

> The definition of "in a defective condition unreasonably dangerous to the user or consumer" ... takes on somewhat different meanings depending on the context of the products liability cause of action, *i.e.*, whether the

cause of action is premised on an alleged defect in the product's design, or in the product's manufacture (the design was not followed in the production phase), or in the product's warning concerning its known dangers.

Toner v. Lederle Labs., 732 P.2d 297, 316 (Idaho 1987).

The Restatement (3d) of Torts: Products Liability in § 2 separately defines each of the three types of defects in "functional" rather than doctrinal terms, as explored in the chapters on the separate types of defects, beginning here. Whereas the Third Restatement's definition of a manufacturing defect is noncontroversial, its definitions of design and warning defects are novel and controversial in a number of ways, a situation that guarantees ferment in the courts for years to come.

A central question is whether courts and legislatures should continue to try to apply truly "strict" liability to design and warning cases, as they continue to do in manufacturing defect cases, or whether they should return to principles more akin to negligence in the former contexts. As will be seen, an increasing majority of jurisdictions have chosen to disaggregate "defectiveness" by providing separate tests for the three types of defect. What this ultimately means is that the conventional theories of liability, developed over the centuries and examined in the last several chapters, may eventually fall by the wayside as unnecessary impediments to a rational determination of the fundamental issues that underlie liability in the different defect contexts. The Iowa Supreme Court, at least, has taken this approach:

> We question the need for or usefulness of *any* traditional doctrinal label in design defect cases because, as comment *n* points out, a court should not submit both a negligence claim and a strict liability claim based on the same design defect since both claims rest on an identical risk-utility evaluation. Moreover, to persist in using two names for the same claim only continues the dysfunction engendered by section 402A. Therefore, we prefer to label a claim based on a defective product design as a design defect claim without reference to strict liability or negligence.

Wright v. Brooke Group Ltd., 652 N.W.2d 159, 169 (Iowa 2002). Many products liability statutes also provide separate standards of liability based on defect type. See, e.g., Ind. Code § 34–20–2–2 (retaining strict liability for manufacturing defects but returning to negligence in design and warning cases); La. Rev. Stat. Ann. §§ 2800.55–57; Miss. Code Ann. § 11–1–63; Ohio Rev. Code Ann. §§ 2307.74–76; Wash. Rev. Code Ann. § 7.72.030. Even if courts continue to ground liability in negligence, strict liability in tort, warranty, or tortious misrepresentation, as most courts in the foreseeable future surely will do, liability under the conventional theories of liability often turns on the particular type of defect at issue in the case.

CHAPTER 6

Manufacturing Defects

A manufacturer may breach its duty to produce and sell products free of *manufacturing* defects in two principal ways. First, the manufacturer may construct the product with raw materials or components that contain physical flaws. For example, the steel used to make a surgical implement or the milk used to make a cake may contain contaminants, or a battery General Motors obtains from a battery manufacturer and installs in a car may contain a leak. Second, although a product's components individually may be free of flaws, the manufacturer may make an error in assembling the components into the final product. For example, an automotive assembly line manager may adjust a die on a punch press improperly so that the press stamps out some number of ashtrays inaccurately, leaving sharp burrs on the edges of the ashtrays, or a battery installer may crush an electrical cable under the battery while installing it in a car. When the manufacturing process goes awry in either manner—when a product contains a defective component or when the components are improperly combined into the final product—the product fails to meet even the manufacturer's own design specification standards. If such a product escapes the manufacturer's quality controls, its flawed condition may lead to its failure, to an accident, and possibly to the injury of the user or another.

When a physically flawed product involved in an accident does end up on trial, its "defectiveness" usually is not contested in any theoretical sense. More typically, since the product may well have been damaged or destroyed in the accident, the crucial issue often is whether the flaw is shown to have resulted from a manufacturing error or from some other cause—such as normal wear and tear; abuse by the user; a mistake by a repair mechanic; or perhaps from the force of the accident itself.

1. Defect Tests

Magnuson v. Kelsey–Hayes Co.

Court of Appeals of Missouri, 1992.
844 S.W.2d 448.

■ Breckenridge, J.

[A wheel and tire broke loose from a pick-up truck and struck and severely injured the plaintiff, 4–year–old Eric Magnuson. Plaintiff sued the manufacturer of the wheel, Kelsey–Hayes, and Chrysler, the manufacturer of the truck. The trial court dismissed Chrysler, and plaintiff proceeded to trial against Kelsey–Hayes on theories of negligence and strict liability, claiming that the wheel was defectively manufactured, abandoning his earlier design defect claim. After the jury rendered a plaintiff's verdict for $4.75 million, the court granted Kelsey–Hayes' motion for a new trial on the ground that it had erred in dismissing Chrysler from the lawsuit. Plaintiff and Chrysler appeal.]

Dr. Robert Bohl, Eric Magnuson's expert metallurgist, testified that the steel forming the wheel had a defective microstructure and that had Kelsey–Hayes microscopically examined the microstructure of the steel, it could have detected the flaw. Dr. Bohl concluded that the design of the wheel was reasonable and that failure was only apt to occur in the case of poor metallurgical structure. He testified that the defective microstructure was related to cooling the steel too slowly during the rolling of the steel [and] that the steel was improperly thinned during the manufacturing process.

* * *

In the instant case Magnuson has made a submissible case on the strict liability theory, demonstrating through the testimony of Dr. Bohl that the wheel was defectively manufactured. Dr. Bohl testified that the steel used in manufacturing the wheel contained carbide films, making the steel brittle, subject to fracture and thereby dangerous. He also testified that the steel was formed too thin, some 30% thinner than original steel blank. Dr. Bohl's testimony makes a submissible case for the jury ... that the steel forming the wheel was dangerously defective and that the wheel contained the defect when [defendants] introduced it into commerce.

[Defendants rely on various cases] for the proposition that in order to make a submissible case as to a manufacturing defect, the plaintiff must establish that the product does not conform to design specifications [citing this court's prior statement that in manufacturing defect cases] "the jury can rather easily determine whether a single product conforms to the intended design." ... This observation does not mandate that a showing of non-conformity to design be made in a strict liability manufacturing defect case. It is illustrative of one form of proof which may be presented, contrasting that to the lack of external standards in design cases.

... Missouri does not require such proof as a threshold of submissibility. The Missouri Supreme Court adopted [§ 402A which] is the standard applied in strict liability cases. Magnuson made a submissible case showing that the [defendants] manufactured the wheel; it was in a defective condition unreasonably dangerous when put to a reasonably anticipated use; was in fact used in such a manner; and that his injuries are a direct result of such defect as existed when the wheel was sold.

[Reversed and remanded for entry of judgment for plaintiff against Kelsey–Hayes.]

NOTES

1. Departure from Specifications. Like *Magnuson*, probably most courts have not yet articulated a separate test specifically applicable to manufacturing defect cases. Some have, however, and the deviation-from-design-specifications test urged on the *Magnuson* court is the well-accepted test. See, e.g., Cooper Tire & Rubber Co. v. Mendez, 204 S.W.3d 797, 800 (Tex. 2006) (manufacturing defect established " 'when a product deviates, in its construction or quality, from the specifications or planned output in a manner that renders it unreasonably dangerous' "); Donegal Mut. Ins. v. White Consol. Indus., 852 N.E.2d 215, 226 (Ohio Ct. App. 2006) ("A product is defective in manufacture or construction if, when it leaves the control of its manufacturer, it deviates in a material way from the design specifications, formula, or performance standards of the manufacturer, or from otherwise identical units manufactured to the same design specifications, formula, or performance standards. R.C. 2307.74."); Johnson v. Black & Decker (U.S.), Inc., 408 F.Supp.2d 353, 357 (E.D. Mich. 2005) (proof "that the allegedly defective product did not conform to the manufacturer's own product standards"); Morson v. Superior Court, 109 Cal. Rptr. 2d 343, 351 (Ct. App. 2001) (quoting Products Liability Restatement § 2). Some states (including La., Miss., N.J., Ohio, & Wash.) have adopted this definition by statute.

2. One decision that applies a departure-from-design-specifications standard is McKenzie v. S K Hand Tool Corp., 650 N.E.2d 612 (Ill. App.1995). Plaintiff sued the manufacturer of a ¾–inch ratchet wrench, the parts of which were held together by a snap ring, for injuries sustained when the wrench came apart and he fell upon the floor. Plaintiff's expert theorized that the snap ring had failed because of defective manufacture respecting both the (1) hardness, and (2) diameter of the ring:

> Defendant has blueprints that contain the specifications of the sizes of each component of the wrench. The components are to comply with these specifications, which have a tolerance for each measurement. The part is acceptable if its actual measurement fits within the tolerance limits. For each part there are figures that represent its upper and lower limits. If the measurement of the part does not fall between the upper and lower limits, the machinist knows the part is not acceptable for use.

* * *

> When measured in various places, the hardness of the ring ranged from 45 to 51 on a Rockwell C scale. Defendant's specifications require a measurement of 48 to 52 on the Rockwell C scale. The outside diameter of the snap ring groove in the handle measured 2.3130 to 2.3125. The specifications required 2.290 inches, with a tolerance of .005 inches, so a measurement between 2.285 to 2.295 inches would be acceptable. Therefore, the outside diameter of the snap ring groove in the handle is larger than the diameter required in the specifications.

Held, evidence sufficient to prove defective manufacture.

3. The Products Liability Restatement. Section 2(a) of the Third Restatement provides that a product "contains a manufacturing defect when the product departs from its intended design even though all possible care was exercised in the preparation and marketing of the product."

4. The Basis of Liability. Under a departure-from-design standard, it is clear that liability is not based on fault but is truly strict. In terms of fairness or policy, should manufacturers be liable for injuries resulting from manufacturing defects in their products if they in fact exercised all due care? After all, perfect quality control is often impossible, and the cost of improving the search for manufacturing flaws at some point becomes prohibitive. Do consumers want to pay higher prices for more products liability quality control "insurance" than is reasonable in the circumstances? If not, should the defendant in a manufacturing flaw case be permitted to demonstrate that the costs of improving quality control procedures sufficiently to have prevented the plaintiff's injuries would have exceeded the resulting benefits? See Brown v. General Foods Corp., 573 P.2d 930 (Ariz. App. 1978). Why or why not? See Products Liability Restatement § 2 cmt. *a*, summarizing the rationales for imposing strict manufacturer responsibility in this context.

The Morality of Strict Liability for Production Flaws*

The very essence of an ordinary exchange transaction involving a new product is the notion that the buyer is paying appropriate value for a certain *type* of "good" comprised of various utility and safety characteristics common to each unit of that type produced by the maker according to a single design. Both the maker and the buyer contemplate (and hence contract for) an exchange of a standard, uniform monetary value for a standard, uniform package of utility and safety. At some level of abstract awareness, most consumers know of course that manufacturers sometimes make mistakes and that the cost of perfect production for many types of products would be exorbitant. However, while consumers may abstractly comprehend the practical necessity of allowing imperfect production, their actual expectation when purchasing a new product is that its important attributes will match those of other similar units. When a purchaser pays full value for a product that appears to be the same as every other, only to receive a product with a dangerous hidden flaw, the product's price and appearance both generate in the buyer false expectations of safety which denies his right to truth.

Manufacturers are accountable for injuries resulting from production flaws, regardless of the maker's efforts or even power to prevent such errors. The manufacturer ordinarily has virtually exclusive power to prevent errors in the manufacturing process. From this enormous imbalance of power springs the demand, from equality, that makers bear responsibility for the consequences of production defects. This is so because the maker, as a legislator, is duty-bound to treat potential victims with equal respect to consumers generally and to shareholders. A consumer injured by a production defect is subjected to a vast disparity in both risk (once the consumer purchases the product) and result from consumers generally. This inequality is unfair and should be rectified because the victim paid an equal price for what was sold as and appeared to be a product of equal quality to those supplied to other consumers. Moreover, since the price charged by the maker and paid by the victim was for a product that was "good," but was

* *From*, Owen, The Moral Foundations of Products Liability Law: Toward First Princi-   ples, 68 Notre Dame L. Rev. 427, 467–74 (1993).

really bad, restitutionary notions behind equality compel the maker to absorb the victim's losses and to transfer them to its shareholders.

2. Proof—Generally

Pouncey v. Ford Motor Co.

United States Court of Appeals, Fifth Circuit, 1972.
464 F.2d 957.

■ Lewis R. Morgan, Circuit Judge.

C.L. Pouncey, the appellee, was injured while putting antifreeze in his 1966 Ford automobile. While he was accelerating the engine with the hood open, a blade broke off the radiator fan, cut through the water hose, and struck him in the face causing permanent facial disfigurement. Pouncey had purchased the car secondhand approximately six months before the accident from Clement Motor Company of Greenville, Alabama. The car had been driven approximately 62,000 miles at the time of the accident.

Pouncey brought this action below against Ford Motor Company, the appellant, seeking damages for the injury on a [negligence] theory. The case was tried to a jury which returned a verdict in favor of Pouncey in the amount of $15,000.00. Ford now appeals. . . .

As is frequently the case in products liability litigation, the trial produced a conflict in expert testimony. The main thrust of Pouncey's case was that the fan blade failure occurred because of a fatigue fracture in the metal fan blade. It was Pouncey's theory that the premature fatigue failure was caused by an excessive number of inclusions in the metal of the blade. An inclusion is a non-metallic impurity in the steel which weakens the metal.

To substantiate this theory, Pouncey called Dr. C.H.T. Wilkins, a metallurgical engineer, as an expert witness. Dr. Wilkins testified that he cut and mounted a specimen of metal from the failed blade. He also cut and mounted specimens from a blade which had not failed and from another Ford fan blade which had failed. On microscopic examination of this mount, Dr. Wilkins found a "surprising number of inclusions" which he did not expect to find in this type steel. These inclusions, he testified, were an identifiable defect in the metal which served as "stress concentrating areas" and "lowered the endurance limit of the fan."

Dr. Wilkins also testified concerning certain bends and deformations in the blade. He conceded that there appeared to be some bends in the blades but he expressed the opinion that the blade which actually failed was not bent. In his opinion, the bends in the blades were not the cause of the fatigue failure.

Not surprisingly, Ford's expert witnesses took a different view of the facts. Ford first called Dr. Robert Hochman, another metallurgical engineer. Dr. Hochman testified that he received and examined the metal specimen that had been mounted by Dr. Wilkins. It was his opinion that the specimen had been mounted in such a way that acid seeped into the cracks between the specimens of metal, causing an exaggerated appearance of large inclusions[.] Dr. Hochman remounted and polished the specimens and took photomicrographs of them. These photomicrographs showed an acceptable inclusion level, testified Dr. Hochman, which conformed with standards established by the Society of Automotive Engineers.

Dr. Hochman attributed the fracture to a different source. He testified that one arm of the blade was bent and that this would have a major effect in throwing the fan out of balance. He also noted that the ends of the blades were bent and cracked and that this condition would also tend to imbalance the fan. An out-of-balance condition, Dr. Hochman testified, could cause the blade to vibrate and set up a high stress pattern which would result in the acceleration of metal fatigue. Dr. Hochman also noted a small notch in the fracture surface which could have been attributed to impact damage.

Ford also called two other expert witnesses, both of whom were Ford employees. Mr. Phillip Burch, a Ford design engineer, testified as to the testing procedures utilized by Ford on newly designed radiator fans. Mr. Robert Riding, another Ford engineer, testified concerning alleged bends in the fan blades. He stated in his opinion that the fan failed because of an unbalanced condition in the fan which may have been caused by a front end collision or by rough handling.

* * *

Initially, Ford argues that the evidence was insufficient because Pouncey's expert testimony, viewed in its best light, does not make any one cause of the blade separation more probable than another. Ford places special emphasis on one portion of the record in which it is said that Dr. Wilkins declined to state that the level of inclusions which he found in the metal was unacceptable. The testimony in question is as follows:

"Q. From what you yourself saw, Doctor, of the inclusions that were in this radiator fan, Exhibit No. 1, that struck Mr. Pouncey, was that an acceptable level of inclusion in that material?

"A. In the sense that I found the number of inclusions that I did, sir, I was very much surprised.

"Q. You were surprised when you saw all that in there?

"MR. MATTHEWS: If the Court please, we move to exclude that answer. That is not what was asked. He said he was surprised. The question was whether it was accept—

"MR. MANCUSO: Why—

"THE COURT: Excuse me. Wait just a minute.

"MR. MATTHEWS: Whether it was an acceptable level of inclusion.

"THE COURT: I think it is appropriate if you can see if you can answer that question, whether it was an acceptable level of inclusion. Can you give an answer to it?

"A. No, sir. Because I do not know what they consider an acceptable level."

It is further contended that Dr. Wilkins' testimony as to the cause of the separation was speculative. Ford asserts that Dr. Wilkins merely stated that the inclusions "could" have caused the fatigue fracture and that he acknowledged that it might have been caused by imbalance of the blades or by other factors such as sludge build-up.

However, a careful reading of Dr. Wilkins' testimony in its entirety requires that we reject Ford's contentions. His testimony went far beyond mere speculation in pinpointing the cause of the fracture. He stated unequivocally that "enormous" inclusions not normally found in spring steel were an "identifiable defect" in the metal which caused premature fatigue failure.[1] Ford's assertion that Dr. Wilkins refused to state that the

---

1. A sampling of Dr. Wilkins' testimony is as follows:

"Q. Is it true the presence of these substances, these foreign substances in metal premature, shorten the life of the metal?

"A. Yes, sir, it can.

"Q. Were these inclusions present and were they an identifiable defect in this particular radiator fan that has been marked as Exhibit No. 1 at the time the thing was installed on the automobile?

"A. Yes, sir.

* * *

"Q. But they [inclusions] were present in the metal?

"A. Yes, sir. And should have been seen at an earlier time.

"Q. Could they have been seen at an earlier time?

"A. Yes, sir.

"Q. If Ford, Dr. Wilkins, had the proper quality control tests run on that metal, would they have discovered that?

"MR. MATTHEWS: Objection to the question, leads to conclusions on the jury.

"THE COURT: I will sustain.

"Q. Dr. Wilkins, with steel which is as you have testified, as dirty as what you saw, could they have reasonably expected this blade to have failed?

"MR. MATTHEWS: Objection to the form of the question.

"THE COURT: Overrule.

"A. Yes, sir.

"Q. All right. Now, Doctor, is it true that the presence of these inclusions would lower the endurance limit of this metal from what it would have been had not the inclusions been present in the metal?

"A. Yes, sir.

"Q. Now does this mean that the blade would break prematurely, and by prematurely I'm referring to what you would normally expect the length of the life of the blade to be?

"MR. MATTHEWS: Objection.

"THE COURT: Overruled.

"A. Yes, sir.

"Q. It would break prematurely with these type—

"A. With respect to what might be considered normal life.

"Q. Now, Doctor, is it true that the presence of these inclusions or these foreign substances or dirty matters, however you want to refer to it, would shorten the fatigue life of the metal in this particular Exhibit No. 1 that we are talking about from what you would expect it to be if it didn't have this matter in it?

"A. Yes, sir. * * *

"Q. Did these inclusions constitute a stress concentrating area?

"A. Yes, sir.

"Q. All right. What are we referring to there?

level of inclusions which he found was "unacceptable" is unfounded. That refusal was merely based on his hesitancy to ascribe the label "unacceptable" to the level of inclusions which he found while not knowing how his questioner defined the term. [Dr. Wilkins] declined to answer the question "[b]ecause I do not know what they consider an acceptable level."

* * *

Ford also contends that the evidence was insufficient to support an inference of negligence either on the part of Ford or Ford's supplier, Fram Corporation. Ford contends that the testimony is undisputed that even under the best quality control program there is always the possibility that isolated pockets of inclusions could be found in metal and that there is no practical means of discovering the particular fans which might have these impurities. Ford argues that [Pouncey's failure to prove] inadequate quality control procedures on the part of Ford or its supplier bars submission of the issue of Ford's negligence to the jury. Again we disagree.

* * *

. . . Under Alabama law, it is settled that a manufacturer's liability for defective product is predicated upon negligence in the manufacture or design of the product. [Citation.] However, the Alabama courts have freely permitted juries to infer manufacturer negligence from circumstantial evidence where there is in the record direct evidence of an actual defect in the product. For example, in Greyhound Corporation v. Brown, 113 So. 2d 916 (Ala. 1959), the plaintiff had been injured while riding in a bus when a tire manufactured by the defendant blew out. In an action against the manufacturer, the plaintiff produced expert testimony that the blowout was due to a defect in the tire, but there was apparently no evidence as to the quality control procedures employed by the manufacturer. The court per-

"A. When you apply a bending stress to a metal, and if an inclusion is located in a highly stressed area, particularly if it is in near the edge, which of course would be highly stressed, then you can have the stress itself concentrated in that particular area. And eventually have this develop into possibly a notch, which could lead into a fracture.

"Q. Doctor, if everything you have testified to, does it have a bearing on what actually happened in this blade that struck Mr. Pouncey?

"A. Yes, sir.

"Q. Now, Doctor, is it true, with regard to these stress concentrated areas, that they did lower the endurance limit of this particular piece of metal that injured Mr. Pouncey from what it would have been had the inclusions or the stress concentrating areas not been in there?

"A. Yes, sir.

"Q. All right. And again would these—would the absence or is it true that the presence of these stress concentrating areas shorten the fatigue life of the metal from what it would have been had they not have been in there?

"A. Yes, sir.

* * *

"Q. You found inclusions in this metal that struck Mr. Pouncey, is that correct?

"A. Yes, sir.

"Q. All right.

"A. We found inclusions, and I might emphasize here, it is not merely a matter of finding inclusions. I think it is the number of them, and the distribution of them enters into it."

* * *

mitted the jury to infer negligence from the direct evidence of the defect in the product....

In the case at bar, there was direct evidence that Ford's supplier manufactured the blades with "dirty" spring steel. There is also testimony by Pouncey's expert that Ford and its supplier could reasonably expect a premature fatigue failure from steel with that level of inclusions. Finally, Ford itself offered no evidence as to the quality control procedures actually employed with regard to the radiator fans produced in 1966. The court below [did not err] in permitting the jury to infer from this evidence negligence on the part of Ford in [marketing] a defective radiator fan which could reasonably have been expected to produce injury or damage.

[Reasonable people could differ on why the blade fractured. Affirmed.]

NOTES

1. For a case on similar facts, see Rudd v. General Motors Corp., 127 F. Supp. 2d 1330 (M.D. Ala. 2001), examined below through a focus on the expert's testimony.

2. In *Pouncey*, why was the court not more interested in the defendant's expert testimony that the fan blade's inclusion level conformed to standards of the Society of Automotive Engineers?

3. How would the plaintiff's case differ in strict tort? Implied warranty? Would evidence on the adequacy of defendant's quality control procedures be relevant?

4. Manufacturing "Defects." "[T]he concept of defect is not self-defining when a product contains a flaw. Since all products are flawed at some technological level, the decision must still be made as to when a flaw emerges as a defect. In order to make this decision, some judgmental standard must be utilized." Weinstein, Twerski, Piehler & Donaher, Product Liability: An Interaction of Law and Technology, 12 Duquesne L. Rev. 425, 430–31 (1974). "To a metallurgist all metallic structures contain flaws or irregularities at some size level. They range from dislocations at the atomic size level to cracks visible to the naked eye.... Since these flaws [unfortunately sometimes called *defects* by metallurgists] can be identified in all products, the critical question to be asked is when can these deviations from structural perfection really lead to a conclusion of [*legal*] defect." Id. n.11. "Materials processing and fabrication are thus based upon flaw or irregularity control to achieve an economically feasible trade-off among all the properties of the material which, together with proper design, serve to achieve a given performance requirement. [Thus], the mere presence of an identifiable irregularity or flaw in a metallic structure is in and of itself an insufficient basis for the establishment of defect." Id. at 432 n.11(4).

Below are two photographs showing metallic flaws in a screw, representative of the type discussed by Professors Weinstein, et al.

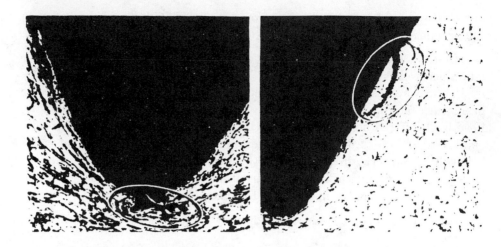

Cross-sections through screw illustrating roll-thread discontinuities at the root as well as the face of the threads. (A) Root discontinuities (250 X); (B) Face discontinuity (135 X).

5. In Keeler v. Richards Mfg. Co., Inc., 817 F.2d 1197 (5th Cir. 1987), a surgeon inserted a compression hip screw into the plaintiff's broken hip to assist the healing process. After several months, the screw broke. Plaintiff sued the screw manufacturer. Her experts testified that the screw had four irregularities, any one of which could have caused plaintiff's injuries by increasing stress concentrations that could have led to fatigue failure in the screw: (1) the internal threads were 1.1875″ in length vs. the 1.125″ maximum length specified in the blueprint specifications; (2) it contained excessive metal debris which could have interfered with the surgeon's ability to compress the screw properly, which could allow the bones excess movement; (3) its radius was slightly less than the exemplar screw furnished by the manufacturer; and (4) it failed to comply with American Society of Testing Materials 35% ductility standard. *Held,* jury verdict for plaintiff affirmed.

6. Faulty Materials. Other cases involving materials produced in a faulty manner include Benitez v. Synthes, Inc., 199 F. Supp. 2d 1339 (M.D. Fla. 2002) (surgical rod containing fractures and cracks); Bell v. T.R. Miller Mill Co., Inc., 768 So. 2d 953 (Ala. 2000) (telephone pole which broke, causing accident, was made of rotten wood); Benson v. Tennessee Valley Elec. Co–op., 868 S.W.2d 630 (Tenn. Ct. App.1993) (defective weld in aerial boom unit).

7. Faulty Assembly. Manufacturing defect cases often involve faulty product assembly. See, e.g., DeWitt v. Eveready Battery Co., 565 S.E.2d 140 (N.C. 2002) (acid leaked from battery case onto plaintiff); Ford Motor Co. v. Massey, 855 S.W.2d 897 (Ark. 1993) (stiff throttle cable caused truck to lurch into plaintiff); Yamaha Motor Co. v. Thornton, 579 So. 2d 619 (Ala. 1991) (motorcycle speed reduction plate left out in manufacture); Hewitt v. B.F. Goodrich Co., 732 F.2d 1554 (11th Cir. 984) (tire bead bundle broke during manufacturing process); Hall v. Chrysler Corp., 526 F.2d 350 (5th Cir.1976) (misrouted transmission cable on truck came into contact with exhaust manifold, which melted cable and caused transmission to lock in "drive" position although gear lever indicated "park").

8. For the Want of a Nail. . . . One simple manufacturing mistake—like failing properly to tighten a nut—can eventually result in a catastrophic accident. Tracing such an accident backwards to such a production error often is exceedingly difficult, but sometimes it can be done. See, e.g., Dieker v. Case Corp., 73 P.3d 133

(Kan. 2003) (improperly tightened nut on hydraulic control valve of combine); Jenkins v. General Motors Corp., 446 F.2d 377 (5th Cir. 1971) (improperly tightened nut on bolt in suspension of car), ch. 2, above. See also Kennelly, Trial of a General Aviation Aircraft Case Against Manufacturer, Component–Part Maker, and Overhaul Company—Defective 5¢ Screws Result in $660,000 Aggregate Awards for Two Deaths, Trial Lawyers Guide 281 (1971).

9. Delegation of Duty of Safe Manufacture. Manufacturers sometimes delegate certain assembly or inspection activities downstream to intermediate sellers, retailers, and even sometimes to the ultimate consumers. If the downstream party fails properly to perform the delegated final steps in the manufacturing process, can the manufacturer shift legal responsibility to that party as well? This was the issue in Vandermark v. Ford Motor Co., 391 P.2d 168, 170–71 (Cal.1964), where Justice Traynor addressed the question whether an automobile manufacturer should be strictly liable in tort for injuries caused by defects that should have been discovered by the dealer under established inspection procedures:

> [The strict liability] rules focus responsibility for defects, whether negligently or nonnegligently caused, on the manufacturer of the completed product, and they apply regardless of what part of the manufacturing process the manufacturer chooses to delegate to third parties. It appears in the present case that Ford delegates the final steps in that process to its authorized dealers. It does not deliver cars to its dealers that are ready to be driven away by the ultimate purchasers but relies on its dealers to make the final inspections, corrections, and adjustments necessary to make the cars ready for use. Since Ford, as the manufacturer of the completed product, cannot delegate its duty to have its cars delivered to the ultimate purchaser free from dangerous defects, it cannot escape liability on the ground that the defect in Vandermark's car may have been caused by something one of its authorized dealers did or failed to do.

10. Proof—The Malfunction Doctrine. Most reported manufacturing flaw cases deal principally with problems of proof—of whether the accident was caused by a product defect or by something else, and of whether any such defect is attributable to the manufacturer. If a plaintiff is unable to prove by direct evidence that a manufacturing defect caused the accident, he or she must turn to circumstantial evidence and inferences to prove the case. Consider the following case.

Ducko v. Chrysler Motors Corp.

Superior Court of Pennsylvania, 1994.
433 Pa. Super. 47, 639 A.2d 1204.

■ WIEAND, JUDGE.

In this product liability action, the sole issue is the sufficiency of the circumstances surrounding a malfunction of an automobile to establish prima facie the existence of a manufacturing defect. The trial court determined the evidence to be insufficient and entered summary judgment in favor of the manufacturer. After careful review, we reverse.

[Plaintiff Ducko was driving a newly purchased 1985 Chrysler Fifth Avenue on a dry road at 55 mph when the car suddenly jerked to the right and the steering felt like it locked. She attempted to apply the brakes, but they also failed to respond. The car crashed, and plaintiff broke her back. The car had been driven 1,655 miles since its purchase less than two months earlier.]

[Plaintiffs' expert] found no specific defect in the vehicle. He opined that Mrs. Ducko's accident had been caused by a transient malfunction of the system providing power to the steering and brakes. Chrysler's expert, however, observed that both steering and brakes were operational, and he found no abnormalities in any of the car's systems. He said that at a speed of 55 m.p.h. even a temporary power failure would not have rendered the steering uncontrollable [and opined] that the accident was a result of operator error.

When advancing a theory of strict product liability, a plaintiff has the burden of showing that the product was defective, that the defect was the proximate cause of his or her injuries and that the defect existed at the time the product left the manufacturer. [Citations.] In certain cases of alleged manufacturing defects, however, the plaintiff need not present direct evidence of the defect. When proceeding on a malfunction theory, the plaintiff may "present a case-in-chief evidencing the occurrence of a malfunction and eliminating abnormal use or reasonable, secondary causes for the malfunction." [Citations.] From this circumstantial evidence, a jury may be permitted to infer that the product was defective at the time of sale. . . .

> Generally, a plaintiff will produce direct evidence of a product's defective condition. In those cases where the plaintiff is unable to prove the precise nature of the product's defect, however, he may, in some cases, rely on the "malfunction theory" of product liability. Rogers v. Johnson & Johnson Products, Inc., 565 A.2d 751, 754 (Pa. 1989). The malfunction theory allows the plaintiff to use circumstantial evidence to establish a defective product. In *Rogers*, the court stated:
>
>> [The malfunction theory] permits a plaintiff to prove a defect in a product with evidence of the occurrence of a malfunction and with evidence eliminating abnormal use or reasonable, secondary causes for the malfunction. [The plaintiff is relieved] from demonstrating precisely the defect yet it permits the trier-of-fact to infer one existed from evidence of the malfunction, of the absence of abnormal use and of the absence of reasonable, secondary causes. [Citations.]
>
> Although proof of a specific defect is not essential to establish liability under this theory, the plaintiff cannot depend upon conjecture or guesswork. "The mere fact that an accident happens, even in this enlightened age, does not take the injured plaintiff to the jury." Stein v. General Motors Corp., 58 D. & C.2d 193, 203 (Bucks 1972), aff'd, 295 A.2d 111 (Pa. 1972).

[Woodin v. J.C. Penney Co., 629 A.2d 974,] 975–976 (Pa. Super. 1993). The malfunction theory, thus, does not relieve the burden of establishing a defect [but] "[t]he malfunction itself is circumstantial evidence of a defective condition, . . ." [Citation.] When a party relies on the malfunction of a product to prove that it was defective, testimony identifying the exact nature of the alleged defect is not essential. "Although it is helpful for a plaintiff to have direct evidence of the defective condition which caused the injury or expert testimony to point to that specific defect, such evidence is *not* essential in a strict liability case based on § 402A." [Citations.] Where the alleged malfunction occurs shortly after the product has been delivered to the user, the inference that the defect originated with the manufacturer is stronger. [Citation.]

* * *

In Brill v. Systems Resources, Inc., 592 A.2d 1377 (Pa. Super. 1991), the [plaintiff was] injured when the chair in which he had been sitting suddenly collapsed. At trial the plaintiff offered his own testimony concerning the events of his fall and the testimony of an eyewitness. The defendant, on the other hand, presented an expert who had examined the chair and opined that it was not defective. He concluded that the accident must have been the result of abnormal use by the plaintiff. The trial court refused to instruct the jury on the malfunction theory, and the jury returned a verdict for the defendant. On appeal, the Superior Court reversed and remanded for a new trial. Because the jury could have inferred a defect from the plaintiff's testimony, the Court held that a jury instruction on the malfunction theory was required [because the evidence on abnormal use was conflicting, making it a question for the jury].

In granting [defendant's] motion for summary judgment in the instant case, the trial court relied upon the deposition testimony and reports submitted by Chrysler's expert. This was error. Mrs. Ducko's testimony of the erratic performance of the vehicle's steering and braking systems, under the circumstances of this case, was sufficient to make out a prima facie case of a manufacturing defect in the vehicle. The issue of strict liability, therefore, was a disputed issue for the jury. Although a jury, after considering the testimony of appellee's expert witnesses, may find that the vehicle was not defective and that the accident was caused by operator error, it was improper for the trial court to make such a determination summarily and as a matter of law.

Our decision [is] consistent with decisions in other jurisdictions which have adopted the malfunction theory and allow proof of a defectively manufactured product by circumstantial evidence. [Citing cases from 3d Cir., D.C. Cir., Ark., Haw., Ill., Nev., N.J., & Or.]

[Reversed and remanded.]

NOTES

1. Defect Ipsa Loquitur. When a product is damaged or destroyed in an accident, the plaintiff often will be unable to prove specifically what defect in the product caused the accident. In such cases, the plaintiff may be required to rely upon some kind of "product malfunction" theory, like *Ducko*, accepted in most states. The Products Liability Restatement addresses this situation:

§ 3.   Circumstantial Evidence Supporting Inference of Product Defect

It may be inferred that the harm sustained by the plaintiff was caused by a product defect existing at the time of sale or distribution, without proof of a specific defect, when the incident that harmed the plaintiff:

(a) was of a kind that ordinarily occurs as a result of product defect; and

(b) was not, in the particular case, solely the result of causes other than product defect existing at the time of sale or distribution.

Comment *b* to § 3 provides in part: "When a product unit contains [a manufacturing] defect, and the defect affects product performance so as to cause a harmful incident, in most instances it will cause the product to malfunction in such a way that the inference of product defect is clear.... Frequently, the plaintiff is able to establish specifically the nature and identify of the defect and may proceed directly under § 2(a). But when the product unit ... is lost or destroyed in the accident, direct evidence of the specific defect may not be available. Under that circumstance, this Section may offer the plaintiff the only fair opportunity to recover." Comment *b* further states that § 3 most often applies to manufacturing defects, and it emphasizes that plaintiffs normally must establish defectiveness under § 2's specific defect tests unless "a product fails to perform its manifestly intended function, thus supporting the conclusion that a defect of some kind is the most probable explanation."

2.   Chair collapse. In Myrlak v. Port Authority of New York and New Jersey, 723 A.2d 45 (N.J. 1999), while plaintiff was seated in a chair performing his duties, he heard a loud noise when the back of the chair cracked and gave way. Plaintiff, who weighed about 325 pounds, fell from the chair and injured his back. *Held,* under § 3 of the Products Liability Restatement, the plaintiff need not prove a specific defect in the chair but may recover against the chair manufacturer if he could establish (1) that the chair collapse was the kind of incident that ordinarily occurs as a result of product defect, and (2) that the collapse was not solely the result of causes other than product defect existing at the time the chair left the manufacturer's control.

3.   Older Products—Failure of Inaccessible Part. Compare Holloway v. General Motors Corp., 271 N.W.2d 777 (Mich. 1978), where plaintiff's car suddenly left the road and hit a utility pole. Plaintiff's theory was that a defective ball joint assembly in the front suspension broke when the car hit a chuckhole in the gravel road, causing the loss of control. Although the car was four years old, had two prior owners, and had been driven 47,000 miles, the break in the ball joint assembly was fresh and metallurgically clean—which tended to negate the possibilities of fatigue, wear and tear, poor maintenance, or misuse. The trial court directed a verdict for the defendant on the ground that Holloway had failed to establish a defect in the ball joint assembly. *Held,* reversed:

Where a failure is caused by a defect in a relatively inaccessible part integral to the structure of the automobile not generally required to be repaired, replaced or maintained, it may be reasonable, absent misuse, to infer that the defect is attributable to the manufacturer.

On rehearing, General Motors argued that a plaintiff, to sustain his burden of proof, must identify the *specific cause* of the defect. The court responded: "Just as a plaintiff injured in an automobile collision need not identify a character or other personality defect which caused the defendant to drive negligently, ... neither need a person injured by product failure identify the specific defect."

4. In accord, that plaintiff need not prove a specific defect, but may establish a prima facie case of defectiveness upon proof of a sudden malfunction, where other plausible causes are absent: Kenkel v. Stanley Works, 665 N.W.2d 490 (Mich. App. 2003) (sliding glass doors closed on plaintiff; implied warranty); Thudium v. Allied Prod. Corp., 36 F.3d 767 (8th Cir. 1994) (grain auger collapsed); Dietz v. Waller, 685 P.2d 744 (Ariz. 1984) (new speed boat "disintegrated" at high speed during normal operation).

5. Burden of Proof. But the burden of proof lies on the plaintiff who must establish the claim by the *probabilities*. Walker v. General Electric Co., 968 F.2d 116 (1st Cir. 1992) (toaster oven caught fire and burned down plaintiff's home). "For circumstantial evidence to make out a prima facie case, it must tend to negate other reasonable causes, or there must be an expert opinion that the product was defective. Because liability in a products liability action cannot be based on mere speculation, guess or conjecture, the circumstances shown must justify an inference of probability as distinguished from mere possibility." Mateika v. LaSalle Thermogas Co., 418 N.E.2d 503, 505 (Ill. App. 1981). Thus, where there is an equal probability that an accident occurred for reasons other than a product defect, the plaintiff fails to make a case. E.g., Mays v. Ciba–Geigy Corp., 661 P.2d 348 (Kan. 1983) (gas pipeline explosion).

6. Spoliation. A plaintiff who loses the product may also lose the lawsuit. See Creazzo v. Medtronic, Inc., 903 A.2d 24, 31 (Pa. Super. Ct. 2006) (implanted neurological pulse generator, with allegedly defective wire, lost after removal from plaintiff; "a claim of manufacturing defect is untenable in the absence of the product itself").

7. While most courts still have not adopted the malfunction doctrine as such by name, a substantial and growing majority of American jurisdictions now accept its principles under the rubric of circumstantial evidence. See generally D. Owen, Products Liability Law §§ 2.2 (res ipsa) and 7.4 (malfunction doctrine) (2d ed. 2008); 1 D. Owen, M.S. Madden, & M. Davis, Madden & Owen on Products Liability §§ 7:9 (res ipsa) and 7:12 (malfunction theory) (3d ed. 2000).

---

3. PROOF—EXPERT TESTIMONY

Expert Testimony and the Rule in *Daubert**

Proof of defectiveness and causation often requires scientific and technical experts to explain the relevant science and engineering of product safety and accidents to a lay jury and the court. Understanding the various aspects of the design, manufacture, and labeling of products normally involves a host of complex, technical considerations requiring specialized expertise. Mechanical, chemical, and materials engineers, chemists, physicists, pharmacologists, epidemiologists, and other technical specialists are often necessary to help the fact finder comprehend how a product was made, how it was supposed to operate, whether and how it may have malfunctioned or otherwise caused an accident, and how it could have been made differently to avoid accidents of that type. Thus, involving as it does

* *From* D. Owen, Products Liability Law § 6.3 (2d ed. 2008).

the inner workings of science and technology, products liability litigation often resolves into a "battle of the experts."

The explosion of expert testimony in products liability litigation during the 1970s and 1980s, fueled by an expanding plaintiffs' bar fed by contingent fees, quite naturally led to a rather rapid increase of lawsuits based on novel, untested, abstract, and occasionally quite fantastic theories of science and technology propounded by "experts" who sometimes were dubiously qualified to testify on issues for which they claimed expertise. As products liability litigation during this period marched along, courts and commentators, always skeptical of this form of witness, increasingly decried a perceived growth in abuses of expert testimony, of "junk science" run amok.[1]

At early common law, courts generally allowed experts to provide relevant testimony about technical matters as a matter of course: once a person was *qualified* as an expert, his or her relevant opinion testimony was simply admitted into evidence. This was the backdrop to *Frye v. United States*, 293 F. 1013 (D.C. Cir. 1923), a murder case in which the defendant offered the results of an early polygraph test to show his innocence. In passing on the merits of a new form of science or technology, ruled the court, the test is whether it is "sufficiently established to have gained general acceptance in the particular field in which it belongs." Shifting the fulcrum of decision from the expert to the expertise, the *Frye* "general acceptance" test tended to exclude testimony on cutting-edge science and technology since new ideas become accepted wisdom only over time. During the next half century, *Frye*'s general acceptance standard, although increasingly criticized for being conservative and vague, evolved into the prevailing test for admissibility of expert testimony.

---

1. The "junk science" moniker was promoted and popularized by Peter W. Huber who worked for the Manhattan Institute, a conservative think-tank:

> Junk science cuts across chemistry and pharmacology, medicine and engineering. . . . It is a catalog of every conceivable kind of error: data dredging, wishful thinking, truculent dogmatism, and, now and again, outright fraud.
>
> On the legal side [is] a speculative theory that expects lawyers, judges, and juries to search for causes at the far fringes of science and beyond. The legal establishment has adjusted rules of evidence accordingly, so that almost any self-styled scientist, no matter how strange or iconoclastic his views, will be welcome to testify in court. The same scientific questions are litigated again and again, in one courtroom after the next, so that error is almost inevitable.

> Junk science is impelled through our courts by a mix of opportunity and incentive. "Let-it-all-in" legal theory creates the opportunity. The incentive is money: the prospect that the Midas-like touch of a credulous jury will now and again transform scientific dust into gold.

P. Huber, Galileo's Revenge: Junk Science in the Courtroom 3 (1991). See also P. Huber, Liability: The Legal Revolution and Its Consequences (1988); Huber, Safety and the Second Best: The Hazards of Public Risk Management in the Courts, 85 Colum. L. Rev. 277, 333 (1985). For a powerful rebuttal, see Chesebro, Galileo's Retort: Peter Huber's Junk Scholarship, 42 Amer. U. L. Rev. 1637 (1993).

As modern products liability and other technical litigation expanded in the late 1960s and early 1970s, coincident with the debate over the Federal Rules of Evidence then under consideration, the *Frye* test substantially gained in prominence. In 1975, the Federal Rules of Evidence were adopted, including Rule 702 which provided for the admission of scientific and technical evidence by a qualified expert if such testimony will "assist the trier of fact"—if it is helpful to the jury,[2] and Rule 703, which allows an expert to rely upon facts and data "reasonably relied upon by experts" in the field.[3] Most jurisdictions interpreted this rule to incorporate *Frye*'s general acceptance standard. During the 1980s and early 1990s, the logic and fairness of *Frye*'s general acceptance test came under increasing scrutiny as the courts increasingly debated whether and to what extent this test made sense and whether it was truly consistent with Rule 702. During this period, the courts struggled to find a balance between the need to open courtrooms to new science, on the one hand, with the problems of allowing experts to propound bad science, on the other. Increasingly, courts began to strike this balance by at least partially shifting the focus away from whether the science was "generally accepted," the *Frye* approach, to an evaluation of the methodology by which the expert reached his or her conclusion.

Daubert v. Merrell Dow Pharmaceuticals

United States Supreme Court, 1993.
509 U.S. 579, 113 S.Ct. 2786, 125 L.Ed.2d 469.

■ JUSTICE BLACKMUN delivered the opinion of the Court.

[In this case, the Supreme Court examined the admissibility of expert testimony on novel scientific theories and the relationship of the *Frye* test to Rule 702. *Daubert* involved the drug Bendectin, an anti-nausea medicine that, from 1956 until 1983, was widely prescribed to pregnant women for morning sickness. From the first Bendectin case filed in 1979, which claimed that the drug had caused the plaintiff's missing and malformed fingers, nearly 2000 similar cases eventually were filed claiming damages for birth defects from the drug. In *Daubert*, filed late in the life cycle of the litigation, the plaintiffs claimed that their birth defects were caused by Bendectin administered to their mothers during pregnancy. The defendant

---

2. Fed. R. Evid. 702 at the time provided: "If scientific, technical, or other specialized knowledge will assist the trier of fact to understand the evidence or to determine a fact in issue, a witness qualified as an expert by knowledge, skill, experience, training, or education, may testify thereto in the form of an opinion or otherwise." As noted below, Rule 702 was amended in 2000 to reflect the holding in Daubert v. Merrell Dow Pharmaceuticals, 509 U.S. 579 (1993).

3. Fed. R. Evid. 703 provides: "The facts or data in the particular case upon which an expert bases an opinion or inference may be those perceived by or made known to him at or before the hearing. If a type reasonably relied upon by experts in the particular field in forming opinions or inferences upon the subject, the facts or data need not be admissible evidence."

moved for summary judgment, arguing that there was no causal link between Bendectin and birth defects. In affidavits from its expert scientists, the defendant showed that none of the thirty-eight epidemiological studies of Bendectin published to that time had found a causal connection between birth defects and the drug. In opposition, plaintiffs offered affidavits from eight witnesses who concluded—on the basis of chemical structure analysis, *in vitro* (test tube) studies of animal cells, *in vivo* (live) animal studies, and a "reanalysis" of the previous epidemiological studies—that Bendectin can in fact cause birth defects. Concluding that the plaintiffs' proffered expert evidence did not meet *Frye*'s "general acceptance" standard of admissibility, the district court granted the defendant's summary judgment motion, and the Ninth Circuit affirmed.

[In the Supreme Court, the petitioning plaintiffs argued that the *Frye* "general acceptance" standard had been superseded by the Federal Rules of Evidence. Vacating and remanding, the Supreme Court agreed that the Rules do not allow a court to use the degree of acceptance of a subject of scientific testimony as the sole determinant of admissibility. Because Rule 702 allows qualified experts to testify about "scientific . . . knowledge," the Court reasoned that a trial judge must determine that proposed expert testimony is both "scientific" and "knowledge"—that the subject of the testimony is "ground[ed] in the methods and procedures of science," that it be "derived by the scientific method." An expert's proposed testimony must be "supported by appropriate validation—i.e., 'good grounds,' . . . ." In short, expert testimony must be "reliable." In addition to requiring expert testimony be *reliable*, the Court further reasoned that Rule 702 requires that such testimony be *relevant*, since the rule provides that expert scientific or technical testimony "assist the trier of fact to understand the evidence or to determine a fact in issue." This is the "helpfulness" requirement of Rule 702, requiring that expert testimony be sufficiently related to disputed facts to help the jury resolve facts or issues in dispute, a requirement that may be simply described as "fit." Thus, when a party proffers expert scientific testimony, the trial court has a vital "gatekeeping function"—a threshold obligation to render a preliminary determination of both the (1) *reliability* (validity), and (2) *relevance* (fit) of the expert's reasoning or methodology underlying the testimony proposed.[1]

[Among the factors a court may use to assess the validity of an expert's proffered testimony on scientific evidence, the Court noted five:[2]

---

1. Thus, "a trial judge must evaluate the proffered testimony to assure that it is at least minimally reliable; concerns about expert testimony cannot simply be referred to the jury as a question of weight." Capra, The *Daubert* Puzzle, 32 Ga. L. Rev. 699, 701–02 (1998). [—Eds.]

2. See *Daubert*, at 593–94. Although the Court lumped factors (3) and (4) together, which has led most observers to a four-factor count, the separation of these two different considerations clarifies analysis. The following five-factor list is adapted from Capra, The *Daubert* Puzzle, 32 Ga. L. Rev. 699, 702 (1998), which is the basis for the formulation in Federal Rule of Evidence 702, Advisory Committee Note to 2000 Amendment. Headings are added for clarification here. [—Eds.]

(1) *Testability*: whether the theory or technique is testable and has been tested—its ability to withstand objective, verifiable challenge and scientific trial;

(2) *Error rate*: whether it has an acceptable known or potential rate of error;

(3) *Control standards*: whether the scientific technique's *application* was subjected to appropriate standards of control; and

(4) *Peer review*: whether it has been subjected to peer review and publication;

(5) *General acceptance*: whether it is widely accepted in the relevant scientific community.

These are *Daubert*'s now-familiar reliability factors. In determining the admissibility of expert testimony under 702, the Court emphasized that the inquiry into pertinent reliability considerations should be flexible, and that the focus of inquiry "must be solely on principles and methodology, not on the conclusions that they generate." Because the lower courts had based their decisions in this case almost exclusively on *Frye*'s general acceptance standard, rather than on the broader reliability and fit requirements of Federal Rule of Evidence 702, the Supreme Court returned the judgment to the Court of Appeals.]

[Vacated and remanded.][3]

———

Daubert's Progeny

Since *Daubert*, the Supreme Court has revisited the expert testimony issue a number of times. In *General Electric Co. v. Joiner*, 522 U.S. 136 (1997), a district court applied *Daubert* to exclude expert testimony that purported to link the plaintiff's exposure to PCBs to his lung cancer, and the court of appeals reversed. Reinstating the district court's ruling, the Supreme Court emphasized that federal trial courts have wide discretion to exclude expert testimony, holding that such determinations are only subject to a permissive "abuse of discretion" standard of review. The Court further noted that *Daubert*'s direction that courts focus on an expert's *methodology* in no way limits a trial judge from scrutinizing the quality of an expert's *conclusions*. There is no reason a district court should "admit opinion evidence which is connected to existing data only by the *ipse dixit* of the expert. A court may conclude that there is simply too great an analytical gap between the data and the opinion preferred."

3. On remand, applying the *Daubert* analysis, the Ninth Circuit ruled again that the district court had properly excluded the plaintiffs' expert testimony, concluding that the testimony of one of the plaintiffs' experts was not reliable and that the testimony of the others was not relevant because they would only testify that Bendectin is "capable of causing" birth defects, not that the drug *in fact* (more likely than not) caused the plaintiffs' birth defects. Daubert v. Merrell Dow Pharmaceuticals, Inc., 43 F.3d 1311 (9th Cir. 1995). [—Eds.]

In *Kumho Tire Co., Ltd. v. Carmichael,* 526 U.S. 137 (1999), the Court ruled that Rule 702's broad reference to expert testimony on "scientific, technical, or other specialized knowledge" means that the *Daubert* gatekeeping principles apply to *all* expert testimony, including engineering testimony of the type ordinarily relied upon in product liability cases involving durable products. See Denbeaux and Risinger, *Kumho Tire* and Expert Reliability: How the Question You Ask Gives the Answer You Get, 34 Seton Hall L. Rev. 15 (2003).

Weisgram v. Marley Co., 528 U.S. 440 (2000), was a wrongful death action arising out of a fire in a home against the manufacturer of a heater. On testimony by three experts that the heater was defective, and that the defect caused the fire, the plaintiffs obtained a judgment on a jury verdict, over the defendant's objection that the testimony was unreliable and therefore inadmissible under Rule 702 and *Daubert.* The circuit court reversed, agreeing with the defendant that the plaintiffs' expert testimony on the heater's defectiveness was speculative and scientifically unsound. Rather than remanding for a retrial, and reasoning that the plaintiffs had had a fair opportunity to prove their claim and so did not deserve a second chance, the circuit court directed judgment for the defendant manufacturer. The Supreme Court affirmed. Rejecting an argument that a plaintiff might hold certain expert testimony in reserve to shore up the claim if the proffered expert testimony were to be found insufficient, the Court noted that *Daubert* put parties relying on expert evidence on notice of "the exacting standards of reliability" demanded of such evidence. "It is implausible to suggest, post-*Daubert,* that parties will initially present less than their best expert evidence in the expectation of a second chance should their first try fail." Id. at 455–56. Reminding parties (usually plaintiffs) that they may well not get a second chance, *Weisgram* underscores *Daubert's* basic message: parties bear responsibility for presenting expert testimony that is rigorously grounded in good science and technology and relevant to the particular issues in the case.

Federal Rule of Evidence 702: The *Daubert* Amendment

In 2000, the Supreme Court approved certain amendments to the rules of evidence (on opinion evidence and expert testimony) to conform them to the principles of *Daubert* and its progeny. In addition to making certain minor changes to Rules 701 and 703, the amendments added an important proviso to Rule 702 that permits expert testimony only if such testimony is grounded on "sufficient facts and data" and is the result of "reliable principles and methods" which are themselves reliably applied to the facts of the case. With the amended language italicized, Federal Rule of Evidence 702 now provides in full:

> If scientific, technical, or other specialized knowledge will assist the trier of fact to understand the evidence or to determine a fact in issue, a witness qualified as an expert by knowledge, skill, experience, training, or education, may testify thereto in the form of an opinion or otherwise *if (1) the testimony is based on sufficient facts and data, (2) the testimony is the*

product of reliable principles and methods, and (3) the witness has applied the principles and methods reliably to the facts of the case.

The Advisory Committee's helpful Note to the 2000 Amendment observes that the amendment requires only that the data, principles, and methods used by an expert are reliable and reliably applied, and that the quality of expert testimony is still largely to be tested by cross examination and the other safeguards of the adversary system. Observing that "[a] review of the caselaw after *Daubert* shows that the rejection of expert testimony is the exception rather than the rule," the Committee Note adds that the amendment "is not intended to provide an excuse for an automatic challenge to the testimony of every expert."

As for the *Daubert* reliability factors, the Advisory Committee's Note reiterates *Daubert*'s five-factor list set forth above and further enumerates several *additional* factors courts have found useful in varying contexts:

(1) Whether experts are "proposing to testify about matters growing naturally and directly out of research they have conducted independent of the litigation, or whether they have developed their opinions expressly for purposes of testifying."

(2) Whether the expert has unjustifiably extrapolated from an accepted premise to an unfounded conclusion.

(3) Whether the expert has adequately accounted for obvious alternative explanations.

(4) Whether the expert "is being as careful as he would be in his regular professional work outside his paid litigation consulting."

(5) Whether the field of expertise claimed by the expert is known to reach reliable results for the type of opinion the expert would give.

While recognizing the importance of these and the original *Daubert* factors, the Committee observed that the Amendments make no attempt to "codify" the factors, which the Supreme Court has emphasized are not exclusive. In sum, the amendments (including the Committee Note) to Federal Rule of Evidence 702 do not provide a conclusive road map for each specific aspect of expert testimony, but they do provide helpful guidance on the fundamental *Daubert* reliability principles.

Daubert in the Lower Federal Courts

Daubert has had its intended effect of forcing courts to examine expert testimony more closely. Post-*Daubert*, the federal district courts, exercising their newly appointed "gatekeeper" function, have plainly heightened their scrutiny of expert testimony, often holding rigorous pre-trial "*Daubert* hearings"—that are often outcome-determinative—to determine the admissibility of proffered expert testimony.

[T]he *Daubert* hearing and ruling have effectively become virtually as case outcome determinative as a class certification hearing and ruling: once decided, a case either shrivels up and goes away, or becomes more dangerous to try. *Daubert* hearings are often every bit as case dispositive, practically speaking, as a summary judgment hearing. Thus, practitioners whose cases rely in any material way on expert testimony must [be] prepared for a full-blown *"trial within a trial"* that the *Daubert* hearing often becomes.

Rudlin, The Judge as Gatekeeper: What Hath *Daubert–Joiner–Kumho* Wrought?, 29 Prod. Safety & Liab. Rep. 329 (BNA Apr. 2, 2001).

Yet heightened judicial scrutiny of expert testimony does not mean that a plaintiff's expert witnesses will necessarily be excluded, even if their testimony is unusual: the circuit courts sometimes affirm plaintiff verdicts in novel contexts in which the traditional scientific indicia on defectiveness or causation is marginal at best, and they will reverse a district court for excluding a plaintiff's expert testimony with excessive zeal. But *Daubert* decisions quite frequently go the other way, by excluding a plaintiff's expert testimony as unreliable or irrelevant. Thus, the lower federal courts have *disallowed* expert testimony on *Daubert* grounds because the expert proposed to testify on a novel causal theory, not generally accepted or subjected to peer review, that was developed only for the litigation; relied too heavily on the temporal proximity of harm to its alleged cause; failed sufficiently to inspect or test the accident product or a proposed alternative design; failed faithfully to reconstruct the circumstances of the accident; failed to provide a theory of causation supported by sufficient confirmatory studies; failed to conduct a differential diagnosis to rule out alternative potential causes, or applied such an approach improperly; failed to show the relevance ("fit") of accepted principles to the plaintiff's case; or otherwise failed to proffer reliable and relevant testimony, supported by reliable data, methods, or conclusions, that were likely to be helpful to the trier of fact. Quite often, an expert's testimony will fail *Daubert* scrutiny for many of these reasons.

———

Booth v. Black & Decker, Inc.

United States District Court, Eastern District of Pennsylvania, 2001.
166 F. Supp. 2d 215.

■ REED, DISTRICT JUDGE.

[This case involved claims of defective manufacture and design against the manufacturer of a toaster oven for negligence, breach of warranty, and strict liability in tort for fire damage to the plaintiffs' house. Although the Fire Marshall determined that the fire was caused by a recently-repaired microwave that had been used shortly before the fire, the plaintiff's expert, Thomas, determined that the fire originated in the defendant's toaster oven located in the same portion of the kitchen. The defendant moved for summary judgment, which hinged on the admissibility of plaintiffs' expert testimony that the toaster oven was defective and caused the fire. For this purpose, the court held a two-day *Daubert* hearing on Thomas' qualifications and the reliability of his opinion that the toaster oven was defective and caused the fire. The court first concluded that Thomas was qualified to offer expert testimony on the electrical aspects of consumer appliances, including toaster ovens, and that he was qualified to interpret the results of a scanning electron microscope examination he had conducted on the oven. On the issues of manufacturing defect and causation, Thomas hypothesized that while the toaster oven was being operated, its power contacts spontaneously welded together, causing the toaster oven to overheat and catch fire. Attempting to confirm this hypothesis, Thomas testified that he used an electron microscope to examine the contacts which showed indications of melting and scoring, which suggested to him that the surfaces had welded together. The toaster oven was defectively designed, in Thomas' view, for two reasons: (1) because it lacked a thermal cut-off device, to cut off power when the oven reached a certain temperature, to prevent it from overheating, and (2) because it was made of an excessive amount of plastic that has a low melting point.

[Applying the Third Circuit's version of the *Daubert* factors,* the court ruled that the evidence failed to establish that Thomas' methodology was reliable. Thomas' manufacturing defect theory was testable, but he had not attempted to get the power contacts of a similar toaster to weld together. While his microscopic investigation was a form of test, he failed to adequately explain why indications of melting and scoring mean that welding has occurred, nor did he offer any other basis for his conclusion other than his personal experience and "broad and circular assertions that such markings simply are what happens when welding occurs." Thomas asserted that his fire investigation methods were generally used by others in the field, but he failed to produce persuasive objective evidence to this effect. Prompted by defense counsel, Thomas claimed to have followed the fire investigation Guidelines of the National Fire Protection Association, but he did not point to any specific procedures in the guidelines that he had followed. Nor was there any credible evidence to show that Thomas' examination method was subject to peer review, had a known or potential rate of error, could be measured by existing standards, or was generally accepted. In short, because Thomas "did not take sufficient care in supporting the credibility or reliability of the methodology he applied, despite the best efforts of counsel to elicit it," his testimony that the toaster contained a manufacturing defect was not admissible. Similarly, Thomas' design defectiveness theories, on which he offered no methodology whatsoever, were equally deficient: he neither sketched nor produced an example of the kind of thermal cut-off device he recommended, nor did he install one on an exemplar oven to test its ability to prevent overheating. While he claimed that such a device was used on a Black & Decker oven sold in Canada, he failed to produce the Canadian model. As for his theory of excessive plastic materials, Thomas never explained how the fire might have been caused or affected by the plastic.

* See Oddi v. Ford Motor Co., 234 F.3d 136, 145 (3d Cir. 2000) (the "haphazard, intuitive inquiry" of plaintiff's expert engineer, who conducted no tests nor calculated forces involved in vehicle accident, failed each of eight reliability factors, including *Daubert's* five plus "(6) the relationship of the technique to methods which have been established to be reliable; (7) the qualifications of the expert witness . . .; and (8) the non-judicial uses to which the method has been put.").

[Thus, whether or not Thomas in fact conducted a reasonable investigation into the cause of the fire, he failed to provide the court with "enough basic, objective information" on the reliability of the investigation and his opinions based thereon. "Thomas performed no tests of his own to determine whether his hypotheses were indeed true; he merely examined the toaster oven and concluded it could have been safer. His testimony ... seemed wholly based on his own training and experience, and he provided the Court with no objective anchor for his conclusions." Based on a review of Thomas' expert reports, deposition testimony, and testimony during the *Daubert* hearing, the court found his inquiry into whether the toaster oven contained a defect that caused the fire to be "intuitive and haphazard, his methodology to be unreliable, and, consequently, his conclusions to be suspect." Since the plaintiffs had failed to meet their burden of establishing the reliability of Thomas' testimony under the principles of Rule 702, *Daubert*, and *Kumho Tire,* Thomas' expert testimony on defectiveness and causation was inadmissible. Nor did plaintiffs have any other evidence to establish that the fire probably was caused by a defect in the toaster oven.]

[Defendant's motion for summary judgment granted.]

Rudd v. General Motors Corp.

United States District Court, Middle District of Alabama, 2001.
127 F. Supp. 2d 1330.

■ THOMPSON, DISTRICT JUDGE.

[The plaintiff was injured when a fan blade from his pickup truck broke lose and struck him while he stood in front of the truck's open hood twisting the distributor housing to adjust the engine's timing. Plaintiff sued the vehicle manufacturer, claiming that the fan blade had been made of defective metal, based largely on the testimony of his expert, Edmondson, a mechanical engineer with extensive experience in failure analysis. GM moved for summary judgment, arguing that plaintiff had offered no admissible evidence of a manufacturing defect. Choosing not to hold a *Daubert* hearing,* the court ruled on the admissibility of Edmondson's testimony on the basis of his expert report and deposition testimony. Edmondson found no direct evidence of a physical flaw in the fan blade but arrived at his conclusion circumstantially by excluding other possible explanations of how the fan blade might have broken. In particular, he first determined that the plaintiff's use of the vehicle at the time the

---

* Normally, the decision whether to hold a *Daubert* hearing is entirely discretionary with the trial court. There may be no need for such a hearing if the parties have developed an extensive evidentiary record, including expert reports, depositions, and the literature that supports the expert opinions, and assuming that the issues are well briefed. As with any discretionary matter, however, a trial court's failure to hold a *Daubert* hearing in particular circumstances, whether or not requested by the losing party, may be an abuse of discretion, particularly if the admissibility issue turns on factual issues and will be determinative of summary judgment.

fan blade broke was entirely proper: the plaintiff's technique in adjusting the timing, while running the engine at 1200 to 1500 rpms, was entirely normal and specifically recommended by GM's tune-up manuals. Next, based on Edmondson's visual examination, his particularized measurements of the accident fan and fan assembly, and his background reading, he determined that prior to the accident the fan blade had not been bent, at the site of the fracture origin or elsewhere, and that there was no visible damage to the blade that might have caused the fatigue fracture and break. Had the fan blade been subjected to a sudden trauma during operation, Edmondson testified that it would have left physical indicia of the trauma, such as broken paint, scarring, or denting, none of which were visible. The absence of any indications that the fan had been subjected to abnormal forces during operation led him to conclude its break was due to a metal-fatigue fracture resulting from a microscopic manufacturing defect, such as a scratch, grind mark, gas bubble, or an inclusion. The court concluded that the expert's systematic elimination of alternative causes led to circumstantial proof of defectiveness *relevant* to a jury's determination of that issue.

[Further, as to the *reliability* of Edmondson's expert testimony, it satisfied each of the three specific reliability standards of new Rule 702—it was based on (1) sufficient data, (2) reliable principles and methods, and (3) reliable application of the methods to the facts. First, the factual basis of Edmondson's testimony was sufficient—based on his visual inspection of the accident fan blade and other fans, his account of the use history of the truck and fan blade, his "total indicator reading" measurements, his reliance on two failure-analysis publications (which included a case study of a car fan fatigue fracture) and GM tune-up manuals, and his background and training analyzing metal fractures,[2] including automotive fan fatigue fractures. Second, the court ascertained that Edmondson's method for determining the cause of the fatigue fracture—by eliminating ("ruling out") other possible causes—is a well-established and reliable scientific method for determining causation (called "differential diagnosis"). Moreover, because a specialty publication had employed the process-of-elimination method in a failure analysis model, which included a case history of a fatigue fracture in an automobile fan, this method further satisfied *Daubert's* reliability factors on publication and acceptance within a relevant community of experts. Third, and finally, the court found that Edmondson reliably applied this method to the accident fan—by determining that the fan's history did not include improper operation and by closely inspecting the fan blade metal for physical indicia of other causes. Noting that Edmondson could not fairly be expected to assign a particular error rate to his techniques, the court concluded that his testimony was reliable, and hence admissible, "because he provides a step-by-step and transparent

---

2. The court quoted the Advisory Committee Note to Rule 702 to the effect that an expert's *experience* (alone or in conjunction with other knowledge, skill, training or education) may provide a sufficient foundation for the expert's testimony if the witness explains "how that experience leads to the conclusion reached, why that experience is a sufficient basis for the opinion, and how that experience is reliably applied to the facts." 127 F. Supp. 2d at 1336.

account" of "reasoning processes and data sources" on which he relies, "the physical indicia he associates with each possible alternative cause, and his reasons for excluding each of the alternative causes." By fully revealing the basis of his opinions, Edmondson's testimony thus supplied the defendant with a fair basis to challenge his opinions by cross examination and the presentation of contrary evidence, the basic tools of the adversary process.]

[Defendant's motion for summary judgment denied.]

NOTES

1. *Daubert* in the State Courts. Because *Daubert* interprets Federal Rule of Evidence 702, it applies by its terms only to the federal courts. Yet, even before the Supreme Court decided *Daubert* in 1993, many state courts had already begun to adopt similar reliability principles, and since 1993 an increasing number of states have abandoned *Frye* and swung over to the *Daubert* point of view. In addition, a large majority of states have adopted codes of evidence patterned on the Federal Rules of Evidence, including Rule 702 on which *Daubert* is based. Moreover, to the extent that *Daubert*'s precepts are grounded in reasoned principles of logic and fair play for adjudicating disputes involving principles of science and technology, those precepts have a certain logical and moral power that is difficult for state courts to ignore. For these reasons, a growing number of state courts, probably a majority, have now adopted the *Daubert* principles of reliability and relevance for expert testimony. See, e.g., Cooper Tire & Rubber Co. v. Mendez, 204 S.W.3d 797 (Tex. 2006); Sandoz Pharmaceuticals Corp. v. Gunderson, ___ S.W.3d ___ (Ky. Ct. App. 2005).

Yet many state courts, now about fifteen, have refused to adopt the *Daubert* principles, still trusting in *Frye* and other conventional rules governing the admissibility of expert testimony. See, e.g., reaffirming *Frye* and rejecting *Daubert*, Howerton v. Arai Helmet, Ltd., 597 S.E.2d 674 (N.C. 2004); Grady v. Frito–Lay, Inc., 839 A.2d 1038 (Pa. 2003); Castillo v. E.I. Du Pont De Nemours & Co., Inc., 854 So. 2d 1264, 1276 (Fla. 2003); Bagley v. Mazda Motor Corp., 864 So. 2d 301 (Ala. 2003); Donaldson v. Central Illinois Public Serv. Co., 767 N.E.2d 314 (Ill. 2002); Goeb v. Tharaldson, 615 N.W.2d 800 (Minn. 2000) (thoroughly examining policy issues).

2. On *Daubert*, see generally Owen, A Decade of *Daubert*, 80 Denver U. L. Rev. 345 (2003); D. Owen, Products Liability Law, § 6.3 (2d ed. 2008).

4.   FOOD AND DRINK

Kolarik v. Cory International Corporation

Supreme Court of Iowa, 2006.
721 N.W.2d 159.

■ CARTER, JUSTICE.

[While eating a salad containing olives from a jar of Italica Spanish Olives, plaintiff bit down on an olive pit or pit fragment and fractured a tooth. He sued the importers and wholesalers of the olives in negligence, warranty (see page 91, above), and strict liability in tort, and the trial court granted defendants' motions for summary judgment. Plaintiff appeals to the Supreme Court. *Held*, affirmed, except for plaintiff's negligent failure to warn claim, which was remanded for trial.]

[Defendants] obtain bulk shipments of pimento-stuffed, green olives shipped in 150–kilogram drums to their plant in Norfolk, Virginia. There, the drums are emptied and the olives are washed and placed in a brine solution in glass jars suitable for retail sale under various names including Italica Spanish Olives. When defendants receive the olives, they are inspected for general appearance, pH, and acid level. Defendants rely on their Spanish suppliers for quality control of the pitting and stuffing. * * *

II. *Strict Liability and Breach of Implied Warranty.*

[The trial court gave summary judgments for defendants on plaintiff's strict liability and implied warranty claims on the basis of a statute that] provides:

1. A person who is not the assembler, designer, or manufacturer, and who wholesales, retails, distributes, or otherwise sells a product is:

a. Immune from any suit based upon strict liability in tort or breach of implied warranty of merchantability which arises solely from an alleged defect in the original design or manufacture of the product.

Iowa Code § 613.18(1)(*a*).

Plaintiff [argues that his strict liability and implied warranty claims survive this statute because defendants, though wholesalers or distributors, were also "assemblers" of the olives under] the statute [because they] remove bulk olives from drums and repackage them in jars. We disagree that this repackaging process excludes defendants from the immunity granted by the statute.

[T]he assemblers exclusion contained in section 613.18(1)(*a*) is aimed at those situations in which an assembling process has some causal connection to a dangerous condition in the product that gives rise to a strict-liability claim or a product condition that constitutes a breach of an implied warranty of merchantability. Because the repackaging of the olives by defendants did not contribute to the condition that underlies plaintiff's product-liability claim, defendants are afforded the immunity granted by the statute.

In the alternative, plaintiff argues that section 613.18(1)(*a*) does not apply because olives are not a "product" [under the statute, but we] are satisfied that agricultural commodities may be products as that term is used in section 613.18(1)(*a*).... *See* Restatement (Third) of Torts: Product Liability § 7 (1998) (one engaged in the business of selling or distributing food products is subject to liability for harm to persons caused by defective product). Consequently, the district court did not err in applying that statute to bar plaintiff's strict-liability and breach-of-implied-warranty-of-merchantability claims.

III.   *Express Warranty.*

[As examined in chapter 4, the court concluded that the words "minced pimento stuffed," contained on the label of the jar of olives, did not constitute an express warranty that the olives had been pitted.]

IV.   *Negligence*

Much of the argument of both parties with regard to plaintiff's negligence claim turns on the decision in *Brown v. Nebiker,* 229 Iowa 1223, 296 N.W. 366 (1941). [There], the plaintiff's decedent, a restaurant patron, swallowed a bone while eating a pork chop. The bone lodged in his esophagus [which] led to the patron's death. [His] personal representative sued the restaurant owner on theories of implied warranty and negligence. At the trial, several witnesses testified that they had ordered pork chops at the same restaurant on the same evening and that the pork chops were served with the bone left intact.

The district court directed a verdict for the defendant on both the [implied] warranty and negligence claims. On appeal this court held that the common-law warranty that flows to patrons of a restaurant protected them against food that was unfit for human consumption and against having foreign objects in the food. The court held that pork chops served with the bones in were not unfit for human consumption and that, because bones are naturally contained in pork, they do not constitute a foreign object. * * *

... *Brown v. Nebiker* decision [merely recognizes] that, when pork chops are served in their natural state with the bone left in the meat, the presence of bone fragments must be anticipated. The opinion sheds little light on the requirements placed on a seller of food products in various stages of preparation or processing. We share the views expressed by the Wisconsin Supreme Court with regard to this matter:

> The "foreign-natural" test ... does not recommend itself to us as being logical or desirable. It is true one can expect a T-bone in T-bone steak, chicken bones in roast chicken, pork bone in a pork chop, pork bone in spare ribs, a rib bone in short ribs of beef, and fish bones in a whole baked or fried fish, but the expectation is based not on the naturalness of the particular bone to the meat, fowl, or fish, but on the type of dish served containing the meat, fowl, or fish. There is a distinction between what a consumer expects to find in a fish stick and in a baked or fried fish, or in a chicken sandwich made from sliced white meat and in roast chicken. The test should be what is reasonably expected by the consumer in the food as served, not what might be natural to the ingredients of that food prior to preparation.

Betehia v. Cape Cod Corp., 10 Wis.2d 323, 103 N.W.2d 64, 68–69 (1960). Other courts [agree, and it] is also the view expressed in Restatement (Third) of Torts: Product Liability section 7, comment *b* (product danger to be determined by reference to reasonable consumer expectations within the relevant context of consumption).

* * *

[I]n the case of processed foods, consumers may develop reasonable expectations that certain components of food products in their natural state that serve to impede human consumption will be removed. Specifically, ... the purchaser of pimento-stuffed olives may reasonably anticipate that the olive pits have been removed. We need not decide whether this expectation would create an implied warranty of merchantability [or subject the sellers here to strict liability in tort] because such [claims are] precluded by statute in the present case. We are convinced, however, that a seller of stuffed olives must be cognizant that consumers will assume that the olives will be free from pits and act on that assumption in consuming the product. Consistent with that expectation, a seller must exercise reasonable care to assure that this expectation is realized. The district court erred in rejecting plaintiff's negligence claim by reliance on the natural component principle that was applied in *Brown v. Nebiker.*

[While there is no suggestion that the defendants were negligent in processing the olives that contained the pit that injured the plaintiff, a question of fact exists] with respect to plaintiff's claim that defendants were negligent in not warning against the possible presence of pits or pit fragments in the jar of olives.

Defendants' quality control officer testified in his deposition that the pitting process is not one hundred percent effective [and] that the presence of an occasional pit or pit fragment in the stuffed olives is inevitable because the machine that does the pitting will fail to remove a pit if the olive has an abnormal shape. [Thus], we conclude that a trier of fact might find that reasonable care by a wholesale seller of stuffed olives would include providing a warning on the label that pits or pit fragments might be encountered. A claim based on that theory should have survived summary judgment. [Hence, we remand to the trial] court for further proceedings on that claim.

Affirmed in Part, Reversed in Part, and Remanded.

NOTES

1. Almost all recent decisions follow *Kolarik*'s replacement of the foreign/natural test with a consumer expectations standard. See, e.g., Schafer v. JLC Food Systems, Inc., 695 N.W.2d 570, 574–575 (Minn.2005) ("the reasonable expectation test focuses on what is reasonably expected by the consumer in the food product as served, not what might be foreign or natural to the ingredients of that product before preparation"). *Schafer* relied on the Third Restatement's use of the reasonable consumer expectations test in food products liability cases:

One ... who sells or distributes a food product that is defective ... is subject to liability for harm to persons or property caused by the defect.... [A] harm-causing ingredient of the food product constitutes a defect if a reasonable consumer would not expect the food product to contain that ingredient.

Restatement (3d) of Torts: Products Liability § 7. The *Schafer* court remarked:

> Under the Restatement approach, consumer expectations are based on culturally defined, widely shared standards allowing a seller's liability to be resolved by judges and triers of fact based on their assessment of what consumers have a right to expect from preparation of the food in question. Id. cmt. *b*. The Reporters to the Restatement note that the majority view is unanimously favored by law review commentators.
>
> . . . Instead of drawing arbitrary distinctions between foreign and natural substances that caused harm, relying on consumers' reasonable expectations is likely to yield a more equitable result. After all, an unexpected natural object or substance contained in a food product, such as a chicken bone in chicken soup, can cause as much harm as a foreign object or substance, such as a piece of glass in the same soup.

2.   Compare Jackson v. Nestle–Beich, Inc., 589 N.E.2d 547, 548–53 (Ill. 1992), where plaintiff broke her tooth when she bit into a Katydid—a chocolate-covered, pecan and caramel candy manufactured by Nestle, whom she sued for breach of implied warranty and strict liability in tort. The trial court granted Nestle's summary judgment motion "on the basis of the foreign-natural doctrine [which] provides that, if a substance in a manufactured food product is natural to any of the ingredients of the product, there is no liability for injuries caused thereby; whereas, if the substance is foreign to any of the ingredients, the manufacturer will be liable for any injury caused thereby." The appellate court reversed in plaintiff's favor, and the Supreme Court affirmed.

Rejecting Nestle's argument that consumers can adequately protect themselves from defective food products, and its proposal that the court adopt Louisiana's modified version of the foreign/natural test, the court responded that the reasonable expectation standard adequately balances the interest of consumers in defect-free products against the interest of manufacturers in doing business at reasonable cost. Rather than imposing a duty on consumers to "think and chew carefully," the court endorsed the following view:

> In an era of consumerism, the foreign-natural standard is an anachronism. It flatly and unjustifiably protects food processors and sellers from liability even when the technology may be readily available to remove injurious natural objects from foods. The consumer expectation test, on the other hand, imposes no greater burden upon processors or sellers than to guarantee that their food products meet the standards of safety that consumers customarily and reasonably have come to expect from the food industry. Note, Products Liability—The Test of Consumer Expectation for "Natural" Defects in Food Products, 37 Ohio St. L.J. 634, 651–52 (1976).

Justice Heiple dissented:

> [Since 1944, Illinois has followed the foreign-natural doctrine, which] provides that the vendor of food is not liable for injuries due to unremoved but naturally occurring ingredients such as nut shells, fruit pits, fish bones and so forth but is liable for foreign objects in the food such as glass shards or pieces of metal. The majority opinion in the instant case discards the foreign-natural doctrine and substitutes the reasonable expectation test. . . .
>
> In truth, the reasonable expectation test is what gave rise to the foreign-natural doctrine. That is to say, since it would be reasonable to expect to find a nut shell in a product containing nuts, there would be no liability. Rather than approach each broken tooth or other injury on a case-

by-case basis, it was deemed more expeditious and efficient to crystallize the matter into the foreign-natural doctrine. That doctrine both did justice and promoted judicial economy.

A reversion to the reasonable expectation test simply means that each food-related injury in this State will be subject to a lawsuit to determine whether the consumer's reasonable expectation was violated. The costs will be significant. . . .

The effects of this decision will go far beyond the defendant Nestle–Beich Company, whose candy caused a broken tooth. It extends to all manufacturers and purveyors of food products including the neighborhood baker, the hot dog vendor and the popcorn man. Watch out Orville Redenbacher!

The continued march towards strict and absolute liability for others (others meaning anyone not injured who has assets) and the absence of any responsibility by the injured for their own welfare takes yet another step with this majority ruling. Accordingly, I dissent.

3. Fish Chowder. The early cases applying the foreign/natural test are nicely illustrated by Webster v. Blue Ship Tea Room, Inc., 198 N.E.2d 309 (Mass. 1964), involving a fish bone in fish chowder. Framing the issue as whether the bone could be considered a foreign object, the court found no liability for breach of implied warranty, concluding that the occasional presence of fish bones in chowder is to be anticipated. Among other delights, the *Webster* opinion reviews the history of chowder, offers several recipes for New England chowder (a "gustatory adventure"), and appeals to regional New England pride in the "hallowed tradition" of fish chowder. What if the chowder had been served in Nebraska?

Suppose a fish bone of one species ends up in a stew containing meat from other kinds of fish. Is the bone a "foreign" or "natural" substance? Cf. Arnaud's Restaurant, Inc. v. Cotter, 212 F.2d 883 (5th Cir. 1954) (crab shell in pompano en papilotte).

How about a broken tooth on a kernel of corn in a box of corn flakes? Would it matter if it were crystallized, and hard as quartz? See Adams v. Great Atl. & Pac. Tea Co., 112 S.E.2d 92 (N.C. 1960).

4. Chewing Gum and Enchiladas. Louisiana (discussed in *Jackson*) and California have adopted half-way approaches that partially retain the foreign-natural distinction. Both states limit liability to negligence in the case of *natural* substances. Consider Hickman v. Wm. Wrigley, Jr. Co., Inc., 768 So. 2d 812, 816 (La. Ct. App. 2000) (screw in stick of chewing gum; manufacturer strictly liable):

Under the "foreign-natural test," if the harmful substance is foreign, the defendant is strictly liable, and the analysis stops. If the substance is natural to the food, then the negligence of the defendant must be determined. [Citation.] A natural substance has been held to include instances where the product does not undergo the manufacturing process and an object with the potential to cause injury remains in the product. An example of this type of situation is the pearl in a fried oyster. [Citation.] However, when a product undergoes the manufacturing process and is marketed as a particular type of product, a foreign substance is any substance not associated with that finished product. Thus, a "fish eye lens," although natural to a tuna fish, is not considered a "natural" object in a can of tuna meat. [Citation.] Likewise, a piece of bone is a "foreign" object in a manufactured boneless chicken breast.

Compare California's curious approach in Mexicali Rose v. Superior Court, 822 P.2d 1292, 1301–02 (Cal.1992) (chicken bone hidden in enchilada): If a substance is *natural* to a particular food, a defendant is subject only to negligence liability, as in Louisiana. But if the substance is *foreign*, the trier of fact must ascertain (1) whether the substance's presence in the food could reasonably be expected by the average consumer, *and* (2) whether that presence rendered the food unmerchantable or defective in warranty or tort.

5.   Fried Chicken. "[T]he plaintiff was contentedly munching away one day on a piece of Roy Rogers take-out fried chicken (a wing) when she bit into something in the chicken that she perceived to be a worm." Yong Cha Hong v. Marriott Corp., 656 F. Supp. 445, 446 (D. Md. 1987). In fact, it was not a worm, but "either one of the chicken's major blood vessels (the aorta) or its trachea, both of which . . . would appear worm-like (although not meaty like a worm, but hollow) to a person unschooled in chicken anatomy." Id. at 447. Plaintiff sued in warranty, and defendants moved for summary judgment on the basis of the foreign/natural doctrine. *Held,* motion denied: (1) the reasonable expectation test should be applied, instead of the foreign/natural test; and (2) a jury, applying the test, could reasonably conclude that a piece of fast food fried chicken is unmerchantable if it contains an inedible item of the chicken's anatomy.

6.   Oysters. The courts impose at least a duty to *warn* of the risk of serious, possibly deadly, infection from contaminated oysters, even though the risk normally is only to persons with cirrhosis of the liver, hepatitis, diabetes, high iron content, or suppressed immune systems, which conditions diminish the ability of the body to destroy the bacteria. See, e.g., Kilpatrick v. Superior Court, 11 Cal. Rptr. 2d 323 (Ct. App. 1992); Simeon v. Doe, 618 So. 2d 848 (La. 1993) (no strict liability, but may be duty in negligence to warn); Cain v. Sheraton Perimeter Park South Hotel, 592 So. 2d 218 (Ala. 1991) (jury might find oyster eater did not reasonably expect contamination that could cause hepatitis).

7.   Trichinosis from Pork. Plaintiff purchases smoked pork, thinking it has already been cooked, eats it without further cooking, contracts trichinosis, and dies. See Scheller v. Wilson Certified Foods, Inc., 559 P.2d 1074 (Ariz. Ct. App. 1976) (liability in strict tort and implied warranty denied; common knowledge that pork must be cooked). What if the consumer does cook the pork yet still contracts trichinosis; should a jury be allowed to decide whether the meat was unfit, or should a court rule as a matter of law that the pork was not properly cooked? See Hollinger v. Shoppers Paradise, Inc., 340 A.2d 687 (N.J. Super. Ct. 1975).

8.   Cloudbirds on Cake. In Harris–Teeter, Inc. v. Burroughs, 399 S.E.2d 801 (Va. 1991), plaintiff's daughter-in-law went to the grocery store and bought a birthday cake decorated with two white plastic birds resting on white "clouds" which were part of the cake's design. Plaintiff ate a piece of the cake, white bird and all, swallowing it whole without chewing. Quite soon she realized that she had a problem, and the bird thereafter was surgically removed from her colon. *Held,* applying the plain view doctrine, no negligence in supplying a cake ornament the same color as the icing.

Shoshone Coca–Cola Bottling Co. v. Dolinski

Supreme Court of Nevada, 1966.
82 Nev. 439, 420 P.2d 855.

■ THOMPSON, JUSTICE.

[Leo Dolinski filed a strict tort liability claim against Shoshone Coca–Cola Bottling Company, the manufacturer and distributor of "Squirt," for physical and mental damage from drinking part of a bottle of "Squirt" that contained a decomposed mouse. The jury returned a verdict in the amount of $2,500 for the plaintiff, and Shoshone appealed. Affirmed.]

[Although a plaintiff may establish strict tort liability against a manufacturer and distributor of a bottled beverage, the plaintiff must] still establish that his injury was caused by a defect in the product, and that such defect existed when the product left the hands of the defendant. The concept of strict liability does not prove causation, nor does it trace cause to the defendant.

In the case at hand Shoshone contends that insufficient proof was offered to establish that the mouse was in the bottle of "Squirt" when it left Shoshone's possession. On this point the evidence was in conflict and the jury was free to choose. The Vice–President and General Manager of Shoshone testified, in substance, that had the mouse been in the bottle while at his plant, it would have been denuded because of the caustic solution used and extreme heat employed in the bottle washing and brushing process. As the mouse had hair when examined following the plaintiff's encounter, the Manager surmises that the rodent must have gotten into the bottle after leaving the defendant's possession. On the other hand, the plaintiff offered the expert testimony of a toxicologist who examined the bottle and contents on the day the plaintiff drank from it. It was his opinion that the mouse "had been dead for a long time" and that the dark stains (mouse feces) which he found on the bottom of the bottle must have been there before the liquid was added. The jury apparently preferred the latter evidence which traced cause to the defendant.

We turn to the question of tampering. Shoshone insists that a burden is cast upon the plaintiff to prove that there was no reasonable opportunity for someone to tamper with the bottle after it left Shoshone's control....

The matter of tampering is inextricably tied to the problem of tracing cause to the defendant. This is so whether the claim for relief is based on negligence or strict liability. Whenever evidence is offered by the plaintiff tending to establish the presence of the mouse in the bottle when it left Shoshone's possession, the defense is encouraged to introduce evidence that the mouse must have gotten there after the bottle left Shoshone's control, thus interjecting the possibility that the bottle and its contents were tampered with by someone, perhaps as a practical joke or for some other reason. In this case, as in most cases, positive proof either way is not available. Inferences must be drawn from the best available evidence produced by each side. We have already alluded to that evidence.

It is apparent that the moment plaintiff produces evidence tending to show that the mouse was in the bottle while in the defendant's control, he has, to some degree, negated tampering by others. The converse is likewise true. A fortiori, once it is decided that enough evidence is present to trace cause to the defendant, that same evidence is sufficient to allow the jury to find an absence of tampering. For this reason, any notion that there is a burden of proof as to tampering, simply does not make sense. The sole burden is upon the plaintiff to prove that his injury was caused by a defect in the product and that such defect existed when the product left the hands of the defendant. The defendant, of course, may offer evidence suggesting tampering under a general denial of liability. . . .

[Affirmed.]

NOTES

1. Litigation in deleterious food and drink cases usually focuses on three major issues: (1) whether the food or drink is wholesome or defective; (2) whether the condition of the product in fact caused plaintiff's damages; and (3) whether the product's condition can be attributed to the defendant.

2. Disgusting Junk in Food. As in *Shoshone,* the first two issues are not often seriously contested where the foreign substance in the product is so obviously harmful or offensive that no one could doubt that the product is unwholesome and capable of causing injury, even without medical testimony. See, e.g., Elliott v. Kraft Foods North America, Inc., 118 S.W.3d 50 (Tex. App. 2003) (rocks in box of Grape Nuts cereal); CEF Enterprises, Inc. v. Betts, 838 So. 2d 999 (Miss. App. 2003) (cockroach in Burger King biscuit and gravy breakfast); Bullara v. Checker's Drive–In Rest., Inc., 736 So. 2d 936 (La. App. 1999) (cockroach in chili dog); Hagan v. Coca–Cola Bottling Co., 804 So. 2d 1234 (Fla. 2001) (condom in soft drink); Jones v. GMRI, Inc., 551 S.E.2d 867 (N.C. App. 2001) (piece of metal in meatball); Kroger Co. v. Beck, 375 N.E.2d 640 (Ind. App. 1978) (prick in throat from tip end of hypodermic needle in steak).

The classic case may be Pillars v. R.J. Reynolds Tobacco Co., 78 So. 365, 366 (Miss.1918) (decomposed human toe in chewing tobacco): "We can imagine no reason why, with ordinary care, human toes could not be left out of chewing tobacco, and if toes are found in chewing tobacco, it seems to us that somebody has been very careless."

3. Responsibility for Junk; Tampering. As in *Shoshone,* whether the defendant is *responsible* for the junk finding its way into the food is contested with some frequency. See also Mears v. H.J. Heinz Co., 1995 WL 37344 (Tenn. App.) (tin plate sliver in bowl of soup could have come from sources other than defendant's control, even though expert testified that 90% of tin plate is used in manufacture of tin cans); Campbell Soup Co. v. Gates, 889 S.W.2d 750 (Ark. 1994) (while eating second bowl of chicken-flavored soup, purchased dry, plaintiff nauseated upon discovering maggots, or "little bitty worms with a black head" floating and squiggling around in the soup; *held,* $24,000 judgment reversed: larvae could have entered the soup in the month between time Campbell sold the soup and plaintiff prepared and ate it).

4. Tampering and Junk; Fingers in Food. Sometimes junk is deliberately put in food products by scam artists who then sue the food producer. See, e.g., Tardella v. RJR Nabisco, Inc., 576 N.Y.S.2d 965 (App. Div. 1991) (pin in Baby Ruth candy bar; in view of defendant's detailed evidence of rigorous quality control procedures, plaintiff failed to meet burden of proof that pin was in candy bar when it left defendant's plant). For a discussion of the bogus case of a finger supposedly found in Wendy's chili in San Jose, California, and other cases, see Richtel, The Media Business: Advertising; Wendy's gets a break in the case of the finger in the chili, but it still has work ahead of it, www.nytimes.com (AP) (April 29, 2005) (also reporting case involving a man's claim to have found a syringe in his Diet Pepsi, later discovered to have been "innocently" deposited there by his diabetic relative, but which led to more than 60 copycat incidents in following week, including incident caught on grocery store's videotape showing woman planting syringe in soda).

Tampering—the insertion of foreign matter into food (or medicinal) products— is a serious problem for manufacturers, as the Wendy's incident illustrates. But sometimes such objects do find their way inadvertently into food, as when a man eating a pint of frozen chocolate custard purchased at a Kohl's frozen custard shop (in Wilmington, N.C.) started sucking on an object in the frozen custard, thinking it was a big piece of candy. It didn't taste as delicious as he expected, and when he washed it off, he discovered that it was part of a finger—later revealed to have belonged to an employee and to have been cut off in the frozen custard machine. See Nation: Customer finds employee's finger in frozen custard www.usatoday.com (May 2, 2005, updated May 3).

5. Keeping the Junk. The plaintiff must prove that the junk was really there, and if he swallows or otherwise disposes of it, his lawsuit may well travel the same route. See, e.g., Schafer v. JLC Food Systems, Inc., 2004 WL 78022 (Minn. Ct. App. 2004) (plaintiff swallowed object with the muffin; *held*, no evidence, no case), rev'd 695 N.W.2d 570 (Minn. 2005) (circumstantial evidence allowed).

Compare the case of one author of this book who, in his second week as a first year law student, drank a glass of milk which smelled and tasted like chewing gum. Upon inspecting the milk container, he discovered a "used" piece of chewing gum stuck to the bottom of the container. Discarding the evidence in disgust, he became nauseated and missed two days of classes only to learn in torts class a few months later that he should have kept the evidence to prove his claim.

6. Ordinary Junk. If the object is not necessarily offensive or commonly regarded as repulsive, the plaintiff must establish that the object's presence rendered the food or beverage unwholesome by contaminating the product. Here, expert testimony normally will be required to establish the plaintiff's case. See Willis v. Safeway Stores, 105 N.Y.S.2d 9 (App. Div. 1951) (pieces of cork from crushed bottle cap in beverage).

7. Invisible Junk. If there is no visible foreign substance in the food, the plaintiff will need to establish the causal connection between his illness and the food, typically requiring expert testimony. See, e.g., Gant v. Lucy Ho's Bamboo Garden, Inc., 460 So. 2d 499 (Fla. App. 1984) (food poisoning from egg rolls; doctor testified that the bacteria involved is usually transmitted from fecal matter of infected person, and that the egg rolls were the probable source); Trapnell v. John Hogan Interests, Inc., 809 S.W.2d 606 (Tex. App. 1991) (expert testimony, based on reasonable medical probability, permitted conclusion that fatal allergic reaction was triggered by sulfite potato whiteners).

8. Uneaten Junk. If a person does not ingest the defective food, but is sickened by observing, touching, or perhaps smelling and thinking about it, he may be able to recover if he can establish the causal connection. See, e.g., Prejean v. Great Atlantic & Pacific Tea Co., 457 So. 2d 60 (La. App. 1984) (consumer nauseated by rotten roast that she saw was "green as grass" when she began to wash it; severe vomiting); Wallace v. Coca–Cola Bottling Plants, Inc., 269 A.2d 117 (Me. 1970) (unpackaged prophylactic in Coke); Sowell v. Hyatt Corp., 623 A.2d 1221 (D.C. App. 1993) (plaintiff sickened by observing worm-like object in rice she almost ate; jury issue).

9. Bottle Junk. See generally Bishop, Trouble in a Bottle, 16 Baylor L. Rev. 337 (1964), an interesting article classifying these cases in various respects. Glass is the most frequent intruder into beverage bottles, followed by mice in the following conditions and numbers: dead—16; dead, fur oozing Coca Cola—1; dead and putrid—2; dead, badly battered—1; decayed—2; decomposed—14; decomposed and swollen—1; skeleton only—1; small—1; unspecified—9. Flies, spiders, worms, and cockroaches also appear with some frequency. Led by Louisiana, the "top" nine states (by number of reported cases) are all in the South.

Just how does the proverbial mouse end up in the bottle? See Spangenberg, Exploding Bottles, 24 Ohio St. L.J. 516 (1963).

10. Damages.

A. The cases of the aspiring litigators. At different times during the 1990s, two law students of one author of this book had separate gross food experiences. Student 1, while contentedly eating a Healthy Choice Beef Burrito Ranchero, munched upon a 3″ piece of plastic cellophane located within the burrito. Student 2, while eating a candy bar, thought that it tasted peculiar and discovered that it was infested with little bugs. Using different techniques (Student 1 wrote a demand letter to the manufacturer; Student 2 showed the remaining candy bar to the store manager), both students demanded $1000 for their disgust. Both suppliers offered to settle for $200 to $300, both students rejected the initial offers, and both cases settled within 2–3 weeks for $500.

B. The cases of the missing mouse heads. Unwanted mice may be worth more than cellophane and bugs, especially if the case is pursued with vigor by someone who has passed the bar. AP reported some time ago that a Yakima, Washington woman found the back half of a mouse in a can of Del Monte green beans. "As I put the beans in a serving bowl I noticed a chunk of something meaty [with] little hocks [and] brown fur." "I keep wondering," she said, "who got the front half, with the little ears and the little nose." The offendee's lawyer settled this case for $2,600.

What if she had gone ahead and bitten into the mouse; how much would her case have been worth then? An Anderson, South Carolina nursing assistant bought a barbecue sandwich from a vending machine late one night, heated it in a microwave oven, and took a bite. She heard "an awful crunch," opened the sandwich and discovered a small mouse with a small tail, but no head. She sued, and the jury awarded damages of $10,000. The Greenville, S.C. News, Feb. 24 & 25, 1993.

Just where do you suppose these little mouse heads really *went*?

11. Regulation. The manufacture of food and drink in some respects is closely regulated. Food and drink marketed in the United States must comply with the Federal Food, Drug, and Cosmetic Act, 21 U.S.C.A. § 301 et seq., which prohibits the sale or distribution in interstate commerce of "adulterated" food or drink. A product may be adulterated under § 342 of the Act if it contains amounts of poisons, pesticide residues, additives, filth, or decomposed matter in excess of administratively established tolerances. For obvious technical and economic reasons, trace amounts of such materials are permitted even though larger amounts would clearly be dangerous to health. Many foods, especially fruits and vegetables, that have been treated with pesticides contain some chemical residue. Some harmful substances cannot be removed during processing but are present at such low levels that they represent no real health hazard. Also, most processed foods contain preservatives or additives necessary for longer shelf life, color, or flavor.

These compounds may not be entirely safe in large concentrations but involve little risk at low concentrations. Tolerance for some impurities reflects a judgment that the health risks from small concentrations of even possibly dangerous substances sometimes are outweighed by the benefits derived from their presence (including cost-savings from not removing them). See generally Merrill, Regulating Carcinogens in Food: A Legislator's Guide to the Food Safety Provisions of the Federal Food, Drug, and Cosmetic Act, 77 Mich. L. Rev. 171 (1978).

12. The Delaney Clause. An important effort by Congress to preclude the FDA from exercising its own judgment exists in the "Delaney Clause" of the Federal Food, Drug, and Cosmetic Act. The Delaney Clause was originally enacted in 1958 out of a belief that "cancer deaths are in some way more to be feared than others." Public Citizen v. Young, 831 F.2d 1108 (D.C. Cir. 1987). It provides that "no additive shall be deemed to be safe if it is found to induce cancer when ingested by man or animal." 21 U.S.C.A. § 348 (c)(3)(A). The plain language of the statute provides for no discretion on the part of the FDA; if a substance is carcinogenic, it must be banned.

In practice, although the Delaney Clause is generally observed quite strictly, the FDA has tried to create an exception for *de minimus* risks, as in the case of Orange No. 17 cosmetic dye, where the risk of cancer was determined to be less than one in 19 billion. The basis for this is the FDA's benchmark standard of allowing a one in a million lifetime risk as acceptable in its risk-utility analysis. Sometimes this exception survives judicial review; sometimes not. The agency's approval of Orange No. 17 as an ingredient in cosmetics was overturned in *Public Citizen,* but approval of acrylonitrile (a known carcinogen used in plastic food containers and believed to migrate into the food) was upheld by the same court in Monsanto Co. v. Kennedy, 613 F.2d 947 (D.C. Cir. 1979). See generally M. Gilhooley, Plain Meaning, Absurd Results and the Legislative Purpose: The Interpretation of the Delaney Clause, 40 Admin. L.J. 267 (1988).

13. Violation of Statute—Negligence Per Se. The states have pure food statutes imposing criminal penalties on those who sell adulterated food, regardless of the seller's knowledge of the adulteration or his ability to discover it. For products liability purposes, some jurisdictions treat violations of pure food statutes as negligence per se. See, e.g., Chambley v. Apple Rest., Inc., 504 S.E.2d 551 (Ga. App. 1998) (condom in chicken salad); Allen v. Delchamps, Inc., 624 So. 2d 1065 (Ala. 1993) (prepackaged celery hearts treated with sulfites in violation of FDA regulations banning their use on fresh produce; asthmatic customer suffered anaphylactic reaction); Koster v. Scotch Assoc., 640 A.2d 1225 (N.J. Super. Ct. Law Div. 1993) (salmonella from Smuggler's Cove); Coward v. Borden Foods, Inc., 229 S.E.2d 262 (S.C. 1976) (hard object in Cracker Jack popcorn). Contra, Jones v. GMRI, Inc., 551 S.E.2d 867 (N.C. App. 2001) (negligence per se doctrine inapplicable to food case).

14. On a seller's liability for defective food and drink, see generally D. Owen, Products Liability Law § 7.5 (2d ed. 2008).

CHAPTER 7

DESIGN DEFECTS

Design defects present the most perplexing problems in the field of strict products liability because there is no readily ascertainable external measure of defectiveness.

Caterpillar Tractor Co. v. Beck, 593 P.2d 871, 880 (Alaska 1979).

[Q]uestions related to "design defects" and the determination of when a product is defective, because of the nature of its design, appear to be the most agitated and controversial issues before the courts in the field of products liability.

Prentis v. Yale Mfg. Co., 365 N.W.2d 176, 182 (Mich. 1984).

————

What are a manufacturer's basic responsibilities in designing its products? What factors must be considered in determining whether enough safety has been built into a product? What should be the role of consumer expectations in making determinations of this sort? What should be the effect of proof that redesigning an accident product to make it safer would have been expensive, or that such a redesign would have reduced its usefulness? May the manufacturer of a multi-purpose industrial press delegate responsibilities for certain safety features to its purchasers, who are themselves manufacturers and who may be better situated to know how best to integrate safety considerations with the particular end uses to which they may variously put the press? As difficult as may be some of the conceptual problems surrounding defects in design, the underlying question of design adequacy is simple enough to state: "How safe is safe enough?"

Design defect litigation is surely the most perplexing part of products liability law for courts and commentators. In part, this reflects the fact that the issues involved in this context more than others involve decisions of major importance concerning the allocation of social resources. Not surprisingly, this is the area where the propriety of judicial action has received the greatest scrutiny. It is also the area of greatest concern to manufacturers, since a judicial declaration that the design of the product on trial is "defective" condemns the entire product line.

The paradigmatic design defect case involves the absence of some type of safety device, such as a guard on a power lawnmower, an electrical interlock cut-off device on an industrial machine, or a "safety" on a gun. In addition to this standard way of thinking about design dangers, there are numerous other ways in which products may be defectively designed—from flammable fabrics not treated with flame-retarding chemicals, and drain cleaners comprised of chemicals that are unnecessarily caustic, to products whose moving parts are made of metal too soft or screws too short to perform the product's normal functions safely over its useful life.

In the design-defect context more than others, both plaintiffs and defendants ordinarily must establish their cases on the central issues of defectiveness and causation through expert witnesses trained in the pertinent areas of engineering or science. How a plaintiff's lawyer constructs a case through expert testimony (including expert affidavits and demonstrative evidence, such as models, charts, videotapes and the like), and how the defendant's lawyer through similar types of evidence attempts to tear it down, is the crux of design defect litigation. The effective use of experts in such cases involves a host of interrelated issues of products liability law, the rules of evidence, practical psychology, and lawyering strategy. These are some of the important issues addressed in this chapter.

1. In General

Matthews v. Lawnlite Co.

Supreme Court of Florida, 1956.
88 So. 2d 299.

■ TERRELL, JUSTICE.

[P]laintiff was in Dean's Tropical Furniture Shop examining furniture with the view of purchasing and sat in a lounge chair manufactured by defendant. "As plaintiff sat in said chair he laid his right hand on the right hand arm rest of said chair and the third finger of said right hand extended over the front of the right hand arm rest and under the front end thereof. Thereupon his said third finger of his right hand was completely severed by the moving parts of said chair and the finger fell upon the floor." A motion to dismiss the complaint was granted and this appeal was prosecuted from said order.

[Restatement of Torts § 398 provides:]

"A manufacturer of a chattel made under a plan or design which makes it dangerous for the uses for which it is manufactured is subject to liability to others whom he should expect to use the chattel lawfully or to be in the vicinity of its probable use, for bodily harm caused by his failure to exercise reasonable care in the adoption of a safe plan or design."

* * *

The chair in question is a rocking chair with moving parts; it rocks back and forth. It was constructed of aluminum and was used for rest and recreation; it looks harmless, every aspect of it suggested ease and comfort. There was no notice of any kind that beneath its restful armrest there were moving metal parts so constructed that they would amputate the occupant's fingers with the ease that one clips a choice flower with pruning shears. It was designed, constructed and delivered to the public with these moving parts that were essential to its use. They were completely concealed from the user and as essential parts of the chair were inherently dangerous. No one would suspect that such a dangerous device would be concealed in such an innocent looking instrumentality.

. . . In our view the facts recited bring this case within the rule recited from Restatement of Torts. If such a mechanism is required for the chair, it should be protected by a housing. . . .

[Reversed and remanded.]

McCormack v. Hankscraft Co.

Supreme Court of Minnesota, 1967.
278 Minn. 322, 154 N.W.2d 488.

■ ROGOSHESKE, JUSTICE.

[Four-year-old Andrea McCormack had a cold, and so her mother set up an electric Hankscraft steam vaporizer manufactured by the defendant in Andrea's bedroom. She set the vaporizer on a 2½ foot high seat-step-type metal kitchen stool, and placed the stool against a chifforobe when she put Andrea to bed about 8 p.m. About 1:30 a.m., Mrs. McCormack replenished the vaporizer's water supply by lifting the cap with a mitt and pouring water from a milk bottle into the jar. During the night, Andrea knocked over the vaporizer on her way to the bathroom. The vaporizer separated into its three component parts—a glass jar, a metal pan, and a plastic top-heating unit—and scalding water spilled onto Andrea, causing third-degree burns over much of her body. Andrea (by her father) sued Hankscraft for negligent design, breach of warranty, and strict liability in tort. The jury returned a verdict for Andrea in the amount of $150,000, the trial court granted the defendant's motion for j.n.o.v. and a conditional new trial, and Andrea appealed. *Held*, reversed; judgment for Andrea reinstated.]

The "automatic-electric" vaporizer in question [similar to the one shown below] is of normal design and consists of three component parts—an aluminum pan which serves as a base, a 1–gallon glass jar or water reservoir which is inserted into the pan, and a black plastic cap to which is fastened a black plastic heating-chamber tube. [The jar, 6⅝ inches square and 8 inches high, was a "standard gallon pickle jar" not specially made for the vaporizer. Its top opening was 4½ inches in diameter, its outer neck had a male-type glass thread, and it held about ¾ gallon of water.]

Hankscraft vaporizer design
at time of McCormack v. Hankscraft

Hankscraft vaporizer disassembled.

... The cap and heating chamber assembly, by its own weight, rests loosely upon the glass jar with the black tube extending down into the jar. There are no threads inside the plastic cap or any other means provided to fasten the cap to the threaded neck of the jar. This design and construction were intended by defendant to serve as a safety measure to avoid any buildup of steam in the glass jar, but it also has the result of allowing the water in the jar to gush out instantaneously when the vaporizer is tipped over. This unit can be tipped over easily by a child through the exertion of about 2 pounds of force.

To operate the vaporizer in accordance with the instructions contained in defendant's booklet, the "entire plastic cover" is removed, the glass jar is filled to the filling marker with tap water containing minerals, and the cord is plugged into an electric outlet, whereupon "[t]he vaporizer will produce a gentle cloud of steam within a few minutes." The heating unit is designed so that it automatically turns off whenever the water in the jar decreases to a certain level. As the booklet pictorially illustrates, the water from the jar enters the lower section of the heating chamber through the small hole at the bottom. Here it is heated until it boils and is vaporized into steam, which passes out of the unit through the hole in the cap.

[Within 4 minutes of operation the water inside the heating chamber reaches 212°; the water outside the chamber reaches 172° after 1 hour and 182° after 5 hours; and water of 140° will burn and 180° water will cause third-degree burns to a small child. While a user by touch can feel that the water in the jar outside the heating unit becomes hot during the operation of the vaporizer, there is no movement of the water in the jar or other indication that it is scalding hot, which Mrs. McCormack did not realize. Moreover, while she understood that it was possible to tip the vaporizer with sufficient force, she relied upon defendant's representations that it was "safe," "practically foolproof," and "tip-proof," which she took] to mean that the unit "was safe to use around [her] children" and that she "didn't have to worry" about dangers when it was left unattended in a child's room since this was the primary purpose for which it was sold.

* * *

Defendant's officers realized that the vaporizers would be primarily used in the treatment of children and usually would be unattended[;] that the water in the jar got scalding hot; that this water would cause third-degree burns on a small child; that the water in the jar would gush out instantaneously if the unit were tipped over; . . . that, prior to plaintiff's injury, at least 10 to 12 children had been burned in this manner[;] and that a user could conclude from their booklet that . . . the reserve water in the jar did not itself become scalding hot.

[Plaintiff's two experts testified that the vaporizer's design was defective in failing] to provide a means for securing the plastic cover to the jar in a manner which would prevent the water in the jar from instantaneously discharging when the unit was tipped over. In the opinion of both, the unit could be tipped over with little force and this defective design created a risk of bodily harm to a child if the unit were left operating and unattended in the room. This defect could have been eradicated by the adoption of any one of several practical and inexpensive alternative designs which utilized simple and well known techniques to secure the top to the jar [including simply threading] the inside of the plastic top so it could screw onto the jar and the putting of two or three small holes in the top, which would take care of any danger that steam would build up inside the jar. . . .

[The evidence justified the jury's finding that the defendant had failed to use reasonable care to inform users of the scalding temperature of the water in the vaporizer.]

We similarly conclude and hold that the evidence is also sufficient to support the jury's verdict of liability on the ground that defendant was negligent in adopting an unsafe design. [A manufacturer] has a duty to use reasonable care in designing its product so that [expected users] are protected from unreasonable risk of harm while the product is being used for its intended use. A breach of such duty renders the manufacturer liable. [Citation.] Clearly, such a duty was owed to plaintiff for defendant admitted that the primary, intended use of the vaporizer was for the treatment of children's colds and croup.

The proof is sufficient to support plaintiff's claim of defective design in that, among other defects,[3] defendant failed to exercise reasonable care in

---

3. Plaintiff claimed there were two other defects in design, but we believe the evidence insufficient to predicate liability upon either. It was argued that the water in the jar was rendered too hot because the design permitted steam and its condensate to escape from the eight ¼–inch holes in the upper section of the heating chamber into the water reservoir. But, plaintiff's experts failed to testify that if suggested changes had been

securing the plastic cover to the jar to guard against the reasonably foreseeable danger that a child would tip the unit over when it was in use and be seriously burned by coming in contact with the scalding water that would instantaneously gush out of the jar.

* * *

[T]he evidence reasonably permits a finding that a simple, practical, inexpensive, alternative design which fastened the top to the jar would have substantially reduced or eliminated the danger which caused plaintiff's injuries. Defendant's experts testified that the design adopted was to guard against an explosion because of a buildup of steam in the heating unit and jar, but the jury could have accepted the testimony of plaintiff's experts which indicated the use of defendant's design was not necessary to accomplish this purpose. Moreover, the fact that at the time [of purchase] many other brands of vaporizers on the market were designed in basically this same manner, while certainly relevant, did not necessarily bar the jury from concluding that the exercise of due care required the adoption of a different design.

[The court also found for the plaintiff on warranty and strict liability in tort, adopting the latter doctrine as the law of Minnesota.]

Reversed with directions to enter judgment upon the verdict.

NOTE

1. Theory of Recovery. As the preceding cases illustrate, plaintiffs in most states typically ground a claim for injuries arising from a product's design on any of the conventional triumvirate of negligence, breach of the implied warranty of merchantability, and strict liability in tort. See, e.g., Bishop v. GenTec Inc., 48 P.3d 218, 225–26 (Utah 2002) ("[a]lternative theories are available to prove [the various types of defect], including negligence, strict liability, or implied warranty of merchantability," citing Products Liability Restatement § 2 cmt. *n*). Compare Stahlecker v. Ford Motor Co., 667 N.W.2d 244 (Neb. 2003) (allowing plaintiff to base design claim on negligence or strict liability in tort, but not on implied warranty which was merged into tort law theories).

2. Strict Liability or Negligence? Which theory of liability is *best* for addressing dangers in design? In the materials that follow, as you observe the law's tortured search for a proper "test" of design defectiveness, observe the conflicting attitudes toward these two bases of products liability law.

————

adopted the water's temperature would have been reduced sufficiently so that it would not have caused third-degree burns to plaintiff. Plaintiff also argued that the vaporizer could be tipped too easily. While it was established that an alternative design would substantially increase the amount of force necessary to tip it over, the experts failed to testify as to how much force plaintiff likely would have exerted when she tipped the vaporizer over and therefore there was no indication whether the suggested changes would have prevented her from doing so. The matters which were omitted are not subjects of common knowledge, and in the absence of expert testimony, the jury could only speculate as to whether these suggested changes in design could have prevented plaintiff's injury. This constituted a failure of proof as to proximate cause. [Citations.]

2.   DEFECT TESTS

Whether a plaintiff's claim is formally based on negligence, implied warranty, or strict liability in tort, the most fundamental question in design defect litigation has long been how to assess whether a product's design was reasonably safe or was, instead, "defective." That is, the central issue in modern products liability law is the evolving search for an appropriate yardstick or "test" for determining design defectiveness.

> [C]ourts continue to flounder while attempting to determine how one decides whether a product is "in a defective condition unreasonably dangerous to the user." . . .
>
> The problem with strict liability of products has been one of limitation. No one wants absolute liability where all the article has to do is to cause injury. To impose liability there has to be something about the article which makes it dangerously defective without regard to whether the manufacturer was or was not at fault for such condition. A test for unreasonable danger is therefore vital.

Phillips v. Kimwood Machine Co., 525 P.2d 1033, 1035–36 (Or. 1974).

The search for a design defect test generates at least two distinct levels of inquiry. The first and more fundamental inquiry concerns the development of theoretical models of defectiveness. To date the courts have propounded two principal *tests* for design defectiveness, (1) consumer expectancy, and (2) risk-utility. The next level of the inquiry involves the problem of *semantics*—how the basis of liability can best be explained to juries charged with the difficult task of deciding whether particular designs of particular products on trial should be deemed "defective." Here the problem is one of administration—of translating the theory into practice, for judging in the courtroom real products involved in real accidents.

———

A.   CONSUMER EXPECTATIONS

R. Pound, Social Control Through Law
114 (1942, 1968 reprint).

In civilized society men must be able to assume that those with whom they deal . . . will act in good faith and hence

(a) will make good reasonable expectations which their promises or other conduct reasonably create; [and]

(b) will carry out their undertakings according to the expectations which the moral sentiment of the community attaches thereto; . . . .

———

Corbin on Contracts*

Vol. 1, at 2–4 (1993).

§ 1.1 The Main Purpose of Contract Law is the Realization of Reasonable Expectations Induced by Promises

The underlying purpose of law and government is human happiness and contentment, to be brought about by the satisfaction of human desires in the highest practicable degree....

[T]he law of contracts attempts the realization of reasonable expectations that have been induced by the making of a promise. Doubtless, this is not the only purpose ... of the law of contracts; but it is believed to be the main underlying purpose, and it is believed that an understanding of many of the existing rules and a determination of their effectiveness require a lively consciousness of this underlying purpose....

The law does not attempt the realization of every expectation that has been induced by a promise; the expectation must be a reasonable one. Under no system of law that has ever existed are all promises enforceable. The expectation must be one that most people would have; and the promise must be one that most people would perform. This necessarily leads to a complexity in the law, to the construction of the various rules determining the circumstances under which a promise is said to be enforceable and those under which its performance will be excused.

[Yet] contract problems [are not] solved by the dictum that expectations must be "reasonable." Reasonableness is no more absolute in character than is justice or morality. Like them, it is an expression of the customs and mores—the customs and mores that are themselves complex, variable with time and place, inconsistent and contradictory. Nevertheless, the term is useful, giving direction to judicial research, and producing workable results. The reasonably prudent person, reasonable care and diligence, reasonable expectations, are terms that are not to be abandoned, at least until we can demonstrate that others will work better.

NOTE

"Many courts have used consumer expectations as a criteria for defining defect. If a consumer reasonably expects a product to be safe to use for a purpose, the product is defective if it does not meet those expectations. The consumer expectations test is natural since strict liability in tort developed from the law of warranty. The law of implied warranty is vitally concerned with protecting justified expectations since this is a fundamental policy of the law of contracts." Fischer, Products Liability—The Meaning of Defect, 39 Mo. L. Rev. 339, 348 (1974).

———

Donegal Mutual Insurance v. White Consolidated Industries, Inc.

Court of Appeals of Ohio, 2006.
166 Ohio App.3d 569, 852 N.E.2d 215.

■ DONOVAN, JUDGE.

[Products liability action by homeowners, David and Susan Nearon, and their insurer for damage to the Nearon's home allegedly caused by a design defect in their Frigidaire electric stove. The jury awarded $104,000 in damages to the plaintiffs. The trial judge granted the defendant's motion for j.n.o.v., and plaintiffs appealed.]

At the close of trial, the court instructed the jury to apply the "consumer-expectation test" pertaining to design defect. Under the consumer-expectation test, a product is defective in design or formulation when it is "more dangerous than an ordinary consumer would expect when used in an intended or reasonably foreseeable manner." [Citing former Ohio statute, Ohio Rev. Code § 2307.75(A)(2).] Moreover, the question of what an ordinary consumer expects in terms of the risks posed by the product is generally one for the trier of fact. [Citation.]

Plaintiffs presented evidence of unsafe, unexpected product performance when they alleged that Susan Nearon merely set the electric stove to self-clean mode before it acted defectively and caused the fire that destroyed the Nearons' residence. This is sufficient evidence from which a trier of fact may infer the existence of a product defect.

[J.n.o.v. reversed and verdict for plaintiffs reinstated.]

Vincer v. Esther Williams All–Aluminum Swimming Pool Co.

Supreme Court of Wisconsin, 1975.
69 Wis.2d 326, 230 N.W.2d 794.

This is a products liability case. The second amended complaint alleges that Curt Vincer, the injured plaintiff-appellant, who was two years old at the time of the July 13, 1970, incident, fell into a swimming pool in the backyard of the home of his grandparents, whom he was visiting. The complaint alleges that a retractable ladder to the above-ground pool had been left in the down position, that the pool was unsupervised, and that Curt climbed the ladder, fell into the water and remained there for an extended period of time, resulting in severe brain damage causing permanent and total disablement. [An action in negligence and strict tort was brought against the manufacturer and the retailer-installer of the pool. The strict tort count alleged in part,] "That the swimming pool was defective and unreasonably dangerous because [defendants] failed to take the reasonable and low-cost precaution of building the swimming pool so that the fencing extended across the deck at the top of the ladder opening, with a self-closing, self-latching gate on the deck of the swimming pool so as to prevent access to the swimming pool area by children of the age of Curt Vincer, even when the ladder from the deck to the ground was in the down position."

[The manufacturer demurred, and the trial court sustained the demurrer and dismissed the complaint. Plaintiff appealed.]

■ CONNOR T. HANSEN, JUSTICE.

* * *

In Dippel v. Sciano, this court adopted sec. 402A of Restatement, 2 Torts 2d, pertaining to strict liability in tort. Under this section, where the plaintiff proves he was injured by a product "in a defective condition unreasonably dangerous to the user" and establishes the other requisite elements listed in the section, he is relieved of the burden of proving specific acts of negligence by the manufacturer who is then deemed negligent per se. . . .

Comment *g* to section 402A of Restatement, Torts 2d, defines "defective condition" in part as follows:

> *g.* ***Defective condition.*** The rule stated in this Section applies only where the product is, at the time it leaves the seller's hands, in a condition not contemplated by the ultimate consumer, which will be unreasonably dangerous to him.

The particular defect in the design of the swimming pool, as alleged in the complaint, is the absence of a self-latching and closing gate to prevent entry to the pool. We are satisfied that the swimming pool is not defective in this respect because, as a matter of law, the swimming pool was as safe as it reasonably could be since it did contain a retractable ladder, which unfortunately was allegedly left down and led to the injury of the small child.

Even if a product is defective, it must be shown to be unreasonably dangerous to the user or consumer. Comment *i* to sec. 402A of the Restatement defines "unreasonably dangerous" in part as follows:

> *i.* ***Unreasonably dangerous.*** The rule stated in this Section applies only where the defective condition of the product makes it unreasonably dangerous to the user or consumer. Many products cannot possibly be made entirely safe for all consumption, and any food or drug necessarily involves some risk of harm, if only from over-consumption. Ordinary sugar is a deadly poison to diabetics, and castor oil found use under Mussolini as an instrument of torture. That is not what is meant by "unreasonably dangerous" in this Section. *The article sold must be dangerous to an extent beyond that which would be contemplated by the ordinary consumer who purchases it, with the ordinary knowledge common to the community as to its characteristics.* (Emphasis supplied.)

* * *

Thus, the test in Wisconsin of whether a product contains an unreasonably dangerous defect depends upon the reasonable expectations of the ordinary consumer concerning the characteristics of this type of product. If the average consumer would reasonably anticipate the dangerous condition of the product and fully appreciate the attendant risk of injury, it would not be unreasonably dangerous and defective. This is an objective test and is not dependent upon the knowledge of the particular injured consumer, although his knowledge may be evidence of contributory negligence under the circumstances.

* * *

Based upon the principles discussed above, we conclude that the swimming pool described in plaintiff's complaint does not contain an unreasonably dangerous defect. The lack of a self-latching gate certainly falls within the category of an obvious rather than a latent condition. Equally important, the average consumer would be completely aware of the risk of harm to small children due to this condition, when the retractable ladder is left in a down position and the children are left unsupervised. We conclude, therefore, that plaintiffs' second amended complaint fails to state a cause of action.

Judgment and order affirmed.

[Dissenting opinion of Wilkie, C.J., omitted.]

NOTES

1. **Obvious Dangers.** When a consumer is injured by an obvious hazard, will his expectations ever be frustrated? The expectancy test plainly precludes liability in most such cases. See, e.g., Bourne v. Marty Gilman, Inc., 452 F.3d 632 (7th Cir. 2006) (risk that aluminum goalpost might snap and fall dangerously when Ball State students rushed on field to celebrate football victory and climbed on post); Chaney v. Hobart Int'l, Inc., 54 F. Supp. 2d 677, 681 (E.D. La. 1999) ("As dangerous as the meat grinder may have been without a feed pan guard, it was clearly 'not dangerous to an extent beyond that which would be contemplated by the ordinary user.' The possibility of injury is glaring."). See also Brown v. Sears, Roebuck & Co., 328 F.3d 1274, 1282–83 (10th Cir. 2003) (Utah law) (ordinary and prudent user would expect danger to toddler standing behind riding mower operated in reverse; hence, mower not defectively designed for failure to have no-mow-in-reverse feature).

2. **Children.** Why did the *Vincer* court test the adequacy of the pool's design against the expectations of the ordinary *adult* consumer? Were not the expectations of the injured *child* deserving of protection? Were they not quite plainly disappointed?

In Bellotte v. Zayre Corp., 352 A.2d 723 (N.H. 1976), a five-year old child was burned when his cotton pajama top ignited while he was playing with matches. In deciding whether the pajamas were "unreasonably dangerous to the user or consumer" because the fabric had not been treated with an effective fire-retardant substance, the court addressed the question of whether the safety characteristics of the pajamas should be measured according to the expectations of the "consuming" child or the "purchasing" parent. Plaintiffs contended that "the test should be whether they were dangerous to an extent beyond that which would be contemplated by the ordinary five-year old child." The court did not agree: "Children of that age do not contemplate even the unavoidable dangers of cotton pajamas and their flammable characteristics. There would therefore be no base from which to determine unreasonableness and the seller would become an insurer." Id. at 725.

Compare Welch v. Scripto–Tokai Corp., 651 N.E.2d 810 (Ind. App. 1995) (3–year–old ignited his pajamas with disposable butane cigarette lighter; held, ordinary consumer is adult, and adults expect lighters to ignite a flame).

Do *Vincer*, *Bellotte*, and *Welch* deny young children the reasonable protection of the law? Do they represent a subtle reversion to the now-discredited doctrine of imputed contributory negligence which barred an injured child's action against a third party tortfeasor if the child's parent was guilty of negligent supervision? What if the child in *Bellotte* had been ten years old? Sixteen? What if Mr. Bellotte had bought his wife an excessively flammable nightgown that ignited as she leaned over the stove? Whose expectations should control, those of the "ultimate consumer," under comment *g*, or those of the "ordinary consumer who purchases" the product, under comment *i*?

3. Patients. Whose expectations should control concerning an injury-producing prescription drug or medical device, those of the *patient* or of the *physician*? V. Mueller & Co. v. Corley, 570 S.W.2d 140, 145 (Tex. Civ. App.1978), was an action against the manufacturer and distributor of a silicone breast prosthesis that broke open inside the plaintiff. Verdict was for the plaintiff, and defendant appealed, arguing that the jury should have been instructed to measure the adequacy of the product against the expectations of the surgeon who had selected the device rather than those of the patient into whom it had been implanted. *Held*, plaintiff's judgment affirmed:

> The defective condition in the prosthesis in question rendered it unreasonably dangerous to Mrs. Corley, not to her physician, Dr. Leeves. The appropriate question for the jury, therefore, was whether the defective condition was one which was not contemplated by the user, the "ultimate consumer." Restatement (2d) of Torts § 402A (1965). The trial court properly keyed its instructions to the mind of the person who would be injured by the dangerous condition of the product.

Is *Corley* consistent with *Vincer* and *Bellotte*?

4. Employees. In Jackson v. Coast Paint & Lacquer Co., 499 F.2d 809, 812 (9th Cir. 1974), plaintiff was injured while spray-painting the inside of a tank car when the accumulated paint fumes ignited unexpectedly. Plaintiff sued the paint manufacturer for failing to warn of this risk. The defendant contended that no warning was necessary since plaintiff's *employer* knew of the risk, even if plaintiff did not. *Held*, for plaintiff. Since warnings could have been placed effectively upon the paint container labels, the "community" whose expectations were relevant consisted of the painters who would be exposed to the danger, not the employers who bought the paint.

5. Bystanders. Suppose plaintiff is walking along a sidewalk when without warning he is hit from the rear by an automobile with an unusual steering characteristic known to the purchaser but not to the operator. Whose expectations should control? Cf. Ewen v. McLean Trucking Co., 706 P.2d 929 (Or. 1985) (pedestrian, struck by truck with poor visibility, not "consumer" under comment *i*).

6. What characteristic do the children, patients, employees and bystanders in these situations all share in common? Should identical expectancy principles accordingly be applied to all four types of plaintiffs? Why or why not?

7.   Expert Consumers. How about the *expert* consumer, the one who knows *more* about a product's dangers, and thus has *lower* expectations as to its safety than the average person in the community? "[A] consumer with less than ordinary expectations, based upon particular expertise, should not gain from having ordinary expectations credited to him." Rheingold, What Are the Consumer's "Reasonable Expectations"?, 22 Bus. Law. 589, 593 n. 16 (1967).

Consider, however, the objective nature of the test prescribed in comment *i*; cf. comment *g*. It is sometimes said that the injured consumer's special knowledge of the danger is not relevant to the defectiveness issue but goes instead to his or her contributory negligence or assumption of risk. Which approach is better? Should the test allow a product to be deemed defective when used by one type of person but not when used by another? What do you think of this type of "shifting defectiveness"?

8.   Consider the broader issue: Why an *objective* basis to the test? "[Are] not the expectations of the specific injured consumer enough? He must be given credit for expecting a product that was reasonably safe. He certainly did not expect an unreasonably dangerous product." L. Green, Strict Liability Under Sections 402A and 402B: A Decade of Litigation, 54 Tex. L. Rev. 1185, 1211 (1976).

9.   Suppose the plaintiff in *Vincer* had been able to establish that dozens of young children are similarly injured or killed each year and that the addition of a self-closing and latching gate would have raised the cost of the $1,000 pool by only $3. Are these facts relevant to consumer expectations?

10.   In addition to a few statutes mandating the consumer expectations test, some courts still adhere to the test as a matter of common law. See, e.g., Green v. Smith & Nephew AHP, Inc., 629 N.W.2d 727, 743 (Wis. 2001) (allergic reactions to latex gloves used by health care workers; reaffirming that state's exclusive reliance on "consumer-contemplation test" in strict products liability cases).

Note that *Donegal* was decided under an Ohio products liability statute that then allowed for liability based solely on a violation of ordinary consumer safety expectations. In 2004, the legislature reduced the role of consumer expectations to one of several factors relevant to the foreseeability of risk in a broad-based risk-utility test for design defect. See Ohio Rev. Code Ann. § 2307.75(B)(5).

11.   Foundations of the Consumer Expectations Test. What is it that lies behind consumer expectations that justifies imposing liability on the basis of their frustration? See Markle v. Mulholland's Inc., 509 P.2d 529, 532–534 (Or. 1973), where the majority remarked that consumer expectations flow from a judicial assumption that a product seller implicitly represents "that the article is not unreasonably dangerous if put to its intended use. . . . These implications are analogous to those underlying a representation of merchantable quality."

See Shapo, A Representational Theory of Consumer Protection: Doctrine, Function and Legal Liability for Product Disappointment, 60 Va. L. Rev. 1109, 1370 (1974):

> Judgments of liability for consumer product disappointment should center initially and principally on the portrayal of the product which is made, caused to be made or permitted by the seller. This portrayal should be viewed in the context of the impression reasonably received by the consumer from representations or other communications made to him about the product by various means: through advertising, by the appearance of the product, and by the other ways in which the product projects an image on the mind of the consumer, including impressions created by widespread social agreement about the product's function.

12.   "Surprise." Judge Roger Traynor perceived the consumer expectations test to be principally directed to the "surprise element of danger." Traynor, The

Ways and Meanings of Defective Products and Strict Liability, 32 Tenn. L. Rev. 363, 370 (1965). How helpful would a test be that based liability on whether the *victim* was "surprised" that the accident occurred? On whether an *ordinary consumer* would be surprised? On whether the *jury*, viewing the accident in retrospect, was surprised?

Problems With the Consumer Expectations Test*

Few courts adhere closely to the letter of section 402A's consumer expectations test in proving design defect. The test has proved unworkable for a variety of reasons. First, it connotes a contract-based liability, encouraging the jury to rely intuitively on principles of bargaining and warranty. Second, if the product contains a defect which is apparent or obvious, the consumer's expectations arguably include the apparent danger, preventing liability and therefore discouraging product improvements which could easily and cost-effectively alleviate the danger. Third, bystanders, who are widely recognized as protected by both tort and contract theories of products liability regardless of privity, cannot be said to have any expectations about a product which causes them injury.

Perhaps the most important criticism of the consumer expectations test as it relates to design defects is the impossibility of the task it requires: to define just what an ordinary consumer expects of the technical design characteristics of a product. While it can be assumed that consumers expect a certain level of safety, how is that level defined when it comes to specific design criteria? For example, what do consumers expect of the structural soundness of one type of metal as opposed to another with slightly different characteristics that, if used, would require changes in still other aspects of the design? If the ordinary consumer can be said reasonably to expect a product to be "strong," how strong is strong? Is a general impression of strength or quality sufficient when it comes to technical design features? If so, how is that impression measurable against the actual condition of the design feature in question? These difficult questions led many courts to reject the consumer expectations test as the sole test for defective design.

NOTES

1. A 5–6 inch rock strikes the wheel of plaintiff's 4–wheel–drive pickup truck at normal highway speed. Thirty minutes later, the wheel comes apart, causing the truck to leave the highway and tip over. Violation of the consumer expectations test under § 402A? See Heaton v. Ford Motor Co., 435 P.2d 806 (Or. 1967).

2. "[A]n attempt to determine the consumer's reasonable expectations of safety concerning a technologically complex product may well be an exercise in futility, for the consumer may have at most only a generalized expectancy—perhaps more accurately only an unconscious hope—that the product will not harm him if

*From, Davis, Design Defect Liability: Wayne L. Rev. 1217, 1236–37 (1993). In Search of a Standard of Responsibility, 39

he treats it with a reasonable amount of care." Montgomery & Owen, Reflections on the Theory and Administration of Strict Tort Liability for Defective Products, 27 S.C. L. Rev. 803, 823 (1976).

"In a sense the ordinary purchaser cannot reasonably expect anything more than that reasonable care in the exercise of the skill and knowledge available to design engineers has been exercised. The test can be utilized to explain most any result that a court or jury chooses to reach. The application of such a vague concept in many situations does not provide much guidance for a jury." W. Page Keeton, Dan B. Dobbs, Robert E. Keeton & David G. Owen, Prosser & Keeton on Torts 699 (5th ed. 1984).

3. How might a plaintiff prove a violation of consumer expectations? By:

A. Testimony by the plaintiff as to his own expectations?

B. Testimony by the dealer as to the expectations of purchasers of such products generally under similar circumstances?

C. The results of an expectations poll taken in the relevant community?

See Turner v. General Motors Corp., 514 S.W.2d 497, 500 (Tex. Civ. App. 1974) (defendant dealer "testified that, based upon his forty-five years of sales experience, the average consumer believes that a sedan vehicle will be a reasonably safe product in a roll-over").

4. Most consumers are savvy enough to know that some percentage of cars leaving the assembly line (perhaps especially those constructed on Mondays) are dangerously defective, and that some pop bottles and "hamburgers" contain foreign matter. How should such expectations of a cynically realistic society be dealt with under the expectancy model when a consumer is injured by one of the many "lemons" spewed out by an imperfect industrial system? See Dickerson, Products Liability: How Good Does a Product Have to Be?, 42 Ind. L.J. 301, 315–16 (1967).

5. If occasional "lemons" are indeed an unavoidable element of our industrial system, given today's resources and technology, should consumers have a "right" to expect anything more? Stated otherwise, is it logical for the legal system to demand more perfection from the industrial system than it in fact is capable of achieving? Or are these the right questions at all?

6. What is your view as to whether any of the following "flaws" in the expectancy model diminish its usefulness as a decision-making tool: "(1) humans lack the data necessary to form expectations; (2) humans are psychologically unable to contemplate injury to themselves and thus underestimate the importance of such injury in making decisions; and (3) people overvalue short-term gains and losses and undervalue long-range considerations." See Hubbard, Reasonable Human Expectations: A Normative Model for Imposing Strict Liability for Defective Products, 29 Mercer L. Rev. 465, 475 (1978).

7. In 1985, the European Community promulgated a Directive "Concerning Liability for Defective Products," providing in Article 6 that:

1. A product is defective when it does not provide the safety which a person is entitled to expect, taking all circumstances into account, including:

(a) the presentation of the product;

(b) the use to which it could reasonably be expected that the product would be put; and

(c) the time when the product was put into circulation.

2. A product shall not be considered defective for the sole reason that a better product is subsequently put into circulation.

See C.J. Miller & R. Goldberg, Product Liability (2d ed. 2004); Howells & Mildred, Is European Products Liability More Protective Than the Restatement (Third) of Torts: products Liability, 65 Tenn. L. Rev. 985 (1998); J. Stapleton, Product Liability, ch. 10 (1994).

8. On the consumer expectations test, see generally Kysar, The Expectations of Consumers, 103 Colum. L. Rev. 1700, 1701 (2003); V. Schwartz & R. Tedesco, The Re–Emergence of "Super Strict" Liability: Slaying the Dragon Again, 71 U. Cin. L. Rev. 917 (2003); Phillips, Consumer Expectations, 53 S.C. L. Rev. 1047 (2002); Korzec, Dashing Consumer Hopes: Strict Products Liability and the Demise of the Consumer Expectations Test, 20 B.C. Int'l & Comp. L. Rev. 227 (1997); Little, The Place of Consumer Expectations in Product Strict Liability Actions for Defectively Designed Products, 61 Tenn. L. Rev. 1189 (1994); D. Owen, Products Liability Law § 8.3 (2d ed. 2008); 1 D. Owen, M.S. Madden, & M. Davis, Madden & Owen on Products Liability § 8:3 (3d ed.2000).

––––––––

B. RISK-UTILITY

Discontent with some of the shortcomings of the consumer expectations test, and hesitant to abandon the familiar calculus of risk principles of negligence law, many courts have employed an approach for ascertaining design defectiveness called "risk-utility," "risk-benefit," or "cost-benefit" analysis. Courts and commentators began to focus on the appropriateness of this form of analysis for design defect determinations in the 1970s. See, e.g., Donaher, Piehler, Twerski & Weinstein, The Technological Expert in Products Liability Litigation, 52 Tex. L. Rev. 1303, 1307 (1974):

> It is time to abandon the perspective of the reasonable consumer ... and formulate the strict liability question for what it is. The issue in every products case is whether the product *qua* product meets society's standards of acceptability. The unreasonable danger question, then, is posed in terms of whether, given the risks and benefits of and possible alternatives to the product, we as a society will live with it in its existing state or will require an altered, less dangerous form. Stated succinctly, the question is whether the product is a reasonable one given the reality of its use in contemporary society.

The basic cost-benefit or "calculus-of-risk" approach to products liability decision-making was initially examined in the negligence context, above. Yet the fundamentals are worth restating. "The basic notion of cost-benefit analysis is not new. Any individual decision is usually the consequence of the actor's assessment of the advantages (benefits) and disadvantages (costs) of the action. Government, no less than individuals, has always made such assessments." H. Green, Cost–Risk–Benefit Assessment and the Law: Introduction and Perspective, 45 Geo. Wash. L. Rev. 901, 903–04 (1977). Consider also Merrill, Risk–Benefit Decision–Making by the Food and Drug Administration, 45 Geo. Wash. L. Rev. 994, 996 (1977): " 'Risk-benefit' ... includes any technique for making choices that explicitly or implicitly attempts to measure the potential adverse consequences of an activity and to predict its benefits. In its most refined form, such an analysis may make use of refined mathematical methods for calculating risks and benefits, attempting to assign uniform values, usually in dollars, to all factors, including human lives."

One early court explained that determining whether a design risk is "unreasonable" involves "a balancing of the probability and seriousness of harm against the costs of taking precautions. Factors to be considered include the availability of alternative designs, the cost and feasibility of adopting alternative designs, and the frequency or infrequency of injury resulting from the design." Raney v. Honeywell, Inc., 540 F.2d 932, 935 (8th Cir. 1976). In short, a product is deemed "defective" under a risk-utility test if the costs of improving its safety are less than the safety benefits resulting from the improvement.

While one purpose of the cost-benefit approach is to provide manufacturers with an incentive to improve the safety of excessively hazardous products, for various reasons the rule in practice may not operate to reduce product accidents to their "optimal" level—the point at which the sum of accident costs and accident avoidance costs is minimized. See, e.g., Calabresi, Optimal Deterrence and Accidents, 84 Yale L.J. 656 (1975); Calabresi & Hirschoff, Toward a Test for Strict Liability in Torts, 81 Yale L.J. 1055 (1972). Nevertheless, many courts have found risk-utility analysis to be a helpful tool in deciding how to allocate losses from product accidents. While economic efficiency may not be precisely optimized through liability determinations based upon risk-benefit analysis, the test may help achieve a roughly efficient allocation of resources by discouraging manufacturers from marketing products in conditions that generate more accident costs than social utility. Moreover, higher prices from liability judgments and settlements should discourage excessive *consumption* of such products by consumers. Finally, judicial use of an efficiency-based standard of liability may have important moral value in punishing and rectifying the wasteful (unjustified) sacrifice of human life and limb and in promoting equality of rights for manufacturers and consumers.

Nichols v. Union Underwear Co.

Supreme Court of Kentucky, 1980.
602 S.W.2d 429.

■ STEPHENS, JUSTICE.

... Four-year-old Richard Nichols was badly burned while playing with matches when his T-shirt caught fire. Through his father, as next friend, he sued Union Underwear Company, Inc., the manufacturer and seller of the shirt. The basis of the suit was strict liability for design defect. [Jury verdict for Union, affirmed by the Court of Appeals. The sole issue before the Supreme Court is whether the trial court erred in instructing the jury on the definition of "unreasonably dangerous" based on comment *i* of § 402A.]

[T]he proof presented concerned itself with the following major areas: (1) the flammability of the fabric of the shirt; (2) the risk of clothing-inflicted burns to children; (3) the availability of commercially feasible, alternative designs and fabrics for this particular article of clothing; (4) the extent of consumer awareness of the danger inherent in flammable children's clothing; (5) the alleged lack of such awareness of danger by this child and his mother; and (6) the significance of the fact that the fabric complies with applicable federal statutory standards for flammability. It is clear that the jury was given ample evidence on which to base its decision.

* * *

[Nichols complains of Instruction #4:]

A product is "unreasonably dangerous" only if it is dangerous to an extent beyond that which would be contemplated by an ordinary adult purchaser thereof, with ordinary knowledge as to its inherent characteristics.

Nichols contends that this instruction was erroneous and prejudicial. He claims that danger beyond an ordinary purchaser's contemplation is only one of several factors to be considered in determining if a product is, in fact, unreasonably dangerous. Further, he argues that a product's danger does not become reasonable simply because it is within the contemplation or actual awareness of the average consumer. Finally, he contends that no definition of the term "unreasonably dangerous" should have been given, but, as one was given, it should not have singled out one factor (consumer awareness) but, instead, should have brought all factors relevant to that determination to the attention of the jury.

* * *

The effect of this instruction is to insulate a product from liability simply because it is patently dangerous, or because it is no more dangerous than would be anticipated by the ordinary person. Some seventeen jurisdictions adhere to this rule, eighteen have repudiated it, and sixteen, including Kentucky, have not addressed the issue. [Citation.] We now join those which have considered and rejected "patent danger" or "consumer expectation" as an absolute defense to strict liability for defective design....

We are immediately met with the difficult problem of describing the standard to which the fact finder should compare the product to decide whether it was in a "defective condition unreasonably dangerous" when sold....

We believe that consumer knowledge, the factor considered below, is only one of the factors that should be before the jury in determining whether a product is unreasonably dangerous. We will not set out an exclusive list of the factors which lead to this determination.... Noted commentators have suggested many factors. But the facts of the individual case will determine what is relevant to each action.

In the event of another trial, the jury should be instructed as follows:

You will find for the plaintiff only if you are satisfied from the evidence that the material of which the T-shirt was made created such a risk of its being accidentally set on fire by a child wearing it that an ordinarily prudent company engaged in the manufacture of clothing, being fully aware of the risk, would not have put it on the market; otherwise, you will find for the defendant.

[Reversed and remanded.]

■ LUKOWSKY, JUSTICE, concurring.

I agree with the opinion of the majority as far as it goes. However, the opinion leaves the law in products liability design defect cases amorphous. It fails to identify the gut issue.

I believe that whether a design is unreasonably dangerous must be determined by a social utility standard—risk versus benefit. If the benefits to be gained by the consuming public outweigh the risks of danger inherent in a particular design, such a product cannot be "unreasonably dangerous." [Citations.] The bottom line is that the trier of fact is required to balance two pairs of factors existing at the time of manufacture: (1) the likelihood that the product would cause the claimants harm or similar harms, and the seriousness of those harms; against (2) the manufacturer's burden of designing a product that would have prevented those harms, and the adverse effect that alternative design would have on the usefulness of the product. That is to say that the manufacturer is not liable unless at the time of manufacture the magnitude of the danger to the claimant out-weighed the utility of the product to the public. [Citations.] The ultimate inquiry is risk versus benefit.

In the event of another trial, I believe the jury should be instructed as follows:

You will find for the Plaintiff if you are satisfied from the evidence that at the time of the manufacture of the cotton and polyester T-shirt the risk of harm from its being accidentally set on fire while being worn by a child outweighed the benefit to the public from its availability in the market-place. Otherwise, you will find for the defendant.

■ STEPHENSON, JUSTICE, dissenting.

In my opinion the only error on the part of the trial court was the failure to give a directed verdict to the defendant here.

Ordinarily in "products liability" cases, I think of design defects as failure to provide proper safety measures in design. For example: lawn mowers, farm machinery, etc. In the machinery cases it is the product itself that has the propensity to cause harm to the user.

Here the T-shirt was manufactured in conformity with applicable federal standards for flammability. In the circumstances of this case, it is absurd to have a jury decide whether the T-shirt is "unreasonably dangerous." Had the manufacturer used highly flammable materials in the garment, I could understand submission of the case to the jury, but not in this situation.

N O T E

Can you restate, precisely, the risk-utility standard Justice Lukowsky proposes?

———

Sperry–New Holland v. Prestage

Supreme Court of Mississippi, 1993.
617 So.2d 248.

■ PRATHER, PRESIDING JUSTICE.

[Plaintiff was injured when his untucked shirt became stuck in the auger of a combine manufactured by the defendant. Plaintiff sued the defendant for negligence and strict liability in tort, alleging that the combine was defectively designed. The jury found for plaintiff on both counts, and defendant appealed. At issue was whether the trial court erred in applying a "risk-utility" instead of a "consumer expectations" analysis.]

This case requires a re-examination of Mississippi products liability law. Two competing theories of strict liability in tort can be extrapolated from our case law. While our older decisions applied a "consumer expectations" analysis in products cases, recent decisions have turned on an analysis under "risk-utility." In this case, Sperry claims that the trial court erred in applying a "risk-utility" theory of recovery, and not a "consumer expectations" theory, when ruling on motions and jury instructions. Prestage argues that while "consumer expectations" was the law at one time, recent cases have embraced "risk-utility."

We today apply a "risk-utility" analysis as adopted in Whittley v. City of Meridian, 530 So. 2d 1341 (Miss. 1988) and Hall v. Mississippi Chemical Exp., Inc., 528 So. 2d 796 (Miss. 1988) and write to clarify our reasons for the adoption for that test.

[Mississippi adopted § 402A in State Stove Manufacturing Co. v. Hodges, 189 So. 2d 113, 119 (Miss. 1966).] *State Stove* explicitly holds that the extent of strict liability of a manufacturer for harm caused by its product is not that of an insurer. However, strict liability does relieve the plaintiff of the onerous burden of proving negligence (i.e. fault). Fault is supplied as a matter of law. [Citation.]

Section 402A is still the law in Mississippi. How this Court defines the phrases "defective condition" and "unreasonably dangerous" used in 402A dictates whether a "consumer expectations" analysis or a "risk-utility" analysis will prevail. Problems have arisen because our past decisions have been unclear and have been misinterpreted in some instances.

"Consumer Expectations" Analysis

* * *

In a "consumer expectations" analysis, "[o]rdinarily the phrase 'defective condition' means that the article has something wrong with it, that it did not function as expected." [Citation.] Comment *g* of Section 402A defines "defective condition" as "a condition not contemplated by the ultimate consumer, which will be unreasonably dangerous to him." Thus, in a "consumer expectations" analysis, for a plaintiff to recover, the defect in a product which causes his injuries must not be one which the plaintiff, as an ordinary consumer, would know to be unreasonably dangerous to him. In other words, if the plaintiff, applying the knowledge of an ordinary consumer, sees a danger and can appreciate that danger, then he cannot recover for any injury resulting from that appreciated danger.

* * *

"Risk–Utility" Analysis

In a "risk-utility" analysis, a product is "unreasonably dangerous" if a reasonable person would conclude that the danger-in-fact, whether foreseeable or not, outweighs the utility of the product. Thus, even if a plaintiff appreciates the danger of a product, he can still recover for any injury resulting from that danger provided that the utility of the product is outweighed by the danger that the product creates. . . .

* * *

Around the country, the test generally employed to determine liability for products defects is the "risk-utility" test developed by Dean Wade. W. Kip Viscusi, Wading Through the Muddle of Risk–Utility Analysis, 39 Amer. L. R. 573, 574 (1990); Kim Larsen, Strict Products Liability and the Risk–Utility Test for Design Defect: An Economic Analysis, 84 Colum. L. R. 2045, 2046 (1984) (stating that in recent years, the "risk-utility" test has replaced the "consumer expectations" test in defective design cases). "Risk-utility" has become the trend in most federal and state jurisdictions.

"Consumer Expectations" vs. "Risk–Utility"

This Court has clearly moved away from a "consumer expectations" analysis and has moved towards "risk-utility." Consistent with the national trend, the two most recent decisions of this Court applied a "risk-utility" analysis to strict products liability. . . .

A "risk-utility" analysis best protects both the manufacturer and the consumer.[3] It does not create a duty on the manufacturer to create a completely safe product. Creating such a product is often impossible or prohibitively expensive. Instead, a manufacturer is charged with the duty to make its product reasonably safe, regardless of whether the plaintiff is aware of the product's dangerousness. This is not to say that a plaintiff is

---

3. In balancing a product's utility against the risk of injury it creates, a trial court may find it helpful to refer to the seven factors enumerated in Professor John Wade's article, On the Nature of Strict Tort Liability for Products, 44 Miss. L.J. 825 (1973). . . .

not responsible for his own actions. In balancing the utility of the product against the risk it creates, an ordinary person's ability to avoid the danger by exercising care is also weighed.[4]

* * *

Affirmed. [Concurring opinion of McRae, J., omitted.]

NOTES

1. Note that both *Nichols* and *Prestage* (n.4) reveal how the risk-utility test arose to a large extent in response to plaintiff's problems with the consumer expectations test when a product danger is open and obvious.

2. In risk-utility determinations, precisely what is to be balanced against what? Reconsider Justice Lukowsky's concurring opinion, in *Nichols*, and the court's opinion in *Prestage*, focusing on this precise issue. Are their formulations of the risk-utility issue correct?

Design Defectiveness: The Risk–Utility Test*
Nature of the Risk–Utility Test

The basic "risk-benefit," "cost-benefit," "risk-utility," or "calculus of risk" approach to products liability decision-making derives from the law of negligence. The fundamentals of this approach are nearly identical in the strict tort context, and they are worth restating here. Most decisions, including design safety decisions of manufacturers, result from an actor's evaluation of the apparent balance of the advantages (benefits) and disadvantages (costs) of some proposed course of action. Under such a cost-benefit (or "risk-utility") test a design is "unreasonable" or "defective" if the costs of eliminating a particular hazard are less than the safety benefits expected to result therefrom.

Thus, the type and amount of safety required is generally a function of the type, likelihood, and amount of harm (together viewed as the magnitude of the risk) that precautions (of a particular cost) may be expected to prevent. If the risk posed by the sale and use of a product in a certain condition is great, substantial precautions must be taken to avert the risk; if the risk is small, precautions may be small as well. Thus, if the risk at issue concerns the possible failure of an automobile's steering, brakes, or tires at highway speeds, or the possibility that a punch press ram may

---

4. [Under the "patent danger" rule, a product with an open and obvious danger is not more dangerous than contemplated by the consumer and hence could not be unreasonably dangerous under the court's former definition of product defect in terms of consumer expectations. However, under the risk-utility test now adopted by the court,] we hold, necessarily, that the "patent danger" bar is no longer applicable in Mississippi. Under a "risk-utility" analysis . . ., the openness and obviousness of a product's design is simply a factor to consider in determining whether a product is unreasonably dangerous. [Citations.]

* *From*, D. Owen, Products Liability Law § 5.7 (2d ed. 2008).

unexpectedly depress upon an operator's hand, the manufacturer must employ the utmost precautions to avert the risk. Yet, if the risk is relatively minimal, reasonably appearing to involve at most the risk of minor harm to person or property—scratches, stains, or the harmless malfunction of the product—then a manufacturer need apply only minimal precautions to reduce such risks. This principle of balance that inheres in tort law generally is sometimes referred to as the "calculus of risk."

The Hand Formula in the Strict Liability Context

The most celebrated formulation of the risk-benefit test, albeit in the context of negligence rather than "strict" products liability, was provided by Judge Learned Hand in the case of *United States v. Carroll Towing Co.*[1] In *Carroll Towing*, Judge Hand reasoned that a determination of the extent of precaution appropriate to an occasion generally reflects a calculus of three factors: the burden of taking precautions to avoid a risk of harm, on the one side, balanced against the likelihood that the actor's conduct will produce the harm multiplied by the seriousness of the harm, on the other. Negligence is implied if an actor fails to adopt a burden of precaution of less magnitude than the harm it is likely to prevent. Judge Hand expressed this concept algebraically: Negligence is suggested if $B < P \times L$, where B is the burden or cost of avoiding accidental loss expected to result if B is not undertaken, P is the increase in the probability of loss if B is not undertaken, and L is the probable magnitude (expected cost) of such loss if it does occur. This is the so-called "Hand formula." If the formula is supplemented with a symbol for the implication of negligence, N, the full formula reads:

$$B < P \times L \Rightarrow N$$

Thus, conceived and applied to negligence determinations in the products liability context, the Hand formula may be explained as follows: if the cost of adopting a particular safety precaution (B) is less than the safety gains expected to result therefrom (P x L), the manufacturer's failure to adopt the precaution implies its negligence (N).

By substituting "defect" for "negligence" (D for N), the Hand formula converts comfortably to the "strict" products liability task of determining defectiveness. So reformulated, the defectiveness "equation" looks like this:

$$B < P \times L \Rightarrow D$$

In cost-benefit terms, the formula states:

(Accident Prevention) Costs < (Safety) Benefits ⇒ Defect

In short, a product is defective if the safety benefits of a particular untaken safety precaution exceed the resulting costs, including any diminished usefulness or diminished safety.[2] Most courts have formulated the risk-

---

1. 159 F.2d 169, 173 (2d Cir. 1947). Perhaps the most helpful study of the test is Gilles, The Invisible Hand Formula, 80 Va. L. Rev. 1015, 1025 (1994).

2. See Owen, Toward a Proper Test for Design Defectiveness: "Micro–Balancing" Costs and Benefits, 75 Tex. L. Rev. 1661, 1690 (1997).

utility test in broader terms, whereby the *product's* risks are weighed against its benefits or utility.[3] Yet the formulation above (the Hand formula in cost-benefit terms) quite accurately describes the test as lawyers and judges properly put it to use in trial courtrooms around the nation. That is, the issue actually litigated almost always concerns the narrow *"micro-balance"* of pros and cons of a manufacturer's failure to adopt some particular design feature that would have prevented the plaintiff's harm—whether the costs of changing the design in some particular (micro) manner would have been worth the resulting safety benefits.[4] Moreover, the more narrow formulation above avoids a number of quite serious problems inherent in the broader test.

The Hand defectiveness formula succinctly captures the common-sense idea that products are unacceptably dangerous if they contain dangers that might cost-effectively (and practicably) be removed. A premise of the formula is that manufacturers may fairly be required to contemplate the consequences to consumers of dangers in their products' safety before they place those products on the market. Thus, in its design and marketing decisions, a responsible manufacturer should consider the risks of injury to consumers and bystanders and should weigh the interests of those parties equally to its own interest in maximizing profits. Manufacturers, of course, may also properly consider such factors as a product's usefulness, its cost, and profitability. But the point of the Hand formula is that manufacturers are also duty-bound to include in the balance a properly proportionate consideration of the various risks of harm that fairly may be expected to result from the product when put to real-world use.

In sum, the risk-utility test demands that manufacturers adopt precautions proportionate to the magnitude of the expected risk. This simple yet fundamental principle of defectiveness, which ties the measure of precaution to the measure of risk, grounds the safety obligations of a manufacturer in strict liability as well as negligence. Because the method for ascertaining responsibility is identical in both negligence and strict liability, many courts and commentators have recognized the "functional" equivalence of the two theories of liability in design and warnings cases,[5] causing the Iowa

---

3. See Owen, Risk–Utility Balancing in Design Defect Cases, 30 U. Mich. J. Law Reform 239 (1997) (surveying risk-utility tests among the states).

4. The more narrow formulation of the test reflects how courts and lawyers actually proceed in assessing liability under the Hand formula. See, e.g., R. Heafey and D. Kennedy, Product Liability: Winning Strategies and Techniques §§ 4.04 and 4.05, and p. 4–9 (1994) (characterizing the manufacturer's choice to forego a reasonable alternative design as "the heart of the plaintiff's case"). See also Rheingold, The Risk/Utility Test in

Product Cases, 18 Trial Lawyers Quarterly 49, 50 (Spring/Fall 1987) (plaintiffs usually and properly offer evidence on alternative designs).

5. See, e.g., Mayor of Baltimore v. Utica Mut. Ins. Co., 802 A.2d 1070, 1089 (Md. App. 2002) ("these two theories—negligence and strict liability failure to warn—have been described as nearly identical"); Cervelli v. Thompson/Center Arms, 183 F. Supp. 2d 1032, 1040 (S.D. Ohio 2002) ("the standard imposed upon the defendant in a strict liability claim grounded upon an inadequate warning is the same as that imposed in a

Supreme Court first to repeal its doctrine of strict products liability in tort in warnings cases in favor of plain negligence[6] and later to abandon liability theory labels altogether in design defect cases.[7] Design defect determinations thus are decided in virtually identical fashion—on cost-benefit ("risk-utility") terms—whether the claim is styled in negligence, implied warranty, or strict liability in tort.

NOTES

1. In Helicoid Gage Div. of Am. Chain & Cable Co. v. Howell, 511 S.W.2d 573, 577 (Tex. Civ. App. 1974), a pressure gauge manufactured by defendant burst, throwing a piece of gauge lens into plaintiff's eye. An "inexpensive" safety shield, that would have protected the plaintiff's eyes at no sacrifice to the gauge's utility, could have been added for about $2.50. *Held*, plaintiff's verdict affirmed.

2. **Burdens, Benefits, and Utility.** Courts often look at risk-utility analysis broadly as involving more than a comparison of the direct dollar costs of safety devices, on the one hand, and consumer injuries, on the other. Thibault v. Sears, Roebuck & Co., 395 A.2d 843 (N.H. 1978), was a strict tort action against the manufacturer of a rotary lawn mower for injuries sustained by plaintiff when his foot slipped under the rear of the mower. Plaintiff claimed that the absence of a rear trailing guard rendered the mower's design unreasonably dangerous. *Held*, verdict for defendant affirmed: "In weighing utility and desirability against danger, courts should also consider whether the risk of danger could have been reduced without significant impact on product effectiveness and manufacturing cost." Moreover, "[i]nquiry into the dangerousness of a product requires a multifaceted balancing process involving evaluation of many conflicting factors.... Reasonableness, foreseeability, utility, and similar factors are questions of fact for jury determination."

If the testimony had revealed that the addition of the rear guard would have added $10 to the $200 price of the mower, could the jury reasonably have found for the plaintiff? What if it would have cost an additional $50? What if the guard would hang up on rocks and tree roots? What if it would detract from the overall "sleekness" of the design?

3. **Ditto—Increased Risks of Other Types.** A number of cases have involved claims by swimmers injured or killed by motorboat propellers claiming that the propellers should have been shrouded with a guard. The benefits from such

negligence claim based upon inadequate warning"); Jones v. NordicTrack, Inc., 550 S.E.2d 101, 103 n.5 (Ga. 2001) (design: "no significant distinction between negligence and strict liability for purposes of the risk-utility analysis"); Ackerman v. American Cyanamid Co., 586 N.W.2d 208, 220 (Iowa 1998) (" 'the strict liability claim depend[s] on virtually the same elements of proof as are required to establish the negligence claim' "and " 'a growing number of courts and commentators have found that, in cases in which the plaintiff's injury is caused by an alleged defect in the design of a product,

there is no practical difference between theories of negligence and strict liability' ").

6. See Olson v. Prosoco, Inc., 522 N.W.2d 284, 289 (Iowa 1994) ("[i]nevitably the conduct of the defendant in a failure to warn case becomes the issue").

7. See Wright v. Brooke Group Ltd., 652 N.W.2d 159, 169 (Iowa 2002) ("We question the need for or usefulness of any traditional doctrinal label in design defect cases because ... a negligence claim and a strict liability claim ... rest on an identical risk-utility evaluation.").

guards would be the large numbers of swimmers saved from harm. But such devices are not without their costs, including reduced speed, reduced fuel efficiency, reduced maneuverability, and an increase in other risks: "[T]he presence of a shroud over the propeller presents its own risks to swimmers [as by creating] a larger target area [and by creating a trap in which human limbs may become wedged], exposing a swimmer to even greater injury." Fitzpatrick v. Madonna, 623 A.2d 322, 325 (Pa. Super. Ct. 1993). Consider comment *f* to § 2(b) of the Products Liability Restatement:

> When evaluating the reasonableness of a design alternative, the overall safety of the product must be considered. It is not sufficient that the alternative design would have reduced or prevented the harm suffered by the plaintiff if it would also have introduced into the product other dangers of equal or greater magnitude.

So, even though an airbag may occasionally break an arm when it explosively deploys in an accident, its design is not defective if it saves more lives and injuries than it causes; and an alternative design, even if it would prevent broken arms, is not "reasonable" unless it is safer overall than the chosen design. Diluzio–Gulino v. Daimler Chrysler Corp., 897 A.2d 438 (N.J. Super. Ct. App. Div. 2006).

4. Ditto—How Broad the Inquiry? How broadly should the law view the benefits from a product, the utility of its production, and the burdens from avoiding its risks? Cipollone v. Liggett Group, Inc., 644 F.Supp. 283, 286 (D.N.J. 1986), was a suit against cigarette manufacturers for the death of plaintiff's wife from lung cancer. The defendants sought to introduce evidence of the collateral social benefits flowing from the *production* of cigarettes, as opposed to from their consumption:

> In essence, defendants argue that in determining liability, a jury engaged in the risk utility analysis may take into consideration profits made, employees hired, benefits to suppliers of goods and services, taxes generated and even charitable activities or contributions made by the defendant manufacturer. The analysis was never meant to balance the risk to the consumer against the general benefit to society.... It is the benefit and utility to the cigarette smoker which is here in issue, and not the benefit to the cigarette industry or those in turn, who benefit from its existence.

A similar approach is adopted in the new Products Liability Restatement, § 2(b), cmt. *f*: "[I]t is not a factor under Subsection (b) that the imposition of liability would have a negative effect on corporate earnings or would reduce employment in a given industry." See Note, 73 Cornell L. Rev. 606, 616–19 (1988).

5. The Wade Factors. In applying the risk-utility (cost-benefit) approach to particular products, many courts (including *Prestage* in an omitted passage) have quoted the famous factors from Wade, On the Nature of Strict Tort Liability for Products, 44 Miss. L.J. 825, 837–38 (1973):

(1) The usefulness and desirability of the product—its utility to the user and to the public as a whole.

(2) The safety aspects of the product—the likelihood that it will cause injury, and the probable seriousness of the injury.

(3) The availability of a substitute product which would meet the same need and not be as unsafe.

(4) The manufacturer's ability to eliminate the unsafe character of the product without impairing its usefulness or making it too expensive to maintain its utility.

(5) The user's ability to avoid danger by the exercise of care in the use of the product.

(6) The user's anticipated awareness of the dangers inherent in the product and their avoidability, because of general public knowledge of the obvious condition of the product, or of the existence of suitable warnings or instructions.

(7) The feasibility, on the part of the manufacturer, of spreading the loss by setting the price of the product or carrying liability insurance.

See, e.g., Roach v. Kononen, 525 P.2d 125, 129 (Or. 1974) ("We agree that these factors should be considered by a court before submitting a design defect case to the jury. Also, proof of these factors bears on the jury's determination of whether or not a given design is defective."). More recently, see, e.g., Bass v. Air Prods. & Chems., Inc., 2006 WL 1419375, at *12 (N.J.Super.App.Div. 2006); Brown v. Crown Equip. Corp., 181 S.W.3d 268, 282–83 (Tenn.2005); George v. Ingersoll–Rand Co., 2005 WL 2588389, at *5 (W.D.Pa.2005).

6. While many courts authoritatively quote Dean Wade's seven factors, few (except in New Jersey and Pennsylvania) actually attempt to apply them to the defectiveness determination. On the infrequent occasions when they do, they tend to get into trouble. See, e.g., Johansen v. Makita U.S.A., Inc., 607 A.2d 637 (N.J. 1992) (trial court should have instructed jury not to consider evidence of plaintiff's lack of care in deciding the question of product defect, because factor (5) pertained only to users generally, not to particular plaintiff's conduct).

7. The "Wade–Keeton" Test: Imputing Knowledge of the Danger. An important variant of the risk-utility test converts negligence into strict liability determinations by doing away with the requirement of foreseeable risk in the latter context. Deans Keeton and Wade in the 1960s independently proposed similar ways of defining strict products liability in this manner:

> "[If a product is unreasonably dangerous,] it is not relevant that [the supplier] neither knew nor could have known nor ought to have known in the exercise of ordinary care that the unreasonable risk actually existed. It is enough that had he known of the risk and dangers he would not have marketed the product at all or he would have done so differently."

W.P. Keeton, Products Liability—Inadequacy of Information, 48 Tex. L. Rev. 398, 404 (1970) (drawing from his earlier discussion in 40 Tex. L. Rev. 193, 210 (1961)).

> "[A]ssuming that the defendant had knowledge of the condition of the product, would he then have been acting unreasonably in placing it on the market?"

Wade, Strict Tort Liability of Manufacturers, 19 Sw. L.J. 5, 15 (1965).

8. Among the many courts adopting the Wade–Keeton test in the 1970s was Phillips v. Kimwood Mach. Co., 525 P.2d 1033, 1036–37 (Or. 1974). A worker injured when a commercial sanding machine ejected a fiberboard sheet sued the manufacturer for failing either to warn of the danger or to equip the machine with an inexpensive line of metal teeth that would have prevented the expulsion without interference with the functioning of the machine. Reversing a summary judgment for the manufacturer, the court formulated the test in the following terms:

A dangerously defective article would be one which a reasonable person would not put into the stream of commerce *if he had knowledge of its harmful character*. The test, therefore, is whether the seller would be negligent if he sold the article *knowing of the risk involved*. Strict liability imposes what amounts to constructive knowledge of the condition of the product.

* * *

The advantage of describing a dangerous defect in the manner of Wade and Keeton is that it preserves the use of familiar terms and thought processes with which courts, lawyers, and jurors customarily deal.

While apparently judging the seller's conduct, the test set out above would actually be a characterization of the product by a jury. If the manufacturer was not acting reasonably in selling the product, knowing of the risks involved, then the product would be dangerously defective when sold and the manufacturer would be subject to liability.

Noting the similarity of this test with negligence, the court pointed out the different focus of the two doctrines—in strict liability, on the condition (dangerousness) of the product; and in negligence, on the reasonableness of the manufacturer's conduct in making and selling it in that condition.

9. Defining Strict Liability in "Constructive Knowledge" Terms. Recall the special use of the "constructive knowledge" term in negligence law, page 73. Note the *Phillips* court's reformulation of the term for use in the strict liability context to mean "imputed knowledge" of facts which may be impossible for a manufacturer to know. Thus, in the 1970s and 1980s, "constructive knowledge" evolved as a term of art in tort law with a very different and special meaning in the products liability context as a means of describing the Wade–Keeton method of defining strict products liability in a manner distinguishing it from negligence. See Brooks v. Beech Aircraft Corp., 902 P.2d 54 (N.M. 1995).

How constructive knowledge is defined is important if a risk is unforeseeable, a problem explored in "state of the art" terms, ch. 11, below. The Wade–Keeton test will be reexamined there, and it will be seen to have fallen in desuetude. But the test is still on the books in many states, and it is still sometimes expressly reaffirmed. E.g., Brooks v. Beech Aircraft Corp., 902 P.2d 54 (N.M. 1995).

10. Product–Specific Tests—Prescription Drugs. Special problems are raised by prescription drugs, comprised of chemical formulations onto which safety devices cannot be installed. Prior to the 1980s, only a small handful of decisions had held that a drug could be defectively designed. Because a growing number of courts began to impose liability on drug manufacturers during the 1990s for defects in design, the Products Liability Restatement carved out a special risk-utility test for design defects in prescription drugs and medical devices. Section 6(c) provides:

A prescription drug or medical device is not reasonably safe due to defective design if the foreseeable risks of harm posed by the drug or medical device are sufficiently great in relation to its foreseeable therapeutic benefits that reasonable health-care providers, knowing of such foreseeable risks and therapeutic benefits, would not prescribe the drug or medical device for any class of patients.

George Conk criticizes the ALI for according the drug industry special, favored protection in this section rather than holding the industry to the ordinary risk-utility principles of § 2(b). See Conk, Is There a Design Defect in the Restatement (Third) of Torts: Products Liability?, 109 Yale L.J. 1087 (2000). The Reporters reply in Henderson and Twerski, Drug Designs Are Different, 111 Yale L.J. 151 (2001), rebutted in Conk, The True Test: Alternative Safer Designs for Drugs and Medical Devices in a Patent–Constrained Market, 49 UCLA L. Rev. 737 (2002).

11. Criticism of Risk–Utility—From the Right. Consider Epstein, The Risks of Risk/Utility, 48 Ohio St. L. Rev. 469, 475–76 (1987):

> Risk/utility represents nothing less than a totally revolutionary way of looking at products liability. [Defect tests that bar recovery if a danger is open and obvious] reinforce market disciplines. The risk/utility test is a massive, if unintended, assault on markets and private ordering, for defendants are now required to *justify independently* every decision that they and their customers have made with respect to a product's use. No longer is it sufficient to say that the defendant informed the plaintiff of the hazards involved. Instead it becomes necessary to go behind the consent of consumers by finding expert testimony to reconstruct their past decisions from the ground up. . . .

* * *

> To see both the magnitude and the weakness of this entire risk/utility approach, it is instructive to ask the questions: Where does the application of the risk/utility test end, and why? . . . There is nothing in the disorganized array of [factors such as Wade's] that prevents a single headstrong jury from making fundamental decisions about what may be marketed and what may not be sold at all.

* * *

> With variables so numerous, the ingenuity of lawyers should never be doubted when the stakes in litigation are very high and discovery underregulated. The test is couched in an offhand way that makes difficult matters [look simple]. It is a utilitarian nightmare. What starts out as a faithful application of the utilitarian calculus ends up as an unprincipled battle of the experts. Everything is admissible; nothing is quantifiable; nothing is dispositive.

12. Ditto—From the Left. Some commentators complain that risk-utility decisionmaking, based on stark economic efficiency, suffers from a lack of richness and humanism. See Klemme, The Enterprise Liability Theory of Torts, 47 U. Colo. L. Rev. 153, 191 n. 106 (1976). Professor Balkin, in Too Good to Be True: The Positive Economic Theory of Law, 87 Colum. L. Rev. 1447, 1475–76 (1987), faults efficiency tests for being incomplete:

> Human values and goals may take wealth maximization into account, but they may not be exclusively or even primarily concerned with it. Human action and human decision may rest only in part on [efficiency analysis. Thus,] the greatest problem with wealth maximization as a theory of human practical reason may be that it is insufficiently rich.

Compare Hubbard, Reasonable *Human* Expectations: A Normative Model for Imposing Strict Liability for Defective Products, 29 Mercer L. Rev. 465, 468–69 (1978):

Which is more important—efficiency or expectation? The answer would seem to depend on the state of society. If the society had such a limited economy that efficiency were necessary for the subsistence of its members, then efficiency would be at least a prima facie candidate to prevail. However, this situation is certainly not the case in the United States. While inefficiency is not desirable in our circumstances, even a considerable amount of inefficiency need not be disastrous. A denial of expectations, on the other hand, would be equally offensive in both a hand-to-mouth and an "affluent" society because such a denial results in a negation of the right of persons to be viewed as ends rather than as mere factors of production involved in achieving an efficient society. From a more general perspective, the entire notion of individual rights becomes highly problematic if social benefit, no matter how slight, can justify a denial of any such right. Thus, human expectation ought to prevail over efficiency in our society.

Do you agree? Which test on balance is the better?

13. On the risk-utility test, see generally Miller, Myth Surrenders to Reality: Design Defect Litigation in Iowa, 51 Drake L. Rev. 549 (2003); M. Green, Negligence = Economic Efficiency: Doubts >, 75 Tex. L. Rev. 1605 (1997); Owen, Toward a Proper Test for Design Defectiveness: "Micro–Balancing" Costs and Benefits, 75 Tex. L. Rev. 1661 (1997); Owen, Risk–Utility Balancing in Design Defect Cases, 30 U. Mich. J.L. Ref. 239 (1997); M. Green, The Schizophrenia of Risk–Benefit Analysis in Design Defect Litigation, 48 Vand. L. Rev. 609 (1995); White, Risk–Utility Analysis and the Learned Hand Formula: A Hand that Helps or a Hand that Hides?, 32 Ariz. L. Rev. 77 (1990); Epstein, The Risks of Risk/Utility, 48 Ohio St. L. J. 469 (1987); D. Owen, Products Liability Law § 8.4 (2d ed. 2008); 1 D. Owen, M.S. Madden, & M. Davis, Madden & Owen on Products Liability § 84:4 (3d ed.2000).

C. ALTERNATIVE TESTS

In searching for a workable test of "defectiveness," most courts focused initially upon the "defective condition unreasonably dangerous" phrase in § 402A. The evolution of this phrase is thus helpful in understanding some of the problems that have arisen in its application.

In 1958 the Reporter for the Restatement, Dean Prosser, prepared a first draft of § 402A imposing strict liability for the sale of food "in a condition dangerous to the consumer." Restatement (Second) of Torts § 402A (Prelim. Draft No. 6, 1958). Another draft was presented to the Council two years later without any change in the crucial "dangerous" condition language. (Council Draft No. 8, 1960). In an effort to address the concern of certain members of the Council that the "dangerous" condition language was over-broad, Dean Prosser changed it to its present form by modifying "dangerous" with the word "unreasonably" and "condition" with the word "defective"—hence, "defective condition unreasonably dangerous to the user or consumer." This was the form in which the section was presented for consideration to the American Law Institute. (Tent.

Draft No. 6, 1961). See generally Wade, On the Nature of Strict Tort Liability for Products, 44 Miss. L.J. 825, 830 (1973).

Consider the following debate over the wording of § 402A that transpired on the floor of the Institute in 1961.

———

The Birth of "Defective Condition Unreasonably Dangerous"

38 ALI Proceedings 86–89 (1961).

PRESIDENT TWEED: Now, as to possible language on Section 402A, I think the reporter has run down—

PROFESSOR DICKERSON: Mr. Chairman, may I make a small point? In this discussion of substantive issues I hesitate to bring up a mere question of draftsmanship, but I think this may have some significance.

I am a little bothered by the phrase "defective condition unreasonably dangerous to the consumer. . . ." This signifies some nondefective conditions unreasonably dangerous to the consumer, and if there are, I would be interested in hearing an example of a product which was at the same time unreasonably dangerous but not defective.

I had always thought that "unreasonably dangerous" was simply the best possible test for what was legally defective. It seems to me . . . that everything we might want to cover here is subsumed under the words "unreasonably dangerous."

Now, the addition of the words "defective condition"—it would seem to me that this involves unnecessary questions of meaning. For example, in addition to "unreasonably dangerous," what would a purchaser have to show in order to make out a defective product? I would think that if he showed that it was unreasonably dangerous, it would per se be legally defective, and it is only gilding the lily to add the word "defective."

For these reasons I move that we strike the word "defective," and consolidate Comments *e* and *f*.

DEAN PROSSER: Mr. Dickerson has stated an original point of view which I first brought into the Council of The American Law Institute in connection with this section. ". . . food in a condition unreasonably[1] dangerous to the consumer" was my language. The Council then proceeded to raise the question of a number of products which, even though not defective, are in fact dangerous to the consumer—whiskey, for example [laughter]; cigarettes, which cause lung cancer; various types of drugs which can be administered with safety up to a point but may be dangerous if carried beyond that—and they raised the question whether "unreason-

---

1. Dean Prosser apparently either misremembered or misspoke in stating that the   *"unreasonably* dangerous" language was his.—Eds.

ably dangerous" was sufficient to protect the defendant against possible liability in such cases.

Therefore, they suggested that there must be something wrong with the product itself, and hence the word "defective" was put in; but the fact that the product itself is dangerous, or even unreasonably dangerous, to people who consume it is not enough. There has to be something wrong with the product.

Now, I was rather indifferent to that. I thought "unreasonably dangerous," on the other hand, carried every meaning that was necessary, as Mr. Dickerson does; but I could see the point, so I accepted the change. "Defective" was put in to head off liability on the part of the seller of whiskey, on the part of the man who consumes it and gets delirium tremens, even though the jury might find that all whiskey is unreasonably dangerous to the consumer.

PROFESSOR DICKERSON: I rest my case entirely on the word "unreasonably." Whenever we gild the lily, I think we just invite difficulty.

PRESIDENT TWEED: The motion is to eliminate "defective" in the black letter. . . .

* * *

DEAN LOCKHART: * * *

It seems to me this ought to come out. I don't know how I voted in the Council.

DEAN PROSSER: Well, I can tell Dean Lockhart that he voted in favor of the word "defective." [Laughter]

PROFESSOR JOINER: I would like to support Mr. Dickerson and Dean Lockhart. It seems to me that the Reporter's case of whiskey is taken care of by the words "unreasonably dangerous."

* * *

We merely confuse the law by adding "defective."

PRESIDENT TWEED: Well, let's have a vote. We have been two hours and twenty-two minutes on this section. The motion is to omit "defective."

[The motion was put to a voice vote.]

PRESIDENT TWEED: The noes seem to me to have it. Does anybody want to keep score?

DIRECTOR GOODRICH: I think the noes have it, but if anybody calls for a division, of course, we will count.

[Nobody called for a division and the motion to strike "defective" failed, leaving the entire phrase "defective condition unreasonably dangerous."]

NOTES

1. Of the two hours and twenty-two minutes devoted to § 402A, the vast bulk of the time had been spent on issues unrelated to the phraseology of its black letter provision.

2. Earlier in the discussion Dean Prosser had indicated that the "unreasonably dangerous" language, too, had been added "to head off liability for a product which is sold where there is nothing wrong with the product as a product, but nevertheless it is going to injure some people. A good many individuals are allergic to strawberries and eggs. That doesn't mean that there is anything wrong with the food. There is something wrong with the individual. 'Defective condition' and 'unreasonably dangerous' are deliberately designed to protect the defendant against undue liability." 38 ALI Proceedings 55 (1961).

3. Section 402A was broadened in 1962 to include "other products for intimate bodily use" in addition to food. Restatement (Second) of Torts § 402A (Tent. Draft No. 7, 1962). Two years later the section was submitted to the Institute in its final form, extending it to the sale of "any product in a defective condition unreasonably dangerous to the user or consumer." Id. (Tent. Draft No. 10, 1964) (emphasis added). The section was approved by the Institute at its meeting that year, and the section was published a year later, 1965, in volume 2 of the Second Restatement.

Cronin v. J.B.E. Olson Corp.

Supreme Court of California, 1972.
8 Cal.3d 121, 104 Cal.Rptr. 433, 501 P.2d 1153.

■ SULLIVAN, JUSTICE.

[The question here] is whether the injured plaintiff seeking recovery upon the theory of strict liability in tort must establish, among other facts, not only that the product contained a defect which proximately caused his injuries but also that such defective condition made the product unreasonably dangerous to the user or consumer. We have concluded that he need not do so. Accordingly, we find no error in the trial court's refusal to so instruct the jury. [Affirmed.]

[In 1963, the court held in Greenman v. Yuba Power Products, Inc., above, that "A manufacturer is strictly liable in tort when an article he places on the market, knowing that it is to be used without inspection for defects, proves to have a defect that causes injury to a human being." This language in *Greenman* was compared to § 402A's standard of liability for selling products in a "defective condition unreasonably dangerous to the user or consumer."]

The almost inextricable intertwining of the *Greenman* and Restatement standards in our jurisprudence was inevitable, considering the simplicity of [the "defect" notion in Greenman compared to the fuller iteration of liability in § 402A, such that we now must] examine and resolve an apparent divergence in the two formulations.

* * *

[The phrase "defective condition unreasonably dangerous" in] Restatement section 402A [is susceptible] to a literal reading [requiring a] finder of fact to conclude that the product is, first, defective and, second, unreasonably dangerous. (Note, 55 Geo. L.J. 286, 296.) A bifurcated standard is of necessity more difficult to prove than a unitary one. [A] requirement that a plaintiff also prove that the defect made the product "unreasonably dangerous" places upon him a significantly increased burden and represents a step backward in the area pioneered by this court. * * * [T]he *Greenman* formulation is consonant with the rationale and development of products liability law in California because it provides a clear and simple test for determining whether the injured plaintiff is entitled to recovery. * * *

NOTES

1. *Cronin*'s purge of the "unreasonably dangerous" phrase from strict liability in tort was blindly followed in a very few cases. Butaud v. Suburban Marine & Sporting Goods, Inc., 543 P.2d 209 (Alaska 1975); Berkebile v. Brantly Helicopter Corp., 337 A.2d 893 (Pa. 1975); Glass v. Ford Motor Co., 304 A.2d 562 (N.J. Super. Ct. Law. Div. 1973). Noting that *"Cronin* has been widely criticized as providing no useful definition of an actionable defect, particularly in relation to a case of a product of unsafe design," the Supreme Court of New Jersey repudiated *Glass* on this point in Cepeda v. Cumberland Eng'g Co., Inc., 386 A.2d 816 (N.J. 1978). Like *Cepeda*, most courts that have passed on the question have rejected the *Cronin* approach. See, e.g., Byrns v. Riddell, Inc., 550 P.2d 1065 (Ariz. 1976); Heldt v. Nicholson Mfg. Co., 240 N.W.2d 154 (Wis. 1976). Law review commentary was generally critical of *Cronin*. See, e.g., Fischer, Products Liability—The Meaning of Defect, 39 Mo. L. Rev. 339 (1974); Keeton, Product Liability and the Meaning of Defect, 5 St. Mary's L.J. 30 (1973); Wade, On the Nature of Strict Tort Liability for Products, 44 Miss. L.J. 825 (1973).

2. Dual Standard. A fair number of courts do in fact *say* that a plaintiff must establish that the product was both "defective" and "unreasonably dangerous". See, e.g., Halliday v. Sturm, Ruger & Co., Inc., 792 A.2d 1145, 1150 (Md. 2002) ("for a seller to be liable under § 402A, the product must be both in a 'defective condition' and 'unreasonably dangerous' at the time it was placed on the market"); American Family Ins. Group v. JVC Ams. Corp., 2001 WL 1618454, at *5 (D. Minn. 2001) ("a plaintiff in a products liability case must establish that the defendant's product was in a defective condition and unreasonably dangerous for its intended use"); Lee v. Martin, 45 S.W.3d 860, 864 (Ark. App. 2001) ("a plaintiff in a strict-liability case must prove that the product is unreasonably dangerous *and* defective"); Farnham v. Bombardier, Inc., 640 A.2d 47, 48 (Vt. 1994) ("To establish strict liability in a products liability action, a plaintiff must show that the defendant's product (1) is defective; (2) is unreasonably dangerous to the consumer in normal use; (3) reached the consumer without undergoing any substantial change in condition; and (4) caused injury to the consumer because of its defective design.").

By statute, Tennessee permits a plaintiff to recover upon a showing that the product was in a defective condition "or" unreasonably dangerous. See Brown v.

Crown Equip. Corp., 181 S.W.3d 268, 281 (Tenn. 2005) ("the Act provides for recovery for injuries caused by a product that either is in a 'defective' condition or is 'unreasonably dangerous' "). Indiana's curious statute adopts the "defective condition unreasonably dangerous" language of § 402A, Ind. Code § 34–20–2–1, and then defines "defective condition" as a condition (1) not contemplated by consumers, and (2) that is "unreasonably dangerous." Ind. Code § 34–20–4–1.

Some jurisdictions state that a defect must "render" or "make" the product unreasonably dangerous. See, e.g., Johnson v. Ford Motor Co., 45 P.3d 86, 91 (Okla. 2002) ("plaintiff must prove . . . that the product was defective when it left the control of the manufacturer, and that the defect made the product unreasonably dangerous").

Notwithstanding these quite frequent dual-standard references, it is difficult to find a case that explicitly addresses the differences between the two elements—perhaps because the comments to § 402A define both phrases congruently (as dangerous beyond a consumer's expectations), or perhaps because there seems to be no good reason to perpetuate a linguistic error grounded in a Restatement that has now been superseded.

   3.   Single Standard. Most courts understand that the basic liability standard of § 402A is "defectiveness" and nothing else. See, e.g., Blue v. Environmental Eng'g, Inc., 828 N.E.2d 1128, 1137–40 (Ill.2005); Sprung v. MTR Ravensburg Inc., 788 N.E.2d 620 (N.Y. 2003); Gramex Corp. v. Green Supply, Inc., 89 S.W.3d 432 (Mo. 2002); Chandler v. Gene Messer Ford, Inc., 81 S.W.3d 493 (Tex. App. 2002). See also Ohio Rev. Code Ann. § 2307.73(A)(1).

   See McAlpine v. Rhone–Poulenc Ag Co., 16 P.3d 1054, 1058 (Mont. 2000), quoting Dean W. Page Keeton of Texas, one of the ALI Advisers for the Second Restatement:

> It is unfortunate perhaps that Section 402A of the Restatement (Second) of Torts provides that as a basis for recovery it must be found that the product was both "defective" and "unreasonably dangerous" when as a matter of fact the term "unreasonably dangerous" was meant only as a definition of defect. The phrase was not intended as setting forth two requirements but only one.

W.P. Keeton, Product Liability and the Meaning of Defect, 5 St. Mary's L.J. 30, 32 (1973). *McAlpine* held that the trial court erred in instructing the jury that liability depended on the product having been in a "defective condition unreasonably dangerous," rather than only in a "defective condition," because the full Restatement phrase could mislead the jury into thinking that liability was based on two requirements rather than just one.

   4.   Alternative Verbalisms. Some states that have rejected the entire Restatement phrase, "defective condition unreasonably dangerous," have adopted the "unreasonably dangerous" phrase as the liability standard. Other states have substituted alternative phrases. See, e.g., La. Rev. Stat. Ann. § 2800.54 ("unreasonably dangerous"); Sollami v. Eaton, 772 N.E.2d 215 (Ill. 2002) ("unreasonably dangerous"); Wash. Rev. Code § 7.72.030 (2) ("not reasonably safe").

   5.   In Azzarello v. Black Bros. Co., Inc., 391 A.2d 1020, 1027 n.12 (Pa. 1978), the court endorsed the following standard jury instruction:

> The [supplier] of a product is the guarantor of its safety. The product must, therefore, be provided with every element necessary to make it safe for [its intended] use, and without any condition that makes it unsafe for

[its intended] use. If you find that the product, at the time it left the defendant's control, lacked any element necessary to make it safe for [its intended] use or contained any condition that made it unsafe for [its intended] use, then the product was defective, and the defendant is liable for all harm caused by such defect.

See Thomas, Defining "Design Defect" in Pennsylvania: Reconciling *Azzarello* and the Restatement (Third) of Torts, 71 Temp. L. Rev. 217 (1998); Wertheimer, *Azzarello* Agonistes: Bucking the Strict Products Liability Tide, 66 Temp. L. Rev. 419 (1993) (endorsing *Azzarello*).

6. No Definition. If the concepts of "defective" and "unreasonably dangerous" are too difficult to define, how about no test at all? Consider Nesselrode v. Executive Beechcraft, Inc., 707 S.W.2d 371, 377–78, 389, 393 (Mo. 1986):

> Though Missouri has adopted the rule of strict tort liability as set forth in the Restatement, we have not yet formally incorporated, in any meaningful way, the Restatement's consumer expectation test into the lexicon of our products liability law. Nor have we yet decided to travel or require plaintiffs to travel the path of risks and utilities....
>
> Under our model of strict tort liability the concept of unreasonable danger, which is determinative of whether a product is defective in a design case, is presented to the jury as an ultimate issue without further definition.[11] Accordingly, our approved jury instruction which governs in a design defect case, MAI 25.04 (3rd) does not contain as one of its component elements a definitional paragraph which gives independent content to the concept of unreasonable danger.
>
> ... The jury gives this concept content by applying their collective intelligence and experience to the broad evidentiary spectrum of facts and circumstances presented by the parties....

See Ford v. GACS, Inc., 265 F.3d 670, 676–77 (8th Cir. 2001) (Mo. law) ("what is unreasonably dangerous 'needs no judicial definition' and is left as an ultimate fact question for the jury").

Barker v. Lull Engineering Co.

Supreme Court of California, 1978.
20 Cal.3d 413, 143 Cal.Rptr. 225, 573 P.2d 443.

■ TOBRINER, ACTING CHIEF JUSTICE.

[Plaintiff, an operator of a high-lift loader manufactured by defendant, was struck by a piece of lumber when he leaped from the loader as the load he was lifting began to shift. Plaintiff's strict liability in tort claim alleged

---

11. Most states, whether they apply a unitary definitional test or a multifactor analysis, define to some extent the appropriate standard to the jury. [Citations.] The subject of how the jury should be instructed and what is the proper role for the jury has been given attention by a number of commentators and courts. See Owens and Montgomery, Reflections on the Theory and Administration of Strict Tort Liability For Defective Products, 27 S.C. L. R. 803, 830–45 (1976) [double sic]; Wade, On the Nature of Strict Tort Liability for Products, 44 Miss. L.J. 825, 838–41 (1973); see also Phillips v. Kimwood Machine Co., 525 P.2d 1033, 1039–40 (Or.1974).

that the loader was deficiently designed in failing to have stabilizing outriggers, a seatbelt and roll bar, an automatic locking device on the leveling lever, and in certain other ways. The trial court instructed the jury that strict liability for defective design is "based on a finding that the product was unreasonably dangerous." The jury found for defendant, and plaintiff appealed. *Held*, under *Cronin*, the design defect instruction was error.]

. . . We held in *Cronin* that a plaintiff satisfies his burden of proof under *Greenman*, in both a "manufacturing defect" and "design defect" context, when he proves the existence of a "defect" and that such defect was a proximate cause of his injuries. In reaching this conclusion, however, *Cronin* did not purport to hold that [a trial court could not define defectiveness appropriate to the circumstances of a particular case, because the term "defect"] is neither self-defining nor susceptible to a single definition applicable in all contexts. . . .

[O]ur cases establish that a product may be found defective in design if the plaintiff demonstrates that the product failed to perform as safely as an ordinary consumer would expect when used in an intended or reasonably foreseeable manner. This initial standard, somewhat analogous to the Uniform Commercial Code's warranty of fitness and merchantability (Cal. U.Com. Code, § 2314), reflects the warranty heritage upon which California product liability doctrine in part rests. As we noted in *Greenman*, "implicit in [a product's] presence on the market . . . [is] a representation that it [will] safely do the jobs for which it was built." When a product fails to satisfy such ordinary consumer expectations as to safety in its intended or reasonably foreseeable operation, a manufacturer is strictly liable for resulting injuries. . . .

. . . [Yet] a product may be found defective in design, even if it satisfies ordinary consumer expectations, if through hindsight the jury determines that the product's design embodies "excessive preventable danger," or, in other words, if the jury finds that the risk of danger inherent in the challenged design outweighs the benefits of such design. [Citations.]

[I]n evaluating the adequacy of a product's design pursuant to this latter standard, a jury may consider, among other relevant factors, the gravity of the danger posed by the challenged design, the likelihood that such danger would occur, the mechanical feasibility of a safer alternative design, the financial cost of an improved design, and the adverse consequences to the product and to the consumer that would result from an alternative design. [Citations.]

[The allocation of the burden of proof] is particularly significant in this context inasmuch as this court's product liability decisions, from *Greenman* to *Cronin*, have repeatedly emphasized that one of the principal purposes behind the strict product liability doctrine is to relieve an injured plaintiff of many of the onerous evidentiary burdens inherent in a negligence cause of action. Because most of the evidentiary matters which may be relevant to the determination of the adequacy of a product's design under the "risk-benefit" standard—e.g., the feasibility and cost of alternative designs— . . .

involve technical matters peculiarly within the knowledge of the manufacturer, we conclude that once the plaintiff makes a prima facie showing that the injury was proximately caused by the product's design, the burden should appropriately shift to the defendant to prove, in light of the relevant factors, that the product is not defective. . . .

[T]o reiterate, a product may be found defective in design, so as to subject a manufacturer to strict liability for resulting injuries, under either of two alternative tests. First, a product may be found defective in design if the plaintiff establishes that the product failed to perform as safely as an ordinary consumer would expect when used in an intended or reasonably foreseeable manner. Second, a product may alternatively be found defective in design if the plaintiff demonstrates that the product's design proximately caused his injury and the defendant fails to establish, in light of the relevant factors, that, on balance, the benefits of the challenged design outweigh the risk of danger inherent in such design.

Although [our] two-pronged definition of design defect [is new, it] is appropriate in light of the rationale and limits of the strict liability doctrine, for it subjects a manufacturer to liability whenever there is something "wrong" with a product's design—either because the product fails to meet ordinary consumer expectations as to safety or because, on balance, the design is not as safe as it should be—while stopping short of making the manufacturer an insurer for all injuries which may result from the use of its product. This test, moreover, explicitly focuses the trier of fact's attention on the adequacy of the product itself, rather than on the manufacturer's conduct, and places the burden on the manufacturer, rather than the plaintiff, to establish that because of the complexity of, and trade-offs implicit in, the design process, an injury-producing product should nevertheless not be found defective.

* * *

The judgment in favor of defendants is reversed.

NOTES

1. "When the ghosts of case and assumpsit walk hand in hand at midnight, it is sometimes a convenient and comforting thing to have a borderland in which they may lose themselves." W. Prosser, The Borderland of Tort and Contract, in Selected Topics on the Law of Torts 380, 452 (1953).

2. The Two–Pronged Test. Courts in a handful of jurisdictions—Alaska, Hawaii, Ohio, and Illinois—explicitly adopted *Barker's* two-pronged definition of product defect, whereas Kansas explicitly rejected it. Arizona and Colorado courts danced around the issue, seemingly adopting *Barker'* s two-pronged approach, but without saying so explicitly. The Ohio legislature eventually merged consumer expectations into a multi-factor risk-utility test for design defect. See Ohio Rev. Code Ann. § 2307.75(B)(5).

Particularly in earlier years, some jurisdictions followed a de facto *Barker* approach, variously applying the consumer expectations and risk-utility tests in different cases without explanation as to why one test was applied in one situation and the other test in some other situation.

3. Shifting the Burden of Proof on Risk–Utility. With a very few exceptions, courts rejected *Barker*'s second-prong shift in the burden of proof. See, e.g., Wilson v. Piper Aircraft Corp. (on rehearing), 579 P.2d 1287 (Or. 1978); Hayes v. Ariens Co., 462 N.E.2d 273 (Mass. 1984); Kallio v. Ford Motor Co., 407 N.W.2d 92 (Minn.1987); Armentrout v. FMC Corp., 842 P.2d 175 (Colo. 1992) (overruling case on point). Most commentators were critical of *Barker's* shift in the burden of proof:

> The rule places an enormous burden on the concept of a "product design that proximately causes injury," a burden which the concept seems ill-equipped to handle.... People fall off ladders all the time, and the fact that ladders are both high and in some general way unstable enables these falls to occur. Does it or doesn't it follow that in every case of a person's falling off a ladder, the ladder's design proximately causes the fall?

G. Schwartz, Foreword: Understanding Products Liability, 67 Calif. L. Rev. 435, 466–67 (1979). See also W.P. Keeton, D. Dobbs, R. Keeton & D. Owen, Prosser and Keeton on Torts 702 (5th ed. 1984); Wade, On Product "Design Defects" and Their Actionability, 33 Vand. L. Rev. 551, 573 (1980).

Soule v. General Motors Corp.

Supreme Court of California, 1994.
8 Cal.4th 548, 34 Cal.Rptr.2d 607, 882 P.2d 298.

■ BAXTER, JUSTICE.

Plaintiff's ankles were badly injured when her General Motors (GM) car collided with another vehicle. She sued GM, asserting that defects in her automobile allowed its left front wheel to break free, collapse rearward, and smash the floorboard into her feet. GM denied any defect and claimed that the force of the collision itself was the sole cause of the injuries. Expert witnesses debated the issues at length. Plaintiff prevailed at trial, and the Court of Appeal affirmed the judgment.

[The court granted review to consider certain issues including whether an "ordinary consumer expectations" instruction is proper in a case where the question of how safely the product should have performed cannot be answered by the common experience of its users. *Held*, the 2–pronged *Barker* design defect instruction in this case was error, but the error was harmless.]

[Another car struck the plaintiff's 1992 Camaro near the left front wheel at a combined closing speed of roughly 50–60 miles per hour, bending the Camaro's frame adjacent to the wheel and tearing loose the bracket that attached the wheel assembly to the frame. When the wheel broke free, the toe pan crushed violently upward against her feet, which fractured both her ankles. Plaintiff sued GM for strict liability in tort, claiming that her ankles were injured when the collapse of the Camaro's wheel She asserted that the Camaro's design was defective in that the frame's bracket design and overall configuration failed to limit the wheel's rearward travel in accidents of this type.]

[At trial, defect and causation were addressed by numerous experts for both sides in such areas as biomechanics, metallurgy, orthopedics, design engineering, and crash-test simulation. Plaintiff's experts testified, on the basis of crash tests, metallurgical analysis, and other bases, as to how the damage to plaintiff's car would have been minimized had it been properly designed and manufactured. G.M.'s experts attempted to refute these claims and explained how the plaintiff's ankle injuries were caused by the force of the collision and her failure to wear a seatbelt rather than any defect in the car.]

[Automotive manufacturers have a duty to consider collision safety in designing their vehicles and are subject to liability for collision injuries from dangers that reasonably should have been designed away. The court reviewed *Cronin* and *Barker*, the latter of which] made clear that when the ultimate issue of design defect calls for a careful assessment of feasibility, practicality, risk, and benefit, the case should not be resolved simply on the basis of ordinary consumer expectations. As *Barker* observed, "... as a practical matter, in many instances it is simply impossible to eliminate the balancing or weighing of competing considerations in determining whether a product is defectively designed or not...."

* * *

Campbell v. General Motors Corp., 649 P.2d 224 (Cal. 1982) (*Campbell*) [explored] the proper use of the ordinary consumer expectations prong of *Barker*. Plaintiff Campbell, a bus passenger, was thrown from her seat and injured during a sharp turn. She sued GM, the manufacturer of the bus, alleging that the vehicle was defectively designed because there was no "grab bar" within easy reach of her seat. Campbell presented no expert testimony, but she submitted photographs of the interior of the bus, showing where safety bars and handles were located in relation to the seat she had occupied. [In that case, we reversed a nonsuit for GM, ruling] that the jurors could employ "[their] own sense of whether the product meets ordinary expectations as to its safety under the circumstances presented by the evidence. Since public transportation is a matter of common experience, no expert testimony was required to enable the jury to reach a decision on this part of the Barker inquiry."

"Indeed, it is difficult to conceive what testimony an 'expert' could provide. The thrust of the first *Barker* test is that the product must meet the safety expectations of the general public as represented by the ordinary consumer, not the industry or a government agency. '[O]ne can hardly imagine what credentials a witness must possess before he can be certified as an expert on the issue of ordinary consumer expectations.'" (*Campbell*, supra, quoting Schwartz, Foreword: Understanding Products Liability (1979) 67 Cal. L. Rev. 435, 480.)

* * *

[I]n Rosburg v. Minnesota Mining & Mfg. Co., 226 Cal. Rptr. 299 (Ct. App.1986), plaintiff claimed she was entitled to judgment under the consumer expectations test because her own testimony that she believed her breast implants would last a lifetime without leaking was the only lay evidence of what consumers expected. However, the Court of Appeal ruled that breast implant performance is beyond common experience, and that expert testimony on what the consumer should expect was therefore relevant and admissible. Here, the court observed, both plaintiff's surgeon and another defense expert had insisted that failures were expectable and patients were not advised otherwise. Hence, there was substantial evidence to support the finding below that no defect was proven under the consumer expectations test.

In *Barker*, we offered two alternative ways to prove a design defect, each appropriate to its own circumstances. The purposes, behaviors, and dangers of certain products are commonly understood by those who ordinarily use them. By the same token, the ordinary users or consumers of a product may have reasonable, widely accepted minimum expectations about the circumstances under which it should perform safely. Consumers govern their own conduct by these expectations, and products on the market should conform to them.

In some cases, therefore, "ordinary knowledge . . . as to [the product's] characteristics" (Rest.2d Torts, supra, § 402A, com. *i.*, p. 352), may permit an inference that the product did not perform as safely as it should. If the facts permit such a conclusion, and if the failure resulted from the product's design, a finding of defect is warranted without any further proof. The manufacturer may not defend a claim that a product's design failed to perform as safely as its ordinary consumers would expect by presenting expert evidence of the design's relative risks and benefits.[3]

However, as we noted in *Barker*, a complex product, even when it is being used as intended, may often cause injury in a way that does not engage its ordinary consumers' reasonable minimum assumptions about safe performance. For example, the ordinary consumer of an automobile simply has "no idea" how it should perform in all foreseeable situations, or how safe it should be made against all foreseeable hazards.

An injured person is not foreclosed from proving a defect in the product's design simply because he cannot show that the reasonable minimum safety expectations of its ordinary consumers were violated. Under *Barker*'s alternative test, a product is still defective if its design embodies "excessive preventable danger," that is, unless "the benefits of the . . . design outweigh the risk of danger inherent in such design." But

---

3. For example, the ordinary consumers of modern automobiles may and do expect that such vehicles will be designed so as not to explode while idling at stoplights, experience sudden steering or brake failure as they leave the dealership, or roll over and catch fire in two-mile-per-hour collisions. If the plaintiff in a product liability action proved that a vehicle's design produced such a result, the jury could find forthwith that the car failed to perform as safely as its ordinary consumers would expect, and was therefore defective.

this determination involves technical issues of feasibility, cost, practicality, risk, and benefit which are "impossible" to avoid. In such cases, the jury must consider the manufacturer's evidence of competing design considerations, and the issue of design defect cannot fairly be resolved by standardless reference to the "expectations" of an "ordinary consumer."

[T]he consumer expectations test is reserved for cases in which the *everyday experience* of the product's users permits a conclusion that the product's design violated *minimum* safety assumptions, and is thus defective *regardless of expert opinion about the merits of the design*. It follows that where the minimum safety of a product is within the common knowledge of lay jurors, expert witnesses may not be used to demonstrate what an ordinary consumer would or should expect. Use of expert testimony for that purpose would invade the jury's function (see Evid. Code, § 801, subd. (a))....

By the same token, the jury may not be left free to find a violation of ordinary consumer expectations whenever it chooses. Unless the facts actually permit an inference that the product's performance did not meet the minimum safety expectations of its ordinary users, the jury must engage in the balancing of risks and benefits required by the second prong of *Barker*.

Accordingly, [unless the accident is of a type that fairly implicates consumer safety expectations,] the jury must be instructed solely on the alternative risk-benefit theory of design defect announced in *Barker*.

GM [argues that "crashworthiness" cases are always complex and technical and so always require an instruction only on *Barker*'s risk-benefit prong. But] the line cannot be drawn as clearly as GM proposes.... The crucial question in each individual case is whether the circumstances of the product's failure permit an inference that the product's design performed below the legitimate, commonly accepted minimum safety assumptions of its ordinary consumers.

* * *

[Applying these principles to the facts of this case,] the instant jury should not have been instructed on ordinary consumer expectations. Plaintiff's theory of design defect was one of technical and mechanical detail. It sought to examine the precise behavior of several obscure components of her car under the complex circumstances of a particular accident. The collision's exact speed, angle, and point of impact were disputed. It seems settled, however, that plaintiff's Camaro received a substantial oblique blow near the left front wheel, and that the adjacent frame members and bracket assembly absorbed considerable inertial force.

An ordinary consumer of automobiles cannot reasonably expect that a car's frame, suspension, or interior will be designed to remain intact in any and all accidents. Nor would ordinary experience and understanding inform such a consumer how safely an automobile's design should perform under the esoteric circumstances of the collision at issue here. Indeed, both parties assumed that quite complicated design considerations were at issue, and that expert testimony was necessary to illuminate these matters. Therefore, injection of ordinary consumer expectations into the design defect equation was improper.

* * *

[However, we] see no reasonable probability that the jury disregarded the voluminous evidence on the risks and benefits of the Camaro's design, and instead rested its verdict on its independent assessment of what an ordinary consumer would expect. [Thus,] the error in presenting that theory to the jury provides no basis for disturbing the trial judgment.

[Affirmed. Concurring and dissenting opinions on other issues omitted.]

NOTE

Courts continue to struggle with the role of consumer expectations in design defect cases, particularly with respect to product performance that fairly may raise certain expectations. For example, in Force v. Ford Motor Company, 879 So.2d 103 (Fla. Dist. Ct. App. 2004), plaintiff challenged the design of an automobile's seatbelt system, alleging that the shoulder restraint did not lock properly in a head-on collision and that excessive slack in the belt resulted in serious injuries. The court ruled that the plaintiff was entitled to a consumer expectations test instruction in such a case in addition to the risk-utility test. As in *Soule*, the court observed that some designs are too complex to be judged by the consumer expectations standard, but it concluded that a seatbelt did not present such a complex case. Id. at 109–110.

What test might the *Soule* court rule should be applied in the case of a seatbelt system design defect issue like the one in *Force*?

Restatement (3d) of Torts: Products Liability § 2(b) (1998)

A product ... is defective in design when the foreseeable risks of harm posed by the product could have been reduced or avoided by the adoption of a reasonable alternative design ... and the omission of the alternative design renders the product not reasonably safe.

NOTES

1. **Syntax.** Paraphrased, § 2(b) provides:

A product is defective in design if its foreseeable risks could have been avoided by a reasonable alternative design, the omission of which renders the product not reasonably safe.

Converted to the active voice:

A product is defective in design if the seller could have reduced the foreseeable risk that harmed the plaintiff by adopting a reasonable alternative design, the omission of which renders the product not reasonably safe.

For a full, linguistic deconstruction of § 2(b), see Owen, Defectiveness Restated: Exploding the "Strict" Products Liability Myth, 1996 U. Ill. L. Rev. 743, 766–77.

2. "Subsection (b) adopts a reasonableness ('risk-utility balancing') test as the standard for judging the defectiveness of product designs. More specifically, the test is whether a reasonable alternative design would, at reasonable cost, have reduced the foreseeable risks of harm posed by the product and, if so, whether the omission of the alternative design ... rendered the product not reasonably safe." The necessary "comparison between an alternative design and the product design that caused the injury [is] undertaken from the viewpoint of a reasonable person. That approach is also used in administering the traditional reasonableness standard in negligence." Products Liability Restatement § 2 cmt. *d*.

3. Factors in the Balance. Comment *f*, "*Design defects: factors relevant in determining whether the omission of a reasonable alternative design renders a product not reasonably safe*," notes the pertinent considerations:

> The factors include, among others, the magnitude and probability of the foreseeable risks of harm, the instructions and warnings accompanying the product, and the nature and strength of consumer expectations regarding the product, including expectations arising from product portrayal and marketing. The relative advantages and disadvantages of the product as designed and as it alternatively could have been designed, may also be considered [including] the likely effects of the alternative design on production costs; the effects of the alternative design on product longevity, maintenance, repair, and esthetics; and the range of consumer choice among products....

4. Comparing Factors. With these Third Restatement factors, compare the seven factors proposed in Dean Wade's celebrated article, On the Nature of Strict Tort Liability for Products, 44 Miss.L.J. 825, 837–38 (1973), set forth above. Which do you prefer? Why?

5. Factoritis. An insidious, infectious, and possibly toxic disease contracted by some courts and commentators is the rendition of long lists of numerous factors. Banks v. ICI Americas, Inc., 450 S.E.2d 671, 675 (Ga. 1994), adopted a risk-benefit test for product design cases: "[N]o finite set of factors can be considered comprehensive or applicable under every factual circumstance, since such matters must necessarily vary according to the unique facts of each case. Such diverse matters as competing cost trade-offs, tactical market decisions, product development and research/testing demands, the idiosyncrasies of individual corporate management styles, and federal and other regulatory restrictions" can properly enter into the determination of the "reasonableness" of the manufacturer's design determination. "[F]or the benefit of bench and bar," the court then set forth a "non-exhaustive list of general factors," beginning with what we might label *risk factors*:

> the usefulness of the product; the gravity and severity of the danger ...; the likelihood of that danger; the avoidability of the danger, i.e., the user's knowledge of the product, publicity surrounding the danger, or the efficacy of warnings, as well as common knowledge and the expectation of danger; the user's ability to avoid danger; the state of the art ...; the ability to eliminate danger without impairing the usefulness of the product or making it too expensive; and the feasibility of spreading the loss in the setting of the product's price or by purchasing insurance.

The court next benefitted bench and bar by outlining the pertinent "*[a]lternative safe design factors*":

the feasibility of an alternative design; the availability of an effective substitute for the product which meets the same need but is safer; the financial cost of the improved design; and the adverse effects from the alternative.

Finally, the court set forth the pertinent *benefit factors* for consideration in the balancing test:

the appearance and aesthetic attractiveness of the product; its utility for multiple uses; the convenience and extent of its use, especially in light of the period of time it could be used [safely]; and the collateral safety of a feature other than the one that harmed the plaintiff.

What is a lawyer or court to *do* with all these factors (33, by our count)? Does the phrase "factor pollution" come to mind? "Fifteen factors or fifty may well be pertinent to the liability determination in every products case, but fifteen factors of varying degrees of importance are too many; a judge attempting to use them all would likely become smothered in factors." Montgomery & Owen, Reflections on the Theory and Administration of Strict Tort Liability for Defective Products, 27 S.C. L. Rev. 803, 817 (1976) (proposing 4 factors).

6. The Triumph of the Risk–Utility Test. Note the Third Restatement's relegation of *consumer expectations* to mere factor status. This is made explicit in comment *f* which, while noting that such expectations are "an important factor" in design defect decisions, explains that "consumer expectations do not constitute an independent standard for judging the defectiveness of product designs."

7. Does Strict Liability = Negligence? Many courts have acknowledged the close similarity, or "functional equivalence," of negligence and "strict" liability in the design context, but most have refused to take the final step and acknowledge that the formal doctrine of negligence is truly the legal standard to be applied in risk-utility determinations. Banks v. ICI Am., Inc., 450 S.E.2d 671, 674 n.3 (Ga. 1994), is typical:

While we recognize that the determination of whether a product was defective (involving the reasonableness of a manufacturer's design decisions), which is a basic inquiry for strict liability purposes, generally will overlap the determination of whether the manufacturer's conduct was reasonable, which is a basic inquiry for negligence purposes, we cannot agree that the use of negligence principles to determine whether the design of a product was "defective" necessarily obliterates under every conceivable factual scenario the distinction Georgia law has long recognized between negligence and strict liability theories of liability. [Citations.] Hence, we see no reason to conclude definitively that the two theories merge in design defect cases. Compare Prentis v. Yale Mfg. Co., 365 N.W.2d 176 (Mich. 1984); Jones v. Hutchinson Mfg. Inc., 502 S.W.2d 66 (Ky. 1973).

Should the courts be honest, and admit their mistake in characterizing this type of liability as "strict"? Or is the Products Liability Restatement correct in asserting that " 'strict products liability' is a term of art that reflects the judgment that products liability is a discrete area of tort law which borrows from both negligence and warranty [and which] is not fully congruent with classical tort or contract law."? See § 1 cmt. *a*.

8. Is Negligence *Better* than "Strict" Liability? Some scholars think so:

Negligence is the ideal standard for product design responsibility. From the start, the concept of negligence has been based on the notion of "reasonableness," predicated on the idea that proper decisions involve selecting the proper *balance* of expected advantages and disadvantages, of expected benefits and risks. Learned Hand, of course, memorialized the essence of this concept in his celebrated

$$B < P \times L \Rightarrow N$$

negligence formula in *United States v. Carroll Towing Co.* This type of "cost-benefit" or "risk utility" analysis nicely describes the decisional calculus that lies at the heart of design defect decisions in products liability law.

"Strict" liability is a rigid absolutist concept premised on an inherent priority of right which is entirely misplaced in evaluating the propriety of design judgments that necessarily involve tradeoffs among conflicting interests of different groups of persons. By contrast, the interrelated concepts of reasonableness, optimality, and balance on which design decisions necessarily rest are captured flawlessly by the flexible negligence concept. This thus explains the widespread judicial practice of applying negligence principles (albeit usually disguised under the rubric of "strict" liability) as the basis of liability for dangers in product design. See Owen, Defectiveness Redefined: Exploding the Myth of "Strict" Products Liability, 1996 U. Ill. L. Rev. 743, 753–55.

Compare the views of Davis, Design Defect Liability: In Search of a Standard of Responsibility, 39 Wayne L. Rev. 1217 (1992), who argues that manufacturers should be held to a care-based standard of responsibility, but heightened beyond ordinary reasonableness to reflect the position of trust held by manufacturers in the modern world.

Indeed, some scholars argue that such a rigorous negligence approach would be better even for plaintiffs. See Miller, Design Defect Litigation in Iowa: The Myths of Strict Liability, 40 Drake L. Rev. 465, 502 (1991), arguing that risk-utility decision-making under negligence is the preferable approach, *if* manufacturers are held to the knowledge and foresight of an expert in the field—a conventional standard applied by many courts when negligence was the dominant theory of recovery. "A toughened negligence standard that truly evaluated the manufacturer's design decisions with exacting scrutiny would better serve plaintiffs and would communicate to defendants that their responsibilities are real, substantial, and framed in a familiar negligence context." See also Miller, Myth Surrenders to Reality: Design Defect Litigation in Iowa, 51 Drake L. Rev. 549 (2003).

Potter v. Chicago Pneumatic Tool Company

Supreme Court of Connecticut, 1997.
694 A.2d 1319.

■ KATZ, ASSOCIATE JUSTICE.

[Appeal from a products liability action in which the plaintiffs, "grinders" at the General Dynamics Electric Boat (Electric Boat) shipyard in Groton, complain of hand-arm vibration syndrome from excessive vibration in pneumatic hand tools manufactured by the defendants which the plaintiffs used for chipping and grinding from the 1960s to the late 1980s. Specifically, plaintiffs allege that the tools were defectively designed and failed to carry adequate warnings. The jury found that the tools had been defectively designed, returning verdicts for the plaintiffs, and the trial court denied the defendants' motions for j.n.o.v. Defendants appeal on the ground that the plaintiffs presented no evidence of feasible alternative designs. *Held*, that, though the case must be reversed and remanded for a new trial for an unrelated procedural error, plaintiffs were *not* required to prove the existence of a feasible alternative design.

[Plaintiffs' experts testified that many of the defendants' tools violated the limits for vibration exposure of both the American National Standards Institute (Institute) and the American Conference of Governmental and Industrial Hygienists (Conference). Plaintiffs' experts further testified that engineers routinely seek to reduce or eliminate the amount of a machine's vibration by "isolation (the use of springs or mass to isolate vibration), dampening (adding weights to dampen vibrational effects), and balancing (adding weights to counterbalance machine imbalances that cause vibration)," and that these techniques have been used for decades. Applying these techniques to the defendants' tools, one expert found their vibration reduced by 35–60%.]

[T]he defendants claim that, in order to establish a prima facie design defect case, the plaintiffs were required to prove that there was a feasible alternative design available at the time that the defendants put their tools into the stream of commerce. We disagree.

* * *

[Noting that some courts apply a consumer expectations test, others a risk-utility test, and some the two-pronged approach of Barker v. Lull Engineering Co., 573 P.2d 443 (Cal. 1978), the court observed that the] "consumer expectation" standard is now well established in Connecticut strict products liability decisions. [Citations.] The defendants propose that it is time for this court to abandon the consumer expectation standard and adopt the requirement that the plaintiff must prove the existence of a reasonable alternative design in order to prevail on a design defect claim. We decline to accept the defendants' invitation.

[Defendants point to a draft of Products Liability Restatement § 2(b)] which provides that, as part of a plaintiff's prima facie case, the plaintiff must establish that "a product is defective in design when the foreseeable risks of harm posed by the product could have been reduced or avoided by the adoption of a reasonable alternative design . . . and the omission of the alternative design renders the product not reasonably safe." The [Restatement Reporters in a comment] state that "[v]ery substantial authority supports the proposition that [the] plaintiff must establish a reasonable alternative design in order for a product to be adjudged defective in design.". . . . Contrary to the [draft Restatement], our independent review of the prevailing common law reveals that the majority of jurisdictions *do not* impose upon plaintiffs an absolute requirement to prove a feasible alternative design.[11]

11. Our research reveals that, of the jurisdictions that have considered the role of feasible alternative designs in design defect cases: (1) six jurisdictions affirmatively state

[A feasible alternative design requirement makes it difficult for plaintiffs to get to the jury without expert witnesses "even in cases in which lay jurors can infer a design defect from circumstantial evidence," and precludes a finding that a product was defective in cases where such evidence is not available even if the product should give rise to strict liability.] See, e.g., O'Brien v. Muskin Corp., 463 A.2d 298 (N.J. 1983) ("other products, including some for which no alternative exists, are so dangerous and of such little use that . . . a manufacturer would bear the cost of liability of harm to others"); [citations.] Accordingly, we decline to adopt the requirement that a plaintiff must prove a feasible alternative design as a sine qua non to establishing a prima facie case of design defect.

Although today we continue to adhere to our long-standing rule that a product's defectiveness is to be determined by the expectations of an ordinary consumer, we nevertheless recognize that there may be instances involving complex product designs in which an ordinary consumer may not be able to form expectations of safety. See 1 M. Madden, Products Liability (2d ed. 1988) § 6.7, p. 209 (noting difficulty in "determining in particular instances the reasonable expectation of the consumer"); W. P. Keeton, D. Dobbs, R. Keeton, & D. Owen, Prosser & Keeton on Torts, § 99, pp. 698–99 (discussing ambiguity of consumer expectation test and shortcomings in its application). In such cases, a consumer's expectations may be viewed in light of various factors that balance the utility of the product's design with the magnitude of its risks. We find persuasive the reasoning of those jurisdictions that have modified their formulation of the consumer expectation test by incorporating risk-utility factors into the ordinary consumer expectation analysis. [Citations]; Seattle–First Nat'l Bank v. Tabert, 542 P.2d 774 (Wash. 1975). Thus, the modified consumer expectation test provides the jury with the product's risks and utility and then inquires whether a reasonable consumer would consider the product unreasonably dangerous. As the Supreme Court of Washington stated in *Tabert*, "[i]n determining the reasonable expectations of the ordinary consumer, a number of factors must be considered. The relative cost of the product, the gravity of the potential harm from the claimed defect and the cost and feasibility of eliminating or minimizing the risk may be relevant in a particular case. In other instances the nature of the product or the nature of the claimed defect may make other factors relevant to the issue." Accordingly, under this modified formulation, the consumer expectation test would establish the product's risks and utility, and the inquiry would then be whether a reasonable consumer would consider the product design unreasonably dangerous.

that a plaintiff need not show a feasible alternative design in order to establish a manufacturer's liability for design defect [citations]; (2) sixteen jurisdictions hold that a feasible alternative design is merely one of several factors that the jury may consider in determining whether a product design is defective [citations]; (3) three jurisdictions require the defendant, not the plaintiff, to prove that the product was not defective [citations]; and (4) eight jurisdictions require that the plaintiff prove a feasible alternative design in order to establish a prima facie case of design defect [citations].

In our view, the relevant factors that a jury may consider include, but are not limited to, the usefulness of the product, the likelihood and severity of the danger posed by the design, the feasibility of an alternative design, the financial cost of an improved design, the ability to reduce the product's danger without impairing its usefulness or making it too expensive, and the feasibility of spreading the loss by increasing the product's price. See Barker v. Lull Engineering Co., 573 P.2d 443 (Cal. 1978); Banks v. ICI Americas, Inc., 450 S.E.2d 671 (Ga. 1994); Wade, On the Nature of Strict Tort Liability for Products, 44 Miss. L.J. 825, 837–38 (1973). The availability of a feasible alternative design is a factor that the plaintiff *may*, rather than must, prove in order to establish that a product's risks outweigh its utility. [Citations. Emphasis added.]

[W]e emphasize that our adoption of a risk-utility balancing component to our consumer expectation test does not signal a retreat from strict tort liability. In weighing a product's risks against its utility, the focus of the jury should be on the product itself, and not on the conduct of the manufacturer. [Citations. And while] today we adopt a modified formulation of the consumer expectation test, we emphasize that we do not require a plaintiff to present evidence relating to the product's risks and utility in every case. As the California Court of Appeals has stated: "There are certain kinds of accidents—even where fairly complex machinery is involved—[that] are so bizarre that the average juror, upon hearing the particulars, might reasonably think: 'Whatever the user may have expected from that contraption, it certainly wasn't that.'" [Citation.] Accordingly, the ordinary consumer expectation test is appropriate when the everyday experience of the particular product's users permits the inference that the product did not meet minimum safety expectations. See Soule v. General Motors Corp., 882 P.2d 298 (Cal. 1994).

Conversely, the jury should engage in the risk-utility balancing required by our modified consumer expectation test when [ordinary consumer expectations of safety are not fairly implicated].... In such circumstances, the jury should be instructed solely on the modified consumer expectation test we have articulated today.

In this respect, it is the function of the trial court to determine whether an instruction based on the ordinary consumer expectation test or the modified consumer expectation test, or both, is appropriate in light of the evidence presented. In making this determination, the trial court must ascertain whether, under each test, there is sufficient evidence as a matter of law to warrant the respective instruction. [Citation.]

With these principles in mind, we now consider whether, in the present case, the trial court [erred in instructing the jury that it could find the defendant manufacturers strictly liable for their design of the tools] based on the reasonable expectations of an ordinary user of [such] tools. Because there was sufficient evidence as a matter of law to support the determination that the tools were unreasonably dangerous based on the ordinary consumer expectation test, we conclude that this instruction was [proper].

[The evidence supported such an instruction. Plaintiff's experts testified that the tools when tested were found to violate the vibration limits of both the Institute and the Conference and further testified on specific, feasible ways—including isolation, dampening and balancing—the tools might have been designed to reduce vibration considerably. Moreover, there was expert testimony that exposure to vibration is a significant contributing factor to the development of hand-arm vibration syndrome and that a clear relationship exists between the level of vibration exposure and the risk of developing the syndrome. The evidence therefore supported the jury's verdicts for plaintiffs on the defective design of the defendants' tools.]

[Reversed and remanded on other grounds.]

NOTES

1. The *Potter* court's redefinition of consumer expectations in risk-utility terms might be viewed as an imaginative way to retain the consumer expectations test while avoiding its various difficulties. The redefinitional approach (calling a pig a mule) may be traced at least to Seattle–First Nat'l Bank v. Tabert, 542 P.2d 774, 779 (Wash. 1975): "In considering the reasonable expectations of the ordinary consumer, a number of factors must be considered including [t]he relative cost of the product, the gravity of the potential harm from the claimed defect and the cost and feasibility of eliminating or minimizing the risk. . . ."

2. However one views the *Tabert–Potter* approach—as imaginative or artful—it has attracted a number of followers, some explicitly, others implicitly. See McCathern v. Toyota Motor Corp., 23 P.3d 320, 330–32 (Or. 2001) (risk-utility evidence may be required to prove consumer expectations); Vautour v. Body Masters Sports Indus., 784 A.2d 1178 (N.H. 2001) (consumer expectations defined in terms of risk-utility); Delaney v. Deere & Co., 999 P.2d 930, 944 (Kan. 2000) (recognizing "the validity of risk/utility analysis as a guide in determining the expectations of consumers in complex cases").

3. Compare the definition of a defective product in the European Community Directive on Defective Products art. 6(1): "A product is defective when it does not provide the safety which a person is entitled to expect, taking all circumstances into account. . . ." How should a person's "entitlement" be determined?

4. Compare and contrast *Soule* and *Potter*. Which is better? Why?

3. PROOF—GENERALLY

Knitz v. Minster Machine Co.

Court of Appeals of Ohio, 1987.
1987 WL 6486.

■ PER CURIAM.

A. *Procedural History*

[Plaintiff lost two fingers when she accidentally activated the press she was operating. Her products liability action against the press manufacturer was initially dismissed by the trial court, but the Ohio Supreme Court reversed and remanded for trial. Knitz v. Minster Machine Co., 432 N.E.2d 814 (Ohio), cert. denied, 459 U.S. 857 (1982). The jury returned a plaintiff's verdict of $150,000, and defendant appealed to the Court of Appeals.]

B. *The Product*

[Plaintiff Virginia Knitz] was employed as a press operator at Toledo Die and Manufacturing Company [TDM]. After initial instructions on the operations of the plant's machinery, plaintiff began operation of various punch presses. [One week later], plaintiff was assigned to operate a sixty-ton OBI Press designed and manufactured by Minster Machine Company [defendant Minster].

[To manufacture an item, the press brought two halves of a die together. At the top was a ram which, when activated, descended with sixty tons of force onto a bolster plate. One die half was attached to the ram, the other to the bolster plate beneath. An operator would insert metal stock between the dies and then activate the ram. When it descended, the ram would force the top die against the bottom die, cutting and shaping the stock into the desired item. The diagram below shows this type of press.]

O. B. I. Press
Flywheel Type

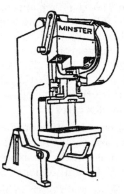

The [accident press] was delivered to TDM in 1971. As originally shipped, the press was delivered with a two-hand button tripping device.* This device permits activation of the press upon simultaneous depression of two buttons, which are placed at shoulder level above the die ram. The buttons, placed several feet apart, do not permit activation of the press unless both buttons are simultaneously depressed. Thus, activation of the press requires [use] of both hands, thereby preventing the operator from inadvertently placing his/her hand in the area where the ram descends.

Along with this device, TDM ordered an optional foot pedal [or "treadle"] tripping device, designed and sold by Minster. The device, attached to

---

* See note 1 following case for diagrams of alternative safety devices.—Eds.

the press, permitted the operator to activate the [ram by depressing a foot treadle in lieu of using] the two-button, tripping device.

Foot Treadle from Accident Press

After [receiving] the press with the optional foot treadle, TDM installed a pull-back safeguard (possum type). These guards were attached to the wrists of the operator and physically pull[ed] the operator's hands out of the die area when the ram descended to the bolster plate. Upon hiring, plaintiff was briefly instructed in the operation of the presses and the pull-back safeguard.

C. The Accident

... The job required [plaintiff to] place, with her hand, a block piece of metal stock in the space between the die halves. While performing this production run, plaintiff [used] the foot treadle to activate the ram, and the pull-back guards to provide safety against the erroneous insertion of her hands into the die area. After two hours, plaintiff, uncomfortable with the [size of the stool on which she was sitting], sought out a more comfortably-sized stool. Upon returning to her job station, she noticed that [someone had moved the foot treadle while emptying] the scrap bin beneath the press. [W]ithout reattaching her pull-backs or deactivating the press, [plaintiff placed her hand on the bolster plate and tried with her foot to slide the foot treadle back into position. Her movement of the treadle activated the ram], severing plaintiff's two fingers.

Plaintiff [claimed the press was defectively designed in not being equipped with safeguards to prevent] activation of the press while a hand was in the die area. . . .

I. TRIAL TESTIMONY

[Plaintiff's design defect expert was] Mr. McCarthy, a safety specialist, previously employed by the Pontiac Division of General Motors. Mr. McCarthy, while employed at Pontiac, was responsible for the development of programs to safeguard machines, including punch presses. Although Mr. McCarthy did not have an engineering degree, he had extensive background with press operations and the necessary safeguards for these machines. His responsibilities included research on how accidents occurred on press operations.

[Mr. McCarthy testified that three separate types of safety systems could protect the point of operation of the press—mechanical, electrical, and pneumatic—and identified five particular safeguards, including] the "sweep," the "interlock gate guard," the "moving/movable barrier," the "photoelectric system," and "pullbacks."

The sweep safeguard operates as a gate in front of the tool die area, which sweeps the operator's hands to the side when the ram is in operation ... similar to the gate protection mechanism seen at a bowling alley. However, [the sweep operates] with such force that an operator's hand, caught in the die area, [is often] struck, breaking or fracturing the operator's arm. . . .

[The interlock gate guard completely encloses the die area before the ram is permitted to descend. If an operator's hands are inside the die area, the guard cannot fully close, and the ram stays in the up position, which protects the user against human error.] The primary disadvantage to this safeguard is that the operator's production rate was substantially reduced. . . .

[T]he moving/movable barrier [guards] the point of operation [by preventing an operator's hands from entering] the die area. [However, such guards preclude the use of different dies and so reduces the utility of a multi-purpose machine like the Minster press involved in this case.] * * *

[The] photo-electric system [sets] forth an electrical field around the die area, which [detects] when an operator's hand [is] within the die area. In such cases, [its] sensing devices [prevent activation of the ram] until the operator remove[s] his hand. This system ... is similar to that seen in the typical grocery store door, which operates when a consumer steps on a mat which contains sensing devices. There are two primary disadvantages to this system, the cost [and] the operator's lack of knowledge as to whether the system is properly working ... until after an accident has occurred [at which point] it would be too late to prevent the injury.

[Another available safeguard,] in fact used on the Minster press, was the possum pull-backs. This safeguard required the operator to strap his wrists into a harness, which, when the press was in operation, pulled the operator's hands out of the die area. While this safeguard was one of the cheapest mechanisms available, it had the decided disadvantage that it required the operator to attach the pull-backs in order to prevent injury. Unlike the [other] safeguards, which would have prevented injury regardless of human error, the pull-backs required that the operator specifically act in order for the safeguard to properly prevent injury. That act required the operator to attach his wrist to the pull-backs.

[Mr. McCarthy concluded that Minster could have equipped the press with the interlock gate guard, the sweep, or the photoelectric system, any one of which would have prevented the plaintiff's injury. The press was the most dangerous machine in the plant, and Mr. McCarthy developed his own safeguard which] was a combination of an interlock guard and a barrier guard. The "McCarthy" guard would [move vertically and provide] an enclosure around the press area which would have deactivated the ram when an operator's hand was within the die area. . . .

On cross-examination, Mr. McCarthy [admitted] that his designed guard was not in use anywhere in the country, and that if it was to be utilized, it would require considerable amount of work by the manufacturer to install the guard and to manufacture it. Counsel for defendant also noted on cross-examination the discrepancy in Mr. McCarthy's testimony from other cases in which he had [testified] that his specific form of safeguard was not always necessary. . . .

[Mr. Jordan, a Minster employee, explained that the company] did not ship the press with any point of operation safeguards other than a two-button tripping device [because] the press, when shipped, generally was not subject to a specific purpose. [T]he press [could be used] for a variety of dies which would need to be attached to the press. . . . The differences in the operation of the press as well as the dies to be attached to the press did not permit the attachment of various safeguards, since the specific safeguards may prevent [using] the press in the desired manner. Therefore, no specific safeguard could be designed for the press.

[Mr. Jordan further testified that the moving/movable barrier was expensive, complex, required additional costly supervision and maintenance, and significantly reduced the rate of production. He also stated that the sweep guard was an unacceptable means of safeguarding the point of operation because it caused numerous injuries to the operator. Although he would not recommend pull-backs, he noted their consistent use throughout the industry. As for the McCarthy guard, Mr. Jordan testified that he was unaware of any manufacturer in the country who used such a device. Finally, when a purchaser ordered a foot pedal with a press, Mr. Jordan observed that the press manufacturer would assume that the purchasing employer intended to add whatever point of operation safeguarding was appropriate for its particular use of the press.][11]

On cross-examination, [Jordan conceded that the press could be feasibly operated with various safeguards attached, and] that the interlocking gate guard, sweep guard, and the photoelectric guard had been available prior to the sale of the Minster press. * * *

[In the earlier appeal of this case, Knitz v. Minster Machine Co., 432 N.E.2d 814 (Ohio 1982), the Ohio Supreme Court adopted the *Barker* two-pronged test for design defect, but not the shift in the burden of proof.

---

11. In recounting Mr. Jordan's testimony, the court is cognizant of the general statement of law which provides that a manufacturer has a nondelegable duty to safeguard the product.

Factors pertinent to the risk-utility prong of design defectiveness include "[1] the gravity of the danger posed by the challenged design, [2] the likelihood that such danger would occur, [3] the mechanical feasibility of a safer alternative design, [4] the financial cost of an improved design, and [5] the adverse consequences to the product and to the consumer that would result from an alternative design." The court also noted the possible relevance of governmental and industry standards as a part of the criteria of the risk benefit analysis.]

[A] key factor in plaintiff's proof is the availability of an alternative design. [M]anufacturers, in defending their action, must consider their best defense to be the costs associated with the alternative design as well as the benefits of the existing design. However, in so defending, the manufacturers are placed in the unenviable position of arguing that the costs of any safety device outweigh the injury to the person's well being. A jury often confronted with the plaintiff, injured, agonizing in pain and perhaps dismembered, will then have to justify that the costs and the benefits outweigh the injury to the plaintiff; not an easy situation for a manufacturer, regardless of its actions in the development and design of the product.

IV. ASSIGNMENTS OF ERROR–SUBSTANTIVE ISSUES

[At trial, the court instructed the jury not only on *Barker*'s two-pronged test for design defect but also that defendant had the burden of proof on the risk-benefit prong. The jury found for the defendant on the consumer expectations prong and for the plaintiff on the risk-benefit prong. *Held*, the instruction partially shifting the burden of proof to the defendant was reversible error.]

V. ASSIGNMENTS OF ERROR–EVIDENTIARY ISSUES

A. *Governmental & Industry Regulations*

Minster argues that the trial court erred [in excluding] governmental and industry regulations concerning available safety devices for presses [because such] regulations are part and parcel of determining the defectiveness under the risk-benefit analysis.

Plaintiff filed a motion *in limine* requesting that the court prohibit the introduction of regulations by the Ohio Industrial Commission,[32] the Occupational Safety and Health Administration, and the American National Standards Institute, ANSI [arguing] that the regulations were irrelevant and would unduly prejudice her case [and that] the regulations, which were promulgated and applied to employers and not manufacturers, cast an unnecessary cloud over the issue of the defective design of the product. [Plaintiff argued that the jury] would be misdirected into focusing on who had the responsibility for supplying the safety devices, i.e., manufacturer or employer, instead of whether the product was defectively designed. [In rebuttal, defendant] argued that the regulations were a necessary component of the risk-benefit analysis test [and] that the manufacturer's reliance

---

32. See Appendix B.

on governmental and industry regulations is a *relevant* factor in analyzing whether the risks of the product outweighed its benefits.

* * *

Congress passed the Occupational Safety and Health Act of 1970 to increase safety in the workplace and prevent workers' injuries [by] imposing civil and criminal penalties against employers failing to comply with OSHA standards[, not by altering the common law. Although the courts are split,] the general trend seems to allow the admission of OSHA standards as long as the standards do not serve as the basis of the cause of action; i.e., violation of OSHA does not equate to a claim for strict products liability. Admission of the standards in the present case would allow the manufacturer to rebut the plaintiff's assertion that the press was unreasonably dangerous. . . .

[Thus, evidence of compliance with OSHA standards, while not conclusive of nonliability, is relevant and admissible (subject to appropriate limiting instructions) to prove feasibility of design, availability of alternative safeguards, and other factors relevant to a risk-benefit determination of defectiveness. Similar principles apply to the admissibility of the Ohio Industrial Commission regulations and ANSI standards. Hence, their exclusion from evidence in this case was error.]

C. *Prior and Subsequent [Acts/Accidents]*

Defendant contends that the trial court erred when it permitted plaintiff to introduce evidence of prior and subsequent acts/accidents which were not substantially similar to the case at bar. At trial, plaintiff's counsel questioned Mr. Jordan, a Minster employee, and Mr. Steinecker[43] about separate accidents, both prior to and subsequent to Ms. Knitz's mishap. To most questions on the accidents, Jordan responded that he could not recall the specific incident relating to the accident. The best that could be discerned from Jordan's testimony, as determined by the leading questions tendered, was that some, if not all of the machine accidents involved Minster presses, without a sweep device, electronic guard, or interlocking gate, and that an injury occurred by some inadvertent hand entry into the die area. No evidence appears to have been adduced as to whether the device which caused the accident was accidentally triggered by the foot pedal.

Defendant, while conceding that the trial court may exercise its discretion in permitting the introduction of evidence on prior accidents, argues that the evidence of prior acts as well as subsequent acts was inadmissible since they were not substantially similar. . . .

---

43. Dennis Steinecker, an employee of Minster Machine Co., investigates press-related injuries. He testified that Minster produces predominantly power presses, which do not contain dies, interlocking gate guards, sweep guards or photoelectric guards. He further testified he was aware of approximately 20 hand injuries on the presses, and another 32 injuries where no interlock gate guards were utilized or installed.

Evidence of *prior acts* is [admissible if it shows notice to the manufacturer of] the hazardous nature of the product. . . . [A] trial court ordinarily is required to determine that the accidents occurred in substantially similar circumstances, so that the evidence is probative, and has a reasonable proximity in time before or after the accident. The factors are then compared with the defendant's potential for unfair surprise and the possibility of confusion of the jury to determine admissibility of the evidence. [Citation.]

Subsequent accident . . . evidence has little relevance as to the issue of notice or knowledge on the part of the manufacturer, but it may have a limited role in establishing the dangerousness or hazardousness of the product [and] the likelihood of injury, relevant factors under the risk-benefit analysis.

* * *

[Plaintiff attempted to show the similarity of the other accidents to the plaintiff's accident by showing that each of the other accidents involved] an inadvertent hand injury on a mechanical press, which contained no bolster plate safeguards, such as an interlock guard, sweep guard or photoelectric guard. [Plaintiff argues] that the purpose for [such evidence] was to establish that Minster had notice of the defect and danger present, as well as knowledge of feasible designs which would prevent the injury. Plaintiff further cries fowl [animal sic #1] in that the manufacturer appears to have either destroyed, lost or mysteriously misplaced records of prior accidents which may have had greater similarity in relationship to the alleged defect, evidence which would have established the defectiveness. [W]e find that the introduction of the evidence was admissible and that defendant, through introduction of its own evidence or by its own questioning, may diminish the credibility of the evidence concerning the prior accidents. . . .

[Even if another accident is substantially similar to the plaintiff's accident, such evidence still must satisfy Evidence Rule 403 which provides that relevant evidence should be excluded if "its probative value is substantially outweighed by the danger of unfair prejudice, of confusion of the issues, or of misleading the jury."]

[I]t was within the trial court's discretion to determine what [other accident] evidence is relevant and admissible in the case at bar. However, we are concerned with the undue prejudice [to the] defendant-manufacturer in this case, for the transcript of proceedings indicates that Mr. Jordan was questioned on well over 30 separate accidents. Similarity of the accidents, bearly [animal sic #2] demonstrated by the leading questions of plaintiff's counsel, was certainly less than desirable and may well have produced undue prejudice to defendant's case. While such evidence, as stated before, is admissible, the constant onslaught of questions, without the plaintiff making some corresponding attempt at relating the accidents to the case at hand, is unduly prejudicial to defendant's case.

* * *

[Reversed and remanded.]

APPENDIX B

**SPECIFIC SAFETY REQUIREMENTS OF THE
  INDUSTRIAL COMMISSION OF OHIO**

* * *

POWER PRESSES, HAMMERS AND MACHINES

IC–5–08.02 DEFINITIONS

* * *

(B) Danger zone. (on power press operations *only*) means the area between the platen and bolster plate.

(C) Ram. Ram means the moving part of the machine referred to as the punch, plunger, ram or slide.

(D) Guards—Power Press:

(1) Electronic. Electronic guard means an electronic safety device so designed and installed that when the operator's hand or any part of body is in the danger zone, the press cannot be tripped and if the hand or any part of the body is inserted while the ram is descending, it will immediately stop the ram.

(2) Fixed Barrier. A fixed barrier guard means an enclosure to prevent the hands or fingers of the operator from entering the danger zone. It may be attached to the dies.

(3) Gate. A gate guard means a movable gate operated by the tripping device which interposes a barrier between the operator and the danger zone, and remains closed until the ram has completed the down stroke.

(4) Magnetic. A magnetic guard means a magnetic safety device so designed and installed that when the operator's hand or any part of body is in the danger zone, the press cannot be tripped and if the hand or any part of the body is inserted while the ram is descending, it will immediately stop the ram.

(5) Photoelectric or Selenium. A photoelectric or selenium guard means a source of light rays together with receiver and other electronic equipment so designed and installed that when the operator's hand or any part of body is in the danger zone the press cannot be tripped and if the hand or any part of the body is inserted while the ram is descending it will immediately stop the ram.

(6) Pull. A pull guard means a device actuated by the ram and attached below the Pittman screw so that movement of the ram will pull the operator's hand or hands from the area between the punch and die (danger zone).

(7) Restraint or Hold–Back. A restraint or hold-back guard means a device with attachment to the hands or wrists of the operator which shall keep the fingers of the operator from entering a pinch point.

(8) Sweep. A sweep guard means a device actuated by some moving part of the press and shall effectively sweep the hands of the operator from the danger zone when the ram or plunger descends.

(9) Two–Hand Tripping Device. A two-hand tripping device means a device designed and constructed to require the simultaneous use of both hands of the operator to trip the press.

(E) Power Press. Power press means a power-driven machine fitted with a ram and dies for the purpose of blanking, trimming, drawing, punching, stamping, coining or forming material. (See IC–5–01.02(G) Feeding: (1) Automatic, (2) Hand or Manual and (3) Semi–Automatic).

IC–5–08.03 POWER PRESSES

(A) GUARDING

(1) Construction

Every power press in use shall be constructed, or shall be guarded to prevent the hands or fingers of the operator from entering the danger zone during the operating cycle.

(B) ACCEPTABLE METHODS OF GUARDING

(1) Manual Feed Presses, by:

(a) Gate Guard

(b) Fixed Barrier Guard

(c) Sweep Guard

(d) Pull and Restraint or Hold–Back Guard

(e) Two–Hand Tripping Device

(f) Limitation of ram stroke

(g) Electronic Guard

(h) Photoelectric or Selenium Guard

(i) Magnetic Guard

(j) Use of Special Tools

N O T E S

1. Consider the various machine guarding approaches illustrated below:

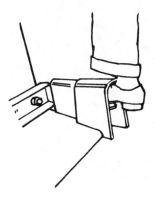 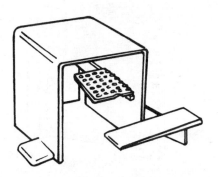

Treadle guards for presses and shears to prevent unintentional tripping

 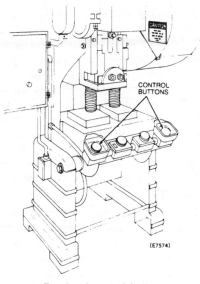

Gate guard on punch press. Guard is interlocked with tripping device of press so that plunger cannot descend until gate is in closed position

Two-hand control buttons
on part-revolution clutch power press

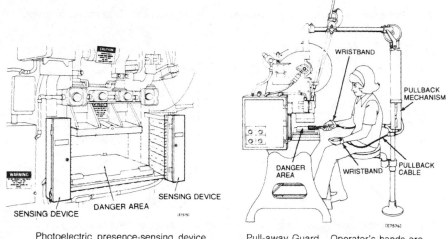

Photoelectric presence-sensing device
on power press

Pull-away Guard. Operator's hands are
pulled away from danger zone before
ram descends

2.   Consider Wilson v. Piper Aircraft Corp., 577 P.2d 1322 (Or. 1978), involving the crash of a small plane possibly caused by carburetor icing which could not have occurred if the plane's engine had been fuel-injected instead of having a carburetor. Although fuel injection systems were available and feasible, some 80–90% of all small airplanes used carbureted engines, a design approach approved by the FAA. Reversing jury verdicts for the plaintiffs, the court observed that "the plaintiff's burden in a design defect case includes a showing that there was an available 'alternative, safer design, practicable under the circumstances,' "which means that the alternative design is *feasible* "in terms of cost, practicality and technological possibility." A trial court should not submit a design case to the jury unless "the jury could find the suggested alternatives are not only technically feasible but also practicable in terms of cost and the over-all design and operation of the product."

3.   Garst v. General Motors Corp., 484 P.2d 47 (Kan. 1971), involved the 40-ton "Euclid" earth-moving scraper pictured below, that ran into and injured a worker at a construction site. The operator saw the plaintiff shortly before he hit him but was unable to brake the scraper to a stop or steer it away to avoid the collision.

Euclid TS–24 Earth–Moving Scraper

Plaintiff claimed that the defendant had been negligent in the design of both the braking and steering systems on the scraper, claiming that they both should have been more effective. The jury returned a verdict for the plaintiff, and defendant appealed.

Plaintiff's expert was John Sevart, an assistant professor of mechanical engineering at Wichita State University studying for his doctorate, whose specialty was in systems and design. His experience on hydraulic systems was limited, and he admitted on cross-examination that he was not a member of the Society of Automotive Engineers (SAE) and was not familiar with its standards relating to earth-moving equipment. Nor was he familiar with the SAE's Construction and Industrial Machines Technical Committee nor any of its standards on heavy equipment. But he did know that the SAE had such standards.

Sevart's challenge to the braking system concerned its open-type construction that allows mud to get into the system, although he admitted that all other manufacturers used similar "open" brakes on similar equipment, and that such brakes had certain advantages. His theory was that "there should be a shield or a guard on the braking system as standard equipment," and he proposed that a flexible seal should have been put over the brake. Although this would not keep mud out, it would reduce the build-up time so that the brakes would not have to be cleaned out so often.

However, Sevart knew of no flexible material that could be used to make the brake seal which his theory postulated. When cross-examined on several materials he mentioned could be used, it was disclosed that these materials would break down at temperatures of 250° Fahrenheit and would fail under the normal brake temperatures of 500 to 800° Fahrenheit. He explained that he was not a "materials expert."

Sevart also testified that the TS–24 scraper's steering system was negligently designed because "it steers too slow at low engine rpm. The way the machine is now designed, the speed of the steering depends upon engine speed." Sevart proposed 3 separate theoretical designs, none of which were in use on any comparable heavy equipment, and none of which had been tested. Moreover, GM experts explained how each of Sevart's solutions would cause a variety of problems for which he had no sufficient solutions. Observing that "All courts agree that as a matter of law, a manufacturer is not obligated to adopt only those features which represent the ultimate in safety or design," the court concluded that the alternatives proposed by plaintiff's expert Sevart were neither available nor feasible.

Held (5–2 decision), judgment for plaintiff reversed.

4. The Ultimate in Safety. Consider Vax v. Albany Lawn & Garden Ctr., 433 S.E.2d 364, 366 (Ga. App. 1993), plaintiff was injured when her riding lawn mower "reared up." She claimed that the absence of a "smooth start clutch" feature and a "deadman control" (that would stop the blade if she left her seat) rendered the mower's design defective. *Held*, summary judgment for defendants affirmed. "The law does not require . . . that a manufacturer produce or sell only the safest products it is capable of making."

Compare Acord v. General Motors Corp., 669 S.W.2d 111 (Tex. 1984), where the trial court instructed the jury that a manufacturer is not an insurer of the product it designs, that an adopted design need not be perfect nor render the product accident-proof, nor must the manufacturer incorporate the ultimate safety features in the product. *Held,* reversible error as an improper comment on the evidence.

5. Feasible Alternative Designs. Recall that § 2(b) of the Products Liability Restatement defines design defectiveness in terms of the availability of a "reasonable" alternative design (a "RAD") that would have prevented the harm. As discussed above, many courts hold (and some state statutes provide) that proof of a *feasible* alternative design is a necessary part of the plaintiff's case. "In order to prove defectiveness, the plaintiff must prove that a safer, practical, alternative design was available to the manufacturer." General Motors Corp. v. Edwards, 482 So.2d 1176, 1191 (Ala. 1985). Accord, Morales v. E.D. Etnyre & Co., 382 F.Supp.2d 1278 (D.N.M. 2005)(adopting Products Liability Restatement § 2(b)); Wright v. Brooke Group Ltd., 652 N.W.2d 159, 169 (Iowa 2002) (same); Williams v. Bennett, 921 So.2d 1269, 1274 (Miss. 2006) (Mississippi Products Liability Act requires proof of a "feasible design alternative" that probably would have "prevented the accident without impairing the utility, usefulness, practicality or desirability of the product").

6. Feasibility Factors. Feasibility may include such factors as technological capability, commercial practicability, cost, commercial availability of materials or components, and the likelihood of consumer acceptance. See, e.g., Rix v. General Motors Corp., 723 P.2d 195 (Mont. 1986); Troja v. Black & Decker Mfg. Co., 488 A.2d 516 (Md. Ct. Spec. App. 1985); Glover v. BIC Corp., 987 F.2d 1410 (9th Cir. 1993) (practicability means economic feasibility in terms of cost, overall design, and operation). Reconsider the kinds of factors pertinent to the "reasonableness" of an alternative design under § 2(b) cmt. *f* of the new Restatement, above.

All significant *disadvantages* of the proposed design are embraced within the feasibility concept, including especially (1) any *decrease* in the product's *utility,* and (2) any *increase* in its *costs* or *risks* of harm. See, e.g., Caterpillar, Inc. v. Shears, 911 S.W.2d 379 (Tex.1995)(front-end loader equipped with detachable rather than permanent "ROPS" rollover protective structure not defective; permanent structure was not "feasible" because it would destroy multi-purpose nature of loader); Monahan v. Toro Co., 856 F.Supp. 955 (E.D. Pa. 1994) (lawn tractor rolled over on steep slope; adding roll-bar and altering center of gravity might diminish utility).

7. Is an Alternative Design Required in Every Case? The consumer expectations test would not seem to require a plaintiff to prove the existence of an alternative design, reasonable vel non. Even some courts that apply the risk-utility test, recognizing that there may be rare products that cannot feasibly be redesigned and which are so dangerous that they should not be sold at all, have stated in dictum that proof of a feasible design alternative is not technically part of the plaintiff's case: "Although normally evidence of a safer design alternative will be presented initially by the plaintiff, it is not necessarily required in all cases." Kallio v. Ford Motor Co., 407 N.W.2d 92, 96–97 (Minn. 1987) (noting, however, that "as a practical matter, successful plaintiffs, almost without fail, introduce evidence of a safer alternative design").

This raises the issue of product category liability for products containing inherent ("generic") dangers, a topic addressed in ch. 10.

8. Delegation of the Duty of Safe Design; Optional Safety Devices. In *Knitz*, at note 11, the court recognizes the general principle that the duty of safe design is "nondelegable." If a product's safety can be substantially enhanced by adding a practical, relatively inexpensive safety device that does not appreciably diminish the product's usefulness, a manufacturer generally will have a duty to add the feature, and to make it mandatory. So, even if a manufacturer offers such a feature as optional equipment, most courts hold that a product sold without such a feasible, safety-enhancing, inexpensive safety feature renders the product defective and the manufacturer negligent for failing to employ the feature as a standard part of the design.

This principle derives largely from Bexiga v. Havir Mfg. Corp., 290 A.2d 281, 285 (N.J. 1972), a punch press case not unlike *Knitz*. Concerned that employers without a common-law tort incentive might often neglect to install safety devices in an effort to economize, the *Bexiga* court ruled:

> Where a manufacturer places into the channels of trade a finished product which can be put to use and which should be provided with safety devices because without such it creates an unreasonable risk of harm, and where such safety devices can feasibly be installed by the manufacturer, the fact that he expects that someone else will install such devices should not immunize him. The public interest in assuring that safety devices are installed demands more from the manufacturer than to permit him to leave such a critical phase of his manufacturing process to the haphazard conduct of the ultimate purchaser. The only way to be certain that such devices will be installed on all machines—which clearly the public interest requires—is to place the duty on the manufacturer where it is feasible for him to do so.

But does the general principle of nondelegability make sense when applied to a multi-function product with various possible safety devices the feasibility of which depends on the use to which the product is put? In this context, should the manufacturer be allowed to sell such products "bare," unequipped with *any* safety device, so that each employer can install whatever safety device may best suit its particular needs?

In fact, the courts on this issue are split. An early case contrary to *Bexiga* was Verge v. Ford Motor Co., 581 F.2d 384 (3d Cir. 1978) (V.I. law), in which a garbage truck without a back-up buzzer backed into and squashed a garbage man against a garbage can. The garbage truck had been assembled by a company that installed a compactor unit on a multi-purpose flat-bed truck cab and chassis it had purchased from Ford Motor Company. In an action against Ford and the garbage truck assembler for failing to equip the vehicle with a back-up buzzer, the Third Circuit ruled that Ford had no duty to install the alarm. Reversing judgment on a verdict for the plaintiff, the court reasoned that the assembler alone should bear responsibility for the selection and installation of appropriate safety equipment on the final truck, based on (1) trade custom, (2) the relative expertise of the parties, and (3) feasibility. What other factors might be relevant to this duty issue?

Bexiga is noted at 86 Harv. L. Rev. 923 (1973); *Verge* at 24 Vill. L. Rev. 406 (1978–79). On optional safety devices, see D. Owen, Products Liability Law § 8.9 (2d ed. 2008).

9. Reform. Requiring proof of a feasible alternative design is a popular form of products liability reform legislation. See, e.g., N.J. Rev. Stat. § 2A:58C–3(1). Compare the elegantly crafted N.C. Gen. Stat. 99B–6(a)(1) (1995).

10. Safety Standards. Design safety standards from a variety of sources may be admissible on the issues of both design defectiveness and design negligence.

A. Governmental standards. *Compliance* with a relevant governmental safety standard is generally considered probative of non-defectiveness or non-negligence. Conversely, *breach* of such standards may show defectiveness or negligence per se.

OSHA standards are peculiar. As in *Knitz*, many courts allow evidence of state and federal OSHA standards in products liability cases, even though such rules are aimed at *employers* rather than manufacturers, because industrial machinery is designed to be used in workplaces covered by OSHA rules.

Compliance with government standards as a defense is a popular type of products liability reform measure. See D. Owen, Products Liability Law § 14.3 (2d ed. 2008).

B. Quasi-public standards organizations. Some quasi-public organizations, such as Underwriters' Laboratories (UL) and the American National Standards Institute (ANSI), set voluntary product safety standards. Both compliance and breach of relevant standards of this type are generally considered probative on the issues of design defectiveness and negligence, but not conclusive.

C. Industry standards; custom. Evidence of compliance with, and breach of customary standards are some evidence, but not conclusive, of due care or negligence. The courts have split, however, on whether a manufacturer's adoption of a customary design is evidence of non-defectiveness in a strict liability case.

On all of these aspects of proof of defectiveness, see D. Owen, Products Liability Law § 6.4 (2d ed. 2008).

11. Proving Risk—Similar Accidents. How is a plaintiff to *prove* the magnitude of the risk for risk–utility purposes? As in both *McCormack* and *Knitz,* plaintiffs often seek to introduce evidence of similar accidents. Most courts hold that such evidence is admissible, in the discretion of the court, provided that the accidents are substantially similar to the case at bar. See Bittner v. American Honda Motor Co., 533 N.W.2d 476 (Wis. 1995) (in ATV case, "comparative risk" evidence on other motorized off-road vehicles, such as snowmobiles, minibikes, & trailbikes, was admissible, but not evidence on other products and activities, such as general aviation, sky diving, swimming, skiing, scuba diving, football, bicycles, motorcycles, and cars). Compare Deans v. Allegheny Int'l (USA), Inc., 590 N.E.2d 825, 827 (Ohio App. 1990) (plaintiff's evidence of 200,000 rotary lawn mower accidents per year properly excluded since "notice" or knowledge of risk is pertinent only to defendant's *conduct* which is not germane to *strict* products liability claim): "[T]he raw number of rotary mower accidents nationwide does not pertain to the risks [of] the specific tractor model under examination [nor to the plaintiff's] allegation that a safer, more cost-beneficial mower could have been designed."

The Consumer Product Safety Commission maintains a National Information Clearinghouse which collects data on injury-producing products. As part of this system, the National Electronic Injury Surveillance System receives data from major hospital emergency rooms throughout the United States, information which may be useful in documenting the frequency and nature of injuries associated with the use of particular products. Similar information may be obtained through the products liability exchange service of the American Association for Justice (formerly called the Association of Trial Lawyers of America), the principal professional association of plaintiffs' lawyers. See Zackey, The ATLA Exchange—Professional Cooperation and Product Safety, Trial 63 (Nov. 1978).

On similar accident evidence, see D. Owen, Products Liability Law § 6.4 (2d ed. 2008).

12. Post–Accident Remedial Measures. Assume that sometime prior to the trial in *Hankscraft*, the vaporizer case, above, the manufacturer had redesigned the plastic top with threads so it could be screwed securely onto the glass container. Should the plaintiff be permitted to introduce evidence of the redesign to prove that the earlier design was defective, or that the manufacturer had been negligent in originally designing the top without threads? The federal rule provides:

Fed. R. Evid. 407, Subsequent Remedial Measures:

> When, after an injury or harm allegedly caused by an event, measures are taken that, if taken previously, would have made the injury or harm less likely to occur, evidence of the subsequent measures is not admissible to prove negligence, culpable conduct, a defect in a product, a defect in a product's design, or a need for a warning or instruction. This rule does not require the exclusion of evidence of subsequent measures when offered for another purpose, such as proving ownership, control, or feasibility of precautionary measures, if controverted, or impeachment.

The Advisory Committee Note gives two reasons in support of the rule: (1) "the rule rejects the notion that 'because the world gets wiser as it gets older, therefore it was foolish before' "; and (2) an attempt to avoid discouraging persons from making safety improvements.

Federal courts. Rule 407 was revised in 1997 to make it clear that, in federal court (1) the rule applies and so bars evidence of safety improvements in strict products liability as well as negligence, and it applies to all three types of defect; and (2) the rule excludes only evidence of safety improvements adopted after the plaintiff's *injury*, leaving the admissibility of safety improvements made after manufacture but before the plaintiff's injury to the general rules of relevancy and prejudice.

State courts. The situation in the states is much less clear: the states agree that the repair doctrine applies to products liability claims based on *negligence*, but they split on whether the rule should be limited to such claims or instead should exclude subsequent remedial measure evidence with respect to *strict* products liability claims as well. The rule on its face traditionally applied only to negligence cases, such that many state courts and rules of evidence hold that it does not apply to strict liability cases. The classic case adopting this view is Ault v. International Harvester Co., 528 P.2d 1148 (Cal. 1974), which reasoned that "it is manifestly unrealistic to suggest that a [mass producer of products] will forego making improvements in its product, and risk innumerable additional lawsuits and the attendant adverse effect upon its public image, simply because evidence of adoption of such improvement may be admitted in an action founded on strict liability for recovery on an injury that preceded the improvement.'' But many state courts follow the modern federal approach in excluding subsequent remedial measure evidence for strict liability claims as well as negligence. See D. Owen, Products Liability Law § 6.4 (2d ed. 2008).

13.   Design Defects in Other Contexts. While the lack of safety features on industrial machinery and durable consumer goods generate recurring design defect litigation, design defect claims arise in other contexts too. See, e.g., Green v. Smith & Nephew AHP, Inc., 629 N.W.2d 727 (Wis. 2001) (allergic reactions to latex gloves possessing excessive levels of proteins and other toxic chemical substances); Morson v. Superior Court, 109 Cal.Rptr.2d 343 (Ct. App. 2001) (same); Arena v. Owens Corning, 74 Cal.Rptr.2d 580 (Ct. App. 1998) (toxic raw asbestos dust inhaled by naval shipyard worker); Nadel v. Burger King Corp., 695 N.E.2d 1185 (Ohio App. 1997) (175° coffee caused second degree burns); Bravman v. Baxter Healthcare Corp., 984 F.2d 71 (2d Cir. 1993) (noisy mechanical heart valve); Strothkamp v. Chesebrough–Pond's, Inc., Prod. Liab. Rep. (CCH) ¶ 13,456 (Mo. App. 1993) (failure to childproof box of cotton swabs); Toner v. Lederle Lab., 828 F.2d 510 (9th Cir. 1987) (DPT vaccine should have been formulated in safer manner); Boyer v. Empiregas, Inc. of Chillicothe, 734 S.W.2d 828 (Mo. App. 1987) (inadequately odorized propane gas exploded); Apels v. Murjani Int'l, Ltd., Prod. Liab. Rep. (CCH) ¶ 11,229 (D. Kan. 1986) (composition of blouse fabric, 80% cotton and 20% polyester, excessively flammable); West v. Johnson & Johnson Prods., Inc., 220 Cal.Rptr. 437 (Ct. App.1985) (extra-high absorbency tampons caused toxic shock syndrome); Hilliard v. A.H. Robins Co., 196 Cal.Rptr. 117 (Ct. App.1983) (Dalkon Shield IUD, with multifilament tail string, facilitated migration of bacteria into uterus); Drayton v. Jiffee Chem. Corp., 395 F.Supp. 1081 (N.D. Ohio 1975), modified 591 F.2d 352 (6th Cir. 1978) (formulation of drain cleaner as 26% lye unnecessarily caustic).

14.   For a small sampling of the design defect literature, see, e.g., Kysar, The Expectations of Consumers, 103 Colum. L. Rev. 1700 (2003); Miller, Myth Surrenders to Reality: Design Defect Litigation in Iowa, 51 Drake L. Rev. 549 (2003); F. Vandall and J. Vandall, A Call for An Accurate Restatement (Third) of Torts: Design Defect, 33 U. Mem. L. Rev. 909 (2003); Owen, Toward a Proper Test for Design Defectiveness: "Micro–Balancing" Costs and Benefits, 75 Tex. L. Rev. 1661 (1997); Owen, Defectiveness Restated: Exploding the "Strict" Products Liability Myth, 1996 U. Ill. L. Rev. 743; Vandall, The Restatement (Third) of Torts, Products Liability, Section 2(b): Design Defect, 68 Temple L. Rev. 167 (1995); M. Green, The Schizophrenia of Risk–Benefit Analysis in Design Defect Litigation, 48 Vand. L. Rev. 609 (1995); Tietz, Strict Products Liability, Design Defects and Corporate Decision–Making: Greater Deterrence Through Stricter Process, 38 Vill. L. Rev. 1361 (1993); Davis, Design Defect Liability: In Search of a Standard of Responsibility, 39 Wayne L. Rev. 1217 (1993). On design defects, see generally D. Owen, Products Liability Law ch. 8 (2d ed. 2008); 1 D. Owen, M.S. Madden, & M. Davis, Madden & Owen on Products Liability ch. 8 (3d ed.2000).

4.   PROOF—EXPERT TESTIMONY

In a design case of any complexity, such as *Knitz*, expert testimony— from an engineer, mechanic, chemist, or other technical specialist—is necessary for the plaintiff to establish design defectiveness, in general, the availability of a feasible alternative design, in particular, and sometimes also causation—the link between the product defect and the plaintiff's harm. On the other hand, if the design defect was clear and easy for the jury to understand—as in Matthews v. Lawnlite Co., 88 So.2d 299 (Fla. 1956), the case that began this chapter—expert testimony may not be needed. This is because the purpose of expert testimony is to educate the jury on matters beyond ordinary experience. See, e.g., Pietrone v. American Honda Motor Co., 235 Cal.Rptr. 137, 139 (Ct. App. 1987) (feasibility of guarding an exposed rear motorcycle wheel was "so self-evident as to obviate the need to present express testimony, expert or otherwise"); Lynd v. Rockwell Mfg. Co., 554 P.2d 1000, 1005 (Or. 1976) ("when the issues presented relate to matters which require only common knowledge and experience to understand them, the testimony of experts is not essential").

The crucial role of expert testimony, and limitations thereon wrought by *Daubert*, was explored in the previous chapter. Yet expert testimony is even more important for design defect claims. Broadly speaking, the parties' experts typically will battle out design defect issues as follows:

Plaintiff's expert: To prove design defectiveness, a *plaintiff's* expert must explain (1) the danger in the chosen design, and (2) how that risk of harm was unreasonable. To establish that the risk in the chosen design was unreasonable, the plaintiff's expert must explain how the injury could have been prevented by an *alternative* design that itself was "reasonable" in that it was (a) feasible, from a technical perspective; (b) safer, overall; (c) cost-effective; and (d) no less useful.

Defendant's expert: In rebuttal, a *defendant's* expert ordinarily must explain (1) the reasonableness of the *chosen* design, and (2) the problems with the plaintiff's proposed *alternative* designs that render them *un*reasonable.

––––

Calhoun v. Yamaha Motor Corp.

United States Court of Appeals, Third Circuit, 2003.
350 F.3d 316.

■ SCIRICA, CHIEF JUDGE.

In this products liability claim under maritime law, a jury rendered a defense verdict. The principal issue on appeal is the proper application of Federal Rule of Evidence 702 to the proffered testimony of plaintiffs' experts. [We affirm.]

[Twelve-year-old Natalie Calhoun was vacationing with her friend and her friend's parents at the Palmas del Mar resort in Puerto Rico where the girls rented a Yamaha Wavejammer WJ500G Personal Water Craft from a beach concessionaire, Roffe. Affixed to the jet ski was a warning that the minimum recommended age for operation was fourteen. Natalie had never ridden a jet ski before. Roffe asked her if she was the requisite fourteen years of age, to which she replied that she was, and Roffe briefly instructed her on how to use the jet ski. Natalie began her ride in the lagoon near the resort. After falling off once while trying to turn, Natalie got back on, made a sudden turn, and planed at high speed across the lagoon toward an anchored boat. As she approached the boat, she screamed but did not appear to attempt to veer away. Roffe testified she appeared "frozen" and "scared stiff." Natalie crashed into the boat and died. Natalie's parents sued Yamaha, the manufacturer of the jet ski, for negligence, breach of implied warranty, and strict liability in tort, alleging a defect in the design of the jet ski's accelerating mechanism, which is called a "squeeze finger throttle" and resembles the braking mechanism on a bicycle.]

Plaintiffs proffered three expert witnesses to testify at trial. After conducting extensive *Daubert* hearings including individual voir dire, the District Court determined that all could testify but limited the extent of their testimony. We review for abuse of discretion. See Gen. Elec. Co. v. Joiner, 522 U.S. 136, 138–39 (1997). . . .

Fed. R. Evid. 702 governs the admissibility of expert testimony. . . . :

> If scientific, technical, or other specialized knowledge will assist the trier of fact to understand the evidence or to determine a fact in issue, a witness qualified as an expert by knowledge, skill, experience, training, or education, may testify thereto in the form of an opinion or otherwise, if (1) the testimony is based upon sufficient facts or data, (2) the testimony is the product of reliable principles and methods, and (3) the witness has applied the principles and methods reliably to the facts of the case.

Fed. R. Evid. 702. Amended in 2000, Fed. R. Evid. 702 represents the logical outgrowth and memorialization of the Supreme Court's landmark cases establishing the standards for admitting expert testimony. In Daubert v. Merrell Dow Pharmaceuticals, Inc., 509 U.S. 579 (1993), the Supreme Court charged trial judges with the responsibility of acting as "gatekeepers" to exclude unreliable expert testimony, and in Kumho Tire Co. v. Carmichael, 526 U.S. 137 (1999), clarified that this "gatekeeper" function applies not only to testimony based on "scientific" knowledge but to testimony based on "technical" and "other specialized" knowledge as well.[9]

. . . Fed. R. Evid. 702 [first requires that the witness] be qualified to testify as an expert. Qualification requires "that the witness possess specialized expertise." Id. "We have interpreted this requirement liberally," holding that "a broad range of knowledge, skills, and training qualify an expert as such." In re Paoli R.R. Yard PCB Litig., 35 F.3d 717, 741 (3d Cir. 1994) (*Paoli II*). Second, the testimony must be reliable [in that] "the expert's opinion must be based on the 'methods and procedures of science' rather than on 'subjective belief or unsupported speculation'; the expert must have 'good grounds' for his or her belief." Id. at 742 (quoting *Daubert*, 509 U.S. at 590). [Assessing] "the reliability of scientific evidence under Rule 702 requires a determination as to its scientific validity." Id. Third,

---

9. Fed. R. Evid. 702 "affirms the trial court's role as gatekeeper and provides some general standards that the trial court must use to assess the reliability and helpfulness of proffered expert testimony." Fed. R. Evid. 702 advisory committee's note.

the expert testimony must "fit," id. at 743, meaning "the expert's testimony must be relevant for the purposes of the case and must assist the trier of fact." [Citation.]

Here, the dispute centers on the second element, whether the proffered testimony of plaintiffs' experts was reliable. While defendants asserted the experts' qualifications were lacking in general, the thrust of their challenge was that the proposed testimony did not derive from scientific methods and procedures, but was simply unsupported opinion. In this respect, the District Court held that certain aspects of the experts' proposed testimony lacked proper foundation and was inadmissible.

In determining whether testimony is reliable, we are guided by several factors:

(1) whether a method consists of a testable hypothesis; (2) whether the method has been subject to peer review; (3) the known or potential rate of error; (4) the existence and maintenance of standards controlling the technique's operation; (5) whether the method is generally accepted; (6) the relationship of the technique to methods which have been established to be reliable; (7) the qualifications of the expert witness testifying based on the methodology; and (8) the non-judicial uses to which the method has been put.

Paoli II, 35 F.3d at 742 n. 8. [These listed items are merely for guidance and should be applied in individual cases only as appropriate. In this case, the District Court carefully applied these standards to restrict the proposed expert testimony only on those specific matters for which the expert had failed to provide a reliable foundation.]

A.

Plaintiffs proffered Dr. Edward W. Karnes to testify that the jet ski was defectively designed because riders would accidentally activate the throttle by clenching their hands as a "stress reaction." . . . The District Court prevented Dr. Karnes from testifying on these matters.

Dr. Karnes holds a doctorate in experimental psychology and is an emeritus professor of psychology at Metropolitan State College in Denver. Among his specialties is human factors engineering.[10] He [was] a human factors engineer at the Martin Marietta Corporation in Denver, serving as head of human factors research for six years. Although defendants stress that Dr. Karnes has no degree in engineering and lacks expertise in marine vessel design or operations, the District Court qualified him as an expert because of his extensive experience in general design and operations.

An expert may be generally qualified but may lack qualifications to testify outside his area of expertise. The District Court allowed Dr. Karnes to describe the squeeze finger throttle on the jet ski and to testify that because of the throttle's similarity to a bicycle brake, a child in a stress situation would naturally squeeze the mechanism in order to stop the jet

---

10. Dr. Karnes explained that human factors engineering "is concerned with an evaluation of the human factors that are in- volved in the design and use of products, equipment, and facilities."

ski. Dr. Karnes's other theory was not permitted—that as a "stress reaction," a person would have a tendency to clench her hands, which would inadvertently activate the squeeze finger throttle of a Yamaha jet ski. Furthermore, Dr. Karnes was not permitted to offer an overall conclusion that the design of the throttle was defective.

... [T]here was no support for Dr. Karnes's opinion on an asserted "tendency" to clench hands as a "stress reaction." There was no literature confirming this theory, nor demonstrable tests. Lacking support, his testimony was speculative and unreliable. With no reliable foundation, the District Court did not abuse its discretion by prohibiting any conclusory statements on the [defectiveness of the] throttle's design....

B.

Plaintiffs proffered Albert Bruton to testify that Yamaha's accelerating mechanism was not as safe as other alternative designs [but the] District Court refused to allow the proffered testimony.

Bruton, a lieutenant for San Diego's Marine Safety Services for sixteen years, had extensive experience with jet skis. [He] had also conducted "aquatic related accident" investigations [but] lacks formal education or training in engineering, psychology, or human factors.

Bruton [was allowed] to explain how jet skis operate and the differences between Yamaha's jet ski and other brands and models [and was] permitted to discuss various accelerating mechanisms, explaining how each type works.... A videotape was played showing Bruton riding a jet ski. But Bruton was prohibited from opining as to which jet skis, and particularly which accelerating mechanisms, were safer because the District Court found his "ranges of experiences" did not give him the expertise or knowledge to make this determination....

These limitations were well considered. [Although] Bruton was knowledgeable about different types of jet skis and their operation, ... [he] had no education or experience in product design of jet skis or accelerating mechanisms; nor did he provide scientific, statistical or other evidence evaluating the relative safety of different jet ski models or their accelerating mechanisms. [Thus, he] had neither the general background nor the specific knowledge to support his proffered testimony that the "squeeze finger throttle" was less safe than other designs....

C.

Plaintiffs proffered Dr. Robert A. Warren to testify that the accelerating mechanism was unsafe because it resembled a bicycle brake and that Yamaha's warnings were inadequate. The District Court restricted Dr. Warren's testimony on these matters.

Dr. Warren has a bachelor's degree in naval architecture and marine engineering, as well as higher degrees in other fields. He worked with the Navy and the Department of Defense and served as an accident reconstruction consultant with a focus on marine engineering and boat accidents.

[While Dr. Warren's background qualified him to testify as an expert, the trial court correctly refused to allow] his proffered testimony that the throttle was unsafe particularly due to its similarity to a bicycle's braking mechanism. . . .

. . . At the time he wrote his expert report, Dr. Warren had never operated a jet ski and, by the time of trial, had only managed to ride a different model. Moreover, [he] admitted he had never examined diagrams of the different throttles used on jet skis [and his] asserted knowledge of possible alternatives to the accelerating mechanism came from his familiarity with outboard motors, which employ a twist grip mechanism, and from his recollection of a friend's motorcycle, which used a thumb throttle. Dr. Warren acknowledged he could have conducted tests to evaluate the relative merits of alternative throttle designs but did not do so. With such a paucity of knowledge regarding the specifics of jet ski accelerating mechanisms, Dr. Warren was unable to give reliable testimony on whether Yamaha improperly employed the squeeze finger throttle on its jet ski. . . .

[Judgment on verdict for defendant affirmed.]

NOTES

1. Why did plaintiffs lose this case? Is plaintiffs' counsel to be faulted for not employing engineers with more experience designing jet skis? How would you go about finding an expert for the plaintiff in a jet ski case like this, one who could testify more credibly and reliably on the defectiveness of the jet ski's acceleration mechanism?

2. Testing. Under *Daubert*, an expert's failure to test his or her alternative design may be fatal to the case. See, e.g., Wagner v. Hesston Corp., 450 F.3d 756 (8th Cir. 2006) (plaintiff's hand caught in unguarded hay baler not equipped with emergency stop device; plaintiff's experts' design defect theories were unreliable in part due to insufficient testing of their proposed alternative design theories); Rypkema v. Time Mfg. Co., 263 F. Supp. 2d 687 (S.D.N.Y. 2003) (plaintiff's expert offered only "a flat opinion, lacking scientific or engineering basis" that was "bereft of any engineering methodology," as contrasted to defendant's "equally qualified expert who had performed tests on the product at issue"); Allen v. LTV Steel Co., 68 F. App'x 718, 721 (7th Cir. 2003) (Ind. law) (expert unreliable because his methodology had not been "verified by testing, subjected to peer review, nor evaluated for its potential rate of error"); Dhillon v. Crown Controls Corp., 269 F.3d 865, 870 (7th Cir. 2001) (no testing of forklift with rear door added; "hands-on testing is not an absolute prerequisite to the admission of expert testimony, but the theory here easily lends itself to testing and substantiation by this method, such that conclusions based only on personal opinion and experience do not suffice"); LaBelle v. Philip Morris, Inc., 243 F. Supp. 2d 508 (D.S.C. 2001) (no testing of supposedly safer cigarette design).

3. Human Factors Experts. As *Calhoun* illustrates, plaintiffs in products liability cases sometimes use "human factors" experts. Compare Bittner v. American Honda Motor Co., 533 N.W.2d 476, 489–90 (Wis. 1995) (3–wheel ATV design defect case; plaintiff's human factors experts explained how a rider must employ complex and counter-intuitive motions and unnatural body position to turn the ATV, contrary to human experience with all other vehicles). See also Prentis v. Yale

Mfg. Co., 365 N.W.2d 176, 179 n. 4 (1984) (expert held Ph.D. in experimental psychology with emphasis on human factors).

In Reiff v. Convergent Technologies, 957 F.Supp. 573 (D. N.J.1997), plaintiff sought to use a human factors expert who was prepared to testify on the feasibility of altering the design of computer keyboards to prevent repetitive stress injuries such as carpal tunnel syndrome. Mrs. Reiff typed on a computer keyboard an average of twenty-five to thirty hours each week from 1988 to the early 1990s when she began to experience numbness and pain in her wrists and hands. She was diagnosed with bilateral carpal tunnel syndrome which required two surgeries to correct. When she returned to work, she began using a new computer keyboard (made by defendant's competitor, Microsoft) that is split into two halves with each half horizontally rotated to form an obtuse angle, arguably an ergonomically superior design. Plaintiff sued the manufacturer of her previous keyboard for design defects in the conventional keyboard configuration.

Plaintiffs sought to use the testimony of an engineer and human factors expert, or ergonomist, an expert in the interaction between humans and machines, to support the design defect claims. Plaintiff's expert argued that a split-angled design reduced musculoskeletal discomfort by easing four unnatural postures: forearm pronation, ulnar deviation, wrist extension, and upper arm abduction, thus reducing the chance for injury. The plaintiff's expert identified one article (that conflicted with his own published research) that concluded on the basis of anecdotal evidence that some split-angle keyboards are more comfortable than conventional keyboards to typists with prior hand and wrist pain. This led the expert to conclude that a conventional keyboard was defective in design because it increased the risk of discomfort, and thus injury, over split-angle keyboards. The trial court excluded this testimony of design defect stating: "In drawing his conclusions, [the expert] performed no scientific study; rather, he merely referenced a single journal article— at odds with his own research—which in truth stands for a proposition much more modest than that for which he cites it." Granting defendant's motion for summary judgment on all claims (including a failure to warn claim), the court remarked:

> Science coexists uneasily with litigation's adversary system, as the imperatives of partisan advocacy coupled with powerful economic incentives often seem to overwhelm good science. Lawyers, judges, and forensic experts sometimes engage in what literature teachers call willing suspension of disbelief. Scientific propositions that would cause even laymen to gasp in disbelief are routinely argued in courts of law. Such are the dangers of a legal system allowing partisan expert testimony.

> Imposing carpal tunnel syndrome liability based on alleged defects in keyboard design would result in a nationwide explosion of litigation at societal costs which are almost unimaginable. In a recent case sent to the jury by Judge Weinstein of the Eastern District of New York, a jury awarded damages in excess of five million dollars. [Geressy v. Digital Equip. Corp., 950 F.Supp. 519 (E.D.N.Y. 1997).] Presumably *Daubert* permit[s] a trial court to be sure that this avalanche of litigation is based on something at least resembling good science. The evidence proffered in this case does not cross that threshold.

Note that the jury verdict in *Geressy* was set aside on a number of grounds as to four of the five plaintiffs. See 980 F.Supp. 640 (E.D.N.Y.1997), aff'd, 152 F.3d 919 (2d Cir.1998) (table).

4. Affidavits and Summary Judgment. Compare Evers v. General Motors Corp., 770 F.2d 984, 986 (11th Cir. 1985), where plaintiff's car was broadsided near the driver's door by a car that ran a stop sign. Plaintiff sued the manufacturer of her own car alleging that it was defective in design due to the absence of an air bag. Defendant moved for summary judgment on the basis of deposition testimony that air bags do not work in side-impact collisions. Two days before the summary judgment hearing, plaintiff filed an affidavit of her expert stating that he had reviewed the evidence and concluded that the absence of an air bag rendered the car's design defective. *Held,* summary judgment for defendant affirmed. "[A] party may not avoid summary judgment solely on the basis of an expert's opinion that fails to provide specific facts from the record to support its conclusory allegations. . . . Most importantly, there is no specific mention of how an 'air bag' would have aided in a side-impact collision." See Fed. R. Civ. P. 56(e).

5. Expert Witness Games. Some expert witnesses testify with less than complete candor. In Sanchez v. Black Brothers Co., 423 N.E.2d 1309 (Ill. App. Ct. 1981), the trial court barred plaintiff from impeaching the credibility of defendant's expert witness on cross-examination with a speech he had given to a group of engineers on how to testify as an expert:

"The way I counteracted the thing, I used another technique. I used the technique of science as a foreign language. I made a statement to the attorney that absolutely nobody could understand. Now, what it amounts to, it's going to terminate the cross examination, and it's going to terminate it in a hurry.

"I want the jury to understand what I say when I feel there are certain conditions. Under direct examination, the jury understands everything that I say. Under cross examination, there are some things I will allow the jury to understand and there are some things which I will not allow the jury to understand.

"If you don't want the jury to understand something, then what you do is you answer the question precisely, you see. . . . I say, 'Do you mean the second bolt above the first bolt,' you know. Just get into something which is a very precise way of saying something.

"The interval of minus infinity to plus infinity of X times X, X^2, and you know the—no one is going to be able to do much with that kind of thing.

"And he says, 'Can you simplify it?' You say, 'See, there's too much simplification already. This is the only way that I can state it to you so there will be no misunderstanding.' " (Emphasis added.)

Held, the trial court's refusal to allow the plaintiff to use the speech for impeachment, on grounds of bias or prejudice, was reversible error. "[T]he expert witness is usually a hired partisan [and] it is unlikely that he could be successfully prosecuted for perjury on the basis of his opinion testimony. [C]ounsel must be given the widest possible latitude during cross examination. . . ." Id. at 1315. Compare Harre v. A.H. Robins Co., 750 F.2d 1501 (11th Cir. 1985) (judgment for defendant reversed and remanded since verdict based in part on perjured testimony by defense expert).

6. On expert witnesses, see generally Owen, A Decade of *Daubert*, 80 Denver L. Rev. 345 (2003); Saks, The Aftermath of *Daubert*: An Evolving Jurisprudence of Expert Evidence, 40 Jurimetrics 229 (2000); Graham, The Expert Witness Predicament: Determining "Reliable" Under the Gatekeeping Test of *Daubert, Kumho,* and Proposed Amended Rule 702 of the Federal Rules of Evidence, 54 Minn. L. Rev. 317 (2000); D. Owen, Products Liability Law § 6.3 (2d ed. 2008); 1 D. Owen, M.S. Madden, & M. Davis, Madden & Owen on Products Liability §§ 27:8–:9 (3d ed. 2000); 3 L. Frumer, M. Friedman, and C. Sklaren, Products Liability ch. 18A.

CHAPTER 8

WARNING DEFECTS

The manufacturer has certain informational obligations with respect to the products it sells. Thus, a product is "reasonably" safe (or non-"defective") only if it carries sufficient informational "software" to permit the consumer to use it with reasonable safety.

From the manufacturer's perspective, it usually is less costly to warn of a danger than to improve quality assurance or to design the danger entirely out of the product. Representing the broader social point of view, courts also tend to make an assumption that supplying warnings and instructions is the easy—and inexpensive—way for a manufacturer to fulfill its obligation to market products that are reasonably safe. And injured plaintiffs often reinforce the importance of safety information by making warning defect claims, since proving a warning "defective" is often a much easier (and less expensive) task than successfully attacking a product's design.

While the direct economic costs of supplying "adequate" warnings and instructions with most products may be minimal, there are some less obvious "costs" involved which raise subtle and important issues. One is the danger of providing too *much* information—the risk of over-warning or "warnings pollution." Moreover, the decision on how much and what types of information a manufacturer should provide with a product can only be answered intelligently if the goals sought to be achieved by the legal requirements are fully understood. Probably the most generally accepted goal of products liability law is deterrence, or risk reduction, predicated on the notion that the consumer who is informed of dangers and methods of safe use will act to protect himself or herself. Behind deterrence lies the more complex goal of economic efficiency, which seeks to maximize social resources by minimizing wasteful injuries.

Another reason for requiring warnings and instructions, but one which reflects a more fundamental human value, has surfaced in recent decades. This is the promotion of individual autonomy in decision-making. Thus, a consumer who is fully informed of the dangers in a product, and methods of safe use, may choose to use it in only a limited manner. Or he or she may choose not to use or buy the product at all. Unlike the risk-reduction rationale, which reflects a utilitarian perspective rooted in economic efficiency, this kind of informed consent idea focuses on protecting the user's individual rights, specifically, his right "to determine his own fate."[1] "The rationale ... is that the user or consumer is entitled to make his own

---

1. Pavlides v. Galveston Yacht Basin, Inc., 727 F.2d 330 (5th Cir. 1984).

choice as to whether the product's utility or benefits justify exposing himself to the risks of harm. Thus, a true choice situation arises, and a duty to warn attaches, whenever a reasonable man would want to be informed of the risk in order to decide whether to expose himself to it."[2] Finally, concerns with paternalism, and efforts to promote individual responsibility, are additional policy factors involved in some warnings cases.

The Products Liability Restatement summarizes the principles of the duty to warn:

> Commercial product sellers must provide reasonable instructions and warnings about risks of injury posed by products. Instructions inform persons how to use and consume products safely. Warnings alert users and consumers to the existence and nature of product risks so that they can prevent harm either by appropriate conduct during use or consumption or by choosing not to use or consume.

Restatement (Third) of Torts: Products Liability § 2(c) cmt *i*.

One important issue concerns the independence of the duty of safe *design* and the duty to provide users with adequate safety information. If a substantial danger could have been designed out of a product at little cost, a large majority of courts hold that even an "adequate" warning does not insulate a manufacturer who failed to employ the safer design.[3] "A warning is not a Band–Aid to cover a gaping wound, and a product is not safe simply because it carries a warning."[4] These and other considerations raised in this section suggest the need for critically examining the tempting conclusion that adding adequate warnings and instructions to dangerous products is a panacea for achieving optimal product safety. Nevertheless, providing sufficient danger and safe-use information with a product is indeed a key obligation of the manufacturer.

The most fundamental, recurring question in this area is whether the information supplied was "adequate," given the nature of the individual product and its probable environments of use. A manufacturer must of course provide sufficient *instructions* with the product on how to use it safely. Yet supplying even adequate instructions will not satisfy the manufacturer's duty to *warn* if the user is not alerted to hidden dangers in the product.[5]

---

2. Borel v. Fibreboard Paper Products Corp., 493 F.2d 1076, 1089 (5th Cir. 1973) (asbestos insulation worker, not warned of risks, contracted asbestosis and mesothelioma).

3. See, e.g., Delaney v. Deere & Co., 999 P.2d 930, 942 (Kan. 2000) ("just because there is a warning on a piece of equipment does not prevent the equipment from being dangerous"); White v. ABCO Eng'g Corp., 221 F.3d 293, 305–06 (2d Cir. 2000) (N.J. law) (notwithstanding clearly adequate warnings, conveyor manufacturer was subject to liability for failing to provide side guarding).

4. Glittenberg v. Doughboy Recreational Indus., 491 N.W.2d 208, 216 (Mich. 1992). See Products Liability Restatement § 2 cmt. *l*; D. Owen, Products Liability Law § 6.2 (2d ed. 2008).

5. Shuras v. Integrated Project Services, Inc., 190 F. Supp. 2d 194, 201 (D. Mass. 2002) ("Instructions on the use of a product does not discharge a manufacturer's duty to warn."); Meisner v. Patton Elec. Co., 781 F.Supp. 1432 (D. Neb. 1990) (instruction to plug space heater directly into wall outlet did not warn of risk of short circuit and fire from using extension cord).

The duty of manufacturers to warn and instruct sometimes is addressed by Congress. The Occupational Safety and Health Act, the Consumer Product Safety Act, the Toxic Substances Control Act, and the Federal Food, Drug and Cosmetic Act are among the more prominent statutes mandating warnings in various situations. See, for example, section 3 of the Toxic Substances Control Act, 15 U.S.C.A. § 2605(a), providing that the Environmental Protection Agency may require that chemical substances or mixtures regulated by the Act "be marked with or accompanied by clear and adequate warnings and instructions. . . . The form and content of such warnings and instructions shall be prescribed by the Administrator." Most of the law on warnings and instructions, however, has come from the courts.

The next section considers what types of information manufacturers must convey to users, how that information may be communicated, and to whom it should be given.

1. In General

Lewis v. Sea Ray Boats, Inc.

Supreme Court of Nevada, 2003.
65 P.3d 245.

■ MAUPIN, J.

Leo Gasse was killed and Robin Lewis catastrophically injured due to carbon monoxide poisoning during an overnight outing in a Sea Ray pleasure boat at the Lake Mead National Recreation Area. Lewis [and Gasse's heirs] brought suit against Sea Ray Boats, Inc., alleging that Sea Ray is strictly liable in tort in connection with the incident. [The jury returned a verdict for Sea Ray, finding that the boat was not defective, and the plaintiffs appealed.]

Plaintiffs' primary contention centers on the district court's failure to adopt plaintiffs' proffered instructions on their theory of liability; that warnings concerning the risk of carbon monoxide migration secondary to use of the boat's air conditioning system were inadequate. Because we conclude that plaintiffs were entitled to more specific instructions with regard to the warnings issue, we reverse the district court's judgment and remand this matter for a new trial.

FACTS

[In 1991, Leo Gasse bought a used Sea Ray pleasure boat from a] Sea Ray dealership. In addition to gasoline propulsion engines, the boat contained a small gasoline generator, which powered the boat's accessories, including the air conditioner.

On May 29, 1993, during a weekend cruise on Lake Mead, Gasse and Lewis "side-tied" the boat to a beach and went to sleep in the boat's cabin, leaving the gasoline generator running to power the air conditioner. The next morning, [a friend staying at the beach] knocked on the cabin door and received no response. He returned later that afternoon, boarded the boat, and found Gasse dead and Lewis barely breathing. [The friend] testified that the engines were not running when he first checked on the couple and when he returned.

Subsequent investigation confirmed that the generator, rather than the engines, was the source of the carbon monoxide, a tasteless odorless gas. This proposition was bolstered by other trial testimony that, had engine exhaust been the source, the couple may have been able to detect the problem because of the distinctive odor of exhaust fumes.

Two warnings regarding carbon monoxide poisoning accompanied the sale of this type of boat in 1981, one written by ... the generator manufacturer:

WARNING

ENGINE EXHAUST GAS (CARBON MONOXIDE) IS DEADLY!

Carbon monoxide is an odorless, colorless gas formed by incomplete combustion of hydrocarbon fuels. Carbon Monoxide is a dangerous gas that can cause unconsciousness and is potentially lethal. Some of the symptoms or signs of carbon monoxide inhalation are:

- Dizziness   - Vomiting

- Intense Headache   - Muscular Twitching

- Weakness and   - Throbbing in Temples
  Sleepiness

If you experience any of the above symptoms, get out into fresh air immediately. The best protection against carbon monoxide inhalation is a regular inspection of the complete exhaust system. If you notice a change in the sound or appearance of the exhaust system, shut the unit down immediately and have it inspected and repaired at once by a competent mechanic.

and the other by the National Marine Manufacturers' Association (NMMA):

WARNING: Use care in running the engine continuously when the boat is closed up in bad weather, particularly when the boat is not in motion. Exhaust fumes and carbon monoxide may accumulate in the passenger areas, so be alert to any indication that exhaust fumes are present, and ventilate accordingly.

... Both warnings primarily addressed the danger of carbon monoxide exposure from engine exhaust.

When Gasse [bought] the boat, the Sea Ray dealership service manager, George Schenk, and the salesman, Curt Snouffer, warned of the danger of exhaust fumes and carbon monoxide, and the necessity of ventilating the boat to remove hazardous fumes. Schenk and Snouffer demonstrated this process by opening a window and the hatch to allow for flow-through ventilation, and explained the need to have the rear door remain open when running the main propulsion engines. Lastly, Schenk indicated that idling the engine with the front hatch closed could cause accumulations of carbon monoxide.

Plaintiffs theorized that a process described as "migrating carbon monoxide" caused the accident. The process occurs when carbon monoxide, although safely exhausted from the boat's gasoline generator into the open air, is blown back into the boat by wind, entering the passenger cabin through small openings. Sea Ray's expert agreed with this theory of causation, but noted that such a phenomenon is quite rare and for carbon monoxide to accumulate to dangerous levels, passenger cabin ventilation must have been obstructed.

Sea Ray's expert testified regarding the safety of sleeping with the air conditioner running. He admitted that although boaters will often sleep with the air conditioner running unless warned not to do so, certain precautions should be taken. These include: (1) posting a watch, since in 1981, the year the boat was manufactured, no carbon monoxide detection devices were available; (2) anchoring the boat from the bow rather than the side, so that any wind currents would blow away from the stern; or (3) creating flow-through ventilation before going to sleep. The expert conceded that Sea Ray's manual contained no such instructions or warnings, but stressed that no incidents of this type resulting in death had ever been reported in connection with the particular pleasure boat model involved in this case. Sea Ray's expert also voiced his opinion that the warnings given were adequate with regard to carbon monoxide exposure, and that the risk of "migrating" carbon monoxide from on-board generators was not a known hazard when the boat was originally purchased in 1981.

Sea Ray's expert additionally relied upon a Nevada Department of Wildlife booklet found on the boat [that] discussed the hazards of exhaust fumes, warned that carbon monoxide itself is tasteless and odorless, that plenty of air flow should be maintained because exhaust fumes can blow back into a boat when running downwind, and that adequate ventilation was required when using catalytic heaters for warmth.

The warnings [involved here] specifically addressed the danger of carbon monoxide exposure from exhaust fumes, generally addressed dangers attendant to carbon monoxide exposure, and only inferentially addressed dangers in connection with generator fumes. This is important because ... the discrete odor from engine exhaust would arguably alert the passengers to the presence of noxious fumes, while emissions from the generator probably would not.

JURY INSTRUCTIONS ON "ADEQUATE WARNING"

Plaintiffs submitted a proposed jury instruction regarding legal requirements for an "adequate warning" based on Pavlides v. Galveston Yacht Basin, Inc., 727 F.2d 330 (5th Cir. 1984), a Fifth Circuit case applying a three-factor test under Texas law [citation] for determining whether a product warning was adequate. The proposed instruction read:

> A warning must (1) be designed so it can reasonably be expected to catch the attention of the consumer; (2) be comprehensible and give a fair indication of the specific risks involved with the product; and (3) be of an intensity justified by the magnitude of the risk.

[Rejecting this proposed instruction, and drawing on some language from *Pavlides*, the district court instructed the jury to use its common sense to decide whether or not the warning was "legally sufficient," which] depends upon the language used and the impression that such language is calculated to make upon the mind of the average user of the product.

[Twice during] deliberations, the jury sent a note to the trial judge, requesting a definition of an "adequate warning." [In addition to asking the court again to give the *Pavlides* instruction, above, plaintiffs proposed the following instruction from a products liability treatise]:

> To be adequate a necessary warning by its size, location, and intensity of language or symbol, must be calculated to impress upon a reasonably prudent user of the product the nature and extent of the hazard involved. The language used must be direct and should, where applicable, describe the method of safe use.

[Both times, the district court rejected these instructions, simply rereading its prior instructions on this point,] and refused to instruct the jury further, despite the confusion.... Shortly thereafter, the jury returned a verdict in favor of Sea Ray. This appeal followed.

DISCUSSION

Failure to give plaintiffs' proposed "adequacy of warnings" instruction

Defendant contends that warnings instructions in cases such as this one should be generally worded and that the adequacy of warnings should be left to the common sense of the finder of facts. Plaintiffs contend that the district court erred by not instructing the jury with their more specific definition of "adequate warning." We agree with plaintiffs.

[A] party is entitled to have the jury instructed on all of his theories of the case that are supported by the evidence, and ... general, abstract or stock instructions on the law are insufficient if a proper request for a specific instruction on an important point has been duly proffered to the court....

[Inherent in strict liability] doctrine is that "a product must include a warning that adequately communicates the dangers that may result from its use or foreseeable misuse." [I]n Fyssakis v. Knight Equipment Corp., 826 P.2d 570 (Nev. 1992), we held that adequacy of warnings was an issue of fact for the jury where an industrial strength soap manufacturer's warnings did not alert the user that the soap could cause blindness. In

Allison v. Merck and Company, 878 P.2d 948 (Nev. 1994), [we held that a manufacturer of a children's vaccine] was required to adequately warn parents of possible side effects of immunization, including blindness, deafness or mental retardation. Accordingly, we held that a general warning that an inoculated child could encounter rashes and possible brain inflammation was arguably inadequate and issues of fact remained as to the sufficiency of the warnings given. In remanding *Allison* for trial on the adequacy of the warnings, we rejected the notion that a drug manufacturer could, via a general warning, avoid liability. . . .

[Here,] the purchasers of the boat were comprehensively warned about the dangers of carbon monoxide poisoning from exhaust fumes, fumes characterized by a distinctive odor. [H]owever, the injuries sustained by Gasse and Lewis were not caused by exhaust fumes; they were caused by odorless and tasteless carbon monoxide fumes from the generator that powered the boat's air conditioner. Whether the warnings described above, which generally addressed dangers and symptoms of carbon monoxide poisoning and specifically addressed carbon monoxide exposure secondary to engine exhaust and running the heater, sufficiently apprised [Gasse] of carbon monoxide poisoning from use of the air conditioner remained the primary issue of fact throughout the trial below. Thus, the text of the "warnings" instruction became critical to the jury's fact-finding mission.

Here, the district court's "warnings" instructions provided very little in the way of guidance, other than to generally state that whether a warning is legally sufficient depends upon the "impression" that the warnings language "is calculated to make upon the mind of the average user of the product," and that the jury should use its common sense in resolving the issue. This instruction was not sufficient to assist the jury in resolving the liability issues based upon Sea Ray's alleged failure to warn. First, in *Fyssakis* and *Allison,* we refused to exonerate products manufacturers as a matter of law from strict tort liability based upon general warnings language. Second, these instructions left lay jurors, persons in much the same position as the users of the product at issue, to search their imaginations to test the adequacy of the warnings. Third, given that experts testified in this case to the nature and quality of the warnings that were given and their supposed behavioral impact, the jurors were entitled to more specific guidance as to the law governing the duty to warn in connection with consumer products.

We therefore embrace the rule of law stated in the *Pavlides* instructions offered by plaintiffs below, and hold that * * * plaintiffs are entitled to have their instruction on the definition of "adequate warning" submitted to the jury. That the jury ultimately became engaged in a dialogue with the district court on this very issue, and that the jury foreman indicated repetition of prior instructions was not helpful to the jury's deliberations, underscores the insufficiency of the instructions that were given.

[Reversed and remanded.]

NOTES

1. No Warning at All. First, of course, a manufacturer breaches its duty to warn by failing altogether to warn of a material, hidden risk. See, e.g., Richter v. Limax Int'l, Inc., 45 F.3d 1464 (10th Cir. 1995) (no warning of risk of stress fractures to ankles from repetitive use of exercise trampoline); Emery v. Federated Foods, Inc., 863 P.2d 426 (Mont. 1993) (no warning of risk to young children from ingesting marshmallows). Nor does warning of one risk satisfy the duty to warn of other material risks. See, e.g., Ayers v. Johnson & Johnson Baby Prod. Co., 818 P.2d 1337 (Wash. 1991) (warning that baby could get diarrhea from ingesting "Baby Oil" did not warn of paralysis).

2. Adequacy—*Insufficient* Warnings. Pursuant to the adequacy principles of *Pavlides*, adopted and applied by the *Lewis* court, a manufacturer's warning against "*prolonged* skin contact" does not sufficiently warn of risks to hands from a *single* use of an "all purpose" cleaner. Hayes v. Spartan Chem. Co., 622 So.2d 1352 (Fla. Dist. Ct. App. 1993). Nor does "toxic" warn of *death*. General Chem. Corp. v. De La Lastra, 815 S.W.2d 750 (Tex. Ct. App. 1991) (sulfur dioxide gas from preservative sprinkled on iced shrimp in hold of boat).

Query, do most parents know the meaning of "ingest," or would an "adequate" warning need to say "swallow"?

3. In Burch v. Amsterdam Corp., 366 A.2d 1079 (D.C. App. 1976), the plaintiff was badly burned in an explosion and flash fire that occurred while he was applying a floor tile adhesive sold by the defendant. The label on the can of mastic adhesive read as follows:

DANGER! EXTREMELY FLAMMABLE:

See Cautions elsewhere on label.

CAUTION: FLAMMABLE MIXTURE. DO NOT USE NEAR FIRE OR FLAME N.Y.F.D.C. of A. No. 2381

USE WITH ADEQUATE VENTILATION

MAY BE HARMFUL OR FATAL IF SWALLOWED—DO NOT INDUCE VOMITING, CALL PHYSICIAN—KEEP AWAY FROM CHILDREN

Plaintiff read the instructions on the label of the mastic adhesive can, opened the windows, and turned on ductal fans and a large air conditioner. He checked the area to be sure there were no flames but did not think of the gas stove pilot light in the kitchen where he was working. After plaintiff applied a first coat of adhesive to the floor, the vapors reached the pilot light and exploded. Plaintiff heard a "whoosh," "had a sense of time being elongated, felt searing heat and saw the skin peeling from his body." The trial court granted summary judgment for defendant on plaintiff's inadequate warnings claim; the Court of Appeals reversed because defendant had failed to warn of the *specific* risk:

> The particular hazard encountered by plaintiffs in using VICO–102 was that fumes or vapors from the product could ignite on contact with a pilot light, resulting in a violent fire or explosion.... Given the potential for serious injury we cannot say as a matter of law that this warning adequately alerted users of the dangers inherent in the product. Among other things, an ordinary user might not have realized that "near fire or flame" included nearby pilot lights or that fumes and vapors, as well as the adhesive itself, were extremely flammable.

Chief Judge Reilly dissented:

> . . . If there was a duty to advert expressly to pilot lights in addition to "fire and flame," it would seem equally incumbent upon the vendors to devise a label warning against lighted pipes, cigars and cigarettes, vigil lights, candles, sparks from an electric lamp switch, a running fan or motor, and the other myriad of things which could possibly ignite vapors. If this is what the law requires, big lettering would have to be discarded for smaller print enumerating details at such length that few users would bother to read it—the warning then [being inadequate in] lacking the requisite "intensity."

4. Compare Murray v. Wilson Oak Flooring Co., 475 F.2d 129, 130–33 (7th Cir. 1973), where plaintiff was burned when the vapors from the mastic flooring adhesive he was applying were ignited by the pilot light of a water heater or stove. In a negligent warning action against the manufacturer, the jury found for the plaintiff, but the court granted the defendant's motion for j.n.o.v. The labels on the can stated in part as follows:

Keep AWAY From Fire,

HEAT and OPEN flame LIGHTS

CAUTION

LEAKING Packages Must be Removed to a Safe Place

DO NOT DROP

Another label was affixed to the opposite side of the can. White with red lettering, it set forth, in part, this message:

CAUTION: INFLAMMABLE MIXTURE
DO NOT USE NEAR FIRE OR FLAME

N. Y. F. D. C. of A. No. 2360

CONTAINS HEPTANE — USE IN WELL VENTILATED AREA
Do not smoke — Extinguish flame — including pilot lights
KEEP LID TIGHTLY CLOSED   KEEP AWAY FROM CHILDREN

"Expert witnesses for both sides testified that Latex '45' emits a heavy and highly combust[i]ble vapor capable (1) of traveling for some distance along a floor from the point at which the mastic is spread, (2) of burning with explosive force upon encountering any form of exposed flame, and (3) of transmitting that flame back to the body of spread adhesive." Reversing the j.n.o.v. and reinstating plaintiff's verdict, the Court of Appeals remarked: "We cannot say as a matter of law that the term 'near' was sufficient to inform Murray that his spreading of adhesive within four feet of a pilot light *located behind a closed door* and within eight feet of stove pilot lights three feet off the floor exposed him to the risk of an explosion."

5. *Overwarning—Warnings "Pollution."* With the preceding cases, contrast Aetna Casualty & Surety Co. v. Ralph Wilson Plastics Co., 509 N.W.2d 520 (Mich. App. 1993), where a glue manufacturer warned of the extreme flammability of its solvents and instructed users to turn off pilot lights, stoves, heaters, flames and electric motors, not to smoke, and to keep away from heat and sparks. Property damage resulted when a worker picked up a piece of foam rubber to mop up some spilled glue solvent and static electricity in the foam rubber set off an explosion. *Held* (2–1), the warning was adequate. "A spark is a spark, and a possible source of ignition of a highly flammable compound irrespective of the means by which the spark was generated, whether by static electricity or otherwise."

> If a manufacturer had to list all sources of friction, or all sources of sparks, as a means of warning of a flammability hazard, its warning would have to be of epic or encyclopedic proportions [because the] combination of circumstances or materials that could create a spark would be almost limitless. [E]xcessive warnings on product labels may be counterproductive, causing "sensory overload" which literally drowns crucial information in a sea of mind-numbing detail.

Cases split on just how precise warning language must be to satisfy the "adequacy" requirement. Sometimes courts rule that even general and quite vague warnings are adequate, whereas others hold that adequacy requires precise and detailed information.

Consider Spillane v. Georgia Pacific Corp., 1995 WL 71183 (E.D. Pa. 1995), which involved a roofing compound which warned: "CAUTION, SLIPPERY WHEN WET. Do not walk on surface unless it is completely dry. Follow proper safety precautions, including using appropriate shoes and safety rope." Plaintiff, a roofer, slipped on the compound, fell off a roof, and sued the manufacturer for failing adequately to warn. *Held*, defendant's motion for summary judgment denied. Although the language "at first seems the epitome of unambiguous clarity," it failed to convey how "appallingly slick" the roof surface was. The court drew an analogy to warning "Beware of cat. Stay Away," which would fail adequately to warn a person "chomped" by "a full-grown, hungry cheetah." "The cheetah is the quickest land-animal in the world, and plaintiffs' papers suggest this was just about the slickest roof in the world."

6. Ditto—*Substance.* Consider Cotton v. Buckeye Gas Products Co., 840 F.2d 935, 937–39 (D.C. Cir. 1988). As a night heater watcher for a construction company, plaintiff's job was to monitor heaters used to cure concrete in cold weather and to change the propane cylinders supplied by defendant as they ran low on gas. The areas being cured were covered with polyethylene curtains to contain the heat. Plaintiff neglected to close the valves on the used cylinders and stored them in the vicinity of the active heaters within the polyethylene enclosed areas. Labels on the cylinders warned that they contained "flammable" gas and should not be used or stored in "living areas." Gas escaping from the used cylinders ignited and severely burned the plaintiff.

Plaintiff sued the suppliers, claiming that the warning was inadequate because it failed (1) to warn that propane was not only flammable but also "explosive"; (2) to instruct users to shut the valves on used cylinders; (3) to advise users not to use or store the cylinders in enclosed, unventilated areas; and (4) to warn that gas might escape from used cylinders believed to be empty. The jury agreed, but the trial court granted the defendant's motion for j.n.o.v. On appeal, *held,* affirmed:

> Failure-to-warn cases have the curious property that, when the episode is examined in hindsight, it appears as though addition of warnings keyed to a particular accident would be virtually cost free. What could be simpler than for the manufacturer to add the few simple items noted above? The primary cost is, in fact, the increase in time and effort required for the user to grasp the message. The inclusion of each extra item dilutes the punch of every other item. Given short attention spans, items crowd each other out; they get lost in fine print. Here, in fact, Buckeye [used] a dual approach: a brief message on the canisters themselves and a more detailed one in the NLPGA pamphlet delivered to Miller & Long (and posted on the bulletin board at the construction site where Cotton was employed).

> . . . If every foreseeable possibility must be covered, "The list of foolish practices warned against would be so long, it would fill a volume." . . .

> [First, there is no] relevant difference between "flammable" and "explosive" [and Cotton's] injuries were exclusively burns, deriving exclusively from the gases' burning [after the explosion. Moreover, the other warnings were in fact] embodied in the NLPGA pamphlet [which] warned that the cylinders should be used only in ventilated areas and that the cylinder valves should be closed. . . . Again, a warning need not dot every i. [In conclusion,] "warnings need not spell out the risk in intricate detail."

7. Ditto—*Prominence.* General Motors Corp. v. Saenz, 873 S.W.2d 353 (Tex. 1993), involved a claim that General Motors' warning against overloading was insufficiently prominent:

> Plaintiffs' argument that the WARNING could have been more prominent does not prove that it was not prominent enough. Every WARNING can always be made bigger, brighter and more obvious. GM could have placed the WARNING where it could not possibly have been overlooked, perhaps engraved upon the dashboard, or backlit on the instrument panel. But it clearly would not be possible for GM to place every important WARNING in such a position of maximum prominence. It can always be argued that a single instruction should have been given more prominence and if it had, an accident might have been prevented. This argument, however, must be considered in the context of the product involved. When, as here, it is important to give a number of instructions concerning the operation of a vehicle, not all of them can be printed on the dashboard. Indeed, the more instructions and WARNINGS that are printed in one place—on the dashboard, on a doorplate, or in the owner's manual—the less likely that any one instruction or WARNING will be noticed.

> The issue is not whether GM could have placed its WARNING against overloading in a more prominent position, such as a sticker near the gear shift lever as plaintiffs argue; rather, the issue is whether the WARNING where it was actually placed was sufficient to give reasonable notice against overloading. GM's WARNING was posted where gross vehicle weights are customarily placed in compliance with federal regulations [to wit] at eye level on the driver's doorjamb [and on page 2 of the] owner's manual [that] was in the glovebox. There is nothing in the record, and nothing in plaintiffs' arguments, to suggest why the WARNING GM gave was not sufficient to give reasonable notice against overloading. . . .

8. Ditto—*Selectivity*. Compare Twerski, Weinstein, Donaher, Piehler, The Use and Abuse of Warnings in Products Liability—Design Defect Litigation Comes of Age, 61 Cornell L. Rev. 495, 514–16 (1976):

> Warnings, in order to be effective, must be selective. They must call the consumer's attention to a danger that has a real probability of occurring and whose impact will be significant. One must warn with discrimination since the consumer is being asked to discriminate and to react accordingly. The story of the boy who cried wolf is an analogy worth contemplating when considering the imposition of a warning in a case of rather marginal risk.... The warning process, in order to have impact, will have to select carefully the items which are to become part of the consumer's mental apparatus while using the product. Making the consumer account mentally for trivia or guard against risks that are not likely to occur imposes a very real societal cost. * * * In short, when calculating the burden of precaution which is part of the risk-utility calculus, it will be necessary to focus on costs other than the cost of label printing. The efficacy of warning is a societal cost of substantial importance.

9. Instructions. "A duty to warn actually consists of two duties: One is to give adequate instructions for safe use, and the other is to give a warning as to dangers...." Ontai v. Straub Clinic & Hosp. Inc., 659 P.2d 734, 743 (Haw. 1983). While warnings and directions for use often blend into each other, they involve separate types of information: A warning provides information on the danger itself; an instruction provides information on how to *avoid* it.

In any particular case, either or both forms of information may be necessary. A plane may crash or a house may burn down if an airplane part or a woodstove chimney pipe is inadvertently installed upside down. See Nesselrode v. Executive Beechcraft, Inc., 707 S.W.2d 371 (Mo. 1986) (plane); Duford v. Sears, Roebuck & Co., 833 F.2d 407 (1st Cir. 1987) (woodstove). See also Piper v. Bear Med. Systems, Inc., 883 P.2d 407 (Ariz. App. 1993) (respirator patient died when therapist, not having been warned of risk, attached one-way valve backwards). Compare Midgley v. S.S. Kresge Co., 127 Cal.Rptr. 217 (Ct. App. 1976) (K–Mart telescope had inadequate written instructions, and no diagrammatic illustrations, on proper method of attaching sun filter).

Even the best of *instructions* will not fulfill the duty to *warn*. "Instructions on the use of a product [do] not discharge a manufacturer's duty to warn." Shuras v. Integrated Project Services, Inc., 190 F. Supp. 2d 194, 201 (D. Mass. 2002). See, e.g., Fuentes v. Shin Caterpillar Mitsubishi, Ltd., 2003 WL 22205665, at *4 (Cal. App. 2003) ("!WARNING Use self-attaching air chuck and stand behind tire tread while inflating." was really an instruction and was an inadequate warning because "there was no description of the fact that the tire assembly or the rim could explode upon inflation or that death or other serious injury could result"); McConnell v. Cosco, Inc., 238 F. Supp. 2d 970 (S.D. Ohio 2003) (highchair instruction to "secure baby with safety straps" does not warn of risk of strangulation); Brown v. Glade & Grove Supply, 647 So.2d 1033 (Fla. App. 1994) (advising driver to operate tractor with lock-out pins in place is instruction, not warning).

10. But compare Todd v. Societe BIC (*Todd II*), 9 F.3d 1216 (7th Cir. 1993), where 2–year–old Tiffany was killed in a fire started by 4–year–old Cori, both of whom lived in a house with cigarette-smoking adults. When Cori awoke one morning, she found a green BIC butane cigarette lighter on the living room table, took it upstairs, and started a fire in Tiffany's room. In an action against the manufacturer, plaintiff asserted that BIC should have warned of the specific risks posed to households with young children. Judge Easterbrook addressed the warnings claim:

> That fire attracts youngsters—and that cigarette lighters in the hands of children can lead to calamity—no one doubts. According to the CPSC, "for the period 1988–90, these fires [set by children under 5 playing with lighters] caused an annual average of 150 deaths, approximately 1,100 injuries, and nearly $70 million in property damages." 58 Fed. Reg. at 37564. BIC recognized this danger, and its lighters were emblazoned: "KEEP OUT OF REACH OF CHILDREN." Plaintiff deems this warning insufficient because BIC did not tell parents that children between three and five are attracted to flame, able and eager to open closets, cabinets, and purses in order to inspect their contents, and unable to follow instructions not to fiddle with what they find there.

Judge Easterbrook noted that BIC's instruction to parents "to make access physically impossible," if heeded, would have prevented the fire in this case.

> Manufacturers could of course provide secondary warnings about the consequences of not following primary warnings. BIC could have written something like: "Keep this lighter out of the reach of children, and be aware that children not only are resourceful in finding things but also are apt to disobey your instructions not to play with lighters they can get their hands on." It could have amplified this longer warning with data about the number of fires children set with lighters, in order to impress on parents the importance of following the primary warning to make the lighters inaccessible (or, perhaps, to induce the parents to quit smoking). Extended warnings present several difficulties, first among them that, the more text must be squeezed onto the product, the smaller the type, and the less likely is the consumer to read or remember any of it. Only pithy and bold warnings can be effective. Long passages in capital letters are next to illegible, and long passages in lower case letters are treated as boilerplate. Plaintiff wants a warning in such detail that a magnifying glass would be necessary to read it.

> Many consumers cannot follow simple instructions (including pictures) describing how to program their video cassette recorders. To be more than a scare tactic, the warning could not stop with the number of fires and deaths. It would have to include the number of lighters sold to households with small children (so that the buyer could determine the risk per lighter) and the number of fires that children set with matches (so that the buyer could evaluate whether it is safer to switch). These numbers are abstract. For a parent determined to smoke, the right question is what to do. BIC provided that information.

> There is a further practical inquiry: will consumers who disdain a bold and (if followed) effective warning be influenced by smaller and more subtle points? If parents leave lighters on living room tables despite "KEEP OUT OF REACH OF CHILDREN," and despite knowing that lighters cause fire (which is why the adults bought them), is a recitation of the CPSC's data likely to alter their conduct? These adults did not heed the Surgeon General's dire warnings, prominent on every package of cigarettes, about the hazards of smoking. They exposed their children to tobacco smoke, which causes more harm than does playing with lighters. Environmental Protection Agency, Respiratory Health Effects of Passive Smoking (1992).... What parent is unaware that children between the

ages of three and five explore and test their surroundings even when told not to? Can it be that only a warning by BIC Corporation will alert parents that kids are at least as successful as cats in getting into cabinets and other hiding places, and that children have minds of their own? Illinois does not require manufacturers to warn consumers about facts they already know, and it does not require manufacturers to dilute the principal warnings with distracting information.

11. Some commentators view warnings pollution claims skeptically. See Latin, Good Warnings, Bad Products, and Cognitive Limitations, 41 UCLA L. Rev. 1193 (1994); Grether, Schwartz & Wilde, The Irrelevance of Information Overload: An Analysis of Search and Disclosure, 59 S. Cal. L. Rev. 277 (1986). See generally Symposium, Rational Actors or Rational Fools? The Implications of Psychology for Products Liability, 6 Roger Williams U. L. Rev. 1 (2000).

12. Overpromotion. An otherwise adequate warning may be nullified by assurances of safety. The classic case is Maize v. Atlantic Refining Co., 41 A.2d 850 (Pa. 1945), where a woman died from inhaling the tetrachloride fumes from a cleaning fluid she used to clean her rugs. The label on the can twice stated, "CAUTION: Do not inhale fumes. Use only in a well ventilated place." However, in letters that were several times larger, the cleaner's name—"Safety-Kleen"—was emblazoned all around the container. *Held,* judgments for plaintiffs affirmed: "[T]he conspicuous display on each of the four sides of a can of the words 'Safety-Kleen' would naturally lull the user [into] a false sense of security [so] as to make the word 'Caution' and the admonition against inhaling fumes and as to use only in a well ventilated place seem of comparatively minor import." Accord, Incollingo v. Ewing, 282 A.2d 206 (Pa. 1971) (pharmaceutical company's detail men minimized drug's hazards and stressed its benefits and widespread acceptance). Compare Ayers v. Johnson & Johnson Baby Prod. Co., 818 P.2d 1337 (Wash. 1991) (warning of diarrhea, but not paralysis, from ingesting "pure and gentle" Baby Oil).

2. DEFECT TESTS

Olson v. Prosoco, Inc.

Supreme Court of Iowa, 1994.
522 N.W.2d 284.

■ SNELL, JUSTICE.

[Plaintiff, a bricklayer foreman, lost the sight in one eye when he dropped a drum of mortar cleaner and the bung closure popped out, splashing hydrochloric acid based cleaner into his eye. Plaintiff sued the manufacturer of the cleaner on various theories, and the court separately instructed the jury on negligence and strict liability for failing adequately to warn or instruct about proper precautions for closing and moving the drums. The jury returned a verdict for the plaintiff, and the defendant appealed, claiming that "the submission of instructions on both strict liability and negligence theories was duplicative and confusing, resulting in prejudicial error."]

[The court noted that it had previously distinguished strict liability from negligence in the design defect context, but that, unlike many courts, it had never explicitly adopted strict liability as a theory of liability for warnings claims.]

Generally, there are two competing views regarding the failure to warn/strict liability question. The first is that there is little, if any, difference between strict liability and negligence in failure to warn cases. [Citing cases from Wis., N.M., N.Y., Ohio, & R.I.] Opposing this view are cases that apply varying forms of a strict liability analysis in failure to warn cases. Some jurisdictions impose strict liability by imputing knowledge of a product's propensity to injure as it did to a defendant-manufacturer, and then asking the jury: With such knowledge would the defendant have been negligent in selling the product without a warning? [Citing cases from Ariz., Ky., Or., Pa. & Wash.]

Other jurisdictions apply strict liability by requiring plaintiffs to prove defendants knew or should have known of the danger. [Citing cases from Cal., Ill., Md., & N.D.] Usually, these courts require plaintiffs to prove that the defendant, "because of the 'present state of human knowledge,' knew or should have known of the danger presented by the use or consumption of a product." [Citations.]

A different analysis is made in some cases to distinguish strict liability from negligence concepts in failure to warn cases on the ground that in negligence the focus is on the defendant's conduct, while in strict liability, the focus is on the condition of the product. [Citations.]

After reviewing the authorities and comments on the failure to warn question, we believe any posited distinction between strict liability and negligence principles is illusory. We fail to see any distinction between negligence and strict liability in the analyses of those jurisdictions injecting a knowledge requirement into their strict liability/failure to warn equation. [Citation.] The standard applied by these "strict liability" jurisdictions is exactly the same in practice as holding defendants to an expert standard of care under a negligence theory. The burden on plaintiffs is the same. They must prove a defendant knew or should have known of potential risks associated with the use of its product, yet failed to provide adequate directions or warnings to users. [As for] jurisdictions imputing to defendants knowledge of its product's propensity to injure as it did, we have refused in the past to impose a duty upon manufacturers to warn of unknowable dangers. Moore v. Vanderloo, 386 N.W.2d 108, 116 (Iowa 1986).

We also find the product/conduct distinction made by several jurisdictions to justify maintaining a strict liability/failure to warn theory of little practical significance. [Some courts reason that] under a strict liability theory the focus is on the unreasonably dangerous condition of the product [in contrast to] the question in negligence cases [of] whether the defendant's conduct breached a duty to exercise reasonable care. [Yet courts applying] this distinction cannot help but slip back into [negligence-type analyses]. Inevitably the conduct of the defendant in a failure to warn case becomes the issue. As one commentator notes regarding the product/conduct distinction, "[i]t is easy enough to assert the manufacturer's conduct is not in issue, but the 'condition of the product' test is hardly self-executing." Keith Miller, Design Defect Litigation in Iowa: The Myths of Strict Liability, 40 Drake L. Rev. 465, 481 (1991).

Maintaining the distinction to justify submission of failure to warn claims under both strict liability and negligence theories is a vain effort. We hold it was error to submit instructions regarding Prosoco's failure to warn under both negligence and strict liability theories. [Because both] instructions essentially required the jury to determine whether Prosoco negligently failed to warn users of the dangers in moving or using Sure Klean 600 in fifteen gallon containers[, they were duplicative.]

[T]he correct submission of instructions regarding a failure to warn claim for damages is under a theory of negligence and the claim should not be submitted as a theory of strict liability. In testing the defendant's liability for negligence in failing to warn, the defendant should be held to the standard of care of an expert in its field. [Citing cases from Iowa, R.I., & Md.] The relevant inquiry therefore is whether the reasonable manufacturer knew or should have known of the danger, in light of the generally recognized and prevailing best scientific knowledge, yet failed to provide adequate warning to users or consumers. [Citing cases from R.I. & Md.]; W. Page Keeton, Dan B. Dobbs, Robert E. Keeton, & David G. Owen, Prosser, and Keeton on the Law of Torts § 99, at 697 (5th ed. 1984).

[The strict liability warnings instruction was error, but not prejudicial.]

Affirmed.

NOTES

1. "In no area of strict products liability has the impact of principles of negligence become more pronounced than in failure-to-warn cases." Anderson v. Owens–Corning Fiberglas Corp., 810 P.2d 549, 561 (Cal. 1991) (Mosk, J., concurring and dissenting). Thus, courts increasingly admit that "the standard imposed upon the defendant in a strict liability claim grounded upon an inadequate warning is the same as that imposed in a negligence claim based upon inadequate warning." Crislip v. TCH Liquidating Co., 556 N.E.2d 1177, 1183 (Ohio 1990) (failure to instruct on strict liability failure to warn claim was harmless error). See also Mohney v. U.S. Hockey, Inc., 300 F. Supp. 2d 556 (N.D. Ohio 2004) ("The standard imposed is the same whether such a claim sounds in negligence or strict liability."). See Hahn v. Richter, 673 A.2d 888 (Pa. 1996) (negligence only basis of liability in prescription drug warning cases). But cf. Carlin v. Superior Court, 920 P.2d 1347 (Cal. 1996) (confusing opinion in which court reaffirmed *Anderson* but refused defendant's call to abandon strict liability cause of action in warnings cases in favor of negligence).

2. Calling a Pig a Mule. Nevertheless, even while acknowledging that liability in the warnings context is really nothing more than negligence, most courts continue to pretend that it is really something more; even in this context, most courts continue to call liability "strict." *Crislip* is one case in point, the court there taking care to explain that "[w]e do not mean to suggest that a cause of action for negligent failure to warn or warn adequately is identical to one brought under strict liability" (principally because a plaintiff's comparative fault may not reduce damages in a strict liability claim in Ohio).

Anderson is another example. In deciding that a defendant in a warnings case may present evidence on state of the art, the majority noted that, "while a manufacturing or design defect *can be* evaluated without reference to the conduct of the manufacturer, the giving of a warning cannot." Nevertheless, the majority asserted that "despite its roots in negligence, failure to warn in strict liability differs markedly from failure to warn in the negligence context." But the majority's frail efforts to explain the supposed differences between the two doctrines in the warnings context rang hollow on the ears of Judge Stanley Mosk, a member of the California Supreme Court since 1964 who personally helped develop " '[t]he pure concepts of products liability so pridefully fashioned and nurtured' "by that court in the 1960s and 1970s. Nevertheless, Judge Mosk rebelled at continuing the subterfuge. Noting that the strict liability focus "has become blurred through the years," he observed that "our past acquiescence in this muddled state of affairs does not justify making matters worse. Misconception compounded cannot result in authenticity." He concluded that the court "should consider the possibility of holding that failure-to-warn actions lie solely on a negligence theory."

3.   Strict Liability Tests. Assuming that a court chooses to retain strict liability doctrine for warnings cases, what *test* should it apply? Consumer expectations? Risk-utility? Why not a simple and straight-forward strict liability test, holding manufacturers to a duty to provide information on all material risks?

4.   The Restatement. The Products Liability Restatement's definition of warnings and instructions defect in § 2(c) is the mirror image of its definition of design defect:

> A product ... is defective because of inadequate instructions or warnings when the foreseeable risks of harm posed by the product could have been reduced or avoided by the provision of reasonable instructions or warnings ... and the omission of the instructions or warnings renders the product not reasonably safe.

The "reasonableness test for judging the adequacy of product instructions and warnings ... parallels [§ 2(b)] which adopts a similar standard for judging the safety of product designs. Although the liability standard is formulated in essentially identical terms, in subsections (b) and (c), the concept is more difficult to apply in the warnings context." Cmt. *i.*

How well does the Restatement's *design* defect test formulation, awkward even in that context, adapt to *warnings* cases?

5.   Tort Reform in the Legislatures. Some state legislatures, tired of all this rubbish, have forthrightly repealed the rule of strict liability in design and warnings cases. Indiana is one example, where § 402A's rule is set forth as the standard of responsibility, with the following proviso: "However, in any action based on an alleged design defect in the product or based on an alleged failure to provide adequate warnings or instructions regarding the use of the product, the [plaintiff] must establish that the [defendant] failed to exercise reasonable care under the circumstances in designing the product or in providing the warnings or instructions." Ind. Code Ann. § 34–20–2–2.

6.   Confusing Ideas, Confusing Tests. And so the hunt for appropriate defect tests goes on—in cases involving dangers from inadequate warnings, as in cases involving dangers in design. Might the inability to find acceptable tests lie in an effort to fit a square peg into a round hole? Might the confusion inhere in the courts' unwillingness to acknowledge that the adoption of "strict" liability in these contexts was, quite simply, a grand mistake? See Owen, Defectiveness Restated: Exploding the "Strict" Products Liability Myth, 1996 U. Ill. L. Rev. 743; Powers, A Modest Proposal to Abandon Strict Products Liability, 1991 U. Ill. L. Rev. 639.

Consider the observations of Professors Henderson and Twerski a couple of years before they were appointed co-reporters for the Products Liability Restatement: "[A]lthough mixing negligence and strict liability concepts is often a game of semantics, the game has more than semantic impact—it breeds confusion and, inevitably, bad law." Henderson & Twerski, Doctrinal Collapse in Products Liability: The Empty Shell of Failure to Warn, 65 N.Y.U. L. Rev. 265, 278 (1990). Note also that the new Restatement, in defining design and warnings defects, does just that: it places a strict-looking "defect" shell over its principles of reasonableness grounded in the law of negligence.

Is this kind of hybrid definitional approach likely to improve clarity in the law? Do you think that most courts will continue to apply principles of negligence while claiming that they are applying a rule of "strict" liability? Do you think they will adopt the Third Restatement test for warnings defects? Or might they instead follow the path of doctrinal purity trod by the Iowa Supreme Court in *Olson*?

3. WARNING METHODS

Meyerhoff v. Michelin Tire Corp.

United States District Court, District of Kansas, 1994.
852 F.Supp. 933.

■ BELOT, DISTRICT JUDGE.

[Kevin Meyerhoff, a truck driver, was killed when a Michelin truck tire he was attempting to repair, reinflate, and remount exploded due to "circumferential wrinkling" caused by driving upon it while underinflated. A jury trial on Michelin's liability for failing adequately to warn Meyerhoff resulted in a verdict for the plaintiff, with fault divided 11% to Michelin, 14% to Meyerhoff, 10% to the tire dealer, and 65% to Fischer, Meyerhoff's employer and the purchaser and owner of the truck and tire. Plaintiff and Michelin both made post-trial motions, plaintiff for a new trial (Fed.R.Civ. Pro. 59), and Michelin for judgment after trial (Fed.R.Civ.Pro. 50(b)). Michelin contends that plaintiff introduced no legally sufficient evidence to support a finding that it negligently failed to provide an adequate warning.]

With respect to sidewall warnings, plaintiffs [theorized] that the following warning [devised by plaintiff's expert, Wells] should have been placed on the Michelin truck tire's sidewall in yellow or some other contrasting color:

WARNING * TIRE MAY EXPLODE WHEN REINFLATED CAUSING SERIOUS INJURY OR DEATH * DO NOT REINFLATE AFTER RUN-

NING UNDERINFLATED—TAKE THE TIRE TO A MICHELIN DEAL-
ER FOR REPAIR

At trial, plaintiffs' yellow warning theory quickly unraveled.

Plaintiffs first called Mr. Forney to testify about the *feasibility* of
placing warnings on a truck tire's sidewall. Mr. Forney, who had worked in
the tire industry, [who was called only to testify about the tire hazard and
Michelin's literature] was unable to give any testimony that it would have
been feasible for Michelin to place a *yellow* or other contrasting colored
warning on its truck tire, particularly a warning with lettering in the size
proposed by plaintiffs.[14] The jury was accordingly instructed that, although
they could consider the wording of plaintiffs' proposed warning, any evidence concerning the color of the warning—that is, a color other than
black—was to be disregarded.[15]

Plaintiffs then called Mr. Wells to testify about the *adequacy* of truck
tire sidewall warnings. Mr. Wells, who had never worked in the tire
industry, testified that the best way to convey a warning is to "put it on the
product" itself. He testified about the warnings other manufacturers placed
on the sidewalls of their tires, and answered questions concerning the
proposed warning that he himself had formulated. With respect to the
Goodyear tire that had been admitted into evidence, Mr. Wells opined that
its sidewall warning was "too small," that "it should be in color," and that
it did not sufficiently describe the hazards and potential injuries associated
with a truck tire nor provide appropriate instructions. He did state,
however, that the Goodyear warning was ["better than nothing," to which
Michelin objected. On cross-examination, Michelin's counsel] elicited several admissions that substantially undermined plaintiffs' case.

First, Mr. Wells admitted that, in his opinion, every warning he had
observed on other manufacturer's tires—truck tires, passenger tires, farm
tractor tires, and others—was inadequate. Hence, according to plaintiffs'
own expert, there were no adequate tire sidewall warnings in use at the
time the Michelin truck tire was sold.

Second, Mr. Wells admitted that there were many dangers associated
with truck tires which the language in his proposed warning failed to
mention: "overloading," "using ether to seat a [tire] bead," "damaged
beads," and a "host of other risks or hazards." He conceded that emphasizing one danger instead of another could be misleading. . . .

Third, Mr. Wells was asked about an experiment he had conducted to
evaluate the effectiveness of his proposed *yellow* warning:

14. The fact that Michelin could have
given a black-on-black sidewall warning was
never in dispute. A Goodyear truck tire with
a raised black-letter warning on it was entered into evidence, and Mr. Forney specifically stated that it would have been feasible
for Michelin to have placed plaintiffs' proposed warning on the sidewall of its truck
tire in raised black letters.

15. This instruction was actually given
during Mr. Wells's testimony, after plaintiffs'
counsel had made a vain attempt to admit
evidence concerning the color of the warning
through him. Mr. Wells simply did not know
whether contrasting colored warnings could
be placed on a tire during the tire manufacturing process.

Q. [By Mr. Hite] Now, let's talk a little bit about the procedure that you went through after you placed this yellow warning on this sidewall of this tire. You wanted to see whether it was adequate and effective, [and so] you devised a test of your own to see whether this warning would be adequate, in effect.

A. That's right.

Q. And with the help of your ... assistant, you took the tire, this exact tire with this yellow warning, to three tire shops in Hutchinson; correct?

A. Yes.

Q. And you had made arrangements with the service manager at each of those places to bring this Michelin tire in with a wheel and ask somebody that did not know this was a test to mount it.

A. That's right.

Q. So that nobody would know what was going on; correct?

A. That's correct.

Q. And you devised a form list of questions to ask those people after they had mounted the tire but before they had started to inflate it; correct? Or as they were starting to inflate it?

A. Right. We stopped them at that point.

Q. As they started to inflate, you would stop them?

A. Correct.

According to Mr. Wells's testimony, each of the three tire repairmen questioned ... were unable to answer simple questions about the meaning of the yellow warning on the tire. Two ... repairmen did not know what the tire warning said; another gave an incorrect response. Mr. Wells testified that he and plaintiffs' counsel decided to terminate the testing because, in their estimation, it had not been "productive."[16]

During redirect, Mr. Wells listed some ways that a tire manufacturer could make a sidewall warning effective even if the warning had to be black in color: "shadowing," "having a different type of a letter that will definitely stand out versus a straight letter," and using larger letters. [Yet,] he never stated that those methods would be adequate. [He] also opined that only the "hidden dangers," not all dangers associated with a truck tire, need to be addressed in a tire sidewall warning [but he failed to] list what dangers were hidden and what dangers were not—what dangers [did and did not need] to be addressed in a sidewall warning.

The question is whether, accepting plaintiffs' experts' opinions concerning sidewall warnings as true, a reasonable jury could have found ... that Michelin *could* have placed an *adequate* warning on the sidewall of its truck.... * * *

[W]ith respect to whether Michelin *could* have placed an *adequate* warning on the sidewall of its truck tire, this court perceives no reasonable

---

16. The jury also heard testimony from fact witnesses experienced in tire repair who stated unequivocally that they never read the sidewalls of tires.

basis for the jury's finding of fault. Mr. Wells was the only expert to testify for plaintiffs on the adequacy of sidewall warnings. He rejected existing sidewall warnings as inadequate because they were too small, not in a contrasting color, and did not sufficiently address tire dangers or provide appropriate tire safety instructions. Mr. Wells offered a warning of his own that was larger, in a contrasting color, and specifically addressed the danger associated with Kevin Meyerhoff's accident. This warning, however, did not stand up to Mr. Wells's own test for adequacy.

First, because Mr. Forney was unable to establish the feasibility of placing a colored warning on a truck tire, Mr. Wells's proposed warning was reduced to black-on-black. He was never asked whether such a warning would be adequate [or] whether such a warning would be effective. His testimony [as] to other manufacturers' warnings, however, seemed to indicate that he believed black-lettered warnings were not adequate.

Second, Mr. Wells conceded that the language in his proposed warning did not address many of the dangers associated with servicing truck tires. He rejected other manufacturers' warnings on this basis. He attempted to explain away the deficiencies in his warning by stating that only the important, hidden dangers need to be included in a warning. But Mr. Wells never stated what those dangers were. In short, he never offered any testimony that a warning sufficiently addressing all of those dangers and prescribing instructions relating to those dangers *could* be crafted, placed on a truck tire's sidewall, and still be effective.

In this court's view, a person cannot, after suffering an accident, simply draw up a warning limited to the dangers involved in that accident and argue that that warning *should* have been conveyed by the manufacturer or seller without first also establishing that that warning is adequate and that it actually *could* have been communicated in the manner proposed. . . .

[A] plaintiff must do more than simply present an expert who espouses a new or different warning. He must establish that warning's feasibility, adequacy, and effectiveness. In this case, plaintiffs' experts' testimony fell woefully short of meeting this criteria. The Supreme Court stated in Daubert v. Merrell Dow Pharmaceuticals, Inc., 509 U.S. 579 (1993):

> The subject of the experts' testimony must be "scientific . . . knowledge." The adjective "scientific" implies a grounding in the methods and procedures of science. Similarly, the word "knowledge" connotes more than subjective belief or unsupported speculation.

Even when viewed in the light most favorable to plaintiffs, the testimony of plaintiffs' experts with respect to sidewall warnings, particularly the testimony of Mr. Wells, was largely unsupported speculation. Mr. Wells's opinions regarding sidewall warnings lacked the underpinnings of "scientific validity" demanded by *Daubert*. To the extent *Daubert* standards were applied by Mr. Wells in his warning label experiment, the results revealed that his opinion lacked scientific validity.

At best, plaintiffs' experts could only state that a raised black-lettered sidewall warning could have been used and that such a warning would have been "better than nothing." "Better than nothing" is not the applicable standard.[17] The standard, instead, is what a reasonably prudent manufacturer would have done. *Garst*. Plaintiffs' experts never focused in on this standard; they never actually testified that a reasonably prudent manufacturer would have placed a black-lettered warning like the one proposed on its tires. Michelin, by contrast, submitted clear evidence that its decision not to place a warning on its truck tire's sidewall was reasonable and prudent. In short, plaintiffs simply never met their burden of proof on the issue of adequate warning.

[Post-trial judgment for Michelin; plaintiff's new trial motion denied.]

NOTES

1. "Procedural" Adequacy—Method of Conveyance. Even if the substantive content of a warning is full, fair, and accurate, it will do no good unless it (1) reaches the user, (2) catches his attention, and (3) penetrates his mind. Hence, the method of conveying warnings and instructions must itself be adequate. The variety of issues here include:

A. Conspicuousness. Like disclaimers, warnings must be printed in type of a sufficient size, style, and color; they often should be headed by appropriate signal words: "Warning," "Danger," "Caution," "Hazard," "Adverse Reactions," "Contraindications," etc.; and they should be located in a prominent position on the label, pamphlet, or other warning medium. See, e.g., Falkner v. Para Chem, 2003 WL 21396693, at *7 (Ohio App. 2003) (warning that carpet adhesive should not be used indoors because its vapors were flammable "could easily be missed," according to defendant's chemist, because it was located on side panel not read by carpet installers).

Contrast Austin v. Will–Burt Co., 361 F.3d 862 (5th Cir. 2004), where a television news producer working out of a news van was electrocuted when his van's telescoping mast hit power lines. Product manuals supplied with the mast warned users not to raise a mast under or near power lines and instructed to check for overhead obstructions near the mast's line of extension and maximum height. Affixed to the base of the mast were yellow labels with red and black lettering, stating:

—DANGER! PLEASE READ INSTRUCTIONS BEFORE RAISING!

—DANGER. WATCH FOR WIRES. YOU CAN BE KILLED IF THIS PRODUCT COMES NEAR ELECTRICAL POWER LINES.

Held, the warnings were adequate.

---

17. The court regrets that it did not sustain Michelin's counsel's objection to the "better than nothing" testimony when it was made. It should be noted that Michelin did not concede that sidewall warnings are "better than nothing." Michelin argued that sidewall warnings are not effective and that because the space on a tire's sidewall is limited, sidewall warnings cannot be as thorough as is necessary, are misleading, and can do more harm than good.

B. Placement on product itself. If feasible, warnings of serious dangers should be permanently located on the product itself, rather than in a pamphlet, booklet, or information sheet that can be damaged, lost or destroyed. Hence, the warning may be located on the container's *label*; on a *warning plate* attached near the ram of a press or other danger point of the machine; or *etched* permanently into the product. See, e.g., Fuentes v. Shin Caterpillar Mitsubishi, Ltd., 2003 WL 22205665, *4 (Cal. App. 2003) (warning of risk that tire rim might explode while putting air in tire should have been stamped on wheel of loader); West v. Broderick & Bascom Rope Co., 197 N.W.2d 202 (Iowa 1972) (metal tag with load limit could have been bonded to collar of metal rope or "sling" that broke); Gordon v. Niagara Machine & Tool Works, 574 F.2d 1182, 1194 (5th Cir. 1978) ("a direct warning attached to the press and conspicuously displayed at eye level would surely be a more effective warning than [words in a] manual").

Depending on the circumstances (and the trier of fact), however, this "direct" form of warning may *not* be required. See, e.g., Freas v. Prater Constr. Corp., 573 N.E.2d 27 (Ohio 1991) (crane manual adequately warned not to stand under boom, and warning did not have to be placed on boom itself); cf. Westry v. Bell Helmets, Inc., 487 N.W.2d 781 (Mich. App. 1992) (warning stickers sufficed; no duty to emboss permanent warnings on helmet).

C. Nonverbal warnings. A *gauge* or *warning light* may be necessary to inform the user that a crane is about to tip or that a rear mounted aircraft engine has stopped operating. See Kay v. Cessna Aircraft Co., 548 F.2d 1370 (9th Cir. 1977) (warning light not necessary because engine gauges on Skymaster instrument panel would have indicated dead engine). A *buzzer*, *bell* or *rear-view mirror* may be necessary for the safe operation of a vehicle in reverse with poor rear visibility. Pike v. Frank G. Hough Co., 467 P.2d 229 (Cal. 1970). *Color* may have to be added to a dangerous, clear, chemical fluid to distinguish it from water. Hayes v. Kay Chem. Co., 482 N.E.2d 611 (Ill. App. 1985) (McDonald's employee wiped face with towel saturated with caustic grill cleaner). Or *odor* added to propane gas. Jones v. Hittle Service, Inc., 549 P.2d 1383 (Kan.1976) (odorized to smell like rotten eggs or dead mice); Donahue v. Phillips Petroleum Co., 866 F.2d 1008 (8th Cir. 1989).

2. Foreign Language Warnings. In an increasingly multi-cultural market-place, should manufacturers be required to warn in languages other than English? What if manufacturers sell large quantities of pesticides in southern Texas, or in Northern Vermont and Maine, adjacent to Québec? Should it matter if they advertise in Spanish (in newspapers or by radio) in Florida or southern California? See Ramirez v. Plough, Inc., 863 P.2d 167 (Cal. 1993) (no); Stanley Indus. v. W.M. Barr & Co., 784 F.Supp. 1570 (S.D. Fla. 1992) (yes). See generally Note, 47 Vand. L. Rev. 1107 (1994); Annot., 27 A.L.R.5th 697 (1995). Compare Fuentes v. Shin Caterpillar Mitsubishi, Ltd., 2003 WL 22205665, at *11 (Cal. App. 2003) ("Determining whether a warning would be feasible and effective necessarily involves a consideration of the language in which a warning must be given. We certainly believe that if a Japanese manufacturer places a product in the stream of commerce, and it is reasonably foreseeable that the product will be used in United States, safety warnings regarding the risks of operation should be in English. However, plaintiff failed to prove manufacturer knew their product, made and sold in Japan, would be resold to a purchaser in U.S.").

3. Pictorial Warnings. Diagrams and pictures increasingly are used to communicate product hazards.

A. Standardized danger symbols—Adults.

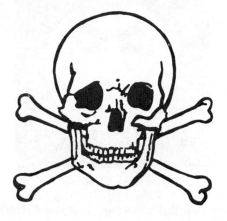

Consider Hubbard–Hall Chem. Co. v. Silverman, 340 F.2d 402 (1st Cir. 1965), where two Spanish-speaking farm workers died from inhalation of insecticide dust. The insecticide bag contained written warnings only. The jury was charged that an adequate warning is one "calculated to bring home to a reasonably prudent person, a reasonably prudent user of the product, the nature and extent of the danger of the product involved." *Held,* a jury could reasonably conclude that even the best of written warnings might not be good enough, since the information foreseeably would be needed by persons of limited education, and that a skull and crossbones or other comparable symbols might fairly be required under the circumstances. See also Campos v. Firestone Tire & Rubber Co., 485 A.2d 305, 310 (N.J. 1984).

With the traditional skull and crossbones pictured above, compare the following stylized version from South Carolina's Palmetto Poison Center:

Which version is preferable? Why?

B. Standardized danger symbols—Children.

MR. YUK

Research at the Pittsburgh Poison Center of the Children's Hospital of Pittsburgh in 1971 revealed that the traditional skull and crossbones symbol tended to *attract* rather than repel small children to hazardous substances so labeled. The children associated the symbol with cartoon pirates, adventure, excitement and, at least in Pittsburgh, with the Pittsburgh Pirates baseball team. So researchers sought a new symbol that would deter young children from playing with (or consuming) toxic substances in the home. Children at daycare centers were shown six bottles of mouthwash, separately labeled with different symbols, and asked to identify bottles they might not like to play with. The symbols included a red stop sign, a skull and crossbones, a scowling green face, and three others. The least popular was the scowling face, which one of the youngsters said "looks yukky." And so "Mr. Yuk" was born. The green-faced Mr. Yuk stickers, to be affixed by parents to toxic substances around the home, are now widely available from poison control centers across the nation. He is a registered trademark and has been copyrighted by the Children's Hospital of Pittsburgh. Mr. Yuk stickers are credited in part with a substantial drop in child poisonings in recent decades.

Should the warnings on toxic chemicals used in the home, such as drain cleaners, be considered defective if pictures of Mr. Yuk are not included on the label?

Should Mr. Yuk be made to look even more revolted? The variation on Mr. Yuk shown below, a registered New Zealand trademark of Quick Stil International, was found in a large field trial to be ineffective in preventing child poisonings. Many of the parents believed the symbol *attracted* children to the labelled substances. 5 Prod. Liab. International 190 (Dec. 1983).

[E7579]

C. Particularized danger symbols—Adults. Empirical research suggests that symbols may be necessary to alert even literate adults to product dangers. See the rather startling article by Dorris and Purswell, Warnings and Human Behavior: Implications for the Design of Product Warnings, 1 J. Prod. Liab. 254 (1977), suggesting that it matters little how completely a warning is worded, or even whether it is given at all, since few people will read or heed it anyway. See also Goldhaber & deTurk, Effects of Consumers' Familiarity With a Product on Attention To and Compliance With Warnings, 11 J. Prod. Liab. 29 (1988). More recent (and more sophisticated) behavioral research lends support to the view that consumers process information irrationally. See, e.g., Symposium: Rational Actors or Rational Fools? The Implications of Psychology for Products Liability, 6 Roger Williams U. L. Rev. 1 (2000); Hanson and Kysar, Taking Behavioralism Seriously: The Problem of Market Manipulation, 74 N.Y.U. L. Rev. 630, 724 (1999); Hanson and Kysar, Taking Behavioralism Seriously: Some Evidence of Market Manipulation, 112 Harv. L. Rev. 1420, 1425 (1999). See generally Sunstein, The Laws of Fear, 115 Harv. L. Rev. 1119, 1123 (2002) (reviewing P. Slovic, The Perception of Risk) ("ordinary people often deal poorly with the topic of risk"). For whatever reasons, people frequently fail to process verbal danger information rationally in a manner that avoids accidents.

A powerful anti-acne drug called Accutane, a synthetic derivative of Vitamin A, has been found to cause birth defects in about 25% of children born to women taking the drug. Rather than totally banning the drug, the FDA has required the manufacturer to provide strong and specific written warnings and instructions, in both the patient and physician information labeling, together with the following diagram on each page of the patient leaflet and on each side of the drug's packaging. In addition, the patient information labeling is to include a drawing of a deformed baby. Willis, New Warning About Accutane and Birth Defects, FDA Consumer 27 (Oct. 1988). See, e.g., Banner v. Hoffmann–La Roche Inc., 891 A.2d 1229, 1239 (N.J.Super.App.Div.2006) ("the warnings given to Debbie Banner in 1995 were 'accurate, clear, and unambiguous,' and were, therefore, adequate as a matter of law").

While warning symbols often help convey danger information, they may be insufficient by themselves. See Fyssakis v. Knight Equip. Corp., 826 P.2d 570 (Nev. 1992) (symbol for corrosiveness on soap dispenser inadequate warning that dishwashing soap could blind).

Several companies and industry associations have been working for some time to improve communications on product hazards in the workplace. The leader in this area has been FMC Corporation, which has developed a sophisticated industrial product warnings system, portions of which follow.

Product Safety Sign and Label System

Copyright © 1993 FMC Corporation.

The limitations associated with words can present serious communication problems. The same words used by different people can have entirely different meanings. People using the same language have differences in terminology, intellect, and literacy that can inhibit common understanding. A person's ability to comprehend a specific language can complicate communication even further.

One method of improving communication among a greater cross-section of population, both nationally and internationally, is to use pictorial or symbolic language in place of, or as a supplement to, written words.

This manual contains a graphic design system for safety signs and labels that uses pictorials as a principal means of communication. The pictorials are combined with words and colors in carefully designed formats intended to present hazard information in an orderly and understandable manner.

The communication system presented in this manual meets or exceeds the requirements of American National Standard Z535.4–1991, *Products Safety Signs and Labels*.

When such safety signs and labels are placed on products in appropriate locations, they can help to reduce the occurrence of accidents through more effective communication.

* * *

The preferred format for product safety labels is a vertically oriented rectangle consisting of three panels encircled by a narrow border. The panels contain four messages which communicate:

1.   The level of hazard seriousness.

2. The nature of the hazard.

3. The consequence of human interaction with the hazard.

4. The instructions on how to avoid the hazard.

The top panel of the format contains a signal word (DANGER, WARNING or CAUTION) which communicates the level of hazard seriousness. [DANGER is printed in white letters, against a red background; WARNING, in black on orange; and CAUTION, in black on yellow.]

The center panel contains the pictorial which communicates the nature of the hazard, and the likely consequence of human interaction with the hazard. In some instances, the pictorial may also depict a preventive action or measure such as wearing protective equipment.

The bottom panel contains the instruction message on how to avoid the hazard. The message may also provide a more explicit description of the hazard and/or the consequence of human interaction with the hazard. [Sometimes a separate box, entitled SAFETY INSTRUCTIONS (white letters on green), is necessary to provide more information on safe use. Examples follow:]

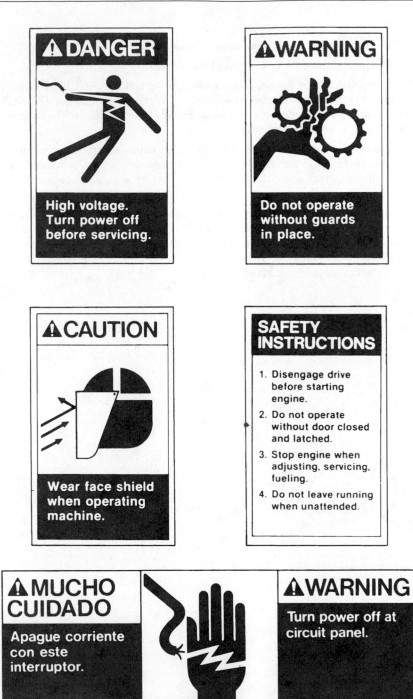

SELECTED PICTORIAL EXAMPLES

[E7581]

What do you think of this form of warning? Do you think it would be more effective than a written warning alone? Is it too paternalistic toward the worker? Should OSHA (or state OSHAs) require that *employers* provide such warnings? If so, should this relieve *manufacturers* of responsibility for so doing? Should similar pictorial warnings be required for hazardous *consumer* products such as lawnmowers? Should the absence of a pictorial representation make a written warning alone legally "defective"?

How might a plaintiff provided only with a written warning *prove* that the absence of a pictorial representation made the warning inadequate?

4. Expert Testimony. Some courts have refused to admit expert testimony on the ultimate issue of the *adequacy* of a warning. E.g., Shell Oil Co. v. Gutierrez, 581 P.2d 271 (Ariz. App.1978) (expert opinion admissible on the properties of chemicals, but not on adequacy of warning).

Other courts permit testimony on this issue by experts with various backgrounds, such as pharmacological labelling, communications psychology, human factors engineering, and others. See, e.g., Benjamin v. Wal–Mart Stores, Inc., 61 P.3d 257, 265 (Or. App. 2002) (mechanical engineering professor, specializing in human factors engineering, could explain how warning was inadequate: "A warning's adequacy is a proper subject of expert testimony."); Smith v. United States Gypsum Co., 612 P.2d 251 (Okla. 1980) (holding admissible testimony of chemical engineer and psychiatrist that manufacturer's warning of heptane flammability was "inadequate" and "vague"); Prevatt v. Pennwalt Corp., 237 Cal.Rptr. 488 (Ct. App. 1987) (cognitive psychologist: labels failed to attract user's attention or to warn appropriately of the danger); Surace v. Caterpillar, Inc., 1995 WL 303895 (E.D. Pa. 1995) (mechanical and safety engineer, and human factors psychologist, both could testify on adequacy of back-up alarm on pavement profiler).

Meyerhoff illustrates how experts proposed to testify on warnings issues now will probably have to meet the *Daubert* admissibility standards (or a state equivalent). See also Kerrigan v. Maxon Ind., 223 F. Supp. 2d 626, 634 (E.D. Pa. 2002) (driver of cement truck injured when mixer unexpectedly raised and struck overpass; expert not qualified to testify as to feasibility of in-cab warning light or buzzer that would have informed driver that mixer was rising while vehicle was in motion; nor was expert's proposed testimony reliable, since he had prepared no plans, drawings, or data showing how feature would work); Johnson v. Manitowoc Boom Trucks, Inc., 406 F.Supp.2d 852, 867 (M.D.Tenn.2005) (plaintiff's expert's warning defect testimony disallowed on *Daubert* grounds). But see Yamaha Motor Co., U.S.A. v. Arnoult, 955 P.2d 661, 668–69 (Nev. 1998) (industrial engineer specializing in human factors and ergonomics allowed to testify; *Daubert* did not apply).

See Note, 76 Ind. L.J. 465 (2001) (applying *Daubert* principles to warning label testimony). As information-related disciplines become increasingly sophisticated, so too should expert testimony on those sciences. See Hardie, Scare Tactics: Motivating Warning Compliance, Prod. Safety & Liab. Rep. (BNA) 935 (Sept. 1, 1995) (reviewing numerous studies on human reactions to warnings).

5. Admissibility of Subsequent Warnings. The subsequent remedial measure admissibility issue, considered in the design context above, arises also in warnings cases when the manufacturer adds or improves a warning after the date of sale, purchase, or the accident. In an omitted portion of *Meyerhoff*, the court ruled inadmissible two of plaintiff's proposed exhibits—(1) a revised edition of a Michelin Truck Tire Warranty, and (2) a Technical Bulletin on Inspection of "Run Flat" Tires—because they were issued after the date of the tire's *sale* (which the court held to be the relevant date, under the Kansas evidence rule, rather than the date of accident). See also John Crane, Inc. v. Jones, 586 S.E.2d 26 (Ga. App. 2003) (subsequent warnings admissible); Fiorentino v. A.E. Staley Mfg. Co., 416 N.E.2d 998, 1005 (Mass. App. 1981) (admissible, but concurring opinion questioned significance of feasibility issue in warnings context, since "it is obviously always 'feasible' to employ a more prominent or more urgent-sounding or more particularized form of warning").

6. On warnings generally, see Latin, Good Warnings, Bad Products, and Cognitive Limitations, 41 UCLA L. Rev. 1193 (1994); Madden, The Duty to Warn in Products Liability: Contours and Criticism, 89 W. Va. L. Rev. 221 (1987) (comprehensive review); Jacobs, Toward a Process Based Approach to Failure-to-Warn Law, 71 N.C. L. Rev. 121 (1992); Henderson and Twerski, Doctrinal Collapse in Products Liability: The Empty Shell of Failure to Warn, 65 N.Y.U. L. Rev. 265 (1990); Comment, Caution: This Superman Suit Will Not Enable You to Fly–Are Consumer Product Warning labels Out of Control?, 38 Ariz. St. L.J. 633 (2006); D. Owen, Products Liability Law ch. 9 (2d ed. 2008); 1 D. Owen, M.S. Madden, & M. Davis, Madden & Owen on Products Liability ch. 9 (3d ed. 2000).

4. DELEGATION OF WARNING OBLIGATION

Defective products often pose risks to persons other than the immediate purchasers: manufacturers sell shampoo to retailers and punch presses to employers, not directly to those who wash their hair and punch the widgets. As seen above, the duty to warn and instruct generally implies an obligation to provide the information to those persons expected to be at risk. Thus, warnings provided in the press manufacturer's sales contract with the employer generally will not satisfy the manufacturer's duty to warn (in negligence, warranty, or strict tort) because such warnings reasonably may not be expected to reach the ultimate users of the press. Instead, most courts today would require a warning plate containing the most important safety information to be affixed directly to the press. Similarly, a shampoo manufacturer can hardly expect to fulfill its warnings obligations other than by placing important safety information directly on the product's label.

Should a manufacturer *ever* escape the burden of providing product warnings and instructions *directly* to the ultimate user? If so, what might be the pertinent considerations and rationales for allowing a manufacturer sometimes to fulfill its obligations by providing the information to its immediate vendee rather than directly to the ultimate user? These are the questions examined in this section.

Higgins v. E.I. DuPont de Nemours & Co.

United States District Court, District of Maryland, 1987.
671 F.Supp. 1055.

■ SMALKIN, DISTRICT JUDGE.

[Plaintiffs sued DuPont, the manufacturer of a paint called Imron, and two suppliers of chemical ingredients (glycol ether acetates) used therein, Eastern and Union Carbide, for failing to warn of the possible teratogenic[1]

---

1. A teratogen is a compound that can cause birth defects, fetal death, or stillbirth.

effects of the paint. The Baltimore City Fire Department purchased Imron from DuPont and distributed it in unmarked cans to its various fire stations throughout the city for use on fire-fighting equipment. The plaintiffs, fire fighters who used the paint, alleged that the glycol ether components of Imron interfered with the fetal development of their children who died at birth. Defendants Eastman and Union Carbide moved for summary judgment.]

Movants' legal position is that, as bulk suppliers of commodity chemicals to a sophisticated chemical and coatings company (DuPont), they had no duty to warn any DuPont customer (much less a customer's employees), of any possible teratogenic effects of the commodity chemicals or the product in which they were incorporated. . . .

In Goodbar v. Whitehead Bros., 591 F. Supp. 552 (W.D. Va. 1984), aff'd sub nom. Beale v. Hardy, 769 F.2d 213 (4th Cir. 1985), the [District Court] recognized the availability of a sophisticated user/bulk supplier defense in a negligent failure to warn claim, asserted under Restatement (Second) Torts § 388 (1965).* There, some 132 present and former employees of the Lynchburg Foundry brought suit against 12 defendants who had supplied silica sand to the Foundry. The sand was supplied unpackaged in railroad car lots, which were emptied onto conveyor belts or pneumatic transporters, where the material was conveyed to large tanks or silos for storage, ultimately to be used in various stages of metal castings production. The suppliers in *Goodbar* were accused of "fail[ing] to advise the Foundry's employees with respect to the dangerous characteristics of silica products and how to protect themselves from them," resulting in the employees' exposure to silica and their eventual illness with silicosis.

In *Goodbar,* Judge Kiser noted that Virginia had not adopted § 402A strict liability, and that the focus therefore was on negligent failure to warn and breach of the implied warranty of merchantability. [On] the negligent failure to warn claim, Judge Kiser [followed the approach of] Restatement

---

* Restatement (2d) of Torts § 388 (1965) provides:

§ 388. Chattel Known to Be Dangerous for Intended Use

One who supplies directly or through a third person a chattel for another to use is subject to liability to [foreseeable victims for foreseeable harms], if the supplier

(a) knows or has reason to know that the chattel is or is likely to be dangerous for the use for which it is supplied, and

(b) has no reason to believe that those for whose use the chattel is supplied will realize its dangerous condition, and

(c) fails to exercise reasonable care to inform them of its dangerous condition or of the facts which make it likely to be dangerous.

§ 388 [in assessing] "whether the Defendants failed to exercise reasonable care in relying upon the Foundry to supply its employees with the necessary information to satisfy the duty to warn." Judge Kiser [relied upon] comment *n* of § 388, entitled "Warnings given to third person," which delineates factors that must be balanced in determining what precautions the supplier must take to satisfy . . . reasonable care including

> (1) the dangerous condition of the product; (2) the purpose for which the product is used; (3) the form of any warnings given; (4) the reliability of the third party as a conduit of necessary information about the product; (5) the magnitude of the risk involved; and (6) the burden imposed on the supplier by requiring that he directly warn all users.

On the basis of § 388 and comment *n* thereto, Judge Kiser recognized the sophisticated user/bulk supplier defense, holding that "there is no duty on product suppliers to warn employees of knowledgeable industrial purchasers as to product-related hazards." Finding "that a plethora of material exists on the Lynchburg Foundry's extensive knowledge of the hazards of inhaling silica dust, the disease of silicosis and proper dust control methods," [he] granted the defendant suppliers' motion for summary judgment regarding the sophisticated user/bulk supplier defense on the § 388 negligent failure to warn claim. [T]he defendant suppliers had no duty to warn Foundry employees, given that the Foundry was the only one in a position to communicate an effective warning to its employees. The Court then listed a number of difficulties faced by the suppliers in trying to warn Foundry employees of silicosis, including "(1) the identification of the users or those exposed to its products would require a constant monitoring by the suppliers in view of the constant turnover of the Foundry's large work force; (2) the manner in which the sand products are delivered in bulk (i.e. unpackaged railroad car lots or truck); (3) no written product warnings placed on the railroad cars would ever reach the workers involved in casting or those in the immediate vicinity due to the way the loose sand is unloaded, conveyed, and kept in storage bins until needed; (4) only the Foundry itself would be in a position to provide the good housekeeping measures, training and warnings to its workers on a continuous and systematic basis necessary to reduce the risk of silicosis; (5) the sand suppliers must rely on the Foundry to convey any safety information to its employees; (6) the confusion arising when twelve different suppliers and the Foundry each try to cope with the awesome task of instructing the Foundry workers; and (7) in a commercial setting, it would be totally unrealistic to assume that the suppliers would be able to exert pressure on a large, industrial customer such as the Foundry to allow the suppliers to come in and educate its workers about the hazards of silicosis."

[For all these reasons, Maryland courts would recognize the sophisticated user/bulk supplier defense in a negligent failure to warn case. Moreover, they would also recognize this defense in a warnings claim brought under § 402A. No Maryland case recognizes] any doctrinal distinction between § 388 negligent, and § 402A strict liability, failure to warn cases [and the] latest edition of the venerable Prosser work on torts states, with respect to failure to warn, that:

> It is commonly said that a product can be defective in the kind of way that makes it unreasonably dangerous by failing to warn or failing adequately to warn about a risk or hazard related to the way a product is designed. But notwithstanding what a few courts have said, a claimant who seeks recovery on this basis must according to the generally accepted view, prove the manufacturer-designer was negligent. There will be no liability without a showing that the defendant designer knew or should have known in the exercise of ordinary care of the risk or hazard about which he failed to warn. Moreover, there will be no liability unless manufacturer failed to take the precautions that a reasonable person would take in presenting the product to the public. Although this ground of recovery is sometimes referred to as strict liability, it is really nothing more than a ground of negligence liability described as the sale of a product in a defective condition, subject, however, only to the defenses and other limitations or liability applicable to strict liability rather than negligence.

W.P. Keeton, D. Dobbs, R. Keeton, D. Owen, Prosser and Keeton on Torts § 99, at 697 (5th ed. 1984) (emphasis supplied). [Thus], in failure to warn cases, whether asserted on negligence or strict liability grounds, there is but one unitary theory of liability which is negligence based—the duty to use reasonable care in promulgating a warning. It logically follows, then, that [Maryland] would recognize the sophisticated user/bulk supplier defense in any failure to warn claim.

* * *

[Next to be considered is] whether Eastman and Union Carbide are entitled to prevail, as a matter of law, on this defense against plaintiffs' failure to warn claims. It is worthwhile to restate the essential premise of this defense: There is no duty on product suppliers to warn ultimate users (whether employees or customers) of product-related hazards in products supplied in bulk to a knowledgeable user.[4] The corollary, of course, is that this is especially the case when the knowledgeable industrial purchaser is the only one in a position to communicate an effective warning to the ultimate user. It is clear from the "plethora of material" before this Court that the possible teratogenic effects of the chemicals were equally within the technical knowledge of DuPont, a very knowledgeable industrial purchaser of the constituent chemicals for its Imron paint, and Eastman and Union Carbide, the suppliers of said chemicals. DuPont acquired its knowl-

---

4. Plaintiffs argue against reliance on *Goodbar,* stating that the sophisticated user/bulk supplier defense should not be expanded beyond cases of employee plaintiffs. [Yet the bulk supplier would confront an even more difficult task in reaching persons not in its employ.]

edge of the possible teratogenic effects of the chemicals known collectively as glycol ether acetates through independent inquiry, as well as from various outside sources including Eastman and Union Carbide. As stated by the plaintiffs themselves, "DuPont was aware of the possible teratogenic effects of the glycol ether acetates used by it in Imron paint as early as 1980. . . . " A DuPont memorandum dated April 23, 1981 makes clear that DuPont at that early date had within its possession reports regarding teratogenicity prepared by Japanese researchers, Dow Chemical, and the National Institute for Occupational Safety and Health (NIOSH). Those reports would be promptly evaluated by DuPont's own Haskell Laboratory. More information on the possible teratogenic effects of glycol ether acetates came to DuPont in the ensuing years. [Thus, DuPont] clearly qualifies as a knowledgeable industrial purchaser with respect to bulk chemicals in general and the possible teratogenic effects of glycol ether acetates in particular. There was, thus, no duty on Eastman and Union Carbide as commodity chemical suppliers to DuPont to warn ultimate purchasers of Imron paint, or the employees thereof, as to teratogenic hazards.

It is patently clear that DuPont was in a far better position than either of the bulk suppliers to communicate an effective warning to its customers, including the Baltimore City Fire Department, and to their customers' employees, including the plaintiff fire fighters. DuPont manufactured (from various chemicals including the glycol ether acetates supplied by Eastman and Union Carbide), packaged, labelled, and distributed the finished product denominated Imron paint. The facility with which DuPont could communicate an effective labelling warning to its customers is apparent. By comparison, Eastman and Union Carbide supplied in bulk, *via* railroad tank cars and tank trucks, vast amounts of liquid chemicals which were subsequently reprocessed and repackaged by DuPont as Imron paint, rendering these bulk suppliers unable, as a practical matter, to communicate any warning to the ultimate purchasers. Contrary to plaintiffs' assertion, there is simply no question of material fact as to whether Eastman and Union Carbide, as suppliers, reasonably relied on the knowledgeable industrial purchaser DuPont to warn customers like Baltimore City. . . . In short, there was no duty upon either Eastman or Union Carbide to communicate any warning to ultimate purchasers of Imron paint, given that only DuPont was ever in any reasonable position to communicate any effective warning. *Goodbar*.

[Eastman's and Union Carbide's motions for summary judgment granted.]

NOTES

1. Distinct Doctrines. Although the sophisticated user and bulk supplier doctrines both relieve an upstream seller of the duty to warn in circumstances where a buyer or user is aware of the risk, and while they often are raised by the same facts, they are in fact distinct legal doctrines. See Carrel v. National Cord & Braid Corp., 852 N.E.2d 100, 108 (Mass. 2006).

A.   The sophisticated user doctrine. This doctrine applies when there is no *need* to warn, because of the expertise of the buyer or user. See, e.g., id. (national Boy Scouts organization that operated camp knew risks of knot on bungee cord becoming untied and recoiling into camper's eye at least as well as cord's manufacturer); Haase v. Badger Mining Corp., 669 N.W.2d 737 (Wis. App. 2003) (silica sand supplier had no duty to warn foundry of risk that foundry workers might contract silicosis); Contranchis v. Travelers Ins. Co., 839 So.2d 301, 304 (La. App. 2003) (supplier of sheet metal had no duty to warn building contractor that metal could be slippery and of dangers of working with metal at heights; "there is no duty to warn 'sophisticated users' of the dangers, which they may be presumed to know about because of their familiarity with the product"); Mohr v. St. Paul Fire & Marine Ins. Co., 674 N.W.2d 576 (Wis. App. 2003) (high school which purchased diving platforms should realize that platforms would be dangerous if used in shallow water, possibly relieving seller of duty to warn; doctrine not limited to purchases by employers).

Many courts have referred to the Restatement (Third) of Products Liability § 5 on the sophisticated user/bulk supplier doctrine as more fully explained in note 9. The Wisconsin Supreme Court declined to endorse § 5 in Haase v. Badger Mining Corp., 682 N.W.2d 389 (Wis. 2004). The court concluded that § 5 was inapplicable because the silica sand at issue was not a component part but, rather, was integrated into the finished parts made by plaintiff's employer. Id. at 394. Further, the court held that the silica was substantially changed before plaintiff was exposed to it so that § 402A strict liability could not be imposed, either. Id. at 398.

For a case endorsing the sophisticated user doctrine in silica sand cases, see Humble Sand & Gravel, Inc. v. Gomez, 146 S.W.3d 170 (Tex. 2004).

B.   The bulk supplier doctrine. This doctrine applies when there is no practical *way* to warn, because of the type of product and method of sale. See, e.g., Wood v. Phillips Petroleum Co., 119 S.W.3d 870, 874 (Tex. App. 2003) (supplier of benzene to petrochemical company had no duty to warn it on why and how to protect workers from its well known toxic effects: "In some instances, a bulk supplier, who has no package of its own on which to place a label, may satisfy its duty to warn ultimate users of its product by proving that the intermediary to whom it sells the product is adequately trained and warned, familiar with the propensities of the product and its safe use, and capable of passing its knowledge on to users in a warning. [Citation.] The question in any case is whether a bulk supplier has a reasonable assurance that its warning will reach those endangered by the use of its product.").

2.   Comment *n* to § 388 provides in part as follows:

> *n.   Warnings given to third person.* Chattels are often supplied for the use of others. . . . In all such cases the question may arise as to whether the person supplying the chattel is exercising that reasonable care, which he owes to those who are to use it, by informing the third person through whom the chattel is supplied of its actual character.
>
> Giving to the third person through whom the chattel is supplied all the information necessary to its safe use is not in all cases sufficient to relieve the supplier from liability. It is merely a means by which this information is to be conveyed to those who are to use the chattel. The question remains whether this method gives a reasonable assurance that the information will reach those whose safety depends upon their having it. * * *

[I]f the danger involved in the ignorant use of a particular chattel is very great, it may be that the supplier does not exercise reasonable care in entrusting the communication of the necessary information even to a person whom he has good reason to believe to be careful. Many such articles can be made to carry their own message to the understanding of those who are likely to use them by the form in which they are put out, by the container in which they are supplied, or by a label or other device, indicating with a substantial sufficiency their dangerous character. Where the danger involved in the ignorant use of their true quality is great and such means of disclosure are practicable and not unduly burdensome, it may well be that the supplier should be required to adopt them. . . .

But the manufacturer *may* rely on the intermediary if it is reasonable to do so. See, e.g., Vines v. Beloit Corp., 631 So.2d 1003 (Ala. 1994) (papermaking machine defendant satisfied duty by warning sophisticated user of machine).

3. Reasonableness of Upstream Seller's Reliance. Whether the upstream supplier is reasonable in relying on the employer or other purchaser to warn the ultimate users depends upon "[1] the reliability of the employer as a conduit of necessary information about the product; [2] the magnitude of the risk involved; and [3] the burdens imposed on the supplier by requiring it to directly warn the ultimate users." Newson v. Monsanto Co., 869 F.Supp. 1255 (E.D. Mich. 1994) (suppliers of chemical to Ford Motor Co. used to make shatterproof windshields could reasonably assume that Ford had or would obtain information "abundantly available in the scientific literature").

Where the upstream supplier has reason to know that its vendee is not passing on important warnings, the reasonableness of the supplier's reliance disappears and its duty to provide warnings directly to the end user is reinstated. See Lakeman v. Otis Elevator Co., 930 F.2d 1547 (11th Cir. 1991) (where manufacturer sold chemical in bulk to repackager who resold chemical to industrial customers with some warnings, but not the most important ones, bulk supplier aware of intermediate seller's inadequate warning labels had duty to warn ultimate users).

4. In Purvis v. PPG Industries, Inc., 502 So.2d 714, 722 (Ala. 1987), a dry cleaner employee was poisoned by a cleaning solvent manufactured by defendant. PPG shipped the solvent in tank trucks to various distributors who then sold the solvent in drums to users such as plaintiff's employer. PPG provided its distributors with warning labels and all relevant danger information in Material Safety Data Sheets. Plaintiff claimed that PPG should have provided the warnings directly to her. *Held,* summary judgment for defendant affirmed:

[Recent decisions] recognize that the manufacturers of some products have no effective way to convey product information or warnings to the ultimate consumer or user of the product. Whether because of bulk sales, repackaging, or product combinations, these manufacturers must rely upon downstream distributors and suppliers to do this. The law has properly evolved to the point where such reliance is permitted, so long as the manufacturer has a reasonable basis to believe that the distributor will pass along the product information or warnings.

See, e.g., In re TMJ Implants Prod. Liab. Litig., 872 F.Supp. 1019, 1029 (D. Minn. 1995) (because DuPont sold Teflon in bulk to knowledgeable medical device manufacturer to make jaw implants, it had no duty to warn ultimate consumers that Teflon might not be suited for human implantation).

5. Rejection of No–Duty Approach. Some courts reject the sophisticated user and bulk supplier no-duty doctrines. See, e.g., Hall v. Ashland Oil Co., 625 F.Supp. 1515 (D. Conn. 1986); Whitehead v. St. Joe Lead Co., 729 F.2d 238 (3d Cir. 1984). Such courts hold that whether there is an obligation to provide warnings directly to ultimate users is a factual question, for jury determination, based on a balance of risk versus feasibility. See, e.g., Bryant v. Technical Research Co., 654 F.2d 1337 (9th Cir. 1981) (bulk supplier might have obtained distributor's customer list and directly warned end users); Shell Oil Co. v. Gutierrez, 581 P.2d 271 (Ariz. App. 1978). See also McCullock v. H.B. Fuller, 981 F.2d 656 (2d Cir.1992) (Vt.) (glue manufacturer had duty to warn book bindery employees directly of dangers of prolonged inhalation of glue pot vapors); Gray v. Badger Mining Corp., 676 N.W.2d 268 (Minn. 2004) (foundry did not have knowledge equal to that of silica supplier that disposable respirators would not protect workers from silica dust, such that sophisticated user no-duty doctrine did not relieve supplier of its duty to provide adequate warnings to foundry).

6. Durable Products. As previously discussed, if the product is a durable good on which a warning may be attached or embossed, the manufacturer usually will have a ready means to provide warnings directly to end users—regardless of whether there is a knowledgeable or "sophisticated" employer or other intermediary involved. See, e.g., Square D Co. v. Hayson, 621 So.2d 1373 (Fla. Dist. App. 1993) (manufacturer of electrical busway system should have placed label on system directly warning workers of backwards installation risks). But see Vines v. Beloit Corp., 631 So.2d 1003 (Ala. 1994) (manufacturer of machine discharged its duty to users by warning sophisticated employer).

How might the manufacturer of fabric, sold in bulk to clothing manufacturers, warn end users of the fabric's flammability characteristics? See Gryc v. Dayton–Hudson Corp., 297 N.W.2d 727 (Minn. 1980); Carter v. E.I. DuPont de Nemours & Co., 456 S.E.2d 661 (Ga. App. 1995).

7. Liability of Intermediate Downstream Supplier. Of course the downstream supplier, unless it is plaintiff's employer and so protected by workers' compensation law, usually will be separately liable for failing to pass on an upstream supplier's warnings. See Goldman v. Walco Tool & Eng'g, 614 N.E.2d 42 (Ill. App. 1993) (intermediate supplier that repackaged oil compound liable for failing to pass on warning it received by upstream supplier's labels).

DuPont was also a defendant in *Higgins*. How might plaintiffs' own proofs against DuPont undercut their case against Eastman and Union Carbide? Could plaintiffs' counsel have avoided this dilemma?

8. Theory of Liability. Most courts apply ordinary negligence principles to "strict" liability warnings cases, including the principles of comment n to § 388. See, e.g., Haase v. Badger Mining Corp., 669 N.W.2d 737 (Wis. App. 2003) (silica sand supplier); Whitehead v. St. Joe Lead Co., 729 F.2d 238 (3d Cir. 1984); Smith v. Walter C. Best, Inc., 927 F.2d 736 (3d Cir. 1990). A few, however, have held that the duty to warn in strict tort is nondelegable as a matter of law. See, e.g., Neal v. Carey Canadian Mines, Ltd., 548 F.Supp. 357, 368 (E.D. Pa. 1982), aff'd sub nom. Van Buskirk v. Carey Canadian Mines, Ltd., 760 F.2d 481, 497 (3d Cir. 1985). At least one court has held that the bulk supplier doctrine does not apply to strict products liability claims so that the supplier must warn the ultimate users directly. Menschik v. Mid–America Pipeline Co., 812 S.W.2d 861 (Mo. App. 1991).

As in other contexts, implied warranty is often considered the functional equivalent of strict tort liability in warnings cases, and "the scope of liability imposed under a breach-of-warranty theory in many if not most duty-to-warn cases will be identical to that imposed under a negligence theory." Bly v. Otis Elevator Co., 713 F.2d 1040, 1045 n.8 (4th Cir. 1983) (Va. law).

9. Products Liability Restatement. The sophisticated user doctrine is submerged in two sections of the Third Restatement.

Comment *i* to § 2 summarizes the principles of Restatement (2d) of Torts § 388, stating that "[T]here is no general rule as to whether one supplying a product for the use of others through an intermediary has a duty to warn the ultimate product user directly or may rely on the intermediary to relay warnings. The standard is one of reasonableness" that includes consideration of (1) the gravity of the risk, (2) "the likelihood that the intermediary will convey the information to the ultimate user," and (3) "the feasibility and effectiveness of giving a warning directly to the user."

Section 5, "Liability of Commercial Seller or Distributor of Product Components for Harm Caused by Products Into Which Components Are Integrated," provides that the supplier of a nondefective component is subject to liability only if it "substantially participates in the integration of the component" into the integrated product, and the integration causes the product to be defective. Suppliers of "raw materials" do not have a duty to investigate end uses nor a duty to warn end users. See cmt. *c*.

10. Bystanders. The broader question in *Higgins* is whether the manufacturer owes a duty to persons not in privity but foreseeably endangered by its products—whether the duty to warn, that is, extends to bystanders. In a variety of contexts, courts have extended the duty to such persons. See, e.g., Georgia–Pacific Corp. v. Pransky, 800 A.2d 722 (Md. 2002) (mesothelioma victim exposed to dust while father worked with asbestos product in basement was a foreseeable bystander); Bohnstedt v. Robscon Leasing L.L.C., 993 P.2d 135 (Okla. Civ. App. 1999) (backup alarm on grader needed to be maintained to protect bystanders); Hayes v. Kay Chem. Co., 482 N.E.2d 611 (Ill. App. 1985) (McDonald's employee wiped face with towel saturated with colorless, odorless, caustic grill cleaner used by another employee; duty extended beyond user to foreseeable persons and "nonusers"); Karns v. Emerson Electric Co., 817 F.2d 1452, 1457 (10th Cir. 1987) (hand-held "Weed Eater" brush-cutting device, with exposed 10–inch circular steel sawblade "capable of suddenly flinging itself through an uncontrolled, 180 degree arc poses a danger to bystanders like Pearce that exceeds the expectations of the ordinary consumer"; blade struck something near ground, causing machine to swing violently around and cut off arm of user's nephew standing 6–10 feet to the rear); Givens v. Lederle, 556 F.2d 1341 (5th Cir. 1977) (mother contracted polio, possibly from contact with diapers of child recently administered vaccine produced by defendant). But see Kirk v. Michael Reese Hosp. & Med. Center, 513 N.E.2d 387 (Ill. 1987) (drug manufacturer had no duty to passenger injured in car accident resulting when driver, who was taking defendant's drug and had been drinking, lost control of car).

11. Regulation. The Hazard Communication Standard promulgated by the Occupational Safety and Health Administration requires manufacturers and importers to label all containers of hazardous chemicals and to provide Material Safety Data Sheets to purchasing employers. In turn, employers must make the MSDS information available to employees, and must train their employees in the safe handling of such substances. 29 C.F.R. § 1910.1200 (2006). The impact of this standard on workplace safety and products liability actions is difficult to determine. See generally M. Green, When Toxic Worlds Collide: Regulatory and Common Law Prescriptions for Risk Communication, 13 Harv. Envt'l L. Rev. 209 (1989); O'Reilly,

Risks of Assumptions: Impacts of Regulatory Label Warnings Upon Industrial Products Liability, 37 Cath. U. L. Rev. 85 (1987).

12. On the sophisticated user and bulk supplier defenses, see Schwartz, Behrens, and Crouse, Getting the Sand Out of the Eyes of the Law: The Need for a Clear Rule for Sand Suppliers in Texas After humble Sand & Gravel, Inc. v. Gomez, 37 St. Mary's L.J. 283 (2006); Korzec, Restating the Obvious in Maryland Products Liability Law: The Restatement (Third) of Torts: Products Liability and Failure to Warn Defenses, 30 U. Balt. L. Rev. 341 (2001); Ausness, Learned Intermediaries and Sophisticated Users: Encouraging the Use of Intermediaries to Transmit Product Safety Information, 46 Syr. L. Rev. 1185 (1996); Mansfield, Reflection on Current Limits on Component and Raw Material Supplier Liability and the Proposed Third Restatement, 84 Ky. L.J. 221 (1996); D. Owen, Products Liability Law § 9.5 (2d ed. 2008); 1 D. Owen, M.S. Madden, & M. Davis, Madden & Owen on Products Liability §§ 9:8 and 9:9 (3d ed. 2000).

5.   PRESCRIPTION DRUGS

"Failure to warn or instruct is the major basis of liability for manufacturers of prescription drugs and medical devices." Restatement (Third) of Torts: Products Liability § 8 cmt. *d*. Many of the same basic warnings and instructions issues at play in other product cases dominate cases involving prescription drugs as well. Yet prescription drugs are a peculiar kind of product reflected by their heavy regulation by the federal Food and Drug Administration, the FDA. Underlying the regulatory scheme are two assumptions that reflect the special types of dangers that inhere in drugs classified as prescription pharmaceuticals. First is the belief that the risks in such drugs are so dangerous and sophisticated that the FDA must determine their effectiveness and safety before they can be marketed at all. Indeed, this agency approves all information the manufacturer intends to provide on the drug's recommended use, contraindications, risks, and side effects. The second premise is that the potential risks of improper prescription drug use are so substantial as to require professional medical judgment and supervision of their use by ordinary consumers. The thought here is that only a medical doctor—a "learned intermediary" between the drug manufacturer and the consuming patient—has the requisite knowledge and professional judgment properly to assess the benefits and risks of matching and monitoring particular dangerous drugs with distinctive medical conditions of individual patients.

Prescription drug litigation gives rise to many of the same warnings issues arising in other products liability contexts. As described in the notes that follow, two major issues that also arise in this context concern (1) *adequacy*, and (2) *delegation*.

N O T E S

1.   Adequacy—In General. All material information on possible risks must be conveyed to the doctor, comprehensible to the general practitioner as well as to the specialist. For a warning to be "adequate":

1.   the warning must adequately indicate the scope of the danger; 2. the warning must reasonably communicate the extent or seriousness of the harm that could result from misuse of the drug; 3. the physical aspects of the warning must be adequate to alert a reasonably prudent person to the danger; 4. a simple directive warning may be inadequate when it fails to indicate the consequences that might result from failure to follow it and, . . . 5. the means to convey the warning must be adequate.

Thom v. Bristol–Myers Squibb Co., 353 F.3d 848, 853 (10th Cir. 2003) (jury question whether manufacturer of Serzone antidepressant adequately warned of seriousness of risk of priapism, a persistent and painful erection of the penis).

2.   Overpromotion. Risks must not be unduly downplayed, nor safety "overpromoted"; instead, the manufacturer's communications to the doctor must present a reasonably balanced portrayal of the effectiveness and dangers of the drug. Compare Stevens v. Parke, Davis & Co., 507 P.2d 653 (Cal. 1973) (overpromotion of Chloromycetin, a broad-spectrum antibiotic, downplaying risk of fatal aplastic anemia), with Spinden v. Johnson & Johnson, 427 A.2d 597 (N.J. Super. Ct. App. Div.1981) (AMA Journal ads did not amount to overpromotion). "An overpromotion theory is one way that a plaintiff in a failure-to-warn case can overcome the manufacturer's argument either (1) that it provided adequate warnings or (2) that the doctor's decision to prescribe a drug despite his awareness of its dangers was an intervening cause sufficient to vitiate the manufacturer's liability." Motus v. Pfizer Inc., 196 F. Supp. 2d 984, 998 (C.D. Cal. 2001).

3.   In Martin v. Hacker, 628 N.E.2d 1308 (N.Y. 1993), a doctor was treating plaintiff's decedent, Mr. Martin, for hypertension (high blood pressure) with two drugs manufactured by the defendant, including reserpine. Martin became severely depressed and fatally shot himself in the head, allegedly because of the reserpine. The issue was whether the information provided by the defendant to physicians on risks of the drug was adequate as a matter of law. The manufacturer's package insert provided in part:

CONTRAINDICATIONS: Known hypersensitivity, mental depression (especially with suicidal tendencies), active peptic ulcer, ulcerative colitis, and patients receiving electroconvulsive therapy.

WARNINGS: Extreme caution should be exercised in treating patients with a history of mental depression. Discontinue the drug at first sign of despondency, early morning insomnia, loss of appetite, impotence, or self-deprecation. Drug-induced depression may persist for several months after drug withdrawal and may be severe enough to result in suicide.

The court outlined the applicable principles of law:

[A] warning "must be commensurate with the risk involved in the ordinary use of the product." Thus, analysis logically starts with an ascertainment of the seriousness of the involved risk. Seriousness depends on the consequences of the side effects. Here, there is no question that the level of the risk is the highest, death from suicide. Accordingly, the adequacy of the package insert for reserpine must be evaluated as a warning of a risk of the most serious degree.

Once the general level of risk is established, the court should evaluate the insert's language for its accuracy, clarity and relative consistency. For a warning to be accurate it must be correct, fully descriptive and complete, and it must convey updated information as to all of the drug's known side effects. In this case, no issue is raised with respect to the correctness or completeness of the reserpine warning.

Clarity in the context of a drug warning means that the language of the warning is direct, unequivocal and sufficiently forceful to convey the risk. A warning that is otherwise clear may be obscured by inconsistencies or contradictory statements made in different sections of the package insert regarding the same side effect or from language in a later section that dilutes the intensity of a caveat made in an earlier section....

Finally, a court should consider the warning as a whole. While a meticulous examination and parsing of individual sentences in the insert may arguably reveal differing nuances in meaning or variations in emphasis as to the seriousness of a side effect, any resulting vagueness may be overcome if, when read as a whole, the warning conveys a meaning as to the consequences that is unmistakable.

Held, based on these standards, the warnings were adequate as a matter of law.

Compare Gerber v. Hoffmann–La Roche Inc., 392 F.Supp.2d 907, 917–918 (S.D.Tex.2005), where plaintiff suffered severe birth defects from his mother's ingestion of Accutane, an acne medication, when she became pregnant despite her use of an IUD. The drug insert warned against use by women who could become pregnant:

The warning specifically and unambiguously mentions the circumstances of which Mr. Gerber complains, "major fetal abnormalities related to Accutane administration." The label ... warns of the dangers of usage of Accutane during pregnancy [and] states that use of the drug is contraindicated for patients who are pregnant, intend to become pregnant, and for women of childbearing age who are not using effective contraception.

Held, the warnings were adequate as a matter of law.

4. Medical devices and implants involve many of the same issues. In Phillips v. Baxter Healthcare Corp., 1993 WL 524688 (Cal. Ct. App. 1993), plaintiff underwent augmentation surgery in which prostheses filled with silicone gel were implanted in her breasts. Several years later, to break up scar tissue that had formed around the implants, she had a closed capsulotomy in which force is applied to the breast. The implants broke and had to be surgically removed and replaced. Plaintiff sued the implant manufacturer on various bases including inadequate warnings. The warning accompanying the implants stated:

The silicone elastomer envelope of these products has a low tear strength and is thin to achieve desired prosthesis softness and mobility. For these reasons, the envelope may be easily cut by a scalpel or rupture by excessive stresses [and] may be easily ruptured when still hot from the autoclave. Care must be exercised during handling to prevent such events.

Heyer–Schulte cannot guarantee the structural integrity of its implant should the surgeon elect to treat capsule firmness by forceful external stress.

Held, the warning was adequate.

Contrast Hufft v. Horowitz, 5 Cal.Rptr.2d 377 (Ct. App. 1992), where plaintiff's penile implant malfunctioned and had to be surgically removed. *Held*, liability for failure to warn that the implant was inappropriate for patients with well-muscled abdomens, that it could cause a continual and painful erection, and that scar tissue might encapsulate its reservoir, preventing it from functioning properly.

Compare Bravman v. Baxter Healthcare Corp., 984 F.2d 71 (2d Cir. 1993) (the case of the tell-tale heart; allowing claim for failing to warn that heart valve might be noisy).

5. Adequacy—Timeliness. A long series of cases involving Aralen, a drug used in the treatment of rheumatoid arthritis and eventually linked to irreversible eye damage in some users, established the following general principles:

A. A warning of side effects to be timely must be made promptly upon discovery of the coexistence of the side effect and use of the drug, even though a causal relationship has not been clearly proved. Basko v. Sterling Drug, Inc., 416 F.2d 417 (2d Cir. 1969).

B. The warning is required as soon as the side effect is documented even in only a very small percentage of users. Sterling Drug, Inc. v. Cornish, 370 F.2d 82 (8th Cir. 1966).

C. Since the drug company is held to have the knowledge of an expert, a warning to be timely must be given as soon as the risks are pointed out in reputable scientific journals. Schenebeck v. Sterling Drug, Inc., 423 F.2d 919 (8th Cir. 1970).

6. Adequacy—Method of Conveyance. The manufacturer must select the best method reasonably available to convey important new information on drug dangers to the doctors who need the information. There are several standard avenues of communication between drug companies and physicians for transmitting information about drugs. The Physician's Desk Reference (PDR), updated periodically, contains copies of package inserts for many prescription drugs. Other sources of information, more complete than the PDR, are Facts and Comparisons (updated monthly), and the annual United States Pharmacopeial Drug Information (USPDI), for the Health Care Professional (vol. IA & IB), and Advice for the Patient—Drug Information in Lay Language (vol. II). Information on warnings and contraindications in the package insert and the PDR ordinarily is adequate to alert physicians to drug risks. However, such information may become out of date due to new developments, and a manufacturer's failure promptly to update the medical profession may subject the company to liability.

Thus, if new information is critically important, a manufacturer may be required to send "Dear Doctor" letters to individual physicians to advise them about it. As to the standards of adequacy for such letters, see, e.g., Lawson v. G.D. Searle & Co., 356 N.E.2d 779 (Ill. 1976). More recently, see Lineberger v. Wyeth, 894 A.2d 141, 143 (Pa.Super.Ct. 2006) (reciting Wyeth's use of Dear Doctor letters to warn of risks of myocardial infarctions and cardiac arrest from fen-phen diet drug). However, a typically busy physician may not routinely read "Dear Doctor" letters or even regularly consult the PDR. If the need to warn is compelling enough, the company may be required to use its drug reps (formerly called "detail men," salespersons who regularly call on physicians) to warn doctors in person of a particular risk. A leading case on the factors bearing on whether a drug company must warn doctors in this manner is Sterling Drug, Inc. v. Yarrow, 408 F.2d 978 (8th Cir. 1969) (Aralen; failure to use detail men to alert doctors of possible eye damage was unreasonable in light of the fact that the PDR and letters might not warn fast enough).

7. Allergic Reactions. "The term *allergy* or *hypersensitivity* refers to the condition or state of an individual who reacts specifically and with unusual symptoms to the administration of, or to contact with, a substance which when given in similar amounts to the majority of all other individuals proves harmless or innocuous." It is not clear, therefore, that anything is "defective" about a product just because it generates an allergic reaction: "A person suffering an allergic reaction to a product is, by definition, abnormal or hypersensitive. The resulting harm, therefore, is arguably more fairly attributable to some 'defect' in the person's body rather than to a 'defect' in the product—a product that is entirely safe for all normal ('nondefective') people." Panel Discussion, Medico–Legal Aspects of Allergies, 24 Tenn. L. Rev. 840–42 (1957).

Two lines of cases address the duty to warn of allergic reactions. One line requires a warning only if the manufacturer can foresee a risk of allergy in *a substantial number of persons*. See Kaempfe v. Lehn & Fink Products Corp., 249 N.Y.S.2d 840 (App. Div. 1964), aff'd 231 N.E.2d 294 (N.Y. 1967) (dermatitis from aluminum sulphate in deodorant; no liability where manufacturer received only 4 sensitivity complaints in 600,000 sales—plaintiff not one "of a substantial number or of an identifiable class" of allergic persons: "the manufacturer is [not] to be held under an absolute duty of giving special warning against a remote possibility of harm due to an unusual allergic reaction from use by a minuscule percentage of the potential customers"). Accord, Griggs v. Combe, Inc., 456 So.2d 790 (Ala. 1984) (first known case of systemic illness from benzocaine in vaginal itch ointment); Morris v. Pathmark Corp., 592 A.2d 331 (Pa. Super. Ct. 1991) (hair straightener).

This is the position of comment *j* to § 402A; see also comment *i* ("unreasonably dangerous" means dangerous to extent beyond contemplation of "ordinary" consumer). It is also the position of the Third Restatement, § 2 cmt. *k*, noting that the "substantial number" logically should decrease as the risk of harm increases.

Another line of cases rejects the *no-duty* approach for "insignificant" or "insubstantial" numbers of allergy victims and instead imposes a duty to warn of *any* foreseeable allergy that may be serious. See Wright v. Carter Prod., Inc., 244 F.2d 53 (2d Cir. 1957) (dermatitis from deodorant; manufacturer might have duty to warn, despite only 373 complaints in 82,000,000 sales, depending on foreseeability of allergy, frequency and seriousness thereof, and feasibility of providing a warning); Kehm v. Procter & Gamble Mfg. Co., 724 F.2d 613 (8th Cir. 1983) (user of defendant's extra absorbent Rely tampon died from toxic shock syndrome; court rejected defense of user's idiosyncratic allergic reaction as inapplicable to strict liability claim).

If there *is* a duty to warn of allergic reaction, the warning must be *adequate*. See Mitchell v. VLI Corp., 786 F.Supp. 966 (M.D. Fla.1992) (package insert for nonprescription "Today" contraceptive sponge stated that approximately 2% of users in studies "discontinued use because of allergic reactions.") Plaintiff suffered severe allergic reaction and ultimately had to have a hysterectomy. *Held*, because it is unclear whether a lay person would understand "allergic reaction" to include a severe reaction requiring major surgery, manufacturer's motion for summary judgment on warnings claim denied.

See generally Barrett, Latex Gloves, 22 J. Legal Med. 263 (2001); Mobilia, Allergic Reactions to Prescription Drugs: A Proposal for Compensation, 48 Alb. L. Rev. 343 (1984); Henderson, Process Norms in Products Litigation: Liability for Allergic Reactions, 51 U. Pitt. L. Rev. 761 (1990); Ortego, Allergic or Idiosyncratic Reactions as a Defense to Strict Products Liability: Recent Developments, 42 Fed'n Ins. & Corp. Couns. Q. 41 (1991); Notes, Suing for Peanuts, 75 Notre Dame L. Rev. 1269 (2000); 18 J.L. & Health 135 (2004) (latex-glove allergies).

8. Delegation—The Learned Intermediary Doctrine. As a general rule of products liability law, a manufacturer is bound to take all reasonable steps to provide necessary warnings to the ultimate user of a hazardous product. Like the bulk sale/sophisticated user doctrines examined above, the learned intermediary doctrine is an exception to that general rule. Its nature and rationale was perhaps best described by Judge Wisdom in Reyes v. Wyeth Laboratories, 498 F.2d 1264, 1276 (5th Cir.), cert. denied, 419 U.S. 1096 (1974):

> [W]here *prescription* drugs are concerned, the manufacturer's duty to warn is limited to an obligation to advise the prescribing physician of any potential dangers that may result from the drug's use. This special standard for prescription drugs is an understandable exception to the Restatement's general rule that one who markets goods must warn foreseeable ultimate users of dangers inherent in his products. See Restatement (Second) of Torts, Section 388 (1965). Prescription drugs are likely to be complex medicines, esoteric in formula and varied in effect. As a medical expert, the prescribing physician can take into account the propensities of the drug, as well as the susceptibilities of his patient. His is the task of weighing the benefits of any medication against its potential dangers. The choice he makes is an informed one, an individualized medical judgment bottomed on a knowledge of both patient and palliative. Pharmaceutical companies then, who must warn ultimate purchasers of dangers inherent in patent drugs sold over the counter, in selling prescription drugs are required to warn only the prescribing physician, who acts as a "learned intermediary" between manufacturer and consumer.

Virtually all jurisdictions have accepted the learned intermediary doctrine as an exception to the general rule. See Thom v. Bristol–Myers Squibb Co., 353 F.3d 848, 852 (10th Cir. 2003) (noting that forty-four jurisdictions adhere to doctrine).

Based on the premise that a manufacturer provides medical practitioners with warnings and instructions that are in fact adequate, the doctrine does not shield manufacturers from liability for providing doctors with warnings that are inadequate or misleading. See, e.g., McNeil v. Wyeth, 462 F.3d 364 (5th Cir. 2006).

9. In addition to prescription drugs, the learned intermediary doctrine has been applied to a cardiac pacemaker, Brooks v. Medtronic, Inc., 750 F.2d 1227 (4th Cir. 1984); an intrauterine device, McKee v. Moore, 648 P.2d 21 (Okla. 1982); a catheter inserted into a patient's heart, Phelps v. Sherwood Medical Indus., 836 F.2d 296 (7th Cir. 1987); an x-ray machine, Kirsch v. Picker Int'l, Inc., 753 F.2d 670 (8th Cir. 1985); an electroconvulsive therapy machine, Andre v. Mecta Corp., 587 N.Y.S.2d 334 (App. Div. 1992); and nicotine chewing gum, Tracy v. Merrell Dow Pharmaceuticals, Inc., 569 N.E.2d 875 (Ohio 1991). The New York Supreme Court seems to have drawn the line at extended-wear contact lenses fitted by an optometrist. See Bukowski v. CooperVision, Inc., 592 N.Y.S.2d 807 (App. Div. 1993) (lenses caused corneal ulcers; no evidence that optometrist has ability to assimilate manufacturer's technical information to fulfill learned intermediary role).

Efforts to apply the doctrine outside the medical field usually have failed. See, e.g., Hall v. Ashland Oil Co., 625 F.Supp. 1515 (D. Conn. 1986) (differences between doctor-patient relationship and employer-employee relationship precluded application of learned intermediary doctrine to chemical manufacturer who warned decedent's employer but not decedent himself). Note, however, that busy courts sometimes mistakenly apply the "learned intermediary" label to other types of "sophisticated user" cases. See, e.g., Burke v. Dow Chemical Co., 797 F.Supp. 1128, 1133 (E.D.N.Y. 1992) (supplier of toxic chemical in "Rid–A–Bug" household insecticide that may have caused brain damage to children of pregnant women).

10.   Learned Intermediary Rule—Exceptions. If a prescription drug is dispensed under circumstances where the doctor does not render the type of individualized balancing of risks and benefits contemplated by the learned intermediary doctrine, the manufacturer may have to provide warnings directly to the patient.

A.   Mass immunization programs. Most courts thus refuse to apply the learned intermediary rule to the mass immunization context, where patients are vaccinated in assembly-line fashion, often by persons other than physicians. See, e.g., Davis v. Wyeth Labs. Inc., 399 F.2d 121 (9th Cir. 1968) (polio); Givens v. Lederle Labs., 556 F.2d 1341 (5th Cir. 1977) (same); Brazzell v. United States, 788 F.2d 1352 (8th Cir. 1986) (swine flu); Petty v. United States, 740 F.2d 1428 (8th Cir. 1984) (same). How if at all could such warnings effectively be given to each participant? See Petty v. United States, 740 F.2d 1428, 1433–34 n. 3 (8th Cir. 1984).

Compare Mazur v. Merck & Co., 964 F.2d 1348 (3d Cir. 1992) (oral rubella vaccine maker satisfied duty by providing information to U.S. Center for Disease Control), with Allison v. Merck & Co., 878 P.2d 948, 959 (Nev. 1994) (measles, mumps, and rubella vaccine manufacturer could *not* delegate its duty to warn to CDC whose information sheet made no mention of risks of blindness, deafness, and brain damage).

Might the provision of truly "effective" warnings directly (and without a doctor's explanation) to every person vaccinated in a mass immunization program needlessly scare many people out of participating in the program? Might such warnings thus increase the incidence of the disease in the community and thereby undercut the effectiveness of the immunization program? Is the legal rule therefore at odds with social policy? See Reyes v. Wyeth Labs., supra, and Allison v. Merck & Co., supra. See generally Franklin & Mais, Tort Law and Mass Immunization Programs: Lessons from the Polio and Flu Episodes, 65 Calif. L. Rev. 754 (1977).

B.   Birth control pills. In MacDonald v. Ortho Pharmaceutical Corp., 475 N.E.2d 65 (Mass. 1985), plaintiff suffered a stroke leaving her partially paralyzed after taking birth control pills, manufactured by the defendant, for an extended time. She had seen her physician once each year. Ortho's warning information given to the consumer via a package insert included a warning on the risks of blood clots but did not specifically mention the possibility of strokes. Plaintiff claimed that the manufacturer had a duty to provide full and adequate warnings directly to her, the patient, and not just to the doctor. Although all 15 prior reported judicial opinions but one had applied the learned intermediary doctrine to birth control pills as other prescription drugs, the *MacDonald* majority reinstated a jury verdict for the plaintiff, reasoning that the basis for the learned intermediary rule is undercut in the birth control pill context:

> The oral contraceptive thus stands apart from other prescription drugs in light of the heightened participation of patients in decisions relating to use of "the pill"; the substantial risks affiliated with the product's use; the feasibility of direct warnings by the manufacturer to the user; the limited participation of the physician (annual prescriptions); and the possibility that oral communications between physicians and consumers may be insufficient or too scanty standing alone fully to apprise consumers of the product's dangers at the time the initial selection of a contraceptive method is made as well as at subsequent points when alternative methods may be considered. We conclude that the manufacturer of oral contraceptives is not justified in relying on warnings to the medical profession to satisfy its common law duty to warn, and that the manufacturer's obli-

gation encompasses a duty to warn the ultimate user. Thus, the manufacturer's duty is to provide the consumer written warnings conveying reasonable notice of the nature, gravity, and likelihood of known or knowable side effects, and advising the consumer to seek fuller explanation from the prescribing physician or other doctor of any such information of concern to the consumer.

Dissenting, Justice O'Connor noted that manufacturers of prescription pharmaceuticals have a duty to provide full information on all material risks to prescribing physicians who, in turn, have a duty (under informed consent doctrine, redressable in a malpractice action) to provide full information on all material risks to patients for whom they prescribe the drug. Arguing that this division of responsibility most fairly and efficiently allocates the risks and responsibilities, he remarked:

[I] believe that those rules [so allocating duties between the manufacturer and doctor] best ensure that a prescription drug user will receive in the most effective manner the information that she needs to make an informed decision as to whether to use the drug. The rules place on drug manufacturers the duty to gather, compile, and provide to doctors data regarding the use of their drugs, tasks for which the manufacturers are best suited, and the rules place on doctors the burden of conveying those data to their patients in a useful and understandable manner, a task for which doctors are best suited. Doctors, unlike printed warnings, can tailor to the needs and abilities of an individual patient the information that that patient needs in order to make an informed decision whether to use a particular drug. Manufacturers are not in position to give adequate advice directly to those consumers whose medical histories and physical conditions, perhaps unknown to the consumers, make them peculiarly susceptible to risk. Prescription drugs—including oral contraceptives—differ from other products because their dangers vary widely depending on characteristics of individual consumers. Exposing a prescription drug manufacturer to liability based on a jury's determination that, despite adequately informing physicians of the drug's risks and complying with FDA regulations, the manufacturer failed reasonably to warn a particular plaintiff-consumer of individualized risks is not essential to reasonable consumer protection and places an unfair burden on prescription drug manufacturers.

MacDonald is often cited as creating a new common-law exception to the learned intermediary rule for birth control pills. While a couple of federal court judges followed *MacDonald*, other courts have uniformly rejected it and held firm to the learned intermediary doctrine in the birth control context. See, e.g., In re Norplant Contraceptive Products Liability Litigation, 955 F.Supp. 700, 704 (E.D. Tex. 1997) ("Only a single jurisdiction, Massachusetts, recognizes an exception to the doctrine for prescription contraceptives.").

Note that the FDA by regulation requires that birth control manufacturers provide warnings of dangers in lay language directly to the user. This means that a *negligence per se* action may be available against such a manufacturer who fails to provide direct and adequate risk information to the user. But the violation-of-regulation approach was explicitly rejected in Martin v. Ortho Pharmaceutical Corp., 661 N.E.2d 352 (Ill. 1996) (risk of birth limb reductions from pills used in first trimester of pregnancy).

C. Direct-to-consumer advertising. Is the learned intermediary doctrine out of touch with the way modern medicine is practiced? More specifically, does a manufacturer of prescription drugs waive its right to rely on the doctrine if it aims

TV and other mass advertising directly at consumers? In Perez v. Wyeth Labs., 734 A.2d 1245 (N.J. 1999), the plaintiff was implanted with the Norplant contraceptive device. Plaintiff sued Wyeth, which had properly warned her doctor of possible complications, for failing to provide warnings directly to her. The trial court granted summary judgment for the manufacturer based on the learned intermediary doctrine as incorporated into the New Jersey statute, and the appellate division affirmed. In the New Jersey Supreme Court, *held*, reversed. The learned intermediary doctrine should no longer insulate prescription drug manufacturers from a duty to warn consumers directly in the case of mass-marketed drugs: "[W]hen mass marketing of prescription drugs seeks to influence a patient's choice of a drug, a pharmaceutical manufacturer that makes direct claims to consumers for the efficacy of its product should not be unqualifiedly relieved of a duty to provide proper warnings of the dangers or side effects of the product." Id. at 1247.

> Our medical-legal jurisprudence is based on images of health care that no longer exist. At an earlier time, medical advice was received in the doctor's office from a physician who most likely made house calls if needed. The patient usually paid a small sum of money to the doctor. Neighborhood pharmacists compounded prescribed medicines. [T]he prevailing attitude of law and medicine was that the "doctor knows best."

> Pharmaceutical manufacturers never advertised their products to patients, but rather directed all sales efforts at physicians. In this comforting setting, the law created an exception to the traditional duty of manufacturers to warn consumers directly of risks associated with the product as long as they warned health-care providers of those risks.

> For good or ill, that has all changed. Medical services are in large measure provided by managed care organizations. Medicines are purchased in the pharmacy department of supermarkets and often paid for by third-party providers. Drug manufacturers now directly advertise products to consumers on the radio, television, the Internet, billboards on public transportation, and in magazines.

Id. at 1246–1247. "The [problems of this type of advertising] practice are manifest. 'The marketing gimmick used by the drug manufacturer often provides the consumer with a diluted variation of the risks associated with the drug product.' Even without such manipulation, '[t]elevision spots lasting 30 or 60 seconds are not conducive to 'fair balance' [in presentation of risks.]' " Id. at 1252–53 (citing Hanson & Kysar, Taking Behaviorialism Seriously: Some Evidence of Market Manipulation, 112 Harv. L. Rev. 1420 (1999)). See also Tham, The Learned Intermediary Doctrine and DTC Advertising, L.A. Law. 16 (Feb. 26, 2004) (GAO estimates that 8.5 million Americans per year receive prescription drugs they ask for by name).

Perez has gone nowhere fast. See In re Meridia Products Liability Litigation, 328 F.Supp.2d 791, 812 n.19 (N.D. Ohio 2004) ("Five years have passed since the New Jersey Supreme Court decided *Perez*. In the intervening period, no other state has followed New Jersey's lead. The Court thus could not apply *Perez*'s logic [in a diversity case, based on other states' law] even if it desired to do so."), aff'd, 447 F.3d 861 (6th Cir. 2006).

Note that of these three exceptions, only the mass immunization program is generally accepted, yet even it is infrequently applied. See Mazur v. Merck & Co., Inc., 742 F.Supp. 239, 253 (E.D.Pa. 1990) ("All of the vaccine cases recognize the theoretical validity of the 'mass immunization exception' to the learned intermediary rule, but very few have found situations where its application is warranted."). Nonetheless, Products Liability Restatement § 6(d)(2) articulates a general exception that arguably embraces all three. See note 12, below. Section 6 cmt. *e* leaves open the question whether a new exception should be created for mass-marketed drugs.

11. Birth Control Pill Risks—Overwarning? A Gallup poll in 1985 showed that "Americans greatly overestimate the risks and understate the effectiveness of birth control methods, particularly the pill, leaving them vulnerable to unintended pregnancies." According to the American College of Obstetricians and Gynecologists, unwanted pregnancies and more than a million abortions each year needlessly threaten women's lives. "The society's survey found that people are particularly misinformed about the birth control pill, which the group said is the most effective and safest contraceptive for many women." Three quarters of the women surveyed thought that the pill presents substantial health risks, despite the fact that the risk of death from taking the pill is about half the mother's risk of death from childbirth. Pill Poll—National Survey Finds Many Have Bad Information, The State (Columbia, S.C.), March 6, 1985, p. 2A, col. 2.

12. The Products Liability Restatement. The Third Restatement adopts the learned intermediary rule, providing in § 6(d) that a prescription drug or medical device is defective if the manufacturer fails to provide reasonable warnings of foreseeable risks to:

(1) the doctor or other health-care provider, or

(2) the patient, if the manufacturer should know that health-care providers are "not in a position to reduce the risks of harm in accordance with the instructions or warnings."

13. See generally Imbroscio and Bell, Adequate Drug Warnings in the Face of Uncertain Causality: The Learned Intermediary Doctrine and the Need for Clarity, 107 W. Va. L. Rev. 847 (2005); Ausness, Will More Aggressive Marketing Practices Lead to Greater Tort Liability for Prescription Drug Manufacturers?, 37 Wake Forest L. Rev. 97 (2002); Madden, The Enduring Paradox of Products Liability Law Relating to Prescription Pharmaceuticals, 21 Pace L. Rev. 313 (2001); Wiseman, Another Factor in the "Decisional Calculus": The Learned Intermediary Doctrine, The Physician–Patient Relationship, and Direct-to-Consumer Marketing, 52 S.C. L. Rev. 993 (2001); Strain and Gaarder, Direct-to-Consumer Advertising and the Learned Intermediary Doctrine: Unsettling a Settled Doctrine, 30 U. Balt. L. Rev. 377 (2001); Heather, Liability for Direct-to-Consumer Advertising and Drug Information on the Internet, 68 Def. Couns. J. 412 (2001); Lear, The Learned Intermediary Doctrine in the Age of Direct Consumer Advertising, 65 Mo. L. Rev. 1101 (2000); Ferguson, Liability for Pharmaceutical Products: A Critique of The Learned Intermediary Rule, 12 Oxford J. Legal Stud. 59 (1992); Notes, 51 Stan. L. Rev. 1543 (2001) (learned intermediary doctrine and patient package inserts); 75 N.Y.U. L. Rev. 1452 (2000) (failure to warn liability for online prescriptions); D. Owen, Products Liability Law § 9.6 (2d ed. 2008); 1 D. Owen, M.S. Madden, & M. Davis, Madden & Owen on Products Liability ch. 22 (3d ed. 2000).

14. Unavoidable Dangers. The issue of responsibility for unforeseeable risks in prescription drugs is treated in ch. 11, below.

CHAPTER 9

REGULATING DEFECTIVENESS

1. DIRECT AGENCY REGULATION

A number of federal agencies directly regulate product safety, notably the CPSC (consumer products), NHTSA (automobiles), OSHA (industrial products), and the FDA (pharmaceutical drugs and medical devices). When an agency promulgates a major safety regulation, particularly if it significantly affects how manufacturers may design a product, the regulation may be challenged in the courts.

Southland Mower Co. v. Consumer Product Safety Commission

United States Court of Appeals, Fifth Circuit, 1980.
619 F.2d 499.

Petitions for Review of an Order of the Consumer Product Safety Commission.

■ GEE, CIRCUIT JUDGE:

Approximately 77,000 people are injured each year in the United States by contacting the blades of walk-behind power mowers.[1] Of these injuries, an estimated 9,900 involve the amputation of at least one finger or toe, 11,400 involve fractures, 2,400 involve avulsions (the tearing of flesh or a body part), 2,300 involve contusions, and 51,400 involve lacerations. The annual economic cost inflicted by the 77,000 yearly blade-contact injuries has been estimated to be about $253 million. This figure does not include monetary compensation for pain and suffering or for the lost use of amputated fingers and toes.[2]

To reduce these blade-contact injuries, the Consumer Product Safety Commission ("CPSC" or "the Commission") promulgated[3] a Safety Stan-

---

1. 44 Fed. Reg. 9990, 10030 (1979). The estimates are based on 1977 data.

2. Id.

3. The gestation period for the safety standard was long and complex. The administrative process was initiated on August 15, 1973, when, pursuant to § 10 of the CPSA, 15 U.S.C. § 2059, the Outdoor Power Equipment Institute, Inc. (OPEI) petitioned the

CPSC to begin a proceeding to develop a consumer product safety standard addressing the hazards of power lawn mowers and asked the Commission to adopt a voluntary standard, ANSI B71.1–1972, "Safety Specifications for Power Lawn Mowers, Lawn & Garden Tractors, & Lawn Tractors," approved by the American National Standards Institute, Inc. as the proposed consumer product

dard for Walk–Behind Power Lawn Mowers, 16 C.F.R. Part 1205 (1979), 44 Fed. Reg. 9990–10031 (Feb. 15, 1979), pursuant to section 7 of the Consumer Product Safety Act ("CPSA" or "the Act"), 15 U.S.C. § 2056 (1976).[4] In the present case we consider petitions by the Outdoor Power Equipment Institute ("OPEI"), manufacturers of power lawn mowers,[5] and an interested consumer to review[6] the Safety Standard for Walk–Behind Power Lawn Mowers.

safety standard. On November 16, 1973, the Commission, after considering information about injuries associated with power lawn mowers, granted that portion of OPEI's petition that requested a proceeding to develop the power lawn mower safety standard. The Commission denied OPEI's request to publish ANSI B71.1–1972, with amendments, as a proposed consumer product safety standard, however.

Instead, the Commission solicited offers to develop a standard pursuant to § 7(b) of the CPSA, 15 U.S.C. § 2056(b). Subsequently, the Commission selected Consumers Union of United States, Inc. (CU) to develop the safety standard. See 39 Fed. Reg. 37803 (1974). As the offeror, CU gave representatives of industry, consumers, and other interests the opportunity to participate in developing the standard. It submitted the resulting proposal to the Commission on July 17, 1975. The recommended standard comprehensively addressed all types of lawn mowers and lawn mower injuries and contained requirements relating to blade-contact and thrown-object injuries, as well as injuries resulting from lawn mowers' slipping, rolling, overturning, or failing to steer or brake, injuries caused by burns from direct contact with exposed heated surfaces of mowers or from fires ignited by lawn mower ignition fluids, and injuries caused by electric shock from electrically powered lawn mowers or electric ignition systems.

After analyzing the recommended CU standard, on May 5, 1977, the Commission published a proposed comprehensive power lawn mower safety standard for public comment. 42 Fed. Reg. 23052 (1977). The proposal elicited more than 100 initial comments, and the Commission solicited and received further comments on these already submitted comments. 42 Fed. Reg. 34892 (1977). On June 7, 1978, the Commission published a notice that it would issue requirements addressing injuries from blade contact with walk-behind power mowers before issuing separate standards dealing with injuries asso-

ciated with thrown objects, fuel and electrical hazards, and riding mowers. 43 Fed. Reg. 24697 (1978). In November 1978, the Commission requested additional comments on the safety and reliability of brake-clutch mechanisms. 43 Fed. Reg. 51638 (1978). On February 26, 1979, Part 1205—Safety Standard for Walk–Behind Power Lawn Mowers, applying only to blade-contact injuries from walk-behind power lawn mowers, was issued, to become effective December 31, 1981.

4. 15 U.S.C. § 2056(a)(1976) provides:

(a) The Commission may by rule, in accordance with this section and section 2058 of this title, promulgate consumer product safety standards. A consumer product safety standard shall consist of one or more of any of the following types of requirements:

(1) Requirements as to performance, composition, contents, design, construction, finish, or packaging of a consumer product.

(2) Requirements that a consumer product be marked with or accompanied by clear and adequate warnings or instructions, or requirements respecting the form of warnings or instructions.

Any requirement of such a standard shall be reasonably necessary to prevent or reduce an unreasonable risk of injury associated with such product. The requirements of such a standard (other than requirements relating to labeling, warnings, or instructions) shall, whenever feasible, be expressed in terms of performance requirements.

5. For convenience, we shall refer to the lawn mower industry petitioners collectively as OPEI.

6. Review of a safety standard by this court is authorized by § 11 of the CPSA, 15

The standard consists of three principal provisions: a requirement that rotary walk-behind power mowers pass a foot-probe test, 16 C.F.R. § 1205.4, 44 Fed. Reg. 10025–26, a requirement that rotary machines have a blade-control system that will stop the mower blade within three seconds after the operator's hands leave their normal operating position, 16 C.F.R. § 1205.5(a), 44 Fed. Reg. 10029, and a requirement, applicable to both rotary and reel-type mowers, that the product have a label of specified design to warn of the danger of blade contact, 16 C.F.R. § 1205.6, 44 Fed. Reg. 10029–30. * * *

Foot-Probe and Shielding Requirements

The standard mandates that walk-behind power rotary mowers pass a foot-probe test designed to assure that the machine guards the operator's feet against injuries caused by contact with the moving blade. The test requires that a probe simulating a human foot be inserted along the rear 120 degrees of the mower and at the discharge chute without coming into contact with the blade when inserted. 16 C.F.R. § 1205.4, 44 Fed. Reg. 10025–26. See also Fed.Reg. 10001–10002. Mowers meet the foot-probe test by having shields that prevent the probe from entering the blade's path. 16 C.F.R. § 1205(a)(1), 44 Fed. Reg. 10025.

OPEI does not deny that a foot-probe test for the rear area of the mower is reasonably necessary to reduce injuries. Rather, it asserts that application of the test to the discharge chute is not supported by substantial record evidence. It alleges that the injury data does not show that foot injuries occur at that location and that it would be theoretically impossible for an operator to suffer a foot injury at the discharge chute while holding the "deadman's" blade-control[17] switch on the mower handle.[18]

The Act requires that safety standards be supported by "substantial evidence on the record as a whole." 15 U.S.C. § 2060(c). The foot-probe provision can be sustained only if the record contains " 'such relevant evidence as a reasonable mind might accept as adequate to support a conclusion' " that an unreasonable risk of foot injury exists from blade-contact at the discharge chute, that the foot-probe test will ameliorate it, and that the benefits of this proposed reform make it reasonable in light of the burdens it imposes on product manufacturers and consumers. Aqua Slide 'N' Dive v. Consumer Product Safety Commission, 569 F.2d 831, 838–

U.S.C. § 2060 (1976).

    17. A deadman control refers to a device on the mower handle that requires continuous pressure to sustain rotation of the mower blades. Only if the operator can reach the discharge chute with his foot while holding the mower handle can he suffer blade-contact injuries at the discharge chute by mowers meeting the blade-stop requirement. Discharge-chute foot injuries suffered after the operator has released the mower handle

and deadman's controls are addressed in the standard's blade-stop provision.

    18. The rear 120 degrees of the mower and the discharge chute were selected for the foot-probe test because the Commission found that they are "areas where foot contact injuries are known to occur while the operator is holding the [mower] handle. Foot contact injuries that occur while the operator is not holding the handle will be addressed by the blade control. . . ." 44 Fed. Reg. 9993.

40 (5th Cir.1978) [hereinafter cited as *Aqua Slide*] (quoting Consolidated Edison Co. v. NLRB, 305 U.S. 197 (1938)).

The determination of whether an unreasonable risk of discharge-chute injury exists involves "a balancing test like that familiar in tort law: The regulation may issue if the severity of the injury that may result from the product, factored by the likelihood of the injury, offsets the harm the regulation imposes upon manufacturers and consumers." *Aqua Slide*, 569 F.2d at 839. [Citations.] Thus, under the unreasonable risk balancing test, even a very remote possibility that a product would inflict an extremely severe injury could pose an "unreasonable risk of injury" if the proposed safety standard promised to reduce the risk effectively without unduly increasing the product's price or decreasing its availability or usefulness. *Aqua Slide,* 569 F.2d at 839–40.[22] Conversely, if the potential injury is less severe, its occurrence must be proven more likely in order to render the risk unreasonable and the safety standard warranted.

In the present case, the discharge-chute probe is intended to reduce the risk of such injuries as amputation of toes, fractures of bones in the feet or toes, avulsions, deep lacerations, and contusions. While the seriousness of these injuries cannot be gainsaid, it does not rise to the level of gravity that would render almost any risk, however remote, unreasonable if the risk could be reduced effectively by the proposed regulation.[23] Substantial evidence that such injury is significantly likely to occur is therefore necessary to sustain this portion of the lawn mower safety standard.

Our examination of the record has failed to reveal substantial evidence that injury at the discharge chute was sufficiently probable that it made the risk addressed by the foot probe of this area unreasonable. In a study of 36 blade-contact foot injuries conducted for the CPSC by the National Electronic Injury Surveillance System (NEISS),[24] one injury occurred when

---

22. For example, in *Aqua Slide* this court ruled that the severity of paraplegic injury from swimming pool slides was so great that a one in ten million risk of such injury, which is less than the risk that an average person will be killed by lightning, would be an "unreasonable risk" if the proposed safety standard "actually promised to reduce the risk without unduly hampering the availability of the slides or decreasing their utility.... "569 F.2d at 840. The court found, however, that the necessary showing of the standard's effectiveness had not been made and that the burdens the regulation would impose had not been adequately evaluated. Id. at 840–44.

23. Cf. *Aqua Slide,* 569 F.2d at 840 (remote risk of paraplegia could be unreasonable under CPSA); Bunny Bear, Inc. v. Peterson, 473 F.2d at 1006–07 (harm of burns or smoke inhalation, including death, from crib

fires was sufficiently great to justify requirement that crib mattress pass a "cigarette test" by not igniting when touched with cigarette, when possibility existed that adult attending child might drop lighted cigarette on mattress) [although possibility of babies smoking, and dropping cigarettes, remote].

24. NEISS collects data from selected hospitals and reports them to the CPSC. The system, which has been operational since July 1, 1972, was designed to develop statistically valid, rationally representative product-related injury data. It employs a computer-based network of 119 statistically selected hospital emergency rooms located throughout the country. 15 U.S.C. §§ 2054, 2055. See "Draft Hazard Analysis of Power Mower Related Injuries & Analysis of Proposed Power Mower Standard," U.S. CPSC, Bureau of Epidemiology (March 1977), at pp. 3–5. The Commission also obtains injury information

the operator inserted his foot into the blade path at the discharge chute while holding the mower handle. This injury represented almost three percent of the blade-contact foot injuries in the sample. However, the study did not involve a random sample, and it is not possible to extrapolate the percentage of total blade-contact injuries represented by discharge-chute incidents involving the operator's feet from the limited information furnished in the record. In any event, trustworthy statistical inferences cannot be drawn from a single incident of discharge-chute injury. Without reliable evidence of the likely number of injuries that would be addressed by application of the foot-probe test to the discharge chute, we are unable to agree that this provision is reasonably necessary to reduce or prevent an unreasonable risk of injury.

* * * We therefore vacate that part of the standard requiring the discharge-chute area of power lawn mowers to pass a foot-probe test. [The court also reviewed and upheld certain shielding requirements that supplemented the foot-probe test.]

Blade-Control System

The second key element of the standard requires a blade-control system that (1) will prevent the blade from rotating unless the operator activates a control, (2) allows the blade to be driven only if the operator remains in continuous contact with the "deadman's" control, and (3) causes the blade to stop moving within three seconds after the deadman's control is released. 16 C.F.R. § 1205.5. * * *

The blade-control system is intended to protect the operator against blade-contact injuries to both hands and feet by stopping the blade before the operator can contact it after he or she leaves the normal operating position and thus releases the deadman's control.[31] The Commission estimates that the blade-control provisions will eliminate approximately 46,500 operator blade-contact injuries a year. This figure represents approximately 60 percent of all blade-contact injuries and nearly 80 percent of all injuries claimed to be reduced by the standard. As OPEI acknowledges, the blade-control requirements thus are the "centerpiece" of the Commission's strategy for reducing blade-contact injuries.

Perhaps as befits its importance in the regulatory scheme promulgated by the Commission, the blade-control system is vigorously attacked by both

from in-depth investigations (IDI's) of particular accidents reported through the NEISS network. IDI's conducted by the Commission, unlike basic NEISS accident data, are not statistically representative of all injuries in a particular product category. IDI's do, however, provide details concerning the sequence of events involved in the injury not available from NEISS surveillance information. Id. at 5. To overcome this deficiency, the Commission weighted IDI cases involving specified types of injuries to derive an adjusted IDI sample that conforms to NEISS data.

31.   For example, when the operator releases the deadman's control and approaches the blade area to clear the path of the mower, unclog a blocked discharge chute, adjust the wheels, or empty a grass catcher, the blade will stop rotating within three seconds. According to the Commission, by the time the operator reached the danger zone the blade would have stopped, or significantly slowed, thus preventing or minimizing injury.

OPEI and consumer proponents of stricter safety requirements. OPEI asserts that the blade-control system provision is expressed as a design requirement, rather than as a performance requirement, in violation of the Act. It argues that a number of alternative requirements are available that are less design restrictive and more performance oriented than the blade-stop criterion and that the Commission therefore erred in adopting the blade-stop approach. OPEI further contends that the standard is unreasonable because it requires the use of mechanisms that allegedly are not safe or reliable. And, OPEI claims, the three-second stopping time is unreasonably short. In contrast, consumer advocate John O. Hayward maintains that the three-second blade-stopping time is too lax and that substantial evidence demonstrates that only a two-second or shorter blade-stopping time is justified.

The CPSA directs that a safety standard's provisions "shall, whenever feasible, be expressed in terms of performance requirements." 15 U.S.C. § 2056(a). The statutory preference[32] for performance requirements is rooted in the belief that this mode of regulation stimulates product innovation, promotes the search for cost-effective means of compliance, and fosters competition by offering consumers a range of choices in the marketplace, while design-restrictive rules tend to freeze technology, stifle research aimed at better and cheaper compliance measures, and deprive consumers of the opportunity to choose among competing designs. See S.Rep.No.92–835, 92d Cong., 2d Sess. 30, U.S.Code Cong. & Admin.News 1972, p. 4573; [citation omitted.]

Although only a limited number of designs can satisfy the blade-stop provision, we find this part of the standard is nonetheless a performance requirement. While the standard mandates that mower blades stop within a specified time period, it does not dictate a specific means of fulfilling this condition. Manufacturers are neither formally nor practically restricted to employing a particular design, since two existing mechanisms, a blade-disengagement system employing a brake-clutch device and an engine-stop system, are capable of passing the blade-stop test.

We also find that the Commission did not act improperly in failing to formulate a safety standard that would have allowed lawn mowers to be equipped with safety devices based on concepts of blade inaccessibility or blade harmlessness[33] as alternatives to blade-stop safety mechanisms. The

32. While the statute favors performance requirements when feasible, it does not prohibit design standards when they are appropriate. 15 U.S.C. § 2056(a)(1) provides that the Commission may promulgate safety standards of the following types: "[r]equirements as to performance, composition, contents, *design,* construction, finish, or packaging of a consumer product" (emphasis added).

33. As their names imply, safety mechanisms based on "blade inaccessibility" are designed to prevent contact with the moving blade by making it virtually impossible for a consumer to reach the blade with hands or feet by removing all controls from the blade area and eliminating the discharge chute. Devices based on "blade harmlessness" would employ grass-cutting means other than the standard rigid or semi-rigid blades that would not inflict serious injury if touched while in operation. It should be noted that the present standard already exempts such innovative, blade-harmless mowers as those

CPSC did consider blade harmlessness and blade inaccessibility requirements but did not develop and adopt these alternative measures as part of the standard because it found that they were not feasible means of reducing or eliminating the risk of blade-contact injury at the time the standard was issued. * * *

We turn now to the issue of whether substantial evidence supports the selection of three seconds as the time limit within which blades must stop. The Commission based the three-second blade-stop time limit primarily upon four time-motion studies of operator-blade access time. These experiments were designed to measure the interval between the moment the operator released the deadman's control and the instant he or she reached the mower blade. One study of operator-blade access data collected at the University of Iowa in 1971 and analyzed by the National Bureau of Standards in 1975 showed that operators reached the blade hazard point after moving directly to it from the mower's rear in times ranging from 2.0 to 3.5 seconds.[38] A second operator-blade access study, using 100 subjects ranging in age from 16–62 with a mean age of 35, was conducted by Consumer's Union at Eckerd College in St. Petersburg, Florida, on March 5–7, 1975. The participants were tested using a reaction-time device designed to simulate a walk-behind power lawn mower. Each participant underwent 25 trials, for a total of 2,500 time-motion incidents. A December 7, 1976, summary of this Eckerd College Study reported that operator access time ranged from 1.66 to 4.90 seconds[39] for normal, as opposed to intentionally fast, movements. This summary cited data from trials using 12 and 15 subjects, aged 18–21. The Final Report on the Eckerd College Study, issued in May 1977, shows operator access time for the 100 participants as ranging from .6 to 3.3 seconds. The discrepancy is not explained. A third blade-access study using five subjects was conducted by the Office of the Medical Director (OMD) of the CPSC. In this experiment, direct, "casual" approach time ranged from 2.35 to 3.3 seconds, with an average time of 2.81 seconds.[40] OMD also recorded intentionally fast direct access times. These ranged from 1.26 to 2.5 seconds, with an average access time

using monofilament "blades" from the standard's safety requirements. 16 C.F.R. § 1205.3(a)(1); 44 Fed.Reg. at 9993.

38. In eight trials, as analyzed in 1975, operators reached the blade in the following times (in seconds): 2, 3, 3, 2.5, 3.5, 2, 2.5, 3. (An earlier analysis performed by the NBS in 1974 and revised by the 1975 analysis had found that the access time ranged from 2.5 to 7.0 seconds. More accurate measurement methods used in the later study appear to account for the discrepancy.) It was recognized that the Iowa study was of limited value, however, because it employed machines that did not conform to the industry's voluntary standard in that they had shorter discharge chutes than the ANSI code now permits for current models. As a result, these

blade-access times may have been shorter than access to the blades of current mower models. It should be noted, however, that figures derived from the other studies are in reasonable agreement with those of the University of Iowa test and that the test was not without some evidentiary value.

39. The data table attached to the summary shows that the longest blade-access time was 5.65 seconds, not 4.90 seconds. The discrepancy is not explained.

40. Blade-access times for the direct, casual approach test were: for subject A, 2.89 and 2.75 seconds; for subject B, 3.14 and 2.95 seconds; for subject C, 2.43 seconds; for subject D, 2.60 and 2.35 seconds; and for subject E, 2.90 and 3.30 seconds.

of 1.79 seconds.[41] In addition, OMD tested subjects' access times when they approached the discharge chute blade area by going around the opposite side and front of the mower. The access time in the indirect, casual approach test ranged from 3.64 to 4.70 seconds, with an average time of 4.25 seconds.[42] Operator-access time in the indirect, hurried approach test fell between 2.48 and 3.68 seconds, with an average of 2.98 seconds.[43] The record contains only preliminary findings from the fourth empirical examination of operator blade-access times. This study was undertaken by the National Bureau of Standards. "[A] superficial examination of the limited observational data" was reported to show an average blade-access time of under three seconds.

In setting the blade-stop time, the Commission considered not only the time in which an operator could reach the blade after releasing the deadman's control but also the incremental cost of successively faster blade-stop times. The record contains substantial evidence that the cost of blade-stop mechanisms varies inversely with the length of time in which the device stops the blade,[44] so that a three-second blade-stop requirement will be cheaper to implement than a one-or two-second time limit.

We find that the three-second blade-stop requirement is not too lax, contrary to petitioner Hayward's claim. The three-second measure will protect consumers against many, although certainly not all, blade-contact injuries. While the Commission may not rely upon mere "common sense" or speculation to establish the *existence* of an *unreasonable risk* of injury, it may exercise considerable discretion in determining an appropriate *remedy*. The Commission was entitled to consider the incremental cost of requiring

---

41. Blade-access times for the direct, intentionally fast approach test were: for subject A, 1.26 and 1.59 seconds; for subject B, 2.21 and 2.20 seconds; for subject C, 1.43 and 1.35 seconds; for subject D, 1.80 and 1.49 seconds; and for subject E, 2.52 and 2.05 seconds.

42. In this test, subject A had access times of 3.64 and 3.88 seconds; subject B, 4.52 and 4.18 seconds; subject C, 4.39 seconds; subject D, no recorded time; and subject E, 4.42 and 4.70 seconds.

43. Here access times were 2.60 and 2.48 for subject A; none recorded for subject B; 3.45 and 3.02 for subject C; 2.63 for subject D; and 3.68 for subject E.

44. A report by the Stanford Research Institute (SRI), "An Economic Analysis of the Proposed Consumers Union Power Mower Safety Standard" (April 1975), stated that the projected cost increases for walk-behind power mowers attributable to the blade-stop requirement would be $90–115 if the stop time were 3.0–4.9 seconds but only $75–100 per mower if the stop time were 5.0–6.0 seconds. In another 1977 study, SRI estimated that a 3–second blade-stop requirement would cost $16.50 more per mower than a 5–second test for manual start rotary mowers and $10.50 more per mower for electric start mowers. The Consumers Union Economic Support Study estimated roughly that the marginal per mower cost of a mechanism would be $10, while a 5–second blade-stop requirement would permit a $2 per mower savings over a 3–second blade clutch. OPEI submitted comparative incremental retail costs in September 1977 that stated that, for gas-powered rotary mowers with electric start mechanisms, a 7–second stop requirement would cost $5 per mower without "easy restart," and a 3–second brake-clutch device would cost $13.50 per mower. For gas-powered rotary mowers with manual starts, OPEI's cost estimate was $10 for a mower meeting a 7–second stop requirement, $15 for a mower having a 5–second engine kill with easy restart, and $34.50 for a 3–second brake-clutch system.

a shorter blade-stop time in rejecting a one-or two-second blade-stop solution. The standard need not guarantee protection for all consumers; it is sufficient that it promises greater safety for consumers and is reasonably necessary to *reduce* the risk of blade-contact injuries.

Correspondingly, we find no merit in OPEI's contention that the requirement of a three-second stopping time is unreasonably demanding. OPEI strenuously urges that the empirical studies cannot support a three-second blade-stop limit because they unrealistically fail to account for such psychological factors as a person's fear of a noisily operating machine and resulting reluctance to approach it. OPEI argues that these conditions would tend to make the operator stay away from the blade area for a longer time than was recorded in the artificial tests and perhaps until all noise and vibration from a moving blade ceases. OPEI also argues that the three-second requirement is not reasonable because a blade that is not moving under power would be decelerating and thus would inflict less damage than a fully powered blade.

The Commission properly rejected these contentions. The record contained neither suggestions for devising a test to measure psychological factors nor evidence indicating that in more "realistic" circumstances operator access to blades would be slower than registered in the time-motion studies. No deceleration curve information was cited to substantiate the claim that between three and seven seconds after power shut-off a blade would be coasting slowly, and no available test can accurately determine the blade velocity at which a risk of injury is reasonable.

We are also unpersuaded by OPEI's contention that current technology is inadequate safely to achieve a three-second blade-stop time. OPEI asserts that this requirement can only be met by using brake-clutch systems, which it alleges are unreliable and unsafe. * * *

Most convincing proof that safe and reliable three-second blade-stop mowers are currently feasible is the fact that, at the time the standard was issued, at least two mower manufacturers were currently producing and marketing mowers that had a brake-clutch mechanism complying with the standard. As one of these manufacturers declared, that such mowers are offered for sale demonstrates their manufacturer's belief in the safety and reliability of this type of brake-clutch mechanism. In addition, the evidence established that a brake clutch is basically a simple device that is widely used with safety and reliability in the production of automobiles and other types of machinery, such as chainsaws. The technology associated with brake clutches is therefore highly developed, and comments presented to the Commission made clear that potential difficulties with the particular application of various types of brake-clutch devices to power lawn mowers can be identified and resolved with present technical knowledge.

This evidence provides substantial support for the Commission's judgment that technology is available to design, produce, and assemble brake-clutch power lawn mowers that are unlikely to fail in an unsafe manner. * * * The three-second blade-stop time is therefore valid. [Citations.]

Labeling Requirement

The safety standard directs that both reel-type and rotary-power walk-behind lawn mowers carry a label of specified design. The label, which is to be placed on the blade housing or other blade shielding, states "DANGER, KEEP HANDS and FEET AWAY." It also contains a pictorial representation of a red, blade-like object cutting into the forefinger of an extended, black hand. 16 C.F.R. § 1205.6. The portrait of the blade and hand does not depict the hand as bleeding or dismembered.

* * * [T]he Commission acted permissibly under section 7 in ordering manufacturers to furnish mowers with warning labels. The record clearly establishes that an unreasonable risk of blade-contact injury exists. The warning label directly addresses this risk of injury by warning operators and bystanders to keep hands and feet from the area in which the blade is accessible. It is true that the standard's shielding and blade-stop requirements also address the risk of blade-contact injury, but there is no claim that these prophylactic measures will be fail-safe. Thus, the Commission properly concluded that there was a *need* for labeling as a safety measure.

The *reasonableness* of the labeling requirement is also supported by the record. The Commission systematically tested various warning labels, and those with designs similar to the label required by the standard were found effective in communicating the risk of danger from moving blades. Significantly, the Commission found that the labeling requirement would impose little, if any, additional cost. The industry's voluntary standard already requires a warning label, and the mandatory label would be no more burdensome. Its contents are not shocking or gruesomely explicit and would not pose an unwarranted deterrent to potential purchasers of lawn mowers. [Citations.]

[W]e hold that the labeling requirement is reasonably necessary to reduce an unreasonable risk of injury.

Finding of Reasonable Necessity and Public Interest

In the preceding discussion, we have examined the petitioners' challenges to specific provisions of the standard and have found several of the complaints unfounded. However, OPEI also contends that the standard as a whole is not supported by substantial record evidence. It claims that the Commission based its determination that the standard was "reasonably necessary" and would produce a net benefit to society upon a document, "Economic Impact of Blade Contact Requirements for Power Mowers" ("the economic report"), which was unreliable because its methodology was fatally flawed, and its findings had never been exposed to public scrutiny in the administrative rule making process. Petitioner Hayward also criticizes the Commission's evaluation of the standard's net social benefit. He argues that the CPSC undervalued the safety benefits of the standard by erroneously failing to place a monetary value on the pain and suffering inflicted by the injuries that the rule was expected to reduce.

The Commission seeks to counter OPEI's broad attack on the standard by defending the final economic report's data and methodology and by asserting that the report was, in essence, merely a revision of earlier cost-benefit analyses of shielding and blade-stop requirements in light of additional evidence introduced into the record by OPEI. The Commission further contends that it adequately considered pain and suffering in evaluating the standard's benefits and that it was not required to quantify these aspects of the cost of lawn mower accidents.

We have carefully scrutinized the record and find that substantial evidence supports the conclusion that the safety benefits expected from the standard bear a reasonable relationship to its costs and make the standard reasonably necessary and in the public interest. The cost-benefit analysis contained in the final economic report and adopted by the standard, 44 Fed.Reg. at 10020–21, 10030, is not methodologically flawed. The Commission estimated that the regulations would raise the retail price of a complying lawn mower $35, costing the consumer $4.40 per year over the projected eight-year life of the mower. Total yearly compliance costs were believed to be $189 million for 5.4 million mower units (1978 production estimate). Blade-contact injuries were calculated to cost $253 million annually, exclusive of pain and suffering. Since, as we have noted, there are approximately 77,000 blade-contact injuries from walk-behind power mowers each year, each injury costs about $3,300, without counting the cost of pain and suffering. Currently there are some 40 million mowers in use by consumers, so that a consumer has about one chance in 500 (1/520) of incurring an injury costing $3,300, exclusive of pain and suffering. The standard's injury cost associated with each mower without the safety features is thus $6.35 per year. The Commission anticipated that implementation of the standard would reduce this injury cost by 83 percent, for an annual savings of $5.30 per mower, exclusive of the savings of pain and suffering costs. Because the standard would result in a net benefit of $.90, a mower meeting the standard's safety requirements would represent a worthwhile investment for the consumer, and the standard's implementation is in the best interests of society.

OPEI questions this analysis by asserting that, given an eight-year mower life, full compliance with the standard will take eight years because only one-eighth of all mowers will be replaced each year. As a result, only one-eighth of the total 83 percent estimated injury cost reduction attributed to the standard will be achieved after the standard's first year, with an additional one-eighth of the projected savings being achieved for each succeeding year until full compliance is had. From this observation, OPEI reasons that a complying mower will reduce injury costs by a mere $.70 after one year and not by the $5.30 projected by the Commission in justifying the standard. OPEI derived the $.70 per mower savings figure by reducing both the number of annual injuries and their total costs by one-eighth in determining a $5.65 per mower injury costs after one year, rather than the Commission's estimated annual injury cost of $6.35 per mower. OPEI then subtracted the $5.65 from the $6.35 to ascertain the savings in per mower injury cost after one year. On the basis of this calculation, OPEI claims that after one year a consumer will have paid $4.40 to reduce his mower injury costs by only $.70 and that the standard thus imposes an unreasonable expense on the consumer.

OPEI's attack on the cost-benefit analysis underpinning the standard is misconceived. It fails to recognize that only purchasers of complying mowers will pay the $4.40 annual cost for the standard's safety features and that these owners will receive the full benefit of the standard's anticipated effectiveness in reducing their injury costs for each year of the mower's life. OPEI's cost-benefit assessment thereby erroneously substitutes a figure representing the injury savings per mower in use, whether complying or not, for the amount of injury savings for owners of complying mowers, which is the relevant calculation. The correct analysis employed by the Commission to support the standard demonstrates its reasonable necessity in reducing the risk of blade-contact accidents. Because the economic findings establish that the standard is in the public interest even absent reliance upon the costs of pain and suffering, we need not determine whether the Commission must assign a dollar value to these aspects of the cost of accidents when precise calculation of their cost is not crucial for determining whether a standard is reasonably necessary and in the public interest. The methodology of the standard's supporting findings as to the costs and benefits of its requirements is sustained.

We also find that the evidence in the 1979 final economic report supporting the standard's cost effectiveness is reliable. In this report the Commission ultimately found that the standard would cost $189 million annually to implement, would prevent $211 million in yearly injury costs when full compliance was achieved, and would save $26.4 million after one year, assuming that the costs of accidents remained constant. The Commission's final economic analysis of the standard used data from fiscal year 1977 to compute an annual blade-contact injury cost of $253 million, exclusive of pain and suffering costs, caused by an estimated 77,000 injuries.

* * *

In summary, the standard's scope and its requirements that mowers pass a rear foot-probe test, shield-strength and obstruction tests, satisfy a three-second blade-stop criterion, and carry a prescribed warning label are upheld. The Commission's conclusion that the standard is reasonably necessary and in the public interest is also valid. The standard's requirement that mowers pass a discharge chute foot-probe test is not justified by substantial evidence on the record as a whole and is therefore vacated.

Affirmed in part, vacated in part.

NOTES

1. The power mower regulations are set forth in 16 CFR Part 1205 (2006). Do they appear to be in the public interest? What do you suppose really motivated the industry to challenge them in court?

2. Burch v. Sears, Roebuck and Co., 467 A.2d 615 (Pa. Super. Ct.1983), held that the absence of a deadman's device could render a power mower defective in design.

3. Reconsider the design defect cases previously covered. Might some of these accidents have been prevented by safety regulations? What might such regulations have provided? How should an agency go about determining (a) what type of safety regulations are needed, and (b) what, specifically, such regulations should provide? The OPEI in *Southland Mower* challenged the blade-contact requirement, in part, because it was a design, and not performance, standard and 15 U.S.C. § 2056(a) stated that standards "shall, whenever feasible, be expressed in terms of performance requirements." See footnote 4. The CPSA was amended in the 1980s to authorize only performance and warning, but not design, requirements. Why would Congress prohibit the CPSA from promulgating design standards?

4. Since its inception in the early 1970s, the CPSC has promulgated only a small number of safety standards, unlike NHTSA regarding automotive safety. In view of the vast number of product hazards, why do you suppose this is so?

5. Europe *vs*. America. Except, perhaps, for drugs and aircraft, product safety regulation plays a much greater role (and post-accident litigation a much smaller role) in the U.K. and Europe than in the U.S. European regulatory efforts, spurred by the thalidomide tragedy in the 1960s, accelerated with a European Community General Product Safety Directive in 1992, extended in 2001. See Directives 92/59/EEC and 2001/95/EC. Should the U.S. devote more resources to accident *prevention* through product safety regulation? Commensurately, should we devote less resources to product accident litigation?

6. Who should set product safety standards? Governmental regulators, subject to judicial review on rationality and fairness grounds? Manufacturers, subject to judicial review on products liability grounds? Both? Or do the existing legal mechanisms need a fundamental restructuring? See generally Pierce, Encouraging Safety: The Limits of Tort Law and Government Regulation, 33 Vand.L.Rev. 1281 (1980); Sugarman, Doing Away with Tort Law, 73 Cal.L.Rev. 555 (1985).

7. Governmental agencies must comply with a variety of administrative procedures in fulfilling their statutory mandates as required by the Administrative Procedures Act, 5 U.S.C. pt. I, ch. 5 (2000). Federal regulatory agency action is occasionally challenged as inconsistent with statutory authority and, therefore, contrary to Congress' intent in adopting the regulatory scheme. A number of product safety standards have been challenged on these grounds. See, e.g., Motor Vehicle Mfrs. Ass'n v. State Farm Mut. Auto Ins. Co., 463 U.S. 29 (1983)(challenge to Federal Motor Vehicle Safety Standard 208 requiring passive restraint systems in automobiles; standard rejected in part); Public Citizen v. Mineta, 340 F.3d 39 (2d Cir. 2003)(challenge to Federal Motor Vehicle Safety Standard 138 requiring tire pressure monitoring systems; standard rejected in part).

8. Other Regulatory Authority. A federal agency may have statutory authority over a regulated industry in addition to standard-setting. A major responsibility of the CPSC, for example, is its authority to recall products that pose a "substantial risk of injury" to the public. 15 U.S.C. § 2064. The CPSA imposes reporting obligations on product manufacturers to "immediately inform the [CPSC]" when it obtains information which "reasonably supports the conclusion that [a] product . . . creates an unreasonable risk of serious injury or death." The CPSC has a variety of remedies to pursue against a manufacturer to address such a risk, including requiring a recall campaign.

In United States v. Mirama Enters., 387 F.3d 983 (9th Cir. 2004), the CPSC filed a civil action against a home products distributor who allegedly knew that a juicer it distributed might shatter during use. The distributor failed to report known accidents immediately to the CPSC. Civil penalties are authorized for "knowingly" violating the Act, including its reporting requirements. 15 U.S.C. § 2069. The CPSC obtained summary judgment against the distributor. The trial court discussed the reporting requirement:

> This reporting requirement was imposed upon consumer product manufacturers to protect the public health and safety—the sooner the Commission knows of a potential problem, the sooner it can investigate and take necessary action. "This notification requirement was statutorily imposed upon manufacturers . . . because they are often the first to receive information about hazardous consumer products." United States v. Athlone Indus., Inc., 746 F.2d 977, 982 (3d Cir.1984). . . . The Commission set forth a "Statement of Enforcement Policy" to provide "additional clarification to help firms meet the reporting requirements" of the Act. 49 Fed. Reg. 13820. The Commission's guidelines instruct companies: "When in doubt, firms should report. Firms should clearly err on the side of over-reporting, rather than under-reporting." Id. at 13822.
>
> The thrust of the Act is clearly for firms to quickly inform the Commission as soon as they might "reasonably believe" that their product, through defect or otherwise, poses a significant threat to consumers. Upon receipt of "first information", a company is required to report *within 24 hours* to the Commission. 16 C.F.R. § 1115.14(c) and (e). Companies are advised that they "should not await complete or accurate risk estimates before reporting. . . ." Id. at (c).

Mirama, 185 F. Supp. 2d 1148, 1158 (S.D. Cal. 2002).

The Court found that the defendant was in receipt of overwhelming evidence which required immediate reporting. For example, one consumer sent a letter in February 1998 stating that his juicer "suddenly exploded, throwing with great violence pieces of the clear plastic cover and shreds of the razor-sharp separator screen as far as eight feet." Id. at 1153. The distributor did not report the hazards to the CPSC until November 1998. The Court of Appeals affirmed the $300,000 in penalties assessed.

9. Regulating Warnings. Agencies are often authorized to require manufacturers use warnings of product hazards as a means to reduce them. As discussed in *Southland Mower,* the CPSC is authorized to promulgate product safety standards requiring products to be accompanied by "clear and adequate" warnings. See 15 U.S.C.A. § 2056. An instructive case brought by a manufacturer against the Commission challenging a proposed warnings requirement was Aqua Slide 'N' Dive Corp. v. Consumer Product Safety Commission, 569 F.2d 831 (5th Cir.1978), discussed and relied on in *Southland Mower.* In 1973, the Commission was petitioned by industry representatives to establish a safety standard for swimming pool slides. In January 1976, the Commission proposed such a standard, citing the fact that adult users of swimming pool slides who slide headfirst into the water encounter a one in ten million risk of spinal injury and paralysis as a result of striking the bottom of the pool. The proposed standard required that such slides be installed in water greater than four feet in depth and that various warning signs be provided. The standard also prescribed that ladder chains be installed on slides used in deeper water, together with an appropriate warning sign concerning the risk of drowning, to discourage use by smaller children. The warnings proposed in the standard provided in part:

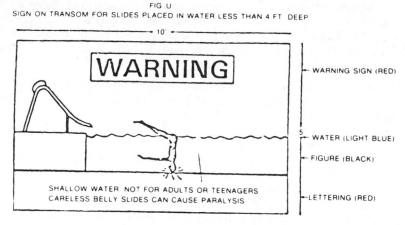

FIG U
SIGN ON TRANSOM FOR SLIDES PLACED IN WATER LESS THAN 4 FT DEEP

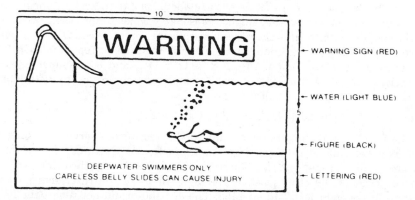

FIG V
SIGN ON TRANSOM FOR SLIDES PLACED IN 4 FT OF WATER OR DEEPER

After promulgation of the standard, Aqua Slide 'N' Dive Corporation, manufacturer of 95% of the 350,000 swimming pool slides then in use in the United States, challenged the standards. Arguing that the Commission had failed to show that the standard was "reasonably necessary to eliminate or reduce an unreasonable risk of injury," as required by § 2058(c)(2), Aqua Slide alleged that neither the warning signs nor the ladder chain had been adequately tested for effectiveness and that the warnings themselves were so explicit as to deter people unnecessarily from using the slide.

Despite the fact that the risk of injury was remote (there being a greater risk of being struck and killed by lightning), the seriousness of the injuries in such accidents led the court to conclude that some kind of safety standard for swimming pool slides might be "reasonably necessary." However, because the Commission had failed to produce "substantial evidence" demonstrating the effectiveness of the warnings proposed, the court concluded that they were not justified. Specific Commission shortcomings included its failure to explain adequately why warnings were chosen over public education campaigns, its failure to extend the warning requirements to slides already in use, and its failure to conduct meaningful tests on the effectiveness of the warnings. Moreover, the court agreed that the warnings appeared sensational in failing to explain that paralysis was only a one in ten million risk, and the CPSC had not examined the possibility that the warnings might unduly deter slide use.

The most promising aspect of the safety standard in reducing the risk of spinal injury was its requirement that large slides be limited to deep water use. But this created a new danger by increasing the risk that small children might drown. In an effort to reduce this new danger, the Commission developed the *ladder chain* requirement. Empirical testing of the ladder chain amounted to an "evaluation" by a CPSC consultant who "tried one out on his neighbors' children at a pool in his own back yard," and the effectiveness of the risk-of-drowning warning sign was not tested at all. *Held*, such testing failed to produce meaningful results and was "not the stuff of which substantial evidence is made." Reasoning that the Commission had failed adequately to evaluate the standard's likely effects on the product's utility, cost, and availability (and its effectiveness in reducing risks of injury), the court concluded that the proposed warnings and ladder chain requirements had to be set aside.

10. After the Aqua–Slide affair, most product safety regulations proposed and adopted by the CPSC and other agencies have been based on more acceptable testing and analysis, but major agency safety studies and programs are always fair game for close scrutiny. Arguably the CPSC learned the Aqua–Slide lesson too well, for the CPSC's test protocol for performance testing of child safety devices on butane cigarette lighters is defined in extraordinary (arguably excruciating) detail. 16 CFR § 1210.4 (2004). Can a regulatory performance test be too good?

11. Cost–Benefit Analysis in Governmental Safety Regulation. As evidenced in *Southland Mower,* governmental product safety agencies make extensive use of risk-benefit analysis in regulatory decision-making. For example, the Consumer Product Safety Act § 15 requires reporting of "defects" that create substantial product hazards. How is such a "defect" to be defined? The CPSC has attempted to introduce a cost-benefit analysis to that effort with limited success. See 71 Fed. Reg. 30350 (May 26, 2006)(proposed revisions to product hazard reporting requirements explain risk-benefit assessment); 16 CFR § 1115.4 (1995)(rejecting cost-benefit analysis in product hazard reporting requirements after objections from commentators). Consider also the defect notification provisions of the National Traffic and Motor Vehicle Safety Act of 1966, where the concepts of "motor vehicle safety" and "defect" have been held "to signify a 'common-sense' balancing of safety benefits and economic costs." See United States v. General Motors Corp., 518 F.2d 420, 435 (D.C.Cir.1975).

Notwithstanding the widespread, perhaps inevitable, use of cost-benefit analysis in safety regulation, it remains a highly politicized issue. In January 2006, the White House Office of Management and Budget issued a proposed Risk Assessment Bulletin intended "to enhance the technical quality and objectivity of risk assessments prepared by federal agencies by establishing uniform, minimum standards." Office of Management and Budget, Proposed Risk Assessment Bulletin at 6 (January 9, 2006). The proposed Bulletin generated wide debate over its necessity, potentially broad scope, and the value of its method of assessing the uncertainties inherent in risk-benefit analysis. See 34 Prod. Safety & Liab. Rep. (BNA) 665 (July 3, 2006). On the value of cost-benefit analysis in product safety regulation, see Geistfeld, Reconciling Cost–Benefit Analysis With the Principle that Safety Matters More Than Money, 76 N.Y.U. L. Rev. 114 (2001).

Even more controversial than the choice of an appropriate cost for safety improvements is the difficult task of determining an appropriate value for a statistical human life. While different agencies use widely varying figures, a study of several years ago found substantial use in the agencies at that time of values in the range of $1–2 million per life. See C. Gillette & T. Hopkins, Federal Agency Valuations of Human Life (Report to the Admin. Conf. of the U.S.)(Oct.1988). Human lives in 1995 were considered to be worth £940,000 in Europe and North America (compared to £62,500 in developing countries and £180,000 in the former Soviet Union), according to UN economists. See One Western Life Is Worth 15 in the Third World, Says UN Report, Daily Telegraph (England, July 23, 1995)("ludicrous," exclaimed Sir Crispin Tickell, the P.M.'s chief environmental advisor). A life in 2004 was valued at around $6.1 million, a figure some would say is too low. Sunstein, Lives, Life–Years, and Willingness to Pay, 104 Colum. L. Rev. 205 (2004).

12. Regulating Prescription Drugs—In General. As discussed in the previous chapter, prescription drugs and medical devices are extensively regulated by the FDA under the Federal Food, Drug and Cosmetic Act, 21 U.S.C.A. §§ 301–392, originally enacted by Congress in 1938. The Act's key provisions prohibit the sale of "any food, drug, device, or cosmetic that is adulterated or misbranded," § 331(a), and require FDA approval prior to the marketing of any new drug, § 355. "Misbranding" occurs when a product's labeling is "false or misleading in any particular," §§ 352 and 353. Adequate information on proper use and possible dangers must be conveyed to the consumer, in the case of over-the-counter drugs, § 352, or to the physician, in the case of prescription drugs, § 353.

13. What is a Drug? "Drugs" and "devices" over which the FDA has authority are defined in § 321(g)(1)(C) as "articles (other than food) intended to affect the structure or any function of the body." A "device" subject to regulation is defined as "an instrument, apparatus, implement, machine, contrivance, ... or other similar or related article [which] is intended to affect the structure or any function of the body."

Are these definitions broad enough to encompass cigarettes and smokeless tobacco products that deliver nicotine which has a pharmacological effect? In 1996, the FDA sought, for the first time, to regulate cigarettes and smokeless tobacco products as drug-delivery devices. The FDA issued restrictions on the sale and distribution of cigarettes to children and adolescents, believing that because most tobacco consumers begin before reaching adulthood, preventing tobacco use by minors could substantially reduce the incidence of tobacco-related death and disease among the U.S. population. The Supreme Court, in Food and Drug Administration v. Brown & Williamson Tobacco Corp., 529 U.S. 120 (2000), overturned the regulation, concluding that the FDA does *not* have jurisdiction to regulate tobacco products. The Court held that, while the FDA exhaustively documented that tobacco products are unsafe, dangerous to health and the "single leading cause of preventable death in the United States," the FDCA's language and Congress' concurrent regulation of tobacco products by other legislative means preclude regulation. The Court found that "if tobacco products were 'devices' under the FDCA, the FDA would be required to remove them from the market" because "there are no directions that could make tobacco products safe for obtaining their intended effects. Thus, were tobacco products within the FDA's jurisdiction, the Act would deem them misbranded devices that could not be introduced into interstate commerce." That result would "plainly contradict congressional policy." Id. at 137–139. Do you agree?

14. Regulating Drug Warnings—Birth Control Pills. As mentioned at the end of the last chapter, the FDA on occasion has deviated from its general pattern and required that information on certain prescription drugs be transmitted directly to users. See, for example, 21 CFR § 310.501 (2006), providing in part as follows:

Patient package inserts for oral contraceptives.

(a) *Requirement for a patient package insert.* The safe and effective use of oral contraceptive drug products requires that patients be fully informed of the benefits and the risks involved in their use. An oral contraceptive drug product that does not comply with the requirements of this section is misbranded under section 502 of the Federal Food, Drug, and Cosmetic Act. Each dispenser of an oral contraceptive drug product shall provide a patient package insert to each patient (or to an agent of the patient) to whom the product is dispensed, except that the dispenser may provide the insert to the parent or legal guardian of a legally incompetent patient (or to the agent of either). The patient package insert is required to be placed in or accompany each package dispensed to the patient.

(b) *Distribution requirements.* (1) For oral contraceptive drug products, the manufacturer and distributor shall provide a patient package insert in or with each package of the drug product that the manufacturer or distributor intends to be dispensed to a patient.

(c) *Contents of patient package insert.* A patient package insert for an oral contraceptive drug product is required to contain the following:

(1) The name of the drug.

(2) A summary including a statement concerning the effectiveness of oral contraceptives in preventing pregnancy, the contraindications to the drug's use, and a statement of the risks and benefits associated with the drug's use.

(3) A statement comparing the effectiveness of oral contraceptives to other methods of contraception.

(4) A boxed warning concerning the increased risks associated with cigarette smoking and oral contraceptive use.

(5) A discussion of the contraindications to use, including information that the patient should provide to the prescriber before taking the drug.

(6) A statement of medical conditions that are not contraindications to use but deserve special consideration in connection with oral contraceptive use and about which the patient should inform the prescriber.

(7) A warning regarding the most serious side effects of oral contraceptives.

(8) A statement of other serious adverse reactions and potential safety hazards that may result from the use of oral contraceptives.

(9) A statement concerning common, but less serious side effects which may help the patient evaluate the benefits and risks from the use of oral contraceptives.

(10) Information on precautions the patients should observe while taking oral contraceptives, including the following:

(i) A statement of risks to the mother and unborn child from the use of oral contraceptives before or during early pregnancy;

(ii) A statement concerning excretion of the drug in human milk and associated risks to the nursing infant;

(iii) A statement about laboratory tests which may be affected by oral contraceptives; and

(iv) A statement that identifies activities and drugs, foods, or other substances the patient should avoid because of their interactions with oral contraceptives.

(11) Information about how to take oral contraceptives properly, including information about what to do if the patient forgets to take the product, information about becoming pregnant after discontinuing use of the drug, a statement that the drug product has been prescribed for the use of the patient and should not be used for other conditions or given to others, and a statement that the patient's pharmacist or practitioner has a more technical leaflet about the drug product that the patient may ask to review.

(12) A statement of the possible benefits associated with oral contraceptive use.

(13) The following information about the drug product and the patient package insert:

(i) The name and place of business of the manufacturer, packer, or distributor, or the name and place of business of the dispenser of the product.

(ii) The date, identified as such, of the most recent revision of the patient package insert placed prominently immediately after the last section of the labeling.

(d) *Other indications.* The patient package insert may identify indications in addition to contraception that are identified in the professional labeling for the drug product.

Prior to 1989, the FDA provided the following tables and graph as satisfying certain of the specified warning requirements. 43 Fed.Reg. 4223–26 (Jan. 31, 1978):

TABLE 1

SUMMARY OF RELATIVE RISK OF
THROMBOEMBOLIC DISORDERS AND
OTHER VASCULAR PROBLEMS IN ORAL
CONTRACEPTIVE USERS COMPARED
TO NONUSERS

	Relative risk, times greater
Idiopathic thromboembolic disease	4-11
Post surgery thromboembolic complications	4-6
Thrombotic stroke	4-9.5
Hemorrhagic stroke	2
Myocardial infarction	2-12

TABLE 2

Estimated annual mortality rate per 100,000 women from myocardial infarction by use of oral contraceptives, smoking habits, and age (in years):

	Myocardial infarction			
	Women aged 30-39		Women aged 40-44	
Smoking habits	Users	Non Users	Users	Non Users
All smokers	10.2	2.6	62.0	15.9
Heavy[1]	13.0	5.1	78.7	31.3
Light	4.7	.9	28.6	5.7
Nonsmokers	1.8	1.2	10.7	7.4
Smokers and nonsmokers	5.4	1.9	32.8	11.7

[1]Heavy smoker: 15 or more cigarettes per day. From Jain AK; Studies in Family Planning, 8:50, 1977.

Figure 1. Estimated annual number of deaths associated with control of fertility and no control per 100,000 nonsterile women, by regimen of control and age of woman.

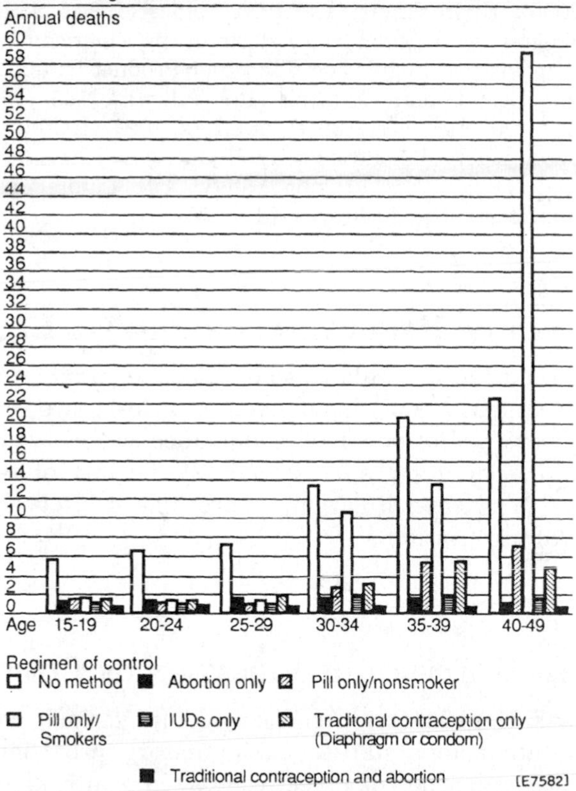

Regimen of control
□ No method   ■ Abortion only   ▨ Pill only/nonsmoker

□ Pill only/ Smokers   ▤ IUDs only   ▧ Traditonal contraception only (Diaphragm or condom)

■ Traditional contraception and abortion   [E7582]

In 1989, the FDA replaced the tables and graph with the information set out above. What do you think of the FDA's decision to abandon the graph and table approach, supplementing written warnings, in favor of the written warnings alone?

Why does the FDA require that users be directly alerted to the dangers of oral contraceptives but not to those of other drugs, say, anti-depressants? Are the risks, usage patterns, public knowledge, or ability of the physician to supervise use significantly different in the two cases?

Why not require user information on *all* prescription drugs? Would such labeling make prescription drugs safer? More dangerous? Would people follow their doctor's orders if they had routine access to information on the dangers associated with their prescription drugs? Are there other issues than safety involved? One may question whether the government should require—or even permit—that health information on the most serious risks be monopolized by the physicians. What is the proper role of government regulation in this area? What is the effect of direct-to-consumer advertising by pharmaceutical companies? See generally Struve, The FDA and the Tort System: Post–Marketing Surveillance, Compensation, and the Role of Litigation, 6 Yale J. Health Pol'y L. & Ethics 587 (2005); Ausness, Will More Aggressive Marketing Practices Lead to Greater Tort Liability for Prescription Drug Manufacturers?, 37 Wake Forest L. Rev. 92 (2002); Noah, Advertising Prescription Drugs to Consumers: Assessing the Regulatory and Liability Issues, 32 Ga. L. Rev. 141 (1997).

15. See generally C. Hodges, European Regulation of Consumer Product Safety (Oxford 2005); H. Burkholz, The FDA Follies (1994); S. Rose–Ackerman, Rethinking the Progressive Agenda: The Reform of the American Regulatory State ch. 8 (1992); W. Kip Viscusi, Regulating Consumer Product Safety (1984); Adler & Posner, Rethinking Cost–Benefit Analysis, 109 Yale L.J. 165 (1999); Gillette & Krier, Risk, Courts, and Agencies, 138 U.Pa.L.Rev. 1027 (1990); T. M. Schwartz, The Role of Federal Safety Regulations in Products Liability Actions, 41 Vand. L.Rev. 1121 (1988); Pierce, Encouraging Safety: The Limits of Tort Law and Government Regulation, 33 Vand.L.Rev. 1281 (1980).

2. THE EFFECT OF REGULATION ON PRIVATE LITIGATION

When a federal agency regulates some aspect of product safety, private products liability litigation may be affected in at least two important ways: (1) a manufacturer's violation of or compliance with a safety regulation may have certain evidentiary effects, and (2) the fact of regulation may restrict the scope of private litigation, or preclude it altogether, under the doctrine of federal preemption.

———

A. EVIDENTIARY EFFECT OF VIOLATION OR COMPLIANCE

Violation of Regulation. As discussed in various contexts above, violation of a state safety statute or regulatory provision amounts to negligence *per se*, and proof of defectiveness, in many jurisdictions. See, e.g., Palmer v. A.H. Robins Co., Inc., 684 P.2d 187 (Colo. 1984)(manufacturer of Dalkon Shield IUD negligent *per se* for advertising product as "safe" in violation of misbranding prohibition of state food and drug act); National Bank of Commerce v. Kimberly–Clark Corp., 38 F.3d 988 (8th Cir.1994)(estate of woman killed by toxic shock syndrome may sue manufacturer for non-compliance with warning requirement of Medical Device Amendments to Food, Drug & Cosmetic Act—type size too small, not written to 6th–to–8th grade level, and absence of boldface or different colors for certain portions demanded by FDA prominence requirement).

The Products Liability Restatement in § 4(a) extends the *per se* principle to strict products liability for design and warnings defects, providing that "a product's noncompliance with an applicable product safety statute or administrative regulation renders the product defective with respect to the risks sought to be reduced by the statute or regulation."

Whether a private right of action is expressly or impliedly *created* under a particular federal statute is another matter, dependent on the language of the statute and the intent of Congress. Compare Swenson v. Emerson Electric Co., 374 N.W.2d 690 (Minn.1985)(private cause of action for violation of CPSC's substantial product hazard reporting regulations), with Drake v. Honeywell, Inc., 797 F.2d 603 (8th Cir.1986)(contra). See generally D. Owen, Products Liability Law § 2.4 (violation as proof of negligence), § 6.4 (as proof of strict liability) (2d ed. 2008).

Compliance With Regulation. Reasoning that governmental safety requirements are generally set at minimally acceptable levels, most courts rule that compliance with a regulatory safety standard, such as a mandated warning, is evidence of due care and non-defectiveness but is not conclusive of either issue. After considering all the evidence, the jury is still free to find the manufacturer negligent or the warning "defective." See, e.g., Lane v. R.A. Sims, Jr., Inc., 241 F.3d 439 (5th Cir. 2001)(Federal Railroad Safety Act); Stevens v. Parke, Davis & Co., 507 P.2d 653, 661 (Cal.1973)(FDCA); Burch v. Amsterdam Corp., 366 A.2d 1079 (D.C.1976)(Federal Hazardous Substances Act); Ferebee v. Chevron Chemical Co., 736 F.2d 1529 (D.C.Cir. 1984)(EPA-approved herbicide label under Federal Insecticide, Fungicide, and Rodenticide Act); Moss v. Parks Corp., 985 F.2d 736 (4th Cir. 1993)(CPSC labeling regulations under Federal Hazardous Substances Act). Products Liability Restatement § 4(b) is in accord.

A number of jurisdictions have enacted reform legislation on the effect of compliance with regulation. See, e.g., Colo.Rev.Stat. § 13–21–403, and Utah Code Ann. § 78–15–6(3), which create a *presumption* of non-defectiveness and non-negligence if the product complies with applicable governmental standards. A Kansas statute provides that a product which complies with a governmental safety standard (for design or warnings) is not defective, unless the plaintiff proves that a reasonably prudent seller would have taken additional precautions (and compliance with mandatory government contract specifications is an absolute defense). Kan.Stat.Ann. § 60–3304.

Which is the better approach? Is it relevant that regulatory agencies often solicit proposals for safety standards from private industry and sometimes use these proposals as the basis for the standards promulgated? See generally Symposium, Regulatory Compliance as a Defense to Products Liability, 88 Geo.L.J. 2049 (2000); D. Owen, Products Liability Law § 14.3 (regulatory compliance as a defense) (2d ed. 2008).

B. PREEMPTION

Perhaps the most important issue in modern products liability law is the role of federal preemption doctrine in private litigation involving product safety issues which Congress has addressed, either directly through statute or indirectly through administrative regulation. A preemption argument is based on a product manufacturer's claim that a federal regulation bearing on a defendant's product forecloses any arguably inconsistent state law regulation of that product, including products liability claims challenging the defendant's exercise of due care or its product's defectiveness. Until the early 1990s, manufacturers had virtually abandoned the preemption argument, for it had been routinely rejected by most courts in most contexts. See, e.g., Ferebee v. Chevron Chem. Co., 736 F.2d 1529 (D.C.Cir. 1984)(EPA-approved label for herbicide, under Federal Insecticide, Fungicide, and Rodenticide Act); Abbot v. American Cyanamid Co., 844 F.2d 1108, 1112 n. 1 (4th Cir.1988)(FDA-approved labeling of DPT vaccine: "The overwhelming majority of courts considering federal preemption of state law as regards vaccines have found no preemption."). The Supreme Court in 1992 infused the preemption doctrine with new power, and it is now a frequent issue in modern products liability litigation.

Preemption doctrine raises questions of federalism that extend far beyond the kinds of problems courts ordinarily confront in product cases. When our Constitution created a federal government of limited, enumerated powers, it created a system of overlapping federal and state legal authority. When Congress legislates in a field within its enumerated powers, conflicts inevitably arise over whether, and how much, state authority has been displaced in the process. The framers of the Constitution recognized that conflicts of law would arise in our federal system and included a provision which defines a basic premise for resolving those conflicts: the Supremacy Clause. The Clause states that federal law "shall be the supreme law of the land." U.S. Const. Art VI, cl. 2. The Supremacy Clause does not further define when federal law is supreme, however. The circumstances in which federal law is supreme over state law are not self-evident. Situations exist in which it might not be desirous for federal legislation to displace state law, but rather that federal and state law should operate concurrently. Furthermore, some situations may require total displacement of even consistent state law. Preemption doctrine provides the method to resolve such conflicts.

Determining the circumstances in which federal law is supreme requires a methodology which the Supreme Court has long framed as a search for congressional intent to preempt. Often intent to preempt is found in an express preemption provision directed to the issue. See Malone v. White Motor Corp., 435 U.S. 497 (1978)(express preemption under ERISA). Sometimes the Court has concluded that an express preemption provision does not reliably indicate the proper scope of Congress' intent to displace state law. When express preemptive scope is not fully defined, the Court determines whether intent to preempt should be implied. The Court has defined two categories of implied preemption: (1) occupation of the field preemption, where Congress's legislation is so comprehensive that it displaces all state law; and (2) conflict preemption, where the federal and state regulations are in such conflict that state law must yield to the federal because either (a) it is impossible for a party to comply with both federal and state regulation, or (b) state law "stands as an obstacle to the accomplishment" of federal objectives and, therefore, must yield. See Hillsborough County v. Automated Med. Labs., Inc., 471 U.S. 707, 712–13 (1985). See generally; Davis, On Preemption, Congressional Intent, and Conflict of Laws, 66 U. Pitt. L. Rev. 181, 182, 198–200 (2004).

A number of issues are presented by the application of federal preemption doctrine to common-law tort actions for damages. Most federal safety statutes expressly prohibit only conflicting state "regulation" and say nothing whatsoever about private damages actions. An example from the CPSC will illustrate the complexity of the problem.

In 1995, a federal appeals court for the first time ruled that the Consumer Product Safety Act (CPSA) preempted a state common-law damages claim. In Moe v. MTD Products, Inc., 73 F.3d 179 (8th Cir.1995), the court examined the preemptive effect of the power lawn mower safety standard upheld in *Southland Mower,* above, which requires (1) that each power lawn mower have a blade-control system that stops the blade rotation within three seconds after the operator's hands leave the handle, and (2) that each mower contain a label warning "DANGER, KEEP HANDS and FEET AWAY" and showing a blade cutting into the forefinger of a hand. Brian Moe's fingers were cut off when he released the control handle on his mower and reached into the side chute to unclog some wet grass. The blade had continued to rotate because the safety clutch control cable had frayed and broken from rubbing against the throttle control housing and possibly because of the sharpness of its turns. Plaintiff alleged that the mower was defective because of (1) the clutch control cable's design, and (2) the manufacturer's failure to warn that the design would cause the cable to fray.

Like most federal safety statutes, the CPSA contains a preemption provision which provides:

> Whenever a consumer product safety standard under this chapter is in effect and applies to a risk of injury associated with a consumer product, no State or political subdivision of a State shall have any authority either to establish or to continue in effect any provision of a safety standard or regulation which prescribes any requirements as to the performance, composition, design, finish, construction, packaging, or labeling of such product which are designed to deal with the same risk of injury associated with such consumer product, unless such requirements are identical to the requirements of the Federal standard.

15 U.S.C. § 2075(a). Also like many federal safety statutes, the Act contains a "savings clause" which provides:

> Compliance with consumer product safety rules or other rules or orders under this Act shall not relieve any person from liability at common law or under State statutory law to any other person.

15 U.S.C. § 2074(a).

Based on the preemption clause, the district court granted the defendant's motion for summary judgment on all the plaintiff's claims. On appeal, the Eighth Circuit held that the plaintiff's warnings claim was preempted but the design claim was not:

> The Moes' failure to warn claim suggests that MTD should have warned consumers that the [clutch control] cable might fray. The risk of injury contemplated by such a warning is the same as that addressed by the labeling requirements in the Mower Standard—injury to the hands by the cutting blade. If the Moes' failure to warn claim were successful, it would create a state standard requiring additional warnings on lawn mowers or in owner manuals related to the same risk of injury addressed by the federal standard. This claim is thus expressly preempted by the CPSA.

> * * *

> The Moes' defective design claim is an example of the type of claim the savings clause preserves, however. A successful tort action based on the defective design of [a clutch control cable] would not create a different standard for mower safety or impose additional requirements on the manufacturer. Instead it would create an incentive for manufacturers to install a [clutch control cable] that works and is properly designed, and thus ensure that the federal standard has meaning. The Moes' defective design claim is not preempted by the CPSA and should not have been dismissed on that ground.

In most federal regulatory contexts, courts conventionally examined such statutes in terms of implied preemption and ordinarily rejected quite summarily defendant claims of express federal preemption. The Supreme Court changed that convention in the following case.

Cipollone v. Liggett Group, Inc.

Supreme Court of the United States, 1992.
505 U.S. 504, 112 S.Ct. 2608, 120 L.Ed.2d 407.

■ STEVENS, J., announced the judgment of the Court and delivered the opinion of the Court with respect to Parts I, II, III, and IV, in which REHNQUIST, C. J., and WHITE, BLACKMUN, O'CONNOR, KENNEDY, and SOUTER, JJ., joined, and an opinion with respect to Parts V and VI, in which REHNQUIST, C. J., and WHITE, and O'CONNOR, JJ., joined. BLACKMUN, J., filed an opinion concurring in part, concurring in the judgment in part, and dissenting in part, in which KENNEDY and SOUTER JJ., joined. SCALIA, J., filed an opinion concurring in the judgment in part and dissenting in part, in which THOMAS, J., joined.

■ JUSTICE STEVENS delivered the opinion of the Court, except as to Parts V and VI.

"WARNING: THE SURGEON GENERAL HAS DETERMINED THAT CIGARETTE SMOKING IS DANGEROUS TO YOUR HEALTH." A federal statute enacted in 1969 requires that warning (or a variation thereof) to appear in a conspicuous place on every package of cigarettes sold in the United States. The questions presented to us by this case are whether that statute, or its 1965 predecessor which required a less alarming label, pre-empted petitioner's common law claims against respondent cigarette manu-facturers.

[Plaintiff, the son of Rose Cipollone, who began smoking in 1942 and who died of lung cancer in 1984, claims that respondents are responsible for his mother's death] because they breached express warranties contained in their advertising, because they failed to warn consumers about the hazards of smoking, because they fraudulently misrepresented those haz-ards to consumers, and because they conspired to deprive the public of medical and scientific information about smoking. The Court of Appeals held that petitioner's state law claims were pre-empted by federal statutes, and other courts have agreed with that analysis. The highest courts of the states of Minnesota and New Jersey, however, have held that the federal statutes did not pre-empt similar common law claims.[6] Because of the manifest importance of the issue, we granted certiorari to resolve the conflict, . . . We now reverse in part and affirm in part.

I

[Defendants contend that the 1965 Federal Cigarette Labeling and Advertising Act, and its successor, the 1969 Public Health Cigarette Smok-ing Act, protect them from any liability based on their post–1965 conduct. The District Court originally concluded that the federal statutes did not pre-empt common law damages based on the adequacy of the federally-mandated warnings. The Court of Appeals reversed, finding that Congress had impliedly pre-empted state law damages actions that "challenge either the adequacy of the warning" or actions based on "the advertising and promotion of cigarettes." The District Court then concluded that the plaintiff's claims were barred to the extent they relied on respondents' advertising and promotions after January 1, 1966. Following extensive discovery and a four month trial, the jury found breach of an express warranty and a failure to warn Mrs. Cipollone prior to 1966. It found that Mrs. Cipollone assumed the risk of her injuries, and denied her damages, but awarded Mr. Cipollone $400,000. The Court of Appeals affirmed.]

II

[After the Surgeon General's 1964 report on the hazards of cigarette smoking, the Federal Trade Commission sought to require health warnings in cigarette advertising, and several states also considered various regula-tions. In 1965, Congress enacted the Federal Cigarette Labeling and Advertising Act which mandated warnings on cigarette packages but not in advertising.]

Section 2 of the 1965 Act declares the statute's two purposes: (1) adequately informing the public that cigarette smoking may be hazardous to health, and (2) protecting the national economy from the burden imposed by diverse, nonuniform and confusing cigarette labeling and adver-

---

6. Forster v. R.J. Reynolds Tobacco Co., 437 N.W.2d 655 (Minn.1989); Dewey v. R. J. Reynolds Tobacco Co., 577 A.2d 1239 (N.J. 1990).

tising regulations. In furtherance of the first purpose, § 4 of the Act made it unlawful to sell or distribute any cigarettes in the United States unless the package bore a conspicuous label stating: "CAUTION: CIGARETTE SMOKING MAY BE HAZARDOUS TO YOUR HEALTH." In furtherance of the second purpose, § 5, captioned "Preemption," provided in part:

"(a) No statement relating to smoking and health, other than the statement required by section 4 of this Act, shall be required on any cigarette package.

"(b) No statement relating to smoking and health shall be required in the advertising of any cigarettes the packages of which are labeled in conformity with the provisions of this Act."

Although the Act took effect January 1, 1966, § 10 of the Act provided that its provisions affecting the regulation of advertising would terminate on July 1, 1969. [As the sunset provision on advertising regulation approached, federal and state authorities prepared to issue regulations on cigarette advertising.] It was in this context that Congress enacted the Public Health Cigarette Smoking Act of 1969, which amended the 1965 Act in several ways. First, the 1969 Act strengthened the warning label, in part by requiring a statement that cigarette smoking "is dangerous" rather than that it "may be hazardous." Second, the 1969 Act banned cigarette advertising in "any medium of electronic communication subject to [FCC] jurisdiction." Third, and related, the 1969 Act modified the pre-emption provision by replacing the original § 5(b) with a provision that reads:

"(b) No requirement or prohibition based on smoking and health shall be imposed under State law with respect to the advertising or promotion of any cigarettes the packages of which are labeled in conformity with the provisions of this Act."

* * *

III

Article VI of the Constitution provides that the laws of the United States "shall be the supreme Law of the Land; ... any Thing in the Constitution or Laws of any state to the Contrary notwithstanding." Art. VI, cl. 2. Thus, since our decision in M'Culloch v. Maryland, 4 Wheat. 316, 427 (1819), it has been settled that state law that conflicts with federal law is "without effect." [Citation.] Consideration of issues arising under the Supremacy Clause "start[s] with the assumption that the historic police powers of the States [are] not to be superseded by ... Federal Act unless that [is] the clear and manifest purpose of Congress." Rice v. Santa Fe Elevator Corp., 331 U.S. 218, 230 (1947). Accordingly, " '[t]he purpose of Congress is the ultimate touchstone' "of pre-emption analysis. Malone v. White Motor Corp., 435 U.S. 497, 504 (1978)(citation).

Congress' intent may be "explicitly stated in the statute's language or implicitly contained in its structure and purpose." Jones v. Rath Packing Co., 430 U.S. 519, 525 (1977). In the absence of an express congressional command, state law is pre-empted if that law actually conflicts with federal law [citation], or if federal law so thoroughly occupies a legislative field " 'as to make reasonable the inference that Congress left no room for the States to supplement it.' " [Citation.]

* * *

In our opinion, the pre-emptive scope of the 1965 Act and the 1969 Act is governed entirely by the express language in § 5 of each Act. When Congress has considered the issue of pre-emption and has included in the enacted legislation a provision explicitly addressing that issue, and when that provision provides a "reliable indicium of congressional intent with respect to state authority," *Malone*, "there is no need to infer congressional intent to pre-empt state laws from the substantive provisions" of the legislation. California Federal Savings & Loan Assn. v. Guerra, 479 U.S. 272, 282 (1987)(opinion of Marshall, J.). Such reasoning is a variant of the familiar principle of *expressio unius est exclusio alterius*: Congress' enactment of a provision defining the pre-emptive reach of a statute implies that matters beyond that reach are not pre-empted. In this case, the other provisions of the 1965 and 1969 Acts offer no cause to look beyond § 5 of each Act. Therefore, we need only identify the domain expressly pre-empted by each of those sections. As the 1965 and 1969 provisions differ substantially, we consider each in turn.

IV

In the 1965 pre-emption provision regarding advertising (§ 5(b)), Congress spoke precisely and narrowly: "No *statement* relating to smoking and health shall be required *in the advertising* of [properly labeled] cigarettes." Section 5(a) used the same phrase ("No *statement* relating to smoking and health") with regard to cigarette labeling. As § 5(a) made clear, that phrase referred to the sort of warning provided for in § 4, which set forth verbatim the warning Congress determined to be appropriate. Thus, on their face, these provisions merely prohibited state and federal rule-making bodies from mandating particular cautionary statements on cigarette labels (§ 5(a)) or in cigarette advertisements (§ 5(b)).

Beyond the precise words of these provisions, this reading is appropriate for several reasons. First, as discussed above, we must construe these provisions in light of the presumption against the pre-emption of state police power regulations. This presumption reinforces the appropriateness of a narrow reading of § 5. Second, the warning required in § 4 does not by its own effect foreclose additional obligations imposed under state law. That Congress requires a particular warning label does not automatically pre-empt a regulatory field. [Citation.] Third, there is no general, inherent conflict between federal pre-emption of state warning requirements and the continued vitality of state common law damages actions.... All of these considerations indicate that § 5 is best read as having superseded only positive enactments by legislatures or administrative agencies that mandate particular warning labels.

This reading comports with the 1965 Act's statement of purpose, which expressed an intent to avoid "diverse, nonuniform, and confusing labeling and advertising *regulations* with respect to any relationship between smoking and health." Read against the backdrop of regulatory activity undertaken by state legislatures and federal agencies in response to the Surgeon General's report, the term "regulation" most naturally refers to positive enactments by those bodies, not to common law damages actions. [Therefore,] § 5 of the 1965 Act only pre-empted state and federal rulemaking bodies from mandating particular cautionary statements and did not pre-empt state law damages actions.[17]

V

Compared to its predecessor in the 1965 Act, the plain language of the pre-emption provision in the 1969 Act is much broader. First, the later Act bars not simply "statements" but rather "requirement[s] or prohibitions . . . imposed under State law." Second, the later Act reaches beyond statements "in the advertising" to obligations "with respect to the advertising or promotion" of cigarettes.

Notwithstanding these substantial differences in language, both petitioner and respondents contend that the 1969 Act did not materially alter the pre-emptive scope of federal law. Their primary support for this contention is a sentence in a Committee Report which states that the 1969 amendment "clarified" the 1965 version of § 5(b). S. Rep. No. 91–566, p. 12 (1969). We reject the parties' reading as incompatible with the language and origins of the amendments. . . . The 1969 Act worked substantial changes in the law: rewriting the label warning, banning broadcast advertising, and allowing the FTC to regulate print advertising. In the context of such revisions and in light of the substantial changes in wording, we cannot accept the parties' claim that the 1969 Act did not alter the reach of § 5(b).[19]

Petitioner next contends that § 5(b), however broadened by the 1969 Act, does not pre-empt *common law* actions. He offers two theories for limiting the reach of the amended § 5(b). First, he argues that common law damages actions do not impose "requirement[s] or prohibitions" and that Congress intended only to trump "state statutes, injunctions, or executive pronouncements." We disagree; such an analysis is at odds both with the plain words of the 1969 Act and with the general understanding of common law damages actions. The phrase "[n]o requirement or prohibition" sweeps

---

17. This interpretation of the 1965 Act appears to be consistent with respondents' contemporaneous understanding of the Act. Although respondents have participated in a great deal of litigation relating to cigarette use beginning in the 1950's, it appears that this case is the first in which they have raised § 5 as a pre-emption defense.

19. As noted above, the 1965 Act's statement of purpose (§ 2) suggested that Congress was concerned primarily with "regulations"—positive enactments, rather than common law damages actions. Although the 1969 Act did not amend § 2, we are not persuaded that the retention of that portion of the 1965 Act is a sufficient basis for rejecting the plain meaning of the broad language that Congress added to § 5(b).

broadly and suggests no distinction between positive enactments and common law; to the contrary, those words easily encompass obligations that take the form of common law rules. As we noted in another context, "[state] regulation can be as effectively exerted through an award of damages as through some form of preventive relief. The obligation to pay compensation can be, indeed is designed to be, a potent method of governing conduct and controlling policy." San Diego Building Trades Council v. Garmon, 359 U.S. 236, 247 (1959).

Although portions of the legislative history of the 1969 Act suggest that Congress was primarily concerned with positive enactments by States and localities, [citation] the language of the Act plainly reaches beyond such enactments. "We must give effect to this plain language unless there is good reason to believe Congress intended the language to have some more restrictive meaning." Shaw v. Delta Air Lines, Inc., 463 U.S. 85, 97 (1983). In this case there is no "good reason to believe" that Congress meant less than what it said; indeed, in light of the narrowness of the 1965 Act, there is "good reason to believe" that Congress meant precisely what it said in amending that Act.

Moreover, common law damages actions of the sort raised by petitioner are premised on the existence of a legal duty and it is difficult to say that such actions do not impose "requirements or prohibitions." [Citations]. It is in this way that the 1969 version of § 5(b) differs from its predecessor: Whereas the common law would not normally require a vendor to use any specific *statement* on its packages or in its advertisements, it is the essence of the common law to enforce duties that are either affirmative *requirements* or negative *prohibitions*. We therefore reject petitioner's argument that the phrase "requirement or prohibition" limits the 1969 Act's preemptive scope to positive enactments by legislatures and agencies. [The Court also rejected petitioner's argument that the phrase "imposed under State law" does not include the common law.]

That the pre-emptive scope of § 5(b) cannot be limited to positive enactments does not mean that that section pre-empts all common law claims. For example, as respondents concede, § 5(b) does not generally pre-empt "state-law obligations to avoid marketing cigarettes with manufacturing defects or to use a demonstrably safer alternative design for cigarettes." For purposes of § 5(b), the common law is not of a piece.

Nor does the statute indicate that any familiar subdivision of common law claims is or is not pre-empted.... [W]e must fairly but—in light of the strong presumption against pre-emption—narrowly construe the precise language of § 5(b) and we must look to each of petitioner's common law claims to determine whether it is in fact pre-empted.[22] The central inquiry

---

22. Petitioner makes much of the fact that Congress did not expressly include common law within § 5's pre-emptive reach, as it has in other statutes. See, *e.g.*, 29 U.S.C. § 1144(c)(1); 12 U.S.C. § 1715z–17(d). Respondents make much of the fact that Congress did not include a savings clause preserving common law claims, again, as it has in other statutes. See, *e.g.*, 17 U.S.C. § 301. Under our analysis of § 5, these omissions

in each case is straightforward: we ask whether the legal duty that is the predicate of the common law damages action constitutes a "requirement or prohibition based on smoking and health . . . imposed under State law with respect to . . . advertising or promotion," giving that clause a fair but narrow reading. As discussed below, each phrase within that clause limits the universe of common law claims pre-empted by the statute. [Based on this analysis, the following claims are therefore preempted: (1) claims based on post–1969 failure to warn allegations; (2) fraudulent misrepresentation claims based on an attempt to neutralize the mandated warning labels. Similarly, the following claims are *not* preempted: (1) claims relying solely on testing, research practices, or other actions not based on advertising or promotion; (2) breach of express warranty; (3) fraudulent misrepresentation claims based on a duty not to deceive; and (4) conspiracy.]

VI

[Judgment of Court of Appeals reversed in part and affirmed in part; remanded.]

■ JUSTICE BLACKMUN, with whom JUSTICE KENNEDY and JUSTICE SOUTER join, concurring in part, concurring in the judgment in part, and dissenting in part.

. . . Our precedents do not allow us to infer a scope of pre-emption beyond that which clearly is mandated by Congress' language. In my view, *neither* version of the federal legislation at issue here provides the kind of unambiguous evidence of congressional intent necessary to displace state common-law damages claims. [Justice Blackmun agreed that the preemptive scope of the statutes is "governed entirely by the express language" of the statutes' pre-emption provisions. He also agreed with the Court's application of those principles to the 1965 Act. He disagreed, however, with the plurality's interpretation of the 1969 Act, concluding that the Act did not "clearly" evidence a congressional mandate to pre-empt state common-law claims.]

More important, the question whether common-law damages actions exert a regulatory effect on manufacturers analogous to that of positive enactments—an assumption crucial to the plurality's conclusion that the phrase "requirement or prohibition" encompasses common-law actions—is significantly more complicated than the plurality's brief quotation from San Diego Building Trades Council v. Garmon, 359 U.S. 236, 247 (1959), . . . would suggest.

The effect of tort law on a manufacturer's behavior is necessarily indirect. Although an award of damages by its very nature attaches additional consequences to the manufacturer's continued unlawful conduct, no particular course of action (e.g., the adoption of a new warning label) is required. A manufacturer found liable on, for example, a failure-to-warn claim may respond in a number of ways. It may decide to accept damages

make perfect sense: Congress was neither pre-empting nor saving common law as a whole—it was simply pre-empting particular common law claims, while saving others.

awards as a cost of doing business and not alter its behavior in any way.... Or, by contrast, it may choose to avoid future awards by dispensing warnings through a variety of alternative mechanisms, such as package inserts, public service advertisements, or general educational programs. The level of choice that a defendant retains in shaping its own behavior distinguishes the indirect regulatory effect of the common law from positive enactments such as statutes and administrative regulations.... Moreover, tort law has an entirely separate function—compensating victims—that sets it apart from direct forms of regulation.... [The Court] has declined on several recent occasions to find the regulatory effects of state tort law direct or substantial enough to warrant pre-emption....

■ Justice Scalia, with whom Justice Thomas joins, concurring in the judgment in part and dissenting in part.

Today's decision announces what, on its face, is an extraordinary and unprecedented principle of federal statutory construction: that express pre-emption provisions must be construed narrowly, "in light of the presumption against the pre-emption of state police power regulations." ... In my view, there is no merit to this newly crafted doctrine of narrow construction. Under the Supremacy Clause, U.S. Const., Art. VI, cl. 2, our job is to interpret Congress's decrees of pre-emption neither narrowly nor broadly, but in accordance with their apparent meaning. [Agreeing with the Court's threshold description of preemption principles, Justice Scalia concludes that the 1965 Act preempts the failure-to-warn claims and the 1969 Act preempts the remaining claims.]

The Court goes beyond ... traditional principles, however, to announce two new ones. First, it says that express pre-emption provisions must be given the narrowest possible construction. This is in its view the consequence of our oft-repeated assumption that, absent convincing evidence of statutory intent to pre-empt, " 'the historic police powers of the States [are] not to be superseded.' " But it seems to me that assumption dissolves once there is conclusive evidence of intent to pre-empt in the express words of the statute itself, and the only remaining question is what the scope of that pre-emption is meant to be. Thereupon, I think, our responsibility is to apply to the text ordinary principles of statutory construction.

* * *

The results seem odder still when one takes into account the second new rule that the Court announces: "When Congress has considered the issue of pre-emption and has included in the enacted legislation a provision explicitly addressing that issue, ... we need only identify the domain expressly pre-empted by [that provision]." Once there is an express pre-emption provision, in other words, all doctrines of implied pre-emption are eliminated. This proposition may be correct insofar as implied "field" pre-emption is concerned: The existence of an express pre-emption provision tends to contradict any inference that Congress intended to occupy a field broader than the statute's express language defines. However, with regard to implied "conflict" pre-emption—i.e., where state regulation actually conflicts with federal law, or where state regulation "stands as an obstacle to the accomplishment and execution" of Congress's purposes [citation], the Court's second new rule works mischief.... When this second novelty is combined with the first, the result is extraordinary: The statute that says *anything* about pre-emption must say *everything*; and it must do so with great exactitude, as any ambiguity concerning its scope will be read in favor of preserving state power. If this is to be the law, surely only the most sporting of congresses will dare to say anything about pre-emption. * * *

NOTES

1. Are you satisfied that Congress, in the preemption language at issue in *Cipollone*, intended to prohibit liability claims by injured smokers? Should a preemption provision which does not expressly prohibit liability for damages be read so broadly? Would it help to know the nature of the deliberative process involved in the drafting of the statute and its preemption provision?

Surely Congress is institutionally aware of the common-law damages claim preemption problem; certainly it could, if it wished, expressly *preclude* such claims in a preemption clause, or, if it so chose, specifically *preserve* such claims in a "savings" clause. See note 22 in Justice Stevens' opinion. Why do you suppose that Congress typically chooses instead to remain mute on this important issue? Which way (if either) should deliberate muteness cut—toward or against the preemption of such claims?

2. Avoiding Preemption—The Cigarette Litigation. Products liability litigation involving cigarettes is now driven by *Cipollone*'s Part V distinction between claims that are preempted and those that are not. See, e.g., Conley v. R.J. Reynolds Tobacco Co., 286 F.Supp.2d 1097 (N.D. Cal. 2002); Carter v. Brown & Williamson Tobacco Corp., 778 So.2d 932 (Fla. 2000); Wright v. Brooke Group Ltd., 652 N.W.2d 159 (Iowa 2002); American Tobacco Co. v. Grinnell, 951 S.W.2d 420 (Tex.1997).

3. Whither *Implied* Preemption? Prior to *Cipollone*, most courts rejected *express* preemption claims, even in cigarette warnings cases, and opted instead to analyze the issue solely in terms of *implied* preemption. Turning that approach on its head, *Cipollone* appeared to reduce the doctrine of implied preemption nearly to a nullity. In Freightliner Corp. v. Myrick, 514 U.S. 280, 288 (1995), involving a claim of preemption under the National Traffic and Motor Vehicle Safety Act, the Court went out of its way to offer the following inscrutable observations: "The fact that an express definition of the pre-emptive reach of a statute 'implies'—i.e. supports a reasonable inference—that Congress did not intend to pre-empt other matters does not mean that the express clause entirely forecloses any possibility of implied pre-emption.... At best, *Cipollone* supports an inference that an express pre-emption clause forecloses implied pre-emption; it does not establish a rule." *Myrick* "is peculiar at best, for it permits courts to use implied-preemption analysis to determine whether there is a need for implied-preemption analysis [which] seems to muddy the waters previously clarified by *Cipollone*." Nader & Page, Automobile–Design Liability and Compliance with Federal Standards, 64 Geo.Wash.L.Rev. 415 (1996).

4. The Preemption Struggle. In the decade after *Cipollone*, the Court decided a number of preemption cases. In each one, the Court seemed to strain under the express preemption analysis required by *Cipollone*. The justices struggled over the statutory interpretation principles to be used in express preemption analysis; the value, if any, to be placed on the presumption against preemption; and the importance of agency action regarding preemption.

For example, in Medtronic, Inc. v. Lohr, 518 U.S. 470 (1996), the Court was asked to determine whether the Medical Device Amendments (MDA) to the Food, Drug, and Cosmetic Act (FDCA) preempted claims arising from a failed pacemaker. Defendant argued that the market approval mechanism it used, known as pre-market notification, contained sufficiently detailed product requirements that a common-law action would conflict with the express preemption provision of the MDA which prohibited States from imposing any "requirement . . . different from, or in addition to, any requirement" which relates to the "safety or effectiveness of the device." 21 U.S.C. § 360(k). The FDA had interpreted this provision to preempt only state requirements that were inconsistent with specific FDA regulations.

The MDA has a classification scheme for medical devices which subjects devices with the greatest risk to the greatest regulatory control. The pacemaker in *Medtronic* is such a device, but because it was "substantially equivalent" to a previously approved device, it could be marketed under a simpler and less expensive approval method known as pre-market notification. The courts of appeals had differed widely on the scope of MDA preemption, but most had found preemption under an express analysis. Compare, Kennedy v. Collagen Corp., 67 F.3d 1453 (9th Cir. 1995)(common-law actions are not "requirements" under the MDA; no preemption) with Lohr v. Medtronic, Inc., 56 F.3d 1335 (11th Cir. 1995)(common-law actions are requirements; preemption).

All the justices in *Medtronic* agreed that the express preemption provision controlled, but that is where their agreement ended. The plurality thought the MDA would "rarely" preempt common-law claims, and tried to interpret the language of the MDA narrowly considering the presumption against preemption, as it had the cigarette labeling statute in *Cipollone*. The plurality determined that common-law claims were not "requirements" under the MDA and found no claims preempted. Justice Breyer, concurring in result, thought the MDA might preempt some common-law claims as "requirements" but expressed serious misgivings about trying to find Congress' intent in such a highly ambiguous preemption provision. In finding no preemption, Justice Breyer gave the Court its majority. Consistent with the plurality, he was influenced by the FDA's own regulation that counseled against preemption. Four justices in dissent thought the MDA did preempt some common-law claims as "requirements," and rejected the majority's reliance on both the presumption against preemption and agency position on preemption.

5. After *Cipollone* and *Medtronic*, are common-law damages claims "requirements" or are they not? Is there anything left of implied preemption after *Medtronic*? And what of the presumption against preemption—does it require a narrow reading of plain meaning, or not? A number of cases involving preemption under regulatory schemes such as the Federal Insecticide, Fungicide and Rodenticide Act (FIFRA), the CPSC, the Federal Boat Safety Act (FBSA), and others, were on the horizon and in need of answers to these questions. Does the following case provide those answers?

Geier v. American Honda Motor Company

Supreme Court of the United States, 2000.
529 U.S. 861, 120 S.Ct. 1913, 146 L.Ed.2d 914.

■ JUSTICE BREYER, delivered the opinion of the court, in which CHIEF JUSTICE REHNQUIST, and JUSTICES O'CONNOR, SCALIA, and KENNEDY, joined. JUSTICE STEVENS, filed a dissenting opinion, in which JUSTICES SOUTER, THOMAS, and GINSBURG, joined.

This case focuses on the 1984 version of a Federal Motor Vehicle Safety Standard promulgated by the Department of Transportation under the authority of the National Traffic and Motor Vehicle Safety Act of 1966, 80 Stat. 718, 15 U.S.C. §§ 1381 et seq. (1988 ed.). The standard, FMVSS 208, required auto manufacturers to equip some but not all of their 1987 vehicles with passive restraints. We ask whether the Act pre-empts a state common-law tort action in which the plaintiff claims that the defendant auto manufacturer, who was in compliance with the standard, should nonetheless have equipped a 1987 automobile with airbags. We conclude that the Act, taken together with FMVSS 208, pre-empts the lawsuit.

I

In 1992, petitioner Alexis Geier, driving a 1987 Honda Accord, collided with a tree and was seriously injured. The car was equipped with manual shoulder and lap belts which Geier had buckled up at the time. The car was not equipped with airbags or other passive restraint devices.

[Geier and her parents sued the car's manufacturer, American Honda Motor Company, Inc., under District of Columbia tort law claiming that Honda had designed its car negligently and defectively because it lacked a driver's side airbag. The District Court dismissed the lawsuit concluding that because FMVSS 208 gave car manufacturers a choice as to whether to install airbags, petitioners' lawsuit sought to establish a different safety standard i.e., an airbag requirement and was, thus, expressly pre-empted by the Act which pre-empts "any safety standard" that is not identical to a federal safety standard, 15 U.S.C. § 1392(d). The Court of Appeals found that, given the existence of the Act's "saving" clause, 15 U.S.C. § 1397(k), plaintiffs' claims were not expressly preempted, but, rather, posed an obstacle to the accomplishment of FMVSS 208's objectives and were there-fore pre-empted under "ordinary pre-emption principles." Acknowledging a split in authority between several state courts which had held that such claims are neither expressly nor impliedly preempted, and all of the federal Circuit Courts of Appeals that had found pre-emption on one theory or the other, the Court] granted certiorari to resolve these differences. We now hold that this kind of "no airbag" lawsuit conflicts with the objectives of FMVSS 208, a standard authorized by the Act, and is therefore pre-empted by the Act.

In reaching our conclusion, we consider three subsidiary questions. First, does the Act's express pre-emption provision pre-empt this lawsuit? We think not. Second, do ordinary pre-emption principles nonetheless apply? We hold that they do. Third, does this lawsuit actually conflict with FMVSS 208, hence with the Act itself? We hold that it does.

II

We first ask whether the Safety Act's express pre-emption provision pre-empts this tort action. The provision reads as follows:

> Whenever a Federal motor vehicle safety standard established under this subchapter is in effect, no State or political subdivision of a State shall have any authority either to establish, or to continue in effect, with respect to any motor vehicle or item of motor vehicle equipment[,] any safety standard applicable to the same aspect of performance of such vehicle or item of equipment which is not identical to the Federal standard.

15 U.S.C. § 1392(d) (1988 ed.). American Honda points out that a majority of this Court has said that a somewhat similar statutory provision in a different federal statute—a provision that uses the word "requirements"—may well expressly pre-empt similar tort actions. See, e.g., Medtronic, Inc. v. Lohr, 518 U.S. 470 (1996). Petitioners reply that this statute speaks of pre-empting a state-law "safety standard," not a "requirement," and that a tort action does not involve a safety standard. Hence, they conclude, the express pre-emption provision does not apply.

We need not determine the precise significance of the use of the word "standard," rather than "requirement," however, for the Act contains another provision, which resolves the disagreement. That provision, a "saving" clause, says that "[c]ompliance with" a federal safety standard "does not exempt any person from any liability under common law." 15 U.S.C. § 1397(k) (1988 ed.). The saving clause assumes that there are some significant number of common-law liability cases to save. And a reading of the express pre-emption provision that excludes common-law tort actions gives actual meaning to the saving clause's literal language, while leaving adequate room for state tort law to operate for example, where federal law creates only a floor, i.e., a minimum safety standard. . . . Without the saving clause, a broad reading of the express pre-emption provision arguably might pre-empt those actions, for, as we have just mentioned, it is possible to read the pre-emption provision, standing alone, as applying to standards imposed in common-law tort actions, as well as standards contained in state legislation or regulations. And if so, it would pre-empt all nonidentical state standards established in tort actions covering the same aspect of performance as an applicable federal standard, even if the federal standard merely established a minimum standard. On that broad reading of the pre-emption clause little, if any, potential "liability at common law" would remain. And few, if any, state tort actions would remain for the saving clause to save. We have found no convincing indication that Congress wanted to pre-empt, not only state statutes and regulations, but also common-law tort actions, in such circumstances. Hence the broad reading cannot be correct. The language of the pre-emption provision permits a narrow reading that excludes common-law actions. Given the presence of the saving clause, we conclude that the pre-emption clause must be so read.

III

We have just said that the saving clause at least removes tort actions from the scope of the express pre-emption clause. Does it do more? In particular, does it foreclose or limit the operation of ordinary pre-emption principles insofar as those principles instruct us to read statutes as pre-empting state laws (including common-law rules) that "actually conflict" with the statute or federal standards promulgated thereunder? [Citations omitted.] Petitioners concede, as they must in light of *Freightliner Corp. v. Myrick*, that the pre-emption provision, by itself, does not foreclose (through negative implication) "any possibility of implied [conflict] pre-emption," (discussing *Cipollone v. Liggett Group, Inc.*). But they argue that the saving clause has that very effect.

We recognize that, when this Court previously considered the pre-emptive effect of the statute's language, it appeared to leave open the question of how, or the extent to which, the saving clause saves state-law tort actions that conflict with federal regulations promulgated under the Act. [Citation.] We now conclude that the saving clause (like the express pre-emption provision) does not bar the ordinary working of conflict pre-emption principles.

Nothing in the language of the saving clause suggests an intent to save state-law tort actions that conflict with federal regulations. The words "[c]ompliance" and "does not exempt," 15 U.S.C. §§ 1397(k) (1988 ed.), sound as if they simply bar a special kind of defense, namely, a defense that compliance with a federal standard automatically exempts a defendant from state law, whether the Federal Government meant that standard to be an absolute requirement or only a minimum one. See Restatement (Third) of Torts: Products Liability § 4(b), cmt. *e* (1997) (distinguishing between state-law compliance defense and a federal claim of pre-emption). It is difficult to understand why Congress would have insisted on a compliance-with-federal-regulation precondition to the provision's applicability had it wished the Act to "save" all state-law tort actions, regardless of their potential threat to the objectives of federal safety standards promulgated under that Act. Nor does our interpretation conflict with the purpose of the saving provision, say by rendering it ineffectual. As we have previously explained, the saving provision still makes clear that the express pre-emption provision does not of its own force pre-empt common-law tort actions. And it thereby preserves those actions that seek to establish greater safety than the minimum safety achieved by a federal regulation intended to provide a floor.

Moreover, this Court has repeatedly "decline[d] to give broad effect to saving clauses where doing so would upset the careful regulatory scheme established by federal law." United States v. Locke, 529 U.S. 89 (2000); [citations omitted.] We find this concern applicable in the present case. And we conclude that the saving clause foresees—it does not foreclose—the possibility that a federal safety standard will pre-empt a state common-law tort action with which it conflicts. We do not understand the dissent to disagree, for it acknowledges that ordinary pre-emption principles apply, at least sometimes.

Neither do we believe that the pre-emption provision, the saving provision, or both together, create some kind of "special burden" [as suggested by the dissent] beyond that inherent in ordinary pre-emption principles which "special burden" would specially disfavor pre-emption here. The two provisions, read together, reflect a neutral policy, not a specially favorable or unfavorable policy, towards the application of ordinary conflict pre-emption principles. On the one hand, the pre-emption provision itself reflects a desire to subject the industry to a single, uniform set of federal safety standards. Its pre-emption of all state standards, even those that might stand in harmony with federal law, suggests an intent to avoid the conflict, uncertainty, cost, and occasional risk to safety itself that too many different safety-standard cooks might otherwise create. [This policy favors pre-emption of state tort suits, for the rules of law that judges and juries apply in such suits may themselves create uncertainty and conflict when different juries in different States reach different decisions on similar facts. On the other hand, the saving clause reflects a congressional determination that occasional nonuniformity is a small price to pay for a system in which juries not only create, but also enforce, safety standards, while simultaneously compensating victims. That policy disfavors pre-emption.] But we can find nothing in any natural reading of the two provisions that would favor one set of policies over the other where a jury-imposed safety standard actually conflicts with a federal safety standard.

Why, in any event, would Congress not have wanted ordinary pre-emption principles to apply where an actual conflict with a federal objective is at stake? Some such principle is needed. In its absence, state law could impose legal duties that would conflict directly with federal regulatory mandates, say, by premising liability upon the presence of the very wind-shield retention requirements that federal law requires. Insofar as petitioners' argument would permit common-law actions that "actually conflict" with federal regulations, it would take from those who would enforce a federal law the very ability to achieve the law's congressionally mandated objectives that the Constitution, through the operation of ordinary pre-emption principles, seeks to protect. To the extent that such an interpretation of the saving provision reads into a particular federal law toleration of a conflict that those principles would otherwise forbid, it permits that law to defeat its own objectives, or potentially, as the Court has put it before, to " 'destroy itself.' " [Citation.] We do not claim that Congress lacks the constitutional power to write a statute that mandates such a complex type of state/federal relationship. But there is no reason to believe Congress has done so here.

[Further, the] Court has not previously driven a legal wedge—only a terminological one—between "conflicts" that prevent or frustrate the accomplishment of a federal objective and "conflicts" that make it "impossible" for private parties to comply with both state and federal law. Rather, it has said that both forms of conflicting state law are "nullified" by the

Supremacy Clause, [citations], and it has assumed that Congress would not want either kind of conflict.... We see no grounds, then, for attempting to distinguish among types of federal-state conflict for purposes of analyzing whether such a conflict warrants pre-emption in a particular case. That kind of analysis, moreover, would engender legal uncertainty with its inevitable systemwide costs (e.g., conflicts, delay, and expense) as courts tried sensibly to distinguish among varieties of "conflict" (which often shade, one into the other) when applying this complicated rule.... In a word, ordinary pre-emption principles, grounded in longstanding precedent, [citation], apply....

IV

The basic question, then, is whether a common-law "no airbag" action like the one before us actually conflicts with FMVSS 208. We hold that it does.

In petitioners' and the dissent's view, FMVSS 208 sets a minimum airbag standard. As far as FMVSS 208 is concerned, the more airbags, and the sooner, the better. But that was not the Secretary's view. DOT's comments, which accompanied the promulgation of FMVSS 208, make clear that the standard deliberately provided the manufacturer with a range of choices among different passive restraint devices. Those choices would bring about a mix of different devices introduced gradually over time; and FMVSS 208 would thereby lower costs, overcome technical safety problems, encourage technological development, and win widespread consumer acceptance, all of which would promote FMVSS 208's safety objectives. See generally 49 Fed.Reg. 28962 (1984).

A

The history of FMVSS 208 helps explain why and how DOT sought these objectives. [In 1967, DOT, understanding that seatbelts would save many lives, required manufacturers to install manual seat belts in all automobiles. Nevertheless, most occupants would not buckle up. DOT then began to investigate "passive restraints," such as airbags and automatic seatbelts. In 1970, it amended FMVSS 208 to include some passive protection requirements, including airbags as one of several "equally acceptable" devices, stating that it neither " 'favored' [n]or expected the introduction of airbag systems." [Citation.] In 1971, it permitted compliance through the use of non-detachable passive belts, and, in 1972, it mandated full passive protection for all front seat occupants for vehicles made after August 15, 1975. For vehicles manufactured in the interim, manufacturers could either install a passive restraint device or retain manual belts and add an "ignition interlock" device that prevented the ignition from engaging if occupants were un-buckled. The interlock, and accompanying buzzer to encourage attachment of the buckle, was popular with manufacturers but not consumers. Congress, responding to public pressure, forbade DOT from requiring such devices. DOT subsequently suspended the passive restraint requirements, sought to win public acceptance of them, and promulgated the 1984 version in issue.]

B

Read in light of this history, DOT's own contemporaneous explanation of FMVSS 208 makes clear that the 1984 version of FMVSS 208 reflected the following significant considerations. First, buckled up seatbelts are a vital ingredient of automobile safety. [Second, despite the enormous and unnecessary risks from not buckling up, more than 80% of front seat passengers would leave their seatbelts unbuckled. Third, airbags could make up for the dangers caused by unbuckled belts, but they could not make up for them entirely. Fourth, automatic restraint systems had their own disadvantages—primarily consumer non-acceptance and dislike. Fifth, airbags introduced special safety risks, primarily to out-of-position occupants (usually children) in small cars. [Citation.] Sixth, airbags were expected to be significantly more expensive, raising the average cost of a vehicle $320 for full frontal airbags. The agency also worried that the high replacement cost—estimated to be $800—could prevent car owners from replacing them after deployment. Seventh, the public, for reasons of cost, fear, or physical intrusiveness, might resist use of any of passive restraint devices, particularly airbags.]

FMVSS 208 reflected these considerations in several ways. Most importantly, that standard deliberately sought variety—a mix of several different passive restraint systems. It did so by setting a performance requirement for passive restraint devices and allowing manufacturers to choose among different passive restraint mechanisms, such as airbags, automatic belts, or other passive restraint technologies ... And DOT explained why FMVSS 208 sought the mix of devices that it expected its performance standard to produce. [DOT rejected an] "all airbag" standard because of safety concerns (perceived or real) associated with airbags, which concerns threatened a "backlash" more easily overcome "if airbags" were "not the only way of complying." [FMVSS 208] deliberately sought a gradual phase-in of passive restraints. [The] phased-in requirement would allow more time for manufacturers to develop airbags or other, better, safer passive restraint systems. It would help develop information about the comparative effectiveness of different systems, would lead to a mix in which airbags and other nonseatbelt passive restraint systems played a more prominent role than would otherwise result, and would promote public acceptance.

* * *

In effect, petitioners' tort action depends upon its claim that manufacturers had a duty to install an airbag when they manufactured the 1987 Honda Accord. Such a state law—i.e., a rule of state tort law imposing such a duty—by its terms would have required manufacturers of all similar cars to install airbags rather than other passive restraint systems, such as automatic belts or passive interiors. It thereby would have presented an obstacle to the variety and mix of devices that the federal regulation sought. It would have required all manufacturers to have installed airbags in respect to the entire District-of-Columbia-related portion of their 1987 new car fleet, even though FMVSS 208 at that time required only that 10% of a manufacturer's nationwide fleet be equipped with any passive restraint device at all. It thereby also would have stood as an obstacle to the gradual passive restraint phase-in that the federal regulation deliberately imposed. In addition, it could have made less likely the adoption of a state mandatory buckle-up law. Because the rule of law for which petitioners contend would have stood "as an obstacle to the accomplishment and execution of" the important means-related federal objectives that we have just discussed, it is pre-empted. [Citations.]

Petitioners ask this Court to calculate the precise size of the "obstacle," with the aim of minimizing it, by considering the risk of tort liability and a successful tort action's incentive-related or timing-related compliance effects.... But this Court's pre-emption cases do not ordinarily turn on such compliance-related considerations as whether a private party in practice would ignore state legal obligations—paying, say, a fine instead—or how likely it is that state law actually would be enforced. Rather, this Court's pre-emption cases ordinarily assume compliance with the state law duty in question. The Court has on occasion suggested that tort law may be somewhat different, and that related considerations—for example, the ability to pay damages instead of modifying one's behavior—may be relevant for pre-emption purposes. See *Cipollone*, 505 U.S., at 536–39 (Blackmun, J., concurring in part). In other cases, the Court has found tort law to conflict with federal law without engaging in that kind of an analysis. [Citations.] We need not try to resolve these differences here.... We simply find unpersuasive their arguments attempting to undermine the Government's demonstration of actual conflict.

One final point: We place some weight upon DOT's interpretation of FMVSS 208's objectives and its conclusion, as set forth in the Government's brief, that a tort suit such as this one would " 'stan[d] as an obstacle to the accomplishment and execution' "of those objectives. Congress has delegated to DOT authority to implement the statute; the subject matter is technical; and the relevant history and background are complex and extensive. The agency is likely to have a thorough understanding of its own regulation and its objectives and is "uniquely qualified" to comprehend the likely impact of state requirements. [Citation.] And DOT has explained FMVSS 208's objectives, and the interference that "no airbag" suits pose thereto, consistently over time. In these circumstances, the agency's own views should make a difference. [Further, we reject the requirement, suggested by the dissent, of] a formal agency statement of pre-emptive intent as a prerequisite to concluding that an actual conflict exists. Indeed, one can assume that Congress or an agency ordinarily would not intend to permit a significant conflict. While we certainly accept the dissent's basic position that a court should not find pre-emption too readily in the absence of clear evidence of a conflict, [citation], ... we find such evidence here. To insist on a specific expression of agency intent to pre-empt, made after notice-and-comment rulemaking, would be in certain cases to tolerate conflicts that an agency, and therefore Congress, is most unlikely to have intended....

Regardless, the language of FMVSS 208 and the contemporaneous 1984 DOT explanation is clear enough—even without giving DOT's own view special weight. FMVSS 208 sought a gradually developing mix of alternative passive restraint devices for safety-related reasons. The rule of state tort law for which petitioners argue would stand as an "obstacle" to the accomplishment of that objective. And the statute foresees the application of ordinary principles of pre-emption in cases of actual conflict. Hence, the tort action is pre-empted.

The judgment of the Court of Appeals is affirmed.

■ JUSTICE STEVENS, with whom JUSTICE SOUTER, JUSTICE THOMAS, and JUSTICE GINSBURG join, dissenting.

Airbag technology has been available to automobile manufacturers for over 30 years. There is now general agreement on the proposition "that, to be safe, a car must have an airbag." Indeed, current federal law imposes that requirement on all automobile manufacturers. See 49 U.S.C. 30127; 49 C.F.R. 571.208, S4.1.5.3 (1998). The question raised by petitioner's common-law tort action is whether that proposition was sufficiently obvious when Honda's 1987 Accord was manufactured to make the failure to install such a safety feature actionable under theories of negligence or defective design. The Court holds that an interim regulation motivated by the Secretary of Transportation's desire to foster gradual development of a variety of passive restraint devices deprives state courts of jurisdiction to answer that question. I respectfully dissent from that holding, and especially from the Court's unprecedented extension of the doctrine of pre-emption.

* * * The rule the Court enforces today was not enacted by Congress and is not to be found in the text of any Executive Order or regulation. It has a unique origin: it is the product of the Court's interpretation of the final commentary accompanying an interim administrative regulation and the history of airbag regulation generally ... It is ... clear to me that the objectives that the Secretary intended to achieve through the adoption of Federal Motor Vehicle Safety Standard 208 would not be frustrated one whit by allowing state courts to determine whether in 1987 the life-saving advantages of airbags had become sufficiently obvious that their omission might constitute a design defect in some new cars. . . .

[It is axiomatic that federal law is supreme in cases of conflict with state law.] On the other hand, it is equally clear that the Supremacy Clause does not give unelected federal judges carte blanche to use federal law as a means of imposing their own ideas of tort reform on the States. Because of the role of States as separate sovereigns in our federal system, we have long presumed that state laws—particularly those, such as the provision of tort remedies to compensate for personal injuries, that are within the scope of the States' historic police powers—are not to be pre-empted by a federal statute unless it is the clear and manifest purpose of Congress to do so. [Citations.]

* * * Given the cumulative force of the fact that 1392(d) does not expressly pre-empt common-law claims and the fact that 1397(k) was

obviously intended to limit the pre-emptive effect of the Secretary's safety standards, it is quite wrong for the Court to assume that a possible implicit conflict with the purposes to be achieved by such a standard should have the same pre-emptive effect " 'as an obstacle to the accomplishment and execution of the full purposes and objectives of Congress.' " Properly construed, the Safety Act imposes a special burden on a party relying on an arguable implicit conflict with a temporary regulatory policy—rather than a conflict with congressional policy or with the text of any regulation—to demonstrate that a common-law claim has been pre-empted. * * * [I]t is evident that Honda has not crossed the high threshold established by our decisions regarding pre-emption of state laws that allegedly frustrate federal purposes: it has not demonstrated that allowing a common-law no-airbag claim to go forward would impose an obligation on manufacturers that directly and irreconcilably contradicts any primary objective that the Secretary set forth with clarity in Standard 208 ... [T]he text of Standard 208 (which the Court does not even bother to quote in its opinion), ... does not contain any expression of an intent to displace state law. Given our repeated emphasis on the importance of the presumption against preemption, [citations], this silence lends additional support to the conclusion that the continuation of whatever common-law liability may exist in a case like this poses no danger of frustrating any of the Secretary's primary purposes in promulgating Standard 208.

* * *

While the presumption is important in assessing the pre-emptive reach of federal statutes, it becomes crucial when the pre-emptive effect of an administrative regulation is at issue. Unlike Congress, administrative agencies are clearly not designed to represent the interests of States, yet with relative ease they can promulgate comprehensive and detailed regulations that have broad pre-emption ramifications for state law. * * * Furthermore, [no case has] upheld a regulatory claim of frustration-of-purposes implied conflict pre-emption based on nothing more than an ex post administrative litigation position and inferences from regulatory history and final commentary. The latter two sources are even more malleable than legislative history. Thus, when snippets from them are combined with the Court's broad conception of a doctrine of frustration-of-purposes preemption untempered by the presumption, a vast, undefined area of state law becomes vulnerable to pre-emption by any related federal law or regulation....

NOTES

1. What is the proper method of preemption analysis after *Geier*? Which of the *Geier* opinions is most persuasive on the result of an express preemption analysis? Is anything left of the express preemption analysis of *Cipollone* and *Medtronic*?

2. What features of the regulatory history of FMVSS 208 weigh in favor of finding an actual conflict between the federal regulatory objectives and state common-law tort claims? What was the nature of the federal regulatory objective in

Geier? Why did Ms. Geier's common-law damages action conflict with that federal objective?

3. Can you identify general considerations that can be applied to implied conflict preemption analysis under other statutes? Does implied conflict preemption analysis require ad hoc balancing in each case? For an effort to identify the general considerations that influence the Court's determination of actual conflict in implied preemption, see Davis, On Preemption, Congressional Intent and Conflict of Laws, 66 U. Pitt. L. Rev. 181 (2004).

4. The Presumption Against Preemption and Implied Preemption. After *Geier*, what is the importance of the presumption against preemption in implied conflict preemption? Does the presumption play any role in express preemption?

More recently, in Bates v. Dow Agrosciences LLC, 544 U.S. 431 (2005), the Court revived the presumption against preemption, as discussed below. In the long run, what will happen to this vital principle of federalism is anyone's guess.

5. Agency Interpretation of Express Preemptive Scope. What effect should an agency's own interpretation of the preemptive scope of its regulations have on preemption analysis? In *Medtronic*, supra, the Court was influenced by the FDA's own narrow interpretation of the preemptive scope of its regulations. See 21 C.F.R. § 808.1. Do you agree with Justice Stevens in *Geier* that for an agency's own interpretation of the preemptive scope of its regulations to be given deference, it should go through the formal rule-making process?

The importance of agency determination of preemptive scope is illustrated by cases involving the MDA and the preemptive effect of the pre-market approval process. Consistent with the holding in *Medtronic* that generalized FDA safety regulations are not preemptive, lower courts have ruled that state common-law claims *are* preempted when the FDA regulations are more exacting and device-specific, as with the pre-market approval process. Brooks v. Howmedica, Inc., 273 F.3d 785 (8th Cir. 2001). Cf., Woods v. Gliatech, Inc., 218 F.Supp.2d 802 (W.D. Va. 2002)(citing split in authority and finding no preemption). Initially, the FDA took the position that the pre-market approval process requirements do not preempt common-law claims. The FDA changed its position in 2002 and argued for express preemption in amici curiae briefs in a number of pending cases. The FDA's new position is influencing courts to find express preemption. Riegel v. Medtronic, Inc., 451 F.3d 104 (2d Cir. 2006); Gomez v. St. Jude Medical Daig Div., Inc., 442 F.3d 919 (5th Cir. 2006); Horn v. Thoratec Corp., 376 F.3d 163 (3d Cir. 2004). Do you agree that such a change in position should have express preemptive effect? For a discussion of whether courts should defer to the FDA's new interpretation of its regulations, see Ausness, "After You, My Dear Alphonse!": Should the Courts Defer to the FDA's New Interpretation of § 360k(a) of the Medical Device Amendments?, 80 Tulane L. Rev. 727 (2006).

Other agencies are also seeking express preemption based on revised positions regarding the effect of their regulations. See e.g., Final Rule: Standard for the Flammability (Open Flame) of Mattress Sets, 16 C.F.R. Part 1633, at preamble ("The Commission intends and expects that the new mattress flammability standard will preempt inconsistent state standards and requirements, whether in the form of positive enactments or court created requirements.")(effective July 2007).

6. Agency Position on Preemption: Implied Conflict Preemption. In cases involving implied conflict preemption, should an agency's assessment of conflict, and thus the preemptive scope of its actions, be given deference as in the express preemption context? How should statements of agency intent regarding preemption affect implied conflict preemption analysis? *Geier* placed "some weight" on the agency's contemporaneous explanation of the federal objectives in issue and its consistent view over time of the negative impact of state tort law on those objectives. The Court declined to require an express statement of preemptive intent to conclude that an actual conflict existed. What aspects of the agency's position were the most influential?

The Food Drug and Cosmetic Act does not contain an express preemption clause relevant to drugs. Historically, courts have found that the FDCA does not impliedly preempt products liability claims regarding warning inadequacy against manufacturers of prescription drugs and have taken the position that FDA drug labeling regulations impose only minimum standards. See Motus v. Pfizer, Inc., 127 F.Supp.2d 1085 (C.D.Cal.2000), aff'd on other grounds, 358 F.3d 659 (9th Cir. 2004); Caraker v. Sandoz Pharm. Corp., 172 F.Supp.2d 1018 (S.D.Ill. 2001). The statute delegates authority to the FDA to preempt state law, but the Agency has not generally done so for prescription drugs.

The FDA's traditional position has been that state tort laws supplement its regulatory scheme. In 2003, in *Motus v. Pfizer, Inc.,* the FDA altered its traditional position and argued in amici curiae briefs that the drug labeling requirement in issue was intended to preempt state common-law damages actions based on the labeling. The FDA has promulgated a new labeling regulation which officially takes this position in its introductory comments, or preamble, but not in the regulation per se. Final Prescription Drug Labeling Regulation, 71 Fed. Reg. 3922, 3934 (January 24, 2006)(effective June 30, 2006)(approved prescription drug labeling preempts conflicting state product liability laws). Apply *Geier*'s implied preemption analysis to this context: what effect will such a statement have on implied conflict preemption? Several trial courts have found preemption based on the FDA's new position. E.g., Colacicco v. Apotex, Inc., 432 F.Supp.2d 514 (E.D. Pa. 2006). Is that conclusion consistent with *Geier*? See Davis, The Battle for Implied Preemption: The FDA and Prescription Drug Products Liability Actions, ___ L.Rev. ___ (forthcoming 2007)(available at http://ssrn.com/author=622762).

7. Preemption Under Other Statutes.

A.   The Consumer Product Safety Act. With an understanding of preemption analysis from *Cipollone* and *Geier*, reconsider *Moe v. MTD Products*, above, on the preemptive effect of the CPSA and the power mower design and warning standards promulgated under it. The *Moe* court found that the CPSA expressly preempted the plaintiff's warning claim but not the design claim. What do you think? The CPSA also contains a "savings clause," not unlike the savings clause in *Geier*. How should the CPSA savings clause operate, according to *Geier*? For an analysis of the CPSA preemption provision relating to regulations for shower glass doors, see Leipart v. Guardian Indus., Inc., 234 F.3d 1063, 1068 (9th Cir. 2000)(finding no preemption of claims alleging design, manufacturing and warning failures in spite of plaintiff's reliance on "a different (and higher) [state] standard of care than that imposed by the applicable CPSA standard").

B.   Federal Insecticide, Fungicide, and Rodenticide Act (FIFRA). FIFRA established a comprehensive regulatory scheme administered by the EPA registering and labeling pesticides, insecticides, herbicides, and other toxic products. 7 U.S.C. §§ 136–136(y) (2000). Under the Act, a manufacturer must submit proposed labels to the EPA to assure that they are "adequate to protect health and environment" and "likely to be read and understood." FIFRA expressly prohibits the states from imposing any "requirements for labeling or packaging in addition to or different from those required" under the Act. Before *Cipollone*, most courts concluded that neither express nor implied preemption under FIFRA prevented claims based on inadequate labeling or defective design. E.g., Ferebee v. Chevron Chemical Co., 736 F.2d 1529 (D.C. Cir. 1984). After *Cipollone*, lower courts reevaluated the preemptive effect of FIFRA, most holding that the Act preempts at least warning claims in such cases. E.g., Lowe's Home Centers, Inc. v. Olin Corp., 313 F.3d 1307 (11th Cir. 2002).

The Supreme Court finally addressed FIFRA preemption in Bates v. Dow Agrosciences LLC, 544 U.S. 431 (2005), where a group of Texas farmers asserted damage claims against Dow, the manufacturer of "Strongarm," a weedkiller conditionally registered by the EPA under FIFRA, for damage the herbicide had caused to their peanut crops. The Court of Appeals ruled that the plaintiffs' defective design and manufacture, negligent testing, and breach of warranty claims were all expressly preempted, based on a broad reading of "requirement" to include common-law tort actions that might "induce" a manufacturer to change its label. Disagreeing with such an expansive reading, the Supreme Court reversed, rejecting the inducement test and cautioning courts not to read *Cipollone*'s discussion of requirement so literally: "A requirement is a rule of law that must be obeyed; an event, such as a jury verdict, that merely motivates an optional decision is not a requirement." Id. at 445. For evidence that lower courts are following *Bates'* guidance and are narrowing FIFRA preemption, see Mortellite v. Novartis Crop Protection Inc., 460 F.3d 483 (3d Cir. 2006).

The *Bates* Court provided guidance on two other important aspects of preemption analysis: the continuing importance of the presumption against preemption and the effect of a change in agency position on preemption analysis. The Court strongly invoked the presumption against preemption, noting that the "long history of tort litigation against manufacturers of poisonous substances adds force to the basic presumption against preemption." 544 U.S. at 449. The history of tort litigation supported a finding of no preemption because had Congress intended "to deprive injured parties of a long available form of compensation," it would have clearly expressed such intent. Id. The Court also frowned upon reliance on the EPA's position on preemption because that position had changed within the past five years, calling the interpretation of preemptive scope "particularly dubious" as a result. Id. at 452.

Neither FIFRA, the MDA, nor the FDCA requires specific warning language. Instead, manufacturers propose certain language, and the regulatory agency (the EPA or the FDA) either approves or disapproves. In the cigarette context, of course, Congress itself specifically mandated the warning language. Cigarettes are essentially a single "product," whereas pesticides, medical devices, and prescription drugs vary enormously in type and risk. How much independent judgment over particular warning language should an agency exercise before a products liability action based thereon should be preempted?

C. Federal Boat Safety Act (FBSA). Congress enacted the Federal Boat Safety Act of 1971 to establish "a coordinated national boating safety program." 46 U.S.C. §§ 4301–431 (2000). The FBSA gives the Coast Guard the authority to promulgate safety standards for boating equipment. In the late 1980s, the Coast Guard studied the advisability of requiring manufacturers to equip motorboats with propeller guards because of the recurring problem of risk to swimmers from impact with them. The Coast Guard declined to require such guards for reasons of safety, economics, and feasibility. The FBSA's preemption provision prohibits state regulations that are not "identical" to federal regulations and a savings clause preserves liability at common law in spite of compliance with a federal standard. 46 U.S.C. § 4306.

In Sprietsma v. Mercury Marine, Inc., 537 U.S. 51 (2002), a unanimous Supreme Court concluded that the FBSA does not preempt design defect claims based on the absence of a propeller guard. First, the express preemption provision was limited to positive state laws and regulations, not common-law damages claims, and the savings clause confirmed that conclusion. The Court, in an opinion by Justice Stevens, followed *Geier*'s implied conflict preemption analysis and found no implied preemption because there was no federal regulation with which a state common-law damages claim could conflict—the Coast Guard's conclusion not to regulate was insufficient to displace state law given that both the Act and state law have the primary goal of safety.

D. Other statutes. A number of other federal regulatory schemes regulate product safety. See, e.g., the Federal Hazardous Substances Act, 15 U.S.C. § 1261–1277; the Occupational Safety and Health Act, 29 U.S.C. § 651 et seq.; the Boiler Inspection Act, 49 U.S.C. § 20701 et seq.; and the National Manufactured Housing Construction and Safety Standards Act, 42 U.S.C. § 5401 et seq., among others. A number of cases interpreting these statutes have been decided, many finding preemption post-*Cipollone*. Compare Milanese v. Rust–Oleum Corp., 244 F.3d 104 (2d Cir. 2001)(FHSA; preemption of warning claims) and Gougler v. Sirius Prods., Inc., 370 F.Supp.2d 1185 (S.D.Ala.2005)(FHSA; no preemption, post-*Bates*). See also, Pinney v. Nokia, Inc., 402 F.3d 430 (4th Cir. 2005)(no express or implied preemption by Federal Communications Act of tort claims related to telephones' radio frequency radiation emissions).

8. Waiver. Is preemption an affirmative defense so that it is *waived* if the defendant fails to plead and prove it? The few decisions addressing this question conclude that it *is* an affirmative defense that is waived if not raised. See Hawkins v. Leslie's Pool Mart, Inc., 184 F.3d 244 (3d Cir. 1999).

9. See generally Eggen, The Normalization of Product Preemption Doctrine, 57 Ala. L. Rev. 725 (2006); Davis, On Preemption, Congressional Intent, and Conflict of Laws, 66 U. Pitt. L. Rev. 181 (2004); Ausness, Preemption of State Law by Federal Safety Statutes: Supreme Court Preemption Jurisprudence since *Cipollone*, 92 Ky.L.J. 911 (2004); Owen, Federal Preemption of Products Liability Claims, 55 S.C.L.Rev. 411 (2003); D. Owen, Products Liability Law, § 14.4 (2d ed. 2008); 2 D. Owen, M. S. Madden, & M. Davis, Madden and Owen on Products Liability, ch. 28 (3d ed. 2000).

CHAPTER 10

LIMITING DEFECTIVENESS: USER CHOICE

The Limits of Law

Law would be reduced to tyranny, and its purposes deprived of a vital dimension, if it were viewed one dimensionally as a good. Law, like most everything known to man, is an evil in excess. Although law must by nature move into the human comedy from time to time to referee disputes between the players, it should cut narrowly and precisely while inside and should move out swiftly when the job is done. A mature respect for law includes a keen respect for its proper limits.*

――――――

The inquiry to this point has centered on factors and rationales that underlie decisions to hold injury-producing products legally defective. In this chapter and the next, the inquiry shifts directions to arguments *against* determinations of defectiveness in varying situations. While the underlying issues—of manufacturer accountability, feasibility, economic efficiency, consumer autonomy, and individual responsibility—remain largely the same, these two chapters look beyond questions of when and why suppliers preliminarily *ought* to be subject to liability for product-caused harm. The perspective here focuses instead on a variety of knotty considerations of when and why product suppliers ought *not* be responsible for such harm. These two chapters thus concern the formulation of proper *limitations* on the principles of manufacturer responsibility developed to this point.

――――――

[Product purchase and use decisions] require personal choices, and it is beyond the province of courts and juries to act as legislators and preordain those choices.

Linegar v. Armour of America, Inc., 909 F.2d 1150, 1154 (8th Cir. 1990).

*From Owen, Respect For Law and Man: The Tort Law of Chief Justice Frank Rowe Kenison, 11 Vt. L. Rev. 389, 407 (1986).

1.   OBVIOUS DANGERS

> [W]e hardly believe it is any more necessary to tell an experienced factory worker that he should not put his hand into a machine that is at that moment breaking glass than it would be necessary to tell a zookeeper to keep his head out of a hippopotamus' mouth.

Bartkewich v. Billinger, 247 A.2d 603, 606 (Pa.1968).

———

Many products liability cases involve dangers that are hidden or "latent." Reconsider Matthews v. Lawnlite Co., in ch. 7, above. Plaintiff sat in a patio furniture store's aluminum lounge chair and placed his hand on the armrest, wrapping his fingers around and underneath it. "[W]ith the ease that one clips a choice flower with pruning shears," the moving metal parts hidden under the armrest amputated his finger, which fell upon the floor. Emphasizing the unexpected nature of the danger, and indicating that a simple and inexpensive housing over the moving parts would have prevented the accident, the court held the manufacturer responsible.

Consider whether the balance of social values and goals listed above might have tipped the other way if Mr. Matthews had known of the shearing action of the moving parts that lurked beneath the armrest, or if the moving parts had been on top of the armrest and hence were open, "patent," and obvious to view. This section examines the effect of such factors on a manufacturer's duty and breach. Their effect on causation and affirmative defenses is examined in chs. 12–14, below.

———

Campo v. Scofield

Court of Appeals of New York, 1950.
301 N.Y. 468, 95 N.E.2d 802.

■ FULD, JUDGE.

Plaintiff, working on his son's farm, was [dumping a crate of] onions into an "onion topping" machine, when his hands became caught in its revolving steel rollers and were [so] badly injured [that they required amputation]. He brought suit against defendants, manufacturers of the machine, alleging that they had been negligent in failing to equip it with a guard or stopping device. . . .

[The trial court denied the defendants' motion to dismiss, the Appellate Division reversed, and the plaintiff appealed. *Held*, plaintiff's failure to allege that the danger was latent or unknown was fatal to the complaint.]

If a manufacturer does everything necessary to make the machine function properly for the purpose for which it is designed, if the machine is without any latent defect, and if its functioning creates no danger or peril that is not known to the user, then the manufacturer has satisfied the law's demands. We have not yet reached the state where a manufacturer is under the duty of making a machine accident proof or foolproof. [T]he manufacturer is under no obligation . . . to guard against injury from a patent peril or from a source manifestly dangerous. [T]he manufacturer who makes, properly and free of defects, an axe or a buzz saw or an airplane with an exposed propeller, is not to be held liable if one using the axe or the buzz saw is cut by it, or if someone working around the airplane comes in contact with the propeller. In such cases, the manufacturer has the right to expect that such persons will do everything necessary to avoid such contact, for the very nature of the article gives notice and warning of the consequences to be expected, of the injuries to be suffered. In other words, the manufacturer is under no duty to render a machine or other article "more" safe—as long as the danger to be avoided is obvious and patent to all.

[Affirmed; complaint dismissed.]

Micallef v. Miehle Co.

Court of Appeals of New York, 1976.
39 N.Y.2d 376, 384 N.Y.S.2d 115, 348 N.E.2d 571.

■ COOKE, JUDGE.

The time has come to depart from the patent danger rule enunciated in Campo v. Scofield, 301 N.Y. 468, 95 N.E.2d 802.

This action [is for] negligent design and breach of an implied warranty. Paul Micallef, plaintiff, was employed by [a graphics arts company where he operated] a photo-offset press, model RU 1, manufactured and sold by defendant Miehle–Gross Dexter, Inc., to his employer. The machine was 150 feet long, 15 feet high and 5 feet wide and [could print] at least 20,000 sheets an hour. [P]laintiff discovered that a foreign object [was on] the plate of the unit. Such a substance, known to the trade as a "hickie", causes a blemish or imperfection on the printed pages. Plaintiff informed his superior of the problem and told him he was going to "chase the hickie" whereupon the foreman warned him to be careful. "Chasing a hickie" consisted of applying, very lightly, a piece of plastic about eight inches wide to the printing plate, which is wrapped around a circular plate cylinder which spins at high speed. The revolving action of the plate against the plastic removes the "hickie". Unsuccessful in his first removal attempt, plaintiff started anew but this time the plastic was drawn into the nip point between the plate cylinder and an ink-form roller along with his hand. The machine had no safety guards to prevent such occurrence. Plaintiff testified that while his hand was trapped he reached for a shut-off button but couldn't contact it because of its location.

Plaintiff was aware of the danger of getting caught in the press in "chasing hickies." However, it was the custom and usage in the industry to "chase hickies on the run", because once the machine was stopped, it required at least three hours to resume printing and, in such event, the financial advantage of the high speed machine would be lessened. . . . Through its representatives and engineers, defendant had observed the machine in operation and was cognizant of the manner in which "hickies were chased" by Lincoln's employees.

[An engineer testified that the press should have had] guards near the rollers where plaintiff's hand entered the machine [and that a number of guards were available that] would not have impeded the practice of "chasing dickies" [and] would have protected an employee from . . . the risk. [The Appellate Division reversed a jury verdict for the plaintiff, relying in part on *Campo v. Scofield*. Plaintiff appealed.]

[D]efendant asserts [that *Campo* requires that the] action must be dismissed because the danger created by the absence of safeguards on the machine was open and obvious and, therefore, as the manufacturer it was under no duty to protect plaintiff from such a patent defect. * * * *Campo* has been the subject of sustained attack [stemming] from the belief that, in our highly complex and technological society, we fall victim to the manufacturer who holds himself out as an expert in his field. . . .

[It has been argued] that the application of *Campo* amounts to an assumption of risk defense as a matter of law "with the added disadvantage that the defendant was relieved of the burden of proving that plaintiff had subjectively appreciated a known risk" (Rheingold, Expanding Liability of the Product Supplier: A Primer, 2 Hofstra L. Rev. 521, 541). *Campo* is viewed as inconsistent because, on the one hand, it places a duty on the manufacturer to develop a reasonably safe product yet eliminates this duty, thereby granting him immunity from answering in damages, if the dangerous character of the product can be readily seen. . . . "The bottom does not logically drop out of a negligence case against the maker when it is shown that the purchaser knew of the dangerous condition. Thus if the product is a carrot-topping machine with exposed moving parts or an electric clothes wringer dangerous to the limbs of the operator, and if it would be feasible for the maker of the product to install a guard or safety release, it should be a question for the jury whether reasonable care demanded such a precaution, though its absence is obvious. Surely [a jury might reasonably find the maker negligent in such as case since the hazard was so readily avoidable]." (2 Harper & James, Torts, § 28.5.)

Other jurisdictions have taken a more liberal position. For example, in Palmer v. Massey–Ferguson, 476 P.2d 713, 719 (Wash. App. 1970), the plaintiff brought an action against the manufacturer of a hay baler for injuries sustained while adjusting a drawbar. In response to the defendant's allegations that the patent peril precluded liability, the court said: "The manufacturer of the obviously defective product ought not to escape because the product was obviously a bad one. The law, we think, ought to discourage misdesign rather than encouraging it in its obvious form." . . .

We find the reasoning of these cases persuasive. *Campo* suffers from its rigidity in precluding recovery whenever it is demonstrated that the defect was patent. Its unwavering view produces harsh results in view of the difficulties in our mechanized way of life.... A casting of increased responsibility upon the manufacturer, who stands in a superior position to recognize and cure defects, ... furthers the public interest. [Thus,] a manufacturer is obligated to exercise that degree of care in his plan or design so as to avoid any unreasonable risk of harm to anyone who is likely to be exposed to the danger when the product is used [as intended or foreseeable].

What constitutes "reasonable care" will, of course, vary with the surrounding circumstances and will involve "a balancing of the likelihood of harm, and the gravity of harm if it happens, against the burden of the precaution which would be effective to avoid the harm" [citations]. * * *

[C]onduct on a plaintiff's part [may] bar recovery from a manufacturer [but] the patent-danger doctrine should not, in and of itself, prevent a plaintiff from establishing his case. [T]he obviousness of the danger [remains] as a factor in the [liability calculus under] ordinary rules of negligence [and contributory negligence, whether both parties] exercised that degree of reasonable care as was required under the circumstances.

[Appellate Division order reversed; new trial granted.]

NOTES

1. *Micallef* was not the first case to reject the patent danger rule. See, e.g., Pike v. Frank G. Hough Co., 467 P.2d 229 (Cal. 1970) (obvious absence of rear-view mirrors, and blind spot behind earthmoving machine, relevant largely to defense of assumption of risk). But *Micallef* hastened the rule's decline. For example, relying on *Micallef*'s overruling of *Campo*, Auburn Machine Works Co. v. Jones, 366 So.2d 1167, 1170 (Fla. 1979), rejected the doctrine: "The patent danger rule encourages manufacturers to be outrageous in their design, to eliminate safety devices, and to make hazards obvious. For example, if the cage which is placed on an electric fan as a safety device were left off and someone put his hand in the fan, under this doctrine there would be no duty on the manufacturer as a matter of law."

2. Status of Patent Danger Rule. The *Micallef* approach is now the law of the land, and the *Campo* patent danger rule is dead. See, e.g., Blue v. Environmental Eng'g, Inc., 828 N.E.2d 1128, 1148 (Ill. 2005) (patent danger rule "not necessarily an absolute bar to recovery either in strict liability design or negligent design cases"). See generally Products Liability Restatement § 2 cmt. *d*; D. Owen, Products Liability Law § 10.2 (2d ed. 2008).

3. Obvious Dangers *vs*. Warned-of Dangers. Should a *warning* of a hazard have more power than the obviousness of a hazard? That is, if a manufacturer fully and fairly *warns* consumers of a latent hazard, should the risk of injury shift to the consumer, absolving the manufacturer of any duty to design away the hazard? A design danger no-duty bar on this ground might be dubbed a "warned-of danger rule." See comment *j* to Restatement (Second) of Torts § 402A:

Where warning is given, the seller may reasonably assume that it will be read and heeded; and a product bearing such a warning, which is safe for use if it is followed, is not in [a] defective condition, nor is it unreasonably dangerous.

When Dean Prosser first attached comment *j* (then labeled comment *f*) to the draft of § 402A (Tentative Draft No. 6, 1961), that proposed new section to the Restatement (Second) of Torts applied only to "food" and similar products (such as tobacco and drugs) "intended for internal human consumption" (see comment *c*). Apart from the possibility that products of this type might contain impurities, the dangers in such products—such as the risk of heart attacks from too much butter or cancer from too much tobacco—are inherent and cannot be removed. The point of comment *j* (and comments *i* and *k* as well) is that sellers of products of this particular type must bear the risks of impurities, and must warn of latent dangers, but that consumers must accept any remaining hazards inherent in such products. See Owen, The Puzzle of Comment *J*, 55 Hastings L.J. 1377 (2004).

Taking the last sentence of comment *j* nakedly out of context, a number of courts and the commentators have interpreted it as meaning that warnings cancel out the duty of safe design, that warnings trump design. See, e.g., Lightolier v. Hoon, 876 A.2d 100, 110–14 (Md. 2005); Curcio v. Caterpillar, Inc., 543 S.E.2d 264 (S.C. App. 2001), rev'd on other grounds, 585 S.E.2d 272 (2003) (adequacy of warning presented jury issue); Freas v. Prater Constr. Corp., 573 N.E.2d 27 (Ohio 1991); Latin, Good Warnings, Bad Products, and Cognitive Limitations, 41 UCLA L. Rev. 1193 (1994).

Quite like the patent danger rule, this approach effectively eviscerates the duty of safe design. So, the great majority of courts and the Third Restatement—though still failing to see the true meaning of comment *j*—have either ignored this sentence in comment *j*, or, reasoning that it represents bad policy, have held that the separate forms of defect give rise to separate obligations that may independently support a products liability claim. See, e.g., Delaney v. Deere & Co., 999 P.2d 930, 942 (Kan. 2000) ("just because there is a warning on a piece of equipment does not prevent the equipment from being dangerous"); Glittenberg v. Doughboy Recreational Indus., 491 N.W.2d 208, 216 (Mich. 1992) ("A warning is not a Band–Aid to cover a gaping wound, and a product is not safe simply because it carries a warning."); Uloth v. City Tank Corp., 384 N.E.2d 1188, 1192 (Mass.1978) (garbageman's foot that slipped into compaction area was severed by descending packer blade) ("If a slight change in design would prevent serious, perhaps fatal, injury, the designer may not avoid liability by simply warning of the possible injury."). See also Products Liability Restatement § 2 cmt. *l*:

In general, when a safer design can reasonably be implemented and risks can reasonably be designed out of a product, adoption of the safer design is required over a warning that leaves a significant residuum of such risks.... Warnings are not ... a substitute for the provision of a reasonably safe design.

See Owen, The Puzzle of Comment *J*, 55 Hastings L.J. 1377 (2004).

Belling v. Haugh's Pools, Ltd.

Supreme Court of New York, Appellate Division, 1987.
126 A.D.2d 958, 511 N.Y.S.2d 732.

MEMORANDUM:

Plaintiff sustained serious injuries when he dove through an inner tube floating in the four-foot, above-ground swimming pool in a friend's yard.

Plaintiff ... was 33 years old, 6 feet, 1 inch tall and 215 pounds at the time, was an experienced swimmer and familiar with above-ground pools including the pool in question, having been swimming in it for several hours on the day the accident occurred. Indeed, he had assisted the owner of the pool in its installation. He [filed] this action ..., claiming that defendants [the manufacturer and retailer] failed to [adequately warn] of the dangers inherent in diving into a four-foot pool. Defendants moved for summary judgment [which the trial court denied].

A manufacturer [may be held strictly liable for failing to provide adequate warnings, but the plaintiff must prove that the failure to warn was a proximate cause of the injury.] Accordingly, there is no liability for failing to warn of obvious dangers, those that would be appreciated by the user to the same extent the warning would have provided (W. Keeton, D. Dobbs, R. Keeton, D. Owen, Prosser & Keeton on Torts [5th ed.], p. 686; [citations]). [In such cases, "a warning would have merely informed [plaintiff] of risks of which he was already aware."]

[Because the danger was obvious, the defendants' failure to warn of the risk was not the proximate cause of plaintiff's harm.]

[Order reversed; defendants' summary judgment motions granted.]

■ GREEN, J., dissenting:

I must dissent [because] "[t]he failure to warn ... is inherently a question for the trier of fact in all but the most egregious instances" [citations].

Defendants maintain that they had no duty to warn plaintiff of the dangers in diving off a deck or ladder into the pool because the dangers are obvious. The obviousness of a danger ..., however, does not militate against a duty to warn, but rather is one of many factors for the jury to take into account in assessing comparative fault [*Micallef*;] New York Pattern Jury Instructions, Vol. I, 2:135; [citations]). "[T]he imposition of the duty to give a warning of some kind involves a balancing test which weighs the seriousness of potential harm to the consumer against the costs to the manufacturer. Since the cost of providing warnings is often minimal, the balance usually weighs in favor of [a duty] to warn" [citation].

This record reveals that defendants knew, or should have known, that similar dives into similar pools had resulted in over 100 quadriplegic injuries per year during the past ten years. Plaintiff's claim is that had defendants adequately warned him of this danger, he would not have taken the dive into the pool. Plaintiff established that it was foreseeable to defendants that people will dive from decks and ladders into the pool. Indeed, the owner's manual [warns] "Do not dive or permit diving or jumping into the pool from the deck or pool rail. Serious injuries can be caused by failure to strictly follow this rule." Moreover, [the] manufacturer provided small warning decals to the pool owner to be attached in an "appropriate place." There is then a question of fact precluding summary judgment whether the warnings given were adequate [and, if not, whether the defendants' breach of their duty to warn] was the proximate cause of plaintiff's injuries . . . . .

NOTES

1. Compare Smith v. Hub Mfg., Inc., 634 F.Supp. 1505, 1508 (N.D.N.Y.1986). While at a party, plaintiffs' 4–year–old son climbed up the ladder of an above-ground pool, fell in, lost consciousness, and two years later died of his injuries. In an action against the manufacturers of the pool and the ladder, the defendants moved for summary judgment. *Held,* the defective design claim could go to the jury because of testimony by plaintiffs' expert "that other swimming pools have ladders that are more effective in preventing pool accidents." Summary judgment was ordered, however, on the failure-to-warn claim:

> [T]here is no duty to warn if the plaintiff knows of the danger or if the danger is well known and should be obvious to anyone. [Citations.] In such situations a warning would be superfluous. Moreover, the elements of a tort claim would not be satisfied in such situations because no plaintiff could establish that the failure to warn caused harm. Whether the danger of a product is obvious is a question for the court. [Citation.]
>
> The danger of swimming pools to small children is obvious and well known. Everyone should know that an accident like the one in this case is liable to happen if a child is left alone near a pool for even a short time. . . .
>
> In addition, the plaintiffs in this case had personal knowledge of the danger of the pool to their son [because] on their way to the party they told him that he was not allowed near the pool without an adult. . . .

2. No Duty to Warn of Obvious Dangers.

A. In general. A great majority of courts hold that there simply is no duty to warn of obvious dangers. See, e.g., Mathews v. University Loft Co., 903 A.2d 1120 (N.J. Super. Ct. App. Div. 2006) (risk that college student might roll out of loft bed located six feet above floor); Bates v. Richland Sales Corp., 803 N.E.2d 977, 986 (Ill. App. 2004) (risk of driving vehicle into guy wire: "If, from an objective point of view, the danger would be apparent, or 'open and obvious,' to an ordinary person, the seller has no duty to warn of it."); Moss v. Wolohan Lumber Co., 1995 WL 348144 (N.D. Ill. 1995) (risk that BB gun could put eye out); Kerr v. Koemm, 557 F.Supp. 283 (S.D.N.Y.1983) (riding 3–year–old child on running board of tractor over bumpy ground); Morgan v. Bethlehem Steel Corp., 481 N.E.2d 836 (Ill. App. 1985) (driving into side of moving train; no duty to light or add reflectors to train cars); Complaint of Diehl, 610 F.Supp. 223 (D. Idaho 1985) (electrocution from sailboat mast hitting power line); Kuras v. International Harvester Co., 820 F.2d 15 (1st Cir.1987) (sticking hand under power lawn mower).

B. Ditto: *Known* dangers. The same is true, in many jurisdictions, with respect to dangers *known* to the user, whether obvious or not. See, e.g., Sprankle v. Bower Ammonia & Chem. Co., 824 F.2d 409 (5th Cir. 1987) (hazards to worker's respiratory system from inhaling ammonia gas; plaintiff had earlier refused to clean storage tanks because of risk); Sherk v. Daisy–Heddon, 450 A.2d 615 (Pa. 1982) (BB gun fired into friend's head at close range could kill); Garrett v. Nissen Corp., 498 P.2d 1359, 1364 (N.M. 1972) (danger of falling off trampoline); Hagans v. Oliver

Mach. Co., 576 F.2d 97 (5th Cir. 1978) (danger of cutting knotted wood with power circular saw).

Some courts lump the two no-duty rules together: "There is no duty to warn where risks are known and obvious to the plaintiff." Olson v. Prosoco, Inc., 522 N.W.2d 284, 291 (Iowa 1994).

C. Ditto: *Commonly known* dangers. Some courts and legislatures extend the no-duty principle to dangers that are a matter of "common knowledge." See, e.g., Coleman v. Cintas Sales Corp., 100 S.W.3d 384 (Tex. App. 2002) (common knowledge that non-flame retardant clothing would burn when exposed to open flame); Mich. Comp. Laws § 600.2948(2). Is this more a variant of known dangers or obvious dangers?

3. Duty to *Remind*? What if the danger is known but *forgotten*? Should there be a duty to *remind*? Compare Tacke v. Vermeer Mfg. Co., 713 P.2d 527 (Mont. 1986) (danger of getting caught in machine's rollers; one purpose of adequate warning is to remind someone of a known hazard) with Berry v. Eckhardt Porsche Audi, Inc., 578 P.2d 1195 (Okla. 1978) (seat belt warning buzzer is "valiant attempt on the part of manufacturer's to nag an occupant into fastening his seat belt," but its absence or failure is not a defect since function of seat belts is generally known).

4. Consider Campos v. Firestone Tire & Rubber Co., 485 A.2d 305 (N.J. 1984), where the court (a) rejected the no-duty-to-warn-of-obvious-dangers doctrine, holding that the obviousness of the hazard was only one factor in the duty to warn analysis, and (b) held that the user's knowledge was relevant to whether the absence of an adequate warning was a cause in fact of the injury, but not to the duty to warn: "Since the duty is to place on the market a product free of defects, and this duty attaches at the time the product is introduced into the stream of commerce, a particular user's subjective knowledge of a danger does not and cannot modify the manufacturer's duty." 485 A.2d at 311.

On the first aspect of *Campos*, very few courts have similarly applied the *Micallef* doctrine to the warnings context. But see Armentrout v. FMC Corp., 842 P.2d 175 (Colo. 1992). Was *Campos* correct in extending *Micallef* to warnings cases, or did the real point zing right past its nose?

Many courts agree with the second aspect of *Campos*, regarding the user's knowledge of the danger as relevant to cause in fact. Should the user's personal knowledge go to duty? To cause in fact? To proximate cause? To affirmative defenses, such as assumption of risk, based on the user's misconduct?

5. What is Obvious? Judge *vs.* Jury.

Consider Corbin v. Coleco Indus., 748 F.2d 411 (7th Cir. 1984), in which the 27–year–old plaintiff jumped up onto the flat, 6–inch rim surrounding the top edge of his 4–foot deep, above-ground pool, "balanced himself, and dove in. He intended to do a 'belly flopper,' but for some reason his waist bent in mid-air and he entered the water head first. He hit his head on the bottom and suffered a fracture dislocation at vertebras C–5 and C–6. From that moment on, he has been quadriplegic."

The trial court dismissed plaintiff's negligence and strict liability claims against the manufacturer, Coleco, because "it was obviously dangerous for a six-foot man to dive into four feet of water, and that Corbin knew it. The court held that Coleco had no duty to warn of open and obvious dangers and that a product is not defectively designed when its dangerous properties are patent. The district court found that the cause of Corbin's injuries was his own error of judgment in executing a shallow dive." Plaintiff appealed, claiming that there were disputed questions of fact on whether the risk of diving was latent or patent, whether Corbin in fact knew of the risk, and on the contemplations of an ordinary consumer toward the risk. *Held,* reversed and remanded:

> Corbin's expert, Gene D. Litwin, testified in his deposition ... that even though people are generally aware of the danger of diving into shallow water, they believe that there is a safe way to do it, namely, by executing a flat, shallow dive. If people do in fact generally hold such a belief, then it cannot be said, as a matter of law, that the risk of spinal injury from diving into shallow water is open and obvious. [I]f people generally believe that there is a danger associated with the use of a product, but that there is a safe way to use it, any danger there may be in using the product in the way generally believed to be safe is not open and obvious.

> * * *

> [Corbin's intention] to do a flat and shallow dive—a "belly flopper"[–] together with the Litwin testimony that people generally believe that flat, shallow dives into shallow water are safe, creates a genuine issue of material fact as to whether Corbin knew that he risked spinal injury by diving into shallow water, even if he attempted a flat, shallow dive. If he did not know this, then a conspicuous warning on the side of the pool could very well have deterred him from diving. Thus summary judgment for Coleco on the basis of Corbin's knowledge of the danger was inappropriate.

Moreover, Corbin's *design* defect "theory is that the lip and sides of the pool are insufficiently rigid, [that it will 'teeter-totter,'] so that a diver attempting a belly flopper from a standing position on the lip is thrown off balance and enters the water at a steeper angle than intended.... This testimony is sufficient to bar the district court from finding as a matter of law" that the pool was not defectively designed. Nor did Indiana's *Campo*-type obvious danger rule, in effect at the time, bar recovery on the design defect claim since the danger posed to divers by the wobbly pool lip might not have been obvious as a matter of law.

See also Klen v. Asahi Pool, Inc., 643 N.E.2d 1360 (Ill. App.1994) (obviousness of risk of permanent and severe neurological injury should be determined, not by court on summary judgment, but by jury on basis of objective knowledge of reasonable 14–year–old minor). *Contra,* explicitly rejecting *Corbin,* Griebler v. Doughboy Recreational, Inc., 466 N.W.2d 897 (Wis. 1991) (ordinarily, obviousness is a question of fact, but expectation of safety in diving into water of an unknown depth is unreasonable as a matter of law).

6. Ditto: Judge or Jury? In contrast to *Corbin,* consider Glittenberg v. Doughboy Recreational Indus., 491 N.W.2d 208 (Mich. 1992) ("*Glittenberg II*"), a consolidation of three cases for review, the Michigan court reaffirmed its no-duty-to-warn-of-dangers-in-simple-products rule and held that the manufacturers of the above-ground pools did not have a duty to warn of the obvious danger of diving head first into the shallow water of such pools:

> The manufacturer of a simple product has no duty to warn of the product's potentially dangerous conditions or characteristics that are readily apparent or visible upon casual inspection and reasonably expected to be recognized by the average user of ordinary intelligence. [W]e conclude that the product is not defective or unreasonably dangerous for want of a warning.
> * * *

> In the failure to warn context, the obvious nature of the simple product's potential danger serves the core purpose of the claim, i.e., it

functions as an inherent warning that the risk is present. Stated otherwise, if the risk is obvious from the characteristics of the product, the product itself telegraphs the precise warning that plaintiffs complain is lacking. . . . The dissent's observation notwithstanding, all properties of the pools in these cases were knowable, and known. The fact that most individuals do not understand how the laws of physics operate during a dive no more alters the perceived danger in the use of this product than failure to understand the medical reasons why a cut with a knife that severed a major artery could lead to death or catastrophic injury.

The court concluded that warnings "that parse the risk are not required. The general danger encompasses the risk of the specific injury sustained. In other words, the [obvious] risk of hitting the bottom encompasses the risk of catastrophic injury."

Dissenting, Judge Levin pointed to the hundreds of annual spinal injuries from such accidents and to the testimony of experts that most people do not appreciate "that diving in shallow water carries the potential for life-threatening injuries." Embracing the reasoning in *Corbin*, Judge Levin faulted the majority for failing to understand that "[i]f there is a specific latent risk, there is an obligation to warn, even if there is a more general obvious risk."

7. Specificity of Risk. As illustrated by the conflicting opinions in *Glittenberg II*, above, courts often disagree on just how specific a plaintiff's knowledge of a danger must be before a warnings claim is defeated, on whatever ground. Compare Tacke v. Vermeer Mfg. Co., 713 P.2d 527 (Mont. 1986) (duty to warn of specific risk of getting caught in machine's rollers; worker's general knowledge that machines were dangerous insufficient), with Shaffer v. AMF, Inc., 842 F.2d 893 (6th Cir. 1988) (since general dangers of motorcycle riding are open and obvious, no duty to warn of specific risks), and Lister v. Bill Kelley Athletic, Inc., 485 N.E.2d 483 (Ill. App. 1985) (helmet manufacturer had no duty to warn football player of risk of broken neck and quadriplegia where coaches told him "not to use his head in making a tackle and that he could injure himself if he used the top of the helmet to make a tackle").

8. Products Liability Restatement. For *design* defectiveness, § 2 cmt. *d* adopts the *Micallef* relevant-but-not-conclusive rule for obvious dangers. For *warnings*, § 2 cmt. *j* provides:

In general, a product seller is not subject to liability for failing to warn or instruct regarding risks and risk avoidance measures that should be obvious to, or generally known by, foreseeable product users.

9. Theory of Liability. Apart from their roles as separate doctrines or as bearing on cause in fact, how might the obviousness of a danger, or the plaintiff's knowledge of it, affect the following theories of recovery:

    A. Negligence.

    B. Tortious misrepresentation. See Rest. (2d) of Torts § 541; cf. id. § 402B, cmt. *j*.

    C. Warranty. See UCC § 2–316(3)(b) and cmt. 8.

    D. Strict liability in tort.

        (1) *Consumer expectations test.*

        (2) *Risk-utility test.*

10. The Consumer Expectations Test. Recall from chapter 7 that the consumer expectations test often operates oppressively in the case of obvious dangers, as in the *Vincer* case examined there in which a 2–year–old child was severely injured when he climbed the ladder and fell into an above-ground swimming pool not equipped with a simple self-latching gate. See also Bourne v. Marty Gilman, Inc., 452 F.3d 632 (7th Cir. 2006) (consumer expectations test barred recovery for injuries from obvious risk that aluminum goalpost might snap and fall dangerously when college students rushed on field to celebrate football victory and climbed on post). A number of courts (and the Third Restatement) cite this as an important reason for rejecting consumer expectations as the basic test of liability for defects in design. See, e.g., Camacho v. Honda Motor Co., 741 P.2d 1240 (Colo. 1987) (motorcycle without crash bars; risk-utility, not consumer expectations, proper test); see also Seymour v. Brunswick Corp., 655 So.2d 892 (Miss. 1995) (swimmer's foot pulled into unguarded motorboat propeller while trying to climb on board).

11. Reform. Statutes provide for a bar to recovery or reduction in damages in the case of obvious, or generally known and inherent dangers, in a large number of states. See Prod. Liab. Rep. (CCH) ¶ ¶ 90,001 et seq.

12. On obvious dangers, see generally D. Owen, Products Liability Law § 10.2 (2d ed. 2008); 1 D. Owen, M.S. Madden, & M. Davis, Madden & Owen on Products Liability § 10:1–:3 (3d ed. 2000).

2. INHERENT DANGERS

[T]he danger that a carving knife will cut the user cannot be eliminated because an exposed, sharp blade is an inherent characteristic of a carving knife, and essential to its intended use.

Roberts v. Rich Foods, Inc., 654 A.2d 1365, 1373 (N.J. 1995).

———

Most products, while useful in some respects, are by nature dangerous in others. That is, virtually all products carry certain inherent dangers when put to use by human beings. The very purpose of the "tests" of product defectiveness, examined above, is to separate *reasonably* dangerous products from the *unreasonably* dangerous kind. As seen in the preceding section, the great majority of courts today hold that the obviousness of a product's danger is but a single consideration in evaluating the safety of a product's design. Does this mean that, when useful products containing inherent dangers result in injury, courts and juries should always decide whether such products pass (or fail) a risk-utility (or consumer expectations) test? Even if the risk were obvious *and* there were no feasible way to design it out of the product? Assuming that the data are available, should courts and juries determine whether particular types or categories of products cause more social harm than good? Alcohol? Hot coffee? Fast foods? Chain saws? Paring knives? Trampolines? Cigarettes? Asbestos? Or should such matters be left to legislatures and administrative agencies?

Injuries from inherent product hazards have raised questions about the advisability of "product category" liability for "generic risks," terms that surfaced only over the last couple of decades. The "generic risk" phrase may be traced to an article by Joseph Page, Generic Product Risks: The Case Against Comment *k* and for Strict Tort Liability, 58 N.Y.U. L. Rev. 853 (1983), the first explicit foray into a variety of the interrelated and knotty issues here involved. Carl Bogus lends a more contemporary perspective to the meaning of these terms:

> Generic liability, or product category liability as it is also called, involves products that remain unreasonably dangerous despite the best possible construction, design and warnings. Some argue that ... a manufacturer who has done everything feasible to make its products reasonably safe ought not to be subject to strict liability. Others contend that a manufacturer has a duty not to [sell] unreasonably dangerous products, *i.e.*, products that have a greater social cost than social benefit, ... and that a manufacturer who cannot feasibly make his product reasonably safe can elect not to [sell the product at all or, alternatively, should pay its accident costs]. To many, generic liability is a radical concept [raising] the specter of courts [legislating which products may be sold].

Bogus, War on the Common Law: The Struggle at the Center of Products Liability, 60 Mo. L. Rev. 1, 8–9 (1995).

Bruner v. Anheuser–Busch, Inc.

United States District Court, Southern District of Florida, 2001.
153 F. Supp. 2d 1358.

■ Middlebrooks, District Judge.

[Plaintiffs sued defendant for "the negative consequences of their own abuse of alcohol" arising out of their being lured during the 1960s and 1970s to consume large quantities of "Budweiser, the King of beers," an alcoholic beverage, a "a known 'psychoactive' substance," produced by the defendant. Plaintiffs alleged that they believed such consumption to be safe in view of the defendant's express warranties of safety, failure to warn of the risks, and its false and fraudulent advertising of the product, and also claimed that the defendant was strictly liable. Plaintiffs sought $1 billion in compensatory damages and $1 billion in punitive damages for personal injuries and other damages from their incarcerations and loss of families, jobs, and income. Defendant moves to dismiss pursuant to Fed.R.Civ.Pro. 12(b)(6).]

[Comment *i* to Restatement (2d) of Torts § 402A provides in part, "Good whiskey is not unreasonably dangerous merely because it will make some people drunk, and is especially dangerous to alcoholics."] Florida courts have recognized that the dangers of alcohol abuse are common knowledge and therefore this product is not considered unreasonably dangerous as defined by the Restatement (Second) of Torts. See [citation] (noting the acceptance of [§ 402A's comments] across jurisdictions, the "universal recognition of all potential dangers associated with alcohol," and holding defendants owed no duty to plaintiffs regarding the well recognized properties of their products).

. . . In this case, plaintiffs cannot meet the prerequisites in establishing a products liability claim since beer is not considered an "unreasonably dangerous" product. Traditionally, courts have recognized that although there are dangers involved in the use of alcoholic beverages, because of the common knowledge of these dangers, the product is not considered unreasonably safe. See [citations]; Joseph E. Seagram & Sons, Inc. v. McGuire, 814 S.W.2d 385 (Tex. 1991) ("From ancient times, the danger of alcoholism from prolonged and excessive consumption of alcoholic beverages has been widely known and recognized."); Greif v. Anheuser–Busch Companies, Inc., 114 F. Supp. 2d 100 (D. Conn. 2000) [defendant's beer not defective because of its intoxicating effects on motorist who struck a biker].

Plaintiffs also assert that as a result of Defendant's product, they have suffered personal injuries [and] "have been caused not to achieve their maximum potential and station in life." They also claim that Defendant's product has caused them to lose their families and has diminished their ability to reason and think. In Florida, however, voluntary drinking of alcohol is the proximate cause of an injury, rather than the manufacture or sale of those intoxicating beverages to that person. [Citation.]

[Defendant's motion to dismiss granted; case dismissed.]

NOTES

1. Comment *i* to § 402A, entitled *"Unreasonably dangerous,"* provides in full:

The rule stated in this Section applies only where the defective condition of the product makes it unreasonably dangerous to the user or consumer. Many products cannot possibly be made entirely safe for all consumption, and any food or drug necessarily involves some risk of harm, if only from over-consumption. Ordinary sugar is a deadly poison to diabetics, and castor oil found use under Mussolini as an instrument of torture. That is not what is meant by "unreasonably dangerous" in this Section. The article sold must be dangerous to an extent beyond that which would be contemplated by the ordinary consumer who purchases it, with the ordinary knowledge common to the community as to its characteristics. Good whiskey is not unreasonably dangerous merely because it will make some people drunk, and is especially dangerous to alcoholics; but bad whiskey, containing a dangerous amount of fusel oil, is unreasonably dangerous. Good tobacco is not unreasonably dangerous merely because the effects of smoking may be harmful; but tobacco containing something like marijuana may be unreasonably dangerous. Good butter is not unreasonably dangerous merely because, if such be the case, it deposits cholesterol in the arteries and leads to heart attacks; but bad butter, contaminated with poisonous fish oil, is unreasonably dangerous.

2. Compare Cochran, "Good Whiskey," Drunk Driving, and Innocent Bystanders: The Responsibility of Manufacturers of Alcohol and Other Dangerous Hedonic Products for Bystander Injury, 45 S.C. L. Rev. 269, 335 (1994):

Manufacturers of alcohol should be liable to innocent bystanders who are injured in traffic accidents arising from drunk driving. They create a very dangerous product that merely provides pleasure. It is dangerous not only because those who consume it are likely to drive negligently but because the product itself inhibits the ability of consumers to judge when they have had too much.... If the drinker cannot pay, then the manufacturer should pay. Most of the cost of liability will ultimately be passed on to consumers in higher prices [which is appropriate] so that those who are injured may be compensated.

3. Alcohol warnings. In 1988, Congress enacted 27 U.S.C. § 215 which requires that alcoholic beverages be labeled as follows:

GOVERNMENT WARNING: (1) According to the Surgeon General, women should not drink alcoholic beverages during pregnancy because of the risk of birth defects.

(2) Consumption of alcoholic beverages impairs your ability to drive a car or operate machinery, and may cause health problems.

4. Peanut butter. In Fraust v. Swift and Co., 610 F.Supp. 711 (W.D. Pa. 1985), 16–month-old Isaac Fraust choked while eating Peter Pan Creamy Peanut Butter spread on bread. Plaintiffs sued, alleging that the texture and consistency of peanut butter made it unreasonably dangerous for children under the age of four. *Held*, defendant's motion for summary judgment denied. The no-defect safe harbor provided certain foods and drink with inherent dangers by comment *i* to § 402A is limited to situations where the dangers are commonly known or warnings have been provided. The court concluded that it could not rule "as a matter of law that the danger of a sixteen month old choking on a peanut butter sandwich is generally known and recognized so that admittedly good peanut butter, without warning of such a danger, is not unreasonably dangerous."

5. Marshmallows. Compare Emery v. Federated Foods, Inc., 863 P.2d 426 (Mont. 1993), where 2½-year-old Chad was munching on some marshmallows which got stuck in his throat, blocking his airway and severely injuring his brain. The trial court granted summary judgment to the marshmallow supplier, Federated Foods, on plaintiff's claim of defectiveness for failure to warn of the risk, finding that "Chad's overindulgence caused his injuries" and that "the manner in which Chad consumed the marshmallows caused his damages" and that there was no evidence that his mother was not cognizant of the potential harm.

Plaintiff's expert's affidavit stated that a marshmallow is particularly dangerous to young children because it is sweet; it appears "soft and innocuous to parents" and so "does not present the same apparent risk" possessed by a piece of hard candy or a jelly bean; that it expands when soaked with liquid secretions in the mouth and continues to swell after entering the trachea (main breathing tube); and that "an aspirated marshmallow fragment might not be reachable with a finger and could be difficult to dislodge with a Heimlich maneuver."

Held (5–2 decision), motion for summary judgment improperly granted; reversed and remanded for trial. Stating the issue as whether a young child's choking on a marshmallow "is the basis for a products liability claim for failure [to warn Chad's] mother of the danger of allowing her son to eat a marshmallow," the Chief Justice (and another judge) dissented: "If marshmallows are unreasonably dangerous to eat without a warning, then so would be nearly every conceivable food item that a two-and-one-half-year-old child would try to eat; and I submit that children of that age will try to eat anything and everything." And "the possibility of young children choking on nearly all food items is, or should be, a matter of common knowledge to all adults."

6. "An Ontario woman died after choking during the Chubby Bunny marshmallow-eating contest. 'It was just an unfortunate incident that happened,' explained a fair manager." [EdmontonSun.com][London Free Press], www.harpers.org/Food.html (Sept. 14, 2006). Does her estate have a products liability claim?

7. Hair Oil. In Greene v. A.P. Prods., Ltd., 717 N.W.2d 855, 861 (Mich. 2006), plaintiff's 11–month-year-old son died from ingesting defendant's Wonder 8 Hair Oil that contained no warning. A state statute provides that product suppliers need not warn of material risks that are obvious to reasonably prudent users or are commonly known to persons in the plaintiff's position. *Held*, as a matter of law, that it "should have been obvious to a reasonably prudent user that ingesting [the product] involved a material risk." In dissent, two judges argued (consistent with the ruling by the Court of Appeals) that whether the risk of *death* from ingesting this product was obvious was a question of fact for the jury.

Is *Greene* consistent with *Fraust* and *Emery*, the peanut butter and marshmallow cases in notes 4 and 5, above?

8. McDonald's Burgers. A number claims were filed against fast food retailers for obesity and other health problems allegedly caused by plaintiffs' consumption of too much "junk food"—high in fat, salt, sugar, and cholesterol—sold by defendants. Pelman v. McDonald's Corp., 237 F. Supp. 2d 512 (S.D.N.Y. 2003), was a class action against McDonald's brought on behalf of obese children, including one 400–pound 15–year–old suffering from Type 2 diabetes who claims to have eaten at McDonald's daily since he was 6. Observing that its failure to act decisively "could spawn thousands of similar 'McLawsuits,'" the court dismissed the *Pelman* complaint, with leave to amend, ruling that fast-food restaurants had no duty to warn consumers of the open, obvious, and well-known fact that such foods contain high levels of cholesterol, fat, salt, and sugar; that the complaint failed adequately to plead proximate cause because it failed to specify how often the children ate such foods and failed to account for factors other than diet that may have contributed to the children's health problems; that it failed to specify how the fats, sugars, and other substances may have been addictive; and that it failed to allege whether the defendants purposefully prepared the fast foods with addictive qualities. At bottom, the court observed that the lawsuit raised vital questions of personal responsibility, an issue highlighted by the derisive popular reactions to the filing of these lawsuits noted by the press.[1] In short, because the complaint failed to allege that consumers are unaware of "the potential ill health effects of eating at

---

1. See id. at 518, quoting: Goldman, "Consumer Republic: Common Sense May Not Be McDonald's Ally for Long," Adweek, Ed. 14 (Dec. 12, 2002), 2002 WL 103089868 ("[T]he masses have expressed their incredulity at and contempt for the litigious kids—and their parents—who won't take responsibility for a lifetime of chowing down Happy Meals. With much tongue-clucking, the vox populi bemoans yet another symptom of the decline of personal responsibility and the rise of the cult of victimhood."); Shlaes, Lawyers Get Fat on McDonald's, Chi. Trib. 25 (Nov. 27, 2002) ("Every now and then America draws a cartoon of herself for the amusement of the rest of the world. Last week's fat lawsuit against McDonald's is one of those occasions."). See also Turley, Editorial, Betcha Can't Sue Just One, L.A. Times, 2002 WL 2492444 (July 24, 2002) ("Finally, there is the question of personal responsibility, which seems often ignored in these massive lawsuits. We may soon see campaigns from the industry reminding us that 'Twinkies don't kill people, people kill people.'"); Parloff, Is Fat the Next Tobacco?, N.Y. Times, www.fortune.com (Jan. 21, 2003) ("News of the lawsuit drew hoots of derision.").

McDonald's, they cannot blame McDonald's if they, nonetheless, choose to satiate their appetite with a surfeit of supersized McDonald's products." Id. at 517–18. The plaintiffs refiled, later abandoned their warnings claim, and the court dismissed the remaining claims of deceptive advertising under the state Consumer Protection Act. Pelman v. McDonald's Corp., 2003 WL 22052778 (S.D.N.Y. 2003). But see Pelman v. McDonald's Corp., 396 F.3d 508 (2d Cir. 2005) (vacated and remanded), 396 F. Supp. 2d 439 (S.D.N.Y. 2005) (motion for more definite statement partially granted).

9. Cheeseburger Legislation. In 2004 (and then again in 2005), the House of Representatives passed the Personal Responsibility in Food Consumption Act (dubbed "the Cheeseburger Bill"), prohibiting such suits. While the Secretary of HHS acknowledged that "overweight and obesity are literally killing us," and that "poor eating habits and obesity are on the verge of surpassing tobacco use as the leading cause of preventable death in America," the House concluded that the matter was one of personal, not legal, responsibility. The chief sponsor of the bill, Rep. Ric Keller (R–FL), stated that the same lawyers who sued the tobacco industry now seek to hold the food industry for $117 billion, the public health costs of obesity as estimated by the Surgeon General. Based on a contingent fee of 40%, "that means these selfless lawyers interested in the public good" would recover $47 billion in attorneys fees, which "is, ultimately, what this is about.... The litigation against the food industry is not going to make a single person any skinnier; it is only going to serve to make the trial attorneys' bank accounts a lot fatter." See 19 Liab. & Ins. Week 1, 14 (March 15, 2004).

In 2005, Senator Mitch McConnell (R–KY) introduced a similar bill in the Senate, but that body has yet to act. If Congress fails to enact this type of legislation, do you think counsel for subsequent plaintiffs can muster sufficiently weighty arguments in McLawsuits of this type?

Nearly half the state legislatures have enacted liability protections for manufacturers, distributors, sellers, or retailers of food and nonalcoholic beverages for weight-related health problems. For example, Me. Rev. Stat. Ann. tit. 14, § 170, enacted in 2005, provides that, apart from misrepresentation or failing to warn pursuant to law, a food provider is not subject to liability for injury or death from "a person's weight gain or obesity resulting from the person's long-term consumption of the food product." For a legislative tally by state, see www.restaurant.org/government/state/nutrition (reporting 23 states as of Feb. 14, 2007).

For analyses of all these issues, see Ausness, Tell Me What you Eat, and I Will Tell You Whom to Sue: Big Problems Ahead for "Big Food"?, 39 Ga. L. Rev. 839 (2005); McMenamin & Tiglio, Not the Next Tobacco: Defenses to Obesity Claims, 61 Food & Drug L.J. 445 (2006).

10. Hot Coffee. How about hot coffee? Should people burned when they spill hot coffee on themselves have claims against the retailers who sold the coffee? Against manufacturers of coffee makers that brew the coffee? Against manufacturers of paper or styrofoam cups in which the coffee is served?

McMahon v. Bunn–O–Matic Corp.

United States Court of Appeals, Seventh Circuit, 1998.
150 F.3d 651.

■ EASTERBROOK, CIRCUIT JUDGE.

During a break from a long-distance auto trip, Jack McMahon bought a cup of coffee from the mini mart at a Mobil station. Jack asked Angelina

McMahon, his wife, to remove the plastic lid while he drove. Angelina decided to pour some of the coffee into a smaller cup that would be easier for Jack to handle. In the process the coffee flooded her lap; Angelina suffered second and third degree burns that caused her pain for months and produced scars on her left thigh and lower abdomen. Angelina believes that the Styrofoam cup collapsed, either because it was poorly made or because inordinately hot coffee weakened its structure. The McMahons' claims against the producers of the cup and lid have been settled. The third defendant is Bunn–O–Matic Corporation, which manufactured the coffee maker. According to the McMahons, the temperatures at which Bunn's apparatus brews and serves coffee—195° F during the brewing cycle and 179° F as the "holding" temperature of a carafe on its hotplate—are excessive, and its design therefore defective. * * *

The McMahons [claim]: (i) that Bunn failed to warn consumers about the severity of burns that hot coffee can produce; and (ii) that any coffee served at more than 140° F is unfit for human consumption (and therefore a defective product) because of its power to cause burns more severe than consumers expect, aggravated by its potential to damage the cup and thus increase the probability of spills. [A magistrate judge entered] summary judgment for the defendants [observing] that both McMahons conceded [in] their depositions that "hotness" was one of the elements they value in coffee and that they sought out hot coffee, knew it could burn, and took precautions as a result. These concessions—which any adult coffee drinker is bound to make—foreclose the possibility of recovery, the opinion concluded. Other, similar suits have come to the same summary end, see [citations], although one published opinion has held that a claim of this sort is triable, see Nadel v. Burger King Corp., 695 N.E.2d 1185 (Ohio App. 1997), and a suit in New Mexico (Liebeck v. McDonald's Restaurants, P.T.S., Inc.) produced a widely publicized jury verdict of some $3 million but not a published opinion (the case was settled before appeal).

* * *

[Should Bunn] have warned the McMahons about the dangers of hot coffee? What would this warning have entailed? A statement that coffee is served hot? That it can cause burns? They already knew these things and did not need to be reminded (as both conceded in their depositions). [Citation.] That this coffee was *unusually* hot and therefore capable of causing severe burns? Warning consumers about a surprising feature that is potentially dangerous yet hard to observe could be useful, but the record lacks any evidence that 179° F *is* unusually hot for coffee. Neither side submitted evidence about the range of temperatures used by commercial coffee makers, or even about the range of temperatures for Bunn's line of products. The McMahons essentially ask us to take judicial notice that 179° is abnormal, but this is not the sort of incontestable fact for which proof is unnecessary. [Courts in prior decisions] reported that the industry-standard serving temperature is between 175° and 185° F, and if this is so then the McMahons' coffee held no surprises. What is more, most consumers prepare and consume hotter beverages at home. Angelina McMahon is a tea drinker, and tea is prepared by pouring boiling water over tea leaves. Until 20 years ago most home coffee was made in percolators, where the water boiled during the brewing cycle and took some time to cool below 180°. Apparently the McMahons believe that home drip brewing machines now in common use are much cooler, but the record does not support this, and a little digging on our own part turned up ANSI/AHAM CM–1–1986, which the American National Standards Institute adopted for home coffee makers. Standard 5.2.1 provides:

> On completion of the brewing cycle and within a 2 minute interval, the beverage temperature in the dispensing vessel of the coffee maker while stirring should be between the limits of 170° F and 205° F (77° C and 96° C).

The upper finished brew temperature limit assures that the coffee does not reach the boiling point which can affect the taste and aroma. The lower temperature limit assures generally acceptable drinking temperature when pouring into a cold cup, adding cream, sugar and spoon.

* * *

Thus home coffee makers that claim to follow the standard (a voluntary step; no statute or regulation requires compliance) must brew and hold coffee at a temperature that does not fall below 170°. Coffee served at 180° by a roadside vendor, which doubtless expects that it will cool during the longer interval before consumption, does not seem so abnormal as to require a heads-up warning.

What remains is the argument that Bunn should have provided a detailed warning about the *severity* of burns that hot liquids can cause, even if 179° F is a standard serving temperature. The McMahons insist that, although they knew that coffee can burn, they thought that the sort of burn involved would be a blister painful for several days (. . . a second degree burn), not a third degree burn of the sort Angelina experienced. An affidavit submitted by Kenneth R. Diller, a professor of biomedical and biomechanical engineering, observed that "full thickness third degree burn injuries would require 60 seconds of exposure [to a liquid at] 140° F, but only 3 seconds of exposure at 179° F." [O]rdinary consumers [probably] do not know this—that, indeed, ordinary consumers do not know what a "full thickness third degree burn" is. But how, precisely, is this information to be conveyed by a coffee maker? Bunn can't deliver a medical education with each cup of coffee. Any person severely injured by any product could make a claim, at least as plausible as the McMahons', that they did not recognize the risks *ex ante* as clearly as they do after the accident.

Insistence on more detail can make any warning, however elaborate, seem inadequate. Indiana courts have expressed considerable reluctance to require ever-more detail in warnings. . . . To be useful, warnings about burns could not stop with abstract information about the relation among a liquid's temperature and volume (which jointly determine not only the number of calories available to impart to the skin but also the maximum rate of delivery), contact time (which determines how many of the available calories are actually delivered), and the severity of burns. [They] would have to address the risk of burns in real life, starting with the number of cups of coffee sold annually, the number of these that spill (... by location, such as home, restaurant, and car), and the probability that any given spill will produce a severe (vs. a mild or average) burn. Only after understanding these things could the consumer determine whether the superior taste of hot coffee justifies the incremental risk. Tradeoffs are complex. Few consumers could understand the numbers and reach an intelligent decision on the spot at a checkout counter. Yet such a detailed warning (equivalent to the package insert that comes with drugs) might obscure the principal point that precautions should be taken to avoid spills. Indiana does not require vendors to [warn] in the detail plaintiffs contemplate. It expects consumers to educate themselves about the hazards of daily life—of matches, knives, and kitchen ranges, of bones in fish, and of hot beverages—by general reading and experience, knowledge they can acquire *before* they enter a mini mart to buy coffee for a journey.

[As for the claim that the *design* of the coffee maker was defective, the court rejected plaintiffs' theory that it brewed coffee at too high a temperature because it could deform the structural integrity of styrofoam cups, reasoning that this was a problem with the cups or the fault of the retailer, not the manufacturer of the coffee maker, and also because Professor Diller failed to explain his reasoning on this point.]

At first glance plaintiffs' alternative theory is stronger. Coffee at 180° F is considerably more likely to cause severe burns than is coffee at 135° to 140° F, the maximum at which Diller believes that coffee should be served. Moreover, because it is costly to serve coffee hot (it takes electricity to keep the hotplate on), risks could be reduced for a *negative* outlay. How can it not be negligent to spend money for the purpose of making a product more injurious? But of course people spend money to increase their risks all the time—they pay steep prices for ski vacations; they go to baseball games where flying bats and balls abound; they buy BB guns for their children knowing that the pellets can maim. They do these things because they perceive benefits from skiing, baseball, and target practice. Moss v. Crosman Corp., 136 F.3d 1169 (7th Cir. 1998), [a] BB gun case, holds that Indiana does not condemn products as defective just because they are designed to do things that create serious hazards. [Citation.] To determine whether a coffee maker is defective because it holds the beverage at 179°, we must understand the benefits of hot coffee in relation to its costs. As for costs, the record is silent. We do not know whether severe burns from coffee are frequent or rare. On the other side of the ledger there are benefits for all coffee drinkers. Jack McMahon testified that he likes his coffee hot. Why did the American National Standards Institute set 170° F as the *minimum* temperature at which coffee should be held ready to serve? Diller does not make any effort to reconcile his "maximum 140° F" position with the ANSI's "minimum 170° F" position—though this is something that an engineer would be sure to do in scholarly work. On this topic, too, Diller's affidavit is worthless because unreasoned. Without some way to compare the benefits of a design change (fewer and less severe burns) against the costs (less pleasure received from drinking coffee), it is impossible to say that designing a coffee maker to hold coffee at 179° F bespeaks negligent inattention to the risks.

. . . The ANSI minimum of 170° F prevents us from treating as obvious the absence of benefits from temperatures above 140°. What is more, even a little investigation (albeit unassisted by the parties) shows that there may be good reasons for selecting a temperature over 170° F, as several other courts have recognized. See Michael Sivetz & H. Elliott Foote, 2 *Coffee Processing Technology* ch. 19.2 (1963). The smell (and therefore the taste) of coffee depends heavily on the oils containing aromatic compounds that are dissolved out of the beans during the brewing process. Brewing temperature should be close to 200° F to dissolve them effectively, but without causing the premature breakdown of these delicate molecules. Coffee smells and tastes best when these aromatic compounds evaporate from the surface of the coffee as it is being drunk. Compounds vital to flavor have boiling points in the range of 150° F to 160° F, and the beverage therefore tastes best when it is this hot and the aromatics vaporize as it is being drunk. For coffee to be 150° F when imbibed, it must be hotter in the pot. Pouring a liquid increases its surface area and cools it; more heat is lost by contact with the cooler container; if the consumer adds cream and sugar (plus a metal spoon to stir them) the liquid's temperature falls again. If the consumer carries the container out for later consumption, the beverage cools still further. Our point in discussing these issues is not to endorse Sivetz & Foote; their position may be scientifically contestable. It is only to demonstrate that without evidence that a holding temperature of 180° F is of little worth to consumers, plaintiffs cannot show that the choice of a high temperature makes coffee defective.

It is easy to sympathize with Angelina McMahon, severely injured by a common household beverage—and, for all we can see, without fault on her part. Using the legal system to shift the costs of this injury to someone else may be attractive to the McMahons, but it would have bad consequences for coffee fanciers who like their beverage hot. First-party health and accident insurance deals with injuries of the kind Angelina suffered without the high costs of adjudication, and without potential side effects such as lukewarm coffee. We do not know whether the McMahons carried such insurance (directly or through an employer's health plan), but we are confident that Indiana law does not make Bunn and similar firms insurers through the tort system of the harms, even grievous ones, that are common to the human existence.

Affirmed.

NOTES

1. **"The Spill Felt Round the World."** Surely the most notorious hot coffee case, mentioned by Judge Easterbrook, was Liebeck v. McDonald's Restaurants,

P.T.S., Inc., 1995 WL 360309 (D.N.M. 1994), in which a jury awarded $2.7 million to a woman scalded by a cup of coffee she purchased at McDonald's. The 81–year–old plaintiff, who spilled the coffee while attempting to remove the lid, suffered third-degree burns over six percent of her body on her inner thighs, buttocks, and genital and groin areas, requiring skin grafts and debridement during a week of hospitalization. The plaintiff's claim was based on McDonald's failure to warn its customers that the company served its coffee exceedingly hot, at 180–90°. At 190°, coffee causes third-degree burns to human skin in less than three seconds. The evidence revealed that McDonald's knew that its coffee was so hot that it was not "fit for consumption" when served, some 20–40° hotter than coffee sold by most other restaurants. The plaintiff also proved that the company continued its policy of keeping the coffee temperature so hot despite receipt of some 700 complaints of burns, some in the third degree. And yet, until after the verdict in this case, the company chose not to warn its customers of the danger. A McDonald's executive testified at trial that the company "had decided not to warn customers about the possibility of severe burns, even though most people wouldn't think it possible," and that the company had no intention to change any of its policies. On post-trial motions, the trial court upheld the jury's finding that punitive damages were warranted on the facts but remitted the jury's punitive damages award, which represented two days of McDonald's national coffee sales, to $480,000—three times the amount of the plaintiff's final compensatory award ($200,000, reduced by 20% to $160,000 on account of the plaintiff's fault). See Mead, Punitive Damages and the Spill Felt Round the World: A U.S. Perspective, 17 Loy. L.A. Int'l & Comp. L.J. 829, 847 (1995); Gerlin, A Matter of Degree: How a Jury Decided That One Coffee Spill Is Worth $2.9 Million, Wall St. J. A1 (Sept. 1, 1994); Morgan, McDonald's Burned Itself, Legal Times, Sept. 19, 1994, at 26; Two Hot Verdicts Were Distorted by Critics, 20 ATLA Advocate 3 (Oct. 1994).

2.   Warning of *Severity* of Risk. Did Judge Easterbrook too casually discard the plaintiff's claim that sellers must inform consumers about the *severity* of a product's hazards? In Coleman v. Cintas Sales Corp., 100 S.W.3d 384 (Tex. App. 2002) (2–1 decision), a golf club groundskeeper was severely burned when his uniform, 65% polyester and 35% cotton, caught fire as he was cooking steaks for the work crew over a barbecue pit. The shirt melted or fused to his body, he could not remove it, nor were his efforts to "stop, drop, and roll" effective, because each time he thought the fire was extinguished he would hear a "poof" and the shirt would reignite. *Held*, although consumers might not know that such a fabric might melt on a person's body and be exceedingly difficult to extinguish, there was no duty to warn because of common knowledge that non-flame-retarded clothing may catch fire from an open flame and that the wearer may be severely injured.

Is this good law? Good policy?

3.   Cigarettes. How about cigarettes? Should juries be allowed to challenge whether the social costs of cigarettes exceed their benefits? Or should courts require that plaintiffs prove design defect claims against the cigarette industry on some more specific basis? See Wertheimer, The Smoke Gets in Their Eyes: Product Category Liability and Alternative Feasible Designs in the Third Restatement, 61 Tenn. L. Rev. 1429, 1445 n.50 (1994) (noting that about 450,000 Americans die each year from the effects of cigarette smoking; that cigarette smoking generates enormous health care costs for this nation, perhaps now as much as $100 billion per year). Worldwide, cigarettes kill about 5 million people per year, and, as cigarette smoking spreads around the globe, the numbers are rapidly increasing. See Bridges, Tobacco Expected to Kill a Billion This Century, www.suntimes.com (July 10, 2006) ("if current trends hold"; the CEO of the American Cancer Society remarked that "[i]n all of world history, this is the largest train wreck not waiting to happen").

Prior to the early 1990s, almost every case ever filed against a cigarette manufacturer was dismissed, usually on the basis of the exemption from liability for cigarettes and other inherently dangerous products in comment *i* to § 402A. Various aspects of the cigarette litigations are examined in ch. 19, but consider the recurring arguments around the inherent risk problem addressed in the case below.

————

Hearn v. R.J. Reynolds Tobacco Co.

United States District Court for the District of Arizona, 2003.
279 F. Supp. 2d 1096.

■ SILVER, DISTRICT JUDGE.

[Winona Hearn began smoking in 1950 at the age of sixteen, allegedly due to the defendants' extensive advertising campaigns. Plaintiffs, her husband and daughter, allege that she was not aware of all of the dangers of smoking when she began the habit and that, by the time she finally became aware of the risks, after the Federal Labeling Act in 1969, she could not stop because of her addiction. Winona was diagnosed with lung cancer in April 2000, resulting in her death seven months later. The plaintiffs sued three cigarette manufacturers, alleging negligence, strict liability, breach of implied warranty, and negligent infliction of emotional distress, and the defendants moved to dismiss, relying principally on the "common knowledge" doctrine and federal preemption.]

* * *

[Defendants argue that the plaintiffs' claims are barred by comment *i* to Restatement (Second) of Torts § 402A, which provides in part, "Good tobacco is not unreasonably dangerous merely because the effects of smoking may be harmful; but tobacco containing something like marijuana may be unreasonably dangerous." Further, defendants argue that plaintiffs claims are barred by the "common knowledge" doctrine, based on comment *i*, which further provides, "The article sold must be dangerous to an extent beyond that which would be contemplated by the ordinary consumer who purchases it, with the ordinary knowledge common to the community as to its characteristics." Rejecting these arguments, the court refuses to dismiss plaintiffs' claims on this basis.]

Defendants argue that their products fall under the Restatement's definition of "good tobacco," rendering plaintiffs unable to state a claim under their various product liability theories. Plaintiffs counter that defendants' products are not "good tobacco" due to the addition of other substances harmful to plaintiffs, and therefore, the claims survive a Motion to Dismiss. Defendants appear to argue that even if plaintiffs make such allegations, their products still fall within the Restatement's definition of "good tobacco."

... [C]ourts differ on whether Comment *i* (or the common knowledge rule in general) bars as a matter of law all tobacco product liability claims.

i.   Courts Granting Motions to Dismiss Based on Comment i

In Lane v. R.J Reynolds, 853 So. 2d 1144 (Miss. 2003), the Supreme Court of Mississippi held that Mississippi product liability law, which is also based on the Restatement § 402A, bars recovery under a products liability theory based on smoking. According to the *Lane* court, "the harm from tobacco use has been well documented, and elimination of the sources of the harm would greatly reduce the desirability of cigarettes." The *Lane* court notes Comment *i* and highlights the fact that the dangers of "good tobacco" are in effect the very qualities that make it good. The court declined to interpret Comment *i* as allowing product liability suits based on smoking where the plaintiff alleges manipulation of the contents of the tobacco in light of the Mississippi Legislature's stated purpose in enacting its products liability law ... to eliminate products liability claims for tobacco. Therefore, it granted a motion to dismiss, in their entirety, the product liability claims.

Similarly, the Northern District of Ohio, applying Ohio law, frequently dismisses smokers' claims under Rule 12(b)(6) based on Comment *i*, and the common knowledge rule in general, even when the smokers allege alteration of the tobacco by addition of "foreign" substances. [Citations] See also Little v. Brown & Williamson Tobacco Corp., 243 F. Supp. 2d 480, 490 (D.S.C. 2001) (listing additional cases that hold that Comment *i* and the common knowledge doctrine bar, as a matter of law, all smoking product liability claims).

ii. Courts Denying Motions to Dismiss Based on Comment i

* * *

[I]n Little v. Brown & Williamson Tobacco Corp., 243 F.Supp.2d 480 (D.S.C. 2001), the court ... denied a motion to dismiss based on Comment *i*. The court noted ... that § 2 of the Restatement (Third) of Torts (1998), which most closely parallels § 402A, excludes tobacco from its list of "commonly and widely distributed products" that may inherently pose substantial risk of harm. The *Little* court postulates this omission reflects the changing attitudes of courts on the status of tobacco as an "unreasonably dangerous" product. [Citations.]

iii. Comment i Fails to Bar as a Matter of Law Plaintiffs' Products Liability Claims

While some courts have found otherwise, this Court finds the Arizona Supreme Court would find that Comment *i* does not bar all smokers' products liability suits. [Citation.]

First, the plain language of Comment *i* refers to "good tobacco," not good cigarettes.... Moreover, "even the majority of cases that have dismissed cigarette product liability claims have done so not based on Comment *i*, but after a thorough analysis of the *specific risks* claimed by the respective plaintiff to have caused his or her injury and whether those risks were 'common knowledge' during the relevant time period." ...

Next, even if the Court was persuaded that the Restatement's definition of "good tobacco" includes manufactured cigarettes containing no additional harmful substances beyond those occurring naturally in tobacco, the Court finds this insufficient to bar plaintiffs' claims. Plaintiffs allege that defendants were involved in a campaign designed "to misrepresent their actual role in manipulating the addictive properties of cigarettes via ammonia and other additives and/or via the engineering of higher nicotine tobaccos." Therefore, [if] the cigarettes smoked by Winona Hearn were manipulated by the addition of some dangerous additive, [they would be removed] from the Restatement's definition of "good tobacco" and rendering them unreasonably dangerous, despite Comment *i*.

Additionally, the Court finds that those cases barring all smokers' products liability claims are distinguishable. In *Lane,* 853 So. 2d 1144 (Miss. 2003), the court relied on the legislative intent of the Mississippi Legislature when it enacted a products liability statute after expressly noting the goals of the statute included "abat[ing] the large volume of tobacco litigation." Similarly, the Northern District of Ohio cases interpreted an Ohio products liability statute as expressing a legislative intent to limit smokers' products liability suits. [Citation.] While the Arizona legislature has enacted statutes addressing products liability, see A.R.S. §§ 12–681, et al., defendants present no evidence that the Arizona legislature intended to limit the availability of this remedy for smokers.

* * *

c. The "Common Knowledge" Doctrine

[Defendants contend that] state and federal courts throughout the country repeatedly dismiss claims brought by smokers because information regarding the risks of smoking, including addiction, has long been available to, and known by, the public. Therefore, Defendants argue that the Court should take judicial notice [under Fed. R. Civ. P. 201] of this past awareness and grant dismissal of all of Plaintiffs' product liability claims.

[The viability of the common knowledge doctrine has not been determined in Arizona, and courts around the country have split on this issue.]

In Hill v. R.J. Reynolds Tobacco Co., 44 F. Supp. 2d 837, 844 (W.D. Ky.1999), the court [concluded that it should not take judicial notice of something as intangible as "the state of popular consciousness" of the risks of cigarettes before 1969, more than three decades in the past, an inherently speculative topic and hence not appropriate for judicial notice. This court agrees that judicial notice should not be used to select "an arbitrary date for when the risks (i.e. lung cancer) associated with smoking became common knowledge," when such a factual matter was hotly in dispute.]

Plaintiffs allege [that Winona did not know of the likelihood or severity of the risks from defendants' tobacco products, including the risk of addiction, when she began smoking; that defendants failed to establish a reasonably safe dose of tobacco for foreseeable users; that they] failed to design a product that when used as intended was reasonably safe for foreseeable users; failed to make such feasible improvements in design and composition of their tobacco products to materially decrease the foreseeable risk to users; [that they designed] "light" cigarettes in such a way that they generate lower tar and nicotine ratings on standard machine smoking tests than regular cigarettes while typically they do not actually deliver less tar or nicotine when smoked by most cigarette smokers; and that defendants controlled and manipulated the amount of ammonia in cigarettes for the purpose and with the intent of creating and sustaining addiction. Moreover, in their design defect claims based on strict liability, the plaintiffs allege that defendants' tobacco products were addictive, habit-forming, and once used caused physical and psychological dependence; the tobacco products failed to perform as safely as an ordinary consumer would expect when used as intended or in a manner reasonably foreseeable by the consumer; and that the risk of danger from the design of defendants' tobacco product outweighed the benefits obtained with the use of the products.

All of these allegations are at war with the claim that consumers knew they were buying a dangerous product. Without factual development, the Court cannot conclude that dismissal based on the common knowledge doctrine is required.

[Defendants' Motion to Dismiss denied in part and granted in part on other grounds.]

N O T E S

1.   Cigarette Litigation. Various aspects of cigarette litigation are addressed below in the punitive damages section of the damages chapter, ch. 15(4), and in the toxic substance and mass tort litigation chapter, ch. 19.

2.   Asbestos. In Halphen v. Johns–Manville Sales Corp., 484 So.2d 110 (La.1986), the court held that an asbestos manufacturer may be held strictly liable if its product fails the risk-utility test, whether or not the risks could be foreseen. Two years later, the legislature enacted a products liability reform statute defining all three types of defect. In La. Rev. Stat. Ann. § 9:2800.56, design defectiveness requires a finding of *both* (1) the availability of "an alternative design" that would have prevented the claimant's harm, *and* (2) the product's failing a risk-utility test. Asbestos litigation is addressed below in the state-of-the-art section of the next chapter, ch. 11(3), and in the toxic substance and mass tort litigation chapter, ch. 19.

3.   Durable Products. So far the inquiry has addressed alcohol, food, coffee, and cigarettes—all consumable substances containing various inherent hazards—

and another toxic substance, asbestos. Are the issues the same for *durable* products that contain inherent dangerous which cannot be designed away?

Parish v. Icon Health & Fitness, Inc.
Supreme Court of Iowa, 2006.
719 N.W.2d 540.

■ Larson, J.

James Parish was severely injured while using a trampoline manufactured by the defendant, Jumpking, Inc. Parish sued Jumpking on theories of defective design of the trampoline, and negligence in failing to warn of the danger in using it. The defendant moved for summary judgment, which was granted, and the plaintiff appealed. We affirm.

[Plaintiff's big brother, Delbert,] and Shelley Tatro purchased a Jumpking fourteen-foot trampoline for use in their backyard. They set up the trampoline, and Delbert tried it out by attempting a somersault. He nearly fell off the trampoline, prompting Delbert and Shelley to purchase a "fun ring"—a netlike enclosure with one entry point onto the trampoline. While [plaintiff was visiting his brother, he attempted] a back somersault on the trampoline, but he landed on his head and was rendered a quadriplegic. . . .

* * *

The Defective Design Claim.

In *Wright v. Brooke Group Ltd.,* 652 N.W.2d 159 (Iowa 2002), we adopted sections 1 and 2 of the Restatement (Third) of Torts: Products Liability [hereinafter Restatement]. . . .

The plaintiff's first argument is that the district court erred in granting summary judgment on his design-defect claim under section 2(b). . . . To succeed under section 2(b), a plaintiff must ordinarily show the existence of a reasonable alternative design, *Wright,* 652 N.W.2d at 169, and that this design would, at a reasonable cost, have reduced the foreseeability of harm posed by the product. Restatement § 2 cmt. *d.*

The Restatement recognizes exceptions to the requirement of a reasonable alternative design, but the plaintiff relies on only one: that the design was "manifestly unreasonable" under Restatement § 2(b) cmt. *e.* Under that comment, [entitled *Design defects: possibility of manifestly unreasonable design,*]

> the designs of some products are so manifestly unreasonable, in that they have low social utility and high degree of danger, that liability should attach even absent proof of a reasonable alternative design. [Comment *e* concludes that a court would declare, in the case of such an "egregiously unacceptable" hazard, the product's design to be defective "because the extremely high degree of danger posed by its use or consumption so substantially outweighs its negligible social utility that no rational, reasonable person, fully aware of the relevant facts, would choose to use, or to allow children to use, the product."]

The plaintiff concedes that he has not offered an alternative design; rather, he argues a trampoline is so inherently dangerous that a reasonable design alternative is not available. He contends there is no safe way to use a trampoline in a backyard, and it must be used only by properly trained and qualified participants under supervision.

The Restatement provides this illustration of a manifestly unreasonable product under comment *e:*

> ABC Co. manufactures novelty items. One item, an exploding cigar, is made to explode with a loud bang and the emission of smoke. Robert purchased the exploding cigar and presented it to his boss, Jack, at a birthday party arranged for him at the office. Jack lit the cigar. When it exploded, the heat from the explosion lit Jack's beard on fire causing serious burns to his face. If a court were to recognize the rule identified in this Comment, the finder of fact might find ABC liable for the defective design of the exploding cigar even if no reasonable alternative design was available that would provide similar prank characteristics. The utility of the exploding cigar is so low and the risk of injury is so high as to warrant a conclusion that the cigar is defective and should not have been marketed at all.

Restatement § 2(b) cmt. *e*, illus. 5.

Application of the "manifestly unreasonable" exception presents an issue of first impression in Iowa. However, the wording of section 2(b) and virtually all commentary on it suggest that this exception should be sparingly applied. In fact, such exceptions to the requirement of a reasonable alternative design were "grudgingly accepted by the Reporters," Keith C. Miller, *Myth Surrenders to Reality: Design Defect Litigation in Iowa*, 51 Drake L.Rev. 549, 564 (2003), suggesting that the drafters did not intend for there to be any exceptions to this requirement. [See] James A. Henderson, Jr., *The Habush Amendment: Section 2(b) comment e*, 8—Fall Kan. J.L. & Pub. Pol'y 86, 86 (1998).

Suits involving common and widely distributed products are more likely than others to require the showing of a reasonable alternative. According to the Restatement,

> Common and widely distributed products such as alcoholic beverages, firearms, and above-ground swimming pools may be found to be defective only upon proof of [a reasonable alternative design]. If such products are [ ] sold without reasonable warnings as to their danger ... then liability under §§ 1 and 2 may attach. Absent proof of defect under those Sections, however, courts have not imposed liability for categories of products that are generally available and widely consumed, even if they pose substantial risks of harm.

Restatement § 2(b) cmt. *d*.

While comment *e* recognizes the possibility that egregiously dangerous products might be held defective for that reason alone, the Restatement has noted that "a clear majority of courts that have faced the issue have refused so to hold." [Reporters' Note to § 2 comment d, which discusses] several cases imposing liability under comment *e* but observe[s] that "[e]ach of these judicial attempts at imposing such liability have either been overturned or sharply curtailed by legislation."

. . . In the present case, the issue is whether a reasonable fact finder could conclude the trampoline was manifestly unreasonable in its design within the meaning of comment *e* as interpreted by the commentary surrounding it and the cases applying it.

In cases involving common and widely distributed products,

> courts generally have concluded that legislatures[3] and administrative agencies can, more appropriately than courts, consider the desirability of commercial distribution of some categories of widely used and consumed, but nevertheless dangerous, products.

Restatement § 2(b) cmt. *d*.

It is undisputed that trampolines are common and widely distributed products. In fact, the evidence showed approximately fourteen million people use them. Even data produced by the plaintiff in his resistance to summary judgment showed that in 2002 only 2.1% of trampolines were associated with injuries, and only one-half of one percent of jumpers were injured. The Consumer Product Safety Commission, based on 1997 and 1998 injury data, concluded trampolines ranked twelfth among recreational use products in terms of injuries. They rated below such common activities as basketball, bicycle riding, football, soccer, and skating.

The benefits of trampolining include use in cardiovascular workouts and other medical treatments, including "bouncing" therapy for children with cystic fibrosis. Trampolining obviously provides valuable exercise and entertainment.

We conclude that the plaintiff has failed to [make out a "manifestly unreasonable" product claim under Restatement § 2 comment *e* as is necessary to] except this product from the alternative-design requirement of section 2(b), and the plaintiff's design-defect claim under that section must therefore be rejected.

The Warnings.

The plaintiff also claims the [defendant's warnings were inadequate.] Three warnings are placed permanently on the pad of the trampoline and advise the user:

---

3. New Jersey recognizes by statute an action for an egregiously dangerous product. However, it has done so in a very limited manner. The official commentary by the New Jersey Senate Judiciary Committee indicates just how limited that exception was intended to be. The commentary notes: "It is intended that such a finding [under the exception] would be made only in genuinely extraordinary cases—for example, in the case of a deadly toy marketed for use by the young children, or of a product marketed for use in dangerous criminal activities." N.J. Senate Judiciary Committee Statement, No. 2805–L.1987, cl. 197.

WARNING

Do not land on head or neck.

Paralysis or death can result, even if you land in the middle of the trampoline mat (bed).

To reduce the chance of landing on your head or neck, do not do somersaults (flips).

Only one person at a time on trampoline.

Multiple jumpers increase the chances of loss of control, collision, and falling off.

This can result in broken head, neck, back, or leg.

This trampoline is not recommended for children under 6 years of age.

These warnings also include nationally recognized warning symbols cautioning against those activities. During manufacture, Jumpking also places one warning on each of the eight legs of the trampoline, and the design is such that the only way to assemble the trampoline is to have these warnings facing out so they are visible to the user. Jumpking further manufactures two printed (nonpictorial) warnings that are sewn onto the trampoline bed itself. It also provides a warning placard for the owner to affix to the trampoline that contains both the pictorial warning and the language regarding safe use of the trampoline, and it provides an owner's manual that contains the warnings as found on the trampoline as well as additional warnings regarding supervision and education. It is undisputed that these warnings exceed the warnings required by the American Society for Testing and Material (ASTM).

Warnings are also provided with the fun ring. Jumpking provides eight warning stickers to be placed on the legs of the fun ring during assembly, and Shelley Tatro recalls installing them as directed. Jumpking provided extra warnings on the fun ring because it was aware that the fun ring may partially cover warnings on the legs of the trampoline. It also provides a warning placard with the fun ring to be placed at the door of the fun ring containing the pictorial warnings and additional language required by the ASTM. The fun ring comes with a separate owner's manual that provides additional warnings.

The Restatement recognizes that users must pay some attention for their own safety:

> Society does not benefit from products that are excessively safe—for example, automobiles designed with maximum speeds of 20 miles per hour—any more than it benefits from products that are too risky. Society benefits most when the right, or optimal, amount of product safety is achieved. *From a fairness perspective, requiring individual users and consumers to bear appropriate responsibility for proper product use prevents careless users and consumers from being subsidized by more careful users and consumers, when the former are paid damages out of funds to which the latter are forced to contribute through higher product prices.*

Restatement § 2 cmt. *a* (emphasis added).

In this case, it is undisputed that the three warnings affixed to the pad of the trampoline and the placards that came with both the trampoline and the fun ring warned against the specific conduct in which the plaintiff was engaged at the time of his injury, i.e., attempting somersaults or flips. We conclude that a reasonable fact finder could not conclude that the defendant's warnings were inadequate, and we affirm the district court's summary judgment on that claim.

[Summary judgment was proper. Affirmed.]

NOTES

1. Snow sleds. In Jordon v. K–Mart Corp., 611 A.2d 1328, 1330–31 (Pa. Super. Ct. 1992), a 10–year–old boy was injured when he lost control of his sled and hit a tree. The sled was a plastic toboggan-like sled purchased for David from defendant K–Mart. David and his parents sued K–Mart (the retailer) and the John Doe Corporation (the unknown manufacturer of the sled), alleging that the sled's design was defective because its runners were molded, rendering the sled difficult to steer, and because it was not equipped with "any independent steering or braking mechanisms." K–Mart's motion for summary judgment was granted, and plaintiffs appealed. *Held*, affirmed. The sled's design, as a matter of law, was not unreasonably dangerous. "[L]ike most recreational activities, sledding involves a degree of risk and even changing the design to require brakes or steering would not remove the inherent risk in the activity." Nor were warnings required, since "the dangers inherent in sledding with a toboggan-like sled with limited steering capacity is one which an ordinary ten-year-old child would recognize and appreciate as part of the risk of sledding."

2. Jungle Gyms. In Cozzi v. North Palos Elementary Sch. District, 597 N.E.2d 683 (Ill. App. 1992), the father of an 11–year–old boy who fell off a jungle gym in the playground sued the manufacturer of the jungle gym for negligently designing it to such a height and in failing to warn of the dangers of using it. The trial judge granted the defendant's motion for summary judgment, and plaintiff appealed. *Held*, affirmed. The danger of falling was obvious, there was no evidence that the jungle gym failed to perform its function of serving as a recreational device, and so it was not unreasonably dangerous. See generally Barton, Tort Reform, Innovation, and Playground Design, 58 Fla.L.Rev. 265 (2006).

3. Baby Walkers. Plaintiff parents put their 7–month-old baby, Tyler, in a Tot Wheels II baby walker, whereupon he scooted backwards to an electric teapot and grabbed its cord. The teapot fell over, scalding Tyler. In a suit against the manufacturer of the walker, *held*, summary judgment for manufacturer on defective design claim affirmed: "The walker was designed to give a baby mobility, the very feature that makes the product dangerous. The only alternative design would be to employ a saucer-type device that would allow a baby to stand, but not allow a baby to move. Such a design, however, completely changes the product. Given the nature and purpose of a baby walker, no feasible alternative design would have prevented the harm here." Thongchoom v. Graco Children's Products, Inc., 71 P.3d 214, 218 (Wash. Ct. App. 2003).

4. Firearms.

A. Gunshot victims. Each year, tens of thousands of Americans are killed by guns—roughly the same number as are killed in car accidents. Gun fatalities divide as follows: 48% suicides, 47% homicides, 4% accidents, and 1% legal justice system. In addition, another 125,000 people are injured by guns each year. Lytton, Tort Claims Against Gun Manufacturers for Crime–Related Injuries: Defining a Suitable Role for the Tort System in Regulating the Firearms Industry, 65 Mo. L. Rev. 1, 3 n.4 (2000). Almost all the gun-shot victim cases were dismissed on such grounds as no duty, no defect (the guns or ammo only did what they were designed to do), and because of the superseding intervention of criminals putting them to improper use (the abuse of guns by people, not the guns themselves, are the proximate cause of harm). The Products Liability Restatement includes firearms in its short list of generically dangerous products that are not inherently defective in design. See Products Liability Restatement § 2 cmt. *d*.

An exception was Kelley v. R.G. Indus., Inc., 497 A.2d 1143 (Md. 1985), an action against the manufacturer of the handgun used by a grocery store robber to shoot the assistant manager in the chest. Although the court decided that the risk-utility test was appropriate only "when something goes wrong with a product," it nevertheless imposed strict liability on sellers of "Saturday Night Specials"—poorly made, cheap, small, inaccurate, and easily concealable handguns, which are useful principally for criminal activity rather than self-protection or other legitimate activity—when used by criminals to harm innocent victims. The N.R.A conducted a multi-million dollar campaign to have *Kelley* overturned, first by the Maryland legislature, and then by the people in a referendum petition. The gun lobby and gun control advocates agreed to compromise legislation overturning *Kelley* but prohibiting the sale of Saturday Night Specials in the state, and the voters by referendum approved the law by a vote of 58% to 42%. See Bogus, Pistols, Politics and Products Liability, 59 U. Cin. L. Rev.1103, 1145–1148 (1991).

B. Municipalities. During the late 1990s and early 2000s, over thirty municipalities brought suit against the handgun industry—on negligent marketing, public nuisance, and other theories—for blanketing their cities with an oversupply of guns, particularly cheap handguns, that far exceeded the lawful market for firearms. Most of the cases were dismissed (or dropped). See, e.g., City of Chicago v. Beretta U.S.A. Corp., 821 N.E.2d 1099 (Ill. 2004) (no duty or proximate cause, and barred by municipal cost recovery rule); People [of State of New York] v. Sturm, Ruger & Co., 761 N.Y.S.2d 192 (App. Div. 2003) (harm too remote); Philadelphia v. Beretta U.S.A. Corp., 277 F.3d 415 (3d Cir. 2002) (no duty, proximate cause, remoteness, and standing). But see James v. Arms Tech., Inc., 820 A.2d 27 (N.J. Super. Ct. App. Div. 2003) (allowing negligent distribution, public nuisance, and punitive damages claims); City of Gary, Indiana v. Smith & Wesson Corp., 801 N.E.2d 1222 (Ind. 2003) (various claims); City of Cincinnati v. Beretta U.S.A. Corp., 768 N.E.2d 1136 (Ohio 2002) (rejecting defenses). See generally Ausness, Public Tort Litigation: Public Benefit or Public Nuisance?, 77 Temp. L. Rev. 825 (2004); Gifford, Public Nuisance as a Mass Products Liability Tort, 71 U. Cincinnati L. Rev. 743 (2003).

C. Legislation. In time, a growing number of state statutes prohibited actions against gun manufacturers in general or, at least in a couple of states, broadly prohibited claims by local governments from suing manufacturers and other sellers for injuries caused by guns. In the end, Congress in 2005 resolved the entire matter with its enactment of The Protection of Lawful Commerce in Arms Act, 15 U.S.C. § 7901 et seq., that bars gun litigation against manufacturers "resulting from the criminal or unlawful misuse" of a firearm or ammunition. Id. at § 7903(5)(A). See, e.g., Ileto v. Glock, Inc., 421 F. Supp. 2d 1274 (C.D. Cal. 2006) (dismissing case pursuant to the Act). See generally Larkin, The "Protection of Lawful Commerce in Arms Act": Immunity for the Firearm Industry is a (Constitutional) Bulls–Eye, 95 Ky. L.J. 187 (2007); D. Owen, Products Liability Law § 10.3 (2d ed. 2008).

5. Above–Ground Swimming Pools. In O'Brien v. Muskin Corp., 463 A.2d 298 (N.J. 1983), ignoring a No–Diving decal on an above-ground pool, plaintiff dove in. His outstretched hands hit and slid apart on the vinyl liner on the bottom of the pool, and his head hit the bottom. He sued the manufacturer, claiming that the slippery liner rendered the pool defective in design and that the warnings were inadequate. The trial judge threw out the plaintiff's defective design claim, and plaintiff appealed. The Appellate Division agreed with the plaintiff, and the Supreme Court affirmed, reasoning that, to prevail on the design defect claim, the plaintiff did not have to prove the existence of an alternative, safer design, but only that the pool's risks, with a slippery liner, exceeded the pool's utility. "[U]nder risk-utility analysis, if the risks outweigh the utility of the product, it is defective."

Concurring and dissenting, Judge Schreiber thought that juries should not be allowed to find a design defective on a *global* balance of all the costs and benefits of the accident product considered as a whole—rather than limiting the risk-utility analysis solely to the costs and benefits of the specific alternative design feature proposed by plaintiff. By so distorting the risk-utility inquiry, the majority effectively converted the basis of liability from "strict" to "absolute" and asked juries to exceed their capabilities by effectively deciding, without adequate tools, when to outlaw whole categories of products. "I must dissent from that conclusion because the jury will not be cognizant of all the elements that should be considered in formulating a policy supporting absolute liability, because it is not satisfactory to have a jury make a value judgment with respect to a type or class of product, and because its judgment will not have precedential effect." 463 A.2d at 310.

Henderson & Twerski, Closing the American Products Liability Frontier: The Rejection of Liability Without Defect

66 N.Y.U. L. Rev. 1263, 1316–31 (1991).

[Particularly after O'Brien v. Muskin Corp., the above-ground pool case in note 5], plaintiffs have urged courts to adopt what we refer to as product-category liability—strict liability for producing and marketing certain categories of risky products, such as handguns, cigarettes, and alcoholic beverages, without regard to whether such products could be designed or marketed more safely.... Courts are not suited to making the sorts of judgments required to be made. Consistent with our analysis, most courts that have considered product-category liability claims have rejected them out of hand. And of the very few decisions that have embraced the notion, each has been reversed by its respective state legislature....

In concluding that courts will not accept product-category liability because they are institutionally incapable of managing the litigation that acceptance would invite, we have not yet addressed the underlying political issues regarding whether any of these product categories ought to be more stringently regulated by nonjudicial institutions, agencies, and markets. We note that these institutions are demonstrably more competent than courts to reach the sorts of decisions called for in product-category liability. Understand that we are not challenging the superior competency of courts to administer most of our existing products liability system. Products liability is a necessary and appropriate response to market failures, such as consumers' lack of adequate information about product-related risks of injury.

However, when one's attention shifts to the products most likely to be deemed socially inappropriate under a system of product-category liability—handguns, cigarettes, alcoholic beverages, and the like—it is frequently difficult to see where the relevant markets have failed in any ordinary sense of the term. Americans may smoke and drink too much, but in substantial measure that is probably because many Americans who do so prefer to engage in those activities knowing of the relevant risks. Those who would prohibit outright or via a crushing liability tax the routine commercial distribution of unavoidably unsafe products may be reacting not so much to society's ignorance of the relevant risks as to society's indifference to them.

Of course, to the extent that smoking and drinking generate externalities or involve addictive behavior, society confronts potentially significant market failure. In those instances, society sensibly may reach collective decisions that this or that activity should be legally regulated—perhaps even proscribed altogether—regardless of the existence of strong consumer demand in the marketplace. But we find no reason to believe that legislatures and administrative agencies are not up to the task of making those decisions. [L]egislatures and regulatory agencies are designed, as courts are not, to address polycentric planning tasks of the sort presented by product-category liability analysis. And the remedies that these regulatory bodies can impose are infinitely more subtle than the "off-on" toggle switch between dramatically high tort liability and practically no liability at all.

NOTE

In 1992, the year after this article was published, Professors Henderson and Twerski were named co-reporters for the Restatement (3d) of Torts: Products Liability. Comments *d* and *e* to § 2 of this Restatement, addressed by the court in *Parish*, examine the inherent danger product-category liability issue. Comment *d* provides that design defect determinations almost always require proof of a reasonable alternative design, even in cases involving such inherently dangerous products as alcoholic beverages, firearms, and above-ground swimming pools, although sellers of such products (as any other) are also subject to liability for defects in manufacture and warnings.

As *Parish* indicates, comment *e* provides a small window of product-category liability for "manifestly unreasonable designs" that are "egregiously unacceptable . . . because the extremely high degree of danger posed by its use or consumption so substantially outweighs its negligible social utility that no rational, reasonable person, fully aware of the relevant facts, would choose to use, or to allow children to use, the product."

The Third Restatement provides two applicable illustrations. *Illustration 4*, following comment *d* and based on *O'Brien*, posits (counterfactually) that the liner was "the best and safest liner available and that no alternative, less slippery liner was feasible." The illustration concludes that the claimant "has failed to establish defective design under Subsection (b)."

Illustration 5, following comment *e*, involves an exploding novelty cigar provided by the purchaser to his boss at a birthday party for the boss who is injured when his beard ignites from the explosion. (No mention is made of the fate of the employee.) The illustration concludes that "[t]he utility of the exploding cigar is so low and the risk of injury is so high as to warrant a conclusion that the cigar is defective and should not have been marketed at all." Accordingly, the factfinder could find the manufacturer liable for defective design, "even if no reasonable alternative design was available that would provide similar prank characteristics."

Rethinking Product Category Liability*

The *Third Restatement* rejects the idea that entire categories of products—perhaps cheap handguns, cigarettes, alcohol, trampolines, above-ground swimming pools, and three-wheel all-terrain vehicles—may be inherently defective in design.[47] The claim of defectiveness in such cases is based upon the idea that some such products may contain excessive inherent danger that cannot be designed or warned away. For example, cheap handguns may kill too many victims of criminal and family assaults. Alcohol and cigarettes, addictive to millions of Americans, may cause more suffering than the perversely addictive "pleasure" they provide. Finally, above-ground pools, trampolines, and three-wheel ATVs may cause more injuries than they are worth. Such products thus may be inherently defective in design, and categorically so, because they fail the basic cost-benefit test: their accident costs exceed the benefits they provide. If the risk-utility calculations are correct, then such products are on balance simply bad; they generate for society a net *dis*utility, more harm than value, more bad than good. This is the concept of product category defectiveness implicitly rejected in § 2(b)'s requirement that the plaintiff establish a reasonable alternative design in virtually every case.

Courts indeed have only infrequently held a product to be defectively designed in the absence of a reasonable alternative design. One may fairly question the appropriateness of product category-wide liability on grounds of judicial competency, on whether courts may properly decide for the public that certain types of products consumers want are simply bad in law. Put this way, a judicial declaration that a certain product type wanted by consumers is "illegal" looks somewhat like judicial prohibition and quite like paternalistic arrogance by the courts. The problem with category defectiveness, then, is that it authorizes courts and juries to interfere with

----

* *From* Owen, The Graying of Products Liability Law: Paths Taken and Untaken in the New Restatement, 61 Tenn. L. Rev. 1241, 1253–57 (1994).

47. The Reporters had argued earlier against this type of categorical design defect liability. *See* James A. Henderson, Jr. & Aaron Twerski, Closing the American Products Liability Frontier: The Rejection of Liability Without Defect, 66 N.Y.U. L. Rev. 1263 (1991).

consumer freedom of choice on the supposition that a court (or jury) knows better than consumers what is good for them.[50]

It just may be, however, that courts do sometimes know what is better for consumers than consumers themselves, or at least that they may sometimes be better positioned to render fair and rational "legislative" type decisions on the balance of risks and benefits in certain types of products. Imagine, for example, a case of a father pestered successfully by his 10–year–old daughter to buy a trampoline for backyard use. Assume further that the daughter thereafter bounces off the trampoline onto her head and is paralyzed for life. Before purchasing the trampoline, the father (unless a public safety epidemiologist for the Consumer Products Safety Commission) probably would have had no meaningful appreciation of the product's balance of trade-offs between fun and danger. Even if the literature accompanying the trampoline fully detailed the numbers, types, and severity of risks from different types of trampoline use and misuse, the father, even as so "informed" probably never could have truly *understood* the real balance of risks and benefits presented by the trampoline, either to society in general or to his family in particular. Nor, of course, was the daughter ever in a position to make any kind of rational cost-benefit decision for herself.

Although a trial court may serve poorly as a legislature or an agency for rendering macro-social determinations on the net value of home trampolines, it provides a better forum for an injured claimant than none at all. After all, courts are the traditional and generally the *only* forums for rendering compensation decisions for consumers after accidents have occurred. While compensation is appropriate only for harm from products that are "defective," what could be more defective than a product that causes more harm than good? It easily is forgotten that ruling such a product as defective does not ban it altogether, but simply taxes to the manufacturer (and thus indirectly to its shareholders and consumers) the true extent of the product's accident costs. It may well be that many courts will want to retain the power to decide that certain high-risk products fairly should be priced to include their excessive costs: costs that consumers are unable to comprehend or avoid, costs inevitably and involuntarily inflicted upon other persons, such as children, passengers in other cars, and the victims of violent crimes. When a product's excessive risks of harm cannot fully and effectively be appreciated and thus dealt with rationally by the persons put at risk, the courts should want to make themselves available to force the manufacturer to internalize the costs of injuries.

Why should not the price of a pack of cigarettes or a can of beer reflect the enormous costs of lung cancer and drunk-driving injuries that are very often borne by innocent third parties and by the public at large through private and public health care insurance mechanisms? To argue that consumer freedom or legislative deference precludes the courts from requir-

---

50. A related process problem concerns the difficulty of principled adjudication of such politicized issues involving broad cost-benefit calculations of values that may be incommensurable.

ing these costs to be included in the price of certain high-risk products of dubious utility—especially those that are addictive—seems to miss the point. If the product in fact is addictive, the issue might be characterized more fairly not as whether to deprive consumers of their freedom, but as whether to protect consumers from *duress*. Moreover, if a legislature or administrative agency actually makes a full and fair determination that a particular type of dangerous product is worth the risks, as Congress may have done with the Swine Flu vaccine in the 1970s and as the National Highway & Traffic Safety Administration arguably did with the various passive restraint alternatives to automotive air bags in the 1980s, then the judiciary should stay its hand. Unfortunately, however, the legislatures are institutionally incapable of addressing the vast majority of product safety problems. Additionally, the various product safety agencies have limited jurisdictions, limited budgets, and often limited skills and wills to address in an effective manner the great majority of product risks. On balance, the *Third Restatement*'s general rejection of the concept of product category defectiveness may reflect an unduly conservative point of view on judicial competency that many courts may choose to reject as an outright rule.

Finally, while it certainly is true that courts infrequently predicate liability on the global disutility of a product, courts have long defined defectiveness in just this global manner, often stating (generally and without qualification) that products are defective if their risks exceed their benefits. In applying this conventional cost-benefit definition of defectiveness, surely the great majority of cases involve products that could have been designed more safely in a variety of alternative ways. The theory of product category defectiveness simply is not relevant to such ordinary product cases in which plaintiffs will quite properly be required to show a reasonable design alternative. For example, automobiles are involved in the deaths of some 40,000 persons, and the maiming of millions of others, in this nation every year. Nonetheless, one would have to search long and hard to find a judge or jury willing to hold that the costs of automotive accidents exceed the many benefits to society that cars provide.[56] By contrast, the benefits of cheap handguns, cheap alcohol, cheap cigarettes, and cheap home trampolines may not on balance fairly be worth their enormous risks. In fact, their low prices[57] may encourage excessive use. Thus, most courts may not wish to tie their hands by outlawing product category defectiveness altogether, but may rather decide to leave this design defectiveness approach within the arsenal of products liability theories as a useful and important tool for special use in certain limited types of cases.

---

56. Accordingly, plaintiffs in automotive design cases must appropriately establish feasible alternative designs.

57. Low relative to the harm they cause since, if product category defectiveness is not allowed, their prices will artificially exclude their arguably excessive accident costs which are instead externalized to a large extent on other persons.

Bogus, War on the Common Law: The Struggle at the Center of Products Liability

60 Mo. L. Rev. 1, 87–88 (1995).

In this age of statutes and of administrative regulation, the common law has receded in importance. Products liability represents the most significant, if not only, area in which the common law [is] a vital and dynamic force. It has become an essential participant in promoting public safety. This is not to deny that the primary role must be played by administrative agencies. We shall live forever more in [a] technologically advancing society, and only a panoply of specialized bureaucracies can attempt to monitor the vast array of new products and services or provide a filtration system that prevents unreasonably dangerous products from entering the stream of commerce. Administrative agencies have their limits, however, and products liability is an essential auxiliary.

Products liability evolved from a system that dealt only with manufacturing defects into one concerned also with design defects because that is where it increasingly was needed. For the same reason, the natural course of evolution will take products liability into a third phase in which it deals forthrightly with generic risks. In a technologically advancing society, the ability to produce new products often outruns the capacity to make them safe. The problem cannot always be solved by warnings because purchasers are not the only ones at risk. There will be an ever-increasing number of nonmechanical products. Chemicals of all kinds will continue to grow in variety, complexity, and potency, and there will more biological, radiological, electromagnetic, and genetic products as well. These products migrate through the environment and put non-users at risk. Between 1971 and 1994, the cancer rate rose eighteen percent rise in the United States; and cancer is expected to surpass heart disease as the leading cause of death by the year 2000. It is almost inevitable that chemicals and other nonmechanical products will increasingly be implicated in cancer and other diseases. Yet chemicals and other nonmechanical products will often be considered exempt from strict liability if generic risks are excluded from products liability. This is why generic liability is so important to the future of products liability.

Products liability now stands at a crossroads. It cannot stand still; it will continue to evolve, progressively or regressively. In an age of statutes and regulatory bureaucracies, products liability is the one flower blooming in the garden of the common law. Either it will continue to thrive—and demonstrate that the common law has a role in modern society—or it will wither, and the garden once lovingly tended by Holmes and Cardozo will be bare.

NOTES

1. Inherent Risks in the Courts. Professor Bogus asserts that "courts are moving slowly yet inexorably toward accepting generic liability." Id. at 9. Do you think that this is likely? More fundamentally, do you think that courts and juries *should* decide liability for generic risks—risks that exceed a product's benefits but that cannot be designed away—when the issue is put to them, or should they forebear deciding cases of this type altogether and leave such matters entirely to markets, legislatures, and product safety regulatory agencies?

2. Inherent Risk Legislation. A number of states and the federal government have enacted legislation addressing in one way or another the issue of products that contain substantial inherent risks. Some state and federal statutes ban the sale to unauthorized persons of such dangerous products as fireworks, cigarettes, alcohol, and controlled substances, while other states have enacted products liability reform statutes that limit a manufacturer's liability for generic product risks. New Jersey's statute, for example, generally shields manufacturers of inherently dangerous products from design defect claims but allows such claims for industrial machinery and products whose design is "egregiously unsafe." N.J. Stat. Ann. § 2A:58C–3. And California and Texas enacted nearly identical reform statutes adopting the safe harbor list of inherently dangerous products of comment *i* to § 402A which shelters manufacturers of such products from most products liability exposure. But California's legislature in 1998 deleted "tobacco" from the safe harbor list of protected products and added new provisions specifically authorizing products liability suits against the tobacco industry. See Cal. Civ. Code § 1714.45(e), (f), and (g).

Miss. Code Ann. § 11–1–63(b) provides that "A product is not defective in design or formulation if the harm for which the claimant seeks to recover . . . was caused by an inherent characteristic of the product which is a generic aspect of the product that cannot be eliminated without substantially compromising the product's usefulness or desirability and which is recognized by the ordinary person with the ordinary knowledge common to the community." In Clark v. Brass Eagle, Inc., 866 So.2d 456 (Miss. 2004), plaintiff was injured in a "paintball war" when hit in the eye with a paintball while riding around with his friends shooting paintballs at each others' cars. *Held*, design and warnings defect claims against the manufacturer of the paintball gun dismissed, where shooter and victim alike knew the inherent risks of using paintball guns without protective eyewear, and where no design alternative could have prevented plaintiff's injury.

3. Negligent Marketing: "Negligent Entrustment." If product "defect" determinations are inappropriate for injuries caused by inherently dangerous products like handguns and trampolines, because such products are socially beneficial when placed in proper hands, how about a claim for "negligent entrustment," or "negligent marketing," when such products are released by manufacturers and retailers into improper hands? See Ausness, Tort Liability for the Sale of Non-Defective Products: An Analysis and Critique of the Concept of Negligent Marketing, 53 S.C. L. Rev. 907, 912–17 (2002); Rachana Bhowmik et al., A Sense of Duty: Retiring the "Special Relationship" Rule and Holding Gun Manufacturers Liable for Negligently Distributing Guns, 4 J. Health Care L. & Pol'y 42 (2000); McClurg, The Tortious Marketing of Handguns: Strict Liability Is Dead, Long Live Negligence, 19 Seton Hall Legis. J. 777, 806–18 (1996) (praising negligent marketing theory).

4. Public Nuisance. How about public nuisance, on the ground that manufacturers who distribute such products substantially and unreasonably interfere with the public health and safety? See, e.g., County of Santa Clara v. Atlantic Richfield Co., 40 Cal.Rptr.3d 313 (Ct. App. 2006) (lead paint); In re Methyl Tertiary Butyl Ether (MTBE) Products, 457 F.Supp.2d 455 (S.D.N.Y. 2006); Johnson v. Bryco Arms, 304 F.Supp.2d 383 (E.D.N.Y. 2004) (Weinstein, J.) (handgun). See generally Sprague & Fitzpatrick, Getting the Lead Out: How Public Nuisance Law Protects Rhode Island's Children, 11 Roger Williams U. L. Rev. 603 (2006); V. Schwartz & Goldberg, The Law of Public Nuisance: Maintaining Rational Boundaries on a Rational Tort, 45 Washburn L.J. 541 (2006); Gifford, Public Nuisance as a Mass Products Liability Tort, 71 U. Cin. L. Rev. 741 (2006).

5. Courts are still uncertain on how best to deal with the inherent risk product-category liability issues, and the scholarship on the subject is still quite sparse and embryonic. In addition to the above, see generally C. Bogus, ed., Symposium on Generic Products Liability, 72 Chi.-Kent L. Rev. 3 (1996) (articles by Bell; Bogus; Hanson, Crowley & Logue; Page; Phillips; Powers; and Wertheimer); D. Owen, Products Liability Law § 10.3 (2d ed. 2008).

3. MISUSE

> We cannot charge the manufacturer of a knife when it is used as a toothpick and the user complains because the sharp edge cuts.

General Motors Corp. v. Hopkins, 548 S.W.2d 344, 349 (Tex. 1977).

———

An original premise of manufacturer liability was that the injury arose out of the *proper* use of the product. Thus, in Greenman v. Yuba Power Products, Inc., 377 P.2d 897, 901 (Cal. 1963):

> Implicit in the machine's presence on the market ... was a representation that it would safely do *the jobs for which it was built*. ... To establish the manufacturer's liability it was sufficient that plaintiff proved that he was injured while using the Shopsmith *in a way it was intended to be used* as a result of the defect in design and manufacture of which plaintiff was not aware that made the Shopsmith *unsafe for its intended use*. (Emphasis added.)

What if the plaintiff in *Greenman* had been injured while using the lathe on a piece of wood that was too big for the machine? Or on a piece of metal, contrary to instructions? Or was running the lathe over its safe maximum speed? Product "misuse" issues like these are explored in this section.

———

Venezia v. Miller Brewing Co.

United States Court of Appeals, First Circuit, 1980.
626 F.2d 188.

■ LEVIN H. CAMPBELL, CIRCUIT JUDGE.

[While playing with friends, the 8–year–old plaintiff found a discarded Miller Beer bottle and threw it against a telephone pole. The bottle shattered, and particles of glass injured his eye. His suit asserting warranty and negligence claims against Miller Brewing Company and three glass manufacturers was dismissed by the trial court for failure to state a claim, under Fed.R.Civ.P. 12(b)(6), and plaintiff appealed. Plaintiff argues that defendants] should have been aware of the dangers inherent in their "thin walled" "non-returnable" bottles and [so should have designed and sold] a product better able to safely withstand such foreseeable misuse as breakage in the course of improper handling by children.

* * *

Plaintiff's allegation of breach of warranty is based upon Mass. G.L. c. 106 § 2–314, which provides that a merchant impliedly warrants that his goods are, *inter alia,* "fit for the *ordinary* purposes for which such goods are used." (Emphasis added.) The linchpin of the warranty claim (and, as will be seen, the negligence claim also) is thus the proper scope of the term ordinary purpose. While at first blush it might appear beyond dispute that throwing a glass container into a telephone pole is by no means an "ordinary" use of that product, some brief examination of recent authority relied on by plaintiff in support of the contrary view may be helpful in explaining just why the initial impression is, in fact, sound.

In Back v. Wickes Corp., 378 N.E.2d 964 (Mass. 1978), the Massachusetts Supreme Judicial Court explored the contours of section 2–314's "ordinary purpose" concept and concluded that the " 'ordinary purposes' contemplated by [that warranty] section include both those uses which the manufacturer intended and those which are reasonably foreseeable." "It is no more than a play on words," the court concluded, "to charge that goods must be fit for 'ordinary' purposes, but not for 'extraordinary' or 'different' or 'unusual' purposes. Such [language] fails to inform ... as to whether the defendant has warranted the goods to be free from the propensity that caused the plaintiff's injuries."

Seizing on these passages and the Supreme Judicial Court's further admonition that a manufacturer must, in designing a product, "anticipate the environment in which [that] product will be used," plaintiff urges that the present defendants might reasonably be found by a jury to have broken a fitness warranty by designing and manufacturing glass bottles unable to safely withstand the arguably foreseeable product abuse that occurred here.

[But] we believe the *Back* court held only that a manufacturer's warranty of product fitness for ordinary use includes a guarantee that such product will withstand, in a reasonably safe manner, foreseeable "misuse" incident to or arising out of the product's intended use. See W. Prosser, The Law of Torts, § 96, p. 646 (1971). We think it would be stretching too far to believe that the Massachusetts courts are presently prepared to expand their definition of "ordinary purposes" to include the deliberate misuse of an otherwise reasonably safe container in a manner totally unrelated to any normal or intended use of that item. The Massachusetts Supreme Judicial Court previously has found no breach of a warranty of merchantability where a plaintiff was injured by glass breakage sustained in an attempt to pry the cover off a glass baby food jar with a beer-type can opener.[2] Vincent v. Nicholas E. Tsiknas Co., 151 N.E.2d 263 (Mass. 1958). *A fortiori*, we can see no possible implied fitness warranty that an empty glass bottle discarded by unknown persons would more safely withstand being intentionally smashed against a solid stationary object. Under Massachusetts law the question of fitness for ordinary purposes is largely one centering around reasonable consumer expectations. *Back,* supra; *Vincent,* supra. "The propensity of glass to break under pressure is common knowledge," *Vincent,* 151 N.E.2d at 265. No reasonable consumer would expect anything but that a glass beer bottle, apparently well suited for its immediate intended use, would fail to safely withstand the type of purposeful abuse involved here. In fact, one would suspect that the present eight year old plaintiff knew well the expected result, if not the potential injury, of his conduct. What, if not the possibility of shattering the bottle, would lead him to throw it against the pole in the first place? [Citation.]

* * *

[With respect to his negligence claim, plaintiff] again, as he did in his warranty argument, attempts to expand the scope of the "intended" use concept by resort to the familiar, and sometimes misleading, rubric of "foreseeability." But reliance on such generality is of limited assistance, for "In a sense, in retrospect almost nothing is unforeseeable." Green v. Volkswagen of America, Inc., 485 F.2d 430, 438 (6th Cir. 1973) [quoting Mieher v. Brown, 301 N.E.2d 307 (Ill.1973)], see also Prosser, supra, § 43, p. 267–68. One with the time and imagination and aided by hindsight no doubt can conjure up all sorts of arguably "foreseeable" misuses of a variety of otherwise reasonable safe products. We see no evidence that the Massachusetts courts have abandoned their previously expressed view that "a common or straight-forward product, if safe for normal uses reasonably to be anticipated at the time of manufacture, is not defective [i.e., unfit for its intended use] simply because it is foreseeable that it may cause injury to someone using it improperly." Tibbetts v. Ford Motor Co., 358 N.E.2d 460, 462 (Mass. App. Ct. 1976). Indeed, the Supreme Judicial Court has recently cited with approval previous decisions of this and other circuit courts which have defined the scope of the concept of "intended use" as encompassing the "probable ancillary consequences of normal use," and the consequences "incident to the normal and expected use" of a particular product. [Citations.] Certainly the present product misuse falls far outside that definition.

Even under the most expansive theories of products liability, a "manufacturer is not an insurer and cannot be held to a standard of duty of guarding against all possible types of accidents and injuries" in any way causally related to the design and manufacture of its products. [Citation.]

---

2. While the jar had included directions to open "gently," the court emphasized in reaching its decision that "glass jars are not sold, or bought, in the expectation that they will be subjected to pressures" of the sort as were in fact exerted. 151 N.E.2d at 265. If a glass container has not been warranted to withstand an attempt to open it with an improper opening device, it hardly could be warranted to safely survive impact with a telephone pole.

The world, as the Massachusetts Appeals Court has noted, is "full of rough edges." *Tibbetts,* supra. [T]he Massachusetts courts would not be prepared to hold a manufacturer liable for injuries sustained by an individual coming into contact with such "rough edges" created by his own intentional misuse of an otherwise "fit" product in a manner in no reasonable way related to the immediate intended uses for which the product was designed, manufactured and marketed. [T]he impact of endorsing a contrary conclusion would be overwhelming, with every discarded glass object holding the potential for generating a future lawsuit.

Affirmed.

Ellsworth v. Sherne Lingerie, Inc.

Court of Appeals of Maryland, 1985.
303 Md. 581, 495 A.2d 348.

■ McAuliffe, Judge.

[Plaintiff was severely burned when the nightgown she was wearing inside out, with the pockets protruding, ignited when it came in contact with her electric range. She had placed a tea kettle on the burner set on "high" and was reaching for a coffee filter in the cupboard over the stove when her pocket touched the edge of the burner and ignited. The gown was designed and manufactured by Sherne Lingerie which bought the cotton flannelette material from a fabric manufacturer, Cone Mills. Plaintiff sued both Sherne and Cone, alleging negligence and strict liability in tort for failing to flame retard the fabric and failing to warn of the flammability hazard. Defendants claimed that the plaintiff had misused the gown, and the judge instructed the jury on the doctrine of misuse. The jury returned a verdict for the defendants, which was upheld by the intermediate appellate court, and plaintiff appealed.]

* * *

The problem of understanding the issue of misuse in strict liability cases is ... compounded by the absence of agreement as to the meaning of the word. Misuse has been defined as: a use not reasonably foreseeable [citations]; a use of the product in a manner which defendant could not reasonably foresee [citations]; ... a use or handling so unusual that the average consumer could not reasonably expect the product to be designed and manufactured to withstand it—a use which the seller, therefore, need not anticipate and provide for [citation]; [and] use of the product which constitutes wilful or reckless misconduct or an invitation of injury [citation]. The Fifth Circuit, in Jones v. Menard, 559 F.2d 1282, 1285 n. 4 (5th Cir. 1977) [La. law], defined misuse in the context of the three types of products cases. That court said,

> [i]n inadequate warning cases misuse means that the seller had no duty to warn against unforeseeable uses of its products, while in design cases misuse means that the manufacturer had no duty to design a product so as

to prevent injuries arising from unforeseeable uses of that product.... In defective manufacture cases, however, misuse means that the injury was not caused by some inherent defect in the product but by the consumer's abnormal use of it....[5]

It has been suggested that misuse means any use not intended by the manufacturer, but this is too narrow and fails to take into account a variety of uses reasonably foreseeable although not subjectively intended. It has also been suggested that virtually anything is possible, and thus arguably foreseeable, so that foreseeability as a test is too broad.

We conclude, as have most courts which have considered the issue, that "reasonable foreseeability" is the appropriate test, and thus a seller is required to provide a product that is not unreasonably dangerous when used for a purpose and in a manner that is reasonably foreseeable.[6] * * *

Applying these principles to the facts of this case, we conclude the evidence was insufficient to generate an issue of misuse, and that the trial judge erred in allowing the jury to consider misuse of the product as a possible bar to recovery. Clearly, and concededly, Appellant was using the nightgown for a reasonably foreseeable purpose. We conclude that her manner of use of the nightgown, though possibly careless, was reasonably foreseeable as a matter of law. It certainly may be foreseen that wearing apparel, such as nightgowns and robes, will occasionally be worn inside out. It is also foreseeable that a loosely fitting gown will come into contact with sources of ignition in the environment where it may be expected to be worn, and particularly when worn in the kitchen and near a stove. Momentary inattention or carelessness on the part of the user, while it may constitute contributory negligence, does not add up to misuse of the product under these circumstances.

[Reversed and remanded for new trial.]

Moran v. Faberge, Inc.

Court of Appeals of Maryland, 1975.
273 Md. 538, 332 A.2d 11.

■ DIGGES, JUDGE.

[Negligence action by Nancy Moran against cologne manufacturer for personal injuries sustained when a bottle of the cologne caught fire. The

---

5. See also W. Keeton, D. Dobbs, R. Keeton, D. Owen, The Law of Torts § 102 (5th ed. 1984)(misuse is defined as a use different in a kind from what was intended, and unforeseeable misuse in the sense of a use that could not reasonably have been anticipated by the manufacturer); J. Dooley, Modern Tort Law § 32.79 (1983 & Cum. Supp. 1984) (misuse is using it for a purpose neither intended nor foreseeable by the defendant); L. Frumer & M. Friedman, Prod-

ucts Liability § 15.01 (1984) (misuse is the abnormal or unintended use of the product if such use was not reasonably foreseeable); P. Sherman, Products Liability for the General Practitioner § 9.06 (1981) (misuse is an unintended and unforeseeable use of a product, by a user, consumer, or third party, that is not in accord with the purpose for which the product was intended).

6. [Citing Moran v. Fabergé, infra.]

jury returned a verdict for plaintiff, but the trial court entered a j.n.o.v. for the defendant. The Court of Special Appeals affirmed, Moran v. Williams, 313 A.2d 527 (Md. App. Ct.1974), and plaintiff appealed.]

. . . [O]n the fateful night of June 8, 1969, Nancy Moran, then 17 years old, visited the home of Mr. and Mrs. Louis P. Grigsby in Hillcrest Heights, Maryland, to meet with a number of friends, including Randy Williams, a young lady of 15 years, who was residing with the Grigsbys at the time. The group congregated in the basement which was being maintained partly as a family clubroom and partly as a laundry room. After listening to music for some time on that warm summer night (estimated to be 72–73° F.), everyone left the basement, except Nancy and Randy. Apparently these two girls were at a loss for entertainment as eventually they centered their attention on a lit Christmas-tree-shaped candle which was positioned on a shelf behind the couch in the clubroom. Possibly because "the idle mind knows not what it is it wants"[3] the girls began to discuss whether the candle was scented. After agreeing that it was not, Randy, while remarking "Well, let's make it scented," impulsively grabbed a "drip bottle" of Fabergé's Tigress cologne, which had been placed by Mrs. Grigsby in the basement for use as a laundry deodorant, and began to pour its contents onto the lower portion of the candle somewhat below the flame. Instantaneously, a burst of fire sprang out and burned Nancy's neck and breasts as she stood nearby watching but not fully aware of what her friend was doing.

[At trial, plaintiff sought] to show that, though no warning of the fact was attached to the bottle or otherwise given, Fabergé's Tigress cologne was highly flammable and, therefore, inherently dangerous.[4] [Plaintiff proved] that this cologne, composed of, by volume, 82.06% alcohol, 5.1% perfume and oils, and 12.84% water, is a dangerously combustible product with a flash point of 73° Fahrenheit, approximately room temperature.[5]

Additionally, the plaintiff evoked testimony from two Fabergé officials, Carl Mann, its Vice President and Chief Perfumer, and Stephen Shernov, a company aerosol chemist, which indicated that not only was the manufac-

---

3. Cicero, De Divinatione, bk. II, ch. 13, quoting the poet Quintus Ennius.

4. Such a warning, however, is placed on Fabergé's Tigress aerosol spray cologne. According to the respondent, the spray container has a warning while the "drip bottle" does not because the spray has a freon propellant and thus is chemically different.

5. Utilizing the American Standard Testing Materials' scientific method of determining the flash point, the tester proceeds as follows: the liquid to be tested is poured into a glass cup surrounded by a water bath; a thermometer is kept in the fluid to check its temperature as the water bath is slowly heated; and, starting at 40° Fahrenheit but increasing the temperature by increments of 2 degrees at a time, the tester passes a wand with an eighth of an inch gas-fed bead flame over the liquid in the cup at a height of one-quarter inch above the surface of the liquid being tested. The temperature of the liquid at which its vapors are ignited constitutes its flash point. In this case the test was run six times by an expert in order to obtain an average flash point.

turer aware of this hazardous quality but also Fabergé foresaw that its product might well be dangerous when placed near flame.

Having produced evidence as to this inherently dangerous characteristic of Tigress cologne, which was known to the company though not to the public generally, as well as the fact that the manufacturer knew it might come in contact with fire and be hazardous in that circumstance, the plaintiff contends that a jury question was presented as to whether Fabergé was negligent for failing to warn against its product's latent flammability characteristic. . . .

[A manufacturer has a duty to warn of all hidden dangers from intended uses and also those which are not intended but which are reasonably foreseeable. If reasonable minds can disagree on foreseeability, it is for the trier of fact, but the courts] have not had an easy time agreeing as to which uses by consumers [might be found foreseeable and those which, as a matter of law, may not]. For example, some courts have ruled that a jury may hold a manufacturer to a duty to warn because it is foreseeable that a baby might consume furniture polish, Spruill v. Boyle–Midway, Inc., 308 F.2d 79 (4th Cir. 1962); that a body rub gives off a vapor which could be ignited under a user's clothing as he attempted to light a cigarette [citation]; that a boy of fifteen might dive into a vinyl lined swimming pool thirty inches deep [citation]; that paint might in some way be splashed into the eye of a painter's helper [citation]; or that use of an automobile includes involvement in collisions [citations]. On the other hand, [other courts have ruled various uses unforeseeable as a matter of law so that no warning of resulting hazards need be provided, such as] that a housewife would splash cleaning fluid into her eye [citation]; that the magnesium alloy legs of its product, a bathinette, when made hot by a fire in a residence would begin to blaze intensely, sending flames across a hallway and thereby greatly increasing the danger to the property and persons present [citation]; that an automobile would participate in collisions [citations]; or that a window casement with steel crossbars might be used either as a handrest or as a ladder by iron and steel workmen [citation].

* * *

[Quoting from Professor Harper's treatise,]

"the courts are perfectly accurate in declaring that there can be no liability where the harm is unforeseeable, if *'foreseeability' refers to the general type of harm sustained.* It is literally true that there is no liability for damage that falls entirely outside the *general threat of harm* which made the conduct of the actor negligent. *The sequence of events, of course, need not be foreseeable. The manner in which the risk culminates in harm may be unusual, improbable and highly unexpectable, from the point of view of the actor at the time of his conduct. And yet, if the harm suffered falls within the general danger area, there may be liability, provided other requisites of legal causation are present.*" Harper, A Treatise on the Law of Torts, § 7 (1933) (emphasis added).

[O]nce the product is used in this "general field of danger," if the manufacturer's conduct is a significant factor in causing harm to another, the fact that the manufacturer neither foresaw nor should have foreseen the severity of the harm or the exact manner in which it occurred, does not prevent it from being liable.

[The law imposes a duty to warn of hidden dangers that may result] when the manufacturer's product comes near ... the elements which are present normally in the environment where the product can reasonably be expected to be brought or used. [Citations.] Under this analysis the unusual and bizarre details of accidents, which human experience shows are far from unlikely, are only significant as background facts to the individual case; it is not necessary that the manufacturer foresee the exact manner in which accidents occur. Thus, in the context of this case, it was not necessary for a cologne manufacturer to foresee that someone would be hurt when a friend poured its product near the flame of a lit candle; it was only necessary that it be foreseeable to the producer that its product, while in its normal environment, may be brought near a catalyst, likely to be found in that environment, which can untie the chattel's inherent danger. For example while seated at a dressing table, a woman might strike a match to light a cigarette close enough to the top of the open cologne bottle so as to cause an explosion, or that while seated in a similar manner she might turn suddenly and accidentally bump the bottle of cologne with her elbow, splashing some cologne on a burning candle placed on the vanity....

In applying this test here, [the plaintiff was not required to establish the foreseeability of the precise use of the product that resulted in injury— that Tigress cologne would be poured] on the lower portion of a lit candle in an attempt to scent it. [R]ather, it was only necessary that the evidence be sufficient to support the conclusion that Fabergé, knowing or deemed to know that its Tigress cologne was a potentially dangerous flammable product, could reasonably foresee that in the environment of its use, such as the home of the Grigsbys, this cologne might come close enough to a flame to cause an explosion of sufficient intensity to burn property or injure bystanders, such as Nancy.

[Thus], especially considering the economic and social climate of our day, the issue of Fabergé's negligence was for the jury....

[Reversed and remanded for entry of judgment on verdict for plaintiff.]

■ O'DONNELL, JUDGE (dissenting).

[The record revealed that this was the first Tigress accident in 27 years.]

Assuming, *arguendo,* that Fabergé may have a duty to warn of a general risk because of a latent danger of flammability of its cologne— where its vapors might be brought within one-quarter of an inch of an open flame—it does not follow that this duty to warn is owed to everyone, howsoever the product might be used or abused. It may well be true that the manufacturer owes a duty to warn of the general risk of fire to a young lady who, while applying the cologne, accidentally should knock over the container and spill it upon a burning candle, but such are not the facts here. [Nor was the use being made at the time of the injury reasonably foreseeable.]

As the counsel for Fabergé observed succinctly:

"There may be some iconoclast who would like their [sic] candles to smell like rum, but if someone were to pour 150 proof rum [75% alcohol] on a lighted candle to give it a rum scent and the vapors of that rum were to catch fire and injure someone, the manufacturer of the rum would not be liable because this is idiosyncratic and unforeseeable use of the product."

A fortiori, if someone undertakes to use a skin freshener or body cologne to perfume a lighted candle and its vapors, in juxtaposition to the open flame, should ignite, its manufacturer should not be liable because of this palpably unanticipated and unforeseeable misuse of its product.

* * *

It seems to me that the majority has fallen into the pitfall, recognized by Professor Prosser, who, in [analyzing] the illusory concept of "foreseeability" and noting the confusion resulting therefrom, states:

"Some 'margin of leeway' has to be left for the unusual and the unexpected. But this has opened a very wide door; and the courts have taken so much advantage of the leeway that it can scarcely be doubted that a great deal of what the ordinary man would regard as freakish, bizarre, and unpredictable has crept within the bounds of liability by the simple device of permitting the jury to foresee at least its very broad, and vague, general outlines." W. Prosser, Torts, § 43, at 269 (4th ed. 1971).

NOTES

1. Are the principal cases correctly decided? Are they consistent?

2. History. The doctrine of product misuse has been around for many years. "It seems quite clearly established where the purchaser, actually knowing the defective nature of the article, puts it to a use for which it is unfit and unsafe, any injury received therefrom is due to his misuse and not to the act of him who created the defect." Bohlen, The Basis of Affirmative Obligations in the Law of Tort (pt. 3), 53 U. Pa. L. Rev. 337, 343 (1905).

3. Rationale. "If a consumer employs a product in some extraordinary manner, and encounters a known danger in the course of his conduct, the doctrine of product misuse will bar recovery from the manufacturer. The adventurous consumer has voluntarily placed himself in a category distinct from the normal consumer who forgoes the pleasure and convenience of using products in novel but dangerous ways. The rationale of loss distribution does not reach his case because it is unfair to force consumers who forego these additional benefits to subsidize those individuals who voluntarily take the additional risks. [The misuse defense] fall[s] into the general category of assumption of risk." Holford, The Limits of Strict Liability for Product Design and Manufacture, 52 Tex. L. Rev. 81, 89 (1973).

4. Doctrine. The misuse doctrine is built into the concept of merchantability, in UCC § 2–314(2)(c) (fitness for "ordinary" purposes), and into the concept of negligence, in Restatement (Second) of Torts § 388 (negligent warnings—liability for harm from "use of the chattel in the manner for which ... it is supplied"); § 395 (negligent manufacture—liability for harm caused by chattel's "lawful use in a manner and for a purpose for which it is supplied"); and § 398 (negligent design—liability for harm from "probable use," special application of § 395). It also defines the limits of strict liability in tort under § 402A, cmt. *g* (defectiveness not established by harm from "mishandling"); cmt. *h* (product not defective when safe for "normal handling"); cmt. *i* (unreasonable danger not established by harm from "over-consumption"); and cmt. *j* (no duty to warn of generally known risks of excessive use; seller may assume warnings will be read and heeded, and product with adequate warning is neither defective nor unreasonably dangerous). The Third Restatement position is found in note 11, below.

5. Quacking Like a Duck: Classifying the Misuse "Defense." It is the defendant, of course, who will try to establish that the plaintiff misused the product. Does this mean, therefore, that misuse is an affirmative defense, on which the defendant has the burden of pleading and proof? This question was considered by the *Ellsworth* court in a portion of the opinion omitted above. See 495 A.2d at 353–56. The trial court had charged the jury that the burden of proving misuse is on the defendant. *Held*, reversed. Noting that the courts are split, some holding that the foreseeability of a product's use is part of the plaintiff's case, others holding that misuse is an affirmative defense, the *Ellsworth* court chose to follow the approach of the Restatement and the scholars, and the trend in court decisions:

[Q]uestions of misuse of the product are involved in the determination of whether the product was defective, and whether a defect was the proximate cause of the injury. Because defectiveness and causation are elements which must be proved by the plaintiff, we conclude that misuse is not an affirmative defense. Misuse, therefore, is a "defense" only in the sense that proof of misuse negates one or more essential elements of a plaintiff's case, and may thereby defeat recovery.

Compare Uptain v. Huntington Lab, Inc., 723 P.2d 1322, 1325 (Colo. 1986): "[T]he defense of misuse ... is a particularized defense requiring that the plaintiff's use of the product be unforeseeable and unintended as well as the cause of the injuries." Further, "[m]isuse ... is a question of causation. Regardless of the defective condition, if any, of a manufacturer's product, a manufacturer will not be liable if an unforeseeable misuse of the product caused the injuries." Id. The dissent referred to misuse as an "affirmative defense." Id. at 1332.

So, what is misuse? Part of plaintiff's case on defect? On cause in fact? On proximate cause? Part of defendant's case as an affirmative defense? Some of the above? All of the above?

6. Under the *Moran* majority's rationale, are there any uses around the home that could not support a verdict for the plaintiff? What result if plaintiff, after cutting grass with a gasoline powered mower on a hot day, decides to splash cologne on her face while standing over the power mower; some of the cologne strikes the hot engine, ignites, and causes serious burns? What result if plaintiff pours cologne into her backyard incinerator because she hopes it will control the odors?

7. Is it reasonably foreseeable, as a matter of fact, or as a matter of law, that:

A. A person will insist on buying shoes that are too small for his feet? See Rest. (2d) of Torts § 395 comment *j*.

B. A person will insist on buying automobile tires too large for his rims? See McDevitt v. Standard Oil Co. of Tex., 391 F.2d 364 (5th Cir. 1968).

C. A person will insist on sitting in a chair too small for his posterior (300 pounds)? See Horne v. Liberty Furniture Co., 452 So.2d 204 (La. App. 1984).

D. A person will stand on an ordinary chair? See Rest. (2d) Torts § 395, comment *k*.

E. A car will be driven at 115 m.p.h., go out of control, and injure a third party? See Schemel v. General Motors Corp., 384 F.2d 802 (7th Cir.1967).

F. A tire, designed for speeds to 85 m.p.h., equipped on a car designed for speeds to 100 m.p.h., will blow out at 100 m.p.h.? See LeBouef v. Goodyear Tire & Rubber Co., 451 F.Supp. 253 (W.D. La. 1978).

G. The emergency brake on a car will be left on during operation, long enough to vaporize the hydraulic brake fluid, causing a brake failure? Knapp v. Hertz Corp., 375 N.E.2d 1349 (Ill. App. 1978).

H. A person will attempt suicide by closing himself in a car trunk without an inside release latch, change his mind, and be trapped inside for 9 days thereafter? Daniell v. Ford Motor Co., Inc., 581 F.Supp. 728 (D.N.M. 1984).

I. An empty Clorox container will be used to store gasoline, will tip over, and the gasoline will be ignited by a spark from the motor of an electric appliance in another room? See Taylor v. General Elec. Co., 505 A.2d 190 (N.J. Super. Ct.1986).

J. A patient will walk, against doctor's orders, on his broken leg held together with a defective surgical pin designed only to stabilize the fracture, not to support the weight of a man? See Stewart v. Von Solbrig Hosp., Inc., 321 N.E.2d 428 (Ill. App. 1974).

K. A machine will not be maintained? See Wilson v. Crouse–Hinds Co., 556 F.2d 870 (8th Cir.), cert. denied, 434 U.S. 968 (1977).

L. A person will pour hot Wesson Oil from the skillet back into the bottle, and then recap the bottle, causing it to explode? See Chandler v. Hunt Food & Indus., Inc., Prod. Liab. Rep. (CCH) ¶ 5969 (Tenn. 1968).

M. Burning alcohol, sold only for professional dental use, will be drunk by penal farm inmate dental assistants, who then will go blind? See Barnes v. Litton Indus. Prod., Inc., 555 F.2d 1184 (4th Cir. 1977).

N. A doctor will transplant synthetic fibers, normally used for rugs and "astroturf," into a patient's scalp as a treatment for baldness, causing irritation and infection? Berg v. Underwood's Hair Adaption Process, Inc., 751 F.2d 136 (2d Cir. 1984).

O. A grocery shopper who trips will hope that a shopping cart does not scoot away when he grabs for it to save himself from falling? Smith v. Technibilt, Inc., 791 S.W.2d 247 (Tex. App. 1990).

P. The owner of a riding lawnmower will give a ride to a 2–year–old in a wooden "dog box" attached to the mower? Erkson v. Sears, Roebuck & Co., 841 S.W.2d 207 (Mo. App. 1992).

Q. A young man will tilt or rock a soft drink vending machine, to dispense a can without paying for it, causing the machine to fall upon and kill him? Oden v. Pepsi Cola Bottling Co., 621 So.2d 953 (Ala. 1993) (person may not impose liability on another for consequences of act of moral turpitude); Morgan v. Cavalier Acquisition Corp., 432 S.E.2d 915 (N.C. App. 1993) (foreseeable).

R. A teenage boy will hang himself with a rope on a swing set as a joke to impress the girls? Smith v. Holmes, 606 N.E.2d 627 (Ill. App. 1992).

Is the legal "test" adequate to resolve these cases in a principled, predictable manner?

8. Common Practice. If persons regularly use the product in a dangerous, unintended manner, the use was probably foreseeable. See Gootee v. Colt Industries, Inc., 712 F.2d 1057, 1065 (6th Cir. 1983)(use of revolver half-cock as safety virtually universal practice); Lamer v. McKee Indus., Inc., 721 P.2d 611, 615 (Alaska 1986) ("a manufacturer should not be relieved of responsibility simply because it closes its eyes to the way its products are actually used by consumers").

9. Children. Both manufacturers and courts have had an especially difficult time with the misuse of products by children. If the children are so young that they fail to appreciate danger, they can be expected to eat, poke, climb into, throw, and otherwise abuse about anything in the household, and the courts have held that many such risks are foreseeable. Spruill v. Boyle–Midway, Inc., 308 F.2d 79 (4th Cir. 1962), is the classic case. Plaintiff's infant decedent died from drinking some of defendant's cherry-red furniture polish left open momentarily on the bureau beside his crib. Plaintiff argued that the "harmful if swallowed, especially by children" warning on the label was inadequate. Defendant argued that the product was not intended to be consumed. Remarking that, " 'Intended use' is but a convenient adaptation of the basic test of 'reasonable foreseeability,' " the court observed that in addition to the literally intended uses of a product a seller "must also be expected to anticipate the environment which is normal for the use of his product and where, as here, that environment is the home, he must anticipate the reasonably foreseeable risks of the use of his product in such an environment. These are risks which are inherent in the proper use for which his product is manufactured. Thus where such a product is an inherently dangerous one, and its danger is not obvious to the average housewife," the manufacturer must warn of the reasonably foreseeable hazards, "though such risks may be incidental to the actual use for which the product was intended." Affirming a judgment for the plaintiff, the court concluded that the manufacturer could fairly have been held to foresee that such a product might be found and drunk by unattended children.

Compare Victory Sparkler & Specialty Co. v. Latimer, 53 F.2d 3 (8th Cir. 1931) (small child ate "spit devil" firework that was wrapped in plain red wrapper and looked like candy); Sherk v. Daisy–Heddon, 450 A.2d 615 (Pa. 1982) (thinking safety was on, 14–year–old pointed BB gun at friend's head and pulled trigger, killing friend); Ritter v. Narragansett Elec. Co., 283 A.2d 255 (R.I. 1971)(4–year–old opened and stood on oven door to see what was cooking on stove, causing range and pot of boiling water to topple over); Larue v. National Union Elec. Corp., 571 F.2d 51 (1st Cir. 1978) (11–year–old boy, riding canister vacuum cleaner like toy car, injured when his penis slipped through opening of filter support into fan whirling at 15,000 rpm); Simpson v. Standard Container Co., 527 A.2d 1337 (Md. Ct. Spec. App. 1987) (children played with gas can designed without child-proof top—no duty); Keller v. Welles Dept. Store of Racine, 276 N.W.2d 319, 324 (Wis. Ct. App.1979) (same—contra):

> Children are incurably curious about their environment. A gasoline can . . . is commonly stored either on the floor or on a low shelf. These are areas readily accessible to children in their "explorations." It is not unforeseeable that a child might attempt to taste the liquid in the can [or,] in the course of playing "mow the lawn" or "gas station," a child might pour the gasoline from the can.

Numerous cases make claims against manufacturers and other sellers of disposable butane cigarette lighters for injuries from fires started by young children. See, e.g., Phillips v. Cricket Lighters, 841 A.2d 1000 (Pa. 2003); Robins v. Kroger Co., 80 S.W.3d 641 (Tex. App. 2002); Colon ex rel. Molina v. BIC USA, Inc., 199 F. Supp. 2d 53 (S.D.N.Y. 2001); Jennings v. BIC Corp., 181 F.3d 1250 (11th Cir. 1999).

What is a manufacturer to do? What is a court to do?

10.   Failure to Follow Directions. What if the user fails to read or heed the warnings or instructions?

> "I had a very bad headache. Bad pain of various kinds. The childproof bottle top gave me some trouble, but by the time a little wave of rage had swept over me, I had defeated it. I tilted some tablets into my left palm, carefully counted off three with my right forefinger, and pushed them into my mouth. I always take three, because the directions say to take one or two." H.F. Saint, Invisible Man 58 (Atheneum 1987).

Many courts follow the approach of Restatement (Second) Torts § 402A comment *j*, discussed above:

> Where warning is given, the seller may reasonably assume that it will be read and heeded; and a product bearing such a warning, which is safe for use if it is followed, is not in a defective condition, nor is it unreasonably dangerous.

See, e.g., Lightolier v. Hoon, 876 A.2d 100 (Md. 2005) (contractor blew cellulose insulation into ceiling in direct contact with light fixtures that warned to keep them at least 3″ away from insulation to prevent heat buildup); Uptain v. Huntington Lab, Inc., 723 P.2d 1322, 1326 (Colo. 1986) (housekeeper used bare hands to wring out mop used to apply bathroom cleaning solution containing 23% hydrochloric acid; label warned against skin contact to avoid chemical burns and to wash skin area well if contact occurred); Watson v. Uniden Corp. of America, 775 F.2d 1514 (11th Cir. 1985) (warranty—failure to follow instructions is not use in "normal" manner; but jury issue on negligence and strict liability warnings adequacy claims); Hughes v. Massey–Ferguson, Inc., 490 N.W.2d 75 (Iowa Ct. App. 1992) (farmer walked on 3″ rim over auger without first shutting off corn head as warnings instructed); Bell v. Montgomery Ward, 792 F.Supp. 500 (W.D. La. 1992) (mower, who lost two toes in lawn mower when he slipped on wet grass, ignored warnings to keep guards in place and feet away from blade, and not to wear tennis shoes or to mow on wet grass or on slopes steeper than 15 degrees).

As mentioned earlier, the problem with interpreting this single sentence of comment *j*, out of context, is that the comment's observations were limited to toxic substances for which there is no design alternative and, hence, where the only way a manufacturer can reduce the risk is to warn of hidden hazards. See Owen, The Puzzle of Comment *J*, 55 Hastings L.J. 1377 (2004).

But what if the warning or instruction disregarded is itself inadequate? "[I]f the injury resulting from foreseeable misuse of a product is one which an adequate warning concerning the use of the product would likely prevent, such misuse is no defense." Bristol–Myers Co. v. Gonzales, 548 S.W.2d 416, 422–23 (Tex. Civ. App. 1976), rev'd on other grounds 561 S.W.2d 801 (1978). See also Harless v. Boyle–Midway Div., American Home Prod., 594 F.2d 1051, 1055 (5th Cir. 1979) ("It seems both confusing and internally inconsistent to ask a jury who has previously concluded that the label was inadequate to consider the defense of failure to read an adequate label."); Johnson v. Johnson Chem. Co., 588 N.Y.S.2d 607 (App. Div. 1992) (failure to read roach bomb instruction to extinguish pilot lights or open flames); Huynh v. Ingersoll–Rand, 20 Cal.Rptr.2d 296 (Ct. App. 1993).

Should it matter whether the inadequacy is one of "substance," or instead is "procedural" in the sense of failing to catch the user's attention? Should it make a difference whether plaintiff read the message and failed to heed it, or simply failed to read it in the first place? See Uptain v. Huntington Lab, Inc., 723 P.2d 1322, 1333 (Colo. 1986) (dissenting opinion).

Notwithstanding vigorous warnings against a particular product use, courts sometimes allow juries to decide whether a user's contrary use was foreseeable. See, e.g., Sanders v. Lull Int'l, Inc., 411 F.3d 1266 (11th Cir. 2005).

11. Products Liability Restatement. The black letter of §§ 2(b) and 2(c) of the Third Restatement limits responsibility to "the foreseeable risks of harm posed by the product." Arguably, for *risks* to be "foreseeable," they must result from foreseeable *use*, as the Reporters suggest in comment *m*:

> *m. Reasonably foreseeable uses and risks in design and warning claims.* Subsections (b) and (c) impose liability only when the product is put to uses that it is reasonable to expect a seller or distributor to foresee. Product sellers and distributors are not required to foresee and take precautions against every conceivable mode of use and abuse to which their products might be put. Increasing the costs of designing and marketing products in order to avoid the consequences of unreasonable modes of use is not required.

Misuse is not "a discrete legal issue," and how it may affect the issues of defect, causation, and comparative responsibility depends on the particulars of the conduct, the type of defect, and other circumstances. See Products Liability Restatement § 2 cmt. *p*.

12. Trial Tactics. What if defense counsel in *Moran* was convinced that the perfume was not particularly flammable and, hence, doubted the veracity of the girls' story as to how the accident occurred? In Howard v. Faberge, Inc., 679 S.W.2d 644 (Tex. App. 1984), the plaintiff claimed that, after dousing his upper body with Brut 33 Splash–On Lotion, he accidentally dropped a match into his waistband, igniting the Brut and burning his body. Plaintiff sued for failure to warn of the lotion's flammability. In closing argument, defense counsel emphasized the weaknesses in the plaintiff's evidence on the lotion's supposed flammability. Suddenly, he produced a bottle purporting to be Brut, poured it over his arm, waved a lit match over his arm, and called on God to burn him if he were wrong. The jury returned a verdict for the defendant. On appeal, *held,* counsel's improper experiment was incurably prejudicial, requiring reversal and a new trial.

13. Reform. At least Arizona, Idaho, Indiana, Michigan, Missouri, Montana, and Tennessee by statute bar or reduce recovery of a person injured due to misuse. Arizona's statute includes conduct in violation of adequate warnings or instructions; Idaho defines misuse in terms of the conduct of an ordinary reasonably prudent person; and Montana treats "unreasonable misuse" as an affirmative defense.

14. On product misuse, see D. Owen, Products Liability Law § 13.5 (2d ed. 2008); 1 D. Owen, M.S. Madden, & M. Davis, Madden & Owen on Products Liability § 14:4 (3d ed. 2000).

CHAPTER 11

LIMITING DEFECTIVENESS: PASSAGE OF TIME

1. DETERIORATION

There is no duty upon a manufacturer to furnish a machine that will not wear out.

Auld v. Sears, Roebuck & Co., 25 N.Y.S.2d 491, 493 (App. Div. 1941), aff'd, 41 N.E.2d 927 (N.Y.1942).

Savage v. Jacobsen Manufacturing Co.

District Court of Appeal of Florida, 1981.
396 So.2d 731.

[Plaintiff, an operator of lawn-mowing tractors at a golf club, slipped and fell from the platform beneath the driver's seat as she was dismounting a tractor manufactured by the defendant and sold to the club a little over three years before. At the time of initial purchase, the platform was covered with a gritty, nonskid paint, but the surface had worn off over time. Several weeks before her accident, the plaintiff's husband, a mechanic who serviced the tractor, had noticed that the platform was slippery from morning dew and hydraulic fluid which had leaked from a reservoir behind the seat, as often happened on such tractors. He asked their supervisor to purchase some nonskid paint to recoat several pieces of equipment, including the tractor in question, but the supervisor had not done so. Plaintiff's strict liability in tort suit against the manufacturer, alleging that her injury was due to the absence of a nonskid surface on the tractor's platform, was dismissed on the defendant's motion for summary judgment. Plaintiff appealed.]

The issue before us here is whether [there is a genuine issue of material fact] as to whether the absence of a nonskid surface on the tractor at the time of appellant's injury constituted a defect. We hold that the trial court properly concluded that there was no showing of a defect. The record before us discloses no evidence that the nonskid painted surface in any way constituted a deviation from the norm, failed to meet the standard of the industry, or constituted a latent, functional defect. In fact, the evidence showed that the purchaser of the tractor was aware at the time of the purchase of the fact that the painted surface would eventually wear off and was aware prior to appellant's accident that the nonskid surface had, in fact, worn off. Thus the platform did not constitute an "unexpected danger" as to such purchaser. In short, there was no showing of a "defect" which would give rise to the application of § 402A. The nonskid surface merely wore off.

[Florida has no law on point, but Louisiana has addressed the issue of whether a manufacturer has a duty to produce a product that will not wear out.] In Foster v. Marshall, 341 So. 2d 1354, 1361 (La. App. 1977), a bolting assembly on the left front axle of a trailer separated, causing the trailer to veer into an oncoming lane of travel and collide with the plaintiff's automobile. The evidence showed that the bolting assembly on the trailer failed primarily because a cotter pin had worn out over time. In affirming the portion of the trial court's decision in favor of the manufacturer, the court of appeal held that the wearing out of a cotter pin did not constitute a "defect," stating:

> A manufacturer cannot be expected to design products with component parts which will never wear out, regardless of the nature of use or maintenance. A manufacturer is entitled to anticipate that a consumer purchasing its product will use reasonable care in maintaining it. The product in this case was a relatively simple piece of agricultural equipment for use by farmers or harvesters who generally have some degree of experience in the maintenance of agricultural equipment. All persons who dealt with this particular wagon testified they knew that cotter keys will wear out and need to be replaced periodically. * * *

> A product is defective when the risks are greater than a reasonable buyer would expect. Welch v. Outboard Marine Corp., 481 F.2d 252 (5th Cir. 1973). A reasonable buyer of a piece of agricultural equipment such as a cotton wagon should expect the product to contain consumable parts which require inspection and maintenance.

We are in accord with the reasoning set out in *Foster*. For us to hold otherwise would be tantamount to saying that a manufacturer is an insurer of his product.

[Summary judgment affirmed.]

NOTES

1. Assume that a weld attaching the platform to the tractor frame had failed, causing the platform to shift and the plaintiff to fall. Same result? What if the failure occurred 10 years after manufacture? 30 years?

2. Compare Blair v. Martin's, 433 N.Y.S.2d 221, 222 (App. Div. 1980). Plaintiff purchased a pair of plastic boots from the defendant for under $10, wore them for months, had new "lifts" installed by her shoemaker, and wore them for several more months. She fell one day, as she was descending the subway steps, and found that the heel had come off one of the boots. *Held,* judgment for defendant, after jury trial, affirmed:

[W]e believe plaintiffs failed to establish, beyond the barest conclusory allegation, that the accident was caused by a defect present in the boots at the time plaintiff purchased them and not by a defect caused as a result of alteration by her shoemaker (who was unavailable to testify at the trial) or by the boots' simply having worn out.

Accord, that manufacturers generally are not liable for accidents from products that wear out from old age, Walker v. General Elec. Co., 968 F.2d 116 (1st Cir. 1992) (solenoid heating element in toaster oven used daily for 6 years); Oquendo v. Teledyne Pines, 602 N.E.2d 56, 58 (Ill. App. 1992) (plaintiff admitted in deposition that hydraulic fluid hose on 33–year–old pipe bending machine ruptured due to "cuts and the wear and tear of old age"). See also Bourgeois v. Garrard Chevrolet, Inc., 811 So.2d 962 (La. App. 2002) (brake pads; wear and tear alone does not establish that product was defective); Hall v. Johnson & Johnson, 2006 WL 1096940, at *3 (D.N.J.2006) (artificial knee, which plaintiff's doctor told him should last 15—20 years, wore out after 5 years; claim dismissed without expert testimony "that the implant should have lasted longer than five years or that its deterioration was due to a defect rather than natural wear").

3. In Mickle v. Blackmon, 166 S.E.2d 173, 188–90 (S.C. 1969), plaintiff was riding in the front passenger seat of a 1949 Ford automobile hit by another car in 1962. The force of the collision threw her against the gearshift lever mounted on the steering wheel, shattering the protective knob and causing the plaintiff's body to become impaled on the spear-like lever. Ford knew that the white plastic material it used for the knob weakened from exposure to ultraviolet rays, but it did not switch to the black material (resistant to such rays) until 1950. In plaintiff's suit against Ford for negligent design, the jury returned a verdict for the plaintiff. The trial court granted Ford's motion for j.n.o.v., and plaintiff appealed. *Held,* reversed (Brailsford, J.):

> It is implicit in the verdict that the gearshift lever presented an unreasonable risk of injury if not adequately guarded. At the time of plaintiff's injury the knob on the Hill car continued to serve its functional purpose as a handhold, but it had become useless as a protective guard. It is inferable that the condition of the knob did not arise from ordinary wear and tear, but from an inherent weakness in the material of which Ford was aware when the selection was made. In the light of the insidious effect on this material of exposure to sunlight in the normal use of an automobile, it could reasonably be concluded that Ford should have foreseen that many thousands of the one million vehicles produced by it in 1949 would, in the course of time, be operated millions of miles with gearshift lever balls which, while yet serving adequately as handholds, would furnish no protection to an occupant who might be thrown against the gearshift lever. The jury could reasonably conclude that Ford's conduct, in manufacturing a needed safety device of a material which could not tolerate a frequently encountered aspect of the environment in which it would be employed, exposed many users of its product to unreasonably great risk of harm.
> * * *

[Plaintiff has] the burden of establishing that the defect complained of existed at the time the product was sold by the defendant. "There is no duty on a manufacturer to furnish a machine that will not wear out." [We agree with Dean Prosser]:

"If the chattel is in good condition when it is sold, the seller is not responsible when it undergoes subsequent changes, or wears out. The mere lapse of time since the sale by the defendant, during which there has been continued safe use of the product, is always relevant, as indicating that the seller was not responsible for the defect. There have been occasional cases in which, upon the particular facts, it has been held to be conclusive. It is, however, quite certain that *neither long continued lapse of time nor changes in ownership will be sufficient in themselves to defeat recovery when there is clear evidence of an original defect in the thing sold.*" (Emphasis added.) Prosser on Torts, 667 (3d ed. 1964).

Here, . . . there was evidence of an original weakness in the gearshift assembly which caused the collapse of the protective knob. The deterioration of the product and its consequent failure was the very risk created by the negligent choice of material, or the jury could so find. The rule relied upon, that a manufacturer is not liable for the failure of a product due to deterioration from ordinary wear and tear or misuse, simply does not fit these facts.

We readily concede that the passage of thirteen years between the marketing of a product and its injury-producing failure is a formidable obstacle to fastening liability upon the manufacturer. However, it may reasonably be inferred in this case that the advanced age of the ball was coincidental with its failure rather than the cause of it, and that the knob would have shattered upon a comparable impact had it occurred much earlier in the life of the car. The important inquiry is not how long the knob lasted but what caused its failure. Mere passage of time should not excuse Ford if its negligence was the cause. Since this conclusion finds support in the evidence, the issue was for the jury.

4. Warning of Failure Hazard. If deterioration is likely to cause a product eventually to fail in a dangerous manner, without warning to the user, the manufacturer will have a duty to give warning of its useful safe life. Strauch v. Gates Rubber Co., 879 F.2d 1282 (5th Cir. 1989).

5. Causation Question for Jury. The life expectancy issue is often treated by the courts as a factual question for the jury of cause in fact or proximate cause, rather than as a question of duty for the court. Cf. Gorath v. Rockwell Int'l, 441 N.W.2d 128, 133 (Minn. App. 1989)(connection between injury and manufacture of 34–year–old used paper cutter "too remote . . . as a matter of public policy"). Consider Balido v. Improved Mach., Inc., 105 Cal.Rptr. 890, 896–97 (Ct. App. 1972), involving an injury due to the failure of a non-moving part in a press about 14 years old:

Passage of time . . . bears only on the third essential of plaintiff's proof—the causal connection between injury and design. The problem arises as a by-product of the inevitability of change, for change brought about by time unravels the connection between prior cause and later effect. Did the product fail because it was badly designed or because it was badly manufactured? Because badly manufactured or badly maintained? Badly maintained or abused in use? Abused in use or because it wore out? Here, we find ourselves deep in the labyrinth of causation, where passage of time almost inevitably brings its concomitant of multiple cause and multiple effect. In working our way out of this labyrinth legal rules, inferences, presumptions furnish little help, for the basic problem is one of reliability of proof.

[When] the problem of time, change, and causation [have] proved particularly troublesome the legislature has provided the courts with arbitrary mechanical solutions, often in the form of statutes of limitation. These statutes ... terminate ... liability by [effectively] decreeing that after the passage of a specified time the causal connection between defect and injury will no longer be legally recognized. But [the knotty problems of causation in products liability cases have required courts] to work out their own [special] solutions.

[Courts normally declare] that the effect of lapse of time on causation is a question for determination by the trier of fact within the limitations of legal cause. Concededly, so loose a rule may not be wholly satisfactory to lawyers advising clients, but for courts and judges it suggests that in most cases the issue of causation should be submitted to the trier of fact, at least whenever a theory of causation can be plausibly sustained.

6. The passage of time gives rise to an enormous web of interrelated issues including foreseeability, defectiveness, changes in the state of the art, consumer abuse, cause in fact, proximate cause (including third party abuse), proof (admissibility of recall campaign letters; evidence of subsequent improvements in warnings or design), statutes of limitations, and statutes of repose.

7. On product deterioration, see generally D. Owen, Products Liability Law § 10.6 (2d ed. 2008); 1 D. Owen, M.S. Madden, & M. Davis, Madden & Owen on Products Liability § 10:9 (3d ed.2000).

---

2.   DISPOSAL AND DESTRUCTION

High v. Westinghouse Electric Corp.

Supreme Court of Florida, 1992.
610 So.2d 1259.

■ OVERTON, JUDGE.

* * * Westinghouse manufactured electrical transformers and sold them to Florida Power and Light Company (FPL). From 1967 to 1983, [when the transformers wore out, FPL sold them] for junk to Pepper's Steel and Alloys (Pepper's), a scrap metal salvage business. To manufacture the electrical transformers sold to FPL, Westinghouse purchased products from Monsanto, a manufacturer of polychlorinated biphenyls (PCBs). In a January 15, 1972, letter and indemnification agreement from Westinghouse to Monsanto, Westinghouse acknowledged that Monsanto had notified Westinghouse that the PCBs used in its products tended to persist in the environment; that care was required in their handling, possession, use, and disposition; and that tolerance limits had been or were being established for PCBs in various food products. In 1976, Westinghouse wrote a letter to its utility company customers, including FPL, disclosing the potential existence of PCBs in their transformers. In that letter, Westinghouse informed them that some oil-filled transformers had been contaminated with PCBs

in the manufacturing process. Westinghouse's letter suggested that when performing repairs, routine maintenance, or disposal, all oil-filled transformers should be checked for the presence of PCBs.

Studies of humans exposed to PCBs have shown numerous adverse effects, including but not limited to chloracne and other epidermal disorders, digestive disturbances, jaundice, impotence, throat and respiratory irritations, and severe headaches. It is undisputed that none of the junk transformers that FPL sold to Pepper's contained any labels, markings, or warnings of any kind that the transformers contained PCBs or that the contents might be hazardous to human health.

Willie J. High was the main truck driver for Pepper's from 1965 to 1983. As part of his duties, he picked up aluminum wire, cable, and other scrap metal. He also picked up transformers from FPL in Miami and other cities around Florida. As part of his job, High loaded and unloaded the transformers onto Pepper's truck with a forklift. Specifically, he hooked and unhooked the forklift cables. During this process, he came into contact with the PCB-contaminated transformer oil.

[From media coverage of environmental agency cleanup proceedings against Pepper's, High learned] that he had been exposed to PCBs while employed at Pepper's and that some of his physical and mental problems might be attributed to this exposure. [In] 1983, High brought this action under strict liability and negligence theories.

The trial court granted Westinghouse's motion for summary judgment, holding as a matter of law that the ultimate disposal of the transformer was not foreseeable to the manufacturer as a reasonably intended "use." On appeal, the district court of appeal, in a split decision, affirmed. . . .

There are two questions we must address. The first is whether strict liability applies under section 402A of the Restatement (Second) of Torts for injuries that occur in dismantling an item. The second is whether the manufacturer, Westinghouse, in this instance was negligent in failing to timely warn of dangerous contents in its product that could cause injuries in its alteration and dismantling.

* * *

While these are questions of first impression in this state, other courts have addressed similar issues. . . . Kalik v. Allis–Chalmers Corp., 658 F. Supp. 631 (W.D. Pa. 1987), [was an action to recover cleanup costs and damages under CERCLA.] In that case, the scrap metal business had purchased junk electrical components as scrap. The electrical components contained, as they did in this instance, PCBs. During the course of dismantling, handling, and storing the junk electrical components, PCB-contaminated oil leaked or spilled onto the site. A furnace used in dismantling and processing the components caused PCBs in the components to allegedly produce dioxins, which also polluted the site. Plaintiff's damage claims were based upon a negligent failure to warn and strict liability in tort. The United States District Court in Pennsylvania . . . held as a matter of law that the recycling of a product after it had been destroyed and the destruction of a product were not reasonably foreseeable uses to the manufacturer.

In Wingett v. Teledyne Industries, Inc., 479 N.E.2d 51 (Ind. 1985), [a worker] hired to remove ductwork in a foundry was injured when a connection between two segments of ductwork failed and a portion [fell on him as he] cut the support hangers. The [worker sued the ductwork manufacturer, claiming] that the connection between the segments of ductwork that failed, consisting of a sheet metal band, screws, and clamps instead of an iron collar and bolts found on the other segments, [was defective and] caused his injury. The Indiana Supreme Court affirmed the summary judgement in favor of the manufacturer, holding as a matter of law that the dismantling and demolishing of the ductwork was not a reasonably foreseeable "use" of the product.

Finally, in Johnson v. Murph Metals, Inc., 562 F. Supp. 246, 249 (N.D. Tex. 1983), a United States District Court in Texas granted a summary judgment and held that fumes and particulates from smelting lead from scrap batteries were not created from a "use" of the batteries. In that case, the employees of various lead-smelting companies who had sued certain automotive battery manufacturers stipulated that their injuries did not result from working with intact batteries or from the destruction of batteries to obtain the lead for smelting. The lead fumes and dust that allegedly injured them were created only after the lead was extracted from the destroyed batteries and used in the smelting process. In determining that the plaintiffs were not "users" of defendants' products, the court held that "the defendants' product had ceased to exist."

With regard to the first question and the applicability of strict liability under section 402A of the Restatement (Second) of Torts, we find that strict liability is not applicable.... In order for strict liability to apply to the manufacturer, the transformers in this instance must have been used for the purpose intended. In the instant case, High's injury resulted from dismantling the transformers and coming into contact with the PCBs as a result of this process. We agree with the district court that section 402A does not apply because of the substantial alteration of the product when High came into contact with the contaminated oil. Secondly, section 402A applies to intended uses of products for which they were produced. When an injury occurs under those circumstances, the manufacturer is strictly liable. We find, under the circumstances in the instant case, that dismantling a product is not an intended use as prescribed by section 402A. Therefore, we find, under these facts, that strict liability does not apply.

The second question ... concerns liability based on negligence. We find that a manufacturer has a duty to warn of dangerous contents in its product which could damage or injure even when the product is not used for its intended purpose. This issue ... is whether Westinghouse was negligent in warning FPL of the possible danger of PCB contamination.

... If Westinghouse knew or should have known from its early 1970s communications with Monsanto that some mineral oil transformers contained PCBs, then it is clear from the record that Westinghouse delayed in warning FPL of the contamination of these transformers. Although we hold that Westinghouse's letter to FPL was adequate notice, we find that Westinghouse had a duty to timely notify FPL so that FPL could timely notify Pepper's of the possible danger that could occur in dismantling the transformers so that it could proceed in the prescribed manner. If this notice was not timely, then the next question is whether the lack of timely notice by Westinghouse was the proximate cause of High's injury. Given the circumstances, we find the knowledge by Westinghouse of the PCB contamination in its transformers and the timeliness of Westinghouse's notice to FPL of that contamination are issues of fact that must be resolved in this case and are not proper for summary judgment.

[Remanded.]

■ BARKETT, J., concurring in part and dissenting in part.

* * *

The majority is correct in stating that section 402A ... "applies to *intended uses* of products for which they were produced." The majority's deficiency, however, is in failing to define "intended uses." The prevailing view recognizes that an "intended use" includes unintended uses of a product if they were reasonably foreseeable by the defendant. [See] M. Stuart Madden, Products Liability § 13.9, at 20 (1988)....

[F]oreseeability is usually a jury question. Neither the majority opinion nor the cases cited therein explain why that determination should be removed from the jury in this instance or why, as a matter of law, the manufacturer would not have reasonably foreseen that its product would be dismantled.

■ KOGAN, J., concurring in part, dissenting in part.

The central premise underlying the law of strict liability is that a for-profit enterprise is better able to shoulder, and therefore must assume strict liability for, the dangerous products it creates:

> The courts [in traditional strict liability contexts, such as workers' compensation and liability for ultra-hazardous activities,] have tended to lay stress upon the fact that the defendant is acting for his own purposes, and is seeking a benefit or a profit from such activities, and that he is in a better position to administer the unusual risk by passing it on to the public than is the innocent victim.

W. Page Keeton, Dan B. Dobbs, Robert E. Keeton, & David G. Owen, Prosser and Keeton on the Law of Torts § 75, at 537 (5th ed. 1984). In other words, the "little man" should not be made to suffer when the for-profit enterprise that released a dangerous product into commerce can absorb the loss.

I see no reason why this principle should not be applied here. The facts disclose that Westinghouse released into commerce a product containing the highly dangerous chemicals called PCBs. While these chemicals were sealed inside transformers, surely Westinghouse cannot now contend that it was "unforeseeable" these transformers would some day be breached and would release their PCBs. It is obvious and foreseeable that whatever is sealed inside a container some day is likely to be released again. If people are injured by that release, then strict liability should exist.

This case is only little different from a toy manufacturer constructing a rubber ball inflated with a poisonous liquid. Obviously, the toy manufacturer does not intend for the liquid to be released; but if a child chews through the rubber coating and is poisoned by the liquid inside, I certainly believe any court in this state would hold the manufacturer strictly liable. We would not resolve such a case, as the majority does here, simply by noting that the manufacturer did not intend its product to be dismantled in this particular manner.

While I agree with the majority on the duty-to-warn issue, I believe the present case also presents a valid claim for strict liability. Here, transformers were created by a for-profit enterprise. Inside these transformers was a dangerous liquid. This plaintiff has alleged that he was injured when that liquid was released again into the environment. In such an instance, any injury that has resulted should be borne by the party best able to absorb the loss—the manufacturer. Accordingly, I would allow the case to proceed on an alternative theory of strict liability.

NOTES

1. Within the context of the growing waste disposal problem, *High* illustrates the confluence of products liability and environmental law. Long after products have outlived their useful lives, "junked" products continue to pose hazards to the community.

2. Strict Liability. How well reasoned and persuasive are the separate opinions in *High*? Note that Judge Kogan transported the Prosser & Keeton quotation from traditional contexts of strict liability for workers' compensation and ultra-hazardous activities to the modern context of liability for the sale of defective products. Except in rare instances, courts have maintained the separate integrity of these independent branches of the law of torts. See, e.g., Richmond, Fredericksburg & Potomac R.R. Co. v. Davis Indus., 787 F.Supp. 572, 575 (E.D. Va. 1992) ("'ultrahazardousness or abnormal dangerousness is ... a property not of substances, but of activities'"; otherwise, the manufacturer would be converted into an insurer). Was Judge Kogan's blending of rationales here confused, or do these separate fields of compensation law in fact converge in the context of this case?

3. Negligence. As in *High*, some courts are more willing to allow negligence claims to go to the jury. See Reed v. Westinghouse Elec. Corp., 1995 WL 96819 (Ky. App. 1995) (allowing negligence claims by 37 salvage workers to go to jury on facts like *High*). Compare Jones v. United Metal Recyclers, 825 F.Supp. 1288 (W.D. Mich. 1993) (jury could determine if manufacturer/seller was negligent in selling scrap aluminum without drying it or warning that it might explode if placed in furnace in wet condition). Note, however, that the appellate court's opinion in *Reed* was reversed by the Kentucky Supreme Court which held that disposal of the electrical transformers in issue was an unforeseeable, substantial alteration of the product. Monsanto Co. v. Reed, 950 S.W.2d 811 (Ky. 1997).

4. CERCLA. Outside of tort law, the primary control for improper disposal of hazardous waste is the Comprehensive Environmental Response, Compensation and

Liability Act of 1980 (CERCLA), 42 U.S.C.A. §§ 9601–75, a regulatory statute designed to clean up the legacy of decades of haphazard hazardous waste disposal and to provide funds to pay for the clean-up costs. One provision of CERCLA permits suits for "necessary costs of response" incurred by a private party against a class of persons that CERCLA deems responsible for cleaning up a waste site. Personal injuries such as Mr. High's are not recoverable under CERCLA. A few courts have suggested that medical monitoring costs for those exposed to hazardous waste are available under CERCLA. Compare Lykins v. Westinghouse Elec. Corp., 27 Env't Rep. Cas. (BNA) 1590 (E.D. Ky. 1988) (medical testing expenses recoverable when incurred in conjunction with a hazardous waste site cleanup), with Coburn v. Sun Chem. Corp., 28 Env't Rep. Cas. (BNA) 1665 (E.D. Pa. 1988) (medical monitoring costs not recoverable under CERCLA).

5. Consider Ashland Oil, Inc. v. Miller Oil Purchasing Co., 678 F.2d 1293 (5th Cir. 1982), holding that a waste disposal contractor was not subject to liability under § 402A, for its disposal of a highly dangerous chemical waste product, because it was not in the business of selling such waste. The contractor tried to incinerate the waste, but it turned into hydrochloric acid which damaged the incinerator. In an attempt to disguise and dispose of the waste, the contractor mixed it with crude oil and had it trucked away. This mixture was eventually sold through wholesale and retail vendors of petroleum products as good crude oil to the plaintiff, whose refinery was damaged when the mixture caught fire and exploded. The two vendors of "crude oil" were both held liable under § 402A.

6. Durables. While the disposal problem is most severe for toxic substances, it exists as well for durable goods. Should General Electric be liable for the suffocation of a child playing in a dump who climbs inside a long-abandoned G.E. refrigerator, manufactured with a latching mechanism in the 1940s, who cannot get out when the door swings shut?

7. Children. See Tucci v. Bossert, 385 N.Y.S.2d 328 (App. Div. 1976), where the purchasers of a can of Drano drain cleaner disposed of it, with some of the contents remaining in the can, in a trash bag placed outside their house. Two children came along, removed the can from the bag, and poured water into the can. The can exploded and injured one of the children. Plaintiffs sued the manufacturer for selling a defectively packaged product with inadequate warnings. The trial court dismissed the complaint. On appeal, *held,* complaint reinstated. See also Hall v. E.I. Du Pont De Nemours & Co., Inc., 345 F.Supp. 353 (E.D.N.Y. 1972) (children injured by lost or abandoned blasting caps; defendants' motion to dismiss denied).

Contrast Venezia v. Miller Brewing Co., 626 F.2d 188, 192 (1st Cir. 1980), examined in connection with misuse, ch. 9(3) above, where a child threw a discarded beer bottle against a telephone pole and suffered injury to his eye. *Held,* dismissal of complaint affirmed: "[T]he impact of endorsing a contrary conclusion would be overwhelming, with every discarded glass object holding the potential for generating a future lawsuit." Right result? Right reasoning? What if plaintiff cuts her foot when she steps on and breaks a discarded beer bottle hidden in the sand at the beach?

8. Policy. On the broader questions raised in this section, consider the remarks of Professor Charles Cantu, who observes that Americans are presently at the end of the "disposable society" era and now must adjust to a new world in which the reclamation and recycling of products is properly addressed by citizens and the law. Cantu, The Recycling, Dismantling, and Destruction of Goods as a Foreseeable Use Under Section 402A of the Restatement (Second) of Torts, 46 Ala. L. Rev. 81 (1994). "If every product has a finite useful life and eventually reaches a point when it should no longer be used, then at the end of that period of time the commodity must necessarily be recycled, dismantled, or demolished." Id. at 100. Challenging arguments that these processes are not "foreseeable" and that the persons injured are not "users" under § 402A, Professor Cantu concludes that manufacturers are best situated to select appropriate materials and provide warnings concerning the risks associated with these terminal stages of a product's life.

9. See generally Cantu, The Recycling, Dismantling, and Destruction of Goods as a Foreseeable Use Under Section 402A of the Restatement (Second) of Torts, 46 Ala. L. Rev. 81 (1994); D. Owen, Products Liability Law § 10.7 (2d ed. 2008); 1 D. Owen, M.S. Madden, & M. Davis, Madden & Owen on Products Liability § 20:6 (3d ed. 2000).

---

3.   STATE OF THE ART

A consumer would not expect a Model T to have the safety features which are incorporated in automobiles made today.

Bruce v. Martin–Marietta Corp., 544 F.2d 442, 447 (10th Cir. 1976).

Some product dangers are discoverable and avoidable under prevailing technology, but only at greater cost than suggested by economic prudence. In production flaw cases of this type, manufacturers are responsible for resulting injuries under strict liability, but not negligence. Other products contain dangers that are simply undiscoverable until after an injury has occurred. Blood infected with serum hepatitis is a prime example. In between lies a vast array of products for which safety attitudes and safety technology evolve over time as manufacturers develop means to discover and reduce product hazards. Changing safety technology poses questions of fairness and efficiency in holding manufacturers accountable for failing to avert injuries they were unable to foresee or prevent.

The terms "undiscoverable," "unknowable," and "unavoidable" have often been used interchangeably by the courts and commentators in describing these types of dangers. Another frequently used phrase is "state of the art," as in the "state of the art defense" or "state of the art evidence." Although the phrase is variously defined by different courts in differing contexts, the basic idea is that a product risk was generally unknown, or the means of avoiding it unknown or unavailable, at the time the product was manufactured and sold.

The very notion of "state of the art" is an undeveloped concept whose meaning in products liability law is still evolving. It has been only loosely defined by most courts, and the doctrine in this area (such as it is) generally has not crystallized into formal rules. Nevertheless, emerging from the cases is a common theme: hesitancy to impose liability on manufacturers for risks they cannot control. The state of the art issue thus is similar to the generic risk issue examined in the preceding chapter in that both problems hinge upon the "unavoidability" of certain product risks. Particularly in more recent years, however, the state of the art problem increasingly has become characterized by the manufacturer's *lack of knowledge* of risks of toxic substances, such as asbestos, drugs, and other chemicals.

Penetrating to the heart of defectiveness and the meaning of "strict" liability, the state of the art issue forces a reexamination of the goals of products liability law. Among the fundamental questions raised in this area are: Who should bear the risks and benefits of changes in technology that develop over time? How should the law deal with changes in public attitudes toward risk, toward institutions such as manufacturers, toward individual responsibility, and toward products liability doctrine? Are present-day juries capable of fairly judging products made before the jurors were born according to the technology, standards, and values of long ago? Is the judicial system capable of addressing these problems in a principled manner, or is the legislature a preferable forum for making the fundamental choices? These are some of the perplexing issues with which courts, legislatures, and commentators must continue to grapple that are on the cutting edge of modern products liability law.

———

A. DURABLE PRODUCTS

Pontifex v. Sears, Roebuck & Co.

United States Court of Appeals, Fourth Circuit, 1955.
226 F.2d 909.

■ PER CURIAM.

This is an appeal from a judgment on a directed verdict for defendant in a personal injury case. Plaintiff was injured when she was struck in the eye by a rope pulled to start the gasoline engine of a lawn mower. Plaintiff contends that there was negligence in the design of the lawn mower in that the rope was not permanently attached to a spring recoil mechanism, such as is found in the latest models of these machines, and that no warning was given of the danger of using it. We do not think, however, that it can be held to be negligence to sell an old model machine not equipped with a safety device of later models, and we find no evidence of negligence in the design or construction of the machine or of any need for warning or of any other negligence upon which a verdict for plaintiff could have been based.

Affirmed.

———

Bruce v. Martin–Marietta Corp.

United States Court of Appeals, Tenth Circuit, 1976.
544 F.2d 442.

■ BREITENSTEIN, CIRCUIT JUDGE.

[Plaintiffs sued for injuries and deaths of persons on an airplane, a Martin 404, manufactured by defendant Martin–Marietta and flown at the time of the crash by Ozark Airlines.] The district court gave summary judgment for the defendants. We affirm.

[The plane was chartered to carry the Wichita State University football team and some of its supporters to a game in Utah.] On October 2, 1970, the plane crashed into a mountain west of Silver Plume, Colorado. The plane first struck trees at an altitude of approximately 10,800 ft. and then travelled 425 ft. before coming to rest. Seats in the passenger cabin broke loose from their floor attachments, were thrown forward against the bulkhead of the plane, and blocked exit. A fire then developed. Of the 40 persons on the plane, 32 died in the crash.

[After Martin manufactured the plane in 1952, it was sold and resold to a number of air carriers, finally to Ozark Airlines in 1965. Defendants] are Martin and Ozark.

[Plaintiffs contend that Martin–Marietta's failure to design] the plane in crashworthy condition caused the deaths, or enhanced the injuries, of the passengers. The alleged defects are the inadequacy of the seat fastenings and the lack of protection against fire. Plaintiffs seek recovery on theories of negligence, implied warranty, and strict liability in tort.

[A defense affidavit showed that the plane's design conformed to all Civil Aeronautics Administration requirements concerning seats and fire protection, in response to which the] plaintiffs presented the affidavit of [a qualified] aircraft accident investigator [who] said:

> [T]here were airline passenger seats in common use on October 2, 1970, which, if installed in the subject Martin 404 aircraft, would have remained in place throughout this otherwise survivable accident and would not have trapped the occupants in the burning aircraft. An occupant in this crash should not have had his escape from the burning aircraft impeded by seat failures. In the crash in question the seat failures constituted an unreasonable dangerous condition to the passengers. . . .

. . . The only fact shown by plaintiffs with regard to the seats is that in 1970, 18 years after Martin made and sold the plane, airplane passenger seats, which would have withstood the crash, were in use. The record establishes that when the plane was made and first sold, its design was within the state of the art. The plaintiffs' affidavit that 18 years after the manufacture and sale of the plane safer passenger seats were in use is not relevant to the determination of whether Martin, by satisfying the 1952 state-of-art requirements, exercised reasonable care and, hence, was not negligent.

Plaintiffs say that state-of-art evidence is not material when the claim is based on strict liability. They argue that a showing of a design defective in 1970 establishes that the plane was defective in 1952, the time of the original sale, absent a subsequent alteration of the plane. . . .

There is authority that state-of-art evidence is not relevant to a strict liability claim. Cunningham v. MacNeal Memorial Hospital, 266 N.E.2d 897, 902, 904 (Ill. 1970) [(because sellers of defective goods are subject to liability under § 402A even if they exercise all due care). But we] respectfully reject [the Illinois approach].

[T]here is "general" agreement that to prove liability under § 402A the plaintiff must show that the product was dangerous beyond the expectation of the ordinary customer. State-of-art evidence helps to determine the expectation of the ordinary consumer. A consumer would not expect a Model T to have the safety features which are incorporated in automobiles made today. The same expectation applies to airplanes. Plaintiffs have not shown that the ordinary consumer would expect a plane made in 1952 to have the safety features of one made in 1970. State-of-art evidence was properly received and considered by the trial court.

[Summary judgments for defendants affirmed.]

Boatland of Houston, Inc. v. Bailey

Supreme Court of Texas, 1980.
609 S.W.2d 743.

■ McGEE, JUSTICE.

[Samuel Bailey was killed in May 1973 when the 16–foot bass boat he was operating struck a partially submerged tree stump, throwing Bailey into the water. Turning sharply, the boat circled back and struck Bailey with its propeller. Bailey's family sued the retail seller of the boat, Boatland of Houston, Inc., in part because of] the failure of the motor to automatically turn off when Bailey was thrown from the boat. [The trial court entered judgment for the defendant on the jury's finding that the boat was not defective.] The court of civil appeals, with one justice dissenting, reversed and remanded[, and the defendant appealed to the supreme court, which reversed the judgment of the court of civil appeals and reinstated the judgment of the trial court in favor of Boatland.]

Whether a product was defectively designed must be judged against the technological context existing at the time of its manufacture. Thus, when the plaintiff alleges that a product was defectively designed because it lacked a specific feature, attention may become focused on the feasibility of that feature—the capacity to provide the feature without greatly increasing the product's cost or impairing usefulness. This feasibility is a relative, not an absolute, concept; the more scientifically and economically feasible the alternative was, the more likely that a jury may find that the product was defectively designed. A plaintiff may advance the argument that a safer alternative was feasible with evidence that it was in actual use or was available at the time of manufacture. Feasibility may also be shown with evidence of the scientific and economic capacity to develop the safer alternative. Thus, evidence of the actual use of, or capacity to use, safer alternatives is relevant insofar as it depicts the available scientific knowledge and the practicalities of applying that knowledge to a product's design. . . .

[The Baileys produced evidence of the scientific and economic feasibility of an automatic cut-off system, known as a "kill switch," which they argued should have been included in the boat. Boat land's president, Nessmith, admitted in his deposition that several types of "kill switches" had become available by the time of the deposition and were then being installed by Boatland on the bass boats it assembles and sells.]

[The Baileys also introduced the deposition] of George Horton, the inventor of a kill switch designed for open-top carriers. . . . Horton began developing his "Quick Kill" in November of 1972 and applied for a patent in January of 1973. According to Horton, his invention required no breakthroughs in the state of the art of manufacturing or production. He stated that his invention was simple: a lanyard connects the operator's body to a device that fits over the ignition key. If the operator moves, the lanyard is pulled, the device rotates, and the ignition switch turns off. When he began to market his "Quick Kill," the response by boat dealers was very positive, which Horton perceived to be due to the filling of a recognized need. He considered the kill switch to be a necessary safety device for a bass boat with stick steering. If the kill switch were hooked up and the operator thrown out, the killing of the motor would prevent the boat from circling back where it came from. Horton also testified that for 30 years racing boats had been using various types of kill switches. Thus, the concept of kill switches was not new.

* * *

Boatland elicited evidence to rebut the Baileys' evidence of the feasibility of equipping boats with kill switches or similar devices in March of 1973, when the boat was assembled and sold. . . . In response to the Baileys' evidence that kill switches were presently used by Boatland, Nessmith testified that he did not know of kill switches until the spring of 1973, and first began to sell them a year later.

In response to the Baileys' evidence that the "Quick Kill" was readily available at the time of trial, Horton stated on cross-examination that until he obtained the patent for his "Quick Kill" in 1974 he kept the idea to himself. Before he began to manufacture them, he investigated the market for competitive devices and found none. The only applications of the automatic engine shut-off concept in use at the time were homemade, such as on racing boats. . . .

Boatland introduced other evidence to show that kill switches were not available when Bailey's boat was sold. . . . Jimmy Wood, a game warden, stated that he first became aware of kill switches in 1975. . . . Willis Hudson, who manufactured the boat operated by Bailey, testified that he first became aware of kill switches in 1974 or 1975 and to his knowledge no such thing was available before then. Ralph Cornelius, the vice-president of a marine appliance dealership, testified that kill switches were not available in 1973. The first kill switch he saw to be sold was in 1974, although homemade "crash throttles" or foot buttons had long been in use.

... The Baileys complained on appeal that the trial court erred in admitting Boatland's evidence that kill switches were unavailable when Bailey's boat was assembled and sold. The court of civil appeals agreed, holding that the evidence was material only to the care exercised by Boatland and thus irrelevant in a strict liability case.

In its appeal to this court, Boatland contends that the court of civil appeals misconstrued the nature and purpose of its evidence. According to Boatland, when the Baileys introduced evidence that kill switches were a feasible safety alternative, Boatland was entitled to introduce evidence that kill switches were not yet available when Bailey's boat was sold and thus were not a feasible design alternative at that time.

The primary dispute concerning the feasibility of an alternative design for Bailey's boat was the "state of the art" when the boat was sold. The admissibility and effect of "state of the art" evidence has been a subject of controversy in both negligence and strict product liability cases. In negligence cases, the reasonableness of the defendant's conduct in placing the product on the market is in issue. Evidence of industry customs at the time of manufacture may be offered by either party for the purpose of comparing the defendant's conduct with industry customs. Defendant's compliance with custom to rebut evidence of its negligence has been described as the "state of the art defense." See generally 2 L. Frumer & M. Friedman, Products Liability § 16A[4][i] (1980). [I]t is argued that the state of the art is equivalent to industry custom and is relevant only to the issue of the defendant's negligence and irrelevant to a strict liability theory of recovery.

In our view, "custom" is distinguishable from "state of the art." The state of the art with respect to a particular product refers to the technological environment at the time of its manufacture. This technological environment includes the scientific knowledge, economic feasibility, and the practicalities of implementation when the product was manufactured. Evidence of this nature is important in determining whether a safer design was feasible. The limitations imposed by the state of the art at the time of manufacture may affect the feasibility of a safer design. [State of the art evidence has been held admissible in other jurisdictions.] In this case, the evidence advanced by both parties was relevant to the feasibility of designing bass boats to shut off automatically if the operator fell out, or more specifically, the feasibility of equipping bass boats with safety switches.

The Baileys offered state of the art evidence to establish the feasibility of a more safely designed boat: They established that when Bailey's boat was sold in 1973, the [concept of an automatic boat motor] cut off had been applied for years on racing boats. One kill switch, the "Quick Kill," was invented at that time and required no mechanical breakthrough. The Baileys [also showed] that other kill switches were presently in use and that the defendant itself presently installed them.

Logically, the plaintiff's strongest evidence of feasibility of an alternative design is its actual use by the defendant or others at the time of manufacture. Even if a safer alternative was not being used, evidence that it was available, known about, or capable of being developed is relevant in determining its feasibility. In contrast, the defendant's strongest rebuttal evidence is that a particular design alternative was impossible due to the state of the art. Yet the defendant's ability to rebut the plaintiff's evidence is not limited to showing that a particular alternative was impossible; it is entitled to rebut the plaintiff's evidence of feasibility with evidence of limitations on feasibility. A suggested alternative may be invented or discovered but not be feasible for use because of the time necessary for its application and implementation. Also, a suggested alternative may be available, but impractical for reasons such as greatly increased cost or impairment of the product's usefulness. When the plaintiff has introduced evidence that a safer alternative was feasible because it was used, the defendant may then introduce contradictory evidence that it was not used.

Thus in response to the Baileys' evidence of kill switch use in 1978, the time of trial, Boatland was properly allowed to show that they were not used when the boat was sold in 1973. To rebut proof that safety switches were possible and feasible when Bailey's boat was sold because the underlying concept was known and the "Quick Kill," a simple, inexpensive device had been invented, Boatland was properly allowed to show that neither the "Quick Kill" nor any other kill switch was available at that time.

It could reasonably be inferred from this evidence that although the underlying concept of automatic motor cut-off devices was not new, kill switches were not as feasible an alternative as the Baileys' evidence implied. Boatland did not offer evidence of technological impossibility or absolute nonfeasibility; its evidence was offered to show limited availability when the boat was sold. Once the jury was informed of the state of the art, it was able to consider the extent to which it was feasible to incorporate an automatic cut-off device or similar design characteristic into Bailey's boat. The feasibility and effectiveness of a safer design and other factors such as utility and risk, were properly considered by the jury before it ultimately concluded that the boat sold to Bailey was not defectively designed.[3]

* * *

CONCLUSION

[T]he judgment of the court of civil appeals is reversed. The ... trial court [judgment for] Boatland, is affirmed.

ON REHEARING

■ CAMPBELL, JUSTICE, dissenting.

I dissent. "State of the art" does not mean "the state of industry practice." "State of the art" means "state of industry knowledge." At the

---

3. This opinion, insofar as it holds that certain evidence of the state of the art is admissible on the issue of defectiveness in product design cases, is not intended to suggest that such evidence constitutes a defense, such as do misuse and assumption of the risk....

time of the manufacture of the boat in question, the device and concept of a circuit breaker, as is at issue in this case, was simple, mechanical, cheap, practical, possible, economically feasible and a concept seventy years old, which required no engineering or technical breakthrough. The concept was known by the industry. This fact removes it from "state of the art."

* * *

In products liability, [t]he focus is on the product, not the reasoning behind the manufacturer's . . . design or the care exercised in making such decisions. Commercial availability . . . to Boatland is not the test. Defectiveness as to the product is the test. . . .

The ["kill switch" is without dispute] one of the simplest mechanical devices and concepts known to man. . . . It is more a concept than an invention. . . . Was an invention required in order to [put] a circuit breaker on a bass boat? Absolutely not! Did the manufacturer have to wait until George Horton invented his specific "Quick Kill" switch before it could [put] a kill switch of some sort on its bass boats? Absolutely not! * * *

NOTES

1. "State of the art" means quite different things to different people. To some (especially manufacturers), the phrase refers to the customary practice in the industry. To others (especially plaintiffs' counsel), it means the ultimate in existing technology, including all knowledge pertinent to the problem existing at the time, regardless of its source, that is published and accessible to researchers.

2. Nebraska's reform act, better than most on this point, defines state of the art as "the best technology reasonably available at the time." Neb.Rev.Stat. § 25–21,182. Would a journal article on point, published in another country in a foreign language, be "reasonably available" to an American manufacturer?

3. Feasibility of Alternative Designs.

A. In General. In evaluating the design of durable products, the state-of-the-art issue often resolves to whether the plaintiff can and must prove that a safer design alternative was feasible at the time of manufacture; or whether, alternatively, the defendant may defend by showing that the plaintiff's proffered alternative design was not feasible at the time of manufacture. In this context, most courts agree that "[m]anufacturers are not to be held strictly liable for failure to design safety features, if the technology to do so is unavailable at the time the product is made." Rexrode v. American Laundry Press Co., 674 F.2d 826 (10th Cir. 1982). Cf. Adams v. Fuqua Indus., Inc., 820 F.2d 271 (8th Cir. 1987) (lawn mower manufacturer should have been permitted to offer rebuttal evidence that safety devices proposed by plaintiff not feasible since not developed at time of manufacture).

B. Consumer Expectations Test. In jurisdictions where design defectiveness is determined by consumer expectations, proof of an alternative design—feasible vel non—is not required. See, e.g., Griffin v. Suzuki Motor Corp., 84 P.3d 1047 (Kan. Ct. App. 2004) ("Although evidence of a reasonable alternative design may be introduced, it is not required because the prevailing test is one of consumer expectations."). In such jurisdictions, is such evidence even relevant?

B. TOXIC SUBSTANCES

Beshada v. Johns–Manville Prod. Corp.

Supreme Court of New Jersey, 1982.
90 N.J. 191, 447 A.2d 539.

■ PASHMAN, J.

The sole question here is whether defendants in a product liability case based on strict liability for failure to warn may raise a "state of the art" defense. Defendants assert that the danger of which they failed to warn was undiscovered at the time the product was marketed and that it was undiscoverable given the state of scientific knowledge at that time. The case comes to us on appeal from the trial court's denial of plaintiffs' motion to strike the state-of-the-art defense. For the reasons stated below, we reverse the trial court judgment and strike the defense.

I

These six consolidated cases are personal injury and wrongful death actions brought against manufacturers and distributors of asbestos products. Plaintiffs are workers, or survivors of deceased workers, who claim to have been exposed to asbestos for varying periods of time. They allege that as a result of that exposure they contracted asbestosis (a non-malignant scarring of the lungs), mesothelioma (a rare cancer of the lining of the chest, the pleura, or the lining of the abdomen, the peritoneum) and other asbestos-related illnesses.

* * *

There is substantial factual dispute about what defendants knew and when they knew it. A trial judge in the Eastern District of Texas, the forum for numerous asbestos-related cases, has concluded that "[k]nowledge of the danger can be attributed to the [asbestos] industry as early as the mid–1930s...." Hardy v. Johns–Manville Sales Corp., 509 F. Supp. 1353, 1355 (E.D. Tex.1981). Defendants respond, however, that it was not until the 1960s that the medical profession in the United States recognized that a potential health hazard arose from the use of insulation products containing asbestos. Before that time, according to defendants, the danger from asbestos was believed limited to workers in asbestos textile mills, who were exposed to much higher concentrations of asbestos dust than were the workers at other sites, such as shipyards. Defendants claim that it was not discovered until recently that the much smaller concentrations those workers faced were also hazardous.

We need not resolve the factual issues raised. For purposes of plaintiffs' motion to strike the defense, we assume the defendants' version of the facts. The issue is whether the medical community's presumed unawareness of the dangers of asbestos is a defense to plaintiffs' claims.

* * *

III

[I]n Freund v. Cellofilm Properties, Inc., 432 A.2d 925 (N.J. 1981) . . . and Cepeda v. Cumberland Engineering Company, Inc., 386 A.2d 816 (N.J. 1978), [we examined] the principle of strict liability. . . .

In *Cepeda,* we explained that in the context of design defect liability, strict liability is identical to liability for negligence, with one important caveat: "The only qualification is as to the requisite of foreseeability by the manufacturer of the dangerous propensity of the chattel manifested at the trial—this being imputed to the manufacturer." [Citations.] In so holding, we adopted the explication of strict liability offered by Dean Wade:

> The time has now come to be forthright in using a tort way of thinking and tort terminology [in cases of strict liability in tort]. There are several ways of doing it, and it is not difficult. The simplest and easiest way, it would seem, is to assume that the defendant knew of the dangerous condition of the product and ask whether he was then negligent in putting it on the market or supplying it to someone else. In other words, the scienter is supplied as a matter of law, and there is no need for the plaintiff to prove its existence as a matter of fact. Once given this notice of the dangerous condition of the chattel, the question then becomes whether the defendant was negligent to people who might be harmed by that condition if they came into contact with it or were in the vicinity of it. Another way of saying this is to ask whether the magnitude of the risk created by the dangerous condition of the product was outweighed by the social utility attained by putting it out in this fashion. Wade, On the Nature of Strict Tort Liability for Products, 44 Miss. L.J. 825 (1973).

Stated differently, negligence is conduct-oriented, asking whether defendant's actions were reasonable; strict liability is product-oriented, asking whether the product was reasonably safe for its foreseeable purposes. *Freund,* supra.[3]

[W]e can distinguish two tests for determining whether a product is safe: (1) does its utility outweigh its risk? and (2) if so, has that risk been reduced to the greatest extent possible consistent with the product's utility? The first question looks to the product as it was in fact marketed. If that product caused more harm than good, it was not reasonably fit for its intended purposes. . . . Whether or not the product passes the initial risk-utility test, it is not reasonably safe if the same product could have been made or marketed more safely.

---

3. The imputation of knowledge is. . . . another way of saying that for purposes of strict liability the defendant's knowledge of the danger is irrelevant. See *Freund,* quoting Keeton, "Products Liability—Inadequacy of Information," 48 Tex. L. Rev. 398, 407–08 (1970). . . .

Warning cases are of this second type.[5] When plaintiffs urge that a product is hazardous because it lacks a warning, they typically look to the second test, saying in effect that regardless of the overall cost-benefit calculation the product is unsafe because a warning could make it safer at virtually no added cost and without limiting its utility. . . .

[We have previously stated the unequivocal difference between negligence and strict liability in warning cases]:

> when a plaintiff sues under strict liability, there is no need to prove that the manufacturer knew or should have known of any dangerous propensities of its product—such knowledge is imputed to the manufacturer. *Freund*.

* * *

IV

As it relates to warning cases, the state-of-the-art defense asserts that distributors of products can be held liable only for injuries resulting from dangers that were scientifically discoverable at the time the product was distributed. Defendants argue that the question of whether the product can be made safer must be limited to consideration of the available technology at the time the product was distributed. Liability would be absolute, defendants argue, if it could be imposed on the basis of a subsequently discovered means to make the product safer since technology will always be developing new ways to make products safer. Such a rule, they assert, would make manufacturers liable whenever their products cause harm, whether or not they are reasonably fit for their foreseeable purposes.

Defendants conceptualize the scientific unknowability of the dangerous propensities of a product as a technological barrier to making the product safer by providing warnings. [Yet] this position [ignores] the *Freund* holding that knowledge of the dangers of the product is imputed to defendants as a matter of law. A state-of-the-art defense would [shift back to the plaintiff the requirement of proving] that knowledge of the dangers was scientifically available [to the defendant] at the time of manufacture.* * *[6]

. . . Essentially, state-of-the-art is a negligence defense. It seeks to explain why defendants are not culpable for failing to provide a warning. They assert, in effect, that because they could not have known the product was dangerous, they acted reasonably in marketing it without a warning.

---

5. This two-part distinction can best be clarified by looking at how it would apply to automobiles without seatbelts. Because of the great utility of cars, few would dispute that even without seatbelts, a car's utility to society outweighs its risks. Thus, cars would be considered safe under the first aspect of the test. However, since seatbelts make cars safer without hindering utility, cars without seatbelts are deemed unsafe by virtue of the second part of the *Freund* test. Warnings are like seatbelts: regardless of the utility and risk of a product without warnings, a warning can generally be added without diminishing utility. *Freund*.

6. [This case holds only] that a state-of-the-art defense should not be allowed in failure to warn cases. . . . We specifically decline to address whether a state-of-the-art defense is appropriate to safety device cases.

But in strict liability cases, culpability is irrelevant. The product was unsafe. That it was unsafe because of the state of technology does not change the fact that it was unsafe. Strict liability focuses on the product, not the fault of the manufacturer. "If the conduct is unreasonably dangerous, then there should be strict liability without reference to what excuse defendant might give for being unaware of the danger." Keeton, Products Liability–Inadequacy of Information, 48 Tex. L. Rev. 398, 408 (1970).

When the defendants argue that it is unreasonable to impose a duty on them to warn of the unknowable, they misconstrue both the purpose and effect of strict liability. By imposing strict liability, we are not requiring defendants to have done something that is impossible. In this sense, the phrase "duty to warn" is misleading. It implies negligence concepts with their attendant focus on the reasonableness of defendant's behavior. However, a major concern of strict liability—ignored by defendants—is the conclusion that if a product was in fact defective, the distributor of the product should compensate its victims for the misfortune that it inflicted on them.

* * *

The most important inquiry [is whether imposing liability for failure to warn of undiscoverable dangers] will advance the [policies of] our strict liability rules. We believe that it will.

Risk Spreading. One of the most important arguments [for] strict liability is that the manufacturers and distributors of defective products can best allocate the costs of the injuries resulting from those products. The premise is that the price of a product should reflect all of its costs, including the cost of injuries caused by the product. This can best be accomplished by imposing liability on the manufacturer and distributors [who] can insure against liability and incorporate the cost of the insurance in the price of the product. In this way, the costs of the product will be borne by those who profit from it: the manufacturers and distributors who profit from its sale and the buyers who profit from its use. "It should be a cost of doing business that in the course of doing that business an unreasonable risk was created." Keeton, 48 Tex. L. Rev. at 408. See Prosser, The Law of Torts, § 75, p. 495 (4th ed.1971).

Defendants argue that this policy is not forwarded by imposition of liability for unknowable hazards. Since such hazards by definition are not predicted, the price of the hazardous product will not be adjusted to reflect the costs of the injuries it will produce. Rather, defendants state, the cost "will be borne by the public at large and reflected in a general, across the board increase in premiums to compensate for unanticipated risks." There is some truth in this assertion, but it is not a bad result.

[S]preading the costs of injuries among all those who produce, distribute and purchase manufactured products is far preferable to imposing it on the innocent victims who suffer illnesses and disability from defective products. This basic normative premise is at the center of our strict liability rules. It is unchanged by the state of scientific knowledge at the time of manufacture.

Finally, contrary to defendants' assertion, this rule will not cause the price and production level of manufactured products to diverge from the so-called economically efficient level. Rather, the rule will force the price of any particular product to reflect the cost of insuring against the possibility that the product will turn out to be defective.

Accident Avoidance. . . . Defendants urge that this argument has no force as to hazards which by definition were undiscoverable. Defendants have treated the level of technological knowledge at a given time as an independent variable not affected by defendants' conduct. But this view ignores the important role of industry in product safety research. The "state-of-the-art" at a given time is partly determined by how much industry invests in safety research. By imposing on manufacturers the costs of failure to discover hazards, we create an incentive for them to invest more actively in safety research.

Fact finding process. The analysis thus far has assumed that it is possible to define what constitutes "undiscoverable" knowledge and that it will be reasonably possible to determine what knowledge was technologically discoverable at a given time. In fact, both assumptions are highly questionable. The vast confusion that is virtually certain to arise from any attempt to deal in a trial setting with the concept of scientific knowability constitutes a strong reason for avoiding the concept altogether by striking the state-of-the-art defense.

. . . Proof of what could have been known will inevitably be complicated, costly, confusing and time-consuming. Each side will have to produce experts in the history of science and technology to speculate as to what knowledge was feasible in a given year. We doubt that juries will be capable of even understanding the concept of scientific knowability, much less be able to resolve such a complex issue. Moreover, we should resist legal rules that will so greatly add to the costs both sides incur in trying a case.

[Moreover, allowing a discussion of state-of-the-art might confuse juries into thinking that blameworthiness is an issue in a strict liability case, which it is not.]

V

[In summary, precluding evidence of state-of-the-art is consistent with] the various policies underlying strict liability. The burden of illness from dangerous products such as asbestos should be placed upon those who profit from its production and, more generally, upon society at large, which reaps the benefits of the various products our economy manufactures. That burden should not be imposed exclusively on the innocent victim. Although victims must in any case suffer the pain involved, they should be spared the burdensome financial consequences of unfit products. At the same time, we believe this position will serve the salutary goals of increasing product safety research and simplifying tort trials.

Defendants have argued that it is unreasonable to impose a duty on them to warn of the unknowable. [Yet] defendants' products were not reasonably safe because they did not have a warning. Without a warning, users of the product were unaware of its hazards and could not protect themselves from injury. We impose strict liability because it is unfair for the distributors of a defective product not to compensate its victims. As between those innocent victims and the distributors, it is the distributors—and the public which consumes their products—which should bear the unforeseen costs of the product.

[Judgment of trial court reversed; plaintiff's motion to strike state-of-the-art defense granted.]

Responsibility for Unforeseeable Product Risks*

When a danger at the time of sale is neither known nor reasonably discoverable, the problem of moral accountability for resulting accidents becomes quite difficult. Failing to warn about an unknowable danger contrasts sharply, in terms of moral accountability, with actively (albeit innocently) misleading consumers by false statements to relinquish their normal levels of self-protection. The "silent" maker, by hypothesis, in no way wills any safety expectation or loss upon the victim; nor does the maker otherwise *cause* the loss, except by providing a product it reasonably thinks is good and by failing to cure a misimpression it neither made nor even knows exists.

Responsibility for harm from undiscoverable product dangers thus may be viewed most fairly as lying with the product—or, perhaps, in nature or in the inadequacies of science or technology—rather than with the manufacturer. That the chemistry and physics of the world contain vast numbers of unknown dangers is a fact well known to consumers who seek the benefits of the products of modern science and technology. Especially when potent chemicals are first developed to treat serious human illnesses, consumers well understand—even if only in a subconscious, "background" kind of way—that unknowable risks may well accompany the benefits expected to result from manipulating the atoms of the universe. And notwithstanding this important background understanding or expectation, most people probably want (or "demand," from the economic perspective of product makers) the benefits of science and technology if and when such benefits reasonably appear to exceed the risks. If a manufacturer does so, and an undiscoverable danger lurking in the product causes injury to a user, the maker cannot fairly be held responsible for the harm. The maker did not choose to put, nor did it unreasonably put, the danger in the product or the world, nor did the maker affirmatively mislead users into surrendering their own responsibility for self-protection. Instead, the manufacturer served in a real sense only as a conduit for consumer preferences,

* *From* Owen, The Moral Foundations of Products Liability Law: Toward First Princi-ples, 68 Notre Dame L. Rev. 427, 465–93 (1993).

providing consumers with what they reasonably appeared to want. Thus, the victim of an accident from an unknowable generic product danger probably should have no claim to hold the manufacture accountable for the loss.

The community may decide to protect its members against the economic costs of statistically inevitable product accidents by sharing such burdens *ex post*. That is to say, *losses* from product accidents may be "spread" throughout the community. The mechanism of loss spreading (or risk spreading, its *ex ante* counterpart) simply is insurance by another name. Risks and losses from product accidents may be spread across society (insured against) in three basic ways. Potential victims (or their employers) may insure themselves against accidental losses by purchasing first-party health, disability, and life insurance from private insurers. Alternatively, the government may "socialize" such losses through various forms of social welfare programs funded by taxation. Finally, product manufacturers may be required to absorb the losses and distribute them among their shareholders and, especially in the long run, consumers (through higher prices and diminished availability of the product). All three mechanisms for distributing risks of and losses from product accidents are used today, to some extent and in varying amounts, in the United States and the British Commonwealth, except New Zealand.

That present insurance mechanisms in this nation, both private and governmental, suffer from serious and increasing weaknesses of course is true. Yet these and other institutions generally do provide at least basic medical protection to the victims of most product accidents. Thus, because communal burden-sharing needs are satisfied at least minimally elsewhere—by institutions specifically designed to administer such programs outside the products liability litigation system—there is little reason even to engage the argument that communal burden-sharing responsibilities should be duplicated within a private litigation system designed to rectify private instances of injustice, rather than the broader public (distributive injustice) kinds.

The specific burden-sharing issue of greatest interest in the products liability context concerns the question of whether manufacturers or users should bear generic product risks unknowable to either party. That most persons forming a community probably would choose *ex ante* to insure against such unforeseeable risks outside the litigation system, suggesting that liability rules should be grounded in principles of fault rather than strict liability, is illuminated by a hypothetical consent analysis. Suppose that a user and a maker negotiate for the exchange of a product, such as a prescription drug, that they both believe to be safe but realize may possess some unknown risk of harm. The parties might well agree, and so price the product accordingly, that the maker should accept the risk of dangers that an ordinary maker should discover through reasonable research, and probably all risks of production defects, for a variety of reasons. The question then would be who, as between the maker and the user, should bear the risks of other dangers, generic to the product's design, that are both unknown and unknowable at the time of sale. Since harm from such risks by hypothesis is unforeseeable and, hence, unavoidable, there appears to be no good reason in social justice to require makers to be responsible. Particularly if the possible danger is very large, such as death, or malformations in the user's offspring, probably neither party would be willing to accept the entire risk, nor feel justified in forcing it on the other party. The victim of such catastrophic harm simply would be unable to bear it all alone, and the manufacturer, not being in the insurance business, would have to raise the drug's price inordinately or stop selling it altogether.

Thus, most persons probably would prefer *ex ante* that unknowable risks of this type be shifted to the community at large, through the fairest and most efficient (and hence the cheapest) forms of insurance. Consumers generally can obtain affordable insurance against unknown (and thus unpredictable) product risks, in types and amounts that suit their individual preferences, from private insurance firms. This type of personalized and reasonably priced first-party insurance must be contrasted to the very rough, incomplete, and expensive kind of third-party insurance obtainable from manufactures in the products liability litigation system. Accordingly, most persons hypothetically would probably choose to leave such risks initially with the user as the better conduit to individualized and efficient insurance mechanisms, and to price the product accordingly without a guarantee against such unknown risks.

NOTES

1. Which is right, the New Jersey Supreme Court opinion in *Beshada*, or this little essay?

2. The defendant in *Beshada*, Johns–Manville ("Manville"), filed for bankruptcy in 1983, followed since then by about 70 other manufacturers of asbestos. See ch. 19, below.

3. Compare Page, Generic Product Risks: The Case Against Comment *k* and for Strict Tort Liability, 58 N.Y.U. L. Rev. 853, 891 (1983) ("Both the satisfaction of justifiable expectations on the part of product victims and the achievement of modest advances in safety justify the application of strict liability to harm from unknowable generic hazards."), with A. Schwartz, Products Liability, Corporate Structure and Bankruptcy: Toxic Substances and the Remote Risk Relationship, 14 J. Legal Stud. 689, 736 (1985) ("The fairness and efficiency objections to imposing remote risks on firms imply the error of such impositions unless strong instrumental or justice reasons exist to hold firms liable. But there are no such reasons.").

Feldman v. Lederle Laboratories

Supreme Court of New Jersey, 1984.
97 N.J. 429, 479 A.2d 374.

■ SCHREIBER, J.

In this case defendants and *amici* drug manufacturers argued that the doctrine of strict products liability should not apply to prescription drugs.

We hold otherwise and conclude that drug manufacturers have a duty to warn of dangers of which they know or should have known on the basis of reasonably obtainable or available knowledge.

Plaintiff, Carol Ann Feldman, has gray teeth as a result of taking a tetracycline drug, Declomycin. Plaintiff's father, a pharmacist and a medical doctor, prescribed and administered the drug to her when she was an infant to control upper respiratory and other secondary types of infections. [Plaintiff sued Lederle Labs, the manufacturer of Declomycin, in strict liability in tort for failing] to warn physicians of the drug's side effect, tooth discoloration.

Defendant contended that . . . it had complied with the state of the art in its warning literature. It had not warned of possible tooth discoloration because, the defendant claimed, the possibility of that side effect was not known at the time its literature was disseminated.

The jury found for the defendant. The Appellate Division affirmed [and plaintiff appealed. Various manufacturers and organizations filed amicus briefs.]

I

[Tetracyclines are a group of antibiotics first introduced in 1948 produced by different drug manufacturers and marketed under various trade names.]

Defendant first marketed Declomycin in 1959. The Physicians' Desk Reference (PDR), a book used by doctors to determine effects of drugs, contains data furnished by drug manufacturers about drugs, their compositions, usages, and reactions. The 1959 PDR entry for Declomycin [described its advantages over other tetracyclines.] The PDR is produced annually. Until the 1965 or 1966 edition, the PDR did not mention that tooth discoloration was a possible side effect of Declomycin. Since 1965 or 1966 the PDR has stated that the drug, when administered to infants and children, could cause tooth discoloration that would be permanent if the drug were given during the developmental stage of the permanent teeth.

Plaintiff, Carol Ann Feldman, was born on February 8, 1960. Her father, Dr. Harold Feldman, [prescribed Declomycin several times from] 1960, when she was eight or nine months old, until the end of 1963. . . . to prevent secondary infections when she had different childhood diseases. [The tetracycline caused plaintiff's teeth (both her baby and permanent teeth) to be discolored gray-brown. The experts] agreed that scientific literature existed by 1960 that referred to tooth staining being caused by tetracycline. [Plaintiff's expert, Dr. Bonda,] specifically mentioned a 1956 article by Dr. Andre reciting that tetracycline accumulated in mineralized portions of growing bones and teeth of mice; an article by Dr. Milch in the July, 1957 Journal of the National Cancer Institute reporting that laboratory animals had yellow fluorescents in bones, including teeth, following dosages of tetracycline; [and several other articles published from 1958–61.] Dr. Bonda concluded the defendant should have begun to investigate the possible effects of all forms of tetracycline on teeth no later than 1956, when the Andre article appeared.

Defendant's expert, Dr. Guggenheimer, on the other hand, noted that before 1962 the literature on tooth discoloration concerned only patients with cystic fibrosis who had been receiving massive doses of tetracyclines. He pointed out that Dr. Milch's papers described only fluorescents, not tooth staining. He testified that Declomycin did not become available until 1959 and that it would take 2½ years for permanent teeth developing in 1959 to erupt. The completion of accurate controlled studies of multiple well-documented cases would have been the only way one could really know whether Declomycin caused tooth discoloration in permanent teeth. [In 1963, after receiving complaints from eight doctors that Declomycin was causing tooth staining, the defendant sought permission from the FDA warn doctors that Declomycin, as other tetracyclines, might discolor the teeth of young children. The FDA agreed, whereupon the defendant began to include the standard tetracycline warnings in their literature later that year.]

The trial court [charged the jury] that if the defendant did not know of the danger of tooth discoloration, and if the application of reasonably developed human skill and foresight consistent with the state of the art and the knowledge of the scientific community [at the time] would not have alerted defendant to the danger, then [the jury should find for the defendant].

II

Does Strict Liability Apply to Manufacturers of Prescription Drugs?

... The defendant and the drug manufacturing *amici curiae* urged that public policy as explicated in comment *k* to section 402A of the Restatement (Second) of Torts (1965) [hereinafter cited as Restatement] should immunize drug manufacturers from liability for side effects of prescription drugs. Comment *k* suggests that strict liability should not apply to certain unavoidably unsafe products. We do not agree that the protective shield of comment *k* immunizes all prescription drugs. Moreover, we are of the opinion that generally the principle of strict liability is applicable to manufacturers of prescription drugs.

* * * Comment *k* reads as follows:

> *Unavoidably unsafe products*. There are some products which, in the present state of human knowledge, are quite incapable of being made *safe* for their intended and ordinary use. These are especially common in the field of drugs. An outstanding example is the vaccine for the Pasteur treatment of rabies, which not uncommonly leads to very serious and damaging consequences when it is injected. Since the disease itself invariably leads to a dreadful death, both the marketing and the use of the vaccine are fully justified, notwithstanding the unavoidable high degree of risk which they involve. Such a product, properly prepared, *and accompa-*

nied by proper directions and warning, is not defective, nor is it *unreasonably* [emphasis in original] dangerous. The same is true of many other drugs, vaccines, and the like, many of which for this very reason cannot legally be sold except to physicians, or under the prescription of a physician. It is also true in particular of many new or experimental drugs as to which, because of lack of time and opportunity for sufficient medical experience, there can be no assurance of safety, or perhaps even of purity of ingredients, but such experience as there is justifies the marketing and use of the drug notwithstanding a medically recognizable risk. The seller of such products, *again with the qualification that they are properly prepared and marketed, and proper warning is given,* where the situation calls for it, is not to be held to strict liability for unfortunate consequences attending their use, merely because he has undertaken to supply the public with an apparently useful and desirable product, attended with a known but apparently reasonable risk. [Emphasis added.]

Comment *k* immunizes from strict liability the manufacturers of some products, including certain drugs, that are unavoidably unsafe. However, we see no reason to hold as a matter of law and policy that all prescription drugs that are unsafe are unavoidably so. Drugs, like any other products, may contain defects that could have been avoided by better manufacturing or design. Whether a drug is unavoidably unsafe should be decided on a case-by-case basis; we perceive no justification [in policy or under comment *k* for immunizing prescription drug manufacturers from their safe manufacturing, warning, and risk-utility design obligations under strict liability in tort.]

III

[In this strict-liability warning case, "the crux of the plaintiff's complaint is that her doctor should have been warned of a possible side effect of the drug in infants, discoloration of teeth." Generally], the doctrine of strict liability assumes that enterprises should be responsible for damages to consumers resulting from defective products regardless of fault. The doctrine differs from a negligence theory, which centers on the defendant's conduct and seeks to determine whether the defendant acted as a reasonably prudent person. This difference between strict liability and negligence is commonly expressed by stating that in a strict liability analysis, the defendant is assumed to know of the dangerous propensity of the product, whereas in a negligence case, the plaintiff must prove that the defendant knew or should have known of the danger. . . .

When the strict liability defect consists of an improper design or warning, reasonableness of the defendant's conduct is a factor in determining liability. [In such cases, the question posed by the Wade–Keeton test] is whether, assuming that the manufacturer knew of the [danger] in the product, he acted in a reasonably prudent manner in marketing the product or in providing the warnings given. Thus, once the defendant's knowledge of the [danger] is imputed, strict liability analysis becomes almost identical to negligence analysis in its focus on the reasonableness of the defendant's conduct. . . .

[A]s to warnings, generally conduct should be measured by knowledge at the time the manufacturer distributed the product. Did the defendant know, or should he have known, of the danger, given the scientific, technological, and other information available when the product was distributed; or, in other words, did he have actual or constructive knowledge of the danger? The Restatement, supra, has adopted this test in comment *j* to section 402A, which reads in pertinent part as follows:

> *Directions or warning.* In order to prevent the product from being unreasonably dangerous, the seller may be required to give directions or warning, on the container, as to its use. . . . Where the product contains an ingredient . . . whose danger is not generally known, or if known is one which the consumer would reasonably not expect to find in the product, the seller is required to give warning against it, *if he has knowledge, or by the application of reasonable, developed human skill and foresight should have knowledge,* of the presence of the ingredient and the danger. [Emphasis added.]

Under this standard negligence and strict liability in warning cases may be deemed to be functional equivalents. [Citations.] Constructive knowledge embraces knowledge that should have been known based on information that was reasonably available or obtainable and should have alerted a reasonably prudent person to act. Put another way, would a person of reasonable intelligence or of the superior expertise of the defendant charged with such knowledge conclude that defendant should have alerted the consuming public? [In answering this question, it should be remembered that "a manufacturer is held to the standard of an expert in the field"] and should keep abreast of scientific advances.

* * *

Furthermore, a reasonably prudent manufacturer will be deemed to know of reliable information generally available or reasonably obtainable in the industry or in the particular field involved. [F]or example, if a substantial number of doctors or consumers had complained to a drug manufacturer of an untoward effect of a drug, that would have constituted sufficient information requiring an appropriate warning. [Citations.]

This test does not conflict with the assumption made in strict liability design defect and warning cases that the defendant knew of the dangerous propensity of the product, if the knowledge that is assumed is reasonably knowable in the sense of actual or constructive knowledge. A warning that a product may have an unknowable danger warns one of nothing. [Our prior decisions did not state] that the manufacturer would be deemed to know of the dangerous propensity of the chattel when the danger was unknowable. [Citation.] In our opinion, Beshada v. Johns–Manville Prod. Corp., 447 A.2d 539 (N.J. 1982), would not demand a contrary conclusion in the typical design defect or warning case. If *Beshada* were deemed to hold generally or in all cases, particularly with respect to a situation like the present one involving drugs vital to health, that in a warning context knowledge of the unknowable is irrelevant in determining the applicability of strict liability, we would not agree. Many commentators have criticized this aspect of the *Beshada* reasoning and the public policies on which it is based. See, e.g., Page, Generic Product Risks: The Case Against Comment K and for Strict Tort Liability, 58 N.Y.U. L. Rev. 853, 877–82 (1983); Schwartz, The Post–Sale Duty to Warn: Two Unfortunate Forks in the Road to a Reasonable Doctrine, id. at 892, 901–05; Wade, On the Effect in Product Liability of Knowledge Unavailable Prior to Marketing, id. at 734, 754–56; Comment, Requiring Omniscience: The Duty to Warn of Scientifically Undiscoverable Product Defects, 71 Geo. L.J. 1635 (1983); Comment, Beshada v. Johns Manville Products Corp.: Adding Uncertainty to Injury, 35 Rutgers L. Rev. 982, 1008–15 (1983); Note, Products Liability—Strict Liability in Tort—State-of-the-Art Defense Inapplicable in Design Defect Cases, 13 Seton Hall L. Rev. 625 (1983). But see Hayes v. Ariens Co., 462 N.E.2d 273, 277–78 (Mass. 1984)(citing *Beshada* with approval for the proposition that in strict liability the seller "is presumed to have been informed at the time of sale of all risks whether or not he actually knew or reasonably should have known of them"). The rationale of *Beshada* is not applicable to this case. We do not overrule *Beshada,* but restrict *Beshada* to the circumstances giving rise to its holding.

* * *

In strict liability warning cases, unlike negligence cases, however, the defendant should properly bear the burden of proving that the information was not reasonably available or obtainable and that it therefore lacked actual or constructive knowledge of the defect. [Citations.] The defendant is in a superior position to know the technological material or data in the particular field or specialty.

* * *

The trial court erred in fixing the date [of] defendant's actual or constructive knowledge [at 1960, the first time plaintiff received Declomycin which she continued to receive until the end of 1963. The evidence reveals] that defendant should have known of the side effect as early as 1960 [and] actually knew of the danger by the end of 1962. Defendant nonetheless continued to market the drug in 1963 and plaintiff continued to ingest the drug that year. [Defendant would at least be responsible for the enhancement of the condition during that period of time.]

We reverse and remand for a new trial.

NOTES

1. "An outstanding example" of an unavoidably dangerous drug, which according to comment *k* should be exempted from strict tort liability, is the rabies vaccine "which not uncommonly leads to very serious and damaging consequences when it is injected. Since the disease itself invariably leads to a dreadful death, both the marketing and use of the vaccine are fully justified, notwithstanding the unavoidable high degree of risk which they involve." Rest. (2d) of Torts § 402A, cmt. *k* (1965). See Calabrese v. Trenton State College, 392 A.2d 600 (N.J. Super. Ct. App. Div. 1978)(brain damage resulting in inability to concentrate on economics such that plaintiff had to drop out of college; manufacturer not liable, but case against doctor remanded for trial on issue of informed consent).

2. Drug *Warnings* and Comment *k*. The great majority of courts applying the comment *k* unavoidable danger concept have done so in the context of warnings of dangers in prescription drugs and vaccines, blood, and medical devices. E.g., Hahn v. Richter, 673 A.2d 888 (Pa. 1996) (negligence only basis of liability for prescription drug warnings cases). A very few cases have applied the doctrine to other products. See, e.g., Purvis v. PPG Indus., Inc., 502 So.2d 714 (Ala. 1987) (dry cleaning solvent); Payne v. Soft Sheen Prod., Inc., 486 A.2d 712 (D.C. App. 1985) (permanent wave solution).

3. *Feldman* spreads to California: *Brown v. Superior Court*. In Brown v. Superior Ct., 751 P.2d 470 (Cal. 1988), a DES case, the California Supreme Court (1) adopted comment *k*'s restriction of a drug manufacturer's duties of design and warnings to *negligence*, rather than strict liability; and (2) applied such negligence principles to *all* prescription drugs, not just to those that are "unavoidably dangerous." In short, the court ruled that "a manufacturer is not strictly liable for injuries caused by a prescription drug so long as the drug was properly prepared and accompanied by warnings of its dangerous propensities that were either known or reasonably scientifically knowable at the time of distribution." Id. at 482–83.

The court reasoned that these holdings were necessary to avoid deterring drug manufacturers from developing and marketing important new drugs as promptly as possible, to help keep prescription drug costs at reasonable levels, and because the extra deterrence of strict liability risk-utility determinations was unnecessary and inappropriate because the FDA makes informed risk-utility judgments on new drugs before they are placed on the market. To illustrate its concerns, the court noted the refusal of drug manufacturers to market a flu vaccine until the federal government took over responsibility for possible adverse consequences, due to the industry's fear "that mass inoculation would subject them to enormous liability [from] lawsuits resulting from injuries caused by the vaccine." The court hastened to add that its ruling did "not mean, of course, that drug manufacturers are free of all liability for defective drugs. They are subject to liability for manufacturing defects, as well as under general principles of negligence, and for failure to warn of known or reasonably knowable side effects." Id. at 483 n.12.

4. A couple of courts followed *Brown*, exempting prescription drugs as a category from strict liability for defective design and warnings. See, e.g., Grundberg v. Upjohn Co., 813 P.2d 89 (Utah 1991); Young v. Key Pharmaceuticals, 922 P.2d 59 (Wash. 1996).

But most courts have rejected *Brown*, ruling that a prescription drug maker, to avoid liability under comment *k*, must establish that its *particular* drug is unavoidably dangerous (that is, that there was no feasible alternative design that could accomplish the same purpose at lesser risk) by passing a judicial risk-utility test. See, e.g., Tansy v. Dacomed Corp., 890 P.2d 881, 886 (Okla. 1994) penile implant that failed from metal fatigue had to be surgically removed; *held*, comment *k* shielded manufacturer: Comment *k* "applies only as an affirmative defense in those cases in which the following criteria are met: (1) the product is properly manufactured and contains adequate warnings, (2) its benefits justify its risks, and (3) the product was at the time of manufacture and distribution incapable of being made more safe. These issues are generally questions for the jury's determination, and must be determined on a case-by-case basis." Accord, Freeman v. Hoffman–La Roche, Inc., 618 N.W.2d 827 (Neb. 2000); Bryant v. Hoffmann–La Roche, Inc., 585 S.E.2d 723 (Ga. Ct. App. 2003) (good summary).

5. The "Wade–Keeton" Test and "Strict" Liability. Recall the "Wade–Keeton" test of defectiveness, examined in ch. 7, above. Apart from the consumer expectations test, the Wade–Keeton test was the clearest way that early courts and commentators found to define liability in a manner that was truly strict. As the notion of true "strict" products liability has been sliding into disfavor in design and warnings cases in recent years, the Wade–Keeton test has declined as well.

In time, both Dean Wade and Dean Keeton repudiated "their" hindsight test(s)—Dean Wade who never meant what he said, and Dean Keeton, who no longer believed what he said. See Wade, On the Effect in Product Liability of Knowledge Unavailable Prior to Marketing, Postscript, 58 N.Y.U.L.Rev. 734, 761 (1983); W.P. Keeton, D. Dobbs, R. Keeton & D. Owen, Prosser and Keeton on the Law of Torts 697–98 n. 21 (5th ed. 1984). The Third Restatement, adopting a negligence-type risk utility approach based on risks which are *foreseeable* at the time of sale, explicitly rejects the Wade–Keeton test. See Reporters' Note to § 2, cmt. *l*: "The idea has not worn well with time."

Is the test such a bad one? See Brooks v. Beech Aircraft Corp., 902 P.2d 54, 63 (N.M. 1995), recognizing that the Wade–Keeton test is now a misnomer, but reaffirming it where the facts did not show a true advancement in the technological state of the art: "[I]n those hypothetical instances in which technology known at the time of trial and technology knowable at the time of distribution differ—and outside of academic rationale we find little to suggest the existence in practice of unknowable design considerations—it is more fair that the manufacturers and suppliers who have profited from the sale of the product bear the risk of loss." See also Denny v. Ford Motor Co., 662 N.E.2d 730 (N.Y.1995) (acknowledging the test as the standard in design defect cases).

The test lives on. See, e.g., Golonka v. General Motors Corp., 65 P.3d 956, 963–64 (Ariz. Ct. App. 2003) (reaffirming and applying hindsight test).

6. The Products Liability Restatement. Section 6 of the Third Restatement prescribes liability rules for sellers of defective prescription drugs and medical devices. Section 6(d) provides noncontroversially that suppliers of such products are subject to liability for failing to provide "reasonable instructions or warnings" of all "foreseeable risks." Section 6(c) provides that manufacturers of such products are subject to liability for design defects

> if the foreseeable risks of harm posed by the drug or medical device are sufficiently great in relation to its foreseeable therapeutic benefits that reasonable health-care providers, knowing of such foreseeable risks and therapeutic benefits, would not prescribe the drug or medical device for any class of patients.

This novel provision has been highly controversial. See, e.g., Conk, Is There a Design Defect in the Restatement (Third) of Torts: Products Liability?, 109 Yale L.J. 1087, 1103–1104 (2000) (the Restatement should have applied the general risk-utility principles of § 2(b) design defect analysis to prescription drugs), to which the reporters responded, Henderson and Twerski, Drug Designs Are Different, 111 Yale L.J. 151 (2001)(prescription drugs are special), to which Mr. Conk replied, Conk, The True Test: Alternative Safer Designs for Drugs and Medical Devices in a Patent–Constrained Market, 49 UCLA L. Rev. 737 (2002) (no, they're not). See also Note, 45 Ariz. L. Rev. 173 (2003).

The courts have not liked § 6(c)'s narrow, and unusual, formulation of the design defect standard. See Freeman v. Hoffman–La Roche, Inc., 618 N.W.2d 827

(Neb. 2000) (criticizing and rejecting § 6(c)); Bryant v. Hoffmann–La Roche, Inc., 585 S.E.2d 723 (Ga. Ct. App. 2003) (same).

————

Anderson v. Owens–Corning Fiberglas Corp.

Supreme Court of California, 1991.
53 Cal.3d 987, 281 Cal.Rptr. 528, 810 P.2d 549.

■ PANELLI, ASSOCIATE JUSTICE.

[Defendants are or were manufacturers of asbestos products. Plaintiff alleged that he contracted asbestosis and other lung ailments through exposure to defendants' asbestos products (i.e., preformed blocks, cloth and cloth tape, cement, and floor tiles) at the Long Beach Naval Shipyard while working from 1941 to 1976 as an electrician in the vicinity of persons removing and installing asbestos insulation products in ships.]

[Plaintiff alleged that defendants, from scientific studies and medical data, knew of the hazards from exposure to asbestos products; that they knew users were not aware of asbestos hazards; and that they failed to warn users of the risks.] Defendants' pleadings raised the state-of-the-art defense, i.e., that even those at the vanguard of scientific knowledge at the time the products were sold could not have known that asbestos was dangerous to users in the concentrations associated with defendants' products.

[The trial court made various confused rulings related to the defendant's state-of-the-art evidence; the jury returned a verdict for the defendants; and the court granted the plaintiff's motion for a new trial. In a split opinion, the Court of Appeal affirmed.]

... Defendants contend that, if knowledge or knowability is irrelevant in a failure-to-warn case, then a manufacturer's potential liability is absolute, rendering it the virtual insurer of the product's safe use. Plaintiff, on the other hand, argues that to impose the requirement of knowledge or knowability improperly infuses a negligence standard into strict liability in contravention of the principles set out in our decisions from Greenman v. Yuba Power Products, Inc., 377 P.2d 897 (Cal.1963), to Brown v. Superior Court, 751 P.2d 470 (Cal.1988). * * *

[I]n Brown v. Superior Court, 751 P.2d 470 (Cal. 1988), [we] concluded that a manufacturer of prescription drugs is exempt from strict liability for defects in design and is not strictly liable for injuries caused by scientifically unknowable dangerous propensities in prescription drugs. [We therefore] refused to extend strict liability to the failure to warn of risks that were unknowable at the time of distribution. As we stated, if a manufacturer could not count on limiting its liability to risks that were known or knowable at the time of manufacture or distribution, it would be discouraged from developing new and improved products for fear that later significant advances in scientific knowledge would increase its liability.

[W]e are now squarely faced with the issue of knowledge and knowability in strict liability for failure to warn in other than the drug context. Whatever the ambiguity of *Brown*, we hereby adopt the requirement [of] the Restatement Second of Torts and acknowledged by ... the majority of jurisdictions, that knowledge or knowability is a component of strict liability for failure to warn.

[Precedent and policy both compel the conclusion that knowability is relevant to imposition of strict liability for failure to warn of a product hazard. An] important goal of strict liability is to spread the risks and costs of injury to those most able to bear them. [Yet commentators have noted that it is not feasible to spread risks by insurance if those risks are unforeseeable, and strict products liability doctrine was never intended to make manufacturers insurers] of the safety of their products. It was never [the] intention to impose *absolute* liability.

[In conclusion], a defendant in a strict products liability action based upon an alleged failure to warn of a risk of harm may present evidence of the state of the art, *i.e.*, evidence that the particular risk was neither known nor knowable by the application of scientific knowledge available at the time of manufacture and/or distribution.

[Affirmed; remanded for new trial.]

■ BROUSSARD, ASSOCIATE JUSTICE, concurring [wrote separately to emphasize that the opinion applied narrowly to claims of warnings defects, not to defects in design, such as West v. Johnson & Johnson Products, Inc., 220 Cal. Rptr. 437 (Ct. App. 1985) (plaintiff developed toxic shock syndrome from use of a tampon permitted to recover for design defect based on consumer expectations test)]. Thus, when the plaintiff in a strict products liability action relies solely on a consumer expectation theory, state-of-the-art evidence may not be relevant or admissible.

■ MOSK, ASSOCIATE JUSTICE, concurring and dissenting.

[P]rinciples of negligence [are no] more pronounced than in failure-to-warn cases. From the inception of the cause of action for strict liability on the theory of failure to warn, courts have impliedly or explicitly held that there can be no liability unless the plaintiff establishes that the defendant knew or should have known of the risk. * * *

We should consider the possibility of holding that failure-to-warn actions lie solely on a negligence theory. "[A]lthough mixing negligence and strict liability concepts is often a game of semantics, the game has more than semantic impact—it breeds confusion and inevitably, bad law." (Henderson & Twerski, Doctrinal Collapse in Products Liability: The Empty Shell of Failure to Warn, supra, 65 N.Y.U. L. Rev. at p. 278.) [H]owever, the majority are not ready to take that step....

NOTES

1. **The Liability Circle: The Rise and Fall of "Strict" Liability.** Beginning in California with *Greenman* in 1963, strict products liability in tort leapt

across the continent two years later to New Jersey, with Santor v. A & M Karagheusian, Inc., 207 A.2d 305 (N.J. 1965), bracketing the doctrine's explosive conquest of America through the early 1980s, reaching its zenith in New Jersey in 1982 with *Beshada* (an asbestos case). With *Feldman* (a drug case), decided in New Jersey in 1984, the strict products liability circle began to close, circling back to California with *Brown* (another drug case) in 1988, and *Anderson* (an asbestos case) in 1991, also in California, where the strict liability journey had all begun. A metaphor for the rise and fall of strict products liability doctrine across the nation, this series of cases mark the return of products liability law from its Great Strict Liability Experiment to its natural home in the Great Pit of Fault. See Owen, The Fault Pit, 26 Ga. L. Rev. 703 (1992).

Yet the common law is never still. Five years later, the California court was asked whether strict products liability in tort and warranty remained viable theories of liability in prescription drug warning cases once *Brown* and *Anderson* had limited a manufacturer's duty to warn to dangers that were known and knowable at the time. *Held*, strict products liability claims still are viable in California. Carlin v. Superior Court, 920 P.2d 1347 (Cal. 1996).

2. Post–Circle Developments: Strict Liability and Unknowable Risks. Beguiled by *Beshada*, a number of courts adopted its true strict liability approach. See Hayes v. Ariens Co., 462 N.E.2d 273 (Mass. 1984); Elmore v. Owens–Illinois, Inc., 673 S.W.2d 434 (Mo. 1984); Kisor v. Johns–Manville Corp., 783 F.2d 1337 (9th Cir. 1986) (Wash. law); Johnson v. Raybestos–Manhattan, Inc., 740 P.2d 548 (Haw. 1987). Other courts, on reasoning similar to *Anderson*'s, have allowed state-of-the-art evidence on "strict" liability failure to warn claims—meaning that the supplier may successfully defend such a case by showing that the risk was "unknowable" or unforeseeable. See, e.g., Fibreboard Corp. v. Fenton, 845 P.2d 1168 (Colo. 1993) (such evidence, admissible on design defect claims with respect to feasibility of alternative design, should also be admissible on failure to warn claims); Owens–Illinois, Inc. v. Zenobia, 601 A.2d 633 (Md.1992) (relying on § 402A cmt. *j*).

3. Rejecting Strict Liability: The Third Restatement. Viewing the *Feldman-Brown–Anderson* approach (and similar approaches in many state legislatures) as the evolving law's proper path, the Products Liability Restatement frames design and warning defect definitions in negligence terms—products are defective under §§ 2(b) and 2(c) only if manufacturers fail to take *"reasonable"* precautions to design away and warn about *"foreseeable"* product dangers.

4. Rejecting Strict Liability: *Vassallo v. Baxter Healthcare*. In Vassallo v. Baxter Healthcare Corp., 696 N.E.2d 909 (Mass. 1998), plaintiff complained of atypical autoimmune disease that she claimed was caused by silicone breast implants manufactured by the defendant's predecessor and implanted in her in 1977, about the time the medical community began to suspect a possible connection between silicone breast implants and systemic disorders.

The jury found for plaintiff, and the Supreme Judicial Court affirmed, ruling that the jury could find the risks foreseeable. But the court took the occasion to reformulate its strict products liability law to align it with "the clear majority rule" on what must be shown to recover in a failure to warn claim based on breach of implied warranty, Massachusetts' version of strict products liability. Accordingly, the Massachusetts court rejected its prior adoption of the Wade–Keeton hindsight approach and adopted a state-of-the-art standard conditioned on foreseeable risk.

Noting "[t]he thin judicial support for a hindsight approach to the duty to warn," for which a Third Restatement Reporters' Note cited only four states (Massachusetts, Hawaii, Pennsylvania, and Washington), the court observed:

> [A] majority of States, either by case law or by statute, follow the principle expressed in Restatement (Second) of Torts § 402A comment *j* (1965), which states that "the seller is required to give warning against [a danger] if he has knowledge, or by the application of reasonable, developed human skill and foresight should have knowledge, of the ... danger." See [citations]; Restatement (Third) of Torts: Products Liability, Reporters' Note to comment *m*, at 104 (1998) ("An overwhelming majority of jurisdictions supports the proposition that a manufacturer has a duty to warn only of risks that were known or should have been known to a reasonable person"). At least three jurisdictions that previously applied strict liability to the duty to warn in a products liability claim have reversed themselves, either by statute or by decision, and now require knowledge, or reasonable knowability as a component of such a claim. See Fibreboard Corp. v. Fenton, 845 P.2d 1168, 1172–1173 (Colo. 1993); Feldman v. Lederle Labs., 479 A.2d 374 (N.J. 1984); La. Rev. Stat. Ann. § 9:2800.59(B) (West 1997). The change in the law of New Jersey is particularly relevant, because we relied in part on New Jersey law in formulating the strict liability standard expressed in [Hayes v. Ariens Co., 462 N.E.2d 273 (Mass.1984), citing Beshada v. Johns–Manville Prods. Corp., 447 A.2d 539 (N.J. 1982)].

Id. at 922. The court concluded:

> In recognition of the clear judicial trend regarding the duty to warn in products liability cases, and the principles stated in Restatement (Third) of Torts: Products Liability, *supra* at § 2(c) and comment *m*, we hereby revise our law to state that a defendant will not be held liable under an implied warranty of merchantability for failure to warn or provide instructions about risks that were not reasonably foreseeable at the time of sale or could not have been discovered by way of reasonable testing prior to marketing the product.

Id. at 923.

5.   The Persistence of Strict Liability: *Sternhagen v. Dow.* In 1981, Charles Sterhagen, a medical doctor, was diagnosed with cancer from which he later died. Sternhagen's estate sued the manufacturers of a herbicide, 2,4–D, alleging that Sternhagen's cancer resulted from his exposure to 2,4–D while he was spraying crops during the summers of 1948–1950. Defendants asserted that "neither they, nor medical science, knew or had reason to know of any alleged cancer-causing properties of the herbicide 2,4–D during the years 1948 through 1950." Sternhagen v. Dow Company, 935 P.2d 1139 (Mont. 1997), involved a certified question from the federal district court to the Supreme Court of Montana:

> In a strict products liability case for injuries caused by an inherently unsafe product, is the manufacturer conclusively presumed to know the dangers inherent in his product, or is state-of-the-art evidence admissible to establish whether the manufacturer knew or through the exercise of reasonable human foresight should have known of the danger?

Id. at 1139. The court concluded that, notwithstanding 402A's position in comment *j* that "the seller is required to give warning [only] if he has knowledge, or by the application of reasonable, developed human skill and foresight should have knowledge, of the presence of the ... danger," Montana law prohibits the admission of state-of-the-art evidence in strict products liability cases. Id. at 1141. Conflicting with comment *j*'s state-of-the-art approach are the strict products liability policies the court had long ago accepted: maximum deterrence of product accidents; cost-spreading; cost-internalization by manufacturers; the difficulty of proving a manufacturer's negligence; and consumer reliance on manufacturers for product safety.

> Under the imputation of knowledge doctrine, which is based on strict liability's focus on the product and not the manufacturer's conduct, knowledge of a product's undiscovered or undiscoverable dangers shall be imputed to the manufacturer. [T]he imputation of knowledge doctrine, and concomitant rejection of the state-of-the-art defense ... reinforces our commitment to provide the maximum protection for consumers....

Id. at 1143.

The court noted its previous acceptance of the Wade–Keeton imputed-knowledge "hindsight test" employed by the Oregon court in Phillips v. Kimwood Machine Co., 525 P.2d 1033, 1036–37 (Or. 1974):

> A dangerously defective article would be one which a reasonable person would not put into the stream of commerce if he had knowledge of its harmful character. The test, therefore, is whether the seller would be negligent if he sold the article knowing of the risk involved. Strict liability imposes what amounts to constructive knowledge of the condition of the product. [Put another way, *Phillips*] explained that a way to determine if a product is unreasonably defective, is to assume that the manufacturer knew of the product's potential dangers and then ask whether a manufacturer with such knowledge should have done something about the danger before the product was sold.

* * *

> Despite the adoption of the state-of-the-art defense in ["an overwhelming majority of"] other jurisdictions, recognition of the defense in the Restatement (Third) of the Law of Torts: Products Liability, and the defendants' assertion that public policy supports adoption of the defense, we choose to continue to adhere to [our clear precedent] which focuses on the core principles and remedial purposes underlying strict products liability. Strict liability without regard to fault is the only doctrine that fulfills the public interest goals of protecting consumers, compensating the injured and making those who profit from the market bear the risks and costs associated with the defective or dangerous products which they place in the stream of commerce.

Id. at 1144–47.

6. Further Persistence: *Green v. Smith & Nephew*. A hospital worker sued the manufacturer of high-protein, powdered latex gloves in strict liability for damages from a severe allergic reaction she suffered from exposure to the proteins in the gloves she wore at work from 1978–91. During this time, the healthcare community generally was unaware that persons could develop latex allergy. The trial court instructed the jury:

> Lack of knowledge on the part of S & N that proteins in natural rubber latex may sensitize and cause allergic reactions to some individuals is not a defense to the claims made by the plaintiff Green in this action. A manufacturer is responsible for harm caused by a defective and unreasonably dangerous product even if the manufacturer had no knowledge or could not have known of the risk of harm presented by the condition of the product.

The jury ruled for the plaintiff, the court of appeals affirmed, and defendant appealed to the Supreme Court of Wisconsin. In Green v. Smith & Nephew AHP,

Inc., 629 N.W.2d 727, 735–36 (Wis. 2001), *held*, under the consumer expectations test, a product may be found defective and unreasonably dangerous regardless of whether manufacturer knew or could have known of the hazard its product presented to consumers.

> [W]e conclude [that] the circuit court did not err in instructing the jury that a product can be deemed defective and unreasonably dangerous regardless of whether the manufacturer of that product knew or could have known of the risk of harm the product presented to consumers. * * *
>
> Foreseeability of harm is an element of negligence [which] hinges in large part on the defendant's conduct under circumstances involving a foreseeable risk of harm [whereas] strict products liability focuses ... on the nature of the defendant's product.... Thus, regardless of whether a manufacturer could foresee potential risks of harm inherent in its defective and unreasonably dangerous product, strict products liability holds that manufacturer responsible for injuries caused by that product.

Id. at 731–46. Dissenting, Justice Sykes argued that the majority opinion was "seriously out of step with product liability law as it has evolved" and that it "keeps Wisconsin in the much-criticized and rapidly dwindling minority" of consumer-expectation test jurisdictions. Id. at 763. Reasoning that the majority's discussion of the role of foreseeability in products liability law was misguided, Justice Sykes favored the Third Restatement's approach in section 2 of defining design and warning defects in terms of foreseeable risk.

7. Burden of Proof. Under the Third Restatement and most case law, a defendant's duty extends only to foreseeable risks and requires only reasonable precautionary measures. This leaves plaintiff with the burden of proof on foreseeability and the availability of feasible precautionary measures to avoid the risks. By contrast, *Feldman* and state-of-the-art defense provisions in a number of state reform statutes place the burden on defendants to prove that a risk was unforeseeable or that no reasonable means was available to avoid it. See Cavanaugh v. Skil Corp., 751 A.2d 518, 521 (N.J.2000) ("in asserting the defense, the defendant must establish the state-of-the-art at the time of distribution [but] the plaintiff must prove the product's non-conformity with the feasible technology to overcome what is otherwise an absolute bar to recovery").

8. The Bad Blood Cases.

A. Hepatitis. The first cases to highlight the state of the art/unavoidable risk issue involved blood transfusions of blood infected with serum hepatitis, causing hepatitis in tens of thousands of transfusion patients each year. The fatality rate of the disease is 5–10% for all cases, and nearly 25% for patients over 40. There is still no reliable blood test to determine whether blood is infected with this disease, making the serum hepatitis risk truly both "undiscoverable" and "unavoidable."

An early case held the supplier of hepatitis-infected blood strictly liable, holding that the blood was undeniably "defective." Cunningham v. MacNeal Mem. Hosp., 266 N.E.2d 897 (Ill. 1970). See also Community Blood Bank v. Russell, 196 So.2d 115 (Fla. 1967). The *Cunningham* case was widely criticized, see, e.g., Notes, 69 Mich. L. Rev. 1172 (1971), and 66 Nw. U. L. Rev. 80 (1971), and it was rejected by virtually every other court. See, e.g., Brody v. Overlook Hosp., 317 A.2d 392 (N.J. Super. Ct. 1974), aff'd, 332 A.2d 596 (N.J. 1975).

To protect the blood supply, almost all jurisdictions have now enacted "blood shield" statutes that limit a supplier's responsibility to negligence, often by defining the provision of blood or blood products as a "service" rather than a "sale." Such statutes often apply broadly to all blood and human tissue products, even if manufactured by commercial enterprises. See, e.g., Scher v. Bayer Corp., 258 F. Supp. 2d 190 (E.D.N.Y. 2003) (strict liability in tort and warranty claims dismissed against commercial supplier of allegedly defective blood derivative product, Hyp–Rho(D), used to prevent hemolytic disease in newborn children of Rh–Negative mothers and Rh–Positive fathers; case allowed to proceed on negligence claims). See Products Liability Restatement § 19(c) ("Human blood and human tissue, even when provided commercially, are not subject to the rules of this Restatement.").

B. AIDS. Many recent cases involve AIDS transmitted by transfused blood and blood products. It was not until 1984 that the medical community learned that AIDS was transmitted by blood (and 1985 when a reliable test for the presence of the virus in blood was first available), so suppliers of blood and blood products sold before that time generally were protected by the blood shield statutes. See, e.g., McKee v. Miles Labs., Inc., 675 F.Supp. 1060 (E.D. Ky.1987). Compare Doe v. Miles Labs., Inc., 927 F.2d 187 (4th Cir. 1991) (statute did not apply; policy considerations precluded use of strict liability, and no negligence on facts); Rogers v. Miles Labs., Inc., 802 P.2d 1346 (Wash. 1991) (ditto). The various collection, testing and heat-treating procedures devised during the mid–1980s now permit virtually 100% assurance of detecting or killing the virus if due care is exercised.

Hence, most such cases today are decided on the basis of negligence, and strict liability in tort or warranty is generally not involved at all. See, e.g., Spann v. Irwin Mem. Blood Centers, 40 Cal.Rptr.2d 360 (Ct. App. 1995); Brown v. United Blood Services, 858 P.2d 391 (Nev. 1993); Zaccone v. American Red Cross, 872 F.Supp. 457 (N.D. Ohio 1994) (summary judgment for defendant on negligence); Christiana v. Southern Baptist Hosp., 867 So.2d 809 (La. Ct. App. 2004) (blood shield law in effect at time of transfusion protected hospital that supplied blood from patient's strict liability claim).

Because of the difficulties of proof of negligence, such claims often fail. See, e.g., Johnson v. American National Red Cross, 578 S.E.2d 106 (Ga. 2003) (negligence claims against blood bank for HIV and fear of HIV failed). Compare Sherwood v. Danbury Hosp., 896 A.2d 777 (Conn.2006)(physician, not hospital, had duty to inform patient of risk that blood used in transfusion during surgery may not have been tested for presence of HIV antibodies); In re Factor VIII or IX Concentrate Blood Prods. Liab. Litig., 408 F.Supp.2d 569 (N.D.Ill.2006) (dismissing negligence claims by hemophiliacs from Italy, Germany, and U.K. for contracting HIV or hepatitis B virus from blood-clotting products manufactured by defendants on grounds of forum non conveniens).

For a history of developments in AIDS research, see Kozup v. Georgetown Univ., 663 F.Supp. 1048 (D.D.C. 1987), rev'd on other grounds, 851 F.2d 437 (D.C. Cir. 1988). For citations to blood shield laws in 48 states, see Roberts v. Suburban Hosp. Ass'n, Inc., 532 A.2d 1081, 1086 n. 3 (Md. Ct. Spec. App.1987) (AIDS) (only jurisdictions then without such statutes were N.J., Vt., & D.C.).

In the face of a blood shield statute, how can you assist a potential client who contracted AIDS or hepatitis from a blood transfusion? Do you decline the case? For an administrative compensation scheme, see Klein, A Legislative Alternative to "No Cause" Liability in Blood Products Litigation, 12 Yale J. on Reg. 107 (1995).

9. Disaggregating Products Liability Law. How about using true strict liability for some products, but not for others? Perhaps strict liability should apply only to the "worst" products, such as asbestos. This, of course, is what *Feldman* effectively did by restricting *Beshada* to its facts. See also Halphen v. Johns–

Manville Sales Corp., 484 So.2d 110 (La. 1986). Or perhaps strict liability should apply to all products except the "best"—such as prescription drugs, as *Brown* did, or the *very* best, as *Feldman* held.

Are prescription drugs and blood really so socially beneficial that they deserve special protection? How about pacemakers? Glasses? Automobiles? Food? Is asbestos really so socially objectionable as to deserve disparate legal treatment? How about cigarettes? Alcohol? Cheap handguns? And how about dangerous prescription drugs, like Thalidomide? Phen–Fen? Vioxx?

The constitutionality of the *Beshada–Feldman* special treatment of asbestos was narrowly upheld in In re Asbestos Litigation, 829 F.2d 1233, 1244 (3d Cir. 1987) (1–1–1) ("the policies of risk spreading, compensation for victims, and simplification of trials in the highly unusual circumstances of asbestos claims furnish an adequate, albeit minimal, basis for eliminating the state-of-the-art defense in these cases"). Concurring, Judge Becker reasoned that "the New Jersey Supreme Court has determined a legislative fact—that the hazards of asbestos exposure were knowable to the industry at all relevant times." Id. at 1245. Judge Hunter concluded: "Today this court has ruled that the manufacturers of one product may not use the state-of-the-art defense. That product is asbestos. . . . This is just plain wrong and I dissent." Id. at 1252.

10.   The Politics of Tort Law.

A.   In general. Do the *Brown* and *Anderson* opinions seem like they came from the same court that decided *Greenman, Cronin, and Barker*? Did they? *Brown* was decided within a few months after Chief Justice Rose Bird and two other "liberal" justices were denied reelection and replaced by judges with more "moderate" views. At least in the Chief Justice's case, the campaign against her centered on her refusal to uphold death penalty convictions.

B.   Tort "reform." Since the late 1970s, insurers and manufacturers have pressed for statutory tort and products liability reform, first focusing on the Congress and then on state legislatures. An important issue in the debate has been the role of "state of the art" and liability for unavoidable dangers, on which many states have passed statutes. Which approaches are best?

(1) Evidence of technological feasibility may be considered by the trier of fact. *Washington*, Wash. Rev. Code Ann. § 7.72.050(1);

(2) Evidence that the product conformed to the state of the art, as distinguished from industry standards, raises a rebuttable presumption that the product was not defective and the defendant not negligent. *Colorado*, Colo. Rev. Stat. Ann. § 13–21–403(1)(a);

(3) A defendant is not liable for a product's design if "there was not a practical and technically feasible alternative design that our have prevented the harm without substantially impairing the" product's function, nor for "an unavoidably unsafe aspect of the product if it was accompanied by" a warning that a reasonably prudent person would provide. *New Jersey*, N.J. Rev. Stat. § 2A:58C–3(1) and (3);

(4) A defendant is not liable for defects in design or warnings unless plaintiff proves that defendant knew or should have known of the risk, "in light of reasonably available knowledge." *Mississippi*, Miss. Code Ann. § 11–1–63;

(5) A manufacturer is not liable for a design defect if it proves that the alternative design proposed by plaintiff "was not feasible, in light of then-existing reasonably available scientific and technological knowledge or then-existing economic practicality." *Louisiana*, La. Rev. Stat. Ann. § 2800.59(A)(3);

(6) State of the art, meaning risk "was not known and could not reasonably be discovered" at time of sale, is an affirmative defense only to warning claims. *Missouri*, Mo. Rev. Stat. § 537.764; or

(7) Conformance to state of the art, meaning knowledge and techniques "in existence and reasonably feasible for use at the time of manufacture," is an affirmative defense. *Arizona*, Ariz. Rev. Stat. Ann. § 12–683(1).

Note the web of interrelationships between state of the art, product deterioration, and the multitude of other issues related to the passage of time.

11. Europe. A close cousin of the state-of-the-art defense in Europe is the "development risk" defense. Article 7(e) of the EC Directive provides that a producer of a defective product shall not be liable if it proves:

> that the state of scientific and technical knowledge at the time when he put the product into circulation was not such as to enable the existence of the defect to be discovered.

See generally Stapleton, Bugs in Anglo–American Products Liability, 53 S.C. L. Rev. 1225 (2002); Howells and Mildred, Is European Products Liability Law More Protective than the Restatement (Third) of Torts: Products Liability?, 65 Tenn. L. Rev. 985 (1998); Newdick, Risk, Uncertainty and "Knowledge" in the Development Risk Defense, 20 Anglo–Am. L. Rev. 309 (1991); Newdick, The Development Risk Defense of the Consumer Protection Act, 47 Cambridge L.J. 455 (1988); Note, Two Roads Diverged in a Yellow Wood: The European Community Stays on the Path to Strict Liability, 27 Fordham Int'l L.J. 1940 (2004).

12. Concluding Reflections: Strict Liability or Negligence? Each year more and more substances—drugs, pesticides, powders, food additives, and untold other types of chemical and other substances—are discovered to be carcinogenic, teratogenic (causing birth defects), or otherwise harmful in unexpected ways. So, which way is it for such toxic substances, strict liability or negligence?

Which way *should* it be? Should manufacturers of such products bear the "unavoidable" losses from previously unknown and "undiscoverable" hazards? Or should consumers? Should the answer be the same for all types of toxic substances? Or should it depend on the type and purpose of the substance?

13. On state of the art, unavoidable dangers, and related issues in American law, see generally Cupp, Rethinking Conscious Design Liability for Prescription Drugs: The New *Restatement* Standard Versus a Negligence Approach, 63 Geo. Wash. L. Rev. 301 (1994); V. Schwartz, Unavoidably Unsafe Products: Clarifying the Meaning and Policy Behind Comment *k*, 42 Wash. & Lee L.Rev. 1139 (1985); Wade, On the Effect in Product Liability of Knowledge Unavailable Prior to Marketing, 58 N.Y.U. L. Rev. 734 (1983); Page, Generic Product Risks: The Case Against Comment *k* and for Strict Tort Liability, 58 N.Y.U. L. Rev. 853 (1983); D. Owen, Products Liability Law § 10.4 (2d ed. 2008); 1 D. Owen, M.S. Madden, & M. Davis, Madden & Owen on Products Liability § 10:4–:8 (3d ed.2000).

4. INTERGENERATIONAL HARM

Chemical compounds and other toxic substances increasingly are discovered to generate chromosomal alteration that may cause genetic defects in subsequent generations. The effects of such defects may spread from generation to generation. If the child, grandchild—or great grandchild—of a person exposed to some toxin is born with a short finger as a result, or a handicap more severe, should the descendant have a products liability claim against the party that manufactured the product generations earlier?

Grover v. Eli Lilly & Co.

Supreme Court of Ohio, 1992.
63 Ohio St.3d 756, 591 N.E.2d 696.

■ WRIGHT, J.

The United States District Court for the Northern District of Ohio has certified the following question to us:

"Does Ohio recognize a cause of action on behalf of a child born prematurely, and with severe birth defects, if it can be established that such injuries were proximately caused by defects in the child's mother's reproductive system, those defects in turn being proximately caused by the child's grandmother ingesting a defective drug (DES) during her pregnancy with the child's mother?"

For purposes of this question, we are required to assume that Charles Grover can prove that his injuries were proximately caused by his mother's exposure to DES. We are not evaluating the facts of this case, but determining, as a matter of law, whether Charles Grover has a legally cognizable cause of action.

DES was prescribed to pregnant women during the 1940s, 1950s and 1960s to prevent miscarriage. The FDA banned its use by pregnant women in 1971 after medical studies discovered that female children exposed to the drug *in utero* had a high incidence of a rare type of vaginal cancer. See 36 Fed. Reg. 21,537 (1971). Candy Grover was exposed to DES as a fetus. Her son, Charles Grover, claims that his mother's DES-induced injuries were the cause of his premature birth and resulting [cerebral palsy].

[T]he child's potential cause of action in such cases [is called] a "preconception tort" [because] a child is pursuing liability against a party for a second injury that flows from an initial injury to the mother that occurred before the child was conceived.

Only a handful of courts have addressed whether a child has a cause of action for a preconception tort. One recurring issue is whether a child has a cause of action if a physician negligently performs a surgical procedure on the mother, such as an abortion or a Caesarean section, and the negligently performed procedure causes complications during childbirth several years later that injure the infant. See Albala v. New York, 429 N.E.2d 786 (N.Y. 1981) (child has no cause of action for doctor's negligence during abortion performed four years prior to his conception); Bergstreser v. Mitchell, 577 F.2d 22 (8th Cir. 1978) (construing Missouri law) (child has a cause of action against a doctor based on the doctor's negligence during a Caesarean section performed two years prior to the child's conception). In another malpractice suit, the Illinois Supreme Court recognized that a child had a cause of action against a hospital that negligently transfused her mother with Rh-positive blood eight years prior to the child's conception. Renslow v. Mennonite Hospital, 367 N.E.2d 1250 (Ill. 1977). As a result, the mother's body produced antibodies to the Rh-positive blood that later injured her fetus during pregnancy. See also Monusko v. Postle, 437 N.W.2d 367 (Mich. App. 1989) (allowing cause of action by child against her mother's physicians for failure to inoculate the mother with rubella vaccine prior to the child's conception).

In McAuley v. Wills, 303 S.E.2d 258 (Ga. 1983), the Supreme Court of Georgia evaluated a wrongful death action brought on behalf of an infant who died during childbirth due to the mother's paralysis. The suit was brought against the driver who had originally caused the mother's paralysis in an automobile accident. The court held that a person may owe a duty of care to a child conceived in the future, but also held that the injury in that case was too remote *as a matter of law* to support recovery. The driver could not reasonably foresee, as a matter of law, that his lack of care in driving a motor vehicle would result in complications during the delivery of a child who was not yet conceived at the time of the accident.

These cases are significantly different from . . . the case before us. The cause of action certified to us involves the scope of liability for the manufacture of a prescription drug that allegedly had devastating side effects on the original patient's female fetus. However, this case is not about the devastating side effects of DES on the women who were exposed to it [but] with the rippling effects of that exposure on yet another generation, when that female child reaches sexual maturity and bears a child. Because a plaintiff in Charles Grover's position cannot be injured until the original patient's child bears children, the second injury [typically occurs] more than sixteen years after the ingestion of the drug.

Several courts have addressed a fact pattern virtually identical to the facts of the case currently before this court. The New York Court of Appeals held that a child does not have a cause of action, in negligence or strict liability, against a prescription drug company based on the manufacture of DES if the child was never exposed to the drug *in utero*. Enright v. Eli Lilly & Co., 570 N.E.2d 198 (N.Y.), cert. denied, 502 U.S. 868 (1991). The court relied in part on its earlier opinion in *Albala*. In both cases, the court was concerned with the "staggering implications of any proposition which would honor claims assuming the breach of an identifiable duty for less than a perfect birth and by what standard and the difficulty in establishing a standard or definition of perfection. . . ." *Albala*. See *Enright*. The court was troubled by the possibility that doctors would forgo certain treatments of great benefit to persons already in existence out of fear of possible effects on future children. *Albala*. In *Enright*, the court noted that "the cause of action plaintiffs ask us to recognize here could not be confined without the drawing of artificial and arbitrary boundaries. For all we know, the rippling effects of DES exposure may extend for genera-

tions. It is our duty to confine liability within manageable limits....
Limiting liability to those who ingested the drug or were exposed to it *in
utero* serves this purpose." See also Loerch v. Eli Lilly & Co., 445 N.W.2d
560 (Minn. 1989) (the evenly divided Supreme Court of Minnesota affirmed, without opinion, a lower court's decision that a child who was not
exposed to DES has no cause of action).

One court has held that a plaintiff situated similarly to Charles Grover
has a cause of action. The United States Court of Appeals for the Seventh
District reversed a lower court's directed verdict on the issue of a pharmaceutical company's liability to a child for injuries caused by a premature
birth. McMahon v. Eli Lilly & Co., 774 F.2d 830 (7th Cir. 1985). The court
concluded that under Illinois law the company could be liable for failing to
warn of the dangerous propensities of the drug, and need not have
anticipated a particular side effect.

We find the reasoning applied by the New York Court of Appeals
persuasive on the issue currently before us. [While the pharmaceutical
companies might have foreseen injuries to the reproductive systems of
fetuses *in utero* of mothers who took DES,] this generalized knowledge is
[not] sufficient to impose liability for injuries to a third party that occur
twenty-eight years later.

Knowledge of a risk to one class of plaintiffs does not necessarily
extend an actor's liability to every potential plaintiff. While we must
assume that DES was the proximate cause of Charles Grover's injuries, an
actor is not liable for every harm that may result from his actions. "...
The plaintiff sues in her own right for a wrong personal to her, and not as
the vicarious beneficiary of a breach of duty to another." Palsgraf v. Long
Island RR. Co., 162 N.E. 99, 100 (N.Y. 1928). An actor does not have a duty
to a particular plaintiff unless the risk to that plaintiff is within the actor's
"range of apprehension." *Id.* "... If the actor's conduct creates such a
recognizable risk of harm only to a particular class of persons, the fact that
it in fact causes harm to a person of a different class, to whom the actor
could not reasonably have anticipated injury, does not make the actor liable
to the persons so injured." Rest. (2d) of Torts (1965), Section 281, Comment *c*; [citation]. The existence of a legal duty is a question for the court,
unless alternate inferences are feasible based on the facts. *Palsgraf.*

When a pharmaceutical company [manufactures drugs that are pre-
scribed] to a woman, the company, under ordinary circumstances, does not
have a duty to her daughter's infant who will be conceived twenty-eight
years later. Charles Grover's injuries are not the result of his own exposure
to the drug, but are allegedly caused by his mother's injuries from her *in
utero* exposure to the drug. Because of the remoteness in time and causation, we hold that Charles Grover does not have an independent cause of
action, and answer the district court's question in the negative. A pharmaceutical company's liability for the distribution or manufacture of a defective prescription drug does not extend to persons who were never exposed
to the drug, either directly or *in utero.*

Judgment accordingly.

■ Moyer, C.J., Holmes and H. Brown, JJ., concur.

■ Sweeney, Douglas and Resnick, JJ., dissent.

■ Alice Robie Resnick, J., dissenting.

I dissent from the result reached in this case, but more importantly from the superficial treatment of the issue which was certified to this court, in light of its complexity. . . .

As the devastating effects of DES continue to mount, so too does the legal debate concerning liability for the damage caused by the drug. * * *

The majority is persuaded by the rationale of the New York Court of Appeals' decision in *Enright*. [T]he majority essentially holds that for public policy reasons there is no legal duty owed to a person who was not *in utero* at the time of injury [blithely accepting] the DES manufacturers' age-old public policy arguments that the imposition of liability would invoke "staggering implications" and "rippling effects," or would require doctors to forgo certain treatments of great benefit to persons already in existence. But as the dissent in *Enright* cogently points out, ". . . this sort of 'floodgates of litigation' [alarm] seems singularly unpersuasive in view of our Court's repeated admonitions that it is not 'a ground for denying a cause of action that there will be a proliferation of claims' and '. . . if a cognizable wrong has been committed, that there must be a remedy, whatever the burden of the courts.' " . . . "Beyond that, however, when defendants' arguments are applied here to urge that although the claims of DES daughters should be allowed the claims of the granddaughters should not be, their forebodings strike a particularly ironic note: i.e., the very fact of the 'insidious nature' of DES which may make the defendants liable for injuries to a future generation is advanced as the reason why they should not be liable for injuries to that generation." *Enright*, supra, 570 N.E.2d at 207 (Hancock, J., dissenting).

I discern no sound basis, in law or public policy, for holding that there is no duty owed to persons in Charles Grover's position. We are dealing with a drug which was widely prescribed for many years to virtually millions of pregnant women. . . . Petitioners aver that, despite warnings from independent researchers dating back to the 1930s that DES caused reproductive tract abnormalities and cancer in exposed animal offspring, that drug companies, including Eli Lilly, performed no tests as to the effects of DES on the developing fetus, either in animals or humans. Petitioners also assert that by 1947 there were twenty-one studies which supported these findings. . . .

In light of the foregoing there can be no question that pharmaceutical companies should have known the dangers of this drug. If in the 1930s and 1940s the manufacturers of DES knew or should have known of the reproductive system defects in the animal fetus exposed to DES, how then is it not foreseeable that this might mean abnormalities in the human fetus' reproductive system? In other words, it would appear that DES manufacturers knew or should have known that the human fetus exposed *in utero* might have a defect in the female reproductive system. Additionally, is it not then foreseeable that that female fetus would at some point seek to employ the defective reproductive system? The answer must be a resounding "yes." Hence, there can be no logic to the holding of the majority that "[b]ecause of the remoteness in time and causation, ... Charles Grover does not have an independent cause of action." What could have a more direct causal connection than a premature birth by a woman who was known to have an incompetent cervix? From this it becomes readily apparent that DES grandchildren were a foreseeable group of plaintiffs. It can hardly be argued that there is no duty owed to a *foreseeable* plaintiff. In the landmark case of *Palsgraf v. Long Island RR. Co.*, the court held that an actor has a duty to all plaintiffs within the actor's "range of apprehension." Indeed, a federal court of appeals had recently stated: "There was sufficient evidence from which a jury could reasonably have found that in 1955 Lilly knew or should have known that DES might cause reproductive abnormalities, such as prematurity, in the female offspring of women exposed to DES during pregnancy." *McMahon.*

While both foreseeability and proximate cause are readily apparent in this case, it is well recognized that in strict products liability claims, unlike causes of action sounding in negligence, the concepts of duty and foreseeability are of diminished significance. See Jorgensen v. Meade Johnson Labs., Inc., 483 F.2d 237 (10th Cir. 1973); [citation]. Even the *Enright* court recognized this concept by citing its decision in *Albala*, for this proposition. Additionally, Prosser & Keeton state: "A perplexing problem that remains in this area is whether claims should be permitted where the harmful contact with the mother occurs even before the child is conceived, as from ingestion of a defective drug causing chromosomal damage to the mother's ovum, or injury to her uterus during a preconception operation. A small number of courts have allowed recovery, but New York in a *thinly reasoned* case has recently ruled that a child has no cause of action for preconception torts upon the mother.... These are indeed staggering problems, that will have to be dealt with *carefully* in future toxic tort contexts such as these, but they by no means require that a blanket no-duty rule be applied in pre-conception injury cases where such problems do not exist." (Emphasis added.) W.P. Keeton, D. Dobbs, R. Keeton, & D. Owen, Prosser & Keeton on Torts (5 Ed. 1984) 369, Section 55.

Conclusion

DES continues to create difficult legal and social problems nationwide. The majority has failed to consider the uniqueness of DES. Instead, it has simply applied an arbitrary "blanket no-duty rule." Today's holding will have profound and devastating effects. To hold under these circumstances that Charles Grover's injuries were not foreseeable is to ignore an entire body of scientific information which was available or could have easily become available with a measure of care concerning the effects of DES on subsequent generations.

[I]ndividuals such as Charles Grover properly have a cause of action for their injuries. This in no way opens the floodgates because litigation can easily be concluded with Charles Grover's generation. Moreover, the majority completely disregards the fact that the petitioners still bear the burden of proving proximate cause. I strenuously dissent.

NOTES

1. Right result?

2. The *Grover* majority referred to Loerch v. Eli Lilly & Co., 445 N.W.2d 560 (Minn. 1989) (3–3 decision), which upheld the trial court's dismissal of a similar third generation DES claim for cerebral palsy damages (rendering the grandchild a spastic quadriplegic) arising out of the grandchild's premature delivery by a DES daughter. In reaching its decision, "the most difficult and challenging of any . . . encountered by this Court in either an official or personal capacity," the trial judge relied heavily on *Palsgraf*:

> A discussion of the concept of duty inevitably beckons a discussion of the landmark decision in Palsgraf v. Long Island R. Co., 162 N.E. 99 (N.Y. 1928). Duty, as defined therein, is a function of the foreseeability of injury to the plaintiff. Chief Judge Cardozo stated:
>
> > The risk reasonably to be perceived defines the duty to be obeyed, and risk imparts relation; it is risk to another or to others within the range of apprehension.
>
> In writing for the majority, Chief Justice Cardozo wrote that the defendant could owe no duty to the plaintiff because the alleged wrong had no relation to her. The majority was of the opinion that the conduct was not a wrong in relation to this particular plaintiff. It was the opinion of the Court that Mrs. Palsgraf was simply too far away; too remote of an individual, for the defendant to have owed any duty.
>
> In his forceful dissent, Justice Andrews rejected Cardozo's view of recovery predicated on duty. Instead, Justice Andrews articulated the standard of "proximate cause." Justice Andrews explained:
>
> > What we do mean by the word "proximate" is, that because of convenience, of public policy, of a rough sense of justice, the law arbitrarily declines to trace a series of events beyond a certain point. This is not logic. It is practical politics. Take our rule as to fires. Sparks from my burning haystack set on fire my house and my neighbor's. I may recover from a negligent railroad. He may not. Yet the wrongful act as directly harmed the one as the other. We may regret that the line was drawn just where it was, but drawn somewhere it had to be.

The *Loerch* court thought that both approaches led to a ruling of no liability. Under a Cardozo analysis, defendant owed no duty to the grandchild, a third-generation plaintiff far removed from the original tortious act who was "simply too remote in time to be justifiably within the zone of danger." The same result would obtain under an Andrews analysis: even conceding a causal link between the grandchild's injuries and the defendant's alleged tortious conduct, as a matter of public policy and "practical politics" (the chilling effect on medical research and development), "a line has to be drawn cutting off liability." Hennepin Cty. Dist. Ct., Minn., 1988.

3. In Catherwood v. American Sterilizer Co., 498 N.Y.S.2d 703 (Sup. Ct. 1986), the plaintiff was allegedly exposed to ethylene oxide in the course of her employment. She subsequently conceived and gave birth to a daughter with chromosomal damage, which she attributed to her previous chemical exposure. The trial court dismissed her complaint against the manufacturer and her employers, reasoning that there is a "policy need for limitation of liability in exposure and ingestion cases." The Appellate Division affirmed, 3–2, 511 N.Y.S.2d 805 (App. Div.), and the Court of Appeals dismissed an appeal, 515 N.E.2d 908 (N.Y. 1987). In a concurring opinion, Lawton, J., remarked:

> I add only my concern over judicial recognition of a cause of action on behalf of a newborn for genetic damage. The occurrence which serves as the basis for liability happened to the parent who, if liability can be established, is entitled to recover for all damages naturally flowing from said occurrence, including genetic injury. No cause of action, however, should accrue to the issue of said person. Many genetic abnormalities pass from generation to generation. Logically, if the second generation is entitled to recovery, so would succeeding generations. The extent and costs of this new cause of action are overwhelming. Such matters cannot be reasonably decided on a case-by-case basis, but rather should be left to the Legislature to fashion relief where appropriate.

511 N.Y.S.2d at 806. Callahan, J.P., and Green, J., dissented:

> We cannot agree that there is no cause of action for an infant for a preconception tort based upon a products liability theory [for failing to warn the mother of] the dangers inherent in her exposure to toxic chemicals at her workplace. [O]nce a causal relationship has been established, the liability of the manufacturer is extended to the entire class of persons thereby affected regardless of privity, foreseeability or due care [citation]. The limits of liability in this case can be defined and limited. [Defendants] would have no greater liability than if they had put a defective product on the market that physically injured a live human being many years hence [citations].

4. *Loerch* was the first of a very few *third* generation cases; *Grover*, decided by a slim 4–3 margin, is one of the more recent. The trial court judge in *Loerch* was clearly torn by his decision; the Minnesota Supreme Court was split in the case 3–3; the New York *Enright* decision, discussed in *Grover*, was split. Other cases will follow. How should they be decided?

5. On intergenerational harm, see Robertson, Toward Rational Boundaries of Tort Liability for Injury to the Unborn: Prenatal Injuries, Preconception Injuries and Wrongful Life, 1978 Duke L.J. 1401; Notes, 69 Fordham L. Rev. 2555 (2001) (preconception tort law); 62 U. Cin. L. Rev. 283 (1993) (noting *Grover*); 17 Am.J.L. & Med. 435 (1991); D. Owen, Products Liability Law § 10.5 (2d ed. 2008).

5. POST-SALE DUTIES

A small number of decisions over the years have imposed on manufacturers a duty "to take all reasonable means to convey effective warning" to consumers threatened by significant hazards discovered in products after they are manufactured and sold. Comstock v. General Motors Corp., 99 N.W.2d 627, 634 (Mich. 1959) (brake failures). Accord, Cover v. Cohen, 461

N.E.2d 864 (N.Y. 1984). Under limited circumstances, a very few courts have even found a common-law duty to *recall*: "It is clear that after such a product has been sold and dangerous defects in design have come to the manufacturer's attention, the manufacturer has a duty either to remedy these or, if complete remedy is not feasible, at least to give users adequate warnings and instructions concerning methods for minimizing the danger." Braniff Airways, Inc. v. Curtiss–Wright Corp., 411 F.2d 451, 453 (2d Cir. 1969) (aircraft engine overheated causing cylinder failure). Cf. doCanto v. Ametek, Inc., 328 N.E.2d 873 (Mass. 1975). Although most courts have not yet addressed the question of a manufacturer's post-sale duties to warn or recall, the topic is receiving increasing attention.

Ostendorf v. Clark Equipment Company

Supreme Court of Kentucky, 2003.
122 S.W.3d 530.

■ JOHNSTONE, JUSTICE.

[Michael Ostendorf, an employee of Delta Airlines, was severely injured in 1994 when the forklift he was driving tipped over when a baggage tug vehicle operated by another employee collided with Ostendorf's forklift. The forklift, a 1980 model C–300Y40 manufactured by Clark Equipment Company, was designed in accordance with OSHA and ANSI standards which at that time did not require forklifts to be equipped with operator restraints. Ostendorf and his wife sued Clark for selling the C–300Y40 without passenger restraints and for not retrofitting it with such restraints.

[Clark and other forklift manufacturers knew since the 1960s of the tendency of forklift trucks to overturn under certain circumstances, causing injury and death to the operator. Yet, there was considerable debate during the 1970s regarding the need to install operator restraints. After a Clark engineer was killed in 1979 when a forklift he was test driving overturned, Clark studied the matter with renewed attention and in 1983 developed a new safety seat for its forklifts that incorporated an operator restraint. In addition, Clark mailed notices of a retrofit program to existing owners of C–300 model forklifts offering to install the new restraint system in their forklifts at no charge. Delta denies receiving such a notice.

[Plaintiffs sued Clark for (1) strict product liability, (2) negligent design, (3) breach of duty to retrofit the forklift with operator restraints, (4) negligent conduct of the retrofit campaign, and (5) breach of warranty. The circuit court granted summary judgment in favor of Clark. The Court of Appeals reversed the summary judgment on the strict liability and negligent design claims but] held that Kentucky does not recognize a common law duty by a seller to retrofit an existing product that was not defective at the time it was manufactured [and that Clark was not liable] for negligent performance of a voluntary retrofit campaign. We affirm the Court of Appeals' decision.]

On appeal to this Court, Ostendorf argues that (1) Clark had a common law duty to retrofit its forklifts; (2) Clark negligently conducted the retrofit program; [and] (3) Clark failed to meet the standard for an appropriate retrofit campaign under the standard set out in the Restatement (Third) of Torts, which this Commonwealth should adopt. . . .

DUTY TO RETROFIT

Ostendorf first argues that a product manufacturer has an affirmative, common law duty to retrofit existing products with safety features that are necessary to make the product reasonably safe. Ostendorf arrives at this duty based on principles of negligence: foreseeability and reasonable care. [T]he Court of Appeals held to the contrary, declaring that Kentucky does not recognize a common law duty by a seller to retrofit an existing product which was not defective at the time it was manufactured with subsequently developed safety features. We agree with the Court of Appeals, with one exception. We think the relevant point in time is not when the product is manufactured, but when it is sold.

* * * A duty to retrofit is a duty to upgrade or improve a product. Some courts have created such a duty in certain, limited circumstances. For example, in Braniff Airways, Inc. v. Curtiss–Wright Corp., 411 F.2d 451 (2d Cir. 1969), plaintiff Braniff purchased an airplane engine from Curtiss–Wright. The engine was installed on one of Braniff's passenger airplanes, which later crashed [due to a defect in the engine.] Finding that an airplane engine was a product involving "human safety," the Second Circuit held: "It is clear that after such a [human-safety] product has been sold and dangerous defects in design have come to the manufacturer's attention, the manufacturer has a duty either to remedy these or . . . at least to give users adequate warnings and instructions concerning methods for minimizing the danger." Accord, Noel v. United Aircraft Corp., 342 F.2d 232, 236–37 (3d Cir. 1964) (duty of care owed by the manufacturer of an airplane propeller system, "an instrumentality likely to endanger the public") [; ditto, with respect to helicopter resold without] an improved tail rotor developed to prevent a known flight hazard. See Bell Helicopter Co. v. Bradshaw, 594 S.W.2d 519 (Tex. Civ. App. 1979). While the few cases finding a duty to retrofit often involve products that directly implicate human safety, that is not always the case. One court found a duty to retrofit a mining shovel where the total number of units sold was so small, 120, that it was easily feasible for the manufacturer to retrofit the product or warn buyers of the danger. See Readenour v. Marion Power Shovel, 719 P.2d 1058 (Ariz. 1986). And one court has even held, without qualification, that "failure to conduct an adequate retrofit campaign may constitute negligence apart from the issue of defective design." Hernandez v. Badger Const. Equip. Co., 34 Cal. Rptr. 2d 732 (1994) (court affirmed jury finding that crane manufacturer could be liable for failing to install later developed safety device on crane that was not defective when sold); but see Tabieros v. Clark Equip. Co., 944 P.2d 1279 (Hawai'i 1997) (concluding there is no duty to retrofit and criticizing both the *Readenour* and *Hernandez* decisions

as wanting "any discernible reason explaining their implicit adoption of a duty to retrofit").

But the majority of jurisdictions reach a different conclusion: there is no duty to retrofit a product not defective when sold. *See* 47 A.L.R. 5th 395. We find the majority reasoning persuasive and we find the result appropriate. There are two main reasons militating against a duty to retrofit. First, in many cases, a duty to retrofit is properly the province of an administrative or legislative body. Second, and more importantly, there is no reason to create a duty to retrofit a product not defective when sold—traditional principles of negligence and strict products liability suffice.

A retrofit campaign may be a costly undertaking. It is typically a multi-step, multi-party process that may cost millions of dollars. *See* Richmond, Expanding Products Liability: Manufacturers' Post–Sale Duties to Warn, Retrofit and Recall, 36 Idaho L. Rev. 7, 10 (1999). The complexity of the decision to retrofit and the ramifications of that decision recommend that courts should not make that determination, but rather should leave it to governmental bodies more suited to the task. See, e.g., Gregory v. Cincinnati Inc., 538 N.W.2d 325, 334 (Mich.1995); Patton v. Hutchinson Wil–Rich Mfg. Co., 861 P.2d 1299, 1315 (Kan. 1993). Professor Schwartz, principal author of The Uniform Product Liability Act, cautions persuasively against a duty to retrofit by judicial fiat:

> [C]ourts that impose a post-sale obligation to remedy or replace products already in the marketplace arrogate to themselves a power equivalent to that of requiring product recall. Product recalls, however, are properly the province of administrative agencies, as the federal statutes that expressly delegate recall authority to various agencies suggest. As Congress has recognized, administrative agencies have the institutional resources to make fully informed assessments of the marginal benefits of recalling a specific product. Because the cost of locating, recalling, and replacing mass-marketed products can be enormous and will likely be passed on to consumers in the form of higher prices, the recall power should not be exercised without extensive consideration of its economic impact. Courts, however, are constituted to define individual cases, and their inquiries are confined to the particular facts and arguments in the cases before them. Decisions to expand a manufacturer's post-sale duty beyond making reasonable efforts to warn product users about newly discovered dangers should be left to administrative agencies, which are better able to weigh the costs and benefits of such action. [Schwartz, The Post–Sale Duty to Warn: Two Unfortunate Forks in the Road to a Reasonable Doctrine, 58 N.Y.U. L. Rev. 892, 901.]

[T]here is a more fundamental reason to eschew imposition of a duty to retrofit: that duty is superfluous in light of existing ... liability doctrines.... When the case involves a retrofit, the plaintiff is claiming the product was defectively designed. Here, for example, Ostendorf claims the C–300 forklift was defectively designed because it did not have operator safety restraints. A plaintiff in Kentucky can bring a defective design claim under either a theory of negligence or strict liability. The foundation of both theories is that the product is "unreasonably dangerous." Ulrich v. Kasco Abrasives Co., 532 S.W.2d 197, 200 (Ky. 1976)....

In *Gregory,* the Michigan Supreme Court considered the propriety of instituting a duty to retrofit. That case involved a worker injured in 1986 by an industrial machine that was not defective when manufactured in 1964. The injured worker argued that the manufacturer had a duty to retrofit its product with later designed safety devices, but the court refused to create such a duty. As the *Gregory* court explained, there are two retrofit scenarios: a retrofit for a latent defect or a retrofit because of a technological advance. *See Gregory.* A latent defect is one that existed undiscovered at the time of manufacture. Because a manufacturer's liability for a design defect hinges on what it knew or should have known at the time of sale, a negligence or strict liability theory can assess liability for a latent defect, so a duty to retrofit is unnecessary. If, however, the retrofit results from a post-sale technological advance, then the product was not originally defective, but has become so due only to the later advancement. That poses a problem under the traditional theories because "[f]ocusing on post[sale] conduct in a negligent design case improperly shifts the focus from point-of-[sale] conduct and considers post[sale] conduct and technology that accordingly has the potential to taint a jury's verdict regarding a defect." The result is that liability for a post-sale defect would have to be premised on some other theory, like an independent duty to retrofit. But[,] "[I]mposing a duty to update technology would place an unreasonable burden on manufacturers. It would discourage manufacturers from developing new designs if this could form the bases for suits or result in costly repair...." Placing such an onerous burden on manufacturers would be tantamount to making strict liability absolute liability and making a manufacturer an insurer. [Citations.] This we decline to do.

A duty to retrofit is an example of a post-sale obligation imposed on a manufacturer. Other examples are the duty to warn of later-discovered defects or foreseeable misuses and the duty to recall a defective product. Numerous cases impose a duty to warn of later discovered defects.[1] See, e.g., Gracyalny v. Westinghouse Elec. Corp., 723 F.2d 1311, 1318 (7th Cir. 1983) (manufacturer's duty to warn extends to dangers that arise after marketing); LaBelle v. McCauley Indus. Corp., 649 F.2d 46, 49 (1st Cir. 1981) (manufacturer's duty to warn extends to purchaser even if defects are discovered after initial sale); Chrysler Corp. v. Batten, 450 S.E.2d 208, 211–13 (Ga. 1994) (duty to warn arises whenever manufacturer knows or reasonably should know of danger arising from product use). When a product is defective, a manufacturer may be subject to one of these post-sale duties. The nature of the defect will dictate the appropriate remedy: a defect that may result in a few minor injuries may only require a warning, whereas a defect that may result in serious injury or death could require more. These remedial measures can be seen as "a continuum of post-sale duties which the law might impose...." *Gregory,* 538 N.W.2d at 341 (Cavanagh, J., dissenting).

---

1. The present case does not present the issue of a duty to warn. Our discussion addresses that topic only generally, as it relates to the issues in this case.

[W]e see no . . . good reason to create an independent duty to retrofit. Accordingly, if Ostendorf can prove what he claims, that Clark's product was defective when sold, then he can recover under existing theories of negligence or strict liability.

LIABILITY FOR VOLUNTARY RETROFIT CAMPAIGN

Ostendorf next argues that Clark is liable to him because of its. . . . voluntary retrofit program Clark began after developing safety improvements in 1983. Although Clark had begun to retrofit its model C–300 forklifts, the forklift involved in the accident injuring Ostendorf was never retrofitted. . . . Ostendorf claims Clark [1] "failed to adequately notify customers of the availability of and the need for the new safety features, and that it [2] failed to provide its dealers with sufficient incentives to implement the retrofit program." Clark maintains that it mailed Delta notice of the program in 1985, but Delta denies ever receiving the notice. Ostendorf first contends that, under the common law principle of voluntary assumption of a duty, Clark negligently conducted its retrofit campaign. Ostendorf next asserts that Clark failed to meet the standard for an appropriate retrofit campaign under the Restatement (Third) of Torts: Products Liability § 11 (1998).

Ostendorf's common law argument is that a manufacturer who voluntarily undertakes a retrofit program can be held liable for negligently performing that program. * * * Ostendorf also quotes well-settled Kentucky case law to support his case: "one who volunteers to act, though under no duty to do so, is charged with the duty of acting with due care." [Citations.] This is an accurate statement of the law, but falls short of attaching liability to Clark. As the Court of Appeals recognized, "traditionally, the purpose of imposing liability upon a party who has assumed a duty to act is premised upon reliance." [Citation.] The Restatement (Second) of Torts § 324A (1965), which considers . . . negligent performance of an undertaking, includes reliance as one of three bases for imposing a duty:

> One who undertakes, gratuitously or for consideration, to render services to another which he should recognize as necessary for the protection of a third person or his things, is subject to liability to the third person for physical harm resulting from his failure to exercise reasonable care to protect his undertaking, if
>
> (a) his failure to exercise reasonable care increases the risk of such harm, or
>
> (b) he has undertaken to perform a duty owed by the other to the third person, or
>
> (c) the harm is suffered because of reliance of the other or the third person upon the undertaking.

Under this framework, Ostendorf would have to demonstrate not only that Clark undertook a retrofit campaign on the C–300 forklifts for the protection of third persons, but also that Clark's negligent performance of that task (a) increased the risk of harm to Ostendorf, (b) was incompatible with the discharge of a duty by Ostendorf's employer, Delta, or (c) caused Ostendorf to suffer harm because either Delta or Ostendorf relied on Clark to complete the retrofit. [Citations.] While it is clear that Clark began a retrofit campaign, there is no evidence that any of the three additional conditions existed. In fact, regarding reliance, Delta and Ostendorf deny ever receiving notice of the retrofit program from Clark. As discussed, *supra*, the existence of a duty is essential to a negligence claim. In the absence of one of these three conditions, Clark owed no duty to Ostendorf based on the voluntary retrofit campaign.

The Restatement (Third) of Torts: Products Liability § 11 (1998), however, does not impose such stringent requirements to establish liability, at least in the context of product recalls. That section provides:

> One engaged in the business of selling or otherwise distributing products is subject to liability for harm to persons or property caused by the seller's failure to recall a product after the time of sale or distribution if:
>
> (a)(1) a governmental directive issued pursuant to a statute or administrative regulation specifically requires the seller or distributor to recall the product; or
>
> (a)(2) the seller or distributor, in the absence of a recall requirement under Subsection (a)(1), undertakes to recall the product; and
>
> (b) the seller or distributor fails to act as a reasonable person in recalling the product.

Ostendorf argues that § 11(a)(2) applies to this case. Ostendorf further alleges that Clark's voluntary recall was merely an attempt to avoid a government mandated recall or retrofit, as explained in Comment c to § 11:

> [V]oluntary recalls are typically undertaken in the anticipation that, if the seller does not recall voluntarily, it will be directed to do so by a governmental regulator. Having presumably forestalled the regulatory recall directive, the seller should be under a common-law duty to follow through on its commitment to recall.

But [Kentucky has not adopted § 11 nor has Ostendorf cited a] single case from any jurisdiction that relies on § 11 to impose liability on a manufacturer for a negligent retrofit campaign. More importantly, adopting the § 11 approach—with its lax requirements—would have the perverse effect of discouraging voluntary retrofits and recalls. A retrofit campaign is a complex process requiring an abundance of technical, administrative, and legal coordination. Imposing liability on a company for a good faith—but perhaps incomplete—effort to undertake that task might dissuade that company from acting until required to by a government directive. . . . [For] the safety of the citizens of this Commonwealth, we decline to adopt § 11.

We think the better course is to impose liability under the dictates of the Restatement (Second) § 324A, which requires proof of reliance, action inconsistent with a duty owed by another party, or increased risk of harm.

As discussed, *supra,* and by the Court of Appeals: "If a product was defective at the time of [sale], then the seller may be liable for injuries resulting from that defect. However if the product was not defective at the time of [sale], the seller's post[sale] conduct must contribute to the injury before liability will be imposed." Based on the facts in this case, we hold that by initiating a voluntary retrofit campaign, Clark did not assume a duty sufficient to impose liability for Ostendorf's injuries.

[Affirmed.]

NOTES

1. **Duty to Recall and Retrofit.** All but a few of the cases agree with *Ostendorf's* conclusion that there is no common-law duty to recall a product to retrofit it with newly developed safety devices. "Generally, a manufacturer is under no duty to modify its product in accordance with the current state of the art safety features." Gregory v. Cincinnati, Inc., 509 N.W.2d 809 (Mich. App. 1993). See also Robinson v. Brandtjen & Kluge, Inc., 2006 WL 2796252 (D.S.D. 2006) (no duty to recall in South Dakota); Padilla v. Black & Decker Corp., 2005 WL 697479 (E.D. Pa. 2005) (no such duty in Pennsylvania).

2. **Post-Sale Duty to Warn.** A number of courts in various contexts have held that manufacturers *do* have a duty to provide warnings of dangers discovered after the product is sold, though the earlier cases often do not focus upon whether the product was originally defective at the time of sale. In Patton v. Hutchinson Wil-Rich Mfg. Co., 861 P.2d 1299 (Kan. 1993), the manufacturer discovered dangers in a cultivator (a piece of heavy farming equipment) after it originally was sold. The manufacturer sold it through a dealership which maintained records of owners and maintained the machine. The court held that there was no duty to recall or retrofit but, following the lead of many courts, that there might be a post-sale duty to warn:

> We recognize a manufacturer's post-sale duty to warn ultimate [purchasers of] the product who can be readily identified or traced when a defect, which originated at the time the product was manufactured and was unforeseeable at the point of sale, is discovered to present a life threatening hazard. . . .

Id. at 1313. Rejecting strict liability in the post-sale context, the *Patton* court noted: "The cardinal inquiry is, was HWR's post-sale conduct reasonable? The reasonableness standard is flexible." Id. at 1314. Refusing to fashion a "bright line" rule for application "to the infinite variety of products that inhabit the marketplace," the court noted that the post-sale warning issue normally should be for the jury:

> The trial judge, in instructing the jury on a post-sale duty to warn, shall utilize the relevant factors referenced herein, including [1] the nature and likelihood of the injury posed by the product, [2] the feasibility and expense of issuing a warning, [3] whether the warning would be effective, and [4] whether ultimate consumers who purchased the product can be identified.

Id. at 1315. Contra, Tober v. Graco Children's Prods., Inc., 431 F.3d 572 (7th Cir. 2005) (no post-sale duty to warn in Indiana).

3. **Nomenclature: "Continuing Duty To Warn."** Many of the earlier decisions speak of a "continuing duty to warn," but this phrase and concept have been rejected by more recent opinions. See *Patton*, 861 P.2d at 1310 ("we choose the label 'post-sale' rather than 'continuing' "); Gregory v. Cincinnati, Inc., 509 N.W.2d

809 (Mich. App. 1993) ("Generally, before there can be any continuing duty—whether it be to warn, repair, or recall—there must be a defect or an actionable problem at the point of manufacture. If there is no [such] problem at this point, then there can be no continuing duty.... ").

4. Post–Sale Misconduct and Punitive Damages. Major recalls of consumer products, such as Rely tampons (associated with toxic shock syndrome) and Tylenol (a number of which were deliberately poisoned in retail shops), often cost the manufacturers tens of millions of dollars. While in most states there is no post-sale duty to recall, manufacturers remain liable for harm from *pre*-sale defects, and *punitive* damages may attach to the failure to take effective post-sale steps to remedy a serious consumer hazard. See Patton v. TIC, 859 F.Supp. 509 (D. Kan. 1994) (manufacturer neglected post-sale *warnings* campaign that would have cost only $110,000; $1 million punitive damages). Even an eventual recall, if belated, may not protect a manufacturer against such damages. Holmes v. Wegman Oil Co., 492 N.W.2d 107 (S.D. 1992) (failure to warn or recall for 10 years during which time problem was fraudulently concealed; $2.5 million punitive damages).

Effective recalls of consumer products rely heavily on the media. Consider the following notice published in 1994 in one author's local newspaper:

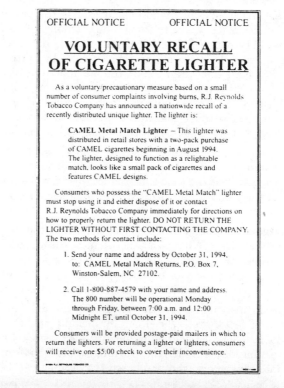

OFFICIAL NOTICE   OFFICIAL NOTICE

VOLUNTARY RECALL OF CIGARETTE LIGHTER

As a voluntary/precautionary measure based on a small number of consumer complaints involving burns, R.J. Reynolds Tobacco Company has announced a nationwide recall of a recently distributed unique lighter. The lighter is:

CAMEL Metal Match Lighter – This lighter was distributed in retail stores with a two-pack purchase of CAMEL cigarettes beginning in August 1994. The lighter, designed to function as a relightable match, looks like a small pack of cigarettes and features CAMEL designs.

Consumers who possess the "CAMEL Metal Match" lighter must stop using it and either dispose of it or contact R.J. Reynolds Tobacco Company immediately for directions on how to properly return the lighter. DO NOT RETURN THE LIGHTER WITHOUT FIRST CONTACTING THE COMPANY. The two methods for contact include:

1. Send your name and address by October 31, 1994, to: CAMEL Metal Match Returns, P.O. Box 7, Winston-Salem, NC 27102.

2. Call 1-800-887-4579 with your name and address. The 800 number will be operational Monday through Friday, between 7:00 a.m. and 12:00 Midnight ET, until October 31, 1994.

Consumers will be provided postage-paid mailers in which to return the lighters. For returning a lighter or lighters, consumers will receive one $5.00 check to cover their inconvenience.

5. Regulatory Recall. Congress has provided various agencies with recall power, for example the CPSC, 15 U.S.C. § 2064(a)("substantial product hazards"); the FDA, 21 U.S.C. § 360(h) (medical devices); the Coast Guard, 46 U.S.C. § 4310(2)(D) (recreational boats with safety defects); Health and Human Services and NHTSA, 49 U.S.C. §§ 30117–21 (automotive recalls treated in ch. 18, below).

6. Products Liability Restatement.

A. Post-sale warnings. Section 10 of the Products Liability Restatement adopts *Patton*'s reasonable duty approach based on similar factors. In addition, § 13 prescribes a duty of reasonable care on a successor corporation to warn of defects in products previously sold by its predecessor if the successor enters into a service or maintenance agreement with purchasers of the predecessor's products.

B. Recall and retrofit. Section 11 of the Products Liability Restatement, set forth in *Ostendorf*, suggests the absence of a *general* duty to recall or retrofit by limiting such a duty to two narrowly described situations.

7. Reform. One of the few pro-plaintiff reform measures in recent years enacted by a few state legislatures is the statutory imposition of a post-sale duty to warn. See, e.g., Dixon v. Jacobsen Mfg. Co., 637 A.2d 915 (N.J. Super. Ct.1994); N.C. Gen. Stat. § 99B–5(a)(2) (duty "to take reasonable steps to give adequate warning" or "take other reasonable action").

8. See generally Ben–Shahar, How Liability Distorts Incentives of Manufacturers to Recall Products, U. Mich. legal Working Paper Series, Paper 37 (2005); D. Owen, Products Liability Law § 10.8 (2d ed. 2008); 1 D. Owen, M.S. Madden, & M. Davis, Madden & Owen on Products Liability ch. 11 (3d ed. 2000).

---

6. STATUTORY REPOSE

How to limit open-ended liability for aging products is perplexing.

Hodder v. Goodyear Tire & Rub. Co., 426 N.W.2d 826, 832 (Minn. 1988).

Lawsuits filed many years after a product was manufactured and sold, and perhaps many years after an accident occurs, involve a large number of problems for the courts and parties. Apart from the various problems of deterioration and changes in the state of the art, the availability and reliability of evidence diminish as time goes by—skid marks fade; burn marks are painted over; debris from the accident is cleaned up and thrown away; the product is repaired, disposed of, or lost; files are destroyed; witnesses forget, move away, get ill, and die. "There comes a time when [a potential defendant] ought to be secure in his reasonable expectation that the slate has been wiped clean of ancient obligations, and he ought not to be called on to resist a claim when 'evidence has been lost, memories have faded, and witnesses have disappeared.' " Raymond v. Eli Lilly & Co., 371 A.2d 170, 173–74 (N.H. 1977) (Kenison, C.J.).

Zamboni v. Aladan Corp.

United States District Court, Massachusetts, 2004.
304 F. Supp. 2d 218.

◾ PONSOR, DISTRICT JUDGE.

[Dino Zamboni suffers from an acute allergy to latex. He and his wife, Susan Zamboni, instituted this suit against Aladan Corp. ("Aladan") and

Bio–Flex International, Inc. ("Bio–Flex"), manufacturers of latex gloves he wore while employed in various positions at Baystate Medical Center ("BMC") in Springfield, Massachusetts. Their complaint alleges negligence and implied warranty breaches for failure to warn of the dangers associated with latex gloves. Plaintiffs also assert statutory unfair trade practice claims. Defendants have moved for summary judgment on all counts based on the statute of limitations. Massachusetts law requires that tort or contract actions to recover for personal injuries be brought within three years after the cause of action accrues and within four years after the cause of action accrues for the statutory unfair trade practice claims.]

. . . On October 4, 1993, Zamboni began work at BMC as a "psych sitter" [where] he oversaw patients under psychiatric evaluation. Occasionally, the job's responsibilities required Zamboni to don latex gloves when handling a patient. A few months after starting work, on February 15, 1994, Zamboni visited the employee health clinic at BMC with a rash on his face. The medical record of that visit documents that Zamboni suspected that the rash developed after his wife began using a new laundry detergent. The attending physician asked Zamboni if he had ever had rashes develop after contact with other latex products, such as toy balloons, to which Zamboni responded in the negative. The physician concluded that the rash may have developed as a reaction to the powder in the latex gloves Zamboni wore. The doctor advised Zamboni to use powder-free gloves in the future.

On April 10, 1994, Zamboni transferred to [an orderly position which] required him to wear gloves almost all the time to protect himself from his increased contact with patients. On June 10, 1994, Zamboni returned to the health clinic, this time with a rash on his hands. The medical records for this visit state that this rash differed from the earlier rash on his face. A few days later, Zamboni again reported . . . for treatment because the rash . . . had worsened.

Zamboni worked as an orderly for approximately one year. Throughout this time, Zamboni continued to suffer great discomfort from the skin [on his hands which contained] "fissures" and "bleeding" and cracking. Prior to his employment at BMC, Zamboni never had suffered from such a skin problem. During this period, BMC repeatedly provided Zamboni with different gloves to try to alleviate his condition. Zamboni generally used powder-free latex gloves, though in an emergency, if no other gloves were on hand, Zamboni used whichever gloves were immediately available.

. . . Three months into his time as an orderly, in June 1994, the employee health clinic referred Zamboni to a dermatologist. Medical records dated June 22, 1994, indicate that the dermatologist tentatively diagnosed his skin problem as eczematous dermatitis. The record also states that "he had an allergic reaction to Latex gloves but not on his hands but rather on his face. In any case he's now using non-powdered gloves." Later, in November of 1994, Zamboni visited the emergency room of BMC for a non-work related burn that he sustained on his arm. In records from that visit, the phrase "latex gloves?" was written under the heading "allergies."

In November 1994, the dermatologist's office noted that Zamboni should be patch tested to [determine if the gloves were related to] his skin condition. After another visit to BMC's employee clinic on December 5, 1994, Zamboni was authorized to return to work with the restriction that he wear powder-free vinyl gloves and cotton liners. Despite [continuing medical treatment], Zamboni's skin condition did not improve.

[In March 1995 Zamboni was transferred to another position, cardiac monitor observer ("CMO"), to remove him from the clinical environment in an effort to stop his skin reactions. Initially, Zamboni's symptoms greatly abated. Within a few weeks, however, his allergy symptoms returned, this time with newly developed respiratory problems. Though he was not using latex gloves (unless no other gloves were on hand in an emergency) a rash reappeared on his skin, his hands swelled, and he began having difficulty breathing.

Defendants have anchored their contention that Zamboni had notice of the cause of his skin problems partly on the timing of his academic pursuits. In 1992, Zamboni enrolled in a two-year nursing program at Springfield Technical Community College ("STCC"). [In fall 1993, Zamboni registered for five classes but soon withdrew from three of them. In the spring of 1994, he registered for only one course and then withdrew from that as well. He then registered for liberal arts courses in the fall of 1994.]

Defendants argue that the undisputed facts of record confirm that Zamboni withdrew from his classes in the spring of 1994 because he knew at that point that he was allergic to latex and, therefore, could not complete the clinical requirements of the nursing program. They point to a portion of Zamboni's deposition testimony where he stated that he eventually left the nursing program altogether because the clinical aspect of the program required him to use gloves. In fact, the deposition testimony is not quite so clear. When asked why he had withdrawn from his classes, Zamboni stated that he quit school because of his hands, adding, "I couldn't concentrate; I was in pain; I had my eczema problem, so-called what they said, and it was just—then I was on medication, and I just lost all concentration and everything; and I was very depressed because of that."

[Zamboni admitted that he had begun to suspect latex gloves caused his skin problems during his work as an orderly, sometime between April 1994 and March 1995. In the fall of 1997, Zamboni was diagnosed with an allergy to latex and moved into an administration position at BMC.] On June 8, 1998, Zamboni and his wife filed this cause of action.

. . . When a defendant raises the statute of limitations, the burden rests on the plaintiff to demonstrate that his claim is not time barred. [Citation.] The plaintiffs must establish the facts that take their case "outside the impact of the statute of limitations." [Citation. The personal injury claims must be brought within three years "after the cause of action accrues" and the unfair trade practice claims within four years from accrual.] Because the phrase "when a cause of action accrues" is not defined in the statute, the courts of Massachusetts have interpreted the phrase as the time when the plaintiffs "(1) knew or had sufficient notice that [they were] harmed; and (2) knew or had sufficient notice of the cause of the harm." [Citation.]

Thus, there are two types of knowledge that the plaintiffs must have for the statute to run. The plaintiffs must have, first, an awareness of the injury and, second, an awareness that the defendants caused the injury. [Citation. Plaintiffs acknowledge that they] knew of the injury more than four years before filing suit. The plaintiffs are adamant, however, that they lacked sufficient notice of the cause of their injury until after June 8, 1995, three years prior to filing this lawsuit.

Under Massachusetts law, the discovery rule tolls the limitations period until a plaintiff recognizes, or reasonably should have recognized, "some causal connection between the defendant's actions and [his] injury." [Citation.] Whether a plaintiff has knowledge or notice of his injury and the causes of the injury is determined by using a reasonable person standard. [Citation.] Therefore, even if a plaintiff does not subjectively know of his injury or the cause of his injury, if . . . the plaintiff reasonably should have known, then the statute of limitations is not tolled.

The discovery rule is designed to protect a plaintiff's cause of action . . . where the plaintiff suffers from an injury whose origin is unknown. [Citation.] The rule tolls the statute of limitations while the plaintiff undertakes a reasonable inquiry into the source of his injury. [Citation.] Thus, the discovery rule, while affording some protection to a plaintiff, also imposes on him an obligation to investigate the cause of his injury. [Citation;] Martinez v. Sherwin Williams Co., 737 N.E.2d 927 (2000) [summary judgment for defendant allowed where plaintiff did not seek answers for more than six years after first symptoms appeared].

[A] cause of action begins to accrue even if the plaintiff does not apprehend the full extent or nature of the injury. [Citation]. It is only while the facts, as opposed to the "legal theory for the cause of action," remain unknown that the discovery rule tolls the statute of limitations. [Citation.] When the discovery rule is at issue, the plaintiff "bears the burden of proving both an actual lack of causal knowledge and the objective reasonableness of that lack of knowledge." [Citation.] . . .

Because plaintiffs filed their complaint on June 8, 1998, their [common law claims are barred] if plaintiffs had reasonable notice of Zamboni's latex allergy before June 8, 1995. [The record supports] that these common law claims are time barred. Medical records from Zamboni's visit to the emergency room in November of 1994 reveal that he believed he suffered from an allergy to latex. In addition, Zamboni admitted at his deposition that he knew of a possible allergy to latex while he was an orderly, a position he left in March of 1995. Thus, the record establishes that plaintiffs knew of the cause of Zamboni's skin reactions by March 1995 at the latest, three years and three months prior to the filing of the lawsuit.

Defendants' Motions for Summary Judgment, therefore, must be allowed with respect to plaintiffs' common law claims.

[Plaintiffs statutory unfair trade practice claims are different. Whether Zamboni knew or should have known that he had an allergy to latex within four years of filing his claim is a closer question. Defendants argue that Zamboni knew in the spring of 1994 that latex caused his skin reactions because, after his first visit to the employee health clinic, the doctor pinpointed the gloves as a possible source of his skin reactions.] Also, Zamboni's skin problems were so severe by the spring of 1994 that he withdrew from his class at STCC. The defendants assert Zamboni withdrew because he knew he could not complete the clinical requirements due to his latex allergy....

Defendants argue alternatively that even if Zamboni did not know he was allergic to latex, he should have known by the spring of 1994 to look into the matter more closely.... The defendants contend that Zamboni had enough information in the spring of 1994 to put him on notice of his cause of action [and therefore the statute began to run before June 8, 1994.]

Strong evidence, however, supports the plaintiffs' contention that they did not have reasonable grounds to conclude that a latex allergy was causing Zamboni's rash until after June 8, 1994. [Zamboni's doctors told him in spring 1994 that he had eczema, not an allergy. On] June 10, 1994, the doctor characterized Zamboni's skin condition on his hands as different from the one he presented in the spring. Therefore, a jury could reasonably conclude that Zamboni and his wife logically regarded his earlier facial rash as unrelated to his later problems with his hands.

[Zamboni stated that he withdrew from his class in the spring of 1994 because of his hand condition, not because of the clinical requirements. Zamboni's testimony is at best ambiguous about his knowledge of the cause of his skin condition. The evidence could support] a jury finding that Zamboni did not withdraw from his class at STCC because he realized he had an allergy to latex.

Likewise, a jury could reasonably conclude that Zamboni did not have sufficient information before June 8, 1994, to put him on notice of his cause of action. The discovery rule protects a plaintiff who conducts a reasonable inquiry into the cause of his injury. [Citation.] Zamboni sought care repeatedly from the employee health clinic at BMC, as well as from dermatologists, all of whom repeatedly diagnosed the cause of his problems as non-latex related. This is not a case where the plaintiff "essentially did nothing to investigate the cause of his injury." ...

[Reasonable inferences must be drawn in plaintiff's favor on summary judgment. The court cannot say with confidence that no reasonable jury could conclude that Zamboni did not know or have notice of the cause of his injury before June 8, 1994. Summary judgment on the unfair trade practice claims is therefore denied.]

NOTES

1.   Statutes of Limitation. The traditional legislative way for addressing the passage-of-time problem has been through statutes of limitations that bar claims brought more than a certain time—from 1 to 6 years, typically 2 or 3—after the claim accrues. Thus, the crucial question is when the claim "accrues."

A.   Tort. Traditionally, courts held that tort claims accrue at the time of the wrong or injury. E.g., Cannon v. Sears, Roebuck & Co., 374 N.E.2d 582 (Mass.1978).

B.   Warranty. Under UCC § 2–725(2), warranty actions accrue on breach—upon tender of delivery—which usually is the date of sale. Patterson v. Her Majesty Indus., Inc., 450 F.Supp. 425 (E.D. Pa. 1978), held that the relevant sale is retail rather than wholesale.

C.   Wrongful death. Such actions generally accrue at the date of death. E.g., Shover v. Cordis Corp., 574 N.E.2d 457 (Ohio 1991) (4–3 decision) (discovery rule inapplicable). Contra, Bressler v. Graco Children's Prod., Inc., 43 F.3d 379 (8th Cir. 1994) (Iowa law).

D.   *Nullum Tempus Regi.* Time does not run against the sovereign, so a school district's abatement claim in an asbestos suit is not barred by the statute of limitations. See Mt. Lebanon School Dist. v. W.R. Grace & Co., 607 A.2d 756 (Pa. Super. Ct. 1992); Tucson Unified School Dist. v. Owens–Corning Fiberglas Corp., 849 P.2d 790 (Ariz. 1993).

2.   The Problem—Unknown Claims. In the event of a violent injury, as from a gas canister explosion or crunched fingers in a press, the plaintiff will know that he has been injured (and often that he may have a legal claim against the defendant) from the moment the limitation period begins to run. But if the damage is a latent disease or condition, caused by a drug, asbestos, or other toxic substance, the plaintiff may not discover—or may not even suffer—his or her injury until after the limitation period has lapsed. See Patterson v. Her Majesty Indus., Inc., 450 F.Supp. 425 (E.D. Pa. 1978), quoting approvingly from Judge Frank's dissenting opinion in Dincher v. Marlin Firearms Co., 198 F.2d 821, 823 (2d Cir. 1952), where he described the "Alice in Wonderland" effect of such a result:

> Except in topsy-turvy land, you can't die before you are conceived, or be divorced before ever you marry, or harvest a crop never planted, or burn down a house never built, or miss a train running on a nonexistent railroad. For substantially similar reasons, it has always heretofore been accepted, as a sort of legal "axiom," that a statute of limitations does not begin to run against a cause of action before that cause of action exists, i.e., before a judicial remedy is available to the plaintiff.

And a judicial remedy may not be "effective" (and hence violate a state's "right-to-a-remedy" constitutional guarantee), unless the statute of limitations affords the plaintiff a period in which to sue after *actually* discovering both the injury and its cause. See Burgess v. Eli Lilly & Co., 609 N.E.2d 140 (Ohio 1993) (DES: "Knowledge of the possibility that an injury may be related to a specific cause simply does not reach the constitutionally mandated threshold granting every person a remedy in due course of law for an injury done."). Compare Orear v. International Paint Co., 796 P.2d 759 (Wash. App. 1990) (no accrual until plaintiff knew or should have known manufacturer's identity). But see Renaud v. Sigma–Aldrich Corp., 662 A.2d 711 (R.I. 1995) (statute of limitations accrual begins on discovery of injury, not identity of manufacturer; *held*, constitutional).

3. The Solution—The Discovery Rule. The problem of statutes of limitations running on unknown claims has been addressed by courts and legislatures in many states by the adoption of the "discovery rule," providing that the statute is tolled until the plaintiff discovers, or reasonably should have discovered, his injury (or, in some states, his legal claim):

> There are at least four points at which a tort cause of action may accrue: (1) when the defendant breaches his duty; (2) when the plaintiff suffers harm; (3) when the plaintiff becomes aware of his injury; and (4) when the plaintiff discovers the causal relationship between his harm and the defendant's misconduct. * * *

> . . . We believe that the proper formulation of the rule and the one that will cause the least confusion is the one adopted by the majority of courts: A cause of action will not accrue under the discovery rule until the plaintiff discovers or in the exercise of reasonable diligence should have discovered not only that he has been injured but also that his injury may have been caused by the defendant's conduct.

Raymond v. Eli Lilly & Co., 371 A.2d 170, 172, 174 (N.H.1977).

4. State Reform—Statutes of Repose. But the discovery rule proves a hardship on defendants who thus become vulnerable to lawsuits indefinitely, sometimes decades after the product originally was produced. As part of the products liability "reform" movement of the late twentieth century, many states adopted "useful life" statutes, or, more commonly, "statutes of repose." A statute of repose is simply a statute of limitation—typically for 8, 10, or 12 years—which begins to run at the date of manufacture or, alternatively, initial sale. The purpose is to give manufacturers a time certain after which they may be confident that their potential liability has ended.

But protecting defendants in this manner subjects plaintiffs once again in some cases to the "Alice in Wonderland" effect of having their rights cut off before they arise. For this and other reasons, repose statutes sometimes make exceptions to the limitations period, for such things as: (1) express warranties; (2) hidden defects; (3) failure to warn; (4) fraud (or even negligence); (5) consumer products (vs. "manufacturing equipment"); and/or (6) harm from asbestos, DES, breast implants, or from some other toxic substance generating a latent disease. See, e.g., Eaton v. Jarvis Prods. Corp., 965 F.2d 922 (10th Cir. 1992) (7–year statute applied only to new manufacturing equipment; exception for hidden defects); Chrysler Corp. v. Batten, 450 S.E.2d 208 (Ga. 1994) (10–years; exceptions for negligence causing disease or birth defects, for willful, reckless, or wanton conduct, and for the duty to warn); Oats v. Nissan Motor Corp., 879 P.2d 1095 (Idaho 1994) (10–year useful safe life statute; exceptions for express warranties and hidden defects).

At the end of the period, repose statutes variously provide for: (1) an absolute bar to all claims; (2) a rebuttable presumption of non-defectiveness and non-negligence, rebuttable by a preponderance of the evidence or, alternatively, by clear and convincing evidence; (3) a bar to strict liability actions only; (4) a limitation of liability to the product's "useful life"; or (5) both a useful life provision and some form of repose provision.

Which of the above approaches best balances the interests of plaintiffs and defendants? Which is the most workable?

5. Statutes of Repose—Constitutionality. While several courts have held their state statutes of repose to be unconstitutional, most courts have upheld then against such challenges. See generally McGovern, The Variety, Policy and Constitutionality of Product Liability Statutes of Repose, 30 Am. U. L. Rev. 579 (1981); 30 A.L.R.5th 1 (1995).

6.   Federal Reform. In 1994, "Congress decided that the economic health of the general aviation aircraft manufacturing industry depended on lifting the requirement that manufacturers abide the possibility of litigation for the indefinite future when they sell an airplane." Lyon v. Agusta S.P.A., 252 F.3d 1078, 1089 (9th Cir. 2001). Accordingly, Congress amended the Federal Aviation Act with the General Aviation Revitalization Act of 1994 (GARA), 49 U.S.C. § 40101, Note. GARA provides an 18–year statute of repose, from the date of first delivery, for manufacturers of "general aviation aircraft and the components, systems, subassemblies, and other parts of such aircraft."

7.   Tort *vs*. Warranty. Since tort and warranty statutes of limitations often differ, a plaintiff's lawyer handling a claim arising out of an older accident will have to be cautious in framing his complaint. Cf. Salvador v. Atlantic Steel Boiler Co., 389 A.2d 1148 (Pa. Super. Ct. 1978) (two year tort statute, not UCC § 2–725, applicable to all third party personal injury actions whether or not pleaded under UCC; "It takes a very strained reading of Section 2–725 to conclude that it was ever meant to apply to persons other than the contracting parties").

8.   John Doe Complaints. A "John Doe complaint" may be filed against an unknown manufacturer during the statute of limitations and amended, after the statute has run, to add the manufacturer's name. Although this procedure is permissible in some states, which hold that the replacement of the John Doe designation with the manufacturer's real name relates back to the original timely suit, it is unclear whether the procedure is permitted in federal courts under Fed. R. Civ. P. 15(c). Compare Britt v. Arvanitis, 590 F.2d 57 (3d Cir. 1978) (not permitted), with Lindley v. General Elec. Co., 780 F.2d 797 (9th Cir.), cert. denied, 476 U.S. 1186 (1986) (procedure, permitted under state law, not prohibited by Rule 15(c)).

9.   Conflict of Laws. Conflict of laws issues are raised by variations among state statutes of limitations and repose. Illustrative is Thornton v. Cessna Aircraft Co., 886 F.2d 85 (4th Cir. 1989), involving the crash in Tennessee of an airplane purchased in South Carolina by the decedent pilot who was a resident of South Carolina. In the ensuing products liability action, the court, applying South Carolina conflicts law, held that the negligence and strict liability counts were barred by the Tennessee statute of repose, applicable as the substantive law of the place of injury; however, the breach of warranty count was not barred by the South Carolina UCC statute of limitations (§ 2–725), applicable under UCC § 1–105 because South Carolina had an "appropriate relation" to the sale transaction. See also Ferens v. John Deere Co., 494 U.S. 516 (1990) (statute of limitations chosen by conflicts law of transferor state applies in transfer of venue under 28 U.S.C. § 1404(a), even when plaintiff seeks transfer); Nesladek v. Ford Motor Co., 46 F.3d 734 (8th Cir. 1995) (2–1) (state of accident law applied, rather than subsequent domicile, in part to discourage forum shopping); Brewer v. Dodson Aviation, 447 F.Supp.2d 1166 (W.D.Wash. 2006) (under "most significant relationship" choice-of-law test of forum state, Washington, separate statutes of repose of Ohio (10 years), North Carolina (6 years), and Kansas (10 years), applied to vacuum pump manufacturer, rebuilder, and installer, respectively, rather than that of Washington (12 years)).

On statutes of limitations in complex litigation, see ALI Complex Litigation Project § 6.04 (P.O.D., Apr. 5, 1993). See generally L. MacDougal, R. Felix, & R. Whitten, American Conflicts Law 425–40 (5th ed. 2001).

10. On statutes of limitations and repose, see generally D. Owen, Products Liability Law § 14.5 (2d ed. 2008); 1 D. Owen, M.S. Madden, & M. Davis, Madden & Owen on Products Liability § 16:1 (3d ed. 2000).

PART III

CAUSATION

The search for causes must have been an incident of the early awakening of primordial man. There is no human who hesitates to identify the cause of any calamity that touches his life. In the highest echelons of social and scientific research, the vain attempts to reduce to control the causes of war, crime, poverty, cancer, and other barriers to man's happy existence continue with unabated zeal. The attraction of causes is as magnetic for people as flames are for insects, and it is frequently as deadly.

L. Green, Strict Liability Under Sections 402A and 402B: A Decade of Litigation, 54 Tex.L.Rev. 1185, 1208 (1976).

————

Two distinct topics are examined in this part of the book: (1) cause in fact, and (2) legal or proximate cause. While many courts reserve the term "proximate cause" exclusively for issues concerning the scope of legal duty, others use it in a broader sense to include the concept of cause in fact as well. See, e.g., Kerns v. Engelke, 369 N.E.2d 1284, 1292 (Ill.1977), rev'd in part on other grounds, 390 N.E.2d 859 (Ill.1979): " 'Proximate cause' is a term of art which encompasses the distinct concepts of cause in fact and legal cause. Determining whether defendant's conduct was a cause of plaintiff's injury involves nothing more than an analysis of the facts. Once it is established that the defendant's conduct has in fact been a cause of the injury, however, there remains the question whether the defendant should be legally responsible for what he has caused. As otherwise stated, the question is whether the policy of the law will extend defendant's responsibility to the consequences which have in fact occurred."

CHAPTER 12

CAUSE IN FACT

1. GENERAL PRINCIPLES

Tests of Cause-in-Fact: "But–For" and "Substantial Factor"

The cause-in-fact element in plaintiff's prima facie case for products liability involves the fact-based inquiry of whether a product defect (or defendant's negligence in allowing the defect) contributed to produce or bring about the harm. Most jurisdictions require that plaintiff prove a connection between the defect and plaintiff's injury such that, without the defect, the plaintiff's injury would not have occurred. In other words, defendant's negligence or a product defect must be a *sine qua non*—a necessary antecedent—of plaintiff's injury. This is the "but-for" test: if plaintiff would not have been harmed but for a defect for which the defendant was responsible, the defendant may be said to have caused the harm. Jurisdictions describe this element in many ways, using phrases like producing cause, substantial factor and the like, but the factual nature of the inquiry is the same.

A number of jurisdictions use an alternative test known as the "substantial factor" test which asks whether the defendant's product was a substantial factor in causing the plaintiff's harm. See Clark v. Leisure Vehicles, Inc., 292 N.W.2d 630 (Wis. 1980). This test evolved in cases of concurrent causation when it would be impossible to decide, based on the but-for test, which of two defendants caused the harm. "The substantial factor standard generally produces the same results as does the 'but for' rule of causation.... The substantial factor standard, however, has been embraced as a clearer rule of causation, one which subsumes the 'but for' test while reaching beyond it to satisfactorily address other situations, such as those involving independent or concurrent causes in fact." Rutherford v. Owens–Illinois, Inc., 941 P.2d 1203 (Cal. 1997) (multiple defendants produced asbestos products, exposure to each of which alone could have caused plaintiff's illness). The Restatement (Second) of Torts § 431(a) endorses a substantial factor test for causation whereas the Restatement (Third) of Torts: Liability for Physical Harm § 26 (Proposed Final Draft No. 1, 2005), employs the traditional but-for test as the primary basis for establishing cause-in-fact ("Conduct is a factual cause of harm when the harm would not have occurred absent the conduct.").

The but-for issue arises quite clearly in some cases. For example, in Stewart v. Von Solbrig Hospital, Inc., 321 N.E.2d 428 (Ill. App. 1974), a stainless steel surgical pin made by defendants was implanted in plaintiff's broken leg to help align and stabilize the bone, and the leg was put in a cast. When the fracture did not heal, plaintiff's doctor removed the cast but instructed plaintiff not to walk on the leg. Plaintiff disobeyed, and the pin broke, causing various complications. Plaintiff presented evidence "that the Rush pin in question had inclusions and scratches which reduced the pin's strength.... Even if the pin had no defects whatsoever, the evidence showed that the pin would have broken if the plaintiff walked on it after his cast was removed." The cause of the break, therefore, was the plaintiff's conduct, not the pin.

The *sine qua non* connection between defect and harm often is also in issue in cases where the product is seriously abused or mishandled. So, for example, even if the gas tank on an automobile is located too close to the rear of the car, this defect in design is not a cause of an explosion following a high speed collision that would have exploded the tank even had it been located in a "proper" position. See Self v. General Motors Corp., 116 Cal.Rptr. 575 (Ct.App.1974).

The but-for test may sometimes wear substantial-factor-test clothing. In Morales v. American Honda Motor Co., Inc., 151 F.3d 500 (6th Cir. 1998), the 9–year–old plaintiff was injured while riding on the back of a motorcycle. Plaintiff alleged that defendant should have attached a red flag to the seat which would have made the motorcycle more visible to other drivers, including the driver who collided with the motorcycle, injuring plaintiff. Defendant argued that the driver would not have seen a safety flag even if one had been in place because of an obstructed view. The Court held that a jury question was presented on whether lack of a red flag was "a substantial factor" in causing the accident.

Whichever test is employed, by far the most important feature of the cause-in-fact inquiry is the nature and quantum of proof necessary to establish the requisite connection between defendant's product and plaintiff's harm. Proof that it was the defendant's product—not some other product or event (even one of the plaintiff's own doing)—that caused the injury, and difficulties in determining the sufficiency of that evidence, are the subject of the next section.

2. PROOF OF CAUSATION

A. IDENTIFYING THE DEFENDANT

Drayton v. Jiffee Chemical Corp.

United States District Court, Northern District of Ohio, 1975.
395 F.Supp. 1081, modified and aff'd, 591 F.2d 352 (6th Cir.1978).

■ BATTISTI, CHIEF JUDGE.

This action arose out of the severe facial disfigurement incurred by the infant plaintiff, Terri Drayton, as a result of a chemical burn. After a trial to the court, the following facts have been established.

The incident in question occurred on December 21, 1968. At that time both plaintiffs, the infant Terri Drayton and her mother Bernice Drayton, lived in a boarding house in Cleveland, Ohio. The house was occupied by several other tenants including James Henderson, the putative father of Terri Drayton.

At approximately 7:00 p.m. on the night of December 21, 1968 Bernice Drayton and her daughter were on the first floor of the boarding house readying it for Christmas by decorating the Christmas tree and retrieving toys and decorations from the basement. At about that time Henderson returned home and obtained a bottle of "liquid-plumr" from his landlady, Mrs. Sorrell, for the purpose of clearing a clogged drain in the second floor bathroom sink. As he ascended the stairs, Henderson had his daughter, Terri, in one arm and the bottle of liquid-plumr in the other. Henderson testified that as he climbed the stairs he read a portion of the label.

At the top of the stairs, Henderson put Terri on the floor in the hall and entered the bathroom alone. According to the testimony, he then poured half of the bottle of liquid-plumr into the drain and placed the uncapped bottle on the back of the sink adjacent to the left faucet. Henderson then placed a towel over the open drain and stepped back from the sink. At that moment Terri grabbed his leg and screamed. When Henderson looked down at the child, she had been doused with the liquid drain cleaner. Henderson testified that he was unaware of the child's presence in the bathroom until the instant he heard her scream.

Immediately after the accident, Henderson took the child downstairs where both Bernice Drayton and Mrs. Sorrell were present. Recalling that the label said "something about burns" and "something about water" Henderson wet his handkerchief and dabbed at Terri's face. After some confusion, Henderson, Mrs. Drayton, Mrs. Sorrell, and Terri drove to Forest City Hospital [which transferred Terri] to University Hospitals for admission, a transfer that entailed an additional twenty-five minute delay. [Terri's injuries were severe.]

The product that allegedly caused Terri Drayton's injuries, liquid-plumr, is designed, manufactured, and marketed by defendant Jiffee Chemical Corporation, an Indiana corporation. [Among other contentions,] Jiffee denies that it was their product (liquid-plumr) that was being used by Henderson at the time of the accident.

With regard to this last contention, it is significant to note that the container which Henderson used to clear the bathroom drain was never recovered nor were the circumstances of its disposal ascertained. Given the emotional atmosphere that surrounded the accident and its aftermath it is most likely that the container was disposed of without regard to what role it might play in possible future litigation. Thus the identity of the injury-causing product must be determined from the testimony of those who were present in the boarding house at the time of the accident.

The landlady of the boarding house, Mrs. Sorrell, testified that she bought a bottle of liquid-plumr in 1966, more than a year before the incident that is the subject of the instant action. She was quite definite in her testimony as was Mrs. Drayton who said that she remembered the name "liquid-plumr" because "those words were large."

Defendant argues that the injury-producing product was not "liquid-plumr" but rather "Mister Plumber", a drain cleaner composed of 92–93% sulfuric acid. The basis for such argument is certain behavior by Henderson that is arguably inconsistent with the recommended procedures for employing liquid-plumr. Great emphasis is placed on Henderson's covering of the drain with a towel immediately after pouring in the drain cleaner. At a 1972 deposition Henderson testified:

> Q. You said, as I understand it, you poured some liquid-plumr into the sink and then put a towel on top of it?
>
> A. Right.
>
> Q. Why did you do that?
>
> A. As I remember reading the label, it said something about odors, you know, giving off a bad odor or something, so I placed a towel over it.
>
> At trial, Henderson's testimony was substantially identical.

The reason for defendant's reliance on Henderson's covering the drain with a towel emanates from the precise wording of the liquid-plumr and Mister Plumber labels. The liquid-plumr label is virtually devoid of any reference to odors. On the front of the label it says merely "No Odor." The Mister Plumber label, however, specifically directs that the drain be covered with a wet cloth. It also states "have plenty of VENTILATION as unpleasant odors may arise. Covering drain with wet cloth will help." Inasmuch as Henderson testified that he had had no prior experience with drain cleaners such behavior is certainly more consistent with having read the Mister Plumber directions than those contained on the liquid-plumr label. Such an inference, however, is not sufficient to offset the uncontroverted (albeit self-serving) testimony of Henderson, Mrs. Drayton, and Mrs. Sorrell. For such an inference to prevail, this Court would have to find the unequivocal testimony of all three of the above witnesses to be incredible—something which it is not prepared to do.

Similarly, defendant [relies upon] Henderson's *dabbing* Terri's face with a wet handkerchief rather than *flushing* it with water [pointing] to the exact wording of the respective labels. The liquid-plumr label calls for the affected area to be flushed or flooded with large amounts of water [whereas Mr. Plumber] directs that the area be wiped gently prior to being flooded with water. This act by Henderson, which was reasonable and prudent under the circumstances, is too fragile an underpinning upon which to find a misidentification of the injurious product.

At trial defendant also made reference to the rapidity with which the liquid drain cleaner burned Terry Drayton as well as the fact that Mrs. Sorrell's shirt was eaten through as a result of holding Terri Drayton's head to her chest while en route to the hospital. Mr. Levy, who is president of Krobaugh Laboratories, testified that sulfuric acid acts much more quickly on human tissue than does sodium hydroxide. Similarly, Mr. Summerfelt, the manager of specialty products for Clorox, testified that the effect of the chemical on Mrs. Sorrell's shirt was inconsistent with exposure to a 30% solution of sodium hydroxide and, in fact, was more consistent with exposure to sulfuric acid.

Such empirical observations, however, are of little significance absent a factual frame of reference. To say that sulfuric acid burns human tissue more quickly than sodium hydroxide is not to say that sodium hydroxide doesn't burn it at all. At trial it was impossible to accurately fix the total elapsed time that the liquid drain cleaner was on Terri Drayton's face. Considering only the twenty-five minute delay in driving from Forest City Hospital to University Hospitals such exposure to the liquid drain cleaner was not insubstantial.

It is also impossible to identify the brand of drain cleaner by its effect on Mrs. Sorrell's shirt. Absent precise information about the shirt's fiber and composition and the duration of the chemical contact any attempt to correlate corrosive effect with a specific chemical compound would be purely speculative. Thus plaintiffs have proven, by a preponderance of the evidence, that it was, in fact, liquid-plumr that came in contact with Terri Drayton and caused her injuries.

[The court found the defendant liable.]

NOTES

1. Was it really liquid-plumr, or was it Mister Plumber? Why did the court rule as it did?

2. If this case had been subsequently reversed and remanded for a new trial, how might defendant have improved its chances of success at retrial?

3. Judge or Jury. Why was there no jury in this case?

4. Identifying the Manufacturer. A plaintiff ordinarily must prove the identity of the manufacturer of the particular injury-producing product. See, e.g., Moore v. Mississippi Valley Gas Co., 863 So.2d 43 (Miss. 2003) (plaintiff failed to identify manufacturer of gas heater that burned her child; product had been replaced and discarded two years after the injury and landlord had no record of the manufacturer at time of suit six years later; summary judgment proper); Brown v. Stone Mfg. Co., 660 F.Supp. 454, 458 (S.D.Miss.1986) (child's pink nightgown that caught fire, the remnants of which were discarded at hospital, was purchased from store that carried several similar brands; child thought defendant's gown purchased by mother at same store one year after accident was "sort of like" accident gown but had different color design; washing instructions remembered by mother differed from those on defendant's subsequently purchased gown—*held,* jury not permitted "to resort to guesswork in identifying . . . proper manufacturer").

5. Direct Evidence. One method of identification is proof that the product bears the defendant's name, as by a label or decal of some sort. See, e.g., Kim v. Ingersoll Rand Co., 921 F.2d 197 (8th Cir.1990) (logo on air hammer); Helm v. Pepsi–Cola Bottling Co., 723 S.W.2d 465 (Mo.App.1986) (plaintiff's wife and lawyer both read "Mead Corporation" on bottom of defective carton subsequently lost by another lawyer).

Another method of identification is proof that the retailer purchased the product sold to the consumer from a particular supplier. Payton v. Abbott Labs., 780 F.2d 147 (1st Cir.1985) (pharmacist purchased generic drug from supplier who generally purchased that type of drug from defendant); Daniels v. GNB, Inc., 629 So.2d 595 (Miss.1993) (batteries always bought from same supplier).

6. Circumstantial Evidence. Where there is no direct identifying information, other evidence may point toward the defendant, such as the product's composition or method of construction (like a garment's stitching) that is unique to the defendant. Cf. C.K.S. Inc. v. Helen Borgenicht Sportswear, Inc., 268 N.Y.S.2d 409 (App.Div.1966) (appearance and composition of blouse). Or its color, English v. Crenshaw Supply Co., 387 S.E.2d 628 (Ga.App.1989) (brackets painted red).

7. Loss of Accident Product—Spoliation of Evidence. What if plaintiff loses or destroys the container or accident product before identification is established? Is the action necessarily destroyed with the product? See Jones v. General Motors Corp., 731 N.Y.S.2d 90 (App.Div.2001)(trial court has discretion on whether or not to strike pleadings).

Some courts treat spoliation of the evidence as an admission against interest when a party with a duty to preserve evidence intentionally, but not negligently, destroys or loses it, raising an inference that the destroyed evidence was unfavorable to that party. Courtney v. Big O Tires, Inc., 87 P.3d 930 (Idaho 2003). And while spoliation may raise inferences in favor of victim of spoliation, independent evidence of defect is required and the plaintiff still has the burden of proof. See Rizzuto v. Davidson Ladders, Inc., 905 A.2d 1165 (Conn. 2006). For these reasons, a few courts have recognized an independent claim for spoliation. Id. at 1178 (recognizing independent claim for intentional spoliation to promote tort law goals, because of insufficiency of other remedies, "when a first party defendant destroys evidence intentionally with the purpose and effect of precluding a plaintiff from fulfilling his burden of production in a pending or impending case").

8. Failure to Produce Identification Evidence—Malpractice. A plaintiff's lawyer who loses, destroys, or fails to obtain or preserve an allegedly defective product for use at trial, leading to dismissal of the underlying products liability action, also may be subject to a legal malpractice action. Galanek v. Wismar, 81 Cal.Rptr.2d 236, 241–242 (Ct.App. 1999); Huber v. Watson, 568 N.W.2d 787 (Iowa 1997) (plaintiff's attorney failed to meet a product identification deadline in asbestos action, leading to summary judgment; plaintiff's subsequent *malpractice* action could proceed on proof that plaintiff's attorney failed to obtain available evidence that asbestos-containing products were present at plaintiff's worksite).

9. Multiple Defendants—Concurrent Causes.

A. Liability. If the actions or products of two or more parties combined to cause the plaintiff's harm, then each such party which was a "substantial factor" in causing the harm may be liable. See, e.g., Bockrath v. Aldrich Chem. Co., 980 P.2d 398 (Cal. 1999) (substantial-factor test permitted worker to maintain products liability complaint against 55 manufacturers of chemicals that allegedly caused his cancer); Basko v. Sterling Drug, Inc., 416 F.2d 417 (2d Cir.1969) (two drugs). This is the classic use of the substantial factor test.

B. **"A" vs. "the" substantial factor.** All that the plaintiff must establish is that the defendant's negligence, or the defect in its product, was "a"—rather than "the"—substantial factor in causing the accident. See, e.g., Vlahovich v. Betts Mach. Co., 242 N.E.2d 17, 20 (Ill.App.1968) (concurring opinion), aff'd, 260 N.E.2d 230 (Ill.1970). Similarly, jury instructions that quantify the requisite "size" of a substantial factor are reversible error. See Jeter v. Owens–Corning Fiberglas Corp., 716 A.2d 633 (Pa. Super. 1998) ("considerable" and "significantly large" improper description of required connection; a substantial factor need not be the sole factor).

C.   Concurrent Causes—Apportionment of damages. It is often difficult to determine which portions of a plaintiff's injuries are attributable to each of two or more responsible parties. If the trier of fact is able to determine which aspects of the plaintiff's loss are attributable to each defendant, then damages ordinarily will be apportioned on that basis. But where no fair and practicable method for apportioning the loss is available, then, traditionally, each defendant whose breach of duty was a substantial factor in producing the damage may be held jointly and severally responsible for the total loss. See, e.g., Smith v. J.C. Penney Co., Inc., 525 P.2d 1299 (Or.1974) (plaintiff suffered severe burns from her excessively flammable imitation fur coat which caught fire when service station operator negligently sprayed gasoline on floor heater).

The doctrine of joint and several liability has increasingly eroded in recent years, as part of the tort reform movement, and most states now have modified or abolished the doctrine. The Restatement (Third) of Torts: Apportionment of Liability (2000), identified at least five variations on the use of joint and several liability. There is no longer a majority rule in the area and much of this law is statutory.

10.   Multiple Defendants—One Cause.

A.   General rule. What should be done if plaintiff can trace his or her injuries to a single product manufactured by A, B, or C, but is unable to identify which of the three culprits manufactured the offending product? Under conventional principles, since plaintiff has the burden of proof on causation, plaintiff's case will fail in this situation.

Plaintiff took one of his two disposable butane lighters from his shirt pocket, lit a cigarette, watched the lighter's flame disappear, and returned it to his pocket. His shirt quickly caught fire, and plaintiff was burned. Unable to recall which lighter he had used, he sued the suppliers of both. The trial court granted summary judgment for defendant since "the best that could be said of this evidence is that it established a 50–50 chance that the fire was started by a particular lighter and this did not qualify as preponderance of the evidence" such that plaintiff failed to sustain his burden of proof. *Held*, affirmed. Martin v. E–Z Mart Stores, Inc., 464 F.3d 827, 829 (8th Cir. 2006).

Compare Garcia v. Joseph Vince Co., 148 Cal.Rptr. 843, 846–47 (Ct. App. 1978) ("Hamlet II"), where a college student's eye was injured during a fencing match when his opponent's sabre penetrated his mask because its tip was thin and sharp instead of round. The sabre was thereafter placed back in the team bag with all the other sabres and was not produced at trial because it had either been lost or "mixed up with the others in the shuffle." The coach had purchased the sabres from two manufacturers. Since there was no evidence pointing to either manufacturer in particular, plaintiff sued both. The nonsuit was affirmed: "The jury on the basis of such evidence would be purely speculating as to who should be liable ... The evidence was evenly divided ...''

Plaintiff argued "that when the evidence is evenly balanced ..., under the rule of Summers v. Tice, 199 P.2d 1 (Cal.1948), the burden of proof should shift to [the defendants] to establish who sold the product. This argument has no merit." Why not? Recall that the rule of alternative liability from *Summers* shifts the burden of proof on causation to two defendants when their tortious but independent actions cause harm to the plaintiff who cannot establish which particular defendant caused the harm. Why is this theory unavailable in *Garcia*?

B. Exception. Contrast Snider v. Bob Thibodeau Ford, Inc., 202 N.W.2d 727 (Mich.Ct.App.1972), where plaintiff was injured when the brakes on his delivery truck failed. Since plaintiff was unable to prove whether the defect had been caused by the manufacturer or the dealer, the trial court dismissed his action against the manufacturer. *Held,* reversed:

> True, the burden of proving which of two possible wrongdoers is responsible is generally assigned to the plaintiff. The courts have, however, shown a willingness to consider special circumstances when allocating the burden of proof. This accords with the general view that the placing of that burden is "merely a question of policy and fairness" based on experience in the different situations.

* * *

> In this case, because of the technical problems involved in a brake system, the superior knowledge and expertise of a manufacturer like Ford, and the close relationship between the manufacturer and retailer Thibodeau, we conclude that the burden of negating individual responsibility for the brake failure should be placed on the defendants.

Id. at 732–33. How is this situation different from *Garcia*? To what other situations might an alternative liability theory apply?

Sutowski v. Eli Lilly & Co.

Supreme Court of Ohio, 1998.
696 N.E.2d 187.

■ Cook, Justice.

[The United States District Court certified the following question of law to this court: Whether market-share liability exists in Ohio as a viable theory of liability in a DES products liability action?] We respond in the negative: In Ohio, market-share liability is not an available theory of recovery in a products liability action.

DES is a form of synthetic estrogen that gained widespread use in the early 1940s. Its uses include hormone replacement during menopause, and the treatment of both senile and gonorrheal vaginitis. By the late 1940s, DES was also being used for the treatment of certain complications of pregnancy. Researchers in the early 1970s, however, discovered a high incidence of clear cell adenocarcinoma, a rare form of cancer, in women exposed to DES *in utero*. As a result, use of DES during pregnancy ceased.

Other reproductive disorders such as a predisposition to miscarry, the injury Sutowski claims, have also been attributed to *in utero* DES exposure. [Citations; Grover v. Eli Lilly & Co., 591 N.E.2d 696 (Ohio 1992), examined in ch. 11(4), above.]

Because DES was not patented, some two hundred to three hundred different drug companies produced DES in the years it was widely prescribed for use during pregnancy. Due to the long interval between DES use and manifestation of its effects a generation later, the great number of possible manufacturer-defendants, and the primarily generic form of the drug, many DES plaintiffs experienced difficulty identifying the particular manufacturer of the drug taken by their mothers years earlier. [Citation.] Many manufacturers were no longer in business, medical and pharmacy records were lost or destroyed, and memories had dulled over time. [Citations.]

In response to the DES plaintiff's inability to establish causation, the California Supreme Court fashioned the market-share theory of liability in its benchmark decision, Sindell v. Abbott Laboratories, 607 P.2d 924 (Cal. 1980). In *Sindell,* the trial court dismissed a DES plaintiff's complaint because she was unable to identify the particular manufacturer of the drug prescribed for her mother. The supreme court reversed, resolving in the plaintiff's favor the conflict between the traditional causation requirement of tort law and the desire to insulate an innocent plaintiff from bearing the cost of injury.

* * * The court cited the following three policy considerations in favor of relieving the plaintiff of the burden of proving causation: (1) the manufacturer should bear the cost of injury as between it and an innocent plaintiff, (2) manufacturers are better able to bear the cost of injury resulting from defective products, and (3) because manufacturers are in a better position to discover and prevent product defects and to warn consumers of harmful effects, imposing liability would further ensure product safety. *Sindell,* 607 P.2d at 936.

Recognizing that "there is a possibility that none of the five defendants in this case produced the offending substance," the California Supreme Court nonetheless justified shifting the burden of proof of causation to the defendant. [Citation.] To this end, the market-share plaintiff need only (1) identify an injury caused by a fungible product, and (2) join in the action a substantial share of the manufacturers of that product. The burden then shifts to each defendant-manufacturer to prove that it did not make the particular injurious product. Market-share liability thus enables a plaintiff who cannot identify a particular tortfeasor to sustain a tort cause of action despite an inability to show proximate causation. [In fairness to manufacturers, each is severally liable for the proportion of the plaintiff's awarded damages that reflects that manufacturer's total share of the product market.] In support of this unique method of damage allocation, the court reasoned that a defendant-manufacturer's percentage share of the total market for a product is proportional to the likelihood that the defendant-manufacturer produced the specific product that injured the plaintiff. The only causation a plaintiff need prove in order to recover under a market-share theory is the causal connection between exposure to, or use of, the product at issue and the injury sustained.

This atypical theory of tort recovery has not gained wide acceptance outside California. Of the courts that have examined market-share liability in the DES context, most have not considered it a plausible theory of recovery. Ohio may now be numbered among those that have considered and rejected market-share theory in the DES context. . . .

Ohio common law has long required a plaintiff to prove that a particular defendant caused his or her injury through negligence. "The rule is elementary, that the defendant in an action for negligence can be held to respond in damages only for the immediate and proximate result of the negligent act complained of" . . . [citations]. The plaintiff must establish a causal connection between the defendant's actions and the plaintiff's injuries, which necessitates identification of the particular tortfeasor.

Under the market-share theory, the plaintiff is discharged from proving this important causal link. The defendant actually responsible for the plaintiff's injuries may not be before the court. Such a result collides with traditional tort notions of liability by virtue of responsibility, and imposes a judicially created form of industry-wide insurance upon those manufacturers subject to market-share liability. In the end, "manufacturers are required to pay or contribute to payment for injuries which their product may not have caused." Mulcahy v. Eli Lilly & Co., 386 N.W.2d 67, 76 (Iowa 1986). This is not the law in Ohio: "Manufacturers are not insurers of their products." [Citation.]

[A review of Ohio cases reveals that the alternative liability theory is available where a plaintiff establishes two negligent defendants and a single cause. Minnich v. Ashland Oil Co., 473 N.E.2d 1199 (Ohio 1984) (citing Summers v. Tice, 199 P.2d 1 (Cal. 1948)). A subsequent case rejected both alternative liability and market share liability in an asbestos action. Goldman v. Johns–Manville Sales Corp., 514 N.E.2d 691 (Ohio 1987).] While in dicta the *Goldman* court presumed that DES litigation was better suited to application of market-share liability, it did not, as Sutowski suggests, state that market-share liability is an available remedy in Ohio. Citing a lack of fungibility, difficulty in defining the asbestos market, and the absence, due to bankruptcy, of the largest asbestos supplier in the world, the court explained that adoption of the market-share theory was a matter singularly suited for the legislature. [Citation.]

[The 1988 Ohio Products Liability Act applicable at the time of Sutowski's claim provides additional support for rejecting market share liability. It subjects a manufacturer to liability only upon proof that a defective product condition was a "proximate cause" of the plaintiff's harm. The current Ohio statute, revised from that applicable to Sutowski's claim, is also instructive. It *prohibits* a products liability claim asserted on a theory of "industrywide or enterprise liability" but *allows* alternative liability "when all possible tortfeasors are named and subject to the jurisdiction of the court." Ohio Rev. Code § 2307.791 (1997)].

Statutory language that is plain and unambiguous, and conveys a clear and definite meaning, needs no interpretation. [Citation.] In this instance, the 1988 version of the Products Liability Act applicable to Sutowski's claim unmistakably required identification of a particular tortfeasor: the successful plaintiff had to establish that the harmful product was defective when it left the manufacturer's control. While not applied retroactively, the 1997 amendments to the Act serve to conclusively reinforce this identification requirement.

[We also rely on a decision by the Sixth Circuit Court of Appeals, *Kurczi v. Eli Lilly & Co.*, 113 F.3d 1426 (6th Cir. 1997), which concluded that the Ohio Supreme Court would not adopt a market-share theory of liability in DES cases based] on the following: (1) Ohio common law embraces the fundamental principle of tort law that a plaintiff must prove that the negligence of a particular defendant caused injury, (2) the 1988 Ohio Products Liability Act "embodies the general common law principle that a plaintiff has to prove an injury proximately caused by a particular defendant," and (3) presuming the General Assembly was aware of the *Minnich* and *Goldman* decisions, alternative and market-share liability schemes are noticeably absent from the 1988 Act. [Citation.] This analysis by the Sixth Circuit is unassailable, . . .

Accordingly, we hold that in Ohio, market-share liability is not an available theory of recovery in a products liability action. . . .

We recognize that the DES plaintiff who, without fault, is unable to identify the manufacturer responsible for her injury engenders sympathy. It is, however, the role of the court to interpret the law, not to legislate. [Citation.] We believe the General Assembly should decide the policy question of whether Sutowski's claims, or others like hers, warrant substantially altering Ohio's tort law.

■ DOUGLAS, J., dissenting.

* * *

The majority's holding in this case is not only contrary to general notions of fairness and equity, but it is also predicated on numerous misstatements and misapplications of law. A reading of today's decision should reveal to any interested person that the majority quite simply does not wish to recognize market-share liability. . . .

The majority's entire decision in this case is built upon the erroneous premise that market-share liability relieves a plaintiff of the obligation to prove proximate causation. . . . The fallacy of this argument is demonstrated by a brief discussion of *Goldman*. . . . At the outset of the *Goldman* decision, this court emphasized that "it is important to understand that both alternative liability and market-share liability are *exceptions* to the general rule that a plaintiff has to prove an injury was caused by the negligence of a *particular* defendant. . . ." *Both theories merely relax the requirement that the plaintiff identify which one of a group of negligent tortfeasors caused the injury to the plaintiff. . . .* As *Goldman* clearly illustrates, market-share liability does not eliminate the need for proof of proximate causation. Rather, the theory of market-share liability merely relaxes the requirement that the injured plaintiff identify which *one* of a group of tortfeasors caused the plaintiff's injuries. The plaintiff still must prove proximate causation, but need not identify the specific party that was actually responsible for the plaintiff's particular injury. Today's majority has gone to great lengths to distort that issue.

[Regarding the majority's analysis of the Ohio statute,] the majority has not applied the "plain and unambiguous" language of any statute, and the majority has certainly not considered the history of the Act. The 1988 version of the [Act] says nothing whatsoever about market-share liability, and the 1997 amendments to the Act serve to "conclusively reinforce" nothing that the majority says. What the majority has done in this case is to *interpret* (or, more appropriately, *misinterpret* the Act). The majority admits as much when it states [that] "[i]t is, however, the role of the court to *interpret the law*, not to legislate." (Emphasis added.) Is this a deathbed confession by the majority that it has interpreted the [A]ct as opposed to applying the "plain and unambiguous" language . . . ?

■ Pfeiffer, J., dissenting.

The right-to-remedy clause of the Ohio Constitution mandates that "every person, for an injury done him in his . . . person, . . . shall have remedy by due course of the law." Section 16, Art. I, Ohio Constitution. [As we have previously stated,] "When the Constitution speaks of remedy and injury to person, property or reputation, it requires an opportunity granted *at a meaningful time and in a meaningful manner*." [Citation]. The majority appears determined to ensure that the plaintiffs do not receive their constitutional right to a remedy. * * *

It is difficult to imagine a case better suited to market-share liability. DES was fungible, virtually impossible to differentiate, and most important, it was all bad. . . . It is unconscionable that any profoundly injured woman of the estimated four hundred thirty thousand Ohio women who took DES should be prohibited from successfully pursuing constitutionally protected compensation for injuries done simply because she can only trace the harm to a group of manufacturers of the same product. . . . Applying market-share liability is the only avenue for DES-injured women to successfully pursue a meaningful remedy.

NOTES

1. Market Share Liability. Variations on market share liability have been adopted by the high courts of several states, notably Washington, Wisconsin, Michigan, New York, Florida (only in negligence), and Hawaii (blood products). In most such states, the doctrine is limited to the DES context, and it has been rejected by the high courts of a number of states, notably Illinois, Missouri, Iowa, and New Jersey (childhood vaccines). The New York case, Hymowitz v. Eli Lilly & Co., 539 N.E.2d 1069 (N.Y. 1989), adopted a national market share theory and, consequently, a large number of DES cases have been filed there. For the history of DES and the *Hymowitz* case in particular, see Bernstein, *Hymowitz v. Eli Lilly and Co.*: Markets of Mothers, Torts Stories 151 (R. Rabin & S. Sugarman, eds., 2003).

2.   The courts that have rejected market share liability consider it too radical a departure from established principles of causation and the burden of proof. The Products Liability Restatement § 15 cmt. *c*, noting the problems of proportional liability, leaves the matter to developing law.

3.   The Wisconsin Supreme Court extended its version of market share liability, the "risk-contribution" theory, to manufacturers of lead-based paint in Thomas v. Mallett, 701 N.W.2d 523 (Wis. 2005). Most courts reject the theory even in such toxic exposure cases despite the often insurmountable defendant identification problems plaintiffs face. Because the market share doctrine applies, if at all, in such cases, it is examined again in ch. 19.

B.   ESTABLISHING CAUSATION: SUFFICIENCY OF THE EVIDENCE

Henderson v. Sunbeam Corp.

United States Court of Appeals, Tenth Circuit, 1995.
46 F.3d 1151.

■ Before ANDERSON, BALDOCK, and BRORBY, CIRCUIT JUDGES.

[Defendants appeal denials of post-trial motions on verdict and judgment for plaintiff in action for property lost in a fire allegedly caused by an electric blanket defendants had manufactured and sold to plaintiff some two years earlier. Affirmed.]

A product liability claim in Oklahoma requires proof that (1) a defective product caused the plaintiff's injury; (2) the defect existed in the product at the time it left the hands of the manufacturer or seller; and (3) the defect made the product unreasonably dangerous to the plaintiff or her property. [Citations.] Defendants contend plaintiff's trial proof, consisting of circumstantial evidence and expert opinion testimony, was legally insufficient to establish that a defect in their electric blanket caused the fire at plaintiff's home. Of course, this type of evidence has always been considered an acceptable, indeed often necessary, means of proof in product cases, [citations] so defendants' objection must go to the weight or probative value of plaintiff's evidence, rather than simply its indirect character. . . .

The parties' stipulations focused the search for the fire's cause on an electrical source in plaintiff's bedroom, specifically on or near the bed. Plaintiff's fire origin expert, L. D. Hallman, testified at length about his first-hand examination of the scene, including the electrical appliances therein, and opined on the basis of his observations that the electric blanket started the fire. This general conclusion was also endorsed by plaintiff's other expert witness, Dr. Croenwett, who specializes in the analysis of malfunctions in electrical devices.

Dr. Croenwett went on to explain what he considered to be the defective component of the blanket and how that defect related causally to the fire. Specifically, he blamed a broken connection in the heating element, which arced and ignited the mantle fabric. His reconstruction of the accident, like that offered by Hallman with which it substantially agreed, was tied to the physical evidence and testimony adduced at trial, and his specification of the design defect responsible was buttressed by testimony that the fire could have been avoided by inclusion of a safety device costing less than $2.50.

Defendants make much of the fact that Hallman found a different defect responsible for the initial arc igniting the blanket, faulting the control unit instead of the heating element in the mantle. The jury, however, was free to believe either expert—or, for that matter, to side with defendants' experts, who blamed the bed vibrator[3].... A jury question is created, not negated, by disagreement among experts, [citation], and the fact that plaintiff's own experts disagreed did not alter the jury's authority to resolve the issue consistently with Dr. Croenwett's view,[4] cf. Poertner v. Swearingen, 695 F.2d 435, 437 (10th Cir.1982) (conflict in expert testimony offered by plaintiff raises issue for jury to resolve). We focus here on Dr. Croenwett's opinions, as he [focused on] the contested elements of plaintiff's claim, including the specification of a defect existing at the time of manufacture [citation].

Defendants contend that the testimony of Dr. Croenwett, who could not identify precisely which connection in the mantle's wiring grid had failed, was, for that reason, legally insufficient to provide a basis for the jury's finding of liability. The case law favors plaintiff on this critical point. Where, as here, an allegedly defective product has largely destroyed itself, making direct evidence of the precise operative defect unavailable, the plaintiff may prove her case with circumstantial evidence, typically including expert testimony, even though she "is unable to point an accusing finger at a particular defective component." [Citations.]

* * * The district court considered the jury's verdict consistent with the evidence presented before it, and nothing urged on this appeal persuades us otherwise.

[Affirmed.]

---

3. The parties stipulated that the vibrator's motor would have to have been on to cause the fire. However, the motor ran for only fifteen-minutes on its timer, and the fire at plaintiff's house was first observed nearly three hours after she left in the morning. Plaintiff's experts considered the obvious timing discrepancy a compelling common-sense corroboration of their common opinion that the vibrator did not cause the fire. Defendants' experts offered no explanation for the delay.

4. There is an important distinction to be drawn here between equivocation by a party's only expert and disagreement among her multiple experts. The former may not provide probative evidence, if the expert never espouses a definite opinion; the latter, however, clearly does provide probative evidence, albeit of conflicting positions that must be assessed by the trier of fact.

Bitler v. A. O. Smith Corp.

United States Court of Appeals, Tenth Circuit, 2004.
391 F.3d 1114.

■ LUCERO, CIRCUIT JUDGE.

Danger lurked in Fred and Peggy Bitler's basement, liability for which is the occasion for the present appeal. Mr. Bitler was severely burned when a gas explosion occurred in the basement of his home. [The Bitlers filed suit against the manufacturer of the water heater, A.O. Smith Corp., and White–Rodgers, manufacturer of the gas control installed in the water heater. The jury found negligence and product defect and awarded damages to the Bitlers. White–Rodgers appeals and assigns as principal error the district court's admission of plaintiffs' expert testimony under *Daubert* principles. We affirm.]

Fred and Peggy Bitler resided in a house provided for their use on the Oldland Ranch outside of Meeker, Colorado where Fred Bitler was a ranch hand. On the evening of the accident, July 25, 1996, Bitler discovered that there was no hot water when he attempted to shower. Hot water was supplied to the Bitlers' home by a liquid propane hot water heater located in the basement. [H]e proceeded to the basement door, unlatched it, and walked approximately two-thirds of the way down the staircase when a large explosion occurred, knocking him backwards. His wife ... was thrown off a sofa and onto the floor, which was later determined to have been raised several inches by the force of the explosion. Fred Bitler sustained severe [injuries.]

There were three gas propane appliances in the Bitlers' home—a cook stove in the kitchen, a furnace in a bedroom, and a space heater in one of the bedrooms. Gas was supplied to the water heater via unsupported, flexible copper tubing that ran along the basement ceiling joints. A "T-fitting" was located above the hot water heater which provided branches running to the hot water heater and the space heater. Post-accident inspection revealed a minor leak at the inlet to the bedroom heater, and a leak at the "T-connector."

White–Rodgers ... manufactured the water heater gas control used in the Bitlers' hot water heater. This gas control regulates the flow of gas to the pilot and main burner of the water heater, and is designed to fulfill a crucial safety role if the pilot light is extinguished. To avoid a gas leak that could lead to an explosion or fire, the gas control is designed to shut off all gas flow to the pilot when the pilot is extinguished.... So long as the pilot is lit, the safety valve remains open. If the pilot goes out, however, [the safety valve snaps shut.] The safety valve seat is made of rubber, and is designed to create a seal ... when closed to prevent the flow of gas to the pilot.

Copper sulfide is a frequent contaminate found in gas and propane lines. If copper sulfide particles of sufficient size become lodged on a safety valve seat when a pilot is extinguished, the particles may prevent the valve from sealing, resulting in a gas leak. [Aware of accidents from copper sulfide contaminants, in 1978 White–Rodgers added a wire mesh screen in the gas inlet of their safety valves to prevent such particles from migrating onto the rubber valve seat and, in 1980, it recalled the pre–1978 controls. Thereafter, White–Rodgers added another safety feature to prevent debris from reaching the valve, but the Bitler's water heater was produced in the interim and so contained the mesh screen but not the additional safety feature.]

As a result of their investigations, plaintiffs' expert Elden Boh, [an insurance company fire investigator,] concluded that the water heater was the source of the accident, and plaintiffs' expert Donald Sommer, [an engineer and accident investigator,] concluded that the leak was caused by copper sulfide contamination on the water heater's safety valve seat.... During post-accident testing of the safety valve [from] the Bitlers' water heater, the device was disassembled in the presence of representatives of both White–Rodgers and the Bitlers. Copper sulfide particulate contamination was discovered downstream of the mesh screen and found on the safety valve seat. During the teardown, a test of the valve revealed that it snapped shut as designed. [Sommer] opined at trial that a mix of copper sulfide particles and grease located on the safety valve seat caused the leak; ... that the valve seat was altered after the accident when the control was turned to the "off" position; [and] that because copper sulfide contamination leads to intermittent leaks, the teardown test could not be determinative. Whether the particles found on the safety valve were large enough or of sufficient quantity to have caused the gas leak in the present case is hotly disputed.

[After denial of its post-trial motions, White–Rodgers appealed and] assigns as a principal source of error the district court's performance of its *Daubert* gatekeeping functions. [Fed. R. Evid. 702 requires *reliability* and *relevance* to support admissibility of expert opinion testimony. Under the reliability prong of Fed. R. Evid. 702, a] plaintiff need not prove that the expert is undisputably correct or that the expert's theory is "generally accepted" in the scientific community. Instead, the plaintiff must show that the method employed by the expert in reaching the conclusion is scientifically sound and that the opinion is based on [sufficient facts]. * * * [While *Daubert* provided factors that might bear on a judge's gatekeeping determination, the Court was clear] that a trial judge has wide discretion both in deciding how to assess an expert's reliability and in making a determination of that reliability....

Accordingly, a trial court's focus generally should not be upon the precise conclusions reached by the expert, but on the methodology employed in reaching those conclusions. *Daubert*. Although it is not always a straightforward exercise to disaggregate method and conclusion, when the conclusion simply does not follow from the data, a district court is free to determine that an impermissible analytical gap exists between premises and conclusion. *Joiner*; [citation]. When examining an expert's method, however, the inquiry should not be aimed at "the exhaustive search for cosmic understanding but for the particularized resolution of legal disputes." *Daubert*. Thus it is the specific relation between an expert's method, the proffered conclusions, and the particular factual circumstances of the dispute, and not asymptotic perfection, that renders testimony both reliable and relevant.

[White Rodgers' appeal focused on the testimony of plaintiffs' accident investigator, Sommer. Regarding the fire investigator, Boh, the court of appeals found his methodology to be sound because he observed the physical evidence at the scene of the accident and deduced the likely cause of the explosion based on his experience and observations. Although such a method is not susceptible to testing or peer review, it does constitute generally acceptable practice as a method for fire investigators to analyze the cause of fire accidents.]

With regard to the testimony of Donald Sommer ..., White–Rodgers argues that his testimony constituted impermissible speculation because he failed to test his theory that copper sulfide particles passed through and around the mesh screen to lodge on the safety valve seat and thereby cause the gas leak. Furthermore, White–Rodgers argues that Sommer's theory fails to "fit" the known facts that no particles of sufficient size to cause a leak were found on the seat of the valve. Finally, White–Rodgers contests the reliability of the so-called "differential diagnosis" method Sommer employed.

[First, no] doubt, *Daubert* noted that a key factor in valid scientific methodology is the practice of testing hypotheses to determine whether they can be falsified. [Citation. Such testing, however,] is aimed at theories purporting to explain the causal relations among regularly occurring natural phenomena. (Ptolemy's theory of the movement of celestial bodies which hypothesized that the Earth was the center of the solar system, later falsified by Copernicus, is a prominent example of such a scientific theory subject to falsification by further inquiry.) No such theory is in question here. The Bitlers need only establish by a preponderance of the evidence that copper sulfide particles caused a one-time occurrence—the gas explosion in their basement. [Citation.] Their experts do not present any controversial or novel explanations concerning regularly occurring natural phenomena. Undoubtedly, had their experts conducted further tests on their water heater's safety valve and established by observation that it did intermittently fail, they would have established causation to a near certainty. But such a high degree of certainty is not required. In fact, the only phenomenon of regular occurrence at issue here is one that is undisputed: copper sulfide particles of sufficient size or quantity if lodged on the valve seat may cause a gas leak. Thus, because testing is not necessary in all instances to establish reliability under *Daubert*, and because it is not required by the particular factual circumstances of this case, we conclude that the district court did not abuse its discretion in finding that the Bitlers' experts' testimony is reliable.

With regard to White–Rodgers' argument that the Bitlers' expert impermissibly relied on a method of "differential diagnosis," we note that the term is being used analogically to its proper use in a medical context;

nonetheless, we conclude that in this circumstance it is a valid scientific technique to establish causation. Concerning the method he employed in his investigation, Sommer testified that he undertook a process of eliminating alternative possible causes, determining that these possibilities were improbable sources of the explosion, and arriving at a highly probable cause for the gas leak, calling it a method of "differential diagnosis." "Differential diagnosis," is "the determination of which of two or more diseases with similar symptoms is the one from which the patient is suffering, by a systematic comparison and contrasting of the clinical findings." Stedman's Medical Dictionary 492 (27th ed.1995). In the medical context, differential diagnosis is a common method of analysis, and federal courts have regularly found it reliable under *Daubert*. [Citations.] What is not so clear is whether "differential diagnosis" is an appropriate method when employed outside of the medical context.

Here, however, the Bitlers' experts use a general method more aptly characterized as a process of reasoning to the best inference.[5] The Bitlers' experts must reason, as it were, backwards to the cause of a single explosion, and to do so requires a process of eliminating possible causes as improbable until the most likely one is identified. For example, Sommer and Boh both testified to how they eliminated the gas leaks in the bedroom and the T-connector above the water heater as likely sources of the accident; the one was not located close enough to the source of the explosion, and the other was itself most likely the result of trauma caused by the explosion. Sommer testified that the force of the explosion lifted the house off its foundation, and accordingly, was the most probable cause of the leak at the T-connector, especially in light of its damaged physical condition. Experts must provide objective reasons for eliminating alternative causes when employing a "differential analysis." [Citation.] Furthermore, the inference to the best explanation must first be in the range of possible causes; there must be some independent evidence that the cause identified is of the type that could have been the cause. *Joiner,* 522 U.S. at 146 ("[N]othing in either *Daubert* or the Federal Rules of Evidence requires a district court to admit opinion evidence that is connected to existing data only by the ipse dixit of the expert."). But more than mere possibility, an inference to the best explanation for the cause of an accident must eliminate other possible sources as highly improbable, and must demonstrate that the cause identified is highly probable. In the present case, it is uncontroverted that if copper sulfide particles of sufficient size became lodged on the safety valve seat, then a gas leak substantial enough to cause the explosion in the Bitlers' basement could occur. Whether or not that actually occurred is a question that may be answered by inference to the best explanation. We see no abuse of discretion, especially in light of

---

5. Unlike a logical inference made by deduction where one proposition can be logically inferred from other known propositions, and unlike induction where a generalized conclusion can be inferred from a range of known particulars, inference to the best ex- planation—or "abductive inferences"—are drawn about a particular proposition or event by a process of eliminating all other possible conclusions to arrive at the most likely one, the one that best explains the available data.

our deferential standard of review, in the district court's admitting expert testimony that employs an expert's physical investigation, professional experience, and technical knowledge to establish causation in this case.

Finally, as to the "fit" between the expert testimony and the material issue at stake in this case, White–Rodgers argues that the theory of copper sulfide particulate contamination does not "fit" the facts that the safety valve at issue is a screened valve, and no screened valve had ever been shown to allow sufficient copper sulfide downstream so as to cause a gas leak; furthermore, the valve functioned properly when tested after the accident. This argument confuses a *Daubert* inquiry into relevant "fit" with the jury question of which theory, plaintiffs' or defendant's, best captures the truth of the matter at issue. The former inquiry is aimed at determining if "a valid scientific connection to the pertinent inquiry," *Daubert*, obtains as a precondition to the admissibility of expert testimony. Here, the expert testimony "fits" because it involves a reliable method that would aid the jury in resolving a factual dispute; whether the jury finds that the testimony "fits" their best assessment of the truth of the matter is an altogether different issue. Accordingly, the district court did not abuse its discretion in admitting the Bitlers' expert testimony.

* * *

[Affirmed.]

NOTES

1. **Practical Problems of Proof.** *Henderson* and *Bitler* illustrate the practical problems of proof of factual causation—whether the accident was caused in fact by some defect in the product as opposed to something else. In cases of this type, circumstantial evidence is the key. Thus, in a case in which the plaintiff does not remember why his fingers were cut off by a power circular saw, testimony as to where the fingers are thrown and where the blood is splattered on the wall may be important evidence in helping determine how the accident occurred—whether it was caused by a product defect or by something else. Werth v. Makita Elec. Works, Ltd., 950 F.2d 643 (10th Cir.1991).

2. **Expert Testimony.** What were defendants' primary complaints about the causal testimony the trial courts allowed in *Henderson* and *Bitler*? In *Bitler*, why isn't Sommers' failure to test the screen (to see if it would intermittently fail to prevent contaminants from migrating to the safety valve) fatal to the admissibility of his testimony?

Review the material on *Daubert* in chapters 6 and 7. In addition to proof of product defect, expert testimony normally is also critical to establishing the causal link between the defendant's product and the plaintiff's harm. In *Bitler*, do you agree with the court's conclusion that Sommers' testimony is reliable? Or is his testimony merely *ipse dixit* and, thus, inadmissible? How about the experts' testimony in *Henderson*?

Note that both cases were decided by the Tenth Circuit Court of Appeals and that other circuits enforce *Daubert*'s admissibility standards more rigorously. In both cases, how do you think plaintiffs' experts' testimony would fare today in a more rigorous circuit?

3. How much proof is required to rule out other possible causes of an accident? In *Henderson* and *Bitler*, the experts provided that testimony. Often, proof is effectively unavailable to the plaintiff, because the product is destroyed or because the plaintiff is not alive or available to testify to what happened.

Consider Calhoun v. Honda Motor Corp., 738 f.2d 126 (6th Cir. 1984), which involved plaintiff's 1977 Honda 750 CB motorcycle. Twenty or thirty minutes after taking the motorcycle to a car wash, plaintiff ran into the back of a tractor trailer, causing him serious head injuries and an inability to remember what happened. There were no witnesses to the accident. For proof of defect, plaintiff relied on a recall letter sent by defendant to motorcycle owners identifying a reduction in the rear brake pad's performance in heavy rain conditions. Plaintiff's expert opined that the car wash amounted to a heavy rain condition that caused the brakes to fail when plaintiff tried to apply them before hitting the tractor trailer. After a jury verdict of $1,250,000 for the plaintiff, defendant obtained a judgment notwithstanding the verdict on the lack of proof of causation.

On appeal, *held*, affirmed. Forty feet of skid marks were consistent with either a defective brake pad or plaintiff's mere failure to brake soon enough to avert the collision. The plaintiff's expert failed to attempt to recreate the wet braking condition, and defendant's expert testified that the brakes would likely have been dry by the time he ran into the tractor trailer. The court reasoned that plaintiff's evidence did not establish that a defective brake pad was a *probable*, as opposed to a *possible*, cause of the collision, and that it was just as likely that the accident was caused by the plaintiff's inattention: "Although it is within the jury's province to determine which expert to believe, plaintiff's expert's opinion as to the cause of the accident was supported by nothing more than conjecture and supposition. It was not based upon evidence which entitled it to be credited by the jury."

Why doesn't *Calhoun* raise a jury question on causation? Should a plaintiff be permitted some relaxation of the causation burden if a defect in the defendant's product created the very risk that injured the plaintiff who, because of the accident, cannot explain what happened? In such cases, should the defendant be required to come forward with an explanation (as the defendant did in *Calhoun*)? Wouldn't this raise a jury question?

4. How do you think a defendant's admission that its product was defective (by recall, in *Calhoun*; or subsequent design change to remedy a danger, in *Bitler*) may affect a finding on causation? More broadly, how do you think proof of *defect* may affect a finding on *causation*?

5. Proof of Causation in State Courts. In Sanchez v. Hillerich & Bradsby Co., 128 Cal.Rptr.2d 529 (Ct.App. 2002), plaintiff baseball pitcher was seriously injured when struck by a ball hit with defendant's Air Attack 2 aluminum bat. Plaintiff alleged that the bat was defective because its composition significantly increased the speed at which the ball leaves the surface of the bat, preventing a pitcher from being able to react in time to protect himself. Plaintiff's expert kinesiologist so concluded in an affidavit, but:

(1) did not explain specifically how fast the batted ball which struck plaintiff was traveling;

(2) did not explain the nature and type of calculations he used to arrive at his conclusion that the bat caused an excessive ball velocity; and

(3) did not review a videotape of the incident or examine plaintiff's injuries.

Nevertheless, the Court of Appeals reversed summary judgment for the defendant, concluding that the expert's conclusions were sufficient because they were based on his review of general data and NCAA reports on the velocity of batted balls. The Court noted that the defendant should have deposed the expert if it wanted to establish that his opinion had no basis.

6.   Product Malfunction. Proof of defect and causation may sometimes be established by a showing that the product malfunctioned, together with the negation of other possible causes. The New York Court of Appeals considered the application of the malfunction theory from the Products Liability Restatement, § 3, to proof of causation in Speller v. Sears, Roebuck & Co., 790 N.E.2d 252 (N.Y. 2003). Plaintiff's spouse died in a house fire which he attributed to defective wiring in a refrigerator. The product had been destroyed in the fire and, after discovery, the defendants moved for summary judgment relying on a report by the Fire Marshall that a stove-top grease fire caused the fire. Recall that, to obtain the benefit of the § 3 malfunction theory, plaintiff must establish that the accident is of a kind that ordinarily results from product defect and was not "solely the result of causes other than product defect." Consequently, once defendant proffered evidence of an alternative cause—the grease fire—plaintiff was "required to come forward with competent evidence excluding the stove as the origin of the fire." Plaintiff responded with testimony of three experts opining that the fire started in the area of the refrigerator, not on the stove top, based on their assessment of the burn patterns and examination of what remained of other kitchen appliances, and interpreting that evidence differently from the fire marshal.

The Court of Appeals reversed summary judgment for the defendants, concluding that the plaintiff raised a fact question by "offering competent evidence which, if credited by the jury, was sufficient to rebut defendants' alternative cause evidence." The Court rejected the defendants' argument that once they produced evidence suggesting an alternative cause of the fire, plaintiffs were foreclosed from establishing product defect circumstantially, reasoning that "such an analysis would allow a defendant who offered minimally sufficient alternative cause evidence in a products liability case to foreclose a plaintiff from proceeding circumstantially without a jury having determined whether defendant's evidence should be credited." Id. at 256.

7.   Obvious Causation. If the causal connection between the use of a product and an injury is apparent to a layperson, many courts will permit the case to go to the jury even without expert testimony on causation. Thus, in Coca Cola Bottling Co. v. Cromwell, 159 S.W.2d 744 (Ark.1942), something stuck in plaintiff's throat as she took a swallow of Coke, and so she took another swig to wash it down. She immediately became ill and was hospitalized. The remaining contents of the bottle were strained and found to contain six spider legs. *Held,* jury verdict for plaintiff affirmed.

8.   When Defect Entered Product. Even if plaintiff is successful in tracing his injury to a product defect, he or she must further prove that the defect was in the product at the time it left the defendant's control. See, e.g., Ford Motor Co. v. Ridgway, 135 S.W.3d 598 (Tex. 2004) (third owner of pick-up truck, injured when his truck caught fire while he was driving, failed to prove that manufacturer was responsible for defect that caused fire; no direct evidence of fire's cause and second owner had repaired fuel system).

3.   THE SPECIAL PROBLEM OF WARNINGS AND RELIANCE

Proving causation in a failure-to-warn case has peculiar difficulties. Proof that a collision between two cars would not have happened had defendant swerved or braked or driven within the speed limit is mostly a matter of physics. Proof that an accident would not have occurred if defendant had provided adequate WARNINGS concerning the use of a product is more psychology and does not admit of the same degree of certainty. A plaintiff must show that adequate WARNINGS would have made a difference in the outcome, that is, that they would have been followed. In the best case a plaintiff can offer evidence of his habitual, careful adherence to all WARNINGS and instructions. In many cases, however, plaintiff's evidence may be little more than the self-serving assertion that whatever his usual practice may have been, in the circumstances critical to his claim for damages he would have been mindful of an adequate WARNING had it been given. In the worst case, where the user of the product is deceased, proof of what the decedent would or would not have done may be virtually impossible.

General Motors Corp. v. Saenz, 873 S.W.2d 353 (Tex.1993).

Greiner v. Volkswagenwerk Aktiengesellschaft

United States District Court, Eastern District Pennsylvania, 1977.
429 F.Supp. 495.

■ JOSEPH S. LORD, III, CHIEF JUDGE.

[Plaintiff was injured when the Volkswagen beetle in which she was riding as a passenger rolled over. The jury found that the vehicle was not defectively designed, and plaintiff appealed the withholding from the jury of her theory on failure to warn. Holding that the jury should have been permitted to pass on this theory, the Court of Appeals vacated judgment for the defendant and remanded the case for further consideration. 540 F.2d 85 (3d Cir.1976). The trial court's decision on remand follows.]

[T]he precise question is: Assuming the necessity of a warning of the Volkswagen's propensity to overturn on sharp steering maneuvers, how did the absence of a warning cause the accident? Or conversely, how would its presence have prevented the accident?

Except for the widely varying estimates of the Volkswagen's speed, the facts of the accident are really not in dispute. Finding herself on her own wrong side of the road facing an oncoming car, the [VW's] driver, Nickel, turned to her right. She immediately found herself headed for a concrete bridge railing approximately ten feet away. Her speed was between 30 and 60 miles per hour. To avoid the bridge railing, Nickel turned sharply to the left and the Volkswagen overturned. Under these circumstances, warning or not, there was no conceivable way that an accident could have been avoided. Even giving Nickel the best possible reading of the evidence, at 30 miles per hour, she would cover ten feet in approximately one-fourth of a second. It is simply not within the bounds of human reason to suppose that, had there been a warning, Nickel would have recalled it, considered it and then intentionally crashed head-on into a concrete rail. We do not, however, rest our determination on this conclusion.

[Comment *j* to § 402A provides: "Where warning is given, the seller may reasonably assume that it will be read and heeded . . ."] Implicit in that comment, however, is the assumption that the warning *could* have been heeded to avoid the peril. Here, it could not. Here, when Nickel found herself ten feet from the railing, a serious accident was inevitable, warning or no warning, and plaintiff made no showing that one would have been less devastating than the other. . . .

Plaintiff points to several cases where recovery was held allowable absent specific evidence of proximate cause. Their factual patterns may be summarized as follows:

1.   [Plaintiff was killed when a helicopter's power failed, resulting in its crash. The accident could have been prevented had the manufacturer warned of the need for an instantaneous shift to autorotation in the event of power failure.]

2.   [A grinding wheel disintegrated while operating at 10,000 rpms, partially blinding plaintiff. There was no warning on the wheel that the maximum safe speed was less than 6,000 rpms.]

3.   [A can of cleaning fluid bore a legend that was insufficient to warn a user of the necessity of ventilating the space in which it was used.]

4.   [A stick of dynamite exploded when inserted into a freshly drilled hole. There was no warning that such an explosion could occur from the heat generated by drilling.]

Defendant argues that in all of those cases, there was no specific proof that the absence or inadequacy of warning was a causative factor in bringing about the harm. Those cases, however, are distinguishable. In the first place, the nature of the required warning was both specific and easily followed—push the autorotation button immediately on engine failure, do not operate in excess of 6,000 revolutions per minute, use only in well-ventilated area, and do not insert dynamite in freshly drilled hole. It requires no guess or conjecture to determine how the accident could have been avoided by following the warnings. In this case, on the other hand, although the propensity to overturn on sudden maneuvers could be described, whether such description could have avoided this accident would call for pure speculation.

Secondly, in the four cases referred to by plaintiff, it was reasonable to infer from the evidence that the simple, easily understood directions and limitations could and would be followed had they been given.

* * * No such inference can be made here, because under the circumstances of this case, a warning, even if read, could not have been heeded.

At oral argument, plaintiff's counsel suggested a more remote causal connection between the failure to warn and the accident: that had the warning been given Nickel might not have bought the car. Such a suggestion, in our opinion, would have invited the jury "to indulge in 'pure conjecture or guess'". Greiner v. Volkswagenwerk Aktiengesellschaft, 540 F.2d 85, 94 (3d Cir.1976). The fine line between "conjecture" on the one hand, and "reasonable inference" on the other, is sometimes hard to draw. As we have said, it is reasonable to infer that a simple warning such as "Do not operate in excess of 6,000 revolutions per minute" would be followed. It is an inference that arises from the factual situation.

[An inference "is a process of reasoning by which a fact or proposition sought to be established is deduced as a logical consequence from other facts, or a state of facts, already proved or admitted."]

There are no proven facts in this record which would lend the dignity of an inference as opposed to a guess, that Nickel would not have purchased the Volkswagen in the face of a warning. Indeed, the impropriety of permitting the jury to make such a finding is intensified by the fact that Nickel testified in plaintiff's case and was totally silent about the effect such a warning would have had. In the face of available, but unproduced evidence, we think it would have been totally improper to permit the jury to guess what Nickel would have said if asked about the effect of the presence of a warning.[2] . . .

Plaintiff also argues that defect means the existence of a characteristic or limitation on the use of a product of which no warning is given, and that causation is proven if a cause and effect relationship between the condition and the harm is established. . . . We find more persuasive the article of Professor Keeton, Products Liability, 48 Tex.L.Rev. 398, 414 (1970):

> "If the basis for recovery under strict liability is inadequacy of warnings or instruction about dangers, then plaintiff would be required to show that an adequate warning or instruction would have prevented the harm."

[Thus, the record does not justify submitting to the jury the question of whether the absence of a warning caused the plaintiff's harm. Judgment for defendant reinstated.]

NOTES

1. Accord Roy v. Volkswagenwerk Aktiengesellschaft, 600 F.Supp. 653 (C.D.Cal.1985) (VW van rolled over when driver swerved to avoid hitting dog). Compare Staymates v. ITT Holub Industries, 527 A.2d 140 (Pa.Super.1987) (warning could not have prevented "instinctive, knee-jerk reaction").

2. What do you think of the *Greiner* court's summary rejection of the plaintiff's claim that, had Nickel (the VW's owner) been adequately warned, she might not have purchased it at all? Accord, Baughn v. Honda Motor Co., Ltd., 727 P.2d 655 (Wash.1986). But see Larsen v. General Motors Corp., 391 F.2d 495, 505–06 (8th Cir.1968); Spruill v. Boyle–Midway, Inc., 308 F.2d 79, 87 (4th Cir.1962) ("had the warning . . . convey[ed] a conception of the true nature of the danger, this mother . . . might not have purchased the product at all").

What if Nickel, after the accident, had sworn off VW Beetles and had in fact testified persuasively that had she known of the risk she never would have bought one?

By rejecting the would-not-have-purchased-the-product argument, does the court frustrate the autonomy-promotion goal of the law of warnings? How can a

2. Indeed, the more reasonable inference is that her testimony would have been unfavorable to plaintiff's case. 2 Wigmore on Evidence (3d ed.) § 285.

consumer meaningfully choose whether to accept a product's hazards, in exchange for the product's benefits, unless he or she is warned of latent hazards prior to purchase in order to decide whether to buy it at all?

3. Consider Jones v. Hittle Service, Inc., 549 P.2d 1383 (Kan.1976), where plaintiffs' decedents were killed in an explosion of gas sold by the defendants. Plaintiffs contended that the defendants had been negligent in adding only one pound of odorant to 10,000 gallons of gas, rather than the nine pounds claimed to be necessary to make the gas reasonably safe. The gas, however, had seeped through the soil prior to passing into the basement where it exploded, and much of the odorizing agent had been leached out as a result. Plaintiffs' expert admitted that even at the nine pound level there would not have been enough odor left in the gas after it had passed through the soil to have been smelled by the victims. *Held*, the inadequate odorization was not a cause of the explosion.

4. Consider also Shell Oil Co. v. Gutierrez, 581 P.2d 271 (Ariz.App.1978), where plaintiffs were injured in an explosion when the vapors in an "empty" 55 gallon drum of xylene were ignited as one plaintiff began welding nearby. Although plaintiffs admitted that they had not read the allegedly inadequate warnings on the drum label, the court affirmed a judgment for the plaintiffs: "Adequate warning could have actuated a policy in handling 'empties' which would have prevented the accident. Had the label stated that the barrel should be washed with an inert solvent, stored with the bung holes covered, and returned immediately, presumably the barrel would not have been where it was."

Nissen Trampoline Co. v. Terre Haute First Nat'l Bank

Court of Appeals of Indiana, 1975.
332 N.E.2d 820 (Ind.Ct.App.1975), rev'd on other grounds, 358 N.E.2d 974 (Ind.1976).

■ LYBROOK, JUDGE.

Defendant–Appellant Nissen Trampoline Company appeals from a granting of a new trial following a jury verdict in its favor in a products liability action initiated by plaintiff-appellee Terre Haute First National Bank as guardian of the estate of Bruno Garzolini, Jr., a minor.

[D]efendant Nissen was the manufacturer of a product know as "Aqua Diver," a circular trampoline with a metal frame thirty-six (36) inches in diameter and a bed of approximately sixteen (16) inches in diameter. The bed is attached to the frame by a network of elastic cables. This circular structure is then attached to a larger metal frame which has a platform approximately twenty-two (22) inches above the bed of the trampoline. The platform is accessible by a ladder attached at the rear. The entire structure, Aqua Diver, was designed and marketed by defendant for use as a diving apparatus at a swimming pool and/or lake. According to literature distributed by defendant, Aqua Diver was "twice as much fun as an old-fashioned diving board at half the cost."

Herbert A. Mason d/b/a Southlake Beach, purchased an Aqua Diver from Nissen and installed it upon a wooden platform at the beach. On June 28, 1970, while attempting to use the Aqua Diver for his first time, plaintiff Bruno Garzolini, Jr., a thirteen (13) year old boy, was injured. Although unable to recall all the specifics of the occurrence, Garzolini testified that he intended to jump from the platform of the Aqua Diver onto the bed of the trampoline and thereby catapult himself into the water. However, plaintiff landed with only one foot on the bed of the trampoline. His other foot either missed or slipped off the bed and passed through the open space between the bed and circular frame, becoming entangled in the elastic cables. As a result, plaintiff fell from the structure and became suspended by his left leg which remained ensnarled in the cables. Ultimately, plaintiff's injuries required amputation of the leg above the knee. Evidence at trial established that in tests conducted prior to marketing the Aqua Diver, defendant had determined that it was possible for a user's foot to pass through the elastic cables which connected the bed to the frame. Nevertheless, Nissen marketed the product without accompanying it with any warnings or instructions for use [rendering it defective under Restatement (Second) of Torts § 402A.]

Plaintiff initiated this action, naming both Nissen and Mason as co-defendants, maintaining that Nissen was liable under the doctrine of strict liability, and that Mason was liable for negligence in failing to furnish supervision and instruction for use of the Aqua Diver. Trial by jury resulted in verdicts in favor of both defendants. [Upon motion,] the trial judge granted a new trial as to Nissen only, thereby prompting this appeal.

* * *

The issue of causation in both negligence and strict liability cases wherein the defect is in design or manufacture differs fundamentally from causation in failure to warn cases. In the former, it is generally required that the plaintiff establish a causal connection in fact by proof that the harm resulted from the condition or ingredient that made the product defective. In the latter case, however, the difference arises in that the factor rendering the product defective is separable from the product itself. Applying the causation in fact test to the failure to warn case would give rise to a doctrine that liability is predicated upon a showing by the plaintiff that he would have suffered no injury but for the absence of warning. Stated differently, the plaintiff would be required to show that he would have heeded a warning had one been given. In our opinion, such an approach would undermine the purpose behind the doctrine of strict tort liability since any such testimony would generally be speculative at best. A more reasonable approach which represents a compromise within the framework of strict liability as suggested in Technical Chemical Co. v. Jacobs 480 S.W.2d 602 (Tex.1972) is that the law should supply the presumption that an adequate warning would have been read and heeded, thereby minimizing the obvious problems of proof of causation. We find such an approach to be meritorious, workable, and desirable.

Comment *j* of Restatement (2d) Torts, § 402A (1965), provides a presumption protecting the manufacturer where a warning is given:

> "Where warning is given, the seller may reasonably assume that it will be read and heeded; ..."

However, where there is no warning, as in the case at bar, the presumption of comment *j* that the user would have read and heeded an adequate warning works in favor of the plaintiff user. In other words, the presumption of causation herein is that Garzolini would have read an adequate warning concerning the danger of a user's foot slipping between the elastic cables of Aqua Diver and heeded it, resulting in his not using the Aqua Diver. This presumption may, however, be rebutted by the manufacturer Nissen with contrary evidence that the presumed fact did not exist. As the Texas Supreme Court said in Technical Chemical Co. v. Jacobs, supra:

> "Depending upon the individual facts, this may be accomplished by the manufacturer's producing evidence that the user was blind, illiterate, intoxicated at the time of use, irresponsible or lax in judgment or by some other circumstance tending to show that the improper use was or would have been made regardless of the warning."

Placing the burden of rebutting the presumption of causation on the manufacturer in failure to warn cases is not inconsistent with the policies behind strict liability. It would encourage manufacturers to provide safe products and to warn of the known dangers in the use of the product which might cause injury. Such a presumption would also discourage those manufacturers who would rather risk liability than provide a warning which would impair the marketability of the product. The presumption of causation in failure to warn cases is not to be taken as an abrogation of the issue of causation, thereby subjecting a manufacturer to liability for almost any injury caused by his product. Rather, it merely shifts to the manufacturer the burden of proof where the fact-finder could only speculate as to whether the injury could have been prevented by a warning.

* * *

Affirmed.

NOTES

1. Nissen was reversed on procedural grounds in 358 N.E.2d 974, 981 (Ind. 1976), where the following picture of the Aqua Diver was set forth:

2. Presuming Causation. Many other courts have similarly "adopted" a rebuttable "heeding presumption" that the plaintiff would have read and heeded an adequate warning. See, e.g., Golonka v. General Motors Corp., 65 P.3d 956 (Ariz. App. 2003) (presumption furthers policy of protecting public from defective products and ensures that legitimate claims of information defect are fairly addressed); General Motors Corp. v. Saenz, 873 S.W.2d 353 (Tex.1993) (reaffirming value of presumption); Eagle–Picher Indus. v. Balbos, 604 A.2d 445 (Md.1992). Some courts, without expressly adopting such a presumption, appear to do so implicitly. See, e.g., DeLuryea v. Winthrop Labs., 697 F.2d 222 (8th Cir.1983) (no need for testimony from prescribing doctors that they would have heeded adequate warnings). Other courts have noted but avoided deciding the issue. Kallio v. Ford Motor Co., 407 N.W.2d 92 (Minn.1987). And at least a couple of courts have expressly rejected the presumption approach. Potthoff v. Alms, 583 P.2d 309, 311 (Colo.App.1978); Riley v. American Honda Motor Co., 856 P.2d 196 (Mont.1993) ("warnings often go unread or, where read, ignored"; the comment *j* presumption "is not appropriate running in either direction").

3. The Meaning of Comment *j*. Does comment *j* really call for a heeding presumption? Not according to a review of its history, which turns its usual interpretation on its head:

> Although it is widely read more broadly, comment *j* in fact pertains only to the narrow category of unavoidably dangerous products such as alcohol, drugs, and cigarettes whose inherently hazardous nature makes warnings the only way to improve their safety. With such products, . . . providing a warning is all a manufacturer or other seller can do to reduce the risk of harm—after which, a seller has nothing else to do except to "assume [read: 'hope'] that [its] warnings will be read and heeded."

D. Owen, Products Liability Law § 11.4 (2d ed. 2008).

4.   Logic or Policy? In a typical case, how legitimate really is a presumption that the plaintiff would have read and heeded an adequate warning? Will such a presumption be inherently speculative in almost every case? If a presumption is not generally true, is it rationally based? May a court properly employ such a presumption?

Consider Coffman v. Keene Corp., 628 A.2d 710, 717–18 (N.J.1993), in which the defendant "provided a plethora of data and studies [showing] that with the proliferation of warnings in our society, it is nearly impossible to go through a day without consciously ignoring [health and safety warnings, so that] there is no common experience on which we can premise the creation of a presumption that the general public reads and heeds warnings." Nevertheless, the New Jersey Supreme Court adopted the heeding presumption in warnings cases, reasoning:

> We agree with defendant that the heeding presumption is not firmly based on empirical evidence. It is not therefore a "natural" or "logical" presumption. * * *

> Nevertheless, the creation of a presumption can be grounded in public policy. [A]n examination of the strong and consistent public policies that have shaped our laws governing strict products liability demonstrates the justification for such a presumption.

Just what "public policies" might justify this "illogical" presumption?

5.   Rebutting the Presumption. Consider Craven v. Niagara Mach. & Tool Works, Inc., 417 N.E.2d 1165, 1171 (Ind.App.1981) (tool and die maker's hand injured in punch press):

> A rebuttable presumption does not shift the burden of proof but it does impose upon the opposing party a burden of producing evidence. If the opponent produces evidence which rebuts the presumption, it serves no further purpose. Niagara offered evidence to rebut the presumption through testimony that Craven had been warned and reminded to use safety blocks, which he failed to do. Once this evidence was offered Craven was then obligated to prove, by direct and circumstantial evidence and reasonable inference therefrom, the ultimate fact that he would have heeded the warning. Craven testified that he would heed a warning of a different nature and that he did use safety blocks when he recognized a danger with heavy dies. He also testified that he heeded warnings on "Roll-in" saws. Other witnesses testified that he was extremely cautious in carrying out his work in terms of safety. From this evidence, a jury could reasonably infer that Craven would have heeded a warning; thus, the issue of cause in fact was ultimately for the jury.

In most states, the heeding presumption shifts the burden of production, not the burden of persuasion. Golonka v. General Motors Corp., 65 P.3d 956 (Ariz.App. 2003) (evidence that plaintiff failed to read portions of her owners manual and ignored other warning devices was enough to rebut the presumption that she would have heeded a warning label in the passenger compartment on the risk of mis-shifting; presumption fell entirely from the case and jury must decide matter based on reasonable inferences from facts without use of presumption). But see Burton v. R.J. Reynolds Tobacco Co., 397 F.3d 906, 918 (10th Cir. 2005) (in Kansas, presumption shifts burden of proof).

Is one instance of inattentiveness enough to rebut the presumption? See Magro v. Ragsdale Bros., Inc., 721 S.W.2d 832 (Tex.1986) (presumption not rebutted by single instance of inattentiveness "unrelated to the plaintiff's ability to perceive or heed warnings ... and which does not rise to the level of habit" under evidence Rule 406); Tenbarge v. Ames Taping Tool Systems, Inc., 190 F.3d 862 (8th Cir. 1999) (jury question on whether presumption rebutted by plaintiff drywall installer returning to work and continuing to use defendant's product after being told it caused his carpal tunnel syndrome).

Of what value is evidence that the plaintiff disregarded *other* kinds of warnings? Compare Graves v. Church & Dwight Co., 631 A.2d 1248 (N.J.App. 1993) (plaintiff's failure to heed health warnings on cigarette labels probative of whether he would have heeded warning of risk of stomach rupture from ingestion of baking soda for indigestion), with Cottam v. CVS Pharmacy, 764 N.E.2d 814 (Mass. 2002) (evidence that plaintiff failed to heed cigarette warnings too remote to rebut inference that he would have heeded warning about side effect of impotence from drug).

6. Plaintiff's Testimony on Hypothetical Reliance. In Blue v. Drackett Products Co., 143 So.2d 897 (Fla.App.1962), the 7–year–old plaintiff was injured in an explosion when he took a can of Drano off the shelf, put water in it, and recapped the can. The manufacturer was sued for failing to warn that the product formed an explosive gas when mixed with water. The mother testified that she had noticed only three words on the label—"Drano," "poison," and "antidotes"—and that she had read neither the admonition to keep the product out of the reach of children nor the words "Keep water out of can." The trial court excluded the mother's testimony that she would have kept the product out of plaintiff's reach had she known it would explode if water were added to the can, and the jury ruled for the defendant. *Held,* reversed:

> "[P]laintiffs were denied their right to prove by direct evidence a material issue raised by the pleadings as to whether the injury was directly caused by the claimed insufficiency of the label to warn the mother that the can had an explosive potential in addition to its danger as a poison. While the question propounded required testimony of what would have been done under circumstances that never existed, the real character of such evidence was the present knowledge of the only witness who knew and could say what would have been done had the explosive propensities of the product been known."

Id. at 898. The dissent disagreed, arguing that since she had read only three words on the label, her testimony as to what she would have done had she read the entire label would be "highly improper and conjectural." The Florida Supreme Court reversed again: "Conjecture has no place in proceedings of this sort." Drackett Prod. Co. v. Blue, 152 So.2d 463, 465 (Fla.1963).

Right result? What result if:

A.   Mother had seen only the two words "Drano" and "Poison"?

B.   Mother had read the entire label and instructed plaintiff not to add water to the can?

C.   Mother had read the entire label and had put the can on the top shelf to keep it out of plaintiff's reach, but plaintiff had climbed up after it?

The courts have split on the admissibility of a plaintiff's self-serving testimony as to whether and how, hypothetically, she would have heeded an adequate warning. *Inadmissible:* Van Dike v. AMF, Inc., 379 N.W.2d 412, 415 (Mich.App. 1985) (evidence Rule 701 on lay witness opinion testimony requires opinions rationally based on witness's perceptions and helpful to a clear understanding of his testimony). *Admissible:* Laaperi v. Sears, Roebuck & Co., Inc., 787 F.2d 726, 732 (1st Cir.1986) ("Self-serving as this testimony was, the jury was free to credit it.").

7. Failure to *Heed* Warnings or Instructions. What result if plaintiff reads but refuses to *heed* the warnings given? "There is no presumption that a plaintiff who ignored instructions that would have kept him from injury would have followed better instructions." General Motors Corp. v. Saenz, 873 S.W.2d 353 (Tex.1993).

Should the effect of a plaintiff's failure to *heed* a warning depend on the how the warning was allegedly inadequate? Petty v. United States, 740 F.2d 1428 (8th Cir. 1984).

8. Failure to *Read* Warnings or Instructions. Will a plaintiff's inadequate warnings claim be defeated for lack of causation if he or she admits failure to *read* the warnings given? See Palmer v. Volkswagen of America, Inc., 904 So.2d 1077 (Miss. 2005) ("The plaintiffs in this case did not read the owner's manual at all. Thus, they hardly can claim to have been harmed or misled by it."); Hiner v. Bridgestone/Firestone, Inc., 978 P.2d 505 (Wash. 1999) (injured motorist claim that she would have heeded a warning imprinted on a wheel to install snow tires on all four wheels, and not only on front wheels, was contrary to her testimony that she never read owners manual which stated "snow tires should be installed on all four wheels; otherwise poor handling may result;" *held*, directed verdict for defendant affirmed).

Should the effect of a plaintiff's failure to *read* a warning depend on how the warning was allegedly inadequate? See E.R. Squibb & Sons, Inc. v. Cox, 477 So.2d 963 (Ala.1985).

9. Known and Obvious Dangers. What happens to the cause in fact issue when the risk is known or obvious to the plaintiff? Reconsider Laaperi v. Sears, Roebuck & Co., Inc., 787 F.2d 726 (1st Cir.1986), supra ch. 10. But what if a "known" risk is momentarily *forgotten*? See Conti v. Ford Motor Co., 743 F.2d 195, 198–99 (3d Cir.1984) (experienced driver injured wife when he started standard transmission car in reverse without engaging clutch):

> [T]he jury's conclusion was based on the mere speculation that if Mr. Conti's eyes had caught a sticker warning him to depress the clutch pedal as he was talking to his wife, he may have remembered to either shift the car to neutral or to disengage the clutch prior to starting the car. Ford cannot be held liable on a failure-to-warn theory merely because a jury concludes that more warnings are needed to remind drivers of the intricacies of standard transmissions.

10. Warnings to Physicians. Because most pharmaceutical warnings are directed to physicians, consistent with the learned intermediary rule, what effect does the physician's knowledge of the risks have on plaintiff's allegations that a better warning would have prevented the harm? Compare Seley v. G.D. Searle & Co., 423 N.E.2d 831 (Ohio 1981)(doctor would have prescribed birth control pills for plaintiff even if warning had been adequate), with Bravman v. Baxter Healthcare Corp., 984 F.2d 71 (2d Cir.1993)(jury could assess credibility of plaintiff's doctor who testified that, even if he had received a warning about noisy condition of heart valve, he would not have passed the warning on to his patient). Why should not the latter case simply be dismissed on causation grounds? What possible credibility issue might the court have had in mind?

11. See generally Geistfeld, Inadequate Product Warnings and Causation, 30 U. Mich. J.L. Reform 309 (1997); Symposium, Rational Actors or Rational Fools? The Implications of Psychology for Products Liability, 6 Roger Williams U.L.Rev. 1 (2000); D. Owen, Products Liability Law § 11.4 (2d ed. 2008); 1 D. Owen, M.S. Madden, & M. Davis, Madden and Owen on Products Liability § 12:6 (3d ed. 2000).

CHAPTER 13

PROXIMATE CAUSE

The issue that is usually called "proximate cause" is very different from "cause in fact." As most courts use the former term, it presupposes (or inquires separately into) some factual connection between defendant's breach of duty and plaintiff's injury and addresses instead the policy question of whether in fairness the defendant ought to be held legally accountable for the plaintiff's harm which in some manner is "remote" from the defendant's breach. Noting that "[p]roximate cause cannot be reduced to absolute rules," Prosser and Keeton quote 1 Street, Foundations of Legal Liability 110 (1906) on the role of proximate cause: "It is always to be determined on the facts of each case upon mixed considerations of logic, common sense, justice, policy and precedent." See W.P. Keeton, D. Dobbs, R. Keeton & D. Owen, Prosser & Keeton on the Law of Torts 279 (5th ed. 1984). Consider also Craig v. Burch, 228 So.2d 723, 729–30 (La.App.1969):

Proximate cause [is] not a factual consideration. It is a legal tool, a legislative and judicial policy. From time immemorial courts have customarily applied two well known tests in determining proximate cause. These are: (1) Was the accident the natural and probable consequence of defendant's act, and (2) Were the results of defendant's conduct reasonably foreseeable? As thusly applied, it appears the proximate cause concept has been employed by the courts to extend or restrict liability at the court's discretion depending upon the circumstances of each case rather than on the basis that the action of the defendant was or was not a cause in fact of the accident. Such application is one of policy....

Further:

Proximate cause presupposes breach of a duty constituting a cause in fact of the accident. When considering proximate cause in connection with a statutory violation, the basic inquiry is what kind of risk or risks does the statute seek to protect against? ... In the absence of statutory duty, proximate cause is determined in the light of the query whether plaintiff's particular interest is protected against defendant's particular conduct. [Thus,] proximate cause is but [another] facet of the duty formula [for] determining when liability attaches to a cause in fact....

The term proximate cause must be used with caution because it does not concern an inquiry into cause. Rather it involves an inquiry into duty, more particularly, the extent of defendant's duty with respect to plaintiff's interest to be protected.

While proximate cause is dealt with here as a separate doctrine, it should be noted that the issue permeates not only duty concepts but indeed *most* of the crucial elements of a products liability case. So, typically, the essential issue in almost every case will be whether—or the degree to which—some "defective" condition of the product, the plaintiff, or some third party "caused" the injury. The court in Palmer v. Ford Motor Co., 498 F.2d 952, 953 (10th Cir.1974), was thus not far off the mark in noting that the labeling of plaintiff's unreasonable encounter of a known danger as contributory negligence or assumption of risk was of little significance since "[t]he controlling factor is causation."

Thought of in this broader sense, proximate cause is at the core of every products liability suit. Dean Leon Green put it well:

> The issues of a 402A action lie as close together as the fingers of one hand, and one issue cannot be considered without holding the other issues in conscious suspense; for all the issues are essential to liability, and each has a part to play in the functioning of all the others. Causal connection runs as a thread through the seller's duty, the violation of its duty, and the use made of the product in its consumption that results in the consumer's injury.

L. Green, Strict Liability Under Sections 402A and 402B: A Decade of Litigation, 54 Tex.L.Rev. 1185, 1208 (1976).

1.   DUTY AND FORESEEABILITY LIMITATIONS ON LIABILITY

The scope of a seller's duty is often limited through application of the principle of "reasonable foreseeability." Manufacturers must act with regard to reasonably foreseeable risks and must produce products that are reasonably safe for their reasonably foreseeable uses and misuses. As foreseeability is a traditional limit on the duty of a product manufacturer, so it is the principal "test" of proximate cause. Foreseeability is used to determine whether responsibility for the defendant's breach of duty should extend to the plaintiff's harm—whether the risks which made the defendant negligent, or its product defective, are the same risks which injured the plaintiff. As one court put it, "foreseeability is the cornerstone of proximate cause." Dillard v. Pittway Corp., 719 So.2d 188 (Ala. 1998).

Yet a few courts hold that foreseeability is relevant only to the breach of duty issue and that liability extends to all direct, or "natural and probable," consequences of the breach. See, e.g., Salazar v. Wolo Manuf. Group, 983 S.W.2d 87 (Tex.App. 1998) (foreseeability not a critical element so long as product is "direct or producing cause"). Most courts recognize that, while the foreseeability of injury is one important factor in determining the proper reach of liability, fairness and policy issues play an important role as well. The cases in this section should be read against the admonition of Dean Wade and others that policy issues are better dealt with in the open, perhaps in the context of duty, than hidden behind a smoke screen of foreseeability and proximate cause. See Wade, On the Nature of Strict Tort Liability for Products, 44 Miss.L.J. 825, 847 (1973).

Crankshaw v. Piedmont Driving Club, Inc.

Court of Appeals of Georgia, 1967.
115 Ga.App. 820, 156 S.E.2d 208.

Plaintiff Elizabeth Crankshaw seeks damages against Piedmont Driving Club, Inc., alleging that on January 15, 1966, she in company with R.M. Harris and Miss Arlene Harris patronized the dining room of the defendant; that Miss Harris ordered shrimp and began eating same at which time she noticed a peculiar odor emanating from the shrimp dish causing her to feel nauseated; that Miss Harris excused herself and proceeded toward the rest room; shortly thereafter plaintiff proceeded toward the rest room to give aid and comfort to Miss Harris and as plaintiff entered the rest room she saw Miss Harris leaning over one of the bowls; that "unbeknownst to plaintiff, Miss Harris had vomited just inside the entrance to the rest room" and that as she hurried toward her she "stepped into the vomit, and her feet flew out from under her," causing her to fall and break her hip. The petition alleged negligence of the defendant in selling unwholesome, deleterious food....

[The trial court dismissed the petition, and plaintiff appeals.]

■ Jordan, Presiding Judge.

... Plaintiff contends [that] "the heart of the legal question presented" is whether or not the negligent serving of unwholesome food to Miss Harris was the proximate cause of [plaintiff's] injury....

"If the damages are only the imaginary or possible result of the tortious act, or other and contingent circumstances preponderate largely in causing the injurious effect, such damages are too remote to be the basis of recovery against the wrongdoer." Code, § 105–2008. Damages must flow from the "legal and natural result of the act done." Code, § 105–2009. [P]roximate cause is one for a jury except in palpably clear and indisputable cases. [T]he facts alleged in this petition bring it within the exception and subject it to be ruled upon as a matter of law. The court must assume this burden where a jury can draw but one reasonable conclusion if the facts alleged are proved, that conclusion being that the acts of the defendant were not the proximate cause of the injury. [Here,] a jury could not reasonably conclude that the plaintiff's injury was proximately caused by the defendant's negligence in serving unwholesome food to another person.

Judgment affirmed.

NOTES

1. Explain the court's reasoning. Same result if the sickened person injures *herself* by slipping on her *own* vomit? Whatever happened to the "Danger invites rescue" doctrine? See Wagner v. International Ry. Co., 133 N.E. 437 (N.Y.1921) (Cardozo, J.); Williams v. Foster, 666 N.E.2d 678 (Ill.App.1996).

2. Plaintiff was driving at 45–50 mph when he hit a horse that suddenly appeared in front of his car. The horse was thrown into the air and onto the roof, collapsing the roof rail (called the "header") on the passenger side of the car, which instantly killed plaintiff's wife. Plaintiff and his son, who was sitting in the back seat, were uninjured; plaintiff's daughter, sitting on her mother's lap in the front, sustained minor cuts and bruises. Plaintiff sued the car manufacturer for defective roof design:

> Defendant argues that the accident was freak and bizarre in that it involved an unusual concentration of forces and an abnormal load on the header, which resulted in the failure of the roof structure. It argues that the support structure is designed to work as a whole but that the horse hit the header at a point where the other roof components could not contribute to its support.... In sum, defendant contends that the design was not defective, because the force and impact of the accident were so unusual that it could not have reasonably been anticipated.

> Product liability for defective design does not extend to cases where the risk of injury from the product's failure is so remote that a reasonable manufacturer would not consider it in design decisions. Plaintiff offered evidence that collisions with large animals, including horses, are common and foreseeable. Defendant countered that it was not foreseeable that such a collision would produce an impact on the roof concentrated at a particular point rather than being more evenly distributed. The problem with that argument is that its converse is equally true: It was just as unpredictable that the impact from a collision would fall evenly on the entire roof rather than land with greater force on its weakest part. That the horse landed with its full weight on the header did not make the accident any more a freak occurrence than if the weight had been distributed evenly.

> There was evidence that the [car's roof design could and should have been made stronger].

Held, "that the accident and the manner of injury were not unforeseeable, as a matter of law, and that plaintiff presented sufficient evidence of defective design to justify submission of the case to the jury." Judgment for plaintiff affirmed. Green v. Denney, 742 P.2d 639 (Or.App.1987).

Not mentioned in the opinion, the jury verdict was for $1.5 million. See Insight, p. 62, col. 3, March 7, 1988. Mentioned in the opinion, the car was a Ford Pinto.

3. Greenfield v. Suzuki Motor Co., 776 F.Supp. 698 (E.D.N.Y.1991), involved a boating accident which began when an outboard motor stalled due to a defective fuel system. Husband attempted to restart the engine, and the anchor line became entangled in the propeller; as he tried to cut the line, he was pulled into the water. While wife tried to rescue him, an onrush of water washed her inside the boat and below deck. The boat capsized, and wife, trapped beneath, drowned. *Held,* foreseeability for the jury.

4. What rule of law should be applied to these cases? Whether the connection between the breach of duty and the harm is "proximate" or "remote"? Whether the result is "natural and probable"? A "freak accident"? "Likely"? "Foreseeable"? See Prosser, Palsgraf Revisited, 52 Mich.L.Rev. 1, 19 (1953) ("too cockeyed and far-fetched").

Winnett v. Winnett

Supreme Court of Illinois, 1974.
310 N.E.2d 1.

■ UNDERWOOD, C.J.

Four-year-old Teresa Kay Winnett was injured when she placed her hand on a moving conveyor belt or screen on a forage wagon then being operated on her grandfather's farm. [She settled a suit against her grandfather and pursued a strict tort action against the manufacturer of the forage wagon, alleging that it was defectively designed because of the absence of rear view mirrors and of a guard or shield to prevent persons from coming in contact with the moving conveyor belt. The circuit court dismissed the action for failure to state a claim, the Appellate Court reversed, and defendant appealed.]

The [parties focus on] whether "use" of this forage wagon by a four-year-old child was "foreseeable" by the manufacturer. Plaintiff urges that foreseeability has no place in strict-tort-liability doctrine but that, in any event, the likelihood of small children being in the vicinity of operating farm equipment is not so unforeseeable as to warrant taking the case from the jury; defendant contends that the product was [unforeseeably] being "used" by a child for whose use it was not intended.... * * *

* * *

Whether [plaintiff] is entitled to the protections afforded by the concepts of strict tort liability depends upon whether it can be fairly said that her conduct in placing her fingers in the moving screen or belt of the forage wagon was reasonably foreseeable. [Yet the foreseeability test is] not intended to bring within the scope of the defendant's liability every injury that might possibly occur. "In a sense, in retrospect almost nothing is entirely unforeseeable." Mieher v. Brown, 301 N.E.2d 307, 309 (Ill.1973). Foreseeability means that which it is *objectively reasonable* to expect, not merely what might conceivably occur. [Citation.]

... While in retrospect it can be asserted that the manufacturer of the forage wagon should have foreseen that the unfortunate event in this case might conceivably occur, we do not believe its occurrence was objectively reasonable to expect. It cannot ... fairly be said that a manufacturer should reasonably foresee that a four-year-old child will be permitted to approach an operating farm forage wagon or that the child will be permitted to place her fingers in or on the holes in its moving screen. [T]he trial court properly dismissed plaintiff's amended complaint. * * *

Appellate court reversed; [plaintiff's case dismissed].

■ GOLDENHERSH, JUSTICE (dissenting).

[W]hether it is reasonably foreseeable that someone might be injured by reason of coming into contact with the inadequately protected and unreasonably dangerous mechanism ... is properly [a question of fact for the jury and should not be decided as a question of law.]

Richelman v. Kewanee Machinery & Conveyor Co.

Appellate Court of Illinois, Fifth District, 1978.
59 Ill.App.3d 578, 16 Ill.Dec. 778, 375 N.E.2d 885.

■ MORAN, JUSTICE.

Defendant appeals [judgment on a verdict for Mark Richelman who was injured in a grain auger designed and manufactured by the defendant and located on his grandfather's farm when Mark was 2 years 9 months old. The auger consists of a 41–foot metal tube, or sleeve, within which a screw-like mechanism revolves extending from a 25–foot high storage silo down to a hopper on the ground. A jury returned a verdict for the plaintiff on both negligence and strict liability, and defendant appealed.]

[Mark and his cousin were put down for their customary mid-day nap whereupon] Donald Richelman started the auger and proceeded to feed some cattle approximately 50 feet away from the operating machinery. As the children were unable to sleep, Mrs. Richelman dressed them and took them to their grandmother's house nearby [which Donald did not notice]. While Mrs. Richelman spoke with her mother-in-law in the living room, the children played on an enclosed porch. Less than five minutes later both parents heard Mark's screams and rushed to the grain elevator in time to pull their son from the hopper. [Mark's right leg had been amputated by the grain auger; no one witnessed the accident.]

[James Suhr, a Kewanee design engineer, testified for plaintiff that in designing the guards he considered only the safety of adult operators, not bystanders or children, although the engineers knew that children frequently play around farms; he used his own size 12 shoe in determining the width of the gap between the guard bars and accordingly spaced the bars 4⅝″ apart; and that he did not contemplate an operator tripping and accidentally thrusting another body part into the auger. In short, the engineers designed the guard for "the majority of users."]

[The issue on appeal is whether Mark Richelman's injury was foreseeable as a matter of law under the rationale of Winnett v. Winnett, 310 N.E.2d 1 (Ill.1974).] In Wenzell v. MTD Products, Inc., 336 N.E.2d 125 (Ill.App.1975), the four-year-old plaintiff was injured when a gasoline-powered lawn mower driven by a seven-year-old came into contact with plaintiff's foot. [In denying liability, the court noted] that the "mower was being used by a group of children virtually as a toy." ... In this case, however, there is no positive evidence that the minor plaintiff was actively playing with or attempting to operate the grain auger. Thus, the jury could have inferred that Mark inadvertently tripped or fell into the open hopper.

Moreover, [most] adults could have been similarly injured because of the 4⅝″ gap between the bars ... in this case; whereas, [in *Winnett*] the holes in the conveyor belt were only of a sufficient size to admit the fingers of a small child. [T]hat the individual injured is a child should not preclude recovery where an adult, with a narrower foot than that of the design engineer, could likewise have sustained injury. [T]he real question is not so much whether the defendant could "objectively expect" that Mark would not take a nap on the day in question but instead would venture outdoors and become entangled in the grain auger, but rather whether the defendant could "objectively expect" that if one with a smaller than 4⅝″ shoe width were to trip or fall near the auger he could be injured because of the inadequate safety guard.

[Foreseeability and defectiveness] are ordinarily for the jury to resolve [and we] cannot say as a matter of law that injury to the plaintiff in this case was not objectively reasonable to expect. [T]he *Winnett* case and its progeny [do not control] this issue.

Affirmed.

■ JONES, JUSTICE, dissenting.

[*Winnett*, having almost identical facts, should control;] it would not be objectively reasonable for the manufacturer to expect plaintiff to be injured by the auger either while playing with it or by accidentally falling into it. As [an earlier Illinois decision stated: "The responsibility for a child's safety lies primarily with its parents, whose duty is to see that his behavior does not involve danger to himself."]

It is likewise irrelevant that an adult might be injured by the machine in question. We are to consider only whether the defendant could reasonably foresee that the plaintiff in question would be injured by the auger. Foreseeability of injury in general simply does not enter into a determination of this particular case. The only question can be whether this particular plaintiff's injury was reasonably foreseeable. The *Winnett* case held that it was not and we should follow it.

NOTES

1. Are *Winnett* and *Richelman* consistent? Are they explainable on the "reasonable foreseeability" of the injuries? On whether the accidents were "objectively reasonable to expect"? How useful are these tests in deciding whether manufacturers of farming machinery or injured children (and their parents) should bear the economic burden of such accidental losses?

What really influenced the majority and dissenting judges in these cases? Should these factors have been made more explicit? Should the jury have been told to consider them? Whether told to or not, *do* juries consider them?

Is there any connection between the real considerations at work in such cases and the "test" of reasonable foreseeability? Should there be?

2. Compare Yassin v. Certified Grocers, Inc., 502 N.E.2d 315 (Ill.App.1986) (3–year–old wandered away from mother to work area in rear of grocery store where she caught her hand in meat tenderizer left on and unattended; *held,* injury *not* objectively reasonable to expect), with Pierce v. Hobart Corp., 512 N.E.2d 14 (Ill.App.1987) (10–year–old, who helped around restaurant after school, caught hand in meat grinder while pushing in piece of cheese; *held,* reversing summary judgment for manufacturer, foreseeability for jury).

3. Foreseeability—Use. Recall that, in strict tort liability, defectiveness rests squarely on the foreseeability of a product's *use*. See Newman v. Utility Trailer & Equipment Co., 564 P.2d 674 (Or.1977). A manufacturer "is not required to foresee, for example, that a lawnmower—which is designed to cut grass—will be used to cut logs or to cut pipe." When a defective elevator stops six feet above a floor, is it a foreseeable use for a passenger to try to jump out? See Egan v. A.J. Construction Corp., 724 N.E.2d 366 (N.Y.1999) (no; hence any defect in the elevator was not a proximate cause of the worker's injury, as a matter of law).

If explosive-grade fertilizer is used as a component in an explosive device, should the manufacturer be able to defend a products liability claim on the unforeseeability of such use? In Port Authority of New York and New Jersey v. Arcadian Corp., 189 F.3d 305, 318 (3d Cir.1999), the owner of the World Trade Center maintained that the manufacturers of fertilizer used to make a terrorist bomb could have used additives to make it more difficult for their products to be turned into explosives. The trial court held that plaintiff's allegations regarding past fertilizer explosions, "as a matter of law, simply do not permit a finding of objective foreseeability" necessary to a determination that the product was defectively designed. The Court of Appeals agreed, holding that "conceivability is not the equivalent of foreseeability."

4. Foreseeability—Risk of Harm.

A. In general. Most courts limit recovery to harm from foreseeable types of risks or hazards. See Rest. (2d) Torts § 442(a), below. See, e.g., Whiteford v. Yamaha Motor Corp., 582 N.W.2d 916 (Minn. 1998), in which a tobogganing child collided headfirst into a snowmobile and suffered facial injuries from a defective metal bracket on the snowmobile; *held*, risk unforeseeable as matter of law.

B. Emotional distress. Should a manufacturer be expected to foresee that some consumers will become distressed, and perhaps even suffer illness as a result, from its defective products? Compare Caputzal v. Lindsay Co., 222 A.2d 513 (N.J.1966) (no: heart attack from fright at sight of rusty brown water caused by defect in defendant's water softener; plaintiff's emotional hypersensitivity was idiosyncratic and hence unforeseeable), with Barnette v. Dickens, 135 S.E.2d 109 (Va.1964) (yes: plaintiff became hysterical, and ultimately suffered traumatic neurosis, when she witnessed her washing machine vibrating violently, like a "robot gone crazy").

C. Suicide. Should a manufacturer be liable for a suicide caused by a defective product? See Kleen v. Homak Manuf. Co., 749 N.E.2d 26 (Ill.App. 2001) (no: manufacturer of defective gun case lock could not foresee that plaintiff's son would break into gun case and commit suicide); Saxton v. McDonnell Douglas Aircraft Co., 428 F.Supp. 1047 (C.D.Cal.1977) (no: mother of passenger killed in plane crash committed suicide from stress of son's death and subsequent products liability trial).

What if the accident victim *himself* commits suicide on account of his injuries? Fuller v. Preis, 322 N.E.2d 263 (N.Y.1974) (yes, if caused by irresistible impulse: surgeon suffered brain damage in car accident).

5. Foreseeability—Manner of Harm. While "certain accidents may occur in such a 'tragically bizarre' and 'unique' manner that no legal duty to guard against them will be imposed upon the defendant," Kerns v. Engelke, 369 N.E.2d 1284, 1293 (Ill.App.1977), rev'd in part on other grounds, 390 N.E.2d 859 (Ill.1979), it generally is agreed that the precise *manner* in which the harm occurs need not be foreseeable. So, a meat packing company that negligently applied a rubber band to bind a shank of lamb need not have foreseen that a butcher would be hit in the eye when the band flew off as he grasped the lamb to pull it forward along a conveyor rail. Katz v. Swift & Co., 276 F.2d 905, 906 (2d Cir.1960) ("It was, of course, not necessary that defendant should have been able to anticipate the particular chain of events that would result in injury in order to be held liable. It was sufficient that it was foreseeable that injury might result if the rubber bands were improperly attached...."").

6. Foreseeability—Extent of Harm. Myrtle Poplar pricked her finger on the jagged point of a silvery metal star adorning a cosmetic gift box she had received for Christmas. An infection developed, and the finger had to be amputated. The manufacturer argued that it should not be held to anticipate "so extraordinary and unpredictable a result" as an amputation "from the otherwise trivial puncturing of her skin." The court disagreed: "[I]f the plaintiff's injury is traceable to the defendant's negligence without intervention of any other independent, legally operative event—the injured person is entitled to recover for the harm actually suffered even though the precise nature and extent of those injuries, as they finally developed, were more severe than could ordinarily have been foreseen. In other words, a defendant is chargeable for all the harm and suffering which his negligent act brought on even though the plaintiff's injuries were aggravated by his own predisposition or weakness or by the intervening mistake or negligence of a physician who treated the original injury." Poplar v. Bourjois, 80 N.E.2d 334, 336–37 (N.Y.1948) (dictum).

7. Foreseeability—Type of Plaintiff. Recall the lesson of the *Palsgraf* case: the defendant's duty extends only to *plaintiffs* who are foreseeable. See Darsan v. Globe Slicing Machine Co., 606 N.Y.S.2d 317 (App.Div.1994) (14–year–old operator of meat-grinder unforeseeable user as matter of law since labor laws prohibited use of machine by persons under 16). But most courts are quite lenient in finding plaintiffs foreseeable. Goree v. Winnebago Indus., 958 F.2d 1537 (11th Cir.1992) (paraplegic with no heat sensitivity in feet drove motor home (with hand controls he had installed) for six hours while his bare feet rested on steel floorboard that reached 175 degrees Fahrenheit; plaintiff was foreseeable consumer).

Recall also the rescue doctrine that defines people who come to the aid of injured persons as foreseeable plaintiffs. See McCoy v. American Suzuki Motor Corp., 961 P.2d 952 (Wash.1998) (motorist, struck by hit-and-run driver during attempt to aid passengers in overturned vehicle, could proceed with design defect action against manufacturer of overturned vehicle even though plaintiff was injured two hours after accident that prompted his rescue and after police had arrived).

8. The Restatements of Torts. Consider the role of foreseeability within the doctrine of proximate causation in the Restatement (Second) of Torts:

§ 435. Foreseeability of Harm or Manner of Its Occurrence

(1) If the actor's conduct is a substantial factor in bringing about harm to another, the fact that the actor neither foresaw nor should have foreseen the extent of the harm or the manner in which it occurred does not prevent him from being liable.

(2) The actor's conduct may be held not to be a legal cause of harm to another where after the event and looking back from the harm to the actor's negligent conduct, it appears to the court highly extraordinary that it should have brought about the harm.

The Products Liability Restatement § 15 incorporates "prevailing rules and principles" for the law governing causation. The Restatement (Third) of Torts: Liability for Physical Harm § 29, "Limitations on Liability for Tortious Conduct" (Proposed Final Draft No. 1, April 6, 2005), provides:

> An actor's liability is limited to those physical harms that result from the risks that made the actor's conduct tortuous.

Comment *j* attempts to distinguish this "risk standard" from foreseeability:

> Although the risk standard in this Section is comparable to the foreseeability standard in actions based on negligence, the risk standard contained in this Section is preferable because it provides greater clarity, facilitates clearer analysis in a given case, and better reveals the reason for its existence [by focusing] attention on the particular circumstances that existed at the time of the actor's conduct and the risks that were posed by that conduct.

Since "risk" must mean "foreseeable risk," the Third Restatement's "risk standard" is little more than a foreseeability standard in risk-standard clothing.

---

2.   INTERVENING CAUSES

The connection between a defendant's breach of duty and the plaintiff's injury may appear tenuous or "remote" because of the intervention of some force other than the plaintiff or defendant. Someone other than the plaintiff may abuse the product, or ignore its warnings or instructions, in a manner that might give rise to a contributory negligence, assumption of risk, or misuse defense had the conduct been that of the plaintiff. As with product misuse by plaintiffs, whether from the vantage point of duty or defense, the principal criterion used to determine whether an intervening cause will be held to "supersede" a seller's breach of duty—and hence relieve the seller of liability—is one of "foreseeability." Yet, as seen in the preceding section, the foreseeability "doctrine" is at best a slippery and incomplete basis for deciding cases, a problem that is magnified in the intervening cause context. "There is no area of tort law that has generated more confusion than the question of superseding or intervening cause [especially] where the claim is based on products liability." Montgomery Elevator Co. v. McCullough, 676 S.W.2d 776 (Ky.1984).

Dugan v. Sears, Roebuck & Co.

Appellate Court of Illinois, 1983.
113 Ill.App.3d 740, 73 Ill.Dec. 320, 454 N.E.2d 64.

■ LORENZ, JUSTICE delivered the opinion of the court upon rehearing:

Plaintiff, Steve Dugan, a minor, filed a strict liability action (by his father and next friend) to recover for injuries suffered when a power lawnmower manufactured and sold by the defendants, Roper Corporation and Sears, Roebuck & Company, picked up a small piece of plastic and ejected it at high velocity, blinding plaintiff's right eye. [Plaintiff appeals a jury verdict for defendants.]

Carol Favia testified that on May 20, 1974, she was mowing the front lawn of her home while five-year-old Steve Dugan, a neighbor, sat on the steps of her front porch. The power mower, which had been manufactured by Roper and purchased from Sears, came with an owner's manual. Favia testified she read the manual, including the following warning:

"Do not allow anyone in the area while cutting. Keep children and pets in the backyard while mowing the front yard. Keep a wary eye out for children or passersby. Stop the engine while they are in the vicinity of your mower ... [A]lthough the area mowed should be completely cleared of all foreign objects, a small object could be accidentally thrown by the mower."

The manual further warned that "[i]t is imperative in [the mower's] use and maintenance that the operator always follow the normal precautions set forth in the Rules for Safe Operation as well as other instructions contained in the Owner's Manual in order to prevent injury or damage."

Despite having read these warnings, Favia continued to mow the lawn while plaintiff sat nearby on the porch steps. Suddenly, while she was about 10 feet from plaintiff, Favia heard a click, then "Stevie cried out and he put his hand over his eye." She took him for first aid, and when she returned she found, on the porch steps, the piece of plastic which hit plaintiff in the eye.

[Plaintiff asserts that the mower's design was unreasonably dangerous because it allowed the random discharge of foreign objects that feasible alternative designs would have prevented. Defendants argued that Carol Favia's conduct [was] the sole proximate cause of plaintiff's injury.]

The jury was instructed [that] plaintiff had the burden of proving that an unreasonably dangerous condition in the mower was a "proximate cause" of plaintiff's injury [and] that: "If you decide that the sole proximate cause of the injury to the plaintiff was the conduct of some person other than the defendants, then your verdict should be for the defendants." See Illinois Pattern Jury Instructions, Civil (2d ed. 1971) § 12.04.

* * *

The difficulty is in where to draw the line between strict liability and absolute liability. This involves a clash between the policy which favors compensating injured consumers, and the policy against imposing on manufacturers and sellers the heavy burden of becoming absolute insurers of the safety of their products. Therefore, "[u]ntil Americans have a comprehensive scheme of social insurance, courts must resolve by a balancing process the head-on collision between the need for adequate recovery and viable enterprises." Helene Curtis Industries, Inc. v. Pruitt, 385 F.2d 841, 862 (5th Cir.1967).

One of the mechanisms used to draw the line between these competing interests[, whether in negligence, warranty, or strict liability in tort,] is the doctrine of proximate cause. As the trial court instructed the jury, "proximate cause" is a "cause which, in natural or probable sequence, produced the injury complained of." (Illinois Pattern Jury Instructions, Civil (2d ed. 1977 Suppl.) § 400.–04.) * * *

[D]efendants argued that Carol Favia's conduct was the "sole proximate cause" of plaintiff's injuries, and that he therefore failed to meet his burden of proving that his injuries were proximately caused by defendants' product. * * * "A superseding cause is an act of a third person or other force which by its intervention prevents the actor from being liable for harm to another which his antecedent [tortious conduct] is a substantial factor in bringing about." (Restatement (Second) of Torts (1965) § 440.) "The concept is that there has intervened between the original wrong and the final injury a new and independent force. The injury is imputed to the new force and not the first and more remote cause." Dooley § 8.05, at 235.

According to plaintiff, however, Favia's conduct was so foreseeable that, as a matter of law, it could not be considered a superseding cause. [However, foreseeability and intervening cause normally require jury determination.]

[A]ssuming for the sake of argument that plaintiff's injury was caused by an unreasonably dangerous condition in defendants' product, the pertinent question is this: could reasonable people disagree about whether the intervening force (Carol Favia's conduct in knowingly disregarding defendants' warnings) was so probable, natural, and foreseeable that the defendants should remain strictly liable for the injury.

There is no doubt that with any given product somebody will eventually disregard the manufacturer's warnings, thereby causing injuries. Nevertheless, ... defendants in strict liability cases are not absolutely liable as insurers, and we find that reasonable people can disagree over whether Favia's conduct was so probable, natural, and foreseeable that the defendants should be held strictly liable for the alleged unreasonably dangerous condition in their product. [Thus, the jury could reasonably conclude that Favia's conduct was a superseding cause that became the sole proximate cause of plaintiff's injuries.]

Affirmed.

Anderson v. Dreis & Krump Manufacturing Corp.

Court of Appeals of Washington, 1987.
739 P.2d 1177.

■ MUNSON, JUDGE.

Steve Anderson brought this [breach of warranty, negligence, and strict liability action for] personal injuries received while operating a Chicago Press Brake (press) manufactured by Dreis & Krump Manufacturing Corporation (Dreis). The trial court entered summary judgment for Dreis, dismissing the action [and plaintiff appealed.]

Mr. Anderson was injured ... while operating a press owned by his employer, Comet Corporation. [Comet bought the Dreis press through a distributor and installed it in its Spokane facility. The press] was designed as a general purpose or "multifunctional" press, capable of performing a variety of functions. Comet used the press for corrugating metal.[2] During

---

2. As utilized by Comet, sheets of aluminum, approximately 100 inches long, were fed into the press from the back of the press moving through the point of operation toward the operator.

operation, the press' "ram," or vertically movable upper section, would descend upon the "bed" or lower section. Shaping tools or "dies" are attached to the ram as well as the bed. When the ram descends, the metal is bent into the desired shape by the upper die pressing the metal against the lower die. The area between the ram die and the bed die is referred to as the "point of operation."

The press, as originally designed, manufactured, and sold to Comet, could be activated by either of two means: the first was a 2–button control located at shoulder level above the ram ... The 2–button system was also the press' principal safety feature because the operator's hands were on the buttons, and thus prevented from entering the point of operation when the ram descended. The second means of activation was by depressing a foot treadle connected to a rod which ran along the base of the press.... Dreis provided no accompanying safety device to prevent the operator's hands from entering the point of operation when the press was activated by the treadle. The operator could choose either the 2–button control or the treadle by flipping a lever on the side of the press.

[Dreis provided manuals with the press explaining how to use it safely, one of which] instructed purchasers never to eliminate or bypass any safety device installed on the press [and requesting] purchasers to contact Dreis with respect to the continued use of the press after any modification. [Further], Dreis attached the following warning sign to the front of the press near the point of operation:

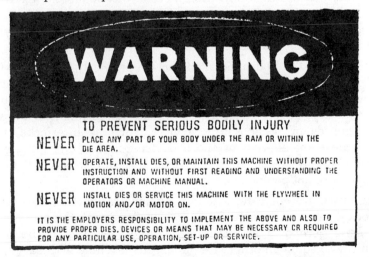

[After delivery, Comet disconnected the 2–button activation device and rewired the press so that it could be activated by pushing a single button] attached to the end of a long, flexible electric cord. This flexible cord, like the adjustable treadle, allowed the operator to move along the length of the press' bed. Because this method of activation required the use of only one hand, the operator's other hand was left free to enter the dangerous point of operation. [Comet installed] no additional "point-of-operation" safety guards.[3] Comet was aware of the danger to operators from use of the unguarded press and discussed these dangers at company meetings prior to the accident. Additionally, the Washington State Department of Labor & Industries inspected the press prior to the accident and found the press to be unsafe. . . . Comet was fined for lack of point-of-operation safety devices on the press.

This accident occurred when Mr. Anderson reached into the point-of-operation area to brush away small circles of aluminum that had accumulated during the stamping process. He was leaning into the die area when his stomach accidently hit the single button activator, the cord of which had been laid nearby. As a result, the ram cycled downward, severely injuring one of his hands.

In moving for summary judgment, Dreis argued: (1) the press was not defective as manufactured and sold since the press included the 2–button (activator) safety feature; (2) adequate warnings were attached to and accompanied the press when it was sold; and (3) Comet's modification of the activation system was the superseding cause of Mr. Anderson's injury.

In response, Mr. Anderson argued the press was designed to be used with the treadle activator. Because use of the treadle allowed the operator to place his hands within the point-of-operation area, the press should have included corresponding point-of-operation or barrier-type guards. He asserted the single button activator, though a modification, did not cut off Dreis' liability because that activation method was no more dangerous than the foot treadle, and the kind of harm which occurred, i.e., accidental injury to hands, was no different than the kind of harm which would have occurred if the treadle had been used.

[The Superior Court dismissed the action primarily because of Comet's modification. The court properly dismissed the breach of warranty and inadequate warnings claims. However, the design defect claims should have gone to the jury.] Dreis contends, however, its installation of point-of-operation guards or other safety devices, such as interlocks, was not feasible because installation of those devices on the multipurpose press would have unduly restricted the myriad uses for which the press was designed. We are not persuaded.

First, Dreis presented no evidence demonstrating that barrier guards or interlock devices would actually have interfered with the press operation *as used here*. Second, a manufacturer cannot delegate to the buyer its responsibility to equip an otherwise dangerous machine with safety guards. [Citations, including Bexiga v. Havir Mfg. Corp., 290 A.2d 281 (N.J. 1972)]. . . .

---

3. The record indicates that several types of point-of-operation guards were available, including: (a) barrier guards, and (b) "light curtains." Either of these guards would have prevented the press from cycling while the operator's hands were in the point-of-operation area.

D. Employer's Modification

The court held Comet's modification from the 2–button device to the single button switch was the superseding cause of Mr. Anderson's injury thereby relieving Dreis of liability as a matter of law. Consequently, the crucial issue is whether the trial court was correct in passing on superseding cause as a matter of law or whether a jury should do so as a matter of fact.

Proximate cause is an essential element of both negligence and products liability theories; it consists of two elements: (1) factual or "but for" causation and (2) legal causation. [Citations.] Unlike factual causation, legal causation "hinges on principles of responsibility, not physics," Van Buskirk v. Carey Canadian Mines, Ltd., 760 F.2d 481, 492 (3d Cir.1985), and the determination of legal causation rests on policy considerations as to how far the legal consequences of a defendant's act should extend....

The doctrine of superseding cause, however, limits the situations in which legal causation can be held to exist between two events. The doctrine applies where the act of a third party intervenes between the defendant's original conduct and the plaintiff's injury such that the defendant may no longer be deemed responsible for the injury. [Citation;] Restatement (Second) of Torts § 440 (1965). Superseding cause thus [breaks the chain of causation] where the intervening act breaks the otherwise natural and continuous causal connection between events. [Citation.]

Whether an act may be considered a superseding cause sufficient to relieve a defendant of liability depends on whether the intervening act can reasonably be foreseen by the defendant; only intervening acts which are *not* reasonably foreseeable are deemed superseding causes. [Citation.] The foreseeability of an intervening act, unlike the determination of legal cause in general, is ordinarily a question of fact for the jury. [Citations.] However, foreseeability is a flexible concept, and a defendant will not be relieved of responsibility simply because the exact manner in which the injury occurred could not be anticipated. Rikstad v. Holmberg, 456 P.2d 355 (Wash.1969); [citation]. Rikstad (quoting McLeod v. Grant Cty. Sch. Dist., 255 P.2d 360 (Wash.1953)), provides:

> It is not, however, the unusualness of the [intervening] act that resulted in injury to plaintiff that is the test of foreseeability, but whether the result of the act is within the ambit of the hazards covered by the duty imposed upon defendant.
>
> * * * It is literally true that there is no liability for damage that falls entirely outside the general threat of harm which made the conduct of the actor negligent. The sequence of events, of course, need not be foreseeable. *The manner in which the risk culminates in harm may be unusual, improbable and highly unexpectable, from the point of view of the actor at the time of his conduct. And yet, if the harm suffered falls within the general danger area, there may be liability, provided other requisites of legal causation are present.*

See also W. P. Keeton, D. Dobbs, R. Keeton, D. Owen, The Law of Torts, at 316 (5th ed. 1984). In this context our Supreme Court has held that generally an intervening act is not a superseding cause where the intervening act (1) does not bring about a different type of harm than otherwise would have resulted from the defendant's conduct; and (2) does not operate independently of the situation created by the defendant's conduct. [Citation]; Restatement (Second) of Torts §§ 442–45 (1965).... The above principles are equally applicable to negligence and strict products liability theories. [Citation.]

Dreis primarily contends Comet's deactivation of the 2–button device and installation of an alternative activation system destroyed the efficacy of the press' safety features. Dreis maintains, and the court found, the deactivation of this safety feature was unforeseeable and constituted a superseding cause of the accident as a matter of law. We disagree.

Contrary to Dreis' argument, a jury could find it was reasonably foreseeable to Dreis that a purchaser of the press would choose an alternative method of activation given the press' myriad uses, see Jiminez v. Dreis & Krump Mfg. Co., 736 F.2d 51 (2d Cir.1984), and because an alternative activation system, i.e., the treadle, was designed into the press and delivered with it to Comet. Obviously, use of an alternative activation method, such as the treadle, rendered the 2–button activation system superfluous and its safety features ineffective since the press operator's hands were no longer occupied.

We are cognizant that the activation method chosen by Comet was not originally designed into the press by Dreis and thus the precise manner in which this accident occurred may not have been foreseeable to Dreis. [Citations.] However, the single button switch, like the treadle, foreseeably allowed the press to be accidentally activated while the operator's free hands were in the unguarded point-of-operation area. Under these circumstances, a jury could find the accidental activation of the press, while Mr. Anderson's hand was in the die area, was within the foreseeable scope of danger created by Dreis' failure to incorporate guards around the point-of-operation area. In the absence of any evidence that Comet's modification enhanced the danger of accidental activation above that found in the treadle, we decline to hold that Comet's modification constitutes a superseding cause as a matter of law. [Citation.]

* * *

E. Comet's Failure to Supply Guards

Notwithstanding the foregoing analysis, Dreis argues ... that Comet had actual, specific knowledge of the danger created by the press' lack of guards and thus had a duty to itself supply such guards. Dreis argues Comet's failure to supply such guards was a negligent act sufficient to constitute a superseding cause as a matter of law. We disagree.

The Restatement (Second) of Torts § 449, at 482 (1965) provides the negligence of a third party does not constitute a superseding cause "[i]f the likelihood that a third person may act in a particular manner is ... one of the hazards which makes the [original] actor negligent." [Citation.] This court has previously held it is foreseeable a small company which purchases dangerous industrial machinery will not install guards on that machinery when the manufacturer delivers that equipment without them. [Citations.] Not only is the manufacturer's duty to supply safety guards on dangerous industrial equipment nondelegable, *Bexiga,* supra, but the failure of the purchaser to supply guards is so likely that it constitutes one of the hazards which makes a manufacturer's failure to supply such guards negligent. Restatement (Second) of Torts § 449 (1965). Moreover, the public interest in assuring that appropriate safety devices be installed on industrial machinery would be undermined if installation was left to the "haphazard conduct of the ultimate purchaser." *Bexiga.* * * *

F. Comet's Continued Use of the Press After the Department of Labor & Industries' Warning

Dreis further contends Comet's continued use of the guardless press after being warned by the Department of Labor & Industries that the press was dangerous without guards constitutes a superseding cause of the injury. [On similar facts, other courts have disagreed. Citations. We agree with] those decisions and likewise hold Comet's failure to heed the Department's warning does not immunize Dreis as a matter of law.

G. Summary

[The trial court erred in ruling that the press was not defectively designed as a matter of law and that Dreis' design was not the legal cause of Mr. Anderson's injury as a matter of law. Reversed and remanded for trial.]

■ Green, Judge (dissenting).

[T]he trial judge was correct in ruling the modification of the activation mechanism of the press was the intervening proximate cause of Mr. Anderson's injuries and dismissing the complaint.

The press was designed to be activated by the use of two buttons or a foot treadle. When the buttons were used, it was impossible for the operator's hands to be under the press. The purchaser, Comet, ... not only modified the press so it could be activated by one button, but placed that button in a position where it could be accidentally activated by the operator's body rubbing against it. That is what happened here. The operator, while removing metal from beneath the press, rubbed against the dangling button setting off the press and injuring his hand.

It is apparent that the sole and proximate cause of this accident was Comet's negligent modification of the button activation system, creating the danger of accidental activation.

If the accident had happened while using the foot treadle, then the issue of defective design as the proximate cause of the injury would create a question for the trier of fact. Here, the treadle was not used and the question of defective design for treadle use is not an issue.

I would affirm.

N O T E S

1. In *Dugan,* do you think that the manufacturer or Sears could foresee that someone might read the operator's manual quickly, when she first purchased the mower, and thereafter forget much of what she read? Might there be something, perhaps one or two minor points, that a student read earlier in this book which has now been forgotten? Is it "foreseeable" that product users will not always remember to, be able to, want to, or know to obey every warning and instruction that accompanies a product? If so, is *Dugan* wrongly decided?

2. In *Anderson,* why should the manufacturer of a multi-purpose press equipped with a perfectly safe (two–button control) activation device be liable for an accident caused by the employer's replacement of the safe device with a dangerous one? Is *Anderson* wrongly decided?

3. Restatement (Second) of Torts. As both *Dugan* and *Anderson* illustrate, many courts rely substantially on the Restatement (Second) of Torts' formulation of principles for intervening and superseding causation:

§ 442.   Considerations Important in Determining Whether an Intervening Force is a Superseding Cause

The following considerations are of importance in determining whether an intervening force is a superseding cause of harm to another:

(a) The fact that its intervention brings about harm different in kind from that which would otherwise have resulted from the actor's negligence;

(b) the fact that its operation or the consequences thereof appear after the event to be extraordinary rather than normal in view of the circumstances existing at the time of its operation;

(c) the fact that the intervening force is operating independently of any situation created by the actor's negligence, or, on the other hand, is or is not a normal result of such a situation;

(d) the fact that the operation of the intervening force is due to a third person's act or to his failure to act;

(e) the fact that the intervening force is due to an act of a third person which is wrongful toward the other and as such subjects the third person to liability to him;

(f) the degree of culpability of a wrongful act of a third person which sets the intervening force in motion.

Consider also the following section on whether and when a third person's nonfeasance will amount to a superseding cause of the plaintiff's harm:

§ 452.   Third Person's Failure to Prevent Harm

(1) Except as stated in Subsection (2), the failure of a third person to act to prevent harm to another threatened by the actor's negligent conduct is not a superseding cause of such harm.

(2) Where, because of lapse of time or otherwise, the duty to prevent harm to another threatened by the actor's negligent conduct is found to have shifted from the actor to a third person, the failure of the third person to prevent such harm is a superseding cause.

Comment *f* to § 452 provides: A court may "find that all duty and responsibility for the prevention of the harm has passed to the third person. It is apparently impossible to state any comprehensive rule as to when such a decision will be made." Relevant factors include "the degree of danger and the magnitude of the risk of harm, the character and position of the third person who is to take the responsibility, his knowledge of the danger and the likelihood that he will or will not exercise proper care, his relation to the plaintiff or to the defendant, the lapse of time, and perhaps other considerations."

Consider the following, recurring forms of third-party intervening misconduct.

4. Parent Misconduct.

A. Passive: Negligent supervision. Many, perhaps most, products liability cases in which young children are injured involve "inadequate" supervision on the part of a parent or other responsible person at the time of the accident. Reconsider *Winnett* and *Richelman* from this perspective. Today, there are virtually no decisions expressly holding that a parent's negligent supervision supersedes the responsibility of a manufacturer of a defective product. In a sense, however, this is implicitly what the court did in *Winnett*, and what the dissent argued should have been done in *Richelman*. Nevertheless, at least with respect to products intended for use in the home, most courts consider parental neglect—and the resulting wandering and mischief of curious youngsters—part of the "foreseeable environment of use" of such products. See, e.g., Spruill v. Boyle–Midway, Inc., 308 F.2d 79 (4th Cir.1962) (unattended infant drank furniture polish that mother left on bureau beside crib); Eshbach v. W.T. Grant's & Co., 481 F.2d 940 (3d Cir.1973) (unbeknownst to father, 9–year–old son drove riding mower with sister riding on back). But see Wenzell v. MTD Prods., Inc., 336 N.E.2d 125, 134 (Ill.App.1975) (unforeseeable that riding mower would be used by group of young children "virtually as a toy").

B. Active: Injuring child with the product. Some of the cases involve more affirmative misconduct by the parent, such as falling asleep at the wheel of a car in which the child is riding, Rossell v. Volkswagen of America, 709 P.2d 517 (Ariz.1985), or knocking over a bottle of liquid drain cleaner onto the child, Drayton v. Jiffee Chem. Corp., 395 F.Supp. 1081 (N.D.Ohio 1975), aff'd, 591 F.2d 352 (6th Cir.1978). Rarely is such conduct held to be a superseding cause.

5. Physician Misconduct.

A. Failing to pass along manufacturer's warnings. Recall that under the "learned intermediary" doctrine, the manufacturer of a prescription drug generally is obligated to warn the doctor, not the patient. See ch. 8, above. What if the doctor negligently, or intentionally, fails to pass along to the patient an important warning or instruction that would have prevented the harm?

In Kirk v. Michael Reese Hosp. & Medical Center, 513 N.E.2d 387, 394 (Ill.1987), plaintiff was injured when the driver of the car in which he was a passenger lost control of the vehicle and crashed into a tree. Earlier in the day, the driver had been discharged from a psychiatric hospital. His doctors had prescribed two drugs, Thorazine and Prolixin, but had failed to warn him of the dangers of mixing alcohol with the drugs. After leaving the hospital, he consumed an alcoholic drink which may have interacted with the drugs to cause the loss of control later in the day. *Held,* the manufacturers could not reasonably have foreseen that "the drugs would be dispensed without the warnings that the two companies provided to the physicians."

B. Active misconduct. What should be the effect of more affirmative misconduct by a medical care provider? A doctor's use of a drug contrary to express warnings will generally terminate the manufacturer's responsibility. See, e.g., Dyer v. Best Pharmacal, 577 P.2d 1084 (Ariz.App. 1978). Nor does the manufacturer have a duty to warn of the risks of prescribing a drug for a non-indicated use. Robak v. Abbott Labs., 797 F.Supp. 475 (D.Md.1992) (renal failure from antibiotic Omniflox prescribed for sinusitis, although drug not indicated for upper respiratory tract conditions).

Compare Pharmaseal Labs., Inc. v. Goffe, 568 P.2d 589 (N.M.1977). As treatment for an internal obstruction, an intestinal tube weighted with a small balloon of mercury was inserted through plaintiff's nostril, down through his stomach, and into his intestines. As the tube began to be removed, it stuck, and the doctor tugged at it forcefully several times to pull it out. The balloon was broken, and plaintiff was discovered to have inhaled the mercury into his lungs. Plaintiff was placed head-down on a tilt table, and "[t]he hospital employees pounded on [his] back for several hours in an attempt to remove the mercury. His head constantly hit the foot of the bed and he experienced chest pain. The next morning he suffered a myocardial infarction." Should the actions of the doctor and hospital employees shield the manufacturer from liability as a matter of law for selling a balloon of inadequate strength? *Held,* no; summary judgment reversed.

6. Employer Misconduct.

A. Failing to pass along manufacturer's warnings. As examined in ch. 8 above, the manufacturer of an industrial product may have a duty to communicate warnings and instructions directly to employees. If the manufacturer has such a duty, and if the manufacturer provides a warning only to the employer (as in a safety information sheet or a technical data manual) and not to the employees (as in a label on the product's container or a warning plate on a machine), the employer's failure to pass along the warning to its employees will not generally supersede the manufacturer's duty to warn them directly. See, e.g., Gordon v. Niagara Mach. & Tool Works, 574 F.2d 1182 (5th Cir.1978).

B. Failing to maintain the product. If an industrial machine malfunctions due to improper maintenance by the employer, should the manufacturer be liable? "The manufacturer is not liable for lack of normal maintenance." Rogers v. Unimac Co., 565 P.2d 181, 184 (Ariz.1977) (failure to replace worn and cracked parts in automatic car wash mechanism). See also La Plante v. American Honda Motor Co., 27 F.3d 731 (1st Cir.1994) (poor maintenance of ATV could constitute statutory defense of alteration).

C. Failing to add guards. Before the 1970s, the custom was for employers—rather than manufacturers—to install appropriate guards on industrial machinery. Yet Bexiga v. Havir Mfg. Corp., 290 A.2d 281 (N.J.1972), ch. 7 above, established the manufacturer's nondelegable duty to equip its machinery with sufficient safety devices. Thus, if the manufacturer fails to provide adequate guards, the employer's failure to remedy the danger will not generally shield the manufacturer. This may be true even if the employer blithely ignores warning letters from the manufacturer urging the employer to cure the defect, explaining how to do so, and offering to provide the employer with the necessary material, for a fee. Balido v. Improved Mach., Inc., 105 Cal.Rptr. 890 (Ct.App.1972). See also Montgomery Elevator Co. v. McCullough, 676 S.W.2d 776 (Ky.1984).

D. Removing or altering guards.

(1) In general. A recurring problem for manufacturers attempting to comply with the *Bexiga* nondelegable duty doctrine occurs when the employer removes or alters a guard provided by the manufacturer. Guards are modified or removed for a variety of reasons: because they malfunction; to facilitate cleaning or maintenance of the machinery; to enhance the usefulness of the machine, as by permitting stock or a particular size or shape to enter the machine; or to speed up production.

Most courts hold the manufacturer accountable for injuries attributable to "foreseeable" modifications, provided that a feasible remedy—such as an electrical interlock—was available. See, e.g., Cepeda v. Cumberland Eng'g Co., 386 A.2d 816 (N.J.1978), rev'g 351 A.2d 22 (N.J.Super.1976) (guard attached to machine with four bolts was not reattached to machine after cleaning; since interlock installation would have cost $25–30, and frequent cleaning was necessary, *held,* foreseeability of removal a jury question); Brown v. United States Stove Co., 484 A.2d 1234, 1240 (N.J.1984) ("a design defect inherent in a safety feature of a product that foreseeably leads to a substantial alteration and an increased risk of danger can be a basis for strict products liability").

In a small number of jurisdictions, even foreseeable alterations may bar recovery. See Hines v. Joy Mfg. Co., 850 F.2d 1146, 1151 (6th Cir.1988) (interpreting Kentucky product liability statute barring recovery for injuries caused by product modifications: "we are not inclined to read the common law concept of foreseeability" into the act).

(2) Substantial change. Courts often examine the alteration question in terms of whether the product was "substantially changed" after it left the manufacturer. This derives from Restatement (Second) of Torts § 402A(b) which provides for liability only if the product "is expected to and does reach the user or consumer without substantial change in the condition in which it is sold." See, e.g., Davis v. Berwind Corp., 690 A.2d 186, 190 (Pa. 1997) (disregarding warnings in the owner's manual and affixed to machine, plaintiff's employer removed the safety devices which "clearly constitutes a substantial change" in the product relieving manufacturer of liability).

Compare Robinson v. Reed–Prentice Div. of Package Mach. Co., 403 N.E.2d 440, 444 (N.Y.1980), where an employee was injured when he stuck his hand through a hole cut in the safety guard by his employer. *Held,* judgment for plaintiff reversed: "The manufacturer's duty . . . does not extend to designing a product that is impossible to abuse or one whose safety features may not be circumvented. . . . Material alterations at the hands of a third party which work a substantial change in the condition in which the product was sold by destroying the functional utility of a key safety feature, however foreseeable that modification may have been, are not within the ambit of a manufacturer's responsibility."

E. Dangerous use of products by other employees. Employees hurt one another with industrial machinery in a variety of ways. A fellow employee's misconduct may or may not supersede the manufacturer's design errors depending on the nature ("foreseeability") of the misconduct and the availability to the manufacturer of a feasible means to prevent it. See Sanders v. Lull Int'l, Inc., 411 F.3d 1266 (11th Cir. 2005) (workers used forklift to transport plaintiff-co-worker contrary to defendant's explicit warnings; summary judgment reversed; reasonable foreseeability of use raised jury question).

F. Shifting responsibility. Particularly in the industrial setting, a proximate cause sub-doctrine relied upon occasionally is that full responsibility for product safety may sometimes be shifted to the employer after the passage of many years and the integration of the product into the employer's operations. Reconsider Rest. (2d) of Torts § 452, note 3, above. See Meuller v. Jeffrey Mfg. Co., 494 F.Supp. 275, 278–79 (E.D.Pa.1980) (plaintiff fell through three foot square hole in floor of 15–year–old sand handling equipment employer had purchased from defendant and installed; relying on § 452, court granted summary judgment: age of product, obvious nature of the danger, ability of the employer to remedy the danger without the manufacturer, and "indisputable duty of the employer to keep the workplace safe and the employer's sole possession and control of the equipment" shifted duty from manufacturer to employer as a matter of law).

7. **Other Party Misconduct.** Although intervening misconduct in products liability cases usually involves parents, doctors, or employers, other parties are sometimes involved. *Dugan,* the lawnmower case, is a good example. Most courts use a foreseeability approach in these cases, too. In Bigbee v. Pacific Tel. & Tel. Co., 665 P.2d 947 (Cal.1983), plaintiff was standing in a telephone booth 15 feet from the street when it was struck by a drunken driver. Plaintiff saw the car coming but could not flee because the door jammed. Plaintiff sued various defendants in connection with the design, location, installation, and maintenance of the booth, and the defendants moved to dismiss, arguing that the drunk driver's conduct was a superseding cause. The trial judge dismissed the complaint and plaintiff appealed. *Held,* reversed and remanded: "the risk that a car might hit the telephone booth could be found to constitute one of the hazards to which plaintiff was exposed."

8. **Plaintiff Misconduct.** Plaintiff misconduct is considered in the next chapter as an affirmative defense that may bar recovery or reduce damages pursuant to contributory negligence or comparative fault. Might plaintiff's misconduct rise to the level of a superseding cause that defeats proximate cause? See Yun v. Ford Motor Co., 647 A.2d 841, 847, 851 (N.J.Super. 1994), rev'd, 669 A.2d 1378 (1996), in which plaintiff's 65–year–old father was killed when he ran across two lanes of a busy, dark, rain-slicked highway to retrieve a defective spare tire assembly, which he had known to need repair. The appellate court upheld summary judgment for defendants stating: "[Decedent's] highly extraordinary and dangerous actions in crossing the Parkway twice with complete disregard for his own personal safety clearly constitute a superseding and intervening cause of his own injuries." The Supreme Court reversed, based on the appellate division's dissent: "A jury could find that it was reasonably foreseeable the tire would dislodge and fall on the roadway while the van was in operation and that the operator or passenger might sustain injuries in his attempt to retrieve it. Indeed, some might think it odd if the operator or passenger were to abandon the tire and drive off."

9. **Statutory Reform—Product Alteration.** A key reform issue, several state products liability reform acts passed in recent decades make product alteration a defense to products liability suits, for example:

Kentucky, **Ky. Rev. Stat. Ann. § 411.320(1):**

> *Circumstances under which defendant is liable.*—(1) In any product liability action, a manufacturer shall be liable only for the personal injury, death or property damage that would have occurred if the product had been used in its original, unaltered and unmodified condition. For the purpose of this section, product alteration or modification shall include failure to observe routine care and maintenance, but shall not include ordinary wear and tear. This section shall apply to alterations or modifications made by any person or entity, except those made in accordance with specifications or instructions furnished by the manufacturer.

Tennessee, **Tenn. Code Ann. § 29–28–108:**

> *Alteration or Improper Use.* If a product is not unreasonably dangerous at the time it leaves the control of the manufacturer or seller but was made unreasonably dangerous by subsequent unforeseeable alteration, change, improper maintenance or abnormal use, the manufacturer or seller is not liable.

Oregon, **Or. Rev. Stat. § 30–915:**

> *Defenses.* It shall be a defense to a product liability civil action that an alteration or modification of a product occurred under the following circumstances:
>
> (1) The alteration or modification was made without the consent of or was made not in accordance with the instructions or specifications of the manufacturer, distributor, seller or lessor;
>
> (2) The alteration or modification was a substantial contributing factor to the personal injury, death or property damage; and
>
> (3) If the alteration or modification was reasonably foreseeable, the manufacturer, distributor, seller or lessor gave adequate warning.

Which approach do you think is preferable? Or should the legislatures stay out of this area, and leave it to the courts?

10.   Should Superseding Cause Doctrine be *Abandoned*? Given the widespread use of apportionment of liability principles, and the difficulty of defining reasonably foreseeable intervening causes which supersede, should the doctrine of superseding cause be abolished entirely in favor of apportionment? In Barry v. Quality Steel Products, Inc., 820 A.2d 258 (Conn. 2003), the Court rejected the doctrine of superceding cause. Plaintiff had appealed from a defense verdict arguing that the jury was improperly instructed that his negligence, combined with his co-workers' and his employer's, could act as a superseding cause of his injury from the defendant's defective roof brackets. The Court explained its rejection of superseding cause doctrine:

> [T]he doctrine of superseding cause no longer serves a useful purpose in our negligence jurisprudence. Historically the doctrine reflects the courts' attempt to limit the defendants' liability to foreseeable and reasonable bounds. See W. P. Keeton, D. Dobbs, R. Keeton, & D. Owen, Prosser & Keeton on The Law of Torts § 44 (5th ed. 1984). In this regard, the doctrine of superseding cause involves a question of policy and foreseeability regarding the actions for which a court will hold a defendant accountable. This aspect of superseding cause is already incorporated in our law regarding proximate causation. [That doctrine requires a determination of the point beyond which the law declines to trace a series of events that exist along a chain signifying actual causation and is a matter of fair judgment and a rough sense of justice.] As some commentators have noted, however, the doctrine was also shaped in response to the harshness of contributory negligence and joint and several liability. See Christlieb, Why Superseding Cause Analysis Should Be Abandoned, 72 Tex. L. Rev. 161 (1993). Under this reasoning, in order to avoid what some courts determined was an undue burden on the plaintiff under contributory negligence regimes, courts developed certain ameliorative doctrines, which identified some aspect of the defendant's negligent act that served as a basis for shifting the plaintiff's negligence to the defendant so that the plaintiff could recover for his losses . . . .

... [I]t is inconsistent to conclude simultaneously that all negligent parties should pay in proportion to their fault, but that one negligent party does not have to pay its share because its negligence was somehow "superseded" by a subsequent negligent act. We also find persuasive ... criticism of the Restatement (Second) method §§ 442–453, which looks to the nature of the subsequent negligent act to determine whether it somehow supersedes the previous act. This approach gives an undue prominence to the temporal order of the allegedly negligent acts. [C]ausal contributions do not operate in neat temporal sequences; rather, most events, such as the events giving rise to the plaintiff's injury in the present case, result from a convergence of many conditions. The Restatement (Second) approach, then, has the potential of misleading the fact finder regarding the determination of whether each allegedly tortious act is a proximate cause of the plaintiff's injury by placing too much emphasis on the timing of the acts.

Moreover, it is no longer necessary to utilize doctrines that aid fact finders in making policy decisions regarding how to assign liability among various defendants and the plaintiff because those decisions already are inherent in our modern scheme of comparative negligence and apportionment. Thus, under the approach we adopt herein, the question to be answered by the fact finder is whether the various actors' allegedly negligent conduct was a cause in fact and a proximate cause of the plaintiff's injury in light of all the relevant circumstances. If found to be both, each actor will be liable for his or her proportionate share of the plaintiff's damages.

Id. at 440–442. The Restatement (Third) of Torts: Liability for Physical Harm § 34 agrees. Do you? See generally, Cupp, Proximate Cause, The Proposed Basic Principles Restatement and Products Liability, 53 S.C.L.Rev. 1085 (2002); M. Green, The Unanticipated Ripples of Comparative Negligence: Superseding Cause in Products Liability and Beyond, 53 S.C.L.Rev. 1103 (2002).

Price v. Blaine Kern Artista, Inc.

Supreme Court of Nevada, 1995.
111 Nev. 515, 893 P.2d 367.

■ PER CURIAM.

Thomas Price [appellant] filed an action in strict tort liability and negligence against Blaine Kern Artista, Inc. ("BKA"), a Louisiana corporation that manufactures oversized masks in the form of caricatures resembling various celebrities and characters (hereafter "caricature mask"). The caricature mask covers the entire head of the wearer. Price alleged in his complaint that the caricature mask of George Bush which he wore during employment as an entertainer at Harrah's Club in Reno was defective due to the absence of a safety harness to support his head and neck under the heavy weight. He also alleged that his injury occurred when a Harrah's patron pushed him from behind, causing the weight of the caricature mask to strain and injure his neck as he fell to the ground.

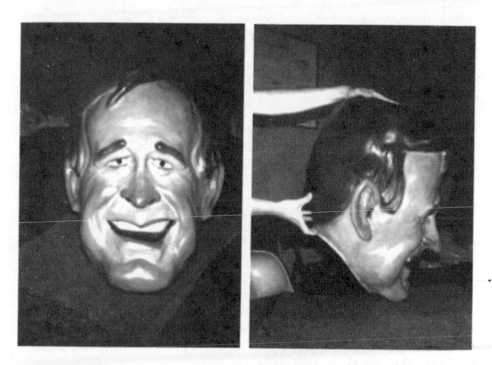

[The district court granted BKA's motion for summary judgment, ruling that the patron's push that precipitated Price's fall constituted an unforeseeable superseding cause absolving BKA of liability. Price appeals.]

[This appeal concerns the question] whether the unknown assailant's push that caused Price to fall to the ground is an intervening, superseding cause of Price's injuries, insulating BKA from liability. * * * Price argues ... that a jury might reasonably infer that a performer wearing a top-heavy, oversized caricature mask may stumble, trip, be pushed, or become imbalanced for numerous reasons [and] may find that BKA proximately caused Price's injury due to its failure to equip the caricature mask of our former President with a safety harness.

BKA ... argues that this is an appropriate case for summary judgment because, by Price's own admission, the third-party attack forming the basis of his complaint was not foreseeable to BKA, and is thus a superseding cause of Price's injuries. [However,] we conclude for two reasons that genuine issues of material fact remain with respect to the issue of legal causation.

[W]hile it is true that criminal or tortious third-party conduct typically severs the chain of proximate causation between a plaintiff and a defendant, the chain remains unbroken when the third party's intervening intentional act is reasonably foreseeable. [Citation.] Under the circumstances of this case, the trier of fact could reasonably find that BKA should have foreseen the possibility or probability of some sort of violent reaction, such as pushing, by intoxicated or politically volatile persons, ignited by the sight of an oversized caricature of a prominent political figure. We certainly cannot preclude such an inference as a matter of law and decline to penalize Price for his attorney's lack of acuity in conceding this issue. Indeed, while the precise force that caused Price's fall is uncertain, shortly before the fall, an irate and perhaps somewhat confused patron of Harrah's took issue with the bedecked Price over Bush's policy on abortion rights.

* * *

For purposes of summary judgment, we note that Price's injuries were not the immediate result of the assailant's push. Rather, the shifting of the weight of the caricature mask was allegedly the immediate cause of Price's injuries, and the risk of such an occurrence and the resulting strain on Price's head and neck may be found to be within the realm of risks that should have been considered and addressed by BKA in the design of its product. In the final analysis, the initial cause of Price's fall appears to be of little consequence, considering the reasonable prospect that among the quantity of users of BKA's products, some of them will sooner or later fall for any number of a variety of reasons.[3]

Assuming, therefore, as we must on appeal, that the caricature mask of George Bush was defective [in design], we are unable to conclude as a matter of law that [the third party's actions precluded the defect from being a proximate cause of Price's injuries, a matter that] is properly within the province of the trier of fact.

[Reversed and remanded for trial.]

Williams v. RCA Corp.

Appellate Court of Illinois, 1978.
59 Ill.App.3d 229, 17 Ill.Dec. 144, 376 N.E.2d 37.

■ SULLIVAN, PRESIDING JUSTICE.

[Plaintiff, a guard employed by a security service, appeals the dismissal of his complaint for injuries arising out of a defective two-way portable receiver manufactured by defendant RCA. During a robbery at a restaurant he was assigned to watch, plaintiff properly radioed patrols in the area for help in apprehending the offender.] Unknown to plaintiff at that time, the receiver did not function—so that his request for assistance was not received. When he attempted to make the arrest by himself, he was wounded by the robber. The complaint [alleges] that the defective condition of the receiver was the proximate cause of his having been wounded.

[D]efendant asserts that as a matter of law the shooting was an independent, intervening cause which broke any causal connection between

---

3. [The court analogizes to the automotive crashworthiness doctrine, which requires manufacturers to design cars to be reasonably safe in collisions from whatever cause. Here, while the particular third party actions causing the mask's wearer to become imbalanced and fall may not have been foreseeable, a jury might reasonably find that BKA had a duty to protect a user against the foreseeable risks of loss of balance and falls.]

the receiver and plaintiff's injury. Plaintiff argues that defendant "should have foreseen that a security guard would be imperiled if [the receiver] failed to function properly." [Citing Winnett v. Winnett, the court observed: "Foreseeability means that which is objectively reasonable to expect, not what might conceivably occur."]

* * * In Klages v. General Ordnance Equipment Corp. 367 A.2d 304 (Pa.Super.1976), a plaintiff suffered severe gunshot wounds when a mace weapon manufactured by defendant failed to function during a confrontation between plaintiff and an armed robber. The court held that since the product was an instrument of crime prevention, the manufacturer could foresee the specific injuries accruing to a user if the product failed to function and, under those circumstances, the intervening criminal act was not a superseding cause absolving the manufacturer from liability. We view this case as distinguishable [because] the product in *Klages* was designed to prevent criminal attack, and therefore the manufacturer could reasonably foresee the injury if it did not function. In the instant case, the portable two-way receiver was a product designed for communication purposes, not the prevention of criminal attack, and therefore the purpose and expected result in the manufacture and use of the respective products are inherently different.

[The shooting here was not] objectively reasonable to expect [because (1) manufacturers normally may assume that people will not violate the criminal law; (2) the two-way receiver is designed for] communication between individuals possessing such units and not the prevention of criminal attack; and (3) it cannot fairly be said, under the circumstances here, that the manufacturer should reasonably foresee that the security guard would approach the armed robber before he became aware of the presence of his support—whether or not he had knowledge of the malfunctioning of the receiver.

[T]he trial court properly found that the intervening criminal act was unforeseeable [as] a matter of law ...

Affirmed.

NOTE

With *Williams*, compare Hollenbeck v. Selectone Corp., 476 N.E.2d 746 (Ill.App. 1985), where plaintiff police officer tried unsuccessfully to activate his mobile pager to call for assistance in making an arrest, and he was injured in the course of the arrest. Plaintiff appealed the the trial court's dismissal of his action against the manufacturer. *Held,* dismissal of the § 402B claim reversed and remanded:

> We find that the intervening criminal acts were not so improbable and unforeseeable as to break the causal connection. As the *Williams* court stated, probable and foreseeable means "objectively reasonable to expect." In the instant case, the plaintiff has alleged that the defendant represented that its product was suitable for use by police agencies and that it marketed its product specifically for use by such agencies. It was, therefore, objectively reasonable to expect that [pagers] would be used by police

officers in emergency situations where communication by pager was necessary. Given the undisputable fact that one of the critical functions of a police officer is to deal with persons violating the law, it was objectively reasonable to expect that the pager would be utilized in a situation involving a criminal offense. In short, we cannot say, as the court in *Williams* did, that the defendant manufacturer could assume that no one will violate the law.

It was also objectively reasonable to expect that the plaintiff, after activating the pager, would proceed to make the arrest. It is a police officer's duty to apprehend and arrest those violating the law. The defendant knew or should have known of this duty when it marketed its product to police departments. Thus, the instant case is distinguishable from *Williams* in that the defendant manufacturer should have foreseen that the plaintiff would act after activating his pager.

Id. at 747–48. The concurring judge thought that the case was indistinguishable from *Williams*, such that *Williams* was effectively overruled.

––––––

In Re September 11 Litigation

United States District Court, Southern District of New York, 2003.
280 F.Supp.2d 279.

OPINION AND ORDER DENYING DEFENDANTS' MOTIONS TO DISMISS

■ HELLERSTEIN, DISTRICT JUDGE.

The injured, and the representatives of the thousands who died from the terrorist-related aircraft crashes of September 11, 2001, are entitled to seek compensation. [Many plaintiffs are pursuing compensation through the Victims Compensation Fund established by the Air Transportation Safety and System Stabilization Act of 2001, 49 U.S.C. § 40101 ("the Act"). Approximately seventy of the injured and representatives of those who died have chosen to bring suit in the traditional manner against a number of defendants, including Boeing Company for its failure to design the cockpit doors of two planes—the aircraft in American Flight 77, which crashed into the Pentagon, and United Flight 93, which crashed in rural Pennsylvania— to prevent entry by the terrorist hijackers.]

[The court resolved a number of preliminary matters including jurisdiction, choice of law, preemption, and duty issues. The governing law of all claims, according to the Act, is "derived from the law, including choice of law principles, of the State in which the crash occurred unless such law is inconsistent with or preempted by Federal law." Thus, as to the defective design claims, the law of Virginia and Pennsylvania controlled. Boeing argued that, under the law of those states, even if the cockpit door could be found defective in design under either negligence or strict liability, the acts of the terrorists constituted a superseding cause which defeated proximate cause as a matter of law.]

Boeing next argues that its design of the cockpit doors on its "757" passenger aircraft, even if held to constitute an "unreasonably dangerous condition," was not the proximate cause of plaintiffs' injuries. Boeing argues that the criminal acts of the terrorists in hijacking the airplanes and using the airplanes as weapons of mass destruction constituted an "efficient intervening cause" which broke the "natural and continuous sequence" of events flowing from Boeing's allegedly inadequate design [under Virginia law. Citation.] Plaintiffs have the burden to prove proximate cause and, generally, the issue is a question of fact to be resolved by a jury. [Citation.] However, when reasonable people cannot differ, the issue becomes a question of law for the court.

The record at this point does not support Boeing's argument that the invasion and take-over of the cockpit by the terrorists must, as a matter of law, be held to constitute an "efficient intervening act" that breaks the "natural and continuous sequence" flowing from Boeing's allegedly inadequate design. Plaintiffs allege that Boeing should have designed its cockpit door to prevent hijackers from invading the cockpit, that acts of terrorism, including hijackings of airplanes, were reasonably foreseeable, and that the lives of passengers, crew and ground victims would be imminently in danger from such hijackings. Virginia law does not require Boeing to have foreseen precisely how the injuries suffered on September 11, 2001 would be caused, as long as Boeing could reasonably have foreseen that "some injury" from its negligence "might probably result." . . . Given the critical nature of the cockpit area, and the inherent danger of crash when a plane is in flight, one cannot say that Boeing could not reasonably have foreseen the risk flowing from an inadequately constructed cockpit door.

[The court distinguished a Virginia case. The] danger that a plane could crash if unauthorized individuals invaded and took over the cockpit was the very risk that Boeing should reasonably have foreseen. "Privacy" within a cockpit means very little if the door intended to provide security is not designed to keep out potential intruders.

Boeing's citation to cases in other jurisdictions are also distinguishable. Two of the cases, Port Authority of N.Y. and N.J. v. Arcadian Corp., 189 F.3d 305 (3d Cir.1999), and Gaines–Tabb v. ICI Explosives USA, Inc., 160 F.3d 613 (10th Cir.1998), [involve inadequate warning claims against the manufacturers of explosive grade fertilizer employed by terrorists to make bombs used in separate terrorist attacks. In both cases, the courts of appeals] held that defendants' actions or inactions were not the "legal proximate cause" of the injuries suffered by the victims of the 1993 World Trade Center and 1995 Oklahoma City bombings. They ruled that the manufacturers of the fertilizer products utilized in the attacks, having made lawful and economically and socially useful fertilizer products, did not have to anticipate that criminals would misappropriate ingredients, mix them with others, and make bombs to bring down a building. The bomb-making by the terrorists were found to be superseding and intervening events and were not natural or probable consequences of any design defect in defendants' products. See *Arcadian Corp.*, 189 F.3d at 318; *Gaines–Tabb*, 160 F.3d at 621.

In re Korean Air Lines Disaster of September 1, 1983, 1985 WL 9447 (D.D.C.1985), involved lawsuits by the legal successors of passengers who died when Korean Airlines passenger flight 007 was shot down by Russian fighter planes. The passenger plane had flown off course and over a sensitive military zone in Russia. Russian fighter pilots intercepted the plane and, instead of following international protocol for causing the plane to return to international routes over the high seas or to land at a selected landing field, shot it down. Plaintiffs sued Boeing, the manufacturer of the airplane, alleging that a product defect in its navigation systems caused it to fly off course and over Soviet territory, and that Boeing's improper and unsafe design was therefore the proximate cause of plaintiffs' damages. The court dismissed the complaint, holding that Boeing could not foresee that the Soviet Union would destroy an intruding aircraft in violation of international conventions, and had no ability to guard against such conduct. The court held, consequently, that Boeing did not owe a duty to passengers with respect to such risks, and that the actions of the Russian pilots were independent and supervening causes that broke the chain of causation.

These three cases do not offer Boeing much support in its motion. In each, the acts of the third-parties were held to be superseding causes because they were not reasonably foreseeable to the product manufacturer. In *Gaines–Tabb* and *Arcadian*, the courts of appeals held that the fertilizer manufacturers could not reasonably foresee that terrorists would mix their products with other ingredients to create explosives to cause buildings to collapse and occupants to be killed. In *KAL*, the court held that the manufacturer of airplane navigational systems could not reasonably foresee that a passenger aircraft that strayed off course would be shot down by hostile military forces in violation of international conventions. In the cases before me, however, plaintiffs allege that Boeing could reasonably have foreseen that terrorists would try to invade the cockpits of airplanes, and that easy success on their part, because cockpit doors were not designed to prevent easy opening, would be imminently dangerous to passengers, crew and ground victims. Plaintiffs' allegations that duty and proximate cause existed cannot be dismissed as a matter of law on the basis of the record now before me.

* * *

[Plaintiffs' claims arising out of United Air Lines flight 93 which crashed in Pennsylvania were similarly resolved.]

NOTES

1. Do you agree with the result in *In re September 11 Litigation*? Are terrorist acts now generally foreseeable as a matter of law? Are there any limits on that foreseeability? See Gash, The Intersection of Proximate Cause and Terrorism: A

Contextual Analysis of the (Proposed) Restatement Third of Torts' Approach to Intervening and Superseding Causes, 91 Ky.L.J. 523 (2003).

Identify the critical facts in each of these cases that explain their results. Are they consistent with one another?

2. In Bellotte v. Zayre Corp., 531 F.2d 1100 (1st Cir.1976), the five–year–old plaintiff suffered burns when his pajamas caught fire from a match. Believing testimony that his twelve–year–old brother had tossed the match on him, the jury in an action against the seller returned a verdict for the defendant. *Held,* affirmed. Although many clothing flammability accidents are caused by children playing with matches, "[t]he deliberate setting afire of a child's pajamas by another would not appear to fall within those acts that ought to be anticipated by a clothing supplier." The court approved the trial court's instruction that such a deliberate act constituted an "absolute defense." See also Briscoe v. Amazing Products, Inc., 23 S.W.3d 228 (Ky.App.2000) (unforeseeable that man would throw defendant's drain cleaning product at plaintiff during altercation); Walcott v. Total Petroleum, Inc., 964 P.2d 609 (Colo.App.1998) (unforeseeable that man purchasing cup of gasoline would throw it on plaintiff and set her on fire).

But see d'Hedouville v. Pioneer Hotel Co., 552 F.2d 886 (9th Cir.1977), in which the court applied "the general principle of foreseeability" to a case where plaintiff's decedent and 27 others perished in a hotel fire set by an arsonist. *Held,* manufacturer of excessively flammable acrylic fiber used in carpeting not relieved of liability where it "was aware of the danger of fire, knew fires are often the result of arson, and knew that in all likelihood its carpeting would be installed in buildings without sprinkler systems, smoke sensors, or fire alarms, and in multi-story homes lacking the safety features the Pioneer Hotel also lacked." Id. at 894.

Which is right, *Bellotte* or *d'Hedouville?* Or are they reconcilable?

3. Crowther v. Ross Chem. & Mfg. Co., 202 N.W.2d 577 (Mich.App.1972), involved allegations of defective warnings against the manufacturer of airplane glue for the deaths of two young girls killed by a person under the effects of "glue sniffing." Plaintiff alleged that defendant knew or should have known that its glue would be sniffed by some users and that sniffers could lose self-control and become insane, thus giving rise to a duty to warn of the dangers involved. Citing to §§ 448 and 449 of the Second Restatement of Torts, the court held that defendant's motion for summary judgment had properly been denied. Section 448 provides that a third person's intentionally tortious or criminal act is a superseding cause, even though the defendant's negligence afforded the opportunity for such misconduct, unless the misconduct was a foreseeable risk of the defendant's negligence. Section 449 provides that an intentionally tortious or criminal act is not a superseding cause if the likelihood of such behavior is one of the hazards which makes the actor negligent.

4. How would §§ 448 and 449 resolve the case of Amy Stahlecker who was driving her Ford Explorer in a remote area of Nebraska in April 2000 when the tread on one of the vehicle's Firestone Wilderness AT radial tires separated due to a defective condition which subsequently led to a nationwide recall of those tires? She was uninjured in the accident, but the flat tire left her stranded. A passerby, finding Amy alone, assaulted and murdered her. Her parents sued Ford and Firestone alleging that Ford and Firestone had long known of the tires' propensity to unexpectedly blow out "causing wide-ranging results that included stranding and rollovers." Stahlecker v. Ford Motor Co., 667 N.W.2d 244 (Neb. 2003). The Stahlecker's alleged that while Amy's particular assault and murder may not have been foreseeable, "the potential for similar dangerous situations arising as a result of a breakdown of a Ford Explorer and/or its tires resulting in danger to its consumers and users from criminal activity, adverse weather conditions, inability to communicate with others or any combination thereof, were known and/or should have been known to Defendants Ford and Firestone." *Held*, relying on *Williams*, summary judgment for defendants affirmed. Is the possibility of criminal conduct against a stranded motorist one of the risks which rendered the tire defective?

5.   Should a dealer, who sells an escaped criminal a used gun without first obtaining information on the purchaser's identity as required by federal gun control law, be held liable for the deaths of persons on whom the gun is subsequently used? See Franco v. Bunyard, 547 S.W.2d 91 (Ark.1977). Cf. Hetherton v. Sears, Roebuck & Co., 593 F.2d 526 (3d Cir.1979) (ammunition sold in violation of state law requiring positive identification).

Should the manufacturer of a pharmaceutical product deliberately contaminated by a third person be liable to the purchaser for failing to render the product tamper-proof? See Wheeler v. Andrew Jergens Co., 696 S.W.2d 326 (Ky.App.1985). Cf. Elsroth v. Johnson & Johnson, 700 F.Supp. 151 (S.D.N.Y.1988) (no liability for providing packaging that was merely tamper-resistant, rather than tamper-proof).

6.   On proximate cause, see generally Cupp, Proximate Cause, The Proposed Basic Principles Restatement and Products Liability, 53 S.C.L.Rev. 1085 (2002); M. Green, The Unanticipated Ripples of Comparative Negligence: Superseding Cause in Products Liability and Beyond, 53 S.C.L. Rev. 1103 (2002); Stapleton, Legal Cause: Cause-in-Fact and the Scope of Liability for Consequences, 54 Vand. L. Rev. 941 (2001); Henderson & Twerski, Intuition and Technology in Product Design Litigation: An Essay on Proximate Causation, 88 Geo.L.J. 659 (2000); Fischer, Products Liability—Proximate Cause, Intervening Cause, and Duty, 52 Mo.L.Rev. 547 (1987); J. Page, Torts: Proximate Cause (2003); D. Owen, Products Liability Law, § 12.3 (2d ed. 2008); 1 D. Owen, M.S. Madden, & M. Davis, Madden and Owen on Products Liability, ch. 13 (3d ed. 2000).

MINI–PROBLEMS

1.   A mountain hiker, injured in a rock slide, dies because a manufacturing defect in his or her cell phone precludes its use to call for rescue. Should the cell phone manufacturer be liable?

2.   Plaintiff is out jogging at night, wearing a whistle (purchased from the local sporting goods store) on a chain around her neck for protection, when an assailant attacks. She blows on the whistle, but it fails to work because the little ball gets stuck in the opening. Should the whistle manufacturer be liable?

PART IV

DEFENSES AND DAMAGES

CHAPTER 14

DEFENSES BASED ON PLAINTIFF'S CONDUCT

"[O]ver ⅔ of all injuries related to consumer products have nothing to do with the design or the performance of the product. They relate to the misuse or abuse of the product."

Byington, Chairman, Consumer Product Safety Commission, Trial Magazine 25 (Feb. 1978).

---

1. CONTRIBUTORY NEGLIGENCE

Reed v. Carlyle & Martin, Inc.

Supreme Court of Virginia, 1974.
214 Va. 592, 202 S.E.2d 874, cert. denied, 419 U.S. 859 (1974).

■ CARRICO, J., delivered the opinion of the court.

The plaintiff, Grayson C. Reed, was injured when he fell into the moving parts of a piece of farm equipment. He [sued the manufacturer, retailer, and repairer of the equipment. The trial court granted defendants' motions for summary judgment on the basis of plaintiff's contributory negligence, and plaintiff appealed. The question before the court was whether the plaintiff was contributorily negligent as a matter of law.]

The depositions disclose that [plaintiff, age 50, was and always had been a farm laborer. Shortly before the accident, the farm owner purchased from one defendant a used ensilage wagon manufactured by another defendant. The wagon was used to transport livestock feed, called ensilage (or silage), from a silo where it fermented to the livestock. It was] pulled by a tractor, from which it also received power to operate its unloading mechanism. In the unloading operation, two moving drag chains carried ensilage forward to the front of the wagon into a pair of exposed beaters—metal rods to which metal spikes were attached. The revolving beaters deposited the ensilage onto a moving conveyor belt, which then discharged the ensilage from the side of the wagon.

[Plaintiff and another farmhand were told to empty the ensilage from the wagon.] Leaving the tractor running and the beaters and conveyor belt in operation, the two employees climbed atop the load of ensilage, estimated to be five feet deep.

Moten proceeded to unload the ensilage by throwing it with a pitchfork from the rear of the wagon [onto the ground]. The plaintiff, however, "decided" to throw the ensilage with a pitchfork into the beaters because, in his words, that was the "easiest" and "quickest" way. In unloading the ensilage, which contained "a good bit of sap" and was "right slippery," the plaintiff created a bank, upon which he was standing, sloping toward the beaters. Suddenly, the ensilage under his feet gave way, and he fell into the beaters [and was injured].

The plaintiff testified.... that he "didn't feel any danger about" working near the beaters [which plaintiff argues establishes] that he was not negligent. But the test is not whether the plaintiff actually knew of the danger confronting him, but whether, in the exercise of reasonable care, he should have known he was in a situation of peril. See Budzinski v. Harris, 189 S.E.2d 372, 375 (Va. 1972). [A reasonable jury would have to conclude that] plaintiff should have known of his peril.

The plaintiff, an experienced farmer, admitted that he was familiar with the operation of the type ensilage wagon in which he was working. Moreover, the revolving beaters were exposed to his plain view. The danger posed by the turning, spike-like mechanism was, therefore, open and obvious to the plaintiff. In exposing himself to this obvious danger, he failed to exercise reasonable care for his own safety. [Citation.]

* * *

[Plaintiff also argued that he created a jury issue by showing an] "established custom and usage among farm laborers to use the same or similar procedure" he used in unloading the ensilage wagon. [But] the existence of a custom or usage cannot excuse conduct which is otherwise negligent where, as here, the custom or usage itself is not "reasonably safe or adequate for its purpose and occasion."

[Summary judgments for defendants affirmed.]

NOTES

1. The Shape of Careless Behavior. All forms of imprudent behavior are reflected in the cases. See, e.g., Lee v. Crest Chem. Co., 583 F.Supp. 131 (M.D.N.C. 1984) (plaintiff failed to wear rubber gloves, contrary to label instructions, and splattered some of defendant's caustic rust stain remover on her hand; defendant's motion for summary judgment granted, pursuant to statutory provision barring recovery for use of product contrary to instructions); Ford Motor Co. v. Bartholomew, 297 S.E.2d 675 (Va. 1982) (gear shift lever, not fully engaged in park, slipped into reverse with motor running; jury's finding of no contributory negligence upheld); J.P.M. & B.M. v. Schmid Labs., Inc., 428 A.2d 515 (N.J. Super. Ct.1981) (negligent use of condom); Duke v. American Olean Tile Co., 400 N.W.2d 677 (Mich. App. 1986) (in slip and fall action against manufacturer of quarry tile used for flooring in fast food restaurant, jury could find that plaintiff was walking unreasonably fast); McClure v. Wilkinson Sword Consumer Prod., Inc., Cook Cty. Cir. Ct., Ill., Prod. Safety & Liab. Rep.(BNA) 394 (Apr. 14, 1995) (carelessly lighting cigarette with disposable lighter, woman ignited her "big hair" bouffant hairdo held in place with excessive hair spray).

2. Contributory Negligence and Failure to Warn. In Parris v. M.A. Bruder & Sons, Inc., 261 F.Supp. 406 (E.D. Pa. 1966), a professional spray painter sued the manufacturer of an epoxy paint for negligently failing to warn that exposure to the paint's fumes could cause a disabling asthmatic condition. Defendant contended that the plaintiff was contributorily negligent in failing to wear a mask while spray painting. The court gave a contributory negligence instruction to the jury which found for the defendant.

On his motion for a new trial, plaintiff argued that the defenses of contributory negligence and assumption of risk cannot bar failure-to-warn claims if the plaintiff's asserted misconduct concerns a risk about which the defendant failed to warn. See Dillard and Hart, Product Liability: Directions for Use and the Duty To Warn, 41 Va. L. Rev. 145, 163 (1955). An exception to this theory, however, allows such defenses when the plaintiff is already aware of the risk from some independent source. Id. Here, plaintiff had been a spray painter for over 20 years; he knew that he needed to wear a mask while spray painting (particularly indoors); his employer furnished masks and replacement filter cartridges; and plaintiff sometimes sprayed without a mask.

But plaintiff argued that the hazards he knew about, from oil and water base paints, were *different* from the risks of the epoxy ingredients in defendant's paint. The court rejected this argument on the basis 2 Harper and James, Torts § 20.5(6) (1956):

> Foreseeability does not mean that the precise hazard or the exact consequences which were encountered should have been foreseen. [When a person] "ought to have foreseen in a general way consequences of a certain kind, it will not avail him to say that he could not foresee the precise course or the full extent of the consequences, being of that kind, which in fact happened."

Motion for new trial denied.

3. Children. In Porter v. United Steel & Wire Co., 436 F.Supp. 1376 (N.D. Iowa 1977), the 5–year–old plaintiff fell and was injured when she attempted to climb into a grocery shopping cart manufactured by the defendant. *Held,* plaintiff was too young to be contributorily negligent, and the parents' negligence in failing to instruct or supervise the child would not be imputed to her.

Compare Phillips, Products Liability for Personal Injury to Minors, 56 Va. L. Rev. 1223, 1225 (1970): "The assumption that children will expose themselves to danger in ways that a reasonable adult would not precludes the manufacturer's reliance on the obviousness of the product's danger to the child plaintiff." Should this principle be applied to adult-type products like power lawn mowers, or just to toys? Professor Phillips concludes that "even the best of educational efforts cannot be expected to change the essential nature of children, and, unless we are prepared to ignore this fact, in many instances better product design presents the only realistic means available for protecting children against injuries." Id. at 1240–41.

Should teenagers receive some type of special protection from their own dangerous conduct? See Morgan v. Cavalier Acquisition Corp., 432 S.E.2d 915 (N.C. App. 1993) (factual dispute existed on contributory negligence of 17–year–old student crushed to death when he tilted soda machine to get soft drink; summary judgment for machine manufacturer and owner reversed).

4. Employees. When a person's job is especially dangerous some courts may "lessen the amount of caution required of him by law in the exercise of reasonable care." Young v. Aro Corp., 111 Cal.Rptr. 535, 537 (Ct. App. 1973) (worker knowingly operating grinding wheel at excessive speed killed when wheel exploded).

5. Warranty—The Case of the Wormy Mr. Goodbar. Plaintiff purchased some groceries including a Hershey "Mr. Goodbar" at the defendant's food store. When she arrived back home, she sat down in a chair to read the newspaper beside a table on which she placed the candy bar. "While reading, she reached with one hand and took the candy bar from the table. Without looking, and with one hand, she opened one end of the wrapper and slid the bar partially out from it. Using this one-handed method, she broke off pieces, one after another, and put them into her mouth."

"From the outset she noticed that the bar 'didn't taste just right,' but she assumed this was because she hadn't eaten all day. She had consumed about one-third of the candy bar by the time she bit into a mushy worm. When she looked at the bar, she saw that it was covered with worms and webbing; worms were crawling out of the chocolate and the webbing had little eggs 'hanging onto it.' " Mrs. Kassouf was sickened and suffered chronic ulcerative colitis as a result of ingesting the contaminated candy.

In an action against the grocery store for breach of warranty of merchantability, the jury returned a verdict for the plaintiff. Defendant appealed the trial court's refusal to instruct the jury that plaintiff had a duty "to take reasonable precautions for her own safety in the handling, inspection, and consumption" of the candy bar. *Held,* affirmed. There is no duty to look at and feel a candy bar prior to biting into it. Kassouf v. Lee Brothers, Inc., 26 Cal.Rptr. 276 (Ct. App. 1962).

6. Warranty—Generally. The warranty provisions of UCC Article 2 do not speak in terms of "contributory negligence" but instead address the issue as one of scope of warranty or proximate cause. See Erdman v. Johnson Bros. Radio & Television Co., 271 A.2d 744 (Md. 1970) (scope of merchantability warranty did not extend to owners' continued use of cantankerous television set which emitted heavy smoke, sparks, and crackling sounds; use of set in such condition, and failure to unplug it before going to bed with knowledge that it sometimes turned itself on, was not "normal" use and supported finding of contributory negligence—defined as using product known to be dangerously defective).

Comment 13 to § 2–314 provides in part: "Action by the buyer following an examination of the goods which ought to have indicated the defect complained of can be shown as matter bearing on whether the breach itself was the cause of the injury."

Section 2–316(3)(b) provides that "when the buyer before entering into the contract has examined the goods ... as fully as he desired or has refused to examine the goods there is no implied warranty with regard to defects which an examination ought in the circumstances to have revealed to him." Comment 8 explains further that "if the buyer discovers the defect and uses the goods anyway, or if he unreasonably fails to examine the goods before he uses them, resulting injuries may be found to result from his own action rather than proximately from a breach of warranty."

Section 2–715(2)(b) defines "consequential damages" (allowable under § 2–714) to include "injury to person or property proximately resulting from any breach of warranty." Comment 5 provides in part: "Where the injury involved follows the use of goods without discovery of the defect causing the damage, the question of 'proximate' cause turns on whether it was reasonable for the buyer to use the goods without such inspection as would have revealed the defects. If it was not reasonable for him to do so, or if he did in fact discover the defect prior to his use, the injury would not proximately result from the breach of warranty."

7. Express Warranty. If the manufacturer expressly warrants the safety of a product, the user's failure to guard against the falsity of the warranty should not bar recovery if an injury results. See Hensley v. Sherman Car Wash Equip. Co., 520 P.2d 146, 148 (Colo. App. 1974) (car wash employee stepped in hole at end of conveyor; equipment manufacturer's information sheet stated that pivoting safety hood "eliminates all possibility of persons stepping into an open pit"): "Contributory negligence is not a defense where plaintiff's conduct only puts the warranty to the test."

8. Tortious Misrepresentation. A consumer's negligent reliance on tortious misrepresentations is usually treated as an issue of the justifiability of reliance, sometimes called the right to rely. Cf. Klages v. General Ordnance Equip. Corp., 367 A.2d 304 (Pa. Super. Ct.1976).

9. On misconduct defenses to warranty claims, see generally D. Owen, Products Liability Law § 13.6 (2d ed. 2008); 2 D. Owen, M.S. Madden, & M. Davis, Madden & Owen on Products Liability § 14:5 (3d ed. 2000).

McCown v. International Harvester Co.

Supreme Court of Pennsylvania, 1975.
463 Pa. 13, 342 A.2d 381.

■ JONES, CHIEF JUSTICE.

[Plaintiff was injured while driving a tractor manufactured by defendant. While entering the highway, his right front tire struck a guardrail which caused the steering wheel to spin rapidly, breaking his arm. A jury held the defendant liable on plaintiff's defective steering claim. The Supreme Court granted review on whether contributory negligence is a defense to an action under § 402A.]

For the purposes of this appeal defendant concedes the defect in the steering system's design, but argues that plaintiff's contributory negligence in colliding with the guardrail should at least be considered in determining plaintiff's recovery. We disagree and affirm.

In Webb v. Zern, 220 A.2d 853 (Pa. 1966), this Court adopted Section 402A of the Restatement and [subsequently] permitted the assertion of assumption of the risk as a defense to a 402A action, citing with approval comment *n* to Section 402A. Today, we complete our acceptance of the principles delineated in comment *n* by rejecting contributory negligence as an available defense in 402A cases.

* * *

Adoption of contributory negligence as a complete defense in 402A actions would defeat one theoretical basis for our acceptance of § 402A. "[A] manufacturer by marketing and advertising his products impliedly represents that it is safe for its intended use." Salvador v. Atlantic Steel Boiler Co., 319 A.2d 903, 907 (Pa. 1974). Based on that implied representation is the consumer's assumption that a manufacturer's goods are safe. Recognition of consumer negligence as a defense to a 402A action would contradict this normal expectation of product safety. One does not inspect a product for defects or guard against the possibility of product defects when one assumes the item to be safe.... We reject contributory negligence as a defense to actions grounded in § 402A.

Judgment affirmed.

■ POMEROY, JUSTICE (concurring).

I agree .. that negligence by the plaintiff should not necessarily bar recovery [to a § 402A claim]; I also agree that McCown's conduct in the instant case—misjudging whether the tractor he was driving would clear a guard rail as he was leaving the parking area—should not bar his recovery....

[T]he answer to the question ... is not to be found altogether in the language of Comment *n* to § 402A [which] provides, on the one hand, that the negligent failure to discover a defect in a product or to guard against the possibility of its existence is not [a] defense to a strict liability action, and, on the other hand, that assumption of risk is a defense. But the [plaintiff's conduct] fits into neither of the above categories. His negligence, if any, was the manner of his operation of an International Harvester tractor [and] Comment *n* is silent with regard to the consequences of negligent use of a product.... I am satisfied that the elimination of the defense of plaintiff's negligence is in accord not only with the weight of authority in other jurisdictions but also with the policy which underlies the concept of strict liability in tort.

The strict liability of Section 402A is founded in part upon the belief that as between the sellers of products and those who use them, the former are the better able to bear the losses caused by defects in the products involved.... It follows that [a user's] negligence should not ordinarily ... preclude recovery in a strict liability case. On the other hand, where assumption of risk is involved, the "loss-bearing" policy underlying Section 402A is outweighed by a countervailing policy, one which refuses recovery to persons who consciously expose themselves to known dangers. * * *

NOTES

1. **Comment *n*.** This comment to § 402A provides in full:

n. ***Contributory negligence.*** Since the liability with which this Section deals is not based upon negligence of the seller, but is strict liability, the rule applied to strict liability cases (see § 524) applies. Contributory negligence of the plaintiff is not a defense when such negligence consists merely in a failure to discover the defect in the product, or to guard against the possibility of its existence. On the other hand the form of contributory negligence which consists in voluntarily and unreasonably proceeding to encounter a known danger, and commonly passes under the name of assumption of risk, is a defense under this Section as in other cases of strict liability. If the user or consumer discovers the defect and is aware of the danger, and nevertheless proceeds unreasonably to make use of the product and is injured by it, he is barred from recovery.

2. In Sheehan v. Anthony Pools, 440 A.2d 1085, 1090–92 (Md. Ct. Spec. App. 1982), the plaintiff was injured when, during a swimming party at his new pool, he fell off the side of the diving board onto the concrete coping of the alcove from which the board projected. The pool was shaped as follows:

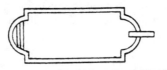

In the plaintiff's strict tort action against the swimming pool company, the plaintiff claimed that the non-skid material on the board should have extended to and over the edges of the board and that the design of the pool's diving board-coping area was unsafe. The trial judge denied the defendant's request to instruct the jury that contributory negligence *was* a defense and also denied the plaintiff's request for a charge that the plaintiff's inadvertence in using the board was *not* a defense. The jury returned a verdict for the defendant, and plaintiff appealed:

In closing argument, [over objection, defense counsel argued]:

You must find that this defect proximately caused the accident. The clear testimony here from Mr. Weiner and using your common sense is that *if someone steps on the board with about an inch of their foot on it, they will fall off the side. That was the proximate cause, the way the board was used, not the design of the board.* I am not willing to concede for a moment that there is anything defective about the board when you use the standards which are customary in the industry and any governmental regulations. Even if you feel there was, I ask you to find that the proximate cause was *the way Mr. Sheehan used it, not the way it was designed.*

. . . *[H]e got ready, and just went right off the side, and no other design of this board would have prevented that unless perhaps a railing along the side of the board.*

He had a little discrepancy in his testimony. He at first said on direct that he didn't teeter. Then I read to him from his deposition where he said *he teetered,* and I asked him what that meant, and I said, did it mean this, and he just threw his arms up and went off.

Mrs. Christenat said that Mr. Sheehan *turned and talked to someone.* That isn't my testimony, it is their witness. She said he turned to talk to someone on the right of the pool. *That again shows that he wasn't looking where he was going.* (Emphasis added.)

The court agreed "that the jury was left without guidance on a point of critical importance, i.e., the type of conduct on the part of the consumer in the use of the product which could or could not afford a valid defense to the seller; the prejudicial effect of this omission was compounded when Anthony Pools' counsel was permitted to argue contributory negligence on the part of Mr. Sheehan under the guise of proximate cause." The court endorsed the view of Cepeda v. Cumberland Eng'g Co., 386 A.2d 816, 832 (N.J. 1978):

> [I]t is implicit in Comment *n* and the generality of the cases that *only a limited range of a plaintiff's conduct—not contributory negligence in the sense of mere carelessness or inadvertence—can be a defense to an action for strict liability in tort for injuries sustained as the result of a product defect, particularly if the defect is one of unsafe design.* We agree that acceptance of "ordinary" contributory negligence as a defense in actions for strict liability in tort would be incompatible with the policy considerations which led to the adoption of strict tort liability in the first instance. *The manufacturer's duty is imposed precisely to avert foreseeable inadvertent injury to a user of a product....*

Held, reversed and remanded: "On the basis of the facts involved and of the Sheehans' specific request, an instruction should have been granted that Mr. Sheehan's inadvertent or careless use of the diving board and pool would not bar his recovery."

Madonna v. Harley Davidson, Inc.

Superior Court of Pennsylvania, 1998.
708 A.2d 507.

■ DEL SOLE, JUDGE:

[Charles Madonna and Dolores Wilson sued Harley Davidson for their injuries from a motorcycle crash. An upper mounting bolt on the brake caliper of the front wheel of the motorcycle was defective and, if it broke during operation, could cause the driver to lose control. Plaintiffs claimed the defective bolt fractured while they were riding, resulting in the accident. The defendant's evidence was that the defective bolt was working properly at the time of the accident and that the collision was solely caused by driver error and intoxication revealed by a blood alcohol level of .14%. Finding for defendant, the jury by special interrogatory found that the defect was not a substantial factor in causing plaintiffs' injuries. The trial court ruled for the defendant on plaintiffs' post-trial motions, and plaintiffs appealed, arguing that the trial court erred in allowing the jury in a strict liability case to consider evidence of driver intoxication and error. *Held,* judgment for defendant affirmed.]

It is true that negligence concepts are not to be introduced into a strict liability case. Evidence of a user's negligence cannot be introduced to excuse a defective product, nor can negligence be used to reduce recovery by comparing fault.... This is not to say however, that plaintiff's conduct in a product's case is always irrelevant. Inquiry into the plaintiff's use of the product may be relevant as it relates to causation. A plaintiff in a strict liability action must prove that the product was defective, and that the defect was a proximate cause of plaintiff's injury. * * *

[Defendant] introduced evidence that despite the bolt defect, the accident occurred solely due to the intoxicated condition of the driver, unrelated in any way to the product.... Defendant's evidence sought to prove that the driver's reckless conduct alone caused the accident regardless of the defect in the bolt. [Because evidence of a user's conduct in using a product can be relevant to legal causation, the evidence as to the user's intoxication and manner of operation] was properly admitted.

[A] user's negligence is not relevant if the product defect contributed in any way to the harm. However, where the defense offers evidence to establish that the accident was *solely* the result of the user's conduct, and not related in any way with a product defect, it is relevant and admissible [to prove] causation. [Here,] the evidence was offered to prove that the driver's conduct was the sole cause of the accident. Since the evidence was relevant and probative of the fact at issue, its introduction was proper.

Because evidence of the driver's conduct was offered to negate the theory that the defect caused the accident, and to establish that the driver's reckless conduct was its sole cause, we affirm.

NOTES

1. Sole Proximate Cause. Scattered decisions agree that a plaintiff's contributory negligence will bar recovery even in strict liability in tort if it is the *sole* proximate cause of the injury. See McCarty v. F.C. Kingston Co., 522 P.2d 778 (Ariz. App. 1974). See also Yun v. Ford Motor Co., 647 A.2d 841 (N.J. Super. Ct. App. Div. 1994) (retrieval from highway of spare tire assembly that fell off van; plaintiff struck by another vehicle while crossing highway), rev'd, 669 A.2d 1378 (N.J. 1996) (question for trier of fact); Bowen v. Cochran, 556 S.E.2d 530, 532 (Ga. App. 2001) ("'A plaintiff's contributory negligence bars any recovery whatsoever if his failure to use ordinary care for his own safety is the sole proximate cause of his injuries, even though such negligence concurs with the negligence of the defendant.'").

2. The Persistence of Contributory Negligence in Strict Liability Cases. Alabama has likened its doctrine of strict liability in tort to negligence per se and has thus held that ordinary contributory negligence—in addition to assumption of risk—acts as a total bar to recovery. Atkins v. American Motors Corp., 335 So.2d 134, 143 (Ala.1976); Campbell v. Cutler Hammer, Inc., 646 So.2d 573 (Ala. 1994) (3 judges dissenting and 1 concurring). Contributory negligence remains a defense to strict liability in tort, operating in one way or another, in a number of other states. See, e.g., Mohr v. St. Paul Fire & Marine Ins. Co., 674 N.W.2d 576, 591 (Wis. Ct. App. 2003) ("contributory negligence may be a defense to a strict product liability claim").

3. Reform Legislation. Many states have enacted products liability "reform" statutes providing various defenses based on a plaintiff's misconduct. The conduct is sometimes defined in terms of "reasonable care," which effectively reintroduces contributory negligence as a defense. Arizona's statute, for example, provides a defense for use of the product contrary to its instructions or warnings "if the injured person knew or with the exercise of reasonable or diligent care should have known of such instructions or warnings."

4. On contributory negligence generally, see D. Owen, Products Liability Law § 13.2 (2d ed. 2008); 1 D. Owen, M.S. Madden, & M. Davis, Madden & Owen on Products Liability § 14:2 (3d ed. 2000).

2. COMPARATIVE FAULT

Daly v. General Motors Corp.

Supreme Court of California, 1978.
20 Cal.3d 725, 144 Cal.Rptr. 380, 575 P.2d 1162.

■ RICHARDSON, JUSTICE.

The [issue] is whether the principles of comparative negligence expressed by us in Li v. Yellow Cab Co. 532 P.2d 1226 (Cal. 1975), apply to actions founded on strict products liability. We will conclude that they do.

* * * In the early hours of October 31, 1970, decedent Kirk Daly, a 36–year–old attorney, was driving his Opel southbound on the Harbor Freeway in Los Angeles. The vehicle, while travelling at a speed of 50–70 miles per hour, collided with and damaged 50 feet of metal divider fence. After the initial impact between the left side of the vehicle and the fence the Opel spun counterclockwise, the driver's door was thrown open, and Daly was forcibly ejected from the car and sustained fatal head injuries. It was equally undisputed that had the deceased remained in the Opel his injuries, in all probability, would have been relatively minor.

[Plaintiff's expert] testified that the Opel's door was caused to open when the latch button on the exterior handle of the driver's door was forcibly depressed by some protruding portion of the divider fence. It was his opinion that the exposed push button on the door constituted a design "defect" which [aggravated Daly's injuries.]

[Defendants introduced evidence] that: (1) the Opel was equipped with a seat belt-shoulder harness system, and a door lock, either of which if used, it was contended, would have prevented Daly's ejection from the vehicle; (2) Daly used neither the harness system nor the lock; (3) the 1970 Opel owner's manual contained warnings that seat belts should be worn and doors locked when the car was in motion for "accident security"; and (4) Daly was intoxicated at the time of collision, which evidence the jury was advised was admitted for the limited purpose of determining whether decedent had used the vehicle's safety equipment. [The jury returned a verdict for defendants, and plaintiffs appeal.]

STRICT PRODUCTS LIABILITY AND COMPARATIVE FAULT

In response to plaintiffs' assertion that the "intoxication-nonuse" evidence was improperly admitted, defendants contend that the deceased's own conduct contributed to his death. Because plaintiffs' case rests upon strict products liability based on improper design of the door latch and because defendants assert a failure in decedent's conduct, namely, his alleged intoxication and nonuse of safety equipment, without which the accident and ensuing death would not have occurred, there is thereby posed the overriding issue in the case, should comparative principles apply in strict products liability actions?

[S]trict liability has never been, and is not now, *absolute* liability....

In Li v. Yellow Cab Co., supra, we.... examined the history of contributory negligence, the massive criticism directed at it because its presence in the slightest degree completely barred plaintiff's recovery, and the increasing defection from the doctrine. [I]n *Li,* [we adopted] a "pure" form of comparative negligence which, when present, reduced but did not prevent plaintiff's recovery. We held that the defense of assumption of risk, insofar as it is no more than a variant of contributory negligence, was merged into the assessment of liability in proportion to fault....

We stand now at the point of confluence of these two conceptual streams....

Those [opposed to applying] comparative fault principles in strict products liability cases vigorously stress [both the conceptual and] semantic difficulties incident to such a course. The task of merging the two concepts is said to be impossible, that "apples and oranges" cannot be compared, that "oil and water" do not mix, and that strict liability, which is not founded on negligence or fault, is inhospitable to comparative principles. The syllogism runs, contributory negligence was only a defense to negligence, comparative negligence only affects contributory negligence, therefore comparative negligence cannot be a defense to strict liability....

The inherent difficulty in the "apples and oranges" argument is its insistence on fixed and precise definitional treatment of legal concepts. In the evolving areas of both products liability and tort defenses, however, there has developed much conceptual overlapping and interweaving in order to attain substantial justice. The concept of strict liability itself, as we have noted, arose from dissatisfaction with the wooden formalisms of traditional tort and contract principles in order to protect the consumer of manufactured goods.

* * *

[Compulsive semantic precision in using the term "comparative negligence"] is less important than [attaining] a just and equitable result. The interweaving of concept and terminology in this area suggests [that courts be] flexible rather than doctrinaire. * * * [When a product injury results from a combination of a product defect and user fault], as in the situation before us, we think the term "equitable apportionment or allocation of loss" may be more descriptive than "comparative fault."

[The policies that support strict products liability in tort] will not be frustrated by the adoption of comparative principles.... The principle of protecting the defenseless is likewise preserved, for plaintiff's recovery will be reduced *only* to the extent that his own lack of reasonable care contributed to his injury. The cost of compensating the victim of a defective product, albeit proportionately reduced, remains on defendant manufacturer, and will, through him, be "spread among society." However, [to the extent that part of a plaintiff's damages] flows from his own fault we discern [no reason why it should] be borne by others. Such a result would directly contravene the principle announced in *Li,* that loss should be assessed equitably in proportion to fault.

[Nor do we think that use of comparative fault] in strict products liability cases [will reduce] a manufacturer's incentive to produce safe products.... [T]he manufacturer's liability, and therefore its incentive to avoid and correct product defects, remains; its exposure will be lessened only to the extent that the trier finds that the victim's conduct contributed to his injury. Second, as a practical matter a manufacturer, in a particular case, cannot assume that the user of a defective product upon whom an injury is visited will be blameworthy....

A third objection to the merger of strict liability and comparative fault [is that jurors cannot effectively] assess, measure, or compare plaintiff's negligence with defendant's strict liability. [But we] are convinced that jurors are able to undertake a fair apportionment of liability.

[T]he majority of our sister states which have addressed the problem, either by statute or judicial decree, have extended comparative principles to strict products liability.

[O]f the more than 30 states which have adopted some form of comparative negligence, three (including California) have done so judicially. The two other states, Alaska and Florida have likewise, judicially, extended comparative principles to strict liability actions. At least five states have adopted comparative fault statutes which are not limited in their language to negligence actions: [citing statutes in Arkansas, Maine, Mississippi, New York, and Rhode Island]. The court noted that two of the three decisions declining to apply comparative negligence to strict liability were bound by comparative fault statutes that expressly limited their applicability to "negligence" actions.

[The court observed that most scholarly commentary approved extending comparative fault to strict products liability, and that the Uniform Comparative Fault Act (Act) explicitly includes strict tort liability in its definition of "fault."]

[P]ersuaded by logic, justice, and fundamental fairness, we conclude that a system of comparative fault should be and it is hereby extended to actions founded on strict products liability. In such cases the separate defense of "assumption of risk," to the extent that it is a form of contributory negligence, is abolished. While ... the term "equitable apportionment of loss" is more accurately descriptive of the process, nonetheless, the term "comparative fault" has gained such wide acceptance by courts and in the literature that we adopt its use herein.

[As one apportionment technique a trial court might employ, the jury might first be asked by interrogatory to answer "yes" or "no" to a series of questions setting forth possible bases for finding the defendant's tortious behavior was a proximate cause of the plaintiff's harm, then ask whether the plaintiff's own negligence contributed to the injuries, followed by a direction to] "state in percentage the extent to which the plaintiff's own negligence contributed to his injuries. (___%)." Finally, the jury [could be] instructed to indicate the amount of plaintiff's damages *without reference* to his own negligence. The *court* then [would reduce] the damage award by the percentage figure [stated by the jury].

[*Held*, the comparative fault ruling was prospective only; judgment reversed because the intoxication and seat belt nonuse evidence was inadmissible under then-prevailing law.]

■ JEFFERSON, JUSTICE, concurring and dissenting.

[The majority engage in] wishful thinking and an application of an impractical, ivory-tower approach. The majority's assumption that a jury is capable of making a fair apportionment between a plaintiff's negligent conduct and a defendant's defective product is no more logical or convincing than if a jury were to be instructed that it should add a quart of milk (representing plaintiff's negligence) and a metal bar three feet in length (representing defendant's strict liability for a defective product), and that the two added together equal 100 percent—the total fault for plaintiff's injuries. [Any such percentages will simply represent "the jurors' instincts, speculations, conjectures and guesses." And the "guessing game" will be aggravated where the fault of several defendants (and perhaps some nonparties) are involved, some of whom are subject to strict liability where others may be subject only to ordinary negligence.]

■ [ROSE] BIRD, C.J., concurs.

■ MOSK, JUSTICE, dissenting.

I dissent.

This will be remembered as the dark day when this court, which heroically took the lead in originating the doctrine of products liability (*Greenman*) . . . , inexplicably turned 180 degrees and beat a hasty retreat almost back to square one. The pure concept of products liability so pridefully fashioned and nurtured by this court for the past decade and a half is reduced to a shambles.

The majority inject a foreign object—the tort of negligence—into the tort of products liability by the simple expedient of calling negligence something else: on some pages their opinion speaks of "comparative fault," on others reference is to "comparative principles," and elsewhere the term "equitable apportionment" is employed, although this is clearly not a proceeding in equity. But a rose is a rose [!] and negligence is negligence * * *.

The defective product is comparable to a time bomb ready to explode; it maims its victims indiscriminately, the righteous and the evil, the careful and the careless. Thus when a faulty design or otherwise defective product is involved, the litigation should not be diverted to consideration of the negligence of the plaintiff. The liability issues are simple: was the product or its design faulty, did the defendant inject the defective product into the stream of commerce, and did the defect cause the injury? The conduct of the ultimate consumer-victim who used the product in the contemplated or foreseeable manner is wholly irrelevant to those issues.

* * *

[Since defendant's negligence] is irrelevant in products liability cases, the negligence—call it contributory or comparative—of the plaintiff is also irrelevant. [T]his decision seriously erodes the pattern of the law which up to now reflected a healthy concern for consumers victimized by defective products [mass marketed and advertised by psychologically subtle means].

NOTES

1. Labeling The Doctrine—Comparative *What*? Justice Richardson suggests that a change in labels from "comparative fault" to something like "equitable apportionment of loss" might help to allay concerns over the apparent inconsistency of mixing apples and oranges, defectiveness and contributory negligence. Do you agree? Are additional problems with the entire scheme highlighted by the new label? How about "comparative causation"? See Butaud v. Suburban Marine & Sporting Goods, Inc., 555 P.2d 42, 47 (Alaska 1976) (Rabinowitz, J., concurring); Duncan v. Cessna Aircraft Co., 665 S.W.2d 414, 427 (Tex. 1984) ("We choose comparative *causation* instead because it is conceptually accurate in cases based on strict liability and breach of warranty theories in which the defendant's 'fault,' in the traditional sense of culpability, is not at issue.").

2. Application of Comparative Fault to Strict Liability. Comparative fault statutes generally provide that the parties' "negligence" or "fault" are to be compared, and the courts have split on whether such language covers *strict* liability actions. When courts are not bound on the issue by legislative decree, "[a]n overwhelming majority ... have adopted the [*Daly*] view that comparative fault should apply to products liability actions based on strict liability." Whitehead v. Toyota Motor Corp., 897 S.W.2d 684, 691 (Tenn. 1995) (comparative fault applies to strict products liability) (citing cases from Conn., Fla., Haw., Idaho, Ill., Kan., La., Me., Mich., Minn., N.H., N.M., N.D., Or., R.I., Tex., Utah, Wash., W.Va., Wis.; and citing as contra cases from S.D., Colo., Ohio, Okla., and Wyo.). *Accord*, holding that a plaintiff's damages should be reduced in a strict tort case in proportion to his fault, Elliot v. Sears, Roebuck & Co., 642 A.2d 709 (Conn. 1994).

Contra, refusing to reduce a plaintiff's damages on account of his negligence in strict tort actions, Shipler v. General Motors Corp., 710 N.W.2d 807 (Neb. 2006) (because comparative fault statute did not cover strict products liability actions, evidence of plaintiff fault barred in such actions); Lutz v. National Crane Corp., 884 P.2d 455 (Mont. 1994); Kimco Dev. Corp. v. Michael D's Carpet Outlets, 637 A.2d 603 (Pa. 1993); Phillips v. Duro–Last Roofing, Inc., 806 P.2d 834 (Wyo.1991); Bowling v. Heil Co., 511 N.E.2d 373 (Ohio 1987).

As mentioned earlier, at least one state continues to treat a plaintiff's contributory negligence as a total bar to recovery, even in strict liability. See Campbell v.

Cutler Hammer, Inc., 646 So.2d 573 (Ala. 1994) (3 justices dissenting and 1 concurring).

3. Modified Comparative Fault. *Daly* was decided in a "pure" comparative fault jurisdiction (as was *Coulter*, below), where a plaintiff is entitled to recover (diminished damages) even if his or her fault exceeded that of the defendant(s). Most states instead have some form of "modified" comparative fault, permitting recovery only if the plaintiff's fault was less than (or, in other states, less than or equal to) the defendant's (or the defendants'). In such states, the plaintiff who is more at fault will be barred from recovering any damages whatsoever. See, e.g., Gratzle v. Sears, Roebuck & Co., 613 N.E.2d 802 (Ill. App. 1993) (60% apportionment of causation to plaintiff reversed; jury should have been instructed on effect of finding that plaintiff's conduct accounted for 50% or more of causation); Taylor v. Square D Co., 2003 WL 23093835 (Tenn. App. 2003) (affirming judgment for manufacturer of electrical substation because negligence of electrician, who was electrocuted when he worked on partially energized circuit contrary to direct orders of his supervisor, was clearly greater than any negligence of manufacturer). See also Coons v. A.F. Chapman Corp., 460 F. Supp. 2d 209 (D.Mass. 2006) (plaintiff's misconduct is sole proximate cause of injury if it is greater than 50% the cause thereof).

General Motors Corporation v. Sanchez

Supreme Court of Texas, 1999.
997 S.W.2d 584.

■ GONZALES, J.

The principal question in this case is when does the doctrine of comparative responsibility apply in a products-liability case. [T]he court of appeals held that the decedent's responsibility for the accident that resulted in his death should not be compared with the manufacturer's responsibility because the decedent's actions merely amounted to the failure to discover or guard against a product defect. We conclude that: (1) comparative responsibility applies in strict liability if a plaintiff's negligence is something other than the mere failure to discover or guard against a product defect, and (2) there was evidence here the decedent was negligent apart from the mere failure to discover or guard against a product defect. . . .

[Lee Sanchez drove his 1990 Chevy pickup truck into a corral, stopped the truck, mis-shifted into what he thought was Park, but which was actually an intermediate, "perched" position between Park and Reverse, and got out of the truck, and walked back to close the gate to prevent cattle from escaping the corral. The gear shift apparently slipped from the perched position into Reverse, and the truck rolled backwards and squashed Sanchez against the gate, killing him. Sanchez' family and estate sued GM and the truck dealership, alleging that the truck's transmission had been defectively designed and that there should have been a better warning of the mis-shift hazard. Finding for the plaintiff on liability, the jury further found that Sanchez was 50% responsible for the accident.

Disregarding this latter finding, the trial court entered judgment for the full amount of plaintiff's damages. A majority of a panel of the court of appeals affirmed the trial court's judgment, and the majority's opinion was adopted by a majority of that court en banc. Both parties appealed.]

The jury found that Sanchez was fifty percent responsible for his accident. G.M. argues that this finding should be applied to reduce its liability for damages whether in negligence or strict liability. However, the plaintiffs argue that Sanchez's actions amounted to no more than a failure to discover or guard against a product defect [and that] such negligence does not constitute a defense to strict liability. * * *

Contributory negligence of the plaintiff is not a defense when such negligence consists merely in a failure to discover the defect in the product, or to guard against the possibility of its existence. On the other hand the form of contributory negligence which consists in voluntarily and unreasonably proceeding to encounter a known danger, and commonly passes under the name of assumption of risk, is a defense under this Section as in other cases of strict liability. If the user or consumer discovers the defect and is aware of the danger, and nevertheless proceeds unreasonably to make use of the product and is injured by it, he is barred from recovery.[46]

We note that comment *n* was not carried forward in the Restatement (Third) of Torts: Products Liability § 17(a) [which broadly provides] that a plaintiff's conduct [of whatever type] should be considered to reduce a damages recovery if it fails to conform to applicable standards of care.... However, comment *d* to the Third Restatement states:

> [W]hen the defendant claims that the plaintiff failed to discover a defect, there must be evidence that the plaintiff's conduct in failing to discover a defect did, in fact, fail to meet a standard of reasonable care. In general, a plaintiff has no reason to expect that a new product contains a defect and would have little reason to be on guard to discover it.

We believe that a duty to discover defects, and to take precautions in constant anticipation that a product might have a defect, would defeat the purposes of strict liability. Thus, we hold [consistent with comment *n* to § 402A of the Second Restatement, and contrary to the Third Restatement] that a consumer has no duty to discover or guard against a product defect, but [that] a consumer's conduct other than the mere failure to discover or guard against a product defect is subject to comparative responsibility. Public policy favors reasonable conduct by consumers regardless of whether a product is defective.... Because we conclude that a consumer has no duty to discover or guard against a product defect, we next determine whether the decedent's conduct in this case was merely the failure to discover or guard against a product defect or some other negligence unrelated to a product defect.

The truck's owner's manual describes safety measures designed to ensure that the truck would not move when parked: (1) set the parking brake; (2) place the truck completely in Park; (3) turn off the engine; (4)

---

46. See Restatement (Second) of Torts § 402A cmt. *n*.

remove the key from the ignition; and (5) check that Park is fully engaged by pulling down on the gear shift. Sanchez's father testified that his son probably read the entire owner's manual. The plaintiff's own experts agreed at trial that Sanchez failed to perform any of the safety measures described in the owner's manual and that performing any one of them would have prevented the accident. This evidence is sufficient to support the jury's negligence finding.

Regardless of any danger of a mis-shift, a driver has a duty to take reasonable precautions to secure his vehicle before getting out of it. The danger that it could roll, or move if the engine is running, exists independently of the possibility of a mis-shift. For instance, the driver could inadvertently leave a vehicle in gear or a mechanical problem unrelated to a product defect could prevent Park from fully engaging. A moving vehicle without a driver is a hazard to public safety.... [A]lthough we do not expect the average driver to have the engineering background to discover defects in their car's transmission, we do expect the reasonably prudent driver to take safety precautions to prevent a runaway car. * * *

Sanchez's actions amounted to conduct other than a mere failure to discover or guard against a product defect [and we hold that such conduct] was legally sufficient evidence to support the jury's verdict that Sanchez breached the duty to use ordinary care and was fifty percent responsible for the accident.

[Court of Appeals judgment reversed, and judgment rendered that plaintiffs recover their actual damages reduced by jury's finding of 50% comparative responsibility.]

Coulter v. American Bakeries Co.

District Court of Appeal of Florida, 1988.
530 So.2d 1009.

■ WIGGINTON, J.

[Appeal from verdict and judgment reducing plaintiff's damages for] comparative negligence. The issue presented is whether the trial court erred in allowing the defendant/appellee to raise comparative negligence as a defense and by [so] instructing the jury.... We reverse.

[Plaintiff/appellant] purchased doughnuts manufactured by defendant and sealed in their original package. [While driving, she opened the package, broke a doughnut into pieces, and popped them] into her mouth. Because of an abscessed tooth and sore jaw, instead of chewing the doughnut with her teeth plaintiff would sip milk through a straw allowing the doughnut to dissolve in her mouth. In fact, it was the dissolving nature of the doughnut which had prompted appellant to purchase that particular product. Shortly after she began consuming the doughnut, she felt something stick in her throat ... later discovered through x-rays [to be] a piece containing a metal wire [that] caus[ed] her subsequent injury.

[Plaintiff sued for] breach of implied warranty in that the doughnuts were unfit for human consumption. Defendant asserted the affirmative defense of comparative negligence, alleging that plaintiff was negligent in the manner in which she had consumed the doughnut by not "chewing" it. The trial court [gave a comparative negligence instruction to the jury which] returned a verdict in favor of plaintiff awarding $12,500 in damages [which, based on the comparative negligence instruction, it reduced by 80%] to $2,500.

[C]omparative negligence is a defense in an implied warranty action. West v. Caterpillar Tractor Co., 336 So. 2d 80 (Fla. 1976); [citation]. However, . . . where there is no evidence tending to prove comparative negligence, the issue should not be submitted to the jury. [Citation.]

In a breach of an implied warranty action based on the presence of a harmful substance in food, the test of whether the presence of the harmful substance constitutes a breach of implied warranty is whether the consumer can reasonably expect to find the substance in the food as served. [W]hen asserting the defense of comparative negligence in [such an] action, the issue pertains to the misuse of the product as opposed to the failure to discover or guard against a defect. [Citation.]

[T]here was simply no evidence that appellant could have expected to find a wire in the doughnut or that she used the doughnut in an abnormal, unintended, or unforeseen way. Indeed, appellant was essentially protecting herself—that is, her abscessed tooth—as best she could by choosing a doughnut that was soft and could easily dissolve with the milk. In that sense, by her use of the milk she was "chewing" the doughnut. [Thus,] there being no evidence tending to prove comparative negligence, the trial court erred in submitting the issue to the jury.

[Reversed and remanded to enter judgment for full damages.]

NOTES

1. Why do you suppose the *Coulter* jury assigned 80% of the fault to the plaintiff? Was it negligent for plaintiff to decide to suck on the doughnuts? Was her particular sucking technique at fault? Or might something else have been at play?

2. Failure to Discover a Defect or Guard Against Its Existence. Like *Sanchez* and *Coulter,* some courts that generally apply comparative fault to strict liability and warranty actions refuse to reduce a plaintiff's damages for this form of negligence. See also Simpson v. General Motors Corp., 483 N.E.2d 1, 3 (Ill. 1985) ("consumer's unobservant, inattentive, ignorant, or awkward failure to discover or guard against a defect should not be compared as a damage-reducing factor").

But note, as did the court in *Sanchez,* that the general principle of Products Liability Restatement § 17 cmt. *d* is to the contrary (though subject to the caveat applied in Sanchez).

3. Warranty. The courts have also split on whether comparative fault applies to warranty actions. Are the arguments pro and con entirely the same as in strict tort? Are the arguments the same in implied warranty as in express warranty?

4. Rescue. In Govich v. North Am. Sys., Inc., 814 P.2d 94 (N.M. 1991), a house caught on fire due to alleged defects in a coffee maker and an electrical component. The son was injured when he ran in the house to save his dog; his mother was injured when she ran in to save her son. *Held,* parties who create unreasonable risks on others have duty toward rescuers, even of property; apportionment of fault and causation for jury.

5. Apportionment Examples. Some examples of comparative fault in application include Busch v. Busch Const., Inc., 262 N.W.2d 377 (Minn. 1977) (defect causing steering to lock, 85%; plaintiff's negligent failure to apply brakes thereafter, 15%); West v. Caterpillar Tractor Co., 336 So.2d 80 (Fla. 1976) (road construction grading machine with poor rear visibility, no rear view mirrors, and no audible warning system for operating in reverse, 65%; failure to maintain proper lookout around such a machine, 35%); Blaw–Knox Food & Chem. Equip. Corp. v. Holmes, 348 So.2d 604 (Fla. App. 1977) (tendency of rotating flow wheel shaft to pop out of bearing in potato chip cooker kettle, 52%; Frito Lay employee's attempt to replace shaft manually while standing on board placed across kettle of hot oil, and slipping in, 48%); Delisa v. Stewart Agency, Inc., 515 So.2d 426 (Fla. Dist. Ct. App. 1987) (defective seat belts, 40%; riding with intoxicated driver, knowing seat belts did not work, 60%); Miller v. Yazoo Mfg. Co., 26 F.3d 81 (8th Cir. 1994) (designing riding mower with blades that stopped 4.2 seconds after clutch released, 0%; riding so close to top edge of ravine that mower tilted and fell in, 100%); Hoeft v. Louisville Ladder Co., 904 S.W.2d 298 (Mo. App. 1995) (manufacturing aluminum ladder without warning against risk of electrocution, 2%; renting such a ladder to work crew, 3%; failing to have power lines de-energized before painting in their vicinity, and failing to use a wooden or fiberglass ladder, 95%); T.H.S. Northstar Assoc. v. W.R. Grace & Co., 860 F.Supp. 640 (D. Minn. 1994) (manufacturing asbestos products, 60%; buying building constructed of such products, 40%); General Motors Corp. v. Castaneda, 980 S.W.2d 777 (Tex. App. 1998) (defective door latch, that allowed door to open in collision with another car, 75%; speeding, 25%); Lakin v. Senco Products, Inc., 987 P.2d 463 (Or. 1999) (defective pneumatic air gun that could discharge multiple nails at once, 95%; use of gun while standing on makeshift sawhorse platform, 5%); Cottam v. CVS Pharmacy, 764 N.E.2d 814 (Mass. 2002) (pharmacy's failure to warn that anti-depression drug could cause permanent impotency, 51%; failing to seek medical attention for erection for 30 hours, 49%); Jett v. Ford Motor Co., 72 P.3d 71 (Or. 2003) (delivery truck transmission that could slip from park to reverse, 85%; plaintiff's failure to wait for alternative truck and disregard of safety protocols, including walking behind truck with engine running, 15%); Blue v. Environmental Eng'g, Inc., 803 N.E.2d 187 (Ill. App. 2003), aff'd, 828 N.E.2d 1128 (Ill. 2005) (failing to equip trash compactor with available safety features, 33%; worker's pushing boxes into compactor by foot, 32%; employer's allowing unsafe use of compactor, 35%).

6. Multiple Parties. Multiple parties multiply the problems. As plaintiff attempted to exit from the rear seat of an automobile driven by D–1 and manufactured by D–2, her foot caught in the safety belt causing her to fall. She sued D–1, for negligently failing to turn the light on, and D–2, for defective design. The jury apportioned total causal negligence as follows: 50% to plaintiff; 25% to D–1; and 25% to D–2. The Vermont comparative negligence statute provided in part: "Contributory negligence shall not bar recovery ... if the negligence was not greater than the causal negligence of the defendant...." *Held,* since plaintiff's negligence exceeded that of each defendant individually, plaintiff could not recover against either one. Stannard v. Harris, 380 A.2d 101 (Vt. 1977). See also Cartel Capital Corp. v. Fireco of New Jersey, 410 A.2d 674 (N.J. 1980) (restaurant owner 41% at fault for allowing paper plates to fall on grill; retailer-installer of fire sprinkler system 30% at fault for inserting screw in wrong place in the activating handle mechanism; manufacturer 29% at fault for designing system presenting risk that installer would make such a mistake); Thompson v. Brown & Williamson Tobacco Corp., 207 S.W.3d 76 (Mo. Ct. App. 2006) (different brands of cigarettes combined to cause throat cancer—Phillip Morris, 40%; Brown and Williamson, 10%; smoker, 50%).

7. Sole Proximate Cause. As mentioned earlier, some courts have ruled that a plaintiff's comparative fault can be the sole proximate cause of an injury, even if the product is defective. Kroon v. Beech Aircraft Corp., 628 F.2d 891 (5th Cir. 1980) (2–1) (Fla. law) (pilot attempted to take off without removing gust lock pin from steering control column). See also Standard Havens Prod., Inc. v. Benitez, 648 So.2d 1192, 1197 (Fla. 1994).

8. Jury Instructions on Effect of Apportionment. Although the prevailing rule formerly was to the contrary, a great majority of (but not all) modified comparative fault jurisdictions (by decision or legislation) now either permit or require instructions and argument to the jury on the *effect* of finding plaintiff fault equal to or greater than the defendant's—*that the plaintiff will take nothing.* E.g., Gratzle v. Sears, Roebuck & Co., 613 N.E.2d 802 (Ill. App. 1993) (failure to so instruct was reversible error). The commentators support this type of "ultimate outcome charge." V. Schwartz, Comparative Negligence § 17–5 (4th ed. 2002); H. Woods and B. Deere, Comparative Fault § 18.2 (3d ed. 1996).

9. Among the many articles on comparative fault in products liability litigation, see, e.g., Henke, Comparative Fault in products Liability: Comparing California and New Jersey, 19 T.M. Cooley l. Rev. 301 (2002); Davis, Individual and Institutional Responsibility: A Vision for Comparative Fault in Products Liability, 39 Vill. L. Rev. 281 (1994); McNichols, The Relevance of the Plaintiff's Misconduct in Strict Tort Products Liability, the Advent of Comparative Responsibility, and the Proposed *Restatement (Third) of Torts*, 47 Okla. L. Rev. 201 (1994) (comprehensive review and consideration of early draft of Products Liability Restatement); Westerbeke & Meltzer, Comparative Fault and Strict Products Liability in Kansas: Reflections on the Distinction Between Initial Liability and Ultimate Loss Allocation, 28 Kan. L. Rev. 25 (1979). See generally Restatement (Third) of Torts: Apportionment of Liability (2000); D. Owen, Products Liability Law § 13.3 (2d ed. 2008); 1 D. Owen, M.S. Madden, & M. Davis, Madden & Owen on Products Liability ch. 15 (3d ed. 2000).

---

3.   ASSUMPTION OF RISK

Moran v. Raymond Corp.

United States Court of Appeals, Seventh Circuit, 1973.
484 F.2d 1008, cert. denied, 415 U.S. 932 (1974).

■ PELL, CIRCUIT JUDGE.

Defendant [Raymond Corporation] appeals from a judgment for $250,000 [on a jury verdict for plaintiff, Juan Moran, for injuries he received while] an employee of Central Steel and Wire Company (Central).

Raymond manufactured a lift truck [a "sideloader"] designed to operate in narrow aisles. It differs from the standard fork lift truck, on which the load is carried fully beyond the front wheels in that . . . the load-lifter is located on one side of the equipment and extends equidistant over the front and rear sets of wheels. At one end [is] an operator's cage with the controls inside. Moran . . . was in the process of returning a tray to a rack approximately eight or nine feet above the ground when some wire rods on the tray slipped therefrom. In attempting to correct this situation, Moran left the operator's cage and first stood on the movable forks and eventually on a platform below the forks. Still not achieving the desired result, he attempted to lower the forks but rather than returning to the cage and while standing on the platform on the lift side of the equipment, he reached through an opening into the cage and pulled the control lever to lower the forks. Although he tried to bring his hand back quickly, it became stuck because of a bandage he had on his wrist. When the cross bar came down with a shearing action, Moran's right arm was seriously injured.

[Moran sued for negligence and strict liability; Raymond defended on Moran's assumption of risk; and the jury found that Moran had not assumed the risk.]

We [find it clear] that Moran assumed the risk. The Illinois Supreme Court adopted the doctrine of strict liability in tort in Suvada v. White Motor Co., 210 N.E.2d 182 (Ill. 1965). In Williams v. Brown Manufacturing Co., 261 N.E.2d 305 (Ill. 1970), the court held that simple contributory negligence, which would bar recovery by a plaintiff in a tort action based on negligence, would not preclude recovery in a suit based on a strict liability theory.

The court held, however, "that a plaintiff who knows a product is in a dangerous condition and proceeds in disregard of this known danger (often termed 'assumption of risk') may not recover for resulting injuries." The [*Williams* court stated:]

> [W]hether a user has assumed the risk of using a product known to be dangerously defective is fundamentally a subjective test, in the sense that it is *his* knowledge, understanding and appreciation of the danger which must be assessed, rather than that of the reasonably prudent person. . . . That determination is not to be made solely on the basis of the user's own statements but rather upon the jury's assessment of all of the facts established by the evidence. No juror is compelled by the subjective nature of this test to accept a user's testimony that he was unaware of the danger, if, in the light of all of the evidence, he could not have been unaware of the hazard [citation]; and the factors of the user's age, experience, knowledge and understanding, as well as the obviousness of the defect and the danger it poses [citation], will all be relevant to the jury's determination of the issue, if raised . . .

Although the test of assumption of risk is a subjective one, depending on the knowledge of the injured party, it is apparent that the question need not always go to the jury. [While] the defense of assumption of the risk ordinarily presents a question [for] the jury [which may] disbelieve the injured party's testimonial denial of knowledge of the danger, even though the test is a subjective one, does not mean that a jury question is presented when the testimony is clear that he did know of the danger.

In Fore v. Vermeer Manufacturing Co., 287 N.E.2d 526 (Ill. App. Ct. 1972), the court affirmed the grant of summary judgment against the plaintiff when the plaintiff admitted in his deposition that he had had numerous past difficulties with the machine: "It appears to be clear [1] that the plaintiff had actual knowledge of the danger; [2] that he understood and appreciated the risk; and [3] that he deliberately exposed himself to such risk, all while he was of full age, well experienced, with complete knowledge and understanding of an obvious defect, and an obvious danger." . . .

[Moran] admitted that he had been instructed to stand in the cage "when you are operating the controls." [S]ignificantly, he recognized the danger in operating the machine in the way he was at the time he was injured since he testified that he knew the bar would hit him if he did not move out of the way: "That's why I pulled the control fast and I withdrew the hand quickly." . . .

[O]ne who stands under the guillotine blade with knowledge of the fact that there will be a descent of the operational part upon activation of the controlling lever would scarcely seem to be in a position to claim that the blade fell faster than he anticipated, [and] we find no support in the record for Moran's contention that the lowering speed of the sideloader he had been operating for several hours . . . was greater than . . . the sideloader he had previously operated.

By way of summary, Moran, standing out of the operator's cage in a position where he would be in the path of the equipment if it was caused to become operative, reached with some effort on his part into the control area and pulled the control lever down as far as it would go. He knew when he did that, the forks would start coming down and would go all the way to the bottom unless he pushed the lever back. This was clearly proven subjective evidence and the verdict . . . cannot stand. Plaintiff argues that "[t]o say that Juan Moran consciously assumed the risk of his own injury would, under the circumstances, be to say that he intended to maim himself, or he was bent upon suicide." This conclusion does not follow. What is clear is that Moran was in a hurry and that he took a calculated risk that he could get his hand out of the way before the forks hit him. Workmen often take risks which they should not take and are fortunate enough to avoid injury. In finding that Moran assumed the risk, we are [dealing] with a hasty, but nonetheless knowing, decision. Obviously Moran, who had operated the machine from the front of the forks before without misadventure, *thought* he could do so again. But that is not the test applied in Illinois. The test, although subjective, relates to knowledge of the risk and not to whether it was a good risk. [Citations.]

[Reversed.]

NOTES

1. In Johnson v. Mid–South Distrib., Inc., Prod. Liab. Rep. (CCH) ¶ 7984 (Tenn. App. 1977), a farmhand was injured when his pants leg became entangled in a rotating shaft behind a tractor as he attempted to mount the tractor. The shaft ran from the power take-off (PTO) outlet at the rear of the tractor to a fertilizer spreader pulled behind the tractor and powered by the rotating shaft. Johnson filed suit against the fertilizer dealer which had supplied the spreader, alleging that the spreader was in a defective condition "because, although originally furnished with a shield device by the manufacturer covering the area where the shaft coupled to the tractor power take-off, there was no shield at the coupling area where Johnson became entangled and that Mid–South had superior knowledge of that defect and danger and failed to warn of it." Mid–South pleaded assumption of risk.

The court noted that "assumption of the risk acts in bar of recovery when the proof shows that the plaintiff has (1) knowledge of the danger, (2) an appreciation of that danger, and (3) voluntarily exposed himself to that danger. Knowledge on the part of the plaintiff is the keystone of the doctrine." At trial, plaintiff had testified in part as follows:

> Q. Now, tell us, if you will, how you go about hooking up this spreader or distributor to the tractor?
>
> A. Well, you back into the tongue of it, put a pin in it, and take the shaft and put it onto the tractor PTO shaft, I recon (sic) is what you call it.
>
> * * *
>
> Q. All right; Mr. Johnson, on the spreader that was delivered to Mr. Taylor's house that morning and which you hooked up behind this tractor, did it have any kind of shield around this shaft?
>
> A. No, sir.
>
> Q. Have you ever seen—well, let me ask you this—have you spread fertilizer with this type of spreader before?
>
> A. Yes, sir.
>
> Q. Have you ever seen one that did have a shield on it?
>
> A. Yes, sir.
>
> Q. Do all of them that come out have shields on them?
>
> A. No, sir.
>
> * * *
>
> Q. Mr. Johnson, I believe you said you tried to be careful around machinery all your life? Is that right?
>
> A. Yes, sir.
>
> * * *
>
> Q. Had you warned people about the dangers of the PTO shaft without a shield?
>
> A. Yes, sir, such as Mr. Henry and hands on the place.
>
> * * *
>
> Q. Did you realize that you might be hurt if you got involved with or got into that turning shaft?

A.   Yes, sir, you would get hurt if you got in it.

* * *

Q.   All right, sir; now when you came back to get on your tractor you knew the PTO was going, didn't you?

A.   Yes, sir, I knew it.

Q.   You knew it didn't have a shield on it?

A.   Yes, sir.

Q.   And, you knew it was dangerous if you got up against it?

A.   If you got against it or stuck your hand in it or foot in it, it was dangerous.

Q.   Or caught your pants leg in it?

A.   Yes, sir.

* * *

Q.   And, at that time, when you hooked it up, I believe you said a while ago, you knew that it would be dangerous if you got up next to it, didn't you?

A.   Yes, sir, if you got against it, it would be dangerous. If you stuck your hand in it, it would be dangerous.

Q.   Just like going in a saw-mill and sticking your hand in a buzz saw?

A.   Yes, sir, that's right.

* * *

Q.   The next question I want to ask you, Mr. Johnson, is, you can put the tractor in neutral, leave it running, and stop the PTO shaft from running, and not cut off the tractor?

A.   Yes, sir, you can do it.

Q.   All right; but you didn't do that?

A.   No, sir. Never had.

What result?

2.   Compare the plaintiff's testimony in O'Neal v. Carolina Farm Supply, Inc., 309 S.E.2d 776, 780 (S.C. App. 1983) (Bell, J.), where his pigs allegedly died from eating toxic corn supplied by the defendant:

Q.   But you went ahead and ground it up and fed it to your hogs knowing it was moldy and knowing it was the worse [sic] corn you had ever bought, is that right?

A.   I did.

What result?

3.   See also Hedgepeth v. Fruehauf Corp., 634 F.Supp. 93 (S.D. Miss. 1986) (oil tanker truck driver, who slipped while walking on top of tanker, testified that top was covered with oil and that he had known it was "real slick and real cruddy"); Bishop v. Firestone Tire & Rubber Co., 814 F.2d 437, 446 (7th Cir. 1987)(truck tire repairman stated, prior to explosion of multi-piece rim, "that he hoped the tire would not explode"); Novak v. Navistar Int'l Transp. Corp., 46 F.3d 844 (8th

Cir.1995)(farmer, run over by tractor he jump-started, knew that jump-starting tractor could move it forward and hence was potentially dangerous).

4. Age, Intelligence, and Experience. An intelligent adult familiar with the product is more likely to be found to have assumed a risk than an inexperienced or dim-witted adult, or a child. Compare Mackowick v. Westinghouse Elec. Corp., 541 A.2d 749 (Pa. Super. Ct. 1988) (experienced electrician stuck screwdriver into energized capacitor box—assumption of risk); Barnes v. Harley–Davidson Motor Co., Inc., 357 S.E.2d 127 (Ga. App. 1987) (motorcyclist of nearly 20 years, who collided with stalled car at night, claimed that motorcycle should have been equipped with crash bars, as standard equipment, and that head-lamp provided too little light at high speed—assumption of risk); and Bakunas v. Life Pack, Inc., 531 F.Supp. 89 (E.D. La. 1982) (movie stuntman performed free fall from 323 feet into air-inflated cushion rated only to 200 feet—assumption of risk), with Nettles v. Electrolux Motor AB, 784 F.2d 1574 (11th Cir. 1986) (experienced but dim-witted woodcutter, injured when chain saw kicked back, had been injured by kick backs before, and knew that he could use a saw equipped with a chain brake—no assumption of risk); and Forrest City Mach. Works, Inc. v. Aderhold, 616 S.W.2d 720 (Ark. 1981) (climbing off grain cart, 8–year–old caught pants in rotating PTO shaft attached to tractor—no assumption of risk).

————

Bowen v. Cochran

Court of Appeals of Georgia, 2001.
252 Ga.App. 457, 556 S.E.2d 530.

■ MILLER, JUDGE.

[David Bowen and his wife sued Fred Cochran for] injuries he sustained when a gas cooking grill manufactured by Cochran exploded, causing severe burns to Bowen's hands and forearms. The jury found in favor of Cochran. On appeal Bowen contends that the court erred in denying his motions [to disallow] Cochran's affirmative defenses of assumption of the risk and contributory negligence, and erred in charging the jury on these defenses. We discern no error and affirm.

[While using the gas cooker grill at his home, Bowen rolled up a newspaper to light the burner and then opened the gas valve. The burner ignited, and Bowen went into his home for about 30 minutes. When he returned,] the flame had extinguished, so he raised the lid and turned off the gas. After waiting for a few minutes for the gas smell to dissipate, Bowen made three attempts to relight the cooker by once again lighting the end of rolled up newspaper and placing it on the burner and then opening the gas valve. During the third attempt, Bowen bent over to look into the cooker when a burst of flame exploded, knocking him to the ground and burning his hands and forearms.

* * *

To show assumption of the risk, "the defendant must present evidence that the plaintiff [1] had actual knowledge of the danger, [2] understood and appreciated the risk, and [3] voluntarily exposed himself to that risk."

Cotton v. Bowen, 524 S.E.2d 737 (Ga. App. 1999). Cochran testified that the cookers are lit by opening the sliding door for ventilation, holding the trigger lighter to the burner to start a flame, and then turning on the gas valve. Although there were no written instructions on how to operate the cooker, Cochran provided Bowen with a trigger lighter and explained to him how to light the cooker. Cochran himself observed Bowen improperly light the cooker by lighting the orifice at the end where the gas enters. He explained to Bowen that he was lighting it improperly and once again showed Bowen the proper lighting procedure.

There must be some evidence that Bowen knew that the cooker could explode if not properly lighted and ventilated, that he understood the risk if the cooker was improperly operated, and that he nevertheless decided to risk operating the cooker improperly. The evidence in fact showed that Bowen lit the cooker improperly on at least two occasions and in two different manners: once by using newspaper instead of the trigger lighter provided by Cochran, and a second time by lighting the end close to where the gas enters. Bowen also left the cooker unattended for 30 minutes with the gas turned on. From this evidence a jury could conclude that Bowen did in fact assume the risk of a flame bursting from the cooker. As there is some evidence to support the affirmative defense of assumption of the risk, the court did not err in denying Bowen's motion for directed verdict on this ground. * * *

[Affirmed.]

■ ELDRIDGE, JUDGE, dissenting.

* * * Bowen placed the burning paper on the burner where it continued to burn without igniting the burner or the pooled gas immediately. However, the single door and the construction of the underside of the cooker with the drip pan allowed gas to pool to the top of the pan wall, because the heavier than air propane collects in a pool in the pan at the bottom of the cooker. The dead space in the burner caused a delayed ignition of the burner, which in turn ignited the accumulated gas pool in the pan, because the design was inadequate to ventilate adequately the cooker of the trapped gas in the pan, and the burner orifices allowed delayed ignition in the dead zone of the burner.

* * *

[T]he trial court erred in [allowing] the defense of assumption of the risk, because the defendant failed to affirmatively prove each essential element of such defense [to] allow the jury to decide the issue.

> The affirmative defense of assumption of the risk bars a plaintiff from recovering on a negligence claim if it is established that he[,] without coercion of circumstances, chooses a course of action with full knowledge of its danger and while exercising a free choice as to whether to engage in the act or not. In Georgia, a defendant asserting an assumption of the risk defense must establish that the plaintiff (1) had actual knowledge of the danger; (2) understood and appreciated the risks associated with such danger; and (3) voluntarily exposed himself to those risks. Knowledge of

the risk is the watchword of assumption of risk, and means both *actual* and *subjective* knowledge on the plaintiff's part. The knowledge that a plaintiff who assumes a risk must subjectively possess is that of the specific, particular risk of harm associated with the activity or condition that proximately causes injury. The knowledge requirement does not refer to a plaintiff's comprehension of general, non-specific risks that might be associated with such conditions or activities. . . . In its simplest and primary sense, assumption of the risk means that the plaintiff, in advance, has given his consent to relieve the defendant of an obligation of conduct toward him, and to take his chances of injury from *a known risk arising from what the defendant is to do or leave undone.*

[Citations. The plaintiff's general awareness that a grill's butane gas could explode if not lit properly fails] to constitute an assumption of the risk, because the specific danger of gas collecting in the grease pit and the dead zone causing delayed ignition was neither actually and subjectively known nor understood and appreciated as a specific hazard. * * *

Thus, the evidence failed to show both an actual and a specific subjective knowledge or understanding and appreciation of the specific risk that the gas would pool in the pan so that normal ventilation would not dissipate the heavy gas from the bottom pan of the cooker and that the gas burner had delayed ignition from a dead zone causing the hazard of a possible flashback upon ultimate ignition of the burner. The trial court erred in treating a comprehension of a general, nonspecific, awareness and understanding of a risk of gas collecting as the actual and subjective knowledge mandated as an essential element of this defense. * * *

NOTES

1. Knowledge of Risk. As plaintiff was mowing his grass up an incline with a rotary lawn mower manufactured by defendant, he approached a barrel in his path. He disengaged the driving clutch and stopped pushing the mower but did not release the clutch controlling the blades. As he worked to move the barrel, his feet slipped on the newly-mown grass and into the machine. Plaintiff sued, claiming the mower was defective because it was not equipped with a "deadman's throttle" that would have stopped the blade automatically when the forward motion of the machine was stopped. *Held,* plaintiff had assumed the risk; directed verdict for defendant affirmed. Denton v. Bachtold Bros., Inc., 291 N.E.2d 229 (Ill. App. 1972).

Compare Burch v. Sears, Roebuck and Co., 467 A.2d 615, 620 (Pa. Super. Ct. 1983). Plaintiff's electric mower shut off twice and would not restart until he pushed the reset button. The third time the motor shut off, plaintiff leaned the mower on its side, without disturbing the reset button, and reached into the blade area to remove the accumulated clumps of grass. The motor unexpectedly restarted and severely injured plaintiff's hand. Plaintiff's suit was based on the mower's failure to have a deadman's device. *Held,* the jury could reasonably find that the plaintiff had not assumed the risk because he believed that the motor was stopped and could be restarted only if the reset button were depressed.

2. Awareness of *Specific* Risks. In Haugen v. Minnesota Min. & Mfg. Co., 550 P.2d 71, 75 (Wash. App. 1976), plaintiff was blinded in one eye when the grinding wheel he was working on exploded into three pieces, one of which hit him in the eye. Plaintiff was not wearing safety goggles at the time of the accident, although two pair were available in the shop, and he knew of their importance from his prior safety training. The trial court instructed the jury as follows: "It is not enough to bar recovery by the plaintiff on the defense of assumption of risk that the plaintiff knew that there was a general danger connected with the use of the product, but rather it must be shown that the plaintiff actually knew, appreciated, and voluntarily and unreasonably exposed himself to the specific defect and danger which caused his injuries." On appeal, *held,* instruction was proper; judgment for plaintiff affirmed:

> [P]laintiff testified that he was aware that dust or small particles of wood were likely to be thrown from the dashboard while he was grinding on it. He further testified that he did not deem it necessary to wear the available safety goggles because he felt that his eyeglasses would provide adequate protection from this danger. If plaintiff assumed any risk at all, it was the risk of having dust or small particles of wood or metal lodged in his eye during the grinding process. He was obviously not aware of the latent defect in the structural integrity of the disc itself and the danger posed by that defect. This latent defect was not and probably could not have been known by the plaintiff. Plaintiff, therefore, could not have assumed the risk engendered by the defect.

Compare Krajewski v. Enderes Tool Co., 396 F. Supp. 2d 1045, 1052 (D. Neb. 2005) (plaintiff "was aware of the specific danger that striking two metal tools together can cause one of them to chip, such that he should wear safety goggles [and when he] removed those safety goggles, he assumed the risk of eye injury").

3. Ditto. Compare Hadar v. AVCO Corp., 886 A.2d 225 (Pa. Super. Ct. 2005), where a farmer was towing a corn picker with his tractor when the picker stopped working. He stopped the tractor but left the power running to the corn picker so he could observe the nature of the problem. Seeing corncobs clogging the husking rollers, he picked up a 3–foot cornstalk and pushed on the cobs to unclog them. Suddenly, the rollers cleared and pulled the cornstalk into the picker before plaintiff had a chance to let it go. *Held* (2–1 decision), defendant's motion for summary judgment based on plaintiff's assumption of risk denied. Although plaintiff was aware of the *general* risk of getting his hand caught in the rollers, a question of fact existed on whether he understood the *specific* risk that the rollers might pull in a 3–foot stalk so quickly that he could not release it before his hand was pulled in as well.

4. Appreciation. Requiring specific-risk awareness is another way of requiring that a risk be "appreciated" to be assumed. Some courts use the specific-risk approach, others use the appreciated-risk approach. Whichever approach is selected, how should the inquiry be affected by the fact that humans have great difficult assessing the true nature and extent of risk? See generally Montgomery, Cognitive Biases and Heuristics in Tort Litigation: A Proposal to Limit Their Effects Without Changing the World, 85 Neb. L. Rev. 15 (2006).

Johnson v. Clark Equipment Co.

Supreme Court of Oregon, 1976.
274 Or. 403, 547 P.2d 132.

■ HOWELL, JUSTICE.

[Plaintiff was injured while operating a forklift] manufactured and designed by defendant Clark [and sold by another defendant to his employer. Plaintiff appeals a verdict for defendants, arguing that the trial court erred in its jury instructions on assumption of risk.]

[A forklift operator at Warrenton Lumber Company, plaintiff's job entailed moving bundles of lumber about the] plant. Because of his various responsibilities, the job was a rather hectic one. The accident occurred . . . shortly after plaintiff's shift began and while he was engaged in feeding the random planer. Plaintiff was in a hurry and was carrying two banded bundles of 2 × 4's which [needed to have the metal bands around them cut]. . . . Although he normally dismounted his machine and moved to the front to cut the bands, on this occasion plaintiff remained in the cab of the forklift and reached through the uprights with the cutters. While he was cutting the bands, his body came in contact with the ascent/descent lever controlling the movement of the forks. The forklift carriage descended and severed his arms just below the elbows.

[T]he forklift consists of a cab attached to uprights along which the forks are raised and lowered. The uprights consist of inner and outer masts: the inner mast is hydraulically raised and lowered within the outer mast. The forks themselves are attached to a chain and sprocket device which causes them to follow the movements of the inner mast. Each mast is tied together at various points with horizontal crossbars. As the inner mast moves within the outer mast, the crossbars of the inner mast pass within ⅜ of an inch of the crossbars of the outer mast. At the time of the accident, plaintiff's arms were between the uprights, and, as the forks descended, the horizontal crossbars of the inner mast sheared plaintiff's arms against the crossbars of the outer mast and severed them.

The ascent/descent lever which caused the inner mast to descend when plaintiff's body came in contact with it is one of three levers controlling the movement of the forks. . . . located at the front of the cab and to the right of the steering wheel. The ascent/descent lever is the nearest of the three to the steering wheel. The operator pushes this lever forward to raise the forks and pulls it back to lower them. Once the lever is released, a spring device returns it to a neutral position. Whenever the ascent/descent lever returns to a neutral position, the movement of the inner mast and forks ceases, and the load remains in mid-air.

[P]laintiff alleged faulty design . . . in that (a) the uprights and cross members were positioned in a manner which allowed them to sever plaintiff's arms; (b) no guard or screen was placed between the cab and the uprights; (c) the ascent/descent lever was located so as to permit the operator's body to unintentionally come in contact with it; (d) the lever was not designed to remain in a neutral position until manually released; and (e) no adequate signs were included to warn the operator of the dangers posed by the machine. [Evidence conflicted on each of these points.]

The concept of assumption of risk in a products liability case differs somewhat from the traditional tort doctrine of assumption of risk. [We previously] adopted the definition of assumption of risk for products liability cases [in Comment *n* to § 402A]. In contrast to the more traditional defense which includes only two elements—subjective knowledge and voluntary encounter—Comment *n* sets forth three elements which must be shown before the plaintiff can be barred from recovery. The defendant must show, first, that the plaintiff *himself* actually knew and appreciated the particular risk or danger created by the defect; second, that plaintiff voluntarily encountered the risk while realizing the danger; and, third, that plaintiff's decision to voluntarily encounter the known risk was unreasonable. . . .[5]

In this case, [the trial court failed to include the third, unreasonableness, element, yet] proof of all three elements is essential to the assumption of the risk defense outlined in Comment *n* . . . .

The reasonableness of any decision to encounter a known danger must depend upon the circumstances surrounding that decision as well as on the relative probability and gravity of the risk incurred. Whenever the jury attempts to ascertain whether a plaintiff's decision to encounter a known risk was reasonable, it will be necessary for them to consider the conditions which motivated the decision, the pressures which were operating on the plaintiff, and the amount of time which he had to make the decision.

It should be emphasized that this element of unreasonableness pertains only to the nature of plaintiff's decision to encounter the known danger. We are not concerned with the apparent reasonableness or unreasonableness of the physical conduct through which plaintiff encountered the danger, but rather the reasonableness of his decision to do so. This distinction, while seemingly theoretical, is significant.

[W]orking conditions and related circumstances are a particularly relevant consideration in an inquiry into the reasonableness of a decision to encounter a job-related danger. Such factors often will have a strong influence on that decision, and, in some cases, they may represent the most important motivational factors. For example, a worker might fear that a slowdown in his individual production would slow down the entire production team and thereby draw the attention of his boss. [A] history of such slowdowns, or of causing excessive spoilage or ruining machine parts, [may lead to his] dismissal. The job market could be tight, and he may have little hope of being able to find a new job. Moreover, the situation may demand an immediate, hurried decision. It is certainly possible that, under such circumstances, a reasonable jury could find that his decision to encounter a known risk was not unreasonable. See [citations]; Brown v. Quick Mix Co., 454 P.2d 205, 208 (Wash. 1969) ("It could never be said as a matter of law that a workman whose job requires him to expose himself to a danger,

---

5. The Comment *n* defense represents a hybrid of contributory negligence and assumption of the risk. It combines both the subjective elements of the traditional assumption of the risk defense and the objective element of contributory negligence. The jury must find that the plaintiff had subjective knowledge and appreciation of the risk and voluntarily assumed it. The jury must also find that plaintiff's decision to assume the risk was objectively unreasonable. . . .

voluntarily and unreasonably encounters the same."). Cf. Rhoads v. Service Mach. Co., 329 F. Supp. 367, 381 (E.D. Ark.1971) ("The 'voluntariness' with which a worker assigned to a dangerous machine in a factory 'assumes the risk of injury' from the machine is illusory.") [citations].

[T]here was considerable testimony about the hectic nature of the forklift driver's job from both the plaintiff himself and from a former driver who had been doing the same work plaintiff was doing at the time of the injury, and who had asked for another position when he found that he was no longer able to keep up that job's demands. Plaintiff indicated that if his forklift had been able to keep up with the heavy loads and the fast pace which he was required to maintain, he would not have been in a rush, time would not have been so important, and he would have been able to get off the machine to cut the wire bands. Plaintiff testified that all he was thinking of at the time of the accident was "[t]he time that I had to do the job in, and the job I was doing." He also stated that if he had had time to think about it he would not have reached through the uprights....

Therefore, even if the jury disbelieved plaintiff's testimony and concluded that he knew and appreciated the danger that the carriage might somehow start to descend while his arms were through the uprights, and, further, that his actions in reaching through the uprights were voluntary, there would still remain an issue for the jury's consideration—whether, under the evidence in this case, his decision to do so was unreasonable. The issue is not whether it might have been more reasonable to have selected another method of cutting the bands around the lumber but rather, whether it was unreasonable, under all the circumstances, for plaintiff to have selected the method he did.

[The trial court's assumption of risk instructions were improper.]

Reversed and remanded for a new trial.

NOTES

1. Compare *Johnson* with *Moran,* at p. 598. Are the cases inconsistent?

2. **Voluntariness—Generally.** If a plaintiff's only or best "choice" is to encounter a known risk, then the encounter is not "voluntary." The voluntary requirement in assumption of risk means that the plaintiff has a true choice, that he or she has *reasonable* options available to avoid the risk. While defining the consensual notions of voluntariness and choice in reasonableness terms may appear to be mixing apples and oranges, it is a useful way to give content to the concept of "voluntary." There is something wrong, indeed illogical and perverse, with a doctrine based on a plaintiff's *consent* that permits a defendant to avoid responsibility for causing harm by forcing a danger upon the plaintiff, "forcing" because the plaintiff has no reasonable means to avoid it. "Where the defendant puts him to a choice of evils, there is a species of duress, which destroys the idea of freedom of election.... By placing him in the dilemma, the defendant has deprived him of his freedom of choice, and so cannot be heard to say that he has voluntarily assumed the risk." Prosser and Keeton on Torts § 68, at 490–91. On the other hand, if a plaintiff has a perfectly reasonable way to avoid a danger created by the defendant,

yet knowingly chooses to encounter it, then he cannot claim that he was compelled to take this path, for the choice is free and voluntary.

Consider Wallace v. Owens–Illinois, Inc., 389 S.E.2d 155, 158–59 (S.C. App. 1989) (Bell, J.) (plaintiff injured while cleaning up effects of soft drink bottle explosion):

> The plaintiff's acceptance of a risk is not voluntary if the defendant's wrongful conduct leaves him no reasonable alternative course of conduct in order to avert harm to himself or another.... [T]he explosion of the defective bottle left him with no reasonable alternative. He had a choice between two evils: he could leave the spill on the floor with the risk that he or others might be injured by its presence or he could undertake to remove the spill with the risk that he or another would be injured in the process of cleaning up. In other words, either choice entailed risk. In these circumstances, his choice to remove the hazard was not a voluntary assumption of risk. The Defendants had created a condition of peril which involved a risk of harm no matter which choice Wallace made. Risk was unavoidable in the circumstances.

3. Voluntariness—Workplace Hazards. With *Johnson,* compare McCalla v. Harnischfeger Corp., 521 A.2d 851, 856 (N.J. Super. Ct. 1987) ("[A]n employee engaged in his assigned task ... has no meaningful choice."). Reasoning that workers as a practical matter are often trapped into performing dangerous activities, destroying the "voluntariness" of many job-related risks, the Ohio Supreme Court abolished the defense in ordinary work-place situations. Cremeans v. Willmar Henderson Mfg. Co., 566 N.E.2d 1203 (Ohio 1991). In some jurisdictions, however, an employer's compulsion will *not* defeat the voluntariness of an employee's assumption of a product risk asserted by the manufacturer. See Hedgepeth v. Fruehauf Corp., 634 F.Supp. 93, 99 n.3 (S.D. Miss. 1986) (relying on Rest. (2d) Torts § 496E cmt. *b*).

4. Unreasonableness. Many courts have followed the approach of comment *n* to § 402A in strict liability cases, requiring that the plaintiff's decision to encounter the risk be shown to have been *unreasonable,* in addition to knowledgeable and voluntary. See, e.g., Allen v. Chance Mfg. Co., Inc., 494 N.E.2d 1324 (Mass.1986) (implied warranty).

5. Warranty. Some courts treat assumption of risk as a defense to warranty claims. See, e.g., Allen v. Chance Mfg. Co., 494 N.E.2d 1324 (Mass.1986) (implied warranty). It may be preferable to inquire whether the conduct falls outside of the warranty, is not in reliance on the warranty, or to examine the issue from the perspective of proximate causation. See Hensley v. Sherman Car Wash Equip. Co., 520 P.2d 146 (Colo. App. 1974).

6. Tortious Misrepresentation. In tortious misrepresentation cases, assumption of risk is subsumed in justifiable reliance. See Klages v. General Ordnance Equip. Corp., 367 A.2d 304 (Pa. Super. Ct. 1976), p. 583, note 8, above.

7. Bystanders. Assumption of risk has been held applicable to bystanders. See Baker v. Chrysler Corp., 127 Cal.Rptr. 745 (Ct. App. 1976) (pedestrian, hit by allegedly uncrashworthy car with protruding metal headlight protector, ran across street trying to beat oncoming car); Brown v. Link Belt Corp., 565 F.2d 1107 (9th Cir. 1977) (worker run over by crane with bad visibility and no warning signal devices). But see Barr v. Rivinius, Inc., 373 N.E.2d 1063 (Ill. App. 1978) (2–1 decision)(worker hit by roadgrader-shoulder spreader machine).

8. The Enigma. "A basic enigma inherent in [the assumption of risk doctrine] is its dependence upon the notion of full appreciation of risk. 'Risk' implies a degree of want of appreciation of the forces that are at work in a given factual setting, since if one knew and understood all these forces he would know that injury was certain to occur or that it was certain not to occur. Thus the expression 'fully appreciated risk' may seem to be a self-contradiction." R. Keeton, Assumption of Risk in Products Liability Cases, 22 La. L. Rev. 122, 124 (1961).

See Campbell v. ITE Imperial Corp., 733 P.2d 969, 976 (Wash. 1987), where a wireman received a severe electrical shock when he began to clean electrical equipment that was not deenergized due to the defective configuration of the equipment. "To conclude that Campbell was aware of the specific defect in this configuration would be tantamount to believing that he intended to commit suicide."

9. Abolition. Some states have abolished assumption of risk by statute. See Hornbeck v. Western States Fire Apparatus, Inc., 572 P.2d 620 (Or. 1977). Other states have abolished it by judicial decision, reasoning that the doctrine is unsound in certain respects or simply incompatible with principles of comparative fault, as discussed below. See Cremeans v. Willmar Henderson Mfg. Co., 566 N.E.2d 1203 (Ohio 1991) (doctrine abolished for workers encountering risks in normal performance of job-related duties).

10. Express Assumption of Risk—Releases. In Diedrich v. Wright, 550 F.Supp. 805 (N.D. Ill. 1982), plaintiff was severely injured when her parachute failed to open fully because the lines were crossed. In her suit against the parachute center for supplying her with an unsafe parachute, the defendant asserted that she had waived her rights by signing a release form that generally exculpated the defendant from liability for injuries from parachuting. *Held,* (1) the release could not bar a strict liability action, and (2) it did not bar the negligence action because it failed clearly to state that the plaintiff was relieving the defendant of liability for *negligence.* Compare Moore v. Sitzmark Corp., 555 N.E.2d 1305 (Ind. App. 1990) (skier's signature on release simply acknowledged laws of physics and did not show she knew of defect in bindings); Ghionis v. Deer Valley Resort Co., 839 F.Supp. 789 (D. Utah 1993) (notwithstanding release, skier not aware that her rented bindings would fail to release because they were incompatible with her boots); Westlye v. Look Sports, Inc., 22 Cal.Rptr.2d 781 (Ct. App. 1993) (ski equipment rental disclaimer against public policy).

11. In Curtis v. Hoosier Racing Tire Corp., 299 F.Supp.2d 777, 779–85 (N.D. Ohio 2004), plaintiff was severely injured in a stock car race at the Talladega Speedway when his right front tire blew out and the car slammed into the track wall. Hoosier Racing Tire Corp., a race sponsor, was responsible for outfitting the cars with tires that it designed, manufactured, and advertised at the races. Prior to the race, plaintiff had signed releases for the speedway and racing association providing in part that plaintiff:

> RELEASE[D], WAIVE[D], DISCHARGE[D], AND COVENANT[ED] NOT TO SUE ... [the] track operator, officials, vehicle owners, drivers, pit crews, ... ***promoters, sponsors, advertisers,*** owners, and lessees of premises ... all ... referred to [below] as "Releasees" ... from all liability to the Applicant ... for any and all loss or damage and any claim ... on account of injury to the person or property ... of the Applicant, whether caused by the negligence of the Releasees or otherwise while ... participating in the [ARCA] EVENT(S). [Emphasis added by court.]

Plaintiff argued that this release was limited to negligence claims and did not cover strict liability claims based on product defects. While plaintiff assumed the risks of car racing, including the risk that his tires might blow out, it was a question of fact whether he also assumed the risk that a tire provided by a sponsor "was unreasonably risky because it was defective. Indeed, under Hoosier's theory, a race-car product supplier could immunize itself from many product liability claims simply by doing what it probably already does—advertise at racing events." Without addressing the fact that Hoosier's sponsorship agreement with ARCA required it to supply tires to all race cars, the court reasoned that, under the release agreement, the plaintiff could sue Hoosier in its role as manufacturer of a defective product rather than in its role as sponsor of the event in which he was injured.

Motion for summary judgment denied.

12. Fireman's Rule. Most states hold that a fire fighter injured in fighting a fire may not recover against a party who tortiously caused the fire because the fire fighter assumes the normal risks incident to the job. See, e.g., Brown v. General Elec. Corp., 648 F.Supp. 470 (M.D. Ga. 1986) (while fighting fire caused by defective coffee pot, fireman injured from jumping off roof of burning building that exploded). The rule may *not* bar recovery if the product does not start or contribute to the fire. Hauboldt v. Union Carbide Corp., 467 N.W.2d 508 (Wis. 1991) (defective acetylene tank exploded, directly injuring firefighter). But see White v. Edmond, 971 F.2d 681 (11th Cir. 1992) (firefighter injured when car's shock absorbers exploded in fire; doctrine barred recovery).

13. Comparative Fault—Retention of Assumption of Risk. Notwithstanding the spread of comparative fault discussed below, some states have retained assumption of risk as a complete bar to recovery, at least for purposes of strict liability. See, e.g., Duncan v. Cessna Aircraft Co., 665 S.W.2d 414, 423 (Tex. 1984). See Milwaukee Elec. Tool Corp. v. San Diego Cty. Super. Ct., 6 Cal.Rptr.2d 423 (Ct. App. 1992) (to bar recovery for breach of warranty, jury must find that plaintiff used product after discovering defect and that a reasonable person would not have used product knowing of its condition).

In Ohio, the Supreme Court merged assumption of risk into its statutory comparative negligence scheme in 1983. Then, in Bowling v. Heil Co., 511 N.E.2d 373 (Ohio 1987), the court declined to apply comparative fault to products liability claims based on *strict liability* in tort, ruling that an unreasonable assumption of risk under comment *n* to § 402A remained an absolute defense to strict tort actions. In Onderko v. Richmond Mfg. Co., 511 N.E.2d 388, 392 (Ohio 1987), the majority reaffirmed this doctrine:

> At first blush, this absolute bar to recovery may seem unnecessarily or insupportably harsh. It must be remembered, however, that this foreclosure of recovery on a strict liability theory does not deprive an injured plaintiff of all possible remedies. A plaintiff injured by a product is not limited to the theory of strict liability as the sole means of redress. An action in negligence may also be available to compensate the plaintiff for his injury.

In dissent, Justice Sweeney argued that the majority's approach denies a person injured by a defective product recovery for any damages, "no matter how slight the plaintiff-victim assumed the risk." Further, applying comparative fault principles to assumption of risk would "dissuade the legal gymnastics that courts and juries endure in [lawyers' attempts] to categorize a plaintiff-victim's conduct as 'assumption of risk' or 'contributory negligence' where a plaintiff's conduct plays a significant role...." Id. at 394.

14. Comparative Fault—Merger. An increasing number of jurisdictions, both by statute and judicial opinion, have merged the assumption of risk doctrine into comparative fault, treating it as a type of fault for damages-reducing purposes, rather than as a complete defense. See, e.g., Perez v. McConkey, 872 S.W.2d 897 (Tenn. 1994) (implied assumption of risk abolished; fault aspects included in comparative fault); Larsen v. Pacesetter Sys., Inc., 837 P.2d 1273 (Haw. 1992) (assumption of risk bar "absurd" in products liability setting); Blackburn v. Dorta, 348 So.2d 287, 292 (Fla. 1977):

> We find no discernable basis analytically or historically to maintain a distinction between the affirmative defense of contributory negligence and assumption of risk. [Would the fault principles of tort law and comparative negligence be advanced by] a doctrine which would totally bar recovery by one who voluntarily, but reasonably, assumes a known risk while one whose conduct is unreasonable but denominated "contributory negligence" is permitted to recover a proportionate amount of his damages for injury? Certainly not. Therefore, we hold that the affirmative defense of implied assumption of risk is merged into the defense of contributory negligence and the principles of comparative negligence ... shall apply....

Contrast Justice Mosk's observations in a portion of his dissenting opinion in *Daly* omitted above:

> The majority note one "felicitous result" of adopting comparative negligence to products liability: the merger of assumption of risk—which they term a "bizarre anomaly"—into their innovative defense. I find that result neither felicitous nor tenable.... If a consumer elects to use a product patently defective when other alternatives are available, or to use a product in a manner clearly not intended or foreseeable, he assumes the risks inherent in his improper utilization and should not be heard to complain about the condition of the object. One who employs a power saw to trim his fingernails—and thereafter finds the number of his fingers reduced—should not prevail to any extent whatever against the manufacturer even if the saw had a defective blade. I would retain assumption of risk as a total defense to products liability, as it always has been.

575 P.2d 1162 at 1185.

Which approach is preferable, *bar* or *merger*? Even if assumption of risk is merged into comparative fault, note that in most jurisdictions the conduct will continue to serve as a total bar—like any other type of plaintiff "fault"—when it exceeds the defendant's fault.

15. On assumption of risk generally, see Simons, Reflections on Assumption of Risk, 50 UCLA L. Rev. 481 (2002); McNichols, The Relevance of the Plaintiff's Misconduct in Strict Tort Products Liability, the Advent of Comparative Responsibility, and the Proposed Restatement (Third) of Torts, 47 Okla. L. Rev. 201 (1994); Twerski, Old Wine in a New Flask—Restructuring Assumption of Risk in the Products Liability Era, 60 Iowa L. Rev. 1 (1974); Note, Assumption of Risk and Strict Products Liability, 95 Harv. L. Rev. 872 (1982); D. Owen, Products Liability Law § 13.4 (2d ed. 2008); 2 D. Owen, M.S. Madden, & M. Davis, Madden & Owen on Products Liability § 14:3 (3d ed. 2000).

4. MISUSE

If a plaintiff's injury results in substantial part from his or her misuse of a product, he may be barred from recovery. This important concept was examined in chapter 10(3) above as a limitation on product defectiveness. Those materials should be reviewed here. We there saw that a plaintiff in most jurisdictions is unable to recover if the injury results from his or her *unforeseeable* misuse of the product. Although the plaintiff in most states must prove, as part of the prima facie case, that the accident arose from a foreseeable use of the product, a number of jurisdictions (mostly by statute) treat product misuse as an affirmative defense.

Whether "product misuse" should be merged into comparative fault, and treated as a damages-reducing factor rather than as a total bar, is a difficult question yet to be deliberatively addressed by most courts and legislatures. Viewing misuse merely as another form of plaintiff misconduct "defense," some courts and legislatures have integrated misuse into the state's comparative fault scheme, to reduce but not bar (if equal to or less than defendant's fault) plaintiff's recovery. See, e.g., Standard Havens Prod., Inc. v. Benitez, 648 So.2d 1192 (Fla. 1994) (negligence action); Elliot v. Sears, Roebuck & Co., 642 A.2d 709 (Conn. 1994) (strict liability).

Logically, injuries produced by *unforeseeable* misuse should remain outside of the scope of recovery, since manufacturers should have no duty to prevent them. Some so hold. E.g., States v. R.D. Werner Co., 799 P.2d 427 (Colo. App. 1990) (unlike comparative negligence, which diminishes recovery, unforeseeable misuse of ladder from which plaintiff fell goes to causation and completely bars recovery, regardless of defective condition); Cigna v. Oy Saunatec Ltd., 241 F.3d 1 (1st Cir. 2001) (unforeseeable misuse totally bars recovery, whereas foreseeable misuse factors into fault and damages allocation).

Mysteriously, a number of courts have ruled to the contrary: "[W]here an unreasonably dangerous defect of a product and the plaintiff's assumption of risk or *unforeseeable misuse* of the product are concurring proximate causes of the injury suffered, the trier of fact must compare those concurring causes to determine the respective percentages" for the apportionment of damages. Mauch v. Manufacturers Sales & Service, Inc., 345 N.W.2d 338, 348 (N.D. 1984) (emphasis added), citing General Motors v. Hopkins, 548 S.W.2d 344 (Tex. 1977) (heroic attempt to explicate and justify this nonsense). See also Barnard v. Saturn Corp., a Div'n of General Motors Corp., 790 N.E.2d 1023 (Ind. App. 2003).

The confusion from combining doctrines (comparative fault and misuse) and sources of law (courts and legislatures) spawns perplexing opinions. See, e.g., Jimenez v. Sears, Roebuck & Co., 904 P.2d 861, 873 (Ariz. 1995) (revealing a glimpse of common sense at least in Martone, J.'s concurrence: "[T]rue misuse (unforeseeable, sole cause) continues to be an all or nothing defense [under Arizona's misuse defense statute]. Foreseeable misuse (concurring cause) is really contributory negligence, and is now a comparative defense to a products case.").

Regardless of how the burden of proof and comparative fault issues are resolved in any particular jurisdiction, product misuse is certain to remain an important "defense" in products liability litigation.

NOTE

See generally Adler, Redesigning People versus Redesigning Products: The Consumer Product Safety Commission Addresses Product Misuse, 11 J.L. & Pol. 79 (1995); McNichols, The Relevance of the Plaintiff's Misconduct in Strict Tort Products Liability, the Advent of Comparative Responsibility, and the Proposed *Restatement (Third) of Torts*, 47 Okla. L. Rev. 201 (1994) (comprehensive review and consideration of early draft of Third Restatement); Fischer, Products Liability—Applicability of Comparative Negligence to Misuse and Assumption of the Risk, 43 Mo.L.Rev. 643 (1978); Twerski, The Many Faces of Misuse: An Inquiry Into the Emerging Doctrine of Comparative Causation, 29 Mercer L. Rev. 403 (1978); D. Owen, Products Liability Law § 13.5 (2d ed. 2008); 2 D. Owen, M.S. Madden, & M. Davis, Madden & Owen on Products Liability § 14:4 (3d ed. 2000).

MINI–PROBLEMS: CONSUMER MISCONDUCT

How might the various defenses based on user misconduct apply to the following situations? Consider what percentage of responsibility you would allocate to the plaintiff if you were a juror in a pure comparative fault state.

1. Plaintiff purchases a lightweight vacuum cleaner designed and manufactured by the defendant. After several hours of intermittent use, it appears to be losing suction. Leaving the vacuum on so that he can evaluate the suction, plaintiff takes off the detachable mouthpiece, leaving exposed the tubular opening into the machine. Plaintiff places his hand over the opening, which reveals that the suction is low, whereupon he inserts his fingers into the opening to extract some dirt which he determines is blocking the tube. His fingers are injured when they are struck by blades of the motor fan hidden behind the dirt. *Defect claims*: fan location and failure to warn.

2. The label on the "Drainclean" can, that contains highly corrosive crystals, warns: "Caution. Not for internal consumption. Keep out of reach of children." Plaintiff is a 12–year–old child who eats a spoonful on a friend's dare, and is badly sickened. *Defect claim*: failure adequately to warn.

3. Plaintiff operates a large punch press manufactured by the defendant. Every 30–40 minutes plaintiff must clear the accumulated metal debris off the press, which involves leaving the point of operation (where the press is activated by means of a foot switch) and going to the other side of the press where there is much better access to the surface area containing the debris. Plaintiff leaves the machine on during these clearing operations to avoid the 5–minute warm-up period necessary if the machine is turned off. When performing this operation, he normally kicks the foot switch under the machine to get it out of the way of traffic. One time he forgets, and another employee accidentally activates the foot control while walking by the press. Plaintiff's hands are injured. *Defect claims*: failure to equip with point of operation guards; inadequately guarded foot treadle.

4. Plaintiff takes a sleeping pill and gets into bed to read, wearing an excessively flammable nightgown manufactured by the defendant. While smoking a cigarette, she falls asleep and drops the cigarette on the nightgown which ignites, burning her severely. Cf. Ross v. Spiegel, Inc., 373 N.E.2d 1288 (Ohio Ct. App. 1977). *Defect claims*: design defect and failure to warn.

5. Plaintiff is a lawyer who knows that many persons are injured annually by projectiles thrown by rotary lawn mowers, sometimes at great distances. While her teenage son is mowing the lawn, plaintiff washes the outside windows on her house, 10 feet from the nearest portion of the lawn. Plaintiff's eye is injured when a pebble is hurled by the lawn mower 15 feet away. *Defect claim*: failure to shield grass ejection chute.

6. Plaintiff is a drunken driver hit by another car when plaintiff goes through a red light at high speed. She is injured in two respects: (1) brain damage, worth $1 million, resulting from her head hitting the roof, which would have been prevented had she been wearing her seat belt, and (2) severe burn injuries, worth $500,000, caused by the uncrashworthy design of the fuel system on her car. Defendant is the manufacturer of plaintiff's car. *Defect claim*: inadequately designed fuel system.

7. Plaintiff's wife goes into labor and he helps her into their car to transport her to the hospital. As he hurries around the front of the car to take his seat behind the wheel, he notices that his right front tire has a large bubble in it. As a tire salesman, he knows that this presents a serious risk of blowout and that the tire could fail at any time, which could cause him to lose control of the car. His wife, however, has had various complications with her pregnancy, and the doctor had advised him that both the mother's and child's lives would be substantially endangered if his wife were not taken to the hospital immediately once she went into labor. Apart from the car, no other means of transportation is available. Plaintiff jumps into the car and proceeds to drive the two miles to the hospital very cautiously, at 25 m.p.h. Unhappily, the tire blows out, the car goes over an embankment, and plaintiff is injured; happily, mother and baby are fine. *Defect claim*: design defect.

8. Adult plaintiff, visiting at friend's house, dives into backyard in-ground swimming pool, half way between shallow and deep ends, and is injured when his head hits bottom. There are no numbers along the edge indicating the depth of the water. See Sciangula v. Mancuso, 612 N.Y.S.2d 645 (App. Div. 1994). *Defect claim*: failure to warn.

CHAPTER 15

DAMAGES

1. PERSONAL INJURY AND DEATH

Anderson v. Sears, Roebuck & Co.

United States District Court, Eastern District of Louisiana, 1974.
377 F.Supp. 136.

■ CASSIBRY, DISTRICT JUDGE.

On April 23, 1970 the Britains' home was completely consumed by a fire which was ignited by a defective Sears' heater. Both Mildred Britain and her infant daughter, Helen Britain, were severely burned and Helen Britain suffered multiple permanent injuries. Thereafter, Mildred Britain and Harry Britain, individually and as administrator of the estate of Helen Britain, brought suit against Sears, Roebuck and Company [as well as against the manufacturers of the heater and of its component parts].

The case was fairly and properly tried, over a period of eight days. . . . and returned a verdict in favor of Mildred Britain, Harry Britain, individually, and Harry Britain, as administrator of the estate of Helen Britain, and against [the defendants], for two hundred fifty thousand dollars, twenty three thousand dollars, and two million dollars respectively. . . .

[By post-trial motion, defendants argue that] the damages awarded to Helen Britain were excessive [merely in view of the size of the verdict.]

The legal standard . . . for remittitur purposes is the "maximum recovery rule" [which] directs the trial judge to determine whether the verdict of the jury exceeds the maximum amount which the jury could reasonably find and if it does, the trial judge may then reduce the verdict to the highest amount that the jury could properly have awarded. Functionally, the maximum recovery rule both preserves the constitutionally protected role of the jury as finder of facts and prevents the predilections of the judge from infecting the jury's determination. . . . In this case there are five cardinal elements of damages: past physical and mental pain; future physical and mental pain; future medical expenses; loss of earning capacity and permanent disability and disfigurement.

PAST PHYSICAL AND MENTAL PAIN

The infant child Helen Britain, was almost burned to death in the tragic fire that swept her home. She was burned over forty per cent of her entire body; third degree burns cover eighty per cent of her scalp and second and third degree burns of the trunk and of her extremities account for the remainder. Helen Britain's immediate post-trauma treatment required hospitalization for twenty-eight days, during which time the child developed pneumonia, required numerous transfusions, suffered fever, vomiting, diarrhea, and infection, and underwent skin graft surgery, under general anesthesia, to her scalp, which was only partially successful. Keloid scarring caused webbing and ankylosis of the child's extremities and severely limited their motion. The child's fingers became adhered together; scarring bent the arm at the elbow in a burdensome, fixed position; and thick scarring on the thighs and on the side of and behind the knees impaired walking.

This child had to undergo subsequent hospitalizations for further major operations and treatment. The second major operation under general anesthesia was undertaken to graft new skin from the back and stomach to the remaining bare areas of the scalp. The third operation under general anesthesia was an attempt to relieve the deformity of her left hand caused by the webbing scars which bound down the fingers of that hand. A fourth operation under general anesthesia was performed to reduce scars which had grown back on the left hand again webbing the fingers. I cannot envisage the breadth and intensity of the pain experienced by Helen Britain throughout this ordeal.

[O]ne of the most tragic aspects of this case is that the horrible mental and emotional trauma caused to this child occurred at an age which medical experts maintain is crucial to a child's entire psyche and personality formation. Helen Britain's persistent emotional and mental disturbance is evidenced by bed wetting, nightmares, refusing to sleep alone, withdrawal, and speech impediments. Dr. Cyril Phillips, a psychiatrist, and Dr. Diamond both indicated that the child manifested to them, even at this early age, emotional illness and retarded mental growth.

[A]n award of $600,000 for this element of damages alone would not be unreasonable.

FUTURE PHYSICAL AND MENTAL PAIN

There is clear evidence that the stretching, pulling, and breaking down of scars inherent in growth will continue to cause severe pain and a crippling limitation of motion in varying degrees to all of Helen Britain's upper and lower extremities. Very little can be done to improve the condition of the scalp which will never be able to breathe, sweat or grow hair. There will be risks, trauma and pain, both physical and mental, with each of the recommended twenty-seven future operations which will extend over most of the child's adult life, if she is in fact fortunate enough to be able to risk undergoing these recommended surgeries. Furthermore, Helen Britain must vigilantly guard against irritation, infection and further injury to the damaged and abnormal skin, scars and grafts because any injury, however slight, can generate cancer in these adynamic areas.

The inherent stresses and tensions of each new phase of life will severely tax this little girl's debilitated and delicate mental and emotional capacity. Throughout her future life expectancy of seventy-five years, it is reasonable to expect, that she will be deprived of a normal social life and that she will never find a husband and raise a family. On top of this, Helen Britain will always be subjected to rejection, stares and tactless inquiries from children and adults.

[A]n award of seven $750,000 for this element of damages alone would not be excessive.

FUTURE MEDICAL EXPENSES

A large award for future medical expenses is justified. The uncontradicted testimony was that Helen Britain would need the guidance, treatment and counseling of a team of doctors, including plastic surgeons, psychiatrists and sociologists, throughout her lifetime. Add to this the cost of the 27 recommended operations and the cost of private tutoring necessitated by the child's mental and emotional needs and the jury could justifiably award $250,000 to cover these future expenses.

LOSS OF EARNING CAPACITY

The evidence of Helen Britain's disabilities both physical, mental and emotional was such that this court holds that the jury could properly find that these disabilities would prevent her from earning a living for the rest of her life. Not only do the physical impairments to her extremities disable her but her emotional limitations require avoiding stress and the combined effect is the permanent incapacity to maintain serious employment.

[A]ctuarial figures . . . accurately calculated both the deduction of interest to be earned and the addition of an inflationary buffer, on any award made for future loss of earning capacity. [The jury could] award as much as $330,000.00 for the loss of earning capacity.

PERMANENT DISABILITY AND DISFIGUREMENT

The award for this element of damage must evaluate in monetary terms the compensation due this plaintiff for the permanent physical, mental and emotional disabilities and disfigurements proved by the evidence adduced at trial. [Miss Britain's permanent disabilities and disfigurements include:]

1. The complete permanent loss of 80% of the scalp caused by the destruction of sweat glands, hair follicles and tissue—all of which effects a grotesque disfigurement and freakish appearance.

2. The permanent loss of the normal use of the legs.

3. The permanent impairment of the left fingers and hand caused by recurring webbing and resulting in limited motion.

4. The permanent impairment of the right hand caused by scars and webbing of the fingers.

5. The permanent injury to the left elbow and left arm with ankylosis and resulting in a crippling deformity.

6. The permanent destruction of 40% of the normal skin. As a result of this a large portion of the body is covered by "pigskin." Pigskin resembles the dry, cracked skin of an aged person and is highly susceptible to irritation from such ordinary things as temperature changes and washing.

7. Permanent scars over the majority of the body where skin donor sites were removed.

8. The permanent impairment of speech.

9. The loss of three years of formative and impressionable childhood.

10. Permanently reduced and impaired emotional capacity.

11. The permanent impairment of normal social, recreational and educational life.

12. The permanent imprint of her mother's hand on her stomach.

Considering each of the foregoing items, the court concludes that the jury had the prerogative of awarding up to $1.1 million for this element of damages.

By totaling the estimated maximum recovery for each element of damages, the jury's actual award is placed in proper perspective. According to my calculations the maximum jury award supported by the evidence in this case could have been $2,980,000. Obviously, the jury's $2 million verdict is well within the periphery established by the maximum award test.

The defendants assert three other grounds for a remittitur. They contend that there was error in the verdict since the verdict exceeded the amount prayed for in the plaintiff's pleadings. This contention fails because the plaintiffs' pleadings were amended subsequent to the jury verdict to conform to the evidence and the verdict of the jury. This amendment was permitted by the court in accordance with law. [Citations]; Fed. R. Civ. P. 54(c).

[Defendants] argue that the introduction of photographs of the plaintiff was inflammatory. Since a part of plaintiff's claim for damages is for disfigurement and the humiliation and embarrassment resulting therefrom, I hold that these photographs were properly admitted to show the condition of the plaintiff as she appeared to others, at the time they were taken. [Citations]; Fed. R. Civ. P. 43.

The defendants suggest that the presence of the child in the courtroom and in the corridors of the courthouse in some way inflamed or prejudiced the jury. This allegation is unfounded; the defendants have not pointed out any wrongful conduct on the part of Helen Britain, her parents, or counsel for plaintiffs. Helen Britain was well behaved and quiet the entire time she was in the courtroom.

... I hold that there was not any bias, prejudice, or any other improper influence which motivated the jury in making its award.

The defendants' motions for a remittitur are denied.

NOTES

1. Valuation. There is perhaps the least law on what may be the most elusive of all issues confronting juries and courts—monetizing injuries and deaths. What is the *maximum* value a jury should be permitted to find for the death of a 15–year–old girl killed in a rollover of a microbus? See MacCuish v. Volkswagenwerk A.G., 494 N.E.2d 390 (Mass.App.1986), aff'd mem. by an equally divided court, 508 N.E.2d 842 (Mass.1987). Is $50,000,000 excessive for a retired FBI agent who suffered a heart attack at age 58 after using the arthritis pain killer Vioxx and has lost nine or ten years of his life? In re Vioxx Products Liability Litig., 448 F.Supp.2d 737 (E.D.La. 2006).

2. Lost Earning Capacity. What kind of testimony is permissible in assessing lost future earnings from damage to earning capacity? In Montgomery v. Mitsubishi Motors Corp., 2006 WL 1147616 (E.D. Pa. 2006), the trial judge concluded that an expert in guidance and counseling could testify that plaintiffs' decedent, their 23 year old son who had completed two years of college, would have completed both his baccalaureate and law degrees and would have earned an average of $75,000 per year until age 89. Defendant argued this testimony was unreliable under *Daubert* because based on pure speculation. How much proof of plaintiff's probable work life should be required?

Expert evidence on the effect of inflation on future earnings is now generally allowed. In Huddell v. Levin, 537 F.2d 726, 743 (3d Cir.1976), expert testimony on this issue was ruled admissible in a wrongful death crashworthiness case:

> In holding that expert economic testimony is admissible in actions for wrongful death on the issue of the effect of inflation on the survivor's future pecuniary loss, we are aware that not all courts share this view. [H]owever, it is simply unrealistic to ignore the problem of inflation in this context. Given the enormity of the potential impact of rising costs over a long period of time, . . . evidence of informed estimates of future inflationary trends will result in damage awards that are fair and just.

Id. at 743 (relying on Tenore v. Nu Car Carriers, Inc., 341 A.2d 613, 621–23 (N.J. 1975)).

3. Noneconomic Damages. "Noneconomic" damages are those that are not readily quantifiable, such as pain and suffering, physical impairment, disfigurement, loss of enjoyment of life, emotional distress, loss of consortium, and other nonpecuniary damage. McGee v. AC & S Inc., 933 So.2d 770 (La. 2006). As part of general tort reform legislation, many states have enacted statutory caps on such damages that range from $250,000 to $500,000; the highest may be $875,000 in New Hampshire. Colorado's is $250,000, or $500,000 if justified by clear and convincing evidence. General Elec. Co. v. Niemet, 866 P.2d 1361 (Colo.1994) (cap applies *severally* to defendants, *after* apportionment; based on a $1 million noneconomic damage award, capped at $500,000, G.E. was liable for 35% of the $1 million actual noneconomic award ($350,000), not 35% of the capped amount ($175,000)). For a general discussion of noneconomic damages, see Symposium, Who Feels Their Pain? The Challenge of Noneconomic Damages in Civil Litigation, 55 DePaul L. Rev. 249 (2006).

4. Loss of Consortium and Companionship. As in other contexts, a spouse may have a claim for loss of consortium arising out of a product accident. Timms v. Verson Allsteel Press Co., 520 F.Supp. 1147 (N.D.Ga.1981) (husband's fingers crushed in press). Most courts have refused, in this context as in others, to permit claims by parents and by children for the loss of companionship arising out of injury to the other. See Siciliano v. Capitol City Shows, Inc., 475 A.2d 19 (N.H.1984) (4–1) (denying parents' claim for loss of society of minor children); Kershner v. Beloit Corp., 611 F.Supp. 943 (D.Me.1985) (denying children's claim for loss of injured parent's society). But see Ford Motor Co. v. Miles, 967 S.W.2d 377 (Tex.1998) (reaffirming its 1990 holding that the parent-child relationship supports loss of consortium, but refusing to extend that holding to include the step-parent-step-child relationship or sibling relationships).

5. Medical Monitoring Expenses. A new form of damages now recoverable in a number of jurisdictions, generally arising out of a person's exposure to a toxic substance, entails future expenses for the costs of monitoring the victim's medical condition over time to catch the onset of a disease—typically a cancerous or precancerous condition—at the earliest possible time. For a review of the cases, see Norwood v. Raytheon Co., 414 F.Supp.2d 659 (W.D. Tex. 2006) (predicting Texas courts would not recognize medical monitoring). See ch. 19, below, for discussion of medical monitoring in the toxic substances context.

6. Wrongful Death. Wrongful death actions in most jurisdictions are creatures of statute and, thus, the statutory language (as interpreted by the courts) governs the coverage of particular claims and the types of damages recoverable. Warranty actions may not be allowed. See Necktas v. General Motors Corp., 259 N.E.2d 234 (Mass.1970). Nor may claims for punitive damages. See Eisert v. Greenberg Roofing & Sheet Metal Co., 314 N.W.2d 226 (Minn.1982).

7. On compensatory damages, see 2 D. Owen, M.S. Madden, & M. Davis, Madden & Owen on Products Liability ch. 17 (3d ed. 2000).

---

2. EMOTIONAL DISTRESS

Kroger Co. v. Beck

Court of Appeals of Indiana, 1978.
176 Ind.App. 202, 375 N.E.2d 640.

■ STATON, JUDGE.

Phyllis Beck [recovered $2700 in small claims court against Kroger, which appeals, raising two issues:]

(1) Was there sufficient evidence of a contemporaneous physical injury to support the [damages award] for mental anguish?

(2) Was $2700 an excessive [award for mental anguish]?

[The judgment is supported by the evidence. Affirmed.]

I. Injury

[Phyllis Beck purchased a prepackaged sirloin steak at a Kroger grocery store.] Later the same day, she prepared the steak for dinner by cutting it into portions and broiling it. After serving the steak to her family for dinner, Phyllis Beck felt a sharp pain in the back of her throat when she placed the second bite of the steak into her mouth. She yanked the piece of steak from her mouth, ran into the bathroom, and vomited violently. In the steak, she found an inch-long piece of metal which was the tip end of a large hypodermic needle used for injecting animals. This sharp end of the hypodermic needle had punctured her throat.

Phyllis Beck testified at trial that she could not swear that she bled as a result of the puncture because of the location of the wound (soft palate at the back of the throat) and the vomiting. She did not go to a doctor, but rather administered first aid to herself for a month by gargling with Listerine. Although her mouth has healed and she does not have a scar, she is afraid that such an incident will reoccur. She further testified that she has not been able to enjoy eating steak or any other kind of meat since.

Her husband [testified] that at one point during dinner his wife screamed and went into the bathroom and vomited. She showed him the needle which she had removed from her mouth. He testified that after the incident "having meat or not having meat" was "a bone of contention." The incident "took, quite frankly, the fun out of eating for some time...."

II. Contemporaneous Physical Injury

Kroger argues, on appeal, that Beck failed to show any contemporaneous physical injury which would justify an award for the psychological injury. Kroger suggests that the "pricking" of Phyllis Beck's throat did not constitute an appreciable physical injury. Kroger maintains that the psychological injury she claims is only related to a fear of what might have happened had the needle been swallowed and was not directly related to the contemporaneous physical "pricking."

* * *

Kroger characterizes her injury as a "prick" followed by an unconnected fear. This framing of the factual basis of the complaint is not even remotely supported by the evidence. Moreover, [Kroger suggests] that a contemporaneous physical injury (which was uncontradicted, in that a "prick" is an injury) must be permanent or substantial to spawn mental distress [but the cases do not support this view].[1]

[Once the injury is proved, it is for the factfinder to decide] whether that injury was the catalyst producing the mental distress.

... Kroger does not maintain that a sharp object in a steak which "pricks" the throat and causes vomiting could not engender emotional distress. Phyllis Beck's testimony was unrefuted, and it established the

---

1. In Clark Restaurant Co. v. Rau, 179 N.E. 196 (Ohio 1931), a man swallowed some glass which scratched the walls of his stomach; he suffered pain and mental distress. The court held that [the swallowing of the glass "itself establishes an injury even though there be no other injury."]

In allowing recovery for mental distress, the courts have uniformly stated that there must be a contemporaneous physical injury which can serve as a predicate to recovery for the ensuing fright, apprehension, and mental anguish suffered. See Tuttle v. Meyer Dairy Products Co., 138 N.E.2d 429 (Ohio Ct.App. 1956). In *Meyer* there was no recovery because the plaintiff "expelled said glass [which had been in cottage cheese] from her mouth *without being cut or scratched thereby....*" (Emphasis added.) But, there is no requirement that the injury be severe to support the parasitic mental anguish claim. A causal connection is [enough].

legally required injury as well as the causal connection. The trial court did not [err in allowing recovery for mental distress] based on an uncontroverted contemporaneous physical injury.

III.   Damages

[Kroger argued that $2700 is excessive in the absence of specific evidence of the damages. However, the plaintiff's husband corroborated her account of the events, and her anxiety] was manifested immediately. She stated that she came back from the bathroom and "pulled everything off the table and was worried that someone else possibly might have had another part of maybe the same thing in their meat." She has had nightmares about the incident. Her husband testified that after the occurrence his wife "wasn't in the state of mind that she wanted to [prepare meat]."

[The factfinder could] consider the mental suffering caused by the anxiety and fear of the ensuing consequences. Phyllis Beck stated, "It lodge up there kind of almost—it almost gagged me. And for a few seconds, which seemed like hours to me, I thought I was going to choke to death. And this is why I vomited." Where realization of the physical effects which *can* be produced by the foreign object *did* produce the total emotional and physical result, recovery is allowed even if there is no showing that the fatal or deleterious consequence resulted in the particular case.

Phyllis Beck's fear of eating meat was also worthy of consideration by the court. She testified that meat had been a staple in her family's [diet,] that she was on a high protein diet and that meat as a source of protein and as a pleasure had been taken from her. [H]er loss should be compensable.

[Affirmed.]

N O T E S

1. Many early products liability mental anguish cases, like *Beck,* involve psychological reactions to foreign or deleterious substances in food and drink. Way v. Tampa Coca Cola Bottling Co., 260 So.2d 288 (Fla.App.1972) (plaintiff, sucking the partially frozen contents out of a bottle of Coke, encountered what "resembled a rat with the hair sucked off;" plaintiff's subsequent nausea, vomiting and physical discomfort lasted two days; recovery permitted).

Compare Ford v. Aldi, Inc., 832 S.W.2d 1 (Mo.App.1992), where a woman eating spinach she prepared became ill and threw up after discovering a ¾ inch insect on her fork. In Missouri, plaintiffs no longer must prove physical harm to recover for emotional distress, but the distress must be "medically diagnosable" or "medically significant." *Held*, because plaintiff admitted to having suffered no injury and to having had insufficient reason to consult a doctor, summary judgment for defendant affirmed.

2.   Physical Injuries. The great majority of courts require plaintiff to establish that the emotional distress was caused by—or that *it* caused—some injury, illness or other physical condition. See Payton v. Abbott Labs., 437 N.E.2d 171, 181 (Mass.1982) (suit by DES daughters for emotional distress due to increased likelihood of suffering future cancer). Most jurisdictions also require that the emotional distress would have been suffered by a reasonable person under the circumstances.

3. In Wilson v. Redken Labs., Inc., 562 S.W.2d 633, 635 (Ky.1978), plaintiff's hair fell out after it was treated with a defective hair conditioner made by the defendant. "Louise had to purchase wigs to cover the ugliness. The damage to her hair made her nervous and upset. When she was asked about it, Louise would cry. She was so distressed about her appearance that she slept in a wig." The jury awarded her $45 for medical expenses, $200 for the cost of wigs, and $30,000 for mental anguish. Reversing as to damages, the intermediate appellate court concluded that the amount awarded for mental anguish appeared at "first blush" to be a product of passion and prejudice. *Held,* reversed and judgment entered on jury verdict: "[I]f any person had a right to a 'first blush' in the real sense of [the] phrase, that person was Louise."

4. Continuing Psychic Harm. Long-term psychological or personality changes may be associated with the sudden trauma of a product-related injury. If the causal connection can be established, damages for such psychological damage may be recovered. In DeSantis v. Parker Feeders, Inc., 547 F.2d 357 (7th Cir.1976), for example, a 12–year–old boy was caught in the auger blades of a cattle feeder manufactured by the defendant. As a result, he lost his left leg below the knee and a portion of his right foot. A psychiatrist testified that the child was, after the accident, inordinately preoccupied with physical injuries and with feet and that it would be difficult for the child to have satisfactory emotional and sexual relationships as he grew older. The defendant objected to the psychiatrist's description of the child's condition as a "neurosis" and to compensation for emotional injuries which were outside the general realm of pain and suffering. The trial court allowed the jury to consider whether the defective product had caused "post-traumatic personality disorder." The jury found the plaintiff's physical and emotional harm, past and future, to be $800,000, and made no attempt to separate the physical from the emotional pain and suffering. *Held,* affirmed on appeal.

5. Pre–Impact Emotional Distress. Should passengers in a defective airplane be permitted to recover damages for their terror prior to an impending crash? What if the plane, shaking violently and hurtling toward the ground at speeds approaching the speed of sound, is pulled out of the impending disaster at the last moment by a skillful pilot? Should it make a difference, in other words, whether the impact actually occurs? Which is the stronger case? See Quill v. Trans World Airlines, Inc., 361 N.W.2d 438 (Minn.App.1985); In re Air Crash Disaster Near Chicago, Illinois on May 25, 1979, 507 F.Supp. 21 (N.D.Ill.1980). See generally Turezyn, When Circumstances Provide a Guarantee of Genuineness: Permitting Recovery for Pre–Impact Emotional Distress, 28 B.C.L.Rev. 881 (1987).

6. Fear of AIDS. In Hagan v. Coca–Cola Bottling Co., 804 So.2d 1234 (Fla.2001), the plaintiff consumed what she thought was a condom in a bottle of Coca–Cola, leading her to worry that she may have been exposed to the HIV virus. The court held that she could recover for emotional distress under the impact rule even though she suffered no accompanying immediate physical injuries, and even though she subsequently tested negative. Compare Johnson v. American National Red Cross, 578 S.E.2d 106 (Ga. 2003) (no emotional distress absent evidence of actual exposure to HIV, though actual injury not required).

7. Strict Liability in Tort. What special problems might there be for claims based not on negligence but upon *strict liability* for emotional distress resulting from a defective product? Cf. Shepard v. Superior Court, 142 Cal.Rptr. 612 (Ct.App. 1977)(2–1)(warranty and strict tort; bystanders). A number of courts have allowed recovery without much analysis. See, e.g., Jeannelle v. Thompson Medical Co., 613 F.Supp. 346 (E.D.Mo.1985); Gnirk v. Ford Motor Co., 572 F.Supp. 1201 (D.S.D. 1983). But see Rahn v. Gerdts, 455 N.E.2d 807 (Ill.App.1983).

How significant is the black letter language of § 402A, which subjects a product seller to liability for "physical harm"? See Walters v. Mintec/Int'l, 758 F.2d 73 (3d Cir.1985), holding that emotional distress is recoverable in strict tort if, but only if, physical harm is also suffered. Although one may assume that most jurisdictions would in any event carry over to strict tort the physical injury requirement from negligence, a number of § 402A jurisdictions have dropped the physical injury requirement in claims for negligent infliction of emotional distress. See, e.g., Culbert v. Sampson's Supermarkets Inc., 444 A.2d 433 (Me.1982).

Khan v. Shiley Inc.

Court of Appeal, Fourth District, 1990.
217 Cal.App.3d 848, 266 Cal.Rptr. 106.

■ SONENSHINE, ASSOCIATE JUSTICE.

[Plaintiffs appeal from a summary judgment against them in their action involving an allegedly defective mechanical heart valve. They contend that the court erred in concluding that because the valve implanted in Judy Khan's heart had not yet malfunctioned, their claims were speculative and their lawsuit premature.]

Judy Khan was 33 years old when, on July 29, 1983, a Bjork–Shiley convexo-concave valve was implanted in her heart to replace a diseased mitral valve. She had first learned about her condition six months earlier and was told she would die without the implant. Before the surgery, Khan had been experiencing fatigue, double vision, exhaustion, and shortness of breath. Within two months of the operation, her symptoms were gone and she was "feeling good about life."

Khan had been advised of the risks associated with mechanical heart valves including the potential for blood clots and the possibility the valve would be rejected by her body. She also knew she would always be a slave to blood thinner medication. She was not, however, told there was a risk the valve might fracture.

In November 1985, Khan's surgeon informed her Shiley had told him the implanted valve was within a group of valves being recalled due to a propensity to fracture.[4] He stated there had been numerous reports the valves were "falling apart and malfunctioning without notice resulting in death to the patients." According to information he received from Shiley, the risk of a second open-heart surgery was even higher than the risk of a malfunction. Further, because any malfunction could be fatal, she should go to the nearest hospital if her valve ceased to operate.

---

4. Shiley's "Dear Doctor" letter dated October 14, 1985, indicates the valve in question had "a statistical fracture rate of 11 per 1,000 through three years of implantation."

Since learning of the recall, Khan's life has not been the same. Although she "made it through the surgery in excellent condition, [she] still face[s] the possibility of the valve falling apart inside of [her] heart and killing [her]. Knowing that [she] face[s] almost certain death without notice has made living a nightmare." She has been treated by three different mental health professionals for her emotional problems and has also experienced physical symptoms associated with her anxiety [including stomach cramps and spasms, headaches, and abnormal heart rhythms.]

[Khan and her husband sued Shiley Inc. and its parent, Pfizer, Inc., seeking both compensatory and punitive damages, and alleging causes of action in negligence, fraud and misrepresentation, breach of warranty, strict liability in tort, and intentional and negligent infliction of emotional distress. The complaint alleged that "an extraordinary number" of the valves implanted to date have malfunctioned causing death or other serious injury. The complaint acknowledged Khan's valve "has not yet malfunctioned," but alleges it] "is defective and likely to malfunction at any moment because of the conduct of the defendant[s] as alleged herein, thereby exposing [Khan] to the constant threat of imminent death or other serious physical injury and the anxiety, fear and emotional distress that results therefrom."

The complaint also alleged [that defendant misrepresented the characteristics and safety of the valve and concealed material and adverse information regarding it.] Examples of defendants' conduct included misrepresentation as to the valve's safety and propensity to fail, failure to adequately test the valve, failure to provide adequate warnings which fairly reflected known risks, making of understatements in reports as to the failure rate when they knew the rate was much higher, and omission of material facts showing the valve had a history of strut fracture....

[Defendants moved for summary judgment, claiming that] all heart valves have an inherent risk of failure and all heart valve recipients always face a risk of death. Further, the risk Khan's valve would fail actually decreased over time; the risk of fracture in heart valve recipients in their sixth postoperative year, such as Khan, is approximately 0.225 percent per annum. In essence, it was defendants' position California law does not recognize plaintiffs' causes of action "based upon their purported emotional distress for an alleged fear of future malfunction." Relying on Khan's 1988 deposition testimony, they asserted the valve had not malfunctioned and, in fact, had "saved [her] life through its effective performance for nearly five years."

Plaintiffs opposed the motion, insisting they had a legitimate claim for all medically verified emotional and physical injuries sustained by Khan after she learned of her dilemma. They argued the valve was defective, had been declared by the Food and Drug Administration (FDA) to be "adulter-ated,"[7] and, to date, had "killed and injured at least 243 people."[8]

[Tentatively granting defendant's summary judgment motion, the trial court noted that] "while some valves of this type have failed, there's no indication this valve has failed or will fail." It found "[t]here's been nobody injured yet." And, just before uttering its final decision, it exclaimed: "We've been asked to speculate about something that may or may not happen, and there is no allegation, nothing that's been presented in the opposition papers, that show any basis now that there is a defect [and] it thus is premature." . . .

Plaintiffs contend [that] the court erred in acquiescing to defendants' argument that "malfunction" is an element in a products liability lawsuit. They insist the owner of a product, functioning as intended but containing an inherent defect which may cause the product to fail in the future, has an action against the manufacturer. Plaintiffs are mistaken.

* * *

No matter which theory [of liability] is utilized, however, where a plaintiff alleges a product is defective, proof that the product has malfunc-tioned is essential to establish liability for an injury *caused by the defect*. Indeed, as stated in Greenman v. Yuba Power Products, Inc., 377 P.2d 897 (Cal.1963), "A manufacturer is strictly liable in tort when an article [it] places on the market, knowing that it is to be used without inspection for defects, proves to have a *defect that causes injury* to a human being." [Citations.]

This essential element of causation is missing here. Khan's alleged injury was not caused by any defect in the valve. Rather, it was caused, if at all, by the knowledge the valve may, at some future time, fracture. As counsel for defendants asserted at the hearing below: "The issue here is whether [the valve has] malfunctioned or not, and all the discovery in the world isn't going to shed any light on that. If her valve does malfunction, she will have a cause of action. She'll still have to prove it was a defective product, but that hasn't happened yet."

[P]laintiffs contend even if product malfunction is a prerequisite in a strict liability context, it has no bearing on causes of action for negligence,[12] breach of warranty, or fraud. They are partly correct. A cause of action does not presently exist under any theory premised on the *risk* the valve

7. Documents which plaintiffs obtained from the FDA disclosed that in December 1985, after Shiley voluntarily recalled the valves, the FDA notified Shiley the recall was classified as Class I [which meant] the FDA found the valve represented "a situation in which there is a reasonable probability that the use of, or exposure to, a violative product will cause serious adverse health conse-quences or death." . . .

8. Of the approximately 81,000 valves implanted as of April 1988, Shiley had re-ceived reports of 243 fractures. Plaintiffs as-sert two-thirds of those implantees have died.

12. Plaintiffs contend Vanoni v. West-ern Airlines, 56 Cal.Rptr. 115 (Ct.App.1967) supports their position that product malfunc-tion is not required to establish negligence. In *Vanoni*, the plaintiffs alleged they suffered shock to their nervous systems when they thought the airplane in which they were trav-eling was going to crash. The trial court sustained a demurrer without leave to amend and the appellate court reversed, noting alle-gations of shock to one's nervous system are sufficient to state a physical injury. The case does not, however, purport to hold that one's fear something may happen in the future is, without more, actionable.

may malfunction in the future. This includes negligence, i.e., failure to warn, and breach of warranty. Allegations of fraud, however, are in a class by themselves.

For purposes of establishing fraud, it matters not that the valve implanted in Khan's heart is still functioning, arguably as intended. Unlike the other theories, in which the safety and efficacy of the *product* is assailed, the fraud claim impugns defendants' *conduct*.

[The plaintiffs assert that the defendants intentionally] misrepresented the characteristics and safety of the valve while concealing other material, adverse information. Specifically, they contend defendants misrepresented the valve's propensity to fail, and omitted material facts showing the product had a history of strut failure even before one was implanted into Khan's heart. . . . Plaintiffs relied on and were induced by these representations in making their selection. They would not otherwise have selected the Shiley valve; indeed, at least six other mechanical heart valves were available at the time of Khan's surgery.

Plaintiffs' complaint contained allegations sufficient to state a cause of action for fraud [and, thus,] summary judgment [thereon] was improper.

We reach this conclusion notwithstanding defendants' position that the unprecedented cause of action plaintiffs seek to establish is contrary to public policy. We recognize the role public policy has played, and continues to play, in the torts arena. However, our decision neither establishes a new cause of action nor drastically extends existing law.[14] It merely confirms that a manufacturer of a product may be liable for fraud when it conceals material product information from potential users. This is true whether the product is a mechanical heart valve or frozen yogurt.

[Reversed.]

NOTES

1. Accord, Angus v. Shiley Inc., 989 F.2d 142 (3d Cir.1993) (plaintiff must prove that his product is defective, "a prerequisite to liability in a products liability action"); Behnke v. Shiley, Inc., 487 N.W.2d 661 (Wis.App.1992) (no evidence that valve, working properly 10 years after implant, was defective).

The first "stress and anxiety" trial over these particular Shiley heart valves was held in late 1993, but the parties settled the litigation as the jury began to deliberate. In a confidential agreement, Shiley Inc., owned by Pfizer, settled 260

---

14. Asserting the implanted valve has saved and, for more than five years, has sustained *Khan's* life, defendants maintain there are compelling reasons why a *new cause of action* should not be created. They contend if manufacturers faced liability to users of products based on product failures experienced by other users, "there would be no incentive to develop or manufacture heart valves or other critical medical devices and drugs. The consequences of such a drastic extension of existing law would be disastrous for health care in this country and would inundate the judicial system with an avalanche of premature and speculative claims." At oral argument, counsel for defendants exclaimed that allowing plaintiffs to proceed with their fraud theory would similarly have a chilling effect on the manufacture of critical medical devices.

claims by plaintiffs worried that their heart valves would break and kill them (4 had already fractured but not yet malfunctioned). Pfizer stated: "[T]here is no basis for people with functioning valves to recover damages, but the company wants to put this time consuming and costly litigation behind it and to focus on more productive issues." Plaintiffs reportedly had depositions from former Shiley employees "alleging the company recycled badly made valves and that employees drank beer and smoked marijuana during working hours." Liab. Week 3 (Sept. 13, 1993).

2. Compare Bravman v. Baxter Healthcare Corp., 984 F.2d 71 (2d Cir.1993), in which the district court dismissed a claim based upon a noisy heart valve that could be heard at a distance of thirty feet, kept the plaintiff from sleeping, and rendered him despondent. Reversing, and allowing the case to proceed, the court concluded that although the life-saving valve was not defectively designed, at some level of noisiness (characterized by the trial court as a "tonitruous jangle") patients would suffer injury and the manufacturer would have a duty to warn (doctors):

> Unlike the purely psychological terror suffered by the protagonist in Edgar Allan Poe's "The Tell–Tale Heart," Bravman's complaint, that his artificial heart valve creates excessive noise . . . is objectively verifiable. While [his] claim is unusual, it is by no means nonsensical. At some level, noise can constitute a cognizable harm.

Id. at 74.

Pearsall v. Emhart Industries, Inc.

United States District Court, Eastern District of Pennsylvania, 1984.
599 F.Supp. 207.

■ KATZ, DISTRICT JUDGE.

[Plaintiff sued the manufacturers of heat and smoke alarms installed in her home, claiming that defects in the alarms were substantial factors in causing the deaths of her husband and two children who died in a fire in their home. The jury found for the plaintiff and awarded substantial damages, including $400,000 for the plaintiff's emotional distress. By post-trial motions, defendants challenged several rulings, including the submission of the emotional distress claim to the jury.]

Defendants argue that plaintiff's claim for emotional distress should not have been submitted to the jury since the plaintiff did not witness the deaths of her husband and children from the fire. In recent years Pennsylvania has expanded the right of a bystander who "witnesses" a traumatic event to recover for emotional distress. In Sinn v. Burd, 404 A.2d 672 (Pa.1979), the Pennsylvania Supreme Court held that a mother who saw her own child struck and killed by a negligently operated vehicle could recover. The Court's decision placed much emphasis on its conclusion that the injuries to the bystander were foreseeable. The Supreme Court has applied a three factor test to determine whether injuries to a bystander from witnessing a wrongful death are foreseeable:

> (1) Whether plaintiff was located near the scene of the accident as contrasted with one who was a distance away from it. (2) Whether the shock

resulted from a direct emotional impact upon plaintiff from the sensory and contemporaneous observance of the accident, as contrasted with learning of the accident from others after its occurrence. (3) Whether plaintiff and the victim were closely related, as contrasted with an absence of any relationship or the presence of only a distant relationship.

Yandrich v. Radic, 433 A.2d 459, 461 (Pa.1981); Sinn v. Burd, 404 A.2d 672, 684 (Pa.1979) (quoting from Dillon v. Legg, 441 P.2d 912 (Cal.1968)). In *Sinn,* the Court found that "[w]here the bystander is a mother who witnessed the violent death of her small child and the emotional shock emanated directly from personal observation of the event, we hold as a matter of law that the mental distress and its effects is a foreseeable injury." The Court specifically noted that it was not considering the case of a parent who was merely notified of an accident but was not present at the scene of the injury or death.

In Yandrich v. Radic, 433 A.2d 459 (Pa.1981) the Pennsylvania Supreme Court addressed the issue it had expressly left open in *Sinn*— whether a parent who was neither a witness to the accident nor in the immediate vicinity thereof, but arrived at the scene after his son had already been taken to the hospital could maintain an action for negligent infliction of emotional distress. Applying the foreseeability standards enunciated in *Sinn* the Court found that the father could not bring such an action. The Court found that the plaintiff was not located near the scene of the accident and that the shock to the plaintiff did not result from the sensory and contemporaneous observance of the accident.

I find that the facts of the instant case support a claim by Mrs. Pearsall for infliction of emotional distress. Upon arriving home, Mrs. Pearsall witnessed the fire-fighters bringing the blaze under control. She testified that she stood near the bodies of her husband and children at the scene of the fire. She arrived at the hospital shortly before the ambulance arrived and witnessed the bodies of her husband and daughter being carried off the ambulance. She testified that she couldn't pick up her daughter because "she [Laurie] was real hot." Mrs. Pearsall also offered substantial evidence proving her claims of subsequent emotional distress.

That Mrs. Pearsall arrived at the scene of the fire shortly after her husband and children had actually died in no way diminishes the foreseeability of her emotional distress. Upon arriving home she witnessed the fire and had no idea whether her husband and children were alive or dead. She saw and later touched the bodies of her family as the fire that took their lives was still smoldering. Her emotional distress was not caused merely by others notifying her of the accident. Instead, plaintiff's shock and emotional distress resulted from the direct impact upon her senses of the fire and its aftermath. I am satisfied that the emotional distress of this mother witnessing the fire and its carnage is foreseeable to a manufacturer of defective alarms and, therefore, meets the standards enunciated in *Sinn* and *Yandrich*. See also Bliss v. Allentown Public Library, 497 F.Supp. 487 (E.D.Pa.1980)(direct visual observation of accident unnecessary to state claim for negligent infliction of emotional distress); General Motors Corp. v.

Grizzle, 642 S.W.2d 837 (Tex.App.1982) (mother arriving upon scene moments after accident may recover for infliction of emotional distress) . . .

[Defendants' post-trial motions denied.]

NOTES

1. "Bystanders"—Dillon v. Legg. Like Pennsylvania, roughly half the states have adopted some form of the *Dillon v. Legg* foreseeability guidelines for the emotional distress of bystanders, although there are only a small number of cases applying the guidelines in the products liability context. See Culbert v. Sampson's Supermarkets Inc., 444 A.2d 433 (Me.1982) (while spoon feeding her infant some Beech Nut turkey and rice baby food, mother observed him choke and gag on, and then spit up, hard object); Shepard v. Superior Court, 142 Cal.Rptr. 612 (Ct.App. 1977) (after being side-swiped by another car, rear door popped open, throwing brother and sister onto highway; parents and brother observed sister being run over and killed by other car).

2. In Thing v. La Chusa, 771 P.2d 814, 829–830 (Cal.1989), in an effort to curb the spread of the *Dillon* foreseeability factors to wider and wider situations, the California Supreme Court converted the factors from "guidelines" into necessary *elements* for a bystander's emotional distress damages claim: "[A] plaintiff may recover damages for emotional distress caused by observing the negligently inflicted injury of a third person if, but only if, said plaintiff: (1) is closely related to the injury victim; (2) is present at the scene of the injury-producing event at the time it occurs and is then aware that it is causing injury to the victim; and (3) as a result suffers serious emotional distress—a reaction beyond that which would be anticipated in a disinterested witness and which is not an abnormal response to the circumstances."

In Ortiz v. HPM Corp., 285 Cal.Rptr. 728 (Ct.App.1991), plaintiff found the limp but alive, oxygen-depleted and bleeding body of her co-worker husband, who had been fixing a plastic injection molding machine, still being crushed between a giant cylinder and a stationary part of the machine. *Held*, the injury-producing event was still occurring when plaintiff found her husband, and she was then aware that it was causing injury to him, such that *Thing*'s contemporaneous observation requirement was met. Note, however, that workers generally will be precluded from recovery of emotional distress damages from observing a co-worker's injuries because they ordinarily are unrelated by blood or marriage. But when the worker is herself operating the defective product at the time a co-worker is killed by it, recovery for emotional damage resulting from witnessing the death is permissible. Bray v. Marathon Corp., 588 S.E.2d 93 (S.C. 2003).

3. Zone of Danger. Some courts still apply the "zone of danger" test to bystander cases. See, e.g., Jeannelle v. Thompson Medical Co., 613 F.Supp. 346 (E.D.Mo.1985) (brother in zone of danger could assert claim for emotional distress from observing mother and brother violently attacked by person deranged by defective drug); Levit v. General Motors Corp., 682 F.Supp. 386 (N.D.Ill.1988)(claim denied where plaintiff was away from home when refrigerator burst into flames).

Are other passengers in the zone of danger when an airbag deploys and kills another occupant of the car? In Sullivan v. Ford Motor Co., 2000 WL 343777 (S.D.N.Y.2000), plaintiff observed the lid of the passenger-side airbag strike her nephew, partially decapitating and killing him. What result under the zone of danger test? Under *Dillon*?

In addition to satisfying a *Dillon* or zone-of-danger proximity test, bystanders must also prove the other elements of an emotional distress claim—including in most jurisdictions physical impact or injury from the emotional distress. E.g., AALAR, Ltd. v. Francis, 716 So.2d 1141 (Ala. 1998).

4. "Users." A couple of decisions have allowed third party recovery, even where the *Dillon* test could not be met, on the theory that the plaintiff was a *user* of the product and hence really a first party to whom a duty was directly owed rather than a bystander. Kately v. Wilkinson, 195 Cal.Rptr. 902 (Ct.App.1983) (father and daughter were towing daughter's best friend on water skis when steering locked, causing boat to circle and hit skier, partially dismembering her; father and daughter, whose presence was legally required to watch skier, were both foreseeable users); Gnirk v. Ford Motor Co., 572 F.Supp. 1201 (D.S.D.1983) (when mother left infant in car to open gate, transmission slipped from park to reverse, and car traveled into pond where it disappeared). But see Slaton v. Vansickle, 872 P.2d 929 (Okl.1994) (no bystander recovery for emotional distress available in Oklahoma; user of rifle that accidentally discharged, killing girl, had no claim).

5. Doctors and Dentists. In Washington State Phys. Ins. Exch. & Assn. v. Fisons Corp., 858 P.2d 1054 (Wash.1993), a doctor prescribed a drug for a 2–year-old patient who suffered a severe reaction as a result. The child's parents sued the manufacturer for failing to provide the doctor with adequate warnings and sued the doctor for malpractice; the doctor cross-claimed against the drug company for contribution, emotional distress (loss of interest in practice, deteriorated relationship with family from despondency), damages for loss of reputation, and attorneys' fees under the unfair trade practices act. Discovery documents which defendant at first suppressed but finally delivered included an internal company memo revealing that the company continued to sell the drug knowing that it was causing a toxicity "epidemic" of brain damage and death and that the dosage recommendations were significantly wrong due to "poor clinical judgment." After the memo was revealed, the defendant promptly settled with the parents for $6.9 million, and the doctor's case proceeded against the manufacturer. *Held* (4–3), the doctor's award of over $2 million for emotional distress damages was not allowable under the definition of "harm" in the state's products liability act; *further held* (7–0), the $1 million verdict for the doctor under the trade practices act for loss of reputation, and the nearly $.5 million award for attorneys' fees (based on a 1.5 lodestar multiple), affirmed.

A dentist administers nitrous oxide to a patient, thinking it is oxygen because the valves on her anesthesia machine are mislabeled. The patient dies. The dentist is sued for malpractice, subjected to a criminal investigation, loses her practice, and as a consequence of all this suffers a deep depression. Should she be permitted to maintain a strict tort action for her emotional distress against the manufacturer of the anesthesia machine? Cf. Kennedy v. McKesson Co., 448 N.E.2d 1332 (N.Y.1983).

6. Strict Liability. As mentioned above, some states hold that emotional distress damages are predicated on fault, precluding their recovery—by bystanders or direct victims—in strict liability. E.g., Pasquale v. Speed Prod. Eng'g, 654 N.E.2d 1365 (Ill.1995) (clutch parts on race car burst through defective bellhousing and flew into crowd of spectators, partially decapitating plaintiff's wife, revealing the interior of her head including the backs of her eyeballs, and spewing bone marrow, blood, and brain matter on plaintiff's face with such force as to leave marks for weeks; *held*, quoting *Shepard* n. 1, no recovery for emotional distress in strict tort).

7. Cancerphobia. Emotional distress concerning future consequences from exposure to toxic substances, also called cancerphobia, is examined in ch. 19 below.

8. See generally Mead, Recovery for Psychic Harm in Strict Products Liability: Has the Interest in Psychic Equilibrium Come the Final Mile?, 59 St. John's L.Rev. 457 (1985); Silverman, Recovery for Emotional Distress in Strict Products Liability, 61 Chi.–Kent L.Rev. 545 (1985).

---

3.   ECONOMIC LOSS AND PROPERTY DAMAGE

Cooperative Power Assn. v. Westinghouse Electric Corp.

Supreme Court of North Dakota, 1992.
493 N.W.2d 661.

■ JOHNSON, JUSTICE.

[Certified question from federal district court on whether manufacturer of machine sold in commercial transaction may be liable in negligence or strict products liability for economic loss caused by failure of a component part which directly damages machine. Question answered: "No."]

Cooperative Power Association (CPA) owns and operates an electrical generating station, the Coal Creek Station, in Underwood, North Dakota. CPA uses step-up transformers to increase the voltage of electricity for transmission over power lines. Westinghouse Electric Corporation manufactures step-up transformers. [Westinghouse sold CPA a defective transformer, resulting in an electrical arc in a bushing that damaged the bushing and contaminated the transformer coils with metal particles, requiring replacement of the bushings and rewinding of the coils. Westinghouse replaced the bushings, but refused to pay for rewinding the coils. CPA sued Westinghouse, alleging breach of express warranty, breach of contract, negligence, and negligent misrepresentation, seeking damages of $1.6 million for the costs of repairing the transformer and temporary replacement.] Westinghouse moved for summary judgment dismissal of CPA's tort claims, asserting that, because CPA claimed damages only to the transformer, CPA's sole remedy was in contract. [The federal court] certified the present question about whether a manufacturer of a machine sold in a commercial transaction may be liable in negligence or strict liability for economic loss for damage to the machine only.[5]

[CPA argues that products liability law in North Dakota focuses on the defective and dangerous product, not the type of damage incurred. Westinghouse responds that contract law, not tort law, applies in a commercial setting when a defective product fails and damages only itself.]

---

5. In the context of products liability cases, economic loss generally means pecuniary damage that occurs through loss of value or use of the goods sold or the cost of repair together with consequential lost profits when there has been no claim of personal injury or damage to other property. E.g., Seely v. White Motor Co., 403 P.2d 145 (Cal.1965). CPA's complaint alleges losses which meet that definition of economic loss.

In East River Steamship Corp. v. Transamerica Delaval, Inc., 476 U.S. 858, 871 (1986), the United States Supreme Court considered a similar issue in the context of admiralty law. The plaintiffs, charterers of four ships, sued the manufacturer of turbines installed in the ships in strict liability and negligence, alleging that the turbines were defectively designed. The plaintiffs alleged that the defects, which caused damage to the turbines themselves, entitled them to damages for the cost of repairs and for lost income while the ships were out of service. The Court, applying products-liability concepts to admiralty law, unanimously held "that a manufacturer in a commercial relationship has no duty under either a negligence or strict products-liability theory to prevent a product from injuring itself."

The Court outlined the three approaches for determining whether an action may be brought in tort for damage to the product itself: (1) the majority approach, which precludes tort actions if a defective product damages only itself, see Seely v. White Motor Co., Jones & Laughlin Steel Corp. v. Johns–Manville Sales Corp., 626 F.2d 280 (3d Cir.1980); (2) the minority approach, which permits tort actions if a defective product damages only itself regardless of whether the defect created an unreasonable risk of harm, see Santor v. A & M Karagheusian, Inc., 207 A.2d 305 (N.J.1965); and (3) the intermediate "degree-of-risk" or "qualitative" approach, which differentiates between disappointed and endangered users and permits only the latter to sue in tort under an analysis focusing on the nature of the defect, the type of risk, and the manner in which the product is damaged. See Pennsylvania Glass Sand Corp. v. Caterpillar Tractor Co., 652 F.2d 1165 (3d Cir.1981) [permits tort action for damage to a defective product resulting from an unreasonably dangerous condition and precludes tort action for damage resulting from a non-dangerous impairment in the quality of the product]; Northern Power & Engineering Corp. v. Caterpillar Tractor Co., 623 P.2d 324 (Alaska 1981) [permits tort action if a defective product creates a potentially dangerous situation and the product is damaged as a proximate result of the danger under calamitous circumstances].

The Supreme Court rejected the intermediate approach, concluding that it was too uncertain to enable manufacturers to structure their business behavior. The Court said that a distinction which rests on the manner in which the product was damaged, either by gradual deterioration and internal breakage or by a calamitous event, was not persuasive, because, by definition, no person or other property was damaged. Economic losses occurring as a result of a calamitous event essentially represented the failure of the purchaser to receive the benefit of the bargain, which is traditionally the core concern of contract law.

In analyzing the minority approach, the Court recognized that it fostered the safety and insurance rationales underlying tort liability and eliminated an arbitrary distinction between a defective product damaging only itself and a defective product causing bodily injury or damage to other property. However, the Court rejected the minority approach because it failed to keep tort liability and contract law in separate spheres and to maintain a realistic limitation on damages.

In adopting the majority approach, the Supreme Court stressed several factors: (1) tort concerns with safety are reduced when a product damages only itself; (2) damage to only the product itself means the product has not met the customer's expectations and is most naturally understood as a warranty claim; (3) warranty law is well suited for commercial controversies, which generally do not involve large disparities in bargaining power, so the parties can contractually set the terms of their agreements and, within limits, disclaim warranties or limit remedies while allowing purchasers to obtain the benefit of their bargain; (4) warranty law has built-in limitations on liability based on privity and the requirement of foreseeability of consequential damages as a result of a breach, whereas tort law confers a duty to the public generally and permits recovery for all foreseeable claims, which could subject manufacturers to indefinite economic losses by a purchaser's customers; and (5) recovery under warranty law establishes a bright line for damages to the product itself and avoids the uncertainty inherent in any attempt by courts to limit purely economic damages in tort.

The Court's rationale focuses on the different types of interests protected by tort and contract law. Tort liability protects a consumer's interest in freedom from injury regardless of the existence of an agreement between the parties. Underlying tort liability is the recognition that buyers and sellers of consumer products are generally in an unequal bargaining position and courts may desire to provide protection for the public from unsafe products beyond that provided by contract law. Tort law imposes responsibility on manufacturers of defective products because they are best able to encourage safer manufacture and design and to allocate the costs of injury arising from unsafe products. [Citations.]

A contractual duty arises from society's interest in the performance of promises and has been traditionally concerned with the fulfillment of reasonable economic expectations. Society's need to spread losses is substantially lessened in commercial transactions where damage is to only the product itself, because those losses essentially relate to the benefit of the bargain between business entities. That loss is most frequently measured by the cost of repairs, the difference in the value of the product, or consequential damages attributable to the failure of the product to perform as expected. See fn. 5. Those losses are based upon, and flow from, the purchaser's loss of the benefit of the contractual bargain and are the type for which a warranty action provides redress.

In *East River* the Supreme Court aptly explained the rationale for distinguishing tort and contract law:

* * *

Damage to a product itself is most naturally understood as a warranty claim. Such damage means simply that the product has not met the customer's expectations, or, in other words, that the customer has received "insufficient product value." See J. White and R. Summers, Uniform Commercial Code 406 (2d ed. 1980). The maintenance of product value and quality is precisely the purpose of express and implied warranties. See UCC § 2–313 (express warranty), § 2–314 (implied warranty of merchantability), and § 2–315 (warranty of fitness for a particular purpose). Therefore, a claim of a nonworking product can be brought as a breach-of-warranty action. Or, if the customer prefers, it can reject the product or revoke its acceptance and sue for breach of contract. See UCC §§ 2–601, 2–608, 2–612.

Since *East River*, other courts have followed the majority approach in commercial transactions and precluded tort actions when a product damages only itself. [Citing cases from 3d Cir., Fla., Nev., N.M., Mich., Ohio, Okla., Pa., & Wyo.]

These cases recognize that, in commercial transactions, the policy considerations for ignoring the parties' contractual obligations are reduced, because the parties are free to negotiate regarding the specifications for a product and the risk of loss. In commercial transactions, those cases preserve the distinction between tort liability and contract law.

CPA nevertheless argues that a "risk of harm" analysis is applicable to commercial transactions because that analysis provides manufacturers with incentive to produce safe products. CPA asserts that it is only through fortuitous circumstances that this defective product did not damage other property or people in the area. Although society has a strong interest in safe products, the rules of negligence and strict liability for damage to property other than the product itself and for personal injury adequately protect that interest and provide manufacturers with incentive to produce safe products.... We should also strive for a statement of liability principles which is capable of being communicated to a jury without intervention by a Professor of Tort Law. We believe the rationale of *East River* is persuasive in commercial transactions involving damage only to the product itself....

We adopt the rationale of *East River* and conclude that a manufacturer of a machine sold in a commercial transaction may not be held liable in negligence or strict liability for economic loss caused by a failure of a component part of the machine which causes damage to the machine only.

Casa Clara Condominium Ass'n, Inc. v. Charley Toppino & Sons, Inc.

Supreme Court of Florida, 1993.
620 So.2d 1244.

■ McDonald, Justice.

[The issue is whether a homeowner can recover for purely economic losses from a concrete supplier under a negligence theory. We agree with the district court that such a recovery cannot be had.]

Charley Toppino & Sons, Inc., a dissolved corporation, supplied concrete for numerous construction projects in Monroe County. Apparently, some of the concrete supplied by Toppino contained a high content of salt that caused the reinforcing steel inserted in the concrete to rust, which, in turn, caused the concrete to crack and break off. The petitioners own condominium units and single-family homes built with, and now allegedly damaged by, Toppino's concrete. In separate actions the homeowners sued numerous defendants and included claims against Toppino for breach of [warranty, products liability, and negligence.] The circuit court dismissed all counts against Toppino in each case. On appeal the district court applied the economic loss rule and held that, because no person was injured and no other property damaged, the homeowners had no cause of action against Toppino in tort. . . .

Plaintiffs find a tort remedy attractive because it often permits the recovery of greater damages than an action on a contract and may avoid the conditions of a contract. William L. Prosser, The Borderland of Tort and Contract in Selected Topics on the Law of Torts, 380, 425 (Thomas M. Cooley Lectures, 4th Series, 1953). The distinction between "tort recovery for physical injuries and warranty recovery for economic loss" rests

> on an understanding of the nature of the responsibility a manufacturer must undertake in distributing his products. He can appropriately be held liable for physical injuries caused by defects by requiring his goods to match a standard of safety defined in terms of conditions that create unreasonable risks of harm. *He cannot be held for the level of performance of his products in the consumer's business unless he agrees that the product was designed to meet the consumer's demands.*

Seely v. White Motor Co., 403 P.2d 145, 151 (Cal.1965) (emphasis supplied). An individual consumer, on the other hand,

> should not be charged at the will of the manufacturer with bearing the risk of physical injury when he buys a product on the market. *He can, however, be fairly charged with the risk that the product will not match his economic expectations unless the manufacturer agrees that it will.*

Id. (emphasis supplied). *Seely* sets out the economic loss rule, which prohibits tort recovery when a product damages itself, causing economic loss, but does not cause personal injury or damage to any property other than itself.[2] E.g., East River Steamship Corp. v. Transamerica Delaval, Inc., 476 U.S. 858 (1986); Florida Power & Light Co. v. Westinghouse Elec. Corp., 510 So.2d 899 (Fla.1987); Danforth v. Acorn Structures, Inc., 608 A.2d 1194 (Del.1992). The rule is "the fundamental boundary between contract law, which is designed to enforce the expectancy interests of the parties, and tort law, which imposes a duty of reasonable care and thereby encourages citizens to avoid causing physical harm to others." Sidney R. Barrett, Jr., Recovery of Economic Loss in Tort for Construction Defects: A Critical Analysis, 40 S.C.L.Rev. 891, 894 (1989).

---

2. The economic loss rule has been adopted in a majority of jurisdictions . . . The rule applies in Florida. [Citations.]

Economic loss has been defined as "damages for inadequate value, costs of repair and replacement of the defective product, or consequent loss of profits—without any claim of personal injury or damage to other property." [Citation.] It includes "the diminution in the value of the product because it is inferior in quality and does not work for the general purposes for which it was manufactured and sold." [Citation.] In other words, economic losses are "disappointed economic expectations," which are protected by contract law, rather than tort law. [Citations.] This is the basic difference between contract law, which protects expectations, and tort law, which is determined by the duty owed to an injured party. For recovery in tort "there must be a showing of harm above and beyond disappointed expectations. A buyer's desire to enjoy the benefit of his bargain is not an interest that tort law traditionally protects." Redarowicz v. Ohlendorf, 441 N.E.2d 324, 327 (Ill.1982).

The homeowners are seeking purely economic damages—no one has sustained any physical injuries and no property, other than the structures built with Toppino's concrete, has sustained any damage. They argue that holding them to contract remedies is unfair and that homeowners in general should be excepted from the operation of the economic loss rule. We disagree.

In tort a manufacturer or producer of goods "is liable whether or not it is negligent because 'public policy demands that responsibility be fixed wherever it will most effectively reduce the hazards to life and health inherent in defective products that reach the market.'" *East River* (quoting Escola v. Coca Cola Bottling Co., 150 P.2d 436, 441 (Cal.1944) (Traynor, J., concurring)). Thus, the "basic function of tort law is to shift the burden of loss from the injured plaintiff to one who is at fault ... or to one who is better able to bear the loss and prevent its occurrence." [Barrett article, above.] The purpose of a duty in tort is to protect society's interest in being free from harm, Spring Motors Distributors, Inc. v. Ford Motor Co., 489 A.2d 660 (N.J.1985), and the cost of protecting society from harm is borne by society in general. Contractual duties, on the other hand, come from society's interest in the performance of promises. When only economic harm is involved, the question becomes "whether the consuming public as a whole should bear the cost of economic losses sustained by those who failed to bargain for adequate contract remedies." [Citation.]

We are urged to make an exception to the economic loss doctrine for homeowners. Buying a house is the largest investment many consumers ever make, see Conklin v. Hurley, 428 So.2d 654 (Fla.1983), and homeowners are an appealing, sympathetic class. If a house causes economic disappointment by not meeting a purchaser's expectations, the resulting failure to receive the benefit of the bargain is a core concern of contract, not tort, law. *East River*. There are protections for homebuyers, however, such as statutory warranties, the general warranty of habitability, and the duty of sellers to disclose defects, as well as the ability of purchasers to inspect houses for defects. Coupled with homebuyers' power to bargain over price, these protections must be viewed as sufficient when compared with the mischief that could be caused by allowing tort recovery for purely economic losses. Therefore, we again "hold contract principles more appropriate than tort principles for recovering economic loss without an accompanying physical injury or property damage." *Florida Power & Light*. If we held otherwise, "contract law would drown in a sea of tort." *East River*. We refuse to hold that homeowners are not subject to the economic loss rule.

The homeowners also argue that Toppino's concrete damaged "other" property because the individual components and items of building material, not the homes themselves, are the products they purchased. We disagree. The character of a loss determines the appropriate remedies, and, to determine the character of a loss, one must look to the product purchased by the plaintiff, not the product sold by the defendant. King v. Hilton–Davis, 855 F.2d 1047 (3d Cir.1988). Generally, house buyers have little or no interest in how or where the individual components of a house are obtained. They are content to let the builder produce the finished product, i.e., a house. These homeowners bought finished products—dwellings—not the individual components of those dwellings. They bargained for the finished products, not their various components. The concrete became an integral part of the finished product and, thus, did not injure "other" property.

We also disagree with the homeowners that the mere possibility that the exploding concrete will cause physical injury is sufficient reason to abrogate the economic loss rule. This argument goes completely against the principle that injury must occur before a negligence action exists. Because an injury has not occurred, its extent and the identity of injured persons is completely speculative. Thus, the degree of risk is indeterminate, with no guarantee that damages will be reasonably related to the risk of injury, and with no possibility for the producer of a product to structure its business behavior to cover that risk. Agreeing with the homeowners' argument would make it difficult "to maintain a realistic limitation on damages." *East River*.

Therefore, we approve the district court's opinions and hold that the economic loss rule applies to the purchase of houses....

It is so ordered.

■ BARKETT, CHIEF JUSTICE, concurring in part, dissenting in part.

If the allegations of the homeowners in this case are true, their homes are literally crumbling around them because the concrete supplied by Toppino was negligently manufactured. The homeowners assert that the concrete is now cracking and breaking apart and poses a danger of serious injury. The courts, including this one, have said "too bad."

I find that answer unacceptable in light of the principle underlying Florida's access to courts provision: that absent compelling, countervailing public policies, wrongs must have remedies. Art. I, s 21, Fla. Const. I understand and accept that sometimes the remedies provided cannot be in the full measure that pure justice unfettered by pragmatism can provide. Thus, some applications of the economic loss doctrine may have acceptable viability. But surely it stretches reason to apply the doctrine in this context to deny these homeowners any remedy.

Their claim for breach of implied warranty has been denied (they lack privity with Toppino); their claim that Toppino violated the Florida Building Codes Act has been denied (Toppino, as a material supplier, is not governed by the Standard Building Code); and now their claim in tort has been denied because, notwithstanding their alleged ability to prove that their houses are falling down around them, they have not suffered any damage to their property on the basis that homes are "products."

A key premise underlying the economic loss rule is that parties in a business context have the ability to allocate economic risks and remedies as part of their contractual negotiations. That premise does not exist here. Moreover, I cannot subscribe to the majority's view that the defective concrete has not damaged "other property" in the form of the houses' individual components.

As Justice Shaw notes, the economic loss doctrine surely cannot and should not apply in a situation such as this.

■ Kogan, J., concurs.

■ Shaw, Justice, concurring and dissenting.

While I basically agree that, under a negligence theory, purely economic loss cannot be recovered by parties to a contract when the loss is to the property that is the subject of the contract, I find the logic of the restriction inapplicable in this instance. The rationale of the economic loss rule is that parties who have bargained for the distribution of risk of loss should not be permitted to circumvent their bargain after loss occurs to the property that was the subject of the bargain. Professors Prosser and Keeton in discussing economic loss make the following observation:

> There were two fundamental doctrines pertaining to the liability of a seller for claims based on the interference with intangible economic interests. These were that (1) privity of contract was normally a prerequisite to recovery leading to the conclusion that only a purchaser or one standing in the shoes of a purchaser as a third party beneficiary could sue for breach of a warranty and then only against his immediate seller and (2) disclaimers and other contract provisions which negate warranties, express or implied, or limit the remedy for breach of a warranty—*if fairly negotiated and bargained about*—were valid and enforceable. There was and is nothing novel or unsound about these propositions *so long as liability is based on a representational theory, and on the theory that the parties should be permitted by contract to allocate the risk of losses as they choose.*

W. Page Keeton, Dan B. Dobbs, Robert E. Keeton, & David G. Owen, Prosser and Keeton on the Law of Torts § 95A, at 681 (5th ed. 1984)(emphasis added).

This works well when the loss is suffered by one who is privy to the contract and involves loss that was the subject matter of the contract. It works a mischief, however, where as in this instance the injured party is not privy to the contract but injury to third parties is reasonably foreseeable. The condominium owners here suffered more than the loss of concrete; they suffered the loss of their homes, a foreseeable consequence of faulty concrete. As the court below noted: "The result of this deterioration process [caused by the defective concrete] is a substantial loss of structural integrity in the homes and buildings requiring vast repair work to or replacement of the homes and buildings." Casa Clara Condominium Ass'n v. Charley Toppino & Sons, Inc., 588 So.2d 631, 632 (Fla. 3d DCA1991).

While I agree with the majority opinion that parties who have freely bargained and entered a contract relative to a particular subject matter should be bound by the terms of that contract including the distribution of loss, I feel that the theory is stretched when it is used to deny a cause of action to an innocent third party who the defendant knew or should have known would be injured by the tortious conduct. Toppino knew that the concrete that was the subject matter of the bargain between Toppino and the general contractor would be incorporated into homes that would be bought and occupied by innocent third parties.

When the concrete proved to be contaminated, damages were not limited to simply the loss of concrete; innocent third parties suffered various degrees of damage to structures using the concrete. In my mind, the economic loss theory was never intended to defeat a tort cause of action that would otherwise lie for damages caused to a third party by a defective product. . . .

■ BARKETT, C.J., and KOGAN, J., concur.

NOTES

1. Economic Loss Rule. The rule generally prohibiting the recovery in tort of economic losses, independent of damage to person or other property, is now very widely accepted, albeit with certain variations. The following are examples. Bocre Leasing Corp. v. General Motors Corp., 645 N.E.2d 1195 (N.Y.1995) (no tort recovery for strict liability or negligence for economic losses in commercial situation); Airport Rent–A–Car, Inc. v. Prevost Car, Inc., 660 So.2d 628 (Fla.1995) (rejecting exceptions for "no alternative remedy," "sudden calamitous events," and post-sale duties to warn). Cf. Duffin v. Idaho Crop Improvement Assn., 895 P.2d 1195 (Idaho 1995) (economic losses recoverable in negligence in "extremely limited" situation where a "special relationship" between parties makes it inequitable to deny tort duty).

Some courts do allow a limited exception for defects creating dangers to persons and other property. E.g., Morris v. Osmose Wood Preserving, 667 A.2d 624 (Md. 1995) (tort recovery precluded unless both the (1) nature of the damage threatened, and (2) the probability of the danger "viewed together, exhibit a clear, serious, and unreasonable risk of death or personal injury"). So does at least Indiana's products liability act. See Martin Rispens & Son v. Hall Farms, Inc., 601 N.E.2d 429 (Ind.App.1992) (recovery allowable for "sudden, major damage to property," but not for "gradually evolving damage to property or economic losses from such damage").

2. Other Property. The courts have had a much easier time justifying recovery for damage to property other than the product itself. The widely prevailing view allows recovery for such damage in tort law as well as warranty. The U.S.

Supreme Court so held in another admiralty case, Saratoga Fishing Co. v. J.M. Martinac & Co., 520 U.S. 875 (1997) in which the owner of a fishing vessel which caught fire and sank brought products liability suit against builder of vessel and designer of vessel's hydraulic system, alleging that system was defectively designed. The Supreme Court held that the plaintiff could recover damages for loss of certain equipment which had been added by previous owner of vessel after its initial purchase from manufacturer because it was not part of the "product itself" that caused physical harm, but was "other property." Accord, A.J. Decoster Co. v. Westinghouse Elec. Corp., 634 A.2d 1330 (Md.1994) (140,000 chickens died when power outage caused ventilation system in chicken house to shut down and defendant's transfer switch failed to activate backup power source).

The important question, then, is what is "other property"? In Gunkel v. Renovations, Inc., 822 N.E.2d 150 (Ind. 2005), plaintiff homeowners brought an action for negligence against the masonry contractor that installed a stone facade on their home, seeking to recover for lost use of the home and repair costs due to extensive moisture damage. The Court held that the homeowners could proceed because the product they purchased was the masonry facade, not the house, and therefore tort recovery for damage to the home was not limited by the economic loss rule. Do you agree?

3. Asbestos Abatement. May a school board recover from the manufacturer of asbestos insulation in tort for the costs of removing that insulation, installed many years before, which must now be removed to avoid health risks to children? Tioga Public School Dist. No. 15 v. United States Gypsum Co., 984 F.2d 915 (8th Cir.1993), involved an action by a school district against a company that manufactured asbestos acoustical plaster known as Audicote during the 1950s and 1960s. The ceilings in two of plaintiff's schools constructed about 1960 were plastered with Audicote. The plaster had begun to crumble, exposing the asbestos in the plaster and causing excessive levels of asbestos in the schools. The cost of removing ("abating") the asbestos was estimated at $400,000 to $1.1 million. Held, the economic loss rule did *not* bar recovery in tort for the costs of abatement:

> Although the North Dakota Supreme Court has adopted the economic loss doctrine, we do not believe that that court would hold that the doctrine precludes Tioga from recovering in this case. The asserted injury here is the presence of Audicote in Tioga's schools and the contamination of the schools by asbestos. The asbestos poses a risk of devastating injury to those whose health may ultimately be harmed by it, a risk best distributed by the seller or manufacturer. Moreover, the presence of asbestos in Audicote and the resulting danger have nothing to do with the level of performance of the product. In fact, the evidence suggests that the Audicote, although encapsulated, is still functioning well as acoustical plaster. * * *

> In sum, Tioga is not seeking to recover the lost benefit of its bargain based on a claim that the plaster is deficient as acoustical plaster; such a claim would clearly be barred by the economic loss doctrine. Instead, Tioga is seeking to recover the cost of removing the asbestos-containing plaster from its schools on the ground that the asbestos poses a risk of injury to those exposed to it. We believe the North Dakota Supreme Court would ... follow the strong majority of reported cases in holding that the economic loss doctrine does not bar Tioga's recovery in tort.

Accord, 80 South Eighth St. Ltd. Partnership v. W.R. Grace Co., 486 N.W.2d 393 (Minn.1992). See generally Ausness, Tort Liability for Asbestos Removal Costs, 73 Or.L.Rev. 505 (1994).

4.   Reform. Comprehensive products liability reform statutes generally exclude recovery for economic loss and property damage, at least indirectly, in definitions of "product liability action [or claim]," or "harm." E.g., *Ariz.:* action for "bodily injury, death or property damage," Ariz. Rev. Stat. Ann. § 12–681; *Conn.:* claim for "personal injury, death or property damage"; " 'Harm' includes damage to property, including the product itself.... As between commercial parties, 'harm' does not include commercial loss," Conn. Gen. Stat. § 52–572m; *N.J.:* "Harm" includes (a) "physical damage to property, other than to the product itself," (b) injury, illness or death, (c) pain and suffering and emotional distress, and (d) loss of consortium or services, N.J. Stat. Ann. § 2A:58C–1; *Ohio:* claim for "death, physical injury to person, serious emotional distress, or physical damage to property other than the product involved. Economic loss is not 'harm.' " Ohio Rev.Code Ann. § 2307.71.

5.   The Products Liability Restatement. Section 21 of the Products Liability Restatement provides for recovery of economic loss only "if caused by harm to: (a) the plaintiff's person; or (b) the person of another [in whom plaintiff has an interest]; or (c) the plaintiff's property other than the defective product itself."

6. See generally Gruning, Pure Economic Loss in American Tort Law: An Unstable Consensus, 54 Am. J. Comp. L. 187 (2006); Comment, 2005 Wis. L. Rev. 225; J. White & R. Summers, Uniform Commercial Code § 10–5 (5th ed. 2000).

---

4.   PUNITIVE DAMAGES

Gryc v. Dayton–Hudson Corp.

Supreme Court of Minnesota, 1980.
297 N.W.2d 727, cert. denied, 449 U.S. 921, 101 S.Ct. 320, 66 L.Ed.2d 149 (1980).

* * *

■ TODD, JUSTICE.

On December 8, 1969, Lee Ann Gryc, then 4 years of age, was clothed in pajamas made from a cotton material manufactured by defendant Riegel Textile Corporation (Riegel). The material was commercially known as "flannelette." It was not treated but did meet the minimum federal standards of product flammability. Lee Ann reached across the electric stove in her home to shut off a timer. Her pajamas were instantly ignited and she received severe burns over her upper body. The jury found Riegel liable for these injuries and awarded Lee Ann $750,000 in compensatory damages and $1,000,000 in punitive damages. We affirm.

[Lee Ann's pajamas] were two-piece, loose-fitting, and the pajama top flared out at the waist. The flannelette used in the pajamas was manufactured by Riegel and distributed to [a clothing manufacturer which made and sold the pajamas to the representative of the defendant retailer, Dayton–Hudson.]

The flannelette used in Lee Ann's pajamas was woven material made from yarns spun from natural cotton fiber. The fabric was brushed on one side which created a nap. Flannelette is light weight, warm, and absorbent.

It has a soft feel or "hand", breathes well, and is launderable and durable. It is relatively inexpensive. Flannelette was very popular during the relevant time period because of these qualities and was the dominant fabric used in children's winter sleepwear.

The flannelette used in Lee Ann's pajamas was not treated with any flame retardant. Its flammable characteristics were demonstrated by one of plaintiffs' expert witnesses, Dr. Robert Johnson, by film at trial. Dr. Johnson reconstructed Lee Ann's accident by making a copy of Lee Ann's pajamas, placing them on a mannequin the size of Lee Ann, and using an ignition source similar to the Gryc electric burner. The film showed that the fabric ignited instantaneously when the hem of the pajama top was placed in contact with the ignition source. The front of the pajama top burned from hem to neck in 4 to 5 seconds. The same experiment was performed on a pair of pajamas of the same design but constructed of newsprint. The newsprint pajamas burned only slightly faster than did the untreated flannelette pajamas.

Plaintiff's experts concluded that the untreated cotton flannelette was unreasonably dangerous for use in children's sleepwear because of the instantaneous manner in which the fabric ignited, the speed at which it burned, the amount of heat produced when it burned, and the difficulty of extinguishing the flames. Defendant's experts characterized these burning characteristics as "normal" for the mass of the fabric and as a "natural" phenomenon for cotton, the characteristics of which had not changed for hundreds of years. They concluded, therefore, that the fabric used in the Gryc pajamas was not defective.

* * *

It was shown at trial that the safety of cotton flannelette could be significantly increased by applying [a chemical flame retardant] to the fabric. Dr. Johnson, by film, demonstrated the flammable characteristics of flame retarded cotton flannelette. He created a pair of pajamas like those which Lee Ann had worn, except that they were treated with a flame-retardant process available in 1967. The pajamas were placed against a heat source similar to an electric burner for 30 seconds. The pajamas blackened, burned, and charred but did not flame in an area 6 inches wide and 8 inches long in that 30 seconds. When the fabric was removed from the heat source, the blackening and charring stopped.

The serious dispute between the experts concerned the availability of flame-retardant processes ... which would not destroy the desirable characteristics of cotton flannelette. Plaintiffs' experts testified that, as early as 1962, there were flame-retardant processes which could be applied to the fabric without adversely affecting its qualities enough to make it unsalable. Plaintiffs also showed that, in England, flannelette-like sleepwear was required by law to be flame retarded since the 1950's.

Defendant's experts [disagreed.] They testified that there were no durable flame retardant chemicals which could be applied to the fabric without severely reducing its tensile and tear strength, its soft feel, increasing its weight and cost, and adversely affecting the color of the fabric.

Plaintiffs' witnesses admitted that there were no mills producing flame retarded flannelette for public consumption in any volume in 1967. However, both of plaintiffs' experts testified that the flame retardant chemicals and the process for applying them could have been made commercially available as early as 1962–1966, if only the textile mills had so desired.

* * *

Defendant's experts contended that no warning of the flammable characteristics of cotton flannelette was necessary on the Gryc pajamas because its burning characteristics are obvious and natural for the mass of the fabric. However, plaintiffs introduced a great amount of testimony tending to show that garment manufacturers, wholesalers, retailers, and consumers were not aware of the highly flammable characteristics of untreated cotton flannelette. Their evidence tended to show that Riegel and other garment manufacturers were uniquely aware of these characteristics.

Defendant's experts were also of the opinion that a warning would not be feasible or practical because Riegel could not be assured that such a warning would get beyond the garment manufacturers. However, there was testimony that for other purposes Riegel could and did use hang tags which were sent through the chain of commerce and did reach consumers.

Defendant's experts were also of the opinion that a warning would "stigmatize" Riegel's flannelette and make it unmarketable as compared with identical flannelette from competitor mills.

Plaintiffs also claimed that defendant Riegel should have instructed consumers of a home remedy which would temporarily flame retard flannelette pajamas. This remedy, a water base solution of boric acid and borax, would come out in the wash, but could be simply sprinkled on clothing after each washing. Dr. Johnson conducted a test with a pair of flannelette pajamas treated with such a solution. The pajamas did not ignite when they were held against a hot plate for 5 seconds.

The issues presented on this appeal are:

(1) Whether the award of punitive damages is an appropriate remedy in a products liability case;

(2) Whether defendant's compliance with an applicable federal safety standard precludes a punitive damages award;

(3) Whether the imposition of punitive damages on a defendant who has complied with the federal Flammable Fabrics Act is prohibited by the preemption provision of that Act or by the Supremacy Clause of the United States Constitution;

(4) Whether the trial court applied the proper legal standard in instructing the jury on the issue of punitive damages;

(5) Whether there was sufficient evidence to support the award of punitive damages in this case;

(6) Whether policy considerations dictate against an award of punitive damages in this case;

(7) Whether ... $1,000,000 in punitive damages is excessive;....

1. This case presents the [novel question] of whether punitive damages may be appropriately awarded in ... a strict liability action. There is ample authority from many jurisdictions approving this remedy in strict liability cases. An exhaustive article, Owen, Punitive Damages in Products Liability Litigation, 74 Mich.L.Rev. 1258 (1976), discusses the pros and cons of allowing such an award. The author concludes that punitive damages are an appropriate remedy in such cases based on the following rationale:

> Manufacturers have a powerful hold over the means for discovering and correcting product hazards. Through the processes of design, testing, inspection and collection of data on product safety performance in the field, the manufacturer has virtually exclusive access to much of the information necessary for effective control of dangers facing product consumers....
>
> Most manufacturers, both from a desire to avoid liability and from a generalized sense of social responsibility, prudently use their resources to prevent excessively hazardous products from reaching or staying on the market. On occasion, however, manufacturers abuse their control over safety information and market defective products in flagrant disregard of the public safety.... A legal tool is needed that will help to expose this type of gross misconduct, punish those manufacturers guilty of such flagrant misbehavior, and deter all manufacturers from acting with similar disregard for the public welfare. The punitive damages remedy is such a tool.

Id. at 1258–60.

Based on this rationale, we recognize today that punitive damages, in an appropriate case, may properly be awarded in a strict liability action.

2. The Flammable Fabrics Act of 1953 ... in effect at the time this cause of action arose,[2] applied to fabrics sold in interstate commerce for wearing apparel. This statute sets forth a test [termed the CS 191–53] to determine whether a fabric is dangerous when used in clothing....

The fabric in the Gryc pajamas passed the CS 191–53 test....

Riegel argues that its compliance with the [Act precludes, as a matter of law, a finding of that guilty state of mind necessary for a punitive damages assessment, arguing that it was justified in relying on the Act to determine which fabrics were safe for dissemination in the marketplace. The trial court disagreed]:

> The difficulty with [Riegel's] argument is that it does not assess the validity of the test. It was proven almost conclusively at trial that this test did not and could not properly determine the flammability of fabrics such

---

2. The Flammable Fabrics Act was subsequently amended to provide for more stringent regulation of fabric used for children's sleepwear. However, these revisions are inapplicable to this cause of action.

as cotton flannelette. Moreover ... defendant Riegel knew not only that the test was invalid but that it could not evaluate the flammability of its products.... Knowing full well at all times after the passage of the Flammable Fabrics Act that CS 191–53 was unreliable, the defendant cannot today say that punitive damages should not be allowed simply because its cotton flannelette passed an unreliable test. Riegel's argument that it had a right to [rely on the Act is specious;] such actions were not taken in good faith [because Riegel knew] that its cotton flannelette was extremely dangerous to the public because of its racing flammability.

[The trial court is correct. The] CS 191–53 test was not a valid indicator of the flammable characteristics of fabrics and did not take into account the uses to which a fabric would be put in determining its safety.[3] It was shown that newspaper passed the CS 191–53 test with a 48–percent margin of safety [and] that the original intent of Congress in passing the CS 191–53 test into law was primarily to protect the public against certain highly flammable synthetic products, not all unreasonably dangerous clothing. 1953 U.S.Code Cong. & Admin.News, p. 1723. [Moreover,] there was evidence that the test was adopted as a result of industry influence and, therefore, served to protect the textile industry rather than the public....

[Riegel knew that the CS 191–53 test was invalid and that] unreasonably dangerous fabrics passed the test. Riegel's head of research, Linton C. Reynolds, knew that newspaper and 19 other samples of paper passed the CS 191–53 test and communicated this to a Riegel top official. In addition, Riegel knew that persons were suffering severe burn injuries when Riegel's flannelette ignited. In 1956, one of Riegel's top officials wrote in a memorandum, "We are always sitting on somewhat of a powder keg as regards our flannelette being so inflammable." The memorandum was entitled "Flammability—Liability."

[We agree with the several courts that have held that a product complying with the invalid CS 191–53 test may still be found unreasonably dangerous and so subject its maker to liability for compensatory damages.] For the same reason, we conclude that while compliance with this test may be relevant to the issue of punitive damages, it does not preclude such an award as a matter of law.

3. [The court rejected the defendant's federal preemption argument based on the Flammable Fabrics Act.]

4. [The court refused to consider Riegel's arguments on the proper legal standard and burden of proof for punitive damages since these issues had not been raised at trial.]

5. In instructing the jury on the issue of punitive damages, the court listed several factors which the jury was to take into account in determining whether Riegel had acted in willful or reckless disregard of plaintiffs' rights:

---

3. The commentators have agreed. See Swartz, Product Liability: The Torch Cases, 76 Case & Comment, No. 1, p. 3 (1971); [citations]; Campbell & Vargo, The Flammable Fabrics Act and Strict Liability in Tort, 9 Ind.L.Rev. 395 (1976).

1.   The existence and magnitude of the product danger to the public;

2.   The cost or feasibility of reducing the danger to an acceptable level;

3.   The manufacturer's awareness of the danger, the magnitude of the danger, and the availability of a feasible remedy;

4.   The nature and duration of, and the reasons for, the manufacturer's failure to act appropriately to discover or reduce the danger;

5.   The extent to which the manufacturer purposefully created the danger;

6.   The extent to which the defendants are subject to federal safety regulation;

7.   The probability that compensatory damages might be awarded against defendants in other cases; and, finally,

8.   The amount of time which has passed since the actions sought to be deterred.

[After reviewing the record and considering] the above-listed factors, [we] have concluded that there was sufficient, in fact substantial, evidence for the jury to find that Riegel acted in willful, wanton and/or malicious disregard of the rights of others in marketing its flannelette.

The Danger

Plaintiffs introduced substantial evidence to show that thousands of people were dying or being seriously injured from clothing fires involving highly flammable fabrics each year. It was shown that the young and the very old were the most susceptible to these injuries. Furthermore, Dr. Johnson, at trial, demonstrated the instantaneous ignition and rapid burning rate of the untreated cotton flannelette manufactured by Riegel.

The Feasibility of Reducing the Hazard

[Notwithstanding Riegel's evidence to the contrary,] plaintiffs introduced a large amount of evidence showing that flame retardant products could have been applied to cotton flannelette well before Riegel manufactured the flannelette used in Lee Ann's pajamas. [E]ven if such evidence had not been sufficient, there was sufficient evidence [to establish Riegel's duty to warn of the high flammability of its cotton flannelette, and that] Riegel was uniquely aware of these flammable characteristics. [Riegel could not seriously dispute its ability to warn consumers because of proof that it] was able to send advertising information concerning the positive attributes of its product through the chain of commerce.

Riegel mainly argued at trial and argues here on appeal that it was not feasible to warn consumers because such a warning would "stigmatize" its product, thereby seemingly admitting that it was protecting the marketing of a product consumers might deem unreasonably hazardous.

Riegel's Knowledge

Riegel's knowledge of the hazard involved and its reason for not taking feasible measures to reduce this hazard was demonstrated at trial. In 1956, one of Riegel's top officials sent to the Riegel head of research a memorandum listing a number of clothing fires and consequent injuries which occurred to persons wearing Riegel flannelette garments. This memorandum stated that the company was sitting on a "powder keg" with respect to the flammability of their flannelette. It was also proven at trial that between 1960 and 1967, Riegel was on notice that approximately 6 lawsuits were brought against it for accidents involving its cotton flannelette.

Riegel introduced a great amount of evidence showing its communications with several chemical companies concerning the availability of flame retardant products and the application of these products to its cotton flannelette. Riegel apparently introduced these items in an effort to show its good faith in attempting to find and apply a viable flame retardant to its cotton flannelette. However, one of Riegel's own letters evidences the reason for its failure in this area. In April 1968, a letter from an official of Riegel explained that satisfactory runs were made with flame-retarded flannelette using various chemicals, but that Riegel was not going to use these products until federal law so required because of the cost factor. Plaintiffs' witnesses testified that the cost of flame-retardant fabrics would not make them unmarketable. Thus, it may be inferred from this letter that the decision not to use flame-retardant cotton flannelette was merely an economic one for the benefit of Riegel.

Plaintiffs' evidence also tended to prove that while Riegel conducted some surveillance of developments in the flame-retardant field, its efforts were minimal. Plaintiffs introduced evidence that prior to 1965, Riegel kept no records on its research and development of nonflammable products and fabrics. Furthermore, from 1967 to 1969, $140,000 was spent on research in this area while the entire research and development spending of the company amounted to $1,831,731.

6. [The court addressed Riegel's arguments on the risk of over-punishment.]

Riegel ... argues that there is no need for the deterrent of punitive damages in this case [because] compensatory damages and loss of sales and reputation act as an adequate deterrent. Riegel also posits that since it no longer manufactures cotton flannelette and since the Flammable Fabrics Act presently has more stringent standards for children's sleepwear, no deterrent is needed. This argument ignores the fact that Riegel was shown to have acted in reckless disregard of the public for purely economic reasons in the past. A punitive damages award serves to deter Riegel from acting in a similar manner with respect to other products manufactured by it in the future. Furthermore, since the potential of compensatory damages awards and loss of sales and reputation did not serve to deter Riegel in the past, Riegel cannot now argue that these considerations act as an adequate deterrent.

Riegel also overlooks the fact that one of the functions of a punitive damages award is to punish past misconduct. This function is well served by a punitive damages award in this case.

7. Riegel contends that the punitive damages award of $1,000,000 was clearly excessive. This court ... will not disturb a punitive damages award unless it appears that the award was actuated by passion and prejudice and is so excessive as to be deemed unreasonable. [In light of the evidence in the record, the punitive damages award is not unreasonable.]

The evidence shows that Riegel created a substantial danger to the public by marketing its highly flammable cotton flannelette. Riegel continued to market this product even though there were economically feasible measures which could have been taken to reduce this danger to a fairly acceptable level. The evidence also showed that Riegel was aware of the danger and the means for reducing this danger. Furthermore, Riegel is a multi-million dollar corporation which reaped substantial profits through the sale of its highly flammable cotton flannelette. We, therefore, do not find that the punitive damages award was excessive as a matter of law.

[Affirmed.]

NOTE

Consider Tetuan v. A.H. Robins Co., 738 P.2d 1210 (Kan.1987), which involved the sale of an IUD contraceptive device called the "Dalkon Shield," marketed by A.H. Robins from 1970 to 1974. The shield was a piece of plastic, roughly oval in shape, which was less than two inches in diameter. Four phalanges on either side, giving it a crab-like appearance, secured it within the uterus. Attached to the bottom of the shield, like most IUDs, was a tail-string, descending from the uterus through the cervix and into the vagina, that permitted the user to know that the device was in place. Unlike other IUDs, which all had monofilament strings, the Dalkon Shield's string was comprised of 200–400 individual filaments covered by a nylon sheath. Much more so than monofilament strings, the shield's multi-filament string acted as a wick for bacteria to travel from the vagina into the uterus, which sometimes resulted in a serious malady called pelvic inflammatory disease (PID).

Barraged with complaints, Robins finally took the shield off the market at the urging of the FDA in 1974. In 1980, the company issued a "Dear Doctor" letter recommending the removal of the shield from asymptomatic users, but refused to pay for such removal. In 1984, Robins sent out its final "Dear Doctor" letter, recommending the removal of any remaining Dalkon Shields, and offering to pay for removal.

The plaintiff's doctor fitted her with a shield in 1971. In September 1979, she began to experience fever and severe pain from PID, caused by the shield. Her doctor, who had received no warnings from A.H. Robins, was unable to diagnose the problem. After antibiotic treatment and hospitalization, the shield was finally removed in March 1980, but the pain persisted. Plaintiff's doctor referred her to a specialist who found it necessary in June 1980 to perform a total hysterectomy—the removal of her uterus, Fallopian tubes, and ovaries. Plaintiff sued Robins, and the jury found in her favor, awarding $1.7 million in compensatory damages, and assessing punitive damages of $7.5 million. Robins appealed:

Robins stresses that no Kansas appellate court has ever upheld a punitive damage award of this magnitude. Neither has any been presented with corporate misconduct of such gravity and duration. We note that, in Palmer v. A.H. Robins Co., Inc., 684 P.2d 187 (Colo.1984), the Colorado Supreme Court upheld an award of punitive damages of $6.2 million....

... In the present case, the jury made a specific finding of fraud. A review of the record indicates that there was substantial evidence tending to show Robins knew the Dalkon Shield was not safe or effective; that Robins knew of the wicking nature of the tail string; that Robins knew of a high rate of PID and septic abortion associated with the Dalkon Shield; that Robins misled doctors through claims of safety and efficacy while it knew there was no basis for a claim of safety, and all responsible tests for the Dalkon Shield's effectiveness showed a much higher pregnancy rate than Dr. Davis' "1.1%" figure; that Robins similarly misled consumers through a misleading lay promotional campaign; that Robins never publicly retracted its claims of "effectiveness" even though it had privately acknowledged the 1.1% rate as invalid; and that Robins knew there were serious problems with its open-ended nylon multi-filament string in maintaining its integrity within the body. But not only was there substantial evidence to conclude that Robins fully comprehended, by 1974 at the latest, the enormity of the dangers it had created, but that it deliberately and intentionally concealed those dangers; that it put money into "favorable" studies; that it tried to neutralize any critics of the Dalkon Shield; that Robins was motivated by a desire to avoid litigation judgments rather than a concern for the safety of the users of the Dalkon Shield; that it consistently denied the dangers of the Dalkon Shield for nearly fifteen years after its original marketing of the Dalkon Shield; that it commissioned studies on the Dalkon Shield which it dropped or concealed when the results were unfavorable; and, ultimately, that it consigned hundreds of documents to the furnace rather than inform women that the Dalkon Shield carried inside their bodies was a bacterial time bomb which could cause septic abortions, PID, and even death.

* * *

The $6.2 million punitive damage award against Robins in *Palmer* was rendered by the jury on July 30, 1979. Loretta Tetuan first experienced symptoms of PID in late September of that year. It is entirely possible that plaintiff's injuries could have been avoided if the company had reacted to the verdict by immediately moving to recall the product or to at least warn of its dangers. Instead, Robins responded with the same position it had taken for the last decade—that the Dalkon Shield was "safe and effective." Robins issued a statement on July 31, 1979, that the verdict was "an aberration" and that it was confident "this unwarranted verdict will not survive" on appeal.

The first Dalkon Shield case to proceed to trial on the merits occurred in Kansas in Deemer v. A.H. Robins Co., Case No. C–26420. On March 1, 1975, the jury awarded punitive damages against Robins in the amount of $75,000. Robins did not recall the product; it did not warn users of the Dalkon Shield's dangers; it did not warn physicians. It certainly did not warn Loretta Tetuan or the physicians who treated her. Instead, it reacted to the modest punitive damages award in *Deemer* by promptly attempting to destroy all evidence of its knowledge of the Dalkon Shield's dangers, consigning hundreds of documents to the draft furnace. To punish Robins for its conduct and to discourage others from committing like wrongs in the future, the punitive damages award is justified.

The judgment is affirmed.

738 P.2d at 1239–40, 1246.

The 1990s counterpart to the Dalkon Shield litigation was the silicone breast implant litigation against Dow Corning. See Hopkins v. Dow Corning Corp., 33 F.3d 1116 (9th Cir.1994)(affirming $6.5 million punitive award). See ch. 19, below. In 1995, a Nevada jury returned a $13.9 million verdict (including $10 million in punitive damages) in a breast implant case against Dow Chemical, one of Dow Corning's two parents. Mahlum v. American Heyer–Schulte Corp., 2d Dist.Ct., Nev., (Oct. 30, 1995); Prod.Liab.Advis. 2 (Nov.1995); Weinstein, Jury Awards $14 Million in Breast–Implant Suit, L. A. Times, Oct. 31, 1995, at A4.

––––––––

Acosta v. Honda Motor Co.

United States Court of Appeals, Third Circuit, 1983.
717 F.2d 828.

■ Becker, Circuit Judge.

[The important question in this case is whether Virgin Islands law permits punitive damages awards against a defendant found strictly liable under § 402A of the Restatement (2d) of Torts for selling a defective product.]

In early 1976, plaintiff purchased a used Honda CB750 motorcycle. At that time the motorcycle was six years old; plaintiff was its third owner. Approximately two months after he bought the motorcycle, plaintiff was injured when he was thrown from the motorcycle while riding at night on a lighted road in St. Thomas. According to his testimony, he was driving at approximately 30–35 miles per hour when he saw in the road a repair ditch approximately four inches deep and ten feet long. He testified that he slowed down, retained control of the motorcycle, and maneuvered it straight through the ditch. As he was exiting the ditch, however, the motorcycle's rear wheel hit the back edge of the ditch and collapsed. Despite plaintiff's efforts to maintain control, the collapsed rear of the motorcycle jerked into the air, tossing him to the ground. Plaintiff sustained multiple injuries, including four fractured vertebrae, a broken femur, and a punctured liver.

[Plaintiff sued the motorcycle manufacturer, Honda, the wheel manufacturer, Daido Kogyo, and another, alleging defects in design and manufacture and failure to warn. The jury returned verdicts against Honda and Daido Kogyo for $175,000 in compensatory damages and assessed each $210,000 in punitive damages. Noting that he was surprised at the modest level of the compensatory award, the trial court denied the defendants' motions for judgment n.o.v. Defendants appealed.]

Defendants' principal contention on appeal is that the evidence was insufficient as a matter of law to sustain the award of punitive damages and that the district court erred in submitting the issue to the jury in the first place. Before turning to that question, however, we first must address their argument that punitive damages are unavailable in this case because, no matter what the evidence, punitive damages are fundamentally inconsistent with a regime of strict products liability in general, and with § 402A in particular.

A. *The Availability of Punitive Damages in the Strict Liability Context.*

* * *

The Restatement (Second) of Torts § 908(2) declares:

> Punitive damages may be awarded for conduct that is outrageous, because of the defendant's evil motive or his reckless indifference to the rights of others. In assessing punitive damages, the trier of fact can properly consider the character of the defendant's act, the nature and extent of the harm to the plaintiff that the defendant caused or intended to cause and the wealth of the defendant.

[There is nothing to] suggest that these principles should not apply to strict products liability, and we concur with the [Fifth Circuit] that "[p]unishment and deterrence, the basis for punitive damages ..., are no less appropriate with respect to a product manufacturer who knowingly ignores safety deficiencies in its product that may endanger human life" than in other cases in which "the defendant's conduct shows wantonness or recklessness or reckless indifference to the rights of others." Dorsey v. Honda Motor Co., 655 F.2d 650, 658 (5th Cir.1981)[Fla. law], opinion modified on rehearing, 670 F.2d 21 (5th Cir.), cert. denied, 103 S.Ct. 177 (1982).

Some courts and commentators, however, have suggested that the policies underlying punitive damages are so incompatible with those animating strict products liability that punitive damage awards should not be permitted against defendants found liable under 402A. These arguments essentially break down into three groups: contentions that punitive damages will upset the delicate balance struck in the creation of a strict products liability regime, assertions that the goals of punitive damages are unachievable in the strict products liability context, and arguments that the imposition of punitive damages in 402A cases will have extremely undesirable economic and social consequences. [These considerations do not warrant our precluding the award of punitive damages.]

1. *Would the Availability of Punitive Damages Disrupt the Regime of Strict Products Liability?*

* * *

We reject the notion that punitive damages are theoretically inconsistent with strict products liability. While it is true that § 402A eschews the culpability of defendants' conduct as a factor in determining liability, it does not do so because focusing on culpability is always inappropriate. Indeed [cmt. *a* notes] that 402A "does not preclude liability based upon the alternative ground of negligence of the seller, where such negligence can be proved." Rather, the rule is intended to expand recovery by circumventing the restrictions imposed by fault-based standards. [Citation.] The fact that some sellers therefore will be found liable in the absence of fault does not mean that those who are at fault—and outrageously so—should not be punished.[10] [Citations.]

* * *

2. Does the Strict Liability Context Limit the Effectiveness of Punitive Damages?

Section 908(1) of the Restatement (Second) of Torts [provides:]

[p]unitive damages are damages, other than compensatory or nominal damages, awarded against a person *to punish him for his outrageous conduct and to deter him and others like him from similar conduct* in the future.

(Emphasis added.); [citation]. While few, if any courts, have challenged these goals, some courts and commentators have suggested that the connection between punitive damages and the goals of punishment and deterrence will be attenuated in the strict products liability context.

Proponents of this argument point out that the magnitude of recent jury verdicts, coupled with the potential for a single design defect to serve as the template for hundreds or thousands of defective, injury-causing products, means that a manufacturer may be liable for many millions of dollars merely as compensation to injured victims [which provides manufacturers with] every incentive to insure that their products are as safe as possible. Indeed [Judge Friendly for] the Court of Appeals for the Second Circuit observed as early as 1967:

Many awards of compensatory damages doubtless contain something of a punitive element, and more would do so if a separate award for exemplary damages were eliminated. Even though products liability insurance blunts the deterrent effect of compensatory awards to a considerable extent, the total coverage under such policies is often limited, bad experience is usually reflected in future rates, and insurance affords no protection to the damage to reputation among [users, consumers, and distributors] which an instance like the present must inevitably produce.

Roginsky v. Richardson–Merrell, Inc., 378 F.2d 832, 841 (2d Cir.1967). Thus the *Roginsky* court concluded that punitive damages were unnecessary to punish and deter the reckless marketing of defective products.

---

10. Defendants also contend that a jury is likely to be confused by the presence of the two concepts in the same case. Accord Gold v. Johns–Manville Sales Corp., 553 F.Supp. 482, 485 (D.N.J.1982). But that argument ignores the fact that many plaintiffs plead alternative theories of negligence and strict products liability. Thus juries are frequently asked, as was the case here, simultaneously to consider both fault and nonfault based standards of liability. Moreover, we are convinced that a properly instructed jury will be able to distinguish between the standards applicable to awards of compensatory and punitive damages.

We are not persuaded that limiting recovery to compensatory damages will, in all cases, provide an effective deterrent against the type of wrongful conduct for which punitive damages are usually available. For example, the cost of litigation relative to the likely recovery may deter victims of product defects from suing the manufacturer, even under a regime of strict liability, where products causing numerous minor injuries are involved. The availability of punitive damages to those who do sue may offset the decreased deterrence attributable to those who thus could but do not. Similarly, consumers will not always be aware of the source of an injury caused by a product defect, see Sturm, Ruger & Co. v. Day, 594 P.2d 38, modified, 615 P.2d 621 (1980) on rehearing, 627 P.2d 204 (Alaska); Owen, Punitive Damages in Products Liability Litigation, 74 Mich.L.Rev. 1258, 1287–95 (1976) (also noting the expense of litigation), or they may wrongfully attribute the accident to their own clumsiness; the manufacturer's reprieve in such cases will be offset by the availability of punitive damages in other cases. Finally, under existing doctrine, compensatory damages may prove an inadequate deterrent even when victims do bring suit.... In addition, those peripherally injured by accidents to another generally are not allowed to bring suit, yet their loss may be, in moral or practical terms, extremely substantial. See Owen, Civil Punishment and the Public Good, 56 So.Cal. L.Rev. 103, 113 (1982). While punitive damages may not be a logically perfect method of remedying these perhaps unavoidable flaws in our system of justice, they are a useful surrogate not necessarily precluded by a strict products liability regime.

3. *Will Punitive Damages Have Undesirable Economic and Social Consequences?*

Perhaps recognizing that mere redundancy would not be sufficient to supersede considerations in favor of allowing punitive damages, the *Roginsky* court predicted that the availability of such damages would have unfortunate results. The court noted that there are frequently numerous potential plaintiffs with claims arising from the same defect in design or manufacture; if each such plaintiff can recover punitive damages, the court warned, the aggregate recovery could be "catastrophic."

> If liability policies can protect against this risk as several courts have held, the cost of providing this probably needless deterrence, not only to the few manufacturers from whom punitive damages for highly negligent conduct are sought but to the thousands from whom it never will be, is passed on to the consuming public; if they cannot, as is held by other courts and recommended by most commentators, a sufficiently egregious error to one product can end the business life of a concern that has wrought much good in the past and might otherwise have continued to do so in the future, with many innocent stockholders suffering extinction of their investments for a single management sin.

Roginsky, 378 F.2d at 841.

Although we recognize that the effect of punitive damages may be harsh, we find somewhat excessive the *Roginsky* court's dire predictions about the consequences of allowing punitive damages. First, even assuming that policy considerations would permit manufacturers to insure against punitive damages, it is not clear that such insurance would necessarily emasculate the effectiveness of the remedy or result in "needless deterrence." Rather, a 1976 study by the Department of Commerce noted that recent increases in the number of products liability claims, policy cancellations, insurance premiums, and average loss per claim have contributed to a situation in which ... many manufacturers are making stronger efforts to improve design and quality control. [Citation.] As one commentator has noted, "these developments compel the conclusion that products liability litigation is increasingly forcing manufacturers to improve product safety even when they are insured against claims for product injuries." Owen, supra, 74 Mich.L.Rev. at 1310.

More importantly, we do not share *Roginsky's* in terrorem vision of the consequences of punitive damages for which insurance is unavailable. It is, of course, possible that "a sufficiently egregious error as to one product" could result in the demise of its manufacturer, but such a result is not inevitable.[15] [For one thing, prior punitive damages awards may be considered in determining the amount of a subsequent award.][16] Moreover, this court has previously recognized that both the wealth of the defendant, [citation],[17] and the size of compensatory damages, [citation], should be

---

15. Nor is such a result necessarily untenable. See infra note 17. We note, however, that no empirical evidence has been offered that Roginsky's forebodings have been realized in the sixteen years since it was written. See State ex rel. Young v. Crookham, 618 P.2d 1268 (Or.1980) (apprehension of corporate annihilation by awards of punitive damages is exaggerated).

16. At least one court has questioned whether these practical problems can be overcome. See *Roginsky,* supra, 378 F.2d at 839–40. In light of our conclusion that plaintiff did not adduce evidence sufficient to sustain his claim for punitive damages, however, see infra Part III.C., we need not determine whether or to what extent a court, before submitting the claim to the jury, should consider prior awards of punitive damages against a defendant for recklessly marketing the same defective product. See generally Owen, supra, 74 Mich.L.Rev. at 1319 (suggesting increased judicial control in the assessment of punitive damages).

17. Although [the cited case] involved a situation in which evidence of the defendant's wealth was introduced by plaintiff in order to get higher punitive damages, such evidence can cut both ways. For example, a jury might decide that a defendant's financial position, as a result of other awards of punitive damages for the same conduct, is so

precarious that a sizeable award of punitive damages would be inappropriate.

Of course, a jury might reasonably decide, when faced with such information, that a bankrupting award is nevertheless appropriate. Although the Second Circuit posited the case in which an otherwise "good" manufacturer is thereby driven out of business, the situation is equally likely in which the manufacturer is one whose success and financial health is directly attributable to its willingness recklessly to market an unsafe, but therefore cheaper and more popular, product. Thus an award of punitive damages may have the effect of redressing an unfair and socially undesirable competitive advantage.

We also take issue with the Second Circuit's hypothesis that the innocent victim of a punitive damages award will be the manufacturing corporation's innocent shareholders. It is true, of course, that the shareholders may ultimately bear the burden of such an award, and it is also true that they are innocent to the extent that it was actually management or an employee who was responsible for the conduct justifying the award. At the same time, it *is* the shareholders who have benefitted from any such conduct that has redounded to the manufacturer's fiscal advantage. Moreover, the loss of investment and the decline in value of invest-

taken into account in assessing punitive damages. "Thus, corporate defendants are protected from excessive punitive damage awards through judicial control both at the district court and appellate levels." Neal v. Carey Canadian Mines, Ltd., 548 F.Supp. 357, 377 (E.D.Pa.1982).

B. Standard of Proof

Although we reject each of the various arguments against awarding punitive damages in the strict liability context, we agree with Judge Friendly's observation in *Roginsky,* supra, that "the consequences of imposing punitive damages in a case like the present are so serious" that "particularly careful scrutiny" is warranted. 378 F.2d at 852 (denying petition for rehearing); cf. Comment, Criminal Safeguards and the Punitive Damages Defendant, 34 U.Chi.L.Rev. 408, 417 (1967)("If one accepts the proposition that the consequences of punitive damages can be 'momentous and serious,' then justice requires increasing the burden of persuasion of the plaintiff in a punitive damages action.") We therefore hold under Virgin Islands law that a plaintiff seeking punitive damages, at least in an action in which liability is predicated on § 402A, must prove the requisite "outrageous" conduct by clear and convincing proof.[18] Accord Wangen v. Ford Motor Co., supra; Model Uniform Product Liability Act § 120(A), 44 Fed.Reg. 62748 (1979).

C. The Standard Applied

Applying the "clear and convincing" standard to the facts of this case, we conclude that the [evidence was insufficient to support the punitive damages awards.]

Plaintiff's evidence allegedly supporting his claim for punitive damages essentially consisted of the following:

> 1. The rear wheel of his motorcycle collapsed from a thirty-five mile per hour impact with a ditch four inches deep;

> 2. The particular wheel of plaintiff's motorcycle suffered from an inherent lack of strength as evidenced by the fact that it weighed sixteen percent less than several other randomly sampled rear wheels of motorcycles of the same model;

---

ments are risks which investors knowingly undertake, and investors should not enjoy ill-gotten gains. There is a public interest to encourage shareholders and corporate management to exercise closer control over the operations of the entity, and the imposition of punitive damages may serve this interest. Wangen v. Ford Motor Co., 294 N.W.2d 437, 453–54 (Wis.1980).

18. Even with such proof, however, a plaintiff is not entitled to recover such damages as a matter of right. Rather the Restatement is quite clear that the award is discretionary with the trier of fact. See § 908 comment *d*.

3. The owner's manual represented the CB750 as a high-speed touring motorcycle but provided no warning that the rear wheel might collapse upon the type of impact that occurred in this case;

4. Although the owner's manual instructed users to set and maintain the tension of the motorcycle's shock absorbers and wheel spokes, the manual did not warn that the failure to do so might result in the collapse of the wheel;

5. Defendants merely spot-checked rear wheels during the assembly process and did not crush test or weigh each wheel;

6. Plaintiff's expert witness testified that the above evidence constituted defective manufacture and a failure adequately to inspect or to warn; and

7. Plaintiff's expert concluded that defendant's conduct manifested a "colossal disregard for the safety of the users of the motor vehicle."[20]

Plaintiff contends that the jury was entitled to infer from this evidence that defendants recklessly disregarded his rights and safety as a user of the motorcycle. We cannot agree. As we have suggested above, § 908 of the Restatement declares that reckless or outrageous conduct on the part of the defendant is the touchstone of punitive damages. [While] § 908 does not elaborate on the kind of conduct for which punitive damages are appropriate, cmt. *b* refers to § 500. . . .

The commentary accompanying § 500 provides:

Recklessness may consist of either of two different types of conduct. In one the actor knows, or has reason to know . . . of facts which create a high degree of risk of physical harm to another, and deliberately proceeds to act, or to fail to act, in conscious disregard of, or indifference to, that risk. In the other the actor has such knowledge, or reason to know, of the facts, but does not realize or appreciate the high degree of risk involved, although a reasonable man in his position would do so. An objective standard is applied to him and he is held to the realization of the aggravated risk which a reasonable man in his place would have, although he does not himself have it.

* * *

For either type of conduct, to be reckless it must be unreasonable; but to be reckless, it must be something more than negligent. It must not only

---

20. Although not raised on appeal, the admissibility of this statement under Fed. R.Evid. 702 or 704 is open to serious question.

be unreasonable, but it must involve a risk of harm to others substantially in excess of that necessary to make the conduct negligent. It must involve an easily perceptible danger of death or substantial physical harm, and the probability that it will so result must be substantially greater than is required for ordinary negligence.

We have examined the evidence; viewed in the light most favorable to plaintiff, it does not show that the conduct of any defendant was outrageous or reckless. Indeed we discern no basis upon which the jury could have concluded that defendants knew or had reason to know that the rear wheel of Acosta's motorcycle was defective in design or manufacture and that they decided not to remedy the defect in conscious disregard of or indifference to the risk thereby created. Although the wheel had been used in over 275,000 motorcycles, and the model first offered in 1970 (six years before plaintiff's accident), there was no evidence of previous consumer complaints or lawsuits that might have called to defendants' attention that there might be a problem. Moreover, plaintiff offered no proof that defendants developed or failed to modify the engineering designs for the rear wheel of the CB750 with any knowledge or reason to know of its alleged lack of safety.[21] Such matters would have been admissible on the punitive damages issues.

In short, a jury could not have reasonably concluded that the evidence by the clear and convincing standard showed defendants to have acted with reckless disregard for the safety of users of the CB750. Accordingly, we hold that the district court should have granted defendants' motions for directed verdicts on the punitive damage claim and that it was error to deny the subsequent motions for judgment n.o.v. on behalf of Honda and Daido Kogyo.

[Punitive damages awards reversed; remanded.]

NOTES

1. Compare Satcher v. Honda Motor Co., 52 F.3d 1311 (5th Cir. 1995)(reversing $2 million punitive award based on manufacturer's failure to equip motorcycle with leg guards; insufficient proof of malice); Butler v. Yamaha Motor Co., 1993 WL 95513 (E.D.Pa.1993)(upholding $250,000 punitive award based on numerous complaints of front-end wobble).

2. Purposes. In addition to punishment and deterrence, punitive or "exemplary" damages further serve to maximize compliance with the rules of law and to provide additional compensation for plaintiffs. They are often criticized for giving plaintiffs undeserved windfalls since they are awarded in addition to compensatory damages. They are, indeed, a powerful tool in the hands of a skillful plaintiff's

---

21. In fact, defendants adduced evidence, which was not contradicted, that pre-production testing followed standard procedures, including on-the-road testing and laboratory testing (including wheel crushing to determine durability), and that samples from each production run of completed motorcycles were subjected to final dynamometer tests before shipping. Apparently, none of these tests suggested that a problem might exist.

lawyer. How appropriate are such damages in the products liability context? In *strict* liability cases?

3. Warranty. Most courts hold that punitive damages will not lie in warranty cases, applying the general rule prohibiting such awards in contract cases. See UCC § 1–106(1): "[N]either consequential or special nor penal damages may be had except as specifically provided in this Act or by any other rule of law."

4. Infrequency of Such Awards. Punitive damages awards were rare in products liability cases until the 1980s. Since then, they have been slightly on a rise in both frequency and size, particularly in asbestos and cigarette litigation. Nevertheless, such awards remain very uncommon, being awarded in only about 2–3% of all products liability cases. Since they are occasionally rendered in automotive and toxic substance litigation, they are considered further in those contexts in chapters 17 and 18, below.

5. Bankruptcy. The threat of punitive damages judgments may have played a role in the bankruptcy of Johns–Manville in 1983, yet punitive damages were only a part of the tens of thousands of claims arising out of the sale of asbestos products over many years without warning of the risks of asbestosis and other lung disorders. Nearly 70 other asbestos companies have followed in Manville's wake so far, also filing for Chapter 11 bankruptcy protection. See Stiglitz et al., The Impact of Asbestos Liabilities on Workers in Bankrupt Firms, 12 J. Bankr. L. & Prac. 51, 52 (2003) (also noting that 47 states have experienced at least one asbestos-related bankruptcy). See also Slawotsky, New York's Article 16 and Multiple Defendant Product Liability Litigation: A Time To Rethink the Impact of Bankrupt Shares on Judgment Molding, 76 St. John's L. Rev. 397 (2002). The problems of punitive damages in the context of toxic substances, such as asbestos and silicone breast implants, are examined in ch. 19, below.

Another company that chose the bankruptcy route (in 1984–85) in the face of massive claims for punitive (and compensatory) damages was A.H. Robins, in connection with the Dalkon Shield litigation, discussed above. A federal court confirmed a reorganization plan for the company in 1988, establishing a $2 billion claimants' trust fund for compensatory damages. Stating that the company's punitive damages liability was "staggering" and "unpredictable," and that such damages would have been a "wild card" undermining a realistic reorganization plan, the court ruled that punitive damages claims would be disallowed. See Prod.Safety & Liab.Rep. (BNA) 793 (Aug. 19, 1988). The *Tetuan* court, among others, questioned whether Robins' bankruptcy petition might have been more of a strategic maneuver, in the management of the thousands of pending cases it confronted around the country, than a true reflection of insolvency (which is not required under Chapter 11). See Tetuan v. A.H. Robins Co., 738 P.2d 1210, 1244 (Kan. 1987).

6. Multiplicity of Awards. *Acosta* touches upon, and the asbestos and breast implant cases illustrate, the problems for manufacturers confronting hundreds or thousands (or tens of thousands) of punitive damages claims all arising out of a single product. The courts generally reject policy-based arguments that such claims should be denied because of the risks of over-punishment, and the appellate decisions unanimously conclude (but often with regret) that such repetitive awards do not violate due process. See Dunn v. HOVIC, 1 F.3d 1371 (3d Cir.)(but reducing $25 million award to $2 million), modified, 13 F.3d 58 (3d Cir.1993); Spaur v. Owens–Corning Fiberglas Corp., 510 N.W.2d 854 (Iowa 1994); W.R. Grace & Co. v. Waters, 638 So.2d 502 (Fla.1994); Ripa v. Owens–Corning Fiberglas, 660 A.2d 521 (N.J.Super.App. Div.1995)(likening punitive damages awards in mass tort cases to a "national lottery," but noting that no appellate court has ever found repetitive awards violative of due process).

7. Expert Testimony. The plaintiff's expert in *Acosta* testified that the defendant's conduct reflected "a colossal disregard for . . . safety." 717 F.2d at 840. What do you think of this form of "expert" testimony on manufacturer reprehensibility as foundational "evidence" for a punitive damages award? See also American Cyanamid Co. v. Roy, 498 So.2d 859, 862 (Fla.1986)("terrible misrepresentation"); Chrysler Corp. v. Wolmer, 499 So.2d 823, 827 (Fla.1986)("an atrocious violation of accepted practices in safety engineering" reflecting "a reckless disregard for safety"); Sliman v. Aluminum Co. of America, 731 P.2d 1267, 1275 (Idaho 1986)("extreme deviation from the customary practice in the industry"); Airco, Inc. v. Simmons First Nat. Bank, 638 S.W.2d 660, 662–63 (Ark.1982)(product was "grossly in violation of safety engineering principles and never should have been put on the market"); Ford Motor Co. v. Stubblefield, 319 S.E.2d 470 (Ga.App.1984) (defendant's actions were "conscious," "deliberate," and "callous").

The last two cases involved the same expert, a "system safety and human factors enginee[r]" who is said to have testified "in over 100 cases with products ranging from toys to airplanes" and whose "field of expertise" is said to be "punitive damages based on engineering management negligence" in a Technical Expert Directory. Products Liability and Transportation Legal Directory 196 (1983). Having apparently made such testimony on corporate "malice" his specialty, this particular expert apparently proved successful in his efforts: in *Airco,* the jury returned a $3 million punitive damages verdict for the sale of a defective anesthesia ventilator and, in *Stubblefield,* the jury assessed punitive damages of $8 million for the sale of an uncrashworthy car.

Most courts, in the few opinions reflecting such expert testimony on corporate malice, either pay little or no attention to its propriety (as in *Airco* and *Stubblefield*), or reason that it is proper. Karns v. Emerson Elec. Co., 817 F.2d 1452, 1459 (10th Cir.1987)("reckless"). In *Acosta,* supra n.20, Judge Becker expressed serious doubts as to its admissibility. What is the problem? What are the relevant rules of evidence? What are the policy issues?

As a plaintiff's lawyer, would you seek to have your expert so testify? As a judge, would you permit such testimony?

8. Judicial Control—Beginnings. *Acosta* is an example of the kind of stricter control over the process of determining punitive damage awards that some courts began to apply as early as the late 1970s as such awards began to increase in frequency and amount. As more punitive assessments were rendered and reviewed, many courts began to appreciate the importance of rigorous oversight of such awards, from discovery safeguards and pretrial rulings through remittitur or reversal on appeal. See Owen, Problems in Assessing Punitive Damages Against Manufacturers of Defective Products, 49 U.Chi.L.Rev. 1, 50 (1982).

9. Judicial Controls—Variety. Today, courts constrain punitive damages in a variety of ways. See, e.g., In re Wilson, 451 F.3d 161, 165 (3d Cir. 2006) (in Multidistrict Diet Drug Product Liability Litigation, involving Pondimin and Redox, class members who opt out may "file suit against Wyeth and others with certain restrictions, the most prominent of which is a bar against seeking an award of punitive damages"); Brown & Williamson Tobacco Corp. v. Gault, 627 S.E.2d 549, 553–54 (Ga. 2006) (individuals prohibited from making punitive damages claims against cigarette manufacturers due to state attorney general's prior settlement agreement with those manufacturers: "The State's release of its punitive damages claim as parens patriae preclude[d] plaintiffs from pursuing the same claim."); Rhode Island v. Lead Indus., 2006 WL 691803 (R.I. Super. Ct. 2006) (lead paint pigment manufacturers liable for public nuisance but not subject to punitive damages because they no longer produced the offending paint and because lead poisoning thresholds have markedly changed in recent years); Phillips v. Cricket Lighters, 883 A.2d 439 (Pa. 2005) (manufacturer's failure to render its butane lighter adequately child-proof was not wanton, particularly since it complied with applicable safety standards).

10. Since the 1990s, the Supreme Court has explicitly required such controls to prevent punitive assessments from violating a defendant's due process rights, as examined below.

———

Henley v. Philip Morris Inc.

California Court of Appeal, 2004.
9 Cal.Rptr.3d 29, 114 Cal.App.4th 1429, cert. denied, 544 U.S. 920 (2005).

■ Sepulveda, J.

Plaintiff brought this action for personal injuries allegedly sustained as a result of defendant's tortious misconduct in the manufacture and marketing of cigarettes. The jury returned a special verdict awarding plaintiff $1.5 million in compensatory damages and $50 million in punitive damages. The trial court denied defendant's motions for new trial and judgment notwithstanding the verdict, except that it ordered a new trial on punitive damages unless plaintiff consented to reduce the punitive award to $25 million. Plaintiff consented to the reduction, and defendant filed a timely appeal.

In our original opinion we affirmed the judgment in its entirety. Henley v. Philip Morris, 113 Cal.Rptr.2d 494 (2001). [On defendant's appeal, the California Supreme Court twice remanded the case to us], this time in light of State Farm Mut. Auto. Ins. Co. v. Campbell, 538 U.S. 408 (2003) (*Campbell*). In that case the United States Supreme Court elaborated considerably upon the federal constitutional principles constraining civil punitive damage awards. We have concluded that in light of that decision, the $25 million in punitive damages awarded in this matter cannot be sustained on the present record, but that an award of $9 million would satisfy the constitutional standards enunciated in that case. Accordingly we will reverse for a new trial on punitive damages unless plaintiff agrees to a reduction of the judgment to reflect such smaller award. * * *

Viewed most favorably to the judgment, the evidence shows that plaintiff, who was born in 1946, began smoking cigarettes in 1961 or 1962, at the age of 15, when she "lit up" with some school friends outside a dance. At that time she felt smoking was "cool" and "grown up," provided the pleasure of the forbidden, made her look older, and served as a "rite of passage." Then and for some years thereafter, nobody told her that cigarettes could cause her serious disease. There were no warnings on cigarette packages or in advertisements. Plaintiff was not taught in school about the dangers of tobacco. As a result she believed that cigarettes, which contained "[t]obacco, pure and simple," were "not a harmful product." Nor did she know that cigarettes or nicotine could be addicting. Nothing in the advertising she saw suggested that if she started smoking she might be unable to stop.

The jury could also find that starting no later than December 1953, defendant and other cigarette manufacturers agreed to act together to counter mounting scientific evidence about the health risks of cigarette smoking. By the time plaintiff began smoking, defendant knew that tobacco contained numerous carcinogenic substances as well as flavoring additives that also produced carcinogenic compounds upon combustion. Tobacco manufacturers were also aware of epidemiological studies that showed a strong correlation between smoking and the incidence of lung cancer. Yet they launched a concerted public relations campaign to deny any link between smoking and serious illness. A major part of this strategy was the creation of a "research institute" that would, as the public was told, attempt to find the truth about smoking and health—though in fact it was permitted to conduct very little research that might confirm a link, serving mainly, as the jury was entitled to find, to gather ammunition against tobacco's detractors. Other strategies included manipulating the mass media to suppress or make light of adverse news developments, such as new studies or reports.

The jury could also find that defendant engaged in saturation advertising, much of it consciously targeting the teenage audience from which new ("replacement") smokers had to come. Defendant knew that persons who did not begin smoking during their teen years were unlikely to do so. In particular, defendant sold the brand of cigarette plaintiff preferred, Marlboro, using symbols of the independence, autonomy, and mature strength for which teenagers were understood to yearn. The jury could find that these targeted teenage consumers possessed less critical judgment, and were more receptive to marketing manipulation generally, than might be the case with adults. The jury could find that teenagers who went past the experimentation phase became addicted to tobacco, as a result of which they found it extremely difficult to stop smoking and often suffered impaired judgment with respect to the consequences of continuing to do so. The jury could find that the strategy of marketing to teenagers and causing them to become addicted to its products was central to the tremendous success and profitability of the Marlboro brand in particular, helping defendant to become one of the largest and most successful corporations in the world.

In 1966, as evidence of health risks mounted, Congress required that cigarette packages bear the relatively mild warning that smoking "may be hazardous." In 1969, Congress required a somewhat stronger warning and required that it appear in advertising as well as on packages. At the same time, Congress explicitly preempted any state law imposing a "requirement or prohibition with respect to advertising or promotion" of cigarettes—language that has since been construed to preempt many but not all common-law tort claims. Although the warnings have since been further strengthened, this partial federal immunity remains in place, and is one of defendant's major defenses [the discussion of which is omitted—Eds.].

In 1988 the tobacco industry acquired a safe harbor under California law when, riding the coattails of a legislative compromise, tobacco was listed among "common consumer products" in former section 1714.45, a statute construed the following year to create an almost complete "immunity" from tort liability.[2] The Legislature repealed that protection effective January 1, 1998, but defendant contended below that it nonetheless applied to bar most or all of plaintiff's claims [the discussion of which is omitted—Eds.].

The jury would have been entitled to find that well before these legislative defenses became applicable, plaintiff had become an addicted smoker with sharply impaired judgment and will where cigarettes were concerned. Plaintiff testified that on the subject of cigarette smoking and health, "my brain wasn't going to register anything that anybody said." When she saw the first package warnings, she minimized the perceived "degree[ ] of danger," thinking to herself that it was also "dangerous to walk across the street." She testified that while she heard the United States Surgeon General was saying things about cigarettes, she also knew "that the tobacco companies were saying different." As a result, the package warning "didn't faze me one way or the other. I wasn't going to give the cigarettes up at that point."

Plaintiff's first regular brand of cigarettes was Marlboro, and it remained her favorite brand throughout almost all of her 35-year smoking history. From age 15 until she was about 43 years old (around 1989), she apparently smoked one-and-a-half to two packs a day of "Marlboro Red," a brand rated to deliver relatively high amounts of tar and nicotine. At that age, however, she switched to Marlboro Lights, a lower-tar brand, on what the jury was entitled to view as the direct advice of a Philip Morris agent. Plaintiff testified that around that time she began to hear that "low-tar cigarettes were better. You wouldn't get as much tar and nicotine and, you know, their advertising on the low-tar cigarettes was really out there."

> I'm thinking, "Well, okay. Maybe there's something to this." So when I was approximately 43, I decided that, "Well, I'll check into this and maybe I'll change from the Reds to the Lights."
>
> So I did indeed call the Marlboro, Philip Morris company and expressed, you know, my concerns as to, "Is it really true? Is there less tar in this or less nicotine?"
>
> And I was assured at the time that if I was concerned that, yes, I could switch to the Lights. . . .

She did so and, in a few weeks, had more or less doubled her intake, to three-and-a-half packs a day. By mid-October 1997 plaintiff "was feeling really bad" and "down for the count with what I thought was heavy-duty

---

2. All references to former section 1714.45 are to the version in effect from January 1, 1988, to January 1, 1998.

flu.'' She was diagnosed in February 1998 with small-cell carcinoma of the lung. The jury was more than entitled to find that this affliction was directly caused by cigarette smoking.

[The court rejected the defendant's arguments on the state immunity statute and on federal preemption, and it found that evidence in the record supported the jury's findings that the defendant's cigarettes were defectively designed (under the consumer expectations test) and that the defendant had failed to provide adequate warnings prior to enactment of the federal statute in 1969. As for the plaintiff's claims of fraud, the court remarked in part:]

* * * Our review of the record satisfies us that there was substantial evidence, which defendant does not cogently dispute for purposes of this appeal, that it engaged in a conscious, deliberate scheme to deceive the public, and individual smokers and potential smokers (many or most of whom it knew to be adolescents), about the health hazards and addictive effects of cigarette smoking. The jury could properly find that commencing no later than 1953 and continuing at least until the time of plaintiff's diagnosis, defendant and other cigarette manufacturers acted both in concert and individually to issue innumerable false denials and assurances concerning the dangers of smoking, deliberately fostering a false impression by the public, or more precisely by smokers and prospective smokers, that assertions of health risk were overblown products of puritanical prejudice, that any real hazards had yet to be shown, and that the industry itself was acting and would act diligently to discover the scientific truth of the matter and promptly disclose its findings, good or bad. The jury could also find that plaintiff heard of these false assurances and denials, if only indirectly, and was falsely led to believe, as defendant intended, that there was a legitimate ''controversy'' about whether cigarettes actually caused cancer or carried any other serious health risks. As a consequence of that information and the distorted judgment brought about by addiction, she was unaffected by reports of adverse health effects because she was unpersuaded they were true or reliable enough to warrant any action by her.

* * *

Defendant attempts to characterize and then attack plaintiff's fraud theory as ''fraud on the market,'' a concept developed under federal securities law, which [our supreme court has] refused to import into our common law of torts. . . . Neither that rule nor its context-specific rationale has any bearing on fraud contended to have been practiced on a vast group of consumers, causing many of them to sustain personal injuries. The facts of this case might be more accurately called ''fraud on the public,'' but even that it is misleading. Plaintiff herself was an intended target and victim of the fraud, through precisely the mechanisms of transmission intended by defendant and its coconspirators. Defendant has failed to show any defect in the jury's verdict on the affirmative fraud claims.

[The court concluded that the jury properly could find for the plaintiff on the breach of express warranty claim, based on the ambiguous telephone representations made to the plaintiff by a Philip Morris agent as described above, which "supported an inference that defendant's representative expressly assured plaintiff that Lights eliminated or reduced whatever risks smoking might otherwise pose." The court also ruled that sufficient evidence supported the plaintiff's fraudulent concealment claim.]

PUNITIVE DAMAGES

A. *Sufficiency of Evidence.*

* * * The jury may award punitive damages "where it is proven by clear and convincing evidence that the defendant has been guilty of oppression, fraud, or malice." Civ.Code, § 3294, subd. (a). " 'Malice' means conduct which is intended by the defendant to cause injury to the plaintiff or despicable conduct which is carried on by the defendant with a willful and conscious disregard of the rights or safety of others." Id., (c)(1). " 'Oppression' means despicable conduct that subjects a person to cruel and unjust hardship in conscious disregard of that person's rights." Id., (c)(2). " 'Fraud' means an intentional misrepresentation, deceit, or concealment of a material fact known to the defendant with the intention on the part of the defendant of thereby depriving a person of property or legal rights or otherwise causing injury." Id., (c)(3).

* * *

Defendant ... attacks the trial court's opinion explaining its denial of defendant's motion to set aside the punitive damages award. The court found the evidence "fully sufficient" to support express or implied jury findings that defendant willfully and consciously marketed its cigarettes to teenagers, violated promises and representations to the public by concealing and suppressing information known to it concerning the addictive and harmful properties of its product, and "affirmatively misled the American public by advertising that there was genuine and legitimate controversy in the scientific community on the subject of smoker health, when in fact there was no such controversy." In responding to these points defendant fails to fairly summarize or address the evidence underlying the judgment.

[Defendant's documents provide a basis for the plaintiff's "targeting of teenagers" claim, including a discussion of the smoking habits and "market penetration" among children as young as 12, and another document reviews the history of Marlboro's success and the business risks posed by a coming decline in the number of teenagers and includes the statement, "Because of our high share of the market among the *youngest* smokers, Philip Morris will suffer more than the other companies...."]

Defendant contends that its failure to disclose that cigarettes are addictive does not support a punitive award because "it is, at bottom, a quibble over definitions." If so, it is a quibble of which the tobacco industry is the chief author and beneficiary. The question is not whether the term "addictive" applies to cigarettes in some narrow medical sense but whether a reasonable effort should have been made to bring home to defendant's mostly teenage "starters" market the extreme difficulty they were likely to encounter in any future attempt to stop smoking. To borrow language used in 1965 congressional hearings, "For many people, the choice to smoke, once it has been made, may as a practical matter be irrevocable." Cigarette Labeling and Advertising Hearings before Sen. Com. on Commerce on Sen. Nos. 559 and 547, 89th Cong., 1st Sess., at p. 500 (1965).

We have examined defendant's remaining points concerning the evidence of oppression, fraud, or malice, and find them to be insufficient to carry defendant's burden of showing that the finding on that subject was marred by error.

B.   Size of Award—Federal Constitutional Constraints.

In our previous opinion we rejected defendant's intertwined arguments that the award was the product of passion and prejudice and was excessive under state and federal law. We are now called upon to reconsider in light of State Farm Mut. Auto. Ins. Co. v. Campbell, 538 U.S. 408 (2003) (*Campbell*), whether the award exceeded the federal constitutional limits articulated in that case. We have concluded that the present award cannot be sustained consistent with *Campbell*, but that an award of $9 million is permissible and appropriate on this record.

"The Due Process Clause of the Fourteenth Amendment prohibits the imposition of grossly excessive or arbitrary punishments on a tortfeasor." *Campbell*; see BMW of North America, Inc. v. Gore, 517 U.S. 559, 562 (1996) (*Gore*). This constraint derives from the fundamental unfairness inherent in arbitrary deprivations of life, liberty, or property, and in the imposition of punishment without fair notice. *Campbell*; *Gore* ["'[e]lementary notions of fairness enshrined in our constitutional jurisprudence dictate that a person receive fair notice not only of the conduct that will subject him to punishment, but also of the severity of the penalty that a State may impose."]. Because civil punitive damage awards present a significant risk of arbitrary punishment exceeding that of which the defendant had fair notice, the Supreme Court has undertaken to "constitutionalize" the field by adopting a variety of substantive and procedural safeguards against excessive awards. Among the procedural safeguards is the requirement, which we assume applies to the present case, that appellate scrutiny of punitive awards be governed by a "de novo" standard of review. *Campbell*; cf. Cooper Industries, Inc. v. Leatherman Tool Group, Inc., 532 U.S. 424, 431, 436 (2001) (*Cooper Industries*).

In determining the sustainability of a punitive award the constitutional "guideposts" to be considered are (1) the degree of the defendant's culpability, i.e., the reprehensibility of his or her conduct, (2) the ratio between the punitive award and the harm to the victim caused by the defendant's actions, and (3) the sanctions imposed in other cases for comparable misconduct. *Campbell*; *Cooper Industries*; see *Gore*.

The "most important" of the three guideposts is the degree of reprehensibility of the defendant's conduct. *Campbell*. The record reflects that defendant touted to children what it knew to be a cumulatively toxic substance, while doing everything it could to prevent them and other addicts and prospective addicts from appreciating the true nature and effects of that product. The result of this conduct was that millions of youngsters, including plaintiff, were persuaded to participate in a habit that was likely to, and did, bring many of them to early illness and death. Such conduct supports a substantial award sufficient to reflect the moral opprobrium in which defendant's conduct can and should be held, and warrants something approaching the maximum punishment consistent with constitutional principles.

The Supreme Court has identified several subsidiary factors which pertain to the degree of reprehensibility of a defendant's conduct: (1) whether the defendant inflicted bodily as opposed to merely economic injury; (2) whether its tortious conduct "evinced an indifference to or a reckless disregard of the health or safety of others"; (3) whether "the target of the conduct had financial vulnerability"; (4) whether the conduct "involved repeated actions or was an isolated incident"; and (5) whether the harm was "the result of intentional malice, trickery, or deceit, or mere accident." *Campbell*. Each of these factors supports finding a high degree of reprehensibility here. The gist of plaintiff's claim was not that defendant inflicted an economic harm but that its conduct caused her severe *bodily* injury in the form of lung cancer. Defendant's malicious infliction of such an injury is, in that respect, substantially more reprehensible than the conduct at issue in *Campbell* (bad faith denial of insurance claim), *Gore* (intentional concealment of repair history in sale of "new" automobile), or *Cooper Industries* (unfair competition, including false advertising, in sale of competing product). Further, defendant's conduct arguably betrayed an attitude characterized not by mere indifference or recklessness, but by a conscious acceptance of the injurious results.

Moreover defendant consciously exploited the known vulnerabilities of *children,* who by its own words comprised its "traditional area of strength." The court in *Campbell* and *Gore* stated the third reprehensibility subfactor in terms of *financial* vulnerability, but that characterization undoubtedly reflects the origins of those opinions in torts of an essentially economic nature. In other cases, such as this one, it makes sense to ask whether and to what extent the defendant took advantage of a known vulnerability on the part of the victim to the conduct triggering the award of punitive damages, or to the resulting harm.[20]

It thus appears that *all five* of the subfactors in *Campbell* point to a high degree of reprehensibility. However defendant emphasizes the court's criticism of the award there under review for resting in major part on conduct which did not resemble, and had no concrete connection with, the conduct which injured the plaintiffs. Justice Kennedy criticized the punitive claim there for not relying on the insurer's wrongful "conduct toward

---

20. Obviously defendant's conduct was also particularly reprehensible on the fourth and fifth axes, i.e., it "involved repeated actions" rather than "an isolated incident," and it inflicted harm by "intentional malice, trickery, or deceit," rather than "mere accident." *Campbell*. These factors are present even when we focus on the conduct contributing to plaintiff's own injuries.

the Campbells," but for instead having been "used as a platform to expose, and punish, the perceived deficiencies of State Farm's operations *throughout the country.*" The court went on to identify three categories of conduct which should have been considered with caution, if at all. It first noted that a state "cannot punish a defendant for conduct that may have been lawful where it occurred." (Jury should be instructed "that it may not use evidence of out-of-state conduct to punish a defendant for action that was lawful in the jurisdiction where it occurred"). Such conduct "may be probative when it demonstrates the deliberateness and culpability of the defendant's action in the State where it is tortious, but that conduct must have a nexus to the specific harm suffered by the plaintiff." Second, a similar constraint will often apply to *unlawful* out-of-state conduct, given that a state ordinarily has no legitimate interest in "imposing punitive damages to punish a defendant for unlawful acts committed outside of the State's jurisdiction." And finally, punitive damages cannot permissibly rest on "dissimilar acts" that "b[ear] no relation to the [plaintiff's] harm."

Defendant contends that these limitations render the award here unconstitutional because the jury heard substantial evidence of wrongful conduct outside California, conduct that may have been lawful where (and when) it occurred, and conduct having no causal connection to the harm suffered by plaintiff. Unlike the defendant in *Campbell*, however, defendant made no attempt to anticipate the Supreme Court's direction by objecting to the evidence or seeking a limiting instruction. See *Campbell*. Defendant also substantially overstates this aspect of *Campbell* by suggesting that it rendered such evidence categorically inadmissible. On the contrary, the court acknowledged that such evidence may be considered if a sufficient "nexus" is shown to the plaintiff's claim. (Id.; see *Gore*, italics added [state "does not have the power . . . to punish [a defendant] for conduct that was lawful where it occurred *and that had no impact on [the forum state] or its residents*"].)

In any event we believe that any error in the consideration of this evidence is sufficiently redressed by the conditional modification we direct here, which reduces the punitive award to a level below which we believe no properly instructed jury was reasonably likely to go. The effect of the evidence affected by these concerns is not nearly as dramatic here as it was in *Campbell*. There the plaintiffs' own cause of action rested on a delay in allowing a single insurance claim, and associated conduct; yet the claim for punitive damages rested on a wholesale attack on many aspects of the defendant's nationwide business practices, including even its assertedly malicious treatment of its employees. Plaintiff's claims, in contrast, rest on a quintessential "mass tort," i.e., a course of more-or-less uniform conduct *directed at the entire public* and maliciously injuring, through a system of interconnected devices, an entire category of persons to which plaintiff squarely belongs.

This brings us to a consideration of the *Campbell* court's discussion of the second *Gore* factor, which is the relationship between the actual damages suffered by the plaintiff and the punitive damage award. It is on this point that we believe the present award of $25 million cannot be sustained. Although the *Campbell* court reiterated its earlier refusals to "impose a bright-line ratio which a punitive damages award cannot exceed" *Campbell*; TXO Production Corp. v. Alliance Resources Corp., 509 U.S. 443, 458 (1993), it went on to suggest several concrete numerical guidelines for considering whether a particular award violates constitutional restraints. Specifically, it stated that (1) "few awards exceeding a single-digit ratio between punitive and compensatory damages, to a significant degree, will satisfy due process"; (2) a "4–to–1 ratio" may typically be "close to the line of constitutional impropriety"; (3) higher ratios may be appropriate where " 'a particularly egregious act has resulted in only a small amount of economic damages,' " where " 'the injury is hard to detect,' " or where " 'the monetary value of noneconomic harm might have been difficult to determine' "; (4) lower ratios—perhaps as low as 1 to 1—may "reach the outermost limit of the due process guarantee" where "compensatory damages are substantial"; but (5) the "precise award in any case . . . must be based upon the facts and circumstances of the defendant's conduct and the harm to the plaintiff.", quoting *Gore*.

The court found the award there, which was 145 times the compensatory damages awarded, constitutionally infirm for a number of reasons: (1) the plaintiffs had been fully compensated by a substantial award of compensatory damages; (2) the harm arose from an economic transaction, "not from some physical assault or trauma," and resulted in no physical injuries; (3) the actual economic damages suffered were "minor" because the defendant insurer had ultimately paid the judgment its conduct caused the plaintiffs to suffer; and (4) the compensatory damages thus probably already included an award for "outrage and humiliation," which was then duplicated in the punitive award. *Campbell*. The court rejected the Utah Supreme Court's conclusion that the award was justified by other factors, notably the wealth of the defendant and the likelihood, according to expert testimony, that other misconduct by the defendant would go unpunished. The court rejected the Utah Supreme Court's justification of the award on grounds that, under the third *Gore* "guidepost," it was proportionate to other sanctions which might have been imposed.[21] The court concluded that the award there "was neither reasonable nor proportionate to the wrong

---

21. . . . We place limited reliance on the proportionality factor here, but note that defendant's earlier arguments on this point seemed to backfire. Defendant suggested analogizing its conduct to furnishing tobacco to a minor under California law (Bus. & Prof.Code, § 22958 [civil penalty from $200 for first offense to $6,000 for fifth offense]; Pen.Code, § 308 [penal fine of $200 for first offense up to $1,000 for third offense]) or to violations of the 1969 Act (15 U.S.C. § 1337 [$10,000 per violation]). By our calculations, and in light of the repetitive nature of defendant's conduct, these statutes could support fines in the range of $6.6 million to $11 million, respectively. Assuming plaintiff smoked for three years before reaching the age of 18, and assuming defendant (by its own analogy) furnished cigarettes to her every day of that time, its conduct would seemingly constitute nearly 1,100 violations of the two California statutes cited, and would arguably constitute as many violations of the federal statutes. Assessing the maximum civil penalties of $6,000 and $10,000, respectively, would yield a total state penalty of some $6.6 million and a federal penalty of some $11 million.

committed, and it was an irrational and arbitrary deprivation of the property of the defendant." It remanded the matter to the Utah courts for a "proper calculation of punitive damages under the principles we have discussed."

In light of *Campbell* we do not believe the 17–to–1 ratio reflected in the present judgment can withstand scrutiny. As we read that case, a double-digit ratio will be justified rarely, and perhaps never in a case where the plaintiff has recovered an ample award of compensatory damages. Indeed, where a plaintiff has been fully compensated with a substantial compensatory award, any ratio over 4 to 1 is "close to the line." [See] *Campbell*. Nonetheless we believe a higher ratio (6 to 1) is justified here by the extraordinarily reprehensible conduct of which plaintiff was a direct victim. There is no reason to believe that the compensatory damages were inflated so as to duplicate elements of the punitive award. Moreover, as we have noted, plaintiff's injuries were not merely economic, but physical, and nothing done by defendant mitigated or ameliorated them in any respect.

C. Size of Award—State Law Constraints.

Under California law, a punitive damage award may be reversed as excessive "only if the entire record, viewed most favorably to the judgment, indicates the award was the result of passion and prejudice." [Citation.] "The purpose of punitive damages is a public one—to punish wrongdoing and deter future misconduct by either the defendant or other potential wrongdoers. The essential question for the jury, the trial court, and the appellate courts is whether the amount of the award substantially serves the public interest in punishment and deterrence. The California Supreme Court has established three criteria for making that determination: (1) the reprehensibility of the defendant's misdeeds; (2) the amount of compensatory damages, though there is no fixed ratio for determining whether punitive damages are reasonable in relation to actual damages; and (3) the defendant's financial condition. [Citations.] The wealthier the wrongdoer, the larger the punitive damage award must be to meet the goals of punishment and deterrence. [Citations.]"

Defendant correctly notes that the constitutional soundness of the third consideration has been rendered uncertain by *Campbell's* seemingly categorical rejection of the Utah Supreme Court's reliance on the defendant's "massive wealth" as one justification for the award there. *Campbell*, quoting Campbell v. State Farm Mut. Auto. Ins. Co., 65 P.3d 1134, 1153 (Utah 2001). The court declared that "[t]he wealth of a defendant cannot justify an otherwise unconstitutional punitive damages award." We need not determine the precise effect of this declaration on California law, however, because in view of our downward reduction of the verdict we do not believe an instruction on this point would have produced a judgment more favorable to defendant.

Defendant also contends that the award is excessive in light of the potential for other actions like this one in which punitive damages may also be awarded, magnifying the deterrent effect. California courts have previously acknowledged the potential multiplicity of awards as a factor that may be weighed, and on proper presentation presumably should or must be weighed, in fixing a punitive damage award. [Citations.] The implementation of *Campbell* will presumably diminish the significance of this factor, however, because it will constrain courts and juries to tailor punitive awards more closely to the harm done to individual plaintiffs, substantially reducing the risk that multiple punitive awards will rest on the same facts and conduct so as to constitute multiple punishment.

Again, however, we need not closely consider the issue because we have already weighed the risk of duplicative punishment in further reducing the award. The trial court did likewise, expressly citing the possibility of future awards as one reason to reduce the jury's award from $50 million to $25 million. The court predicted that numerous suits would be filed against defendant, that the costs of defense and any resulting judgments would be substantial, that punitive damages "undoubtedly will be requested and may well be awarded in many such suits," and that this reinforced the court's conclusion "that $25 million is enough to punish and deter in the present context." Defendant has argued that that the award should have been reduced even further, and with our remittitur today it has. We also reiterate our earlier observation that the risk of multiple punitive awards against defendant remains highly speculative. . . .

Insofar as the award is challenged under California law, we cannot say that, as reduced by the trial court and further reduced by this court, it is the product of passion and prejudice.

[Affirmed, except that the amount of punitive damages is reduced to $9 million if plaintiff consents and, if not, judgment reversed and remanded solely on issue of punitive damages.]

NOTES

1. Compare Boeken v. Philip Morris Inc., 26 Cal.Rptr.3d 638, 686–87 (Ct. App. 2005), cert. denied, 126 S. Ct. 1567 (2006), where a jury awarded about $5.5 million compensatory and $3 *billion* punitive damages to a smoker who contracted cancer. The trial court reduced the punitive damages to $100 million, and the Court of Appeals further remitted the punitive damages judgment to $50 million, about 9:1 ratio which it held was not excessive under *Campbell*.

2. Determining Amount. One of the most perplexing problems for courts and juries has been the determination of appropriate amounts for punitive damages awards. The Restatement common-law formulation is widely accepted, but not too helpful, in directing the factfinder to consider: (1) the character of the defendant's act, (2) the nature and extent of the plaintiff's harm, and (3) the defendant's wealth. Rest. (2d) of Torts § 908(2).

3. Defendant's Wealth and Related Factors. Perhaps the most interesting, and certainly most controversial, type of evidence generally allowable on the amount issue concerns the wealth of the defendant. Evidence of this type—with a corporate defendant, usually data on net income and net worth—is generally admitted on the theory that it takes more to punish a rich person than a poor person. Most courts allow (but do not require) either party to introduce such evidence—the plaintiff, to show the vastness of defendant's resources, the defendant, to show its poverty. Defendants argue that wealth evidence contaminates the deliberative process and biases juries against large corporations. As *Henley* points out, the Supreme Court tends to agree but has yet to declare such evidence constitutionally infirm. A small number of states, including California, *require* proof of wealth as a predicate for a punitive damages award. See, e.g., Adams v. Murakami, 813 P.2d 1348, 1352 (Cal.1991)(holding that the burden of producing evidence of the defendant's wealth lies on the plaintiff: "Without such evidence, a reviewing court can only speculate as to whether the award is appropriate or excessive.").

Some plaintiffs' lawyers ask for, and some juries award, some number of days of profit from the sale of the offending product, or some percentage of the defendant's profits (perhaps in days) or of its net worth. And sometimes juries look to other factors. In a recent asbestos case in New York, the jury awarded each of three plaintiffs $18 million, which the jury tentatively selected as between one-third and one-half the company's annual profit, "to send a message to the company." They settled on these amounts when one juror observed, "Oh, that's such a good number. It means 'life'" in Hebrew. Interviewed after the trial, another juror recalled, "When we heard that, we were like, 'Yes, this is what we want.'" Lambert, Jurors Calculate Punitive Damages In Unusual Manner, Wall St.J., Apr. 14, 1994, at B10.

Compare Ammerman v. Ford Motor Co., Marion Cty.Super.Ct., Ind., Oct. 30, 1995, where the jury awarded $58 million in punitive damages to two girls severely injured in the roll-over of a Bronco II with a high center of gravity and a narrow track width, giving it a propensity to roll over. The award was apparently based on the plaintiffs' lawyers' suggestion that the jury multiply the number of Bronco II vehicles on the road, 700,000, by the $83 Ford estimated (in documents in evidence) that it would cost to modify each vehicle to make it safer. Prod.Liab.Advis. 3 (Nov.1995).

4. **Award Size Factors.** Expanding upon the three Restatement factors in note 1, above, a number of courts and legislatures have adopted some version of the following list of factors in determining appropriate amounts for such awards:

(1) the amount of the plaintiff's litigation expenses;

(2) the seriousness of the hazard to the public;

(3) the profitability of the marketing misconduct (increased by an appropriate multiple);

(4) the attitude and conduct of the enterprise upon discovery of the misconduct;

(5) the degree of the manufacturer's awareness of the hazard and of its excessiveness;

(6) the number and level of employees involved in causing or covering up the marketing misconduct;

(7) the duration of both the improper marketing behavior and its cover-up;

(8) the financial condition of the enterprise and the probable effect thereon of a particular judgment; and

(9) the total punishment the enterprise will probably receive from other sources.

Owen, Punitive Damages in Products Liability Litigation, 74 Mich.L.Rev. 1257, 1319 (1976). What do you think of these factors?

5. Reversal and Remittitur. Because large awards of punitive damages often reflect passion or prejudice by the jury, they are frequently reversed or remitted by the trial or appellate court. Perhaps the most famous award of this type was the $125 million punitive damages verdict against Ford Motor Company in a Pinto fuel system case, Grimshaw v. Ford Motor Co., 174 Cal.Rptr. 348 (Ct.App. 1981), ch. 18 below. The trial court's remittitur to $3.5 million was upheld on appeal. See also Ford Motor Co. v. Durrill, 714 S.W.2d 329 (Tex.App.1986), vac'd and remanded on settlement of parties, 754 S.W.2d 646 (Tex.1988)(Mustang II fuel system) ($100 million punitive damages verdict, remitted by trial court to $20 million, further remitted on appeal to $10 million); General Motors Corp. v. Moseley, 447 S.E.2d 302 (Ga.App.1994) ($101 million punitive verdict for death of youth in fiery crash of GM pickup truck reversed for improper argument by plaintiff's counsel); Hodder v. Goodyear Tire & Rubber Co., 426 N.W.2d 826 (Minn.1988) (multi-piece tire rim exploded; $12.5 million punitive damages verdict reduced to $4 million). "[I]t is because of the unique, public aspect of punitive damages that the court exercises a much closer supervision over these awards than is the case with compensatory awards." Id. at 837.

The most dramatic recent reversal of a punitive damages award came in a Florida smokers' class action that generated a punitive damages award for the entire class of $145 billion. See Liggett Group Inc. v. Engle, 853 So.2d 434 (Fla. Dist. Ct. App. 2003) (award excessive and otherwise improper under both state and federal law), approved and quashed in part, Engle v. Liggett Group, Inc., 2006 WL 3742610 (Fla. 2006) (tort liability finding required before punitive damages liability may be determined; classwide punitive damages not properly assessed prior to determining total compensatory damages for class, so reasonableness of relationship could be evaluated; and amount of punitive award was clearly excessive).

An even more celebrated example is the notorious McDonald's hot coffee case, discussed in ch. 10(2), above, where the jury awarded an elderly woman $2.7 million in punitive damages for the third-degree burns she suffered when she spilled a cup of McDonald's exceedingly hot (reported as 190 degrees) coffee that she was holding between her legs. The jury reportedly fixed on the figure for punitive damages as equaling 2 days of McDonald's gross coffee sales. The jury also awarded $160,000 in compensatory damages for the third degree burns, so severe as to require skin grafts. Less publicized than the verdict was the fact that the trial court remitted the punitive award to $480,000, 3 times the actual damages. See generally Mead, Punitive Damages and the Spill Felt Round the World: A U.S. Perspective, 17 Loy. L.A. Int'l & Comp. L.J. 829 (1995).

6. Reversal—Size and Argument. Very large awards by nature suggest the possibility that bias and prejudice, as opposed to principle and reason, governed the award. In Jadlowski v. Owens–Corning Fiberglas Corp., 661 A.2d 814, 821 (N.J.Super.App.Div.1995), an asbestos wrongful death action, jury 1 returned a compensatory damages verdict before Christmas of somewhat under $800,000 and was discharged. The second, punitive damages phase of the bifurcated case was heard thereafter by jury 2. At the end of 16 days of trial 2, the plaintiff's lawyer exhorted the jury in summation:

Whatever decision you make, you're going to send Owens–Corning Fiberglas a message. If you find them not responsible, they will hear a message that their conduct past and present is excusable, that what they did to Mr. Jadlowski and others is okay. Maybe more importantly, they'll hear that it is okay to do the same thing with another product in the future.

If you find them responsible, they'll get the message stop paying the lawyers, start paying the victims. If you still have asbestos in that Kaylo, get it out. That's the message they'll get.

What you did was wrong will be the message they get. They'll get a message that we here in Middlesex County want confidence that the products that we buy are safe. That we here in Middlesex County want confidence that the workplace is safe.

If you should find that punitive damages are appropriate, the message has to be loud and it has to be clear. A small slap on the wrist is not going to affect this billion dollar company. They'll spend another billion to fight these cases, to come in here and say they didn't know. Let this be the last case that this is done in.

Send a message to Toledo, the tower, that says to Owens–Corning and to the Owens–Cornings of the world that in New Jersey we won't tolerate it anymore.

The jury deliberated and returned a punitive damages verdict of $15 million, which the trial judge remitted on post-trial motion to $2.5 million. Both parties appealed, and the appellate court remarked:

The rhetoric is excellent, but its aim was for the jury to punish Owens–Corning in this case for what it did in all cases. The sheer size of the verdict demonstrates to us that the jury perceived its role as punishing Owens–Corning for the course of conduct that was demonstrated in this case that affected tens of thousands if not hundreds of thousands of workers.

Characterizing the award as "anomalous," and citing its decision six weeks earlier in another asbestos case where it likened the recovery of such an award to winning a "national lottery," the court reversed and remanded for a new trial.

7. Reform—Statutory and Judicial. Punitive damages have been the subject of substantial recent reform by state legislatures and courts. Consider the following approaches:

A. Raising the standard of proof to "clear and convincing evidence." As *Acosta,* many courts and legislatures have so raised the standard of proof; e.g., Kan.Stat.Ann. § 60–3701; Ohio Rev.Code Ann. § 2307.80(A); Owens–Illinois, Inc. v. Zenobia, 601 A.2d 633 (Md.1992).

B. Capping punitive awards. E.g., Ala.Code 6–11–21 ($500,000 unless misconduct was "highly aggravated"); Colo.Rev.Stat. 13–21–102(1)(a) (punitive damages may not exceed compensatory damages); Ind. Code § 34–51–3–4 (such awards may not be more than the greater of 3 times compensatory damages or $50,000).

C. Payment of portion of award to public treasury. E.g., Iowa Code § 668A.1 (75%); Ga. (75%), see Georgia v. Moseley, 436 S.E.2d 632 (Ga.1993)(upholding statute's constitutionality in connection with $101 million award for death in fiery crash of GMC pickup truck); Life Ins. Co. of Georgia v. Johnson, 1995 WL 683857 (Ala.1995) (50% by judicial declaration).

D. Bifurcating trials. E.g., Mo.Ann.Stat. § 510.263 (Vernon 1995 Supp.) (bifurcation required; net worth evidence admissible only in punitive damages portion of trial); W.R. Grace & Co. v. Waters, 638 So.2d 502 (Fla.1994) (bifurcation on motion by party).

E. Shifting determination of amount from jury to judge. E.g., Ohio Rev.Code Ann. § 2307.80(B); Kan.Stat.Ann. § 60–3701(b)(7), upheld in Smith v. Printup, 866 P.2d 985 (Kan.1993).

F. Barring punitive damages where defendant complied with government regulations. E.g., N.J.Stat.Ann. § 2a:58C–5(c) (FDA regulations); Ohio Rev.Code Ann. § 2307.80(c) (same).

G. Allowing punitive damages to be pleaded only upon proper showing and amendment to complaint. E.g., Minn.Stat. § 549.191; Fla.Stat. § 768.72.

8. Constitutional Reform. *Henley* illustrates how powerfully the Supreme Court's recent constitutionalization of punitive damages law has altered judicial decisionmaking on punitive damages issues, particularly the size of such awards. Defendants and commentators have long questioned the fairness of a civil penalty system based on standards as vague as "malice," "reckless," or "willful and wanton" that has no real ceiling on the size of the assessments and that has none of the procedural safeguards designed to assure the propriety of punishment in criminal cases. See, e.g., Comment, Criminal Safeguards and the Punitive Damages Defendant, 34 U.Chi.L.Rev. 408 (1967). Due process and other constitutional challenges to punitive damages fared poorly in the courts until the United States Supreme Court entered the debate, beginning in 1989, with a string of decisions, the last one of which is pending as this edition goes to press.

A. Browning–Ferris Indus. v. Kelco Disposal, Inc., 492 U.S. 257 (1989). In this case, the Court ruled that the Excessive Fines Clause of the 8th Amendment does not apply to such assessments in civil cases where the state does not share in the recovery.

B. Pacific Mutual Life Ins. Co. v. Haslip, 499 U.S. 1 (1991). In *Haslip*, the Court held that due process does not permit juries to have unbridled discretion in awarding punitive damages. *Haslip* and subsequent cases have focused on three procedural due process controls over jury discretion: (1) trial courts should *instruct* juries on the nature and purposes of punitive damages—punishment, deterrence, and possibly compensation or vindication; (2) trial courts should apply a meaningful *post-trial review* of the law and the evidence underlying such awards, to assure that the jury properly applied the legal standards to the facts of the case; and (3) *appellate review* should provide another layer of meaningful control. In addition, each of the justices except Scalia and Thomas has endorsed the view that substantive due process notions limit punitive damages awards according to principles of "reasonableness" and/or the underlying goals of such awards.

C. BMW of North America, Inc. v. Gore, 517 U.S. 559 (1996). Until 1996, the Court had been vague about how such due process standards might be applied either to justify or strike down a particular award. But in *Gore*, the Court provided more guidance on the issue. An Alabama dentist recovered $4,000 in compensatory damages against BMW for its selling as new a car that had been partially repainted to repair damage in transit from acid rain. In calculating punitive damages, following the suggestion of the plaintiff's lawyer, the jury multiplied the compensatory damages times 1000, the number of cars BMW allegedly had refinished and sold as new, for a total punitive award of $4 million. Concluding that the jury could not properly have based its award on the defendant's conduct outside the state, the Alabama Supreme Court reduced the punitive damages award to a "constitutionally reasonable" amount of $2 million, 646 So.2d 619 (1994). An important issue before the Supreme Court was the appropriateness of extraterritorial punishment in such a case. This issue is important in products liability litigation where a manufacturer's sale of thousands or millions of similarly defective products across the nation (or throughout the world) is often argued by plaintiff's counsel as aggravating the misconduct, and as providing in the aggregate a proper foundation for calculating a punitive assessment proportionate to the totality of the defendant's wrong.

The U.S. Supreme Court, 5–4, reversed, on grounds that the $2 million punitive award was "grossly excessive" and thus offended due process of law. Ruling that principles of state sovereignty and comity preclude one state from imposing extra-territorial punishment on a defendant for lawful conduct in other states, the majority viewed the penalty assessed in this case as impermissibly large when Alabama's state interests alone were considered. Actors are entitled to fair notice of the severity of a potential penalty, and certain "guideposts" or "indicia" may indicate whether a punitive award in a particular case is unfairly large: (1) the degree of reprehensibility of the defendant's conduct, the most important guidepost; (2) the reasonableness of the relationship (the "ratio") of the punitive to the compensatory award; and (3) a comparison of the punitive award with other civil and criminal penalties authorized in such cases. On the facts, each of these indicia suggested that the $2 million punitive damages award was out of all proportion to its proper purposes, rendering the award constitutionally defective.

D. Cooper Indus., Inc. v. Leatherman Tool Group, Inc., 532 U.S. 424 (2001). In this case, the Supreme Court continued its definition of the procedures required for constitutional imposition of punitive damages by holding that trial court determinations of whether jury verdicts awarding punitive damages satisfy due process are to be reviewed by appellate courts *de novo*, not under the more limited, conventional abuse-of-discretion standard.

E. State Farm Mutual Automobile Insurance Co. v. Campbell, 538 U.S. 408 (2003). *Campbell* involved a bad faith failure to settle a claim in which the plaintiff's insurance company, State Farm, failed to settle within the policy limits tort claims against the plaintiff arising out of a serious car accident. Although plaintiff was clearly negligent in causing the accident in which one driver died and another was disabled, State Farm told him that he did not need independent representation, assured him that his personal assets were safe, and refused to settle the case for the policy limits of $50,000. The jury returned a verdict for more than $185,000, leaving plaintiff with excess liability of more than $135,000.

Initially, State Farm refused to cover the plaintiff's excess liability or even to post bond to permit the plaintiff to appeal. Thereafter, plaintiff and his wife sued the company for bad faith failure to settle, fraud, and intentional infliction of emotional distress. At the trial of these claims, plaintiff introduced evidence that State Farm's denial of the plaintiff's claim was part of the company's nation-wide scheme over 20 years to limit claim payouts improperly to improve profitability. On this evidence, the jury returned verdicts of $2.6 million in compensatory damages and $145 million in punitive damages which the trial judge remitted, respectively, to $1 million and $25 million. Reinstating the full $145 million punitive damages verdict, the Utah Supreme Court concluded that it was warranted under the three *Gore* guideposts because of the reprehensibility of the defendant's nation-wide scheme to cheat its policyholders, coupled with the company's "massive wealth" and the improbability of its being caught and punished due to the clandestine nature of its activities. Campbell v. State Farm Mut. Auto. Ins. Co., 65 P.3d 1134, 1153 (Utah 2001).

State Farm appealed the case to the Supreme Court, arguing that the $145 million punitive damages assessment was excessive and violated due process because the Utah courts had improperly considered conduct outside the state and otherwise violated the due process principles set forth in *Gore*. Agreeing, the Supreme Court reversed and remanded, stating that the case was "neither close nor difficult" under *Gore*'s guideposts for avoiding constitutionally excessive punitive damages awards. 538 U.S. at 418. As for reprehensibility, the first and most important guidepost, the Court acknowledged the impropriety of the defendant's scheme but explained that due process precluded courts from basing punitive awards on misconduct, especially conduct outside the state, unrelated to the plaintiff's harm. The Court explained, "Lawful out-of-state conduct may be probative when it demonstrates the deliberateness and culpability of the defendant's action in the State where it is tortious, but that conduct must have a nexus to the specific harm suffered by the plaintiff." 538 U.S. at 422. Nor did the Court think that a punitive damages award could be supported by substantially dissimilar conduct by the defendant that harmed persons other than the plaintiffs:

> A defendant should be punished for the conduct that harmed the plaintiff, not for being an unsavory individual or business. Due process does not permit courts, in the calculation of punitive damages, to adjudicate the merits of other parties' hypothetical claims against a defendant under the guise of the reprehensibility analysis.... Punishment on these bases creates the possibility of multiple punitive damages awards for the same conduct....

Id. at 423. So long as a defendant's misconduct to other persons is similar to the conduct that harmed the plaintiff, courts and juries may properly consider it as showing that the defendant is a repeat offender and, hence, deserving of greater punishment, but the majority concluded that the record in this case revealed scant evidence of repeated misconduct of the kind that injured the plaintiff—the denial of third-party liability claims. Noting that a much lower award would have adequately protected Utah's interest in punishing and deterring State Farm's relevant misconduct that occurred in Utah, the Court observed that the case was improperly "used as a platform to expose, and punish, the perceived deficiencies of State Farm's operations throughout the country." Id. at 420. The court concluded its analysis of reprehensibility:

> The reprehensibility guidepost does not permit courts to expand the scope of the case so that a defendant may be punished for any malfeasance, which in this case extended for a 20–year period. In this case, because the Campbell's have shown no conduct by State Farm similar to that which harmed them, the conduct that harmed them is the only conduct relevant to the reprehensibility analysis.

Id. at 424.

In dissent, Justice Ginsburg noted additional evidence of the defendant's abusive business practices. "[O]n the key criterion 'reprehensibility,' there is a good deal more to the story than the Court's abbreviated account tells." Id. at 431. The evidence revealed an ongoing, company-wide scheme to falsify records and use trickery and other dishonest techniques—such as unjustly attacking a claimant's character, reputation, and credibility by making false and prejudicial notations in the file—to pay both first-party and third-party claims at less than fair value. Two of the defendant's Utah employees testified to "intolerable" and "recurrent" pressure to reduce payouts below fair value, and the local manager ordered the adjuster for the Campbell case to falsify company records by inventing a story that the driver who died in the accident was speeding to see a pregnant girlfriend who did not exist. Several former State Farm employees testified "that they were trained to target 'the weakest of the herd'—'the elderly, the poor, and other consumers who are least knowledgeable about their rights and thus most vulnerable to trickery or deceit, or who have little money and hence have no real alternative but to accept an inadequate offer to settle a claim at much less than fair value.' " The plaintiffs fell into this vulnerable claimant category—economically, emotionally, and physically, Mr. Campbell (since deceased) having suffered from a stroke and Parkinson's disease. Id. at 432–433.

As for the second guidepost, the ratio between punitive and compensatory damages, the Court "decline[d] again to impose a bright-line ratio which a punitive damages award cannot exceed." 538 U.S. at 424. While signaling that "few awards exceeding a single-digit ratio ... will satisfy due process," the Court observed that due process may permit greater ratios in certain circumstances—for particularly egregious misconduct resulting in small economic damages, where the injury is hard to detect, or where the misconduct causes physical injuries. In all cases, however, "courts must ensure that the measure of punishment is both reasonable and proportionate to the amount of harm to the plaintiff and to the general damages recovered." Id. at 426. Because State Farm eventually paid the plaintiffs' excess liability, their losses were mostly emotional, leading the Court to determine that the generous $1 million compensatory damages award contained a substantial punitive component such that a large punitive award would be constitutionally inappropriate. Finally, the Court explained that the very large punitive damages award was unjustified by the final *Gore* guidepost which compares the punitive award to other civil and criminal penalties that may also apply to the defendant's misconduct which, in Utah, was a mere $10,000 fine for fraud. For these reasons, the Court concluded that the $145 million punitive damages assessment in this case was "neither reasonable nor proportionate to the wrong committed, and it was an irrational and arbitrary deprivation of the property of the defendant." Id. at 429.

F. Philip Morris v. Williams, 2007 WL 505781, ___ U.S. ___ (2007). After *Campbell*, the Supreme Court vacated and remanded a number of products liability cases, including Williams v. Philip Morris, Inc., 48 P.3d 824 (Or. Ct. App. 2002), a smoker cancer death case against a cigarette manufacturer on culpability facts similar to Henley v. Philip Morris Inc., 9 Cal.Rptr.3d 29 (Ct. App. 2004), the last principal case above. In *Williams*, a jury awarded slightly over $800,000 in compensatory damages and $79.5 million in punitive damages to the smoker's widow. The trial court remitted the punitive award to $32 million, but the Oregon Court of Appeals reinstated the jury's full verdict. After the United States Supreme Court vacated and remanded the Court of Appeals' decision, that court reinstated the full $79.5 punitive damages award, reasoning that the defendant's reprehensibility justified a punitive damages award well in excess of a single-digit ratio and met the *Gore/Campbell* due process guidelines. 92 P.3d 126, 143–46 (Or. Ct. App. 2004) ("it is difficult to conceive of more reprehensible misconduct for a longer duration of time on the part of a supplier of consumer products to the Oregon public than what occurred in this case"). The Oregon Supreme Court, 127 P.3d 1165, 1181–82 (Or. 2006), affirmed:

> Philip Morris's conduct here was extraordinarily reprehensible, [putting] a significant number of victims at profound risk for an extended period of time. [Even Oregon's criminalization of] such conduct ... did not dissuade Philip Morris from pursuing its.... massive, continuous, near-half-century scheme to defraud the plaintiff and many others, even when [it] always had reason to suspect—and for two or more decades absolutely knew—that the scheme was damaging the health of a very large group of Oregonians—the smoking public—and was killing a number of that group. Under such extreme and outrageous circumstances, we conclude that the jury's $79.5 million punitive damage award ... comported with due process.

Vacating and remanding, the United States Supreme Court side-stepped the excessiveness issue and ruled (5–4) that the Oregon court should have instructed the jury that, in considering the *reprehensibility* of the defendant's conduct (relevant to assessing a proper amount of punishment), the jury could consider the defendant's conduct on other Oregonians, but that the jury could not *punish* the defendant "directly" for harming such "nonparty victims." To do the latter, reasoned the Court, would contravene due process by magnifying the risks of arbitrariness, uncertainty, and lack of notice that surround awards of punitive damages. In dissent, Justice Stevens remarked, "This nuance eludes me."

9. Application of *Campbell* to Other Products Liability Cases. In addition to *Williams*, the Supreme Court vacated and remanded several other products liability decisions after *Campbell* for reconsideration in light of that decision: Sand Hill Energy, Inc. v. Ford Motor Co., 83 S.W.3d 483 (Ky.2002), which had approved a $15 million punitive damages award, on a compensatory award of $3 million, in a park-to-reverse transmission slip case; Romo v. Ford Motor Co., 122 Cal.Rptr.2d 139 (Ct.App.2002), which had approved a $290 million punitive damages award, on a compensatory award of $5 million, in a Ford Bronco roll-over case; Bocci v. Key Pharmaceuticals, Inc., 35 P.3d 1106 (Or. App. 2001), which had approved a punitive damage award for $22.5 million, in a drug fraud case, on a compensatory award of $500,000; and Clark v. Chrysler Corp., 310 F.3d 461 (6th Cir. 2002), which had approved a $3 million punitive damages award, on a compensatory award of $235,629.13 (half of the total compensatory award, due to 50% plaintiff fault), in a pickup truck crashworthiness case.

On remand in *Sand Hill*, the Kentucky Supreme Court vacated the $15 million punitive award and remanded for a new trial on punitive damages to exclude extraterritorial punishment, Sand Hill Energy, Inc. v. Smith, 142 S.W.3d 153 (Ky. 2004); in *Romo*, the California Court of Appeals remitted the punitive award from $290 million to $23.7 million, Romo v. Ford Motor Co., 6 Cal.Rptr.3d 793 (Ct. App. 2003); in *Bocci*, the Oregon Court of Appeals reduced the punitive award from $22.5 million to $3.5 million, Bocci v. Key Pharm. Inc., 79 P.3d 908 (Or. Ct. App. 2003); and, in *Clark*, the district court upheld the jury's $3 million award, but the court of appeals remitted it to $471,258.26, a ratio of 2:1, Clark v. Chrysler Corp., 436 F.3d 594 (6th Cir. 2006).

10. Procedural Requirements. After *Haslip*, many courts began to impose a variety of procedural requirements in an effort to tighten up the standards by which punitive damages are assessed and reviewed, such as requiring judges to provide written (or record) justification of such awards in ruling on post-trial motions. E.g., Gamble v. Stevenson, 406 S.E.2d 350 (S.C.1991)(trial judges); Transportation Ins. Co. v. Moriel, 879 S.W.2d 10 (Tex.1994) (appellate judges; trials to be bifurcated).

11. See generally Gash, Solving the Multiple Punishments Problem: A Call for a National Punitive Damages Registry, 99 Nw. U. L. Rev. 1613 (2005); Eaton, Mustard, and Talarico, The Effects of Seeking Punitive Damages on the Processing of Tort Claims, 34 J. Legal Stud. 343 (2005); Sharkey, Punitive Damages as Societal Damages, 113 Yale L.J. 347 (2003); D. Owen, Products Liability Law ch. 18 (2d ed. 2008).

Punitive damages are examined further in the contexts of automotive litigation, ch. 18, and toxic substance litigation, ch. 19, below.

*

PART V

SPECIAL TYPES OF DEFENDANTS, PRODUCTS, AND TRANSACTIONS

CHAPTER 16

SPECIAL TYPES OF DEFENDANTS

> The Manufacturer is the father of the transaction. He makes the article and puts it in the channels of trade for sale to the public. No one questions the justice of a rule which holds him liable for defects arising out of the design or manufacture.

Santor v. A & M Karagheusian, Inc., 207 A.2d 305, 309 (1965).

Parties in the distribution chain other than manufacturers play significant roles in moving defective products from factories to consumers. The justice of holding these secondary, non-manufacturing, defendants liable for defects in products they sell is less clear. While similar liability principles often operate regardless of the defendant's position in the distribution chain, a number of important variations in policy (and sometimes doctrine) arise in litigation involving non-manufacturing defendants that merit attention here.

In reading this chapter, bear in mind the diversity of interests, concentrations of economic power, and methods of doing business of the various types of non-manufacturing defendants. Retailers, for example, vary in size from small, corner stores to major and even multi-national enterprises like Wal–Mart; in function from serving primarily as conduits for products made by others to imposing on manufacturers their own design specifications and quality control programs; and in range of services from sale alone to sale plus substantial services. Wholesalers, distributors, and component part manufacturers are similarly diverse. One step further removed from the distribution chain are product endorsers who convey the product's image to consumers and shape their expectations. Other defendants examined in this chapter include the federal government, government contractors, parent and apparent manufacturers, successor corporations, and employers.

Despite the variations among these and other parties participating in the distribution of new products, certain common problems have occupied the attention of the courts in addressing the liability of non-manufacturers. The most significant issue is the extent to which strict liability in tort should be applied to such defendants. It will be seen that negligence principles have retained a significant role in these contexts. Suits against non-manufacturers inevitably foster attempts to shift the losses back up the distribution chain to the manufacturer. Accordingly, courts in recent years have increasingly focused on the variety of issues involved in the adjustment of losses among defendants.

1.   RETAILERS, WHOLESALERS, AND DISTRIBUTORS

Zamora v. Mobil Corp.

Supreme Court of Washington, 1985.
104 Wash.2d 199, 704 P.2d 584.

■ PEARSON, JUSTICE.

The primary issue presented by this appeal is whether a seller of propane, who never had physical possession or control of the gas, should be held liable under either common law negligence or strict product liability theories for injuries resulting from a propane explosion and fire. We hold that as a matter of law respondent was not negligent, but that the principles of common law strict liability do place respondent in the chain of distribution of the propane. . . .

[A propane gas leak in the house of plaintiff-appellants went undetected because insufficient odorant had been added to the gas. A resulting fire killed 5 of appellants' children. Appellants sued the manufacturer (Mobil), distributor (Cal Gas, the respondent), and retailer (Northwest). The trial judge granted respondent's motion for summary judgment. Appellants settled with the other parties and appealed the entry of summary judgment for Cal Gas.]

Mobil manufactured the propane involved here at its Ferndale, Washington refinery. Propane is an odorless, colorless, highly flammable gas; a foul-smelling odorant is added to increase the safety of the product. Pennwalt manufactured this odorant (thiophane) and sold it to Mobil for use at Mobil's Ferndale refinery. Respondent Cal Gas, a Delaware corporation headquartered in California, bought the propane from Mobil and sold it to Northwest Propane, a retailer who delivered the propane directly to appellants. Significantly, respondent never had possession or control of the propane here. It bought and sold the gas completely as a paper transaction. Northwest Propane took delivery of the gas it purchased from respondent directly from Mobil's Ferndale refinery.

The fact that respondent never physically handled, modified, altered, transported, or refined the propane ultimately sold to appellants is uncontroverted. At issue here is the legal effect of respondent's role in the marketing of the gas.

I. Negligence

Appellants allege that respondent was negligent in failing to inspect the propane for odorization and in failing to warn appellants of the dangers of the propane. We find that because respondent never had possession or control of the gas and had no reason to believe that the gas was not properly odorized, it had no duty to inspect or warn appellants.

The general rule is that where a product is sold in the original package or container, in the condition in which it was received from a reputable manufacturer, and the seller had no opportunity to inspect or test before resale, no liability attaches to that seller for such failure to test or inspect. [Davis v. Siloo, Inc., 267 S.E.2d 354 (N.C.App.1980).] The rationale of that rule fully applies to respondent, who never handled the product and therefore had no opportunity to test or inspect it.

Further, a seller of an item which was manufactured by a third party is not generally liable for harm caused by the dangerous character of the item *if* the seller did not know or had no reason to know that the item was, or was likely to be, dangerous. Restatement of Torts § 402 (1948 Supp.); [Ringstad v. I. Magnin & Co., 239 P.2d 848 (Wash.1952).] A seller is not obligated to test a product unless he has notice that it may be dangerous or defective. *Ringstad*. [Here, Mobil, from whom Cal–Gas purchased the propane, had contracted with Mobil to odorize the propane in accordance with governmental regulations or industry practice. Cal–Gas could reasonably rely on Mobil, a reputable manufacturer, to odorize the propane. Further, Cal–Gas had no opportunity to inspect the gas itself, and thus cannot be held to have known or to have had reason to know that the propane was inadequately odorized.]

Appellants, however, urge that because propane is an inherently dangerous product, respondent should be held to have a duty to *obtain* control or possession in order to inspect it. We disagree.

* * *

The rule stated in Martin v. Schoonover, 533 P.2d 438 (Wash.App. 1975), applicable not only to retailers, but also to other product sellers, is appropriate here:

> The more the retailer [seller] is only a conduit for the product, the less likely he can be held in negligence.... Conversely, the more the [seller] takes an active part in preparing the product for final use and takes the role of a manufacturer or assembler, the more likely he can be found liable in negligence.... If a [seller] adopts a product as his own, he is subject to the same liability for negligence as is the manufacturer.... The [seller] can be found negligent in cases where he has failed to make an inspection ... prior to sale when it was reasonable for him to do so in light of the nature of the product, the reputability of the supplier and the scope of the risk.

Here, respondent never touched the product, took no active part in its manufacture, did not adopt the product as its own, and was dealing with reputable manufacturers (Mobil and Pennwalt). In spite of the inherently dangerous nature of propane, it appears respondent had no notice that the product was unreasonably dangerous due to a defect (inadequate odorization). Thus, respondent had no duty to test or inspect in this case.

[In addition, the court found that the bulk supplier defense, from Restatement (Second) of Torts § 388, applied. The court held, consistent with Jones v. Hittle Serv., Inc., 549 P.2d 1383 (Kan. 1976), that the distributors of bulk propane to a retailer had no independent duty to warn the ultimate consumer. Rather, the distributor had only a duty to insure that the *retailer* was knowledgeable regarding the dangers and was able to warn the ultimate buyers. Thus, a seller of bulk propane can delegate to the retailer its duty to warn the ultimate consumer.] Furthermore, the bulk seller has no duty to warn the retailer of the dangers of a product if that retailer is already aware "through common knowledge or learning" of a specific hazard. . . .

Accordingly, respondent could rely on Northwest Propane to warn the ultimate consumer (appellants). Additionally, because Northwest Propane is a well-established propane distributor, the largest in Whatcom County and in business for many years, respondent had no duty to warn Northwest Propane of the obvious dangers of its business.

II. Strict Liability

The product liability act is inapplicable to this case because the fire occurred prior to the effective date of that act. See RCW 7.72.060 and 4.22.920. Applying only the common law principles of strict liability for a defective product, we hold that respondent is properly regarded as a member in the chain of distribution of the propane. . . .

This court adopted section 402A as the law of this state and applied it to claims against manufacturers in Ulmer v. Ford Motor Co., 452 P.2d 729 (Wash.1969). In a broad interpretation of section 402A, this court later extended strict liability beyond manufacturers to all others in the chain of distribution. Seattle–First Nat'l Bank v. Tabert, 542 P.2d 774 (Wash.1975).

Section 402A, by its literal terms, imposes strict liability for *any* sale of a defective product. [As well,] the policies underlying the imposition of strict liability justify its imposition in this case. The primary policy justification recognized by this court for the extension of strict liability to all sellers in the chain of distribution is provision of the "maximum of protection" to the consumer. The sellers are then required to argue among themselves any questions as to their respective liability. *Seattle–First Nat'l Bank v. Tabert, supra.* That policy rationale is as applicable to sellers who never handle or control the product as it is to those sellers who do possess or control the product. . . .

Accordingly, the fact that respondent never physically handled the gas is not dispositive of the question whether it should be regarded to be a member in the chain of distribution. Respondent has not provided this court with any case, nor has our research revealed any case, which holds that handling or possession of the product is a requisite of strict liability. Respondent's reliance on Lyons v. Premo Pharmaceutical Labs, Inc., 406 A.2d 185 (N.J.Super.1979) to support such a proposition is misplaced.

In *Lyons,* the court held that a broker, who never had possession of the product, could not be held strictly liable. This holding was based on the fact that the product was subsequently sold in an *altered form* and for *unsafe uses,* those ultimate uses being beyond the broker's knowledge and control. Conversely, in the present case the gas was marketed exactly as sold by respondent and respondent had full knowledge of the uses to which the ultimate consumer would put the gas. Thus, the *Lyons* case is inapposite here.

Furthermore, respondent cannot be held to be merely a "passive conduit" in the marketing of the propane, as it claims. Respondent did agree to hold its buyer, Northwest Propane, harmless for liability resulting from improper odorization. Therefore, respondent's role in the marketing of the propane was certainly more active than that of an uninvolved conduit. Moreover, as we indicated in *Tabert,* the *degree* of a seller's participation in the marketing process is less important to our decision than the public protection consideration where, as here, a seller has had *some* identifiable role in placing a defective product on the market.

Accordingly, based upon the literal terms of section 402A and upon the public protection rationale for our broad interpretation of that section, we find that respondent is appropriately included within the chain of distribution of the propane sold to appellants.

[Reversed and remanded.]

NOTES

1. Retailers—Negligence. Retailers conventionally have a duty to test or inspect only if they have *notice* that the product is likely to be dangerous. See Rest. (2d) Torts § 402; Schweich v. Ziegler, Inc., 463 N.W.2d 722 (Minn.1990) (tractor retailer negligently failed to inspect). The retailer has a duty to warn if it knows or should know that the product is likely to be dangerous when put to normal use. See Frey v. Montgomery Ward & Co., 258 N.W.2d 782 (Minn.1977). See also In re Asbestos Litig., 832 A.2d 705 (Del. 2003)(discussing applicability of § 402 to asbestos products sellers).

2. Should the retailer's economic power relative to that of the manufacturer bear on whether it should be required to test or inspect its products prior to sale? What if the retailer is a major national chain—such as Target or K–Mart—which may be in a position to extract indemnification agreements from manufacturers as a condition of marketing their products? Conversely, what if the retailer is small and highly dependent on a single product manufactured by a large company? Do purchasers have different expectations when purchasing products from large chain stores versus small merchants?

3. Tortious Misrepresentation. Many of the products liability cases involving tortious misrepresentation have involved retailers as defendants, as discussed in ch. 3, above. Note, however, that retailer communications to consumers ordinarily are not "public" representations for purposes of strict liability under Restatement (Second) of Torts § 402B (1965).

4. Express Warranty. Retailers may of course expressly warrant the quality of the products they sell under UCC § 2–313. In addition, a retailer will be subject to liability under the manufacturer's express warranty if the retailer "adopts" the manufacturer's warranty. E.g., Scovil v. Chilcoat, 424 P.2d 87 (Okla.1967)(new VW engine). Mere resale of a product carrying a manufacturer express warranty does not alone constitute adoption, nor does explaining its terms to the buyer. See Import Motors, Inc. v. Matthews, 557 S.W.2d 807 (Tex.Civ.App.1977). Nor does making repairs on behalf of the manufacturer pursuant to the latter's warranty. Carbo Indus. Inc. v. Becker Chevrolet, Inc., 491 N.Y.S.2d 786 (App.Div.1985).

5.   Implied Warranty.

A.   In general. Retailers may be liable for breach of implied warranties under UCC §§ 2–314 and 2–315. E.g., Pierce v. Liberty Furniture Co., Inc., 233 S.E.2d 33 (Ga.App.1977) (§ 2–314) (defective porch swing collapsed; retailer liable although swing kit purchased in sealed container from reputable manufacturer and resold to plaintiff in original package). In the consumer goods products liability context, the § 2–315 warranty of fitness for a particular purpose is principally applicable to retailers. Why?

B.   Restaurateurs. As a holdover from days when an innkeeper would provide a traveler with food, lodging, and a stable for his horse all for a single fee, some courts formerly held that the sale of food for consumption on the premises was the provision of a service to which implied warranties did not attach. The modern rule is to the contrary. See UCC § 2–314(1); Ray v. Deas, 144 S.E.2d 468 (Ga.App.1965); Sofman v. Denham Food Service, Inc., 181 A.2d 168 (N.J.1962).

Should a restaurant be liable under UCC § 2–314 for injuries from a wine glass breaking in a patron's hand? What are the issues? See Shaffer v. Victoria Station, Inc., 588 P.2d 233 (Wash.1978), rev'g, 572 P.2d 737 (Wash.App.1977).

6.   Strict Liability in Tort. Until the advent of products liability reform in the state legislatures, see note 9 below, ordinary strict liability in tort was widely applied to retailers. E.g., Mead v. Warner Pruyn Div., 394 N.Y.S.2d 483 (App.Div. 1977). Comment *f* to § 402A provides: "The rule stated in this Section applies to any person engaged in the business of selling products for use or consumption. It therefore applies to any manufacturer of such a product, to any wholesale or retail dealer or distributor, and to the operator of a restaurant."

An early, influential case on point was Vandermark v. Ford Motor Co., 391 P.2d 168, 171–72 (Cal.1964) (Traynor, J.):

Retailers like manufacturers are engaged in the business of distributing goods to the public. They are an integral part of the overall producing and marketing enterprise that should bear the cost of injuries resulting from defective products. (*Greenman.*) In some cases the retailer may be the only member of that enterprise reasonably available to the injured plaintiff. In other cases the retailer himself may play a substantial part in insuring that the product is safe or may be in a position to exert pressure on the manufacturer to that end; the retailer's strict liability thus serves as an added incentive to safety. Strict liability on the manufacturer and retailer alike affords maximum protection to the injured plaintiff and works no injustice to the defendants, for they can adjust the costs of such protection between them in the course of their continuing business relationship.

In jurisdictions where the legislatures have not reformed the common-law rules, § 402A still generally applies to retailers as well as manufacturers. See Adkins v. K–Mart Corp., 511 S.E.2d 840 (W.Va. 1998).

The Products Liability Restatement speaks approvingly of the reform statutes but reaffirms the Second Restatement's unqualified rule of strict tort liability for retailers and other parties in the chain of distribution. Products Liability Restatement, § 1 cmt. *e.*

7.   Wholesalers and Distributors. As illustrated by *Zamora,* and stated in comment *f* to § 402A above, the strict liability rules applicable to retailers have generally been applied to wholesalers and distributors as well, although the reform statutes protect these non-manufacturing defendants as well. For a case endorsing strict liability, see Fuchsgruber v. Custom Accessories, Inc., 628 N.W.2d 833 (Wis. 2001) (confirming strict liability applies to distributors even after adoption of comparative fault statute). Contra, Kolarik v. Cory Intern. Corp., 721 N.W.2d 159, 162 (Iowa 2006) (reform statute immunized stuffed olive importer/wholesaler from strict liability in tort and from implied warranty liability for defects in product's original design or manufacture).

8. Occasional Sellers. The seller must be in the business of selling the product under § 402A, cmt. *f*. A number of cases explore the distinction between the occasional, or casual, seller and the type of seller to whom strict liability should apply. Compare Gebo v. Black Clawson Co., 703 N.E.2d 1234 (N.Y. 1998) (prior owner of embossing machine, who had designed, assembled, installed, and sold modified machine not subject to strict liability; owner's single act of design and assembly did not make it equivalent to product manufacturer), with Sprung v. MTR Ravensburg, Inc., 788 N.E.2d 620 (N.Y. 2003)(manufacturer of specialty sheet metal products who custom fabricated retractable floor for factory not a casual manufacturer).

9. Reform. Relieving retailers of strict liability has been a popular legislative reform. The general approach has been to relieve such sellers of strict liability, except for express warranty (and possibly manufacturing flaws), unless the manufacturer (1) cannot be identified, (2) is insolvent, or (3) is not subject to the jurisdiction of the court. See Marcon v. K–Mart Corp., 573 N.W.2d 728 (Minn.App. 1998) (seller strictly liable if manufacturer not available to satisfy judgment; seller found 0% at fault and manufacturer 100% but bankrupt; seller liable under statute); Hester v. Human, 439 S.E.2d 50 (Ga.App.1993) (passive retailer, unaware of any defects, not strictly liable).

A small number of reform statutes include a "sealed container" defense, a common law doctrine that had withered away with the advent of UCC § 2–314. See *Pierce v. Liberty Furniture Co.*, supra note 5. This defense protects the retail seller (or other non-manufacturing seller) if the seller buys and resells the product in a sealed container and the seller has no reason to believe it is defective.

Non-manufacturer reform statutes are collected at 2 Prod.Liab.Rep. (CCH) ¶ 90,000. A couple of states have statutes protecting motor vehicle dealers, as between such dealers and the manufacturers. See Del. Code Ann. tit. 6 § 4905; Idaho Code Ann. § 49–1622.

10. See generally Sachs, Product Liability Reform and Seller Liability: A Proposal for Change, 55 Baylor L.Rev. 1031 (2003); D. Owen, Products Liability Law, § 15.2 (2d ed. 2008); 2 D. Owen, M.S. Madden, & M. Davis, Madden & Owen on Products Liability § 19:1 (3d ed. 2000).

2. COMPONENT PART MANUFACTURERS

City of Franklin v. Badger Ford Truck Sales, Inc.

Supreme Court of Wisconsin, 1973.
58 Wis.2d 641, 207 N.W.2d 866.

■ ROBERT W. HANSEN, JUSTICE.

The municipality (Franklin) sued the sales company (Badger), the chassis maker (Ford), and the wheel maker (Gunite), alleging each liable under products liability for the sale to the city of a fire truck chassis with a defective wheel. The fire truck was damaged when it tipped over while negotiating a turn in responding to a fire call.

* * *

BASIS OF LIABILITY. The case against all three defendants went to the jury on the basis of strict liability. Ford and Gunite contend that they were manufacturers of component parts and, as such, were not subject to the rule of strict liability. Some states hold component manufacturers and suppliers subject to strict liability; some do not. Where there is no change in the component part itself, but it is merely incorporated into something larger, and where the cause of harm or injury is found, as here, to be a defect in the component part, we hold that, as to the ultimate user or consumer, the strict liability standard applies to the maker and supplier of the defective component part. Where the component part is subject to further processing or substantial change, or where the causing of injury is not directly attributable to defective construction of the component part, the result might be different. We agree with the comment: "... The question is essentially one of whether the responsibility for discovery and prevention of the dangerous defect is shifted to the intermediate party who is to make the changes...."[1] In the case before us, we do not see responsibility for the defective construction of the wheel shifting from the maker of the wheel or from the assembler of wheel and chassis so as to make only the seller, who was in no position to detect the hidden defect, strictly liable.[7]

[Remanded for trial for determination of relative negligence of defendants for purposes of contribution.]

1.   [Rest. (2d) Torts § 402A, comment *p.* See also comment *q*:] "*Component parts.* The same problem [referring to products requiring further processing] arises in cases of the sale of a component part of a product to be assembled by another, as for example a tire to be placed on a new automobile, a brake cylinder for the same purpose, or an instrument for the panel of an airplane. Again the question arises, whether the responsibility is not shifted to the assembler. It is no doubt to be expected that where there is no change in the component part itself, but it is merely incorporated into something larger, the strict liability will be found to carry through to the ultimate user or consumer. But in the absence of a sufficient number of decisions on the matter to justify a conclusion, the Institute expresses no opinion on the matter."

7.   In Howes v. Hansen, 201 N.W.2d 825 (Wis.1972), in extending strict liability protection beyond a user or consumer to a bystander, this court stated one of the reasons for the strict liability concept was stated [to be] "... the manufacturer has the greatest ability to control the risk created by his products since he may initiate or adopt inspection and quality control measures thereby preventing defective products...." See also: Frumer and Friedman, 2 Products Liability, sec. 16.04[2] [f], pages 3–151–152, stating: "There seems to be no good reason why ... the part manufacturer as well as the assembler should not be liable to the injured person.... While it may be true that the assembler is in a better position to distribute the risk in a particular case, and will ordinarily be the supplier to whom the injured person will look for redress, the part manufacturer did, after all, supply a defective product."

Lee v. Butcher Boy

California Court of Appeal, 1985.
169 Cal.App.3d 375, 215 Cal.Rptr. 195, review denied.

■ THOMPSON, J.

[Plaintiff's hand was caught and injured in a meat grinding machine. In addition to suing the manufacturer of the grinder, plaintiff and her husband sued the manufacturer of the motor used in the grinder, contending (1) that the motor should have stopped immediately when turned off, and (2) that the motor manufacturer should have warned that it took a while for the motor to stop. The court granted the motor manufacturer's motion for summary judgment, and plaintiffs appeal.]

We have found no case in which a component part manufacturer who had no role in designing the finished product and who supplied a non-defective component part, was held liable for the defective design of the finished product. . . .

. . . The evidence establishes that defendant had no role in the design of the machine, and that defendant reasonably relied on [the grinder manufacturer] to take appropriate measures to insure proper design and installation of the motor. [Thus, the defendant's] design of the non-defective motor could not have proximately caused the injury.

[Nor did defendant have a duty to warn because it] gave no input and had no control over the design, manufacture, and packaging of the finished product. The cases . . . demonstrate a reluctance against imposing liability for the component part manufacturer's failure to warn the consumer where the final product is subsequently packaged, labeled and marketed by another manufacturer. (Walker v. Stauffer Chemical Corp., 96 Cal.Rptr. 803 (Ct.App.1971)) [manufacturer of sulfuric acid supplied to manufacturer of drain cleaner had no duty to warn consumers].

[Affirmed.]

————

Apperson v. E.I. Du Pont De Nemours & Co.

United States Court of Appeals, Seventh Circuit, 1994.
41 F.3d 1103.

■ CUDAHY, CIRCUIT JUDGE.

[Plaintiffs brought separate products liability actions against DuPont claiming they were injured by medical prostheses manufactured with DuPont materials. The district court granted summary judgment for Du-Pont, and plaintiffs' suits were consolidated on appeal.]

After experiencing problems with their temporomandibular joints (TMJ)(the joint connecting the upper and lower jaw), the plaintiffs received a medical prosthesis known as the Proplast TMJ Interpositional Implant. After implantation, plaintiffs allege that the Proplast TMJ Implants failed, abrading the surrounding bone and triggering immune system reactions. The plaintiffs were required to undergo further surgery to remove the implants and, in some cases, to reconstruct the facial bones.

The Proplast TMJ Implant was designed, manufactured and sold by Vitek, Inc., a now-bankrupt company founded by Dr. Charles Homsy, a former DuPont scientist. In the late 1960s, Homsy developed and patented the biomaterial "Proplast," a spongy implant material designed to encourage tissue ingrowth. Proplast is made by combining carbon and soluble ingredients with polytetrafluorethylene (PTFE), better known by its tradename Teflon, a safe and inert plastic sold in resin, powder or fiber form. Although the physical and mechanical properties of Teflon change during the multi-stage Proplast manufacturing process, its chemical composition remains the same. The Proplast TMJ Implant is a pre-formed Proplast device, and received FDA approval for sale in 1983.

DuPont supplied Vitek with the Teflon for the Proplast TMJ Implants. Plaintiffs allege that DuPont knew that Vitek intended to use the Teflon to manufacture Proplast TMJ Implants, and at one point considered entering into a joint marketing agreement with Vitek. DuPont also knew that Teflon implants had met with mixed success. In particular, published studies in the 1960s had shown that Teflon tended to abrade when used in hip implants.

When Vitek first sought to purchase Teflon from DuPont, DuPont informed Vitek of these studies of hip implants. DuPont also advised Vitek that its Teflon was industrial grade and had not been manufactured for medical applications, and that DuPont had not studied its suitability for medical use. DuPont conditioned the sale of Teflon on Vitek's acknowledgement of DuPont's disclaimers and agreement to use its own medical judgment as to the safety of Teflon in the TMJ Implant. . . .

The plaintiffs contend that DuPont knew that Teflon was not appropriate for use in the Proplast TMJ Implant. The plaintiffs alleged three theories of liability: that DuPont was strictly liable for selling an unreasonably dangerous product; that DuPont was strictly liable for failing to warn both Vitek and the plaintiffs that Teflon was unsuitable for use as a TMJ Implant; and that DuPont was negligent in supplying Teflon to Vitek and failing to warn plaintiffs when it knew that it was unsafe in human implants. DuPont responded that it owed no duty to the plaintiffs for injury caused by a specialized end-use of its product; that the Teflon in Proplast was substantially altered; that DuPont satisfied any duties since Vitek was a sophisticated purchaser; and that any state claims were preempted by federal drug laws.

The district court granted summary judgment to DuPont, finding that it owed no duty of care to the plaintiffs since "it is simply not responsible for a product that it did not create." [Plaintiffs claim that DuPont's Teflon was unreasonably dangerous in design and warning and that DuPont should have refused to sell Teflon to Vitek.]

A.

. . . Strict liability may extend to manufacturers of component parts for injuries caused by design or manufacturing defects in the component part itself. [Citations.] It will also extend to a manufacturer of an inherently dangerous raw material. Hammond v. North American Asbestos Corp., 454 N.E.2d 210, 215–16 (Ill.1983)(raw asbestos inherently dangerous). The plaintiffs contend that Teflon was unreasonably dangerous when used in TMJ Implants, since the "ordinary" consumer would not expect Teflon to disintegrate and cause injury.

But the plaintiffs do not contend that Teflon is an inherently dangerous product with no safe applications. Clearly, Teflon is a raw material with many safe uses; it only became dangerous when Vitek incorporated it into a highly specialized medical device, the Proplast TMJ Implant. The drafters of the Restatement took no position on whether § 402A applies in this context, but did offer some commentary:

> If, for example, raw coffee beans are sold to a buyer who roasts and packs them for sale to the ultimate consumer, it cannot be supposed that the seller will be relieved of all liability when the raw beans are contaminated with arsenic, or some other poison. . . . On the other hand, the manufacturer of pigiron, which is capable of a wide variety of uses, is not so likely to be held to strict liability when it turns out to be unsuitable for the child's tricycle into which it is finally made by a remote buyer. The question is essentially one of whether the responsibility for discovery and prevention of the dangerous defect is shifted to the intermediate party who is to make the changes.

Restatement (2d), § 402A, cmt. *p.*

Illinois courts have largely followed the logic of the Restatement. While manufacturers of inherently dangerous raw materials will be held liable for injury caused by their product, *Hammond*, courts have treated differently manufacturers of inherently *safe* components when the final assembly, rather than a manufacturing or design defect in the component itself, renders the component dangerous. "[S]uch a manufacturer will not be held liable if the injury resulted from a dangerous condition created by the party who created the final product. 'The obligation that generates the duty to avoid injury to another which is reasonably foreseeable does not . . . extend to the anticipation of how manufactured components not in and of themselves dangerous or defective can become potentially dangerous dependent upon the nature of their integration into a unit designed, assembled, installed, and sold by another.' " Woods v. Graham Engineering Corp., 539 N.E.2d 316, 319 (Ill.1989); [citations].

The rule is particularly applicable when an inherently safe raw material is used in the manufacture of a highly specialized finished product. Illinois adopted the doctrine of strict products liability to ensure that the loss caused by unsafe products is borne by those who created the harm, who derive economic benefits from them, and, importantly, "who are in a position to eliminate the unsafe character of the product and prevent the loss." Hebel v. Sherman Equip., 442 N.E.2d 199, 205 (Ill.1982). A rule placing liability for a defective product on the manufacturer of a specialized end-product, rather than the supplier of safe raw materials follows from these policies. The manufacturer of a finished product knows the precise use it intends to make of the raw material or component part, and is in a far better position than the manufacturer of raw materials to determine whether it is safe for that purpose.

We believe that, in this case, the Illinois courts would not place that burden on DuPont. Teflon was a safe, raw material. DuPont informed Vitek that Teflon was not manufactured and had not been tested for use in medical devices. Although the plaintiffs allege that DuPont was intimately aware of Vitek's plans for developing and marketing a Proplast TMJ Implant, they have not alleged that DuPont had any control over the design or composition of the Proplast TMJ Implants, or that there was a manufacturing defect in the Teflon. . . . Clearly Vitek—an FDA-regulated manufacturer of medical devices—was in a better position than DuPont to determine whether an inert raw material could be safely implanted in the human body, it seems clear that Illinois would not hold DuPont liable for the eventual failure of Teflon in the Proplast TMJ Implant. [Citation.]

B.

A product that is not inherently dangerous may be considered defective if the manufacturer fails to warn of its non-obvious dangers. A manufacturer need warn only of dangers of which it knows or should know. Woodill v. Parke Davis & Co., 402 N.E.2d 194 (Ill.1980). The plaintiffs alleged that DuPont breached its duty by failing to warn Vitek, physicians and the plaintiffs that Teflon was unsuitable for use in the Proplast TMJ Implant. Clearly, DuPont told Vitek everything that it knew: in addition to the warnings that DuPont had not tested Teflon for medical use, DuPont pointed Vitek to the studies showing that Teflon had failed when used in hip implants. The plaintiffs rely in great part on their expert's affidavit stating (unsurprisingly) that the hip and jaw implants could be expected to perform similarly, and thus DuPont should have discerned from the studies on hip implants that Teflon was unsuitable for TMJ Implants.

We find that DuPont's warnings to Vitek were sufficient as a matter of law. DuPont warned Vitek of everything that it knew; the plaintiffs have put forth no evidence from which a jury could find that DuPont should have known anything more. Indeed, when DuPont told Vitek about the studies on hip implants, Dr. Homsy replied that he was familiar with those studies, had been in contact with their author, but believed for numerous reasons that a Proplast TMJ Implant would function better than the pure Teflon hip implant. Moreover, a duty to warn arises only when there is unequal knowledge with respect to the risk of harm, [citations]; and while DuPont had superior knowledge of any of Teflon's hidden dangers, Vitek clearly had superior knowledge of its suitability for use in joint implants.

DuPont's duty to warn did not, however, require it to warn physicians and the plaintiffs. Were Teflon an inherently dangerous raw material,

DuPont would have a duty to warn the plaintiffs, as well as Vitek, of its hazards. *Hammond*. But, as a supplier of raw materials, DuPont cannot warn plaintiffs of dangers created by the faulty design of a finished product manufacturer. "The alleged foreseeability of the risk of the finished product is irrelevant to determining the liability of the component part manufacturer because imposing such a duty forces the supplier to retain an expert in every finished product manufacturer's line of business." Kealoha v. E.I. Du Pont de Nemours & Co., 844 F.Supp. 590, 594 (D.Haw.1994). . . . We believe that after DuPont has warned Vitek of any dangers, and so long as there are no inherent dangers, Illinois would shift the burden of subsequent warnings to Vitek.

[Plaintiffs negligence claims, essentially the same as their strict liability claims, also fail. District court's summary judgment is affirmed.]

NOTES

1. Troubled in part by the absence of privity of contract, some early decisions questioned whether strict liability should lie against the manufacturer of a defective component part. See Goldberg v. Kollsman Instrument Corp., 191 N.E.2d 81 (N.Y.1963)(warranty)(defective altimeter caused crash of plane). See generally Hunt, A Reporter at Large: The Case of Flight 320, The New Yorker, (Apr. 30, 1960, at 119) (recounting investigation into *Goldberg* crash).

Virtually all modern courts, however, agree with the *City of Franklin* approach holding the manufacturer of the defective component part liable. E.g., Jimenez v. Superior Court, 98 Cal.Rptr.2d 587 (Ct. App. 2000)(manufacturers of defective windows for mass-produced homes strictly liable to homeowners); d'Hedouville v. Pioneer Hotel Co., 552 F.2d 886 (9th Cir.1977) (flammable acrylic fiber made into carpeting). Liability is recognized regardless of the type of product defect. E.g., Fleck v. KDI Sylvan Pools, Inc., 981 F.2d 107 (3d Cir.1992)(replacement pool-liner manufacturer had duty to provide diving warnings and depth markers).

2. Substantial Change. The component part manufacturer will not be held responsible if the part is subjected to *substantial change* by an assembler, and the changed condition causes an accident. Liability in strict tort will lie only if the product "is expected to and does reach the user or consumer without substantial change in the condition in which it is sold." Rest. (2d) Torts § 402A(1)(b). The *further processing* and *substantial change* issues are addressed in cmt. *p* to § 402A, excerpted in the celebrated pig-iron-in-the-tricycle example found in *Apperson*.

Compare, with comment *p*'s pig-iron-in-the-tricycle example, States Steamship Co. v. Stone Manganese Marine, Ltd., 371 F.Supp. 500 (D.N.J.1973). Shipowner sued the manufacturer of alloy ingots which were cast into propellers and installed on plaintiff's ships by a third party shipyard. The alloy was inadequate for the job, and several of the propeller blades fractured causing various damage. Defendant argued that casting the ingots into propellers was a "substantial change" in their condition, precluding liability under § 402A. The court thought this "too simplistic a reading of Section 402A(1)(b)," pointing out that at issue were "the qualities of the alloy, regardless of its shape."

3. Assembly Process Errors. Problems arise when an apparently safe component is assembled into the final product in a dangerous manner or the final product is marketed by the assembler without proper warnings of its dangers. Thus, no liability for selling dual operating buttons to plaintiff's employer who installed them on a power press, facing *upwards,* creating risk that stock could fall upon and accidentally activate the buttons. Temple v. Wean United, Inc., 364 N.E.2d 267, 272 (Ohio 1977): "[T]he obligation that generates the duty to warn does not extend to the speculative anticipation of how manufactured components, not in and of themselves dangerous or defective, can become potentially dangerous dependent upon the nature of their integration into a unit designed and assembled by another."

4. Raw Materials vs. Component Parts. Is there a distinction between "raw materials" and "component parts"? Should there be? In the TMJ implant situation in *Apperson*, was Teflon a raw material or a component part? If you were representing duPont in such a case, for which of the two classifications would you argue?

5. Is *Apperson* rightly decided? In the TMJ implant cases, portions of the jaws (and in some cases skulls) of thousands of persons disintegrated from foreign-body reactions to commercial-grade plastic implanted in their heads. Should DuPont be allowed to close its eyes to the known risk, and be shielded by the courts from the consequences of selling a product which appears dangerous for its intended use, simply because there is an intermediary assembler who claims that he has studied the risks and found them inconsequential? Compare Gryc v. Dayton–Hudson Corp., ch. 15(4) above, where Riegel Textile Corporation was held liable for *punitive* damages for selling untreated cotton flannelette fabric to a garment manufacturer knowing that it would be used in making young girls' nightgowns.

Which is right, *Apperson* or *Gryc*? Compare *Apperson* to Products Liability Restatement § 5, illustration 4.

6. Third Restatement. The Products Liability Restatement § 5 adopts the *Apperson* no-duty approach. Liability is limited to manufacturing defects and to component manufacturers who "substantially participate in the integration of the component into the design of the product." Nor, usually, does a component supplier have a duty to warn end users. See § 5 cmt. *b.*

7. Negligent Entrustment. Does *negligent entrustment* seem an appropriate doctrine for use in such cases? See generally Prosser & Keeton on Torts, at 197; Rest. (2d) of Torts §§ 308, 390, Products Liability Restatement § 5 cmt. *b* (principles of negligent entrustment govern component seller liability if purchaser likely to utilize component dangerously).

On the other hand, consider the implications of requiring a manufacturer of a component material—such as plastic, pigiron, or a basic chemical—to ascertain the variety of risks, and ways of minimizing them, arising out of the myriad specialized end-uses of their component materials, a policy issue noted by the court in another TMJ implant case:

> [T]he common law cannot countenance [making] raw material suppliers guarantors of finished products over which they have little control. [C]ompanies like DuPont would have no choice but to take their products off the market entirely or to double-check their suitability in many new applications before making any sales. [One case explained that] imposing responsibility for a completed product on a component part supplier "would be contrary to public policy, as it would encourage ignorance on the part of component part manufacturers [of the ultimate use of the component part] or alternatively require them to 'retain an expert in the client's field of business to determine whether the client intends to develop a safe product.'"

Jacobs v. E.I. du Pont de Nemours & Co., 67 F.3d 1219, 1241 (6th Cir. 1995)(concluding that, if liability were allowed, "access to raw materials like Teflon for entrepreneurs seeking new applications would either disappear or be undermined by an inevitable increase in price [which would] stymie the kind of beneficial scientific innovation which, sadly, did not take place here, but which has occurred in many other areas of human endeavor").

8.   Warnings. In Schwark v. Total Vinyl Products, Inc., 2006 WL 988640, at *3 (N.D. Ohio 2006), a teenager was paralyzed when he dove into an in-ground pool and struck his head on the transition wall separating the deep and shallow ends of the pool. The owner had purchased and installed a pool replacement liner sometime before the accident, and the plaintiff sued the liner manufacturer for failing to warn of the risk. *Held*, summary judgment granted for defendant:

> Ohio has adopted the component part manufacturer rule in "failure to warn" cases. According to the rule, "[t]here is no duty to warn extending to the speculative anticipation of how manufactured components, not in and of themselves dangerous or defective, can become potentially dangerous dependent upon their integration into a unit designed and assembled by another." ... Thus, such manufacturers are not liable unless (1) the component part itself is defective, or (2) the manufacturer substantially participated in the integration of the component part into the system and the component part proximately caused injury to the plaintiff.... [T]o hold otherwise would be to encourage ignorance on the part of component part manufacturers, or alternatively, require them to retain an expert to determine the safety of the final integrated product.

Contra, Fleck v. KDI Sylvan Pools, Inc., 981 F.2d 107 (3d Cir.1992) (pool liner manufacturers are in best position to affix labels warning of diving dangers; component part manufacturer rule does not apply to such liners because of their specific purpose).

9.   For the Want of a Nail.... What advice would you have for a chemical company which sells hundreds of different compounds to several hundred commercial users? To a screw manufacturer which has thousands of commercial purchasers? Cf. Kennelly, Trial of a General Aviation Aircraft Case Against Manufacturer, Component–Part Maker, and Overhaul Company—Defective Screws Result in $660,000 Aggregate Awards for Two Deaths, Trial Lawyers Guide 281 (1971).

Compare the litigation some years ago against Amoco for oil pollution damages to the French Coast from an oil tanker that ran aground when a single defective bolt failed in the tanker's steering system during a storm. When the dust had finally settled, after more than a decade of litigation, Amoco's costs totalled about $100 million—all for a defective bolt made by someone else, placed in a tanker made by someone else again.

10.   See generally Fischer, Product Liability: A Commentary on the Liability of Suppliers of Component Parts and Raw Materials, 53 S.C. L. Rev. 1137 (2002); Madden, Component Parts and Raw Materials Sellers: From the Titanic to the New Restatement, 26 N.Ky.L.Rev. 535 (1999); Mansfield, Reflections on Current Limits on Component and Raw Material Supplier Liability and the Proposed Third Restatement, 84 Ky.L.J. 22 (1996); D. Owen, Products Liability Law § 15.3 (2d ed. 2008).

---

3. THE FEDERAL GOVERNMENT

Berkovitz v. United States

United States Supreme Court, 1988.
486 U.S. 531, 108 S.Ct. 1954, 100 L.Ed.2d 531.

■ JUSTICE MARSHALL delivered the opinion of the Court.

The question in this case is whether the discretionary function exception of the Federal Tort Claims Act (FTCA or Act), 28 U.S.C. § 2680(a), bars a suit based on the Government's licensing of an oral polio vaccine and on its subsequent approval of the release of a specific lot of that vaccine to the public.

I

On May 10, 1979, Kevan Berkovitz, then a 2–month-old infant, ingested a dose of Orimune, an oral polio vaccine manufactured by Lederle Laboratories. Within one month, he contracted a severe case of polio. The disease left Berkovitz almost completely paralyzed and unable to breathe without the assistance of a respirator. The Communicable Disease Center, an agency of the Federal Government, determined that Berkovitz had contracted polio from the vaccine.

Berkovitz['s parents] subsequently filed suit against the United States[1] [in district court alleging] that the United States was liable for his injuries under the FTCA, 28 U.S.C. §§ 1346(b), 2674, because the Division of Biologic Standards (DBS), then a part of the National Institutes of Health, had acted wrongfully in licensing Lederle Laboratories to produce Orimune and because the Bureau of Biologics of the Food and Drug Administration (FDA)* had acted wrongfully in approving release to the public of the particular lot of vaccine containing Berkovitz's dose. According to petitioners, these actions violated federal law and policy regarding the inspection and approval of polio vaccines.

The Government moved to dismiss the suit for lack of subject-matter jurisdiction on the ground that the agency actions fell within the discretionary function exception of the FTCA. The District Court denied this motion, concluding that neither the licensing of Orimune nor the release of a specific lot of that vaccine to the public was a "discretionary function" within the meaning of the FTCA. At the Government's request, the District Court certified its decision for immediate appeal to the Third Circuit

---

1. Petitioners also sued Lederle Laboratories in a separate civil action. That suit was settled before the instant case was filed.

* In 1963, the DBS issued a license to Lederle to produce Orimune. The DBS was transferred in 1972 from the National Institutes of Health to the FDA and renamed the Bureau of Biologics, and in 1984 it was renamed the Office of Biologics Research and Review.—Eds.

pursuant to 28 U.S.C. § 1292(b), and the Court of Appeals accepted jurisdiction. [The divided panel of the Court of Appeals reversed, and we granted certiorari to] resolve a conflict in the Circuits regarding the effect of the discretionary function exception on claims arising from the Government's regulation of polio vaccines. . . .

II

The FTCA, 28 U.S.C. § 1346(b), generally authorizes suits against the United States for damages

> "for injury or loss of property, or personal injury or death caused by the negligent or wrongful act or omission of any employee of the Government while acting within the scope of his office or employment, under circumstances where the United States, if a private person, would be liable to the claimant in accordance with the law of the place where the act or omission occurred."

The Act includes a number of exceptions to this broad waiver of sovereign immunity. The exception relevant to this case provides that no liability shall lie for

> "[a]ny claim . . . based upon the exercise or performance or the failure to exercise or perform a discretionary function or duty on the part of a federal agency or an employee of the Government, whether or not the discretion involved be abused." 28 U.S.C. § 2680(a).

This exception, as we stated in our most recent opinion on the subject, "marks the boundary between Congress' willingness to impose tort liability upon the United States and its desire to protect certain governmental activities from exposure to suit by private individuals." United States v. Varig Airlines, 467 U.S. 797, 808 (1984).

The determination of whether the discretionary function exception bars a suit against the Government is guided by several established principles. This Court stated in *Varig* that "it is the nature of the conduct, rather than the status of the actor, that governs whether the discretionary function exception applies in a given case." Id. at 813. In examining the nature of the challenged conduct, a court must first consider whether the action is a matter of choice for the acting employee. This inquiry is mandated by the language of the exception; conduct cannot be discretionary unless it involves an element of judgment or choice. See Dalehite v. United States, 346 U.S. 15, 34 (1953) (stating that the exception protects "the discretion of the executive or the administrator to act according to one's judgment of the best course"). Thus, the discretionary function exception will not apply when a federal statute, regulation, or policy specifically prescribes a course of action for an employee to follow. In this event, the employee has no rightful option but to adhere to the directive. And if the employee's conduct cannot appropriately be the product of judgment or choice, then there is no discretion in the conduct for the discretionary function exception to protect. [Citation.]

Moreover, assuming the challenged conduct involves an element of judgment, a court must determine whether that judgment is of the kind that the discretionary function exception was designed to shield. The basis for the discretionary function exception was Congress' desire to "prevent judicial 'second-guessing' of legislative and administrative decisions grounded in social, economic, and political policy through the medium of an action in tort." *Varig Airlines*. The exception, properly construed, therefore protects only governmental actions and decisions based on considerations of public policy....

This Court's decision in *Varig Airlines* illustrates these propositions. The two cases resolved in that decision were tort suits by the victims of airplane accidents who alleged that the Federal Aviation Administration (FAA) had acted negligently in certifying certain airplanes for operation. The Court characterized the suits as challenging the FAA's decision to certify the airplanes without first inspecting them and held that this decision was a discretionary act for which the Government was immune from liability. In reaching this result, the Court carefully reviewed the statutory and regulatory scheme governing the inspection and certification of airplanes. Congress had given the Secretary of Transportation broad authority to establish and implement a program for enforcing compliance with airplane safety standards. In the exercise of that authority, the FAA, as the Secretary's designee, had devised a system of "spot-checking" airplanes for compliance. This Court first held that the establishment of that system was a discretionary function within the meaning of the FTCA because it represented a policy determination as to how best to "accommo-dat[e] the goal of air transportation safety and the reality of finite agency resources." 467 U.S. at 820. The Court then stated that the discretionary function exception also protected "the acts of FAA employees in executing the 'spot-check' program" because under this program the employees "were specifically empowered to make policy judgments regarding the degree of confidence that might reasonably be placed in a given manufac-turer, the need to maximize compliance with FAA regulations, and the efficient allocation of agency resources." Ibid. Thus, the Court held the challenged acts protected from liability because they were within the range of choice accorded by federal policy and law and were the results of policy determinations.

In restating and clarifying the scope of the discretionary function exception, we intend specifically to reject the Government's argument, pressed both in this Court and the Court of Appeals, that the exception precludes liability for any and all acts arising out of the regulatory programs of federal agencies. That argument is rebutted first by the language of the exception, which protects "discretionary" functions, rather than "regulatory" functions. The significance of Congress' choice of lan-guage is supported by the legislative history.... The discretionary function exception applies only to conduct that involves the permissible exercise of policy judgment. The question in this case is whether the governmental activities challenged by petitioners are of this discretionary nature.

III

Petitioners' suit raises two broad claims. First, petitioners assert that the DBS violated a federal statute and accompanying regulations in issuing a license to Lederle Laboratories to produce Orimune. Second, petitioners argue that the Bureau of Biologics of the FDA violated federal regulations and policy in approving the release of the particular lot of Orimune that contained Kevan Berkovitz's dose....

A

[The Court reviewed several specific statutory and regulatory provisions governing the development, testing, and licensing of vaccines. These provisions] require the DBS, prior to issuing a product license, to receive all data the manufacturer is required to submit, examine the product, and make a determination that the product complies with safety standards.

Petitioners' first allegation with regard to the licensing of Orimune is that the DBS issued a product license without first receiving data that the manufacturer must submit showing how the product, at the various stages of the manufacturing process, matched up against regulatory safety standards. The discretionary function exception does not bar a cause of action based on this allegation. The statute and regulations described above require, as a precondition to licensing, that the DBS receive certain test data from the manufacturer relating to the product's compliance with regulatory standards.... The DBS has no discretion to issue a license without first receiving the required test data; to do so would violate a specific statutory and regulatory directive. Accordingly, to the extent that petitioners' licensing claim is based on a decision of the DBS to issue a license without having received the required test data, the discretionary function exception imposes no bar.

Petitioners' other allegation regarding the licensing of Orimune is difficult to describe with precision. Petitioners contend that the DBS licensed Orimune even though the vaccine did not comply with certain regulatory safety standards.[9]

If petitioners aver that the DBS licensed Orimune either without determining whether the vaccine complied with regulatory standards or after determining that the vaccine failed to comply, the discretionary function exception does not bar the claim. Under the scheme governing the DBS's regulation of polio vaccines, the DBS [has no discretion to deviate from its mandated procedures requiring a determination that the product complies with all regulatory standards.] Petitioners' claim, if interpreted as alleging that the DBS licensed Orimune in the absence of a determination that the vaccine complied with regulatory standards, therefore does not challenge a discretionary function. Rather, the claim charges a failure on

---

9. Petitioners point to two specific regulatory standards that the product allegedly failed to satisfy. First, petitioners claim that an original virus strain from which the vaccine was made did not comply with the requirement that the strain be "free of harmful effect upon administration in the recommended dosage to at least 100,000 people susceptible to poliomyelitis." [Citations.] Second, petitioners assert that the strain, ..., and the ultimate vaccine product failed to comply with the regulatory scheme's neurovirulence requirement. [The neurovirulence of the polio vaccine is its ability to cause poliomyelitis. The vaccine must be tested on animals to determine if it meets the neurovirulence criterion.]

the part of the agency to perform its clear duty under federal law.... [and thus] the discretionary function exception does not apply.

If petitioners' claim is that the DBS made a determination that Orimune complied with regulatory standards, but that the determination was incorrect, the question of the applicability of the discretionary function exception requires a somewhat different analysis. In that event, the question turns on whether the manner and method of determining compliance with the safety standards at issue involves agency judgment of the kind protected by the discretionary function exception.[11] Petitioners contend that the determination involves the application of objective scientific standards, whereas the Government asserts that the determination incorporates considerable "policy judgment." [The record is incomplete on this issue, and the District Court should decide] whether agency officials appropriately exercise policy judgment in determining that a vaccine product complies with the relevant safety standards.

B

The regulatory scheme governing release of vaccine lots is distinct from that governing the issuance of licenses. [The vaccine release regulations require manufacturers to examine all vaccine lots prior to distribution to ensure that they comply with regulatory standards, but do not impose a corresponding duty on the Bureau of Biologics.] Although the regulations empower the Bureau to examine any vaccine lot and prevent the distribution of a noncomplying lot, see 21 CFR § 610.2(a) (1978), they do not require the Bureau to take such action in all cases. The regulations generally allow the Bureau to determine the appropriate manner in which to regulate the release of vaccine lots, rather than mandating certain kinds of agency action. The regulatory scheme governing the release of vaccine lots is substantially similar in this respect to the scheme discussed in *Varig Airlines*.

Given this regulatory context, the discretionary function exception bars any claims that challenge the Bureau's formulation of policy as to the appropriate way in which to regulate the release of vaccine lots. Cf. *Varig Airlines* (holding that discretionary function exception barred claim challenging FAA's decision to establish a spot-checking program). [Further, if the formulated policies and programs allow implementing officials to make independent policy judgments, the discretionary function exception protects those acts as well.] Thus, if the Bureau's policy leaves no room for an official to exercise policy judgment in performing a given act, or if the act simply does not involve the exercise of such judgment, the discretionary function exception does not bar a claim that the act was negligent or wrongful. Cf. Indian Towing Co. v. United States, 350 U.S. at 69 (holding

---

11. As noted, see n. 9, infra, the regulatory standards that petitioners claim were not satisfied in this case are the neurovirulence criterion and the requirement that virus strains be free from harmful effect. The question presented is thus whether the determination that a vaccine product complies with each of these regulatory standards involves judgment of the kind that the discretionary function exception protects.

that a negligent failure to maintain a lighthouse in good working order subjected Government to suit under the FTCA even though the initial decision to undertake and maintain lighthouse service was a discretionary policy judgment).

Viewed in light of these principles, petitioners' claim regarding the release of the vaccine lot from which Kevan Berkovitz received his dose survives the Government's motion to dismiss. Petitioners allege that, under the authority granted by the regulations, the Bureau of Biologics has adopted a policy of testing all vaccine lots for compliance with safety standards and preventing the distribution to the public of any lots that fail to comply. Petitioners further allege that notwithstanding this policy, which allegedly leaves no room for implementing officials to exercise independent policy judgment, employees of the Bureau knowingly approved the release of a lot that did not comply with safety standards. Thus, petitioners' complaint is directed at a governmental action that allegedly involved no policy discretion. [If petitioners are able to substantiate this claim,] the discretionary function exception does not bar the claim.[13] ...

IV

[The judgment of the Court of Appeals is accordingly reversed, and the case is remanded for further proceedings consistent with this opinion.]

NOTES

1. In the interest of justice, why does it matter whether the plaintiff's injury resulted from the government's erroneous policy or from the government's erroneous failure to follow its regulatory rule? Indeed, is not an error in policy the more objectionable of the two? Or are the courts in these cases concerned with something other than justice?

2. The Supreme Court addressed the nature of discretionary actions again in United States v. Gaubert, 499 U.S. 315, 324–25 (1991), where the Court established a presumption that, when following established governmental policy, whether derived from statute, regulation, or agency guidelines, "the agent's acts are grounded in policy" and thus qualify for protection under the Federal Tort Claims Act—provided that the agent's acts are "based on the purposes that the regulatory scheme seeks to accomplish." In *Gaubert*, the Court held that the day-to-day decisions made at an agency's operational level were protected, thus widening the FTCA's discretionary function exception beyond policy decisions.

3. **National Childhood Vaccine Injury Act of 1986.** This statute, 42 U.S.C. §§ 300aa–10 et seq., creates a no-fault compensation program for "vaccine related" injuries and authorizes actions to be brought against the federal government through the Secretary of Health and Human Services. The purposes of the Act are (1) to offer fair compensation to victims of childhood vaccine-related illnesses,

---

13. The Government's own argument before this Court provides some support for petitioners' allegation regarding the Bureau's policy. The Government indicated that the Bureau reviews each lot of vaccine and decides whether it complies with safety standards. The Government further suggested that if an employee knew that a lot did not comply with these standards, he would have no discretion to approve the release of the lot.

and (2) to insure the continued supply of vaccines by limiting litigation against vaccine manufacturers. See McGowan v. Secretary of Dep't of Health & Human Servs., 31 Fed.Cl. 734, 738–39 (1994).

Under the Act, a claimant is entitled to recover on a showing that (1) he contracted a statutorily defined condition, (2) after receiving one of the covered vaccines, (3) within the time period specified. No further showing of causation is required. The federal government may defend by proving that the condition "is due to factors unrelated to the administration of the vaccine." Allowable compensation includes "actual unreimbursable expenses," an award for pain and suffering and emotional distress of no more than $250,000, and lost earnings after the age of 18 based on a statutorily defined formula. The claimant may sue the vaccine manufacturer in limited circumstances, but only if he has first pursued the statutory remedy and rejected a Court of Claims judgment. See, e.g., Rooks v. Secretary of Dep't of Health & Human Servs., 35 Fed.Cl. 1 (1996).

See generally Rabin, Some Thoughts on the Efficacy of a Mass Toxics Administrative Compensation Scheme, 52 Md.L.Rev. 951 (1993); V. Schwartz & Mahshigian, National Childhood Vaccine Injury Act of 1986: An Ad Hoc Remedy or a Window for the Future?, 48 Ohio St.L.J. 387 (1987).

4. On the discretionary function exception to the Federal Tort Claims Act, see generally Niles, "Nothing but Mischief:" The Federal Tort Claims Act and the Scope of Discretionary Immunity, 54 Admin.L.Rev. 1275 (2002); Zillman, Protecting Discretion: Judicial Interpretation of the Discretionary Function Exception to the Federal Tort Claims Act, 47 Me.L.Rev. 365 (1995). The Court of Appeals decision in *Berkovitz* is noted at 61 Temp.L.Rev. 281 (1988).

---

4. GOVERNMENT CONTRACTORS

Kerstetter v. Pacific Scientific Co.

United States Court of Appeals, Fifth Circuit, 2000.
210 F.3d 431

■ ROBERT M. PARKER, CIRCUIT JUDGE.

Plaintiff–Appellant brought suit on behalf of her son, a deceased naval pilot, contending that the pilot restraint system in the T–34C aircraft he was flying at the time of his death was defectively designed. The defendants moved for summary judgment based on, *inter alia,* the government contractor defense. Because we find that the government contractor defense applies and that no genuine issues of material fact exist which would preclude summary judgment, we affirm.

This case arises from the 1995 death of Navy instructor pilot Lt. David Joseph Huber, who died while conducting a familiarization flight with a student pilot off Padre Island, Texas. Lt. Huber was inadvertently ejected from a T–34C aircraft during a training maneuver when his pilot restraint system ("PRS") released without command. Pacific Scientific Company manufactured the PRS on board the aircraft. The Navy conducted an investigation of the incident and concluded that a possible cause for the ejection was contact between the aircraft control stick grip and the rotary buckle that releases the restraint belts.

In late 1973, the Navy began Phase I testing of the T–34C [a modification of its previous flight trainer] and specifically observed several deficiencies in the pilot restraint system (PRS). The Navy concluded that these deficiencies should be corrected. In mid–1974, Phase II testing focused on the PRS and concluded in a final report that the PRS was uncomfortable and functioned poorly during negative G testing. The report recommended corrective action.

By 1975, Beech Aircraft [the manufacturer] had not yet corrected the PRS difficulties identified in Phase II testing; however, Beech proposed a fifth "crotch strap" with a quick release buckle in preparation for further testing. A preliminary evaluation in September of 1976 gave this new PRS a positive evaluation. The Navy performed further tests and found that "The pilot restraint system in the T–34C airplane is an enhancing characteristic which significantly improves airplane controllability during spins and should be included in future designs." In 1982, the Navy ordered 120 T–34Cs with this "crotch strap" design. All drawings were approved by the Navy through thorough review and training sessions. Once approved, these drawings could not be modified without Navy approval. The PRS design resulting from this review and testing process was the same as that in the victim's plane.

In a 1985 Field Engineering Action Team (FEAT) meeting, Beech heard reports for the first time of a phenomenon called "uncommanded seat harness release." The next year's meeting included an agenda item [on this phenomenon which was ultimately not addressed.] This is the last time Beech heard about the problem until after the [plaintiff's accident.]

The Navy instructed students training in the T–34C to position their harness buckles under their life preservers to prevent inadvertent release of the PRS and also created a form for pilots to report occurrences of inadvertent releases. The Navy took no further actions in response to this problem before the accident in this case. After this accident, a Navy official noted that the PRS posed a "severe flight hazard."

Kerstetter brought this suit on behalf of Lt. Huber against the named defendants. All defendants filed motions for summary judgment based on the government contractor defense ... The district court granted defendants' motions [and plaintiff appealed].

* * *

Government contractor immunity is derived from the government's immunity from suit where the performance of a discretionary function is at issue. See Boyle v. United Tech. Corp., 487 U.S. 500, 511 (1988). The Supreme Court has noted that "the selection of the appropriate design for military equipment to be used by our Armed Forces is assuredly a discretionary function." Id.

In order for a contractor to claim the government contractor defense, (1) the government must have approved "reasonably precise" specifications; (2) the equipment must have conformed to those specifications; and (3) the supplier/contractor must have warned of those equipment dangers that were known to the supplier/contractor, but not to the government. See *Boyle*; [citation].

The government need not prepare the specifications to be considered to have approved them. See Trevino v. General Dynamics, 865 F.2d 1474, 1480 (5th Cir.1989) (holding that "substantive review" is adequate). To determine whether "substantive review" occurred, a court must take into consideration a number of factors. The factors involve examining drawings, evaluation from time to time, criticism and extensive government testing—a "continuous back and forth" between the contractor and the government. [Citation.] The specifications need not address the specific defect alleged; the government need only evaluate the design feature in question. *Boyle*; *Trevino* ("The government contractor defense as reformulated in *Boyle* protects government contractors from liability for defective designs if discretion over the feature in question was exercised by the government.").

Nonconformance with a specification means more than that the ultimate design feature does not achieve its intended goal. The alleged defect must exist independently of the design itself, and must result from a deviation from the required military specifications. [Citation.] Extensive government involvement in the design, review, development and testing of a product, as well as extensive acceptance and use of the product following production, is evidence that the product line generally conformed with the government-approved specifications. [Citation.]

The third part of the *Boyle* test requires the contractor to warn the government about those equipment dangers that were known to the contractor, but not to the government. The purpose of this element is *not* to create an incentive to discover latent defects in a product designed for the government. *Boyle* ("The third condition is necessary because, in its absence, the displacement of state tort law would create some incentive for the manufacturer to withhold knowledge of risks, since conveying that knowledge might disrupt the contract but withholding it would produce no liability."). The government contractor defense does not require a contractor to warn the government of defects about which it only should have known. "After *Boyle*, government contractor is only responsible for warning the government of dangers about which it has actual knowledge." *Trevino*.

Plaintiff argues that, in the approval process, the government must have considered and rejected a safer design alternative proposed by the plaintiff, or at least must have itself prospectively limited the discretion of the contractor to include a safer alternative design.... [T]his argument is well suited for presentation to Congress or to the Supreme Court rather than the district court but it *is contrary to the case law*. *Boyle*. The *Boyle* court noted that, while this is perhaps a reasonable rule of tort law, it did not sufficiently protect the federal interest in the selection of appropriate military equipment.

> The design ultimately selected may well reflect a significant policy judgment by Government officials whether or not the contractor rather than those officials developed the design. In addition, it does not seem to us sound policy to penalize, and thus deter, active contractor participation in the design process, placing the contractor at risk unless it identifies all design defects.

[Citation.] The district court noted that this last sentence can mean only that the defense applies even when the contractor did not warn the government of latent defects-in other words, defects that neither the contractor nor the government considered it at all. We agree. The articulation of the government contractor defense offered by the plaintiff is contrary to the case law.

* * *

Defendants claim that the government contractor defense immunizes them from [design defect] liability in this case. The primary issue with regard to an alleged design defect in this case is whether the government approved reasonably precise specifications. The district court held that the unrebutted summary judgment evidence establishes that the government approved reasonably precise specifications for the design features in this case.

First, the T–34C originated as a modification of the T–34B, a plane the Navy had been using to train pilots for 20 years. The T–34B had the same PRS, the same control stick and the same cockpit design as the T–34C. Second, the government was extensively involved in the approval process. The record reveals a clear pattern of government-contractor interaction over at least eight years. Third, approval of the T–34C's design included the specific features at issue in this case. The defendants argue that "[t]he *defective nature* of the features may have been latent to the Navy as well as the contractors, but the features themselves were obvious to anyone who flew the T–34C." Fourth, the Navy specifically addressed the design features at issue in this case throughout the approval process.

... [P]laintiff's arguments that the government contract defense is not available are unavailing. First, plaintiffs argue that the defendants purchased the PRS "off the shelf." As noted by the district court, the government procurement officer did not order a quantity of restraint systems in the same way he would order light bulbs, but rather, government engineers approved the inclusion of these specific components into a complex piece of equipment. In addition, the Navy specifically tested the T–34C's PRS during its evaluation of the aircraft following Phase II testing. Furthermore, neither counsel for the plaintiff nor counsel for the defendant were able to name or otherwise identify another aircraft which uses the PRS involved in this case.

Second, plaintiffs argue that the T–34C's PRS specifications conflict with another, more general specification. [The specifications cited by the plaintiff were not implicated by the facts of this case.] Lastly, the plaintiffs argue that the defense should not apply because the government did not actively limit the contractor's ability to develop a safer design. Basically, plaintiffs argue that a safer design could have been developed "without violating any specification." This argument focuses on an incorrect standard which is whether the government approved a specification that did not contain a safer design. The inapplicability of this standard to the case at bar has been addressed.

The defendants argue that the government approved reasonably precise specifications. They reference numerous documents involving the PRS in general and the buckle in particular. The "reasonably precise" standard is satisfied as long as the specifications address, in reasonable detail, the product design feature, alleged to be defective. *Boyle*, Bailey v. McDonnell Douglas Corp., 989 F.2d 794, 799 (5th Cir.1993) (noting that the specifications need not address the specific design defect alleged, just the specific feature). Defendants alternatively allege that even if the Navy is found not to have approved the PRS during T–34C design process, it did approve the allegedly defective design at issue far before the accident by subsequent testing and use. The 1985 and 1986 FEAT meetings are evidence of this.

We find that the district court's conclusion that the Navy approved reasonably precise specifications for the T–34C's seat harness was appropriate under the facts of this case. Therefore, the government contractor defense applies.[9]

[Plaintiff raises failure to warn allegations in addition to design claims. Regarding the failure to warn claims, this court has previously] held that a "conflict between state law and federal policy might arise if there is evidence that the government was involved in the decision to give, or not to give, a warning." [Citation.] This is a modified *Boyle* test. State law is displaced if (1) the United States exercised discretion and approved the warnings; (2) the contractor provided a warning that conformed to the approved warnings; and (3) the contractor warned about dangers it knew, but the government did not.

The district court found that the first element was satisfied in that the Navy approved, changed and edited warnings in the T–34C ... Flight Manual. Although the manual contained no express evaluation of a warning of the specific hazard of inadvertent seat release, the government contractor defense applies because the Navy exercised discretion in approving warnings in the flight manual. See *Tate*, 140 F.3d at 660 (holding that the government contractor defense applies in "situations in which the government makes the informed decision not to include a specification or require a warning because, in the government's view, one would be

---

9. The second element of the defense is satisfied as there was no evidence of a manufacturing defect—i.e., the product conformed to the government specifications. The third element is also satisfied because there is no evidence that Beech knew information about the inadvertent seat harness release that was not known to the government. Evidence exists that the Navy knew as early as 1985 of this inadvertent risk—i.e., the Navy knew at least as much as the contractors.

unnecessary or problematic."). Inadequacy is not an issue when it is the government's warning in the first place. The district court found that there ~~was no failure to warn claim under Texas law either because the Navy~~ added a release warning to the flight manual 3 years before the incident in this case.

Plaintiff argues that BASI [the maintenance contractor] and Beech were under a continuing duty to advise and warn the Navy because they continued to exercise the necessary degree of continuing control, thus creating a continuing duty to advise. [Citation.] The degree of control necessary to give rise to a continuing duty to advise was not present in this case. [Citation].

[The undisputed fact is] that the Navy knew about the problem at least 10 years before the accident. Existence of a duty to warn is a question of law and since the Navy knew, contractors had no duty to warn. Contractors need not warn the victim directly. [Citation.] Since the Navy knew of the danger of the "uncommanded seat release" on the T–34C's PRS, the contractors did not have a duty to warn of that danger.

* * *

Because we find that the government contractor defense applies and that no genuine issue of material fact exists, we affirm the decision of the district court.

NOTES

1. The government contractor defense from *Boyle* is not premised on any federal statute, but rather on a more general notion "that a few areas, involving 'uniquely federal interests,' [citation], are so committed by the Constitution and laws of the United States to federal control that state law is pre-empted and replaced, where necessary, by federal law of a content prescribed (absent explicit statutory directive) by the courts—so-called 'federal common law.' " *Boyle*, 487 U.S. at 504. Preemption of this kind is warranted only when the imposition of liability under state law would create a "significant conflict" with those "unique federal interests." Id. at 507. To provide a "limiting principle to identify those situations in which a 'significant conflict' with federal policy or interests does arise," the Court relied on its line of cases defining an exception to the Federal Tort Claims Act for injuries to military personnel in the course of military service. See Feres v. United States, 340 U.S. 135 (1950). The Court also considered the operation of the discretionary function exception to the FTCA and concluded that "the selection of the appropriate design for military equipment to be used by our Armed Forces is assuredly a discretionary function within the meaning of that provision."

2. How, if at all, do you think *Boyle* affects the cost of products purchased by the government? The availability of such products? Their quality? Safety?

3. The Scope of the Government Contractor Defense. After *Boyle*, the lower courts had to determine the scope of the defense and the contours of its three components, defined in *Kerstetter*.

A. Does the defense encompass nonmilitary products, such as lawn mowers, purchased by the military? Nonmilitary products purchased by other branches of government, such as mail trucks or mail sorting machines? Compare Carley v. Wheeled Coach, 991 F.2d 1117 (3d Cir.1993), with Nielsen v. George Diamond Vogel Paint Co., 892 F.2d 1450 (9th Cir.1990).

B.   Does it apply to nondeliberative approvals of "reasonably precise specifications"? For a discussion of a "rubber stamp" exception to the defense, see Trevino v. General Dynamics Corp., 865 F.2d 1474 (5th Cir.1989), relied upon in *Kerstetter*, and Maguire v. Hughes Aircraft Corp., 912 F.2d 67 (3d Cir.1990). How much deliberation is enough to avoid characterization as a "rubber stamp" approval? Does the deliberation in *Kerstetter* strike you as a "rubber stamp?" Is a simple signature on a form enough to raise the defense? See Snell v. Bell Helicopter Textron, Inc., 107 F.3d 744 (9th Cir. 1997).

C.   Does the defense apply when the "reasonably precise specifications" that are actually reviewed and approved do not include the design danger that causes the harm? In other words, if the government approves precise specifications for most aspects of a helicopter, but the specifications do not specify which way the doors open, does the defense apply? See Lewis v. Babcock Ind., 985 F.2d 83 (2d Cir.1993); Gray v. Lockheed Aeronautical Systems Co., 125 F.3d 1371 (11th Cir. 1997).

D.   What result when reasonably necessary safety features are not called for in the specifications? Anzalone v. Westech Gear Corp., 661 A.2d 796 (N.J. 1995)(plaintiff tripped near unguarded device which partially amputated his hand, defendant argued that the device was manufactured in strict conformance with specific and detailed government specifications; summary judgment reversed, defense not applicable because the defendant was not prohibited from including safety devices).

E.   Does the defense apply to manufacturing defect claims? Review carefully the three elements of the defense. See McGonigal v. Gearhart Indus., 851 F.2d 774 (5th Cir.1988). Inadequate warning claims? See In re Joint Eastern and Southern District New York Asbestos Litigation, 897 F.2d 626 (2d Cir.1990).

F.   Does the defense apply to a maintenance service contract? Hudgens v. Bell Helicopters/Textron, 328 F.3d 1329 (11th Cir. 2003)(helicopter pilot injured in crash alleging negligent maintenance by defendant; *held*, defense applies).

G.   If a government contractor otherwise entitled to the defense reasonably chooses to settle a case because of uncertainty over whether the defense will apply, is the contractor entitled to indemnity from the Federal Government? No, according to the Supreme Court in Hercules Inc. v. United States, 516 U.S. 417 (1996). Chemical manufacturers who previously had settled actions brought by Vietnam veterans for injuries suffered from exposure to Agent Orange sought implied indemnification from the Government for the amounts paid in settlement. Virtually ignoring *Boyle,* the Supreme Court ruled that although the Government had required the defendants to make Agent Orange pursuant to the Defense Production Act of 1950, the Government neither expressly nor impliedly promised to reimburse the manufacturers for claims by third parties allegedly injured by the defoliant.

4.   Why is the third prong of the defense defined so narrowly? Should not the manufacturer be liable for failing to warn the government about all risks of which the manufacturer reasonably *should* have known?

5.   See generally Cantu and Young, The Government Contractor Defense: Breaking the *Boyle* Barrier, 62 Alb. L. Rev. 403 (1998); Cass & Gillette, The Government Contractor Defense: Contractual Allocation of Public Risk, 77 Va. L.Rev. 257 (1991); M. Green & Matasar, The Supreme Court and the Products

Liability Crisis: Lesson's from *Boyle's* Government Contractor Defense, 63 S.Cal. L. Rev. 637 (1990).

---

5. PARENT AND APPARENT MANUFACTURERS

Fletcher v. Atex, Inc.

United States Court of Appeals, Second Circuit, 1995.
68 F.3d 1451.

■ Before: KEARSE, CALABRESI, and CABRANES, CIRCUIT JUDGES.

■ JOSE A. CABRANES, CIRCUIT JUDGE:

[Plaintiffs sued Atex, Inc. ("Atex") and its parent, defendant Eastman Kodak Company ("Kodak"), for repetitive stress injuries caused by their use of computer keyboards manufactured by Atex. The district court entered summary judgment for Kodak, dismissing all claims against it, and plaintiffs appeal.]

... From 1981 until December 1992, Atex was a wholly-owned subsidiary of Kodak. In 1987, Atex's name was changed to Electronic Pre–Press Systems, Inc., ("EPPS"), but its name was changed back to Atex in 1990. In December 1992, Atex sold substantially all of its assets to an independent third party and again changed its name to 805 Middlesex Corp., which holds the proceeds from the sale. Kodak continues to be the sole shareholder of 805 Middlesex Corp.

After extensive discovery, Kodak moved for summary judgment [which plaintiffs opposed], arguing that genuine issues of material fact existed as to Kodak's liability under any number of theories, including (1) that Atex was merely Kodak's alter ego or instrumentality; (2) that Atex was Kodak's agent in the manufacture and marketing of the keyboards; (3) that Kodak was the "apparent manufacturer" of the Atex keyboards; and (4) that Kodak acted in tortious concert with Atex in manufacturing and marketing the allegedly defective keyboards.

[The district court rejected each of plaintiffs' theories of Kodak's liability. First, regarding the allegation of alter ego liability, it] found that Kodak and Atex observed all corporate formalities and maintained separate corporate existence. It held that Atex's participation in Kodak's cash management system and Kodak's control over Atex's major expenditures and asset sales were insufficient to raise an issue of material fact regarding Kodak's liability under an alter ego theory. Second, it held that [the agency theory failed because Kodak's] representations in various advertisements, promotional literature, and annual reports were ... insufficient as a matter of law to [establish an agency relationship.] Third, [it held that the] apparent manufacturer theory [failed] because [Kodak] was not involved in the sale or distribution of the keyboards. Finally, the court found that the plaintiffs' concerted action theory failed [for want of] evidence indicating that Kodak and Atex had agreed to commit a tortious act. This appeal followed.

1. *Alter Ego Liability*

[Under New York conflict of laws principles, the law of Kodak's state of incorporation, Delaware, determines whether its corporate form may be disregarded.]

Delaware law permits a court to pierce the corporate veil of a company "where there is fraud or where [it] is in fact a mere instrumentality or alter ego of its owner." Geyer v. Ingersoll Publications Co., 621 A.2d 784, 793 (Del.Ch.1992).... To prevail on an alter ego claim under Delaware law, a plaintiff must show (1) that the parent and the subsidiary "operated as a single economic entity" and (2) that an "overall element of injustice or unfairness ... [is] present." [Citations.]

* * * Among the factors to be considered in determining whether a subsidiary and parent operate as a "single economic entity" are: "[W]hether the corporation was adequately capitalized for the corporate undertaking; whether the corporation was solvent; whether dividends were paid, corporate records kept, officers and directors functioned properly, and other corporate formalities were observed; whether the dominant shareholder siphoned corporate funds; and whether, in general, the corporation simply functioned as a facade for the dominant shareholder." ... [A] showing of fraud or wrongdoing is not necessary under an alter ego theory, but the plaintiff must demonstrate an overall element of injustice or unfairness. [Citation.]

A plaintiff seeking to persuade a Delaware court to disregard the corporate structure faces "a difficult task." ...

Kodak has shown that Atex followed corporate formalities, and the plaintiffs have offered no evidence to the contrary. [P]laintiffs have not challenged Kodak's assertions that Atex's board of directors held regular meetings, that minutes from those meetings were routinely prepared and maintained in corporate minute books, that appropriate financial records and other files were maintained by Atex, that Atex filed its own tax returns and paid its own taxes, and that Atex had its own employees and management executives who were responsible for the corporation's day-to-day business. The plaintiffs' primary arguments regarding domination concern (1) the defendant's use of a cash management system; (2) Kodak's exertion of control over Atex's major expenditures, stock sales, and the sale of Atex's assets to a third party; (3) Kodak's "dominating presence" on Atex's board of directors; (4) descriptions of the relationship between Atex and Kodak in the corporations' advertising, promotional literature, and annual reports; and (5) Atex's assignment of one of its former officer's mortgage to Kodak in order to close Atex's asset-purchase agreement with a third party. [I]n light of the undisputed factors of independence cited [above, plaintiff cannot] establish the degree of domination necessary to disregard Atex's [corporate identity].

First, the district court correctly held that "Atex's participation in Kodak's cash management system is consistent with sound business practice and does not show undue domination or control." . . . [A]ll of Kodak's domestic subsidiaries participate in the system and maintain zero-balance bank accounts. All funds transferred from the subsidiary accounts are recorded as credits to the subsidiary, and when a subsidiary is in need of funds, a transfer is made. At all times, a strict accounting is kept of each subsidiary's funds.

Courts have generally declined to find alter ego liability based on a parent corporation's use of a cash management system. [Instead, courts have considered such systems legitimate techniques for administrative convenience and economy, rather than regarding them as manifesting control or as a device for intermingling funds. Plaintiffs] offer no facts to support their speculation that Kodak's centralized cash management system was actually a "complete commingling" of funds or a means by which Kodak sought to "siphon all of Atex's revenues into its own account."

Second, [domination is not established by] evidence that Kodak's approval was required for Atex's real estate leases, major capital expenditures, negotiations for a sale of minority stock ownership to IBM, or the fact that Kodak played a significant role in the ultimate sale of Atex's assets to a third party. . . . [T]his evidence [does not show that] the two corporations constituted "a single economic entity." Indeed, this type of conduct is typical of a majority shareholder or parent corporation. See *Phoenix Canada Oil Co. v. Texaco*, 842 F.2d 1466, 1476 (3d Cir.1988) (declining to pierce the corporate veil where subsidiary required to secure approval from parent for "large investments and acquisitions or disposals of major assets"); [citations]. . . .

The plaintiffs' third argument, that Kodak dominated the Atex board of directors, also fails. Although a number of Kodak employees have sat on the Atex board, it is undisputed that between 1981 and 1988, only one director of Atex was also a director of Kodak. Between 1989 and 1992, Atex and Kodak had no directors in common. Parents and subsidiaries frequently have overlapping boards of directors while maintaining separate business operations. . . .

Fourth, the descriptions of the relationship between Atex and Kodak and the presence of the Kodak logo in Atex's promotional literature [fail to] justify piercing the corporate veil. The plaintiffs point to several statements in both Kodak's and Atex's literature to evidence Kodak's domination of its subsidiary[, including] (1) a promotional pamphlet produced by EPPS (a/k/a Atex) describing Atex as a business unit of EPPS and noting that EPPS was an "agent" of Kodak; (2) a document produced by Atex entitled "An Introduction to Atex Systems," which describes a "merger" between Kodak and Atex; (3) a statement in Kodak's 1985 and 1986 annual reports describing Atex as a "recent acquisition" and a "subsidiar[y] . . . combined in a new division"; and (4) a statement in an Atex/EPPS document [referring to Atex as a division of EPPS, a Kodak company]. [Plaintiffs also note] that Atex's paperwork and packaging materials frequently displayed the Kodak logo.

[But Atex never merged with Kodak or operated as a Kodak division, and the documentary] statements and the use of the Kodak logo are not evidence that the two companies operated as a "single economic entity." See Coleman v. Corning Glass Works, 619 F.Supp. 950, 956 (W.D.N.Y.1985) (upholding corporate form despite "loose language" in annual report about "merger" and parent's reference to subsidiary as a "division"); [citations].

Fifth, the plaintiffs contend that Atex's assignment of its former CEO's mortgage to Kodak [for business reasons] is evidence of Kodak's domination of Atex. We reject this argument as [rubbish].

Finally, even if [plaintiffs had shown] Kodak's domination of Atex, summary judgment would still be appropriate because the plaintiffs offer no evidence on the second prong of the alter ego analysis. [Plaintiffs have not shown] an "overall element of injustice or unfairness" that would result from respecting the two companies' corporate separateness.... [T]he plaintiffs offer nothing more than the bare assertion that Kodak "exploited" Atex "to generate profits but not to safeguard safety." There is no indication that Kodak sought to defraud creditors and consumers or to siphon funds from its subsidiary. [Summary judgment for defendant on plaintiffs' alter ego theory affirmed.]

2. Agency Liability

[Next is plaintiffs'] agency theory—that is, whether Kodak, as principal, could be liable for the tortious acts of Atex, its agent. The plaintiffs rely on statements in Atex/EPPS literature to support their theory: (1) the statement in the Atex document "Setting Up TPE 6000 on the Sun 3 Workstation" that "Atex is an unincorporated division of Electronic Pre–Press Systems, Inc., a Kodak company"; and (2) the statements in the EPPS promotional pamphlet that "EPPS serves as Kodak's primary agent to supply electronic pre-press products" and that "Atex is the largest of the EPPS business units." [T]he district court rejected the plaintiffs' agency theory of liability, finding that there was no evidence that Kodak authorized the statements.

[Plaintiffs argue that Kodak permitted the use of its logo on these documents, suggesting that] Kodak authorized or appeared to authorize the references to Atex/EPPS as its agent. First, the plaintiffs' argument fails under a theory of actual authority. The Restatement (Second) of Agency states: "Authority is the power of the agent to affect the legal relations of the principal by acts done in accordance with the principal's manifestations of consent to him." Restatement (2d) of Agency § 7 (1958). [There is no evidence that Kodak manifested consent that Atex act on its behalf.] The presence of a parent's logo on documents created and distributed by a subsidiary, standing alone, does not confer authority upon the subsidiary to act as an agent.

For similar reasons, plaintiffs' arguments fail under a theory of apparent authority. ["Apparent] authority is dependent upon verbal or other acts *by a principal* which reasonably give an appearance of authority to conduct the transaction." Greene v. Hellman, 412 N.E.2d 1301, 1306 (N.Y. 1980)(emphasis added)(citing Restatement (2d) of Agency § 8 cmts. *a, c*). "Key to the creation of apparent authority," the court continued, "is that the third person, accepting the appearance of authority as true, has relied upon it." The plaintiffs offer no evidence that Kodak authorized or gave the appearance of having authorized the statements in the Atex/EPPS documents. Atex's/EPPS's use of the Kodak logo is not a "verbal or other act[ ] by a *principal*," but rather, an act by the purported agent. [There is no evidence] plaintiffs relied on the documents at issue.... We affirm [summary judgment for defendant on] plaintiffs' agency theory of liability.

3. *Apparent Manufacturer*

The plaintiffs' third theory of liability is that Kodak should be held liable as the "apparent manufacturer" of the Atex keyboards. Restatement (2d) of Torts § 400 (1965), [defines this theory and states:] "One who puts out as his own product a chattel manufactured by another is subject to the same liability as though he were its manufacturer." This theory of liability is well-established under New York law. See Commissioners of State Ins. Fund v. City Chem. Corp., 48 N.E.2d 262 (N.Y.1943); [citation].

The district court held that Kodak could not be held liable under the apparent manufacturer doctrine because "[t]here is no indication in the Restatement [or New York case law] that § 400 was intended to apply to a party which is not a seller of chattel, or is [not] otherwise involved in the chain of distribution of a product." ... See Torres v. Goodyear Tire and Rubber Co., 867 F.2d 1234, 1236 (9th Cir.1989)(parent not liable under § 400 for subsidiary's product where it was not manufacturer or seller); Affiliated FM Ins. Co. v. Trane Co., 831 F.2d 153, 156 (7th Cir.1987) (parent not liable under § 400 [if not] involved in manufacture, sale, or installation of product); [citation].

Kodak argues that the district court's conclusion is supportable on three different theories. First, § 400 cannot apply because Kodak was neither the seller nor the distributor of the allegedly defective keyboards. Second, ... it does not apply to Kodak [here] because the Kodak logo was not affixed to the keyboards or their packages, only to promotional and advertising materials. Finally, [the promotional and packaging materials at issue here] do not suggest that Kodak, rather than Atex, manufactured the keyboards. We agree.

First, New York courts have only applied the apparent manufacturer doctrine to sellers of a product or parties otherwise involved in the chain of distribution. [Citation;] *State Ins. Fund* (finding chemical vendor could be held liable under earlier version of § 400 where vendor purchased chemicals from a distributor, removed distributor's label, and affixed its own); *Markel* (finding defendant Ford Motor Company liable for malfunctioning brake pedal arm that it sold as a component part of a Ford automobile); [citations].

[Although some cases] hold that participation in the chain of distribution is not essential to liability under the apparent manufacturer doctrine, each involved a licensing agreement in which the defendant allowed the use of its name in exchange for control over (or involvement in) the manufacture of the product. See [citation]; City of Hartford v. Associated Constr. Co., 384 A.2d 390 (Conn.1978) (licensor who "retained and exercised rights of control as to the quality and the methods and manner of application of the product" could be held liable under § 400); [citation].

[Plaintiffs have produced no evidence that Kodak participated in any way in the development, design, sale or distribution of the keyboards, nor that it had a keyboard licensing agreement with Atex.]

Second, [there is] no evidence that Kodak held itself out as the manufacturer of the Atex keyboard. See Restatement (2d) of Torts § 400. [The keyboards prominently display the name of Atex, the true manufacturer, and the Kodak logo was not affixed either to the keyboards or their packages. Under these circumstances, no] defendant could be held liable on an apparent manufacturer theory. Indeed, the cases cited by the plaintiffs only extend § 400 liability to defendants who placed their names directly on the product or the product packaging at issue. [Citations.]

Third, [plaintiffs' evidence does] not suggest that Kodak manufactured the Atex keyboards. Many of the documents ... make reference only to Atex computer *software*, such as the Atex "Color Imaging System" and the "PC Custom Display Software User Manual." Furthermore, Atex is repeatedly identified as the manufacturer ... in all the documents identified by the plaintiffs. [Thus,] plaintiffs' argument—that the presence of the Kodak logo on these documents [shows that] Kodak represented itself as the manufacturer of the keyboards—must fail. [Summary judgment for defendant on plaintiffs' apparent manufacturer theory affirmed.]

4. Concerted Tortious Action

The plaintiffs' final theory of liability is that Kodak acted in tortious concert with Atex in designing and marketing of the allegedly defective keyboards. [Plaintiffs argue that Kodak (1) directly participated in, or (2) "substantially assisted" Atex in marketing the defective keyboard equipment, thus proving that Kodak "acted in concert" with Atex.]

Section 876 of the Restatement (Second) of Torts provides that:

For harm resulting to a third person from the tortious conduct of another, one is subject to liability if he

(a) does a tortious act in concert with the other or pursuant to a common design with him, or

(b) knows that the other's conduct constitutes a breach of duty and gives substantial assistance or encouragement to the other ...

[P]laintiffs' claim fails as a matter of law under either theory.

Under the first theory of concerted action, New York law "provides for joint and several liability on the part of all defendants having an understanding, express or tacit, to participate in a common plan or design to commit a tortious act." Rastelli v. Goodyear Tire & Rubber Co., 591 N.E.2d 222, 224 (N.Y.1992). [*Rastelli* held that each defendant charged with acting in concert must have "acted tortiously and that one of the defendants committed an act in pursuance of the agreement which constitutes a tort." P]laintiffs argue that various statements in the Atex/EPPS literature and the use of the Kodak logo on certain documents packaged with Atex products [demonstrates] Kodak's "full collaboration" in the marketing of the keyboards. In addition, the plaintiffs present various reports and documents on ergonomics[1] and repetitive stress injuries that Kodak created for the use of its own employees as evidence that "Kodak was fully aware of both the hazards associated with keyboard use and the means of reducing or eliminating those hazards." Finally, they rely on the Kodak Design Resource Center's evaluation of the ergonomics of three Atex keyboards in 1990 as evidence that "Kodak was a full participant with Atex in the deliberations about whether to warn users of the Kodak/Atex equipment, exactly what such warnings should state, and what would be the risks of not issuing such warnings."

As the district court correctly held, "none of this tends to show that Kodak and Atex had 'an understanding . . . to participate in a common plan or design to commit a tortious act.' " [P]laintiffs have offered no [proof] that Kodak actually participated in the design or manufacture of the Atex keyboards. The documents offered by the plaintiffs do not suggest any "agreement" between Kodak and Atex to act "jointly and tortiously." They merely refer to general statements about the "merger" between Atex and Kodak and the "marriage" between the two companies.

Furthermore, none of the evidence demonstrates that Kodak's actions were tortious. [The guidelines prepared for Kodak employees regarding computer workstations does not constitute tortious conduct regarding keyboards made and sold by Atex because Kodak's internal guidelines were not used by Atex. Although] Atex retained Kodak's Design Resource Center to evaluate the ergonomics of various Atex keyboards in 1990, [this was] only after all of the keyboards at issue had been designed, developed, and manufactured. [P]laintiffs have offered no shred of evidence to support their speculation that "Kodak was a full participant with Atex in the deliberations about whether to warn users of the Kodak/Atex equipment." Nothing contradicts the defendant's evidence that Atex retained Kodak as an "independent organization" solely to conduct a single evaluation of three Atex keyboards. Finally, there is no allegation that Kodak's laboratory performed the tests on the Atex equipment negligently or provided Atex with false information about its evaluation of Atex's keyboards.

[P]laintiffs contend that even if there was no agreement between the parties to act tortiously, Kodak [provided] "substantial assistance or encouragement" to Atex in furtherance of its tortious conduct. A "substantial

---

1. "Ergonomics is the study of the design of requirements of work in relation to the physical and psychological capabilities and limitations of people . . . The aim of the discipline is to prevent the development of occupational disorders and to reduce the potential for fatigue, error, or unsafe acts through the evaluation and design of facilities, environments, jobs, tasks, tools, equipment, processes, and training methods to match the capabilities of specific workers." See 57 Fed.Reg. 34192, 34199 app. A (Aug. 3, 1992) (OSHA advance notice of proposed rulemaking on ergonomics safety).

assistance'' claim based on [§ 876] requires evidence that (1) the defendant knows that the other's conduct constitutes a breach of duty and (2) the defendant gives substantial assistance or encouragement to the other's conduct. Restatement (2d) of Torts § 876(b).

[Kodak's] general awareness of the hazards of repetitive stress injuries and the Kodak laboratory's evaluation of the Atex keyboards in 1990 are insufficient to raise a question of material fact regarding Kodak's knowledge of or substantial assistance in Atex's allegedly tortious conduct. Kodak's knowledge about repetitive stress injuries generally cannot be construed as knowledge of the alleged defective design of the Atex keyboard or Atex's alleged failure to warn keyboard users of the hazards of repetitive stress injuries. Furthermore, [Kodak's] one-time evaluation of the keyboards in 1990 occurred years after the keyboards in question were designed and distributed. Finally, the plaintiffs present no evidence to suggest that Kodak was involved—either before or after the 1990 evaluation—in the decision to include warnings about repetitive stress disorders or user guidelines with Atex keyboards. Thus, we find that summary judgment on this claim was also appropriate.

* * *

[District court's order granting summary judgment for defendant on each of plaintiffs' four theories of liability affirmed.]

N O T E S

1. Which of the plaintiffs' four theories was the strongest? Should parent corporations, such as Dow Chemical, be shielded from the products liability responsibilities of their subsidiaries, such as Dow Corning, which went bankrupt from claims for manufacturing silicone breast implants? Is there something inherently unfair in a legal regime which allows a parent company to absorb all of its subsidiary's profits but which does not require it to absorb all of its losses?

2. The parent corporation may have direct liability for its negligence in undertaking to provide services for the subsidiary, giving rise to a duty to third persons injured by the subsidiary's products. Dow Chemical Co. v. Mahlum, 970 P.2d 98 (Nev. 1998), rejected concert of action liability under Rest. (2d) of Torts § 876, as had *Fletcher,* but approved application of Rest. (2d) of Torts § 324A, negligent undertaking, permitting a negligence action to proceed based on Dow Chemical's testing of silicone for use by Dow Corning in medical devices. The court stated:

> Because the jury could reasonably conclude that Dow Chemical undertook to completely test the safety of the liquid later used in Dow Corning's silicone breast implants, Dow Chemical had a duty to exercise reasonable care in the performance of this undertaking. Comment *b* to section 324A explains that the section "applies to any undertaking to render services to another, where the actor's negligent conduct in the manner of performance of his undertaking, or his failure to exercise reasonable care to complete it, or to protect the third person when he discontinues it, results in physical harm to the third person." Thus, under section 324A, once Dow Chemical undertook to test and advise Dow Corning on the safety of liquid silicone, it was obligated to fully complete this course of conduct.

Id. at 118–119. A jury verdict for plaintiff was upheld.

Compare In re TMJ Implants Prods. Liab. Litig., 113 F.3d 1484, 1495 (8th Cir. 1997), addressing the alleged direct liability of Dow Chemical for its negligent performance of testing from 1943 to the 1970s of silicone for use by Dow Corning. Though none of the testing was performed to determine whether the specific compound could be used safely as a TMJ medical implant, summary judgment for Dow Chemical was affirmed: "Plaintiffs can point only to Dow Chemical's perform-ance of approximately a dozen tests involving silicone (but not its use in medical implants) performed over four decades at the request of Dow Corning, a 1967 meeting attended by a Dow Chemical employee in which the idea of a tooth implant was discussed, a 1948 and a 1950 article published by three Dow Chemical scientists discussing toxicological research on various silicones and a trademark agreement allowing Dow Chemical to inspect the quality of Dow Corning's products. These Dow Chemical actions ... are insufficient to establish an undertaking of such breadth and magnitude as to create a duty on the part of Dow Chemical to ensure the safety of all of Dow Corning's silicone products."

Would this theory have been useful against Kodak in *Fletcher*?

3.   Alter Ego Liability—Piercing the Corporate Veil. If the parent and subsidiary are so closely related as to be essentially identical, the limited liability provided by incorporation may be disregarded. See In re Birmingham Asbestos Litig., 619 So.2d 1360 (Ala.1993)(no liability for subsidiary's actions unless parent exerts so much control over subsidiary's operations as to render parent its alter ego).

An important factor in determining whether the corporate veil may be pierced is the adequacy of the subsidiary corporation's capitalization. See Nelson v. Interna-tional Paint Co., 734 F.2d 1084, 1091–93 (5th Cir.1984)(attempt to impose liability on parent for defective paint sold by subsidiary). In *Fletcher*, the Kodak–Atex cash management accounting system seemed to provide Atex with a bottomless well of funds for operations: "when a subsidiary is in need of funds, a transfer is made." Why should not the well also be available for satisfying judgments against the subsidiary? See generally Hackney & Benson, Shareholder Liability for Inadequate Capital, 43 U.Pitt.L.Rev. 837 (1982).

4.   Concert of Action. Consider plaintiff's concert-of-action theory. Assume that Kodak's 1990 tests revealed ergonomic problems with the keyboards, suggest-ing that users confronted a repetitive stress risk of which they had not been warned. Do you suppose that Kodak would have discussed this problem with Atex? What if they did discuss the problem and, further, decided not to provide post-sale warnings to former purchasers of the keyboards? Might such facts provide a basis for a concert-of-action claim against Kodak?

5.   The Apparent Manufacturer Doctrine. "The rationale for imposing liability on the apparent manufacturer was a species of estoppel: the vendor who, through its labeling or advertising of a product, caused the public to believe that it was the manufacturer and to buy the product in reliance on the vendor's reputation and care in making it, was held to have assumed the obligations of a manufacturer and to be estopped to deny its identity as the manufacturer." Hebel v. Sherman Equip., 442 N.E.2d 199 (Ill.1982). The doctrine is embodied in § 400 of the Restatement (Second) of Torts, and § 14 of the Products Liability Restatement.

6.   Liability for Harm from Copycat Products. Should the originator of a product's design or labeling be liable for injuries to a person from another manufac-turer's copycat product? See Foster v. American Home Prods. Corp., 29 F.3d 165 (4th Cir.1994)(manufacturer of brand name drug not subject to liability on negligent misrepresentation theory for inadequate labeling by manufacturer of generic equivalent); Arceneaux v. Lykes Bros. S.S. Co., 890 S.W.2d 191 (Tex.App.1994)(no liability for copycat design of ship ladder).

7.   Franchisers; Trademark Licensors. If a franchiser consents to the use of its name on an unsafe product, its liability may hinge on the extent of its control over the creation of the unsafe condition. In Kosters v. Seven–Up Co., 595 F.2d 347 (6th Cir.1979), plaintiff was blinded in one eye when a bottle of 7–Up slipped out of a defectively designed carton that had been supplied to the franchisee bottling company from a third party. The Seven–Up Company had contractually retained control over the design of such cartons, and the particular carton involved had been submitted to and approved by Seven–Up.

Held, Seven–Up was subject to strict liability (in implied warranty) for the carton's design. Whether this duty arises depends upon a combination of factors: "(1) the risk created by approving for distribution an unsafe product likely to cause injury, (2) the franchiser's ability and opportunity to eliminate the unsafe character of the product and prevent the loss, (3) the consumer's lack of knowledge of danger, and (4) the consumer's reliance on the trade name which gives the intended impression that the franchiser is responsible and stands behind the product." Id. at 353. In sum, "Liability is based on the franchiser's control and the public's assumption, induced by the franchiser's conduct, that it does in fact control and vouch for the product." Id. Of course the case for liability is even stronger if the franchiser itself designs the product. See Cook v. Branick Mfg., Inc., 736 F.2d 1442 (11th Cir.1984).

In Torres v. Goodyear Tire & Rubber Co., 786 P.2d 939, 944 (Ariz.1990), the court found that Goodyear participated significantly in the design, manufacture, promotion, and sale of a Goodyear Great Britain tire and so concluded that it was subject to strict liability for its subsidiary's tire. "To hold ... that when the product is [defective] it should not be considered a 'Goodyear' tire but a 'Goodyear GB' tire would be to espouse a doctrine that would no doubt surprise most Goodyear customers, and perhaps some officers of Goodyear itself."

8.   Trade Associations. Should trade associations—which help their members with product design development, public relations, and possibly lobbying (against regulation)—be subject to liability for a product's bad design? *Yes, negligence*: Meneely v. S.R. Smith, Inc., 5 P.3d 49 (Wash. App. 2000)(defendant undertook to complete testing and set standards for pools and diving boards; relying on Restatement (Second) of Torts §§ 323, 324); FNS Mortgage Serv. Corp. v. Pacific General Group, Inc., 29 Cal.Rptr.2d 916 (Ct.App.1994) (assumed responsibility for approving plumbing products). Compare, Bailey v. Edward Hines Lumber, 719 N.E.2d 178 (Ill.App. 1999)(no duty to workers who relied on trade association pamphlet on construction). *No, strict liability*: Swartzbauer v. Lead Indus. Ass'n, Inc., 794 F.Supp. 142 (E.D.Pa.1992)(association did not make or sell lead pigment or lead paint products).

9.   See generally King, Limiting the Vicarious Liability of Franchisers for the Torts of Their Franchisees, 62 Wash. & Lee L. Rev. 417 (2005); Weinmann, Trademark Licensors and Product Liability Claims–A European Perspective, 95 Trademark Rep. 1394 (2005); LoPucki, Toward a Trademark–Based Liability System, 49 UCLA L. Rev. 1099 (2002); Franklyn, The Apparent Manufacturer Doctrine, Trademark Licensors and the Third Restatement of Torts, 49 Case W. Res. L. Rev. 671 (1999); Franklyn, Toward a Coherent Theory of Strict Tort Liability for Trademark Licensors, 72 So. Cal. L. Rev. 1 (1998); Comment, 25 St. Louis U. Pub. L. Rev. 247 (2006) (liability of trademark licensors for defective products bearing its name); D. Owen, Products Liability Law § 15.4 (2d ed. 2008); 2 D. Owen, M.S. Madden & M. Davis, Madden & Owen on Products Liability § 19:5 (3d ed. 2000).

6. CERTIFIERS AND ENDORSERS

Hanberry v. Hearst Corp.

Court of Appeals of California, 1969.
276 Cal.App.2d 680, 81 Cal.Rptr. 519.

■ AULT, ASSOCIATE JUSTICE, PRO TEM.

[Plaintiff purchased a pair of shoes that were defective in manufacture and design in that they had a low co-efficient of friction on vinyl, and were slippery and unsafe, causing her to slip and fall on the vinyl floor of her kitchen resulting in severe personal injuries. Her complaint against Hearst Corporation was dismissed on demurrer, and she appeals.]

[Hearst] publishes a monthly magazine known as Good Housekeeping in which products, including the shoes she purchased, were advertised as meeting the "Good Housekeeping's Consumers' Guaranty Seal." With respect to the seal the magazine stated: "This is Good Housekeeping's Consumers' Guaranty" and "We satisfy ourselves that products advertised in Good Housekeeping are good ones and that the advertising claims made for them in our magazine are truthful." The seal itself contained the promise, "If the product or performance is defective, Good Housekeeping guarantees replacement or refund to consumer."

[Plaintiff alleged that] prior to purchasing the shoes she had seen an advertisement of them, either in Good Housekeeping Magazine or in a newspaper ad [with a] Good Housekeeping endorsement; Good Housekeeping seal was affixed to the shoes and the container for the shoes with Hearst's consent; Hearst was paid for the advertising of the shoes which appeared in its magazine and for the use of its seal; plaintiff relied upon respondent's representation and seal and purchased the shoes because of them. Plaintiff further alleges Hearst made no examination, test or investigation of the shoes, or a sample thereof, or if such tests were made they were done in a careless and negligent manner and that Hearst's issuance of its seal and certification as to the shoes was not warranted by the information it possessed.

* * *

The [question] on this appeal is whether one who endorses a product for his own economic gain, and for the purpose of encouraging and inducing the public to buy it, may be liable to a purchaser who, relying on the endorsement, buys the product and is injured because it is defective and not as represented in the endorsement. We conclude such liability may exist and a cause of action has been pleaded in the instant case. . . .

[Hearst permits a] manufacturer or retailer of a product which has been approved by Good Housekeeping Magazine to advertise that fact in other advertising media and permits its seal to appear in such ads and to be attached to the product itself. While the device used by respondent enhances the value of Good Housekeeping Magazine for advertising purposes, it does so because its seal and certification tend to induce and encourage consumers to purchase products advertised in the magazine and which bear that seal and certification. Implicit in the seal and certification is the representation respondent has taken reasonable steps to make an independent examination of the product endorsed, with some degree of expertise, and found it satisfactory. Since the very purpose of respondent's seal and certification is to induce consumers to purchase products so endorsed, it is foreseeable certain consumers will do so, relying upon respondent's representations concerning them, in some instances, even more than upon statements made by the retailer, manufacturer or distributor.

Having voluntarily involved itself into the marketing process, having in effect loaned its reputation to promote and induce the sale of a given product, . . . we think respondent Hearst has placed itself in the position where public policy imposes upon it the duty to use ordinary care in the issuance of its seal and certification of quality so that members of the consuming public who rely on its endorsement are not unreasonably exposed to the risk of harm. [Citation.]

* * *

While we have held plaintiff has stated a cause of action for negligent misrepresentation against Hearst, we reject her contention she may also proceed in warranty or on the theory of strict liability in tort. [No court] has extended either theory of recovery to one not directly involved in manufacturing products for, or supplying products to, the consuming public. To invoke either theory of recovery here would subject respondent to liability not warranted by the circumstances. Plaintiff does not contend, nor do respondent's representations permit the interpretation, it examined or tested the particular pair of shoes involved. The most that can be implied from respondent's representation is that it has examined or tested samples of the product and found the general design and materials used to be satisfactory. Application of either warranty or strict liability in tort would subject respondent to liability even if the general design and material used in making this brand of shoe were good, but the particular pair became defective through some mishap in the manufacturing process. We believe this kind of liability for individually defective items should be limited to those directly involved in the manufacturing and supplying process, and should not be extended through warranty or strict liability to a general endorser who makes no representation it has examined or tested each item marketed.

[Dismissal of negligent misrepresentation claim reversed.]

N O T E S

1. Accord, U.S. Lighting Service, Inc. v. Llerrad Corp., 800 F.Supp. 1513, 1517 (N.D.Ohio 1992)(defective lighting equipment approved by Underwriters Laboratories, a nonprofit testing organization, which was negligent in applying its own internal testing procedures: "The raison d'etre of the UL mark is to show that a product has met safety standards. By offering its mark to manufacturers, UL has placed itself into the stream of commerce.... The UL seal does not guarantee that a manufacturer has acted with ordinary care but sound public policy requires that UL act with ordinary care in the conduct of its own business—the certification process.").

Should certifiers be subject to *strict* liability?

2. Celebrity Endorsements. Assume that a movie or sports star or other public figure is paid to endorse a product which is defective in some respect. Plaintiff purchases it on the strength of the endorsement and is injured by the defect. Should the endorser be liable? Suppose that the plaintiff is injured when the roof of his uncrashworthy Chrysler is crushed in a roll-over in which the roof should have maintained its integrity. If plaintiff purchased the car on the strength of a celebrity endorsement, say, a famous golfer, should the celebrity be subject to liability for the injuries? If so, on what theories of liability? Should it make a difference if the celebrity is a renowned race car driver? Former Chrysler chairman Lee Iacocca?

3. Safety and Accident Inspections. Insurance companies and gas utilities which inspect products such as industrial machinery, furnaces, or service lines, may be liable for negligent inspection. See, e.g., O'Laughlin v. Minnesota Natural Gas Co., 253 N.W.2d 826 (Minn.1977)(gas furnace); Jackson v. New Jersey Mfrs. Ins. Co., 400 A.2d 81 (N.J.App.Div.1979)(insurer liable to third persons only if it has undertaken to make safety inspections upon which insured has relied). Should such an inspection be held to carry an implied warranty of sufficiency?

4. See generally D. Owen, Products Liability Law, § 15.7 (2d ed. 2008); 2 D. Owen, M.S. Madden & M. Davis, Madden & Owen on Products Liability § 19:5 (3d ed. 2000).

7. SUCCESSOR CORPORATIONS

Semenetz v. Sherling & Walden, Inc.

New York Court of Appeals, 2006.
851 N.E.2d 1170.

■ READ, J.

A corporation that purchases another corporation's assets is not liable for the seller's torts, subject to four exceptions outlined in Schumacher v. Richards Shear Co., 451 N.E.2d 195 (N.Y.1983). Plaintiff Bridget Semenetz asks us to revisit *Schumacher* to endorse a fifth exception—the "product line" exception in cases of strict products liability. For the reasons that follow, we reject the "product line" exception.

I.

In May 1998, defendant S & W Edger Works, Inc., an Alabama corporation, sold a 10,000–pound band sawmill to Semenetz Lumber Mill, Inc., located in Jeffersonville, New York. The sawmill, which cost $45,000, was capable of sawing logs 36 inches in diameter and 20 feet long. On July 26, 1999, Sean Semenetz, an infant, caught his right hand and fingers between a sprocket and chain apparatus in the sawmill, causing partial amputation of several fingers.

On October 5, 2000, Edger Works sold most of its assets, including real property, goodwill, trade names and inventory, to Sawmills & Edgers, Inc., another Alabama corporation, for $300,000. [The contract expressly stated that Sawmills did not assume any of Edger Works' liabilities except for the payment of ordered inventory. Edger Works changed its name to Sherling & Walden which paid Edger Works' outstanding corporate debts.]

Sawmills manufactured sawmills at the same plant in Alabama where Edger Works had formerly produced them, and retained at least some of Edger Works' former employees. Its advertising described Sawmills as "formerly S & W Edger Works," stating that it "opened [its] doors for business in 1990," which is the date Edger Works first sold its products in the marketplace. Sawmills has made only two sales in New York, both to Semenetz Lumber at its request and for less than $100.

[Plaintiff commenced this products liability action against Sawmills, Edger Works and Sherling & Walden. Sawmills pleaded lack of personal jurisdiction and moved to dismiss the complaint on this ground. The Supreme Court denied Sawmills' motion for summary judgment, relying on the exceptions to successor non-liability rule from *Schumacher*.] These exceptions arise where a successor corporation "expressly or impliedly assume[s] [its] predecessor's tort liability"; or "there [is] a consolidation or merger of seller and purchaser"; or "the purchasing corporation [is] a mere continuation of the selling corporation"; or "the transaction is entered into fraudulently to escape such obligations." *Schumacher*. The court determined that Sawmills did not fit within any of the four *Schumacher* exceptions, [but that the Appellate Division's decision in Hart v. Bruno Mach. Corp.,679 N.Y.S.2d 740 (App. Div. 1998) expanded *Schumacher*] to encompass two additional exceptions in cases alleging strict products liability—the "product line" exception, ... and the "continuing enterprise" exception. [The court concluded that both exceptions applied to Sawmills, subjecting it to long-arm jurisdiction. The Appellate Division reversed and dismissed the complaint but did not reach the question of successor liability. We permitted plaintiff to appeal] and now affirm, but on a different ground altogether.

II.

The "product line" exception to the general rule against successor liability originated with the California Supreme Court's decision in Ray v. Alad Corp., 560 P.2d 3 (Cal. 1977). In *Ray*, the court imposed liability on the successor corporation for an injury sustained by a plaintiff who fell off a ladder manufactured by its predecessor. The court concluded that successor liability was proper because "a party which acquires a manufacturing business and continues the output of its line of products under the circumstances here presented assumes strict tort liability for defects in units of the same product line previously manufactured and distributed by the entity from which the business was acquired" [Citation.]

The court articulated three rationales for the "product line" exception:

(1) the virtual destruction of the plaintiff's remedies against the original manufacturer caused by the successor's acquisition of the business, (2) the successor's ability to assume the original manufacturer's risk-spreading role, and (3) the fairness of requiring the successor to assume a responsibility for [its predecessor's] defective products that was a burden necessarily attached to the original manufacturer's good will being enjoyed by the successor in the continued operation of the business. [Citation.]

As for the *Ray* court's first rationale—the virtual destruction of the products liability plaintiff's remedies against the original manufacturer—this "is not a justification for suing the successor, but rather ... merely a statement of the problem.... More than just a statement of the problem is required to justify a change in the corporate law." Fish v. Amsted Indus., Inc., 376 N.W.2d 820, 826 (Wis. 1985) (rejecting "product line" exception).

As the Wisconsin Supreme Court has pointed out, the successor may lack capacity to spread the risk of injuries because

[s]mall manufacturers have a difficult problem obtaining products liability insurance and find it impossible to cover the risks by raising prices because they have to compete with large manufacturers who can keep the price down.... [I]t is one thing to assume that a manufacturer can acquire insurance against potential liability for its own products and another to assume it can acquire such insurance for the products made by a different manufacturer. [Citation.]

As for whether liability should be imposed upon the successor corporation because it enjoys the benefit of its predecessor's goodwill,

any benefit the successor acquired through the goodwill or reputation of the predecessor's product line was considered and negotiated for at the time of the sale and constituted part of the sale price. To hold the successor liable for defects in products manufactured by the predecessor would be forcing the successor to pay twice for ... goodwill. [Citation.]

Importantly, the "product line" exception threatens "economic annihilation" for small businesses (Bernard v. Kee Mfg. Co., Inc., 409 So.2d 1047, 1049 (Fla. 1982) (rejecting "product line" exception)). Because small businesses have limited assets, they face potential financial destruction if saddled with liability for their predecessors' torts. This threat would deter the purchase of ongoing businesses that manufacture products and, instead, force potential sellers to liquidate their companies. As the Florida Supreme Court has observed, 90% of the nation's manufacturing enterprises are small businesses, and "[i]f small manufacturing corporations liquidate rather than transfer ownership, the chances that the corporations will be replaced by other successful small corporations are decreased." [Citation.]

Further, extending liability to the corporate successor places responsibility for a defective product on a party that did not put the product into the stream of commerce. This is inconsistent with the basic justification for strict products liability,

> which is to place responsibility for a defective product on the manufacturer who placed that product into commerce. The corporate successor has not created the risk, and only remotely benefits from the product. The successor has not invited usage of the product or implied its safety. Since the successor was never in a position to eliminate the risk, a major purpose of strict liability in modifying a manufacturer's behavior is also lost. [Citation.]

In short, adoption of the "product line" exception would mark "a radical change from existing law implicating complex economic considerations better left to be addressed by the Legislature" [citing Restatement (Third) of Torts: Products Liability § 12, com. *b*].

We therefore join the majority of courts declining to adopt the "product line" exception. [The Appellate Division decision is affirmed.]

NOTES

1. "A corporate successor is not a seller and bears no blame in bringing the product and the user together. It seems patently unfair to require such a party to bear the cost of unassumed and uncontemplated products liability claims primarily because it is still in business and is perceived as a 'deep pocket.' " Nissen Corp. v. Miller, 594 A.2d 564, 569 (Md.1991).

2. The Product Line Exception. What do you think of the product line exception to the general rule of nonliability? In Ray v. Alad, 560 P.2d 3, 9 (Cal.1977), discussed in *Semenetz*, the court explained its first rationale concerning the destruction of the plaintiff's remedies:

> [T]he practical value of [plaintiff's right to recover] against the original manufacturer was vitiated by the purchase of Alad I's tangible assets, trade name and good will on behalf of Alad II and the dissolution of Alad I within two months thereafter in accordance with the purchase agreement. The injury giving rise to plaintiff's claim against Alad did not occur until more than six months after the filing of the dissolution certificate declaring that Alad I's "known debts and liabilities have been actually paid" and its "known assets have been distributed to its shareholders." This distribution of assets was perfectly proper as there was no requirement that provision be made for claims such as plaintiff's that had not yet come into existence. Thus, even if plaintiff could obtain a judgment on his claim against the dissolved and assetless Alad I, he would face formidable and probably insuperable obstacles in attempting to obtain satisfaction of the judgment from former stockholders or directors.

How about amending the dissolution statutes to condition the corporation's ability to liquidate and dissolve upon its making adequate provision for future products liability claims? See M. Green, Successor Liability: The Superiority of Statutory Reform to Protect Products Liability Claimants, 72 Cornell L.Rev. 17 (1986); Roe, Mergers, Acquisitions, and Tort: A Comment on the Problem of Successor Corporation Liability, 70 Va.L.Rev. 1559 (1984).

Like *Semenetz*, most courts reject the product line exception. See Guerrero v. Allison Engine Co., 725 N.E.2d 479, 483–484 (Ind.App. 2000) (listing majority of states rejecting exception); Guzman v. MRM/Elgin, 567 N.E.2d 929 (Mass. 1991). But see Mettinger v. Globe Slicing Machine Co., 709 A.2d 779 (N.J. 1998) (extending product line exception to cover distributors and other sellers of the product with claim for indemnity or contribution against successor).

3. How compelling is Ray's second rationale, based on the successor's ability to spread the risk?

4. What do you think of the third rationale, that the successor ought to bear the burdens along with the benefits of the predecessor's goodwill? See Garcia v. Coe Manuf'g Co., 933 P.2d 243, 249 (N.M. 1997) (adopting product line exception: "[T]he successor is positioned to assess the risks before purchasing the assets, and to then decide whether to assume the potential burden associated with its acceptance of the predecessor's goodwill by continuing to produce the same product line."). Might *Ray* have been referring to "goodwill" in a broader sense than the corporate-accounting law perspective of a property right in an intangible asset?

5. The "Continuity of Enterprise" Exception. As an alternative to the *product line* exception to the rule of non-liability of successor corporations, several courts have opted for a "continuity of enterprise" approach, recognizing that if the business activities remain constant pre-and post-acquisition of the assets, there is no reason to protect the successor corporation simply because of the change in ownership. Like the product line exception, the continuity of enterprise exception expands upon and extends well beyond the "mere continuation" exception to successor non-liability. Turner v. Bituminous Cas. Co., 244 N.W.2d 873 (Mich. 1976)(3–2), was the leading case adopting this exception, and its approach has been followed in Ala., Miss., and Ohio, with three or four other states flirting with the notion. The *Turner* majority summarized its rationale for expanding upon the traditional four exceptions:

> [I]t seems both unfair and unbelievable that a corporate combination or acquisition decision would be principally or exclusively made on the basis of cutting off the contingent right to sue of a products liability victim. . . .
> First, it would seem illogical that a merger or de facto merger be encumbered by liability for a products liability suit while a cash acquisition of corporate assets is free from such liability. [Second], if there are no real business reasons for choosing a cash acquisition of corporate assets and the only real reason is to avoid products liability suits, then it would seem that the machinery of corporate law is unreasonably geared up to accomplish a purpose not really intended for it or in the public interest.

Nissen Corp. v. Miller, 594 A.2d 564 (Md.1991), rejected the continuity of enterprise exception, concluding that it is fundamentally unfair to make one entity liable for the acts of another.

6. Duty to Warn. A number of courts have concluded that a successor may have an independent duty to *warn,* dependent upon various factors, even if none of the four traditional exceptions apply. E.g., Leannais v. Cincinnati, Inc., 565 F.2d 437 (7th Cir.1977); Kaleta v. Whittaker Corp., 583 N.E.2d 567 (Ill.App.1991).

The Products Liability Restatement § 13(a) recognizes a duty to warn by successor corporation's of risks in products sold by a predecessor if (1) the successor enters into a maintenance, repair, or similar product service relationship with its predecessor's customers, and (2) "a reasonable person in the position of the successor would provide a warning." A reasonable person would provide a warning depending on (1) knowledge of the danger; (2) whether those who might be affected are both identifiable and unlikely to know the danger; (3) whether there is an effective way to convey a warning, and (4) the gravity of the risk. Id. at § 13(b).

7.   See generally Kuney, A Taxonomy and Evaluation of Successor Liability, 3 Fla. St. Bus. L. Rev. 1 (2006); Kuney, Jerry Phillips' Product Line Continuity and Successor Corporation Liability: Where Are We Twenty Years Later?, 72 Tenn. L. Rev. 777 (2005); Reilly, Making Sense of Successor Liability, 31 Hofstra L.Rev. 745 (2003); Epstein, Imperfect Liability Regimes: Individual and Corporate Issues, 53 S.C. L. Rev. 1153 (2002); Cupp, Redesigning Successor Liability, 1999 U.Ill.L.Rev. 845; D. Owen, Products Liability Law § 15.5 (2d ed. 2008).

---

8.   EMPLOYERS

Employers as Manufacturers: Product Safety in the Industrial Setting*

In bringing products and workers together, employers stand at the "nip point" of product safety in the industrial setting. Employers have virtually exclusive control over many product safety matters, such as selecting industrial machinery and specifying guards for that machinery; allocating particular employees to operate particular machines; training workers to use dangerous chemicals and machinery; designing the production process, including the speed of the assembly line; and supervising all of the production activities. With such extensive control over product safety in the workplace, employers bear principal responsibility for many injuries to workers from industrial tools, chemicals and machines.

Because of their commercial exploitation of workers, together with their tenacious hold on industrial safety, employers are properly held responsible for on-the-job injuries to workers from dangerous products supplied by the employer. Indeed, it was for this reason that state legislatures enacted "workmen's compensation" acts in the early 1900s. Prior to such legislation, a worker injured on the job could sue his or her employer for negligence, but the difficulties of proving an employer's fault, together with the rigorous defenses of contributory negligence, assumption of risk, and the fellow-servant rule, prevented recovery in [most] cases. In place of protracted common-law actions which had little chance of success, workers' compensation statutes substituted speedy and assured no-fault compensation from employers for workplace accidents. The legislative trade-offs for providing workers with these benefits was to restrict the amounts of compensation paid and to abolish negligence and other common-law claims against employers for workplace accidents. Thus, a central feature of all workers' compensation statutes is that the benefits legislatively prescribed are the worker's "exclusive remedy" against the employer for injuries on the job. Workers frequently sue the manufacturer of the industrial products

*From 2 D. Owen, M.S. Madden & M.   § 19:7 (3d ed. 2000).
Davis, Madden & Owen on Products Liability

which injure them to supplement workers compensation benefits. Employers are usually not directly involved in such actions.

Not infrequently, however, industrial employers design and manufacture products for their own use. Often these are specialty tools used only in the employer's own business and not manufactured and sold widely to the public. Yet, some manufacturers make products not only for their own use but also for sale to the general public. So, a press manufacturer may use its own presses on its own assembly line to make parts for presses sold to others, and a tire manufacturer may equip the trucks it uses around its factories with tires from its normal production inventory. Because such an enterprise in a real sense wears two hats, it may be said to act in a "dual capacity"—both as a manufacturer and employer. What types of claims does an injured employee have in such a case? Is workers compensation still an exclusive remedy or may the employee sue his employer as a manufacturer under products liability?

The dual capacity doctrine had an interesting but quite short and narrow life in products liability law. The dual capacity doctrine was first recognized in Duprey v. Shane, 249 P.2d 8 (Cal.1952). Defendant chiropractor treated his nurse for an injury. The treatment aggravated the injury, and the nurse sued for malpractice. The court permitted the suit, notwithstanding the exclusive remedy rule of the workers' compensation statute, because the defendant had assumed the obligations of a chiropractor when he undertook to treat his employee as a patient.

A quarter of a century later, the doctrine was extended to the products liability context in Douglas v. E. & J. Gallo Winery, 137 Cal.Rptr. 797, 802–03 (Ct.App. 1977). Plaintiffs were injured when the scaffolding on which they were working collapsed. Their employer had manufactured the scaffolding as well as other scaffolding sold to the general public. The court of appeals held that plaintiffs could maintain a products liability action against their employer on the dual capacity doctrine:

> When an employer becomes a manufacturer for sale to the public, and assumes the risk of being a manufacturer, he has the opportunity to spread his costs for product liability and transfer it to the ultimate consumer. The fact that he himself as an employer may be one of those ultimate consumers is a factor he must consider in whether or not he becomes a manufacturer for sale to the public. The obligations of a manufacturer exist even if the manufacturer had not employed workers such as plaintiff.

> Limitations on the remedy of an injured employee should not be extended beyond the purposes of the Workers' Compensation Law. Failure to apply the dual capacity doctrine to the manufacturer who sells to the public would unduly restrict the injured person's remedy. There is no reason to relieve a manufacturer who sells to the public of liability *as a manufacturer* by the chance circumstance that the defendant manufacturer also happens to be an employer of the injured person.

In the same year as *Douglas,* Ohio also applied the doctrine to a products liability case, Mercer v. Uniroyal, Inc., 361 N.E.2d 492 (Ohio App.1976), in which a truckdriver for Uniroyal was injured in a crash when a defective

Uniroyal tire on his truck blew out. Four years later, the doctrine was reaffirmed and extended in California, in Bell v. Industrial Vangas, Inc., 637 P.2d 266 (Cal.1981).

Outside of California and Ohio, however, the doctrine experienced quite a different reception. Troubled by the doctrine's obvious conflict with the exclusive remedy rule, and fearful that it would undermine the long-established balance the legislatures had struck in the workers' compensation legislation, courts in other states widely rejected it. In 1980, for example, characterizing the dual capacity doctrine as "fundamentally unsound," the New York Court of Appeals explained that "[w]e would be seriously undermining the salutary social purposes underlying the existing workers' compensation scheme if we were to permit common-law recovery outside of that scheme on the basis of such illusory distinctions." Billy v. Consolidated Mach. Tool Corp., 412 N.E.2d 934, 939 (N.Y. 1980). A federal district court agreed, and noted: "Imagine how much would remain of employer immunity if it were forfeited every time an employer adjusted or tinkered with a machine." Rader v. U.S. Rubber Reclaiming Co., Inc., 617 F.Supp. 1045, 1046 (S.D. Miss. 1985).

Even in California and Ohio, the states that spawned the dual capacity doctrine in products liability cases, it quickly ran out of steam. The California legislature abolished the doctrine two years after the Supreme Court approved it, Cal. Lab. Code § 3602; and the Ohio Supreme Court restricted the doctrine substantially the following year. Freese v. Consolidated Rail Corp., 445 N.E.2d 1110 (Ohio 1983). Thus, the doctrine operated in only two states for only a few years, from 1977 to 1983. Courts continue to reject the rule, and it seems safe to proclaim that the dual capacity doctrine essentially is dead.

NOTES

1. See Billy v. Consolidated Mach. Tool Corp., 412 N.E.2d 934, 939 (N.Y. 1980):

> The Workers' Compensation Law was designed to spread the risk of industrial accidents through [insurance] coverage and, more specifically, to [provide a swift and sure source of benefits to injured employees] without regard to fault in most instances. In exchange for the security of knowing that fixed benefits will be paid without the need to resort to expensive and sometimes risky litigation, however, the employee has been asked to pay a price [by surrendering] his common-law right to sue his employer in tort and perhaps to enjoy a more substantial recovery through a jury award. . . .

> We cannot sanction the circumvention of this clear legislative plan by approving a theory which would permit the employer to be sued in his capacity as property owner or manufacturer of equipment used on the job site. As we have previously observed, "an employer remains an employer in his relations with his employees as to all matters arising from and connected with their employment. He may not be treated as a dual legal personality, 'a sort of Dr. Jekyl and Mr. Hyde.'" Employers are expected to

provide their employees with a safe workplace that is reasonably free of hazards. This obligation to provide a safe workplace simply cannot be separated in a logical and orderly fashion from the duties owed by the employer to his employees by reason of his ownership of the premises or his manufacture of the equipment with which the employees must work.

2. Is the doctrine really such a bad idea? See Note, 96 Harv.L.Rev. 1641, 1661 (1983):

> [M]ost courts have yielded to a perception that any breach in the exclusive remedy rule would betray the bargain implicit in the enactment of the original workers' compensation laws and thereby impair, if not destroy, the compensation system itself. In view of the outdated terms of the bargain and the inconsistency of these terms with major goals of compensation law, courts should not feel compelled to apply the exclusive remedy rule rigidly in the borderline cases not squarely within the scope of the bargain. Judicial recognition of reasonable exceptions to the rule would itself contribute to the achievement of safety, compensation, and equity goals while encouraging legislatures to undertake necessary reform of the workers' compensation system.

3. Intentional Employer Misconduct. Another means of avoiding the exclusive remedy rule in some states is to demonstrate that the employer *intentionally* caused harm to the employee. Compare Birklid v. Boeing Co., 904 P.2d 278 (Wash.1995)(toxic chemicals; intentional infliction of emotional distress falls outside of normal bar as exempt "deliberate intent to injure"); Blankenship v. Cincinnati Milacron Chem., Inc., 433 N.E.2d 572 (Ohio 1982) (employees exposed to noxious chemicals; tort action allowed).

4. Defining the Scope of the Exclusive Remedy Rule. The rule bars recovery if plaintiff is a "statutory employee," DuBose v. Flightsafety Int'l, Inc., 824 S.W.2d 486 (Mo.App.1992), but not if he is not. See, Duvon v. Rockwell Int'l, 807 P.2d 876 (Wash.1991)(former employee); Willison v. Texaco Refining & Marketing, Inc., 848 P.2d 1062 (Nev.1993)(defendant might not have had requisite control over employee of wholly-owned subsidiary).

5. Allocation of Comparative Fault. Even if the employer is not liable, should the factfinder be permitted or required to determine the employer's fault and to reduce the manufacturer's responsibility accordingly? Compare Lake v. Construction Mach., Inc., 787 P.2d 1027 (Alaska 1990)(no), with Snyder v. LTG Lufttechnische GmbH, 955 S.W.2d 252 (Tenn. 1997)(employer conduct may be admissible evidence but no fault may be allocated to employer).

6. See generally 6 A. Larson & L. Larson, Workers' Compensation Law §§ 117.01 et. seq. (2000); Weiler, Workers' Compensation and Product Liability: The Interaction of a Tort and Non–Tort Regime, 50 Ohio St.L.J. 825 (1989).

9. ALLOCATING RESPONSIBILITY AND LOSS: CONTRIBUTION AND INDEMNITY

A. IN GENERAL

Modern products liability litigation frequently involves multiple defendants, each of whom may bear some responsibility for a plaintiff's harm.

The dramatic expansion of multi-party litigation may be attributed to the expanded liability of those within the chain of distribution (such as retailers, distributors, successors, and certifiers) and the broadened use of joinder of parties, including persons outside the chain of distribution who may have contributed to the plaintiff's harm.

Tactical considerations often induce plaintiffs' lawyers to join all potentially liable parties, and third party joinder rules afford defendants the opportunity to join others who may contribute to a settlement or judgment. With multiple defendants come important questions of how liability will be allocated among them. Even if a potentially liable person is not joined in the underlying action, the defendant(s) in that action may bring a subsequent action against him for indemnity or contribution.

Loss allocation issues have become increasingly complicated in recent years as most jurisdictions have adopted rules providing for comparative fault and contribution among joint tortfeasors. In many states, statutes altering the traditional rules allowing joint and several liability have only added to the complications. Because such schemes vary considerably, it is vital to focus closely on the statutes and decisions of the particular jurisdiction. The Restatement (Third) of Torts: Apportionment of Liability (1999) provides a comprehensive treatment of the different ways jurisdictions have altered the traditional common law rules of apportionment under joint and several liability and their effect on contribution and indemnity principles, comparative fault allocation, settlement by joint tortfeasors, and other issues.

Phillips, Contribution and Indemnity in Products Liability
42 Tenn.L.Rev. 85, 87–94 (1974).

II. CONTRIBUTION AND INDEMNITY COMPARED

A. *Express Agreements*

Rights of contribution or indemnity may arise either by express contract or by implication of law. Where they are based on express contract, they are usually in the form of indemnity: one party agrees to hold another harmless from any damage arising out of use of a product, or to reimburse the other for liability he may incur as a result of such use. Such agreements are usually not held to be against public policy even when they provide for nonliability or reimbursement for injuries caused by the promisee's own negligence, although courts generally construe the agreement quite strictly and require that it make very clear that the promisee is being released from the consequences of his own fault.

* * *

Express agreements appear relatively rarely, however, and the lack of more frequent use may be explained in part by two significant considerations. As a practical matter it may not be good business to attempt to negotiate the shifting of risks at the bargaining stage, particularly where the agreement expressly releases one from liability for his own fault, thereby perhaps raising questions about the reliability of the product or of the contracting party. Also, the parties may not stand in a contractual relationship with one another, in which event no express agreement can be negotiated. More commonly indemnity or contribution is sought not on the basis of express agreement, but rather on principles of implied contract or equitable loss apportionment.

B. *Implied or Equitable Apportionment*

Implied indemnity or contribution is basically equitable in nature, although it is sometimes described in terms of implied contract. It is based on a determination that, where there is more than one party who may be liable for the same wrong or loss to another, liability should in fairness be apportioned between or among all such parties. There may of course be any number of joint tortfeasors, but the basic situation analyzed here will include only the injured party, A, and two co-tortfeasors, X and Y, against whom A has a claim; X, in turn, has a claim over against Y for indemnity or contribution.

The amount of X's claim against Y will depend on whether X is asserting a claim for indemnity or contribution. Traditionally, a claim in indemnity by X against Y is for the full amount X has been required to pay A. In contribution, however, the claim is for less than the full amount. In Tennessee, for example, each tortfeasor shares equally with the other tortfeasors under the Contribution Among Tortfeasors Act adopted in this state. So, if there are only two tortfeasors, X and Y, each would bear one-half of the liability to A; if there are three tortfeasors, each would bear one-third, and so on. In other jurisdictions, however, shares of liability for contribution may be computed on the basis of comparative responsibility for the loss, rather than on a strict pro rata basis. This method of apportioning loss resembles that used in jurisdictions applying a comparative negligence approach to adjusting claims by the injured party, A, against either X or Y.

Whenever A is permitted to recover against X or Y for a single injury caused by both X and Y, the extent of A's judgment against the tortfeasors is normally for the full amount of his loss, subject to any reduction that may be made for A's own negligence in a comparative negligence jurisdiction. Although A can collect the entire judgment only once, either from X or Y or in part from both depending on the availability of executable assets, the judgment itself is for the full amount of recoverable damages against each. The apportionment of liability, either on the basis of contribution or indemnity, occurs if at all as between X and Y. It would be possible, of course, to apportion liability at the front end, in determining A's claim against X and Y, rather than in determining the latter parties's rights *inter sese*, but this is not usually done unless the damages can be reasonably allocated between X and Y on the basis of relative causation.

Essentially, then, there are three main approaches to allocating loss among several tortfeasors, each of whom is responsible for the same wrong to a third party: (1) pro rata division of liability, (2) allocation of liability on the basis of comparative fault, and (3) a complete shifting of liability from one tortfeasor to the other. The first and second approaches are typical of claims for contribution, and the third of claims in indemnity. The first approach can be criticized for its arbitrariness but defended for its predictability and ease of application. The second can be supported on the basis of its equitable orientation which is the theoretical basis for allocation of loss among tortfeasors, and conversely can be attacked for its uncertainty of application, especially where differences in degrees of fault are divided by very fine lines. The third is the subject of the following section.

III.   THE ROLE OF FAULT IN INDEMNITY RECOVERY

The indemnity approach of completely shifting the loss from one tortfeasor to another would seem to make sense only where the entire actual fault lies with the indemnitor (Y), and the indemnitee (X) is free from actual fault and is held liable to the injured party (A) only because of some duty strictly imposed by statute or case law. In fact, many of the situations where indemnity is imposed involve nonfault, or only "technical" fault, on the part of the indemnitee, and actual fault on the part of the indemnitor. This indemnity pattern is not uniform, however, and there is a large body of cases where indemnity has been allowed even though both the indemnitee and the indemnitor are at fault. The courts' approach in such cases has been to characterize the indemnitee's fault as merely "passive" or secondary, while that of the indemnitor is described as "active" or primary.

———

B.   INDEMNITY AND CONTRIBUTION

Before the conceptual merger of warranty and negligence theories of liability into strict products liability in tort, actions based on warranty provided the primary basis for the application of indemnity principles in products liability cases. Express contractual provisions creating rights of indemnity have always been enforceable. But more often such rights were recognized as arising out of an implied warranty. A retail seller liable for a breach of implied warranty to an injured consumer usually could then bring an action against its own supplier based on breach of the seller's implied warranty to the retailer. Recall Justice Traynor's concurring opinion in *Escola*, above ch. 5: "The courts recognize, however, that the retailer cannot bear the burden of this [implied] warranty, and allow him to recoup any losses by means of the warranty of safety attending the wholesaler's or manufacturer's sale to him."

———

DiGregorio v. Champlain Valley Fruit Co.

Supreme Court of Vermont, 1969.
127 Vt. 562, 255 A.2d 183.

■ HOLDEN, CHIEF JUSTICE.

The plaintiffs, who operate the Quality Market in Burlington, purchased some bananas from the defendant Champlain Valley Fruit Company. One of the bananas contained a glass fruit thermometer which had been inserted by the defendant wholesaler. The fruit that contained the thermometer, or fragments of the instrument, was retailed by the plaintiffs to Mrs. Barbara Malloy who injured her teeth when she undertook to eat the banana. She later brought an action to recover for the injury against the plaintiffs, alleging breach of warranty and negligence. The plaintiffs called upon the defendant Champlain Valley Fruit Company to enter and defend the action. Upon its refusal, it became necessary for the plaintiffs to employ counsel to defend them. The Champlain Valley Fruit Company was later joined as a party defendant. The personal injury action was settled without trial. Of the amount paid to compromise the claim, the plaintiffs contributed $300 and the defendant Champlain Valley paid $1,200.

On the strength of these facts, which were submitted as an agreed case, the plaintiffs seek to recover their contribution to the settlement and reasonable expenses. The lower court ordered judgment for the plaintiffs in the amount of $968.23. The defendants, who we refer to in the singular, bring this appeal.

The defendant challenges the plaintiffs' right to contribution on the contention that the plaintiffs have only the standing of joint tortfeasors, relying on Spalding v. Administrator of Oakes, 42 Vt. 343. It seeks to support this position by stating that the evidence would have disclosed active fault by the plaintiffs had the Malloy action gone to full trial. The argument is based on facts beyond those agreed upon and entirely foreign to the record in this appeal. . . .

In this light the most that can be said for the plaintiffs' misconduct is a failure to discover, in its retail operation, the presence of the thermometer which the defendant Champlain Valley had inserted in the banana. This shortage, of itself, will not defeat the plaintiffs' right to indemnity against the seller who put the harmful cause in motion. Boston Woven–Hose and Rubber Co. v. Kendall, 59 N.E. 657 (Mass)(opinion by Holmes, C.J.).

Under the Uniform Sales Act, the sale of the bananas—first by the defendant Champlain Valley Fruit Company and later by the plaintiffs, as the Quality Market, carried an implied warranty that the food was wholesome and fit for human consumption at the time of purchase. [Citation.] The fact that the injured consumer had a right of action against either the wholesaler or retailer, or both, does not disrupt the defendant's undertaking with the plaintiffs. On the showing made in the stipulated facts, there is no policy of the law which prevents the plaintiffs from holding the defendant to its implied warranty for such damage as the plaintiffs sustained from the purchase and resale of the dangerous commodity. [Citation.]

In the framework of this appeal we are not concerned with the contributions among wrongdoers who have violated equivalent duties, as in *Spalding*. See also Oakes v. Spaulding, 40 Vt. 347. We are dealing with successive warranties implied by law which attended the initial, as well as the subsequent sale of defective foodstuff. Both parties to this controversy, as sellers, had duties and obligations to the injured consumer. [Citation.] The plaintiffs were also buyers. And the defendant's warranty and duty extended to them, as well as to the person injured. Whether the original action was brought in contract or tort is of no consequence. [Citations.]

As between themselves, the parties to the present action are not in equal fault for the plaintiffs were entitled to rely on the defendant's warranty to them. In these circumstances indemnity is not precluded by the rule against contribution among wrongdoers. [Citations.] Since it appears that the plaintiffs' fault in its duty to the injured person was secondary to the initial negligence of the defendant, its right to restitution is established. Restatement, Restitution §§ 76, 93(1).

The defense offers further resistance. It urges that the plaintiffs' defense of the personal injury action and its contribution to the settlement were voluntarily undertaken and not subject to indemnity. The findings do not support the argument.

To protect the indemnitor's right to defend against liability, a voluntary payment by an indemnitee, without notice to the person sought to be charged, may foreclose restitution. [Citation.] The letter from plaintiffs' counsel to Champlain Valley, which is incorporated in the findings, fully protected its right to defend the action and called upon it to do so. According to the findings, the defendant's refusal to defend in the first instance, made it necessary for the plaintiffs to undertake the defense. At this point the plaintiffs were entitled to proceed in good faith to reach a reasonable settlement. [Citation.]

The fact that the defendant finally participated in the compromise indicates its acquiescence in the result it achieved. There is nothing in the findings to indicate the plaintiffs' contribution was unreasonable. And we cannot infer from the facts presented that the joint compromise with the claimant discharged the defendant from the obligation of its warranty to the retailer.

[Affirmed as modified per stipulation.]

NOTES

1. In agreement with *DiGregorio*, consider Frey v. Montgomery Ward & Co., 258 N.W.2d 782, 790 (Minn.1977): "Retailers generally are at the mercy of manufacturers with respect to knowledge of dangers that inhere in the products they sell. Standing at the head of the stream of commerce, we may presume a manufacturer to be familiar with its product and the dangers it presents the public. Not only is it

reasonable for a retailer to rely on the manufacturer's greater knowledge of its product, but that reliance is recognized by the law of implied warranties."

~~See also Kelly v. Hanscom Bros., Inc., 331 A.2d 737, 740~~ (Pa.Super.1974)(retailer of defective toy could recover against wholesaler in warranty, and wholesaler could use same procedure against Japanese manufacturer even if manufacturer insolvent or beyond reach of court: "It is not unusual for liability to move transactionally up the chain of distribution until the manufacturer ultimately pays for its breach of its implied warranty of merchantability to the distributor to whom it initially sold the goods. Indeed, [when privity of contract was still required,] this was precisely how everyone assumed the causes of action would develop."). Accord UCC § 2–314, cmt. 8, providing that the implied warranty of "merchantability" affords "protection [to] the person buying for resale to the ultimate consumer" See also comment 1.

2. Vouching In. The retailer will often want to follow the "vouching in" procedures of UCC § 2–607(5): "Where the buyer is sued for breach of a warranty or other obligation for which his seller is answerable over (a) he may give his seller written notice of the litigation. If the notice states that the seller may come in and defend and that if the seller does not do so he will be bound in any action against him by his buyer by any determination of fact common to the two litigations, then unless the seller after seasonable receipt of the notice does come in and defend he is so bound."

3. Effect of Joint Tortfeasor Contribution Rules. With the adoption in most jurisdictions of principles of strict products liability, contribution among joint tortfeasors, and comparative fault, courts began to question the need for complete indemnity. The issue in *DiGregorio* was treated differently in a case where comparative fault and contribution rules were in effect. See Frazer v. A.F. Munsterman, Inc., 527 N.E.2d 1248 (Ill.1988). In *Frazer*, a person injured by a defective trailer hitch sued the lessor, for failing to discover a defect in the hitch, and the manufacturer, for selling it in a defective condition. The lessor cross-claimed against the manufacturer for indemnity. The manufacturer settled with plaintiff. The jury returned a verdict of negligence and strict liability against the lessor, and the trial court dismissed the lessor's indemnity action. The legislature had enacted a law permitting contribution among joint tortfeasors, Ill. Rev. Stat. ch. 70, pars. 302(a), 303 (1979) and determining the "pro rata share" based on "relative culpability."

On appeal, the *Frazer* court had to decide whether indemnity survived the adoption of comparative fault and contribution among tortfeasors. The trial court's dismissal of the indemnity action was affirmed, even though the lessor's only conduct giving rise to liability was its failure to discover the defect. The adoption of both comparative fault and contribution rules precluded indemnity, even though the lessor's liability was based simply on its lease of the product and failure to discover the product defect, 527 N.E.2d at 1256–58:

> There is nothing in the policy underlying strict liability to require that the manufacturer of a defective product bear the entire loss in situations where the negligence of a distributor contributes to causing the loss or harm. The imposition of strict liability was not intended to make the manufacturer an absolute insurer of the product, requiring it to bear the full burden of damages resulting from not only the defective product but from the contributing fault of other parties as well. It should be borne in mind that the rule of indemnification ... was adopted in part to ameliorate the harshness of the rule prohibiting contribution.... [I]f the injured person sued and recovered from the immediate seller of the defective

product, the manufacturer, because of the then-existing rule against contribution, would be free from liability if the seller were denied indemnity. With the adoption of contribution, however, if the negligent conduct of the intermediate seller played a role in proximately causing the plaintiff's injuries, there is no reason that the negligent conduct should not be compared with the conduct of the manufacturer and the responsibility for damages shared.

* * *

[I]n strict liability actions the principle of comparative fault is applicable to joint tortfeasors. Thus, here the distributor of a product who negligently failed to inspect for defects in the product cannot under strict liability recover in indemnity from the manufacturer. [A] majority of the courts in other jurisdictions that have considered the issue have held that a negligent failure to inspect and discover a product defect by an intermediate seller bars a claim for indemnity from the manufacturer.

Unlike the retailer in *DiGregorio*, the lessor in *Frazer* was found negligent by a jury. The retailer in *DiGregorio* first settled with the plaintiff and then proceeded with its indemnity action. What result in *DiGregorio* if the retailer had been adjudged negligent? What if the lessor in *Frazer* had settled with the plaintiff first and then sued the manufacturer for indemnity? See Thatcher v. Commonwealth Edison Co., 527 N.E.2d 1261 (Ill.1988).

For jurisdictions continuing to rely on notions of "active/passive" fault in determining indemnity, the Rest. (Second) of Torts § 886B and the Products Liability Restatement § 32 may continue to be instructive. See Franklin v. Morrison, 711 A.2d 177 (Md. 1998).

4. Should a *strictly* liable downstream seller be able to maintain an indemnity action against the upstream manufacturer responsible for creating the defect?

Promaulayko v. Johns Manville Sales Corp.

Supreme Court of New Jersey, 1989.
116 N.J. 505, 562 A.2d 202.

■ POLLOCK, J.

The sole issue on this appeal is whether an intermediate distributor in a chain of distribution should indemnify the ultimate distributor when both are strictly liable in tort to the injured plaintiff. The Law Division granted indemnification to the ultimate distributor, but the Appellate Division reversed, 540 A.2d 893 (N.J.Super.1988). We ... now reverse the judgment of the Appellate Division.

I

The underlying facts are that the decedent, John Promaulayko (Promaulayko), contracted asbestosis while working for Ruberoid Corporation from 1934 to 1978 at its South Bound Brook plant. During that period, Ruberoid purchased asbestos from Leonard J. Buck, Inc. (Buck), Asbestos Corporation Limited (Asbestos), and various other suppliers. Included in the asbestos sold by Buck to Ruberoid's South Bound Brook plant was 96.5

tons of Soviet asbestos, which Buck purchased from Amtorg Trading Corporation (Amtorg). The asbestos was packaged in 100–pound bags that did not warn of the dangers of asbestosis. Apparently neither Amtorg nor Buck ever took possession of the bags, which were shipped from the Soviet Union to the United States where Ruberoid took possession of them.

The jury determined in answer to a special interrogatory that Amtorg had supplied all of the Soviet asbestos that caused Promaulayko's injuries. After Promaulayko's death, his wife, plaintiff, [instituted wrongful death and survival actions against] Amtorg, Buck, and Asbestos. Only Buck and Amtorg are involved in the present appeal.

Buck, a corporation of the State of Delaware, is a broker of mineral products, whose brokerage of asbestos at the time of its sales to Ruberoid accounted for less than one percent of its business. Amtorg is a New York corporation founded in 1924 to promote trade between the United States and the Soviet Union. Its employees are Soviet citizens, the majority of whom remain in the United States for three or four years before returning to jobs in the Soviet Ministry of Foreign Trade. By 1930, Amtorg served as broker for eighty-six percent of the Soviet products entering the United States. At present, Amtorg serves as a direct agent for Soviet business interests and channels the majority of Soviet trade to the United States.

At the conclusion of the trial, the jury [awarded $100,000 to the plaintiff.] In reaching that result, the jury provided the following answers to special interrogatories:

6. Considering that all of the fault that proximately contributed to John Promaulayko's asbestosis is 100%, what percentage of that total fault is attributable to:

(a) Leonard J. Buck, Inc.	25%
(b) Amtorg Trading Corp.	10%
(c) Asbestos Corp. Ltd. (also known as Johnson's Company Ltd.)	65%
TOTAL	100%

7a. Was all (100%) of the asbestos fiber sold by Leonard J. Buck, Inc., which proximately contributed to John Promaulayko's asbestosis sold to Buck by Amtorg Trading Corp.?

Yes X No ___

Based on the jury's answer that Amtorg had supplied Buck with all of the asbestos that had caused Promaulayko's asbestosis, the trial court granted Buck indemnification from Amtorg [rejecting] Amtorg's argument that Buck was not entitled to indemnification because the jury's answer to interrogatory 6 indicated that Buck was more at fault than Amtorg. Although the court acknowledged the inconsistencies in the answers to interrogatories 6 and 7a, it concluded that if the jury made a mistake, it was in answer to interrogatory 6, which dealt with the difficult issue of the allocation of fault. By contrast, the answer to the simple factual issue posed by interrogatory 7a established that Amtorg had supplied all the Soviet asbestos that Buck sold to Ruberoid's South Bound Brook plant.

The Appellate Division reversed, ruling that one in the position of a retailer, such as Buck, could obtain indemnification only from the manufacturer who produced the defective product and not from an intermediate distributor such as Amtorg. Underlying that determination was the court's conclusion that indemnity is based on the difference between the primary liability of the manufacturer and the secondary liability of distributors lower in the chain of distribution. The court reasoned that [requiring Amtorg to indemnity Buck is based on Amtorg's proximity to the manufacturer, not on Amtorg's primary fault. Both Amtorg and Buck were blameless in terms of conduct creating the product's defect. The appellate division rejected indemnity:]

> The purpose of indemnification is restitution to prevent an active wrongdoer from being unjustly enriched by having another party discharge the obligation of the active wrongdoer. . . . Where, as here, the distributors' liability is based upon a common failure to detect the defect in the product and this failure merely continued the defect created by the manufacturer, we perceive of no valid reason to shift the liability of one distributor to another distributor through common law indemnification. Because Buck and Amtorg were both without personal fault, indemnification would create, rather than prevent, unjust enrichment.

The court concluded that the proper method ameliorating its otherwise "harsh" result was to modify the award based on the Comparative Negligence Act, N.J.S.A. 2A:15–5.1 to–5.3. Consequently, it molded the verdict in accordance with the jury's answer to interrogatory 6, the result of which is that Asbestos would pay sixty-five percent; Buck, twenty-five percent; and Amtorg, ten percent of the total $100,000 award.

II

Two basic principles underlie the development of strict liability in tort. [First, the allocation of the risk of loss to the party best able to *control* it, and, second, allocation of that risk to the party best able to *distribute* it. Consequently, the essence of a strict liability case is proof that defendant placed a defective product in the stream of commerce and liability extends beyond the manufacturer to all entities in the chain of distribution.] Although a distributor and a retailer may be innocent conduits in the sale of the defective product, they remain liable to the injured party. [Citations.] The net result is that the absence of the original manufacturer or producer need not deprive the injured party of a cause of action. . . .

In the absence of an express agreement between them, allocation of the risk of loss between the parties in the chain of distribution is achieved through common-law indemnity, an equitable doctrine that allows a court to shift the cost from one tortfeasor to another. The right to common-law indemnity arises "without agreement, and by operation of law to prevent a result which is regarded as unjust or unsatisfactory." W. Keeton, D. Dobbs, R. Keeton, & D. Owen, Prosser & Keeton on The Law of Torts § 51 at 341 (5th ed. 1984) (Prosser & Keeton). One branch of common-law indemnity shifts the cost of liability from one who is constructively or vicariously liable to the tortfeasor who is primarily liable. [Citation.] A corollary to this principle is that one who is primarily at fault may not obtain indemnity from another tortfeasor. Cartel Capital Corp. v. Fireco of New Jersey, 410 A.2d 674 (N.J.1980). Consistent with this principle, actions by retailers against manufacturers have been recognized in this State for twenty years. Newmark v. Gimbel's Inc., 258 A.2d 697 (N.J.1969); *Cartel Capital.*

* * *

[T]he effect of requiring the party closest to the original producer to indemnify parties farther down the chain is to shift the risk of loss to the most efficient accident avoider. See R. Posner, Economic Analysis of the Law 173–74 (1986)(Posner). Passing the cost of the risk up the distributive chain also fulfills, as a general rule, the goal of distributing the risk to the party best able to bear it. [Citations.] The manufacturer to whom the cost is shifted can distribute that cost among all purchasers of its product. Similarly, a wholesale distributor can generally pass the risk among a greater number of potential users than a distributor farther down the chain. When viewed in terms of these economic consequences, the principle of unjust enrichment, on which the Appellate Division relied, [citation], similarly supports the allocation of the risk to the distributor closest to the manufacturer. [Citations.]

[This analysis applies equally to strict liability in tort and warranty law under the UCC.] Other jurisdictions have also allowed recovery on implied warranties that extend from one party to another down the chain of distribution. See Klein v. Asgrow Seed Co., 246 Cal.App.2d 87, 54 Cal.Rptr. 609 (1966)(tomato grower recovered judgment for breach of warranty against seed grower; indemnification allowed by each party in the chain of distribution against party higher in the chain); [citations]; see also N.J.S.A. 12A:2–607(5)(a)(permits buyer to vouch in its seller when third party brings suit against buyer based on the product).

III

In the present case, Amtorg was closer than Buck to the producer of the asbestos in the Soviet Union. As between the two of them, Amtorg is better positioned "to put pressure on" the producer to make the product safe. *Newmark.* Here, the defect was the absence of a warning of the dangers of asbestosis when the bags were placed in the stream of commerce. Because of Amtorg's relationship to Soviet commerce in general and to the producer in particular, it is more likely that it, rather than Buck, will be able to persuade the producer to provide an adequate warning. Further, Amtorg is better able to shift the cost of the loss to the asbestos producer and to require that producer to reflect the cost of injury in the price of its product.

Conceivably, a set of facts might arise in which the party at the end of the distributive chain will be a better risk-bearer than a party higher in the chain. As a general rule, however, we expect indemnification to follow the chain of distribution. Finally, we recognize that parties in a distributive chain may contract for a different allocation of the risk of loss. For example, one distributor may expressly agree to disclaim or waive any right of indemnification against a distributor farther up the chain. In the present case, the parties did not make any such agreement, and we are satisfied that Buck is entitled to indemnification from Amtorg, the distributor that was interposed between Buck and the producer of the product.

Amtorg contends that it should not be obliged to indemnify Buck because of the answer to special interrogatory 6, in which the jury found Buck twenty-five percent at fault and Amtorg only ten per cent at fault for Promaulayko's injuries. The trial court apparently submitted this interrogatory because of the crossclaims for contribution. According to the trial court, the jury's determination did not represent a finding of fault in the negligence sense. Instead, it was a finding of "sterile fault" assigned in a strict-liability case to intermediate parties in a distributive chain. This finding led the trial court to conclude that the jury's allocation of fault was probably based on the fact that Buck was closer in the chain to Ruberoid. As previously indicated, however, the liability of Buck and Amtorg to plaintiff stems from their relative roles as conduits for the distribution of the defective product. In answer to interrogatory 7, the jury found that Amtorg had supplied to Buck 100% of that product. As between Buck and Amtorg, then, Amtorg should accept the responsibility for Buck's liability to plaintiff. Thus, the jury's finding of fault with respect to a possible claim for contribution does not change Buck's right to indemnification from Amtorg. Nothing in the Joint Tortfeasors Contribution Act, N.J.S.A. 2A:53A–1 to –5, or the Comparative Negligence Act, N.J.S.A. 2A:15–5.1 to –5.3, would alter that result. [Citation.]

Here, the injured party sued two distributors, neither of which altered or even possessed the product as it proceeded from the producer to the ultimate purchaser. In this context, the appropriate vehicle for allocating responsibility between the distributors is indemnification, not contribution. It follows that the trial court should not have asked the jury to determine the various percentages of fault attributable to Buck and Amtorg. The right of the downstream distributor to indemnification from the upstream distributor existed as a matter of law. Consequently, the court should have determined that right following the entry of the jury verdict against defendants.

The judgment of the Appellate Division is reversed, and the matter is remanded to the Law Division for the entry of judgment permitting indemnification by Buck against Amtorg.

N O T E S

1. Were Amtorg and Buck as blameless as the court asserts? The "manufacturer" apparently provided raw asbestos that it had mined. Who within the distribution chain was best suited to provide adequate warnings of the dangers of asbestos fibers? Will it always be true, as the court suggests, that the distributor closest to the manufacturer is in the best position " 'to put pressure on' the producer to make the product safe"? If not, is there something more equitable about the Appellate Division's result?

2. Effect of Comparative Fault. The appellate division in *Promaulayko* rejected indemnity in favor of application of the Comparative Negligence Act, held applicable to strict liability actions, which required sharing of liability between the distributors based on the jury's allocation of percentages of responsibility to them. That Act, N.J. Stat. Ann. § 2A:15–5.2, provides that the fact finder must determine "[t]he extent, in the form of a percentage, of each party's negligence . . . and the total of all percentages of negligence of all the parties to a suit shall be 100%." The judge is commanded to "mold the judgment from the finding of fact." Do you agree with the principal case that this statute did not apply?

3. Comparative ("Equitable") Indemnity. Although indemnity traditionally shifted the loss entirely from one tortfeasor to another, some courts have applied comparative fault principles even while claiming to apply principles of indemnity. Safeway Stores, Inc. v. Nest–Kart, 579 P.2d 441, 445 (Cal.1978): "With the advent of the common law comparative indemnity doctrine, we achieve a more precise apportionment of liability in circumstances such as the instant case by allocating damages on a comparative fault or a comparative responsibility basis, rather than by fixing an inflexible pro rata apportionment pursuant to the contribution statutes." See also Schneider National, Inc. v. Holland Hitch Co., 843 P.2d 561 (Wyo.1992) (modified comparative equitable indemnity adopted partially because court had previously concluded its comparative negligence statute did not reach strict liability actions.) But see Vermeer Carolina's, Inc. v. Wood/Chuck Chipper Corp., 518 S.E.2d 301 (S.C.App. 1999) (no indemnity where both parties are at fault).

4. How Far Upstream—Manufacturers of Component Parts. Should manufacturers be entitled to indemnity from their suppliers of component parts? If responsibility were placed on the party best able to bear and distribute the loss, assemblers who incorporate defective components into the finished product often would be left with the loss. Is this a sound policy? Is it fair? See Jones v. Aero–Chem Corp., 680 F.Supp. 338 (D.Mont.1987).

5. Recoverable Expenses. Some jurisdictions hold that "generally an indemnitee is entitled to recover, as part of his damages, reasonable attorney's fees, and reasonable and proper legal costs and expenses, which he is compelled to pay as the result of suits by or against him in reference to the matter against which he is indemnified." Insurance Co. of North America v. King, 340 So.2d 1175, 1176 (Fla.App.1976). Contra, Kerns v. Engelke, 390 N.E.2d 859 (Ill.1979). The indemnitee should logically be permitted to recover such expenses even (or, especially) if judgment is rendered in his favor in the first action, leaving only the attorney's fees and litigation expenses to be recovered in the indemnity action. See Pender v. Skillcraft Indus., 358 So.2d 45 (Fla.App.1978). Notice of the first action and tender of its defense to the supplier may be necessary to the recovery of such expenses.

What if the jury finds no defendant liable and a distributor seeks indemnity from the manufacturer for its costs and attorneys fees in defending the action? As a predicate for such indemnity, some courts require a contractual provision, a statutory duty, or that the manufacturer be found at fault. See Krasny–Kaplan Corp. v. Flo–Tork, Inc., 609 N.E.2d 152 (Ohio 1993). Other jurisdictions ground such recovery on the unjust enrichment of the manufacturer by the retailer's successful support. Pullman Standard, Inc. v. Abex Corp., 693 S.W.2d 336 (Tenn. 1985).

6. Express Indemnification Agreements. A retailer may have enough bargaining power to require the manufacturer to agree contractually to indemnify it for losses resulting from defective products. Such agreements are generally enforced, and the requirements to establish indemnity are controlled by the contract. See Kelly–Springfield Tire Co. v. Mobil Oil Corp., 551 P.2d 671 (Okla.App. 1975)(agreement provided that retailer would be indemnified against "every claim" from defective workmanship in tires; retailer need only establish that it incurred liability, and good faith settlement with consumer sufficient). Express indemnification provisions are usually narrowly interpreted. See Concast, Inc. v. AMCA Systems, Inc., 959 F.2d 631 (7th Cir.1992).

7. Loss Allocation Outside the Distribution Chain. May a defendant sued on theories of negligence and strict products liability join as third-party defendants those persons whose acts of negligence contributed to cause the injuries? Any number of non-product defendants may be contributors to a product-related accident. Whether a product defendant can sue a non-product defendant for contribution/indemnity involves both strategic and procedural joinder considerations. See Fed.R.Civ.Pro. 14(a)(third-party practice). Most jurisdictions under modern liberal joinder practices, and with the advent of comparative fault statutes seeking wide allocation of liability, permit joinder of such non-product defendants. See Svetz v. Land Tool Co., 513 A.2d 403, 408 (Pa.Super.1986)(manufacturer of defective helmet sought to join another motorcycle racer and hotel where the decedent had allegedly been drinking alcohol just before the accident; joinder permitted: a person's right to contribution derives from the "equitable principle that once the joint liability of several tortfeasors has been determined, it would be unfair to impose the financial burden of the plaintiff's loss on one tortfeasor to the exclusion of the other. It matters not on which theory a tortfeasor has been held responsible").

8. Dividing Damages: Computation of Shares. Regardless of whether some of the parties are outside the chain of distribution, and assuming that contribution is appropriate, how should responsibility for the damages be divided between multiple actors? Traditionally, contribution generally was prescribed on a pro rata, equal division basis. See Unif. Contribution Among Tortfeasors Act § 2, 12 U.L.A. 57, 87 (1955 rev.). With the advent of the comparative fault doctrine, many courts and legislatures have switched to a comparative approach for contribution purposes, dividing responsibility for damages in proportion to the defendants' fault, causation, or responsibility. See Unif. Comparative Fault Act § 4, 12 U.L.A. 37, 47 (1977, Supp.1988).

The Apportionment of Liability Restatement § 8 describes factors to be used in assigning shares of responsibility including the character and nature of each person's risk-creating conduct and the causal connection. In allocating damages among those responsible for the plaintiff's loss, should the trier-of-fact consider the fault of a person not brought into the lawsuit? Compare Ladwig v. Ermanco Inc., 504 F.Supp. 1229 (E.D.Wis.1981) (yes), with Ryden v. Johns–Manville Products, 518 F.Supp. 311 (W.D.Pa.1981) (no). Since the non-party is not present to explain and defend its actions, how can the jury rationally allocate fault to it? Will the parties before the court have adequate *incentives* to present the jury with sufficient information about the non-party's participation in the accident? Will the parties have adequate *means* to find and prove these facts? What about negligent employers who are immune from suit under workers' compensation laws?

9. Reform. A significant effect of the legislative tort reform movement begun in the mid–1980s has been a dramatic curtailment in the joint and several liability rules in various states. The Apportionment of Liability Restatement has usefully broken down the approaches to joint and several liability and apportionment into five alternatives, or tracks. See §§ 28A, 28B, 28C, 28D, 28E. While pure joint and several liability is no longer the majority, it continues to be the most widely employed method of joint liability. See § 28A, cmt. *a*.

10. See generally Cetkovic, Loss Shifting: Upstream Common Law Indemnity in Products Liability, 61 Def. Couns. J. 75 (1994); 2 D. Owen, M.S. Madden & M. Davis, Madden & Owen on Products Liability §§ 24:2 (basic principles of joint and several liability); 25:2 (indemnity generally); 25:7 (contribution generally) (3d ed. 2000).

C. WORK-RELATED INJURIES

Perhaps the most evenly-balanced controversy in all of workmen's compensation law is the question whether a third party in an action by the employee can recover over against the employer, when the employer's fault has caused or contributed to the injury.

Larson, Workmen's Compensation: Third Party's Action Over Against Employer, 65 Nw.U.L.Rev. 351 (1970).

Eaton, Revisiting the Intersection of Workers' Compensation and Product Liability

64 Tenn. L. Rev. 881 (1997).

A. Characteristics of Workplace Product Liability Claims

* * * Given that workplace product-related injuries constitute a major liability concern for both manufacturers and employers, it is not surprising that each has a significant interest in how such injury costs are apportioned between the two systems. The manufacturers' interest is heightened by the employer's central role in many workplace product-related injuries. Employers select workplace products, determine the sorts of safety guards or other protective devices that are placed on the product, train and supervise employees, maintain equipment, and communicate warnings and instructions. This degree of involvement lends credence to manufacturers' claims that employers are at least partially responsible for many workplace product-related injuries. In fact, some insurance industry studies estimate that employers are "at fault" in approximately 50% of employees' product-related suits.[22]

* * *

B. The Basic Dilemma in Workplace Product Liability Litigation: The Exclusive Remedy Doctrine, Third Party Suits, Subrogation, and Contribution

... The basic dilemma is how to apply [the products liability and workers' compensation systems] in a way that gives effect to the major

22. Insurance Services Office, Product Liability Closed Claims Survey: A Technical Analysis of Survey Results, 10 (1977).

policies of each one without sacrificing important policies of the other. One defining feature of all workers' compensation systems is limited employer liability, embodied in the exclusive remedy doctrine. The workers' compensation system is conceptualized as a quid pro quo bargain between employees and employers. In exchange for giving up the right to recover full tort compensatory damages from negligent employers, employees receive guaranteed, but limited benefits without having to prove employer fault and without being subject to common law tort defenses. In exchange for incurring no-fault liability and surrendering conduct-based defenses, employers are shielded from tort liability by the exclusive remedy doctrine. Under the laws of every state, workers' compensation benefits are the injured employee's exclusive remedy against even a negligent employer.[28] Thus, a cornerstone of every state's workers' compensation system is the guarantee of limited liability for the employer.

Noticeably absent from this conception of the workers' compensation bargain is any mention of third parties, such as product manufacturers. Either by court decision or explicit legislation, employees in every state retain the right to bring tort suits against third parties who injure them in the course of employment.[30] Should employees be allowed to secure workers' compensation benefits from the employer and tort damages from the product manufacturer? If the answer is "yes," what steps, if any, should be taken to prevent a double recovery? Employers and their insurers maintain that they should be reimbursed for workers' compensation payments out of any tort recovery the employee secures from the product manufacturer. The employers' interest in reimbursement is most often framed as a right of subrogation. On the other hand, product manufacturers argue that their tort liability should be reduced by the amount of benefits employees receive under workers' compensation. The manufacturers' equitable claim for some sort of reduction of tort liability is especially cogent when the employer's negligence contributed to the employee's injury.

C.   Various Approaches to Resolving the Dilemma

[H]ow should the law accommodate the employee's interest in full recovery, the employer's interests in subrogation and limited liability, and the product manufacturer's interest in reducing its tort liability, especially when employer fault is involved? . . . To illustrate the practical impact of the various approaches described below, consider the following hypothetical:

> Assume an employee is injured on the job while using a defective punch press. Also, assume the employer was negligent in training and supervising the employee [but the employee was not at fault.] The product manufacturer and the employer would be deemed equally at fault. Full tort damages would be $100,000 and workers' compensation benefits would be $25,000.

28.   2A A. Larson & L. Larson, The Law of Workmen's Compensation § 65.111.10 (1995).

30.   Id. § 71.

1. The Majority Approach: Employer Subrogation and No Contribution

In an overwhelming majority of states,[37] the hypothetical employee could first recover the $25,000 in workers' compensation benefits, and then pursue the tort claim against the product manufacturer. The employee could recover the full $100,000 in tort damages, subject to the employee reimbursing the employer or the insurer the $25,000 paid in workers' compensation benefits. Although there are procedural differences among these states, all provide for such reimbursement, usually through a formal right of subrogation. At the same time, product manufacturers and other third party tortfeasors are denied a right of contribution against the negligent employer. The prevailing rationale justifying this result is that because of the exclusive remedy doctrine, the employer is immune from tort liability vis-a-vis the employee. Since the employer is not a "tortfeasor," there is no "common liability" with the product manufacturer upon which to base a claim for contribution. The ultimate result is that the employee recovers workers' compensation benefits from the employer, recovers full tort damages from the product manufacturer, and reimburses the employer or its insurer for compensation benefits received out of the tort recovery. Thus, the product manufacturer ends up paying for the total cost of the injury and the workers' compensation system pays nothing. [Tabular material set forth in the original article here and throughout this excerpt is omitted. Eds.]

... The majority approach is deemed unfair in that it saddles the product manufacturer with liability that is disproportionate to its culpability. It also reduces the employer's incentive to invest appropriate resources in injury avoidance. Despite decades of criticism from prominent academics, the employer subrogation-no contribution approach continues to operate in more than forty states.

2. Contribution Proportionate to Fault

Another approach is to retain the employer's right of subrogation, but to allow third party tortfeasors to assert contribution claims against employers based on proportional fault.[48] Today, only New York follows this approach.[49] Under the proportional contribution approach, the employee recovers workers' compensation benefits from the employer, full tort damages from the product manufacturer, and reimburses the employer or its

---

37. See 2B Larson & Larson, supra note 28, § 76.20. For citations to supporting cases from 45 jurisdictions, see Clifford, Kotecki v. Cyclops Welding Corp.: The Efficacy of a Limited Contribution Rule and its Effect on Good Faith Settlements, 68 Chi.-Kent. L.Rev. 479, 492 n.84 (1992).

48. Dole v. Dow Chem. Co., 282 N.E.2d 288, 292–94 (N.Y. 1972).

49. New York recently enacted legislation that reportedly limits the scope of the proportional contribution rule to cases involving "grave injury." N.Y. Work.Comp.Law § 635 (McKinney 1996); ... Illinois previously allowed proportional contribution against negligent employers. See, e.g., Skinner v. Reed–Prentice Div. Package Mach. Co., 374 N.E.2d 437, 442–43 (Ill. 1977). The current Illinois practice is more accurately described as one of limited contribution. See, e.g., Kotecki v. Cyclops Welding Corp., 585 N.E.2d 1023, 1027–28 (Ill. 1991).

insurer for compensation benefits received out of the tort recovery, and the product manufacturer secures contribution from the employer proportionate to its fault. . . .

The primary criticism of this approach is that it exposes an employer to liability in excess of its workers' compensation obligation. In the above hypothetical, the employer would pay the product manufacturer $50,000 in contribution despite the fact that its workers' compensation obligation was limited by statute to $25,000. This extended liability is thought to undermine the basic quid pro quo bargain and jeopardize the economic foundation of the workers' compensation system.

3. Limited Contribution

A few states allow product manufacturers and other third party tortfeasors to secure contribution from negligent employers, but limit the amount of contribution to the employer's workers' compensation obligation.[54] If this approach were applied to the hypothetical, the employee would recover workers' compensation benefits from the employer, recover full tort damages from the product manufacturer, and reimburse the employer for compensation benefits received out of the tort recovery, and the product manufacturer would secure contribution from the employer up to the $25,000 limit of workers' compensation benefits.

This approach embodies a clear compromise between the policies and values underlying the workers' compensation and tort systems. It does not give as much protection to the product manufacturer's interest in proportional liability as does the New York approach, but it gives such interest more weight than does the majority "no contribution" rule. At the same time, it limits the employer's financial exposure to that set by the workers' compensation system, and thus gives some effect to the policies and values underlying the exclusive remedy doctrine.

4. Direct Reduction of the Tort Recovery by the Amount of the Workers' Compensation Benefits

A consequence of recognizing both the employer's right of subrogation and the product manufacturer's right of contribution is that money may change hands several times, thus increasing the transaction costs of processing claims. These transaction costs could be reduced if the workers' compensation benefits were directly subtracted from the tort judgment and the rights of subrogation and contribution were eliminated. . . .

One variation [of this approach] reduces the third party's tort liability and eliminates the employer's subrogation lien only when there is a finding of employer fault.[58] This approach is followed in California and North

---

54. See, e.g., Ky. Rev. Stat. Ann. § 342.690(1)(1993); Runcorn v. Shearer Lumber Prod., Inc., 690 P.2d 324, 330 (Idaho 1984); Kotecki, 585 N.E.2d at 1027; Lambertson v. Cincinnati Welding Corp., 257 N.W.2d 679, 689 (Minn. 1977).

58. See Witt v. Jackson, 366 P.2d 641, 648–50 (Cal. 1961); Hunsucker v. High Point Bending & Chair Co., 75 S.E.2d 768, 777 (N.C. 1953).

Carolina. It reflects the view that the employer should retain its right of subrogation when it has not been negligent....

[Another variation would reduce tort recovery] in all cases [regardless of "employer fault"]. Conditioning direct reduction on a finding of employer fault [would increase transaction costs by requiring the involvement of the jury to resolve apportionment questions which may be especially difficult. Under either version of the direct reduction approach,] the employee in the hypothetical would receive full compensation, with a portion ($25,000) paid by the employer under workers' compensation and the remainder ($75,000) paid by the product manufacturer.

5. Complete Separation of Workers' Compensation and Product Liability Systems

One approach that has attracted some judicial and academic support is to structure a complete separation of the workers' compensation and product liability systems. Such a separation would be achieved by eliminating the employer's right of subrogation and limiting the manufacturer's liability to its proportional share of fault. If applied to the hypothetical case, this approach would authorize the employee to recover $25,000 from the employer under workers' compensation and $50,000 from the product manufacturer under product liability.

This proposal would give full effect to the manufacturer's interest in proportional liability and employer's interest in limited liability. The employee, however, would not recover full tort compensation. Is this fair to the employee? Proponents of the complete separation approach maintain that this allocation of injury costs is consistent with the quid pro quo premise of workers' compensation. Under workers' compensation, the employee has agreed to broader (no-fault) coverage, but limited recovery. This distributional pattern allows benefits to:

> be spread across the broader pool of all injured workers. It is not unfair, therefore, to apply the same [workers' compensation] principle of limited but guaranteed compensation so as to reduce somewhat the size of an employee's tort recovery in a case which happens to intersect in this way with the [workers' compensation] system.[68]

Another consequence of the complete separation proposal is that it requires the adjudication of employer fault in a context in which the employer has no interest in the issue. The product manufacturer would have a significant incentive to persuade the jury to allocate a large percentage of fault to the employer. [The employer, however, would not have any incentive to participate actively in the employee's product liability suit because its liability is limited in any event to the workers' compensation benefits already paid. The employee would have to defend the employer's conduct.] The employer not having any real stake in the litigation raises the danger of distorting the allocation of fault.

---

68. Weiler, Workers' Compensation and Product Liability: The Interaction of a Tort and a Non–Tort Regime, 50 Ohio St.L.J. 825, 845 (1989).

6. Eliminate Third Party Tort Claims and Increase Workers' Compensation Benefits

Another proposal would combine the elimination of third party tort suits with an increase in workers' compensation benefits.[69] The transaction costs of claiming under these two systems would be reduced substantially, thereby allowing a higher percentage of aggregate insurance premiums to be used for the compensation of injured workers. All injured workers—not just those who have potential third party tort claims—would gain from increased workers' compensation benefits. The employee's loss of the third party tort claim could be justified as part of a re-conceptualized quid pro quo bargain, [enlarging the scope of the underlying workers' compensation benefits for all injured workers by trading the right of a few injured workers to sue third-party manufacturers.[70]] Under this proposal, the hypothetically injured worker would receive workers' compensation benefits, presumably greater than $25,000, but would not have a tort claim against the product manufacturer.

7. Eliminate the Exclusive Remedy Doctrine

The final proposal ... is one to abolish or reduce the scope of the exclusive remedy doctrine.[73] Under this approach, injured employees would be allowed to pursue tort claims they might have against employers—at least if damages exceed a minimum threshold above the workers' compensation benefits payable for the injury. The hypothetical employee could sue both the employer and product manufacturer in tort and recover $100,000. The precise division of responsibility between the two defendants would turn on the nuances of state law regarding joint and several liability.

This approach reflects a dissatisfaction with the current equity of the quid pro quo bargain and the perceived need to provide employers with greater incentives to improve workplace safety. Whether employees as a group would benefit from expanded employer tort liability is hard to say.... This undoubtedly would increase transaction costs and deliver compensation to fewer injured workers as compared to the existing system.

N O T E S

1. Many courts have expressed frustration at the lack of legislative leadership on the conflict between workers' compensation and products liability. See, Kotecki v. Cyclops Welding Corp., 585 N.E.2d 1023, 1026 (Ill.1991):

> There are, however, times when there exists a mutual state of inaction in which the court awaits action by the legislature and the legislature awaits guidance

---

69. 1 American Law Institute, Reporters' Study on Enterprise Responsibility 192–98 (1991); 2 Interagency Task Force on Prod. Liab., U.S. Dep't of Commerce, Final Report 112 (1979); ...; J. O'Connell, Supplementing Workers' Compensation Benefits in Return for an Assignment of Third–Party Tort Claims—Without an Enabling Statute, 56 Tex.L.Rev. 537 (1978); [citation.]

70. 2 ALI Reporters' Study, supra note 69, at 195.

73. T. Haas, On Reintegrating Workers' Compensation and Employers' Liability, 21 Ga.L.Rev. 843, 897–98 (1987); [citation].

from the court. Such a stalemate is a manifest injustice to the public. When such a stalemate exists and the legislature has for whatever reason, failed to [act], it is the imperative duty of the court to repair that injustice and reform the law to be responsive to the demands of society.

The *Kotecki* court endorsed a limited contribution rule.

2. No Contribution—Fairness. Is the majority no-contribution approach fair to manufacturers? In Unique Equipment Co. v. TRW Vehicle Safety Systems, 3 P.3d 970 (Ariz. App. 1999), the manufacturer of a product made according to the employer's design specifications was held liable in products liability for making a defective product but could not receive indemnity or contribution from the employer.

3. The Goose v. the Gander. Although the manufacturer generally is barred from suing the employer, the converse is not true; that is, the employer typically *is* permitted to maintain a subrogation action against the manufacturer, even though the employer's fault also contributed to the employee's injury. Florida's workers' compensation statutory procedures are typical. See Sunspan Eng'g & Constr. Co. v. Spring–Lock Scaffolding Co., 310 So.2d 4, 6 (Fla.1975) (employer subrogated to the rights of the employee as against a third party tortfeasor to the extent of compensation benefits paid to employee; employer has lien on proceeds recovered by employee; employer may sue if employee does not sue within a year). See also Barry v. Quality Steel Prods., Inc., 905 A.2d 55 (Conn. 2006) (employer who has intervened in case to recoup workers' compensation benefits paid to a plaintiff is not a "party" against which proportional liability may be assigned).

4. Express Indemnification Agreements. Contractual provisions whereby an employer expressly agrees to indemnify a supplier for any liability it may incur as a result of the use of the product are generally enforced despite the exclusive remedy provision. See, e.g., Dutchmen Mfg., Inc. v. Reynolds, 849 N.E.2d 516 (Ind. 2006); Mosley Mach. Co. v. Gray Supply Co., 833 S.W.2d 772 (Ark.1992).

5. Reform. Prof. Eaton's article also addressed the proposed Product Liability Legal Reform Act, S.B. 565, § 111, 104th Cong., 1st Sess. (1995), which sought to (1) create a federal right of subrogation in favor of an employer or its insurer, and (2) authorize a direct reduction of the employee's product liability recovery when the manufacturer proves by clear and convincing evidence that the injury was caused either by employer or co-employee fault. What incentives do these reform proposals create?

6. See generally 2 D. Owen, M.S. Madden, & M. Davis, Madden & Owen on Products Liability §§ 19:7, 25:12 (3d ed. 2000).

D. PARTIAL SETTLEMENTS

Cartel Capital Corp. v. Fireco of New Jersey

Supreme Court of New Jersey, 1980.
81 N.J. 548, 410 A.2d 674.

■ SCHREIBER, J.

[Plaintiff, Country Burger, sued Fireco, the retailer, installer and servicer of plaintiff's fire extinguishing equipment, and Ansul], manufacturer of that equipment, for property damage caused by a fire during which the equipment allegedly failed to operate. Plaintiff's cause of action against Ansul was based upon negligence and strict liability arising out of a design defect. The action against Fireco involved [1] strict liability because of the same design defect and [2] negligence in improperly servicing the system. The codefendants asserted cross-claims against each other under the Joint Tortfeasors Contribution Act, N.J.S.A. 2A:53A–1 et seq., and for indemnification.

At the outset of the trial Ansul settled with plaintiff for $50,000, voluntarily dismissed its cross-claims and successfully moved for dismissal of Fireco's cross-claims. Plaintiff then proceeded against Fireco alone. In response to a set of special interrogatories, the jury found that Fireco was negligent, that Ansul had defectively designed the equipment, and that both the negligence and defect were proximate causes of plaintiff's damages. The jury determined that plaintiff had also been guilty of negligence. It fixed damages due to the malfunctioning of the fire extinguishing equipment to operate at $113,400 and the percentages of fault as follows: Plaintiff—41%, Fireco—30%, and Ansul—29%. The trial court then entered a judgment in favor of plaintiff for $34,020, plus interest and costs.

[Plaintiff and Fireco both appealed, first to the Superior Court, which reversed, and then to the Supreme Court. The issues here] are [1] the effect to be given to plaintiff's settlement with defendant Ansul, [2] the existence of plaintiff's negligence, and [3] the propriety of dismissing Fireco's cross-claims for indemnification and contribution.

I.

Defendants Ansul and Fireco argue that Country Burger's settlement with Ansul eliminated plaintiff's strict liability cause of action against Fireco, on the theory that the release of Ansul operated to remove any basis for the derivative claim against Fireco. Additionally, it is contended that Country Burger had, in fact, abandoned its strict product liability claim against Fireco. We find neither of these arguments persuasive.

Ansul contends that when it settled plaintiff's strict product liability claim, any cause of action predicated on that defect had been extinguished. However, a plaintiff may be entitled to and obtain several judgments against different persons for the same obligation or liability so long as there is only one satisfaction or recovery. . . .

Even when liability of one defendant is wholly vicarious, settlement with the primarily liable defendant may not necessarily release the other. For example, when an employer is liable for an employee's negligence, both the employer and employee are jointly and severally liable to the injured party until full satisfaction is received. . . .

This rationale is also apposite when one joint tortfeasor has settled. Over 20 years ago Justice Jacobs in Breen v. Peck, 146 A.2d 665 (N.J.1958), discussed and rejected the common law doctrine that the release of one joint tortfeasor automatically released all. Instead the Court adopted the principle that the legal effect of a release on other parties should be determined by the intent of the parties to the release, with due consideration being given to whether the compensation paid was fully adequate. That eminently more just rule has been consistently followed. * * *

It follows that we must look to the parties' intention when the settlement was made. *Breen*. Before the jury was impaneled and sworn, Ansul announced that it had settled with plaintiff for $50,000; its total damage claim exceeded $180,000. Ansul's attorney stated that he would "be receiving settlement papers probably in the nature of a covenant not to sue" and "that the settlement with Ansul is not intended to release the other defendant, Fireco of New Jersey." The general release delivered conformed with that intent. Recited therein was the following:

> It is the intention of this Release to release Ansul, Inc., only, and this Release shall not affect in any way any and all claims the Releasor has against Fireco of New Jersey.

Further, plaintiff relinquished its claim against Ansul for only partial satisfaction of its alleged damages. The settlement was less than one-third the amount of damages claimed. The jury award of $113,400 confirmed that plaintiff's losses substantially exceeded the $50,000 settlement figure. Thus, plaintiff's action against Fireco, in which plaintiff sought damages based upon strict liability and negligence, remained viable. Release of Ansul as a primary tortfeasor did not release Fireco from either its vicarious or direct responsibility.

* * *

II.

[The court concluded that the plaintiff's conduct was insufficient as a matter of law to diminish its recovery.]

III.

We turn next to Fireco's cross-claims for indemnity or contribution from Ansul as a joint tortfeasor. [Because Fireco's liability arose from selling a defective product manufactured by Ansul, Fireco's cross-claim against Ansul for indemnity was viable.]

Fireco's cross-claim also sought contribution under the Joint Tortfeasors Contribution Law, N.J.S.A. 2A:53A–1 et seq. That act established a right of contribution among joint tortfeasors, N.J.S.A. 2A:53A–2, when the "injury or damage is suffered by any person as a result of the wrongful act, neglect or default of joint tortfeasors ..." N.J.S.A. 2A:53A–3. When that has occurred a joint tortfeasor can recover contribution from another tortfeasor for any excess paid in satisfaction of a judgment "over his pro rata share ..." N.J.S.A. 2A:53A–3. That law applies here.

The statute defines "joint tortfeasors" to mean two or more persons jointly or severally "liable in tort for the same injury." N.J.S.A. 2A:53A–1.

Ansul and Fireco satisfy that definition. Both were found to be at fault and liable in tort—Ansul because of its production and distribution of a defective product, [citation], and Fireco because of its negligent servicing and because of its role in the distributive chain of a defective product.

[The Joint Tortfeasors Contribution Law] does not require that joint tortfeasors be liable on the same theory of recovery, so that a defendant whose responsibility arises out of strict liability and another defendant whose responsibility is due to negligence may be joint tortfeasors under [the Law. Under that statute, a joint tortfeasor's recovery is limited] to any excess paid over "his pro rata share." N.J.S.A. 2A:53A–3. [I]t is important to note [here that] the Comparative Negligence Act, N.J.S.A. 2A:15–5.1 et seq. [requires determining] the percentage of each party's fault . . . and "[a]ny party who is so compelled to pay more than such party's percentage share may seek contribution from the other joint tortfeasors." N.J.S.A. 2A:15–5.3. Thus the Legislature has seen fit to redefine the "pro rata" allocation to be a party's "percentage share" in the contribution scheme between and among joint tortfeasors. [Citation.]

Under the joint tortfeasors law we had held that a settlement with a joint tortfeasor, even though for less than a pro rata share of the total claim, reduced the plaintiff's total claim against the nonsettling codefendant or codefendants by the pro rata share and thus barred contribution from the settling tortfeasor. [Citations.] Now the effect on the plaintiff of a joint tortfeasor's settlement will depend upon the percentage of fault found against him. When one defendant settles, the remaining codefendant or codefendants are chargeable with the total verdict less that attributable to the settling defendant's percentage share.

Other jurisdictions have reached similar results. [Citations.] Cf. Frey v. Snelgrove, 269 N.W.2d 918 (Minn.1978)(involving a "Pierringer-type" release); Pierringer v. Hoger, 124 N.W.2d 106 (Wis.1963)(release of codefendant expressly states that nonsettling tortfeasors would not be liable for that percentage of fault to be attributed to settling tortfeasor). Our holding also comports with Section 6 of the Uniform Comparative Fault Act (1977).

Applying the foregoing principles, we find that the total relevant fault is that of Ansul and Fireco, there being no contributory negligence as a matter of law. Ansul's 29% and Fireco's 30%, or 59%, constitute the total fault in the case. In a sense, the 59% is 100%. Thus, Fireco's responsibility is 30/59ths or 50.8% and Ansul's is 29/59ths or 49.2%. It follows that Fireco's proportionate share of the entire damages of $113,400 is $57,661.01 and Ansul's proportionate share is $55,738.99. Ansul, however, had settled its obligation to the plaintiff for $50,000. Fireco remains liable for its share, namely $57,661.01.

[Remanded for entry of judgment for] plaintiff and against Fireco in the sum of $57,661.01 plus costs and interest.

NOTES

1. Effect of Settlement by One Defendant—Alternative Approaches. In most jurisdictions, the basic settlement rules are now governed by statute. New

Jersey's approach reflects that of § 6 of the Uniform Comparative Fault Act, which reduces a plaintiff's recovery against non-settling defendants by the percentage fault ("equitable share") of any settling defendants. The Apportionment of Liability Restatement takes the same approach in § 26.

In California, the plaintiff's claim is reduced by the dollar value of a "good faith" settlement. See American Motorcycle Ass'n v. Superior Court, 578 P.2d 899, 916 (Cal.1978); Espinoza v. Machonga, 11 Cal.Rptr.2d 498 (Ct.App.1992) (analyzing effect on settlement of Proposition 51 which imposes several liability for noneconomic damages). For the procedures used to determine whether a settlement was made in good faith, see Price Pfister, Inc. v. William Lyon Co., 18 Cal.Rptr.2d 437 (Ct.App.1993) (applying Cal. Code Civ. Pro. §§ 877, 877.6).

In New York, the plaintiff's claim is reduced by the greater of the settlement amount or the settling defendant's equitable share of the damages. N.Y. Gen. Oblig. Law § 15–108. See Williams v. Niske, 615 N.E.2d 1003, 1007 (N.Y.1993) (plaintiff infant burned when clothing caught fire settled before trial with four manufacturing defendants for $900,000; during trial, plaintiff settled with a playmate (Niske) for $100,000 and with clothing manufacturer on a "high-low" basis, with manufacturer agreeing to pay $100,000 as a base and up to $500,000 if the plaintiff did not recover at least $500,000 against the remaining defendant at trial, the clothing retailer; jury returned verdict of $2,600,000, apportioning liability 35% to retailer 30% to friend and 35% to manufacturer; Court of Appeals first reduced the award by the settlement amounts, then apportioned the remaining portion of the award ($1,700,000) according to the equitable fault of the remaining defendants, even though two of them had already settled).

Which approach is best—New Jersey's, California's, or New York's?

2. Should the jury be informed of the fact of settlement and its effect on the remaining defendants? See Slayton v. Ford Motor Co., 435 A.2d 946 (Vt.1981) (no). See also Brewer v. Payless Stations, Inc., 316 N.W.2d 702 (Mich.1982) (unless the parties agree otherwise, crediting to be performed by the court). Should the answer depend on whether the settling defendant has remained in the case to have its liability and comparative share determined?

3. In a dollar-for-dollar credit jurisdiction, matters are complicated when the total award must be reduced by some percentage of a plaintiff's fault as well as by a prior settlement. How should such computations be made? See Whalen v. Kawasaki Motors Corp., 703 N.E.2d 246 (N.Y. 1998) (when plaintiff comparatively at fault and a defendant has settled prior to trial, settlement deducted from verdict first, then plaintiff's fault is allocated to remaining verdict).

4. In *Cartel Capital*, the court reduced the judgment by the settling defendant's equitable share as determined by the jury. In *Promaulayko*, although the jury assessed a percentage of fault against both defendant-distributors in strict liability, the court allowed the downstream distributor to recover indemnity against its upstream co-defendant. Does *Promaulayko* make sense in light of *Cartel Capital*? Does a good faith settlement between a plaintiff and a product defendant extinguish rights of indemnity other defendants might have against the settling defendant? Compare Dunn v. Kanawha County Board of Education, 459 S.E.2d 151 (W.Va. 1995) (no), with Frazer v. A.F. Munsterman, Inc., 527 N.E.2d 1248 (Ill.1988) (yes).

5. Releases. Does a general release given by a plaintiff to one defendant release other potential defendants not parties to nor mentioned in the release? In Hansen v. Ford Motor Co., 900 P.2d 952 (N.M.1995), plaintiff, who had been injured in an automobile accident in 1990 and signed a general release in settlement with the driver, subsequently sued Ford claiming a defective air bag caused her injuries. Ford claimed it was released from liability by the general release plaintiff executed with the driver. The court canvassed the different positions courts have taken and adopted the majority rule—that the parties' *intent* (rather than the form of the agreement) controls whether a general release includes unnamed parties, and that a rebuttable presumption exists that a release benefits only those persons specifically identified.

6. "Mary Carter" Agreements. "Mary Carter" agreements, a type of settlement device used in multi-party litigation, owe their name to the case of Booth v. Mary Carter Paint Co., 202 So.2d 8 (Fla.App.1967). Since that case, the term has come to mean "any agreement between the plaintiff and some (but less than all) defendants whereby the parties place limitations on the financial responsibility of the agreeing defendants, the amount of which is variable and usually in some inverse ratio to the amount of recovery which the plaintiff is able to make against the non-agreeing defendant or defendants." Maule Indus., Inc. v. Rountree, 264 So.2d 445 (Fla.App.1972). The Supreme Court of Florida described such agreements in Ward v. Ochoa, 284 So.2d 385 (Fla.1973):

> A "Mary Carter Agreement" ... is basically a contract by which one co-defendant secretly agrees with the plaintiff that, if such defendant will proceed to defend himself in court, his own maximum liability will be diminished proportionately by increasing the liability of the other co-defendants. Secrecy is the essence of such an arrangement because the court or jury as trier of the facts, if apprised of this, would likely weigh differently the testimony and conduct of the signing defendant as related to the non-signing defendant. By painting a gruesome testimonial picture of the other defendant's misconduct or, in some cases, by admissions against himself and the other defendants, he could diminish or eliminate his own liability by use of the secret "Mary Carter Agreement."

These agreements resemble covenants not to sue in that the plaintiff relinquishes his cause of action against the settling defendant. They have, however, two characteristics not found in covenants not to sue. First, the settling defendant remains an active participant in the litigation, in appearance but not in fact a true adversary of the plaintiff. Second, because of the refund provision, the settling defendant has an incentive to increase the plaintiff's recovery by presenting damaging testimony against the non-settling defendants. Freedman, The Expected Demise of "Mary Carter": She Never Was Well, 1975 Ins.L.J. 602, 609.

Most states require that such agreements be *disclosed* so that the bias of the settling defendant is revealed. See, e.g., Gatto v. Walgreen Drug Co., 337 N.E.2d 23 (Ill.1975); Carter v. Tom's Truck Repair, Inc., 857 S.W.2d 172 (Mo.banc 1993); Hatfield v. Continental Imports, Inc., 610 A.2d 446 (Pa.1992).

After giving birth to the "Mary Carter" agreement, the Florida Supreme Court subsequently concluded that such agreements are simply too injurious to the litigation process and refused to permit them. Dosdourian v. Carsten, 624 So.2d 241, 245 (Fla.1993). Accord, Elbaor v. Smith, 845 S.W.2d 240 (Tex.1992) (Mary Carter Agreements void as against public policy). Entman, Mary Carter Agreements: An Assessment of Attempted Solutions, 38 U.Fla.L.Rev. 521 (1986).

7. See generally Restatement (Third) of Torts: Apportionment §§ 26, 33; Uniform Comparative Fault Act; Bernstein and Klerman, An Economic Analysis of Mary Carter Agreements, 83 Geo.L.J. 2215 (1995); 2 D.Owen, M.S. Madden & M. Davis, Madden & Owen on Products Liability § 25:13 (3d ed. 2000).

CHAPTER 17

SPECIAL TYPES OF PRODUCTS AND TRANSACTIONS

Some products liability litigation involves transactions other than the typical sale of a new chattel. The principal issue involved in many of these cases is whether the principles of products liability law, particularly the doctrine of strict liability in tort, should be extended from the new chattel sale situation to another transactional context in which other policies and principles may predominate. In some of these situations, the differing objectives and doctrinal borderlines of products liability, premises liability, professional malpractice, environmental protection, and other areas of the law are brought into sharp relief.

As in the previous chapter, the essential question here is, How far should strict "products" liability law be extended?

1. LEASES AND BAILMENTS

Samuel Friedland Family Enterprises v. Amoroso

Supreme Court of Florida, 1994.
630 So.2d 1067.

■ GRIMES, J.

[The following question was certified by the District Court of Appeals:]

WHETHER THE DOCTRINE OF STRICT LIABILITY AS TO DEFECTIVE PRODUCTS EXTENDS TO COMMERCIAL LEASE TRANSACTIONS OF THOSE PRODUCTS?

* * *

The Diplomat Hotel is a waterfront property in Hollywood, Florida. Sunrise Water Sports, Inc. (Sunrise) leased part of the Diplomat's property and operated a sailboat rental stand there. The boats are owned by Sunrise. However, the actual rentals are handled by Atlantic Sailing Center, Inc. (Atlantic) which subleases the rental stand and was organized to operate the rental business at the Diplomat.

The Amorosos were guests at the Diplomat and rented sailboats on three occasions. The third time, Mrs. Amoroso was injured when the sailboat's crossbar broke. As a result of her injuries, Mr. and Mrs. Amoroso sued the Diplomat, Sunrise, Atlantic, and a welder who had repaired the crossbar a few days before the accident.

The Amorosos asserted a claim in strict liability against the Diplomat, Sunrise, and Atlantic. The trial court directed verdicts [for all] defendants on this claim. The district court of appeal reversed [holding] that the doctrine of strict liability extends to commercial lease transactions.[2]

The underlying basis for the doctrine of strict liability is that those entities within a product's distributive chain "who profit from the sale or distribution of [the product] to the public, rather than an innocent person injured by it, should bear the financial burden of even an undetectable product defect." [Citation.] Those entities are in a better position to ensure the safety of the products they market, to insure against defects in those products, and to spread the cost of any injuries resulting from a defect.

This Court adopted [§ 402A] in West v. Caterpillar Tractor Co., 336 So.2d 80, 87 (Fla.1976). In *West*, ... we recognized that a manufacturer, who places a potentially dangerous product on the market and encourages its use, undertakes a special responsibility toward members of the public who may be injured by the product. Since *West*, Florida courts have expanded the doctrine of strict liability to others in the distributive chain including retailers, wholesalers, and distributors. [In this case], we must decide whether the doctrine of strict liability applies to commercial lessors.

[Many courts have] held that commercial lessors can be held strictly liable for defective products they lease. . . . In Cintrone v. Hertz Truck Leasing & Rental Service, 212 A.2d 769, 778–79 (N.J.1965), the New Jersey Supreme Court held that a truck rental company could be held strictly liable for injuries caused by a defective condition in one of the trucks it leased. In reaching this conclusion, the court found little difference between sales and lease transactions, and recognized that, like a purchaser of new goods, a lessee is entitled to expect that a product is being delivered in a nondefective condition. In fact, after taking note of the growth of the car and truck rental business, the court suggested that the rationale for imposing strict liability on manufacturers and sellers may even be greater in the context of leased goods as a lessee usually has less opportunity to inspect items and lessors, by repeatedly introducing and reintroducing products into the stream of commerce, are exposing the public to a proportionately greater risk of injury.

In Price v. Shell Oil Co., 466 P.2d 722, 723 (Cal.1970), the Supreme Court of California also addressed the application of strict liability to commercial lease transactions. *Price* involved an aircraft mechanic who was injured when a ladder, which was attached to a gasoline truck, broke. The truck was leased by the mechanic's employer from Shell Oil Company.

Prior to *Price*, California courts had applied the doctrine of strict tort liability to manufacturers, retailers, suppliers of personal property, and

---

2. While the Diplomat was not the lessor of the sailboat, as such, the court held that there was sufficient evidence to prove that Sunrise was operating its business under the apparent authority of the Diplomat.

residential builders. In determining whether to further expand the strict liability cause of action, the court reasoned:

> Such a broad philosophy evolves naturally from the purpose of imposing strict liability which "is to insure that the costs of injuries resulting from defective products are borne by the manufacturers that put such products on the market rather than by the injured persons who are powerless to protect themselves." [Greenman v. Yuba Power Products, Inc., 377 P.2d 897, 901 (Cal.1963).] Essentially the paramount policy to be promoted by the rule is the protection of otherwise defenseless victims of manufacturing defects and the spreading throughout society of the cost of compensating them. . . .
>
> . . . We can perceive no substantial difference between *sellers* of personal property and *non-sellers*, such as bailors and lessors. In each instance, the seller or non-seller "places [an article] on the market, knowing that it is to be used without inspection for defects, . . ." [*Greenman.*] In light of the policy to be subserved, it should make no difference that the party distributing the article has retained title to it. Nor can we see how the risk of harm associated with the use of the chattel can vary with the legal form under which it is held. Having in mind the market realities and the widespread use of the lease of personalty in today's business world, we think it makes good sense to impose on the lessors of chattels the same liability for physical harm which has been imposed on the manufacturers and retailers. The former, like the latter, are able to bear the cost of compensating for injuries resulting from defects by spreading the loss through an adjustment of the rental.

Price, 466 P.2d at 725–26. The court concluded that lessors can be held strictly liable. However, this holding was limited to those lessors "found to be in the business of leasing, in the same general sense as the seller of personalty is found to be in the business of manufacturing or retailing." To do otherwise would work an injustice on those lessors who cannot adjust the costs associated with strict liability in an economically viable manner, such as where the lease is an isolated transaction.

The Diplomat argues that the district court opinion in the instant case "casts too wide a net." They contend that applying the doctrine of strict liability to *all* commercial lease transactions is unfair. It would cause a vast increase in potential liability which small businesses in Florida would be unable to bear. Thus, if we were to apply the doctrine of strict liability to commercial lease transactions, the Diplomat urges us to limit our holding to those lessors who are "mass dealers in chattel."

However, we note that no state which has applied strict liability to lessors has retreated from this view because of its economic consequences on commercial leasing. Also, we can find no express authority for the proposition that the doctrine of strict liability should be limited to those lessors who can be called "mass dealers in chattel," and, if such authority does exist, it is certainly a minority view. For purposes of applying strict liability, we can discern no reason to differentiate between a business which is a mass dealer in a product and one which is not, provided each is actually engaged in the business of leasing the defective product.

* * *

Mindful of the recent growth of the commercial leasing business in recent years, we believe that the rationale justifying the imposition of strict liability on manufacturers and sellers is also applicable to commercial lessors. Thus, we hold that the doctrine of strict liability is applicable to commercial lease transactions in Florida. However, we limit our holding to those lessors who are engaged in the business of leasing the allegedly defective product. The strict liability cause of action is not applicable to those leases which are isolated or infrequent transactions not related to the principal business of the lessor. [Citations.]

We turn now to the facts presented by the instant case. Sunrise leased the property on which the sailboat rental stand was located and owned the sailboats which were rented from the stand. The company was clearly engaged in the business of leasing sailboats and, therefore, could properly be held strictly liable for leasing a defective boat to the Amorosos.

The question of the Diplomat's liability is more difficult. The Diplomat is, of course, a hotel, and would not commonly be considered to be in the business of renting sailboats. On the other hand, the Diplomat leased its property to Sunrise specifically for the purpose of establishing a sailboat rental business and the hotel was actively involved in marketing the boats to its guests. The district court noted:

> The Diplomat placed brochures in each room advertising the availability of sailing at the hotel. The rental stand was on the Diplomat Beach. . . . [N]either Sunrise nor Atlantic were identified as the owner or operator at the beach. The sailboats were paid for by charging them to the room and leaving the room key as security for the rental. Mrs. Amoroso also testified that she saw in the brochure a sail with the Diplomat logo on it. . . . [T]his evidence taken together was sufficient to show that *the Diplomat represented to their guests that the sailboat rental stand was a part of the hotel operations.*

604 So.2d at 831. The emphasized portion is particularly significant. The record reflects that, when the Amorosos, and presumably the other hotel guests, rented a boat, they reasonably believed that they were renting it from the Diplomat. Further, the Amorosos were entitled to expect that the sailboat was being delivered to them in a safe, nondefective condition. We find that, under the circumstances presented here, the hotel's involvement was sufficient to sustain a strict liability cause of action against it as a lessor engaged in the business of leasing the sailboats.

Accordingly, we answer the certified question in the affirmative. [S]trict liability is applicable to commercial lease transactions, subject to the limitations set forth in this opinion, and [applies] to Sunrise and the Diplomat in this case.

■ McDONALD, J., concurring in part, dissenting in part; [OVERTON, J., concurs].

I fully concur with the decision under review insofar as it holds that the Diplomat and Sunrise may be held liable under the theories of implied warranty of fitness and negligence. There clearly is an implied warranty of fitness for ordinary use in the leasing of boats by a hotel, its agents, or its franchisees, to members of the public. Strict liability, on the other hand, has serious overtones. I do not feel it is appropriate to apply this doctrine to a hotel where the furnishing of rental boats is an incidental part of its business. I thus dissent to that part of the majority opinion extending strict liability to the Diplomat in this case. The implied warranty of fitness and negligence theories are adequate to protect the public.

NOTES

1. Cintrone v. Hertz Truck Leasing and Rental Service, 212 A.2d 769 (N.J. 1965), discussed by the court was the path-breaking case extending liability without fault to commercial lease transactions. It has been widely followed. E.g., Ruzzo v. LaRose Enter., 748 A.2d 261 (R.I. 2000); Francioni v. Gibsonia Truck Corp., 372 A.2d 736 (Pa.1977); Stang v. Hertz Corp., 497 P.2d 732 (N.M.1972).

2. Ski resorts and ski equipment lessors have been held strictly liable for leasing defective ski equipment, notwithstanding contractual efforts to release themselves from liability. See, e.g., Ghionis v. Deer Valley Resort Co., 839 F.Supp. 789 (D.Utah 1993); Westlye v. Look Sports, Inc., 22 Cal.Rptr.2d 781 (Ct.App.1993). Compare Katz v. Slade, 460 S.W.2d 608 (Mo.1970) (strict liability claim against municipality dismissed where golf cart leased from municipal golf course malfunctioned; course was operated as a recreational resource for city residents, not a commercial venture).

3. Should a laundromat be strictly liable in tort as a "lessor" of defective washers and dryers that injure its patrons? See Garcia v. Halsett, 82 Cal.Rptr. 420, 423 (Ct.App.1970). A young boy's arm became entangled in clothing and was injured when a defective washing machine at defendant's laundromat unexpectedly began to spin. *Held,* although this was a license rather than a lease transaction, a strict tort action against the laundromat owner would lie:

> Although respondent is not engaged in the distribution of the product, in the same manner as a manufacturer, retailer or lessor, he does provide the product to the public for use by the public, and consequently does play more than a random and accidental role in the overall marketing enterprise of the product in question.

Keen v. Dominick's Finer Foods, Inc.

Appellate Court of Illinois, 1977.
49 Ill.App.3d 480, 7 Ill.Dec. 341, 364 N.E.2d 502.

■ McNAMARA, JUSTICE.

[Plaintiff, Eleanore Keen, sued Dominick's Finer Foods seeking damages for injuries sustained while she was using a shopping cart in a Dominick's grocery store. Her complaint alleged theories of negligence, strict products liability, breach of implied warranty, and breach of duty of care by a bailor. The trial court granted Dominick's motion to strike all counts except that based upon negligence. Plaintiff appeals the dismissal of her claim for strict tort liability.]

[Plaintiff alleged that while she was using a grocery cart, it began to tip over, and she was injured while attempting to prevent it from overturning. She claimed that it was not reasonably safe for use in that it was inclined to collapse in a manner which would cause it to roll onto its side and injure its user. Dominick's defended on the ground that it could not be held strictly liable since it had not placed the cart into the stream of commerce, and the trial court agreed.]

The nature of a manufacturer's liability for placing a defective product into the stream of commerce was set out in Suvada v. White Motor Co., 210 N.E.2d 182, 188 (Ill.1965):

> "... The plaintiffs must prove that their injury or damage resulted from a condition of the product, that the condition was an unreasonably dangerous one and that the condition existed at the time it left the manufacturer's control...."

The rule promulgated in *Suvada* is in accordance with the Restatement (Second) of Torts § 402A (1964)....

In Dunham v. Vaughan and Bushnell Mfg. Co., 247 N.E.2d 401 (Ill.1969), the court stated that [strict products liability in tort] applies [equally] to all the parties in a chain who place the article into commerce. While liability does not depend upon whether there was an actual sales transaction [citation], ... the party to be charged with liability [must] be in the business of placing the allegedly defective product into the stream of commerce. [L]iability rests upon the defendant's active participation in placing the product into commerce for use and consumption by others. [An important reason for] strict liability is to ensure that losses are borne by those who have created the risk and subsequently reaped the profit of marketing the allegedly defective product....

In the present case, plaintiff concedes that Dominick's is not in the business of either selling or renting shopping carts. She maintains, however, that although Dominick's gratuitously furnishes the carts to its customers, such is done as an incident of the sale of the items which constitutes Dominick's business. In attempting to hold Dominick's strictly liable, plaintiff relies [on] Bainter v. Lamoine LP Gas Co., 321 N.E.2d 744 (Ill.1974). [This court there] permitted a cause of action in strict products liability against a defendant who supplied a defective tank for storage of gas sold to the plaintiff. The tank was characterized as an incident of the sale of the gas and the consideration given for the gas was deemed to include the use of the tank.

The facts in *Bainter* differ demonstrably from those in the present case. In *Bainter* the fluidity of the product compelled supplying the tank as a necessary concomitant of the sale of gas. The shopping cart, on the other hand, can be classified only as a convenient receptacle which the customer may temporarily utilize to move groceries to the checkout or outside to the customer's automobile. Not every customer will use a shopping cart. It is our opinion that to hold Dominick's liable under the principles of strict products liability would [extend the principles too far].... [Unlike *Bainter*, i]n the present case, plaintiff's use of the allegedly defective shopping cart could only be considered as a use of a convenience furnished by Dominick's to facilitate its customers' shopping. Any mishap which might occur from availing oneself of such a convenience does not render the store liable under the principles of strict products liability. In this case, the allegedly defective shopping cart was placed into the stream of commerce by the parties responsible for its distribution to Dominick's. The store, like its customer, is merely a user of the shopping cart.

Public policy considerations do not demand that the duty of a storekeeper to keep its premises in a safe condition be elevated beyond the traditional standard of reasonable care. [Citation.] Plaintiff [may make a] strict products liability [claim] against the manufacturer of the shopping cart and others who placed the shopping cart into the stream of commerce and reaped the profits therefrom. We simply hold that Dominick's [is not] part of the distributive chain within the ambit of the principles of strict products liability.

[Dismissal of the strict products liability count affirmed.]

■ SIMON, PRESIDING JUSTICE, dissenting.

[P]laintiff should be permitted to proceed to trial on her strict products liability count. Dominick's was part of the stream of commerce flowing from the cart's manufacturer to the plaintiff. The cart was intended for use by customers of grocery supermarkets. It reached the plaintiff through Dominick's. Therefore, the stream of commerce did not stop, as the majority views it, with the parties who distributed the cart to Dominick's, but continued until the cart reached the customers who were intended to use it and for whose use Dominick's supplied it. The approach of the majority is that Dominick's is the consumer or user of the carts. On the other hand, I regard Dominick's as the supplier of the carts to its customers and, therefore, as a conduit in the marketing chain which brought the carts to their ultimate users, Dominick's customers.

... It would be virtually impossible for a customer to make substantial purchases at Dominick's supermarts without the use of a cart. The customer may be regarded as paying for this use because the cart is a cost of doing business which no doubt is reflected in the charge Dominick's makes for its merchandise. Strict liability [seeks] to ensure that losses are borne by those who reap the profit of marketing an allegedly defective product. By supplying the carts, Dominick's fits within this rationale....

NOTES

1. In Safeway Stores, Inc. v. Nest–Kart, 579 P.2d 441 (Cal.1978), a supermarket shopping cart broke and fell on plaintiff's foot. The jury found the supermarket 80% liable, in negligence and strict liability in tort, and the cart manufacturer 20% liable in strict liability. Without discussing the propriety of the strict liability claim against the supermarket, the Supreme Court approved the verdict.

2. With Bainter v. Lamoine LP Gas Co., 321 N.E.2d 744 (Ill.App.1974), discussed in *Keen,* compare Shaffer v. Victoria Station, Inc., 588 P.2d 233 (Wash. 1978)(restaurant liable in both warranty and strict tort for injuries to patron from wine glass shattering in his hand).

3. Warranty—Generally. In Garfield v. Furniture Fair–Hanover, 274 A.2d 325 (N.J.Super.Ct. Law Div.1971), a woman was injured when a bed collapsed that had been loaned to her and her husband by the defendant furniture store pending the delivery of a new bed they had purchased. *Held,* since plaintiffs had never taken title to the loaned bed, and since they were bound to return it upon delivery of the purchased bed, the transaction was a bailment rather than a sale under U.C.C. § 2–106(1). Nor had the bailment become integrated into the sale of the new bed so as to extend the warranties attaching to the sale to the bailment as well. See also Ferrucci v. Atlantic City Showboat, Inc., 51 F.Supp.2d 129 (D.Conn. 1999)(hotel not liable under bailment for bed which allegedly caused plaintiff to trip).

4. Warranty—UCC Article 2A. A number of cases had applied Article 2 to the lease context, but in 1987, NCCUSL and the ALI promulgated UCC Article 2A, Leases, which was quickly enacted in a significant number of states. The key warranty provisions closely mimic those in Article 2: § 2A–210 (express warranties), § 2A–212 (implied warranty of merchantability), § 2A–213 (implied warranty of fitness for a particular purpose), § 2A–214 (exclusion or modification of warranties), § 2A–216 (third party beneficiaries, including alternatives A, B, and C), § 2A–503 (modification or impairment of rights and remedies, including prima facie unconscionability for injury to the person in the case of consumer goods), § 2A–520 (lessee's incidental and consequential damages, including injury to person or property proximately resulting from breach). In 2003, Article 2A was revised to reflect debate over issues regarding security interests and the remedy structure under Article 2A. The warranty provisions were modified consistently with revisions to the mirror provisions in Article 2.

5. On leases and bailments generally, see Products Liability Restatement § 20; Ausness, Strict Liability for Chattel Leasing, 48 U. Pitt. L. Rev. 273 (1987); D. Owen, Products Liability Law, § 16.2 (2d ed. 2008).

---

2. SERVICES

Cafazzo v. Central Medical Health Services, Inc.

Supreme Court of Pennsylvania, 1995.
542 Pa. 526, 668 A.2d 521.

■ MONTEMURO, JUSTICE.

[The question of first impression is whether a hospital and a doctor can be held subject to strict liability under § 402A] for defects in a product incidental to the provision of medical services.

In 1986, appellant Albert Cafazzo underwent surgery for implantation of a mandibular prosthesis. In 1992, some time after it was discovered that this device was defective, a complaint was filed [against] the physician who performed the surgery and the hospital where the operation took place, claiming that "all defendants sell, provide or use certain prosthetic devices," and that they should be held strictly liable as having "provided, sold or otherwise placed in the stream of commerce products manufactured by Vitek, Inc., known as Proplast TMJ Implants." The complaint alleged that the prosthesis was defectively designed, unsafe for its intended use, and lacked any warning necessary in order to ensure safety.

[The trial court granted the defendants' demurrer, the Superior Court affirmed, and plaintiff appealed. This Court finds that defendants are not "sellers" for purposes of § 402A, and] that even if defendants could be shown to have "marketed" the prosthesis, strict liability does not apply.

Section 402A of the Restatement (Second) of Torts, provides [strict liability for "one who sells" any product in a defective condition unreasonably dangerous. The plaintiff's effort to have us slavishly adhere to the language of 402A] makes a mockery of the idea behind strict liability, i.e., that it inheres only in situations where a defective product has been provided by a seller "engaged in the business of selling such a product."

In Musser v. Vilsmeier Auction Co., Inc., 562 A.2d 279 (Pa.1989), this Court observed that "the broadened concept of" supplier, "for purposes of predicating strict liability, is not without practical limits. The limits obtain in the purposes of the policy. When those purposes will not be served, persons whose implication in supplying products is tangential to that undertaking will not be subjected to strict liability for the harms caused by defects in those products." The policy behind strict liability is "to insure that the costs of injuries resulting from defective products are borne by the manufacturers who put such products on the market rather than by the injured persons who are powerless to help themselves." Shepard v. Alexian Brothers Hosp., 109 Cal.Rptr. 132, 132 (Ct.App.1973), and to further insure that defective products are removed from the market.

In this instance, the manufacturer is in bankruptcy, and unable to sustain liability. Thus, an alternative, and solvent, payor was sought. All other considerations were subordinated to this objective, hence the unequivocal necessity, in plaintiff's view, for defendants to be designated as sellers irrespective of the actual facts of this matter. However, to ignore the ancillary nature of the association of product with activity is to posit surgery, or indeed any medical service requiring the use of a physical object, as a marketing device for the incorporated object. This is tantamount to deciding that the surgical skills necessary for the implantation of [the TMJ prostheses] are an adjunct to the sale of the implants. Moreover, under such a theory, no product of which a patient in any medical setting is the ultimate consumer, from CT scanners to cotton balls, could escape the assignment of strict liability. Clearly, the relationship of hospital and/or doctor to patients is not dictated by the distribution of such products, even if there is some surcharge on the price of the product. As the New York Court of Appeals has aptly stated,

> Concepts of purchase and sale cannot be separately attached to the healing materials ... supplied by the hospital for a price as part of the medical services. That the property or title to certain items of medical material may be transferred, so to speak, from the hospital to the patient during the

course of medical treatment does not serve to make such a transaction a sale. "Sale" and "transfer" are not synonymous, and not every transfer of personal property constitutes a sale.

Perlmutter v. Beth David Hospital, 123 N.E.2d 792, 794 (N.Y.1954).

The thrust of the inquiry is thus not on whether a separate consideration is charged for the physical material used in the exercise of medical skill, but what service is performed to restore or maintain the patient's health. The determinative question becomes not what is being charged, but what is being done. See Hoff v. Zimmer, 746 F.Supp. 872 (W.D.Wis.1990) (strict liability not applied to hospital for failure of hip prosthesis); [citations]; Magrine v. Krasnica, 250 A.2d 129 (N.J.1969)(strict liability not applied to dentist whose drill broke while in use on patient).

The cases cited above have been labeled by some the exponents of a "service exception" to 402A. However, the very term "service exception" is misleading, since it presupposes that the distinction drawn where medical personnel/hospitals are involved is an artificial one. The cases, however, make clear that provision of medical services is regarded as qualitatively different from the sale of products, and, rather than being an exception to 402A, is unaffected by it. [Case law applying this distinction under 402A make clear that] what has been provided is not medical service or products connected with diagnosis and treatment, but rather materials related to mechanical or administrative functions. See Thomas v. St. Joseph Hospital, 618 S.W.2d 791 (Tex.Civ.App.1981) (hospital held strictly liable where hospital gown ignited when lighted match fell on it); [citation].

In this connection, it must be noted that the "seller" need not be engaged solely in the business of selling products such as the defective one to be held strictly liable. An example supporting this proposition appears in comment f of the Restatement (Second) of Torts, § 402A and concerns the owner of a motion picture theater who offers edibles such as popcorn and candy for sale to movie patrons. The analogue to the instant case is valid in one respect only: both the candy and the TMJ implant are ancillary to the primary activity, viewing a film or undergoing surgery respectively. However, beyond that any comparison is specious. A movie audience is free to purchase or not any food items on offer, and regardless of which option is exercised the primary activity is unaffected. On the other hand, while the implant was incidental to the surgical procedure here, it was a necessary adjunct to the treatment administered, as were the scalpel used to make the incision, and any other material objects involved in performing the operation, all of which fulfill a particular role in provision of medical service, the primary activity. Once the illness became evident, treatment of some kind became a matter of necessity to regain health. [W]hen one enters the hospital as a patient[,] he goes there, not to buy medicines or pills, not to purchase bandages or iodine or serum or blood, but to obtain a course of treatment in the hope of being cured of what ails him. Perlmutter v. Beth David Hospital, 123 N.E.2d 792, 795 (N.Y.1954).

[Consistent with these decisions, which distinguish medical services from merchandising, we conclude that defendants are not sellers, providers, suppliers or distributors of products so as to activate 402A. Yet, even if providers of medical services could reasonably be termed sellers,] the policy reasons for strict liability are not present.

[This court applied a policy test] in Francioni v. Gibsonia Truck Corp., 372 A.2d 736 (Pa. 1977), to determine whether a particular supplier of products, whose status as a supplier is already determined, is to be held liable for damages caused by defects in the products supplied. It was first concluded that a lessor of hauling equipment could properly be considered a supplier after the application of a four part inquiry, which focuses initially on [1] which members of the marketing chain are available for redress; then asks [2] whether imposition of liability would serve as an incentive to safety; [3] whether the supplier is in a better position than the consumer to prevent the circulation of defective products; and, finally, [4] whether the supplier can distribute the cost of compensation for injuries by charging for it in his business.

[Plaintiff's case fails this test.] First, as to the availability of some entity for redress, medical personnel and hospitals are already subject to liability, albeit only where the quality or quantity of the services they provide may be called into question. It is perfectly reasonable to assume, for example, that a physician or hospital possesses the necessary skill and expertise to select a product for use in medical treatment which is fit for its intended purpose. An error of choice might indeed be attributed to negligence or ignorance. However, no allegation has been made that the selection of the Vitek TMJ was made either carelessly or intentionally despite knowledge of its defects. To assign liability for no reason other than the ability to pay damages is inconsistent with our jurisprudence. . . .

Next comes the matter of whether applying strict liability would provide an incentive to safety. The safety of the product depends on the judgment of those connected to the research, development, manufacture, marketing and sale of the product. [Citation.] Moreover, the safety testing and licensing for use of medical devices is a responsibility specifically undertaken by the federal government. Therefore, imposing liability for a poorly designed or manufactured product on the hospitals and doctors who use them on the assurances of the FDA is highly unlikely to effect changes of this sort. Again, selection of the wrong product becomes a matter of professional negligence for which recovery is available.

As to the related matter of restricting circulation of defective products, defendants and those similarly situated have no control over distribution. In *Musser*, this Court noted that the "[control] factor implies the existence of some ongoing relationship with the manufacturer from which some financial advantage inures to the benefit of the latter and which confers some degree of influence on the [putative seller.]"

The influence described is that of the putative seller, i.e., doctor/hospital, on the manufacturing process. However, in finding the relationship between auctioneer and product too tenuous to justify assignment of liability, the *Musser* Court notes that the catalogue of items for sale listed more than ninety different tractors, for each of which the auctioneer would have to be held strictly liable were 402A applied in the auction context. The list is easily comparable to the many items employed in surgery, which includes but is not limited to surgical instruments, medical devices such as the implant, anesthesia machine and accoutrements, drugs, bandages and dressings, surgical apparel and operating suite furniture, such as the table on which the procedure is performed.

The implications of the ruling espoused by plaintiff extend far beyond responsibility for a defective TMJ [implant], and thus bring into sharp relief the problems surrounding [such an extension]. The difficulties inherent in such a course are obvious; particularly in medicine, the changes in technology are such that even definitional problems may arise. As an example, for purposes of 402A, is gene therapy a drug, and thus exempt under comment k, or a device, or something else altogether? . . .

The fourth question posed is whether the supplier of the product can distribute the cost of compensating for injuries resulting from defects by spreading the charges therefor. The Superior Court, in addressing this element [noted that the use of the compensation and cost spreading rationales as the only considerations] would result in absolute rather than strict liability [and] would confine the focus of the 402A principle to the search for a deep pocket. The net effect of this cost spreading would further endanger the already beleaguered health care system. As a practical matter costs would merely be absorbed by the insurers of physicians and hospitals, whose charges would reflect the increase in policy rates without corresponding improvement to any aspect of the health care system. . . . In short, medical services are distinguished by factors which make them significantly different in kind from the retail marketing enterprise at which 402A is directed.

[B]efore a change in the law is made, a court, [should strive to anticipate] the results of its decision and to say with reasonable certainty that the change will serve the best interests of society.

The consequences of a step such as plaintiff would have us take are of such magnitude, and of such potentially negative effect as to require more examination than has yet been afforded this issue. It is, for example, not clear enough that strict liability has afforded the hoped for panacea in the conventional products area that it should be extended so cavalierly in cases such as the present one.

[Affirmed.]

■ CAPPY, JUSTICE, dissents.

I am deeply troubled by the majority's opinion and therefore must respectfully dissent.

[By mistakenly deferring] to the law of foreign jurisdictions, the majority has also distorted our established case law. In analyzing the *Francioni* test, the majority has presented a muddled view of the test's purpose and an imperfect application of the test's prongs.

[The majority misapplies the four prongs of the *Francioni* test. It sidesteps the first prong by redefining it;] ostensibly applying this test, [the majority] concludes that the defendants are not amenable to strict liability because "medical personnel and hospitals are already subject to liability, albeit only where the quality or quantity of the services they provide may be called into question." This answer is a non-sequitur; the majority has sidestepped, rather than answered, the pertinent query of whether doctors and hospitals are in the marketing chain of this prosthesis. Furthermore, . . . it seems not to matter to the majority whether the plaintiff in the case before the court actually has that "other" cause of action available to it. I find this "test" perplexing for I can think of no entity which would not be excluded under the test fashioned by the majority. Thus, what purpose would this new "test" serve other than to eradicate strict liability?

Second, the majority also distorts the *Francioni* prong which directs the Court to ascertain whether this defendant is in a better position than the consumer to prevent the circulation of defective products. The majority commences its analysis of this point by recognizing that the focus of this inquiry is on whether there is "some ongoing relationship with the manufacturer from which some financial advantage inures to the benefit of the latter and which confers some degree of influence on the [putative seller]." *Musser.* The majority, however, rapidly loses sight of its objective. It deduces that since the defendants here have an extensive list of products at their disposal, as did the defendant in *Musser*, then the defendants here should also be held immune from strict liability as was the defendant in *Musser*. This distortion of *Musser* could have frighteningly far-reaching implications. Such reasoning would lead to the absurd result that a department store, with an inventory of tens of thousands of items, would be less likely to be held strictly liable than the local, family-run convenience store with its modest inventory. Such a "test" does not advance the goals of strict liability, but rather perverts them.

I am gravely concerned that the majority's opinion will have an unwanted and adverse impact on our strict liability law. In an effort to reach its result in the area of medical services, the majority has failed to advance with caution. . . .

NOTES

1. Also ruling that strict products liability does *not* apply to such transactions, see Royer v. Catholic Med. Ctr., 741 A.2d 74 (N.H. 1999) (prosthetic knee); In re Breast Implant Prod. Liab. Litig., 503 S.E.2d 445 (S.C. 1998) (breast implants); St. Mary Med. Ctr. v. Casko, 639 N.E.2d 312 (Ind.App.1994) (pacemaker). Missouri courts had permitted such actions, but the Missouri legislature subsequently prohibited strict liability against health care providers. Budding v. SSM Healthcare Sys., 19 S.W.3d 678 (Mo. 2000).

2. The classic case on the responsibility of a provider of pure services is Gagne v. Bertran, 275 P.2d 15, 20–21 (Cal.1954) (Traynor, J.), which involved the liability of a soil tester for an erroneous report:

The evidence in the present case does not justify the imposition of the strict liability of a warranty. There was no express warranty agreement, and there is nothing in the evidence to indicate that defendant assumed responsibility for the accuracy of his statements.... The amount of his fee and the fact that he was paid by the hour also indicate that he was selling service and not insurance. Thus the general rule is applicable that those who sell their services for the guidance of others in their economic, financial, and personal affairs are not liable in the absence of negligence or intentional misconduct.

* * *

The services of experts are sought because of their special skill. They have a duty to exercise the ordinary skill and competence of members of their profession, and a failure to discharge that duty will subject them to liability for negligence. Those who hire such persons are not justified in expecting infallibility, but can expect only reasonable care and competence. They purchase service, not insurance.

Thus, doctors uniformly have been held not subject to strict liability for medical accidents arising out of their treatment. Barton v. Owen, 139 Cal.Rptr. 494 (Ct.App.1977); Hoven v. Kelble, 256 N.W.2d 379 (Wis.1977).

3. Sales–Service Hybrid Transactions. The difficulty arises when a transaction partakes both of a sale component and a services component. What then? Most courts search for the " *'essence'* of the transaction" to ascertain whether the sale or service aspect predominates. See Sapp v. Morton Buildings, Inc., 973 F.2d 539 (7th Cir.1992) (Indiana Product Liability Act does not apply to "a transaction that, by its nature, involves wholly or predominantly the sale of a service rather than a product"; *held*, providing customized horse stable was a "service"). See generally Products Liability Restatement § 20 (c), cmt. *d*.

4. Pharmacists. Assuming that the *Cafazzo* majority is correct in holding that doctors and hospitals should not be liable for "selling" patients defective medical implants, should pharmacists be liable for selling drugs that are defective in design or have inadequate warnings? Considering the types and amounts of ordinary merchandise sold by pharmacies, are they more like hospitals and doctors or more like K–Mart? Or should the question be narrowed to the particular transaction giving rise to the plaintiff's injury? See Murphy v. E.R. Squibb & Sons, Inc., 710 P.2d 247 (Cal.1985) (DES causing cancer in daughter—no strict liability); Coyle v. Richardson–Merrell, Inc., 584 A.2d 1383 (Pa.1991) (no strict liability duty to warn); Frye v. Medicare–Glaser Corp., 605 N.E.2d 557 (Ill.1992) (no strict liability or negligence duty to warn of all dangerous side effects). Contra, Hooks SuperX, Inc. v. McLaughlin, 642 N.E.2d 514 (Ind.1994) (pharmacist knew patient using addictive pain killer improperly); Heredia v. Johnson, 827 F.Supp. 1522 (D.Nev. 1993) (pharmacist in distribution chain—strict liability duty to warn).

5. Professionals. Consider the broader issue of whether *nonmedical* professionals—architects, engineers, lawyers, and law professors—should be exempted from strict liability coverage when they provide defective "products" in the course of providing their professional services. There is broad agreement that such "professionals" should *not* be strictly liable for their errors. The architect cases are illustrative. In Bruzga v. PMR Architects, P.C., 693 A.2d 401, 405 (N.H. 1997), the court remarked:

[W]e are not convinced that architects and contractors are able to spread their economic losses as easily as manufacturers are able to spread their losses to the consumers of their mass-produced goods. While manufacturers "have ample opportunity to test their products for defects before marketing them, the same cannot be said of architects. Normally, an architect has but a single chance to create a design for a client which will produce a defect-free structure." City of Mounds View v. Walijarvi, 263 N.W.2d 420, 425 (Minn. 1978).

Architects and building contractors are not in the business of "mass production and distribution of goods to a large body of distant consumers." [Citations]. Simply stated, "the raising of a building and the assembly-line manufacturing of a product are not analogous processes." Comment, Strict Liability and the Building Industry, 33 Emory L.J. 175 (1984); [citations].

Consider also City of Mounds View v. Walijarvi, 263 N.W.2d 420, 424–25 (Minn. 1978), reconsidering the majority rule:

> The reasoning underlying the general rule as it applies both to architects and other vendors of professional services is relatively straightforward. Architects, doctors, engineers, attorneys, and others deal in somewhat inexact sciences and are continually called upon to exercise their skilled judgment in order to anticipate and provide for random factors which are incapable of precise measurement. The indeterminate nature of these factors makes it impossible for professional service people to gauge them with complete accuracy in every instance. Thus, doctors cannot promise that every operation will be successful; a lawyer can never be certain that a contract he drafts is without latent ambiguity; and an architect cannot be certain that a structural design will interact with natural forces as anticipated. Because of the inescapable possibility of error which inheres in these services, the law has traditionally required, not perfect results, but rather the exercise of that skill and judgment which can be reasonably expected from similarly situated professionals. * * *

Contra, holding that a design professional impliedly warrants that the structure will be reasonably fit for its intended use, Broyles v. Brown Engineering Co., 151 So.2d 767 (Ala.1963) (as to routine engineering survey of subdivision drainage requirements); Bloomsburg Mills, Inc. v. Sordoni Const. Co., 164 A.2d 201 (Pa.1960). Professionals are liable for their negligent mistakes.

6. Nonprofessional Services. Compare Newmark v. Gimbel's Inc., 246 A.2d 11 (N.J.Super.Ct.App.Div. 1968), where the customer of a beauty parlor lost her hair and developed contact dermatitis due to a permanent wave solution applied by the defendant beautician. Plaintiff's warranty claims were dismissed by the trial court, and plaintiff appealed:

> Mrs. Newmark was a regular customer of defendant and had a weekly appointment to have her hair washed and set. On the day in question she received something in addition—a permanent wave. In essence, it involved application of a permanent wave lotion or solution and thereafter a neutralizer. The lotion was selected by one of defendant's operators who was familiar with her scalp and hair from current examination and prior visits. The product was secured from sources known to defendant and only defendant knew of any special instructions concerning its use. The risk from use of the lotion was incident to the operation of defendant's business ... yielded it a profit and placed it in a position to promote safety through pressure on suppliers. It was in a position to protect itself by making inquiry or tests to determine the susceptibility of customers to the use of

the product, or by using another lotion which did not present the possibility of an adverse effect. It could secure indemnity from its suppliers through legal proceedings or otherwise. The fact that there was no separate charge for the product did not preclude its being considered [a supplier] to the customer in a sense justifying the imposition of an implied warranty against injurious defects therein.

The facts in Magrine v. Krasnica, [227 A.2d 539 (N.J.Super.Ct.1967)], on which defendant principally relies, are clearly distinguishable. That case involved a hypodermic needle, a tool of the dental profession, which was never intended to be supplied to the patient or consumed in the course of dental treatment. Here the product supplied to Mrs. Newmark was used up in the process of giving her a permanent wave. While it was later rinsed out, its effect was intended to remain and be part of the finished product. * * *

The Appellate Division reversed the trial court's dismissal and the Supreme Court affirmed. 258 A.2d 697, 702–03. Justice Francis, who had penned *Henningsen* nearly a decade earlier, spoke for a unanimous court:

Defendants suggest that there is no doctrinal basis for distinguishing the services rendered by a beauty parlor operator from those rendered by a dentist or a doctor, and that consequently the liability of all three should be tested by the same principles. On the contrary there is a vast difference in the relationships. The beautician is engaged in a commercial enterprise; the dentist and doctor in a profession. The former caters publicly not to a need but to a form of aesthetic convenience or luxury, involving the rendition of non-professional services and the application of products for which a charge is made. The dentist or doctor does not and cannot advertise for patients; the demand for his services stems from a felt necessity of the patient. In response to such a call the doctor, and to a somewhat lesser degree the dentist, exercises his best judgment in diagnosing the patient's ailment or disability, prescribing and sometimes furnishing medicines or other methods of treatment which he believes, and in some measure hopes, will relieve or cure the condition. His performance is not mechanical or routine because each patient requires individual study and formulation of an informed judgment as to the physical or mental disability or condition presented, and the course of treatment needed.... Practitioners of such callings, licensed by the State to practice after years of study and preparation, must be deemed to have a special and essential role in our society, that of studying our physical and mental ills and ways to alleviate or cure them, and that of applying their knowledge, empirical judgment and skill in an effort to diagnose and then to relieve or to cure the ailment of a particular patient. Thus their paramount function—the essence of their function—ought to be regarded as the furnishing of opinions and services. Their unique status and the rendition of these *sui generis* services bear such a necessary and intimate relationship to public health and welfare that their obligation ought to be grounded and expressed in a duty to exercise reasonable competence and care toward their patients. In our judgment, the nature of the services, the utility of and the need for them, involving as they do, the health and even survival of many people, are so important to the general welfare as to outweigh in the policy scale any need for the imposition on dentists and doctors of the rules of strict liability in tort.

7. Policy or Politics? Are you persuaded of the fundamental difference between professional and nonprofessional services? Do you sense a kernel of class consciousness between the rulers and the ruled? See Murphy v. E.R. Squibb & Sons, Inc., 710 P.2d 247, 258 (Cal.1985)(Bird, J., dissenting)(protecting pharmacists as "professionals" creates "elitist distinctions"). Do you see an analogy to the reluctance of managers of industrial enterprises to have their design decisions second-guessed in a courtroom? To the discretionary function exception of the FTCA?

8. Line–Drawing. Putting aside the merits of the distinction, drawing the line between "professional" and "nonprofessional" services is not always easy. Should the prescription, fitting and sale of contact lenses result in strict liability on the optometrist for eye damage caused by an improper curvature in the lenses? Is it relevant that optometrists must be licensed? That the defendant operates a chain of 84 offices throughout the state? That it advertises in newspapers, radio and television? That a standard fee is charged, regardless of the complexity of the individual's eye problems or the number of fittings required? See Barbee v. Rogers, 425 S.W.2d 342 (Tex.1968).

9. Installers. Do the policies underlying strict liability for sellers of defective goods apply to those who *install* the goods in a faulty manner? Most courts hold not. E.g., Saddler v. Alaska Marine Lines, Inc., 856 P.2d 784 (Alaska 1993)(common carrier that pumped explosive asphalt materials into tanks); Monte Vista Dev. Corp. v. Superior Ct., 277 Cal.Rptr. 608 (Ct.App.1991) (tile subcontractor not liable for bathtub soap dish that broke). Some apply strict liability in warranty or tort, particularly if the installer participates in the product's design or manufacture. E.g., Prompt Air, Inc. v. Firewall Forward, Inc., 707 N.E.2d 235 (Ill.App. 1999)(installer of defective turbocharger in airplane strictly liable); Miller v. Solaglas California, Inc., 870 P.2d 559 (Colo.App.1993)(auto windshield installation service which used faulty sealant was product "seller" because it substantially "altered" the product).

10. Repairers. Should strict liability principles apply to faulty *repair*? *No*: Micciche v. Eastern Elevator Co., 645 A.2d 278 (Pa.Super.Ct.1994)(elevator); Rolph v. EBI Companies, 464 N.W.2d 667 (Wis.1991)(reconditioner of bending roll machine); Winans v. Rockwell Int'l Corp., 705 F.2d 1449 (5th Cir.1983)(jet plane). What if the repairer was the original seller or manufacturer and alters the product? Young v. Aro Corp., 111 Cal.Rptr. 535 (Ct.App.1973). Or if repairs create a deceptive appearance of safety? Anderson v. Glynn Const. Co., 421 N.W.2d 141 (Iowa 1988).

Rossetti v. Busch Entertainment Corp.

United States District Court, Eastern District of Pennsylvania, 2000.
87 F.Supp.2d 415.

■ ROBRENO, DISTRICT JUDGE.

[Plaintiff seeks damages for injuries she sustained while riding on an attraction at an amusement park. Defendant Busch Entertainment Corporation d/b/a Sesame Place ("Busch"), the amusement park owner, seeks partial summary judgment on plaintiff's breach of warranty and strict liability claims. Plaintiff has also sued Waterworld, the manufacturer of the water ride on which she was injured, but it has not appeared. Judgment against it was rendered in favor of plaintiff.]

... Plaintiff, accompanied by friends and family, went to Sesame Place, an amusement park, which is owned and operated by Busch. Like all park patrons, plaintiff paid an admission fee to enter the park. While at the park, plaintiff went for a ride on what is known as the "Sky Splash" attraction. The "Sky Splash" consists of a water slide on which small groups of park patrons descend in oversized rafts. At one point, the raft rose and came down hard, jolting plaintiff. As a result of that "jolt," plaintiff suffered serious injury to her back.

[The court dismissed plaintiff's breach of warranty claim against Busch rejecting plaintiff's assertion that Busch, by selling an admission ticket to her, which allowed her to ride on the park's attractions, was selling her a "good."] Busch next contends that it is entitled to summary judgment on plaintiff's strict liability claim.... under section 402A because "it is not engaged in the business of selling a product, rather, it is in the business of proving amusement rides to its patrons," (citing Malloy v. Doty Conveyor, 820 F.Supp. 217, 220 (E.D.Pa.1993)("federal courts applying Pennsylvania law have made clear that strict products liability has not been expanded to include persons who provide only services")). Busch further argues that a consideration of the policy reasons behind imposing strict liability and the lack of evidence put forth by plaintiff dictate a finding in its favor.

In her response to Busch's motion, plaintiff argues that Busch "could be deemed a 'seller' or 'supplier' under section 402A" as interpreted by the Pennsylvania courts. Plaintiff then argues that a balancing of the policy considerations behind the imposition of strict liability weigh in favor of imposing strict liability on Busch.

The Pennsylvania Supreme Court has stated that "[t]he affixation of strict liability for damages caused by defective products to sellers of those products is based on policy which has as its purpose the protection of the public against the harms such defects engender." Musser v. Vilsmeier Auction Co., 562 A.2d 279, 281 (Pa. 1989). With that policy in mind, under Pennsylvania law, a "seller" pursuant to section 402A includes "anyone who, as a supplier, enters into the business of supplying the public with products, which may endanger them." Id. (citing Francioni v. Gibsonia Truck Corp., 372 A.2d 736 (Pa. 1977)). Nonetheless, this seemingly broad definition is not without limits. When the purposes of the policy "will not be served, persons whose implication in supplying products is tangential to that undertaking will not be subjected to strict liability for the harms caused by defects in the products."

[T]he Pennsylvania Supreme Court has stated that the following four factors [from *Francioni*] should be considered: (1) whether the defendant is the only member of the marketing chain available to the injured plaintiff for redress; (2) whether the imposition of strict liability would serve as an incentive to safety; (3) whether the defendant is in a better position than the consumer to prevent circulation of defective products; and (4) whether the defendant can distribute the cost of compensating for injuries resulting from defects by charging for it in the business.

... [P]laintiff has offered no evidence ... on any of these factors. Consequently, this court is left with nothing but sheer speculation on which to base a finding that the extension of strict liability upon Busch is warranted in this case. See Cafazzo v. Central Med. Health Servs., Inc., 668 A.2d 521, 525 (Pa. 1995).

As way of illustration, turning to the first factor, plaintiff argues ... that Busch is realistically the only member of the marketing chain available to plaintiff for redress. In other words, plaintiff is stating that recovery against defendant Waterworld is unlikely. During oral argument, however, plaintiff's counsel conceded that, in fact, plaintiff's chances of recovery against Waterworld are unknown at this point in time and offered no evidence regarding the prospects of recovering a money judgment against either Waterworld or Busch, for that matter. Moreover, "[t]o assign liability for no reason other than the ability to pay damages is inconsistent with [Pennsylvania] jurisprudence." *Cafazzo*.

With respect to the second and third factors, plaintiff similarly has put forth no evidence of record demonstrating that Busch was involved in, or influenced in any way, the design or manufacturing of the "Sky Splash." Nor has plaintiff offered any evidence of an ongoing relationship between defendants Busch and Waterworld from which Busch would have some leverage to insist that the rides be free from defect.

Finally, it is undisputed that Busch charges park patrons an admission fee. Therefore, Busch could "conceivably" pass on the costs that the imposition of strict liability may have on it by raising that fee. The court finds, however, that this factor only marginally furthers the purposes of the policy behind strict liability. Again, the court cannot effectively weigh this "conceivability" argument against the other three factors because of plaintiff's complete failure to proffer any evidence concerning those factors.

[Summary judgment for defendant is granted].

NOTES

1. What kind of evidence would support strict liability? The court placed the burden on plaintiff to establish the *Francioni* factors, also applied in *Cafazzo*, to show that Busch was a seller. See also Greenwood v. Busch Entertainment Corp., 101 F.Supp.2d 292 (E.D.Pa. 2000) (Busch not a seller; no title to water slide passed, no attributes of sale present in admission ticket).

2. On liability of ski resorts for injuries from products incident to operation, see Lewis v. Big Powderhorn Mountain Ski Corp., 245 N.W.2d 81 (Mich. App. 1976)(no implied warranty; "only product in this case that could conceivably be divined by the exercise of ingenuity is 'a weekend of skiing'"); Bolduc v. Herbert Schneider Corp., 374 A.2d 1187 (N.H.1977)(no implied warranty or strict tort liability for fall from ski lift tramway; moreover, statute prohibited holding ski lift operator as common carrier with specially high duty of care).

3. Lending Transactions. Courts have refused to apply strict liability principles to those who finance sales or leases of products, including lease-for-purchase transactions. See, e.g., Starobin v. Niagara Mach. & Tool Works Corp., 577 N.Y.S.2d

327 (App.Div.1991); Rivera v. Mahogony Corp., 494 N.E.2d 660 (Ill.App.1986)(lease-purchase of plastic molding machine); AgriStor Leasing v. Meuli, 634 F.Supp. 1208, 1216 (D.Kan.1986)("A distinction is drawn ... between 'commercial' lessors and 'finance' lessors, with strict liability being imposed on the former but not the latter."). Nor have the courts allowed negligence claims against lenders, provided that the lender does not involve itself with the product other than is necessary to protect its interests as a lender. See, e.g., Wright v. Newman, 735 F.2d 1073 (8th Cir.1984) (Ford Motor Credit Co. not a distributor of product it had re-financed, but was subject to negligence as a supplier for failing to inspect the truck for defects so that it could inform the driver of the danger).

4. Reform. A number of products liability reform statutes, such as Idaho's, *exclude* service providers from their definitions of "product sellers." Idaho Code Ann. § 6–1402(1)(b). "Finance lessors" may also be excluded. Id.

5. Miscellaneous Transactions. How do the policies behind strict products liability answer whether common carriers should be strictly liable for injuries from "defective" transport by plane, train, bus, or subway? Should there be strict liability for defective computer programming? See Smith, Suing the Provider of Computer Software: How Courts Are Applying U.C.C. Article Two, Strict Tort Liability, and Professional Malpractice, 24 Willamette L.Rev. 743 (1988).

6. See generally Cantu, A New Look at an Old Conundrum: The Determinative Test for the Hybrid Sales/Service Transaction under Section 402A of the Restatement (Second) of Torts, 45 Ark. L. Rev. 913 (1993); Powers, Distinguishing Between Products and Services in Strict Liability, 62 N.C.L.Rev. 415 (1984); D. Owen, Products Liability Law § 16.3 (2d ed. 2008); 2 D. Owen, M.S. Madden, & M. Davis, Madden & Owen on Products Liability § 20:3 (3d ed. 2000).

3. USED PRODUCTS

Jordan v. Sunnyslope Appliance Propane & Plumbing Supplies Company

Arizona Court of Appeals, 1983.
135 Ariz. 309, 660 P.2d 1236.

■ MEYERSON, JUDGE.

The sole issue on this appeal from summary judgment is whether the trial court correctly held that dealers in used products cannot be held strictly liable for harm resulting from defective goods which may be unreasonably dangerous. We hold that a dealer in used goods may be held strictly liable under the Restatement (Second) of Torts § 402A (1965)(hereinafter cited as § 402A) as adopted by our supreme court.

I. FACTS

[Plaintiff's father purchased a used propane storage tank, manufactured in 1947, from a propane tank dealer Canyon Gas and Appliance Co. (Canyon Gas), and had it installed at his rental property adjacent to his son's home. The seller provided no guarantees or representations concerning the tank's condition. A year and a half later, while the tank was being filled with liquid propane gas, the hose used in filling the tank disconnected. The propane exploded, totally destroying the plaintiff's house next door. Plaintiffs sued Canyon Gas for strict liability in tort, alleging that a defect in the tank's shut-off valve malfunctioned by failing to close, thereby allowing the propane to escape from the tank when the hose disconnected. Plaintiffs also sued Sunnyslope for negligently filling the tank and allowing the propane to escape.]

[Canyon Gas moved for summary judgment, arguing that the doctrine of strict liability in tort did not extend to a seller of used goods. The trial court agreed and dismissed Canyon Gas from the case. Plaintiffs appeal.]

II. CONTENTIONS OF THE PARTIES

[P]laintiffs urge that § 402A and the comments thereto can be read to show the drafters meant to include used goods or at least did not mean to exclude them from the section. Section 402A states that one who sells "any" product is liable, not one who sells "any new" product. Comment *f* specifies there is an exception for one who is an "occasional" seller, not engaged in the business of selling the particular kind of product. It does not state that an exception applies to those in the business of selling particular used goods.

Plaintiff urges that the requirement that the product be "unreasonably dangerous" allows the trier of fact to inquire into the age and condition of the product and the knowledge of the buyer, and serves to limit liability to those cases where injury was caused by a defect below the degree of safety which the ordinary purchaser of a used product could reasonably expect. Plaintiff points out that strict liability is a cost spreading device to shift the cost of injuries from the injured party to those responsible for placing the product on the market and who are more aware and better able to control the actual risks involved. [P]laintiff urges that a seller of used goods, just like a seller of new goods, is able to distribute the cost of doing business among his customers or shift liability to others in the chain of production.

In urging this court not to impose the doctrine of strict liability on used good dealers, Canyon Gas stresses the differences between dealers in used and new goods. It argues that the dealer in used products is not an integral part of the producing and marketing chain, having had no part in placing the product into the hands of consumers in the first instance. Because he has no continuing relationship with the manufacturer, Canyon Gas argues that a dealer in used products cannot exert pressure on the manufacturer nor adjust the cost of liability imposed upon him during the course of such relationship. Furthermore, according to Canyon Gas, the dealer in used goods cannot obtain indemnity because the product has changed hands since leaving the manufacturer. Finally, Canyon Gas argues that the cost of insurance would be prohibitive and trying to pass liability and insurance costs on to customers would drive used good dealers out of the market.

III. DECISIONS FROM OTHER JURISDICTIONS

Most of the arguments proffered by the parties have been discussed at length by those courts which have faced this issue to date. The question of whether or in what circumstances a dealer in used products should be held strictly liable for a defect attributable to the initial design or manufacturing of the used product has produced a split in authority. . . .

In Hovenden v. Tenbush, 529 S.W.2d 302 (Tex.App.1975), a plaintiff sought to impose strict liability upon a dealer in used brick. Relying on its understanding of the language in § 402A and the policy behind it as set forth in the official comments, the court held that a seller of used products is not insulated from liability. [B]ecause enterprise liability is the basis for the rule, dealers in used goods should be treated the same for strict liability purposes as dealers in new goods. According to the court, both obtain profit from selling the product and often are able to distribute the cost and shift liability. The court observed that "Sec. 402A imposed liability on sellers of used products where the evidence showed that the injury resulted from an inherent defect in the product, rather than from a condition brought about by normal use of the chattel."

In Turner v. International Harvester Company, 336 A.2d 62 (N.J.Super.Ct.1975), a New Jersey court held that § 402A applied to dealers in used goods; the plaintiff was fatally injured when a truck collapsed on him. The court found enterprise liability to be the justification for the products liability doctrine and found that the same considerations for holding sellers of new goods strictly liable applied to dealers in used goods:

> An economic analysis of enterprise liability, which includes direct as well as indirect costs, would charge those in the business of selling a defective product with responsibility for all harms, physical and economic, which result from its use. To a considerable extent—with respect to *new* goods— the manufacturer bases the cost of his product on his expenses, which include damages caused by the product and insurance to cover those damages. This cost is spread among all the customers for that product; it reflects the justifiable expectations of customers regarding safety, quality and durability of new goods. Sellers of used goods may similarly distribute their costs of doing business which, in turn, will reflect what is considered by the public to be justifiable expectations regarding safety, quality and durability of used goods.

(citations omitted).

The *Turner* court rejected the notion that the public did not expect used products to be safe from manufacturing and design defects when purchasing a serviceable product as opposed to junk parts. The court observed that while buyers of used products could not expect the same quality and durability as would be found in a new product, their expectations of *safety* were not generally lessened simply because the product is used:

> [R]ealistic expectations of quality and durability will be lower for used goods, commensurate with their age, appearance and price. However, safety of the general public demands that when a used motor vehicle, for

example, is sold for use *as a serviceable motor vehicle* (and not as junk parts), absent special circumstances, the seller be responsible for safety defects whether known or unknown at time of sale, present while the machine was under his control. Otherwise, the buyer and the general public are bearing the enterprise liability stemming from introduction of the dangerously defective used vehicle onto the public highways. Public policy demands that the buyer receive a used chattel safe for the purpose intended (where no substantial change will occur prior to reaching the buyer or foreseeable consumer).

Finally, the *Turner* court observed that the requirement that the defect in the product be "unreasonably dangerous" permits the court or jury to inquire into the nature of the product, its age and condition, creating a standard against which the defect can be measured. The unreasonably dangerous standard also allows an inquiry into the particular relationship of the parties or the degree of sophistication of the purchaser which might show that the product did not present an unreasonable danger in the particular situation.... As explained in Section IV, infra, we agree with the reasoning of the court in *Turner* ...

One of the first courts to conclude that sellers of used goods should not be strictly liable for defects created by the manufacturer was the Oregon court in Tillman v. Vance Equipment Co., 596 P.2d 1299 (Or.1979). The plaintiff sought to impose strict liability on the seller for injuries from a defect in a used crane. The court noted that *"if a jurisdiction has adopted the principle of strict liability on the basis of enterprise liability, the liability of the seller of either a new or used product would logically follow."* (emphasis added). The court noted, however, that it had never been willing to rely on enterprise liability alone as a justification for strict liability for defective products. Along with enterprise liability, the Oregon court identified three other justifications for the doctrine—implied representation of safety made by the seller to the consumer, risk reduction and compensation.

The court first considered whether an inference can be made that a dealer makes any representation with regard to safety when selling a used product. The court decided that a buyer of used goods does not expect the same quality as a buyer of new goods:

> Those markets, generally speaking, operate on the apparent understanding that the seller, even though he is in the business of selling such goods, makes no particular representation about their quality simply by offering them for sale. If a buyer wants some assurance of quality, he typically either bargains for it in the specific transaction or seeks out a dealer who routinely offers it....

The court then concluded that the sale of a used product, without more, does not generate the kind of expectations of safety which are created when the product is first put on the market. In our view, this reasoning misses the mark because we have found no empirical evidence to warrant the conclusion that the purchaser of a used product from a commercial dealer engaged in the business of selling that product, necessarily expects the product to contain *unreasonably dangerous* defects. Furthermore, this contention ignores the plight of the innocent bystander, such as the plaintiffs herein, who may suffer loss or injury without ever having purchased the product themselves.

The Oregon court also noted that the risk-reduction aspect of strict liability would not be served where a used product was sold. The court observed that a dealer in used products is normally outside the original chain of distribution of the product. It saw no ready channel of communication by which the dealer and the manufacturer may exchange information about possible or actual dangerous defects with a view to eliminating the defects.

Admittedly, the relationship between a dealer in used products and the manufacturer is more attenuated than the relationship between the dealer in new products and the manufacturer. But we reject the view that the seller of used goods is outside the chain of distribution. He offers the goods for sale and profits therefrom. Thus, he is an integral part of the marketing system. At any rate, imposing strict liability on the commercial dealer of used products should result in increased maintenance and inspection of such products before they are offered for sale. [Citation.]

* * *

IV. ARIZONA CASES

Arizona courts have touched on the question of whether strict liability is to be imposed on dealers in used goods in only one case. In Rix v. Reeves, 532 P.2d 185 (Ariz.App.1975) [we refused] to impose strict liability on an auto salvage yard operator from whom the plaintiff had obtained a used wheel which later caused injury. . . . We found "no justification . . . for extending the strict liability in tort theory to the operator of an auto salvage yard where a tire rim of unknown age and use fails."[3] [W]e observed that it would be a severe economic blow to force dealers in junk parts—parts which are often obviously worn and damaged—to inspect and repair the parts, warn against dangers, and insure against possible liability. We pointed out, though, that "[b]y used products we do not refer to products rebuilt by a manufacturer, nor do we mean to imply that there is never any liability when used products are sold."

[W]e conclude that a dealer engaged in the business of selling used goods of the type in question may be held strictly liable under the terms of the Restatement rule. . . . It is the plaintiff's burden in Arizona, in a strict liability case, to prove that the product is unreasonably dangerous; thus, the nature of the good—whether it is new or used—becomes relevant. As the *Turner* court found, the unreasonably dangerous standard which allows inquiry into matters such as age and condition of a used product, specific representations made, and sophistication of the buyer, provides sufficient protection to the dealer in used goods. [Citations.]

3. In addition to salvage yard sales, strict liability should not extend to "random and accidental" sales such as garage sales or swap meets. § 402A comment (f).

* * * There is no justification for finding that used good dealers as a class cannot shift losses, distribute costs, or insure against losses. [Canyon Gas' final argument, that the dealer will not be able to obtain indemnity from the manufacturer because of substantial change to the product, is unpersuasive. That is true, however, whether the product is new or used.] Indeed, Arizona law authorizes a seller to seek indemnity from a manufacturer without any limitation on whether the product is new or used. A.R.S. §§ 12–681–86. In addition, no product liability action may be filed more than twelve years after the product was first sold. A.R.S. § 12–551.

[Reversed.]

NOTES

1. The courts are badly split on whether strict liability in tort should apply to sellers of used products. See Cataldo v. Lazy Days R.V. Center, Inc., 920 So.2d 174, 179 (Fla. Dist. Ct. App. 2006) ("No national consensus exists on the refusal to extend strict liability claims to the sellers of used goods."). In accord with *Jordan*, see Stanton v. Carlson Sales, Inc., 728 A.2d 534 (Conn.Super.Ct. 1998); Nelson v. Nelson Hardware, Inc., 467 N.W.2d 518 (Wis.1991). Turner v. International Harvester Co., 336 A.2d 62 (N.J.Super.Ct.1975), was the early leading case for this position.

For the opposite view, that strict liability does *not* generally apply, Tillman v. Vance Equip. Co., 596 P.2d 1299 (Or.1979), discussed in *Jordan*, was the early leading case. See also Peterson v. Idaho First Nat'l Bank, 791 P.2d 1303 (Idaho 1990); Keith v. Russell T. Bundy & Assocs., Inc., 495 So.2d 1223 (Fla.App.1986).

Do the policies behind strict liability explored in ch. 5 weigh in favor or against strict liability for used products?

2. Rebuilding or Reconditioning. Some courts will impose strict liability if the used product dealer rebuilds or reconditions the product. E.g., Crandell v. Larkin & Jones Appliance Co., Inc., 334 N.W.2d 31 (S.D.1983) (dealer, who reconditioned and guaranteed used clothes dryer which caught fire, liable in strict tort, express warranty, and implied warranty of merchantability). Compare Cataldo v. Lazy Days R.V. Center, Inc., 920 So.2d 174 (Fla.Dist.Ct.App. 2006), in which the Lazy Days R.V. Center, advertising itself as the "world's largest R.V. dealer," sold the plaintiffs a reconditioned 1988 motor home manufactured originally by a now bankrupt company. Lazy Days had taken possession of the Cataldo's motor home as a trade-in. Lazy Days usually performed extensive inspections on vehicles both at the time they are received in trade and prior to delivery on resale to insure that the systems are working properly. The Cataldo's motor home apparently underwent two separate pre-delivery inspections and several walk-through inspections prior to sale, which resulted in some reconditioning of the vehicle but did not affect the retractable steps that ultimately caused Mr. Cataldo's injuries. The appellate court rejected strict liability based on precedent, but asked the Florida Supreme Court to address the question, which it refused to do. 929 So.2d 1051 (Fla. 2006).

3. Occasional Sellers. If the seller does not regularly deal in used good sales, but only does so infrequently, it will not be considered a "seller" of the used goods. See, e.g., Griffin Indus., Inc. v. Jones, 975 S.W.2d 100 (Ky. 1998); Gebo v. Black Clawson Co., 703 N.E.2d 1234 (N.Y. 1998).

4. Latent Defects. Some courts shield the seller in the case of latent defects. See Grimes v. Axtell Ford Lincoln–Mercury, 403 N.W.2d 781 (Iowa 1987)(no strict liability); Stump v. Indiana Equip. Co., 601 N.E.2d 398 (Ind.App.1992)(former owner had hot-wired starter on grader that cut off operator's legs; duty of due care to inspect and warn not breached since defect was latent).

5. Warranty. Early courts held that the sale of a used product did not carry an implied warranty. See Bayer v. Winton Motor Car Co., 160 N.W. 642 (Mich. 1916). Today, however, an implied warranty of merchantability will attach in certain situations. See U.C.C. § 2–314, comment 3: "A contract for the sale of second-hand goods, however, involves only such obligation as is appropriate to such goods …"; Roupp v. Acor, 384 A.2d 968 (Pa.Super.Ct.1978)(both implied warranties accompanied sale of used truck). But see Valley Datsun v. Martinez, 578 S.W.2d 485 (Tex.Civ.App.1979)(no implied warranty of merchantability where purchaser knows goods are used).

6. The Products Liability Restatement. The Products Liability Restatement provides in § 8 that commercial sellers of defective used products are liable for resulting harm if the defect (a) arises from the seller's negligence; or (b) is a manufacturing defect or a defect under the malfunction theory of § 3 and "the seller's marketing of the product would cause a reasonable person … to expect the used product to present no greater risk of defect than if the product were new;" or (c) is from a product remanufactured by the seller; or (d) arises from failure to comply with a safety regulation.

7. See generally D. Owen, Products Liability Law §§ 16.4 (repaired and rebuilt products), 16.5 (used products) (2d ed. 2008); 2 D. Owen, M.S. Madden, & M. Davis, Madden & Owen on Products Liability, § 20:5 (3d ed. 2000).

---

4. REAL ESTATE

Menendez v. Paddock Pool Construction Co.

Arizona Court of Appeals, 1991.
172 Ariz. 258, 836 P.2d 968.

■ TAYLOR, PRESIDING JUDGE.

[Plaintiff] Luis Menendez was an employee and kitchen training supervisor for TGI Friday's, Inc. (TGIF). On the evening of June 29, 1985, TGIF hosted a private party at the La Casita recreational common area of the Dobson Ranch subdivision in Mesa, Arizona. This facility, which included a large in-ground swimming pool and other amenities, was rented that evening by TGIF from 8:00 p.m. to midnight so that about two hundred of its new employees could celebrate their completion of a two-week company training program.

TGIF furnished beer and wine to the partygoers that night. Further, trainees had been told they could "get crazy" at the party and even throw their training supervisors into the swimming pool. By 9:00 p.m., the effects of alcohol consumption became noticeable. At about 9:30 p.m., after at least four supervisors had been pushed or thrown into the La Casita pool, Luis Menendez was seized by several trainees as he was leaving the party. He was then forcibly carried to the pool and thrown headlong into its shallow end where he sustained spinal injuries resulting in quadriplegia.

[Plaintiff and his family sued the various parties, including the company that designed and built the pool (Paddock Pool) on grounds of strict liability in tort. The trial court dismissed the strict tort claim, and plaintiffs appeal.]

[A real estate developer solicited bids for the design and construction of a custom, non-diving lap pool of specified dimensions to be built at its residential development known as Dobson Ranch. Paddock was awarded the contract, which provided that the pool would be custom designed and have a maximum water depth of 3–4½ feet. The developer deeded the La Casita recreational property, including the pool, to the Dobson Homeowners' Association which thereafter managed the facility, renting it regularly to homeowners' groups.]

... The trial court found that the in-ground pool was not, as a matter of law, a "product" for purposes of strict liability in tort. Noting that such a pool is not manufactured and then introduced into the stream of commerce for sale, the trial court characterized it as a structural improvement to real property rather than as a product incorporated into an improvement to a structure.

* * *

A seller engaged in the business of selling a product in a defective condition unreasonably dangerous to the user or consumer is subject to strict liability in tort for physical harm or property damage caused thereby. O.S. Stapley Co. v. Miller, 447 P.2d 248, 251 (Ariz.1968)(citing Rest. (2d) of Torts § 402A). [An implicit condition to such liability] requires the plaintiff to show that the object or instrumentality claimed to be defective is a "product" as defined either by § 402A, legislation, or case law. [Citation.] Whether an object or instrumentality is a "product" is a question of law. [Citations.]

... Although strict liability in tort under the Restatement has long been recognized in Arizona, [citation] the question of whether an in-ground swimming pool falls within the definition of a product is an issue of first impression in this state.

Neither the Restatement, Arizona Revised Statutes Annotated ("A.R.S."), nor our case law provide a comprehensive definition of product for characterization purposes. The trial court resolved the issue against Menendez by applying a principle of strict liability recited in Craft v. Wet 'N Wild, Inc., 489 So.2d 1221 (Fla.App.1986). This principle states that a structural improvement to realty is not itself subject to strict liability, although manufactured components incorporated into it could be. The trial court [concluded] that an in-ground pool is not manufactured and then introduced into the stream of commerce for sale.

Menendez argues on appeal that the principle announced in *Craft* and adopted by the trial court is unreasonably restrictive. This principle,

Menendez contends, conflicts with the broad application of strict liability in tort which is inherent in the Restatement and which is reflected in the case law of Arizona[4] and other jurisdictions. . . .

A *per se* rule excluding structural improvements to realty has found support in cases from various jurisdictions. See [cases from Cal., Ga., Miss., Mo., N.M., Pa.]. Some courts have reasoned, however, that since the doctrine of strict liability is based upon a defect in a product, injuries arising either from an unsafe design or from a product manufactured by a defendant and incorporated into an improvement to realty may support a strict liability in tort action. See [cases from Pa., Cal., Iowa, N.J., N.Y., citations].

Moreover, numerous cases in other jurisdictions have excluded specific structures as well as improvements to realty after weighing the policy considerations for imposing strict liability in tort. See [cases from Colo., Fla., Haw., Ill., Mo., Mont., Ohio. Some courts, however,] have found strict liability in tort applicable to specific realty improvements after taking into account the policy considerations underlying the doctrine. See [cases from Pa., Ill., Haw.;] see generally Lindsay, Strict Liability and the Building Industry, 33 Emory L.J. 175, 191–210 (1984).

[W]e do not deem it necessary to assess the validity of the *per se* rule adopted by the trial court in which it characterized an in-ground pool as a structural improvement and therefore not a product. Rather, we examine the policy reasons underlying the strict liability doctrine to see if it should be applied to this case. . . .

. . . One authority has identified three main policy reasons driving the development of strict liability in tort[. These policies can be summarized as the now familiar cost-shifting, accident reduction, and increased recovery because of ease of proof. We examine the applicability of these policies to determine whether to apply strict liability in tort principles to the in-ground pool at issue, focusing especially on the adequacy of a remedy. Defendants argue that plaintiff] had an adequate remedy through the negligence counts brought against them and others in this action with no difficulty of access to a remote manufacturer. Indeed, [defendants note and Menendez admits] that prior to this appeal, Dobson Homeowners' Association, originally named as a co-defendant and identified as the pool landowner, had settled Menendez's negligence and gross negligence claims.

. . . Although we decline to make recovery alone dispositive of strict liability, we are persuaded at least that the nature of the La Casita pool as a realty improvement did not inherently foreclose Menendez from [any remedy].

---

4. [Menendez relies on the Supreme Court opinion which] recognized a builder-vendor's implied warranty to remote home-owners in Richards v. Powercraft Homes, 678 P.2d 427 (Ariz.1984). . . . *Richards*, however, involved an implied warranty of workmanship and habitability in the construction of dwellings, which the supreme court subsequently determined . . . to sound only in contract. . . .

Claiming that the La Casita pool was custom-built, defendants also argue against shifting the injury cost to them because unique projects limit a builder's ability to absorb and spread the cost of risk through mass-production volume. If risk is to be shifted, defendants contend that the landowners are in the best position to control the use of a realty improvement, to discover defects and assess risks arising from its use, and to procure appropriate insurance for protection. In reply, Menendez responds that cost-shifting against the corporate defendants is warranted because they are "large companies which produce large numbers of similar products."

The cost-shifting arguments advanced by defendants ... are grounded on the uniqueness of a constructed structure [and] lose their force when [a structure is mass-produced].

In the landmark case of Schipper v. Levitt & Sons, Inc., 207 A.2d 314 (N.J.1965), the New Jersey Supreme Court held that a builder-vendor of mass-produced tract homes could be found strictly liable for injuries resulting from a defect in a water distribution system design which allowed excessively hot water into a bathroom faucet. The builder was a mass developer of planned communities and marketed residential homes through advertised models constructed with standardized specifications. The court found "that there [were] no meaningful distinctions between Levitt's mass production and sale of homes and the mass production and sale of automobiles and that the pertinent overriding policy considerations [were] the same."

> If there is improper construction such as a defective heating system or a defective ceiling, stairway and the like, the well-being of the vendee and others is seriously endangered and serious injury is foreseeable. The public interest dictates that if such injury does result from the defective construction, its cost should be borne by the responsible developer who created the danger and who is in the better economic position to bear the loss rather than by the injured party who justifiably relied on the developer's skill and implied representation.

Id. at 326. This same reasoning was adopted by a California appellate court. In Kriegler v. Eichler Homes, 74 Cal.Rptr. 749 (Ct.App.1969), the court extended strict liability in tort to a builder of mass-produced tract homes for economic damages resulting from a defectively installed radiant heating system. [Citations.] Therefore, even if we were to adopt the reasoning of *Schipper*, cost-shifting can be justified in this case only if the pool at issue was a mass-produced rather than a unique structure.

Finally, defendants argue against the public safety justification. Defendants assert that the construction process for structures such as this pool limits the ability of the builder to eliminate or minimize design defects by means of the testing, refinement, and quality-control procedures compatible with mass production. Because we find the evidence supports the contention of defendants that this pool was individually designed and custom built, this argument is persuasive. Defendant Paddock further contends that public safety is already protected by governmental regulation of the construction process through builder licensing, mandatory building codes, and project permit requirements, including plan review and site inspection approvals. We also find merit in this latter argument.

We conclude from this review that policy reasons do not justify characterizing the La Casita pool as a product for purposes of strict liability in tort. . . .

[Affirmed.]

NOTES

1. **Mass–Produced Homes—Strict Liability.** As *Menendez* indicates, there is growing authority for applying strict tort principles to the sale of new homes, especially those constructed by mass production developers as was the case in the landmark decision, Schipper v. Levitt & Sons, Inc., 207 A.2d 314 (N.J.1965)(infant severely scalded by excessively hot water from faucet in bathroom sink due to failure of developer to add inexpensive mixing valve to reduce temperature of water drawn from boiler). Contra, Calloway v. City of Reno, 993 P.2d 1259 (Nev. 2000) (townhouses not products for purposes of strict products liability). Should a medium-sized builder which constructs 6 or 8 houses be strictly liable in tort? See Patitucci v. Drelich, 379 A.2d 297 (N.J.Super.Ct.Law Div. 1977) (defective sewage disposal system; yes). How about the custom builder who works on only two or three houses at a time? For a case refusing to follow *Schipper,* see Chapman v. Lily Cache Builders, Inc., 362 N.E.2d 811 (Ill.App.Ct.1977)(building contractors generally not as financially capable as manufacturers of mass produced chattels to act as insurers).

Strict tort has been applied to "defective" house *lots* which subsided from inadequate compaction of the fill, Avner v. Longridge Estates, 77 Cal.Rptr. 633 (Ct.App.1969); and to the defective foundation of a home, Stearman v. Centex Homes, 92 Cal.Rptr.2d 761 (Ct.App. 2000); and to defective components that cause additional property damage, Jiminez v. Superior Court, 58 P.3d 450 (Cal. 2002).

2. **Homes—Implied Warranty.** Most states have now replaced the traditional rule of caveat emptor in the sale of new homes with an implied warranty of reasonable quality, or "habitability." See, e.g., Hoke v. Beck, 587 N.E.2d 4 (Ill.App. 1992) (leaky pipes, smelly floors and toilets, and a dozen other problems); Lane v. Trenholm Bldg. Co., 229 S.E.2d 728, 729 (S.C.1976)(summarizing policy reasons: "the transaction was primarily a sale of a house and not a conveyance of land, the disparity of bargaining positions between the seller and purchaser, reliance by the purchaser on the skill of the builder, and the inability of the purchaser to inspect the house for latent defects"); Council of Unit Owners of Breakwater House Condominium v. Simpler, 603 A.2d 792 (Del.1992) (warranty of good quality and workmanship, distinguishing warranty of habitability).

3. **Landlords. A. Negligence.** For centuries, the rule of caveat emptor, or more precisely "caveat lessee," dominated the law of real estate leases as it did the law of real estate sales. Because of the dominant position of the landowner in medieval society, the landlord was cloaked at an early date in a mantle of immunity from liability for injuries caused by defective conditions in the leased premises. As time progressed, however, various exceptions grew up around the general rule of nonliability, so that landlords became subject to liability in negligence for (1) hidden dangers known to the lessor but not to the lessee, (2) injuries to persons off the premises, (3) defects in premises leased for admission of the public, (4) defects in

"common areas" retained under the landlord's control, (5) failure to keep the premises in good repair when the landlord had covenanted so to do, (6) negligence in making repairs, and (7) defects constituting violations of building or housing code provisions. Then, in 1973, the New Hampshire Supreme Court turned the general rule of nonliability on its head and held that landlords would be subject to the general principles of negligence liability. Sargent v. Ross, 308 A.2d 528 (N.H. 1973) (Kenison, C.J.). A number of courts have followed.

B. Warranty. While a warranty of habitability had been implied into short-term leases of furnished dwellings by a few courts for some time, courts began to find a general implied warranty of habitability in leases of residential premises in the 1960s and early 1970s. E.g., Pines v. Perssion, 111 N.W.2d 409 (Wis.1961). While most of the cases involve contractual disputes surrounding the nonpayment of rent and other economic complaints, e.g., Wade v. Jobe, 818 P.2d 1006 (Utah 1991), some have involved more typical products liability claims. E.g., Alharb v. Sayegh, 604 N.Y.S.2d 243 (App.Div.1993)(plaintiff's infant contracted lead poisoning from ingesting paint chips that fell from ceiling; lack of notice of dangerous condition may be defense); Brooks v. Lewin Realty III, Inc., 835 A.2d 616 (Md. 2003)(lead poisoning claim; notice not required under applicable housing code).

C. Strict Liability. At the end (perhaps height) of the tort law expansionary era, the California Supreme Court in 1985 adopted a rule of landlord strict tort liability for injuries from defects in leased dwellings, reasoning that an apartment itself may be considered a "product" placed in the stream of commerce by the landlord. Becker v. IRM Corp., 698 P.2d 116 (Cal.1985). Louisiana, by statute, was the only other state with such a rule. Marcantel v. Karam, 601 So.2d 1 (La.App. 1992). No court followed *Becker*, and many courts and commentators rejected it as an excessive extension of the principles of products liability law. See Armstrong v. Cione, 738 P.2d 79 (Hawaii 1987). The composition of the California Supreme Court changed substantially after *Becker* was decided, and the newly constituted court found an opportunity to revisit the decision when asked to rule on whether *Becker* should be extended to hoteliers. In Peterson v. Superior Court, 899 P.2d 905, 906 (Cal.1995), the court noted that no other jurisdiction had followed *Becker* and concluded that it had "erred in *Becker* in applying the doctrine of strict products liability to a residential landlord that is not a part of the manufacturing or marketing enterprise of the allegedly defective product" in question. Consequently, strict liability also did not apply to a hotel proprietor for injuries caused by an alleged defect in the hotel premises that the hotel proprietor did not create or market.

4. Emotional Distress. Although damages for emotional distress do not usually attach to claims for "mere" property damage or economic loss, the situation is arguably different in respect to such damages caused by the defective construction of a home. See Salka v. Dean Homes of Beverly Hills, Inc., 864 P.2d 1037 (Cal.1993)(plaintiff suffered grief and distress from water problems, lasting 7 years until corrected, in her defective "dream house"). "The significant distinction [from cases denying recovery for emotional harm in economic loss cases] is that the purchase of a home is not only the largest investment most people make in their lifetime, it is also a highly personal choice concerning how and where one lives his or her life. Generally, no other material acquisition is of equivalent personal importance.... The purchase of a home involves an individual's personal values and private life." *Salka*, 22 Cal.Rptr.2d 902, 910 (Ct.App.), superseded by 864 P.2d 1037 (Cal. 1993). See also Liberty Homes, Inc. v. Epperson, 581 So.2d 449 (Ala. 1991)(warranty claim for extremely defective mobile home; mental-distress claims allowable in exceptional cases arising out of contract).

5. Statutes of Repose. Many states have special statutes of repose for improvements to real property. These statutes protect building contractors from suits long after a structure has been completed, but manufacturers of component products used in the structure may not be protected. See, e.g., Noll v. Harrisburg Area YMCA, 643 A.2d 81 (Pa.1994). Statutes drawn more broadly may protect component manufacturers. Krull v. Thermogas Co., 522 N.W.2d 607 (Iowa 1994). Most such statutes withstand constitutional challenge. Coleman v. United Eng'r & Constr., Inc., 878 P.2d 996 (N.M.1994); but see Brennaman v. R.M.I. Co., 639 N.E.2d 425 (Ohio 1994)(statute unconstitutional). The limitations period in a few such statutes is quite short. See Trust Co. Bank v. U.S. Gypsum Co., 950 F.2d 1144 (5th Cir.1992)(Miss. 6-year statute barred claim for asbestos abatement costs against manufacturer of the materials).

6. See generally Love, Landlord's Liability for Defective Premises: Caveat Lessee, Negligence, or Strict Liability?, 1975 Wis.L.Rev. 19; Products Liability Restatement § 19(a), cmt. *e*; D. Owen, Products Liability Law 16:7 (2d ed. 2008); 2 D. Owen, M.S. Madden & M. Davis, Madden & Owen on Products Liability § 20:8 (3d ed. 2000).

---

5. MISCELLANEOUS "PRODUCTS"

Latham v. Wal–Mart Stores, Inc.
Missouri Court of Appeals, 1991.
818 S.W.2d 673.

■ GAERTNER, PRESIDING JUDGE.

[Plaintiffs appeal a summary judgment for defendants on plaintiffs' products-liability claim.] We affirm.

[Plaintiff Roberta Latham special ordered a parrot at the Wal–Mart store where she worked. When the parrot arrived, it was left in its container, and Ms. Latham took it home. The bird was infected with psittacosis, a disease much like pneumonia, transmittable to humans. James Latham, Roberta Latham's husband, contracted psittacosis from the bird, and consequently suffered various pneumonic symptoms (fever, nausea, loss of appetite, etc.). Mr. and Mrs. Latham sued Wal–Mart and its manager, Charles Bezoni, for strict products liability under § 402A. The trial court granted summary judgment for defendants, and plaintiffs appeal.]

[T]he issue presented is whether a living animal can be a "product" under the Restatement. This question, though a subject of some controversy in several states, is one of first impression in Missouri. We begin our analysis by reviewing the decisions reached by other courts.

The issue of whether an animal fits within § 402A's definition of a product first arose in Whitmer v. Schneble, 331 N.E.2d 115 (Ill.App.1975). In this dog-bite case, the plaintiffs alleged that the defendants were strictly liable for selling them an unreasonably dangerous product. The Illinois court disagreed, holding [that while] a product under § 402A need not be manufactured, and may be a viable thing, its nature must be fixed when it leaves the defendant's control. The [*Whitmer* court relied on the policies of strict liability], that the costs of injuries resulting from defective products be borne by those who market such products, rather than by the injured persons, who are powerless to protect themselves [and concluded that this] purpose would be defeated if strict liability were applied to products whose character could be changed and shaped by the purchaser rather than the seller. Thus, the Illinois court held, as a matter of law, that animals could not be "products" under the Restatement.

Two years later, a New York court reached a different result on the same issue, this time in the guise of diseased hamsters. Beyer v. Aquarium Supply Co., 404 N.Y.S.2d 778 (Sup.Ct.1977). Denying a motion to dismiss, the New York court noted that the reason for strict products liability is to equitably distribute the inevitable consequences of commercial enterprise and to promote the marketing of safe products. [The court reasoned] that there is no reason why a breeder, distributor or vendor who places a diseased animal in the stream of commerce should be less accountable for his actions than one who markets a defective manufactured product. "The risk presented to human well being by a diseased animal is as great and probably greater than that created by a defectively manufactured product."

Thus, the court held that the diseased hamsters were products within the meaning of the Restatement. . . .

. . . In Anderson v. Farmers Hybrid Cos., Inc., 408 N.E.2d 1194 (Ill.App.1980), the court held that diseased gilts (unbred female pigs used for breeding purposes) were not products under the Restatement due to their mutability. The court [reasoned] that living creatures, such as [swine], are by their nature in a constant process of internal development and growth and they are also participants in a constant interaction with the environment around them as part of their development. Thus, living creatures have no fixed nature and cannot be products as a matter of law. Recovery under [strict liability thus was] disallowed in *Anderson*.

Since [*Anderson*], only two other jurisdictions have been presented with the instant issue. In 1985, Oregon adopted the New York view and specifically rejected Illinois's analysis. Sease v. Taylor's Pets, Inc., 700 P.2d 1054 (Or.Ct.App.1985)[pet shop skunk—"product"]. In that same year, the United States District Court of Colorado adopted the Illinois position. Kaplan v. C Lazy U Ranch, 615 F.Supp. 234 (D.Colo.1985)[dude ranch patron fell off "fractious" horse with tendency to expand chest while being saddled—the "contention that a horse and saddle constitute a 'product,' while a novel idea, is rebutted by case law and the basic underlying policies of the strict tort liability doctrine which requires that a product's nature be fixed when it leaves the manufacturer's or seller's control"].

We tend to agree with the Illinois view, that due to their mutability and their tendency to be affected by the purchaser, animals should not be products under § 402A as a matter of law. [A seller should not be] liable for changes potentially wrought upon a "product" by the purchaser, while the item was completely outside the seller's control. Also we question that § 402A was intended to apply as broadly as plaintiffs argue.

[Moreover,] defendants were not in the business of selling parrots, nor were plaintiffs their normal type of customer. Plaintiff Roberta Latham was an employee of the store, who asked that the parrot be specially ordered as a special favor. In addition, [the] bird was in Wal–Mart's possession for only a short time (less than one hour). . . .

Defendants have asserted in their affidavit that neither Wal–Mart nor Charles Bezoni sell parrots to the general public in the ordinary course of business [as required under § 402A]. This assertion is uncontradicted by plaintiffs in their affidavit [thereby defeating plaintiff's claim].

[Summary judgment for Wal–Mart and Bezoni affirmed.]

N O T E

"[W]hen a living animal is sold commercially in a diseased condition and causes harm to other property or to persons, the animal constitutes a product for purposes of this Restatement." Products Liability Restatement § 19 cmt. *b.* Contra, Malicki v. Koci, 700 N.E.2d 913 (Ohio App. 1997) (diseased parakeet not a product).

Winter v. G.P. Putnam's Sons
United States Court of Appeals, Ninth Circuit, 1991.
938 F.2d 1033.

■ SNEED, C.J.

Plaintiffs are mushroom enthusiasts who became severely ill from picking and eating mushrooms after relying on information in The Encyclopedia of Mushrooms, a book published by the defendant. Plaintiffs sued the publisher and sought damages under various theories. The district court granted summary judgment for the defendant. We affirm.

I.   FACTS AND PROCEEDINGS BELOW

The Encyclopedia of Mushrooms is a reference guide containing information on the habitat, collection, and cooking of mushrooms. It was written by two British authors and originally published by a British publishing company. Defendant Putnam, an American book publisher, purchased copies of the book from the British publisher and distributed the finished product in the United States. Putnam neither wrote nor edited the book.

Plaintiffs purchased the book to help them collect and eat wild mushrooms. In 1988, plaintiffs went mushroom hunting and relied on the descriptions in the book in determining which mushrooms were safe to eat. After cooking and eating their harvest, plaintiffs became critically ill. Both have required liver transplants.

Plaintiffs allege that the book contained erroneous and misleading information concerning the identification of the most deadly species of mushrooms. In their suit against the book publisher, plaintiffs allege liability based on products liability, breach of warranty, negligence, negligent misrepresentation, and false representations. Defendant moved for summary judgment asserting that plaintiffs' claims failed as a matter of law because 1) the information contained in a book is not a product for the purposes of strict liability under products liability law; and 2) defendant is not liable under any remaining theories because a publisher does not have a duty to investigate the accuracy of the text it publishes. The district court granted summary judgment for the defendant. Plaintiffs appeal. We affirm.

II. DISCUSSION

A book containing Shakespeare's sonnets consists of two parts, the material and print therein, and the ideas and expression thereof. The first may be a product, but the second is not. The latter, were Shakespeare alive, would be governed by copyright laws; the laws of libel, to the extent consistent with the First Amendment; and the laws of misrepresentation, negligent misrepresentation, negligence, and mistake. These doctrines applicable to the second part are aimed at the delicate issues that arise with respect to intangibles such as ideas and expression. Products liability law is geared to the tangible world.

A. Products Liability

The language of products liability law reflects its focus on tangible items. In describing the scope of products liability law, the Restatement (Second) of Torts lists examples of items that are covered. All of these are tangible items, such as tires, automobiles, and insecticides. The American Law Institute clearly was concerned with including all physical items but gave no indication that the doctrine should be expanded beyond that area.

The purposes served by products liability law also are focused on the tangible world and do not take into consideration the unique characteristics of ideas and expression. Under products liability law, strict liability is imposed on the theory that "[t]he costs of damaging events due to defectively dangerous products can best be borne by the enterprisers who make and sell these products." Prosser & Keeton on The Law of Torts, § 98, at 692–93 (5th ed. 1984). Strict liability principles have been adopted to further the "cause of accident prevention . . . [by] the elimination of the necessity of proving negligence." Id. at 693. Additionally, because of the difficulty of establishing fault or negligence in products liability cases, strict liability is the appropriate legal theory to hold manufacturers liable for defective products. Id. Thus, the seller is subject to liability "even though he has exercised all possible care in the preparation and sale of the product." Restatement § 402A cmt. a. It is not a question of fault but simply a determination of how society wishes to assess certain costs that arise from the creation and distribution of products in a complex technological society in which the consumer thereof is unable to protect himself against certain product defects.

Although there is always some appeal to the involuntary spreading of costs of injuries in any area, the costs in any comprehensive cost/benefit analysis would be quite different were strict liability concepts applied to words and ideas. We place a high priority on the unfettered exchange of ideas. We accept the risk that words and ideas have wings we cannot clip and which carry them we know not where. The threat of liability without fault (financial responsibility for our words and ideas in the absence of fault or a special undertaking or responsibility) could seriously inhibit those who wish to share thoughts and theories. As a New York court commented, with the specter of strict liability, "[w]ould any author wish to be exposed ... for writing on a topic which might result in physical injury? e.g., How to cut trees; How to keep bees?" Walter v. Bauer, 439 N.Y.S.2d 821, 823 (Sup.Ct.1981)(student injured doing science project described in textbook; court held that the book was not a product for purposes of products liability law).... One might add: "Would anyone undertake to guide by ideas expressed in words either a discrete group, a nation, or humanity in general?"

Strict liability principles even when applied to products are not without their costs. Innovation may be inhibited. We tolerate these losses. They are much less disturbing than the prospect that we might be deprived of the latest ideas and theories.

Plaintiffs suggest, however, that our fears would be groundless were strict liability rules applied only to books that give instruction on how to accomplish a physical activity and that are intended to be used as part of an activity that is inherently dangerous. We find such a limitation illusory. Ideas are often intimately linked with proposed action, and it would be difficult to draw such a bright line. While "How To" books are a special genre, we decline to attempt to draw a line that puts "How To Live A Good Life" books beyond the reach of strict liability while leaving "How To Exercise Properly" books within its reach.

Plaintiffs' argument is stronger when they assert that The Encyclopedia of Mushrooms should be analogized to aeronautical charts. Several jurisdictions have held that charts which graphically depict geographic features or instrument approach information for airplanes are "products" for the purpose of products liability law. [Cases discussed in note 2, below.] Plaintiffs suggest that The Encyclopedia of Mushrooms can be compared to aeronautical charts because both items contain representations of natural features and both are intended to be used while engaging in a hazardous activity. We are not persuaded.

Aeronautical charts are highly technical tools. They are graphic depictions of technical, mechanical data. The best analogy to an aeronautical chart is a compass. Both may be used to guide an individual who is engaged in an activity requiring certain knowledge of natural features. Computer software that fails to yield the result for which it was designed may be another. In contrast, The Encyclopedia of Mushrooms is like a book on how to use a compass or an aeronautical chart. The chart itself is like a physical "product" while the "How to Use" book is pure thought and expression.

Given these considerations, we decline to expand products liability law to embrace the ideas and expression in a book.

We know of no court that has chosen the path to which the plaintiffs point.[6]

* * *

Finally, plaintiffs ask us to find that a publisher should be required to give a warning 1) that the information in the book is not complete and that the consumer may not fully rely on it or 2) that this publisher has not investigated the text and cannot guarantee its accuracy. With respect to the first, a publisher would not know what warnings, if any, were required without engaging in a detailed analysis of the factual contents of the book. This would force the publisher to do exactly what we have said he has no duty to do—that is, independently investigate the accuracy of the text. We will not introduce a duty we have just rejected by renaming it a "mere" warning label. With respect to the second, such a warning is unnecessary given that *no* publisher has a duty as a guarantor.

[Affirmed.]

NOTES

1. Accord, Birmingham v. Fodor's Travel Publications, Inc., 833 P.2d 70 (Haw.1992)(travel guide not a "product;" no strict liability for failing to warn body-surfing tourist of ocean surf conditions at beach); Way v. Boy Scouts of America, 856 S.W.2d 230 (Tex.App.1993)(content of *Boys Life* magazine, and advertising supplement for shooting sports, not "products").

2. Aeronautical Chart Cases. The aeronautical chart cases are treated differently. In Brocklesby v. United States, 767 F.2d 1288 (9th Cir.1985), plaintiffs brought wrongful death and property damage claims against the publisher of an aircraft instrument approach chart and the federal government. An error in the chart, based on inaccurate data supplied by the FAA to the chart publisher, caused an airline jet to crash into a mountain. Plaintiffs argued that strict liability should apply. The publisher obtained from the FAA information on the technical details of an instrument approach, including directional heading, distances, minimum altitudes, and approach procedures, and presented it in its approach plates in a unique graphic format. *Held,* the chart was a "product," the publisher its "manufacturer," and strict liability applied.

Accord, Fluor Corp. v. Jeppesen & Co., 216 Cal.Rptr. 68 (Ct.App.1985)(jet pilot crashed into mountain not depicted on approach chart); Saloomey v. Jeppesen & Co., 707 F.2d 671 (2d Cir.1983)(chart showed Martinsburg, W.Va. airport as having full ILS instrument approach; plaintiff crashed into ridge as a result). Jeppesen, the defendant in all three cases, mass produces and sells world-wide many thousands of aeronautical charts, periodically up-dated, to commercial and private pilots, including one author of this book who would rather be flying now.

6. See Jones v. J.B. Lippincott Co., 694 F.Supp. 1216 (D.Md.1988)(nursing student injured treating self with constipation remedy listed in nursing textbook; court held that Restatement § 402A does not extend to dissemination of an idea of knowledge); [citations]; Smith v. Linn, 563 A.2d 123 (Pa.Super.1989) (reader of Last Chance Diet book died from diet complications; book is not a product under Restatement § 402A); [citations].

3. Is the *Winter* rule correct? Do you agree that aeronautical charts should be treated differently? Are the First Amendment considerations the same or different in the two situations? Should the rule be a blanket one for all publications?

4. In Eimann v. Soldier of Fortune Magazine, Inc., 680 F.Supp. 863 (S.D.Tex. 1988), plaintiffs sued the magazine in negligence for publishing the following ad:

> EX–MARINES—67–69 'Nam vets—ex-DI-weapons specialist—jungle warfare, pilot, M.E., high risk assignments U.S. or overseas. (404) 991–2684.

A husband hired the person who placed the ad to kill his wife, and the job was done. *Held*, a negligence action for failure to investigate could be maintained, in view of the nature of the magazine and the fact that other ads explicitly offered criminal services. The first amendment was not a bar because this form of commercial speech was not as stringently protected as core speech. The jury subsequently awarded plaintiffs $9.4 million, but the court of appeals reversed, 880 F.2d 830, 838 (5th Cir. 1989), "declin[ing] to impose on publishers the obligation to reject all ambiguous advertisements for products or services that might pose a threat of harm."

5. In Rice v. Paladin Enter., 128 F.3d 233 (4th Cir. 1997) (Md. law), the Fourth Circuit allowed a tort-law aiding-and-abetting claim against the publisher of a "how-to" book for contract killers, including precise instructions on every gruesome detail of such projects. "[R]eadied by these instructions and steeled by these seductive adjurations from *Hit Man: A Technical Manual for Independent Contractors*, a copy of which was subsequently found in his apartment, James Perry brutally murdered Mildred Horn, her eight-year-old quadriplegic son Trevor, and Trevor's nurse." Id. at 239. Mildred Horn's ex-husband had hired Perry, the contract killer, so he could receive his son's $2 million settlement for injuries that had left him paralyzed. In conducting the murders, Perry meticulously followed numerous details from the *Hit Man* manual. Since the defendant publisher stipulated that it targeted the book to murderers and would-be murderers and that it knew and intended that the manual would be used for contract murders, the court found no difficulty in ruling that a jury could find that *Hit Man* had "little, if any, purpose beyond the unlawful one of facilitating murder," and so was unprotected by the First Amendment. After the court allowed the action to proceed, the publisher settled the case for millions of dollars. See also Wilson v. Paladin Enters., 186 F.Supp.2d 1140, 1144 (D. Or. 2001)(also involving *Hit Man*).

6. In James v. Meow Media, Inc., 300 F.3d 683 (6th Cir. 2002), parents of students killed when a classmate, acting allegedly based on movies, video games, and Internet websites that desensitized him to violence, discharged firearms at a group of students in their high school lobby sued the producers of the material. The court of appeals affirmed summary judgment for defendants, holding that the offending materials are not products for purposes of strict products liability.

7. See generally Gilles, Poisonous Publications and Other False Speech Physical Harm Cases, 37 Wake Forest L. Rev. 1073 (2002); Ausness, The Application of Product Liability Principles to Publishers of Violent or Sexually Explicit Material, 52 Fla.L.Rev. 603 (2000); Products Liability Restatement § 19, cmt. *d*; D. Owen, Products Liability Law § 16.8 (2d ed. 2008).

Bryant v. Tri–County Electric Membership Corp.

United States District Court, Western District of Kentucky, 1994.
844 F.Supp. 347.

■ HEYBURN, DISTRICT JUDGE.

[Plaintiffs brought an action in negligence, warranty and strict liability against their local utility company, Tri–County Electric Membership Corporation, and the manufacturer of electrical transformers, Kuhlman Corporation, for property damage sustained in connection with a fire that consumed plaintiffs' sawmill. Defendant Tri–County Electric moved for summary judgment on the implied warranty and strict liability claims on the ground that Kentucky law imposes only negligence liability on a utility company for careless transmissions of an electric current. Defendant Kuhlman moved for summary judgment contending that plaintiffs' evidence failed to show that it manufactured the electrical transformers that caused the fire.]

... The fire began when a switch attached to a lumber-surfacing machine exploded. Plaintiffs suspect that the switch's failure resulted from a series of voltage surges that plagued the sawmill in the years preceding the fire. These voltage spikes, plaintiffs contend, passed through their electric meter and gradually destroyed the switch's insulation.

[Significant irregularities in plaintiffs' electrical supply frequently burned out motors in their equipment and computers.] The transformers regulating the current entering plaintiffs' facility emitted an unusually loud hum. An oscilloscope registered voltage surges when attached to plaintiffs' machinery. In October 1986, Tri–County sought to eliminate these problems by removing the transformers then in service and installing transformers manufactured by Kuhlman.

This replacement improved plaintiffs' power supply, but did not successfully eliminate all symptoms of erratic voltage. Plaintiffs continued to suffer occasional voltage-related motor failures [until the April 1988 fire which plaintiffs claim resulted from the failure of Tri–County properly and adequately to supply them with electric power, and from the failure of or a defect in the transformers manufactured by Kuhlman and installed at plaintiffs' mill.]

Tri–County contends that Kentucky law does not impose liability on a producer of defective electrical current absent proof of negligence.[2] Since Kentucky has not yet declared whether principles of strict liability might apply to injuries caused by electricity, [this] Court has examined numerous decisions of other state courts [and] concludes that Kentucky would apply strict liability concepts in the circumstances of this case.

---

2. A utility clearly faces liability if its negligence results in injury. Kentucky law requires producers of electricity to "exercise the utmost care and skill to protect their patrons and the public against danger and harm." [Citations.]

A.

["Strict product liability"] applies generally to an entity that *"sells any product* in a *defective* condition [which renders the product] *unreasonably dangerous"* causing injuries. Restatement (2d) Torts § 402A, adopted by Dealers Transp. Co. v. Battery Distrib. Co., 402 S.W.2d 441 (Ky.1965). Opinions applying [§ 402A] to distributors of electricity focus on three dispositive legal questions: (1) Is electricity a "product"? If so, (2) When is electricity "sold", such that the principles of product liability might first apply? And finally, (3) When does electricity contain a "defect" that renders it "unreasonably dangerous"?[3]

The majority of the state courts considering this issue have encountered little difficulty deciding that electricity is a product. [E]lectricity is "a form of energy that can be made or produced by men, confined, controlled, transmitted and distributed...." Ransome v. Wisconsin Elec. Power Co., 275 N.W.2d 641, 643 (Wis.1979).[5]

Even so, electricity is subject to product liability rules only after it is "sold" to the consumer. Although identifying the moment of sale is a more challenging task, a reasonable consensus prevails: electricity is typically held to be "sold" when it passes through the customer's meter. See, e.g., *Ransome*. It is at this moment that the customer's charges are computed, the seller relinquishes control over its product, and the electricity has been reduced to a voltage suitable for ordinary use. [Citations.] Put another way, strict liability typically applies, if at all, only to injuries suffered *inside* the home or business, not to those experienced *outside*. See, e.g., Pierce v. Pacific Gas & Elec. Co., 212 Cal.Rptr. 283 (Ct.App.1985)(excluding "antenna" and "downed-power-line" injuries from product liability's scope).[6]

A product is sold in a "defective condition unreasonably dangerous" under Kentucky law when "the product creates such a risk of accident that an ordinarily prudent company ... would not have put it on the market." Montgomery Elevator Co. v. McCullough, 676 S.W.2d 776, 780 (Ky.1984). Courts in other jurisdictions generally declare that electric voltage far in excess of the level intended by the utility and expected by the customer is dangerously defective. [Citations.] On the other hand, a defective current might not reach "unreasonably dangerous" proportions if the threat posed

---

3. Strict liability in warranty exists when a manufacturer enters a contract for the *sale of goods* that are *unfit* for ordinary use. Ky.Rev.Stat. § 355.2–314(2)(c). [W]arranty relief in this case should therefore depend upon the same analysis that governs strict liability in tort: Tri–County [is not liable] unless it *sold* a *product* that was *defective*. [Citation.]

5. At least two states, however, flatly reject this definition, declaring instead that customers of electric utilities purchase a service, not a product. See Otte v. Dayton Power & Light Co., 523 N.E.2d 835 (Ohio 1988); Bowen v. Niagara Mohawk Power Corp., 590

N.Y.S.2d 628 (App.Div.1992). Injuries caused by voltage surges in these states are governed exclusively by negligence standards. See McKee v. Cutter Lab., 866 F.2d 219, 222 (6th Cir.1989).

6. At least ten states have considered the applicability of strict liability principles to electricity. Of these ten, eight states have determined that electricity is a "product", and that electricity is "sold" by its passage through the customer's meter. [Citing cases from Calif., Colo., Conn., Ind., N.J., Pa., Tex., and Wis.] ...

by the defect can be minimized most economically by the consumer rather than by the utility. [Citation.] Where the consumer is better able to eliminate the defect, the policies underlying the assignment of liability without fault—placing liability on the party best able to prevent the damage, and spreading the risk of loss—would not justify penalizing the utility.[7]

B.

The Kentucky courts have shown themselves willing to permit recovery under negligence standards when a utility transmits voltage either in excess of, or far below, ordinary levels, and such voltage causes harm inside or outside the home. [Citing cases of low voltage causing injury in the home, and high tension wire causing injury outside the home]. But would the Kentucky courts follow the concerns of other jurisdictions and apply strict liability principles to injuries resulting from a defective power supply? . . .

[Another federal district judge has] declared that Kentucky law would not hold the defendant utility strictly liable for damage caused to a farmer's cattle by the utility's "stray voltage" transmissions. G & K Dairy v. Princeton Elec. Plant Bd., 781 F.Supp. 485 (W.D.Ky.1991)(Siler, J.). Depending heavily on . . . the Ohio Supreme Court's analysis in *Otte*, Judge Siler concluded that . . . the service of distributing energy may be measured solely by negligence standards. . . .

Given the different circumstances of this case, however, this Court does not believe that the *G & K Dairy* opinion calls for the same result. Judge Siler contemplated the liability of a power company for stray voltage in *G & K Dairy*; that is, he evaluated the liability of a producer of electric power for injuries caused by stray electricity that did not form part of the current ordinarily purchased and used by the company's customers. He observed that "[s]tray voltage is an inherent by-product of every electrical transmission system" which is "neither marketed nor marketable"; the defendant utility was "not in the business of selling stray voltage, and it did not sell stray voltage to the plaintiffs." He concluded that such voltage was not a "product" subject to strict liability oversight.[9]

The unique characteristics of the stray voltage limit the applicability of *G & K Dairy* [to cases such as this where] injury results from ordinary

---

7. Consider in this context the Wisconsin court's finding in *Ransome* that a current of 4800 volts is unreasonably dangerous because the circuit breakers used by ordinary consumers cannot protect homes from currents in excess of 600 volts. *Ransome*. [The *Ransome* court may have reached a different conclusion if the damaging current had been 500 volts. That voltage, since it would have exceeded the ordinary supply of 120–240 volts, would be "defective"; however, since currents of up to 600 volts could be controlled most economically by the consumer, the electricity might not have been held "unreasonably dangerous."]

9. The stray voltage in *G & K Dairy* apparently had not passed through the plaintiff's meter before causing injury. Thus the majority rule described above would have dictated the result reached by *G & K Dairy*: strict liability does not govern injuries caused by *non-metered electricity* . . . .

electricity. Stray voltage is not an independently useable product. It is more by-product than product.... The current that allegedly caused injury in this lawsuit, by contrast, was ordinary electricity. Tri–County markets such electricity and its customers purchase and use that current. Ordinary electricity is therefore a "product" in virtually every respect that stray voltage is *not* a product....

C.

[This Court concludes that Kentucky courts] would follow the majority rule that considers ordinary electricity to be a "product", and would adopt the view that electricity is "sold", and first becomes subject to strict liability oversight, when it passes through a customer's meter. These rules provide a logical basis for determining the electric company's liability. The general view holding electricity to be a "product" sensibly accounts for the fact that electricity is created, harnessed, measured, transported, bought and sold, like products generally. The "meter as the point of sale" rule has the merit of creating a bright line between injuries resulting from the *service* of transmitting electricity—that is, injuries due to contact with electricity *before* the current reaches its intended destination—and damage resulting from the *product* of electricity itself—that is, injuries caused by defective electricity after the current has been purchased by the customer.

Kentucky's longstanding policies of protecting consumers and spreading risk encourage the state's courts to apply product liability standards to electricity. The citizen's dependence upon, and vulnerability to, electricity is almost without parallel in modern life. The consumer must purchase electricity and yet cannot possibly inspect the product before buying it or putting it to use. Indeed, a defect in electrical current often reveals itself only when it causes a catastrophe. Consumers therefore cannot avoid the purchase of defective electricity and cannot protect themselves from harm in the event the utility sells them a dangerous current.... The Kentucky courts would therefore probably conclude, in concert with the decisions of most other states, that the imposition of strict liability upon electric utilities will advance the twin policies of spreading the risk of loss among all product consumers and discouraging the sale of defective goods. [Citations.]

[T]he Court has considered whether any characteristics of electric power make the application of strict liability inappropriate to it.... Like other well made products, electricity presents an intermittent and haphazard risk to consumers. Consumers are encouraged to believe that electric power is safe and are given assurance in this belief by government regulation. Because electric companies deliver their product as part of a government regulated monopoly, consumers have no reason to be suspicious of the product nor any method to change their source if they are dissatisfied. Consequently, the theory of strict liability and the policy of risk spreading apply in the same manner to electricity as it does to any traditional product.

Some courts have found an unfairness in the imposition of strict liability upon a utility which must seek government approval to raise its rates and which may not be entitled to include these expenses as part of its costs. See Otte v. Dayton Power & Light Co., 523 N.E.2d 835, 838 (Ohio 1988). But the application of this rule is neither unfair nor overburdensome to utilities, even without the ability to pass along its expenses. For one thing, the "unreasonably dangerous" standard is a particularly difficult hurdle as applied to electricity. The law recognizes that electric power is not completely uniform and correctly allows a greater deviation before determining that it may be unreasonably dangerous. Moreover, Plaintiffs must still show a defect. The self-destroying character of electricity and the usual absence of electricity monitoring devices are additional hurdles of proof making these difficult cases. These factors also argue for the fairness in the strict liability approach.

In sum, the court perceives no policy rationale for not applying strict liability in these circumstances. The Court shall accordingly deny Tri–County's Motion to Dismiss.

D.

The fact that Plaintiffs *may* recover from Tri–County under strict liability principles is not to say that Plaintiffs *will* recover on the basis of the evidence presented thus far in this lawsuit. The Court recognizes that in some respects electricity is different from traditional products. These real differences will be considered by the Court and by the jury.

Although the definition of electricity as a "product" is a legal question, the distinction between ordinary electricity (a "product") and stray voltage (an incident of the service of transmission) is fact-oriented. Thus, if the evidence is such that reasonable persons could differ on the nature of the electricity that caused Plaintiffs' injuries, that issue is properly one for the jury's attention, and might ultimately lead to a verdict in Tri–County's favor. Whether the injurious current passed through Plaintiffs' meter before causing harm is likewise a question of fact.

The most interesting legal and factual question will focus on whether the allegedly damaging electricity was so "defective" as to be "unreasonably dangerous." The Court will not now attempt to design a precise definition of "unreasonably dangerous defect" in the context of electricity. The Court will propose, however, that if the defect established by Plaintiffs could have been mitigated most economically by Plaintiffs rather than Tri–County—if the voltage surges allegedly entering Plaintiffs' business varied only minimally from the normal current, for example, and occurred only rarely—then that defect might not be sufficient to render the current unreasonably dangerous. [Citation.]

[Plaintiffs are unable to identify the manufacturer of the transformers that triggered the fire. Tri–County purchased transformers from several suppliers, and its records do not show who manufactured the transformers used before October 1986. Nor, after diligent search, can plaintiffs locate them. Defendant Kuhlman's motion for summary judgment is granted.]

NOTES

1. "What is electricity? Simply stated, it is a force, like the wind. . . ." Pierce v. Pacific Gas & Elec. Co., 212 Cal.Rptr. 283, 288 n. 3 (Ct.App.1985)(holding that electricity is a product under § 402A).

2. Compare Balke v. Central Missouri Electric Cooperative, 966 S.W.2d 15 (Mo.App. 1997) (over-voltage from defective transformer; electricity not a good and not subject to strict products liability); Monroe v. Savannah Electric & Power Co., 471 S.E.2d 854 (Ga. 1996) (electricity is a product; sale element of strict liability requires "the manufacturer to have relinquished control" and that product was "in a usable or marketable condition"); Fuller v. Central Maine Power Co., 598 A.2d 457 (Me.1991) (house painter's aluminum ladder hit 7200–volt power line between residences; adopting nearly unanimous view that electricity in high-power lines not a "product").

3. See generally Cantu, A Continuing Whimsical Search for the True Meaning of the Term "Product" in Products Liability Litigation, 35 St. Mary's L.J. 341 (2004); Cantu, The Illusive Meaning of the Term "Product" Under Section 402A of the Restatement (Second) of Torts, 44 Okla.L.Rev. 635 (1991); Products Liability Restatement § 19, cmt. *d*; D. Owen, Products Liability Law § 16.6 (2d ed. 2008).

PART VI

SPECIAL TYPES OF LITIGATION

CHAPTER 18

SPECIAL ISSUES IN AUTOMOTIVE LITIGATION

* from The New York Times, March 10, 1985, § 3, at 1. Art by Niculae Asciu

Much products liability litigation involves claims against manufacturers of cars, vans, trucks, motorcycles, and other vehicles alleging that defects in the vehicles injured the plaintiffs. The usual victims in such accidents are the drivers and passengers, but sometimes bystanders are struck by the vehicle or some component thereof—such as a runaway tire from an 18–wheeler truck.

The automotive cases examined so far have for the most part involved manufacturing flaws: MacPherson v. Buick Motor Co., ch. 2(1), involved a wheel made of defective wood; Jenkins v. General Motors Corp., ch. 2(2), involved an improperly tightened nut in the suspension system; Ford Motor Co. v. Zahn, ch. 2(2), involved a jagged edge or burr on the corner of the ash tray; and Henningsen v. Bloomfield Motors, ch. 4(5), involved a mechanical defect in the steering mechanism. One of the cases involved a warnings claim: Greiner v. Volkswagenwerk A.G., ch. 11(3), where there was no warning of the VW beetle's propensity to roll over on sharp steering maneuvers. Most of the cases examined so far have involved claims of defect that caused the accident.

Not yet examined closely are automotive cases involving defects in design. The two principal types of automotive design cases are (1) those where the design defect *causes the accident,* and (2) those where the design defect *aggravates the injuries* in an accident caused by something else, such as driver error. Examples of the first type are design defects in the vehicle's steering, e.g., Smith v. Ford Motor Co., 215 F.3d 713 (7th Cir. 2000), or brakes, e.g., Santos v. Chrysler Corp., 715 N.E.2d 47 (Mass. 1999). Cf. Brooks v. Chrysler Corp., 786 F.2d 1191 (D.C. Cir. 1986) (brake defect claim dismissed where lip-in dust boot permitted junk to enter caliper bore). Since design defects by their nature infect the entire product line, threatening the safety of thousands of persons, some have become quite notorious. The control problems with the Corvair, publicized by Ralph Nader in "Unsafe at Any Speed" in the 1960s, is one example. Other examples in recent decades include the accelerator sticking problems of certain Audis, see Perona v. Volkswagen of America, Inc., 658 N.E.2d 1349 (Ill. App. 1995), and the roll-over tendencies of the Suzuki Samurai, the Ford Bronco II, and certain other SUVs, in the 1990s, and Ford Explorers equipped with Firestone tires in the early 2000s.

One design problem of the first type that began in the 1970s and 1980s involved the tendency of the transmissions in certain vehicles to slip from Park to Reverse. Accidents could occur when the driver tried to place the gear shift in Park but mispositioned the lever on the gatepost between Park and Reverse. If the driver then left the car with the engine running, the vibration from the engine or the door slamming could cause the transmission to slip into Reverse. See, e.g., General Motors Corp. v. Sanchez, 997 S.W.2d 584 (Tex. 1999), examined in ch. 14(1), above. In many cases, plaintiffs' experts testified that the shape and height of the gatepost, and the design of the springs involved, made it much more likely that the Ford FMX transmission would accidentally slip into Reverse than the transmissions in other cars. See, e.g., Ford Motor Co. v. Nowak, 638 S.W.2d 582 (Tex. App. 1982) (5–1) (affirming $400,000 pecuniary damages and $4,000,000 punitive damages awards for death of person run over when she went behind her car to close the driveway gate); Ford Motor Co. v. Bartholomew, 297 S.E.2d 675 (Va. 1982) (plaintiff fell while chasing car that slipped into reverse while she was loading groceries); Sandhill Energy, Inc. v. Ford Motor Co., 33 S.W.3d 483 (Ky. 2002), punitive damages verdict vacated, 538 U.S. 1028 (2003). See generally Branton, From "Park" to "Reverse"—The Costly Slip, Trial 42 (Nov. 1978).

The second type of automotive design defect, examined in the cases that follow, causes an occupant's injuries in an accident to be unnecessarily severe. This type of defect causing "aggravated injuries" can also become quite notorious, as illustrated by the Ford Pinto fuel tank problem in the 1970s and early 1980s, and the GM pick-up truck side-saddle gas tank problem in the mid–1990s. These "second collision" or "crashworthiness" cases are the focus of this chapter because they involve a variety of special issues unique to automotive litigation.

---

1. CRASHWORTHINESS

"Crashworthiness" is defined in the Motor Vehicle Information and Cost Savings Act, 49 U.S.C.A. § 32301(1) (2006), as "the protection a passenger motor vehicle gives its passengers against personal injury or death from a motor vehicle accident." A vehicle's crash worthiness concerns its capacity to withstand the physical stresses of a collision and to minimize additional or "enhanced" injuries the passengers may sustain as a result of the "second collision" between the occupants and the interior of the vehicle. The cause of the accident (the first collision, or roll-over) is largely irrelevant to the crashworthiness issue and, specifically, the accident need not have been caused by a defect in the car.

Whether manufacturers should be obligated to design crashworthy vehicles was one of the major debates in products liability law in the late 1960s and early 1970s. The origin of the controversy was Evans v. General Motors Corp., 359 F.2d 822 (7th Cir. 1966), where the driver was killed when another vehicle struck the side of his vehicle which collapsed in on him. Plaintiff alleged that the death was attributable to the vehicle's "X" frame design which afforded occupants less protection in side-impact collisions than the side frame rail design used by other manufacturers as shown in the advertisement of a rival manufacturer set forth below.

Which frame is stronger?

Reasoning that the purpose of automobiles is not to collide with other objects, the *Evans* 2–1 majority ruled that the manufacturer had breached no duty in failing to design a safer car. Two years later, Larsen v. General Motors Corp., 391 F.2d 495 (8th Cir.1968) ruled to the contrary. There, plaintiff was injured in a head-on collision when his steering mechanism, the front shaft of which protruded 2.7 inches in front of the forward tires, was propelled back into his head. In view of the clear foreseeability of automobile accidents, and data demonstrating that many if not most vehicles are involved in at least one accident which causes injury or death, the court ruled that car manufacturers must be held accountable for vehicular safety in the crash environment. "The sole function of an automobile is not just to provide a means of transportation, it is to provide a safe means of transportation or as safe as is reasonably possible under the present state of the art." Id. at 502.

Although a small handful of cases followed the *Evans* no-duty approach, the vast majority followed *Larsen.* If there was any doubt as to the final outcome of the issue, it was put to rest in 1977 when the Seventh Circuit repudiated its decision in *Evans,* in Huff v. White Motor Corp., 565 F.2d 104, 109 (7th Cir.1977)(death by fire from rupture of fuel tank): "[There] is no rational basis for limiting the manufacturer's liability to those instances where a structural defect has caused the collision and a resulting injury.... Since collisions [from] whatever cause are foreseeable events, the scope of liability should be commensurate with the scope of foreseeable risks." This is now an axiom of products liability law. See Products Liability Restatement § 16 cmt. *a.*

Settling the crashworthiness duty issue does not of course resolve the more difficult problem of deciding just what the scope and limits of a manufacturer's design obligations should be. What kinds of accidents should a vehicle reasonably be able to withstand? How severe and what types of injuries are acceptable? In some situations these questions are easy to resolve. Thus, if a low-speed collision causes the covering over the center hub on the steering wheel to pop off, exposing sharp prongs that injure a passenger's face, the car is plainly uncrashworthy. See Ellithorpe v. Ford Motor Co., 503 S.W.2d 516 (Tenn. 1973). Yet, difficult issues arise when the initial impact is more severe, as in Soule v. General Motors Corp., 882 P.2d 298 (Cal. 1994), examined in ch. 7(2), above, and in the materials below.

The difficult problem of apportioning damages in crashworthiness cases gives rise to certain problems of proof. Since usually an uncrashworthy design does not cause the initial accident, the defendant logically should be liable only for those additional ("aggravated" or "enhanced") injuries caused in the "second collision." Yet, difficulties arise in this situation when a plaintiff dies or otherwise cannot prove that his or her serious injuries are attributable only to the uncrashworthy nature of the vehicle's design.

A final problem arises with respect to airbags, safety devices that normally add considerable safety to a car's performance in some crash situations but that sometimes activate so as to injure an occupant who otherwise would have been unharmed.

Burgos v. Lutz

New York Supreme Court, Appellate Division, 1987.
128 A.D.2d 496, 512 N.Y.S.2d 424.

■ [PER CURIAM.]

[Plaintiff's decedent was killed while driving his Honda Civic 1200 when he made a left turn at an intersection and his car was struck by an oncoming vehicle, a Ford LTD. The decedent suffered a transection (laceration) of his thoracic aorta, and apparently died instantly. Plaintiff brought this action against the driver of the Ford, alleging negligence, and against Honda, alleging defective design of the steering column and seat belt system of the Civic. The jury and trial court found for the defendants. The trial lasted three months.]

The plaintiff's evidence concerning the defective seatbelt system consisted of expert testimony to the effect that, upon inspection of the actual seatbelt in the decedent's Honda, the locking device performed erratically. The plaintiff failed to establish that the erratic performance was caused by the design of the locking device. Furthermore, the plaintiff's expert did not testify that there was an alternative, safer design of the seatbelt locking system. Moreover, none of the plaintiff's evidence established, either directly or circumstantially, that the decedent was wearing his lap or shoulder belts at the time of the collision. Thus, the plaintiff failed to meet her obligation to present evidence that it was feasible to design a seatbelt system in a safer manner, see Voss v. Black & Decker Mfg. Co., 450 N.E.2d 204 (N.Y. 1983), or that the alleged defect was the cause in fact of the decedent's death. Accordingly, the plaintiff failed to establish a prima facie case of a defectively designed seatbelt system.

The plaintiff's theory with respect to her claim of a defectively designed steering column was that the system lacked an adequate energy absorbing capability, and that when the decedent came into contact with the steering wheel, his chest sustained an intolerable impact from the force of the collision, causing the injuries which resulted in his death. Although the plaintiff's expert testified to the characteristics and qualities of an alternative, feasible steering column energy absorption system, the expert failed to explain how the proposed design would have prevented any of the decedent's injuries under the circumstances of the actual collision. Significantly, the plaintiff's expert failed to indicate how the alternative design would have absorbed more energy than the steering column design used in the decedent's vehicle. Thus, the plaintiff failed to show that the alternative design was any safer or more capable of preventing the harm that the decedent suffered than Honda's design. . . .

Because the plaintiff failed to establish a prima facie case with respect to either of her defective design claims, the trial court properly granted the respondents' motions to dismiss those claims.

[Affirmed.]

NOTES

1. This "short" case, which took *three months* to try, raises many of the issues in litigation involving automobiles. Consider, in studying the cases and materials in this chapter, why it would take so long to try such a case. Consider also the resources consumed in this type of litigation.

2.   The typical automobile defect case usually involves a complex interrelationship of proof of design defect, including the feasibility of alternative designs, the role of safety devices such as seat belts and airbags, and difficult issues of causation. All require extensive expert testimony on what typically are complex and sometimes largely indeterminate matters on which there is little hard evidence and much uncertainty. For example, how can anyone really know what would have happened had the plaintiff been wearing a seatbelt? Or had the steering column absorbed more energy? How much certainty should be required from the evidence, and who should bear the risk of the evidence being insufficient?

Had you represented plaintiff in *Burgos,* what might you have done differently?

3.   There is extensive federal regulation of automotive design by the National Highway Traffic Safety Administration (NHTSA) of the Department of Transportation. How should this pervasive regulatory system affect the common law process of products liability litigation?

Sumnicht v. Toyota Motor Sales, U.S.A., Inc.

Wisconsin Supreme Court, 1984.
121 Wis.2d 338, 360 N.W.2d 2.

■ CECI, JUSTICE.

[Vernon Sumnicht was rendered a quadriplegic when the car in which he was riding as a back seat passenger left the roadway on a curve and collided with a tree. Immediately before the accident, which occurred at 2 o'clock in the morning,] Sumnicht was lying down, with his head behind the driver's seat, in the back seat of a 1975 Toyota Corolla two-door sedan operated by Edmund C. O'Connor, Jr. Sumnicht was not using the available seat belt. Jack Vallerugo was riding in the front passenger's seat of the Toyota, which was equipped with bucket seats. Sumnicht, O'Connor, and Vallerugo were returning to the University of Wisconsin–Whitewater, where they were students.

[As the Toyota entered a large curve in the roadway, it] drifted off the highway, traveling approximately 303 feet along the shoulder. It then crossed a drainage ditch and climbed a grass incline before hitting the tree head-on. At the moment of impact with the tree, the Toyota was estimated to be traveling between thirty and fifty miles per hour.

O'Connor sustained chest injuries, from which he fully recovered. Vallerugo also received chest injuries and died en route to the hospital. Sumnicht suffered a fractured dislocation of his cervical spine at C6–7, which caused his quadriplegia. Other than his severed spinal cord, Sumnicht had relatively minor injuries, which consisted of two chipped teeth, a possible fractured rib, and two leg lacerations.

Sumnicht initially commenced suit against the driver of the Toyota, his father, and their insurers, later amending his complaint to include three sellers and distributors of the 1975 Toyota involved in the accident (collectively referred to herein as "Toyota"). The complaint alleged causes of action on the theories of strict products liability and negligence.

The trial commenced on January 31, 1983, lasting over three weeks. Sumnicht's liability case revolved around the theories that the front seat system of the Toyota was both defective and unreasonably dangerous and negligently designed and manufactured. His liability experts included an accident reconstructionist, a mechanical engineer, a biomedical engineer, a safety engineer, a neurosurgeon, and a metallurgist.

These experts testified that, at the time of the collision, Sumnicht was lying down in the back seat, with his head toward the driver's side of the Toyota. They theorized that upon impact of the car with the tree, Sumnicht was propelled forward and his head became entrapped in the cutout portion of the back of the driver's seat, while his lower torso swung forward, smashing into the back of the front passenger's seat. The inboard hinge on the passenger's seat broke loose, allowing Sumnicht's lower torso to wrap around the seat. The continued movement forward of his lower torso, while his head was stationary, created the shearing forces which injured his spinal cord and resulted in his quadriplegic condition.

Sumnicht's experts opined that the 1975 Toyota was defective and unreasonably dangerous and negligently designed and manufactured insofar as the back of the bucket seat did not have any energy-absorbing material beneath the vinyl seat cover. Instead of the bucket seat's serving as a shock absorber, it permitted Sumnicht's head to become captured in the hollow cutout portion of the back of the driver's seat.

The hinges on the passenger's seat which connect the bottom of the seat to the seat back were also criticized. There was testimony that the inboard bracket on the passenger's seat broke upon impact because it was made of the weakest steel available. This allowed Sumnicht's lower torso to propel around and enter the front seat area of the Toyota. Sumnicht's experts concluded that had the seat backs not been so designed and had the bracket not broken, Sumnicht would not have sustained the paralyzing injuries.

Conversely, Toyota was of the opinion that the seat system was not defective and did not cause Sumnicht's injuries. Toyota's liability experts included an engineer specializing in crash analysis, a biomechanical engineer, an accident reconstructionist, and a metallurgist. These experts theorized that Sumnicht's head did not become entrapped in the seat at all. It was reasoned that just prior to the collision, Sumnicht sat up and was injured when he was thrown over and between the front bucket seats, striking his head on the dashboard area of the automobile.

At the verdict formulation phase of the trial, the court dismissed the negligence claim at Toyota's request, and the case went to the jury solely on the theory of strict liability. The jury found that the 1975 Toyota automobile contained such a defect in the design of the seat system as to be unreasonably dangerous to a prospective passenger in the rear seat of the automobile and found that such defective design was a cause of injuries to the plaintiff over and above those injuries which he probably would have sustained as a result of the collision without such defective design. The jury also found that O'Connor was negligent at the time of the collision and that his negligence was also a cause of plaintiff's injuries. The jury found that plaintiff was not negligent in his own conduct prior to the collision. The jury apportioned the negligence at 50% to the defective seat system and 50% to the driver, Edmund C. O'Connor, Jr. The jury awarded $4.7 million for the plaintiff's personal injuries, including his pain and suffering, past and future; his permanent disability; his loss of earnings, past and future; and his medical, hospital, drugs, and nursing care, past and future. These damages were awarded specifically for injuries which plaintiff sustained over and above injuries which he would have probably sustained from the collision without the defective design in the seat system. The trial court reduced the damage award by the percentage of negligence attributed to O'Connor, denied Toyota's motions after verdict, and entered judgment against Toyota in the amount of $2.35 million. Toyota now appeals.

I.

A. *Introduction*

This suit falls within a class of cases commonly referred to as "second collision" or "crashworthy" cases. The crashworthiness doctrine imposes liability upon a manufacturer in a vehicular collision case for design defects which do not cause the initial accident but which cause additional or more severe injuries when the driver or passenger subsequently impacts with the defective interior or exterior of the vehicle. This double-collision distinction is clarified by the following:

> "An automobile collision is really two collisions. In the first phase of the accident, the plaintiff's automobile collides with another automobile or with a stationary object. Most of the property damage results from the first collision, but the occupants of the vehicle usually sustain little or no injury at this stage. Personal injuries occur most frequently in the second collision, in which the occupants are thrown against or collide with some part of their automobile. Courts will hold the manufacturer liable for the plaintiff's loss in the second collision only if defective design of the automobile caused or exacerbated the plaintiff's injury. Yet, if a court finds that defective automobile design did cause some injury, determining where one defendant's liability ends and another's begins may be virtually impossible. Both those injuries for which the manufacturer should be liable and those attributable to other causes, such as another driver's negligence, occurred during the very brief time span of the second collision." Note, Apportionment of Damages in the "Second Collision" Case, 63 Va. L. Rev. 475, 476 (1977).

The instant case can be termed a "second collision" case because the plaintiff's claim is not that Toyota's defective seat system caused the accident ("first collision"), but, rather, that as a result of his impact with the defective seats ("second collision"), he sustained injuries which he otherwise would not have sustained.

The case generally credited with extending liability to manufacturers for injuries resulting from a defectively designed automobile that is uncrashworthy is Larsen v. General Motors Corporation, 391 F.2d 495, 503 (8th Cir. 1968). That court pioneered the benchmark that,

> "Any design defect not causing the accident would not subject the manufacturer to liability for the entire damage, but the manufacturer should be liable for that portion of the damage or injury caused by the defective design *over and above* the damage or injury that probably would have occurred as a result of the impact or collision absent the defective design." (Emphasis added.)

This ruling is consistent with the basic [tort law premise limiting] a defendant's liability to that portion of harm which he has in fact caused, as distinguished from harm arising from other sources.

The issue of a manufacturer's liability in a "second collision" case was first decided by this court in Arbet v. Gussarson, 225 N.W.2d 431 (Wis. 1975), a case arising out of an automobile accident in which the plaintiffs were burned following the rupture of their vehicle's gasoline tank and ignition of the fuel. The plaintiffs alleged in their complaint that the defectively designed gasoline tank, although not a cause of the accident, was the proximate cause of their burns. The trial court dismissed the complaint, and we reversed, holding that the automobile manufacturer may incur liability for injuries to occupants of a vehicle arising from its negligence in designing the vehicle such that it is unreasonably unsafe in an accident.

* * *

B. Burden of Proof

The standard of proof issue in "second collision" products liability cases has been phrased by some as being an issue of which party bears the burden of proving the apportionment of damages. Apportionment of damages should not be confused with plaintiff's burden of proving causation. [Prosser] explains,

> "Once it is determined that the defendant's conduct has been a cause of some damage suffered by the plaintiff, a further question may arise as to the portion of the total damage sustained which may properly be assigned to the defendant, as distinguished from other causes. The question is primarily not one of the fact of causation, but of the feasibility and practical convenience of splitting up the total harm into separate parts which may be attributed to each of two or more causes."

W. Keeton, D. Dobbs, R. Keeton, & D. Owen, Prosser and Keeton on Torts § 52 at 345 (5th ed. 1984).

The *Arbet* decision tells us that Sumnicht has a cause of action in strict liability against Toyota for all injuries which the defective seat system was a substantial factor in causing. This premise forecloses recovery against Toyota for injuries sustained solely in the "first collision," because Toyota's defective seat system was not a proximate cause of the accident. Requiring Sumnicht to distinguish between the damages sustained in the "first collision" and the "second collision" is part and parcel of his burden of proving causation. However, only after Sumnicht has proven what injuries were caused by Toyota is the issue of apportionment of damages properly raised. The precise issue here is not which party bears the burden of apportioning damages in cases involving joint tortfeasors, but what quantum of evidence must a plaintiff bring forth in a "second collision" products liability case to prove that his injuries were proximately caused by the manufacturer's defect.

A divergence in opinion on this issue stems from the following language in Larsen v. General Motors Corporation, 391 F.2d 495, 503 [cited in *Arbet*]:

> "[T]he manufacturer should be liable for that portion of the damage or injury caused by the defective design *over and above* the damage or injury that probably would have occurred as a result of the impact or collision absent the defective design." (Emphasis added).

Based on this language, defendants take the position that in a "second collision" case the plaintiff must not only prove that the defective product was a substantial factor in causing the injuries, but also must prove what the injuries would have been had there been no defect. Toyota asserts that its liability is nonexistent until Sumnicht shows the extent to which the injuries were enhanced by the defect.

Two opposing views on the plaintiff's standard of proof are set forth in Huddell v. Levin, 537 F.2d 726, 737–38 (3d Cir. 1976), and Fox v. Ford Motor Co., 575 F.2d 774 (10th Cir. 1978). Toyota relies on *Huddell,* wherein that court held that the plaintiff must prove three elements in order to recover in a crashworthy case.

> "We have set forth, supra, the basic elements of proof in an orthodox strict liability case under New Jersey law: a *defective* product *causing* injury. The simplicity of the general formulation belies the difficulty of applying it in ... crashworthy or second collision cases.... First, in establishing that the design in question was defective, the plaintiff must offer proof of an alternative, safer design, practicable under the circumstances.... Second, the plaintiff must offer proof of what injuries, if any, would have resulted had the alternative, safer design been used. [The court is correct] in Yetter v. Rajeski, 364 F. Supp. 105, 109 (D.N.J. 1973) that 'it is absolutely necessary that the jury be presented with some evidence as to the extent of injuries, if any, which would have been suffered [if] the plaintiff's hypothetical design [had been installed.]' Third, as a corollary to the second aspect of proof, the plaintiff must offer some method of establishing the extent of enhanced injuries attributable to the defective design."

The *Huddell* court has been criticized for requiring the plaintiff to assume an impossible burden of proving a negative fact. [Mitchell v. Volkswagenwerk, AG, 669 F.2d 1199, 1204–05 (8th Cir. 1982),] declares,

> "The primary difficulty we have with [the *Huddell*] analysis is that it forces not only the parties but the jury as well to try a hypothetical case. Liability and damage questions are difficult enough within orthodox principles of tort law without extending consideration to a case of a hypothetical victim. More realistically, the parties and juries should direct their attentions to what actually happened rather than what might have happened."

> "[*Larsen*] was not intended to create a rule which requires the plaintiff to assume an impossible burden of proving a negative fact. A rule of law which requires a plaintiff to prove what portion of indivisible harm was

caused by each party and what might have happened in lieu of what did happen requires obvious speculation and proof of the impossible. This approach converts the common law rules governing principles of legal causation into a morass of confusion and uncertainty."

Sumnicht relies on a second approach to the standard of proof in a "second collision" case, enumerated in *Fox,* 575 F.2d 774, 787, which places a significantly lesser burden of proof on a plaintiff. In *Fox,* the tenth circuit found no reason to require plaintiffs in second collision cases to bring forth proof in addition to that required of plaintiffs in all tort cases, i.e., that the plaintiff suffered a legally cognizable injury proximately caused by the defendant. The court reasoned,

> "Generally this duty to prove so-called enhanced damages is simply a part of the plaintiff's responsibility to prove proximate cause, that is, that the defendant in such a case is liable only for those damages which are within the orbit of risk created by him, but Ford would have us say that the plaintiffs were required to prove with specificity the injuries which flowed specifically from its deficiencies.

> "The case which is relied on by Ford to illustrate its position is Huddell v. Levin, 537 F.2d 726 (3d Cir. 1976). There the holding was that plaintiff in a collision case such as the present one had the burden of proving enhanced injuries and that the presentation of evidence that the accident was survivable did not meet this burden. The thesis of this case was that collision cases are to be treated differently from other liability or negligence cases as far as the specificity of proof is concerned. It refused to follow the orthodox doctrines of joint liability of concurrent tort-feasors for injuries which flow from their concurring in one impact.

> "We fail to see any difference between this type of case and the other case in which two parties, one passive, the other active, cooperate in the production of an injury. Each one's contribution in a causal sense must be established. Damages may be apportioned between the two causes if there are distinct harms or a reasonable basis for determining the causes of injury. Rest. (2d) of Torts § 433A."

[As for apportionment of damages, *Fox* held] that death "is not a divisible injury in which apportionment is either appropriate or possible."

For the reasons set out in *Mitchell* and *Fox,* this court also rejects the two requirements enumerated in *Huddell* that the plaintiff in a "second collision" case must offer proof of what injuries, if any, would have resulted had an alternative, safer design been used and that the plaintiff must offer some method of establishing the extent of enhanced injuries attributable to the defective design.

[Strict liability] requires proof that the product was in a defective condition, unreasonably dangerous, which caused the plaintiff's harm. The long-standing test for cause in Wisconsin is whether the defect was a substantial factor in producing the injury[:]

> "It need not be the sole factor or the primary factor, only a 'substantial factor.' The phrase 'substantial factor' denotes that the defendant's conduct has such an effect in producing the harm as to lead the trier of fact, as a reasonable person, to regard it as a cause, using that word in the popular sense. There may be several substantial factors contributing to the same result." Clark v. Leisure Vehicles, Inc., 292 N.W.2d 630 (Wis. 1980).

The requirement in *Huddell* that the plaintiff prove the extent of enhancement of injuries would, in some cases, require the plaintiff to isolate that portion of injuries caused solely by the manufacturer. This may be an impossible task and is not required by the law of this state. We affirm the applicability of the substantial factor test in proving causation.

* * *

In any event, once the plaintiff has proven that the defect was a cause of his injuries, he need not prove what portion of indivisible harm is attributable solely to the manufacturer. If there is more than one tortfeasor who contributed to the injury, Wisconsin's law concerning joint and several liability applies.

> " 'When two actors negligently conduct themselves so as to injure another, they become jointly and severally liable to the other if their actions concur in time to directly produce injury or to create an injury-producing situation. [Citations.]' "Wis. Natural Gas v. Ford, Bacon & Davis Constr., 291 N.W.2d 825 (Wis. 1980).

[O]nly after the plaintiff establishes that there are joint tortfeasors can the issue of apportionment of damages be raised.

C.   *Sufficiency of Evidence*

[Plaintiff called six experts, four of whom testified on causation:] Bruce Enz, a safety engineer and accident reconstructionist; Dr. Anthony Sances, a biomedical engineer; Dr. Patrick Walsh, a neurosurgeon; and Dr. Robert Brenner, a safety engineer.

Bruce Enz, vice president of the Institute for Safety Analysis, testified regarding the accident reconstruction and the plaintiff's kinematics at the time of the collision. Based on his thorough examination of the Toyota, he concluded that, at the time of the impact, the plaintiff was lying in the back seat of the vehicle on his left side, with his head toward the driver's side. In a simultaneous progression, his upper torso struck the driver's seat, entrapping his head in the cutout portion of the driver's seat, while his legs flew forward, striking the passenger's seat. His lower torso then continued forward as a result of the failure of the seat's bracket that holds together the seat's back rest and bottom. This movement caused Sumnicht's body to rotate around his upper thorax area. Enz's examination of the Toyota eliminated other possible kinematic scenarios by which Sumnicht could have sustained his injuries. Enz concluded,

> "It's my opinion that the entrapment and capturing capability of the seat backs and the failure of the bracket enhanced and created the injury mechanism."

Dr. Anthony Sances [analyzed] Sumnicht's injury sequence. Based on his inspection of the Toyota and his evaluation of the medical reports, Sances attested that the upper portion of Sumnicht's spinal column became fixed as his legs swung forward. This created a shear force between the sixth and seventh cervical elements that [tore] the spinal cord. He opined that Sumnicht would not have sustained his paralyzing injuries if the driver's seat had not allowed his head to become entrapped and if the seat's bracket had not failed.

Dr. Walsh testified mainly from the plaintiff's X-rays ... that Sumnicht's paralyzing injuries were caused by a number of forces on his spine, including flexion, compression, shear, and possible rotation. [Walsh stated that these findings were consistent with the hypothesis that plaintiff's] head became entrapped in the back of the driver's seat while his lower torso continued to move forward.

Finally, Robert Brenner, president of the Institute for Safety Analysis, testified [on] the design of Toyota's seat system. He initially assigned Mr. Enz with the responsibility of taking the crash vehicle apart to analyze what happened in the crash. He subsequently studied a number of documents and reports and examined the vehicle himself to analyze the crashworthiness of Toyota's seat system. He [opined] that the defective seat design was a substantial factor in causing Sumnicht's injuries.

We hold that there is credible evidence to support a finding that the defective seat design was a substantial factor in causing Sumnicht's injuries. Two separate theories were presented at trial as to how Sumnicht's spinal cord was severed. Toyota opined that the plaintiff's injuries were caused by Sumnicht's hitting his head on the dashboard of the Toyota. The jury obviously chose not to believe Toyota's theory and, instead, relied on Sumnicht's theory of causation. We agree with the jury's determination, which is supported by expert testimony and the physical facts of this case.

Second, although Sumnicht was not required to prove what extent of his injury was over and above any injury which he probably would have sustained as a result of the collision without the defective design, in essence this was proven at trial. There is sufficient evidence to support Sumnicht's theory that the portion of indivisible harm attributable solely to the defective design was his fractured cervical spine. The plaintiff adequately distinguished between the injuries he would have sustained without the defect (his minor injuries) and those injuries caused by the defect (his fractured spine).... Technically, the defective seat system did not "enhance" Sumnicht's injuries because, but for the defect, there were no injuries to enhance. The defect in this case was latent until activated by the negligence of the driver of the car; acting together, this produced Sumnicht's quadriplegia. Toyota's defective seat system did not enhance the plaintiff's injury; it was a substantial factor in causing it.

II.

Sumnicht's entire liability case concentrated on the alleged design defects in Toyota's seat system.

* * *

Question number one of the special verdict asks,

"Did the 1975 Toyota automobile contain such a defect in the design of the seat system as to be unreasonably dangerous to a prospective passenger in the rear seat of the automobile?"

[The jury's affirmative answer is supported by credible evidence.]

Toyota contends that there is no credible evidence to support the jury's finding that the defect in the design of the seat system was unreasonably dangerous because the plaintiff brought forth no proof of "an alternative, safer design, practicable under the circumstances." *Huddell*. We disagree with Toyota for two reasons. First, although evidence of an alternative safer design may be relevant and admissible in a products liability case, our state's strict products liability rule does not mandate such evidence. A product may be defective and unreasonably dangerous even though there are no alternative, safer designs available. [We have] held that a whole industry may be negligent in failing to adopt new and available devices. The question is not whether any other manufacturer has produced a safer design, but whether the specific product in question is defective and unreasonably dangerous. Second, although not required, the evidence in this case proves that there was an alternative safer design available for Toyota's seat system. There was a confirmation by one witness that there are numerous energy-absorbing materials available to fill in the cutout section of the driver's seat and that these materials were being used in the industry. Also, another witness stated that the bracket on the passenger's seat failed because it was made of low-grade steel instead of a material that would stand up to forces in a reasonably foreseeable collision.

[Design defectiveness] can be established through expert opinion testimony that was formed after an examination of the product. [Citation.]. Four of the plaintiff's experts—Enz, Sances, Brenner, and Weiss—gave their opinions with respect to the defectiveness and unreasonableness of Toyota's seat design.

Enz examined the Toyota and stated that the seat system was defective [due to] the open cutout section of the driver's seat, which has the capability of capturing and entrapping, and the inadequate metal selected for the bracket, which allowed it to break upon impact. Dr. Sances also testified that the seat design was defective and unreasonably dangerous and that many energy-absorbing materials were available to cover the cutout portion of the driver's seat. Dr. Brenner, an automobile safety engineer with substantial credentials, testified at great length as to how a properly designed seat system would compartmentalize an unbelted rear seat occupant and manage the energy caused in a foreseeable collision. It was his opinion that the seat system failed and was, therefore, defective and unreasonably dangerous because of the hollow cutout portion in the driver's seat, the lack of energy-absorbing material in the cutout section, and the weak steel from which the bracket was made. Finally, Stanley Weiss, a metallurgist, testified [on] the seat bracket that had failed. [He] performed a fractographic analysis (to determine the nature of the fracture), a stress analysis, and a hardness test on the bracket [and] concluded that the seat bracket was defective because it was made of the weakest steel available and would not withstand the force of a rear seat occupant's impacting it in a reasonably foreseeable crash.

In addition to expert testimony, [design defectiveness] can be established by the presentation of circumstantial evidence. "Evidence of a malfunction is one type of circumstantial evidence that can be used in establishing a defective condition." [Citation.] In this case, it was undisputed that there was severe damage to the interior of the Toyota: the bracket on the passenger's seat broke, the seats were displaced, the floor buckled, and the vinyl covering the back of the driver's seat showed an imprint from a body. Second, there was testimony that from a safety standpoint, a primary function of a seat system is to compartmentalize unbelted rear seat occupants and not to enhance injuries that may occur in a reasonably foreseeable collision. The plaintiff brought forth evidence that Toyota's seat system did not serve the function of compartmentalizing unbelted rear seat occupants. Also, although controverted by other evidence, the plaintiff introduced an article co-authored by Arnold Siegel, Toyota's chief expert, which included a study of 54 frontal collisions resulting in 135 incidents of injuries to unbelted rear seat occupants. Only twenty percent of the rear seat passengers suffered serious injuries in crashes occurring at speeds over forty miles per hour; eighty percent of those injured suffered only moderate or minor injuries. Sumnicht inferred that absent the defective seat system, it was probable that he would have suffered only moderate or minor injuries, but in this case the Toyota was defective in that it failed to protect him from further injuries.

Finally, Toyota showed two films of full-scale crash tests conducted on 1975 Toyota Corollas. [There was testimony] that the seat brackets in the film broke upon impact, just as the bracket did in this case, and that the films supported the plaintiff's theory of liability and not Toyota's theory.

[T]he risk that a car may be in an accident is reasonably foreseeable [such that defendants] have a duty to anticipate that risk. *Arbet*. We reemphasize the following from [*Larsen*, relied on by *Arbet*]:

> "We perceive of no sound reason, either in logic or experience, nor any command in precedent, why the manufacturer should not be held to a reasonable duty of care in the design of its vehicle consonant with the state of the art to minimize the effect of accidents. The manufacturers are not insurers but should be held to a standard of reasonable care in design to provide a reasonably safe vehicle in which to travel.... While all risks cannot be eliminated nor can a crash-proof vehicle be designed under the present state of the art, there are many common-sense factors in design, which are or should be well known to the manufacturer that will minimize or lessen the injurious effects of a collision. The standard of reasonable care is applied in many other negligence situations and should be applied here."

[T]here is credible evidence to sustain the jury's finding that Toyota's seat system was both defective and unreasonably dangerous. [The jury could] conclude that Toyota's seat system was defective in that it failed to compartmentalize the plaintiff in a foreseeable frontal collision and, thus, failed to minimize his injuries, and that the defect was unreasonably dangerous because rear seat occupants would not realize the risk of harm that they are subjected to if an accident does occur. The defect in the design of the seat system was not open and obvious to an ordinary passenger. It is rational to hold that Toyota's seat system was not as safe as it reasonably could have been or as safe as reasonably contemplated by rear seat occupants.

[Affirmed.]

[Concurring opinion of HEFFERNAN, C.J., omitted.]

■ STEINMETZ, JUSTICE (dissenting).

* * * The injuries to plaintiff are awesome and due deliberation should be given to allow him the right to a fair trial and to receive damages if he is entitled to them. I find it incomprehensible that the jury found under the facts of this case the plaintiff was not negligent for his own care and safety by failing to wear the available rear seat belt. The finding of no negligence is inconsistent with the facts of a head-on crash at a speed of 30 to 50 miles per hour while not wearing a seat belt and sustaining very serious injuries as a result of being propelled forward. The fact that plaintiff was affected by his failure to wear a seat belt is obvious and a finding of no negligence is inconsistent with the evidence and therefore is perverse. * * *

NOTES

1. **Proof of Apportionment.** A sizable majority of courts have followed the *Sumnicht* path and adopted the *Fox–Mitchell* approach of requiring apportionment proof from the defendant in crashworthiness cases involving indivisible harm. See, e.g., Harsh v. Petroll, 887 A.2d 209, 218–19 n.20 (Pa. 2005); Trull v. Volkswagon of Am., Inc., 761 A.2d 477 (N.H. 2000). The cases are collected in D. Owen, Products Liability Law § 17.4 (2d ed. 2008).

2. **Defectiveness and Crashworthiness.** The test for defectiveness in crashworthiness cases involves the same basic considerations arising in design defect cases generally. An influential early case was Dreisonstok v. Volkswagen-werk, A.G., 489 F.2d 1066, 1073–74 (4th Cir. 1974). Plaintiff was injured while riding as a passenger in the front seat of a Volkswagen microbus when the vehicle collided with a telephone pole at 40 m.p.h. The district court found for the plaintiff, concluding that the vehicle's design was defective for failure to have "sufficient energy-absorbing materials or devices or 'crush space' . . . so that at 40 miles an hour the integrity of the passenger compartment would not be violated." Plaintiff's case was built upon a comparison of the structural integrity of the passenger compartment in front-end collisions of the VW microbus with that of a standard American passenger car. Rejecting this comparison, the appeals court reversed:

> The defendant's vehicle, described as "a van type multipurpose vehicle", was of a special type and particular design. This design was uniquely developed in order to provide the owner with the maximum amount of either cargo or passenger space in a vehicle inexpensively priced and of such dimensions as to make possible easy maneuverability. To achieve this, it advanced the driver's seat forward, bringing such seat in close proximity to the front of the vehicle, thereby adding to the cargo or passenger space. This, of course, reduced considerably the space between the exact front of the vehicle and the driver's compartment. All of this was readily discernible to any one using the vehicle; in fact, it was, as we have said, the unique feature of the vehicle. The usefulness of the design is vouchsafed by the popularity of the type. [Indeed, the driver's father immediately purchased another microbus to replace the one destroyed in this accident.] It was of special utility as a van for the transportation of light cargo, as a family camper, as a station wagon and for use by passenger groups too large for the average passenger car. . . . There was no evidence in the record that there was any practical way of improving the "crashability" of the vehicle that would have been consistent with the peculiar purposes of its design.

The court also noted the importance of cost in crashworthiness risk-benefit analysis, observing that "if a change in design would appreciably add to cost, add little to safety, and take an article out of the price range of the market to which it was intended to appeal, it may be 'unreasonable' as well as 'impractical' for the Courts to require the manufacturer to adopt such change." The public, thought the court, expects less crashworthiness in an economy car than in a Cadillac. See Products Liability Restatement § 2 cmt. *f*, Illus. 8; § 16 cmt. *b*, Illus. 5.

Compare Seattle–First National Bank v. Volkswagen of America, Inc., 525 P.2d 286 (Wash. App. 1974), aff'd, 542 P.2d 774 (Wash. 1975), where the court held that a jury should be permitted to pass on the crashworthiness of the front end of a VW microbus which struck the rear end of a flatbed truck at a relative speed of 20 m.p.h. *Dreisonstock* was distinguished on the basis of the difference in speed at the time of the collisions. Are the cases reconcilable?

Virginia may be the only state to reject the crashworthiness doctrine altogether for conflicting with the principle that a manufacturer need not provide an "accident-proof" product. Slone v. General Motors Corp., 457 S.E.2d 51 (Va. 1995).

3. Types of Claims. Automotive design litigation has involved virtually every aspect of vehicle safety. For example:

A. Inadvertent design mistakes. Nay v. General Motors Corp., 850 P.2d 1260 (Utah 1993)(pinch point between steering coupling and steering box susceptible to catching rock); Ford Motor Co. v. Nowak, 638 S.W.2d 582 (Tex. App. 1982) (tendency of transmission to slip from Park to Reverse).

B. Structural integrity. Shipler v. General Motors Corp., 710 N.W.2d 807 (Neb. 2006) (Blazer's roof crushed in rollover); Dawson v. Chrysler Corp., 630 F.2d 950 (3d Cir. 1980) (side frame collapsed on impact with pole); Grimshaw v. Ford Motor Co., 174 Cal.Rptr. 348 (Ct. App. 1981) (fuel tank located within flimsy rear structure).

C. Interior design. Mickle v. Blackmon, 166 S.E.2d 173 (S.C.1969) (passenger impaled on gear shift lever mounted on steering column when plastic knob shattered in side-impact collision); Rossell v. Volkswagen of America, 709 P.2d 517 (Ariz. 1985) (battery located inside passenger compartment of VW beetle where it could drip acid on occupants if vehicle rolled on back).

D. Safety devices. Camacho v. Honda Motor Co., Ltd., 741 P.2d 1240 (Colo. 1987) (crash bar to protect legs on motorcycle); Leichtamer v. American Motors Corp., 424 N.E.2d 568 (Ohio 1981) (Jeep roll bar collapsed); Huddell v. Levin, 537 F.2d 726 (3d Cir. 1976) (death from head hitting sharp metal edge inside head restraint); Garrett v. Ford Motor Co., 684 F.Supp. 407 (D. Md. 1987) (severe abdominal injuries to rear passengers wearing lap belts, causing paralysis and death); Kupetz v. Deere & Co., 644 A.2d 1213 (Pa. Super. 1994) (bulldozer without ROPS); Dannenfelser v. DaimlerChrysler Corp., 370 F.Supp.2d 1091 (D. Hawai'i 2005) (airbag failed to deploy).

Hundreds of cases have been based on whether the standard rear seat lap belt, as opposed to the three point shoulder belt used in the front, renders a vehicle uncrashworthy. See, e.g., Johnson v. General Motors Corp., 438 S.E.2d 28 (W. Va. 1993). See generally Sakayan, Holtz & Kelley, More Than a Case About a Car—An Analysis of Garrett v. Ford Motor Company, Trial 34 (Feb.1989); Swartz, Swartz & Cantor, Seat–Belt Injury Litigation, Trial 47 (Nov.1988).

E. Exterior design. Green v. Volkswagen of America, Inc., 485 F.2d 430 (6th Cir. 1973) (as young girl was walking by parked van, finger severed by sharp vent on side); Knippen v. Ford Motor Co., 546 F.2d 993 (D.C.Cir.1976); Passwaters v.

General Motors Corp., 454 F.2d 1270 (8th Cir. 1972) (motorcycle passenger's leg injured when struck by Ben–Hur type wheel cover); Threats v. General Motors Corp., 890 S.W.2d 327 (Mo. Ct. App. 1994) (rigid side-view mirror unreasonably dangerous to pedestrians).

   4. Statistical Evidence. In Seese v. Volkswagenwerk A.G., 648 F.2d 833 (3d Cir. 1981), the court addressed the evidentiary use of accident statistics collected by the federal government. The National Highway Traffic Safety Administration operates a Fatal Accident Reporting System (FARS) which collects information on fatal accidents by vehicle type and make. The plaintiff in *Seese* attempted to introduce FARS data into evidence to show the greater likelihood of ejection from a VW van than from competitive vehicles. The defendant objected on the ground that the government data were not official records, nor was proof offered that the data represented accidents similar to the accident in question. Defendant's objections were overruled on the basis that FARS data offered in the form of certified copies of official records were admissible as public records under Fed.R.Evid. 1005, as part of the basis of an expert's opinion under Fed. R. Evid. 703, and under the Business Records Act, 28 U.S.C.A. § 1732, and that differences between the plaintiff's accident and FARS data went to the weight of the evidence and not to its admissibility.

   5. Crash Test Evidence. Defendants often, and plaintiffs sometimes, stage reconstructed crashes in an attempt to prove how the accident occurred. See, e.g., General Motors Corp. v. Jernigan, 883 So.2d 646, 655 (Ala. 2003) ("GM says that it runs 500 to 600 crash tests per year"); Shipp v. General Motors Corp., 750 F.2d 418 (5th Cir. 1985) (Pontiac TransAm roof collapsed in rollover accident, injuring plaintiff; drop test results used by plaintiff to show roof defect admitted over defense objections that test conditions differed from actual accident conditions). *Held,* the test was relevant to roof strength, and its admission by the trial judge was not an abuse of discretion, even without an instruction to the jury to consider any differences between the drop test and accident conditions. Note, however, that to be admissible the crashes tested must be similar to the hypothesized accident vehicle crash. Hinds v. General Motors Corp., 988 F.2d 1039 (10th Cir. 1993) (videotapes of government crash-performance tests dissimilar to plaintiff's crash).

   6. Design Safety and the Litigation Process. In Dawson v. Chrysler Corp., 630 F.2d 950 (3d Cir. 1980), cert. denied, 450 U.S. 959 (1981), plaintiff lost control of his 1974 Dodge Monaco which "slid off the highway, over a curb, through a small sign, and into an unyielding steel pole that was fifteen inches in diameter. The car struck the pole in a backwards direction at a forty-five degree angle on the left side of the vehicle; the point of impact was the left rear wheel well. As a result of the force of the collision, the vehicle literally wrapped itself around the pole. The pole ripped through the body of the car and crushed Dawson between the seat and the 'header' area of the roof, located just above the windshield." Dawson's collision with the interior of the car ruptured his fifth and sixth cervical vertebrae, rendering him a quadriplegic.

   Plaintiffs alleged the car was defectively designed "because it did not have a full, continuous steel frame extending through the door panels, and a cross-member running through the floor board between the posts located between the front and rear doors of the vehicle. Had the vehicle been so designed, the Dawsons alleged, it would have 'bounced' off the pole following relatively slight penetration by the pole into the passenger space." Chrysler's experts testified that:

[T]he design and construction of the 1974 Dodge Monaco complied with all federal vehicle safety standards, and that deformation of the body of the vehicle is desirable in most crashes because it absorbs the impact of the crash and decreases the rate of deceleration on the occupants of the vehicle. Thus, Chrysler's experts asserted that, for most types of automobile accidents, the design offered by the Dawsons would be less safe than the existing design. They also estimated that the steel parts that would be required in the model suggested by the Dawsons would have added between 200 and 250 pounds to the weight, and approximately $300 to the price of the vehicle. It was also established that the 1974 Dodge Monaco's unibody construction was stronger than comparable Ford and Chevrolet vehicles.

The jury awarded plaintiffs over $2 million in damages, and Chrysler appealed. Chrysler argued that the jury could not reasonably have found that plaintiffs' alternative design was safer than the existing design, or that it was cost effective, practicable, or marketable. "In short, Chrysler urges that the substitute design would be less socially beneficial than was the actual design [emphasizing] that the design of the [car] complied with all [NHTSA standards]." The court responded:

> Compliance with the safety standards promulgated pursuant to the National Traffic and Motor Vehicle Safety Act, however, does not relieve Chrysler of liability in this action. For, in authorizing the Secretary of Transportation to enact these standards, Congress explicitly provided, "Compliance with any Federal motor vehicle safety standard issued under this subchapter does not exempt any person from any liability under common law." 15 U.S.C. § 1397(c) (1976).

Dawson, 630 F.2d at 958. *Held,* affirmed. The jury could reasonably have found that the car was "not reasonably fit, suitable and safe" under New Jersey law. The court concluded, at 962–63:

> Although we affirm the judgment of the district court, we do so with uneasiness regarding the consequences of our decision and of the decisions of other courts throughout the country in cases of this kind.
>
> As we observed earlier, Congress, in enacting the National Traffic and Motor Vehicle Safety Act, provided that compliance with the Act does not exempt any person from liability under the common law of the state of injury. The effect of this provision is that the states are free, not only to create various standards of liability for automobile manufacturers with respect to design and structure, but also to delegate to the triers of fact in civil cases arising out of automobile accidents the power to determine whether a particular product conforms to such standards. In the present situation, for example, the New Jersey Supreme Court has instituted a strict liability standard for cases involving defective products, has defined the term "defective product" to mean any such item that is not "reasonably fit, suitable and safe for its intended or reasonably foreseeable purposes," and has left to the jury the task of determining whether the product at issue measures up to this standard.
>
> The result of such arrangement is that while the jury found Chrysler liable for not producing a rigid enough vehicular frame, a factfinder in another case might well hold the manufacturer liable for producing a frame that is too rigid. Yet, as pointed out at trial, in certain types of accidents— head-on collisions—it is desirable to have a car designed to collapse upon

impact because the deformation would absorb much of the shock of the collision, and divert the force of deceleration away from the vehicle's passengers. In effect, this permits individual juries applying varying laws in different jurisdictions to set nationwide automobile safety standards and to impose on automobile manufacturers conflicting requirements. It would be difficult for members of the industry to alter their design and production behavior in response to jury verdicts in such cases, because their response might well be at variance with what some other jury decides is a defective design. Under these circumstances, the law imposes on the industry the responsibility of insuring vast numbers of persons involved in automobile accidents.

Equally serious is the impact on other national social and economic goals of the existing case-by-case system of establishing automobile safety requirements. As we have become more dependent on foreign sources of energy, and as the price of that energy has increased, the attention of the federal government has been drawn to a search to find alternative supplies and the means of conserving energy. More recently, the domestic automobile industry has been struggling to compete with foreign manufacturers which have stressed smaller, more fuel-efficient cars. Yet, during this same period, Congress has permitted a system of regulation by ad hoc adjudications under which a jury can hold an automobile manufacturer culpable for not producing a car that is considerably heavier, and likely to have less fuel efficiency.

In sum, this appeal has brought to our attention an important conflict that implicates broad national concerns. Although it is important that society devise a proper system for compensating those injured in automobile collisions, it is not at all clear that the present arrangement of permitting individual juries, under varying standards of liability, to impose this obligation on manufacturers is fair or efficient. Inasmuch as it was the Congress that designed this system, and because Congress is the body best suited to evaluate and, if appropriate, to change that system, we decline today to do anything in this regard except to bring the problem to the attention of the legislative branch.

Bound as we are to adjudicate this appeal according to the substantive law of New Jersey, and because we find no basis in that law to overturn the jury's verdict, the judgment of the district court will be affirmed.

7. Fixing the *Dawson* Problem. As a matter of substantive defectiveness theory, most courts today would probably conclude that a manufacturer is protected from *Dawson*-type claims, on the ground that reasonable automotive design safety necessarily involves tradeoffs that will result in injury to certain occupants in certain crash situations in order to protect against more serious types of risks to other occupants in other crash situations. "When evaluating the reasonableness of a design alternative, the overall safety of the product must be considered. It is not sufficient that the alternative design would have reduced or prevented the harm suffered by the plaintiff if it would also have introduced into the product other dangers of equal or greater magnitude." Products Liability Restatement § 2 cmt. *f*; § 16 cmt. *b*, Illus. 5.

8. Strategy and Ethics. In automotive products liability cases, however, manufacturers typically confront a much more serious *practical* problem—not concerning the *theory* of defectiveness but its fair *administration* by juries sympathetic to humans severely injured in crashes and antagonistic to profit-motivated multi-national automotive companies whose design engineers pre-planned for just such accident scenarios. A jury returned an $8.7 million verdict to a woman who was rendered paraplegic because of defectively designed seat belts in a 1987 Isuzu Trooper II. Dorsett v. American Isuzu Motors, Inc., 805 F.Supp. 1212 (E.D. Pa. 1992), aff'd, 977 F.2d 567 (3d Cir. 1992). After the verdict, the company stated: "[T]he verdict was based on sympathy and against the great weight of the evidence which showed no defect in the vehicle's design and that the design of the vehicle did not cause her injuries." Prod.Safety & Liab.Rep. (BNA) 1152 (1991).

If you represent an automotive manufacturer in a serious crash case, anticipating a strong jury bias for the plaintiff and against your client, how might you address this daunting disadvantage?

If you represent the plaintiff in such a case, how might you exploit your jury advantage? Should a plaintiff's lawyer take automotive design cases that are marginal on the merits—on defectiveness, causation, or because of limited damages—banking on jury sympathy and empathy to bridge the evidentiary gap?

9. Legislative Reform. A number of states have enacted laws that provide for indemnification between the automobile manufacturer and dealer for products liability claims. See, e.g., Idaho Code § 49–1623 (vehicle manufacturer must indemnify dealer for all products liability judgments and settlements); Maine Rev. Stat. Ann. § 10–1175 (manufacturer, if held liable, must indemnify dealer for costs and attorney's fees incurred in defending suit).

10. On automotive products liability, see generally Latin, Bad Designs, Lethal Profits: The Duty to Protect Other Motorists Against SUV Collision Risks, 82 B.U. L. Rev. 1161 (2002); Nader & Page, Automobile–Design Liability and Compliance with Federal Standards, 64 Geo. Wash. L. Rev. 414 (1996); Note, 48 Case W. Res. L. Rev. 659 (1998) (airbag injuries); D. Owen, Products Liability Law ch. 17 (2d ed. 2008); 2 D. Owen, M.S. Madden, & M. Davis, Madden & Owen on Products Liability ch. 21 (3d ed. 2000).

———

Quintana–Ruiz v. Hyundai Motor Corp.

United States Court of Appeals, First Circuit, 2002.
303 F.3d 62.

■ LYNCH, CIRCUIT JUDGE.

This product design case tests some of the limits of the minority rule, adopted by Puerto Rico and California, that the defendant bears the burden of proving that the utility of a product's design outweighs the risks. Aponte Rivera v. Sears Roebuck de P.R., Inc., 1998 WL 198857 (P.R. 1998); Barker v. Lull Eng'r Co., 573 P.2d 443 (Cal. 1978). The question here is whether a jury may find for a plaintiff, injured when her airbag properly deployed in an auto accident, when the evidence is that the overall utility of the design exceeds the overall risk, there is no evidence of the existence of an alternative safer design, and the jury verdict is based either on a misunderstanding of the law or solely on the jury's rejection of the testimony of the experts retained by the defendant. We hold that such a jury verdict is not sustainable. It effectively, in these circumstances, either converts the defendant to the status of an insurer or creates liability based on a consumer expectation theory. Since neither of these outcomes is permissible under Puerto Rican law, we reverse and direct entry of judgment for defendant.

I. FACTS

[Fifteen-year-old Ines Reyes–Quintana was riding in the front passenger's seat of a 1996 Hundai Accent manufactured by the defendant and driven by her brother, possibly wearing her seatbelt but maybe not. When a much slower Nissan pulled in front of them, her brother braked the Hyundai but rear-ended the Nissan at a speed differential of about 30 miles per hour. The passenger-side airbag deployed, striking Reyes–Quintana's hand, which she had raised as if to brace herself, fracturing her arm and wrist in four places. The fractures required three surgeries, including the permanent attachment of two metal plates and sixteen metal screws, and Reyes–Quintana has lost some strength in and has scarring on the arm. The damage to the Hyundai was about $11,300. Suit was brought by Reyes–Quintana's mother, Quintana–Ruiz.]

II. TRIAL PROCEEDINGS

[Two experts testified on the airbag's design, both retained by Hyundai, and a medical expert testified for the plaintiff as to the extent of her injuries.]

A.   Testimony of Dr. Martinez

Dr. Jose Martinez, formerly of Texas A & M University, testified as an accident reconstruction expert [for the defendant], providing the probable explanation of how the accident took place. He testified that the police reports showed 163 feet of braking marks before impact. Based on the damage sustained by the Hyundai, Dr. Martinez concluded that it was traveling thirty miles per hour faster than the Nissan at the point of impact. Based on this conclusion and the length of the skid marks, Dr. Martinez opined that the Hyundai had to be traveling at least 63 miles per hour before the driver began to brake.

Dr. Martinez explained the mechanics of accident reconstruction, a short summary of which is necessary in order to understand the issues in this case. Barrier equivalent velocity, referred to as BEV, is the speed at which a vehicle goes into a barrier, measured in miles per hour. BEV is used for setting the deployment level for airbags, and it is the measurement used in the relevant federal regulations. Delta V, a related but not identical concept, is the change in velocity of a vehicle, usually at the center of gravity, also measured in miles per hour. Generally, accident reconstruction experts measure the Delta V of the car environment, rather than that of a specific occupant. In accidents involving impact into a barrier, the BEV is often slightly less than the Delta V.

The higher the Delta V is, the more serious the injuries are likely to be. Conversely, the lower the Delta V, the less serious the injuries are likely to be. The majority of accidents occur in the 10 to 15 Delta V range. Generally, accidents with a Delta V under 15 are considered to be of lower severity. Middle severity accidents are in the 15 to 25 Delta V range; above

25 is considered high severity. Dr. Martinez testified that a BEV of 15 "is where you start to get serious injuries, according to the statistics" and that is "where you want that air bag to go off." He also testified that even an accident referred to as "low severity" is not mild because, if you are unrestrained, such an accident can "put your head in the windshield" and cause serious injuries. Although he could not provide the specific percentiles of how many people would get hurt in an accident with a BEV under 14, he stated that "people do get hurt and will get hurt" in those types of accidents. Dr. Martinez testified that an accident with a BEV of 12 would cause an unbelted test dummy to go through the windshield. Based on his reconstruction of the plaintiff's accident, Dr. Martinez estimated the BEV of the accident at "14 to 16, or maybe thirteen and change" and the Delta V at "15 to 16, could be 15 to 17."

The airbag in this Hyundai model is designed to always deploy in accidents with a BEV of 12 or greater, and so the deployment of the airbag was in keeping with its intended design. Dr. Martinez testified that, in any American car with an airbag, the airbag would have deployed in an accident of the type at issue here. Nothing in the cross-examination impeached any of these conclusions. [Plaintiff's counsel unsuccessfully tried to get Dr. Martinez to] concede that airbag deployment Hyundai could have chosen an airbag design that would deploy at a higher BEV; Dr. Martinez responded that he did not know whether it was possible to create a design that would only deploy at a BEV of over 14 and still meet the federal performance standards.

[Plaintiff's counsel also tried] to get Dr. Martinez to concede that he knew of studies indicating that airbag deployment at a BEV of less than 15 causes more injuries than it prevents; Dr. Martinez responded that he had no knowledge of such studies. No such studies were introduced. Dr. Martinez's overall conclusion was that, even at accidents with a BEV of 14 and less, the airbag "does more good than harm."

B. Testimony of Dr. Benedict

Dr. James Benedict, an expert in the response of the human body to acceleration and impact forces, such as in accidents, also testified. Specifically, he is an expert in biomechanical analysis, occupant kinematics, injury causation, and airbag performance. Although the defense retained Dr. Benedict, the plaintiff called him as a witness and presented his testimony. [He testified that] the airbag deploys when sensors in the car detect a change in acceleration level; the airbag is essentially "predictive in nature," in that it must predict the severity of the collision based on the initial change in acceleration. The airbag deploys in about ¼ of the time it takes to blink an eye. Dr. Benedict testified that he knew of no way for an airbag to deploy more slowly and still provide the required protection. As for the Hyundai involved in this particular accident, Dr. Benedict testified that the airbag was designed to deploy in every accident with a BEV of 12 or higher (which he referred to as the "must fire" level), but because of variances in vehicle tolerances, could deploy at a BEV of as low as 8.9. He agreed that in any car in America in 1996, the airbag would deploy during a crash with a BEV of 15[, and that accidents occurring from 0–14 or–15 Delta V should be classified as "low" severity accidents; those from 15–25 Delta V as "moderate" severity; those from 25 to 35 Delta V as "severe"; and those over 35 Delta V as "very severe"].

Dr. Benedict testified that the effects of a crash with a BEV of 15 could vary. Some occupants will emerge from such an accident with minor or moderate injuries, referred to as "AIS–I" or "AIS–II" injuries, in reference to the Abbreviated Injury Scale system for categorizing the severity of injuries. Perhaps as many as half of those involved in such crashes would walk away from the accident with no injuries. An unbelted individual without an airbag in the type of crash experienced by Reyes–Quintana, however, could hit and shatter the windshield, sustaining facial bone fractures, lacerations to the face, and perhaps neck injuries. Death could even result. Accidents with a Delta V of 15 account for twenty percent of all AIS–III or greater injuries. AIS–III injuries are severe, serious or critical, including injuries such as contusions to the lung or a penetrating injury to the skull, and may pose a threat to life.

Dr. Benedict acknowledged that there have been injuries and some deaths caused by deployment of airbags. At the same time, over six thousand lives had been saved by the presence of airbags. He characterized this as a "trade-off." Airbags are meant to protect the primary systems that keep people alive: the head, neck, spine, chest, heart, and lungs. Airbag systems are most effective in preventing these head, neck, and chest injuries, although they may increase the risk of less severe injuries in some crashes.

[Plaintiff's counsel tried] to get Dr. Benedict to admit that reports had concluded that, in low severity crashes, occupants are more likely to be injured by the airbag than by the accident itself. Dr. Benedict responded that he knew of one study concerning driver's side airbags, but denied that he knew of any such conclusion. At no point did any expert testify that such a conclusion would be accurate.

[As for the issue of the risks to belted passengers raised by plaintiff's counsel,] Dr. Benedict testified that "you can have significant injury in Delta Vs of 15, 14, 13," even when wearing a seat belt, although he conceded that "it's less likely wearing a seat belt" and the "probability of the head hitting something [when a passenger is wearing a seat belt] is low." According to Dr. Benedict, however, federal law requires that airbags be designed to protect unrestrained passengers as well as restrained passengers.

Quintana–Ruiz offered no evidence to contradict any of the evidence described.

C. *Proceedings After Close of Evidence*

After all the evidence had been introduced, Hyundai moved for judgment as a matter of law. The district court granted the motion on the plaintiff's failure to warn claim,[2] but denied it on the plaintiff's design defect claim.

In closing, the plaintiff's attorney argued that the "only question" for the jury was "whether the damages suffered by Ines [Reyes–Quintana] would have been less had the airbag not been in the car or not deployed in the car." He argued that the Delta V was around 15 and the BEV was in the 12 to 14 range, classifying the accident as a "minor collision,"[3] and that there should not be airbag deployment "at these speeds." [He told the jury that both Dr. Martinez and Dr. Benedict were credible witnesses. The judge instructed the jury in part:]

[A] plaintiff may bring an action against a manufacturer who defectively designed a product, or in the alternative, failed to provide instructions or warnings.

Under the design theory, a plaintiff must establish that, first, the product failed to perform as safely as an ordinary consumer would expect when used in an intended or reasonably foreseeable manner; or the product's design is the proximate cause of the plaintiff's injury and the defendant failed to establish, in light of the relevant factors, that, on balance, the benefits of the challenged design outweigh the risk of danger inherent in such a design [and if] you find that the benefits surpass the risks, then the defendants are not liable under this theory.

On the other hand, if you find that the benefits do not surpass the risks, then you find for the plaintiffs.

[T]he jury found for the plaintiff, [awarding] $400,000 to Ines Reyes–Quintana ... and $150,000 in emotional distress damages to [her mother].

[The district court denied Hyundai's post-trial motions except that he remitted the mother's damages to $90,000.] In denying the motion for judgment as a matter of law, the district court held that there was sufficient evidence for the jury to conclude "that the deployment of the airbag in an accident of this type was unwarranted given the risks posed by the high speed at which the airbag deploys" or that, given the evidence that airbags are designed to protect the upper body areas, "the jury may have reasonably found that the risk posed to other parts of the body, like plaintiff's arm, were too high and that the overall design was defective." He further reasoned that, even if all the experts testified that the utility of the airbag design outweighed the risk, "there was testimony from which the jury could have found that defendant's experts' testimony was biased and unreliable." The judge also found that Hyundai had forfeited any claim of error regarding the consumer expectation test by not specifically objecting to its inclusion in the jury instructions, and that, regardless, the fleeting

---

2. The judge held that federal law preempted any failure to warn claim, because the federal regulations specify what warnings manufacturers must provide.

3. There was no evidence that the BEV could have been as low as 12. The expert testimony was that the BEV was "14 to 16, or maybe thirteen and change." The experts classified this accident as a "moderate" severity accident.

reference to consumer expectations in the jury instructions was harmless error.[4]

III.

On appeal, Hyundai argues that there is insufficient evidence, as a matter of law, to support the jury verdict. . . .

A. *Evidence of Design Defect*

Under Puerto Rican tort law governing design defect claims, if the plaintiff proves that "the product's design is the proximate cause of the damage," the burden shifts to the defendant to prove that "the benefits of the design at issue outweigh the risk of danger inherent in such a design." [Citations.] This rule, which follows California law as established in Barker v. Lull Eng'r Co., 573 P.2d 443 (Cal. 1978), [was designed] to "lighten the plaintiff's burden" in proving a design defect . . . not to radically expand the scope of products considered defective by design.

In this case, the defendant concedes that the plaintiff has met her burden of establishing that the airbag was the proximate cause of Reyes–Quintana's injuries. The question is whether the defendant has met its burden of showing that the benefits accruing from the airbag's design outweigh the risks.

The defect claimed in this case is that the airbag was designed to deploy at a BEV of 14, the BEV level of the crash in this case[, rather than at a higher speed that might have prevented Reyes–Quintana's injuries.]

The plaintiff's attorney argued in his closing that the question was "whether the damages suffered by Ines would have been less had the air bag not been in the car or not deployed in the car." That, however, is not the correct question in a design defect case. The question posed by the plaintiff's attorney unfairly stacks the deck in the risk-utility equation—when the question is based on the plaintiff's particular circumstances, the "risk" of injury is 100%, as the plaintiff in question has by definition been injured, and therefore the risk will almost always outweigh the utility for that particular plaintiff in that particular instance. Similarly, the trial court's conclusion that, given the evidence that airbags are designed to protect the upper body areas, "the jury may have reasonably found that the risk posed to other parts of the body, like plaintiff's arm, were too high and that the overall design was defective," misstates the test. The issue is not whether the design posed too great a risk to the passenger's arm, or any one specific body part.

Instead, the question for the jury was whether, generally, the benefits imposed by the airbag's challenged design aspect (here, the fact that the passenger side airbag deploys in accidents with a BEV in the range of 14 to 16) outweigh its risks. In this inquiry, the jury should have considered the

---

4. Hyundai had specifically opposed the consumer expectation theory in its pre-verdict motion for judgment as a matter of law, arguing that "the ordinary consumer has no knowledge or expectation as to how an airbag could or should perform" and therefore it is not a proper theory for a defect claim based on an airbag's design.

risk and utility to unbelted passengers, as well as the risk to belted passengers. The evidence was that unbelted passengers receive a considerable utility from airbags in such accidents, as, absent the airbag, there is a substantial risk of severe facial, head and spinal injuries.[5]

There was much evidence presented at trial on the risks posed by, and the utility created by, airbag deployment at a BEV of 14. The uncontradicted evidence was that the benefits outweighed the risks. No expert testified that the risk of harm posed to passengers by airbags in accidents with a BEV of 14 exceeded the benefits of airbags deploying in those types of crashes. In fact, both Dr. Martinez and Dr. Benedict testified that they knew of no studies coming to such a conclusion. Dr. Martinez specifically testified that, at accidents with a BEV of 14 and under, the airbag "does more good than harm." The evidence was that airbags are designed to prevent the most serious types of injuries and therefore to preserve lives, although the cost of preserving these lives may be an increased risk of injuries of a less serious variety in some crashes.

The plaintiff's argument that these serious injuries do not occur in the type of accident she had was not supported by the evidence. The evidence was that 20% of all AIS–III injuries occur at a Delta V of 15 or below—therefore, a significant percentage of serious injuries are the result of these "moderate" severity accidents. Reyes–Quintana had the benefit of the protection against these types of injuries afforded by the airbag. She did not suffer any head, face or brain injuries, precisely the types of injuries an airbag protects against in an accident with a Delta V of 15.

* * *

Many products, like airbags, involve a "trade off" between the benefits offered to the consumer and the risk created by the product. The risk-utility balancing test is designed to avoid converting the manufacturer into the insurer of every harm that arises out of a product from which the consumer derives utility. [Citations.] The plaintiff is entitled to compensation only if the challenged design aspect does more harm than good, overall, for the consumer.

2. *Alternative Design*

An important part of the risk-utility test is the question of whether there is a mechanically feasible safer alternative design. See *Barker*; [citation. But] no expert presented any evidence that there was any alternative design that would have posed less of a risk to passengers while still providing the same level of protection. In fact, the expert testimony was just the opposite. The only alternative design suggested by the plaintiff was an airbag with a higher deployment level (presumably a deployment level at a BEV greater than 16, given that the expert testimony placed the BEV of this accident at between 14 and 16). The expert testimony effective-

---

5. Reyes–Quintana herself admitted that, until just prior to the accident, she was not wearing her seatbelt. Had the accident occurred at an earlier point in the evening, when she was not belted, she would have benefitted tremendously from the airbag deployment.

ly refuted this as a feasible alternative that would decrease overall risk to passengers. "[F]easibility [is] not the sole issue, for another relevant consideration [is] whether an alternative design of the car, while averting the particular [harm here], would have created a greater risk of injury in other ... situations." *Barker*. Expert testimony established that a deployment trigger above a BEV of 12 would leave many individuals unprotected from serious injuries of AIS–III and higher.

Further, Dr. Benedict testified that airbags cannot be designed to trigger at one specific BEV level. Rather, because of variations in cars, any one design will result in a range of deployment levels. If a designer wants an airbag to definitely deploy at a BEV of 12 (what Dr. Benedict referred to as a "must fire" level), the airbag will sometimes deploy at as low as a BEV of 8.9. The plaintiff's suggestion in closing arguments that Hyundai should have designed a bag that would deploy at a BEV of 16 and above, but never at a BEV of 14 or 15, is inconsistent with the evidence presented at trial on mechanical feasibility.

[We conclude that no rational jury could have found] on these facts that the risks of the airbag design outweighed the benefits.

* * *

A consumer expectations theory was not available to the plaintiff here.[12] "*Barker* ... made clear that when the ultimate issue of design defect calls for a careful assessment of feasibility, practicality, risk and benefit, the case should not be resolved simply on the basis of ordinary consumer expectations." Soule v. Gen. Motors Corp., 882 P.2d 298, 305 (Cal. 1994) (holding that the consumer expectations test was not appropriate for a claim that a car was defective because the wheel assembly detached in accident). The California Supreme Court has held that "the consumer expectations test is reserved for cases in which the *everyday experience* of the product's users permit a conclusion that the product's designs violated *minimum* safety assumptions." Id. The court specifically observed that "the ordinary consumer of an automobile simply has 'no idea' how it should perform in all foreseeable situations, or how safe it should be made against all foreseeable hazards." *Id.* In one airbag design defect suit, a California appellate court held that:

> The deployment of an air bag is, quite fortunately, not part of the "everyday experience" of the consuming public. Minimum safety standards for air bags are not within the common knowledge of lay jurors. Jurors are in need of expert testimony to evaluate the risks and benefits of the challenged design.... [I]n designing air bags there are tradeoffs involving complex technical issues.

Pruitt v. Gen. Motors Corp., 86 Cal. Rptr. 2d 4 (Cal. App. 1999). [But other California cases are contra.]

---

12. The district court erroneously instructed the jury on the consumer expectation theory. But Hyundai failed to object after the instruction was given and therefore failed to preserve its objection....

IV. CONCLUSION

[Verdict vacated and case remanded to enter judgment for defendant.]

NOTES

1. Compare Crespo v. Chrysler Corp., 75 F. Supp.2d 225, 226–27 (S.D.N.Y. 1999), which held that the mother of 5–year–old son killed when her Dodge Caravan minivan's airbag deployed in a minor automobile accident (a BEV of 9–12 mph) could not recover because she failed to prove that her proposed alternative designs were safer than the vehicle manufacturer's airbag design. Her alternatives included higher "no fire" and "threshold" deployment points and the removal of the airbag altogether, but she offered no evidence showing that the number of lives saved and injuries avoided if her alternatives were adopted would have exceeded the corresponding numbers of persons protected by the manufacturer's chosen design:

> Automobile airbags are the proverbial mixed blessing. To inflate rapidly and forcefully enough to save lives they create a lethal hazard to young children and other small persons sitting too close to the point of deployment. Thus, according to the latest government data, while airbags saved the lives of more than 4,700 people through October 1, 1999, in the same period they killed 146 people, of whom 84 were out-of-position children. To be sure, those deaths could have been avoided if the victims had worn seat belts; but part of the need for airbags derives from the unpalatable but undeniable fact that a significant number of people simply refuse to wear such belts. Airbags respond to this improvidence, but not without creating risks of their own: risks that can be reduced but not eliminated.

See also Diluzio–Gulino v. Daimler Chrysler Corp., 897 A.2d 438, 440 (N.J. Super. Ct. App. Div. 2006), where plaintiff's expert candidly testified:

> [Air bags] are intended to reduce injuries in collisions. It is known that the air bags will cause injuries. [I]f the air bag causes more injuries than it prevents then it should not deploy. The deployment should only occur when the air bag reduces the injury, which is to say that when the injuries caused by the accident and the air bag [are] less than the injuries you would have sustained without the air bag there, then the air bag should deploy.

2. In McCabe v. American Honda Motor Co., 123 Cal.Rptr.2d 303 (Ct. App. 2002), plaintiff was injured when her airbag failed to deploy in a collision. Plaintiff claimed that the other car struck her Civic "head on" at 35 mph whereas defendant's expert concluded that the crash was at a 35° angle, outside of the 30° frontal collision range, at a longitudinal speed of 4 mph, substantially below the 12 mph speed at which the airbag was designed to deploy. The trial court granted Honda's motion for summary judgment. On appeal, *held*, reversed, since there were genuine issues of material fact as to (1) whether airbag performed according to representations in the owners manual, (2) whether the airbag's nondeployment violated an ordinary consumer's minimum safety expectations, and (3) whether the benefits of the airbag design outweighed its risk.

3. Note that no-airbag claims for second-collision injuries in early model cars without air bags are preempted by a federal motor vehicle safety standard. See ch. 9.

2.   DRIVER FAULT

Lowe v. Estate Motors, Ltd.

Supreme Court of Michigan, 1987.
428 Mich. 439, 410 N.W.2d 706.

■ RILEY, CHIEF JUSTICE.

In this automobile products liability action, we [rule upon] the admissibility of evidence concerning the existence of and failure to use seat belts for the purpose of (1) attempting to establish the affirmative defense of comparative negligence, and (2) defending the design of the vehicle in cases in which the "crashworthiness" doctrine is asserted as a theory of liability. We hold that the introduction of evidence concerning the existence of and failure to use seat belts is not to be treated differently than evidence concerning the existence of and failure to use safety devices generally, and, therefore, that such evidence may be admissible for either purpose provided a proper foundation is established. For purposes of comparative negligence, applicable in all products liability cases by legislative act, evidence of a plaintiff's failure to use an available seat belt may raise a factual issue to be submitted for jury consideration. In crashworthiness cases evidence of restraint systems is relevant to whether the vehicle as a whole was defective in design.

FACTS AND PROCEDURES

[Plaintiff was a passenger in the rear seat of a 1979 Mercedes 300D owned and driven by her son, third-party defendant Rayburnell Neighbors. Mr. Neighbors lost control of the car, sideswiped a parked truck,] and struck a concrete dividing barrier. At some point after the initial impact, the right rear door opened, and plaintiff was ejected from the vehicle, sustaining multiple injuries.

Plaintiff commenced this action asserting negligent design and breach of implied warranty theories of liability. She alleged that the cause of the accident was attributable to a defectively designed floor mat which had wedged under the brake pedal, contributing to the driver's loss of control of the automobile, and further that her injuries were also caused by a defectively designed door and door-locking mechanism which rendered the automobile uncrashworthy. Defendants include Mercedes–Benz of North America (MBNA), Estate Motors Limited, a local distributor from which the automobile was purchased, and Newark Auto Products, manufacturer of the floor mat.

Defendant MBNA asserted an affirmative defense of comparative negligence on the basis of the plaintiff's failure to use the available three-point seat restraint provided for rear seat passengers. Plaintiff moved to strike that affirmative defense and to exclude at trial the admission of any evidence concerning that safety device, and her failure to use it. In support of her motions, plaintiff argued that, as a matter of law, her failure to wear a seat belt did not constitute negligence because plaintiff "owed no duty" to defendant to wear a seat belt, that her failure to wear a seat belt did not contribute to the cause of the accident, and that it did not violate her duty to avoid consequences or minimize damages. [The trial court denied both of plaintiff's motions to exclude the seat belt evidence. In an interlocutory appeal, the Court of Appeals reversed (2–1), holding that the seat belt evidence should be excluded. 382 N.W.2d 811 (Mich. Ct. App. 1985). Defendants appeal.]

I

[The appeal in this automobile products liability action involves the admissibility of seat belt] evidence for two entirely independent purposes: [1] to attempt to establish the partial defense of comparative negligence; [2] to defend the crashworthiness design of the vehicle. All relevant evidence is generally admissible, MRE 402. * * *

II

The doctrinal origin of the judicially created rule disallowing evidence of a plaintiff's failure to use a seat belt in this jurisdiction may be traced to the Court of Appeals decision in Romankewiz v. Black, 167 N.W.2d 606 (Mich. Ct. App. 1969) [an ordinary automobile negligence case decided in 1969, ten years before this Court adopted pure comparative negligence] in Placek v. Sterling Heights, 275 N.W.2d 511 (Mich. 1979). In *Romankewiz,* the Court rejected claims that a plaintiff's failure to use a seat belt could amount to contributory negligence as a total bar to recovery or a failure to mitigate damages.

With regard to the issue of contributory negligence, the Court held "that as a matter of law, [plaintiff] had no duty to wear a seat belt," and that "plaintiff's failure to fasten his seat belt was not such negligence as to contribute to the cause of the accident [because] [u]nbuckled plaintiffs do not *cause* accidents." *Romankewiz.* [The *Romankewiz* Court reasoned, first,] that the then-recently enacted statute requiring automobiles to be equipped with seat belts did not obligate individuals to use them. Second, the Court mentioned "statistics demonstrating the general non-use of seat belts, indicating that only 15% of the nation's drivers 'buckle up' [and] that belts can [actually] exacerbate injuries." Finally, the Court reasoned that the failure to buckle a seat belt could not amount to "a failure to exercise the [ordinary care *under the circumstances* [because] until one has, or should have, notice of another's negligence, he is not required to anticipate it. On the contrary, he is entitled to assume that others will use due care for his safety and their own." *Romankewiz.*

The Court disposed of the issue of avoidable consequences or mitigation of damages by "a very simple bit of logic: if there is no duty to buckle a seat belt, failure to do so cannot be held a breach of duty to avoid consequences or minimize damages." [The *Romankewiz* Court concluded that it was for the legislature "to prescribe any required use" of seat belts.]

* * *

[The current] majority view in comparative negligence jurisdictions in which the issue has been addressed requires allowing the jury to consider the seat belt nonuse defense. See Note, The Seat Belt Defense: Must the Reasonable Man Wear a Seat Belt?, 50 Mo. L. Rev. 968, 976 n.83 (1985).

In Ins. Co. of North America v. Pasakarnis, 451 So. 2d 447 (Fla.1984), for example, the Florida Supreme Court rejected the reasoning adopted in *Schmitzer.* The court first addressed the assertion that whether failure to use a seat belt could constitute comparative negligence was more appropriate for legislative consideration. Noting that tort law is peculiarly nonstatutory and that the court had not hesitated in the past in overturning unsound precedent in the area of tort law, the court viewed the issue as most appropriate for judicial decision, and concluded that "[t]o abstain from acting responsibly in the present case on the basis of legislative deference would be to [ignore an illogical exception to comparative negligence created by our lower courts.]"

[Based on] pure comparative fault which it had judicially adopted in Hoffman v. Jones, 280 So. 2d 431 (Fla. 1973), the court concluded that the failure to wear an available seat belt could be a pertinent factor appropriate for consideration by a jury in deciding whether the plaintiff exercised due care for his own safety. *Pasakarnis.* [T]he court flatly rejected the contention that seat belt effectiveness as a safety precaution is too "speculative," stating that the evidence of seat belt effectiveness "in reducing deaths and injury severity is substantial and unequivocal."

[Rejecting the argument that automobile accidents are unforeseeable,] the *Pasakarnis* court relied upon Ford Motor Co. v. Evancho, 327 So. 2d 201 (Fla. 1976), [which adopted for Florida] the "crashworthiness" doctrine and rationale of Larsen v. General Motors Corp., 391 F.2d 495 (8th Cir. 1968), [where] it "expressly acknowledged [that] automobile collisions are foreseeable as are the so-called 'second collisions' with the interior of the automobile." *Pasakarnis.* * * *

[Following]   Spier v. Barker, 323 N.E.2d 164 (N.Y. 1974),[12] the [*Pasakarnis* court] concluded that failure to use a seat belt may not be deemed negligent or nonnegligent as a matter of law, but that it is "necessarily a matter to be determined in each instance by the jury" in all cases in which there is "competent evidence to show that the plaintiff's failure to use an available seat belt bore a causal relation to the plaintiff's injuries."

---

12. When *Spier* was decided, contributory negligence as a total bar to recovery had not yet been replaced with the doctrine of comparative fault. The court premised its decision upon the doctrine of avoidable consequences, which it reasoned was similar to the doctrine of mitigation of damages. Whether failure to use an available seat belt constituted a breach of the duty to avoid consequences or mitigate damages was deemed a question for the jury.

III

[We agree with *Pasakarnis* that the trier of fact should be permitted to consider] a failure to use a seat belt for the purpose of the affirmative defense of comparative negligence. * * *

[For comparative negligence,] the standard of conduct to which one must conform for his own protection is that of "a reasonable [person] under like circumstances." [Under this standard], every person has an obligation to exercise reasonable care for his own safety. * * *

The "no duty" formulation adopted in *Romankewiz* may have been a product of the all or nothing analyses surrounding the abrogated doctrine of contributory negligence as a total bar to recovery [in order to avoid "the potentially harsh and inequitable consequences of that complete defense."] It was precisely that concern which led this Court to judicially adopt the doctrine of pure comparative fault in *Placek,* supra, to move toward "accomplish[ing] the goal of a fair system of apportionment of damages."

In contrast to the abrogated defense of contributory negligence, comparative negligence never allows an otherwise liable defendant to entirely "avoid" liability and thus "escape" the duty of due care. [Citation.] That significant difference [counsels against creating] aberrational exceptions inherently inconsistent with general negligence principles. . . .

IV

[The basis for the Court of Appeals'] decision—that one need not anticipate the negligence of others, even if foreseeable, that a high percentage of automobile occupants do not use seat belts, that seat belt effectiveness is too speculative, and that the imposition of a duty to use them for purposes of the common-law doctrine of comparative negligence is more appropriate for legislative consideration—is flawed and inconsistent with modern and traditional principles of negligence law. That analysis, furthermore, substantially obscures the appropriate functions of the court and the jury.

While evidence of the high percentage of failures to use seat belts is relevant to the issue of reasonableness, such evidence does not support withholding the issue from the jury. The assertion that certain conduct is customary, or that a majority engage in the conduct in question, does not in and of itself make such conduct reasonable. The determinative evaluation requires contemplating the fictitious objective "reasonable person," not the subjective "average person." For customary conduct to be reasonable under the circumstances, it must be a product [of] "learned reason." That is, as first articulated by Judge Learned Hand in United States v. Carroll Towing Co., 159 F.2d 169, 173 (C.A.2, 1947), and consistently applied by the courts of this [state], such conduct may be found to be unreasonable if the magnitude of the risk of harm created (probability of harm multiplied by the gravity of that harm) is greater than the burden of adequate precautions or the utility of the conduct in question.

In light of the uniform applicability of that formula, whether considering a defendant's conduct for purposes of liability or a plaintiff's for purposes of reducing his recovery, we agree with the reasoning of the New York Court of Appeals in *Spier* that "the burden of buckling an available seat belt may, under the facts of the particular case, be found by the jury to be less than the likelihood of injury when multiplied by its accompanying severity."

[However, we] are not persuaded that all reasonable persons would agree that the burden of seat belt use, or the utility of seat belt nonuse, outweighs the resulting magnitude of the risk of injury. [Nor are we persuaded that such an approach should] be adopted and applied in all cases. Accordingly, we hold that whether failure to use a seat belt constitutes comparative negligence so as to require the proportionate reduction of a plaintiff's recovery is an evaluative issue [of fact for the jury]. . . .

V

[T]he recent enactment of the mandatory seat belt usage legislation, M.C.L. § 257.710e; M.S.A. § 9.2410(5), . . . which took effect on July 1, 1985, requires drivers and front-seat passengers of motor vehicles operated in this state to wear seat belts, making the failure to use them unlawful. Section [5 provides] that failure to use a seat belt in violation of the statute may be considered evidence of negligence, [and] that such negligence shall not reduce a plaintiff's recovery by more than 5%. The [statute is not applicable here] because: (1) the accident occurred prior to the statute's effective date, (2) plaintiff was a rear-seat passenger to whom the statute, by its terms, would not have applied, and (3) the accident occurred [outside the state where the statute does not apply].

VI

The Court of Appeals did not address that portion of the trial court's ruling allowing the admission of seat belt evidence for the purpose of defending the crashworthiness design of the automobile as a whole. Plaintiff has asserted, as an independent theory of liability, that the design of the vehicle in question was a cause of her injuries because that design created an unreasonable risk of harm to its occupants resulting from an impact or collision. Plaintiff's theory in this regard is based upon the manufacturer's duty of designing crashworthy vehicles. . . .

MBNA argues that seat belt evidence should be admissible in crashworthiness cases to defend the safety design of the vehicle, and the relation of that design to the plaintiff's injuries, entirely independent of the comparative negligence issue. We agree with one-half of that argument completely.

By its nature, the defective crashworthiness design theory of liability requires that the vehicle be considered as a whole. . . . Accordingly, the jury should consider the vehicle's overall design, including safety features, in order to determine the crashworthiness issue, and, thus, whether the vehicle was defective in design. . . .

Evidence of the seat-restraint system goes to the heart of the issue in crashworthiness cases in which the plaintiff's injuries were sustained after being ejected from the vehicle, a result which seat belts are specifically designed to prevent. Whether the [plaintiff's case is predicated on negligent design—whether the design created an unreasonable risk of injury, or whether it is breach of implied warranty—that the car was not reasonably fit for its intended and foreseeable uses, the determinative liability issue is whether the car] was unreasonably unsafe because of its design. Evidence of product safety features specifically designed to prevent the injuries complained of is entirely relevant to this issue. No reason, even arguably sound, exists for excluding such evidence on this liability issue. Plaintiff has provided us with none.

[However, seat belt evidence is appropriate only for limited purposes, which compels us to reject the second part of defendant's argument. Mixing up causation and duty, MBNA argues] that, independent of the comparative negligence issue, it may properly seek to establish that plaintiff's failure to use a seat belt was *the* cause in fact and sole proximate cause of her enhanced injuries rather than any design defect in the vehicle. [Intertwining the issue of causation with the separate] issue of negligent design tends to confuse the purposes for which defendant seeks to introduce seat belt evidence, as well as the elements of plaintiff's cause of action....

The plaintiff's conduct and its causal relation to her injuries is not relevant to the issue of the vehicle's design. While it is true that plaintiff must establish both that the vehicle was defective in design and that that defect proximately caused her enhanced injuries, those elements are entirely distinct. In considering whether the insufficient crashworthiness design of the vehicle was *a* proximate cause of plaintiff's injuries, the focus is upon the vehicle's design and its relation to the plaintiff's injuries. [Consideration of the plaintiff's conduct and the relation of that conduct to her injuries should be deferred to the determination] of the comparative fault issue.

[If the vehicle is determined to be uncrashworthy, the argument that plaintiff's failure to use a seat belt could be the only cause of her enhanced injuries, without regard to comparative negligence, is a curious causal claim.]

... Whether, and to what extent, plaintiff's failure to use an available seat restraint proximately caused her enhanced injuries may properly be considered within the context of the comparative fault issue, and even then only after [resolution of the defendant's liability on the plaintiff's crashworthiness claims].

VII

In conclusion, we hold that evidence of a failure to use a seat belt may be admissible to support an affirmative defense of comparative negligence.... Additionally, we hold that in crashworthiness cases, seat-restraint evidence is admissible for the purpose of defending the design of the vehicle as a whole, entirely independently of the comparative negligence defense. . . .

. . . We express no opinion concerning the future applicability of M.C.L. § 257.710e; M.S.A. § 9.2410(5) with regard to cases in which the injury occurred after the effective date of that statute and a plaintiff's failure to use a seat belt was in violation of its provisions.

Thus, we reverse the decision of the Court of Appeals and reinstate the trial court's denial of plaintiff's motions to exclude all evidence of the existence of and failure to use seat belts, with the appropriate limitations expressed in part VI.

■ ARCHER, JUSTICE (dissenting).

* * *

While other jurisdictions have reached contrary conclusions when considering the admissibility of evidence of a plaintiff's nonuse of a seat belt, Michigan's [former] rule of prohibiting the admissibility of such evidence is the better [rule.]

Historically, passengers in automobiles have been considered to be free of contributory or comparative negligence unless exceptional circumstances were present.

Furthermore, the injured plaintiff in this case was a passenger in the rear seat. The risks of nonuse of a seat belt for a rear-seat passenger are unclear, and even the Legislature has not required rear-seat passengers to use seat belts.

The Legislature, during its recent tort law reforms, addressed the issue of seat belt use. During its review, the Legislature was informed of the statistics relating to the effect of seat belt use on reducing injuries and deaths in automobile accidents.

* * *

After its evaluation, the Legislature did two things. First, the Legislature made seat belt use mandatory only for the driver and the front-seat passenger. The Legislature also provided that a plaintiff's recovery could not be reduced by more than 5% for his failure to wear a seat belt. Second, the Legislature was silent about the issue of seat belt use by rear-seat passengers.

Although Michigan's mandatory seat belt statute has been criticized for failing to apportion the damages for injuries in collisions and for creating a windfall for plaintiffs, the seat belt defense [creates a windfall for tortfeasors who pay only partially for the harm their negligence causes.]

A majority of courts, including contributory negligence jurisdictions, prohibit the introduction of a plaintiff's nonuse of a seat belt to reduce a plaintiff's recovery. [Citation.] Among the reasons cited are that a "defendant's fault in causing the accident distributed risks to the world at large and was capable of causing some degree of damage to any plaintiff within the sphere of foreseeability. Conversely, a plaintiff's failure to use a seat belt creates no risks to others, but merely exposes himself to a risk." [Citation.]

[Although the majority is correct] that in crashworthiness cases the vehicle should be considered as a whole, I would, nevertheless, bar testimony regarding the nonuse of seat belts subject to the applicability of M.C.L. § 257.710e; M.S.A. § 9.2410(5).

* * *

■ Levin, Justice (separate opinion).

* * *

I agree with the [lead opinion] that evidence concerning the seat-restraint system may be considered by the trier of fact in determining whether a motor vehicle was defective in design [with respect to its crashworthiness].

After this cause was argued in the Court of Appeals, the Legislature enacted Act 1, generally requiring the driver and front-seat passenger of a motor vehicle to wear seat belts. No such obligation is imposed on rear-seat passengers. The act provides that "[f]ailure to wear a safety belt in violation of this section may be considered evidence of negligence and may reduce the recovery for damages arising out of the ownership, maintenance, or operation of a motor vehicle. However, such negligence shall not reduce the recovery for damages by more than 5%."[9]

9. M.C.L. § 257.710e(5); M.S.A. § 9.2410(5)(5).

A large majority of the statutes requiring adults to wear seat belts provide either that a violation cannot be grounds for reducing an award on the basis of comparative or contributory negligence, or limit the possible reduction to a small percentage of the award. Of the approximately twenty-six states other than Michigan that have statutes presently in effect, three follow Michigan in limiting the possible reduction to a small percentage. See Iowa Code Ann., § 321.445(4)(b)(2)(5%); La. Rev. Stat. Ann., § 32.295.1(E)(4)(2%); Mo. Ann.Stat., § 307.178(3)(2)(1%).

Of the remaining twenty-three statutes, sixteen provide either that evidence of nonuse is not admissible in a civil action, or that it cannot be used to reduce an award. See Conn. Gen. Stat., § 14–100a(c)(4); D.C. Code, § 40–1607; Ill. Ann. Stat., ch. 95 1/2, § 12–603.1(c); Ind. Stat. Ann., § 9–8–13–9; Kan. Stat. Ann., § 8–2504(c); Md. Code Ann., § 22–412.3(g); Nev. Rev. Stat., § 484.641(3); N.M. Stat. Ann., § 66–7–373(B); N.C. Gen. Stat., § 20–135.2A(d); Ohio Rev. Code Ann., § 4513.26.3(G); Okla. Stat. Ann., tit. 47, § 12–420; Tenn. Code Ann., § 55–9–604; Tex.

Rev. Civ. Stat. Ann., art. 6701d, § 107C(j); Utah Code Ann., § 41–6–186; Va. Code, § 46.1–309.2(E); Wash. Rev. Code, § 46.61.688(6). Only two of the statutes specifically allow evidence of nonuse to reduce an award. See Cal. Veh. Code, ¶ 27315(i); N.Y. Veh. & Traf. Law, § 1229–c(8) (McKinney). Four of the remaining five statutes do not specifically state whether evidence of nonuse can be used to reduce an award. See Hawaii Rev. Stat., § 291–11.6; Idaho Code, § 49–764; Minn. Stat. Ann., § 169.686; N.J. Stat. Ann., § 39:3–76.2h. One statute provides that evidence of nonuse cannot be used as "prima-facie" evidence of negligence. See Fla. Stat. Ann. § 316.614(10).

The Michigan statute is also consistent with the overwhelming majority of statutes in restricting the duty to drivers and front-seat passengers. See Conn. Gen. Stat. Ann., § 14–100a(c)(1); D.C. Code, § 40–1602; Fla. Stat. Ann., § 316.614(4)(a); Hawaii Rev. Stat., § 291–11.6(a); Idaho Code, § 49–764(1); Ill. Ann. Stat., ch. 95½1/2, § 12–603.1(a); Ind. Stat. Ann., § 9–8–14–1; Iowa Code Ann., § 321.445(2); Kan. Stat. Ann., § 8–2503(b); La. Rev. Stat. Ann.,

The enactment of Act 1 should be viewed in the context of the consistent fifteen-year adherence by the Court of Appeals to the view that the failure to use a seat belt was not evidence of contributory or comparative negligence and could not be used in either an ordinary automobile negligence case or in an automobile products liability case to reduce the damages otherwise to be awarded to an injured person, and in light of this Court's decisions to decline to review those decisions of the Court of Appeals.

[In Act 1, the Legislature] codified the common-law rule,[10] established by the Court of Appeals, that damages may not be reduced for failure to wear a seat belt with a "narrow exception" permitting reduction of a damage award by not more than 5% for failure of a front-seat occupant to wear a seat belt.

The July 1, 1985, effective date of Act 1 was the date selected by the Legislature on which the narrow 5% exception for front-seat occupants was to become effective, not the date on which a possible 100% reduction of damages was to be reduced to no more than five percent [which is the effect of the lead opinion.]

The Legislature, like bench and bar, may consider and rely on [court decisions] when enacting new legislation. At times the common law is uncertain, and it may not be appropriate to attribute to the Legislature any particular reading of the common law. Where the common law is well-established and uncontradicted, however, and the Legislature essentially accepts the common-law rule, a proper respect for legislative supremacy on substantive issues requires, in our opinion, that the judiciary ordinarily defer to the legislative decision to enter the field, abide by the legislative solution, and refrain from further and belated refinement of the substantive law.

[T]he Legislature, when it enacted Act 1, had no reason to suppose that the common-law no-reduction-of-damages rule that had been stated and restated in [several court opinions], might in effect be overruled by this Court two years after [Act 1 was enacted].

§ 32.295.1(B); Md. Code Ann., § 22–412.3(b); Minn. Stat. Ann., § 169.686(1); Mo. Ann. Stat., § 307.178(2); Nev. Rev. Stat., § 484.641(2); N.J. Stat. Ann., § 39:3–76.2f(a); N.M. Stat. Ann., § 66–7–372(A); N.Y. Veh. & Traf. Law, § 1229–c(3) (McKinney); N.C. Gen. Stat., § 20–135–2A(a); Ohio Rev. Code Ann., § 4513.26.3(B)(3); Okla. Stat. Ann., tit. 47, § 12–417(A); Tenn. Code Ann., § 55–9–603(b)(1); Utah Code Ann., § 41–6–182; Tex. Rev. Civ. Stat. Ann., art. 6701d, § 107C(b)(2); Va. Code, § 46.1–309.2(A). Only two states, California and Washington, require adult, rear-seat passengers to wear seat belts. See Cal. Veh. Code,

§ 27315(d); Wash. Rev. Code, § 46.61.688(3). Only the California statute provides that evidence of nonuse by a rear-seat passenger may be used to show negligence or to mitigate damages.

10. [Although the Legislature did not adopt the precise terms of common-law rule, it did so in substance.] Act 1, viewed in terms of the tort significance and consequence of its enactment, in effect codified the common-law rule of no reduction of damages for failure to wear a seat belt with the narrow five-percent exception.

NOTES

1. Courts are split on the admissibility of evidence that the plaintiff was not wearing his or her seat belt. See D. Owen, Products Liability Law § 17.5 (2d ed. 2008). The Restatement (Third) of Torts: Apportionment of Liability § 3 Illus. 3 takes the position that a plaintiff's failure to use a seat belt is relevant to plaintiff's fault and to apportioning damages. See also Products Liability Restatement § 16 cmt. *f.*

2. Assume that (1) the comparative fault statute in the jurisdiction bars plaintiff's recovery entirely if his fault exceeds the defendant's; (2) the jury finds the plaintiff driver 20% responsible, and the defendant manufacturer 80%, for causing the *accident*; (3) the jury finds that the plaintiff's failure to wear a seat belt was 60% responsible for causing the *injuries*; and (4) the plaintiff's total injuries are $100,000.

Should plaintiff be allowed to recover anything? If so, how much? See Waterson v. General Motors Corp., 544 A.2d 357, 374–77 (N.J. 1988).

3. Seat belt usage continues to rise. By 1988, usage rates had risen to a then all-time high of 43.4%, according to a NHTSA survey, saving 4,000 lives per year. See Prod. Safety & Liab. Rep.(BNA) 810–11 (Aug. 19, 1988). By 2005, seat belt usage had risen to 82%. www.buckleupamerica.org

4. Should failure to buckle a seat belt be considered contributory negligence as a matter of law? Contributory negligence per se? See Hutchins v. Schwartz, 724 P.2d 1194 (Alaska 1986); Note, 102 Harv. L. Rev. 925 (1989).

5. Legislative Reform. The varieties of seat belt laws are described in n.9 of Justice Levin's "separate" opinion. Why do you suppose that most of the laws preclude nonuse evidence in civil actions? Because the legislatures think it reasonable not to buckle up? To enhance the deterrent effect of tort suits on manufacturers? Or for some other, non-substantive, reason?

6. Driver Misconduct—Intoxication & Negligent Driving. Should a negligent driver's intoxication or other fault that contributes to cause the collision reduce his or her damages for aggravated injuries in a claim against the manufacturer of an uncrashworthy car? Some courts hold that the manufacturer's duty to build crashworthy cars should protect occupants no matter what the cause of the crash. E.g., Andrews v. Harley Davidson, Inc., 796 P.2d 1092 (Nev.1990)(4–1 decision); Reed v. Chrysler Corp., 494 N.W.2d 224, 230 (Iowa 1992) (5–4 decision):

> The [crashworthiness] theory, which presupposes the occurrence of accidents precipitated for myriad reasons, focuses [only] on the enhancement of resulting injuries. The rule does not pretend that the design defect had anything to do with causing the accident. It is enough if the design defect increased the damages. So any participation by the plaintiff in bringing the accident about is quite beside the point.

But the decisions are sharply split, and many courts disagree. "The majority [view] is that comparative fault should be applied to such an enhanced injury case." Whitehead v. Toyota Motor Corp., 897 S.W.2d 684, 693 (Tenn. 1995). See also V. Schwartz, Comparative Negligence § 11.05[a] (4th ed. 2002) ("in the interests of fairness, courts should have the power to reduce a plaintiff's award for his share of fault in causing his injuries when that fault consists of negligent driving").

The Products Liability Restatement, in § 17 cmt. *d*, sides with the latter approach, said (perhaps incorrectly) to be the majority view.

7. In Shipler v. General Motors Corp., 710 N.W.2d 807, 824 (Neb. 2006), plaintiff was injured when the driver of the vehicle she was riding in lost control and the vehicle rolled over at least four times. Plaintiff and driver had both been drinking and plaintiff misused her seatbelt by fastening it over both herself and her infant son who was sitting in her lap. *Held*, "The inherent nature of the crashworthiness or enhanced injury theory of liability disallows the submission of issues of contributory negligence to a jury.... Any negligence by [the driver or plaintiff passanger], in connection with the original crash cannot be used by the manufacturer in defending against [the plaintiff's] enhancement claim."

8. On comparing design defectiveness with a driver's contributory negligence, reconsider Daly v. General Motors Corp., supra ch. 14(1).

9. See generally D. Owen, Products Liability Law § 17.5 (2d ed. 2008).

3. Punitive Damages

Grimshaw v. Ford Motor Co.

Court of Appeals of California, 1981.
119 Cal.App.3d 757, 174 Cal.Rptr. 348.

■ Tamura, Acting Presiding Justice.

A 1972 Ford Pinto hatchback automobile unexpectedly stalled on a freeway, erupting into flames when it was rear ended by a car proceeding in the same direction. Mrs. Lilly Gray, the driver of the Pinto, suffered fatal burns and 13–year–old Richard Grimshaw, a passenger in the Pinto, suffered severe and permanently disfiguring burns on his face and entire body. Grimshaw and the heirs of Mrs. Gray (Grays) sued Ford Motor Company and others. Following a six-month jury trial, verdicts were returned in favor of plaintiffs against Ford Motor Company. Grimshaw was awarded $2,516,000 compensatory damages and $125 million punitive damages; the Grays were awarded $559,680 in compensatory damages. On Ford's motion for a new trial, Grimshaw was required to remit all but $3½ million of the punitive award as a condition of denial of the motion.

[Ford appealed the punitive damages award and Grimshaw appealed the remittitur.]

FACTS

[Due to a defective carburetor float, Mrs. Gray's 6–month old Pinto suddenly stalled on an interstate highway and coasted to a stop. The Pinto was struck from the rear by another car that had braked to a speed of 28–37 mph.]

At the moment of impact, the Pinto caught fire and its interior was engulfed in flames. According to plaintiffs' expert, the impact of the Galaxie had driven the Pinto's gas tank forward and caused it to be punctured by the flange or one of the bolts on the differential housing so that fuel sprayed from the punctured tank and entered the passenger compartment through gaps resulting from the separation of the rear wheel well sections from the floor pan. By the time the Pinto came to rest after the collision, both occupants had sustained serious burns. When they emerged from the vehicle, their clothing was almost completely burned off. Mrs. Gray died a few days later of congestive heart failure as a result of the burns. Grimshaw managed to survive but only through heroic medical measures. He has undergone numerous and extensive surgeries and skin grafts and must undergo additional surgeries over the next 10 years. He lost portions of several fingers on his left hand and portions of his left ear, while his face required many skin grafts from various portions of his body....

Design of the Pinto Fuel System:

In 1968, Ford began designing a new subcompact automobile which ultimately became the Pinto. Mr. Iacocca, then a Ford Vice President, conceived the project and was its moving force. Ford's objective was to build a car at or below 2,000 pounds to sell for no more than $2,000.

Ordinarily marketing surveys and preliminary engineering studies precede the styling of a new automobile line. Pinto, however, was a rush project, so that styling preceded engineering and dictated engineering design to a greater degree than usual. Among the engineering decisions dictated by styling was the placement of the fuel tank. It was then the preferred practice in Europe and Japan to locate the gas tank over the rear axle in subcompacts because a small vehicle has less "crush space" between the rear axle and the bumper than larger cars. The Pinto's styling, however, required the tank to be placed behind the rear axle leaving only 9 or 10 inches of "crush space"—far less than in any other American automobile or Ford overseas subcompact. In addition, the Pinto was designed so that its bumper was little more than a chrome strip, less substantial than the bumper of any other American car produced then or later. The Pinto's rear structure also lacked reinforcing members known as "hat sections" (2 longitudinal side members) and horizontal cross-members running between them such as were found in cars of larger unitized construction and in all automobiles produced by Ford's overseas operations. The absence of the reinforcing members rendered the Pinto less crush resistant than other vehicles. Finally, the differential housing selected for the Pinto had an exposed flange and a line of exposed bolt heads. These protrusions were sufficient to puncture a gas tank driven forward against the differential upon rear impact.

Crash Tests:

During the development of the Pinto, prototypes were built and tested. Some were "mechanical prototypes" which duplicated mechanical features of the design but not its appearance while others, referred to as "engineering prototypes," were true duplicates of the design car. These prototypes as well as two production Pintos were crash tested by Ford to determine, among other things, the integrity of the fuel system in rear-end accidents. Ford also conducted the tests to see if the Pinto as designed would meet a proposed federal regulation requiring all automobiles manufactured in 1972 to be able to withstand a 20–mile–per–hour fixed barrier impact without significant fuel spillage and all automobiles manufactured after January 1, 1973, to withstand a 30–mile–per–hour fixed barrier impact without significant fuel spillage.

The crash tests revealed that the Pinto's fuel system as designed could not meet the 20–mile–per–hour proposed standard. Mechanical prototypes struck from the rear with a moving barrier at 21–miles–per–hour caused the fuel tank to be driven forward and to be punctured, causing fuel leakage in excess of the standard prescribed by the proposed regulation. A production Pinto crash tested at 21–miles–per–hour into a fixed barrier caused the fuel neck to be torn from the gas tank and the tank to be punctured by a bolt head on the differential housing. In at least one test, spilled fuel entered the driver's compartment through gaps resulting from the separation of the seams joining the rear wheel wells to the floor pan. The seam separation was occasioned by the lack of reinforcement in the rear structure and insufficient welds of the wheel wells to the floor pan.

Tests conducted by Ford on other vehicles, including modified or reinforced mechanical Pinto prototypes, proved safe at speeds at which the Pinto failed. Where rubber bladders had been installed in the tank, crash tests into fixed barriers at 21–miles–per–hour withstood leakage from punctures in the gas tank. Vehicles with fuel tanks installed above rather than behind the rear axle passed the fuel system integrity test at 31–miles–per–hour fixed barrier. A Pinto with two longitudinal hat sections added to firm up the rear structure passed a 20–mile–per–hour rear impact fixed barrier test with no fuel leakage.

The Cost to Remedy Design Deficiencies:

When a prototype failed the fuel system integrity test, the standard of care for engineers in the industry was to redesign and retest it. The vulnerability of the production Pinto's fuel tank at speeds of 20 and 30–miles-per-hour fixed barrier tests could have been remedied by inexpensive "fixes," but Ford produced and sold the Pinto to the public without doing anything to remedy the defects. Design changes that would have enhanced the integrity of the fuel tank system at relatively little cost per car included the following: Longitudinal side members and cross members at $2.40 and $1.80, respectively; a single shock absorbent "flak suit" to protect the tank at $4; a tank within a tank and placement of the tank over the axle at $5.08 to $5.79; a nylon bladder within the tank at $5.25 to $8; placement of the tank over the axle surrounded with a protective barrier at a cost of $9.95 per car; substitution of a rear axle with a smooth differential housing at a cost of $2.10; imposition of a protective shield between the differential housing and the tank at $2.35; improvement and reinforcement of the bumper at $2.60; addition of eight inches of crush space at a cost of $6.40. Equipping the car with a reinforced rear structure, smooth axle, improved bumper and additional crush space at a total cost of $15.30 would have made the fuel tank safe in a 34 to 38–mile–per–hour rear end collision by a vehicle the size of the Ford Galaxie. If, in addition to the foregoing, a bladder or tank within a tank were used or if the tank were protected with a shield, it would have been safe in a 40 to 45–mile–per–hour rear impact.

If the tank had been located over the rear axle, it would have been safe in a rear impact at 50–miles–per–hour or more.

Management's Decision to Go Forward With Knowledge of Defects:

The idea for the Pinto, as has been noted, was conceived by Mr. Iacocca, then Executive Vice President of Ford. The feasibility study was conducted under the supervision of Mr. Robert Alexander, Vice President of Car Engineering. Ford's Product Planning Committee, whose members included Mr. Iacocca, Mr. Robert Alexander, and Mr. Harold MacDonald, Ford's Group Vice President of Car Engineering, approved the Pinto's concept and made the decision to go forward with the project.... The Pinto crash tests results had been forwarded up the chain of command to the ultimate decision-makers and were known to the Ford officials who decided to go forward with production.

Harley Copp, a former Ford engineer and executive in charge of the crash testing program, testified [on behalf of the plaintiff] that the highest level of Ford's management made the decision to go forward with the production of the Pinto, knowing that the gas tank was vulnerable to puncture and rupture at low rear impact speeds creating a significant risk of death or injury from fire and knowing that "fixes" were feasible at nominal cost. He testified that management's decision was based on the cost savings which would inure from omitting or delaying the "fixes."

Mr. Copp's testimony concerning management's awareness of the crash tests results and the vulnerability of the Pinto fuel system was corroborated by other evidence. At an April 1971 product review meeting chaired by Mr. MacDonald, those present received and discussed a report (Exhibit 125) prepared by Ford engineers pertaining to the financial impact of a proposed federal standard on fuel system integrity and the cost savings which would accrue from deferring even minimal "fixes."[2]

* * *

2. The "FUEL SYSTEM INTEGRITY PROGRAM FINANCIAL REVIEW" report included the following:

"PRODUCT ASSUMPTIONS

"To meet 20 mph movable barrier requirements in 1973, fuel filler neck modifications to provide breakaway capability and minor upgrading of structure are required.

"To meet 30 mph movable barrier requirements, original fuel system integrity program assumptions provided for relocation of the fuel tanks to over the axle on all car lines beginning in 1974. Major tearup of rear and center floor pans, added rear end structure, and new fuel tanks were believed necessary for all car lines. These engineering assumptions were developed from limited vehicle crash test data and design and development work.

"Since these original assumptions, seven vehicle crash tests have been run which now indicate fuel tank relocation is probably not required. Although still based heavily on judgment, Chassis Engineering currently estimates that the 30 mph movable barrier requirement is achievable with a reduced level of rear end tearup.

"In addition to added rear-end structure, Chassis Engineering believes that either rubber 'flak' suits (similar to a tire carcass), or alternatively, a bladder lining within the fuel tank may be required on all cars with flat fuel tanks located under the luggage compartment floor (all cars, except Ford/Mercury/Lincoln and Torino/Montego station wag-

Finally, Mr. Copp testified to conversations in late 1968 or early 1969 with the chief assistant research engineer in charge of cost-weight evaluation of the Pinto, and to a later conversation with the chief chassis engineer who was then in charge of crash testing the early prototype. In these conversations, both men expressed concern about the integrity of the Pinto's fuel system and complained about management's unwillingness to deviate from the design if the change would cost money.

[FORD'S APPEAL]

[EVIDENTIARY RULINGS]

(1) Exhibit No. 125:

Exhibit No. 125 was a report presented at a Ford production review meeting in April 1971, recommending action to be taken in anticipation of the promulgation of federal standards on fuel system integrity. The report recommended, *inter alia,* deferral from 1974 to 1976 of the adoption of "flak suits" or "bladders" in all Ford cars, including the Pinto, in order to realize a savings of $20.9 million. The report stated that the cost of the flak suit or bladder would be $4 to $8 per car. The meeting at which the report was presented was chaired by Vice President Harold MacDonald and attended by Vice President Robert Alexander and occurred sometime before the 1972 Pinto was placed on the market. A reasonable inference may be drawn from the evidence that despite management's knowledge that the Pinto's fuel system could be made safe at a cost of but $4 to $8 per car, it decided to defer corrective measures to save money and enhance profits. The evidence was thus highly relevant and properly received. (See Evid. Code §§ 210, 351.)

Ford's contention appears to be addressed not so much to the admissibility of Exhibit No. 125 but to the use which Grimshaw's counsel made of it in his argument to the jury. Ford complains that while Exhibit No. 125 recommended "that $100 million dollars [sic] be spent," Grimshaw's counsel argued that the report showed $100 million would be saved and urged the jury to award that sum as punitive damages. It is not clear that Exhibit

---

ons). Although further crash tests may show that added structure alone is adequate to meet the 30 mph movable barrier requirement, provisions for flak suits or bladders must be provided. The design cost of a single flak suit, located between the fuel tank and the axle, is currently estimated at $(4) per vehicle. If two flak suits (second located at the rear of the fuel tank), or a bladder are required, the design cost is estimated at $(8) per vehicle. Based on these estimates, it is recommended that the addition of the flak suit/bladder be delayed on all affected cars until 1976. However, package provision for both the flak suits and the bladder should be included when other changes are made to incorporate 30 mph movable barrier capabili-

ty. A design cost savings $10.9 million (1974–1975) can be realized by this delay. Although a design cost provision of $(8) per affected vehicle has been made in 1976 program levels to cover contingencies, it is hoped that cost reductions can be achieved, or the need for any flak suit or bladder eliminated after further engineering development.

"Current assumptions indicate that fuel system integrity modifications and 1973 bumper improvement requirements are nearly independent. However, bumper requirements for 1974 and beyond may require additional rear end structure which could benefit fuel system integrity programs."

No. 125 recommended that "$100 million be spent"; it states that over the period 1973 to 1976 the cost estimates to meet the federal standards would be $100 million. Nor is the record clear that Grimshaw's counsel was referring to Exhibit No. 125 when he urged the jury to award punitive damages in the sum of $100 million. In any event, Ford failed to object to counsel's argument as a misstatement of the evidence. In the absence of an objection and a request for admonition where an admonition would have cured the harm, the issue may not be raised on appeal. . . .

PUNITIVE DAMAGES

Ford contends that it was entitled to a judgment notwithstanding the verdict on the issue of punitive damages on two grounds: First, punitive damages are statutorily and constitutionally impermissible in a design defect case; second, there was no evidentiary support for a finding of malice or of corporate responsibility for malice. In any event, Ford maintains that the punitive damage award must be reversed because of erroneous instructions and excessiveness of the award.

(1) "Malice" Under Civil Code Section 3294:

The concept of punitive damages is rooted in the English common law and is a settled principle of the common law of this country. (Owen, Punitive Damages in Products Liability Litigation, 74 Mich. L. Rev. 1258, 1262–1263 (hereafter Owen); Mallor & Roberts, Punitive Damages, Towards A Principled Approach, 31 Hastings L.J. 639, 642–643 (hereafter Mallor & Roberts); note, Exemplary Damages in the Law of Torts, 70 Harv. L. Rev. 517, 518–520.) The doctrine was a part of the common law of this state long before the Civil Code was adopted. [Citations.] When our laws were codified in 1872, the doctrine was incorporated in Civil Code section 3294, which at the time of trial read: "In an action for the breach of an obligation not arising from contract, where the defendant has been guilty of oppression, fraud, or malice, express or implied, the plaintiff, in addition to the actual damages, may recover damages for the sake of example and by way of punishing the defendant."[11]

---

11. Section 3294 was amended in 1980 (Stats.1980, ch. 1242, § 1, p. 4217, eff. Jan. 1, 1981) to read:

"(a) In an action for the breach of an obligation not arising from contract, where the defendant has been guilty of oppression, fraud, or malice, the plaintiff, in addition to the actual damages, may recover damages for the sake of example and by way of punishing the defendant.

"(b) an employer shall not be liable for damages pursuant to subdivision (a), based upon acts of an employee of the employer, unless the employer had advance knowledge of the unfitness of the employee and employed him or her with a conscious disregard of the rights or safety of others or authorized or ratified the wrongful conduct for which the damages are awarded or was personally guilty of oppression, fraud, or malice. With respect to a corporate employer, the advance knowledge, ratification, or act of oppression, fraud, or malice must be on the part of an officer, director, or managing agent of the corporation.

"(c) As used in this section, the following definitions shall apply:

"(1) 'Malice' means conduct which is intended by the defendant to cause injury to the plaintiff or conduct which is carried on by the defendant with a conscious disregard of the rights or safety of others.

Ford argues that "malice" as used in section 3294 and as interpreted by our Supreme Court in Davis v. Hearst, 160 Cal. 143, 116 P. 530, requires *animus malus* or evil motive—an intention to injure the person harmed—and that the term is therefore conceptually incompatible with an unintentional tort such as the manufacture and marketing of a defectively designed product. This contention runs counter to our decisional law. As this court recently noted, numerous California cases after Davis v. Hearst, supra, have interpreted the term "malice" as used in section 3294 to include, not only a malicious intention to injure the specific person harmed, but conduct evincing "a conscious disregard of the probability that the actor's conduct will result in injury to others." [Citations.]

* * *

The interpretation of the word "malice" as used in section 3294 to encompass conduct evincing callous and conscious disregard of public safety by those who manufacture and market mass produced articles is consonant with and furthers the objectives of punitive damages. The primary purposes of punitive damages are punishment and deterrence of like conduct by the wrongdoer and others. (Civ. Code, § 3294; Owen, supra, pp. 1277, 1279–1287; Mallor & Roberts, supra, pp. 648–650.) In the traditional noncommercial intentional tort, compensatory damages alone may serve as an effective deterrent against future wrongful conduct but in commerce related torts, the manufacturer may find it more profitable to treat compensatory damages as a part of the cost of doing business rather than to remedy the defect. (Owen, supra, p. 1291; Note, Mass Liability and Punitive Damages Overkill, 30 Hastings L.J. 1797, 1802.) Deterrence of such "objectionable corporate policies" serves one of the principal purposes of Civil Code section 3294. [Citation.] Governmental safety standards and the criminal law have failed to provide adequate consumer protection against the manufacture and distribution of defective products. (Owen, supra, pp. 1288–1289; Mallor & Roberts, supra, pp. 655–656; Developments in the Law: Corporate Crime, 92 Harvard L. Rev. 1227, 1369.) [Citations.] Punitive damages thus remain as the most effective remedy for consumer protection against defectively designed mass produced articles. They provide a motive for private individuals to enforce rules of law and enable them to recoup the expenses of doing so which can be considerable and not otherwise recoverable.

We find no statutory impediments to the application of Civil Code section 3294 to a strict products liability case based on design defect.

(2) Constitutional Attacks on Civil Code Section 3294:

Ford's contention that the statute is unconstitutional has been repeatedly rejected. [Citations.] Ford's argument that its due process rights

"(2) 'Oppression' means subjecting a person to cruel and unjust hardship in conscious disregard of that person's rights.

"(3) 'Fraud' means an intentional misrepresentation, deceit, or concealment of a material fact known to the defendant with the intention on the part of the defendant of thereby depriving a person of property or legal rights or otherwise causing injury."

were violated because it did not have "fair warning" that its conduct would render it liable for punitive damages under Civil Code section 3294 ignores the long line of decisions in this state ... holding that punitive damages are recoverable in a nondeliberate or unintentional tort where the defendant's conduct constitutes a conscious disregard of the probability of injury to others. * * *

The argument that application of Civil Code section 3294 violates the constitutional prohibition against double jeopardy is equally fallacious. This prohibition like the ex post facto concept is applicable only to criminal proceedings. [Citations.]

The related contention that the potential liability for punitive damages in other cases for the same design defect renders the imposition of such damages violative of Ford's due process rights also lacks merit. Followed to its logical conclusion, it would mean that punitive damages could never be assessed against a manufacturer of a mass produced article. No authorities are cited for such a proposition; indeed, as we have seen, the cases are to the contrary. We recognize the fact that multiplicity of awards may present a problem, but the mere possibility of a future award in a different case is not a ground for setting aside the award in this case, particularly as reduced by the trial judge. If Ford should be confronted with the possibility of an award in another case for the same conduct, it may raise the issue in that case. We add, moreover, that there is no necessary unfairness should the plaintiff in this case be rewarded to a greater extent than later plaintiffs. As Professor Owen has said in response to such a charge of unfairness: "This conception ignores the enormous diligence, imagination, and financial outlay required of initial plaintiffs to uncover and to prove the flagrant misconduct of a product manufacturer. In fact, subsequent plaintiffs will often ride to favorable verdicts and settlements on the coattails of the firstcomers." (Owen, supra, at p. 1325, fn. omitted.) That observation fits the instant case.

(3) Sufficiency of the Evidence to Support the Finding of Malice and Corporate Responsibility:

* * *

Through the results of the crash tests Ford knew that the Pinto's fuel tank and rear structure would expose consumers to serious injury or death in a 20 to 30 mile–per–hour collision. There was evidence that Ford could have corrected the hazardous design defects at minimal cost but decided to defer correction of the shortcomings by engaging in a cost-benefit analysis balancing human lives and limbs against corporate profits. Ford's institutional mentality was shown to be one of callous indifference to public safety. There was substantial evidence that Ford's conduct constituted "conscious disregard" of the probability of injury to members of the consuming public.

Ford's argument that there can be no liability for punitive damages because there was no evidence of corporate ratification of malicious misconduct is equally without merit. California follows the Restatement rule that punitive damages can be awarded against a principal because of an action of an agent if, but only if, " '(a) the principal authorized the doing and the manner of the act, or (b) the agent was unfit and the principal was reckless in employing him, or (c) the agent was employed in a managerial capacity and was acting in the scope of employment, or (d) the principal or a managerial agent of the principal ratified or approved the act.' (Rest.2d Torts (Tent. Draft No. 19, 1973) § 909.)" [Citations.] The present case comes within one or both of the categories described in subdivisions (c) and (d).

[The court held that there was no basis for reversal for the instructions on malice or the burden of proof, and that the amount of the award was "far from excessive as a deterrent against future wrongful conduct by Ford and others."]

GRIMSHAW'S APPEAL

[Grimshaw argued that the punitive damages award was not excessive, as a matter of law, and that the trial court erred in cutting the award so drastically.]

[T]he judge, exercising his independent judgment on the evidence, determined that a punitive award of 3½ million dollars was "fair and reasonable." Evidence pertaining to Ford's conduct, its wealth and the savings it realized in deferring design modifications in the Pinto's fuel system might have persuaded a different fact finder that a larger award should have been allowed to stand. [But we cannot say that the judge abused his discretion.] Finally, while the trial judge may not have taken into account Ford's potential liability for punitive damages in other cases involving the same tortious conduct in reducing the award, it is a factor we may consider in passing on the request to increase the award. Considering such potential liability, we find the amount as reduced by the trial judge to be reasonable and just. We therefore decline the invitation to modify the judgment by reducing the amount of the remittitur.

[Affirmed.]

Owen, Problems in Assessing Punitive Damages Against Manufacturers of Defective Products

49 U.Chi.L.Rev. 1, 16–47 (1982).

The key to winning a punitive damages case against a manufacturer is often said to lie in finding a "smoking gun" in the defendant's files. The "powder keg" memorandum, for example, was pivotal in the *Gryc* flammable fabrics case [see ch. 15], as was Ford's cost-feasibility memorandum—examining various design improvements for the Pinto fuel system—in the *Grimshaw* case. On rare occasions such documents may in themselves prove a callous disregard by corporate executives of human health or safety.

In many cases, however, there are significant dangers of abuse in the manipulation of documentary evidence. Manufacturers necessarily create massive documentation of their design and production processes, sometimes amounting to millions of pages of notes, memoranda, and correspondence over the life of a product. Especially during the initial design of the product, but also as information returns on the product's performance in the field, reports of many instances of one problem or another will be documented, acted upon, and filed away. In fact, the more a manufacturer is truly concerned about its product's safety, the more it will encourage self-criticism and "negative" analyses of the product within the company.[83] For example, it often is desirable during the initial stages of a product's design to test it to its limits to discover what those limits are: cars may thus be crash-tested until their gas tanks burst, and rats may be injected with a drug in ever higher doses until some die. Documentary evidence (especially films) of such tests can later return to haunt the manufacturer, as they did in the *Grimshaw* Pinto case.[85] * * *

---

83. One may postulate that the most safety-conscious manufacturer will direct its employees to search out and investigate even remotely possible dangers, to explore even barely plausible remedial measures, and to document the possibilities that dangers may be present and cured. Among the range of dangers and remedies so documented, a manager with "due" regard for consumer safety will act to reduce or eliminate such risks only to the extent that it is reasonable to do so. Such a manager may therefore "consciously" yet reasonably choose to leave in the product remote dangers that are too expensive to remove, and sometimes even substantial dangers for which there is no practicable remedy. The documentation of such a choice should not, of course, support a punitive award.

Another dimension of this problem concerns the variety of psychological make-ups of the manufacturer's employees. The employees of a large manufacturing concern will entertain a broad spectrum of diverse political and practical viewpoints on how much safety is enough. At one extreme may be an engineer or marketing person who will decry any loss of utility for safety, while at the other extreme may be an employee to whom safety is paramount. One might characterize the persons at these extremes as "alarmists": the "utility alarmists"—who characteristically will criticize the prototype or final product as "too safe," and the "safety alarmists"—who characteristically will find an "excess" of danger. While memoranda from either type of alarmist will likely appear incriminating after a product accident years later, the conscientious manufacturer may find the dialectical presentation of such extreme viewpoints especially useful in establishing a counterpoint for informed decision making, somewhere toward the center of which will usually lie the "correct" decision as to the level of safety. Tribunals must be cautious, therefore, not to place excessive weight on internal memoranda criticizing product safety performance or proposing (or questioning) improvements, for the source of such criticism may have been an alarmist whose advice was properly rejected after due consideration. Although such documentation may, of course, be highly relevant to the culpability issue, it will usually represent only a part of the much larger puzzle of institutional motivation and rationale. Cf. Dorsey v. Honda Motor Corp., 655 F.2d 650, 653 (5th Cir. 1981) (noting Honda's rejection of an employee's proposal to enlarge the car's size or strength to increase safety).

85. One piece of evidence that made a particular impact on the jury in *Grimshaw* was Exhibit 122, a motion picture showing a prototype Pinto being crash tested. When the vehicle was backed into a fixed barrier at 21.5 miles per hour, "the filler neck of the fuel tank separated allowing fluid to spill from the tank." 119 Cal. App. 3d at 791, 174 Cal. Rptr. at 370. A juror who was interviewed shortly after the verdict pointed to the dramatic impact this film had made at trial: "The gas tank, filled with a nonflammable substance, ruptured with such force . . . that 'it looked like a fireman had stuck a hose

. . . An important aggravating factor in some cases is the manufacturer's awareness of an easy solution to the problem plainly demanded by its simplicity and economy. The *Grimshaw* court thus was impressed that there were a variety of "inexpensive fixes," each costing only several dollars, that supposedly could have solved the Pinto's gas tank problem.

* * *

One must be somewhat skeptical of the *Grimshaw* court's heavy reliance on an array of purported "cheap fixes," some of which may not have been feasible at all. For example, the court appeared to be impressed with the concept of adding a rubber or nylon bladder to the inside of the gas tank. Yet such bladders apparently are still not generally used in commercially produced cars; one thus must wonder whether they are feasible even today or, if they are, whether they would do much good. Similar problems of feasibility are raised by the court's reliance on testimony that an over-the-axle location of the fuel tank would have been a preferable design, because such a tank apparently cannot be built into a small hatchback car such as the model of Pinto involved in *Grimshaw*.

. . . In a complex product such as a car, there are always hundreds of design changes that can be made to enhance the safety of the vehicle in a particular type of a crash situation, ranging in cost per unit from pennies to hundreds of dollars. Although the cost of any one change may be small in isolation, all we can fairly ask of management and its engineers in the punitive damages context is that safety considerations not be deliberately excluded or shunted far to the rear in deciding on the total design mix involved. Each separate design choice is of course only a small sub-decision in the overall safety-cost-utility mix that must be tailored to the special needs and limitations of each different type of product.

* * *

Cost-benefit analysis is fundamental to the design engineer's trade. The depth of the rubber on an automobile's bumper forever may be increased by another one-tenth inch. One more cross-beam always may be added to protect the occupants in certain types of collisions. The configuration of crossbeams may be changed to increase their strength; thicker or harder steel may be used in the beams; perhaps they may be made of another metal, or perhaps even of a form of plastic. Many hundreds of such choices are made by design engineers in the production of a single complex product, and each such decision involves a range of trade-offs between cost, weight, appearance, performance capabilities (for separate functions in varying environments), and safety in one type of accident versus another. A steel beam that protects an occupant in one type of accident may endanger him in another, as by rendering that portion of the vehicle less energy

inside the car and turned it on.' " Wall St. J., Feb. 14, 1978, at 1, col. 4. Ford's objections to the relevance of the film, a particularly sensitive issue in view of the substantial prejudice it obviously was bound to engender, were based upon the fact that the *Grimshaw* car's filler neck did not separate, unlike the crash test car. These objections were rejected by the court. 119 Cal. App. 3d at 791, 174 Cal. Rptr. at 370.

absorbent, and may endanger pedestrians and the occupants of other vehicles as well.[112] Although much of this decision making involves the application of proven scientific principles, much is art, and some by its nature can be little more than trial and error.

* * * [T]he design and warnings "defect" notions ... are surrounded by shrouds of mist. The mist exists, of course, only in the middle of the spectrum, and cases do arise at either extreme, where the product is clearly defective or not. Yet for the great number of cases in the middle, the legal "tests" of liability for such defects are by their nature so vague that they are often effectively meaningless as guides for design engineers attempting to comply with the law. There is therefore a vast defect "no man's land" where a manufacturer has no idea whether it is on the right or wrong side of the law. One indeed may ask whether "law" itself exists in such terrain, or whether "lawless" is the better word to describe the prevailing "rule" of random guilt. The very notion of how much design safety is enough, and to a lesser extent how much safety information is enough, involves a morass of conceptual, political, and practical issues on which juries, courts, commentators, and legislatures strongly disagree. * * *

... A rose is often not a rose in such an environment, and what looks like acceptable if not praiseworthy conduct to one person may look flagrantly improper to another: one person's sound engineering is another person's trading lives for profits.

NOTES

1. For a variety of reasons, the *Grimshaw* Ford Pinto case is the classic punitive damages automotive products liability case. See generally G. Schwartz, The Myth of the Ford Pinto Case, 43 Rutgers L. Rev. 1013 (1990–91).

2. One document excluded by the *Grimshaw* trial court, on grounds that its relevance would be outweighed by undue prejudice, was the so-called Grush–Saunby Report which analyzed a proposed NHTSA standard that set a maximum allowable rate of fuel leakage in roll-overs. The report evaluated the expected costs and benefits of meeting the proposed standard by installing a carburetor valve. The report, entitled "Fatalities Associated with Crash Induced Fuel Leakage and Fires," was circulated as an inter-office memorandum in Ford's Environmental and Safety Engineering Department. The Grush–Saunby Report contained the key cost-benefit calculations in Table 3:

---

112. This is to say nothing of the increases in weight and cost and decreases in roominess, maneuverability, and fuel efficiency that may result. See also Dawson v. Chrysler Corp., 630 F.2d 950, 962–63 (3d Cir. 1980), cert. denied, 450 U.S. 959 (1981).

BENEFITS AND COSTS RELATING TO FUEL LEAKAGE ASSOCIATED WITH THE STATIC ROLLOVER TEST PORTION OF FMVSS 208

BENEFITS:

Savings—180 burn deaths, 180 serious burn injuries, 2,100 burned vehicles.

Unit Cost—$200,000 per death, $67,000 per injury, $700 per vehicle.

Total Benefit—180 × ($200,000) + 180 × ($67,000) + 2,100 × ($700) =

$49.5 million

COSTS:

Sales—11 million cars, 1.5 million light trucks.

Unit Cost—$11 per car, $11 per truck.

Total Cost—11,000,000 × ($11) æ 1,500,000 × ($11) =

$137 million

Employing the $200,000 per life value used at the time by NHTSA, the memo concluded that the proposed design requirements would not be cost effective: "The cost of implementing the rollover portion of the amended Standard has been calculated to be almost three times the expected benefit, even using very favorable benefit assumptions. The yearly benefits of compliance were estimated at just under $50 million, with an associated customer cost of $137 million. Analyses of other portions of the proposed regulation would also be expected to yield poor benefit-to-cost ratios."

Although the above memorandum was excluded from evidence in *Grimshaw*, it has been cited in justification of the large punitive damages award as proof of Ford's callous attitude toward the safety of consumers. For example, in an interview with Ford Vice President of Environmental and Safety Engineering and others, CBS News Correspondent Mike Wallace referred to this same report: "I find it difficult to believe that top management of the Ford Motor Company is going to sit there and say, 'Oh, we'll buy 2,000 deaths, 10,000 injuries, because we want to make some money or we want to bring in a cheaper car." See "Is Your Car Safe?," 60 Minutes, vol. 10, no. 40, at p. 7 (June 11, 1978).

What precisely was it that troubled Mike Wallace? Are you similarly troubled? Are there implications for the usefulness of risk-benefit analysis as a decision-making tool?

3. Fuel Tank Litigation—Ford. Ford did not fare well with its gas tank cases. See also Ford Motor Co. v. Durrill, 714 S.W.2d 329 (Tex. App. 1986), vac'd on motion of the parties, 754 S.W.2d 646 (Tex. 1988) ($100 million punitive damages verdict, remitted by trial court to $20 million, further remitted on appeal to $10 million, and then settled, for design of Ford Mustang II fuel system); Ford Motor Co. v. Stubblefield, 319 S.E.2d 470 (Ga. App. 1984) ($8 million: Mustang II). The design of the Mustang II was in many respects the same as the Pinto.

4. Criminal Prosecution. In 1978, Ford was prosecuted in Indiana for the deaths of three teenage sisters in a Pinto that burst into flames when it was struck from the rear. After a long, dramatic trial, Ford was acquitted. For an account of the trial, see L. Stobel, Reckless Homicide? (1980).

5. Fuel Tank Safety—Comparisons. In fairness to Ford, it should be noted that the Pinto gas tanks appear to have been no more hazardous than those of most other subcompacts at the time. NHTSA (FARS) statistics for post–1970 cars in fatal fire accidents, per million cars in operation, for 1975 & 1976, are as follows: all vehicles—6.8; all compacts—7.3; Pinto—7.0; VW—9.3; Vega—7.0; Datsun—9.7; Toyota—4.9; Gremlin—9.8; Dodge Colt—5.3; Opel—8.8; Honda—11.1. Defendant's Exhibit EE, State v. Ford Motor Co., No. 5324 (Super. Ct. Elkart Cty., Ind., Sept. 13, 1978).

6. Fuel Tank Litigation—Other Manufacturers. Other manufacturers have had similar problems with fuel tank litigation. General Motors has been troubled by fire cases involving the side-saddle gas tank design on its pickup trucks. See, e.g., General Motors Corp. v. Moseley, 447 S.E.2d 302 (Ga. App. 1994) ($101 million punitive verdict for death of youth in fiery crash of GM side-saddle pickup truck reversed for improper argument by plaintiff's counsel); cf. In re General Motors Corporation Pick–Up Truck Fuel Tank Products Liability Litigation, 55 F.3d 768 (3d Cir.1995) (rejecting coupon settlement with owners of pickups equipped with dangerous side-saddle fuel tanks). See also Toyota Motor Co. v. Moll, 438 So.2d 192 (Fla. App. 1983) ($3 million punitive damages award upheld); American Motors Corp. v. Ellis, 403 So.2d 459 (Fla. App. 1981) (punitive damages claim for jury); Chrysler Corp. v. Wolmer, 499 So.2d 823 (Fla.1986)($3 million punitive damages award reversed), quashing Wolmer v. Chrysler Corp., 474 So.2d 834 (Fla. App. 1985).

7. Non–Fuel Tank Litigation—Ford. Punitive damage awards have proved nettlesome to Ford beyond the Pinto (and Mustang II) fuel tank cases. In Ammerman v. Ford Motor Co., No. 93–2690 (Marion Cty., Ind., Super. Ct., Oct. 30, 1995), a rollover case, the plaintiffs "contended that Ford had known in 1982 that the Bronco II was unstable, but had decided against spending extra money to widen the vehicle and lower its center of gravity in order to meet a production schedule," and thereafter sought to cover up the danger. *Jury verdict*, $58 million in punitive damages against Ford, divided equally between the driver and passenger who were both severely injured. Prod. Liab. Advisory 3 (Nov.1995). A Texas jury assessed $22.5 million against Ford in another Bronco II rollover case, reduced by the trial court to the statutory maximum of $4 million, four times the compensatory award. Cammack v. Ford Motor Co., Tex. Dist. Ct., 61st Dist. Harris Cty. (Aug.25, 1995). Prod. Safety & Liab. Rep. (BNA) 958 (Sept. 8, 1995).

See also Buell–Wilson v. Ford Motor Co., 46 Cal.Rptr.3d 147, 175 (Ct. App. 2006)($246 million punitive damages award, reduced by trial court to $75 million and by appellate court to $55 million (a 2:1 ratio with compensatory damages), where plaintiff paralyzed when SUV's roof crushed in rollover; award sustained notwithstanding " 'reasonable disagreement' among experts concerning the propriety of [the manufacturer's] design decisions"); Karlsson v. Ford Motor Co., 45 Cal.Rptr.3d 265 (Ct. App. 2006) ($15 million punitive damages award sustained for paralysis in collision of young child riding on third row bench of minivan not equipped with 3–point harness).

8. Non–Fuel–Tank Litigation—Other Manufacturers. But other manufacturers have fared little better in the non-fuel-tank litigation. See, e.g., Rodriguez v. American Suzuki Motor Co., Mo.Cir.Ct., 22d Cir. (verdict July 7, 1995) ($60 million punitive damages to passenger for rollover of Suzuki Samurai); General Motors Corp. v. Johnston, 592 So.2d 1054 (Ala. 1992) ($15 million punitive damages award reduced to $7.5 million for stalling problem on which GM issued only a "silent" or "unpublished" recall); Dorsey v. Honda Motor Co., Ltd., 655 F.2d 650 (5th Cir.1981) ($5 million punitive damages upheld for frontal design of small Honda).

But see Montgomery v. Mitsubishi Motors Corp., 2006 WL 1030272, at *4–5 (E.D. Pa. 2006) (no punitive damages for death in rollover: "the alleged design flaw posited by the Plaintiffs' experts [does not rise] to the level of outrageous conduct . . . from which a reasonable jury could find that [the defendant] acted with an evil motive or with reckless indifference to the rights of others in designing" the vehicle); Peters v. General Motors Corp., 200 S.W.3d 1, 27 (Mo. Ct. App. 2006) (reversing $50 million punitive damages verdict for severe injuries from sudden acceleration from malfunctioning cruise control device; evidence did not reveal that defendant's "conduct was outrageous because of evil motive or reckless indifference").

9. On the Pinto fuel system design problem, see generally G. Schwartz, The Myth of the Ford Pinto Case, 43 Rutgers L.Rev. 1013 (1991); Bruck, How Ford Stalled the Pinto Litigation, The American Lawyer 23 (June 1979); Kunen, Reckless Disregard 249 et seq. (1994); Schmitt & May, Beyond Products Liability: The Legal, Social, and Ethical Problems Facing the Automobile Industry in Producing Safe Products, 56 U. Det. J. Urb. L. 1021 (1979); and the Pulitzer Prize-winning article by Dowie, Pinto Madness, Mother Jones 18 (Sept./Oct.1977).

On the criminal prosecution, see L. Stobel, Reckless Homicide? (1980); Epstein, Is Pinto a Criminal? Regulation 15 (Mar./Apr.1980); Tybor, How Ford Won Pinto Trial, Nat'l L.J. 1 (Mar. 24, 1980); and a series of 5 articles by Wheeler, beginning with In Pinto's Wake, Criminal Trials Loom for More Manufacturers, Nat'l L.J. 27 (Oct. 6, 1980).

---

4.   RECALL

As observed in the context of post-sale duties of manufacturers generally in ch. 11(5), above, only a small handful of cases have found a *common-law* duty to recall. See, e.g., Hammes v. Yamaha Motor Corp. U.S.A., 2006 WL 1195907, at *11 (D. Minn. 2006) (granting summary judgment to defendant on plaintiff's failure to recall claim: "the overwhelming majority of jurisdictions have rejected ... an obligation" to "institute a product recall or retrofit").

Yet Congress has statutorily imposed substantial post-marketing obligations on the automobile industry to warn consumers of defects and provide for their repair. The National Traffic & Motor Vehicle Safety Act requires manufacturers to notify motor vehicle purchasers of defects "related to motor vehicle safety," 49 U.S.C. § 30118, as determined by the Secretary of Transportation (through the National Highway Traffic Administration, NHTSA) or by the manufacturer. See generally 49 U.S.C. §§ 30117–21. Automotive recalls are now an every-day occurrence: during January–March 2004, there were 56 automotive recall campaigns (some involving numerous models and years) by 21 separate manufacturers of cars, motorcycles, trucks, vans, trailers, buses, and automotive equipment. See Quarterly Index, Prod. Safety & Liab. Rep(BNA) Table of Recalls 15–16 (Apr. 12, 2004).

United States v. General Motors Corp.

United States Court of Appeals, District of Columbia Circuit, 1977.
565 F.2d 754.

■ J. Skelly Wright, Circuit Judge.

On December 19, 1974 the Administrator of the National Highway Traffic Safety Administration (NHTSA), acting pursuant to his authority under the National Traffic and Motor Vehicle Safety Act, determined that Rochester Quadrajet carburetors installed in 1965 Chevrolets and 1966 Chevrolets and Buicks contained a "defect which relates to motor vehicle safety" and that the manufacturer was therefore required to notify owners of the potential danger. See 15 U.S.C.A. §§ 1391, 1397, 1402 (1970).[1] General Motors did not comply with the notice order; instead, it filed suit to have the order declared null and void. At the same time the Administrator brought suit to enforce the order and to impose a civil penalty on General Motors for its refusal to comply. The two cases were consolidated and, after substantial discovery, the District Court granted the Government's motion for summary judgment and fined General Motors $400,-000—the maximum statutory penalty. This appeal followed. It is our conclusion that the grant of summary judgment was appropriate, but that the penalty should not have been imposed absent briefs or argument on point, or any form of hearing. We therefore remand this case to the District Court for further consideration of the penalty question.

I.

Under the National Traffic and Motor Vehicle Safety Act (Safety Act), manufacturers are required to notify purchasers of motor vehicles containing "a defect which relates to motor vehicle safety," 15 U.S.C.A. § 1402(e) (1970), as determined by the Administrator of NHTSA. General Motors has conceded, both in the District Court and in this appeal, that the Government successfully established the existence of a "defect" in the Rochester Quadrajet carburetors. When these carburetors were manufactured holes were drilled into them; these holes were later sealed by inserting metal plugs. One of the holes, in the fuel inlet portion of the carburetor, was sealed by a plug known as the "fuel inlet plug." If this plug becomes dislodged gasoline can spill directly into the engine, resulting in a fire under the hood. According to the affidavit of one of General Motors' own employees, a number of these fuel inlet plugs were improperly inserted during the assembly process. While only figures maintained in General Motors' central—as opposed to its regional—offices have been available in this litigation, and while all incidents of carburetor failures clearly may not be reported, the record discloses *at least* 665 reported incidents of engine compartment fires in vehicles equipped with the Rochester Quadrajet carburetor. As General Motors recognized, under prior case law this evi-

---

1. The Act was amended on October 27, 1974 by Pub. L. No. 93–492, 88 Stat. 1477. The defect notification provision in § 1402 was replaced by 15 U.S.C.A. §§ 1411–1420, which explicitly require manufacturers to repair or replace defective parts at no charge when the notification order is issued within eight years of the first purchase. However, the definitions of "defect" and "motor vehi- cle safety," which are central to this litiga- tion, were not altered by the 1974 amend- ments. Those amendments do not apply to this case, since the order here was issued prior to the effective date of the Act, see Pub. L. No. 93–492, § 102(c), 88 Stat. 1477. [Note that the Act has been recodified at 49 U.S.C. §§ 30101 et seq.—Eds.]

dence clearly establishes as a matter of law that the vehicles in question contain a "defect" within the meaning of the Act.

General Motors, however, argues that summary judgment was inappropriate because material questions of fact exist as to whether this defect "relates to motor vehicle safety." "Motor vehicle safety" is defined in the Act to mean

> the performance of motor vehicles or motor vehicle equipment in such a manner that the public is protected against unreasonable risk of accidents occurring as a result of the design, construction or performance of motor vehicles and is also protected against unreasonable risk of death or injury to persons in the event accidents do occur, and includes nonoperational safety of such vehicles.

15 U.S.C.A. § 1391(1)(1970). According to General Motors, the defect in the Rochester Quadrajet carburetor does not—or at least may not—pose an "unreasonable risk" of accidents or injuries.

In United States v. General Motors Corp. (*Wheels*), 171 U.S. App. D.C. 27, 518 F.2d 420, 435 (1975), we held that a "commonsense" approach must be adopted in construing the Safety Act and, particularly, the term "unreasonable."[6] Applying such an approach, we can see no question but that engine fires, which may occur on thoroughfares where pulling over and standing outside the car is difficult or dangerous, or which may take the driver by surprise and quickly spread to the passenger compartment, are extremely dangerous for all involved and should be considered an unreasonable risk to safety....

In appealing the summary judgment in this case, General Motors seeks to call into question this commonsense conclusion as to what is an unreasonable risk by relying on affidavits of two of its employees presenting predictions as to the likely number of carburetor failures and resulting injuries in the future.... Our affirmance of the District Court's summary judgment order rests on the fact that, even if the numbers contained in these affidavits were established to be accurate predictions, this would not relieve General Motors of its obligation to inform the vehicle owners in question of the admitted defect in the cars they are operating.

General Motors' first affidavit seeks to predict the number of injuries likely to be suffered in the future as a result of dislodgment of fuel inlet plugs in 1965 Chevrolets and 1966 Chevrolets and Buicks. Taking into account the number of such vehicles still on the road, and assuming 665

---

6. The definition of "motor vehicle safety" in the Act applies not only to defect notification procedures, but also to promulgation of mandatory motor vehicle safety standards under the Act. According to Senator Magnuson, chairman of the Senate Commerce Committee, "The reason the word 'unreasonable' was put in there is that we hope that there will be some common sense applied to this." Hearings on Traffic Safety Before the Senate Commerce Committee, 89th Cong., 2d sess. 56 (1966). While safety was considered by the committee to be the "overriding consideration," the committee report noted that in promulgating standards "the Secretary will necessarily consider reasonableness of cost, feasibility and adequate lead time." S. Rep. No. 1301, 89 Cong., 2d Sess. 6 (1966), U.S. Code Cong. & Admin. News 1966, pp. 2709, 2714.

prior fires and between one and 15 prior injuries as a result of these fires, General Motors' manager of Analysis and Product Assurance predicts between less than one and three injuries in the future. The second affidavit is addressed not to the likely number of injuries, but rather to predictions of instances of future plug failure. In this affidavit a General Motors Staff Analysis Engineer concludes that dislodgment of the fuel inlet plugs is due in part to a process of thermal expansion known as "creep" and that, given the age of the cars in question, "*virtually* all creep to which they were theoretically subject has already occurred." Thus it is his view "that the number of future plug failures will be *negligible.*"

Apparently General Motors' position is that since, given the passage of time and the reduction in the number of vehicles on the road, many or most of the failures and injuries resulting from this defective carburetor have already occurred, it is no longer required to take any action to protect against those failures that it *admits* will occur in the future.... We disagree.

The basic purpose of the Safety Act is to reduce motor vehicle accidents, injuries, and property damage. In adopting the notification provisions of the Act the Senate Commerce Committee found that "[d]eficiencies in past industry practices relating to the notification and curing of manufacturing defects necessitate the imposition of mandatory procedures to insure such notification of purchasers and correction of *all* safety-related defects." S. Rep. No. 1301, 89th Cong., 2d Sess. 4 (1966), U.S. Code Cong. & Admin. News 1966, p. 2712 (emphasis added). In our view, where a defect—a term used in the sense of an "error or mistake"—has been established in a motor vehicle, and where this defect results in hazards as potentially dangerous as a sudden engine fire, and where there is no dispute that at least some such hazards, in this case fires, can definitely be expected to occur in the future, then the defect must be viewed as one "related to motor vehicle safety," and the Act's basic purpose of protecting the public requires that notification be provided.

In this case it is clear, with the gift of hindsight, that this purpose would have been best served had a notification order been issued some seven years ago. At that time NHTSA, relying substantially on information provided by General Motors predicting a substantial decrease in future carburetor failures, decided not to require notification. General Motors' predictions later proved wholly inaccurate, and the order was finally issued in 1974.[13] Our purpose in noting this is not to assign any fault for this unfortunate delay, or to cast doubt upon the trustworthiness of General Motors' instant predictions on the basis of their past record of inaccuracy.

---

13. The case was first opened in November 1967 on the basis of a single consumer complaint, and was closed shortly thereafter. It was reactivated in September 1969 after receipt of three additional complaint letters and publication of an article in *Product Engineering* relating to inlet plug failures. See JA 93. At that time General Motors predicted a total of 43 carburetor failures in the vehicles in question during 1970 and 1971; it later reported that 167 failures had in fact occurred during this period. See JA 103, 134.

Rather, it is only to point out that if the consumer safety would have been best served by an order in the first instance, it would be most ill served by extending this delay based on new predictions that the number of injuries caused by the defect will diminish.

The fact remains that some of these cars continue to be driven and that, according to General Motors, some "negligible" number of them will burst into flames in the future.... The purpose of the Safety Act, however, is ... to prevent serious injuries stemming from established defects before they occur. To now hold that General Motors, having managed to avoid issuance of an order in 1970, was not required to notify those operators who remain subject to risk since most of the failures have already occurred would be to leave this purpose permanently unfulfilled and to establish a system which encourages manufacturers to delay proceedings whenever possible—at the expense of those endangered by defective vehicles.

This conclusion is in no way undercut, as General Motors suggests, by our view of the " 'commonsense' balancing of safety benefits and economic cost" articulated in *Wheels,* supra, 518 F.2d at 435. In *Wheels* we stated:

> The commonsense limitation reflects an awareness that costs must be considered in determining what safety measures are required by the Act. While some margin of safety must be built-in [*sic*]to protect against failures during day-to-day operation, manufacturers are not required to design vehicles or components that never fail. It would appear economically, if not technologically, infeasible for manufacturers to use tires that do not wear out, lights that never burn out, and brakes that do not need adjusting or relining. Such parts cannot reasonably be termed defective if they fail because of age and wear.

Id. at 436. Here we do not deal with a part which is subject to failure because of age and wear, or a part which drivers reasonably expect to have to check and replace because of the particular problem involved. Nor is there involved any question of requiring General Motors to produce perfect, accident-free vehicles at any expense. Rather, we are merely requiring General Motors to notify owners as to a carburetor which did not, from the beginning, meet the manufacturer's own standards for proper assembly and which, absent notification, will in the future cause *at least* some operators and passengers to be confronted with the clear dangers attending a sudden fire in the engine.

[Remanded for a hearing on the amount of penalty.]

Mitchell, Ford: Faulty Capri Wipers Safer Than Recall Hazards

Charlotte Observer, Observer Washington Bureau, June 3, 1978, p. 2A, col. 4.

WASHINGTON—The Ford Motor Co. claims a government-ordered recall of 150,000 Mercury Capris would create a greater safety risk for owners than the defective windshield wipers which prompted the recall.

Ford, arguing in federal court, estimates the owners would be exposed to 10 times greater risk of accident by driving back and forth from dealers for the repair work than by continuing to drive with wipers that could fall off in a storm.

This estimate assumes owners would drive an average of 15 miles round-trip to get their wipers fixed. Ford cited national statistics to support its prediction 20 accidents would occur during the 2 million miles of driving required by the recall.

Permitting owners to continue driving with their present wipers would cause only two accidents, the company claims.

The National Highway Traffic and Safety Administration, which has been trying to get the 1971–73 model Capris recalled since January 1976, dismissed Ford's argument as "silly" and "ludicrous."

The case could be the first court test of the kind of "risk analysis" employed by Ford.

N O T E S

1. Establishing a definition for "defect" under the National Traffic and Motor Vehicle Safety Act proved troublesome for vehicle manufacturers, administrative agencies, and the courts, especially in the context of vehicle misuse. See, e.g., United States v. General Motors Corp., 841 F.2d 400 (D.C. Cir. 1988). Consider United States v. General Motors Corp., 518 F.2d 420, 427 (D.C. Cir. 1975):

> We find that a vehicle or component "contains a defect" if it is subject to a significant number of failures in normal operation, including failures either occurring during specified use or resulting from owner abuse (including inadequate maintenance) that is reasonably foreseeable (ordinary abuse), but excluding failures attributable to normal deterioration of a component as a result of age and wear. Whether a defect exists in a particular case thus turns on the nature of the component involved, the circumstances in which the failures occurred, and the number of failures experienced. Where, as here, the component is designed to function without replacement over the lifetime of the vehicle, the Government may discharge its burden of establishing a defect by showing a significant number of failures without making any showing of cause. But in all cases the manufacturer may prove, as an affirmative defense, that the failures resulted from unforeseeable owner abuse (gross abuse) or unforeseeable neglect of vehicle maintenance.

2. The National Traffic and Motor Vehicle Safety Act sets minimum informational standards which manufacturers must meet in their recall letters. See 49 U.S.C. § 30119 which requires, inter alia, that the recall notice clearly describe the defect, evaluate the risk, specify measures to remedy the defect, and inform the purchaser that repairs will be made without charge. See 49 C.F.R § 577 (1994). A manufacturer failing to comply with these standards may be required to mail another notice at its expense. See United States v. Ford Motor Co., 574 F.2d 534 (D.C. Cir.1978).

3. A major recall may cost the manufacturer many millions of dollars. The recall of Ford Pintos to modify the fuel system design called for adding a longer neck on the filler tube, improving a seal, substituting a new gas cap, and inserting a plastic shield between the gas tank and the car's gear housing. If all 1.5 million of the 1971–76 Pintos had been returned for repair, the cost to Ford would have been approximately $30–45 million. More recently, Ford estimates that its recall of 8.7 million autos will cost $300 million after taxes. Often, however, only about 60% of the cars recalled are in fact taken in for repair. See Christian & Nomani, Ford Recalls 8.7 Million Cars To Fix Ignitions, Wall St. J., p. B1, col. 6 (Apr. 26, 1996).

4. Consider Ford's objections to NHTSA's order requiring that it recall 150,000 Mercury Capris to fix the windshield wipers, reported above. General Motors made a similar argument in response to a recall order for 5.3 million mid-sized cars that allegedly had a defect making them prone to lose their rear wheels. A GM economist testified that the costs to owners of returning all the cars to the dealers, including gasoline, oil, depreciation, and time consumed in the trip, would amount to $117 million. By comparison, the company calculated that the repairs were likely to prevent 16 accidents, thus putting the cost of preventing each accident at nearly $8 million. Wall Street Journal, May 5, 1983, at 4, col. 2.

Are such economic arguments "silly," as NHTSA reportedly said? Conversely, does requiring such recalls make sense?

5. Consider the following recall notices, pertaining to a carburetor malfunction problem, that were sent by a manufacturer* to its dealers and purchasers pursuant to the National Traffic and Motor Vehicle Safety Act:

DEALER RECALL NOTICE

To: All Dealers

Subject: Service Recall 248, Certain 1977 and 1978 Vehicles Equipped with a 460 C.I.D. Engine and Model 4350–4V Carburetor for Inspection and Possible Replacement of the Carburetor.

We have found that a potential for secondary throttle "hang-up" is present on some of subject vehicles equipped with 4350–4V carburetors and 460 C.I.D. engines. The condition may cause the vehicle to continue to accelerate after the accelerator pedal is released. To stop the vehicle if the secondary throttle should stick open, the transmission must be placed in neutral or the engine ignition must be turned off and the brakes applied. Vehicles' speed could be retarded momentarily by applying the brakes, but it would be resumed when the brakes are released. Each vehicle identified on the enclosed list must have the carburetor inspected and functionally checked according to the following instructions. If the results of this review indicate a potential for secondary throttle hang-up, the carburetor must be replaced....

Notification

No vehicle affected by this recall that is currently in your possession is to be delivered until the required correction has been completed. The owners of vehicles for whom names and addresses are shown are being notified directly. In those instances where an affected vehicle has been sold, but the owner's name and address is not listed, you should contact the owner immediately and advise him of this campaign. If the owner of any vehicle cannot be contacted or does not make an appointment to have his vehicle inspected, the Form 1864 must be returned to us with the owner's name and address indicated so that we can handle further notification. Federal law requires that we advise the owner of the procedure to be

---

* Manufacturer's name withheld by request.—Eds.

followed by him in informing the National Highway Traffic Safety Administration if the defect is not remedied without charge within a reasonable time after the vehicle is tendered for repair. This has been done in the owner letter. It is also important, however, that you promptly report any instance in which an owner will not allow you to complete this recall because of objections to scheduling, or for any other reason.

PURCHASER RECALL LETTER

Dear Owner:

This notice is sent to you in accordance with the requirements of the National Traffic and Motor Vehicle Safety Act. [The company] has determined that a defect which relates to motor vehicle safety exists in certain 1977 and 1978 vehicles equipped with 460 C.I.D. engines and 4–V carburetors.

Some of these vehicles may have defective carburetors in which under certain circumstances the secondary throttle plates may stick open. Should this occur the vehicle may continue to accelerate after the accelerator pedal is released. Since such an occurrence could take place without warning, it could lead to a vehicle crash.

The likelihood of the condition occurring can be reduced by avoiding full or nearly full depressions of the accelerator pedal as during high acceleration of full power operations. To stop the vehicle if the secondary throttle plates stick open, the driver should apply the brakes and either turn the ignition switch to "off" or place the transmission selector lever in "neutral." With the ignition "off" you may experience the need to exert extra effort on the brake pedal and steering wheel.

We ask that you contact your dealer after October 12, 1977, to arrange for inspection and, if necessary, replacement of the carburetor. Your dealer has instructions for inspection and correction of this defect without charge.

* * *

In the interest of your safety and satisfaction with your vehicle, we want to emphasize the importance of having this service performed.

Sincerely,

[Company Representative]

6. Admissibility of Recall Letters. A recurring issue on which there has been some disagreement is the admissibility of evidence of recall campaigns, especially recall letters. Defense counsel have raised a variety of objections to such evidence, including the statutory and public policy arguments examined in *Ault*, irrelevance, and hearsay. Addressing most of the arguments, the court in Manieri v. Volkswagenwerk A.G., 376 A.2d 1317 (App. Div. 1977), held admissible recall letters pertaining to the defect that plaintiff's expert testified had caused the automobile accident. The court opined that admission of such evidence would not deter manufacturers from reporting defects to NHTSA since such reports were required by law. Nor was the state's evidentiary rule against evidence of subsequent remedial measures to prove negligence or culpable conduct applicable since the issues in the case were defect and control, not fault. And the letters were relevant since they pertained to the specific defect that plaintiff asserted had caused his accident. The court also relied on the following observations from Fields v. Volkswagen of America, Inc., 555 P.2d 48, 57 (Okla. 1976):

The recall letter by itself does not make a prima facie case or shift the burden of proof. It does not prove that the defect existed at the time of the accident. This must be proved independently. But if a defect contributing to or causing the accident is the defect that is the subject of the recall letter, then the letter would be some evidence that the "defect existed at the time the product left the manufacturer." This is an element that the plaintiff is required to prove.

Accord, Farner v. Paccar, Inc., 562 F.2d 518 (8th Cir. 1977), where the defendant argued that the recall letter should have been excluded under the hearsay rule. *Held,* pursuant to Fed.R.Evid. 801(d)(2), such documents are treated as "admissions falling outside of the hearsay rule as prior statements by a party opponent or its employee offered against that party at trial." This was so despite the fact that the admission was made under the compulsion of the National Traffic and Motor Vehicle Safety Act. *Further held,* Fed. R. Evid. 407 does not apply to strict liability actions and thus did not bar admission of the recall letter.

Compare Hammes v. Yamaha Motor Corp. U.S.A., 2006 WL 1195907, at *1 (D. Minn. 2006) (plaintiff injured when motorcyle "revved up and 'took off like a rocket' " due to throttle-cable problem for which it had been recalled: even if recall evidence not itself admissible, plaintiff's expert may rely partially on recall in forming his opinion).

7. In addition to the general post-sale duty materials cited in ch. 10(5), see generally McDonald, Shifting Out of Neutral: A New Approach to Global Road Safety, 38 Vand. J. Transnat'l L. 743 (2005); McDonald, Separations, Blow–Outs, and Fallout: A Treatise on the Regulatory Aftermath of the Ford–Firestone Tire Recall, 37 J. Marshall L. Rev. 1073 (2004); McDonald, Federal Preemption of Automotive Recalls: A Case of Too many Backseat Drivers?, 71 Tenn. L. Rev. 471 (2004); McDonald, Judicial Review of NHTSA–Ordered Recalls, 47 Wayne L. Rev. 1301 (2002); Annot., 84 A.L.R.3d 1220 (1978) (admissibility of recall letters).

CHAPTER 19

SPECIAL ISSUES IN TOXIC SUBSTANCE AND MASS TORT LITIGATION

* Poster from ''The Toxic Avenger'', a horror/comedy film on the consequences of toxic waste. See Acknowledgments, supra.—Eds.

1.   THE NATURE OF TOXIC SUBSTANCE LITIGATION

Since 1973, when the first asbestos case was upheld on appeal, Borel v. Fibreboard Corp., 493 F.2d 1076 (5th Cir. 1973), toxic substance litigation has become a significant part of the products liability landscape. The widely proclaimed "litigation explosion" of recent decades is almost entirely the result of asbestos, and other toxic substance, case filings. In the federal courts alone, the annual rate of asbestos case filings increased tenfold in the early 1980s, to approximately 10,000 cases; during the late 1980s, approximately 37,000 cases were filed; and in 1990 alone, 13,000 new cases were filed. See Hensler, Fashioning a National Resolution of Asbestos Personal Injury Litigation, 13 Cardozo L. Rev. 1967, 1971 (1992). By 2002, approximately 730,000 people had filed compensation claims for asbestos-related injuries. At least 8,400 defendants have been sued and paid $70 billion to settle these claims. Both plaintiffs' and defendants' lawyers express concern over whether compensation is being fairly allocated and whether there will be funds available in the future to compensate the remaining unknown number of persons likely to be afflicted with an asbestos-related injury who have not yet filed suit. By all accounts, however, at most only about three-fourths of the total number of claimants have come forward. S. Carroll, et. al., Asbestos Litigation: Summary, at xvii, xxiv-xxvi (RAND Institute for Civil Justice 2005)(hereinafter 2005 RAND Report Summary).

With such enormous numbers of cases affecting the judicial system, it is important to determine what makes litigation involving toxic substances like asbestos unique. "Toxic tort cases typically involve claims against manufacturers for a variety of harms that result from occupational, environmental, or consumer exposures to toxic products or wastes. In most toxic tort cases, a person is exposed to a toxic product and decades later becomes afflicted with cancer or another ailment that cannot always be traced to a single substance or cause." Wagner, Choosing Ignorance in the Manufacture of Toxic Products, 82 Cornell L. Rev. 773, 777 (1997). Examples of toxic products abound: chemicals such as pesticides, Agent Orange, or DDT; pharmaceutical products such as Vioxx, DES, and silicone gel breast implants; consumer products like cigarettes; and industrial products made of asbestos, PCBs, and lead. Substances such as these can cause chronic diseases that are not manifested until years, even decades, after original exposure.

The latent nature of the underlying injuries makes it especially difficult for a plaintiff to prove a number of the traditional elements in products liability claims. For example, proving causation—an actual causal connection between the plaintiff's exposure to a toxic agent and his or her illness or injury—is established very differently in science and the law. Proof of causation in such cases almost always must be established by scientific experts, on *Daubert* standards of good science, yet scientific models of causation fit awkwardly with the but-for and substantial factor standards of products liability law. In addition, assessing product defectiveness or manufacturer negligence requires asking thorny state-of-the-art questions involving what the manufacturer and others knew about the risks of exposure at the operative times. The natural time lag between the time producers begin to suspect the possibility that a substance may cause particular deleterious effects on humans and the time when those effects become widely known and appreciated by consumers, coupled with the long latency periods of many such illnesses and injuries, means that many thousands of people may be exposed to and injured by a substance before anything can be done to prevent it. See generally Comment, Affirmative Judicial Case Management: A Viable Solution to the Toxic Product Litigation Crisis, 38 Me. L. Rev. 339–344 (1986).

Toxic substances often give rise to mass tort litigation. The impact on the judicial system of such "mass torts" has been dramatic, giving rise to calls for non-traditional resolution techniques to process the thousands of claims inundating the court system. Apart from the sheer number of claimants in absolute terms, mass tort victims are far more likely to file claims than ordinary tort victims. In typical tort contexts, only between 10–20% of potential plaintiffs pursue a claim at all (and merely 2–7% of product accident victims, as noted in ch.2), whereas 100–200% of mass tort victims actually file suit. McGovern, An Analysis of Mass Torts for Judges, 73 Tex.L.Rev. 1821, 1823 (1995)(citing D. Hensler, et al., Compensation for Accidental Injuries in the United States 110 (RAND 1991)). Consumers on a daily basis are exposed to myriad substances at home and in the workplace—pharmaceuticals, chemicals, and other substances in food, clothing, housing, cars, and at work—many of which may contribute to as-yet-unknown illnesses and injuries. When such substances eventually are shown to be unreasonably deleterious to consumers and workers, the legal system must confront the challenge of how to structure and resolve the hundreds or thousands (or tens of thousands) of resulting lawsuits in a fair and practicable manner for all concerned.

Hensler & Peterson, Understanding Mass Personal Injury Litigation: A Socio–Legal Analysis

59 Brook. L. Rev. 961 (1993).

The 1980s marked the era of mass personal injury litigation. Hundreds of thousands of people sued scores of corporations for losses due to injuries or diseases that they attributed to catastrophic events, pharmaceutical products, medical devices or toxic substances.... In some parts of the country, mass tort claims threatened to overwhelm the civil justice system, accounting for more than one-quarter of the entire civil caseload in certain courts. As a result of this wave of litigation, some businesses found that products once regarded as significant marketing successes now had the potential to drive them into bankruptcy. The specter of mass liability frightened insurers from some markets, and manufacturers from research and development in some product lines.

* * *

Although there is a disagreement about the causes and legitimacy of this litigation, almost all of those involved would agree that the civil justice system has not performed well in response to the challenge of mass torts. The litany of criticisms is long and familiar: cases take an inordinately long time to reach disposition, sometimes concluding long after a plaintiff's death; outcomes are highly variable, often seeming to have little relationship to plaintiffs' injuries or defendants' culpability; transaction costs are excessive, far outstripping the amounts paid out in compensation.

Why the civil justice system has had such problems responding to mass personal injury litigation is itself a matter of some controversy. Some attribute these problems to a lack of fit between traditional civil procedure, with its reliance on individualized case treatment, and the demands imposed on courts by massive numbers of claims which, in practice, cannot be treated individually. This view has led to myriad proposals to facilitate aggregative treatment of mass tort claims, by amending Rule 23; extending multi-districting to include trial as well as pretrial preparation and state as well as federal cases; encourage informal coordination between state and federal courts; creating a new "national disaster court," or removing some or all mass torts from the court system entirely.

* * *

Three factors distinguish mass torts from ordinary personal injury litigation: the large number of claims associated with a single "litigation;" the commonality of issues and actors among claims within a litigation; and the interdependence of claim values. Numerosity is the primary defining characteristic of a mass tort litigation. The best known examples of mass litigation, such as asbestos workers' personal injury suits and the Dalkon Shield bankruptcy litigation, have involved hundreds of thousands of cases; the most recent examples of mass torts involve at least a thousand individual claims. . . . The high visibility of mass torts and the burdens they impose on courts and parties are direct consequences of the large numbers of claims in each litigation.

But numerosity, by itself, is not sufficient to distinguish mass tort litigation from ordinary tort litigation. The court system routinely disposes of half a million or so automobile accident cases per year, far more than the number involved in any single mass tort. Mass torts are distinguished from automobile accident litigation and other ordinary, high-volume litigation by the commonality of issues and actors among individual mass tort claims. Mass torts involve a common set of injuries which are incurred in the same or similar circumstances. Most plaintiffs are represented by a relatively small number of law firms, each of which may represent hundreds or thousands of claimants. Claims are brought against one or a few defendants, and a relatively small number of law firms defend or at least control the defense of thousands of claims. In addition, mass tort litigation is usually concentrated in a few jurisdictions, either as a result of the circumstances of injury or as a result of court action.

For example, almost all asbestos personal injury cases involve claims of either respiratory or gastro-intestinal cancers or other respiratory injuries incurred in the course of handling asbestos in shipyards or maritime industries, petrochemical factories or other workplaces. Each asbestos case typically names about twenty of the same thirty to forty asbestos manufacturers and distributors as defendants. Most of the hundreds of thousands of claimants are represented by fewer than fifty plaintiffs' law firms that specialize in this litigation, and their law suits are concentrated in a dozen courts. . . .

Because of their high degree of commonality, similar factual issues and legal questions will arise in all claims in a mass tort litigation, or at least in significant subsets of claims. The same injuries will involve similar causation issues. Liability issues will be similar among claims alleging similar exposures to a particular defendant's products. Because of the common legal representation within each side, even the litigation strategies will be similar among large groups of claims.

* * *

This commonality produces the third defining characteristic of mass tort litigation: the monetary values of mass tort claims are highly interdependent. In mass litigation, the likely amount that one plaintiff will receive for a claim depends upon the values of other claims. Indeed, the claims are so similar that the prospective value of many claims will rise or fall sharply with a large plaintiff award, a defense verdict or even a signal discovery event or evidentiary decision in a single case that is part of the mass of pending claims.

The interdependence of values in mass tort claims is . . . striking. No claim in a mass tort litigation will have value until plaintiffs are able to establish causation, liability and damages for at least a few representative claims. For example, asbestos claims became viable only after the United States Court of Appeals for the Fifth Circuit in *Borel v. Fibreboard Paper Products* held that asbestos manufacturers could be held strictly liable for workers' injuries. Moreover, a large award in one case increases the value of other, similar mass tort claims. Following a $7.3 million San Francisco jury award to a plaintiff claiming injuries from silicone breast implants, every breast implant claim pending nationwide became much more valuable. Conversely the adverse disposition of some mass tort claims can sharply reduce the values of all other claims. For example, when jurors delivered a defense verdict in a consolidated trial of about 1000 Bendectin cases, thousands of Bendectin claims that were not directly involved in the trial lost their value. Similarly, the several hundred pending claims for cigarette-related lung cancer still have little value because plaintiffs have not been able to win and sustain a significant verdict in any such case.

Critical events other than trial outcomes also can greatly change the value of all other claims in the same mass tort. For example, the discovery of the "Sumner–Simpson" papers, indicating knowledge among major defendants of asbestos' injurious effects, exposed these defendants to significant punitive damages. This increased the value of all asbestos claims against those defendants, not simply those claims directly involved in the relevant discovery. Similarly, the Food and Drug Administration's ("FDA") decision to prohibit silicone breast implantation under most circumstances likely increased the value of pending and future breast implantation claims and encouraged a large number of new claims.

The enormous social and financial consequences of mass torts derive from the combination of large numbers of claims and interdependency of case values. In ordinary litigation a major adverse outcome—a multimillion dollar plaintiff award or a defendant victory in a high stakes case—may be a significant blow to the parties. But such outcomes take on far greater significance when they are multiplied many times over through their impact on other mass claims. Numerosity and interdependency create incentives for plaintiff's attorneys to seek out potential mass tort claims, for defendants to invest enormous sums in defending against these claims and for judges to devise strategies to arrive at global resolution of mass claims. . . .

NOTES

1. "Asbestos litigation is the longest-running mass tort litigation in the United States. The litigation arose as a result of individuals' long-term and widespread exposure to asbestos, which can cause serious and sometimes fatal injuries, and as a result of many asbestos product manufacturers' failure to protect workers against exposure and failure to warn their workers to take adequate precautions against exposure. Over time, the history of the litigation has been shaped by changes in substance and procedural law, the rise of a sophisticated and well-capitalized plaintiff bar, heightened media attention to litigation in general and toxic tort litigation in particular, and the information science revolution. In turn, asbestos litigation has made a significant contribution to the evolution of mass civil litigation." 2005 RAND Report Summary at xvii.

2. What are the substantive issues that presented hurdles to early plaintiffs? Toxic workplace exposure presented many legal difficulties because products liability principles had not theretofore been applied in such a context. For example, did the manufacturer of industrial materials have to warn the employees directly of hazards in their products or was it sufficient that the employer knew or should have known of the hazards? What does "state-of-the-art" knowledge include for industrial product manufacturers when the scientific knowledge in the field is arguably constantly evolving? Should strict liability apply in such cases? How can an exposed worker establish causation when he or she has been exposed to a number of manufacturers' products of a variety of types, all with different levels of asbestos? This last question, dealing with causation in toxic exposure cases, is possibly the most enduring problem for toxic exposure plaintiffs and is the subject of section 3, infra.

Borel summarizes the extensive history of the state-of-the-art of industry knowledge of the risks of asbestos exposure. It concluded that the manufacturers, as experts in the field, were obligated under both strict liability and negligence to warn of foreseeable risks in their products, particularly because those risks are unavoidable: "The rationale for this rule is that the user or consumer is entitled to make his own choice as to whether the product's utility or benefits justify exposing himself to the risk of harm. Thus, a true choice situation arises and a duty to warn attaches, whenever a reasonable man would want to be informed of the risk in order to decide whether to expose himself to it." 493 F.2d at 1089. This decision seems hardly innovative by today's standards but it was ground-breaking at the time.

Recall the discussion of the duty to warn of unavoidable risks in ch. 11 and the New Jersey Supreme Court's dramatic reversal on the viability of a state-of-the-art "defense" from its ruling in an asbestos case, *Beshada*, to its ruling in *Feldman v. Lederle Labs.*, which restricted *Beshada* to its facts. The *Feldman* ruling was challenged on equal protection grounds, and narrowly upheld, in In re Asbestos Litigation, 829 F.2d 1233 (3d Cir.1987) (1–1–1). In the lead opinion, Judge Weis remarked in part:

> Administrative convenience standing alone is not an adequate ground for the elimination of a substantive defense. [Citation.] However, we cannot help but be conscious of the extraordinary size of the asbestos personal injury litigation.... [T]his unprecedented phenomenon in American tort law requires states be given some leeway in devising their own solutions.

Judge Becker concurred on the basis that the New Jersey Supreme Court had determined a legislative (as opposed to an adjudicative) fact that "at all relevant times, asbestosis harms were knowable to the industry. That being the case, the New Jersey Supreme Court has reasonably decided to preclude endless re-litigation of what was 'knowable' to the asbestos industry." Judge Hunter dissented:

> My review of the *Beshada–Feldman* line of cases leads me to conclude that the challenged classification represents nothing more than an unprincipled, expedient, and ineffective response to widespread criticism of the *Beshada* doctrine combined with an unwillingness to give up the application of *Beshada* to asbestos manufacturers. If so, the *Beshada–Feldman* classification is undeniably arbitrary. Worse yet, I fear that the New Jersey Supreme Court's sole purpose may have been to inflict a special punishment on asbestos manufacturers. The Constitution does not permit the New Jersey courts to level either an arbitrary or a punitive sanction against asbestos manufacturers (or the manufacturer of any other product, for that matter).

Johns–Manville Sales Corp., the leading asbestos producer before it filed bankruptcy in 1982 because of the number of personal injury claims pending against it, had its main manufacturing facility in New Jersey. See P. Brodeur, Outrageous Misconduct (1985)(chronicling history of manufacturer misconduct leading to asbestos litigation).

3. Almost all of the claimants in the early asbestos litigation were occupationally exposed in industries such as asbestos mining and manufacturing, shipyards, railroads and construction. Litigation involving workers in these "traditional" industries tended to be concentrated in a limited number of courts in a handful of states: Texas, Pennsylvania, New Jersey, California, and Massachusetts, where asbestos cases constitute a significant percentage of the total civil docket. Cases migrated to different states in the late 1990s where claims are increasingly being brought by workers in industries such as textiles, paper, glass and food because asbestos is present in the workplace.

Of the $70 billion that had been spent on asbestos litigation by 2002, 42% was dedicated to plaintiffs' net compensation, 27% went to plaintiffs' transaction costs including attorneys' fees, and 31% to defense costs. At least 73 companies named in asbestos litigation have filed for bankruptcy through mid–2004. See 2005 RAND Report Summary at xxvii.

4. *Borel* also held that the defendants to whose asbestos plaintiffs were exposed could each be found to have been a contributing cause of the plaintiff's asbestosis and they would be held jointly and severally liable. 493 F.2d at 1095–96. This holding in *Borel* led to a significant increase in the number of defendants against whom asbestos cases were pursued, compounding the complexity of the litigation and increasing the difficulty courts had in administering the claims.

---

2. JUDICIAL ADMINISTRATION

Weinstein, Ethical Dilemmas in Mass Tort Litigation

88 Nw. U. L.Rev. 469, 469 (1994).

When Abraham Lincoln took office there were about thirty million people in the United States. The population had increased about ten times since 1776. Nevertheless, in Lincoln's day the usual attorney-client relationship still consisted of a single attorney serving a single client.

Today there are approximately one quarter of a billion people in the United States, soon to be ten times what it was in Lincoln's time, and the justice system has grown proportionately. Contrast the individual client of Lincoln with the 10,000 asbestos claimants represented by a Baltimore lawyer, the 45,000 present claims represented by a consortium of lawyers in asbestos cases, or the representative in the Manville Personal Injury Settlement Trust of future claimants estimated to number in the hundreds of thousands. Can a structure of justice crafted for three million and conceived in liberty continue to meet our needs in our time and beyond? Can we handle the problems now presented while preserving the sense of individual justice that Lincoln assumed? Can we apply assumptions about individual litigants and evidentiary analysis to the massive multiparty litigations of today, more likely to be decided outside the courtroom than in it?

The avalanche of toxic substance cases in the judicial system has dumped an avalanche of administrative problems on the courts. In 1984, ten years after *Borel* was decided, tens of thousands of asbestos-related personal injury cases were pending across the country. Many of those plaintiffs had waited years for trial, and new cases were being filed every day. Increasingly trial judges sought ways to process these claims more efficiently, so that plaintiffs did not have to wait years for compensation and the court did not have backlogs of cases waiting to be resolved. Each of these cases involved litigation of the same issues such as state of the art, product identification, and product defectiveness. Courts quickly recognized the value of resolving these issues "en masse" instead of individually.

The most likely method for resolving large numbers of toxic or mass tort claims would seem to be the class action, based on Fed. R. Civ. P. 23 or a state equivalent. The class action method for resolving large numbers of tort claims has been the subject of great debate over the past twenty years, however. The debate has centered around the propriety of mass torts for class treatment because of the individual issues, such as causation and damages, that predominate. In addition, courts and commentators are wary of the coercive effect of class action status to compel defendants to settle non-meritorious claims, and, thus, the incentive for unscrupulous plaintiffs' lawyers to manufacture such classes for that purpose. Because so few class actions are actually litigated, and virtually all settle either before or soon after certification, understanding the requirements for certifying a class is paramount.

A. Class Actions—Certification and Settlement

The Federal Rules of Civil Procedure authorize class actions in Rule 23. Most states have a comparable procedural rule. Fed. R. Civ. P. 23 states:

> **(a) Prerequisites to a Class Action.** One or more members of a class may sue or be sued as representative parties on behalf of all only if (1) the class is so numerous that joinder of all members is impracticable, (2) there are questions of law or fact common to the class, (3) the claims or defenses of the representative parties are typical of the claims or defenses of the class, and (4) the representative parties will fairly and adequately protect the interests of the class.

> **(b) Class Actions Maintainable.** An action may be maintained as a class action if the prerequisites of subdivision (a) are satisfied, and in addition:

> (1) the prosecution of separate actions by or against individual members of the class would create a risk of

> (A) inconsistent or varying adjudications with respect to individual members of the class which would establish incompatible standards of conduct for the party opposing the class, or

> (B) adjudications with respect to individual members of the class which would as a practical matter be dispositive of the interests of the other members not parties to the adjudications or substantially impair or impede their ability to protect their interests; or

> (2) the party opposing the class has acted or refused to act on grounds generally applicable to the class, thereby making appropriate final injunctive relief or corresponding declaratory relief with respect to the class as a whole; or

> (3) the court finds that the questions of law or fact common to the members of the class predominate over any questions affecting only individual members, and that a class action is superior to other available methods for the fair and efficient adjudication of the controversy. The

matters pertinent to the findings include: (A) the interest of members of the class in individually controlling the prosecution or defense of separate actions; (B) the extent and nature of any litigation concerning the controversy already commenced by or against members of the class; (C) the desirability or undesirability of concentrating the litigation of the claims in the particular forum; (D) the difficulties likely to be encountered in the management of a class action.

Other subsections address notice requirements and sub-classing (Rule 23(c)), the conduct of class actions (Rule 23(d)), the process for dismissal or compromise (Rule 23(e)), appeal methods (Rule 23(f)), and appointment of class counsel (Rule 23(g)).

In one of the earliest attempted mass tort class actions, the court of appeals in Jenkins v. Raymark Industries, 782 F.2d 468 (5th Cir.1986), upheld an order certifying a class of 900 asbestos cases from the Eastern District of Texas, where *Borel* had been filed. Regarding the propriety of using Rule 23 for mass tort class actions, the court remarked:

> Courts have usually avoided class actions in the mass accident or tort setting. Because of differences between individual plaintiffs on issues of liability and defenses of liability, as well as damages, it has been feared that separate trials would overshadow the common disposition for the class. The courts are now being forced to rethink the alternatives and priorities by the current volume of litigation and more frequent mass disasters. If Congress leaves us to our own devices we may be forced to abandon repetitive hearings and arguments for each claimant's attorney to the extent enjoyed by the profession in the past.

After five weeks of trial, *Jenkins* settled for $137 million. See M. Peterson & M. Selvin, Resolution of Mass Torts: Toward a Framework for Evaluation of Aggregative Procedures 39–48 (RAND 1988).

The *Jenkins* class broke ground for class actions in mass torts which most courts were, and continue to be, reluctant to certify. Of those that are certified, the pressure to settle is enormous because the financial stakes are so high. To save unnecessary time spent seeking a litigation class that would never be litigated, the class action for "settlement only" evolved. One such class action attempted to resolve all claims in the asbestos litigation and put the use of the class action for mass torts to the test.

––––––––––

Amchem Products, Inc. v. Windsor

Supreme Court of the United States, 1997.
521 U.S. 591, 117 S.Ct. 2231, 138 L.Ed.2d 689.

■ JUSTICE GINSBURG delivered the opinion of the Court.

This case concerns the legitimacy under Rule 23 of the Federal Rules of Civil Procedure of a class-action certification sought to achieve global settlement of current and future asbestos-related claims. The class proposed for certification potentially encompasses hundreds of thousands, perhaps millions, of individuals tied together by this commonality: each was, or some day may be, adversely affected by past exposure to asbestos products manufactured by one or more of 20 companies. Those companies, defendants in the lower courts, are petitioners here. The United States District Court for the Eastern District of Pennsylvania certified the class for settlement only, finding that the proposed settlement was fair and that representation and notice had been adequate. That court enjoined class members from separately pursuing asbestos-related personal-injury suits in any court, federal or state, pending the issuance of a final order. The Court of Appeals for the Third Circuit vacated the District Court's orders, holding that the class certification failed to satisfy Rule 23's requirements in several critical respects. We affirm the Court of Appeals' judgment.

I

A

The settlement-class certification we confront evolved in response to an asbestos-litigation crisis. See Georgine v. Amchem Products, Inc., 83 F.3d 610, 618, and n. 2 (3d Cir.1996) (citing commentary). A United States Judicial Conference Ad Hoc Committee on Asbestos Litigation, appointed by the Chief Justice in September 1990, described facets of the problem in a 1991 report:

> [This] is a tale of danger known in the 1930s, exposure inflicted upon millions of Americans in the 1940s and 1950s, injuries that began to take their toll in the 1960s, and a flood of lawsuits beginning in the 1970s. On the basis of past and current filing data, and because of a latency period that may last as long as 40 years for some asbestos related diseases, a continuing stream of claims can be expected. The final toll of asbestos related injuries is unknown. Predictions have been made of 200,000 asbestos disease deaths before the year 2000 and as many as 265,000 by the year 2015. "The most objectionable aspects of asbestos litigation can be briefly summarized: dockets in both federal and state courts continue to grow; long delays are routine; trials are too long; the same issues are litigated over and over; transaction costs exceed the victims' recovery by nearly two to one; exhaustion of assets threatens and distorts the process; and future claimants may lose altogether." Report of The Judicial Conference Ad Hoc Committee on Asbestos Litigation 23 (Mar.1991).

Real reform, the report concluded, required federal legislation creating a national asbestos dispute-resolution scheme. [Citation.] As recommended by the Ad Hoc Committee, the Judicial Conference of the United States urged Congress to act. See Report of the Proceedings of the Judicial Conference of the United States 33 (Mar. 12, 1991). To this date, no congressional response has emerged.

In the face of legislative inaction, the federal courts—lacking authority to replace state tort systems with a national toxic tort compensation regime—endeavored to work with the procedural tools available to improve management of federal asbestos litigation. Eight federal judges, experienced in the superintendence of asbestos cases, urged the Judicial Panel on Multidistrict Litigation (MDL Panel), to consolidate in a single district all asbestos complaints then pending in federal courts. Accepting the recommendation, the MDL Panel transferred all asbestos cases then filed, but not yet on trial in federal courts to a single district, the United States District Court for the Eastern District of Pennsylvania; pursuant to the transfer order, the collected cases were consolidated for pretrial proceedings before Judge Weiner. [Citation.] The order aggregated pending cases only; no authority resides in the MDL Panel to license for consolidated proceedings claims not yet filed.

B

After the consolidation, attorneys for plaintiffs and defendants formed separate steering committees and began settlement negotiations. Ronald L. Motley and Gene Locks—later appointed, along with Motley's law partner Joseph F. Rice, to represent the plaintiff class in this action—co-chaired the Plaintiffs' Steering Committee. Counsel for the Center for Claims Resolution (CCR), the consortium of 20 former asbestos manufacturers now before us as petitioners, participated in the Defendants' Steering Committee. Although the MDL order collected, transferred, and consolidated only cases already commenced in federal courts, settlement negotiations included efforts to find a "means of resolving ... future cases." [Citations; see also Georgine v. Amchem Products, Inc., 157 F.R.D. 246, 266 (E.D.Pa.1994) ("primary purpose of the settlement talks in the consolidated MDL litigation was to craft a national settlement that would provide an alternative resolution mechanism for asbestos claims," including claims that might be filed in the future)].

In November 1991, the Defendants' Steering Committee made an offer designed to settle all pending and future asbestos cases by providing a fund for distribution by plaintiffs' counsel among asbestos-exposed individuals. The Plaintiffs' Steering Committee rejected this offer, and negotiations fell apart. CCR, however, continued to pursue "a workable administrative system for the handling of future claims." [Citation.] To that end, CCR counsel approached the lawyers who had headed the Plaintiffs' Steering Committee in the unsuccessful negotiations, and a new round of negotiations began; that round yielded the mass settlement agreement now in controversy. At the time, the former heads of the Plaintiffs' Steering Committee represented thousands of plaintiffs with then-pending asbestos-related claims—claimants the parties to this suit call "inventory" plaintiffs. CCR indicated in these discussions that it would resist settlement of inventory cases absent "some kind of protection for the future." [Citation.]

Settlement talks thus concentrated on devising an administrative scheme for disposition of asbestos claims not yet in litigation. In these negotiations, counsel for masses of inventory plaintiffs endeavored to represent the interests of the anticipated future claimants, although those lawyers then had no attorney-client relationship with such claimants. Once negotiations seemed likely to produce an agreement purporting to bind potential plaintiffs, CCR agreed to settle, through separate agreements, the claims of plaintiffs who had already filed asbestos-related lawsuits. In one such agreement, CCR defendants promised to pay more than $200 million to gain release of the claims of numerous inventory plaintiffs. After settling the inventory claims, CCR, together with the plaintiffs' lawyers CCR had approached, launched this case, exclusively involving persons outside the MDL Panel's province—plaintiffs without already pending lawsuits.[3]

C

The class action thus instituted was not intended to be litigated. Rather, within the space of a single day, January 15, 1993, the settling parties—CCR defendants and the representatives of the plaintiff class described below—presented to the District Court a complaint, an answer, a proposed settlement agreement, and a joint motion for conditional class certification.

The complaint identified nine lead plaintiffs, designating them and members of their families as representatives of a class comprising all persons who had not filed an asbestos-related lawsuit against a CCR defendant as of the date the class action commenced, but who [had been occupationally exposed to asbestos-containing products of a CCR defendant or whose spouse or family member had been so exposed.] Untold numbers of individuals may fall within this description. [All named plaintiffs fulfilled the class definition and many alleged currently manifested physical injuries from the exposure.] The complaint delineated no subclasses; all named plaintiffs were designated as representatives of the class as a whole. [Jurisdiction was based on diversity and alleged various claims for relief including negligent and strict liability failure to warn, breach of warranty and enhanced risk and medical monitoring causes of action. Each plaintiff requested unspecified damages in excess of $100,000. The answers denied the principal allegations of the complaint and asserted various affirmative defenses.]

A stipulation of settlement accompanied the pleadings; it proposed to settle, and to preclude nearly all class members from litigating against CCR companies, all claims not filed before January 15, 1993, involving compensation for present and future asbestos-related personal injury or death. An exhaustive document exceeding 100 pages, the stipulation presents in detail an administrative mechanism and a schedule of payments to compensate class members who meet defined asbestos-exposure and medical requirements. The stipulation describes four categories of compensable disease: mesothelioma; lung cancer; certain "other cancers" . . .; and "non-malignant conditions" (asbestosis and bilateral pleural thickening) . . . For each qualifying disease category, the stipulation specifies the range of damages CCR will pay to qualifying claimants. Payments under the settlement are not adjustable for inflation. Mesothelioma claimants—the most highly compensated category—are scheduled to receive between $20,000 and $200,000. [The stipulation] also establishes procedures to resolve disputes over medical diagnoses and levels of compensation [which may be obtained

---

3. It is basic to comprehension of this proceeding to notice that no transferred case is included in the settlement at issue, and no case covered by the settlement existed as a civil action at the time of the MDL Panel transfer.

over the ranges in limited circumstances.] But the settlement places both numerical caps and dollar limits on such claims. [The number of claims payable for each disease in a given year is also capped. Certain claims are not compensable at all even if otherwise applicable state law recognizes them. Non-compensable claims include all loss of consortium claims, "exposure-only" claimants' increased risk of cancer, fear of future injury and medical monitoring claims, and all "pleural" claims, which might be asserted by persons with asbestos-related plaques on their lungs but no accompanying physical impairment, are also excluded.] Although not entitled to present compensation, exposure-only claimants and pleural claimants may qualify for benefits when and if they develop a compensable disease and meet the relevant exposure and medical criteria. Defendants forgo defenses to liability, including statute of limitations pleas.

Class members, in the main, are bound by the settlement in perpetuity, while CCR defendants may choose to withdraw from the settlement after ten years. A small number of class members—only a few per year—may reject the settlement and pursue their claims in court. Those permitted to exercise this option, however, may not assert any punitive damages claim or any claim for increased risk of cancer. Aspects of the administration of the settlement are to be monitored by the AFL–CIO and class counsel. Class counsel are to receive attorneys' fees in an amount to be approved by the District Court.

D

[In 1993, the District Court conditionally certified an encompassing opt-out class under Federal Rule of Civil Procedure 23(b)(3). The court conducted fairness hearings at which objectors claimed, inter alia, that the settlement unfairly disadvantaged those with currently compensable conditions and that the compensation levels were intolerably low compared to awards available in litigation or paid to the inventory plaintiffs. The court found the settlement terms fair, negotiated in good faith, and the prerequisites of Rule 23 fulfilled. The Court of Appeals for the Third Circuit vacated the certification, holding that the requirements of Rule 23 had not been satisfied. See Georgine v. Amchem Products, Inc., 83 F.3d 610 (3d Cir. 1996)]. We granted certiorari, and now affirm.

II

Objectors assert in this Court, as they did in the District Court and Court of Appeals, an array of jurisdictional barriers. [The Third Circuit declined to address these issues because they "would not exist but for the [class action] certification." The class certification issues are dispositive, and because their resolution here is logically antecedent to the existence of any Article III issues, it is appropriate to reach them first.] We therefore follow the path taken by the Court of Appeals, mindful that Rule 23's requirements must be interpreted in keeping with Article III constraints, and with the Rules Enabling Act, which instructs that rules of procedure "shall not abridge, enlarge or modify any substantive right," 28 U.S.C. 2072(b), [citation.]

III

* * * In addition to satisfying Rule 23(a)'s prerequisites, parties seeking class certification must show that the action is maintainable under Rule 23(b)(1), (2), or (3). In the 1966 class-action amendments, Rule 23(b)(3), the category at issue here, was "the most adventuresome" innovation. [Citation.] Rule 23(b)(3) added to the complex-litigation arsenal class actions for damages designed to secure judgments binding all class members save those who affirmatively elected to be excluded. See 7A Wright, Miller & Kane, Federal Practice and Procedure 1777; [citation.]

Framed for situations in which "class-action treatment is not as clearly called for" as it is in Rule 23(b)(1) and (b)(2) situations, Rule 23(b)(3) permits certification where class suit "may nevertheless be convenient and desirable." Adv. Comm. Notes. To qualify for certification under Rule 23(b)(3), a class must meet two requirements beyond the Rule 23(a) prerequisites: Common questions must "predominate over any questions affecting only individual members"; and class resolution must be "superior to other available methods for the fair and efficient adjudication of the controversy." In adding "predominance" and "superiority" to the qualification-for-certification list, the Advisory Committee sought to cover cases "in which a class action would achieve economies of time, effort, and expense, and promote ... uniformity of decision as to persons similarly situated, without sacrificing procedural fairness or bringing about other undesirable results." ...

Rule 23(b)(3) includes a non-exhaustive list of factors pertinent to a court's "close look" at the predominance and superiority criteria [set forth above]. In setting out these factors, the Advisory Committee for the 1966 reform anticipated that in each case, courts would "consider the interests of individual members of the class in controlling their own litigations and carrying them on as they see fit." Adv. Comm. Notes. They elaborated:

> The interests of individuals in conducting separate lawsuits may be so strong as to call for denial of a class action. On the other hand, these interests may be theoretic rather than practical; the class may have a high degree of cohesion and prosecution of the action through representatives would be quite unobjectionable, or the amounts at stake for individuals may be so small that separate suits would be impracticable.

[The Third Circuit observed in the instant case that "[e]ach [personal injury] plaintiff has a significant interest in individually controlling the prosecution of [his case]." While the Rule does not exclude by its terms personal injury actions in which damages might be high, the Advisory Committee had dominantly in mind vindication of "the rights of groups of people who individually would be without effective strength to bring their opponents into court at all." The Rule also requires individual notice of the "opt out" right in (b)(3) classes. Eisen v. Carlisle and Jacquelin, 417 U.S. 156, 173–77 (1974).]

In the decades since the 1966 revision of Rule 23, class action practice has become ever more "adventuresome" as a means of coping with claims too numerous to secure their "just, speedy, and inexpensive determination" one by one. F.R.C.P. 1. The development reflects concerns about the efficient use of court resources and the conservation of funds to compensate claimants who do not line up early in a litigation queue. [Citations.] Among current applications of Rule 23(b)(3), the "settlement only" class has become a stock device. [Citations.] Although all Federal Circuits recognize the utility of Rule 23(b)(3) settlement classes, courts have divided on the extent to which a proffered settlement affects court surveillance under Rule 23's certification criteria ... A proposed amendment to Rule 23 would authorize settlement class certifications even though the requirements of 23(b)(3) might not otherwise be met. The Committee has not yet acted on the matter. We consider the certification at issue under the rule as it is currently framed.

IV

We granted review to decide the role settlement may play, under existing Rule 23, in determining the propriety of class certification. The Third Circuit's opinion stated that each of the requirements of Rule 23(a) and (b)(3) "must be satisfied without taking into account the settlement." That statement, petitioners urge, is incorrect.

We agree with petitioners to this limited extent: settlement is relevant to a class certification. The Third Circuit's opinion bears modification in that respect. But, as we earlier observed, the Court of Appeals in fact did not ignore the settlement; instead, that court honed in on settlement terms in explaining why it found the absentees' interests inadequately represented. The Third Circuit's close inspection of the settlement in that regard was altogether proper.

Confronted with a request for settlement-only class certification, a district court need not inquire whether the case, if tried, would present intractable management problems, for the proposal is that there be no trial. But other specifications of the Rule—those designed to protect absentees by blocking unwarranted or overbroad class definitions—demand undiluted, even heightened, attention in the settlement context. Such attention is of vital importance, for a court asked to certify a settlement class will lack the opportunity, present when a case is litigated, to adjust the class, informed by the proceedings as they unfold.

And, of overriding importance, courts must be mindful that the rule as now composed sets the requirements they are bound to enforce. Federal Rules take effect after an extensive deliberative process involving many reviewers: a Rules Advisory Committee, public commenters, the Judicial Conference, this Court, the Congress. See 28 U.S.C. 2073, 2074. The text of a rule thus proposed and reviewed limits judicial inventiveness. Courts are not free to amend a rule outside the process Congress ordered, a process properly tuned to the instruction that rules of procedure "shall not abridge ... any substantive right." 2072(b).

Rule 23(e), on settlement of class actions, reads in its entirety: "A class action shall not be dismissed or compromised without the approval of the court, and notice of the proposed dismissal or compromise shall be given to all members of the class in such manner as the court directs." This prescription was designed to function as an additional requirement, not a superseding direction, for the "class action" to which Rule 23(e) refers is one qualified for certification under Rule 23(a) and (b). [Citation.] Subdivisions (a) and (b) focus court attention on whether a proposed class has sufficient unity so that absent members can fairly be bound by decisions of class representatives. That dominant concern persists when settlement, rather than trial, is proposed.

The safeguards provided by the Rule 23(a) and (b) class-qualifying criteria, we emphasize, are not impractical impediments—checks shorn of utility—in the settlement class context. First, the standards set for the protection of absent class members serve to inhibit appraisals of the chancellor's foot kind—class certifications dependent upon the court's gestalt judgment or overarching impression of the settlement's fairness. Second, if a fairness inquiry under Rule 23(e) controlled certification, eclipsing Rule 23(a) and (b), and permitting class designation despite the impossibility of litigation, both class counsel and court would be disarmed. Class counsel confined to settlement negotiations could not use the threat of litigation to press for a better offer, [citations], and the court would face a bargain proffered for its approval without benefit of adversarial investigation, [citation].

Federal courts, in any case, lack authority to substitute for Rule 23's certification criteria a standard never adopted—that if a settlement is "fair," then certification is proper. Applying to this case criteria the rulemakers set, we conclude that the Third Circuit's appraisal is essentially correct. Although that court should have acknowledged that settlement is a factor in the calculus, a remand is not warranted on that account. The Court of Appeals' opinion amply demonstrates why, with or without a settlement on the table, the sprawling class the District Court certified does not satisfy Rule 23's requirements.

A

We address first the requirement of Rule 23(b)(3) that "[common] questions of law or fact ... predominate over any questions affecting only individual members." The District Court concluded that predominance was satisfied based on two factors: class members' shared experience of asbestos exposure and their common [desire to be compensated fairly, with little risk and cost.] The settling parties also contend that the settlement's fairness is a common question, predominating over disparate legal issues that might be pivotal in litigation but become irrelevant under the settlement.

The predominance requirement stated in Rule 23(b)(3), we hold, is not met by the factors on which the District Court relied. The benefits asbestos-exposed persons might gain from the establishment of a grand-scale compensation scheme is a matter fit for legislative consideration, but it is not pertinent to the predominance inquiry. That inquiry trains on the legal or factual questions that qualify each class member's case as a genuine controversy, questions that preexist any settlement.

The Rule 23(b)(3) predominance inquiry tests whether proposed classes are sufficiently cohesive to warrant adjudication by representation. [Citations.] The inquiry appropriate under Rule 23(e), on the other hand, protects unnamed class members "from unjust or unfair settlements affecting their rights when the representatives become fainthearted before the action is adjudicated or are able to secure satisfaction of their individual claims by a compromise." [Citation.] But it is not the mission of Rule 23(e) to assure the class cohesion that legitimizes representative action in the first place. If a common interest in a fair compromise could satisfy the predominance requirement of Rule 23(b)(3), that vital prescription would be stripped of any meaning in the settlement context.

The District Court also relied upon th[e commonality of shared asbestos exposure to defendants' products.] Even if Rule 23(a)'s commonality requirement may be satisfied by that shared experience, the predominance criterion is far more demanding. [Citation.] Given the greater number of questions peculiar to the several categories of class members, and to individuals within each category, and the significance of those uncommon questions, any overarching dispute about the health consequences of asbestos exposure cannot satisfy [Rule 23(b)(3)'s predominance requirement. The disparate questions undermining class cohesion and defeating predominance include the different time, manner and amount of exposures to different products producing widely varying injuries, particularly regarding the exposure-only plaintiffs who may never contract asbestos-related disease.] Differences in state law, the Court of Appeals observed, compound these disparities. Phillips Petroleum Co. v. Shutts, 472 U.S. 797, 823 (1985).

No settlement class called to our attention is as sprawling as this one. [Citation.] Predominance is a test readily met in certain cases alleging consumer or securities fraud or violations of the antitrust laws. [Citation.] Even mass tort cases arising from a common cause or disaster may, depending upon the circumstances, satisfy the predominance requirement. The Advisory Committee for the 1966 revision of Rule 23, it is true, noted that "mass accident" cases are likely to present "significant questions, not only of damages but of liability and defenses of liability, . . . affecting the individuals in different ways." And the Committee advised that such cases are "ordinarily not appropriate" for class treatment. But the text of the rule does not categorically exclude mass tort cases from class certification, and district courts, since the late 1970s, have been certifying such cases in increasing number. [Citation.] The Committee's warning, however, continues to call for caution when individual stakes are high and disparities among class members great. As the Third Circuit's opinion makes plain, the certification in this case does not follow the counsel of caution. That certification cannot be upheld, for it rests on a conception of Rule 23(b)(3)'s predominance requirement irreconcilable with the rule's design.

B

Nor can the class approved by the District Court satisfy Rule 23(a)(4)'s requirement that the named parties "will fairly and adequately protect the interests of the class." The adequacy inquiry under Rule 23(a)(4) serves to uncover conflicts of interest between named parties and the class they seek to represent. See General Telephone Co. of Southwest v. Falcon, 457 U.S. 147, 157158 (1982). "[A] class representative must be part of the class and 'possess the same interest and suffer the same injury' as the class members." East Tex. Motor Freight System, Inc. v. Rodriguez, 431 U.S. 395, 403 (1977).

As the Third Circuit pointed out, named parties with diverse medical conditions sought to act on behalf of a single giant class rather than on behalf of discrete subclasses. In significant respects, the interests of those within the single class are not aligned. Most saliently, for the currently injured, the critical goal is generous immediate payments. That goal tugs against the interest of exposure-only plaintiffs in ensuring an ample, inflation-protected fund for the future. [Citation. The adequacy of defendants' assets to pay the claims, despite the disparity between those claims, does not render the disparity insignificant.] Although this is not a "limited fund" case certified under Rule 23(b)(1)(B), the terms of the settlement reflect essential allocation decisions designed to confine compensation and to limit defendants' liability. For example, . . . the settlement includes no adjustment for inflation; only a few claimants per year can opt out at the back end; and loss-of-consortium claims are extinguished with no compensation.

The settling parties, in sum, achieved a global compromise with no structural assurance of fair and adequate representation for the diverse groups and individuals affected. Although the named parties alleged a range of complaints, each served generally as representative for the whole, not for a separate constituency. In an asbestos class action, the Second Circuit spoke precisely to this point: "[W]here differences among members of a class are such that subclasses must be established, we know of no authority that permits a court to approve a settlement without creating subclasses on the basis of consents by members of a unitary class, some of whom happen to be members of the distinct subgroups. . . . [T]he adversity among subgroups requires that the members of each subgroup cannot be bound to a settlement except by consents given by those who understand that their role is to represent solely the members of their respective subgroups." In re Joint E. & S. Dist. Asbestos Litig., 982 F.2d 721, 742743 (2d Cir.1992). The Third Circuit found no assurance here either in the terms of the settlement or in the structure of the negotiations that the named plaintiffs operated under a proper understanding of their representational responsibilities. That assessment, we conclude, is on the mark.

C

Impediments to the provision of adequate notice, the Third Circuit emphasized, rendered highly problematic any endeavor to tie to a settlement class persons with no perceptible asbestos-related disease at the time of the settlement. [Citation.] Many persons in the exposure-only category, the Court of Appeals stressed, may not even know of their exposure, or realize the extent of the harm they may incur. Even if they fully appreciate the significance of class notice, those without current afflictions may not have the information or foresight needed to decide, intelligently, whether to stay in or opt out.

Family members of asbestos-exposed individuals may themselves fall prey to disease or may ultimately have ripe claims for loss of consortium. Yet large numbers of people in this category—future spouses and children of asbestos victims—could not be alerted to their class membership. And current spouses and children of the occupationally exposed may know nothing of that exposure. Because we have concluded that the class in this case cannot satisfy the requirements of common issue predominance and adequacy of representation, we need not rule, definitively, on the notice given here. In accord with the Third Circuit, however, we recognize the gravity of the question whether class action notice sufficient under the Constitution and Rule 23 could ever be given to legions so unselfconscious and amorphous.

V

The argument is sensibly made that a nationwide administrative claims processing regime would provide the most secure, fair, and efficient means of compensating victims of asbestos exposure. Congress, however, has not adopted such a solution. And Rule 23, which must be interpreted with fidelity to the Rules Enabling Act and applied with the interests of absent class members in close view, cannot carry the large load CCR, class counsel, and the District Court heaped upon it. As this case exemplifies, the rulemakers' prescriptions for class actions may be endangered by "those who embrace [Rule 23] too enthusiastically just as [they are by] those who approach [the rule] with distaste." [Wright, Law of Federal Courts at 508. The judgment of the Third Circuit is Affirmed.]

NOTES

1. Because class actions typically settle after certification, much of the concern over class action practice has centered around insuring settlements are fairly constructed. Rule 23 was amended in 2003 to include additional safeguards in Rule 23(e), such as the requirement of additional notice of a settlement, a fairness hearing on the terms of settlement, and permitting a new opportunity to opt-out after settlement.

2. Over the years, a number of legislative proposals to set up a no-fault compensation system for asbestos victims have been proposed but none has succeeded. See, e.g., Fairness in Asbestos Injury Resolution Act of 2003, S. 1125, 108th Cong. 1st Sess (2003). The Federal Coal Mine Health and Safety Act, 30 U.S.C.A. §§ 801–62 (1982), popularly known as the Black Lung Act, is one example of a federalized no-fault scheme for a particular class of victims. Another is the National Childhood Vaccine Injury Act of 1986, 42 U.S.C.A. § 300aa et seq.

Why has Congress not enacted asbestos compensation legislation?

3. Bankruptcy. To date, about seventy asbestos manufacturers have filed bankruptcy as a result of litigation expenses. Might consolidating cases in a bankruptcy proceeding be an effective method for resolving thousands of similar toxic substance claims? See 2005 RAND Report Summary, at xxvii (costs of bankruptcy substantial); McGovern, The Tragedy of the Asbestos Commons, 88 Va.L.Rev. 1721, 1754 (2002)(bankruptcy is "current nirvana" for asbestos defendants).

4. MDL Consolidations and Class Action Certification. As in *Amchem Products*, consolidations under the Multi–District Litigation statute, 28 U.S.C. § 1407, often result in efforts to certify a class action under Fed.R.Civ.P. 23, and then settlement of the claims. Cases involving injuries from silicone gel breast implants were consolidated in the MDL process which eventually led to efforts at class certification and settlement. In re Silicone Gel Breast Implants Liab. Litig., 793 F.Supp. 1098 (J.P.M.L.1992). After consolidation, a proposed $4.2 billion settlement fund was established. The settlement eventually fell apart after many more claims were presented than had been anticipated and the principal defendant, Dow Corning, filed for bankruptcy. Claimants Given Option to Pursue Individual Lawsuits, Prod. Liab. Rep. (CCH) No. 843 (Oct. 16, 1995).

Consolidation under the MDL is appropriate when the cases share common questions and transfer will serve the convenience of the parties and witnesses. The transferee court may only decide pre-trial issues and may not try the cases in a consolidated manner. 28 U.S.C. §§ 1407 (a), (c)(i)-(ii). See Lexecon Inc. v. Milberg Weiss Bershad Hynes & Lerach, 523 U.S. 26 (1998).

The Judicial Panel for Multi–District Litigation, which consists of seven circuit and district judges appointed by the Chief Justice of the United States, may transfer cases to a particular district court for consolidated discovery and pre-trial rulings, according to the needs of the litigation. See generally Manual for Complex Litigation (4th ed. 2003). While many consolidated cases lead to settlement, the transferee court often decides dispositive pre-trial motions, like summary judgment, preliminary to any class certification decision or settlement agreement. Meridia Prods. Liab. Litig. v. Abbott Labs., 447 F.3d 861 (6th Cir. 2006)(trial court granted manufacturer's motion for summary judgment on the adequacy of its drug's warning label, binding all consolidation claimants and previously certified class action claimants); In re Temporomandibular Joint (TMJ) Implants Prods. Liab. Litig., 880 F.Supp. 1311 (D. Minn. 1995)(summary judgment on warning claims granted to two suppliers of Teflon products used in TMJ implants).

5. Rule 23(a)—Prerequisites. The Court in *Amchem Products* made clear that settlement classes must satisfy each of the requirements of Rule 23(a) and (b), with an understanding that the class will not be litigated as part of the analysis. Rule 23(a)'s requirements are typically not in issue in most mass torts, except for the heightened concern for adequacy of representation raised in *Amchem Products*.

A. Numerosity and typicality. For example, there is no set number of claimants to satisfy the numerosity requirement of rule 23(a) and most mass torts easily satisfy it. In re Serzone Prods. Liab. Litig., 231 F.R.D. 221, 237 (S.D.W.Va. 2005) (settlement class certified; 8 million claimants). The typicality requirement is often subsumed under commonality which is often subsumed under the fuller analysis of Rule 23(b)(3)'s predominance requirement, as was the case in *Amchem Products*. See *In re Serzone Prods.*, 231 F.R.D. at 238 (discussing typicality).

B. Commonality and predominance. Opponents of class certification most frequently challenge the commonality and predominance requirements of Rules 23(a) and 23(b)(3), respectively. The main argument that toxic substance cases are not appropriate for class actions under the commonality and predominance requirements is that the factual issues might appear similar but, in truth, are very particular because of the individual circumstances of exposure and causation present in such cases.

Amchem Products explains the central inquiry: sufficient cohesiveness to warrant adjudication by representation. What caused the class in *Amchem Products* to fail this test? Could it be rectified in a subsequent asbestos case? Early cases rejecting class action status based on a lack of commonality include: In re Northern Dist. of Calif., Dalkon Shield IUD Prods. Liab. Litig., 693 F.2d 847 (9th Cir. 1982)(different advertisements seen over time by various plaintiffs, affecting warranty claims; different injuries suffered, different defenses available); In re American Medical Sys., Inc., 75 F.3d 1069 (6th Cir.1996) (general allegations of commonality in penile implant cases insufficient; district court's "total disregard" of Rule 23 requirements required mandamus to decertify class).

C. Adequacy of Representation. What was the main concern over adequacy of representation in *Amchem Products*? The adequacy of representation requirement has two components: whether the named plaintiffs' interests are sufficiently aligned with the absentees to insure the claims of all will receive attention and whether counsel is/are qualified to represent the class. The potential conflicts of interest that are presented between class members who have different exposure or damages circumstances may call into question the fairness of any apportionment of a settlement.

Most mass tort class actions involve plaintiffs lawyers with substantial experience in products liability litigation. See In re Diet Drugs Prods. Liab. Litig., 385 F.3d 386 (3d Cir. 2004) (discussing lawyers efforts in diet drug settlement in relation to fee setting; interim fee award not appealable). After the 2003 amendment to Rule 23 which required trial judges to select lead counsel in class actions, the concern for adequate legal representation is reduced. The Manual for Complex Litigation §§ 10.224, 21.271 (Federal Judicial Center, 4th ed. 2004), describes a number of factors that a court should consider in determining who the lead plaintiffs' counsel will be under new Rule 23(g). For a discussion of the application of Rule 23(g) and its affect on the adequacy of representation requirement, see *In re Serzone Prods.*, 231 F.R.D. at 239, discussed below.

How can class members challenge the adequacy of their representation, especially those who may not know they are class members? Notice requirements provide some due process protections certainly. The class certification decision itself can be challenged. Class members in Rule 23(b)(3) classes may opt out, and now have a second opt out opportunity after the class is certified. Once a settlement is achieved, may class members collaterally attack an entered settlement judgment? Compare In re Diet Drugs Prods. Liab. Litig., 431 F.3d 141 (3d Cir. 2005)(no) with Stephenson v. Dow Chem. Co., 273 F.3d 249 (2d Cir. 2001)(yes). On the value of the fairness hearing, see Rubenstein, The Fairness Hearing, Adversarial and Regulatory Approaches, 53 UCLA L.Rev. 1435 (2006).

The proliferation of class actions because of the lure of large fees, and the perceived abuse of the device by plaintiffs' lawyers seeking that fee at the expense of a fair settlement for the class members are a focus of critics of class actions. A settlement class in In re Serzone Prods. Liab. Litig., 231 F.R.D. 221 (S.D. W. Va. 2005), involving allegations of failure to warn of liver injuries from taking the anti-depressant serzone manufactured by Bristol–Myers–Squibb, established $70,000,000 in two funds based on the nature of the illnesses alleged and an opportunity to draw upon $8,000,000 more in the event the original fund is depleted. Attorneys fees are to be awarded separately, not to exceed $20,000,000. What do you need to know to assess the proper amount of fees the court should award?

The American Law Institute's project on the Principles of the Law of Aggregate Litigation is addressing the inherent problems in aggregate litigation when control of litigation and ownership of the underlying claim become separated. See Discussion Draft § 1.06 (adequate representation a goal in all aggregate lawsuits). For discussions of the ethical issues involved, see Kahne, Curbing the Abuser, Not the Abuse; A Call for Greater Professional Accountability and Stricter Ethical Guidelines for Class Action Lawyers, 19 Geo.J.L.Ethics 741 (2006); Nagareda, Administering Adequacy in Class Representation, 82 Tex.L.Rev. 287 (2003).

6. Rule 23(b)(1) and (2) Class Categories. Of the three class alternatives in Rule 23(b), those in (b)(1) and (b)(2) are known as the mandatory classes: not subject to the strict notice or opt-out provisions in Rule 23(c). Courts have considered 23(b)(1)(B) classes, established to handle claims to a limited fund, generally inappropriate for mass tort cases. A nationwide 23(b)(1)(B) class action on punitive damages against the tobacco industry was decertified in In re Simon II Litig., 407 F.3d 125 (2d Cir. 2005). The trial judge considered the constitutional cap on punitive damages to constitute a limited fund because it limited the amount of punishment that could be meted out nationwide. The Second Circuit disagreed. Id. at 138. The Supreme Court has held that a theoretical limited fund is not sufficient. See, e.g., Ortiz v. Fibreboard Corp., 527 U.S. 815 (1999) (limited fund must exist independent of litigation). See also In re Telectronics Pacing Systems, Inc., 221 F.3d 870 (6th Cir.2000) (threat of bankruptcy insufficient basis for finding limited fund).

Rule 23(b)(2) classes are appropriate where injunctive relief (and not monetary damages) is the primary relief sought. Classes for medical monitoring of claimants exposed to defendants toxins or pharmaceuticals have been successfully certified. See In re Diet Drugs Prods. Liab. Litig., 1999 WL 673066 (E.D. Pa. 1999)(MDL consolidated cases from fen-phen diet cocktail, settlement class certified and approved), reviewed in 431 F.3d 141 (3d Cir. 2005). Not all jurisdictions recognize medical monitoring, however. See Barnes v. American Tobacco Co. 176 F.R.D. 479 (E.D.Pa. 1997), aff'd, 161 F.3d 127 (3d Cir. 1998)(rejecting medical monitoring class for nicotine addicted smokers).

7. Rule 23(b)(3) Common Issues Classes—Predominance and Superiority. *Amchem Products* was a 23(b)(3) class in which it is asserted that common issues predominate over individual ones and the class action method is a superior method of adjudication. In *Amchem Products*, the Court recognized that, since the case was never to be litigated, superiority of the class action litigation method was not a critical concern. The Court discussed predominance and concluded that the class there did not satisfy that requirement because the District Court's analysis "rests on a conception of Rule 23(b)(3)'s predominance requirement irreconcilable with the rule's design." To what is the Court referring? Do you agree? Consider the next case which discusses predominance and superiority in the context of a litigation class.

Castano v. American Tobacco Co.

United States Court of Appeals, Fifth Circuit, 1996.
84 F.3d 734.

■ Jerry E. Smith, Judge:

In what may be the largest class action ever attempted in federal court, the district court in this case embarked "on a road certainly less traveled, if ever taken at all," Castano v. American Tobacco Co., 160 F.R.D. 544, 560 (E.D.La.1995) (citing Edward C. Latham, The Poetry of Robert Frost, "The Road Not Taken" 105 (1969)), and entered a class certification order. [The trial court defined the class as "All nicotine-dependent persons in the United States ... who have purchased and smoked cigarettes manufactured by the defendants" since 1943, and their estates and families. The trial court certified its order for interlocutory appeal.] Concluding that the district court abused its discretion in certifying the class, we reverse.

[Plaintiffs complaint against the tobacco companies sought compensation solely for the injury of nicotine addiction.] The gravamen of their complaint is the novel and wholly untested theory that the defendants fraudulently failed to inform consumers that nicotine is addictive and manipulated the level of nicotine in cigarettes to sustain their addictive nature. [A number of causes of action were alleged including primarily fraud and deceit. The plaintiffs seek damages, compensatory and punitive, attorneys' fees, equitable relief, including disgorgement of profits and a medical monitoring fund. Plaintiffs agreed that addiction would have to be proven by each class member.]

[Plaintiffs proposed a four-phase trial plan with early determination of common issues of "core liability." Subsequent trial phases would address causation and damages. The district court granted the motion for class certification under Fed. R. Civ. P. 23(b)(3) and, using its power to sever issues for certification under Fed. R. Civ. P. 23(c)(4), certified the class on core liability and punitive damages conditionally pursuant to Fed. R. Civ. P. 23(c)(1). The court defined core liability issues as "common factual issues [of] whether defendants knew cigarette smoking was addictive, failed to inform cigarette smokers of such, and took actions to addict cigarette smokers," and found that the predominance requirement of Rule 23(b)(3) was satisfied for the core liability issues.] Without any specific analysis regarding the multitude of issues that make up "core liability," the court found that under Jenkins v. Raymark Indus., 782 F.2d 468 (5th Cir.1986), common issues predominate because resolution of core liability issues would significantly advance the individual cases. The court did not discuss why "core liability" issues would be a significant, rather than just common, part of each individual trial, nor why the individual issues in the remaining categories did not predominate over the common "core liability" issues.

The only specific analysis on predominance was on the plaintiffs' fraud claim. The court determined that it would be premature to hold that individual reliance issues predominate over common issues. Relying on Eisen v. Carlisle & Jacquelin, 417 U.S. 156 (1974), the court stated that it could not inquire into the merits of the plaintiffs' claim to determine whether reliance would be an issue in individual trials. Moreover, the court recognized the possibility that under state law, reliance can be inferred when a fraud claim is based on an omission. Accordingly, the court was convinced that it could certify the class and defer the consideration of how reliance would affect predominance.

The court also deferred substantial consideration of how variations in state law would affect predominance. Relying on two district court opinions,[11] the court concluded that issues of fraud, breach of warranty, negligence, intentional tort, and strict liability do not vary so much from state to state as to cause individual issues to predominate [and] noted that any determination of how state law variations affect predominance was premature, as [it] had yet to make a choice of law determination. . . .

The court also concluded that a class action is superior to other methods for adjudication of the core liability issues. Relying heavily on *Jenkins*, the court noted that having this common issue litigated in a class action was superior to repeated trials of the same evidence. Recognizing serious problems with manageability, it determined that such problems were outweighed by "the specter of thousands, if not millions, of similar trials of liability proceeding in thousands of courtrooms around the nation." [The trial court also certified punitive damages for class treatment.]

II.

A district court must conduct a rigorous analysis of the Rule 23 prerequisites before certifying a class. General Tel. Co. v. Falcon, 457 U.S. 147, 161 (1982); [citation]. The decision to certify is within the broad discretion of the court, but that discretion must be exercised within the framework of Rule 23. Gulf Oil Co. v. Bernard, 452 U.S. 89 (1981). The party seeking certification bears the burden of proof. [Citation.]

The district court erred in its analysis in two distinct ways. First, it failed to consider how variations in state law affect predominance and superiority. Second, its predominance inquiry did not include consideration of how a trial on the merits would be conducted. [These failures require] reversal. Moreover, at this time, while the tort is immature, the class complaint must be dismissed, as class certification cannot be found to be a superior method of adjudication.

A. Variations in State Law

* * * In a multi-state class action, variations in state law may swamp any common issues and defeat predominance. See Georgine v. Amchem Prods., 83 F.3d 610 (3d Cir.1996); [citation]. [A] district court must consider how variations in state law affect predominance and superiority. Walsh v. Ford Motor Co., 807 F.2d 1000 (D.C.Cir.1986). The *Walsh* court rejected the notion that a district court may defer considering variations in state law:

---

11. The court cited In re Asbestos Sch. Litig., 104 F.R.D. 422, 434 (E.D.Pa.1984) (discussing the similarity of negligence and strict liability in U.S. jurisdictions), aff'd and rev'd in part, 789 F.2d 996, 1010 (3d Cir. 1986), and In re Cordis Cardiac Pacemaker Prod. Liability Litig., No. C–390–374 (S.D.Ohio Dec.23, 1992) (unpublished) (discussing similarities among negligence, strict liability, and fraud).

> Appellees see the "which law" matter as academic. They say no variations in state warranty laws relevant to this case exist. A court cannot accept such an assertion "on faith." Appellees, as class action proponents, must show that it is accurate. We have made no inquiry of our own on this score and, for the current purpose, simply note the general unstartling statement made in a leading treatise: "The Uniform Commercial Code is not uniform."

[Citation].

A district court's duty to determine whether the plaintiff has borne its burden on class certification requires that a court consider variations in state law when a class action involves multiple jurisdictions. [A trial court must not only identify the substantive law issues which will control the outcome of the litigation, but must know which law will apply. This requirement] is especially important when there may be differences in state law. See In re Rhone–Poulenc Rorer, Inc. 51 F.3d 1293, 1299–1302 (7th Cir.1995); [citation.] Given the plaintiffs' burden, a court cannot rely on assurances of counsel that any problems with predominance or superiority can be overcome. . . .

The able opinion in *School Asbestos* demonstrates what is required from a district court when variations in state law exist. There, the court affirmed class certification, despite variations in state law, because:

> To meet the problem of diversity in applicable state law, class plaintiffs have undertaken an extensive analysis of the variances in products liability among the jurisdictions. That review separates the law into four categories. Even assuming additional permutations and combinations, plaintiffs have made a creditable showing, which apparently satisfied the district court, that class certification does not present insuperable obstacles. Although we have some doubt on this score, the effort may nonetheless prove successful.

[Citations].

The district court's review of state law variances can hardly be considered extensive; it conducted a cursory review of state law variations and gave short shrift to the defendants' arguments concerning variations. In response to the defendants' extensive analysis of how state law varied on fraud, products liability, affirmative defenses, negligent infliction of emotional distress, consumer protection statutes, and punitive damages[15], the

---

15. We find it difficult to fathom how common issues could predominate in this case when variations in state law are thoroughly considered. . . . The *Castano* class suffers from many of the difficulties [other courts have] found dispositive. The class members were exposed to nicotine through different products, for different amounts of time, and over different time periods. Each class member's knowledge about the effects of smoking differs, and each plaintiff began smoking for different reasons. Each of these factual differences impacts the application of legal rules such as causation, reliance, comparative fault, and other affirmative defenses.

Variations in state law magnify the differences. [In a fraud claim, some states require justifiable reliance on a misrepresentation while others require reasonable reliance. States impose varying standards to determine when there is a duty to disclose facts. Products liability law also differs among states, Restatement (Second) of Torts § 402A. Affirmative defenses vary widely as does the availability of comparative fault doctrine.]

court examined a sample phase 1 jury interrogatory and verdict form, a survey of medical monitoring decisions, a survey of consumer fraud class actions, and a survey of punitive damages law in the defendants' home states. The court also relied on two district court opinions granting certification in multi-state class actions.

The district court's consideration of state law variations was inadequate. The surveys provided by the plaintiffs failed to discuss, in any meaningful way, how the court could deal with variations in state law. The consumer fraud survey simply quoted a few state courts that had certified state class actions. The survey of punitive damages was limited to the defendants' home states.

* * *

The court also failed to perform its duty to determine whether the class action would be manageable in light of state law variations. The court's only discussion of manageability is a citation to *Jenkins* and the claim that "while manageability of the liability issues in this case may well prove to be difficult, the Court finds that any such difficulties pale in comparison to the specter of thousands, if not millions, of similar trials of liability proceeding in thousands of courtrooms around the nation."

The problem with this approach is that it substitutes case-specific analysis with a generalized reference to *Jenkins*. The *Jenkins* court, however, was not faced with managing a novel claim involving eight causes of action, multiple jurisdictions, millions of plaintiffs, eight defendants, and over fifty years of alleged wrongful conduct. Instead, *Jenkins* involved only 893 personal injury asbestos cases, the law of only one state, and the prospect of trial occurring in only one district. Accordingly, for purposes of the instant case, *Jenkins* is largely inapposite.

In summary, whether the specter of millions of cases outweighs any manageability problems in this class is uncertain when the scope of any manageability problems is unknown. Absent considered judgment on the manageability of the class, a comparison to millions of individual trials is meaningless.

B. Predominance

The district court's second error was that it failed to consider how the plaintiffs' addiction claims would be tried, individually or on a class basis. The district court, based on Eisen v. Carlisle & Jacquelin, 417 U.S. 156 (1974), and Miller v. Mackey Int'l, 452 F.2d 424 (5th Cir.1971), believed that it could not go past the pleadings for the certification decision. The result was an incomplete and inadequate predominance inquiry.

[Neither *Eisen* nor *Miller*] suggests that a court is limited to the pleadings when deciding on certification. Both, instead, stand for the unremarkable proposition that the strength of a plaintiff's claim should not affect the certification decision. In *Eisen*, the Court held that it was improper to make a preliminary inquiry into the merits of a case, determine that the plaintiff was likely to succeed, and consequently shift the cost of providing notice to the defendant. In *Miller*, this court held that a district court could not deny certification based on its belief that the plaintiff could not prevail on the merits.

A district court certainly may look past the pleadings to determine whether the requirements of Rule 23 have been met. Going beyond the pleadings is necessary, as a court must understand the claims, defenses, relevant facts, and applicable substantive law in order to make a meaningful determination of the certification issues. See Manual for Complex Litigation § 30.11 (3d ed. 1995).

The district court's predominance inquiry demonstrates why such an understanding is necessary. The premise of the court's opinion is a citation to *Jenkins* and a conclusion that class treatment of common issues would significantly advance the individual trials. Absent knowledge of how addiction-as-injury cases would actually be tried, however, it was impossible for the court to know whether the common issues would be a "significant" portion of the individual trials. The court just assumed that because the common issues would play a part in every trial, they must be significant.[18] The court's synthesis of *Jenkins* and *Eisen* would write the predominance requirement out of the rule, and any common issue would predominate if it were common to all the individual trials.

The court's treatment of the fraud claim also demonstrates the error inherent in its approach. According to both the advisory committee's notes to Rule 23(b)(3) and this court's decision in Simon v. Merrill Lynch, Pierce, Fenner & Smith, Inc., 482 F.2d 880 (5th Cir.1973), a fraud class action cannot be certified when individual reliance will be an issue. The district court avoided [*Simon* by refusing to consider whether reliance would be an individual issue. The problem with this approach is] that after the class trial, it might have decided that reliance must be proven in individual trials. The court then would have been faced with the difficult choice of decertifying the class after phase I and wasting judicial resources, or continuing with a class action that would have failed the predominance requirement of Rule 23(b)(3).[21]

---

18. The district court's approach to predominance stands in stark contrast to the methodology the district court used in *Jenkins*. There, the district judge had a vast amount of experience with asbestos cases. He certified the state of the art defense because it was the most significant contested issue in each case. *Jenkins*, 109 F.R.D. 269 at 279. To the contrary, however, the district court in the instant case did not, and could not, have determined that the common issues would be a significant part of each case. Unlike the judge in *Jenkins*, the district judge a quo had no experience with this type of case and did not even inquire into how a case would be tried to determine whether the defendants'

conduct would be a significant portion of each case.

21. Severing the defendants' conduct from reliance under Rule 23(c)(4) does not save the class action. A district court cannot manufacture predominance through the nimble use of subdivision (c)(4). The proper interpretation of the interaction between subdivisions (b)(3) and (c)(4) is that a cause of action, as a whole, must satisfy the predominance requirement of (b)(3) and that (c)(4) is a housekeeping rule that allows courts to sever the common issues for a class trial. [Citation omitted.] Reading Rule 23(c)(4) as allowing a court to sever issues until the remaining common issue predominates over

III.

In addition to the reasons given above . . ., this class must be decertified because it independently fails the superiority requirement of Rule 23(b)(3). In the context of mass tort class actions, certification dramatically affects the stakes for defendants. Class certification magnifies and strengthens the number of unmeritorious claims. Aggregation of claims also makes it more likely that a defendant will be found liable and results in significantly higher damage awards. [Citations].

In addition to skewing trial outcomes, class certification creates insurmountable pressure on defendants to settle, whereas individual trials would not. [Citation.] The risk of facing an all-or-nothing verdict presents too high a risk, even when the probability of an adverse judgment is low. [Citation.] These settlements have been referred to as judicial blackmail.

It is no surprise then, that historically, certification of mass tort litigation classes has been disfavored. The traditional concern over the rights of defendants in mass tort class actions is magnified in the instant case. Our specific concern is that a mass tort cannot be properly certified without a prior track record of trials from which the district court can draw the information necessary to make the predominance and superiority requirements required by Rule 23. This is because certification of an immature tort results in a higher than normal risk that the class action may not be superior to individual adjudication.

* * *

The district court's rationale for certification in spite of [recognized extensive manageability problems], that a class trial would preserve judicial resources in the millions of inevitable individual trials is based on pure speculation. Not every mass tort is asbestos, and not every mass tort will result in the same judicial crises. The judicial crisis to which the district court referred is only theoretical. [W]hat no court can determine at this time, is the very real possibility that the judicial crisis may fail to materialize.[25] The plaintiffs' claims are based on a new theory of liability and the

---

the remaining individual issues would eviscerate the predominance requirement of Rule 23(b)(3); the result would be automatic certification in every case where there is a common issue, a result that could not have been intended.

25. The plaintiffs, in seemingly inconsistent positions, argue that the lack of a judicial crisis justifies certification; they assert that the reason why individual plaintiffs have not filed claims is that the tobacco industry makes individual trials far too expensive and plaintiffs are rarely successful. The fact that a party continuously loses at trial does not justify class certification, however. [Citation.] The plaintiffs' argument, if accepted, would justify class treatment whenever a

defendant has better attorneys and resources at its disposal.

The plaintiffs' claim also overstates the defendants' ability to outspend plaintiffs. Assuming arguendo that the defendants pool resources and outspend plaintiffs in individual trials, there is no reason why plaintiffs still cannot prevail. The class is represented by a consortium of well-financed plaintiffs' lawyers who, over time, can develop the expertise and specialized knowledge sufficient to beat the tobacco companies at their own game. [Citation.] Courts can also overcome the defendant's alleged advantages through coordination or consolidation of cases for discovery and other pretrial matters. [Citation.]

existence of new evidence. Until plaintiffs decide to file individual claims, a court cannot, from the existence of injury, presume that all or even any plaintiffs will pursue legal remedies. Nor can a court make a superiority determination based on such speculation. [Citation.]

Severe manageability problems and the lack of a judicial crisis are not the only reasons why superiority is lacking. The most compelling rationale for finding superiority in a class action—the existence of a negative value suit—is missing in this case. Accord Phillips Petroleum Co. v. Shutts, 472 U.S. 797, 809 (1985); *Rhone–Poulenc*, 51 F.3d at 1299.

As he stated in the record, plaintiffs' counsel in this case has promised to inundate the courts with individual claims if class certification is denied. Independently of the reliability of this self-serving promise, there is reason to believe that individual suits are feasible. First, individual damage claims are high, and punitive damages are available in most states. The expense of litigation does not necessarily turn this case into a negative value suit, in part because the prevailing party may recover attorneys' fees under many consumer protection statutes. [Citation.]

In a case such as this one, where each plaintiff may receive a large award, and fee shifting often is available, we find Chief Judge Posner's analysis of superiority to be persuasive:

> For this consensus or maturing of judgment the district judge proposes to substitute a single trial before a single jury.... One jury ... will hold the fate of an industry in the palm of its hand.... That kind of thing can happen in our system of civil justice.... But it need not be tolerated when the alternative exists of submitting an issue to multiple juries constituting in the aggregate a much larger and more diverse sample of decision-makers. That would not be a feasible option if the stakes to each class member were too slight to repay the cost of suit.... But this is not the case.... Each plaintiff if successful is apt to receive a judgment in the millions. With the aggregate stakes in the tens or hundreds of millions of dollars, or even in the billions, it is not a waste of judicial resources to conduct more than one trial, before more than six jurors, to determine whether a major segment of the international pharmaceutical industry is to follow the asbestos manufacturers into Chapter 11.

Rhone–Poulenc, 51 F.3d at 1300. So too here, we cannot say that it would be a waste to allow individual trials to proceed, before a district court engages in the complicated predominance and superiority analysis necessary to certify a class.

Fairness may demand that mass torts with few prior verdicts or judgments be litigated first in smaller units even single-plaintiff, single-defendant trials until general causation, typical injuries, and levels of damages become established. Thus, "mature" mass torts like asbestos or Dalkon Shield may call for procedures that are not appropriate for incipient mass tort cases, such as those involving injuries arising from new products, chemical substances, or pharmaceuticals.

The remaining rationale for superiority, judicial efficiency, is also lacking. In the context of an immature tort, any savings in judicial resources is speculative, and any imagined savings would be overwhelmed by the procedural problems that certification of a sui generis cause of action brings with it. [There is only a speculative basis for assuming that there will be a saving in judicial resources. Only after the courts have more experience with this type of case can a court certify issues in a way that preserves judicial resources, as in *Jenkins*, certifying state of the art defense.]

[C]ertification of an immature tort brings with it unique problems that may consume more judicial resources than certification will save.... Determining whether the common issues are a "significant" part of each individual case has an abstract quality to it when no court in this country has ever tried an injury-as-addiction claim.... It may turn out that the defendant's conduct, while common, is a minor part of each trial. Premature certification deprives the defendant of the opportunity to present that argument to any court and risks decertification after considerable resources have been expended. [Similarly, the complexity of the choice of law inquiry makes individual adjudication superior to class treatment. Individual adjudication will permit plaintiffs to] winnow their claims to the strongest causes of action. The result will be an easier choice of law inquiry and a less complicated predominance inquiry. State courts can address the more novel of the plaintiffs' claims, making the federal court's *Erie* guesses less complicated. * * *

Another factor weighing heavily in favor of individual trials is the risk that in order to make this class action manageable, the court will be forced to bifurcate issues in violation of the Seventh Amendment. [The Seventh Amendment prohibits a second jury from reexamining facts and issues decided by a first jury. The district court proposed to empanel a class jury to adjudicate common issues. A second jury, or a number of "second" juries, will pass on the individual issues, either on a case-by-case basis or through group trials of individual plaintiffs.] Thus, the Constitution allows bifurcation of issues that are so separable that the second jury will not be called upon to reconsider findings of fact by the first. [The Seventh Circuit in *Rhone–Poulenc*,] described the constitutional limitation as one requiring a court to "carve at the joint" in such a way so that the same issue is not reexamined by different juries. [Citation.]

* * *

The plaintiffs' final retort is that individual trials are inadequate because time is running out for many of the plaintiffs[, noting] that prior litigation against the tobacco companies has taken up to ten years to wind through the legal system. While a compelling rhetorical argument, it is ultimately inconsistent with the plaintiffs' own arguments and ignores the realities of the legal system. First, the plaintiffs' reliance on prior personal injury cases is unpersuasive [because] they have new evidence and are pursuing a claim entirely different from that of past plaintiffs.

Second, the plaintiffs' claim that time is running out ignores the reality of the class action device. In a complicated case involving multiple jurisdictions, the conflict of law question itself could take decades to work its way through the courts. Once that issue has been resolved, discovery, subclassing, and ultimately the class trial would take place. Next would come the appellate process. After the class trial, the individual trials and appeals on comparative negligence and damages would have to take place. The net result could be that the class action device would lengthen, not shorten, the time it takes for the plaintiffs to reach final judgment.

IV.

The district court abused its discretion by ignoring variations in state law and how a trial on the alleged causes of action would be tried. Those errors cannot be corrected on remand because of the novelty of the plaintiffs' claims. Accordingly, class treatment is not superior to individual adjudication.

We have once before stated that "traditional ways of proceeding reflect far more than habit. They reflect the very culture of the jury trial. . . ." In re Fibreboard Corp., 893 F.2d 706, 711 (5th Cir.1990). The collective wisdom of individual juries is necessary before this court commits the fate of an entire industry or, indeed, the fate of a class of millions, to a single jury. For the forgoing reasons, we REVERSE and REMAND with instructions that the district court dismiss the class complaint.

NOTES

1. Did the Court of Appeals overstate the case against class decertification? If the cigarette companies market their product nationally, and uniformly, does not the issue of whether that conduct constitutes fraud, or negligent misrepresentation, predominate? Why should not one trial of those issues be enough? Would the *Amchem Products'* court agree with *Castano*'s discussion of predominance?

2. Plaintiffs, as promised after the *Castano* decertification, filed at least ten state class action lawsuits against the tobacco industry alleging addiction-as-injury claims. The state class actions generally have fared poorly. E.g., Philip Morris Inc. v. Angeletti, 752 A.2d 200 (Md. 2000)(class action not superior, claims not mature); Small v. Lorillard Tobacco Co., 720 N.E.2d 892 (N.Y.1999) (class action improper for state tobacco claims). A settlement class action against only one defendant, The Liggett Group, was decertified in Walker v. Liggett Group Inc., 175 F.R.D. 226 (S.D.W.Va.1997). A class action of only Pennsylvania plaintiffs was not proper because of the individual causation and damages problems. Barnes v. American Tobacco Co., 176 F.R.D. 479 (E.D.Pa.1997), aff'd, 161 F.3d 127 (3d Cir.1998).

In the first state class action to go to trial, a Florida jury found the tobacco industry liable for defrauding smokers about the health effects of smoking. Class-wide punitive damages were assessed at $145 billion and upheld by the trial judge. In Engle v. R.J. Reynolds Tobacco Co., 853 So.2d 434 (Fla. App. 2003), the Florida Court of Appeals struck down the historic judgment concluding that certification was not proper after all. The court of appeals noted that "virtually all courts that have addressed the issue have concluded that certification of smokers' cases is unworkable and improper." The court of appeals was particularly concerned with the "multitude of individual issues" based on the choice of law analysis required. Id.

at 448–49. The Florida Supreme Court agreed, 2006 WL 3742610 (Fla. 2006), and upheld the reversal of class action status.

A Rule 23(b)(1)(B) limited fund nationwide class on punitive damages against the tobacco industry was decertified in In re Simon II Litig., 407 F.3d 125 (2d Cir. 2005). Another nationwide tobacco class action was recently certified alleging that the tobacco industry made false representations about the safety of light cigarettes. Schwab v. Philip Morris USA Inc., 449 F.Supp.2d 992 (E.D.N.Y. 2006). This class was certified under Rule 23(b)(3). Will it suffer the same fate as *Castano*?

3. Cigarette Litigation. Since 1954, more than 300 lawsuits have been filed against cigarette manufacturers, and the defendants successfully defended them for forty years. An example of that early success is Ross v. Philip Morris Co., 328 F.2d 3 (8th Cir.1964). *Cipollone v. Liggett Group, Inc.,* above ch. 9(2), the first monetary award rendered against the industry, was eventually dismissed by the plaintiffs without ever being retried. Commentators observed that the *Cipollone* verdict was more a success for the defendants than the plaintiffs because the $400,000 verdict was "simply not enough to encourage other plaintiffs' attorneys to pursue tobacco products liability cases, especially when compared to the estimated $2 million which plaintiffs' attorneys spent to try the *Cipollone* case." *Tobacco on Trial*, Tobacco Prod. Liab. Project Newsletter, 1–8 (Oct. 15, 1988).

A. Smokers claims. The last decade has seen a significant change in the climate for tobacco litigation. A fair number of individual cases have been successful, based on pre–1965 warning failures, fraud and conspiracy claims, and others that survive *Cipollone*: Grinnell v. American Tobacco Co., 883 S.W.2d 791 (Tex.App. 1994)(strict liability claims for defective design survive *Cipollone*); Horton v. American Tobacco Co., 667 So.2d 1289 (Miss.1995) (risk-utility test applies to cigarette design; jury may assess unreasonable danger of cigarettes as designed). Plaintiffs won their first jury verdict since *Cipollone* in Carter v. Brown & Williamson Tobacco Corp., 778 So.2d 932 (Fla. 2000). Evidence of concealment of tobacco smoking hazards by the industry has led to some high verdicts. As previously discussed in the punitive damages section of the book, a punitive damages verdict of $79.5 million against Philip Morris was upheld by the Oregon Supreme Court which called Philip Morris's decades of deception "extraordinarily reprehensible." Williams v. Philip Morris, Inc., 127 P.3d 1165 (Or. 2006), cert. granted, 126 S.Ct. 2329 (U.S. May 30, 2006) (see Case and Statutory Supplement).

B. Second–hand smoke claims. One new source of cigarette litigation arises out of so-called environmental tobacco smoke (ETS). Persons allegedly injured as a result of exposure to such second-hand smoke do not face the typical assumption of the risk defense. Plaintiffs may face significant causation hurdles, but some suits have already been filed. See Broin v. Philip Morris Cos., 641 So.2d 888 (Fla.App.1994)(class action by 60,000 flight attendants against cigarette manufacturers alleging injuries from passenger smoke in airline cabins). The case settled for a $300 million contribution to fund tobacco research. The first individual flight attendant to attempt to establish causation based on exposure to ETS was successful. 33 Prod. Safety & Liab. Rep. (BNA) 35 (Jan. 10, 2005).

C. Public claims. To recoup some of the many millions of dollars of Medicaid and Medicare health care costs spent annually on tobacco-caused harm, the states began suing the industry on a variety of theories, primarily fraud, and violations of state antitrust and consumer protection statutes, in the late 1990s. Eventually, all the states joined in a $246 billion settlement of those claims. See D. Owen, Products Liability Law § 10.3 (2d ed. 2008).

Another type of public claim is based on consumer fraud and deceptive trade practices statutes. A consumer fraud class action tried in Illinois resulted in a $10.1 billion verdict against the tobacco industry for misleading smokers into believing "light" cigarettes are less harmful, but the Illinois Supreme Court reversed the verdict based on applicable statutory defenses. Price v. Philip Morris, Inc., 848 N.E.2d 1 (Ill. 2005).

The final public claim involves civil RICO liability. The United States filed suit against nine cigarette manufacturers to recover health care expenditures the federal government had paid or would pay to treat tobacco-related illnesses. In U.S. v. Philip Morris USA, Inc., 396 F.3d 1190 (D.C. Cir. 2005), the court of appeals held that the federal government could not seek disgorgement of profits as a remedy because RICO provides only for forward-looking remedies. The district court then found that the manufacturers were liable under RICO for conspiring to deceive the public about the health effects of smoking, the addictiveness of nicotine, the health benefits of "light" cigarettes, and by manipulating the design and composition of cigarettes to sustain nicotine addiction:

> The Defendants have marketed and sold their lethal products with zeal, with deception, with single-minded focus on their financial success, and without regard for the human tragedy or social costs that success exacted.

United States v. Philip Morris USA, Inc., 449 F.Supp.2d 1 (D.D.C. 2006).

On tobacco litigation generally, see P. Hilts, Smokescreen: The Truth Behind the Tobacco Industry Cover-up (1996); Gantz, et.al., The Cigarette papers (1996); Rabin, The Third Wave of Tobacco Tort Litigation, in Regulating Tobacco, ch. 7 (R. Rabin & S. Sugarman eds., 2001); Ausness and LeBel, Toward Justice in Tobacco Policymaking: A Critique of Hanson and Logue and an Alternative Approach to the Costs of Cigarettes, 33 Ga. L.Rev. 693 (1999); A Sociolegal History of the Tobacco Tort Litigation, 44 Stan.L.Rev. 853 (1992); D. Owen, Products Liability Law § 10.3 (2d ed. 2008).

4. Rule 23(b)(3)—Predominance. Nationwide classes like *Castano* present special predominance issues because of the variations in state law that may be applicable. Even when only one state's law applies, predominance issues arise. In Howland v. Purdue Pharma L.P., 821 N.E.2d 141 (Ohio 2004), the trial court certified a class based on failure to warn claims over the prescription pain killer Oxycontin. The Supreme Court reversed, finding that the trial court did not consider the individual issues that arose from the learned intermediary doctrine and its effect on the defendant's liability. Can such concerns be overcome?

Why do variations in state law matter so much in determining predominance? How many variations could there be in how, say, fraud is established? Considering the number of products liability issues which often split the 51 separate jurisdictions in various directions, can a court ruling on a motion for nationwide class certification *ever* conclude that class issues are common and predominate? Should this problem alone prohibit the certification of nationwide mass toxic substance classes?

How did the *Castano* trial court attempt to resolve this problem? *Amchem Products* stated "the predominance inquiry trains on the legal or factual questions that qualify each class member's case as a genuine controversy, . . . The predominance inquiry tests whether proposed classes are sufficiently cohesive to warrant adjudication by representation." 521 U.S. at 598. Does this concern require as exact a choice of law inquiry as the *Castano* court deemed necessary? See In re Bridgestone/Firestone, Inc., 288 F.3d 1012 (7th Cir. 2002) (no class action is proper unless all litigants are governed by the same legal rules, otherwise the commonality and superiority requirements cannot be met).

What about a class smaller in geographic scope? See Chemtall, Inc. v. Madden, 607 S.E.2d 772 (W. Va. 2004)(class seeking medical monitoring and punitive damages arising out of toxic exposure at coal preparation plant decertified because trial court did not consider variety of applicable laws to plaintiffs from seven state area).

Phillips Petroleum Co. v. Shutts, 472 U.S. 797 (1985), held, in the context of a state breach of contract class action, that the due process clause prohibits a state from applying its own law to all claims in a class action when some claims have no legitimate connection to that state. *Shutts*, thus, raises the variations in state law issue in Rule 23(b)(3) certifications. The problems *Shutts* raises are addressed in Class Action Symposium, The Twentieth Anniversary of Phillips Petroleum Co. v. Shutts, 74 U.M.K.C. L. Rev. 487 (2006).

5. Rule 23(b)(3)—Superiority of the Class Method of Resolution. Are there other, better ways to resolve mass toxic tort litigation than through class action treatment? Rule 23(b)(3) requires that the class action be the superior method of adjudication "to other available methods for the fair and efficient adjudication of the controversy." The superiority requirement in toxic substance cases demands an evaluation of whether individualized case resolution is a reasonable way of resolving complex mass litigation problems. The waste of resources necessary to litigate the same issues, factual and legal, over and over again, troubles many courts and commentators.

In re Rhone–Poulenc Rorer, Inc., 51 F.3d 1293, 1299 (7th Cir. 1995), mentioned in *Castano,* has been influential. Plaintiffs were hemophiliacs who received HIV-contaminated blood solids manufactured and sold by defendant drug companies before the presence of the virus in the blood supply was discovered and remedied in 1984–85. A large percentage of the 20,000 hemophiliacs in this country may be HIV-positive and (due to the long incubation period) not yet aware of it. A nation-wide class was certified to determine negligence. If liability was found, individual members of the class could rely on the verdict and, using collateral estoppel, try the remainder of the individual issues such as causation and damages. The Court of Appeals decertified the class, in part because of the irreparable harm the defendants would suffer if forced to try the case in the class action form.

> [One reason for decertification] is a concern with forcing these defendants to stake their companies on the outcome of a single jury trial, or be forced by fear of the risk of bankruptcy to settle even if they have no legal liability, when it is entirely feasible to allow a final, authoritative determination of their liability for the colossal misfortune that has befallen the hemophiliac population to emerge from a decentralized process of multiple trials.... A notable feature of this case.... is the demonstrated great likelihood that the plaintiffs' claims, despite their human appeal, lack legal merit. This is the inference from the defendants' having won 92.3 percent (12/13) of the cases to have gone to judgment....

Is Judge Posner overstating the plaintiffs' leverage? Sometimes it is the defendants who want class certification in an effort to rid themselves of repetitive litigation. See, e.g., In re TMJ Implants Prod. Liab. Litig., 880 F.Supp. 1311 (D.Minn. 1995)(summary judgment for suppliers of jaw implant plastic materials in MDL).

Should the financial future of the defendants be an issue in the superiority inquiry? The dissent in *Rhone–Poulenc Rorer* argued that the defendants' financial health was "at odds with Fed.R.Civ.P. 23 itself [which] expressly permits class treatment of such claims when its requirements are met, regardless of the magnitude of potential liability." Id. at 1308. After the *Rhone–Poulenc Rorer* class was decertified, the case settled. See also Valentino v. Carter–Wallace, Inc., 97 F.3d 1227 (9th Cir. 1996)(defendant's financial stake not a proper consideration); In re Copley Pharmaceutical, Inc., 161 F.R.D. 456 (D.Wyo.1995)(same). See Silver, We're Scared to Death—Does Class Certification Subject Defendants to Blackmail?, 78 N.Y.U.L.Rev. 1357 (2003).

6.   Limited Common Issue Classes. Rule 23(c)(4)(A) provides that, when appropriate, a class may be maintained with respect to a particular issue, but the rule does not indicate when this approach is appropriate. In toxic substance cases, when might such limited issue class treatment be inappropriate? Do you consider the *Castano* court's reading of Rule 23(c)(4) appropriate? See Manual For Complex Litigation § 22.75 (4th ed. 2004) (listing factors courts consider in deciding whether issues class will materially advance the disposition of a mass tort).

Examples of toxic substance classes certified under Rule 23(c)(4)(A) include Mejdrech v. Met–Coil Sys. Corp., 319 F.3d 910, 912 (7th Cir. 2003) (leakage of contaminants common issue in environmental damage action); In re School Asbestos Litig., 789 F.2d 996, 1008 (3d Cir.1986)("[d]etermination of liability issues in one suit may represent a substantial savings in time and resources"); Central Wesleyan College v. W.R. Grace & Co., 6 F.3d 177, 185 (4th Cir.1993)("Significant economies may be achieved by relieving educational institutions of the need to prove over and over when defendants knew or should have known of asbestos' hazards, or whether defendants engaged in concerted efforts to conceal this knowledge.") Commentators have proposed limited issue classes as an appropriate way to use class actions to resolve common mass tort issues. Davis, Toward the Proper Role for Mass Tort Class Actions, 77 Or.L.Rev. 157 (1998). But See Hines, Challenging the Issue Class Action End Run, 52 Emory L.J. 709 (2003).

7.   Issue Preclusion. If a limited issue class is permitted, and certain factual issues resolved, are the parties against whom the issue is decided precluded from raising the issue again? Are absent class members precluded from re-litigating issues decided adversely? The use of collateral estoppel to prevent the relitigation of previously decided factual issues is another traditional litigation management technique. Especially in the early days of the asbestos litigation, some commentators argued that collateral estoppel should be used to lighten the burdens created by asbestos and other toxic substance litigation, but the potential benefit of collateral estoppel has never been realized.

The Fifth Circuit Court of Appeals refused its use in the asbestos context in Hardy v. Johns–Manville Sales Corp., 681 F.2d 334, 342 (5th Cir.1982). The purposes behind issue preclusion—protecting litigants from the burden of relitigating issues and promoting judicial economy by preventing needless litigation—might be served, but the existence of inconsistent verdicts and ambiguity about the jury's fact findings prevented it. The requirements of identity of issues and actual litigation of that issue are often not satisfied. See Parklane Hosiery Co. v. Shore, 439 U.S. 322 (1979); Whalen v. Ansell Perry, Inc., 2004 WL 840286 (S.D.N.Y. 2004).

After affirming the decertification of the tobacco class action in *Engle v. R.J.Reynolds Tobacco Co.*, the Florida Supreme Court affirmed the jury's fact findings regarding the defendants' liability so that subsequent plaintiffs might be able to use them in individual litigation. 2006 WL 3742610 (Fla. 2006). The defendants litigated the issues fully in the class action trial, but what limitations should there be on the use of such findings when the class is subsequently decertified? See generally Wolff, Preclusion in Class Action Litigation, 105 Colum. L. Rev. 717 (2005); Madden, Issue Preclusion in Products Liability, 11 Pace L.Rev. 87 (1994)(issue preclusion exalts judicial economy over fairness to the opponent).

8. Class Action Fairness Act of 2005. While federal courts became increasingly inhospitable to mass-tort class actions because of the rigor of Rule 23 analysis, as evidenced by cases like *Amchem Products* and *Castano,* some state courts appeared to become more hospitable to them. Large class action judgments were rendered and some state jurisdictions earned the reputation of being magnets for non-meritorious litigation that attracted plaintiffs' lawyers interested principally in large fees. Consumer fraud class actions in which small claims were aggregated to achieve class action status became popular, but critics alleged that only the plaintiffs' lawyers made any money; class members received coupons. These trends in class action practice led Congress to enact the Class Action Fairness Act of 2005, Pub. L. No. 109–2, 119 Stat. 4 (2005) (CAFA).

CAFA's purposes include preventing forum shopping for "magnet" jurisdictions that have little or no connection to a controversy, keeping cases of national importance in federal court, and ensuring that class action settlements are fair and reasonable and the fees proportional to the class benefit conferred. Thus, CAFA amended Title 28, the Judiciary Act, to require only minimal diversity and an aggregate amount in controversy of $5,000,000 for class actions whether filed originally in federal court or removed there. 28 U.S.C. § 1332(d)(2). CAFA also contained exceptions for those class actions that are truly limited in nature to one state, § 1332(d)(4)(B), or which involve a local controversy, § 1332(d)(4)(A). The exceptions are likely to require years of litigation to clarify.

Once a class action makes it to federal court, Rule 23 applies to class certification and, as noted, Rule 23 is difficult to satisfy. The ultimate result, therefore, is likely to be many fewer class actions certified in both state and federal court. Recent data suggests that CAFA is having its intended effect: more state law based class actions are being removed to federal court. See Class Actions Moving to Federal Courts as Result of New Legislation, 75 U.S.L.W. 2149 (Sept. 19, 2006).

CAFA also creates a category of multi-party action called a "mass action" which is to be treated like a class action. § 1332 (d)(11). A "mass action" is one "in which monetary relief claims of 100 or more persons are proposed to be tried jointly on the ground that plaintiffs' claims involve common questions of law or fact." Id. Exemptions attempt to keep truly local claims out of federal court. The "mass action" provision has already produced confusion: one court calling it "muddled," Abrego Abrego v. Dow Chem. Co., 443 F.3d 676, 678 (9th Cir. 2006) (burden of proof on manufacturer to establish "mass action" removal jurisdiction; not satisfied). Courts are just beginning to interpret the scope of CAFA. See generally Vance, A Primer on the Class Action Fairness Act of 2005, 80 Tul. L. Rev. 1617 (2006); Sherman, Class Actions After the Class Action Fairness Act of 2005, 80 Tul. L. Rev. 1593 (2006).

9. What is the future of the mass tort class action? See McGovern, A Proposed Settlement Rule for Mass Torts, 74 UMKC L. Rev. 623 (2006); Symposium, Emerging Issues in Class Actions, 54 UCLA L. Rev No. 3 (2006); Rosenberg, Mandatory Litigation Class Action: The Only Option for Mass Tort Cases, 115 Harv. L.Rev. 831 (2002); D. Hensler, et al., Class Action Dilemmas: Pursing Public Goals for Private Gain (RAND Institute for Civil Justice 2000).

———

B.   Class Actions—Management

Mass-tort class action practice is so consumed with settlement that it is the rare class action that is litigated, even on limited issues. Manageability is an important consideration, nonetheless, in deciding whether a class action is a superior method of adjudication. A second attempt to certify a 23(b)(3) class for asbestos cases in the Fifth Circuit was rejected in In re Fibreboard Corp., 893 F.2d 706 (5th Cir.1990). The trial court had certified a class of approximately 3,000 asbestos plaintiffs in *Cimino v. Raymark Indus.*, 1989 WL 253889 (E.D.Tex.1989). The court planned to try the case in three phases with the same jury deciding issues of (I) product defectiveness, (II) general causation, and (III) damages apportionment. The Court of Appeals in *Fibreboard* decertified the class as to general causation in Phase II. *Castano* relied on *Fibreboard* for the following proposition:

> [At some point] cumulative changes in procedure work a change in the very character of a trial. [C]hanges in "procedure" involving the mode of proof may alter the liability of the defendants in fundamental ways. We do not suggest that procedure becomes substance whenever outcomes are changed. Rather, we suggest that changes in substantive duty can come dressed as a change in procedure. We are persuaded that Phase II would work such a change.

On remand, the trial court modified its trial plan. The following opinion explains the trial plan that the trial court eventually implemented which, again, was rejected by the court of appeals. As you read the following, consider what a trial court is to do to resolve thousands of similar claims like those involved in asbestos and other toxic substance cases.

Cimino v. Raymark Industries, Inc.

United States Court of Appeals, Fifth Circuit, 1998.
151 F.3d 297.

■ Garwood, Circuit Judge:

Before us are appeals and cross-appeals in personal injury and wrongful death damage suits against several manufacturers of asbestos-containing insulation products and some of their suppliers, the district court's jurisdiction being based on diversity of citizenship and the governing substantive law being that of Texas. This is the same set of cases addressed in In re Fibreboard, 893 F.2d 706 (5th Cir.1990), but the judgments now before us result from a trial plan modified following that decision. Principally at issue on this appeal is the validity of that modified trial plan. [The trial judge observed on remand that its "task appears to be insurmountable," but stated that it would nonetheless "take[] its place behind the old mule and start down that long row." The trial court utilized the following trial plan.]

[T]he court determined to employ new phases II and III: "asking the jury in Phase Two to make findings on exposure that are specific to job site, craft and time; and then by submitting to a jury in Phase Three individual damage cases of a statistically significant, randomly selected sample from each of the five disease categories." For purposes of phase II, twenty-two different worksites [including refineries, shipyards, and chemical plants in several Texas and Louisiana communities] would be considered. The district court contemplated that the phase II jury (the same jury as in phase I) would [hear evidence concerning (a) the presence of the defendants' products at the worksites; (b) the presence of asbestos dust at the worksites; and (c) the nature of the various crafts at the worksites and the relationship between these crafts and the presence of asbestos dust at these facilities. The jury was to make a determination as to which crafts at the worksites were exposed to which defendants' asbestos products (if any) for a sufficient period of time to cause injury, and during which decades the exposure took place. The trial judge was to make a determination as to which plaintiffs worked for long enough to be considered members of the different worksite groups.]

In Phase III, two other juries would determine for 160 sample cases only "two damage issues," namely "(a) whether the Plaintiffs suffered from an asbestos-related injury or disease and, if so, (b) what damages the Plaintiffs incurred." The court ultimately determined, based on information from plaintiffs, that the entire class of 2,298 cases could be broken down into the 5 disease categories, and the court then randomly selected 160 sample cases, some from each disease category, as follows:

	SAMPLE SIZE	**DISEASE CATEGORY POPULATION**
Mesothelioma	15	32
Lung Cancer	25	186
Other Cancer	20	58
Asbestosis	50	1,050
Pleural Disease	50	972
TOTAL	160	2,298

Individual judgment would be entered in each of the 160 sample cases based on the phase III verdict in that particular sample case. After phase III, the district court would assign each of the remaining 2,298 cases to one of the 5 disease categories, and in each case make an award of actual damages equal to the average of the awards in the phase III cases involving the same disease.

Phase I

The phase I trial lasted approximately eight weeks. [The jury found in answer to the first four questions when the defendants knew or should have known that their "asbestos-containing insulation products" posed a risk of asbestos-related disease. Pittsburgh Corning knew or should have known this since 1962 (when it first entered the business; it left it in 1972); the other three defendants since 1935 as to insulators and since 1955 as to other crafts; all four defendants as to household members since 1965. The jury found that, since 1962 as to Pittsburgh Corning and since 1935 as to the other defendants, the defendants' products "were defective and unreasonably dangerous as a result of not having an adequate warning." The jury found each defendant guilty of gross negligence warranting punitive damages and assigned a punitive damages multiplier of $3.00 per $1.00 of actual damages to Pittsburgh Corning, $2.00 to Celotex, and $1.50 each to Fibreboard and Carey Canada.]

Phase III

Following completion of the phase I trial (and a continuance), the district court proceeded directly into phase III, without any phase II trial. It was not until approximately seven weeks into the phase III trials that the stipulation—which ultimately replaced phase II—was entered into. It was clear from the beginning of, and throughout, the phase III trials that the two juries were not to, and did not, determine whether exposure to any of defendants' products was a cause of the sample plaintiffs' complained-of condition. In phase III, the court instructed the jury that they were to assume exposure was sufficient to be a producing cause of all the disease categories. As plaintiffs admit in their brief here, in the phase III trial "the juries were told to assume that the claimants had sufficient exposure." Indeed, for the most part evidence of exposure and its likely or possible results was not allowed. Simply stated, whether there was exposure to Pittsburgh Corning's—or any other defendant's—asbestos, and, if so, whether that exposure was a cause of any of the 160 sample plaintiffs' illness, disease, or damages, was neither litigated nor determined in any of the phase III trials....

Following the phase III jury verdicts (including 12 zero verdicts) in the 160 sample cases, the district court ordered remittiturs in 35 of these cases ("34 of the pulmonary and pleural cases and in one mesothelioma case"), and calculated the average actual damage award, after remittitur (and considering the zero verdicts), in each disease category to be the following: mesothelioma, $1,224,333; lung cancer, $545,200; other cancer, $917,785; asbestosis, $543,783; pleural disease, $558,900. These were the figures to be applied to the extrapolation cases.

Phase II stipulation

We now turn to the written stipulation ... which replaced phase II. It was executed by all the plaintiffs and by Pittsburgh Corning, Fibreboard, and Celotex ..., and was approved "so ordered" by the district court.

Attached to the stipulation as an exhibit was a special verdict form that would consist of separate interrogatories, each with a part (a) and a part (b), one each for each of the twenty-two worksites at issue. For example, question 1(a) would ask "For Worksite No. 1, do you find that the following crafts had sufficient exposure to asbestos during the specified time periods to be a producing cause of the disease of asbestosis." The jury would answer yes or no separately as to each of over fifty listed crafts for each of four specified decades, namely 1942–52, 1952–62, 1962–72, and

1972–82. Question 1(b) would state, "For the crafts and the time periods which were answered 'yes' in question 1(a), causation is apportioned as follows." This question would be answered by stating separately for each listed craft a percentage applicable to each of the current defendants and each of the former defendants who had settled as to each of the same four decades (as to each decade the percentages were to total one hundred percent). This process would be repeated, with questions 2(a) and 2(b), 3(a) and 3(b), and so forth, separately as to each of the remaining worksites.

The stipulation provides in part that [some individuals working at the worksites from 1942 to 1982 were exposed to asbestos during their employment in an amount of sufficient length and intensity to cause pulmonary asbestosis of varying degrees. Asbestos-containing products of predecessors to Celotex and Fibreboard were present during each of those decades and an asbestos-containing product of Pittsburgh Corning was present from 1962–1982. Further, "The defendants do not stipulate that any members of the various crafts at the various worksites had the same exposure to any products or that any such individuals had the same susceptibility to asbestos-related diseases in the various crafts and worksites." The stipulation provides that "it shall be deemed that the Phase Two jury" assigned in all instances the following comparative causation shares: Pittsburgh Corning, ten percent; Fibreboard, ten percent; Celotex, ten percent; and Manville Personal Injury Settlement Trust, thirteen percent. The court would use these percentages to fashion judgments in the 160 phase III sample cases and in the extrapolation cases.]

Before setting out these percentages, however, the stipulation had made clear that defendants were not thereby agreeing that the trial plan—either the originally planned phase II or the contemplated extrapolation procedure—was a permissible way to adjudicate their liability and damages. [Defendants' continued to object to these extrapolation procedures, and paragraph 8 states "Defendants reserve all rights to object to all past and future aspects of the *Cimino* trial plan and to assign as error all prior, present, and future rulings of the Court."]

After the stipulation, the phase III trials continued for approximately five more weeks, conducted in all material respects on the same basis and in the same manner as they had been during the some seven weeks before the stipulation was entered into.

Extrapolation

The final phase was that of extrapolation. [A one-day non-jury hearing was held in which the district court heard evidence concerning the degree to which the 160 sample cases were representative, in their respective disease categories, of the cases in the same disease category among the 2,128 extrapolation cases. Three expert witnesses called by the plaintiffs testified. Professor Frankewitz stated that he was furnished by someone in the offices of plaintiffs' counsel computerized written data reflecting, as to each of the 160 sample cases and each of the 2,128 extrapolation cases, which of the 5 disease categories the case involved, and an answer to each of 12 specific variables pertaining to the particular plaintiff—gender, race, smoker, deceased, employment, age, first and last year of exposure, and the like. Professor Frankewitz testified that the sample cases in each of the five disease categories were representative of the extrapolation cases in the same disease category "in terms of the variables that I've analyzed.," so that random selection would produce, 99 out of 100 times, "the same mix of variables" as the 50 asbestosis cases which were a part of the 160 sample phase III cases. Dr. Frankewitz did not choose the variables and, in some cases, admitted he did not know what they meant.]

[Pittsburgh Corning challenged the trial plan on the basis that it fails to properly determine individual causation, and in the extrapolation cases also fails to properly determine individual damages, as to any plaintiffs other than the ten class representatives whose individual cases were fully tried in phase I. The Court of Appeals reversed.]

With one exception, we are aware of no appellate decision approving such a group, rather than individual determination of cause in a damage suit for personal injuries to individuals at widely different times and places.... In sum, as *Fibreboard* held, under Texas law causation must be determined as to "individuals, not groups." And the Seventh Amendment gives the right to a jury trial to make that determination. There was no such trial and determination made, and no jury determined, that exposure to Pittsburgh Corning's products was a cause of the asbestos disease of any of the 160 phase III plaintiffs. Nor does the stipulation determine or establish that. [Thus,] the judgments in all the 143 phase III cases before us must be reversed. [The same result applied to the extrapolation cases.]

NOTES

1. How might the causation issue be resolved other than by an individual trial for each plaintiff? Many plaintiffs in asbestos cases die before their trial can be completed. Many defendants file bankruptcy because of the weight of the pending liability and the costs to defend. It has been estimated that almost 60% of each dollar paid in compensation to asbestos plaintiffs goes to transaction costs. 2005 RAND Report Summary at xxvi.

2. The Manual for Complex Litigation (4th ed. 2004) is published by the Federal Judicial Center to assist judges in the management of complex litigation. Chapter 22 is devoted to mass tort litigation. "[C]ourts recognize that the complexity, diversity, and volume of mass tort claims require adapting traditional procedures to new contexts, to achieve both fairness and efficiency." Id. § 22.1. Despite the availability of a variety of litigation management techniques, are the courts equipped (even through the class action device) to deal with mass toxic substance litigation? The Fifth Circuit was skeptical:

> We are told that [class certification] is the only realistic way of trying these cases; that the difficulties faced by the courts as well as the rights of the class members to have their cases tried cry powerfully for innovation and judicial creativity. The arguments are compelling, but they are better addressed to the representative branches—Congress and the State Legislature. The Judicial Branch can offer the trial of lawsuits. It has no power or competence to do more. We are persuaded on reflection that the procedures here called for comprise something other than a trial within our authority. It is called a trial, but it is not.

In re Fibreboard, 893 F.2d at 712.

3. See generally Advisory Comm. on Civil Rules and Working Group on Mass Torts, Report on Mass Tort Litigation (1999); Willging, Beyond Maturity; Mass Tort Case Management in the Manual for Complex Litigation, 148 U.Pa.L.Rev. 2225 (2000); Symposium, Toxic Torts: Issues of Mass Litigation, Case Management and Ethics, 26 Wm. & Mary Envtl.L. & Policy Rev. 1 (2001); 2 D. Owen, M.S. Madden, & M. Davis, Madden & Owen on Products Liability ch. 26 (3d ed. 2000).

3. CAUSATION

> Many commentators recognize proof of causation as the paramount obstacle to just resolution of tort claims based on injury from toxic substances.

Brennan, Causal Chains–Statistical Links: The Role of Scientific Uncertainty in Hazardous Substance Litigation, 73 Cornell L.Rev. 469, 469 (1988).

A toxic substance plaintiff must show that (1) the allegedly toxic substance is capable of causing the illness from which plaintiff suffers—the so-called general causation issue; (2) the plaintiff has been exposed to the toxic substance in sufficient quantities to cause the alleged illness; and (3) exposure to the defendant's toxic substance, and not exposure to some other toxic substance or even plaintiff's natural predisposition to disease, caused the plaintiff's illness. The second two inquiries combine to define the "specific causation" inquiry.

A. General Causation—The Capacity of the Agent to Cause Plaintiff's Disease

While most casual observers (and many lawyers) think of general causation as an all-or-nothing proposition, the connection between diseases and toxic substances rarely provides such categorical certainty. The problem runs very deep and goes to the ability of non-scientist lawyers and judges to understand scientific method and theory:

> The courts' difficulty with handling evidence linking a hazardous substance to a disease is largely the result of the courts' inability to understand scientific notions of causation. The assumptions that courts make about causation very much resemble those that provide the foundation for Newtonian physics. Over the past century, science has come to rely on new assumptions about cause and effect. These new assumptions have not been integrated into legal reasoning. As a result, lawyers and judges are often confused when they address scientific causation issues.

Brennan, Causal Chains and Statistical Links: The Role of Scientific Uncertainty in Hazardous–Substance Litigation, 73 Cornell L.Rev. 469, 478 (1988). The Restatement (Third) of Torts: Liability for Physical Harm, § 28, cmt *c*, (Tentative Draft No. 3, April 7, 2003), discusses the tension between law and science in toxic substance causation problems:

[C]ourts may be relying on a view that "science" presents an "objective method of establishing that, in all cases reasonable minds cannot differ on the issue of factual causation." Such a view is incorrect. First, scientific standards for the sufficiency of the evidence to establish a proposition may be inappropriate for the law, which itself must decide the minimum amount of evidence permitting a reasonable (and therefore permissible) inference as opposed to speculation that is not permitted. Second, scientists report that an evaluation of data and scientific evidence to determine whether an inference of causation is appropriate requires judgment and interpretation. Scientists are subject to their own value judgments and preexisting biases that may affect their view of a body of evidence. There are instances in which although one scientist or group of scientists comes to one conclusion about factual causation, they recognize that another group that comes to a contrary conclusion might still be "reasonable." Judgments about causation may also be affected by the comparative costs of errors, as when caution counsels in favor of declaring an uncertain agent toxic because the potential harm it may cause if toxic is so much greater than the benefit foregone if it were permitted to be introduced. Courts, thus, should be cautious about adopting specific "scientific" principles, taken out of context, to formulate bright-line legal rules or conclude that reasonable minds cannot differ about factual causation.

See Feldman, Science & Uncertainty in Mass Exposure Litigation, 73 Tex. L. Rev. 1, 2–3 (1995)(observing how frequently "science is severely uncertain about the causal effects of the substances and products that figure so prominently in contemporary tort litigation."); Cheng, Changing Scientific Evidence, 88 Minn.L.Rev. 315 (2003) ("Whenever litigation occurs before the scientific community has developed a substantial literature on the harmful effects of a substance, there is a significant probability that fact finders will reach ultimately inaccurate conclusions."). As you read these materials, consider the roles of the judge, the jury, and the expert in determining the causal connection between toxic substances and harm.

Black & Lilienfeld, Epidemiologic Proof in Toxic Tort Litigation

52 Fordham L. Rev. 732, 750–62 (1984).

II. Epidemiologic Principles

The elucidation of the relationship between a disease and a factor (e.g., a toxic substance) suspected of causing it lies within the domain of epidemiology.[76] The epidemiologist examines this relationship in the context of populations, comparing the disease experiences of people exposed to the factor with those not so exposed.[77] Although the epidemiologist utilizes

---

76. Epidemiology has been defined as "the science dealing with the environmental causes of diseases of humans as inferred from observations of human beings." Cole, The Evolving Case–Control Study, 32 J.Chronic Dis. 15 (1979).—Eds.

77. See A. Lilienfeld & D. Lilienfeld, Foundations of Epidemiology 3 (2d ed. 1980).

statistical methods, the ultimate goal is to draw a biological inference concerning the relationship of the factor to the disease's etiology and/or to its natural history. * * *

B.   *Determining the Relationship between Incidence of Disease and Exposure to a Factor*

Once the epidemiologist has defined the disease of interest, he seeks to compare the rate of disease development (incidence rate) among those exposed to the factor of interest with the rate among those not so exposed. The incidence rate is a measure of the probability that an individual will develop the disease. Hence, the epidemiologist is interested in determining if exposure to the factor changes the probability that an individual will develop the disease. If there is a gradation in the degree of exposure, the possibility of a corresponding gradation in incidence rates exists and merits investigation. The two principal approaches to collecting and analyzing morbidity/mortality data for exposed and non-exposed individuals are the demographic study and the epidemiologic study. In the former, the subjects within the two groups are viewed in the aggregate, while in the latter the subjects are viewed individually. The results of demographic studies are used to generate etiologic hypotheses, which are then tested through epidemiologic studies.

1.   The Demographic Study

Demographic studies explore either morbidity, if the investigator seeks to explain sickness, or mortality, if the investigator seeks to explain death. In either case, a study initially seeks to determine the accuracy and completeness of the statistics being analyzed and then attempts to ascertain how such statistics are related to possible etiologic factors, such as age, sex, cigarette consumption or asbestos exposure. One might, for example, examine the relationship between annual asbestos use in the United States from 1910–1950 and the annual mortality rates for mesothelioma in the United States from 1940–1980. Before drawing conclusions from the relationship between asbestos exposure and mesothelioma, however, the epidemiologist must determine the accuracy of the available mortality and exposure data in order to ensure that there has not been under- or over-reporting of either asbestos use or mesothelioma mortality. Studies have indicated that such data are available and accurate and that there is a positive relationship between asbestos use and mortality from mesothelioma. Although such a positive correlation is supportive of a possible causal relationship between the two, it is by no means conclusive.

No matter how compelling the findings in a demographic study, it must be recognized that such observations refer to groups and not to the individuals within the groups. A correlation may exist between a factor and the incidence of a disease even though no causal relationship exists. The classic example of this phenomenon is the linear relationship between pig iron production in the United States and the birth rate in Great Britain. Clearly, such an association is spurious. This problem is known as an "ecological fallacy," and it imposes an inherent limitation on the use of demographic studies in inferring a causal relationship between a factor and a disease. Demographic studies are used mainly to focus attention on a possible association between a factor and a disease, the elucidation of which requires further, more refined modes of study. In order to demonstrate the association in terms of the individual members of a group, the investigator utilizes the epidemiologic study.

2.　The Epidemiologic Study

The epidemiologic study attempts to explore and clarify a possible association between a factor and a disease within individuals in a population. For epidemiologists, it represents the application of the scientific method to human populations. In the scientific method, the investigator observes the effect of a single modification in the environment of one of two otherwise identical animals. Similarly, in an epidemiologic study, one seeks to observe the effect of exposure to a single factor upon the incidence of disease in two otherwise identical populations.

. . . One might, for example, be interested in determining the difference in lung cancer incidence between smokers and non-smokers. If the epidemiologist views the population in terms of the individuals' exposure, the study type is "prospective." The investigator first determines if the individuals are cigarette smokers, then follows them over a sufficient number of years to see if their lung cancer incidence rate differs from that of non-smokers. If the epidemiologist views the populations in terms of individual disease status, the study is either "retrospective" or "cross-sectional." Retrospective studies focus on past exposure while cross-sectional studies consider current exposure. The investigator selects individuals who have or do not have lung cancer and then determines whether or not they are or have been cigarette smokers.

a.　Prospective Studies

The prospective study is a powerful way to investigate the relationship between a factor and a disease because it closely approximates the classical scientific method. The investigator identifies two populations (or representative samples thereof), one composed of individuals who have been exposed to the factor and one of individuals who have not been so exposed. Ideally, these populations will be otherwise identical. The investigator follows these populations for a period of time (possibly many years), observing the incidence rates of disease in each population. If the two groups are comparable, any difference in disease incidence can then be related either to the factor or to the sampling process, that is, to chance. . . . After eliminating chance and determining that a statistically significant relationship between the disease and the factor exists, the epidemiologist's next task is to estimate the magnitude of the association. The accepted means of measuring such an association is the calculation of the relative risk, which is the ratio of the incidence rate of disease in the exposed group divided by that rate in the non-exposed "control" group.[105] If there is no association

---

105.　EXAMPLE OF COMPUTATION OF RELATIVE RISK

1.　Groups A and B are assumed identical except for exposure to Factor F.

between the factor and the disease, the relative risk is 1.0; that is, the incidence rates for the exposed and non-exposed groups are equal.

The greater the magnitude of the observed relative risk, the stronger the association between the factor and the disease. If the factor were the only cause of the disease, the relative risk would be infinite because the incidence of disease in the unexposed group would be zero. Because most diseases have multi-factorial etiologies, however, it is rare to observe a relative risk greater than 10. When a relative risk of 10 or more is observed, one can be reasonably certain that it represents a causal relationship. For example, the relative risk for mesothelioma from asbestos exposure, which is widely recognized as causal, is between 50 and 80. By comparison, the relative risk for leukemia in children who have been irradiated *in utero* is only 1.6 times that of children who were not so irradiated. This represents a relatively small increase in the risk of developing leukemia for the irradiated children, which reflects a relatively weak causal relationship.

The prospective study, although very reliable, is difficult and expensive to conduct. It is not always possible to identify populations that are exposed and not exposed to a factor. Frequently, the epidemiologist is unable to follow the two groups for the period of time required. Hence, epidemiologists have developed and extensively used the retrospective study.

b.   *Retrospective Studies*

Whereas a prospective study investigates the disease experience of exposed and non-exposed groups, the epidemiologist performing a retrospective study begins with individuals who already have (cases) or do not have (controls) the disease under investigation. He then determines whether or not each individual has a past exposure to the factor, presumably prior to the onset of the pathologic process resulting in the disease. Cases are usually ascertained in a hospital setting. * * *

d.   *Attributable Risk*

Observational studies are all directed at determining the relative risk of developing a disease that is associated with exposure to a factor. The relative risk, however, expresses only the magnitude of that association. The statistical measure of a factor's relationship to a disease in the population is the "attributable risk." It was originally described as the percentage decline in the population's disease incidence that would occur if the population's exposure to the factor were eliminated. For example, the risk of lung cancer attributable to smoking in the United States today is approximately eighty percent. In other words, if smoking were eliminated

(If not identical, there are methods of adjustment that still allow valid comparisons).

2.   Incidence of disease D in Group A (exposed to Factor F) is 50 per 100,000 population. Incidence of the disease in Group B (not exposed) is 5 per 100,000.

3.   Relative risk (r) of exposed to non-exposed is 50/5 = 10.0.

in the United States, the incidence of lung cancer would decline by about eighty percent.

* * *

C. *Biological Inferences From Epidemiologic Data*

Demographic and epidemiologic studies both facilitate the elucidation of the statistical association between a factor and a disease. In order to draw the biological inference that a causal relationship exists, however, the epidemiologist must integrate additional scientific information. The derivation of such an inference requires rigorous consideration of laboratory, experimental, demographic and epidemiologic data.[124]

Daubert v. Merrell Dow Pharmaceuticals, Inc.

Supreme Court of the United States, 1993.
509 U.S. 579, 113 S.Ct. 2786, 125 L.Ed.2d 469.

■ JUSTICE BLACKMUN delivered the opinion of the Court.

In this case we are called upon to determine the standard for admitting expert scientific testimony in a federal trial.

I

Petitioners Jason Daubert and Eric Schuller are minor children born with serious birth defects. They and their parents sued respondent in California state court, alleging that the birth defects had been caused by the mothers' ingestion of Bendectin, a prescription anti-nausea drug marketed by respondent. Respondent removed the suits to federal court on diversity grounds.

After extensive discovery, respondent moved for summary judgment, contending that Bendectin does not cause birth defects in humans and that petitioners would be unable to come forward with any admissible evidence that it does. In support of its motion, respondent submitted an affidavit of Steven H. Lamm, physician and epidemiologist, who is a well-credentialed expert on the risks from exposure to various chemical substances. Doctor Lamm stated that he had reviewed all the literature on Bendectin and human birth defects—more than 30 published studies involving over 130,000 patients. No study had found Bendectin to be a human teratogen (i.e.,

---

124. It should be noted that it is possible to have an inadequately developed biological inference regarding the relationship between a factor and a disease, yet still have a statistically plausible relationship. See A. Lilienfeld & D. Lilienfeld, supra note 77, at 315–16. The necessary biological knowledge may not be available at the time that the statistical association is found. An example of this occurrence is the relationship between oral contraceptives and various circulatory diseases. Id. at 315–16. When an association was discovered, there was no laboratory evidence to support a causal inference. However, the statistical association provided direction for laboratory workers in their research. The resulting laboratory data provided the necessary biological facts for the causal relationship to be stated. Id. at 316.

a substance capable of causing malformations in fetuses). On the basis of this review, Doctor Lamm concluded that maternal use of Bendectin during the first trimester of pregnancy has not been shown to be a risk factor for human birth defects.

Petitioners did not (and do not) contest this characterization of the published record regarding Bendectin. Instead, they responded to respondent's motion with the testimony of eight experts of their own, each of whom also possessed impressive credentials. These experts had concluded that Bendectin can cause birth defects. Their conclusions were based upon "in vitro" (test tube) and "in vivo" (live) animal studies that found a link between Bendectin and malformations; pharmacological studies of the chemical structure of Bendectin that purported to show similarities between the structure of the drug and that of other substances known to cause birth defects; and the "reanalysis" of previously published epidemiological (human statistical) studies.

[The District Court granted respondent's motion for summary judgment, ruling that scientific evidence is admissible only if the principle upon which it is based has general acceptance in the field to which it belongs. Given the vast body of epidemiological data concerning Bendectin, the trial court held that petitioners' expert opinions were not admissible to establish causation because not based on epidemiological evidence. The animal-cell studies, live-animal studies, and chemical-structure analyses relied upon by petitioners' experts were insufficient to raise a jury issue; their epidemiological analyses, based on recalculations of data in previously published studies that had found no causal link, were inadmissible because they had not been published or subjected to peer review. The Court of Appeals for the Ninth Circuit affirmed, 951 F.2d 1128 (9th Cir.1991), relying on Frye v. United States, 293 F. 1013, 1014 (App.Cir.1923), which requires that an expert's opinion, to be admissible, must be based on a scientific technique that is "generally accepted" as reliable in the relevant scientific community, and petitioners' experts' opinions were not. Other courts of appeals had refused to admit re-analyses of Bendectin epidemiological studies that had been neither published nor subjected to peer review because "the massive weight of the original published studies" found no causal connection. Moreover, the re-analyses on which petitioners' experts' relied were generated solely for litigation purposes.]

We granted certiorari in light of sharp divisions among the courts regarding the proper standard for the admission of expert testimony. Compare, e.g., United States v. Shorter, 809 F.2d 54, 59–60 (D.C.Cir.)(applying the "general acceptance" standard), cert. denied, 484 U.S. 817 (1987), with DeLuca v. Merrell Dow Pharmaceuticals, Inc., 911 F.2d 941, 955 (3d Cir.1990) (rejecting the "general acceptance" standard).

II

[The Court rejected the *Frye* general acceptance standard and endorsed a test requiring an assessment of reliability of the expert testimony and its relevance to the underlying case. This test stems from the language of Rule

702 which requires that the expert's testimony be both "scientific" and "helpful to the trier of fact."]

The primary locus of this obligation is Rule 702, which clearly contemplates some degree of regulation of the subjects and theories about which an expert may testify. "If scientific, technical, or other specialized knowledge will assist the trier of fact to understand the evidence or to determine a fact in issue" an expert "may testify thereto." The subject of an expert's testimony must be "scientific ... knowledge." The adjective "scientific" implies a grounding in the methods and procedures of science. Similarly, the word "knowledge" connotes more than subjective belief or unsupported speculation. The term "applies to any body of known facts or to any body of ideas inferred from such facts or accepted as truths on good grounds." [Citation.] Of course, it would be unreasonable to conclude that the subject of scientific testimony must be "known" to a certainty; arguably, there are no certainties in science.... But, in order to qualify as "scientific knowledge," an inference or assertion must be derived by the scientific method. Proposed testimony must be supported by appropriate validation—i.e., "good grounds," based on what is known. In short, the requirement that an expert's testimony pertain to "scientific knowledge" establishes a standard of evidentiary reliability.

Rule 702 further requires that the evidence or testimony "assist the trier of fact to understand the evidence or to determine a fact in issue." This condition goes primarily to relevance.... [See] United States v. Downing, 753 F.2d 1224, 1242 (3d Cir.1985). The consideration has been aptly described by Judge Becker as one of "fit." "Fit" is not always obvious, and scientific validity for one purpose is not necessarily scientific validity for other, unrelated purposes. [Citation.] The study of the phases of the moon, for example, may provide valid scientific "knowledge" about whether a certain night was dark, and if darkness is a fact in issue, the knowledge will assist the trier of fact. However (absent creditable grounds supporting such a link), evidence that the moon was full on a certain night will not assist the trier of fact in determining whether an individual was unusually likely to have behaved irrationally on that night. Rule 702's "helpfulness" standard requires a valid scientific connection to the pertinent inquiry as a precondition to admissibility.

[The Court describes the trial court's inquiry on reliability to entail] preliminary assessment of whether the reasoning or methodology underlying the testimony is scientifically valid and of whether that reasoning or methodology properly can be applied to the facts in issue. We are confident that federal judges possess the capacity to undertake this review. Many factors will bear on the inquiry, and we do not presume to set out a definitive checklist or test. But some general observations are appropriate.

[The Court sets out a list of factors, identified above in ch. 6, that will assist the trial court in its "gatekeeping" role. Those factors include (1) whether the theory or technique can and has been tested; (2) whether the theory or technique has been subjected to peer review; (3) whether there is a known or potential rate of error; (4) whether there are standards controlling the technique's operation; and (5) whether there is general acceptance of the theory or technique.]

The inquiry envisioned by Rule 702 is, we emphasize, a flexible one. Its overarching subject is the scientific validity—and thus the evidentiary relevance and reliability—of the principles that underlie a proposed submission. The focus, of course, must be solely on principles and methodology, not on the conclusions that they generate.

[The judgment of the Court of Appeals is vacated and the case remanded. The Opinion of CHIEF JUSTICE REHNQUIST concurring and dissenting in part is omitted.]

NOTES

1. Bendectin Litigation. The Bendectin litigation is often cited as an example of how poorly toxic substance litigation interacts with scientific discovery. In a pre-*Daubert* Bendectin decision, DeLuca v. Merrell Dow Pharmaceuticals, Inc., 911 F.2d 941, 946–48 (3d Cir.1990), the Third Circuit allowed the plaintiff's expert's opinion under a non-*Frye* admissibility standard and explained the nature of that expert testimony:

> [Plaintiff's expert] Dr. Done's opinion that Bendectin is a teratogen largely rests on inferences he draws from epidemiological data, most of which he contends are the same that was utilized by the experts, including the FDA committee, to whom Merrell Dow cites to bolster its contention that Bendectin does not cause birth defects. The principal difference is that Dr. Done analyzes that data using an approach, advocated by Professor Kenneth Rothman of the University of Massachusetts Medical School, that places diminished weight on so-called "significance testing." *See* K.J. Rothman, Modern Epidemiology (1986)("Rothman").

> Epidemiological studies, of necessity, look to the experience of sample groups as indicative of the experience of a far larger population. Epidemiologists recognize, however, that the experience of the sample groups may vary from that of the larger population by chance.... As a result of the acknowledged risk of this so-called "sampling error," researchers typically have rejected the associations suggested by epidemiological data unless those associations survive the rigors of "significance testing." ...

> Significance testing has a "P value" focus; the P value "indicates the probability, assuming the null hypothesis is true, that the observed data will depart from the absence of association to the extent that they actually do, or to a greater extent, by actual chance." Rothman, *supra*, at 116. [The null hypothesis in Bendectin cases is that Bendectin is not a teratogen.] If P is less than .05 (or 5%) a study's finding of a relationship supportive of the alternative hypothesis is considered statistically significant, if P is greater than 5% the relationship is rejected as insignificant. Accordingly, the results of a particular study are reported as simply "significant" or "not significant" or as P < .05 or P > .05.

> Use of a .05 P value to determine whether to accept or reject the null hypothesis necessarily enhances one of two types of possible error. Type one error is when the null hypothesis is rejected when it is in fact true. Type two error is when the null hypothesis is in fact false but is not rejected. Rothman notes that at .05, the null hypothesis will "be rejected

about 5 per cent of the time when it is true," a relatively small risk of type one error. Unfortunately, the relationship between type one error and type two error is not simple; however, one study ... concluded that when the risk of type one error equalled 5%, the risk of type two error was 50%. Cohen, Confidence in Probability: Burdens of Persuasion in a World of Imperfect Knowledge, 60 N.Y.U.L. Rev. 329, 411 & n. 116 (1985). Type one error may be viewed here as the risk of concluding that Bendectin is a teratogen when it is not. Type two error is the risk of concluding that Bendectin is not a teratogen, when it in fact is.

Rothman contends that there is nothing magical or inherently important about .05 significance; rather this is just a common value on the tables scholars use to calculate significance. He stresses that the data in a certain study may indicate a strong relationship between two variables but still not be "statistically significant" and that the level of significance which should be required depends on the type of decision being made and the relative values placed on avoiding the two types of risk.

* * *

Rothman suggests a less rigid approach in which researchers look at the confidence intervals produced by various studies. [Confidence intervals graphically represent the probability that an actual relationship exists between two variables.] By charting the range of possibilities consistent with the data found in different studies it is possible to evaluate whether the collective data is more supportive of the proposition that the null hypothesis is false than that it is true. At the same time, the use of confidence intervals indicates the risks inherent in generating any estimate of the true parameter from the data, and allows the decisionmaker to adjust the confidence level depending on the context in which a decision is required. [Dr. Done's reanalysis concludes that a 95% confidence interval exists that Bendectin is a teratogen.]

Does this evidence meet the reliability test of *Daubert*? How likely is it that judges, lawyers, and jurors are going to understand the significance testing P-value focus and confidence intervals at issue here? If your answer is that lawyers and laypersons cannot adequately understand this fundamental tool of scientific analysis, how can the law fairly adjudicate disputes involving scientific problems?

Early cases found no causal connection between Bendectin and the birth defects for which it was blamed but cases continued to be filed. In re Bendectin Litig., 857 F.2d 290 (6th Cir.1988), cert. denied, 488 U.S. 1006 (1989); Richardson v. Richardson–Merrell, Inc., 857 F.2d 823 (D.C.Cir.1988)(no causation, notwithstanding plaintiffs' expert testimony to the contrary to a "reasonable medical certainty;" for more than two decades of research, no epidemiological study had found causation); Ealy v. Richardson–Merrell, Inc., 897 F.2d 1159 (D.C.Cir. 1990)(expert opinion that Bendectin is teratogenic inadmissible; $20,000,000 verdict reversed).

2. After remand, *Daubert* returned once again to the Ninth Circuit:

... The first prong of *Daubert* puts federal judges in an uncomfortable position. The question of admissibility only arises if it is first established that the individuals whose testimony is being proffered are experts in a particular scientific field; here, for example, the Supreme Court waxed eloquent on the impressive qualification of plaintiffs' experts. Yet something doesn't become "scientific knowledge" just because it's uttered by a scientist; nor can an expert's self-serving assertion that his conclusions were "derived by the scientific method" be deemed conclusive, else the Supreme Court's opinion could have ended with footnote two. As we read [*Daubert*], therefore, though we are largely untrained in science and certainly no match for any of the witnesses whose testimony we are reviewing, it is our responsibility to determine whether those experts' proposed testimony amounts to "scientific knowledge," constitutes "good science," and was "derived by the scientific method."

* * *

Our responsibility, then unless we badly misread the Supreme Court's opinion, is to resolve disputes among respected, well-credentialed scientists about matters squarely within their expertise, in areas where there is no scientific consensus as to what is and what is not "good science," and occasionally to reject such expert testimony because it was not "derived by the scientific method." Mindful of our position in the hierarchy of the federal judiciary, we take a deep breath and proceed with this heady task.

43 F.3d 1311, 1315–18 (9th Cir.1995). The Court of Appeals concluded that the expert testimony was unreliable because it was developed for use in litigation, was not based on preexisting or independent research, and was never published. Affirming once again defendant's motion for summary judgment, the court noted that, "Despite the many years the controversy has been brewing, no one in the scientific community—except defendant's experts—has deemed these studies worthy of verification, refutation or even comment. It's as if there were a tacit understanding within the scientific community that what's going on here is not science at all, but litigation."

Why do you suppose Dr. Done's findings have not been published? Why are not findings prepared for use in litigation just as "helpful to the jury" as any other opinion? They are, after all, subject to cross-examination on credibility. Why not let the jury decide what weight the expert's opinion deserves?

On the Bendectin litigation, see generally M. Green, Bendectin and Birth Defects (1996); Sanders, From Science to Evidence: The Testimony of Causation in the Bendectin Cases, 46 Stan. L. Rev. 1 (1995).

3. Silicone Gel Breast Implant Litigation—Culpability vs. Causation. Cases involving the use of silicone gel breast implants and their alleged connection to a variety of illnesses are another example of the tension between science and law. Early cases found a connection between the implants and the auto-immune diseases alleged to stem from them though no research concerning the long-term health effects of the implants had been conducted. Hopkins v. Dow Corning Corp., 33 F.3d 1116 (9th Cir. 1994): "The longest study to address possible adverse health effects of the implants took place over only 80 days and revealed evidence of inflammatory immune response cause by the gel. Dow continued to market these implants ... without the benefit of a lifetime study to demonstrate the safety of its product." The jury's verdict for plaintiff was affirmed. After the *Hopkins* verdict, the FDA imposed a moratorium on cosmetic silicone gel breast implants and opened the first major investigation into their safety. See Feldman, Science and Uncertainty in Mass Exposure Litigation, 73 Tex. L. Rev. 1, 23–25 (1995)(describing studies of silicone gel breast implants).

There may not have been strong causal evidence but there was compelling evidence of Dow Corning's culpability: "Plaintiff presented evidence that Dow created a Mammary Task Force charged with getting the new gel implant to market in less than five months." Even after a task force member presented his concerns about "a possible gel bleed situation" Dow ignored proposed design modifications that would reduce the likelihood of leakage. Dow instructed salesmen to wash the implants with "soap and water" in the nearest rest room, and to "dry with hand towels as the implants become oily after being handled and [bleed] on the velvet in the showcase." *Hopkins*, 33 F.3d at 1123. Does compelling evidence of culpability taint evidence of causation? How do defendants keep evidence of culpability from potentially affecting the jury's determination of causation? From affecting the court's determinations on admissibility? Eventually Dow Corning filed bankruptcy from the potentially staggering liability based on early large verdicts.

After several large verdicts, the scientific evidence began to suggest there was no causal connection after all. Implant Global Settlement in Jeopardy, 81 A.B.A. J., August 1995, at 34 (National Institutes of Health (NIH)/Harvard study, most definitive study to date on health effects of implants, finds no connection); New Study Finds No Link Between Implants and Illnesses, N.Y. Times, June 22, 1995, at A12 (NIH study finds no major link but cautions that such diseases occur infrequently and study cannot be considered definitive). The NIH Study was prospective; it studied 87,500 nurses, beginning in 1976, 1100 of whom had implants. The researchers found that women with implants were, if anything, slightly less likely to develop connective tissue diseases. See Angell, Science on Trial: The Clash of Medical Evidence and the Law in the Breast Implant Cases (1996). The studies still do not "fully answer the question of whether the implants might lead to atypical symptoms related to the immune system in some women." New Study Finds No Link, N.Y. Times, June 22, 1995, at A12.

One court used a panel of experts to review the scientific evidence of causation. After the report, the court granted summary judgment to the defendants because the plaintiff's testimony of causation was inadmissible under *Daubert*. Hall v. Baxter Healthcare Corp., 947 F.Supp. 1387 (D.Ore. 1996). Another court affirmed summary judgment for defendant when plaintiff's experts did not deal at all with the adverse epidemiological studies and tried to establish causation on differential diagnosis theory alone. Norris v. Baxter Healthcare Corp., 397 F.3d 878 (10th Cir.2005). A national advisory panel appointed to evaluate the evidence for the federal MDL litigation concluded that silicone does not cause the immunologic illnesses claimed, though it can cause serious side effects from it leakage. Institute of Medicine, Safety of Silicone Breast Implants (1999). Six months after this report, the Bankruptcy Court in which the reorganization of Dow Corning was pending approved a $3.2 billion payment plan for the silicone-related injuries filed against the company. 27 Prod.Safety & Liab.Rep. (BNA) at 1157 (Dec. 3, 1999).

Was the Court of Appeals in *Daubert* right about the inability of courts to assess the reliability of scientific evidence?

4. For some toxic substances, the causal link to a particular disease is well established. Diseases for which a specified agent is the only cause are called "signature diseases," because the existence of the disease indicates the agent's causal role. Asbestos and its signature diseases asbestosis and mesothelioma are good examples. For other toxic substances, scientific methods lead only to the conclusion of strong uncertainty about general causation, as with Bendectin and silicone. For others, the dose-response relationship will be a primary factor. McClain v. Metabolife Int'l, Inc., 401 F.3d 1233 (11th Cir. 2005). Consider the following conclusions of one author:

> Perhaps the most striking characteristic of toxic causation cases is their diversity. In some, the defendant's responsibility for the plaintiff's injury is nearly indisputable; in others, defendants may be clearly innocent

of causal responsibility. Some cases involve individual plaintiffs who were exposed to rare chemicals; others involve thousands of plaintiffs and imperil the financial stability of entire industries. It is the beginning of wisdom to realize that no one approach can do justice under such diverse circumstances.

Farber, Toxic Causation, 71 Minn.L.Rev. 1219, 1259 (1987). The absence of epidemiologic evidence does not necessarily sound the death knell for general causation. See Restatement (3d) of Torts: Liability for Physical and Emotional Harm § 28, cmt. *c* ("[M]ost courts have appropriately declined to impose a threshold requirement that a plaintiff always must prove causation with epidemiologic evidence, and, in some cases, the evidence bearing on specific causation may be sufficient to pretermit the need to assess general causation."); Hollander v. Sandoz Pharms. Corp., 289 F.3d 1193 (10th Cir. 2002) (general causation need not in all cases require epidemiologic proof).

Should courts permit general causation to be established on the differential diagnoses of physicians alone, however, absent independent assessment of the toxicity of the agent? See Ruggiero v. Warner–Lambert Co., 424 F.3d 249 (2d Cir. 2005)(differential diagnosis testimony, alone, insufficient to establish general causation). See also Feldman, Science and Uncertainty in Mass Exposure Litigation, 73 Tex.L.Rev. 1 (1995)(strong scientific uncertainty about general causation dictates finding alternative approaches for proving causation; accepting uncertainty as conclusive of no causation frustrates tort law goals).

5. *Daubert*'s Effect. While many commentators believed that *Daubert* would make a plaintiff's case easier, reasoning that more testimony would be admissible under the Federal Rules of Evidence than under *Frye*, the post-*Daubert* experience has been to the contrary. See Owen, A Decade of *Daubert*, 80 Denv.U.L.Rev. 345, 365 (2002) ("[T]he fact remains that only infrequently do courts invoke *Daubert* to exclude expert testimony by defendants. Instead, courts almost always apply *Daubert* principles (often with good reason) to exclude a plaintiff's experts, and, hence, to bar the plaintiff's claim.").

6. See generally Golanski, General Causation at a Crossroads in Toxic Tort Cases, 108 Penn. St. L. Rev. 479 (2003); Cheng, Changing Scientific Evidence, 88 Minn.L.Rev. 315 (2003); Geistfeld, Scientific Uncertainty and Causation in Tort Law, 54 Vand.L.Rev. 1011 (2001); D. Owen, Products Liability Law § 11.5 (2d ed. 2008); 1 D. Owen, M.S. Madden, & M. Davis, Madden & Owen on Products Liability § 12:5 (3d ed. 2000).

———

B. Specific Causation—Whether Plaintiff's Disease Was Caused by the Agent

In Re Agent Orange Product Liability Litigation

United States District Court, Eastern District of New York, 1984.
597 F.Supp. 740, aff'd, 818 F.2d 145 (2d Cir.1987).

■ Weinstein, Chief Judge.

* * *

PREFACE AND SUMMARY

In 1979 a class action was commenced charging the United States government and a major portion of the chemical industry with deaths and dreadful injuries to tens of thousands of Vietnam veterans who came in contact with herbicides used in the war in Southeast Asia. The suit also claimed that as a result of the veterans' exposure, their children suffer severe birth defects. After five years of numerous motions and extensive discovery a tentative settlement was reached on the eve of trial.

The sole question before this court is whether the case against the chemical companies should now be settled. Eleven days of nationwide hearings were conducted to give the class members themselves an opportunity to be heard on the merits of the settlement. After weighing the uncertainties and legal obstacles that would accompany years of protracted litigation were the case to go to trial, the court has concluded that the settlement should be approved.

* * *

The many legal issues are unique and the factual issues unresolved by the scientific communities addressing them. But it is neither fact nor law that makes this decision such a difficult one—rather, it is the deeply charged emotions that surround and engulf the litigation.

In listening to hundreds of witnesses around the country and reading the poignant letters of many veterans, their wives and parents, a repeated refrain makes it clear that more than money is at stake. The veterans feel that out of love of country they went to its aid and fought bravely in a brutal war. In return, they believe, they were sprayed with chemicals that insidiously are destroying them. They were vilified by their countrymen on their return because the war became unpopular. Their perception is that they are denied proper treatment by the Veterans Administration to the point where many of them shun the VA's medical and other facilities. Their families suffer as they waste away. And, perhaps even more important, they fear that they have been damaged genetically so that many choose to have no children or live in the despair of having sired children with birth defects who may spread this genetic damage to future generations.

Vietnam veterans and their families desperately want this suit to demonstrate how they have been mistreated by the country they love. They want it to give them the respect they have earned. They want it to protect the public against future harm by the government and chemical companies. They want a jury "once-and-for-all" to demonstrate the connection between Agent Orange and the physical, mental and emotional problems from which many of them clearly do suffer.

The court has been deeply moved by its contact with members of the plaintiffs' class from all over the nation and abroad. Many do deserve better of their country. Had this court the power to rectify past wrongs—actual or perceived—it would do so. But no single litigation can lift all of plaintiffs' burdens. The legislative and executive branches of government—state and federal—and the Veterans Administration, as well as our many private and quasi-public medical and social agencies, are far more capable than this court of shaping the larger remedies and emotional compensation plaintiffs seek.

Within the sharply limited judicial role we must ask whether the settlement of the litigation proposed by the parties' representatives is acceptable. For the reasons indicated below we tentatively hold that it is. It gives the class more than it would likely achieve by attempting to litigate to the death. It provides funds to help at least some men, women and children whose hardships will be reduced in some small degree. It does represent a major step in the essential process of reconciliation among ourselves.

[Sections III and IV discuss the factual and legal obstacles confronting the parties if the case were to go to trial. Section III, Factual Problems with Claims, summarizes the inconclusive evidence of causation that the plaintiffs have adduced in support of their allegations. This is due in part to the difficulty of proof in any toxic substance litigation and in part to the weakness in proof of causal relationship as demonstrated in the epidemiological studies completed to date. Because of the epidemiological nature of much of the evidence, no *individual plaintiff* would likely be able to prove that his or her particular adverse health effects are due to Agent Orange exposure.] It may be possible—through the use of the class action device— to overcome this obstacle by making a single, class-wide determination of liability and by distributing the damages charged to all defendants as a group among all class members on a pro rata basis. At the present time, however, it is doubtful whether the legal system is ready to employ this device except, perhaps, as part of an overall settlement plan voluntarily entered into by the parties.

IV. LEGAL PROBLEMS WITH CLAIMS

[Plaintiffs face enormous legal problems before they could succeed in obtaining relief.]

B. Failure to Determine Who Was Harmed and Who Caused Harm

Defendants contend that even if anyone was injured by Agent Orange, plaintiffs cannot establish that the harm to any one of them was caused by any [of the defendants.]

(b) The Problem of the Indeterminate Plaintiff

[E]ven if plaintiffs as a class could prove that they were injured by Agent Orange, no individual class member would be able to prove that his or her injuries were caused by Agent Orange. For example, plaintiffs as a class may be able to show that statistically, X% of the population not exposed to Agent Orange could have been expected to develop soft-tissue sarcoma, but that among those veterans who were exposed to Agent Orange, X + Y% suffer from soft-tissue sarcoma. If Y is equal to or less than X and there is no meaningful "particularistic" or anecdotal proof as to the vast majority of plaintiffs, virtually no plaintiff would be able to show by a preponderance of the evidence that his or her cancer is attributable to the Agent Orange rather than being part of the "background" level of cancer in the population as a whole. The probability of specific cause would necessarily be less than 50% based upon the evidence submitted.

(1) Scope of the Problem

The problem just noted is one that has received a significant amount of scholarly discussion as well as some attention from the United States Congress. See, e.g., Rosenberg, The Causal Connection in Mass Exposure Cases: A "Public Law" Vision of the Tort System, 97 Harv.L.Rev. 849 (1984); Black and Lilienfeld, Epidemiological Proof in Toxic Tort Litigation, 52 Fordham L.Rev. 732, 782–83 (1984); [citations]. Because of the rarity of the situation until recently scant attention has been given to the issue by the courts. There has apparently been only one other mass exposure decision that has discussed the indeterminate plaintiff problem explicitly, *viz.* Allen v. United States, 588 F.Supp. 247 (D.Utah 1984), a case where injury was claimed as a result of radiation exposure from testing of atomic explosive devices.

In our complex industrialized society it is unfortunately possible that some products used on a widespread scale will cause significant harm to the public. While it may be possible to prove, through the use of such proof as laboratory tests on animals and epidemiological evidence, that such harm— for example cancer—can be "caused" by a particular substance, it may be impossible to pinpoint which particular person's cancer would have occurred naturally and which would not have occurred but for exposure to the substance.

* * *

In two of the largest and most widely publicized mass tort litigations, those involving DES and asbestos, the problem outlined above does not pose a serious obstacle since at least some of the damage caused by the harmful substance was, it has been claimed, unique to that substance. Adenosis and clear cell adenocarcinoma of the vagina and uterus, the conditions associated with DES, are, it is said, almost unknown among women whose mothers had not taken DES. [Citation.] The situation is similar, in the asbestos litigation, albeit to a lesser extent. Although lung cancer is associated with cigarette smoking and other factors as well as asbestos exposure and mesothelioma may have causes other than asbestos, [citation] asbestosis is alleged to be uniquely associated with asbestos exposure. Borel v. Fibreboard Paper Products Corp., 493 F.2d 1076, 1083 (5th Cir.1973). In most other mass exposure cases, however, the harm caused by the toxic substance is indistinguishable from the naturally occurring disease or condition. [Citations].

The recent case of *Allen v. United States*, illustrates the problem well. Plaintiffs claimed that they developed various forms of cancer as a result of their exposure to radiation from nuclear explosions. While some forms of cancer can, it is contended, with some certainty be attributed to factors other than exposure to radiation, many others "cannot be distinguished from cancer of the same organ arising from ... unknown causes", i.e., the "background" cancers. J. Gofman, Radiation and Human Health 59 (1981), quoted in *Allen*. The statistical evidence in *Allen* apparently made it clear that there was a strong positive association between exposure to low-level ionizing radiation, presumably the result of atomic explosions, and various forms of cancer suffered by plaintiffs. Thus, the *Allen* case has some of the characteristics of the DES and asbestos cases in addition to persuasive statistical correlations.

(2) Preponderance Rule

Even if there were near certainty as to general causation, if there were significant uncertainty as to individual causation, traditional tort principles would dictate that causation be determined on a case-by-case basis using the preponderance-of-the-evidence rule. Santosky v. Kramer, 455 U.S. 745, 755 (1982); [citations]. The rule provides an " 'all or nothing' approach, whereby [assuming all other elements of the cause of action are proven], the plaintiff becomes entitled to full compensation for those . . . damages that are proved to be 'probable' (a greater than 50 percent chance), but is not entitled to any compensation if the proof does not establish a greater than 50 percent chance." Jackson v. Johns–Manville Sales Corp., 727 F.2d 506, 516 (5th Cir.1984).

Under the "strong" version of the preponderance rule, statistical correlations alone indicating that the probability of causation exceeds fifty percent are insufficient; some "particularistic" or anecdotal evidence, that is, "proof that can provide direct and actual knowledge of the causal relationship between the defendant's tortious conduct and the plaintiff's injury," is required. Rosenberg, *supra*. [Citations.] As Professor Jaffee has put it,

> If all that can be said is that there are 55 chances of negligence out of 100, that is not enough. There must be a *rational,* i.e., evidentiary basis on which the jury can choose the competing probabilities. If there is not, the finding will be based . . . on mere speculation and conjecture.

Jaffee, Res Ipsa Loquitur Vindicated, 1 Buffalo L.Rev. 1, 4 (1951). The "weak" version of the preponderance rule would allow a verdict solely on statistical evidence; the "all-or-nothing" approach converts the statistical probability into a legally absolute finding that the causal connection did or did not exist in the case. . . .

There would appear to be little harm in retaining the requirement for "particularistic" evidence of causation in sporadic accident cases since such evidence is almost always available in such litigation. In mass exposure cases, however, where the chance that there would be particularistic evidence is in most cases quite small, the consequence of retaining the requirement might be to allow defendants who, it is virtually certain, have injured thousands of people and caused billions of dollars in damages, to escape liability. Because of this fact and the fact that "particularistic evidence . . . is . . . no less probabilistic than . . . statistical evidence," the "weak" version of the preponderance rule appears to be the preferable standard to apply in mass exposure cases—particularly where, as here, all claimants and defendants are joined in one suit.

(a) Application of the Preponderance Rule to Mass Exposure Cases

Conventional application of the "weak" version of the preponderance rule would dictate that, if the toxic substance caused the incidence of the injury to rise more than 100% above the "background" level, each plaintiff exposed to the substance could recover if he or she is suffering from that type of injury. If, however, to put it in somewhat graphic, albeit artificial terms, the incidence rose only 100% or less, no plaintiff could recover—i.e., the probability of specific causation would not be more than 50%.

Where a plaintiff's injuries result from a series of unrelated sporadic accidents, this "all-or-nothing" rule is justifiably rationalized on the ground that it is the fairest and most efficient result. In mass exposure cases, however, this all-or-nothing rule results in either a tortious defendant being relieved of all liability or overcompensation to many plaintiffs and a crushing liability on the defendant. These results are especially troublesome because, unlike the sporadic accident cases, it may be possible to ascertain with a fair degree of assurance that the defendant did cause damage, and, albeit with somewhat less certainty, the total amount of that damage.

The problem is both illustrated and further compounded by the fact that lack of precision in the data and models used may cause the range of the probabilities estimated by the statistical proof to lie on either or both sides of the 100% line. Because the statistical proof will almost never be as complete or as free from confounding factors as desirable, it may be possible to infer, for example, that the toxic substance caused the incidence to rise over the background level somewhere between 80 and 120%. [Citation.] Moreover, issues of credibility and varying inferences drawn by the trier based upon varying assessments of probative force may cause reasonable people to assess these percentages in a range from almost zero to well over 120. [Citation.]

Under the traditional application of the preponderance rule, whether individual plaintiffs recover will depend on where the probability percentage line is drawn despite the fact that a reasonable trier would conclude that a large proportion of the plaintiffs were injured by the defendant and a large number were not. Even if the statistical increase attributed to the substance in question is just a few percentage points, if statistical theory supports a finding of correlation there is no reason why the industry as a whole should not pay for the damages it probably caused.

A simple hypothetical will illustrate why too heavy a burden should not be placed on plaintiffs by requiring a high percentage or incidence of a disease to be attributable to a particular product. Let us assume that there are 10 manufacturers and a population of 10 million persons exposed to their product. Assume that among this population 1,000 cancers of a certain type could be expected, but that 1,100 exist, and that this increase is "statistically significant," permitting a reasonable conclusion that 100 cancers are due to the product of the manufacturers. In the absence of other evidence, it might be argued that as to any one of the 1100 there is only a chance of about 9% (100/1100) that the product caused the cancer. Under traditional tort principles no plaintiff could recover.

(b) *Inadequacy of Individualized Solutions*

Any attempt to resolve the problem on a plaintiff-by-plaintiff basis cannot be fully satisfactory. The solution that would most readily suggest itself is a burden shifting approach, analogous to that used in the indeterminate defendant situation already discussed. *Allen* provides a good example of how burden-shifting would be applied in an indeterminate plaintiff case. A plaintiff must show that the defendant, in that case the United States, negligently put "an identifiable population group" of which he was a member at "increased risk" and that his injury is

> consistent with having been caused by the hazard to which he has been negligently subjected, such consistency having been demonstrated by substantial, appropriate, persuasive and connecting factors....

At that point, the burden shifts to the defendant which will be held liable unless it can offer "persuasive proof" of noncausation.

Generally courts have shifted the burden to the defendant to prove that it was not responsible for plaintiff's injury only in sporadic accident cases where it was certain that one of a very limited number of defendants injured the plaintiff, see, e.g., Summers v. Tice, 199 P.2d 1 (Cal.1948); Ybarra v. Spangard, 154 P.2d 687 (Cal.1944), or in mass exposure cases where general causation was certain and liability was apportioned in accordance with some market-share theory. See, e.g., Sindell v. Abbott Laboratories, 607 P.2d 924 (Cal.1980); [citations].

Shifting the burden of proof in such cases will, at least theoretically, not result in crushing liability for the defendant either because the litigation only involves a sporadic accident, as in *Summers* and *Ybarra,* or because the defendant will only be held liable for the amount of damage it caused based on market share ... By contrast, shifting the burden of proof in the indeterminate plaintiff situation could result in liability far out of proportion to damage caused. It is not helpful in most situations to say that the defendant will not be liable for "those harms which [he] can reasonably prove were *not* in fact a consequence of his risk-creating, negligent conduct," *Allen,* since, were such individualized proof available, there would have been no need to shift the burden.

(3) Possible Solution in Class Action

Since the problem results from a plaintiff-by-plaintiff method of adjudication, one solution is to try all plaintiffs' claims together in a class action thereby arriving at a single, class-wide determination of the total harm to the community of plaintiffs. Given the necessarily heavy reliance on statistical evidence in mass exposure cases, such a determination seems feasible. The defendant would then be liable to each exposed plaintiff for a pro rata share of that plaintiff's injuries.

This approach can be illustrated using the hypothetical given above. Suppose all 1,100 of those who were exposed to the harmful substance and who developed the cancer in the example join in a class action against all 10 manufacturers. Let us say that damages average $1,000,000 per cancer. A recovery of $100,000,000 (100 × $1,000,000) in favor of the class would be allowed with the percentage of the award to be paid by each manufacturer depending on the toxicity of its product. For example, if a company produced only 20% of the substance in question but, because of the greater toxicity of its product, likely caused 60% of the harm, it would contribute 60% of the total amount. If accurate records are available on the composition of each defendant's product, that analysis should be possible.

Since no plaintiff can show that his or her cancer was caused by any one of the defendants, they should divide the $100,000,000 by 1,100, giving each a recovery of about $90,000. While any plaintiff might feel that his or her recovery denigrated the degree of harm, the alternative of receiving nothing is far worse. The latter is, of course, the necessary result in any plaintiff's individual suit. Moreover, the deterrent effect of this result on producers would be significant. See Delgado, Beyond *Sindell:* Relaxation of Cause-in-Fact Rules for Indeterminate Plaintiffs, 70 Cal.L.Rev. 881, 893 (1982).

If the number of cases were only 1,050, most statisticians would say the difference was not statistically significant and a court using the pro rata approach might find that the defendant is not legally responsible for any of the increased incidence. But see *Allen*, 588 F.Supp. at 416–17 (noting that although increased incidence might be deemed "insignificant" by a scientist or statistician, it may well be that it "is still far more likely than not" that "the observed increase is related to its hypothetical cause rather than mere chance"). . . .

Putting a dollar amount on the damages suffered by individual plaintiffs is, from a real-world standpoint, a critical part of the solution. If the judicial and monetary economies of the class action are not to be lost through lengthy and expensive individual trials on damages, some mechanism must be devised to decide damage claims without the need for a full-fledged trial for each plaintiff. As Professor Rosenberg points out, "[p]ossibly the greatest source of litigation expense [in mass exposure tort litigation] is the individual assessment and distribution of damages that must follow trial of common liability questions." Rosenberg, *supra.*

* * *

Every effort should be made to reduce questions of fact to a bare minimum. A preferred solution is to pay claims on a fixed and somewhat arbitrary schedule using a ministerial agency as is done with the Medicaid and Medicare programs where disbursements are made by insurance agencies acting for the United States.

No matter what system is used the purpose is to hold a defendant liable for no more than the aggregate loss fairly attributable to its tortious conduct. As long as that goal is met a defendant can have no valid objection that its rights have been violated.

* * *

Conclusion as to Indeterminate Plaintiffs and Defendants

The vexing problems of toxic torts probably would be best dealt with by legislation. In the absence of legislative and executive action courts must attempt to devise the most effective and equitable means of dealing with them through approaches that are consonant with present law and reasonable predictions about trends in the law. . . .

There is a strong likelihood that even if some causal link could be established between Agent Orange and the diseases and conditions from which plaintiffs claim they are suffering, it would be impossible in most cases to identify the individual class members who were injured by Agent Orange. Given the desirability of resolving the indeterminate plaintiff problem using a form of proportional liability or some other acceptable method, a dismissal of the class action would be unwarranted. The statistical theory, available data, and public policy are far from settled. Particularly during this period of rapidly changing scientific approaches and increased threats to the environment, we should not unduly restrict development of legal theory and practice—both substantive and procedural—by dismissing a class action such as the one now before us although the hazards of an ultimate dismissal must be considered in assessing the fairness of the settlement. [Like inhibitions against dismissal of individual actions do not exist.]

VIII. CONCLUSION

In conclusion it is well to remind ourselves of President Lincoln's admonition which is as relevant now, almost fifteen years after the end of the Vietnam war, as it was six score years ago. In his Second Inaugural Address he urged us "to bind up the nation's wounds; to care for him who shall have borne the battle and for his widow, and his orphan—to do all which may achieve and cherish a just and lasting peace among ourselves. . . . It is time for the government to join with plaintiffs and defendants in even greater efforts toward this noble goal. Whether their hurt can be traced to Agent Orange or whether they are merely 'casually unfortunate,' " C.L. Black, Jr., The Human Imagination in the Great Society, 5 (1983), is beside the point in the broader context of the nation's obligations to Vietnam veterans and their families.

IX. ORDER

The settlement is approved subject to hearings on fees and preliminary consideration of plans for distribution. This order is not final.

So Ordered.

NOTES

1. In 1986, the New York Times reported that "the medical case against Agent Orange is but a shadow." Agent Orange—Let it Lie, N.Y. Times, Sept. 4, 1986, at 26. The debate over a causal link between Agent Orange and the veterans' ailments continues, however. The Centers for Disease Control concluded in 1990 that no causal connection existed. Clean Bill for Agent Orange, Time, April 9, 1990, at 82. Critics charged that the CDC's work had been a fraud. A Cover–Up on Agent Orange?, Time, July 23, 1990, at 27. Three years later, the National Academy of Sciences' Institute of Medicine concluded that Agent Orange can be linked conclusively to three cancers, including Hodgkin's disease. Agent Orange Redux, Time, August 9, 1993, at 51.

How should the legal system respond to the evolving nature of scientific evidence of causation? Should the courts stay proceedings until the science is there? Should parties whose cases are decided on what is ultimately proved to have been bad science be given relief from the judgment? See Fed.R.Civ.P.60. In Stephenson v. Dow Chemical, 273 F.3d 249 (2d Cir. 2001), plaintiffs whose Agent Orange illnesses manifested themselves after the settlement expired in 1994 sued, challenging the adequacy of representation in the prior class action. Judge Weinstein held the claims were barred, but the court of appeals reversed. A divided Supreme Court affirmed in part and reversed in part. 539 U.S. 111 (2003).

2. *Agent Orange* aside, it is rare for a case to be litigated on "naked statistical evidence." See Parascandola, What is Wrong with the Probability of Causation, 39 Jurimetrics J. 29 (1998). Inadequacies in available epidemiological studies and idiosyncratic factors peculiar to the plaintiff's case must be evaluated in addition to any probabilities generated by epidemiological evidence. These individual factors may include a medical history indicating the possibility of increased susceptibility, an alternative disease with the same or similar clinical symptoms, or conflicting evidence about plaintiff's diagnosis, symptoms, or their onset. See, e.g., In re Hanford Nuclear Reservation Litig., 292 F.3d 1124 (9th Cir. 2002)(recognizing importance of individual circumstances); Donaldson v. Central Ill. Pub. Serv. Co., 767 N.E.2d 314 (Ill. 2002) (limited exposure; very few cases of disease).

3. The literature evaluating the use and the appropriateness of statistics and probability theory as aspects of the fact-finding process in the civil justice system is rich. One common theme is the legal system's need to provide an answer in the face of uncertainty. Another is the existence of social policies that may conflict with the principle of maximizing accurate fact-finding. A third is the extent to which jurors, in assessing evidence and reaching a verdict, might be assisted (or, alternatively, misled) by formal models of statistical decision-making theory. See, e.g., Kaye & Freedman, Reference Guide on Statistics, in Federal Judicial Center, Reference Manual on Scientific Evidence 83 (2d ed. 2000) (explaining problems in using statistical evidence to determine an individual's causal connection to an agent). See generally Barnes, Too Many Probabilities: Statistical Evidence of Tort Causation, 64 Law & Contemp. Probs. 191 (2001); Finkelstein and Levin, Statistics for Lawyers and Law for Statistics, 89 Mich. L. Rev. 1520 (1991).

4. Proof of Exposure. Plaintiff has the burden of proving exposure to the toxic substance. The matter is complicated when multiple defendants and their toxic agents are involved. Dosage is an important variable in the effect that a toxic agent has on any individual. Minimal exposures may not play any (or any significant) role in the plaintiff's disease. This concern was reflected in Lohrmann v. Pittsburgh Corning Corp., 782 F.2d 1156, 1162–64 (4th Cir.1986). The court there held that a plaintiff who had been employed as a shipyard pipefitter for 39 years could not recover against three asbestos defendants. Although the three defendants' products were present at the shipyard, there was no evidence to demonstrate that plaintiff was exposed to those products. Without proof of regular use of products, proximity to them by the plaintiff, and over an extended period of time, plaintiff could not meet his burden to show that the products were a substantial cause of his injury.

Lohrmann's tripartite *regularity, proximity*, and *frequency* standard has been adopted by a number of other courts. Chism v. W.R. Grace & Co., 158 F.3d 988 (8th Cir. 1998); James v. Bessemer Processing Co., 714 A.2d 898 (N.J. 1998) (*Lohrmann* test also applies to non-asbestos products). Compare Horton v. Harwick Chemical Corp., 653 N.E.2d 1196 (Ohio 1995) (*Lohrmann* test rejected; creates overly burdensome standard).

Plaintiffs also developed the "fiber drift" theory to connect a defendant's asbestos products at a worksite with a plaintiff's exposure and consequent disease. The theory relies on the fact that asbestos fibers easily travel through the air and thus migrate around a worksite. Robertson v. Allied Signal, Inc., 914 F.2d 360 (3d Cir.1990), the leading case adopting the fiber drift theory, held that expert witness testimony of fiber migration could satisfy the "proximity" aspect of the *Lohrmann* test, but that plaintiff would still be required to prove *regular use* of the product and *frequent presence* by the plaintiff in an area to which the asbestos might have migrated. See generally Celotex Corp. v. Catrett, 477 U.S. 317 (1986)(summary judgment proper where claimant failed to meet burden of proof on asbestos exposure).

5. Experts and Sufficiency. If all a plaintiff has is an expert's opinion on the statistical link between an agent and a disease, like those in *Daubert* and *DeLuca*, that may not be enough to prove that *plaintiff's* disease was caused by the agent. Recall that the issue here is not the *admissibility* of the evidence but its *sufficiency* to establish causation by the requisite standard of proof. See, e.g., In re Joint E. & S. Dist. Asbestos Litig., 52 F.3d 1124 (2d Cir.1995), in which a jury found that a plaintiff's colon cancer had been caused by asbestos, and the district court granted the defendants' motion for j.n.o.v.:

> Although we conclude that *Daubert* did not alter the traditional sufficiency standard, . . . we acknowledge that sufficiency poses unique difficulties for trial courts in toxic or carcinogenic tort cases, such as the one before us, which hinge on competing interpretations of epidemiological evidence. . . . In light of the inherent uncertainty shrouding issues of probabilistic causation, the decision of a district court on whether plaintiff's epidemiological evidence is sufficient to get to the jury should be guided by the well-established standards governing judgment as a matter of law. . . .

> Applied to epidemiological studies, the question is not whether there is some dispute about the validity or force of a given study, but rather, whether it would be unreasonable for a rational jury to rely on that study to find causation by a preponderance of the evidence. . . . Unlike admissibility assessments, which involve decisions about individual pieces of evidence, sufficiency assessments entail a review of the sum total of a plaintiff's evidence.

Held, j.n.o.v. reversed, and plaintiff's verdict reinstated. A number of state courts have relaxed the sufficiency requirement on toxic substance causation. See, e.g., Bloomquist v. Wapello County, 500 N.W.2d 1 (Iowa 1993)(epidemiological studies not required to present jury question on causation; court reiterated commitment to principle that issues of proximate cause are only rarely decided as a matter of law); Landrigan v. Celotex Corp., 605 A.2d 1079 (N.J.1992)(relaxed causation standard approved; proof that a toxic substance caused decedent's injuries more subtle and sophisticated than proof in traditional torts). See generally Faigman, How Good is Good Enough?: Expert Evidence Under *Daubert* and *Kumho*, 50 Case. W. Res.L.Rev. 645 (2000).

6. Proportional Recovery. Has the time come, at least in toxic substance cases, to consider arguments for proportional recovery? Recall the cases recognizing recovery for increased risk of harm in medical negligence cases. Herskovits v. Group Health Co-op. of Puget Sound, 664 P.2d 474, 479–87 (Wash.1983). In terms of the practical politics of toxic substance litigation, the strength of the causation evidence is likely to play a prominent—perhaps the predominant—role in establishing a settlement value for the litigation. For a comprehensive discussion, see Gifford, The Challenge to the Individual Causation Requirement in Mass Products Torts, 62 Wash. & Lee L.Rev. 873 (2005).

C. IDENTIFYING THE PARTY RESPONSIBLE FOR THE AGENT

If a plaintiff can successfully establish that a toxic substance to which he was exposed caused his particular disease, and that he was exposed to that toxic substance in an amount sufficient to permit a jury to conclude that he more likely than not acquired the disease through his exposure, he must then identify the defendant(s) that produced the toxic substance to which he was exposed. In many toxic substance cases involving workplace exposure, like asbestos cases, this product identification requirement means plaintiff must obtain records of the products used at the worksites where plaintiff was exposed, perhaps spanning decades. While this is a daunting task, records may exist that will assist the plaintiff in establishing the defendants who made the products to which he was exposed. What tools are available for plaintiffs for whom evidence of the identity of the relevant defendant(s) is not possible?

The most promising defendant identification theory in toxic substance cases has undoubtedly been market share liability, discussed in chapter 12. The DES cases, with hundreds of manufacturers using a generic prescription drug formula which injured plaintiffs in utero, begged for a solution to the insurmountable defendant identification hurdles plaintiffs faced. Nevertheless, most jurisdictions rejected the theory. Smith v. Eli Lilly & Co., 560 N.E.2d (Ill. 1990)(summarizing the variety of approaches to the issue and concluding the theory posed too great a change from traditional practice). The New York Court of Appeals in Hymowitz v. Eli Lilly & Co., 539 N.E.2d 1069 (N.Y. 1989), endorsed the theory in the face of a legislative extension of the statute of limitations in DES cases. The Court acknowledged that the national market approach it chose could not provide a reasonable link between liability and the risk created by a defendant to a particular plaintiff. Rather, the liability corresponded to the over-all culpability of each defendant to the public-at-large. A radical departure from traditional tort principles? Fair nevertheless? For a thorough study of the history of DES and the *Hymowitz* case in particular, see Bernstein, *Hymowitz v. Eli Lilly and Co.*: Markets of Mothers, Torts Stories, 151 (R. Rabin & S. Sugarman eds. 2003).

Should the market share concept be extended to other toxic substances?

Thomas v. Mallett

Supreme Court of Wisconsin, 2005.
285 Wis.2d 236, 701 N.W.2d 523.

■ BUTLER, J.

Steven Thomas, by his guardian ad litem, seeks review of a court of appeals decision that declined to extend the risk-contribution theory announced in Collins v. Eli Lilly Co., 342 N.W.2d 37 (Wis. 1984), to the defendant lead pigment manufacturers [including American Cyanamid Co., Atlantic Richfield Co., DuPont, and Sherwin–Williams Co. (collectively "Pigment Manufacturers"). We find that the lead pigment] claims at issue in this case are factually similar enough to *Collins* to warrant extension of the risk-contribution theory....

Because this case is before us on summary judgment, we construe all facts and reasonable inferences in the light most favorable to [Thomas. He] was born on June 23, 1990. He claims that he sustained lead poisoning by ingesting lead paint from accessible painted surfaces, paint chips, and paint flakes and dust at two different houses he lived in during the early 1990's. [Both houses were built between 1900 and 1905. Thomas exhibited symptoms of early onset of childhood lead poisoning since he was 14 months old when testing of his cognitive skills identified deficits in perceptual organization, visual motor integration, expressive language, academic and fine motor skills coupled with an attention deficit hyperactivity disorder. His blood lead levels were well above recommended minimums throughout his early life. The City of Milwaukee Health Department documented lead-based violations at both homes where he lived during the time.]

According to Dr. John F. Rosen, a professor of pediatrics ..., Thomas's cognitive deficits are a "signature or constellation of cognitive effects" that are typical of lead poisoning, [and, in Thomas' case, permanent.] In addition, due to Thomas's elevated [blood lead levels] over the extended period of time, Thomas will require lifetime medical monitoring surveillance for physical disorders, as he is now at a high risk for developing future medical complications, including kidney and cardiovascular disease. Rosen opines that Thomas's high lead levels are exclusively derived from ingesting lead based pigments in paint. [The Pigment Manufacturers agreed, for purposes of summary judgment, that Thomas could present enough evidence to create a jury question on whether his claimed injuries were caused by his ingestion of lead.]

[Thomas' expert toxicologist, Dr. Mushak, chemically analyzed various paint samples collected from the prior residences. He concluded that all contained detectable levels of only the lead contaminant known as white lead carbonate. Chromium and sulfate pigments along with white lead carbonate pigments were the essential lead pigments used for residences. White lead carbonate was the principal pigment used, however.... Dr. Mushak opines to a reasonable degree of scientific certainty that the houses contain lead paint made with white lead carbonate pigment. He also testified that "while lead exposure may qualitatively and potentially arise from various sources of the toxic element, the qualitative and quantitative nature of the lead source at issue in this case, lead paint, is such that (i) it dwarfs other lead sources in terms of lead concentration and intensity of exposure and (ii) it comprises the lead source most actively providing lead exposure and poisoning in the exposure settings here: lead paint present in properties occupied or visited by Thomas."]

As noted, the houses where Thomas alleges he ingested lead paint were built in 1900 and 1905. During that period, use of lead paint for residences was common. Lead paint contained up to 50 percent lead pigment and maintained widespread use through the 1940s. The use and manufacturing of interior lead-based paints declined during the 1950s, and in 1955, the lead industry voluntarily adopted a standard of the American National Standards Institute that limited lead content to a maximum of one percent in paints intended for children's toys, furniture, and interior surfaces. However, lead paint for interiors continued to be available until the 1970s. [Lead paint for interior and exterior household use was regulated in the early 1970s so that by 1978, use of lead paint for residential interiors containing more than 0.06 percent lead by weight was banned. 16 C.F.R. § 1303.2(b)(2) (2005).]

Although all of the Pigment Manufacturers ... manufactured white lead carbonate at various times during the existence of Thomas's prior residences, Thomas conceded that he cannot identify the specific pigment manufacturer that produced the white lead carbonate he ingested. The Pigment Manufacturers moved for summary judgment, arguing, as relevant here, that Thomas could not prove causation in fact or proximate cause; [and that] *Collins v. Eli Lilly* [which recognized a version of market share liability called risk contribution] should not be extended outside the unique circumstances of diethylstilbestrol (DES). [The trial court granted the defendants' summary judgment and the court of appeals affirmed.]

A problem facing Thomas, who alleges that he was injured by white lead carbonate pigment, is that he is unable to identify the precise producer of the white lead carbonate pigment he ingested at his prior residences due to the generic nature of the pigment, the number of producers, the lack of pertinent records, and the passage of time.... Some courts have simply denied extension of market-share liability under these circumstances and thus denied lead pigment plaintiffs recovery. [E.g., Santiago v. Sherwin Williams Co., 3 F.3d 546 (1st Cir. 1993)]. However, the question presented is whether *Collins'* risk-contribution theory should be extended to white lead carbonate claims. We agree that it should.

The following backdrop provides the relevant context for determining whether *Collins'* risk contribution theory should be recognized for white lead carbonate claims.... According to the Center for Disease Control, ...

it is well-recognized that given children's rapidly developing nervous systems, "[c]hildren are particularly susceptible to lead's toxic effects." [Citation.] Because the human body cannot differentiate between lead and calcium, after lead has remained in the bloodstream for a few weeks, it is then absorbed into bones, where it can collect for a lifetime. [Citation.] Once lead enters the child's system, more lead is absorbed than would be in adults. [Citation. Because of the normal hand-to-mouth activities of children, they are exposed to more non-food items in their gastrointestinal tract than adults. The ingestion of more non-food substances has been implicated in cases of lead poisoning; however, a child does not have to eat paint chips to become poisoned. It is more common for children to ingest dust and soil contaminated with lead from paint that either has flaked or chalked as it aged or has been otherwise disturbed during home maintenance or renovation.] "This lead-contaminated house dust, ingested via normal repetitive hand-to-mouth activity, is now recognized as a major contributor to the total body burden of lead in children." [Citation.] Thus, "[b]ecause of the critical role of dust as an exposure pathway, children living in sub-standard housing and in homes undergoing renovation are at particular risk for lead poisoning." ... Although lead can originate from many different materials, such as food, soil, water, or air, lead paint is the primary culprit....

[Plaintiff introduced evidence that the Pigment Manufacturers or their predecessors knew, since the 1880s, of the significant risks of exposure from lead-based paint. Parallel with the emergence of the knowledge of the dangers caused by lead in industrial and residential settings was the awareness of childhood lead poisoning. During the mid–1800s, child lead poisoning was already linked to mouthing lead-painted toys. During the mid to late 1920s, the view that children were more susceptible to lead poisoning was "almost universal." In 1928, rising alarms regarding the hazards of lead spurred lead producers and manufacturers to form the Lead Industries Association (LIA) to respond to "the undesirable publicity regarding lead poisoning." Throughout the next several decades, the LIA considered the problem of childhood lead poisoning as "a major headache." The LIA and the Pigment Manufacturers continued to promote and sell white lead paints for interior use well after the mid 1940s. In 1957, the LIA recognized that lead paint was the major source of childhood lead poisoning. Nevertheless, the promotion and marketing of paint containing white lead continued well into the 1960s.]

According to [plaintiff's public health experts,] the Pigment Manufacturers' marketing and ad campaigns created an enduring belief among consumers that the best paint was lead paint—as National Lead stated, "Remember, also that the more white-lead you use, the better the paint." They further opine that "notwithstanding repeated statements over the years that it no longer produced white lead paint for interior use, the industry continued to sell white lead paints that were applied on interiors."

IV

We begin our analysis with a discussion of *Collins.* In that case, the plaintiff developed adenocarcinoma of the vagina and benign adenosis of the vagina in 1975. [Citation.] While she was in utero in 1957, her mother used diethylstilbestrol (DES) to prevent miscarriage. In 1971, medical researchers established "a possible statistical link between fetal exposure to DES during pregnancy and the development many years later of adenocarcinoma of the vagina." The plaintiff's mother could not remember where she purchased the DES or who manufactured it. By that time, many mothers had taken DES during their pregnancies. [Plaintiff sued 12 drug companies, all of which produced or marketed DES. She was unable to identify the precise manufacturer of the DES taken by her mother due to its generic status, the number of producers, the lack of pertinent records, and the passage of time. This court recognized that the traditional causation requirement posed an insurmountable obstacle for her.]

Thus, this court was faced "with a choice of either fashioning a method of recovery for the DES case which will deviate from traditional notions of tort law, or permitting possibly negligent defendants to escape liability to an innocent, injured plaintiff." [Citation.] "In the interests of justice and fundamental fairness," this court chose the former.

* * * First, "[e]ach defendant contributed to the *risk* of injury to the public and, consequently, the risk of injury to individual plaintiffs...." [Citation.] In this sense, each shared some measure of culpability in producing or marketing the drug. Second, because the drug companies were in a better position to absorb the cost of the injury (through either insurance, incorporation of the damage awards, or by passing the cost along to the public as "a cost of doing business"), this court concluded that "it is better to have drug companies or consumers share the cost of the injury than to place the burden solely on the innocent plaintiff." Third, the court recognized that "the cost of damages awards will act as an incentive for drug companies to test adequately the drugs they place on the market for general medical use."

Under the risk-contribution theory as stated in *Collins,* a plaintiff need commence an action against only one defendant, [with the burden on that defendant to implead other culpable defendants], but the plaintiff will have to allege the following elements and prove each to the satisfaction of the trier of fact: [T]hat the plaintiff's mother took DES; that DES caused the plaintiff's subsequent injuries; that the defendant produced or marketed the type of DES taken by the plaintiff's mother; and that the defendant's conduct in producing or marketing the DES constituted a breach of a legally recognized duty to the plaintiff. It was not fatal to a plaintiff's claim if he or she could not identify the type of DES taken by the mother. The *Collins* court held that "[i]n the situation where the plaintiff cannot allege and prove what type of DES the mother took, as to the third element the plaintiff need only allege and prove that the defendant drug company produced or marketed the drug DES for use in preventing miscarriages during pregnancy." If these elements could be proven, the plaintiff could recover all damages from the named defendant....

However, this court was concerned that "only those defendant drug companies that *reasonably could have* contributed *in some way* to the actual injury" be held accountable. Thus, after the plaintiff made a prima facie case under either negligence or strict products liability theory, a defendant could escape liability if it proved by a preponderance of evidence that the DES it produced or marketed could not have reached the plaintiff's mother. A defendant could accomplish this by establishing "that it did not produce or market the subject DES either during the time period the plaintiff was exposed to DES or in the relevant geographical market area in which the plaintiff's mother acquired the DES."

Providing defendants the ability to prove their way out of liability "will result in a pool of defendants which it can reasonably be assumed could have caused the plaintiff's injuries." This procedure, however, was imprecise, as it could mean that some of the remaining defendants may still be innocent. Nevertheless, this court accepted that possibility "as the price the defendants, and perhaps ultimately society, must pay to provide the plaintiff an adequate remedy under the law."

For those defendants that could not exculpate themselves, this court concluded that the application of comparative negligence "provide[d] the most equitable means to assign liability and apportion damages among the liable defendants." In assigning liability among the defendants, this court determined that the jury may consider the following nonexhaustive list of factors:

> [W]hether the drug company conducted tests on DES for safety and efficacy in use for pregnancies; to what degree the company took a role in gaining FDA approval of DES for use in pregnancies; whether the company had a small or large market share in the relevant area; whether the company took the lead or merely followed the lead of others in producing or marketing DES; whether the company issued warnings about the dangers of DES; whether the company produced or marketed DES after it knew or should have known of the possible hazards DES presented to the public; and whether the company took any affirmative steps to reduce the risk of injury to the public.

[Citation.] Through the trial court's exercise of discretion, the jury could be permitted to consider other relevant factors to apportioning liability.

* * *

[After determining that the Wisconsin Constitution did not bar the plaintiff's claim against the Pigment Manufacturers simply because the plaintiff may also have a remedy against the landlords,] we now consider whether Thomas's suit is factually similar to that in *Collins*. This court in *Collins* authorized the expansion of the theory in other factually similar scenarios. [Citation.] Although this case is not identical to *Collins,* we conclude that it is factually similar such that the risk-contribution theory applies.

As a prefatory note, as this court did in *Collins* with DES cases, we recognize that cases involving lead poisoning stemming from lead pigment pose difficult problems. The entirely innocent plaintiffs may have been severely harmed by a substance they had no control over, and they may never know or be able to prove with certainty which manufacturer produced or promoted the white lead carbonate that caused the injuries. The Pigment Manufacturers are faced with possible liability for white lead carbonate they may not have produced or marketed. As this court did in *Collins,* we again conclude "that as between the plaintiff, who probably is not at fault, and the defendants, who may have provided the product which caused the injury, the interests of justice and fundamental fairness demand that the latter should bear the cost of injury."

There is no dispute that Thomas is an innocent plaintiff who is probably not at fault and will be forced to bear a significant cost of his injuries if he is not allowed to sue the possibly negligent Pigment Manufacturers. Further, given the disturbing numbers of victims of lead poisoning from ingesting lead paint, and given that white lead carbonate was the overwhelming pigment added to that paint, it is clear from the summary judgment record that we are not dealing with an isolated or unique set of circumstances. As far as the summary judgment record reveals, the problem of lead poisoning from white lead carbonate is real; it is widespread; and it is a public health catastrophe that is poised to linger for quite some time.

The main policy reasons identified by *Collins* warrant extension of the risk-contribution theory here.

First, the record makes clear that the Pigment Manufacturers "contributed to the *risk* of injury to the public and, consequently, the risk of injury to individual plaintiffs such as" Thomas. Many of the individual defendants or their predecessors-in-interest did more than simply contribute to a risk; they knew of the harm white lead carbonate pigments caused and continued production and promotion of the pigment notwithstanding that knowledge. Some manufacturers, paradoxically, even promoted their nonleaded based pigments as alternatives that were safe in that they did not pose the risk of lead poisoning. For those that did not have explicit knowledge of the harm they were engendering, given the growing medical literature in the early part of the century, Thomas's historical [public health] experts submit that by the 1920s the entire industry knew or should have known of the dangers of its products and should have ceased producing the lead pigments, including white lead carbonate. In short, we agree with Thomas that the record easily establishes the Pigment Manufacturers' culpability for, at a minimum, contributing to creating a risk of injury to the public.

Second, as compared to Thomas, the Pigment Manufacturers are in a better position to absorb the cost of the injury. They can insure themselves against liability, absorb the damage award, or pass the cost along to the consuming public as a cost of doing business. As we concluded in *Collins,* it is better to have the Pigment Manufacturers or consumers share the cost of the injury rather than place the burden on the innocent plaintiff. [The] *Collins* court identified another policy reason, which was providing an incentive for drug companies to test adequately the drugs they place on the market for general medical use. This policy is not implicated here because lead pigment in paint has been banned for some time now. Although the *Collins* court recognized that the "sting" from damage awards might spur better research and development for the drug companies, it does not seem that this formed a pillar for the court's articulation of the risk-contribution theory. We read *Collins* as establishing that the predominant policy reasons undergirding the risk-contribution theory were that the defendants contributed to the risk of harm and that the defendants were in a better position to absorb the cost.

* * *

Thomas is also unable to identify the precise manufacturer of the white lead carbonate that caused his injuries due to the number of manufacturers, the passage of time, and the loss of records. Additionally, he cannot identify which of the three types of white lead carbonate he ingested. On this failure of proof, the Pigment Manufacturers contend, Thomas's claim must fall. They argue that because white lead carbonate was not "fungible" or manufactured from a chemically identical formula, *Collins*' risk-contribution cannot be applied here. We disagree.

One of the proof problems the *Collins* court recognized the plaintiff had was that she was unable to identify the precise producer or marketer of the DES her mother took due to, among other things, "the generic status of some DES." In different terms, this court stated that the plaintiff could not identify the drug company that caused her injury because "DES was, for the most part, produced in a 'generic' form which did not contain any clearly identifiable shape, color, or markings." This court also observed that "DES was a fungible drug produced with a chemically identical formula, and often pharmacists would fill DES prescriptions from whatever stock they had on hand, whether or not a particular brand was specified in the prescription."

There is no denying that *Collins* involved a situation where a chemically identical formula allegedly caused harm. It is also true that white lead carbonate was made from three different chemical formulas. However, *Collins* did not address whether DES was fungible because of its chemical identity, because of its interchangeability due to its generic status, or because of both. The question is, does fungibility require chemical identity? We conclude that it does not.

Chemical identity was a feature that DES apparently shared, and it was that chemical formula that created a possibility of causing harm. Here, although the chemical formulas for white lead carbonate are not the same, Thomas's toxicologist, Mushak, opines that it is the common denominator in the formulas that counts: lead. According to Mushak, the formulary differences between white lead carbonates do not affect the bioavailability of, and hence the consequences caused by, the lead pigment. Thus, the formulas for both DES and the white lead carbonate are in a sense on the same footing as being inherently hazardous. Therefore, it would be imprudent to conclude that chemical identity is a touchstone for fungibility and, in turn, for the risk-contribution theory. To prevent the triumph of form over substance, we conclude that chemical identity is not required.

But the question still remains: what does fungibility mean? It has been noted that "[w]hile 'fungibility' [has] become an obsession for courts discussing market share liability, no court has ever explained thoroughly what 'fungibility' means or why it is important." Allen Rostron, Beyond Market Share Liability: A Theory of Proportional Share Liability for Nonfungible Products, 52 UCLA L.Rev. 151, 163 (2004). Rostron writes that a product can be fungible in at least three different senses.

First, a product can be "functionally interchangeable." Under this meaning, whether a product is fungible is a matter of degree and heavily dependent on the context of whatever "function" is at issue. For example, " 'for signaling New Year's Eve, a blast from an auto horn and one from a saxophone may be equivalent as noise, but few would want to dance to the former.' " *Id.* at 163–64 (quoting Hamilton v. Accu–Tek, 32 F.Supp.2d 47, 51 (E.D.N.Y.1998)). This type of fungibility is significant "because it is a reason why a product may pose unusually severe identification problems."

Second, a product can be fungible in the sense that it is "physically indistinguishable." Because appearances can be deceiving, the degree of physical similarity required, as with functional interchangeability, depends heavily on context: "For example, the difference between two brands of a cola drink in their original packaging will be obvious. After being poured from the can or bottle, they might be completely indistinguishable in appearance, distinguishable by taste for some consumers and not others, and easily distinguishable to chemists analyzing them in a laboratory." As with functional interchangeability, fungibility in the sense that a product is physically indistinguishable is significant because it is also a reason why a product may pose identification problems.

Third, a product can be fungible as it presents a "uniformity of risk." Under this meaning, "[a]s a result of sharing an identical or virtually identical chemical formula, each manufacturer's product posed the same amount of risk as every other manufacturer's product. The products therefore were 'identically defective,' with none being more or less defective than the rest." However, "whether a product poses a uniform risk can depend on the choice of the unit for which risk is measured. While each milligram of DES presented the same amount of risk, each DES pill did not, because the pills came in different dosages." Thus, as products may contain different concentrations of the hazardous substance, there is leeway to conclude that strict chemical uniformity does not render all substances fungible. Nevertheless, this was important to market-share liability as it defined "the market" by concretely establishing the risk undertaken by the manufacturers.

Fungibility, therefore, is not a term that is capable of being defined with categorical precision. Its character will depend on the context of the injury, its cause, and the particular obstacles encountered in linking the causation to the possibly negligent defendants. [Citation.] The facts presented in this case, when construed in the light most favorable to Thomas, however, establish that white lead carbonate is fungible under any of the above meanings.

First, white lead carbonate was functionally interchangeable. All forms of white lead carbonate were lead pigments, which constituted one of the two necessary components of paint (the other being the "vehicle"). The pigment is what provided the hiding power of the paint. Although there may be varying grades of hiding powers based on differing physical properties and concentrations of the particular pigments, those are differences of degree, not function.

Second, based on the summary judgment record, white lead carbonates are physically indistinguishable. As far as Thomas has been able to tell, the pigment at issue is white lead carbonate pigment. And as far as Thomas has been able to tell, there appears to be no difference between the various white lead carbonates. Although the Pigment Manufacturers contend that white lead carbonates were manufactured according to different processes, which resulted in white lead carbonates of different physical properties, these physical differences are available only on the microscopic scale. Our concern here is whether the white lead carbonates are physically indistinguishable in the context in which it is used (in paint) and to whom is using it (the consumer or injured party). We acknowledge that the physical identity in this case is markedly different from that in *Collins*. Whereas in *Collins*, the plaintiff's mother could identify certain characteristics about the particular DES pill she ingested, that type of analysis is not possible here, as pigment in paint by its nature and concentration defy more specific identification. Nevertheless, we conclude the factual circumstances of physical interchangeability that are present are still sufficiently similar to remain within *Collins'* confines.

Third, we have already noted that white lead carbonates were produced utilizing "virtually identical chemical formulas" such that all white lead carbonates were "identically defective." [Citation; see also Wheeler v. Raybestos–Manhattan, 8 Cal.App.4th 1152, 11 Cal.Rptr.2d 109, 111 (1992)] (concluding that although brake pads containing asbestos chrysotile fibers were not all manufactured from one single chemical formula, "they are fungible ... by virtue of containing roughly comparable quantities of the single asbestos fiber, chrysotile."). It is the common denominator in the various white lead carbonate formulas that matters; namely, lead.

Therefore, based on the factors identified in *Collins*, we conclude that Thomas's case is factually similar to warrant extension of the risk-contribution theory.

The Pigment Manufacturers, however, contend that there are a number of factual dissimilarities between this case and *Collins* that should preclude recognizing the risk-contribution theory here. While there are dissimilarities between the two, we do not agree that these defeat the extension of *Collins* in this case.

First, the Pigment Manufacturers note that the paint Thomas allegedly ingested could have been applied at any time between construction of the two houses in 1900 and 1905 and the ban on lead paint in 1978. This significant time span greatly exceeds the nine-month window during which a plaintiff's mother would have taken DES, the Pigment Manufacturers note. Given that *Collins* attempted to strike a balance between assuring a DES plaintiff had a remedy and providing a realistic opportunity to each DES pill manufacturer to prove that it could not have caused the plaintiff's harm (by establishing its DES could not have reached the mother during her pregnancy), the Pigment Manufacturers contend that *Collins* should not be extended given that they have no reasonable ability to exculpate themselves.

We recognize that the window during which the possible injury causing white lead carbonate was placed in a house that eventually harmed Thomas is drastically larger than a nine-month window for pregnancy. However, the window will not always be potentially as large as appears in this case. Even if it routinely will be, the Pigment Manufacturers' argument must be put into perspective: they are essentially arguing that their negligent conduct should be excused because they got away with it for too long. As Thomas says, the Pigment Manufacturers "are arguing that they should not be held liable under the risk contribution doctrine because of the magnitude of their wrongful conduct."

Collins was concerned with providing possibly innocent defendants a means to exculpate themselves by establishing their product could not have caused the injury. If they could not do so, this court stated that the equities "favor placing the consequences on the defendants." Equity does not support reversing that balance simply because the Pigment Manufacturers benefitted from manufacturing and marketing white lead carbonate for a significant period of time.

Next, the Pigment Manufacturers contend that the risk-contribution theory should not be extended because Thomas's lead poisoning could have been caused from many different sources. We agree that the record indicates that lead poisoning can stem from the ambient air, many foods, drinking water, soil, and dust.

Further, the Pigment Manufacturers argue that the risk-contribution theory should not be extended because lead poisoning does not produce a "signature injury." As alternate explanations for Thomas's cognitive deficits, the Pigment Manufacturers have brought forth evidence that genetics, birth complications causing damage to the central nervous system, severe environmental deprivation, inadequate parenting, parental emotional disorders, and child abuse could all, in varying ways, cause such impairments.

These arguments have no bearing on whether the risk-contribution theory should be extended to white lead carbonate claims. Harm is harm, whether it be "signature" or otherwise. Even under the risk-contribution theory, the plaintiff still retains a burden of establishing causation. To establish a . . . claim under the risk-contribution theory, this court concluded that the plaintiff nonetheless needed to prove that "DES caused the plaintiff's subsequent injuries." Similarly, on a products liability claim, the *Collins* court held that the plaintiff has to prove "that the defect was a cause of the plaintiff's injuries or damages." On whatever theory the plaintiff chooses to proceed, this causation showing must be made by a preponderance of the evidence, and ultimately "to the satisfaction of the trier of fact." The plaintiff's burden is relaxed only with respect to establishing the specific type of DES the plaintiff's mother took, which, in this case, translates into the specific type of white lead carbonate Thomas ingested.

While *Collins* concerned a plaintiff who had injuries of a "signature" nature, that merely means that Thomas may have a harder case to make to his jury. Further, while the Pigment Manufacturers are correct to argue that Thomas's lead poisoning could have come from any number of sources, that is an argument to be made before the jury.

Finally, the Pigment Manufacturers argue that because they were not in exclusive control of the risk their product created, the risk-contribution model should not apply to them. We again disagree.

This was again not a distinction relevant in *Collins*. Further, we see no reason why it should be for at least two reasons. First, as doctors were the ones who prescribed the dosage of DES, so too were the paint manufacturers that mixed the amount of white lead carbonate in the paint. However, the paint did not alter the toxicity of the white lead carbonate anymore than the pharmacist did by filling a prescription. To the contrary, at best, the paint manufacturers actually diluted the white lead carbonate's toxicity. In other words, the inherent dangerousness of the white lead carbonate pigment existed the moment the Pigment Manufacturers created it.

Second, the record is replete with evidence that shows the Pigment Manufacturers actually magnified the risk through their aggressive promotion of white lead carbonate, even despite the awareness of the toxicity of lead. In either case, whoever had "exclusive" control over the white lead carbonate is immaterial.

Thomas has brought claims for both negligence and strict products liability. Applying the risk-contribution theory to Thomas's . . . claim[s], he will have to prove the following elements to the satisfaction of the trier of fact:

(1) That he ingested white lead carbonate;

(2) That the white lead carbonate caused his injuries;

(3) That the Pigment Manufacturers produced or marketed the type of white lead carbonate he ingested; and

(4) That the Pigment Manufacturers' conduct in producing or marketing the white lead carbonate constituted a breach of a legally recognized duty to Thomas [or that the product was defective under strict liability doctrines].

Because Thomas cannot prove the specific type of white lead carbonate he ingested, he need only prove that the Pigment Manufacturers produced or marketed white lead carbonate for use during the relevant time period: the duration of the houses' existence. . . .

Once Thomas makes a prima facie case under either claim, the burden of proof shifts to each defendant to prove by a preponderance of the evidence that it did not produce or market white lead carbonate either during the relevant time period or in the geographical market where the house is located. However, if relevant records do not exist that can substantiate either defense, "we believe that the equities of [white lead carbonate] cases favor placing the consequences on the [Pigment Manufacturers]." In addition to these specific defenses, and unlike in the DES cases, the Pigment Manufacturers here may have ample grounds to attack and eviscerate Thomas's prima facie case, with some of those grounds including that lead poisoning could stem from any number of substances (since lead itself is ubiquitous) and that it is difficult to know whether Thomas's injuries stem from lead poisoning as they are not signature injuries.

We continue to believe that this procedure will result in a pool of defendants which can reasonably be assumed "could have caused the plaintiff's injuries." The alarmist tone of the dissents aside, our application of *Collins* here achieves *Collins'* requirement that it be shown that the defendant pigment manufacturer "reasonably *could have* contributed *in some way* to the actual injury." [Citation.] The procedure is not perfect and could result in drawing in some defendants who are actually innocent, particularly given the significantly larger time span at issue in this particular case. However, *Collins* declared that "we accept this as the price the defendants, and perhaps ultimately society, must pay to provide the plaintiff an adequate remedy under the law."

[The Pigment Manufacturers raised a number of constitutional challenges which the Court found not to be ripe for decision. Thomas also argued that he should be able to present the alternative theories of enterprise liability and civil conspiracy. The court rejected those claims.]

■ WILCOX, J., dissenting.

It is often said that bad facts make bad law. Today's decision epitomizes that ancient legal axiom. The end result of the majority opinion is that the defendants, lead pigment manufacturers, can be held liable for a product they may or may not have produced, which may or may not have caused the plaintiff's injuries, based on conduct that may have occurred over 100 years ago when some of the defendants were not even part of the relevant market. Even though the injury in this case is tragic, the plaintiff cannot demonstrate that he was lead poisoned as a result of white lead carbonate, much less the type of white lead carbonate produced by any of the respective defendants. More importantly, he cannot prove *when* the supposed white lead carbonate that allegedly poisoned him was manufactured or applied to the houses in which he was supposedly lead poisoned. However, none of these facts seem to matter to the majority.

Subjecting the defendants in this case to liability under these circumstances amounts to an unwarranted and unprecedented relaxation of the traditional rules governing tort liability, and raises serious concerns of fundamental fairness, as the defendants will be unable to realistically exculpate themselves. The majority opinion not only creates the risk that liability may be wholly out of proportion with the culpability of each individual defendant; it raises a distinct possibility that some defendants may be held liable for an injury that they did not and could not have caused. The majority seems content to run roughshod over established principles of causation and the rights of each defendant to present a defense and be judged based on its own actions. The majority's decision renders Wisconsin the only state to apply some form of collective liability in lead paint suits under similar facts.

* * *

A legitimate system of law requires adherence to established legal principles, even if such adherence does not produce a result deemed desirable by the collective wisdom of four members of this court. Our common law used to require a plaintiff to prove four elements in order to recover under a theory of negligence: duty, breach, causation, and damages. Throughout the years, this court has essentially eliminated the requirement that a plaintiff prove the second element by holding that in Wisconsin, everyone owes a duty of reasonable care to the entire world. [Citation.] Today, the majority proclaims that if a plaintiff is sympathetic enough and the "industry" of which a defendant was a part is culpable enough, a plaintiff may dispense with proof of the third element and recover against a party even though it has not been shown that the party reasonably could have contributed in someway to the plaintiff's actual injury. Simply put, the majority opinion amounts to little more than this court dictating social policy to achieve a desired result. . . .

NOTES

1. Most courts have rejected market share outside the DES context. *Thomas* is the first to recognize it in the case of lead paint poisoning. Cases rejecting market share in lead paint cases include *Santiago*, 3 F.3d 546 (1st Cir. 1993), mentioned in *Thomas*: "[A]llowing plaintiff's market share claim to proceed despite plaintiff's inability to pinpoint with any degree of precision the time the injury-causing paint was applied to the house . . . would significantly undermine both of the articulated reasons for the identification requirement [the interests in holding wrongdoers liable only for the harm they have caused, and in separating tortfeasors from innocent actors]." Accord, Jefferson v. Lead Industries Ass'n, 106 F.3d 1245 (5th Cir. 1997).

2. Do you consider cases involving lead paint exposure appropriate for some kind of market share liability? Why or why not? Which of the majority's explanations for extending *Collins* do you find the most persuasive? Do you find the dissent's traditional arguments compelling? See generally Gifford & Pasicolan, Market Share Liability Beyond DES Cases: The Solution to the Causation Dilemma in Lead Paint Litigation?, 58 S.C.L.Rev. 115 (2006); Geistfeld, The Doctrinal Unity of Alternative Liability and Market–Share Liability, 155 U.Pa.L.Rev. 447 (2006).

3. Beyond DES.

A. Asbestos. In Celotex Corp. v. Copeland, 471 So.2d 533 (Fla.1985), the Florida Supreme Court held that the plaintiff, who during his 33 year career as a boilermaker was exposed to various asbestos products, could not rely on a market share theory. First, plaintiff was able to identify some of the specific products (and their manufacturers) to which he had been exposed. Second, asbestos products, unlike DES, have a wide divergence of toxicity. Most courts have agreed. See, e.g., University System of New Hampshire v. United States Gypsum Co., 756 F.Supp. 640 (D.N.H.1991); Case v. Fibreboard Corp., 743 P.2d 1062 (Okl.1987)(citing cases).

In California, the court of appeals in Mullen v. Armstrong World Indus., Inc., 246 Cal.Rptr. 32 (Ct.App. 1988) "align[ed] California, the progenitor of the market share theory of liability, with the great majority of jurisdictions which have declined to extend it to the field of asbestos-related injuries." Five years later, the same court of appeals decided Wheeler v. Raybestos–Manhattan, 11 Cal.Rptr.2d 109 (Ct.App. 1992), relied on in *Thomas*, in which market share liability was applied to injuries resulting from asbestos-containing brake pads which contain "a single type of asbestos fiber, chrysotile, . . . and the amount of asbestos by weight in the pads varied within a limited range." The California Supreme Court denied the application of alternative liability theory from *Summers v. Tice* to asbestos cases in Rutherford v. Owens–Illinois, Inc., 941 P.2d 1203 (Cal. 1997).

B. Benzene. Benzene, a component of gasoline, is thought to cause leukemia and other blood diseases. Workers in the automotive industry are unlikely to be able to identify the manufacturers of all the gasoline to which they are exposed. One court has nonetheless refused to apply market share liability in such a case. Bly v. Tri–Continental Indus., 663 A.2d 1232, 1244 (D.C.App.1995). Plaintiff, whose husband died of leukemia after 25 years as an automotive mechanic, produced testimony from an economist experienced in the gasoline market who testified that "[G]asoline is manufactured by more than 100 refining companies in the United States, and it is possible that the products of these manufacturers could end up in one of the terminals in the District of Columbia area. . . . [T]he gasoline to which Bly . . . may have been exposed could have come from anywhere in the United States or even from other countries and that it would not be possible to know which refiner manufactured the gasoline." The trial court granted the defendants' motion for summary judgment, and the Court of Appeals affirmed, stating: "Market share liability is a remedy of last resort which was developed to provide a remedy to injured parties who could not identify the manufacturer of the product which caused them harm. . . . Mere difficulty in identifying the source of the product is insufficient; plaintiff must make a genuine attempt to identify the party responsible for the harm. [Citation.] It does not appear from the record in this case that the suppliers of the gasoline could not be identified or that there was an extensive effort to ascertain their identities." Did the court not understand the expert's testimony?

C. Blood products. Smith v. Cutter Biological, Inc., 823 P.2d 717, 727–28 (Haw.1991), recognized market share liability in the case of a hemophiliac who had contracted AIDS but could not identify the source of the contaminated blood factor which caused his AIDS. He sued the four manufacturers of blood products that supplied the Army Medical Hospital where he had received all his transfusions during the pertinent time. The court adopted the market share theory from *Hymowitz*. Accord, Ray v. Cutter Labs., 754 F.Supp. 193 (M.D.Fla.1991). See Klein, Beyond DES: Rejecting the Application of Market Share Liability in Blood Products Litigation, 68 Tul. L. Rev. 883, 918–21 (1994).

D. Handguns. Is market share liability applicable to claims arising out of the negligent marketing and distribution of handguns? See Hamilton v. Beretta U.S.A. Corp., 750 N.E.2d 1055 (N.Y. 2001) (no.)

4. Public Nuisance Theory. Along with the individual plaintiff cases involving lead paint contamination, a number of municipalities have pursued claims against the manufacturers under a public nuisance theory, claiming that the manufacturers should be required to help remedy the lead paint contamination in public buildings, particularly in public housing. The public nuisance theory claims that the defendant has unreasonably interfered with a right held in common by the general public. Restatement (Second) of Torts § 821B. An unreasonable interference is one that affects the public's health, safety, peace, comfort, or convenience; violates a statute or ordinance prohibiting the conduct; and/or has produced a permanent effect on the public right. Id. See generally Ausness, Public Tort Litigation: Public Benefit or Public Nuisance?, 77 Temp. L. Rev. 825 (2004).

A number of jurisdictions have rejected the use of the public nuisance theory in handgun marketing cases, see City of Chicago v. Beretta U.S.A. Corp., 821 N.E.2d 1099 (Ill. 2004), and the theory has had mixed reception on its application to lead paint, see, Ausness, 77 Temp. L. Rev. at 854–55, but at least a couple of jurisdictions now recognize it in the lead paint context. See Rhode Island v. Lead Indus., 2006 WL 691803 (R.I. Super. Ct. 2006); County of Santa Clara v. Atlantic Richfield Co., 40 Cal.Rptr.3d 313 (Ct. App. 2006); City of Milwaukee v. NL Indus., Inc., 691 N.W.2d 888 (Wis. Ct. App. 2004). Is this the more appropriate theory for dealing with lead paint contamination and similar product-related social ills? See V. Schwartz, The Law of Public Nuisance: Maintaining Rational Boundaries on a Rational Tort, 45 Washburn L.J. 541 (2006).

5. Products Liability Restatement. The Products Liability Restatement § 15 does not take a position on the availability of market share liability but identifies a series of factors that courts have considered when determining whether to adopt some form of "proportional liability." Those factors include the generic nature of the product, the long latency period of harm, the plaintiff's inability to identify the product's manufacturer after extensive discovery, the clarity of the causal connection, and the availability of market share data to support reasonable apportionment. Id. cmt. *c*.

6. See generally Gifford, The Death of Causation: Mass Products Torts' Incomplete Incorporation of Social Welfare Principles, 41 Wake Forest L.Rev. 943 (2006); D. Owen, Products Liability Law § 11.3 (multiple defendants) and § 11.5 (toxic substances) (2d ed. 2008); 2 D. Owen, M.S. Madden, & M. Davis, Madden & Owen on Products Liability §§ 24:6, 24:7 (3d ed. 2000).

---

4. DAMAGES, APPORTIONMENT, AND MISCELLANY

Norfolk & Western Railway v. Ayers

Supreme Court of the United States, 2003.
538 U.S. 135, 123 S.Ct. 1210, 155 L.Ed.2d 261.

■ JUSTICE GINSBURG delivered the opinion of the Court.

The Federal Employers' Liability Act (FELA or Act), 45 U.S.C. § 51–60, makes common carrier railroads liable in damages to employees who suffer work-related injuries caused "in whole or in part" by the railroad's negligence. This case, brought against Norfolk & Western Railway Company (Norfolk) by six former employees now suffering from asbestosis (asbestosis claimants), presents two issues involving the FELA's application. The first issue concerns the damages recoverable by a railroad worker who suffers from the disease asbestosis: When the cause of that disease, in whole or in part, was exposure to asbestos while on the job, may the worker's recovery for his asbestosis-related "pain and suffering" include damages for fear of developing cancer?

The second issue concerns the extent of the railroad's liability when third parties not before the court—for example, prior or subsequent employers or asbestos manufacturers or suppliers—may have contributed to the worker's injury. Is the railroad answerable in full to the employee, so that pursuit of contribution or indemnity from other potentially liable enterprises is the railroad's sole damages-award-sharing recourse? Or is the railroad initially entitled to an apportionment among injury-causing tort-feasors, *i.e.,* a division of damages limiting the railroad's liability to the injured employee to a proportionate share?

In resolving the first issue, we follow the line drawn by Metro–North Commuter R. Co. v. Buckley, 521 U.S. 424 (1997), a decision that relied on and complemented Consolidated Rail Corporation v. Gottshall, 512 U.S. 532 (1994). In *Metro-North,* we held that emotional distress damages may not be recovered under the FELA by disease-free asbestos-exposed workers; in contrast, we observed, workers who "suffe[r] from a disease" (here, asbestosis) may "recover for related negligently caused emotional distress." [Citation.] We decline to blur, blend, or reconfigure our FELA jurisprudence in the manner urged by the defendant; instead, we adhere to the clear line our recent decisions delineate. Accordingly, we hold that mental anguish damages resulting from the fear of developing cancer may be recovered under the FELA by a railroad worker suffering from the actionable injury asbestosis caused by work-related exposure to asbestos.

As to the second issue, we similarly decline to write new law by requiring an initial apportionment of damages among potential tortfeasors. The FELA's express terms, reinforced by consistent judicial applications of the Act, allow a worker to recover his entire damages from a railroad whose negligence jointly caused an injury (here, the chronic disease asbestosis), thus placing on the railroad the burden of seeking contribution from other tortfeasors.

I

[Plaintiffs brought this FELA action against Norfolk alleging negligent exposure to asbestos which caused their asbestosis. As an element of their damages, plaintiffs sought recovery for mental anguish based on their fear of developing cancer. The trial court permitted evidence on the link between asbestos exposure and cancer, including expert testimony that asbestosis sufferers with smoking histories have a significantly increased risk of developing lung cancer—one in ten risk of dying of mesothelioma, a fatal cancer of the lining of the lung or abdominal cavity. Concluding that no plaintiff had shown he was reasonably certain to develop cancer, the trial court found that damages could not be awarded for cancer or any increased risk of cancer, but the testimony about cancer was relevant "only to judge the genuineness of plaintiffs' claims of fear of developing cancer." The trial court refused to permit apportionment of damages between Norfolk and other employers or manufacturers who may have contributed to the plaintiffs' disease. The jury returned verdicts for all plaintiffs, ranging from $770,000 to $1.2 million. The Court of Appeals of West Virginia denied review and we granted certiorari. We now affirm.]

II

Section 1 of the FELA renders common carrier railroads "liable in damages to any person suffering injury while ... employed by [the] carrier" if the "injury or death result[ed] in whole or in part from the [carrier's] negligence." 45 U.S.C. § 51. [FELA abolished a number of common law defenses.] When the Court confronts a dispute regarding what injuries are compensable under the statute, *Gottshall* instructs common-law principles "are entitled to great weight in our analysis."

III

A

We turn first to the question whether the trial judge correctly stated the law when he charged the jury that an asbestosis claimant, upon demonstrating a reasonable fear of cancer stemming from his present disease, could recover for that fear as part of asbestosis-related pain and suffering damages. In answering this question, we follow the path marked by the Court's decisions in *Gottshall,* and *Metro–North Commuter R. Co. v. Buckley.*

The FELA plaintiff in *Gottshall* alleged that he witnessed the death of a co-worker while on the job, and that the episode caused him severe emotional distress. [Citation.] He sought to recover damages from his employer, Conrail, for "mental or emotional harm ... not directly brought about by a physical injury." [T]his Court stated that uncabined recognition of claims for negligently inflicted emotional distress would "hol[d] out the very real possibility of nearly infinite and unpredictable liability for defendants." [Citations.] Of the "limiting tests ... developed in the common law," the Court selected the zone-of-danger test to delineate "the proper scope of an employer's duty under [the] FELA to avoid subjecting its employees to negligently inflicted emotional injury." That test confines recovery for stand-alone emotional distress claims to plaintiffs who: (1) "sustain a physical impact as a result of a defendant's negligent conduct"; or (2) "are placed in immediate risk of physical harm by that conduct"— that is, those who escaped instant physical harm, but were "within the zone of danger of physical impact." ...

In *Metro–North*, the Court applied the zone-of-danger test to a claim for damages under the FELA, one element of which was fear of cancer stemming from exposure to asbestos. The plaintiff in *Metro–North* had been intensively exposed to asbestos while working as a pipefitter for Metro–North in New York City's Grand Central Terminal. At the time of his lawsuit, however, he had a clean bill of health. The Court rejected his entire claim for relief. Exposure alone, the Court held, is insufficient to show "physical impact" under the zone-of-danger test. "[A] simple (though extensive) contact with a carcinogenic substance," the Court observed, "does not . . . offer much help in separating valid from invalid emotional distress claims." The evaluation problem would be formidable, the Court explained, "because contacts, even extensive contacts, with serious carcinogens are common . . . The large number of those exposed and the uncertainties that may surround recovery," the Court added, "suggest what *Gottshall* called the problem of 'unlimited and unpredictable liability.' "

As in *Gottshall,* the Court distinguished stand-alone distress claims from prayers for damages for emotional pain and suffering tied to a physical injury: "Common-law courts," the Court recognized, "*do* permit a plaintiff *who suffers from a disease* to recover for related negligently caused emotional distress...." [Citation]. When a plaintiff suffers from a disease, the Court noted, common-law courts have made "a special effort" to value related emotional distress, "perhaps from a desire to make a physically injured victim whole or because the parties are likely to be in court in any event."

In sum, our decisions in *Gottshall* and *Metro–North* describe two categories: Stand-alone emotional distress claims not provoked by any physical injury, for which recovery is sharply circumscribed by the zone-of-danger test; and emotional distress claims brought on by a physical injury, for which pain and suffering recovery is permitted.... The claimants before us ... complain of a negligently inflicted physical injury (asbestosis) and attendant pain and suffering.

B

Unlike stand-alone claims for negligently inflicted emotional distress, claims for pain and suffering associated with, or "parasitic" on, a physical injury are traditionally compensable. The Restatement (Second) of Torts § 456 (1963–1964) states the general rule:

> "If the actor's negligent conduct has so caused *any* bodily harm to another as to make him liable for it, the actor is also subject to liability for '(a) fright, shock, *or other emotional disturbance*' resulting from the bodily harm or from the conduct which causes it...." (Emphases added.)

A plaintiff suffering bodily harm need not allege physical manifestations of her mental anguish. Id., cmt *c.* "The plaintiff must of course present evidence that she has suffered, but otherwise her emotional distress claims, in whatever form, are fully recoverable." D. Dobbs, Law of Torts 822 (2000).

By 1908, when the FELA was enacted, the common law had evolved to encompass apprehension of future harm as a component of pain and suffering. The future harm, genuinely feared, need not be more likely than not to materialize. [Citation.] Physically injured plaintiffs, it is now recognized, may recover for "reasonable fears" of a future disease.... In the course of the 20th century, courts sustained a variety of other "fear-of" claims. Among them have been claims for fear of cancer. Heightened vulnerability to cancer, as one court observed, "must necessarily have a most depressing effect upon the injured person. Like the sword of Damocles," he knows it is there, but not whether or when it will fall. Alley v. Charlotte Pipe & Foundry Co., 74 S.E. 885 (1912); [citation].

Many courts in recent years have considered the question presented here—whether an asbestosis claimant may be compensated for fear of cancer. Of decisions that address the issue, a clear majority sustain recovery. See, e.g., Hoerner v. Anco Insulations, Inc., 812 So.2d 45, 77 (La. App. 2002)(fear of cancer testimony "appropriately presented in order to prove [asbestosis claimant's] general damage claim"); [citations, including the two influential cases of Mauro v. Raymark Indus., Inc., 561 A.2d 257 (N.J. 1989); and Jackson v. Johns–Manville Sales Corp., 781 F.2d 394 (5th Cir. 1986), and additional cases from Iowa, Tenn., Del., Fla., Ky., N.Y., Tex., and Wash.]

Arguing against the trend in the lower courts, Norfolk ... asserts that the asbestosis claimants' alleged cancer fears are too remote from asbestosis to warrant inclusion in their pain and suffering awards. In support of this contention, the United States, [in support of Norfolk], refers to the "separate disease rule," under which most courts have held that the statute of limitations runs separately for each asbestos-related disease.... Pustejovsky v. Rapid–American Corp., 35 S.W.3d 643, 649, n. 3 (Tex.2000) (listing cases).[12] Because the asbestosis claimants may bring a second action if cancer develops, Norfolk and the Government argue, cancer-related damages are unwarranted in their asbestosis suit. The question, as the Government frames it, is not *whether* the asbestosis claimants can recover for fear of cancer, but *when*. ...

But the asbestosis claimants did not seek, and the trial court did not allow, discrete damages for their *increased risk* of future cancer. Instead, the claimants sought damages for their *current* injury, which, they allege, encompasses a *present fear* that the toxic exposure causative of asbestosis may later result in cancer. The Government's *"when, not whether,"* argument has a large gap; it excludes recovery for the fear experienced by an asbestosis sufferer who never gets cancer. For such a person, the question is *whether,* not *when,* he may recover for his fear.

* * *

There is an undisputed relationship between exposure to asbestos sufficient to cause asbestosis, and asbestos-related cancer. Norfolk's own expert acknowledged that asbestosis puts a worker in a heightened risk category for asbestos-related lung cancer. [Plaintiffs' expert testified] without contradiction to a risk notably "different in kind from the background risks that all individuals face." [Citation.] Some "ten percent of the people who have the disease, asbestosis, have died of mesothelioma." ... In light

---

12. The rule evolved as a response to the special problem posed by latent-disease cases. Under the single-action rule, a plaintiff who recovered for asbestosis would then be precluded from bringing suit for later developed mesothelioma. Allowing separate complaints for each disease, courts determined, properly balanced a defendant's interest in repose and a plaintiff's interest in recovering adequate compensation for negligently inflicted injuries.

of this evidence, an asbestosis sufferer would have good cause for increased apprehension about his vulnerability to another illness from his exposure, a disease that inflicts "agonizing, unremitting pain," relieved only by death.

Norfolk understandably underscores a point central to the Court's decision in *Metro–North*. The Court's opinion in *Metro–North* stressed that holding employers liable to workers merely exposed to asbestos would risk "unlimited and unpredictable liability." But as earlier observed, *Metro–North* sharply distinguished exposure-only plaintiffs from "plaintiffs who suffer from a disease," and stated, unambiguously, that "[t]he common law permits emotional distress recovery for [the latter] category." Commentary similarly distinguishes asymptomatic asbestos plaintiffs from plaintiffs who "developed asbestosis and thus suffered real physical harm." Henderson & Twerski, Asbestos Litigation Gone Mad: Exposure–Based Recovery for Increased Risk, Mental Distress, and Medical Monitoring, 53 S.C.L.Rev. 815, 830 (2002)....

C

Norfolk presented the question "[w]hether a plaintiff who has asbestosis but not cancer can recover damages for fear of cancer under the [FELA] without proof of physical manifestations of the claimed emotional distress." Our answer is yes, with an important reservation. We affirm only the qualification of an asbestosis sufferer to seek compensation for fear of cancer as an element of his asbestosis-related pain and suffering damages. It is incumbent upon such a complainant, however, to prove that his alleged fear is genuine and serious.... In this case, proof directed to that matter was notably thin, and might well have succumbed to a straightforward sufficiency-of-the-evidence objection, had Norfolk so targeted its attack.

* * * We did not grant review, in any event, to judge the sufficiency of the evidence or the reasonableness of the damages awards. We rule, specifically and only, on the question whether this case should be aligned with those in which fear of future injury stems from a current injury, or with those presenting a stand-alone claim for negligent infliction of emotional distress. We hold that the former categorization is the proper one under the FELA.

IV

We turn next to Norfolk's contention that the trial court erred in instructing the jury "not to make a deduction [from damages awards] for the contribution of non-railroad [asbestos] exposures" to the asbestosis claimants' injuries. The statutory language, however, supports the trial court's understanding that the FELA does not authorize apportionment of damages between railroad and non-railroad causes.... Nothing in the statutory text instructs that the amount of damages payable by a liable employer bears reduction when the negligence of a third party also contributed in part to the injury-in-suit.

* * * Norfolk asks us to narrow employer liability without a textual warrant. Reining in employer liability as Norfolk proposes, however, is both unprovided for by the language of the FELA and inconsistent with the Act's overall recovery facilitating thrust. Accordingly, we find Norfolk's plea an untenable reading of the congressional silence. . . . Norfolk's view also runs counter to a century of FELA jurisprudence. No FELA decision made by this Court so much as hints that the statute mandates apportionment of damages among potentially liable tortfeasors. . . . Also significant is the paucity of lower court authority for the proposition that the FELA contemplates apportionment. * * *

The conclusion that the FELA does not mandate apportionment is also in harmony with this Court's repeated statements that joint and several liability is the traditional rule. . . . Looking beyond historical practice, Norfolk contends that the modern trend is to apportion damages between multiple tortfeasors. The state of affairs when the FELA was enacted, however, is the more important inquiry. . . . At any rate, many States retain full joint and several liability, see Restatement (Third) of Torts, Apportionment of Liability § 17, Reporters' Note, table, pp. 151–152 (1999), even more retain it in certain circumstances, and most of the recent changes away from the traditional rule have come through legislative enactments rather than judicial development of common-law principles. Congress, however, has not amended the FELA. . . .

Finally, reading the FELA to require apportionment would handicap plaintiffs and could vastly complicate adjudications, all the more so if, as Norfolk sometimes suggests, manufacturers and suppliers, as well as other employers, should come within the apportionment pool. [Citation.] Once an employer has been adjudged negligent with respect to a given injury, it accords with the FELA's overarching purpose to require the employer to bear the burden of identifying other responsible parties and demonstrating that some of the costs of the injury should be spread to them. * * *

The "elephantine mass of asbestos cases" lodged in state and federal courts, we again recognize, "defies customary judicial administration and calls for national legislation." Ortiz v. Fibreboard Corp., 527 U.S. 815 (1999); [citations]. Courts, however, must resist pleas of the kind Norfolk has made, essentially to reconfigure established liability rules because they do not serve to abate today's asbestos litigation crisis.

For the reasons stated, the judgment of the [lower court] is *Affirmed*.

■ JUSTICE KENNEDY, with whom THE CHIEF JUSTICE, JUSTICE O'CONNOR, and JUSTICE BREYER join, concurring in part and dissenting in part.

. . . The Court allows compensation for fear of cancer to those who manifest symptoms of some other disease, not itself causative of cancer, though stemming from asbestos exposure. The Court's precedents interpreting FELA neither compel nor justify this result. The Court's ruling is not based upon a sound application of the common-law principles that should inform our decisions implementing FELA. On the contrary, those principles call for a different rule, one which does not yield such aberrant results in asbestos exposure cases. These reasons require my respectful dissent.

* * * This Court has recognized the danger that no compensation will be available for those with severe injuries caused by asbestos. Amchem Products, Inc. v. Windsor, 521 U.S. 591, 598 (1997) (" '[E]xhaustion of assets threatens and distorts the process; and future claimants may lose altogether' "). In fact the Court already has framed the question that should guide its resolution of this case: "In a world of limited resources, would a rule permitting immediate large-scale recoveries for widespread emotional distress caused by fear of future disease diminish the likelihood of recovery by those who later suffer from the disease?" *Metro-North*. The Court ignores this question and its warning. It is only a matter of time before inability to pay for real illness comes to pass. The Court's imprudent ruling will have been a contributing cause to this injustice.

* * * When the Court asks whether the rule it adopts has been settled by the common law, the answer, in my view, must be no. The issue before us is new and unsettled, as is evident from the diverse approaches of state and federal courts to this problem.... The result it reaches ... is far from inevitable, and the rule the majority derives does not comport with our responsibility to develop a federal common law that administers FELA in an effective, principled way. [The dissent would follow those cases, such as Simmons v. Pacor, Inc., 674 A.2d 232 (Pa. 1996), that permit claimants to sue for cancer damages if cancer develops.]

[Justice BREYER, concurring and dissenting in part, mentioned additional reasons why the Court should not recognize fear of cancer damages under FELA: (1) limitations are needed that separate valid, important emotional distress claims from less important, or trivial claims; (2) limitations are needed that avoid pure jury speculation that can produce unpredictable liability; and (3) "it would be perverse to apply tort law's basic compensatory objectives in a way that compensated less serious injuries at the expense of more serious harms."]

NOTES

The issues addressed in *Ayers* have long puzzled courts in toxic substance cases. The long latency period between exposure and final manifestation of injury raises questions regarding the types of damages that may be recoverable, and when. In addition, the availability of apportionment is a recurring theme. These issues, and others, are addressed below.

DAMAGES

1. Future Disease. As in *Ayers*, most courts refuse to permit plaintiffs to recover for an increased risk of cancer unless that risk has a greater than 50% probability to occur. See, e.g., Herber v. Johns–Manville Corp., 785 F.2d 79 (3d Cir.1986); Lohrmann v. Pittsburgh Corning Corp., 782 F.2d 1156 (4th Cir.1986); Sorenson v. Raymark Indus., Inc., 756 P.2d 740 (Wash.App.1988). In each of the previously cited cases, plaintiff failed to recover for the risk of future injury because he could not establish the requisite probability.

2.   Emotional Distress. While there is some debate over the propriety of claims for fear of cancer, or cancerphobia, most decisions have allowed such claims to be submitted to the jury, at least if plaintiff already suffers from asbestosis or other injury. Capital Holding Corp. v. Bailey, 873 S.W.2d 187 (Ky.1994) (present physical injury prerequisite to recovery for fear of cancer); In re Moorenovich, 634 F.Supp. 634 (D.Me.1986)(recovery for cancerphobia recoverable without proof that plaintiff had suffered any physical harm); Potter v. Firestone Tire & Rubber Co., 863 P.2d 795 (Cal.1993) (cancerphobia recovery permitted, even without present disease, but only if it is more likely than not that plaintiff will suffer future cancer); Watkins v. Fibreboard Corp., 994 F.2d 253 (5th Cir.1993) (cancerphobia recoverable even without present asbestos-related disease, and even if it was not medically probable that such a disease would sometime result).

Should a spouse or child be permitted to recover damages for emotional distress from observing a spouse or parent die from cancer caused by a toxic agent? See Wisniewski v. Johns–Manville Corp., 812 F.2d 81 (3d Cir.1987); Ochoa v. Superior Court, 703 P.2d 1 (Cal.1985).

See generally Klein, Fear of Disease and the Puzzle of Futures Cases in Tort, 35 U.C. Davis L.Rev. 965 (2002).

3.   Medical Monitoring Expenses. Plaintiffs exposed to a toxic agent putting them at risk of developing a latent disease have sometimes sought and recovered for medical expenses incurred in monitoring their condition to facilitate early diagnosis and treatment. See, e.g., Miranda v. Shell Oil Co., 15 Cal.Rptr.2d 569 (Ct.App.1993) (reasonably necessary medical monitoring costs recoverable by plaintiffs exposed to pesticide); Meyerhoff v. Turner Const. Co., 534 N.W.2d 204, 206 (Mich.App.1995) ("medical-monitoring expenses are a compensable item of damages [where] such surveillance to monitor the effect of exposure to toxic substances, such as asbestos, is reasonable and necessary"); Ayers v. Township of Jackson, 525 A.2d 287 (N.J.1987); Herber v. Johns–Manville Corp., 785 F.2d 79 (3d Cir.1986); Potter v. Firestone Tire & Rubber Co., 863 P.2d 795 (Cal.1993)(plaintiff need not show risk of cancer probable, but only significant, and must also show that such costs are reasonable and necessary).

Some decisions condition recovery of such damages somewhat restrictively, making it clear that the courts will insist on good evidence of exposure and the commensurate need for monitoring. See Barnes v. American Tobacco Co., 161 F.3d 127 (3d Cir. 1998) (collecting authority); In re Paoli Railroad Yard PCB Litig., 35 F.3d 717, 786–87 (3d Cir.1994)(Pa. law; rejecting threshold requirements imposed by some courts that plaintiffs show significant increase in their risk of disease); Theer v. Philip Carey Co., 628 A.2d 724 (N.J.1993) (limited recovery to persons who had been directly exposed to an agent and who suffer from a direct and discrete injury clearly related to that exposure); Hansen v. Mountain Fuel Supply Co., 858 P.2d 970 (Utah 1993)(medical monitoring costs recoverable based on 8 factors to weed out spurious claims).

4.   Property Damage. Property damage claims arising out of the need to remove toxic substances from buildings are common. Insulation containing asbestos has been installed in thousands of school buildings, other public facilities, and private residences. In 1980, Congress enacted the Asbestos School Hazard Detection and Control Act, 20 U.S.C.A. §§ 3601–11 (1982), mandating testing for the presence of asbestos in schools. Numerous lawsuits have been brought by school districts and other building owners against asbestos producers to recover damages for the costs of removing or enclosing asbestos insulation. Most courts allow recovery for such costs. E.g., T.H.S. Northstar Assoc. v. W.R. Grace & Co., 66 F.3d 173 (8th Cir.1995) (upholding award of $6.2 million in compensatory damages); City of Greenville v. W.R. Grace & Co., 827 F.2d 975 (4th Cir.1987) (upholding award of compensatory damages, remitted to $4.8 million, and $2 million punitive damages).

5. Punitive Damages. Many asbestos cases involve claims for punitive damages. Consider the following report, by Dr. Kenneth Smith, a physician who worked with Johns–Manville in the mid–1940s, of the dust conditions at a Johns–Manville mining and milling facility in 1949, recommending against informing workers that they had contracted asbestosis:

> It must be remembered that although these men have the x-ray evidence of asbestosis, they are working today and definitely are not disabled from asbestosis. They have not been told of this diagnosis for it is felt that as long as the man feels well, is happy at home and at work, and his physical condition remains good, nothing should be said. When he becomes disabled and sick, then the diagnosis should be made and the claim submitted *by the Company*. The fibrosis of this disease is irreversible and permanent so that eventually compensation will be paid to each of these men. But as long as the man is not disabled it is felt that he should not be told of his condition so that he can live and work in peace and the Company can benefit by his many years of experience. Should the man be told of his condition today there is a very definite possibility that he would become mentally and physically ill, simply through the knowledge that he has asbestosis.

Does such information support punitive damages? See Motley, The Lid Comes Off, 16 Trial 21, 24 (April 1980). Should contemporary notions of tort responsibility be applied to conduct which, in all likelihood, was considered appropriate at the time it occurred? For discussion of proof supporting punitive damages in asbestos litigation, see Jackson v. Johns–Manville Sales Corp., 781 F.2d 394 (5th Cir. 1986); Spaur v. Owens–Corning Fiberglas Corp., 510 N.W.2d 854 (Iowa 1994). See Page, Asbestos and the Dalkon Shield: Corporate America on Trial, 85 Mich. L.Rev. 1324 (1985).

Should punitive damages claims be allowed to send a company, or an industry, into bankruptcy? In Engle v. R.J.Reynolds Tobacco Co., 853 So.2d 434 (Fla.App. 2003), the first state class action tried to verdict, the jury assessed punitive damages against the tobacco defendants of $145 billion, far more than the combined assets of the entire industry. The court of appeals reversed on a number of issues, including the excessiveness of the punitive damages award.

> It is well established that punitive damages may not be assessed in an amount which will financially destroy or bankrupt a defendant. See Arab Termite & Pest Control of Florida, Inc. v. Jenkins, 409 So.2d 1039, 1043 (Fla.1982); [citations omitted]. And yet, that is precisely what occurred in the instant case.

> This trial produced the largest punitive damage verdict in American legal history. As acknowledged by even the plaintiffs' purported experts, the $145 billion punitive award will extract all value from the defendants and put them out of business, in violation of established Florida law that prohibits bankrupting punitive awards.

> The defendants established that their combined net worth was no more than $8.3 billion. Their collective capacity to pay any punitive award while still remaining in business was far less. The $145 billion verdict is roughly 18 times the defendants' proven net worth.

There is no precedential authority for such an award. No Florida decision endorses even a remotely comparable award. The largest reported awards involved only a fraction of a defendant's net worth. See Wackenhut Corp. v. Canty, 359 So.2d 430 (Fla.1978) (2%); Smith v. Telophase Nat'l Cremation Soc'y, Inc., 471 So.2d 163 (Fla. 2d Dist. App. 1985) (20%); [citations omitted]. No case has awarded punitive damages based upon multiples of net worth, as was done in the present case.

A defendant's financial capacity is a crucial factor in determining the appropriateness of a punitive damages award. The amount awarded should be large enough to provide retribution and deterrence, but cannot be so great as to result in bankruptcy. Punitive damages are imposed to benefit society's interests. Because society has an interest in protecting future claimants' demands, the importance of the relationship between the amount of punitive damages and the ability of the defendant to pay the award cannot be ignored.

The excessive award in the present case will frustrate the societal interest in protecting all injured claimants' rights to at least recover compensatory damages for their smoking related injuries. Smokers with viable compensable claims will have no remedy if the bankrupting punitive award in the instant case is upheld.

For the several reasons stated above, we find the trial court abused its discretion when it denied the defendants' motion for either a remittitur or a new trial. This unprecedented punitive damages award is excessive as a matter of law, and thus does not promote a valid societal interest. See State Farm Mutual Automobile Ins. Co. v. Campbell, 538 U.S. 408 (2003)(punitive award of $145 million on a $1 million compensatory judgment held excessive) . . .

The Florida Supreme Court upheld the reversal of punitive damages. 2006 WL 3742610 (Fla. 2006). On punitive damages generally, see ch. 15(4), above.

APPORTIONMENT OF CAUSATION

1. Between Defendants. When a plaintiff sues a number of responsible defendants for an indivisible toxic substance injury, such as cancer or death, traditional tort law principles (now largely reformed by apportionment statutes) hold the defendants jointly and severally liable for the harm. Juries are typically are asked to apportion responsibility to each defendant in such cases, based on fault or causation. The defendants may be jointly and severally liable for the harm, and possess a right of contribution if they pay more than their apportioned share, or they may be only severally liable if the legislature has limited or abolished joint liability. See Contribution and Indemnity, ch. 16(9), above, and the Apportionment of Liability Restatement. The Court in *Ayers* endorsed the traditional rule of joint and several liability for FELA, permitting a plaintiff to recover 100% of his damages from the railroad, who then must seek contribution or indemnity from third-parties.

Occasionally, asbestos defendants will seek reimbursement from tobacco defendants when plaintiff's lung cancer may have been caused, in part, by smoking. In Owens Corning v. R.J. Reynolds Tobacco Co., 868 So.2d 331 (Miss. 2004), the plaintiff asbestos producers sought recovery from tobacco companies on claims of fraud and unjust enrichment alleging that the tobacco companies were liable for producer's expenditures on past and future asbestos claims where the asbestos claimants also smoked. The court upheld summary judgment, concluding that the asbestos producers did not suffer a direct injury and thus were barred by doctrines of proximate cause.

2. Plaintiff's Non–Fault Conduct. If the defendants claim that plaintiff's conduct is partially at fault for the injuries suffered, comparative fault schemes ordinarily allow the jury to assess plaintiff's percentage of responsibility as well, also on the basis of fault or causation.

Is plaintiff's smoking a matter of comparative fault that should reduce liability under comparative fault, or a fact that should be considered in apportionment regardless of fault? In asbestos cases, defendants often seek to have causation apportioned to plaintiffs for lung diseases attributable at least partially to smoking. Courts typically permit apportionment of damages in such cases. In Dafler v. Raymark Industries, Inc., 611 A.2d 136 (N.J.Super. App. Div.1992), plaintiff was exposed to large quantities of asbestos during his work as a shipfitter from 1939 to 1945 and, for 45 years, he smoked a pack of cigarettes a day until he was diagnosed with asbestosis in 1984. He was subsequently diagnosed as having lung cancer, for which he sought recovery in this case. Plaintiff's medical experts testified that apportionment between the asbestos and the smoking was impossible, but that both were "significant contributing factors." As in *Ayers*, there was testimony that smoking alone increases a person's chances of suffering lung cancer 5–fold, occupational exposure to asbestos alone increases such chances 10–fold, and that the two together generate a "multiplicative or synergistic" result, increasing the risk by a factor of 50. Defendant's expert testified that plaintiff's smoking was the sole cause of his cancer. The jury found that plaintiff contributed 70% to his lung cancer and the defendant asbestos manufacturer 30%, and plaintiff appealed the apportionment of responsibility.

The apportionment was upheld on appeal. The court relied on Restatement (Second) of Torts § 433A which recognizes apportionment when there are distinct harms or "there is a reasonable basis for determining the contribution of each cause to a single harm." Comment *a* to the Restatement indicates that "the rules stated apply also where one of the causes in question is the conduct of the plaintiff himself, whether it be negligent or innocent." The court noted that the party seeking apportionment is responsible for proving that the harm is capable of apportionment. See Martin v. Owens–Corning Fiberglas Corp., 528 A.2d 947, 949 (Pa.1987). This approach is also consistent with comparative fault and contribution among tortfeasor statutes.

In a typical asbestos case, an asbestos worker sues more than a dozen manufacturers of various asbestos products to which he was exposed for periods ranging from days to decades. Should damages in such cases be apportioned among the defendants? How? See Moore v. Johns–Manville Sales Corp., 781 F.2d 1061 (5th Cir.1986)(comparative causation to be apportioned by the jury).

See generally Strassfeld, Causal Comparisons, 60 Fordham L. Rev. 913 (1992); 2 D. Owen, M.S. Madden & M. Davis, Madden & Owen on Products Liability §§ 25:8, 25:9 (3d ed. 2000).

STATUTES OF LIMITATIONS

1. Discovery Rule. Because of the latency period of many toxic substance diseases, plaintiffs may not know the full extent of their injuries before the statute of limitations runs. Normally a tort claim accrues when the plaintiff is injured. However, when the injury is a disease, especially a slowly progressing one, and not a traumatic event, years may pass before the fact of injury is known. Most courts (and, increasingly, legislatures) have responded by adopting some form of "discovery rule" for accrual of the cause of action—starting the limitations clock ticking when the plaintiff becomes aware, or in the exercise of reasonable diligence should become aware, of information about his claim. Brown v. E.I. duPont de Nemours & Co, 820 A.2d 362 (Del. 2003)(limitations for toxic substance injury begins to run when plaintiffs are on notice that harmful effects of toxic substance were possibly caused by wrongful conduct).

A number of states have enacted statutes applying more lenient discovery rules to asbestos or other toxic substance cases, or to latent disease cases generally, than are applied to other types of products liability actions. New York is one example. See N.Y. CPLR § 214–c (3–year discovery rule). Maryland has enacted a statute extending the limitations period for breast implant claims. Md. Code Ann. Cts. & Jud. Proc. § 5–116 (1995).

2. Knowledge that Triggers. At least five separate forms of knowledge may be relevant to determining when the plaintiff's claim accrues under the discovery rule—knowledge (1) of symptoms of the injury, such as shortness of breath or pain; (2) of the injury (or impairment); (3) that the injury was caused by a particular substance; (4) that it was caused by a particular party; and (5) that the law may provide a remedy for the injury. There is considerable variation among jurisdictions as to just what type of knowledge will start the statute running. See, e.g., Brown v. E.I. duPont de Nemours, 820 A.2d 362 (Del. 2003); Orear v. International Paint Co., 796 P.2d 759 (Wash.App.1990) (statute begins to run when plaintiff on notice of tortious cause of illness); Soliman v. Philip Morris Inc., 311 F.3d 966 (9th Cir. 2002) (smoker's claims accrued on date smoker should have known of addiction); Jolly v. Eli Lilly & Co., 751 P.2d 923 (Cal.1988)(statute begins to run when plaintiff does or should suspect that her injury was caused by wrongdoing).

The question of when the plaintiff in the exercise of reasonable diligence should have made the requisite discovery is often debated. See, e.g., Cowgill v. Raymark Indus., Inc., 832 F.2d 798, 801 (3d Cir.1987)(seven-day jury trial required to resolve issue of whether decedent should have known of pleural thickening more than two years before suit was filed); Moll v. Abbott Labs., 506 N.W.2d 816 (Mich. 1993)(limitations period triggered as a matter of law by doctor's suggestion that plaintiff's mother's use of DES caused plaintiff's malformed cervix; summary judgment proper).

3. In light of the widespread adoption of the discovery rule, the multi-decade latency period of many toxic substance diseases, the improvement (rather than deterioration) of evidence on causation and damages over time, and the perverse incentives created by statutes of limitations for premature filing of claims and forum shopping, many courts have recognized the value of permitting a plaintiff to split his cause of action, suing for separate diseases as they manifest themselves. *Ayers* acknowledged the value and widespread use of such "separate diseases" rules. See also M. Green, The Paradox of Statutes of Limitations in Toxic Substances Litigation, 76 Calif.L.Rev. 965 (1988) (limitations statutes should be allowed in toxic substance cases to promote more accurate fact finding, efficiency, and fairness).

4. Wrongful Death. In the event of death, should the statute run from the date the plaintiff in the wrongful death action discovers or should have discovered the claim, or from the date of death? The date of death may be required by statute. See Pastierik v. Duquesne Light Co., 526 A.2d 323 (Pa.1987)(5–2), rev'g 491 A.2d 841 (Pa.Super.1985).

5. Statutes of Repose. In addition to statutes of limitations, a number of jurisdictions have enacted statutes of repose, which begin to run at the time a product is first manufactured or sold. Typically such statutes have 8–12 year limits, after which an injured party is barred from suing, confronts an enhanced evidentiary burden, or can recover only upon proof of fault. See Martin, A Statute of Repose for Product Liability Claims, 50 Fordham L.Rev. 745 (1982). Application of statutes of repose to insidious diseases with lengthy latency periods often causes harsh results. In Wilder v. Amatex Corp., 336 S.E.2d 66 (N.C.1985), the court strained mightily to interpret a ten-year statute of repose as inapplicable to latent disease claims. See also Black v. ACandS, Inc., 752 N.E.2d 148 (Ind. App. 2001)(applying Indiana statute of repose protecting sellers of asbestos).

WORKERS' COMPENSATION

1. One might think that asbestos workers suffering diseases from toxic substances in the workplace could recover compensation for their illnesses through workers' compensation. Yet the workers' compensation system has poorly served persons who have suffered occupational diseases. Estimates are that only 5–15% of those who suffer from workplace diseases ever receive workers' compensation, although recent reforms have probably increased that number. The explanations vary but begin with the historical conception of workers' compensation as a system designed to assist employees suffering traumatic injury. In that regard, the difficulties that workers' compensation has had in accommodating occupational disease parallel, in many ways, the problems the tort system has encountered in addressing toxic substances. Thus, statutes of limitations for compensation claims often begin running on termination of employment or cessation of exposure. The only causation requirement in workers' compensation is to demonstrate that the injury arose out of employment, but that has been an impossible burden for many workers. Workers' compensation statutes also typically require that the worker's injury occur "by accident," a term that has been read to require a sudden calamitous event. Finally, employers contest occupational disease claims much more frequently than traumatic injury claims, and recovery of compensation is accordingly much slower (almost a year, as opposed to 6 weeks for injury claims). See D. Rosner & G. Markowitz, Deadly Dust: Silicosis and the Politics of Occupational Disease in Twentieth–Century America 78–86 (1991). See generally 2 D. Owen, M.S. Madden, & M. Davis, Madden & Owen on Products Liability § 19:7 (3d ed. 2000).

2. One ironic explanation for the infrequent recourse to workers' compensation by injured toxic substance workers is the adverse impact such a proceeding may have on a subsequent products liability case. Some products liability plaintiffs have had claims dismissed, on statutes of limitations grounds, because a prior workers' compensation claim established a date by which they clearly knew of their condition and its cause. See Chandler v. Johns–Manville Corp., 507 A.2d 1253 (Pa.Super.1986).

3. Intentional Exposure to Toxic Substances. A number of courts that have recognized an intentional tort exception to the exclusivity of workers' compensation have narrowly circumscribed the exception, requiring that the employer actually intend to injure the employee. See, e.g., Wilson v. Asten–Hill Mfg. Co., 791 F.2d 30 (3d Cir.1986)(Pennsylvania law). Compare Birklid v. Boeing Co., 904 P.2d 278 (Wash.1995)(toxic chemicals; intentional infliction of emotional distress exempt as "deliberate intent to injure"); Blankenship v. Cincinnati Milacron Chem., Inc., 433 N.E.2d 572 (Ohio 1982)(employees exposed to noxious chemicals; tort action allowed). Some jurisdictions refuse the intentional exposure claim but permit a fraudulent concealment of medical condition claim. Millison v. E.I. du Pont de Nemours & Co., 501 A.2d 505, 516 (N.J.1985); Johns–Manville Products Corp. v.

Contra Costa Superior Court, 612 P.2d 948 (Cal.1980). See, Comment, Intentional Disregard: Remedies for the Toxic Workplace, 30 Envtl. L. 811 (2000).

4.   Despite widespread agreement on the desirability of a legislative solution to asbestos litigation, and repeated judicial calls for legislative action, Congress has not even come close to enacting such a statute, although a number of bills have been introduced. See, e.g., Asbestos Fund Negotiations Halted After No Compromise Found, 19 Liab. & Ins. Week 1 (May 10, 2004). What social, economic, and political factors might be involved?

*

INDEX

References are to pages.

†